# The Heath Introduction to LITERATURE

# The Heath Introduction to LITERATURE

Third Edition

Alice S. Landy

D. C. Heath and Company
*Lexington, Massachusetts · Toronto*

Cover photo © David Muench.



Published simultaneously in Canada.

Printed in the United States of America.

International Standard Book Number: 0–669–14809–1

Library of Congress Catalog Card Number: 87–80091

# *Acknowledgments*

Sherwood Anderson. "I'm a Fool." Reprinted by permission of Harold Ober Associates Incorporated. Copyright 1922 by Dial Publishing Company, Inc. Copyright renewed 1949 by Eleanor Copenhaver Anderson.

W. H. Auden. "The Unknown Citizen" and "Musée des Beaux Arts." Copyright 1940 and renewed 1968 by W. H. Auden. Reprinted from *W. H. Auden: Collected Poems,* by W. H. Auden, edited by Edward Mendelson, by permission of Random House, Inc.

James Baldwin. "Sonny's Blues" from *Going to Meet the Man* by James Baldwin. Copyright © 1948, 1951, 1957, 1958, 1960, 1965 by James Baldwin. Permission granted by The Dial Press.

Amiri Baraka (LeRoi Jones). "W. W." from *Black Magic Poetry 1961–1967,* copyright © 1969 by LeRoi Jones. Reprinted by permission of Ronald Hobbs Literary Agency.

Donald Barthelme. "The Balloon" from *Unspeakable Practices, Unnatural Acts* by Donald Barthelme. Copyright © 1966, 1968 by Donald Barthelme. This story originally appeared in *The New Yorker.* Reprinted here by permission of Farrar, Straus & Giroux, Inc.

Jorge Luis Borges. "The South" from *Ficciones* by Jorge Luis Borges. Reprinted by permission of Grove Press, Inc. Translated from the Spanish by Anthony Kerrigan. Copyright © 1962 by Grove Press, Inc. Spanish copyright © 1956 by Emece Edítores, S.A., Buenos Aires.

Gwendolyn Brooks. From *The World of Gwendolyn Brooks* by Gwendolyn Brooks: "The Bean Eaters," copyright © 1959 and "We Real Cool" copyright © 1959. Reprinted by permission of Gwendolyn Brooks.

Albert Camus. "The Guest" from *Exile and the Kingdom,* by Albert Camus, translated by Justin O'Brien. Copyright © 1957, 1958 by Alfred A. Knopf, Inc. Reprinted by permission of Alfred A. Knopf, Inc.

John Cheever. "The Swimmer" from *The Stories of John Cheever,* copyright © 1964 by John Cheever. Reprinted by permission of Alfred A. Knopf, Inc.

Anton Chekhov. *A Marriage Proposal;* English version by Hilmar Baukhage and Barrett H. Clark. Copyright © 1914 by Barrett H. Clark. Copyright © 1942 (In Renewal) by Barrett H. Clark. Reprinted by permission of Samuel French, Inc. CAUTION: Professionals and amateurs are hereby warned that *A Marriage Proposal,* being fully protected under the copyright laws of the United States of America, the British Commonwealth countries, including Canada, and the other countries of the Copyright Union, is subject to a royalty. All rights, including professional, amateur, motion picture, recitation, public reading, radio, television, and cablevision broadcasting, and the rights of translation into foreign languages, are strictly reserved. Amateurs may give stage production of this play without the payment of royalty. For all other rights contact Samuel French, Inc., 45 West 25th Street, New York, NY 10010.

Joseph Conrad. "The Secret Sharer" from *Twixt Land and Sea* by Joseph Conrad. Copyright 1910 by Harper & Brothers. Reprinted by permission of Doubleday & Company, Inc.

Countee Cullen. "For a Lady I Know" from *On These I Stand* by Countee Cullen. Copyright 1925 by Harper & Row, Publishers, Inc. Renewed 1953 by Ida M. Cullen. Reprinted by permission of Harper & Row, Publishers, Inc.

E. E. Cummings. Selections are reprinted from *Tulips & Chimneys* and *IS 5 Poems* by E. E. Cummings by permission of Liveright Publishing Corporation. Copyright 1923, 1925 and renewed 1951, 1953 by E. E. Cummings. Copyright © 1973, 1976 by George James Firmage.

Emily Dickinson. All selections reprinted by permission of the publishers and The Trustees of Amherst College from *The Poems of Emily Dickinson,* edited by Thomas H. Johnson, Cambridge, Mass.: The Belknap Press of Harvard University Press, copyright © 1951, 1955, 1979, 1983 by the President and Fellows of Harvard College.

T. S. Eliot. "The Love Song of J. Alfred Prufrock" from *Collected Poems 1909–1962* by T. S. Eliot, copyright © 1936 by Harcourt Brace Jovanovich, Inc.; copyright © 1963, 1964 by T. S. Eliot. Reprinted by permission of the publisher.

William Faulkner. "A Rose for Emily." Copyright 1930 and renewed 1958 by William Faulkner. Reprinted from *Collected Stories of William Faulkner,* by William Faulkner, by permission of Random House, Inc.

Lawrence Ferlinghetti. "The Pennycandy store beyond the El" from *A Coney Island of the Mind,* © 1958 by Lawrence Ferlinghetti. Reprinted by permission of New Directions Publishing Corporation.

Robert Frost. "Provide, Provide," "Two Tramps in Mud Time," "Design," "Out, Out—" and "Birches." From *The Poetry of Robert Frost,* edited by Edward Connery Lathem. Copyright © 1969 by Holt, Rinehart and Winston, Inc. Copyright © 1958 by Robert Frost. Copyright © 1967 by Leslie Frost Ballantine. Reprinted by permission of Henry Holt and Company, Inc.

Allen Ginsberg. "A Supermarket in California." Copyright © 1955 by Allen Ginsberg. "In back of the real." Copyright © 1954 by Allen Ginsberg, from *Collected Poems 1947–1980* by Allen Ginsberg. Reprinted by permission of Harper & Row, Publishers, Inc.

Nikki Giovanni. "Woman" and "The Beep Beep Poem" from *Cotton Candy on a Rainy Day* by Nikki Giovanni. Copyright © 1978 by Nikki Giovanni. Reprinted by permission of William Morrow & Company, Inc.

Susan Glaspell. "Trifles" from *Plays* by Susan Glaspell. Copyright 1920 by Dodd, Mead & Company, Inc. Copyright renewed 1948 by Susan Glaspell. Reprinted by permission of Dodd, Mead & Company, Inc.

Robert Graves. "Down, Wanton, Down!" from *Collected Poems 1975* by Robert Graves. Reprinted by permission of Robert Graves.

Thomas Hardy. "The Ruined Maid" and "The Man He Killed" are reprinted from *Complete Poems of Thomas Hardy,* edited by James Gibson (New York: Macmillan, 1978).

Robert Hayden. "Those Winter Sundays." Reprinted from *Angle of Ascent, New and Selected Poems* by Robert Hayden, by permission of Liveright Publishing Corporation. Copyright © 1975, 1972, 1970, 1966 by Robert Hayden.

Seamus Heaney. "Docker" from *Poems 1965–1975* by Seamus Heaney. Copyright © 1966, 1969, 1972, 1975, 1980 by Seamus Heaney. Reprinted by permission of Farrar, Straus & Giroux, Inc.

H. D. (Hilda Doolittle). "Heat" from *Selected Poems.* Copyright © 1957 by Norman Holmes Pearson. Reprinted with permission of New Directions Publishing Corporation.

Ernest Hemingway. "The Snows of Kilimanjaro." Copyright 1936 Ernest Hemingway; copyright renewed 1964 Mary Hemingway. Reprinted with permission of Charles Scribner's Sons from *The Short Stories of Ernest Hemingway.*

A. E. Housman. "With Rue My Heart Is Laden," "When I Was One-and-Twenty," "Terence, This Is Stupid Stuff," and "To an Athlete Dying Young" from "A Shropshire Lad," Authorized Edition, from *The Collected Poems of A. E. Housman.* Copyright 1939, 1940, © 1965 by Holt, Rinehart and Winston. Copyright © 1967, 1968 by Robert E. Symons. Reprinted by permission of Henry Holt and Company, Inc.

Langston Hughes. "Harlem." Copyright 1951 by Langston Hughes. Reprinted from *Selected Poems of Langston Hughes,* by Langston Hughes, by permission of Alfred A. Knopf, Inc.

Ted Hughes. "Pike" from *New Selected Poems* by Ted Hughes. Copyright © 1959 by Ted Hughes. By permission of Harper & Row, Publishers, Inc.

Henrik Ibsen. *A Doll's House* by Henrik Ibsen, translation by Otto Reinert. Copyright © 1977 by Otto Reinert. Reprinted from *Thirteen Plays: An Introductory Anthology,* edited by Otto Reinert and Peter Arnott, by permission of Little, Brown and Company.

Eugène Ionesco. *The Gap,* translated by Rosette Lamont. Reprinted from *The Massachusetts Review,* © 1969 The Massachusetts Review, Inc.

Shirley Jackson. "The Lottery" from *The Lottery and Other Stories* by Shirley Jackson. Copyright 1948, 1949 by Shirley Jackson. Copyright renewed © 1976, 1977 by Laurence Hyman, Barry Hyman, Mrs. Sarah Webster, and Mrs. Joanne Schnurer. This story originally appeared in *The New Yorker.* Reprinted here by permission of Farrar, Straus & Giroux, Inc.

Robinson Jeffers. "Love the Wild Swan." Copyright 1935 and renewed 1963 by Donnan Jeffers and Garth Jeffers. Reprinted from *The Selected Poetry of Robinson Jeffers,* by Robinson Jeffers, by permission of Random House, Inc.

James Weldon Johnson. "O Black and Unknown Bards" from *St. Peter Relates an Incident* by James Weldon Johnson. Copyright 1935 by James Weldon Johnson, © renewed 1963 by Grace Nail Johnson. Reprinted by permission of Viking Penguin Inc.

James Joyce. "Araby" from *Dubliners* by James Joyce. Copyright 1916 by B. W. Huebsch. Definitive text copyright © 1967 by the Estate of James Joyce. Reprinted by permission of Viking Penguin Inc.

Franz Kafka. "The Bucket Rider." Reprinted by permission of Schocken Books Inc. from *The Penal Colony* by Franz Kafka. Copyright © 1948 by Schocken Books Inc. Copyright renewed 1976 by Schocken Books Inc.

Ring Lardner. "Haircut" in *The Love Nest and Other Stories.* Copyright 1925 Ellis A. Lardner; copyright renewed. Reprinted with the permission of Charles Scribner's Sons.

D. H. Lawrence. "The Rocking-Horse Winner" from *The Complete Stories of D. H. Lawrence,* vol. III. Copyright 1933 by The Estate of D. H. Lawrence, © 1961 by Angelo Ravagli and C. M. Weekley, Executors of The Estate of Frieda Lawrence Ravagli. "Piano" from *The Complete Poems of D. H. Lawrence,* edited by Vivian de Sola Pinto and F. Warren Roberts. Copyright © 1964, 1971 by Angelo Ravagli and C. M. Weekley, Executors of The Estate of Frieda Lawrence Ravagli. Reprinted by permission of Viking Penguin Inc.

Denise Levertov. "Six Variations (part iii)" from *The Jacob's Ladder.* Copyright © 1960 by Denise Levertov Goodman. "Six Variations" was first published in *Poetry.* Reprinted by permission of New Directions Publishing Corporation.

Amy Lowell. "Wind and Silver" and "Patterns" from *The Complete Poetical Works of Amy Lowell.* Copyright © 1955 by Houghton Mifflin Company. Copyright © 1983 renewed by Houghton Mifflin Company, Brinton P. Roberts, Esquire and G. D'Andelot Belin, Esquire. Reprinted by permission of Houghton Mifflin Company.

Robert Lowell. "For the Union Dead" from *For the Union Dead* by Robert Lowell. Copyright © 1960, 1964 by Robert Lowell. Reprinted by permission of Farrar, Straus & Giroux, Inc.

Carson McCullers. "A Tree, A Rock, A Cloud" from *The Ballad of the Sad Café and Collected Short Stories* by Carson McCullers. Copyright 1936, 1941, 1942, 1950, 1951, 1955 by Carson McCullers. Reprinted by permission of Houghton Mifflin Company.

Archibald MacLeish. "Ars Poetica" from *New and Collected Poems, 1917–1976* by Archibald MacLeish. Reprinted by permission of Houghton Mifflin Company.

Katherine Mansfield. "Miss Brill." Copyright 1922 by Alfred A. Knopf, Inc. and renewed 1950 by John Middleton Murry. Reprinted from *The Short Stories of Katherine Mansfield,* by Katherine Mansfield, by permission of the publisher.

Edna St. Vincent Millay. Sonnet *xcix* by Edna St. Vincent Millay. From *Collected Poems,* Harper & Row. Copyright © 1931, 1958 by Edna St. Vincent Millay and Norma Millay Ellis. Sonnet *xlii* by Edna St. Vincent Millay. From *Collected Poems,* Harper & Row. Copyright © 1923, 1951 by Edna St. Vincent Millay and Norma Millay Ellis. Reprinted by permission.

Arthur Miller. *Death of a Salesman* by Arthur Miller. Copyright 1949 by Arthur Miller. Copyright renewed © 1977 by Arthur Miller. Reprinted by permission of Viking Penguin Inc.

Marianne Moore. "The Mind Is an Enchanting Thing." Reprinted with permission of Macmillan Publishing Co. Inc. from *Collected Poems* by Marianne Moore. Copyright 1944 and renewed 1972 by Marianne Moore. "Poetry." Reprinted with permission of Macmillan Publishing Co. Inc. from *Collected Poems* by Marianne Moore. Copyright 1935 by Marianne Moore, renewed 1963 by Marianne Moore and T. S. Eliot.

Flannery O'Connor. "A Good Man Is Hard to Find." Copyright 1953 by Flannery O'Connor; copyright renewed 1981 by Mrs. Regina O'Connor. Reprinted from *A Good Man Is Hard to Find and Other Stories* by permission of Harcourt Brace Jovanovich, Inc.

Tillie Olsen. "Tell Me a Riddle," excerpted from the book *Tell Me a Riddle* by Tillie Olsen.

Copyright © 1956, 1957, 1960, 1961 by Tillie Olsen. Reprinted by permission of Delacorte Press/Seymour Lawrence.

Wilfred Owen. "Anthem for Doomed Youth" from *The Collected Poems of Wilfred Owen* by Wilfred Owen. Copyright © 1963 Chatto & Windus Ltd. Reprinted by permission of New Directions Publishing Corporation.

Grace Paley. "The Loudest Voice" from *Little Disturbances of Man* by Grace Paley. Copyright © 1956, 1958, 1959 by Grace Paley. Reprinted by permission of Viking Penguin Inc.

Dorothy Parker. "Résumé" from *The Portable Dorothy Parker,* revised and enlarged edition by Brendan Gill. Copyright 1926 by Dorothy Parker. Copyright renewed 1954 by Dorothy Parker. Reprinted by permission of Viking Penguin Inc.

I. L. Peretz. "If Not Higher" from *A Treasury of Yiddish Stories,* edited by Irving Howe and Eliezer Greenberg. Copyright 1953, 1954 by The Viking Press, Inc. Reprinted by permission of Viking Penguin Inc.

Sylvia Plath. "Morning Song" from *The Collected Poems of Sylvia Plath,* edited by Ted Hughes. Copyright © 1961 by Ted Hughes. "Metaphors" from *The Collected Poems of Sylvia Plath,* edited by Ted Hughes. Copyright © 1960 by Ted Hughes. Reprinted by permission of Harper & Row, Publishers, Inc.

Katherine Anne Porter. "The Jilting of Granny Weatherall." Copyright 1930, 1958 by Katherine Anne Porter. Reprinted from her volume *Flowering Judas and Other Stories* by permission of Harcourt Brace Jovanovich, Inc.

Ezra Pound. "In a Station of the Metro," "L'Art 1910," "These Fought in Any Case," "Ancient Music," "The Seafarer," from *Personae.* Copyright 1926 by Ezra Pound. Reprinted by permission of New Directions Publishing Corporation.

Dudley Randall. "Ballad of Birmingham." Reprinted by permission of Dudley Randall.

John Crowe Ransom. "Bells for John Whiteside's Daughter." Copyright 1924 by Alfred A. Knopf, Inc., and renewed 1952 by John Crowe Ransom. Reprinted from *Selected Poems,* Third Edition, Revised and Enlarged, by John Crowe Ransom, by permission of Alfred A. Knopf, Inc.

Adrienne Rich. "Aunt Jennifer's Tigers" is reprinted from *Poems, Selected and New, 1950–1974,* by Adrienne Rich, by permission of W. W. Norton & Company, Inc. Copyright © 1975, 1973, 1971, 1969, 1966 by W. W. Norton & Company, Inc. Copyright © 1951 by Adrienne Rich.

Edwin Arlington Robinson. "Mr. Flood's Party." Reprinted with permission of Macmillan Publishing Co., Inc. from *Collected Poems* by Edwin Arlington Robinson. Copyright 1921 by Edwin Arlington Robinson, renewed 1949 by Ruth Nivison.

Theodore Roethke. "My Papa's Waltz," copyright 1942 by Hearst Magazines, Inc. "I Knew a Woman," copyright 1954 by Theodore Roethke from the book *The Collected Poems of Theodore Roethke.* Both reprinted by permission of Doubleday & Company, Inc.

Saki (H. H. Munro). "The Story Teller" from *The Complete Short Stories of Saki* (H. H. Munro). Copyright 1930 by The Viking Press, Inc. Copyright renewed 1958 by The Viking Press, Inc. Reprinted by permission of Viking Penguin Inc.

Carl Sandburg. "Cool Tombs" from *Cornhuskers* by Carl Sandburg, copyright 1918 by Holt, Rinehart and Winston, Inc., copyright 1946 by Carl Sandburg. "Fog" from *Chicago Poems* by Carl Sandburg, copyright 1916 by Holt, Rinehart and Winston, copyright 1944 by Carl Sandburg. Both selections reprinted by permission of Harcourt Brace Jovanovich, Inc.

Anne Sexton. "Her Kind" from *To Bedlam and Part Way Back,* by Anne Sexton. Copyright © 1960 by Anne Sexton. Reprinted by permission of Houghton Mifflin Company.

William Shakespeare. *Hamlet,* edited by Willard Farnham, in *The Pelican Shakespeare.* General Editor: Alfred Harbage (rev. ed.; New York: Penguin Books, 1970). Copyright © Penguin Books Inc., 1957, 1970. Reprinted by permission of Penguin Books.

Sophocles. *Oedipus Rex,* an English version by Dudley Fitts and Robert Fitzgerald, copyright 1949 by Harcourt Brace Jovanovich, Inc.; renewed 1977 by Cornelia Fitts and Robert Fitzgerald. *The Antigonê of Sophocles,* an English version by Dudley Fitts and Robert

Fitzgerald, copyright 1939 by Harcourt Brace Jovanovich, Inc.; renewed 1967 by Dudley Fitts and Robert Fitzgerald. Both reprinted by permission of the publisher. CAUTION: All rights, including professional, amateur, motion picture, recitation, lecturing, public reading, radio broadcasting, and television are strictly reserved. Inquiries on all rights should be addressed to Harcourt Brace Jovanovich, Inc., Orlando, FL 32887.

Wallace Stevens. "Thirteen Ways of Looking at a Blackbird." Copyright 1923 and renewed 1951 by Wallace Stevens. Reprinted from *The Collected Poems of Wallace Stevens,* by Wallace Stevens, by permission of Alfred A. Knopf, Inc.

Dylan Thomas. "Fern Hill," "Do Not Go Gentle into That Good Night," and "In My Craft or Sullen Art" from *The Poems of Dylan Thomas.* Copyright 1946 by New Directions Publishing Corporation, copyright 1952 by Dylan Thomas. Reprinted by permission of New Directions Publishing Corporation.

James Thurber. "The Secret Life of Walter Mitty" from *My World—and Welcome To It* by James Thurber, published by Harcourt Brace Jovanovich. Copyright © 1942 James Thurber, copyright 1970 Helen W. Thurber and Rosemary A. Thurber.

Alice Walker. "Really, *Doesn't* Crime Pay?" Copyright © 1972 by Alice Walker. Reprinted from her volume *In Love & Trouble* by permission of Harcourt Brace Jovanovich, Inc.

Eudora Welty. "A Worn Path." Copyright 1941, 1969 by Eudora Welty. Reprinted from her volume *A Curtain of Green and Other Stories* by permission of Harcourt Brace Jovanovich, Inc.

Richard Wilbur. "Love Calls Us to the Things of This World" from *Things of This World,* © 1956 by Richard Wilbur, and "Place Pigalle" from *The Beautiful Changes,* © 1947, 1975 by Richard Wilbur. Reprinted by permission of Harcourt Brace Jovanovich, Inc.

William Carlos Williams. "The Dance" from *Collected Poems of William Carlos Williams.* Reprinted by permission of New Directions Publishing Corporation.

Richard Wright. "The Man Who Was Almost a Man," © Ellen Wright. Reprinted by permission of Ellen Wright.

William Butler Yeats. "An Irish Airman Foresees His Death." Reprinted with permission of Macmillan Publishing Co., Inc., from *Collected Poems* by William Butler Yeats. Copyright 1919 by Macmillan Publishing Co., Inc., renewed 1947 by Bertha Georgie Yeats. "The Folly of Being Comforted" from *Collected Poems* by William Butler Yeats (New York: Macmillan, 1956). "Sailing to Byzantium." Reprinted with permission of Macmillan Publishing Co., Inc., from *Collected Poems* by William Butler Yeats. Copyright 1928 by Macmillan Publishing Co., Inc., renewed 1956 by Georgie Yeats. "The Circus Animals' Desertion." Reprinted with permission of Macmillan Publishing Company from *Collected Poems* by William Butler Yeats. Copyright 1940 by Georgie Yeats, renewed 1968 by Bertha Georgie Yeats, Michael Butler Yeats and Anne Yeats.

# PREFACE

In designing and writing *The Heath Introduction to Literature,* we began from the groundwork laid by The Heath Introductions to Fiction, Poetry, and Drama—books that themselves drew on the help and expertise of scores of teachers of English and the humanities. This book differs from those other texts in bringing together all three genres within one volume; in ordering its material in thematic rather than chronological fashion (except in the case of drama); and in providing new introductions and study questions that make the book not just an anthology, but a unified teaching plan.

The book is divided into four parts. The first part supplies a general introduction to the study of literature. Its opening chapter, on reading literature, introduces the student to the basic components of literature—plot, character, and theme—and to basic critical concepts such as unity and inevitability. This chapter also introduces the philosophy of the text: that literature is a dialogue between writer and reader, an art form whose subject is a vision of humanity and the universe. The second chapter, on writing about literature, reiterates these fundamentals and shows how they underlie the skills and techniques of writing about literature. While the first chapter is philosophical in bent, the second is practical. Work plans, lists of questions, and a diagram make the idea of writing concrete and comprehensible and provide "how-to's" for the assignments in the rest of the book.

Although these introductory chapters precede the structured parts on fiction, poetry, and drama, they need not be read first. The instructor who wishes to begin with short stories or poems can elicit spontaneous student responses, unguided by study questions. The questions raised in the introductory chapters can then be applied to works everyone has recently read, and the focus of the course will be clearly defined as being the reading *of* (rather than *about*) literature.

The first genre to be studied is fiction. Its presentation is organized around modes of narration and narrative techniques. The interplay of listener and narrator is thus highlighted, and the basic framework of the text is kept simple. Within this framework, other concepts appear as a natural outgrowth of the subject under discussion and easily become a part of the student's critical vocabulary. The presentation provides a variety of critical concepts within a firmly structured framework—a more satisfying organization than the "grasshopper" approach in which each chapter, or each story, heralds a new topic and leaves students and instructors alike negotiating the jumps between topics as best they can.

Poetry follows fiction, this being the order preferred by most instructors. In response to requests, the third edition has added a chapter devoted wholly to sonnets. Otherwise, the ordering of chapters remains constant. Throughout the poetry section we use well-known and highly readable works to introduce the student to the technical aspects of poetry, such as rhythm and verse form, and then to the genre's subtler concerns, among them the voice of the speaker, imagery, and the use of sound. This movement allows the student to begin with a general overview of what a poem *is*, and then to delve more deeply into the specific characteristics that *make* it a poem. For those instructors who wish to offer their students works free of critical commentary, an anthology of poems completes the part.

Drama now receives greater coverage than it did in the second edition. We have expanded the number of plays from nine to eleven, including works from comedy, tragedy, realism, and the theatre of the absurd. After the introductory chapter on reading drama, the drama section, unlike the parts on fiction and poetry is organized chronologically, to illustrate clearly the important structural and historical developments in this genre.

Within each section there are plentiful study aids: introductory essays, study questions, essay suggestions, and questions for further thought. Objective and subjective responses both have their place as answers to our questions; the emphasis is on knowing which is which and on achieving a judicious balance between the two. In general, questions near the beginning of a section will offer more guidance than those that come later, thus tacitly encouraging students to greater independence as their skills and familiarity with literature grow. Some sets of questions are constructed so that they form an example of how to organize an essay; others concentrate on showing how to follow a theme through a story, poem, or play; still others encourage students to look at a work from as many angles as possible.

In short, we feel that a good textbook, like the literature it contains, must offer variety within unity, and we have done our best to achieve that goal. Our thanks to the many colleagues who have helped us: especially to Ethel Bonds, Virginia Western Community College; Robert Burke, Joliet Junior College; John Driscoll, Phoenix College; Allan Duane, Ulster County Community College; James F. Gordon, Jr., Mississippi Delta Junior College; Maria Haman, Louisiana Technical University; Jeff Jeske, University of

California, Los Angeles; Vernon Miles, University of Arkansas, Margaret Shepherd, Surry Community College; Rebecca Shuttleworth, Mississippi Delta Junior College; and Margaret Sullivan, University of California, Los Angeles. Finally, we thank you, the users of this book, who have helped us revise the selections and commentary and who bring to it your own love of literature and skills in teaching. May you enjoy using it, and may it serve you well.

ALICE LANDY
H. HOLTON JOHNSON

# CONTENTS

# The Heath Introduction to LITERATURE

# ON LITERATURE

# 1 *The Bases of Literature*

Literature has its roots in one of the most basic human desires—the desire for pleasure. Its writers find one source of pleasure in mastering the difficult demands of their craft. If they do well, they then reap a second delight from witnessing the pleasure their work gives to others. Readers, meanwhile, derive pleasure from literature's power to imitate life. A truly good book can speak of imaginary people so vividly that they seem more alive than people we meet on the street, and can make us care about its characters as if they were close friends.

We are always curious about each other, and usually curious about ourselves as well. Why do we behave as we do? What are the causes of our actions? Literature is far from having all the answers. But it does offer hints, suggestions, and flashes of insight. Moreover, it offers them in such a way as to refresh and encourage our own thinking, and so leads us to insights of our own. Readers have many standards for judging writers. But one enduring standard is the writers' power to interpret us, as humans, to ourselves. The greater the writers' knowledge of people seems to be, the more openly they share their knowledge with us, the higher we rate them. We speak with disdain of shallow or insincere writers; we demand truth and sincerity even in the most fantastic fiction.

Literature, then, exists because it pleases us. And it pleases us by imitating life—or, more precisely, by displaying its writers' visions of life as it is or as the writers think it should be. But how does it contrive its imitation? Its only medium is words; and we know how hard it is to make words say what we want them to say. How do writers handle their words to get such powerful effects from them? What guidelines help them make the million-and-one choices that result in a play, a poem, or a story?

The first necessities for any work of literature—and therefore the first things that writers must consider—are **plot** and **character.** These may occur to a writer in either order. That is, a writer may first imagine some characters, and then decide what actions they are to perform; or a writer may envision some action, and then decide on the people who must perform it. Every work of literature, however, must have both action and characters. It cannot please us, or hold our interest, otherwise.

It may seem that poetry is an exception to this rule. While stories and plays tend to present fully developed plots with sequences of actions with discernable beginnings, middles, and ends, poems more often plunge us into the middle of an event, and may tell us neither what came before the event nor what comes after it. Here, for instance, is a poem with no physical action at all. Yet it shows us one person, at least, and gives us some insight into his actions and feelings.

GEORGE GORDON, LORD BYRON (1788–1824)

**So We'll Go No More A-Roving**

So we'll go no more a-roving
  So late into the night,
Though the heart be still as loving,
  And the moon be still as bright.

5 For the sword outwears its sheath,
  And the soul wears out the breast,
And the heart must pause to breathe,
  And Love itelf have rest.

Though the night was made for loving,
10   And the day returns too soon,
Yet we'll go no more a-roving
  By the light of the moon.

We know several things about the speaker of this poem. We know that he has enjoyed "roving," and that he still thinks warmly of it, since he declares that "the night was made for loving, / And the day returns too soon." We know that he feels weary, like a sheath worn out by the motions of the sword within it. We hear him declare that his roving days are done. But we also hear him speak of pausing and resting, verbs that imply an eventual return to action. And so we begin to wonder: is he really finished with love, as he says he is? The action of the poem might thus be described as the act of the lover forswearing love. Its interest arises from our recognition of the complex emotions the renunciation reveals. It is the action, and the emotion, of a moment; but it is none the less real—and none the less action—for its momentary nature.

For now, however, let us return to the more thoroughly developed plots of drama and fiction. These, too, must find some balance between action and emotion, some method of telling us both what the characters do and how they feel. A given story may emphasize action or feeling; that choice, like so many others, is up to its writer. But it must contain some of both. We have no interest in unfeeling characters, or in characters who do nothing.

In addition to a plot and to characters who act and feel, a work of literature must have **unity** and **coherence.** It must make us believe that its characters really would have committed the actions it says they commit, and that the actions could really have taken place. At its best, the movement of a play, a poem, or a story must make us feel that the tale could have reached no other end, and that it could have reached it in no other way. When this happens, the story's ending seems inevitable. Its characters and its actions have convinced us wholly. A sense of inevitability is thus another hallmark of a fine work of literature. Works so marked tend to be moving and powerful.

The **language** of a work of literature is also important. Words have so many undercurrents of meaning that the change of one word may change our image of a scene or a character. Consider, for instance, the difference between *a thin, tense man; a thin, nervous man;* and *a thin harried man*—or the difference between *a plump woman, a well-rounded woman,* and *an overweight woman.* A writer's language must be chosen with care. It should carry overtones that enrich our sense of the story, thus adding to the pleasure we get from the tale. And it must avoid all false tones, for those would diminish our pleasure. Again, we demand at least that the words fit the actions and characters of which they tell. And again, we shall find that the best seem almost inevitable. Reading them, we cannot imagine the author having used any other words.

When we read, we don't want to be aware of these choices of words and acts and characters. We don't want to hear the author muttering behind the scenes: "I need this word, not that one. This character must say this; that description must carry this message." Rather, we want to be able to concentrate on the story itself, accepting everything within it as valid and necessary parts of its world. When we discuss and analyze works of literature, however, we do become aware of the choices the writers made in constructing them. We note who the characters are and how they relate to each other. We observe how the action begins, how it ends, and how it is carried from beginning to ending. We study the ways in which the language characterizes people and events and consider the broader or deeper meanings it suggests.

These questions, we may note, are **questions of fact.** Their answers can be found, decided, and agreed upon. We can count the characters in *Hamlet,* and we will learn that Hamlet is a prince of Denmark, that Gertrude is his mother and Claudius his stepfather, and that the ghost who appears from time to time is the ghost of Hamlet's murdered father. Similarly, we learn that eight people are killed during the course of the play (one by stabbing, one by drowning, two by beheading, one by poison, and three by some combination of sword wounds and poison) and that virtually none of the major characters is still alive when the play ends. There is no question about any of these happenings and no reason to argue about them.

Questions of fact, however, are only a beginning in thinking about a work of literature. They tell us certain choices a writer has made, but they rarely tell us why the writer has made those particular choices. To learn that, we must go on to **questions of interpretation,** questions that deal with the artistic vision underlying the work and thus with such issues as theme, pattern, message, and meaning.

**Message** and **meaning** are not universal to literature. They belong to one school of literature, the **didactic.** When writers or critics demand that a story carry a message to its readers, that it "mean something" to them, they are saying that literature should teach us something and that it should appeal to our sense of moral values. At its simplest, this approach ends in pat morals: "Always tell the truth; stop beating up on your fellow humans." On a more sophisticated level, however, didacticism becomes what the critic Matthew Arnold called "high seriousness" and produces literature that deals with such complex questions as the value of human life and the sources of human ideals and aspirations.

Not all literature is didactic. Some writers believe that literature does not need to make a moral statement. For these writers, a work of literature is important for its own sake, not for any message it might carry. As one modern poet put it, "A poem should not mean, but be."[1] In works like these, the concept of message does not apply; to impose it upon them is to falsify the intent of the writer.

The questions of **theme** and **pattern,** however, concern all literature. Within any work of literature that strikes us as unified and complete we will find some sort of pattern into which its parts fit or through which they are perceived. Didactic tales, for example, present acts and people in terms of a moral order. Hence the tales tend to be built around patterns of good and evil, temptation and response. In contrast, a Romantic poem

[1] Archibald MacLeish, "Ars Poetica," p. 609.

describing a summer day might have sensory impressions of light and shade, coolness and warmth, as its unifying vision.

There may be many patterns—patterns of action, characterization, language, or metaphor—within a single work. Sometimes each will work separately; sometimes several will be intertwined to bear on a single theme. Sometimes, too, several themes will be interwoven within one work to create a complexity of vision that no single theme could contain. But always there will be that sense of a single ordered vision embracing and unifying all the patterns or themes.

Sometimes the main theme of a work is announced by its author. Joseph Conrad, whose story "The Secret Sharer" appears on pages 131–164, also wrote a well-known story that tells of a twenty-year-old man's first voyage to the East. He titled the story "Youth." He had its hero tell the tale himself, looking back on his voyage from the age of forty-two, and had him interrupt his story from time to time with exclamations such as, "O youth! The strength of it, the faith of it, the imagination of it!" By doing so, Conrad made it perfectly clear that the hero's vision of what youth was and what his own youth had meant to him would be the main theme of his story. More often, however, deciding what themes are being worked out is our affair; and here interpretation becomes most individual and most varied.

We all read the same words when we read a story. We observe the same characters acting out the same deeds and passions. But we each interpret them a little differently because of our individual views of life, our interests, and our experience. When we try to explain how the story works, therefore, or decide what themes are being emphasized, we read some of our own perceptions into the story.

If we realize that we are interpreting, all is well. Then we can say, "This is how it seems to me." We can look for patterns of language or imagery and details of action or characterization to support our view. We can listen to others who have other views and evaluate the support they bring for their arguments; and, in the end, we can probably come to a pretty fair idea of what the story does have to offer and how it is able to offer it.

On the other hand, if we do not recognize the extent to which we are active interpreters of what we read, we may have trouble when we try to deal with such subjective issues as theme or message. For then we may make the error of saying, "I see this. Therefore the author intended it that way and I have found the only correct interpretation this story can possibly have." Since very few works of literature will not admit some variance of interpretation, definitive statements such as this are wrong more often than not. It is true that there are limits to the range of interpretations we can apply to a work of literature if we are to read it honestly on its own terms. Within those limits, however, we must be willing to acknowledge various ways of looking at it.

We must also be willing to allow our perceptions to change. It often happens that what we notice the first time we read a story is not what seems most important to us later on. Nor would it make sense to talk or write about a poem or a story if our perception of it could not be enriched by the discussion. Too, we must be willing to use our full judgment, to read the story carefully and attentively. We must be sure we are trying to discover what it really does say rather than simply assuming that it says what we want it to say. Once we have done this, however, we should be able to feel comfortable with our judgments and our responses. Above all, we must not undervalue ourselves. We are the people for whom these stories, plays, and poems are written. If we cannot trust ourselves, we will have a hard time trusting them.

# 2 *Writing About Literature*

Literature allows writers to share their ideas and visions with their readers. Their work is not complete until someone has read it and responded to it.

As readers, we too have something to say. At the very least, we have opinions about the work itself, but we also may have other ideas to express. Perhaps we are moved to compare this story with others, or perhaps it has given us some new ideas that we want to explore further. Sometimes we share our ideas directly with others in face-to-face discussions. At other times, we become writers in order to communicate our thoughts and opinions.

The first part of writing about literature, therefore, is thinking about it. This step is perhaps the most vital part of the process, for we need to know not only what we think but why we think as we do. Which of our thoughts come from the work itself? Which have been inspired by it? Which come from our predispositions and preconceptions about literature?

We enjoy stories for many reasons. Some are intrinsic to the story itself: language artfully used, characters we believe in and care about, actions that carry significant messages for us or give us new insight into ourselves and our society. (Whether the story provides that insight by answering questions for us or by urging us into asking our own questions does not matter here. What does matter is that the impetus for question or answer comes from within the story itself.) Other causes of enjoyment are external, coming not from the artistry of the story, but from the fact that the story fits our current notions of what a story should be like, or calls forth some pleasant personal memories. In short, the external factors in our response to a story come from things we already think or feel. Intrinsic factors come from the writer's craftsmanship and art.*

When we read for pleasure alone, we need not care where our pleasure comes from. Any appeal a story may have will be welcome. When we study literature, however, we want to concentrate on the intrinsic qualities of the works we read, for they can teach us most about the craft and the workings of literature. It is a story's intrinsic qualities, therefore, and our response to them, that we want to write about when we write about literature.

When we rule out external responses to literature, and say that we are only going to talk and write about its intrinsic qualities, we are not denying the individuality of our responses. In fact, only when we escape from our prejudices and preconceptions about literature can we respond most freely to the stories we read. Even when we write most directly of the story itself and the art that created it, our writing will contain an emotional component as well as an intellectual one. Emotion and intellect together answer such questions as, "Does the hero's death seem inevitable?" and "How has it been made to seem so?"

All analysis ends in judgment. All questions of, "How is this done?" begin or end with, "Is it a success?" It would be useless to ask, "How has the writer characterized his heroine?" if we could not also ask, "Has he made me care what happens to her?" Literature appeals to mind and emotions alike; our response, therefore, must be both analytic and emotional, objective and subjective. Concentrating on those things that are intrinsic to the story does not deny the subjective component of our response. Rather, it frees us for more truly personal reactions, subjective and objective alike, even while it helps us recognize how and why we are responding.

Before we begin to write about a story, therefore, we should ask ourselves some version of the following questions:

1. Which aspects of the story had the greatest impact on me?
2. What did they seem to be saying? How did they say it? (Or what did they make me think that seemed new to me? How did they make me think it?)

---

* What is true for stories is true for plays and poems as well. For the rest of this chapter, therefore, I shall use the word "stories" to stand for all types of literature, rather than repeating the more awkward phrases "stories, plays, and poems" and "works of literature."

3. How did other aspects of the story support or contribute to my response?
4. How did these particular aspects of the story help create the story's total effect?

We start, that is, with our response to the story; we move from there to an analysis of the art that creates the response; and then we return to the overall impression or effect.

When we write, we follow the same pattern of response, analysis, and final judgment. Unless we have unlimited time and paper, however, we will not be able to write down all that we have thought about the story. Choices must be made: What shall I include? What shall I emphasize? To make those choices, we must consider not only the story and our response to it, but the purpose of our paper and the audience for which we are writing it.

Let's look at two extreme examples. Let's imagine, first, that we keep a journal or diary and that we want to record in it the fact that we read and enjoyed a story. In this case, our main interest would be our own reaction to the story; our writing, therefore, would concentrate on our subjective response. We would mention only those incidents or characters that impressed us most strongly; and we could write in whatever style we pleased, for we would be our only audience.

At the other extreme, suppose we were writing a paper for a scholarly journal. In this case, we would write in an objective, balanced style, presenting carefully worked out analyses of each aspect of the story that related to our topic. We would define our terms carefully and provide adequate illustrations to support our thesis. In fact, we would be writing almost like a debater, trying to make our points as clear, convincing, and firmly based on factual evidence as possible.

Somewhere between these extremes lie most writing assignments. Two we might look at are book reviews and English papers. Let's consider what these types of writing most often say. Then let's look at how they can go about saying it.

Book reviews tend to be frankly subjective, focusing on "What I liked and why I liked it." (Or, alternatively, "Why you shouldn't waste time or money on this book.") By its very nature, a review commits the reviewer to making judgments: the book may be "one of the year's best," or "not up to this author's usual standards," or simply "a pleasant afternoon's reading." Too, the reviewer may try to judge what type of reader would enjoy the book most: "Readers with a taste for psychological studies will enjoy . . .", or "Mystery fans will welcome the appearance of. . . ."

A brief review may contain little more than these judgments. A more thorough review will usually provide evidence to support them, by discussing some particularly outstanding character or episode or by quoting a few lines of description or dialogue as a sample of the writer's style. Readers of reviews are presumed to be asking themselves, "Is this a book I want to read?" Through judgments and illustrations supporting the judgments, reviews are designed to help readers answer that question.

A review, therefore, will generally begin in one of two ways. It will either start right out with its broadest judgment to show exactly where the reviewer stands, or it will start out with a "teaser," a quote or detail from the book that seems striking enough to catch the readers' attention and "tease" them into reading at least the review, if not the book itself.

Then will come the explanation, details, and analyses. What was it that made the experience of reading the book so enjoyable? Why is the teaser a good sample of what the book has to offer? Reviews may focus on one aspect of a book, such as its characters, or they may glance at many aspects in turn. But they must maintain a balance between the personal interest of the reviewers' subjective comments and the objective analyses with which they try to convince us that they are sound judges of books whose opinions should be respected. And they must bring their comments and analyses together again in a final summary, judgment, or call to action: "Rush right out and buy this book; you won't be disappointed."

Reviewers, then, consider their audience (potential readers of the book being reviewed) and their purpose (telling their readers that the book exists and helping them decide whether or not they want to read it). They offer their own judgments, support them with relevant evidence, and draw all together to a logical conclusion.

English papers demand many of the same techniques as reviews and are often written in similar formats. They vary in scope and purpose, however, more than reviews do. The assignments in this book provide a range of possible types of papers.

Many of the assignments are quite narrowly defined. Their purpose is to make you look closely at some particular technique of the writer's—the role of the narrator in a story, for example, or the way a theme is carried through a tale. In this case your writing, too, must be tightly focused, your style almost wholly objective. Your first sentence will probably state your basic theme; and every sentence that follows, down to your final summation, will bear directly on that theme. The particular points you discuss, and the order in which you present them, may be suggested by the questions or instructions of the assignment itself. The evidence with which you support your answers will come from within the story. But the finished product will be very much your own: a tight, coherent piece of writing built on your own handling of the material given to you by the story.

Other assignments are broader, or ask that you define your own subject. (For example, "What do you think is the major theme of this story? How would you support your view?") Now your own judgments must be more boldly expressed. You must decide which aspects of the story should be

**FIGURE ONE**

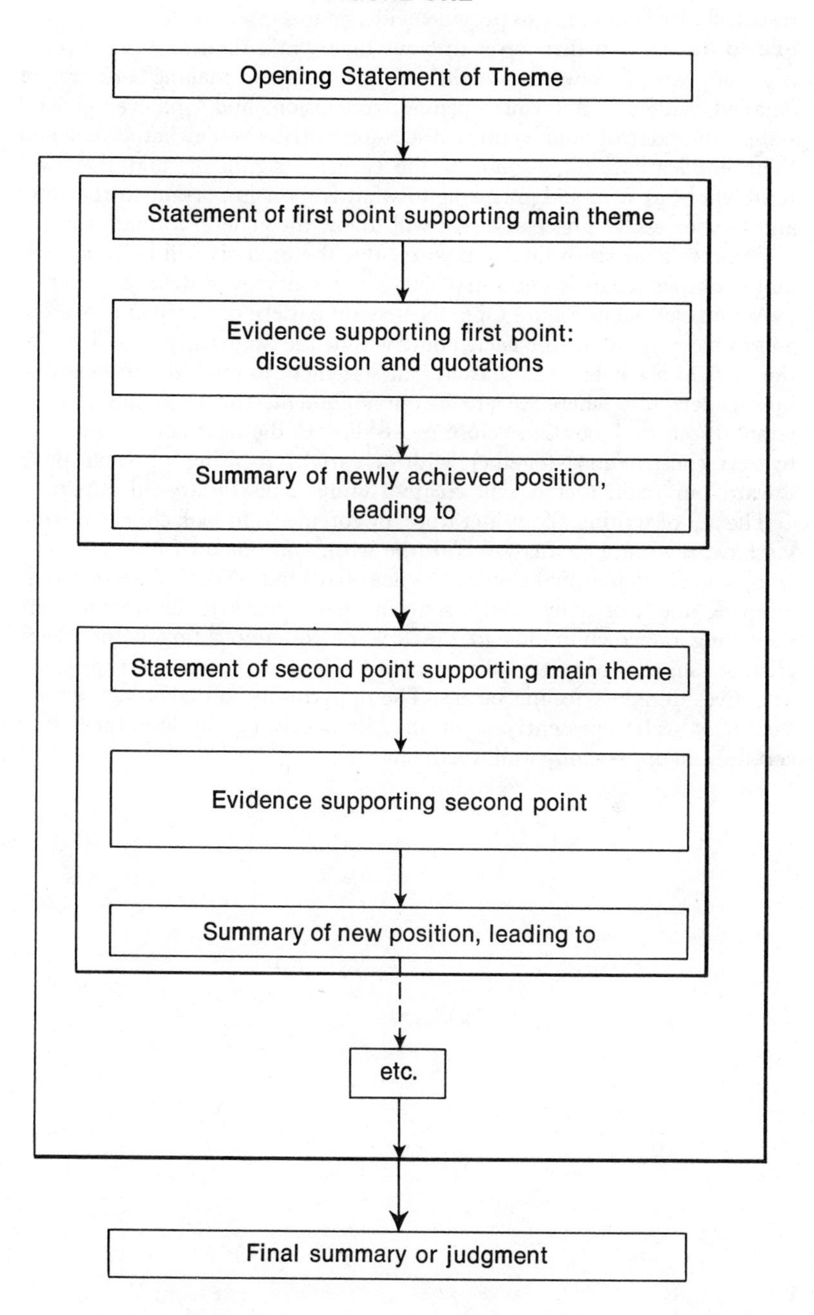

Opening Statement of Theme
Statement of first point supporting main theme
Evidence supporting first point: discussion and quotations
Summary of newly achieved position, leading to
Statement of second point supporting main theme
Evidence supporting second point
Summary of new position, leading to
etc.
Final summary or judgment

emphasized, and which are irrelevant to the question at hand. Your responsibility is not only to provide evidence to support a theory you were told to discuss, but first to set up your theory and then to support it.

Again, you will want a tightly focused paper, making full use of detailed evidence. But your opening, conclusion, and whatever general statements control your central discussion will be somewhat broader in their implications than those of the earlier assignment, and they will represent your own judgments as to what is most important to the story and to your essay. This essay, too, will follow the general format of initial response → analysis → final summary. But the analysis will be fuller and more complex than is necessary with a more narrowly defined paper.

As you can see in Figure One, the general pattern of statement → proof → summary is useful for each point within the analysis, just as it is for the essay as a whole. We use each new statement to remind ourselves and our readers just where we are in our argument, and each summary to establish our new position before proceeding to the next point. This step-by-step construction, together with a careful focusing of each point toward our main theme, will create a unified, tightly argued paper.

The act of writing about literature, by forcing us to look closely at what we have read and to analyze both the work and our own responses, can thus be seen as the final step in the act of reading. Now we are not only enjoying the words by which someone else speaks to us, we also are stretching our own minds to the task of communicating with others. Reading and writing, we take an active role and thus reassert ourselves as active, thinking, feeling beings. The opportunity to make that reassertion may well represent one of the deepest values of literature. It is certainly an opportunity well worth our taking.

# FICTION

# FICTION AS NARRATIVE

## 1 *The Art of Narration: Giving Meaning to Action*

There are two elements that are essential to a work of literature: someone to speak, and someone to listen. In the short story that follows, Saki's "The Story-Teller," the plot is shaped by two stories that are narrated *within* Saki's larger story by a woman and a man who have met by chance on a train. As a prologue to our study of literature, let us look then at this very short story that swiftly, skillfully, and humorously examines speakers and listeners and the ways in which they relate to each other. Note the comparative absence of physical action in Saki's tale—it is dialogue that dominates "The Story-Teller."

## SAKI (H. H. MUNRO) (1870–1916)

# *The Story-Teller*

It was a hot afternoon, and the railway carriage was correspondingly sultry, and the next stop was at Templecombe, nearly an hour ahead. The occupants of the carriage were a small girl, and a smaller girl, and a small boy. An aunt belonging to the children occupied one corner seat, and the further corner seat on the opposite side was occupied by a bachelor who was a stranger to their party, but the small girls and the small boy emphatically occupied the compartment. Both the aunt and the children were conversational in a limited, persistent way, reminding one of the attentions of a housefly that refused to be discouraged. Most of the aunt's remarks seemed to begin with "Don't," and nearly all of the children's remarks began with "Why?" The bachelor said nothing out loud.

"Don't, Cyril, don't," exclaimed the aunt, as the small boy began smacking the cushions of the seat, producing a cloud of dust at each blow.

"Come and look out of the window," she added.

The child moved reluctantly to the window. "Why are those sheep being driven out of that field?" he asked.

"I expect they are being driven to another field where there is more grass," said the aunt weakly.

"But there is lots of grass in that field," protested the boy; "there's nothing else but grass there. Aunt, there's lots of grass in that field."

"Perhaps the grass in the other field is better," suggested the aunt fatuously.

"Why is it better?" came the swift, inevitable question.

"Oh, look at those cows!" exclaimed the aunt. Nearly every field along the line had contained cows or bullocks, but she spoke as though she were drawing attention to a rarity.

"Why is the grass in the other field better?" persisted Cyril.

The frown on the bachelor's face was deepening to a scowl. He was a hard, unsympathetic man, the aunt decided in her mind. She was utterly unable to come to any satisfactory decision about the grass in the other field.

The smaller girl created a diversion by beginning to recite "On the Road to Mandalay." She only knew the first line, but she put her limited knowledge to the fullest possible use. She repeated the line over and over again in a dreamy but resolute and very audible voice; it seemed to the bachelor as though some one had had a bet with her that she could not repeat the line aloud two thousand times without stopping. Whoever it was who had made the wager was likely to lose his bet.

"Come over here and listen to a story," said the aunt, when the bachelor had looked twice at her and once at the communication cord.

The children moved listlessly towards the aunt's end of the carriage. Evidently her reputation as a story-teller did not rank high in their estimation.

In a low, confidential voice, interrupted at frequent intervals by loud, petulant questions from her listeners, she began an unenterprising and deplorably uninteresting story about a little girl who was good, and made friends with every one on account of her goodness, and was finally saved from a mad bull by a number of rescuers who admired her moral character.

"Wouldn't they have saved her if she hadn't been good?" demanded the bigger of the small girls. It was exactly the question that the bachelor had wanted to ask.

"Well, yes," admitted the aunt lamely, "but I don't think they would have run quite so fast to her help if they had not liked her so much."

"It's the stupidest story I've ever heard," said the bigger of the small girls, with immense conviction.

"I didn't listen after the first bit, it was so stupid," said Cyril.

The smaller girl made no actual comment on the story, but she had long ago recommenced a murmured repetition of her favourite line.

"You don't seem to be a success as a story-teller," said the bachelor suddenly from his corner.

The aunt bristled in instant defence of this unexpected attack.

"It's a very difficult thing to tell stories that children can both understand and appreciate," she said stiffly.

"I don't agree with you," said the bachelor.

"Perhaps *you* would like to tell them a story," was the aunt's retort.

"Tell us a story," demanded the bigger of the small girls.

"Once upon a time," began the bachelor, "there was a little girl called Bertha, who was extraordinarily good."

The children's momentarily-aroused interest began at once to flicker; all stories seemed dreadfully alike, no matter who told them.

"She did all that she was told, she was always truthful, she kept her clothes clean, ate milk puddings as though they were jam tarts, learned her lessons perfectly, and was polite in her manners."

"Was she pretty?" asked the bigger of the small girls.

"Not as pretty as any of you," said the bachelor, "but she was horribly good."

There was a wave of reaction in favour of the story; the word *horrible* in connection with goodness was a novelty that commended itself. It seemed to introduce a ring of truth that was absent from the aunt's tales of infant life.

"She was so good," continued the bachelor, "that she won several medals for goodness, which she always wore, pinned on to her dress. There was a medal for obedience, another medal for punctuality, and a third for good behaviour. They were large metal medals and they clicked against one another as she walked. No other child in the town where she lived had as many as three medals, so everybody knew that she must be an extra good child."

"Horribly good," quoted Cyril.

"Everybody talked about her goodness, and the Prince of the country got to hear about it, and he said that as she was so very good she might be allowed once a week to walk in his park, which was just outside the town. It was a beautiful park, and no children were ever allowed in it, so it was a great honour for Bertha to be allowed to go there."

"Were there any sheep in the park?" demanded Cyril.

"No," said the bachelor, "there were no sheep."

"Why weren't there any sheep?" came the inevitable question arising out of that answer.

The aunt permitted herself a smile, which might almost have been described as a grin.

"There were no sheep in the park," said the bachelor, "because the Prince's mother had once had a dream that her son would either be killed by a sheep or else by a clock falling on him. For that reason the Prince never kept a sheep in his park or a clock in his palace."

The aunt suppressed a gasp of admiration.

"Was the Prince killed by a sheep or by a clock?" asked Cyril.

"He is still alive so we can't tell whether the dream will come true," said the bachelor unconcernedly; "anyway, there were no sheep in the park, but there were lots of little pigs running all over the place."

"What colour were they?"

"Black with white faces, white with black spots, black all over, grey with white patches, and some were white all over."

The story-teller paused to let a full idea of the park's treasures sink into the children's imaginations; then he resumed:

"Bertha was rather sorry to find that there were no flowers in the park. She had promised her aunts, with tears in her eyes, that she would not pick any of the kind Prince's flowers, and she had meant to keep her promise, so of course it made her feel silly to find that there were no flowers to pick."

"Why weren't there any flowers?"

"Because the pigs had eaten them all," said the bachelor promptly. "The gardeners had told the Prince that you couldn't have pigs and flowers, so he decided to have pigs and no flowers."

There was a murmur of approval at the excellence of the Prince's decision; so many people would have decided the other way.

"There were lots of other delightful things in the park. There were ponds with gold and blue and green fish in them, and trees with beautiful parrots that said clever things at a moment's notice, and humming birds that hummed all the popular tunes of the day. Bertha walked up and down and enjoyed herself immensely, and thought to herself: 'If I were not so extraordinarily good I should not have been allowed to come into this beautiful park and enjoy all that there is to be seen in it,' and her three medals clinked against one another as she walked and helped to remind her how very good she really was. Just then an enormous wolf came prowling into the park to see if it could catch a fat little pig for its supper."

"What colour was it?" asked the children, amid an immediate quickening of interest.

"Mud-colour all over, with a black tongue and pale grey eyes that gleamed with unspeakable ferocity. The first thing that it saw in the park was Bertha; her pinafore was so spotlessly white and clean that it could be seen from a great distance. Bertha saw the wolf and saw that it was stealing towards her, and she began to wish that she had never been allowed to come into the park. She ran as hard as she could, and the wolf came after her with huge leaps and bounds. She managed to reach a shrubbery of myrtle bushes and she hid herself in one of the thickets of the bushes. The wolf came sniffing among the branches, its black tongue lolling out of its mouth and its pale grey eyes glaring with rage. Bertha was terribly frightened, and thought to herself: 'If I had not been so extraordinarily good I should have been safe in the town at this moment.' However, the scent of the myrtle was so strong that the wolf could not sniff out where Bertha was hiding, and the bushes were so thick that he might have hunted about in them for a long time without catching sight of her, so he thought he might as well go off and catch a little pig instead. Bertha was trembling very much at having the wolf prowling and sniffing so near her, and as she trembled the medal for obedience clinked against the medals for good conduct and punctuality. The wolf was just moving away when he heard the sound of the medals clinking and stopped to listen; they clinked again in a bush quite near him. He dashed into the bush, his pale grey eyes gleaming with ferocity and triumph, and dragged Bertha out and devoured her to the last morsel. All that were left of her were her shoes, bits of clothing, and the three medals for goodness."

"Were any of the little pigs killed?"

"No, they all escaped."

"The story began badly," said the smaller of the small girls, "but it had a beautiful ending."

"It is the most beautiful story that I ever heard," said the bigger of the small girls, with immense decision.

"It is the *only* beautiful story I have ever heard," said Cyril.

A dissentient opinion came from the aunt.

"A most improper story to tell to young children! You have undermined the effect of years of careful teaching."

"At any rate," said the bachelor, collecting his belongings preparatory to leaving the carriage, "I kept them quiet for ten minutes, which was more than you were able to do."

"Unhappy woman!" he observed to himself as he walked down the platform of Templecombe station; "for the next six months or so those children will assail her in public with demands for an improper story!"

## QUESTIONS

1. How do the tales of the two storytellers differ? What motives are behind each tale? How do the motives differ from each other?
2. Although Saki calls this story "The Story-Teller," *two* people within it tell stories. Which of the two do you think is the storyteller of the title? Why do you think so?
3. Saki's story, like the bachelor's, is meant to amuse its audience. Do you think that, like the aunt, Saki also hopes to teach his readers something? If you do, what do you think this something might be?

---

As Saki's tale suggests, fiction is the art of the storyteller. Not only are writers of fiction storytellers themselves, but within every story they create a new storyteller, the narrator of the tale. It is the narrator's voice we hear speaking as we read a novel or short story. The narrator introduces the tale to us, keeps us amused during its telling, and dismisses us at its end. The narrator describes scenes and characters, relates events, sets the tone of the tale, and supplies whatever meanings or explanations the author sees fit to provide.

Reader and story are thus brought together by the narrator. For this reason, the study of fiction usually begins with a study of types of narrators and narrations. Let us now look at a very brief story, a modern tale that, strongly reminiscent of folk tales, suggests some of the oldest traditions of storytelling. Notice the simplicity of the action and the sharp contrasts drawn among the few characters. Listen to the voice of the storyteller as he builds his tale.

## I. L. PERETZ (1851–1915)

# *If Not Higher*

Early every Friday morning, at the time of the Penitential Prayers, the Rabbi of Nemirov would vanish.

He was nowhere to be seen—neither in the synagogue nor in the two Houses of Study nor at a *minyan*. And he was certainly not at home. His door stood open; whoever wished could go in and out; no one would steal from the rabbi. But not a living creature was within.

Where could the rabbi be? Where should he be? In heaven, no doubt. A rabbi has plenty of business to take care of just before the Days of Awe. Jews, God bless them, need livelihood, peace, health, and good matches. They want to be pious and good, but our sins are so great, and Satan of the thousand eyes watches the whole earth from one end to the other. What he sees he reports; he denounces, informs. Who can help us if not the rabbi!

That's what the people thought.

But once a Litvak came, and he laughed. You know the Litvaks. They think little of the Holy Books but stuff themselves with Talmud and law. So this Litvak points to a passage in the *Gemarah* —it sticks in your eyes—where it is written that even Moses, our Teacher, did not ascend to heaven during his lifetime but remained suspended two and a half feet below. Go argue with a Litvak!

So where can the rabbi be?

"That's not my business," said the Litvak, shrugging. Yet all the while—what a Litvak can do!—he is scheming to find out.

That same night, right after the evening prayers, the Litvak steals into the rabbi's room, slides under the rabbi's bed, and waits. He'll watch all night and discover where the rabbi vanishes and what he does during the Pentitential Prayers.

Someone else might have got drowsy and fallen asleep, but a Litvak is never at a loss; he recites a whole tractate of the Talmud by heart.

At dawn he hears the call to prayers.

The rabbi has already been awake for a long time. The Litvak has heard him groaning for a whole hour.

Whoever has heard the Rabbi of Nemirov groan knows how much

sorrow for all Israel, how much suffering, lies in each groan. A man's heart might break, hearing it. But a Litvak is made of iron; he listens and remains where he is. The rabbi, long life to him, lies on the bed, and the Litvak under the bed.

Then the Litvak hears the beds in the house begin to creak; he hears people jumping out of their beds, mumbling a few Jewish words, pouring water on their fingernails, banging doors. Everyone has left. It is again quiet and dark; a bit of light from the moon shines through the shutters.

(Afterward the Litvak admitted that when he found himself alone with the rabbi a great fear took hold of him. Goose pimples spread across his skin, and the roots of his earlocks pricked him like needles. A trifle: to be alone with the rabbi at the time of the Penitential Prayers! But a Litvak is stubborn. So he quivered like a fish in water and remained where he was.)

Finally the rabbi, long life to him, arises. First he does what befits a Jew. Then he goes to the clothes closet and takes out a bundle of peasant clothes: linen trousers, high boots, a coat, a big felt hat, and a long wide leather belt studded with brass nails. The rabbi gets dressed. From his coat pocket dangles the end of a heavy peasant rope.

The rabbi goes out, and the Litvak follows him.

On the way the rabbi stops in the kitchen, bends down, takes an ax from under the bed, puts it in his belt, and leaves the house. The Litvak trembles but continues to follow.

The hushed dread of the Days of Awe hangs over the dark streets. Every once in a while a cry rises from some *minyan* reciting the Penitential Prayers, or from a sickbed. The rabbi hugs the sides of the streets, keeping to the shade of the houses. He glides from house to house, and the Litvak after him. The Litvak hears the sound of his heartbeats mingling with the sound of the rabbi's heavy steps. But he keeps on going and follows the rabbi to the outskirts of the town.

A small wood stands behind the town.

The rabbi, long life to him, enters the wood. He takes thirty or forty steps and stops by a small tree. The Litvak, overcome with amazement, watches the rabbi take the ax out of his belt and strike the tree. He hears the tree creak and fall. The rabbi chops the tree into logs and the logs into sticks. Then he makes a bundle of the wood and ties it with the rope in his pocket. He puts the bundle of wood on his back, shoves the ax back into his belt, and returns to the town.

He stops at a back street beside a small broken-down shack and knocks at the window.

"Who is there?" asks a frightened voice. The Litvak recognizes it as the voice of a sick Jewish woman.

"I," answers the rabbi in the accent of a peasant.

"Who is I?"

Again the rabbi answers in Russian. "Vassil."

"Who is Vassil, and what do you want?"

"I have wood to sell, very cheap." And, not waiting for the woman's reply, he goes into the house.

The Litvak steals in after him. In the gray light of early morning he sees a poor room with broken, miserable furnishings. A sick woman, wrapped in rags, lies on the bed. She complains bitterly, "Buy? How can I buy? Where will a poor widow get money?"

"I'll lend it to you," answers the supposed Vassil. "It's only six cents."

"And how will I ever pay you back?" said the poor woman, groaning.

"Foolish one," says the rabbi reproachfully. "See, you are a poor sick Jew, and I am ready to trust you with a little wood. I am sure you'll pay. While you, you have such a great and mighty God and you don't trust him for six cents."

"And who will kindle the fire?" said the widow. "Have I the strength to get up? My son is at work."

"I'll kindle the fire," answers the rabbi.

As the rabbi put the wood into the oven he recited, in a groan, the first portion of the Penitential Prayers.

As he kindled the fire and the wood burned brightly, he recited, a bit more joyously, the second portion of the Penitential Prayers. When the fire was set he recited the third portion, and then he shut the stove.

The Litvak who saw all this became a disciple of the rabbi.

And ever after, when another disciple tells how the Rabbi of Nemirov ascends to heaven at the time of the Penitential Prayers, the Litvak does not laugh. He only adds quietly, "If not higher."

---

"Early every Friday morning . . . the Rabbi of Nemirov would vanish." The statement is blunt and surprising. Rabbis do not usually vanish. We read on, expecting some explanation for the rabbi's behavior. But we find only more mystery. First the narrator tells us where the rabbi isn't. Then he tells us where the townspeople think he is; then he introduces the Litvak who argues that the rabbi can't be there, either. "So where can the rabbi be?" By the time the Litvak sets out to discover the answer, we may be pardoned for being curious ourselves. The narrator has certainly done his best to catch our interest and make us curious.

We notice, meanwhile, that the narrator is not unbiased. Although he takes no direct part in the tale, he does identify himself somewhat with the townspeople, slipping from the statement that "*they* want to be pious and good" to the recognition that "*our* sins are so great. . . . Who can help us if not the rabbi!" He pulls back in the next sentence: "That's what the people thought"; but the identification remains in our minds.

That "our" and "us", in fact, might almost include us, the readers. Certainly the narrator treats us as people who share with him knowledge of rabbis and religious matters and Litvaks—especially Litvaks. "You know the Litvaks . . . . Go argue with a Litvak!" The Litvak has an important role in the story. In contrast to the townspeople, who are ready to spread and believe miraculous rumors, the Litvak is a sceptic. He is a well-read man, so studied in law and religious books that he can keep himself awake all night by reciting Biblical commentaries; but he is a sceptic, nonetheless. It is precisely because he is sceptical, however, that the Litvak becomes curious enough to find out the real answer to the mystery; and it is he who has the final word at the end of the tale.

The Litvak is almost a type or symbol of the person with more knowledge than faith. The narrator, in fact, insists on seeing him as a type—"the Litvak" rather than a man with a name. At the same time, his prejudice characterizes the narrator. We feel that he'd like to see the Litvak shown up, the rabbi and townsfolk triumphant; we feel he himself has a stake in the outcome of the tale.

As the tale continues, the suspense builds. The narrator helps it along by his talk of "groaning" and "hushed dread," his relation of how even the Litvak suffers "goose pimples" and "a great fear," how he "trembles" and quivers "like a fish in water."

Finally, the mystery is revealed. Now, for the first time, we hear voices other than the narrator's. We hear the rabbi (the only words we do hear from him) and the sick woman (the only characterization we have of her; and it's enough). We see what the Litvak sees, hear what he hears; and we are not told what to think about any of it. The narrator, who heretofore has been generous with his comments, is now letting actions and characters speak for themselves.

Even the conclusion is restrained. We learn that "the Litvak who saw all this became a disciple of the rabbi," and we learn his new attitude toward the tale that the rabbi ascends to heaven on Fridays. Note that this is the Litvak's attitude; it is he, not the narrator, who says, "If not higher," and so makes the final judgment on the rabbi's actions. Note, too, that we are told nothing else of how the Litvak's life may have changed. What does becoming the rabbi's disciple mean for him? That we must figure out for ourselves.

The tale is rich in interpretive value. There is no need for the narrator to characterize the rabbi's actions; we can all supply our own view of their significance. Similarly, we can all tell what the Litvak means by his comment, "If not higher," though we might each phrase the meaning somewhat differently. At the start of the story, the Litvak was looking for something. At the end, he has found it, and we feel the value to him of the discovery. Yet even this is lightly handled, in keeping with the slightly humorous tone of the story. The narrator continues to focus on his one question, "Where does the rabbi go early Friday mornings?" It is the solution of that mystery, the resolution of that conflict between Litvak and the townspeople, that he presents as the "quietly" triumphant ending of his story. Anything else we choose to read into it is our own affair.

"If Not Higher," then, is a tale (almost a "tall tale") told by a narrator who takes no direct part in the action, but who has some concern that the story come out well. His voice is a speaking voice, sometimes humorous, sometimes emphatic, sometimes exasperated. Clearly, this is a practiced speaker, a man who enjoys telling stories. We sense his enjoyment in every line of the tale.

In contrast, look at this next story. It too is told by a narrator who remains outside the action; it too is a tale that lends itself to symbolic interpretation. But notice the differences in tone and technique. What attitudes does this narrator convey? How far does she go in interpreting actions and characters for us?

## SHIRLEY JACKSON (1919–1965)

# *The Lottery*

The morning of June 27th was clear and sunny, with the fresh warmth of a full-summer day; the flowers were blossoming profusely and the grass was richly green. The people of the village began to gather in the square, between the post office and the bank, around ten o'clock; in some towns there were so many people that the lottery took two days and had to be started on June 26th, but in this village, where there were only about three hundred people, the whole lottery took less than two hours, so it could begin at ten o'clock in the morning and still be through in time to allow the villagers to get home for noon dinner.

The children assembled first, of course. School was recently over for the summer, and the feeling of liberty sat uneasily on most of them; they tended to gather together quietly for a while before they broke into boisterous play, and their talk was still of the classroom and the teacher, of books and reprimands. Bobby Martin had already stuffed his pockets full of stones, and the other boys soon followed his example, selecting the smoothest and roundest stones; Bobby and Harry Jones and Dickie Delacroix—the villagers pronounced this name "Dellacroy"—eventually made a great pile of stones in one corner of the square and guarded it against the raids of the other boys. The girls stood aside, talking among themselves, looking over their shoulders at the boys, and the very small children rolled in the dust or clung to the hands of their older brothers or sisters.

Soon the men began to gather, surveying their own children, speaking of planting and rain, tractors and taxes. They stood together, away from the pile of stones in the corner, and their jokes were quiet and they smiled rather than laughed. The women, wearing faded house dresses and sweaters, came shortly after their menfolk. They greeted one another and exchanged bits of gossip as they went to join their husbands. Soon the women, standing by their husbands, began to call to their children, and the children came reluctantly, having to be called four or five times. Bobby Martin ducked under his mother's grasping hand and ran, laughing, back to the pile of stones. His father spoke up sharply, and Bobby came quickly and took his place between his father and his oldest brother.

The lottery was conducted—as were the square dances, the teen-age club, the Halloween program—by Mr. Summers, who had time and energy to devote to civic activities. He was a round-faced, jovial man and he ran the coal business, and people were sorry for him, because he had no children and his wife was a scold. When he arrived in the square, carrying the black wooden box, there was a murmur of conversation among the villagers, and he waved and called, "Little late today, folks." The postmaster, Mr. Graves, followed him, carrying a three-legged stool, and the stool was put in the center of the square and Mr. Summers set the black box down on it. The villagers kept their distance, leaving a space between themselves and the stool, and when Mr. Summers said, "Some of you fellows want to give me a hand?" there was a hesitation before two men, Mr. Martin and his oldest son, Baxter, came forward to hold the box steady on the stool while Mr. Summers stirred up the papers inside it.

The original paraphernalia for the lottery had been lost long ago, and the black box now resting on the stool had been put into use even before Old Man Warner, the oldest man in town, was born. Mr. Summers spoke frequently to the villagers about making a new box, but no one liked to upset even as much tradition as was represented by the black box. There was a story that the present box had been made with some pieces of the box that had preceded it, the one that had been constructed when the first people settled down to make a village here. Every year, after the lottery, Mr. Summers began talking again about a new box, but every year the subject was allowed to fade off without anything's being done. The black box grew shabbier each year; by now it was no longer completely black but splintered badly along one side to show the original wood color, and in some places faded or stained.

Mr. Martin and his oldest son, Baxter, held the black box securely on the stool until Mr. Summers had stirred the papers thoroughly with his hand. Because so much of the ritual had been forgotten or discarded, Mr. Summers had been successful in having slips of paper substituted for the chips of wood that had been used for generations. Chips of wood, Mr. Summers had argued, had been all very well when the village was tiny, but now that the population was more than three hundred and likely to keep on growing, it was necessary to use something that would fit more easily into the black box. The night before the lottery, Mr. Summers and Mr. Graves made up the slips of paper and put them in the box, and it was then taken to the safe of Mr. Summers' coal company and locked up until Mr. Summers was ready to take it to the square next morning. The rest of the year, the box was put away, sometimes one place, sometimes another; it had spent one year in Mr. Graves's barn and another year underfoot in the post office, and sometimes it was set on a shelf in the Martin grocery and left there.

There was a great deal of fussing to be done before Mr. Summers declared the lottery open. There were the lists to make up—of heads of families, heads of households in each family, members of each household in each family. There was the proper swearing-in of Mr. Summers by the postmaster, as the official of the lottery; at one time, some people remembered, there had been a recital of some sort, performed by the official of the lottery, a perfunctory, tuneless chant that had been rattled off duly each year; some people believed that the official of the lottery used to stand just so when he said or sang it, others believed that he was supposed to walk among the people, but years and years ago this part of the ritual had been allowed to lapse. There had been, also, a ritual salute, which the official of the lottery had had to use in addressing each person who came up to draw from the box, but this also had changed with time, until now it was felt necessary only for the official to speak to each person approaching. Mr. Summers was very good at all this; in his clean white shirt and blue jeans, with one hand resting carelessly on the black box. he seemed very proper and important as he talked interminably to Mr. Graves and the Martins.

Just as Mr. Summers finally left off talking and turned to the assembled villagers, Mrs. Hutchinson came hurriedly along the path to the square, her sweater thrown over her shoulders, and slid into place in the back of the crowd. "Clean forgot what day it was," she said to Mrs. Delacroix, who stood next to her, and they both laughed softly. "Thought my old man was out back stacking wood," Mrs. Hutchinson went on, "and then I looked out the window and the kids were gone, and then I remembered it was the twenty-seventh and came a-running." She dried her hands on her apron, and Mrs. Delacroix said, "You're in time, though. They're still talking away up there."

Mrs. Hutchinson craned her neck to see through the crowd and found her husband and children standing near the front. She tapped Mrs. Delacroix on the arm as a farewell and began to make her way through the crowd. The people separated good-humoredly to let her through; two or three people said, in voices just loud enough to be heard across the crowd, "Here comes your Missus, Hutchinson," and "Bill, she made it after all." Mrs. Hutchinson reached her husband, and Mr. Summers, who had been waiting, said cheerfully, "Thought we were going to have to get on without you, Tessie." Mrs. Hutchinson said, grinning, "Wouldn't have me leave m'dishes in the sink, now, would you, Joe?" and soft laughter ran through the crowd as the people stirred back into position after Mrs. Hutchinson's arrival.

"Well, now," Mr. Summers said soberly, "guess we better get started, get this over with, so's we can go back to work. Anybody ain't here?"

"Dunbar," several people said. "Dunbar, Dunbar."

Mr. Summers consulted his list. "Clyde Dunbar," he said. "That's right. He's broke his leg, hasn't he? Who's drawing for him?"

"Me, I guess," a woman said, and Mr. Summers turned to look at her. "Wife draws for her husband," Mrs. Summers said. "Don't you have a grown boy to do it for you, Janey?" Although Mr. Summers and everyone else in the village knew the answer perfectly well, it was the business of the official of the lottery to ask such questions formally. Mr. Summers waited with an expression of polite interest while Mrs. Dunbar answered.

"Horace's not but sixteen yet," Mrs. Dunbar said regretfully. "Guess I gotta fill in for the old man this year."

"Right," Mr. Summers said. He made a note on the list he was holding. Then he asked, "Watson boy drawing this year?"

A tall boy in the crowd raised his hand. "Here," he said. "I'm drawing for m'mother and me." He blinked his eyes nervously and ducked his head as several voices in the crowd said things like "Good fellow, Jack," and "Glad to see your mother's got a man to do it."

"Well," Mr. Summers said, "guess that's everyone. Old Man Warner make it?"

"Here," a voice said, and Mr. Summers nodded.

A sudden hush fell on the crowd as Mr. Summers cleared his throat and looked at the list. "All ready?" he called. "Now, I'll read the names—heads of families first—and the men come up and take a paper out of the box. Keep the paper folded in your hand without looking at it until everyone has had a turn. Everything clear?"

The people had done it so many times that they only half listened to the directions; most of them were quiet, wetting their lips, not looking around. Then Mr. Summers raised one hand high and said, "Adams." A man disengaged himself from the crowd and came forward. "Hi, Steve," Mr. Summers said, and Mr. Adams said, "Hi, Joe." They grinned at one another humorlessly and nervously. Then Mr. Adams reached into the black box and took out a folded paper. He held it firmly by one corner as he turned and went hastily back to his place in the crowd, where he stood a little apart from his family, not looking down at his hand.

"Allen," Mr. Summers said. "Anderson . . . Bentham."

"Seems like there's no time at all between lotteries any more," Mrs. Delacroix said to Mrs. Graves in the back row. "Seems like we got through with the last one only last week."

"Time sure goes fast," Mrs. Graves said.

"Clark . . . Delacroix."

"There goes my old man," Mrs. Delacroix said. She held her breath while her husband went forward.

"Dunbar," Mr. Summers said, and Mrs. Dunbar went steadily to the box while one of the women said, "Go on, Janey," and another said, "There she goes."

"We're next," Mrs. Graves said. She watched while Mr. Graves came around from the side of the box, greeted Mr. Summers gravely, and selected a slip of paper from the box. By now, all through the crowd there were men holding the small folded papers in their large hands, turning them over and over nervously. Mrs. Dunbar and her two sons stood together, Mrs. Dunbar holding the slip of paper.

"Harburt . . . Hutchinson."

"Get up there, Bill," Mrs. Hutchinson said, and the people near her laughed.

"Jones."

"They do say," Mr. Adams said to Old Man Warner, who stood next to him, "that over in the north village they're talking of giving up the lottery."

Old Man Warner snorted. "Pack of crazy fools," he said. "Listening to the young folks, nothing's good enough for *them*. Next thing you know, they'll be wanting to go back to living in caves, nobody work any more, live *that* way for a while. Used to be a saying about 'Lottery in June, corn be heavy soon.' First thing you know, we'd all be eating stewed chickweed and acorns. There's *always* been a lottery," he added petulantly. "Bad enough to see young Joe Summers up there joking with everybody."

"Some places have already quit lotteries," Mrs. Adams said.

"Nothing but trouble in *that*," Old Man Warner said stoutly. "Pack of young fools."

"Martin." And Bobby Martin watched his father go forward. "Overdyke . . . Percy."

"I wish they'd hurry," Mrs. Dunbar said to her older son. "I wish they'd hurry."

"They're almost through," her son said.

"You get ready to run tell Dad," Mrs. Dunbar said.

Mr. Summers called his own name and then stepped forward precisely and selected a slip from the box. Then he called, "Warner."

"Seventy-seventh year I been in the lottery," Old Man Warner said as he went through the crowd. "Seventy-seventh time."

"Watson." The tall boy came awkwardly through the crowd. Someone said, "Don't be nervous, Jack," and Mr. Summers said, "Take your time, son."

"Zanini."

After that, there was a long pause, a breathless pause, until Mr. Summers, holding his slip of paper in the air, said, "All right, fellows." For a minute, no one moved, and then all the slips of paper were opened. Suddenly, all the women began to speak at once, saying, "Who is it?" "Who's got it?" "Is it the Dunbars?" "Is it the Watsons?" Then the voices began to say, "It's Hutchinson. It's Bill," "Bill Hutchinson's got it."

"Go tell your father," Mrs. Dunbar said to her older son.

People began to look around to see the Hutchinsons. Bill Hutchinson was standing quiet, staring down at the paper in his hand. Suddenly, Tessie Hutchinson shouted to Mr. Summers, "You didn't give him time enough to take any paper he wanted. I saw you. It wasn't fair."

"Be a good sport, Tessie," Mrs. Delacroix called, and Mrs. Graves said, "All of us took the same chance."

"Shut up, Tessie," Bill Hutchinson said.

"Well, everyone," Mr. Summers said, "that was done pretty fast, and now we've got to be hurrying a little more to get done in time." He consulted his next list. "Bill," he said, "you draw for the Hutchinson family. You got any other households in the Hutchinsons?"

"There's Don and Eva," Mrs. Hutchinson yelled. "Make *them* take their chance!"

"Daughters draw with their husbands' families, Tessie," Mr. Summers said gently. "You know that as well as anyone else."

"It wasn't *fair,*" Tessie said.

"I guess not, Joe," Bill Hutchinson said regretfully. "My daughter draws with her husband's family, that's only fair. And I've got no other family except the kids."

"Then, as far as drawing for families is concerned, it's you," Mr. Summers said in explanation, "and as far as drawing for households is concerned, that's you, too. Right?"

"Right," Bill Hutchinson said.

"How many kids, Bill?" Mr. Summers asked formally.

"Three," Bill Hutchinson said. "There's Bill, Jr., and Nancy, and little Dave. And Tessie and me."

"All right, then," Mr. Summers said. "Harry, you got their tickets back?"

Mr. Graves nodded and held up the slips of paper. "Put them in the box, then," Mr. Summers directed. "Take Bill's and put it in."

"I think we ought to start over," Mrs. Hutchinson said, as quietly as she could. "I tell you it wasn't *fair*. You didn't give him time enough to choose. *Every*body saw that."

Mr. Graves had selected the five slips and put them in the box, and he dropped all the papers but those onto the ground, where the breeze caught them and lifted them off.

"Listen, everybody," Mrs. Hutchinson was saying to the people around her.

"Ready, Bill?" Mr. Summers asked, and Bill Hutchinson, with one quick glance around at his wife and children, nodded.

"Remember," Mr. Summers said, "take the slips and keep them folded until each person has taken one. Harry, you help little Dave." Mr. Graves took the hand of the little boy, who came willingly with him up to the box. "Take a paper out of the box, Davy," Mr. Summers said. Davy put his hand into the box and laughed. "Take just *one* paper," Mr. Summers said. "Harry, you hold it for him." Mr. Graves took the child's hand and removed the folded paper from the tight fist and held it while little Dave stood next to him and looked up at him wonderingly.

"Nancy next," Mr. Summers said. Nancy was twelve, and her school friends breathed heavily as she went forward, switching her skirt, and took a slip daintily from the box. "Bill, Jr.," Mr. Summers said, and Billy, his face red and his feet over-large, nearly knocked the box over as he got a paper out. "Tessie," Mr. Summers said. She hesitated for a minute, looking around defiantly, and then set her lips and went up to the box. She snatched a paper out and held it behind her.

"Bill," Mr. Summers said, and Bill Hutchinson reached into the box and felt around, bringing his hand out at last with the slip of paper in it.

The crowd was quiet. A girl whispered, "I hope it's not Nancy," and the sound of the whisper reached the edges of the crowd.

"It's not the way it used to be," Old Man Warner said clearly. "People ain't the way they used to be."

"All right," Mr. Summers said. "Open the papers. Harry, you open little Dave's."

Mr. Graves opened the slip of paper and there was a general sigh through the crowd as he held it up and everyone could see that it was blank. Nancy and Bill, Jr., opened theirs at the same time, and both beamed and laughed, turning around to the crowd and holding their slips of paper above their heads.

"Tessie," Mr. Summers said. There was a pause, and then Mr. Summers looked at Bill Hutchinson, and Bill unfolded his paper and showed it. It was blank.

"It's Tessie," Mr. Summers said, and his voice was hushed. "Show us her paper, Bill."

Bill Hutchinson went over to his wife and forced the slip of paper out of her hand. It had a black spot on it, the black spot Mr. Summers had made the night before with the heavy pencil in the coal-company office. Bill Hutchinson held it up, and there was a stir in the crowd.

"All right, folks," Mr. Summers said. "Let's finish quickly."

Although the villagers had forgotten the ritual and lost the original black box, they still remembered to use stones. The pile of stones the boys had made earlier was ready; there were stones on the ground with the blowing scraps of paper that had come out of the box. Mrs. Delacroix selected a stone so large she had to pick it up with both hands and turned to Mrs. Dunbar. "Come on," she said. "Hurry up."

Mrs. Dunbar had small stones in both hands, and she said, gasping for breath, "I can't run at all. You'll have to go ahead and I'll catch up with you."

The children had stones already, and someone gave little Davy Hutchinson a few pebbles.

Tessie Hutchinson was in the center of a cleared space by now, and she held her hands out desperately as the villagers moved in on her. "It isn't fair," she said. A stone hit her on the side of the head.

Old Man Warner was saying, "Come on, come on, everyone." Steve Adams was in the front of the crowd of villagers, with Mrs. Graves beside him.

"It isn't fair, it isn't right," Mrs. Hutchinson screamed, and then they were upon her.

---

"If Not Higher" concentrates on action: the rabbi's mysterious Friday morning activities, the Litvak's detective work. Characterization is less important. The rabbi, the Litvak, and the sick woman are types rather than fully characterized individuals; and, except for the Litvak's conversion (about which we are told very little) they do not change or develop during the story.

"The Lottery," too, centers on action and mystery almost to the exclusion of individual characterization. Of all the townspeople, Old Man Warner alone stands out as a distinguishable figure. Even he is a type: the "Old Man," fiercely proud of his past, dismissing as "young fools" all those who would change things. The rest are simply members of a small farming community, so like each other that one description often serves for all. Thus, "the children came reluctantly, having to be called four or five times," and "the people . . . only half listened to the directions; most of them were quiet, wetting their lips, not looking around." These descriptions, moreover, center on observable facts: the number of times the children have to be called, the posture and nervous motions of the villagers. We were given some inside knowledge of the Litvak's sensations, being told that "a great fear took hold of him," that he "hears the sound of his heartbeats mingling with the sound of the rabbi's heavy steps." We are told almost nothing about the villagers' thoughts and emotions that any reporter at the scene of the lottery could not have told us.

The narrator can tell us facts about the lottery, however, that only a very well informed reporter could supply. She can inform us that "the original paraphernalia for the lottery had been lost long ago," that the current black box (which "had been put into use even before Old Man Warner, the oldest man in the town, was born") is still used because "no one liked to upset even as much tradition as was represented by the black box." She knows what parts of the ritual have been lost and what parts are imperfectly remembered; and from time to time, she doles out some bit of this information as background to the unfolding ritual.

Does the narrator also know why the lottery was originally instituted, or what this group of villagers, who have lost so much of its history, think it accomplishes? If she does, she doesn't tell us. The narrator of "If Not Higher" made a great mystery of the rabbi's whereabouts by insisting that they were a great mystery and by depicting all the townspeople as being in a state of wonder and suspense. The narrator of "The Lottery" creates suspense by describing in a calm, matter-of-fact way the matter-of-fact behavior of a group of undemonstrative people. The people are engaged in some poorly defined event that seems to represent a mildly exciting once-a-year break in their normal routine. Therefore, our suspense comes largely from the fact that we feel ourselves to be the only people who don't know what's going on. (Until Tessie Hutchinson first cries "It wasn't fair," for instance, we don't even know whether the "winner" of this lottery is lucky or unlucky.) And so we keep waiting for the explanation, which never comes.

We are given some clues as to what's going on; but the author slips them in so quietly that we may not realize that they are clues until we read the story a second time. The "pile of stones," for instance, is introduced as though it were merely part of the children's "boisterous play": "Bobby and Harry Jones and Dickie Delacroix . . . eventually made a great pile of stones in one corner of the square and guarded it against the raids of the other boys." Not until the very end of the story do we find out the significance of those stones: "Although the villagers had forgotten the ritual and lost the original black box, they still remembered to use stones." But we still are not told what meaning—if any—the townsfolk find in their use.

We are not even told directly that Tessie is killed. We have to fill in that fact for ourselves, an act of participation that for some readers adds a last gruesome twist to the end of the story. Tessie's protests have warned us that the lottery ends badly for the chosen one. But many readers still have trouble at first realizing just how badly it does end, especially since the narrator's calm, reportorial voice never changes its tone, reporting as objectively as ever the women's conversation and the fact that "someone gave little Davy Hutchinson a few pebbles."

The almost casual acceptance by villagers and narrator alike of the stoning to death of a woman by her neighbors and family throws the full burden of reaction on us, while the "just plain folks" characterization of the villagers forces us to interpret the action in the broadest possible terms, asking not only, "Can these villagers really be doing this?" but also "Do people really act this way?"

All the unanswered questions rise at this point. Why are these people doing this thing? How do they justify it to themselves? All the action in "If Not Higher" was slightly unrealistic (one man hiding under a bed, another disguising himself), so the not-quite-realistic ending came as no shock. But the style of "The Lottery" has been unrelentingly realistic throughout, and its ending is a deliberate shock. All along we've been feeling, "Yes, a group of neighbors would behave as this group behaves. What a careful observer this writer is; what a fine eye for details of behavior she has." Now we want to say, "No; she's mistaken; they wouldn't do that." But the acceptance we've given the story so far, linked with our own knowledge of the ways people do behave toward each other, makes our rebellion all but impossible. We can dismiss the actual details; ritual stonings rarely occur in the twentieth century. But we cannot dismiss the symbolic import of the action, nor escape the grim vision of human nature that "The Lottery" 's action and narrator thrust upon us. Good humor and neighborliness are part of that vision; but what else is there? How would you personally interpret "The Lottery?"

## QUESTIONS FOR FURTHER THOUGHT

When we study literature, we first look at each story as an entity in itself, existing on its own terms. We enter the world of the story and speak of its characters and narrator as though they were living people. Eventually, however, we begin to wonder about the writers of the stories. Why did they choose to create these characters, to have them perform these actions, to tell their tales from this particular point of view?

We can never know exactly what writers had in mind when they were writing their stories. The process of writing is too complex, with too much of it hidden even from the writers themselves, to allow any sure or simple answers to that question. But we should examine our own ideas on the subject—our sense of what the writers seem to consider important and what values or feelings of ours they seem to be invoking; for our impression of the writers' values and intentions plays an important part in our response to their work.

If we look back at "The Lottery" and "If Not Higher," for instance, we notice that these stories project nearly opposite views of their characters. To define the contrast, we can ask such questions as, "What things seem most important to the characters in each story? What mood are we in at the end of the story?" Judging from this opposition, we can then ask what aspects of human life each author seems to consider important. We can ask, "To what feelings of mine does each story appeal? To what values?" And we can then try to decide whether our own values and feelings, and our sense of the authors', are as sharply opposed as our sense of the characters' values, or whether our interpretations of the authors' views and of the appeals their tales make to us do in fact share some common elements.

# 2 *The Omniscient Narrator*

"If Not Higher" and "The Lottery" are tales related by omniscient narrators. As the term implies, these narrators "know all" about the characters and events of which they tell. Somewhat distanced by their greater knowledge from action and actors alike, omniscient narrators project an air of authority over their material.

Their relation to the readers is a more variable matter. Peretz's narrator treats us familiarly, sharing occasional asides with us ("You know the Litvaks") or letting us into his characters' secrets. Jackson's narrator keeps us at the same distance that she keeps her material. (This type of narrator, who takes no sides, makes no interpretations, and lets us watch only the characters' public actions, rather than letting us into their private thoughts and feelings, is sometimes called an **objective narrator,** with the term **omniscient narrator** being reserved for those who do relate their characters' thoughts or interpret their actions for us.)

We begin this chapter with two more stories told by omniscient narrators. Read them through and read the questions that follow them. Then read them again with the questions in mind, seeing how the narrators' voices help shape your view of the stories' action and characters.

## NATHANIEL HAWTHORNE (1804–1864)

# *Young Goodman Brown*

Young Goodman Brown came forth at sunset, into the street of Salem village, but put his head back, after crossing the threshold, to exchange a parting kiss with his young wife. And Faith, as the wife was aptly named, thrust her own pretty head into the street, letting the wind play with the pink ribbons of her cap, while she called to Goodman Brown.

"Dearest heart," whispered she, softly and rather sadly, when her lips were close to his ear, "prithee, put off your journey until sunrise, and sleep in your own bed to-night. A lone woman is troubled with such dreams and such thoughts, that she's afeard of herself, sometimes. Pray, tarry with me this night, dear husband, of all nights in the year!"

"My love and my Faith," replied young Goodman Brown, "of all nights in the year, this one night must I tarry away from thee. My journey, as thou callest it, forth and back again, must needs be done 'twixt now and sunrise. What, my sweet, pretty wife, dost thou doubt me already, and we but three months married!"

"Then God bless you!" said Faith with the pink ribbons, "and may you find all well, when you come back."

"Amen!" cried Goodman Brown. "Say thy prayers, dear Faith, and go to bed at dusk, and no harm will come to thee."

So they parted; and the young man pursued his way, until, being about to turn the corner by the meeting-house, he looked back and saw the head of Faith still peeping after him, with a melancholy air, in spite of her pink ribbons.

"Poor little Faith!" thought he, for his heart smote him. "What a wretch am I, to leave her on such an errand! She talks of dreams, too. Methought, as she spoke, there was trouble in her face, as if a dream had warned her what work is to be done to-night. But no, no! 't would kill her to think it. Well; she's a blessed angel on earth; and after this one night, I'll cling to her skirts and follow her to Heaven."

With this excellent resolve for the future, Goodman Brown felt himself justified in making more haste on his present evil purpose. He had taken a dreary road, darkened by all the gloomiest trees of the forest, which barely stood aside to let the narrow path creep through, and closed immediately behind. It was all as lonely as could be; and there is this peculiarity in such a solitude, that the traveller knows not who may be concealed by the innumerable trunks and the thick boughs overhead; so that, with lonely footsteps, he may yet be passing through an unseen multitude.

"There may be a devilish Indian behind every tree," said Goodman Brown to himself; and he glanced fearfully behind him, as he added, "What if the devil himself should be at my very elbow!"

His head being turned back, he passed a crook of the road, and looking forward again, beheld the figure of a man, in grave and decent attire, seated at the foot of an old tree. He arose at Goodman Brown's approach, and walked onward, side by side with him.

"You are late, Goodman Brown," said he. "The clock of the Old South was striking, as I came through Boston; and that is full fifteen minutes agone."

"Faith kept me back awhile," replied the young man, with a tremor in his voice, caused by the sudden appearance of his companion, though not wholly unexpected.

It was now deep dusk in the forest, and deepest in that part of it where these two were journeying. As nearly as could be discerned, the second traveller was about fifty years old, apparently in the same rank of life as Goodman Brown, and bearing a considerable resemblance to him, though perhaps more in expression than features. Still, they might have been taken for father and son. And yet, though the elder person was as simply clad as the younger, and as simple in manner too, he had an indescribable air of one who knew the world, and would not have felt abashed at the governor's dinner-table, or in King William's court, were it possible that his affairs should call him thither. But the only thing about him that could be fixed upon as remarkable, was his staff, which bore the likeness of a great black snake, so curiously wrought, that it might almost be seen to twist and wriggle itself like a living serpent. This, of course, must have been an ocular deception, assisted by the uncertain light.

"Come, Goodman Brown!" cried his fellow-traveller, "this is a dull pace for the beginning of a journey. Take my staff, if you are so soon weary."

"Friend," said the other, exchanging his slow pace for a full stop, "having kept covenant by meeting thee here, it is my purpose now to return whence I came. I have scruples, touching the matter thou wot'st of."

"Sayest thou so?" replied he of the serpent, smiling apart. "Let us walk on, nevertheless, reasoning as we go, and if I convince thee not, thou shalt turn back. We are but a little way in the forest, yet."

"Too far, too far!" exclaimed the goodman, unconsciously resuming his walk. "My father never went into the woods on such an errand, nor his father before him. We have been a race of honest men and good Christians, since the days of the martyrs. And shall I be the first of the name of Brown that ever took this path and kept—"

"Such company, thou wouldst say," observed the elder person, interrupting his pause. "Well said, Goodman Brown! I have been as well acquainted with your family as with ever a one among the Puritans; and that's no trifle to say. I helped your grandfather, the constable, when he lashed the Quaker woman so smartly through the streets of Salem. And it was I that brought your father a pitch-pine knot, kindled at my own hearth, to set fire to an Indian village, in King Philip's war. They were my good friends, both; and many a pleasant walk have we had along this path, and returned merrily after midnight. I would fain be friends with you, for their sake."

"If it be as thou sayest," replied Goodman Brown, "I marvel they never spoke of these matters. Or, verily, I marvel not, seeing that the least rumor of the sort would have driven them from New England. We are a people of prayer, and good works to boot, and abide no such wickedness."

"Wickedness or not," said the traveller with twisted staff, "I have a very general acquaintance here in New England. The deacons of many a church have drunk the communion wine with me; the selectmen, of divers towns, make me their chairman; and a majority of the Great and General Court are firm supporters of my interest. The governor and I, too—but these are state secrets."

"Can this be so!" cried Goodman Brown, with a stare of amazement at his undisturbed companion. "Howbeit, I have nothing to do with the governor and council; they have their own ways, and are no rule for a simple husbandman like me. But, were I to go on with thee, how should I meet the eye of that good old man, our minister, at Salem village? Oh, his voice would make me tremble, both Sabbath-day and lecture-day!"

Thus far, the elder traveller had listened with due gravity, but now burst into a fit of irrepressible mirth, shaking himself so violently, that his snakelike staff actually seemed to wriggle in sympathy.

"Ha! ha! ha!" shouted he, again and again; then composing himself, "Well, go on, Goodman Brown, go on; but, prithee, don't kill me with laughing!"

"Well, then, to end the matter at once," said Goodman Brown, considerably nettled, "there is my wife, Faith. It would break her dear little heart; and I'd rather break my own!"

"Nay, if that be the case," answered the other, "e'en go thy ways, Goodman Brown. I would not, for twenty old women like the one hobbling before us, that Faith should come to any harm."

As he spoke, he pointed his staff at a female figure on the path, in whom Goodman Brown recognized a very pious and exemplary dame, who had taught him his catechism in youth, and was still his moral and spiritual adviser, jointly with the minister and Deacon Gookin.

"A marvel, truly, that Goody Cloyse should be so far in the

wilderness, at nightfall!" said he. "But, with your leave, friend, I shall take a cut through the woods, until we have left this Christian woman behind. Being a stranger to you, she might ask whom I was consorting with, and whither I was going."

"Be it so," said his fellow-traveller. "Betake you to the woods, and let me keep the path."

Accordingly, the young man turned aside, but took care to watch his companion, who advanced softly along the road, until he had come within a staff's length of the old dame. She, meanwhile, was making the best of her way, with singular speed for so aged a woman, and mumbling some indistinct words, a prayer, doubtless, as she went. The traveller put forth his staff, and touched her withered neck with what seemed the serpent's tail.

"The devil!" screamed the pious old lady.

"Then Goody Cloyse knows her old friend?" observed the traveller, confronting her, and leaning on his writhing stick.

"Ah, forsooth, and is it your worship, indeed?" cried the good dame. "Yea, truly is it, and in the very image of my old gossip, Goodman Brown, the grandfather of the silly fellow that now is. But, would your worship believe it? my broomstick hath strangely disappeared, stolen, as I suspect, by that unhanged witch, Goody Cory, and that, too, when I was all anointed with the juice of smallage and cinque-foil and wolf's-bane—"

"Mingled with fine wheat and the fat of a new-born babe," said the shape of old Goodman Brown.

"Ah, your worship knows the recipe," cried the old lady, cackling aloud. "So, as I was saying, being all ready for the meeting, and no horse to ride on, I made up my mind to foot it; for they tell me there is a nice young man to be taken into communion to-night. But now your good worship will lend me your arm, and we shall be there in a twinkling."

"That can hardly be," answered her friend. "I may not spare you my arm, Goody Cloyse, but here is my staff, if you will."

So saying, he threw it down at her feet, where, perhaps, it assumed life, being one of the rods which its owner had formerly lent to the Egyptian Magi. Of this fact, however, Goodman Brown could not take cognizance. He had cast up his eyes in astonishment, and looking down again, beheld neither Goody Cloyse nor the serpentine staff, but his fellow-traveller alone, who waited for him as calmly as if nothing had happened.

"That old woman taught me my catechism!" said the young man; and there was a world of meaning in this simple comment.

They continued to walk onward, while the elder traveller exhorted his companion to make good speed and persevere in the path, discoursing so aptly, that his arguments seemed rather to spring up in the bosom of his auditor, than to be suggested by himself. As they went he plucked a branch of maple, to serve for a walking-stick, and began to strip it of the twigs and little boughs, which were wet with evening dew. The moment his fingers touched them, they became strangely withered and dried up, as with a week's sunshine. Thus the pair proceeded, at a good free pace, until suddenly, in a gloomy hollow of the road, Goodman Brown sat himself down on the stump of a tree, and refused to go any farther.

"Friend," said he, stubbornly, "my mind is made up. Not another step will I budge on this errand. What if a wretched old woman do choose to go to the devil, when I thought she was going to Heaven! Is that any reason why I should quit my dear Faith, and go after her?"

"You will think better of this by and by," said his acquaintance, composedly. "Sit here and rest yourself awhile; and when you feel like moving again, there is my staff to help you along."

Without more words, he threw his companion the maple stick, and was as speedily out of sight as if he had vanished into the deepening gloom. The young man sat a few moments by the roadside, applauding himself greatly, and thinking with how clear a conscience he should meet the minister, in his morning walk, nor shrink from the eye of good old Deacon Gookin. And what calm sleep would be his, that very night, which was to have been spent so wickedly, but purely and sweetly now, in the arms of Faith! Amidst these pleasant and praiseworthy meditations, Goodman Brown heard the tramp of horses along the road, and deemed it advisable to conceal himself within the verge of the forest, conscious of the guilty purpose that had brought him thither, though now so happily turned from it.

On came the hoof-tramps and the voices of the riders, two grave old voices, conversing soberly as they drew near. These mingled sounds appeared to pass along the road, within a few yards of the young man's hiding-place; but owing, doubtless, to the depth of the gloom, at that particular spot, neither the travellers nor their steeds were visible. Though their figures brushed the small boughs by the wayside, it could not be seen that they intercepted, even for a moment, the faint gleam from the strip of bright sky, athwart which they must have passed. Goodman Brown alternately crouched and stood on tiptoe, pulling aside the branches, and thrusting forth his head as far as he durst, without discerning so much as a shadow. It vexed him the more, because he could have sworn, were such a thing possible, that he recognized the voices of the minister and Deacon Gookin, jogging along quietly, as they were wont to do, when bound to some ordination or ecclesiastical council. While yet within hearing, one of the riders stopped to pluck a switch.

"Of the two, reverend Sir," said the voice like the deacon's, "I had rather miss an ordination dinner than to-night's meeting. They tell me that some of our community are to be here from Falmouth and beyond, and others from Connecticut and Rhode Island; besides several of the Indian powwows, who, after their fashion, know almost as much deviltry as the best of us. Moreover, there is a goodly young woman to be taken into communion."

"Mighty well, Deacon Gookin!" replied the solemn old tones of the minister. "Spur up, or we shall be late. Nothing can be done, you know, until I get on the ground."

The hoofs clattered again, and the voices, talking so strangely in the empty air, passed on through the forest, where no church had ever been gathered, nor solitary Christian prayed. Whither, then, could these holy men be journeying, so deep into the heathen wilderness? Young Goodman Brown caught hold of a tree, for support, being ready to sink down on the ground, faint and overburthened with the heavy sickness of his heart. He looked up to the sky, doubting whether there really was a Heaven above him. Yet, there was the blue arch, and the stars brightening in it.

"With Heaven above, and Faith below, I will yet stand firm against the devil!" cried Goodman Brown.

While he still gazed upward, into the deep arch of the firmament, and had lifted his hands to pray, a cloud, though no wind was stirring, hurried across the zenith, and hid the brightening stars. The blue sky was still visible, except directly overhead, where this black mass of cloud was sweeping swiftly northward. Aloft in the air, as if from the depths of the cloud, came a confused and doubtful sound of voices. Once, the listener fancied that he could distinguish the accents of town's-people of his own, men and women, both pious and ungodly, many of whom he had met at the communion-table, and had seen others rioting at the tavern. The next moment, so indistinct were the sounds, he doubted whether he had heard aught but the murmur of the old forest, whispering without a wind. Then came a stronger swell of those familiar tones, heard daily in the sunshine, at Salem village, but never, until now, from a cloud at night. There was one voice, of a young woman, uttering lamentations, yet with an uncertain sorrow, and entreating for some favor, which, perhaps, it would grieve her to obtain. And all the unseen multitude, both saints and sinners, seemed to encourage her onward.

"Faith!" shouted Goodman Brown, in a voice of agony and desperation; and the echoes of the forest mocked him, crying—"Faith! Faith!" as if bewildered wretches were seeking her, all through the wilderness.

The cry of grief, rage, and terror was yet piercing the night, when the unhappy husband held his breath for a response. There was a scream, drowned immediately in a louder murmur of voices fading into far-off laughter, as the dark cloud swept away, leaving the clear and silent sky above Goodman Brown. But something fluttered lightly down through the air, and caught on the branch of a tree. The young man seized it and beheld a pink ribbon.

"My Faith is gone!" cried he, after one stupefied moment. "There is no good on earth, and sin is but a name. Come, devil! for to thee is this world given."

And maddened with despair, so that he laughed loud and long, did Goodman Brown grasp his staff and set forth again, at such a rate, that he seemed to fly along the forest path, rather than to walk or run. The road grew wilder and drearier, and more faintly traced, and vanished at length, leaving him in the heart of the dark wilderness, still rushing onward, with the instinct that guides mortal man to evil. The whole forest was peopled with frightful sounds; the creaking of the trees, the howling of wild beasts, and the yell of Indians; while, sometimes, the wind tolled like a distant church bell, and sometimes gave a broad roar around the traveller, as if all Nature were laughing him to scorn. But he was himself the chief horror of the scene, and shrank not from its other horrors.

"Ha! ha! ha!" roared Goodman Brown, when the wind laughed at him. "Let us hear which will laugh loudest! Think not to frighten me with your deviltry! Come witch, come wizard, come Indian powwow, come devil himself! and here comes Goodman Brown. You may as well fear him as he fear you!"

In truth, all through the haunted forest, there could be nothing more frightful than the figure of Goodman Brown. On he flew, among the black pines, brandishing his staff with frenzied gestures, now giving vent to an inspiration of horrid blasphemy, and now shouting forth such laughter, as set all the echoes of the forest laughing like demons around him. The fiend in his own shape is less hideous, than when he rages in the breast of man. Thus sped the demoniac on his course, until, quivering among the trees, he saw a red light before him, as when the felled trunks and branches of a clearing have been set on fire, and throw up their lurid blaze against the sky, at the hour of midnight. He paused, in a lull of the tempest that had driven him onward, and heard the swell of what seemed a hymn, rolling solemnly from a distance, with the weight of many voices. He knew the tune. It was a familiar one in the choir of the village meeting-house. The verse died heavily away, and was lengthened by a chorus, not of human voices, but of all the sounds of the benighted wilderness, pealing in awful harmony together. Goodman Brown cried out; and his cry was lost to his own ear, by its unison with the cry of the desert.

In the interval of silence, he stole forward, until the light glared full upon his eyes. At one extremity of an open space, hemmed in by the dark wall of the forest, arose a rock, bearing some rude, natural resemblance either to an altar or a pulpit, and surrounded by four blazing pines, their tops aflame, their stems untouched, like candles at an evening meeting. The mass of foliage, that had overgrown the summit of the rock, was all on fire, blazing high into the night, and fitfully illuminating the whole field. Each pendent twig and leafy festoon was in a blaze. As the red light arose and fell, a numerous congregation alternately shone forth, then disappeared in shadow, and again grew, as it were, out of the darkness, peopling the heart of the solitary woods at once.

"A grave and dark-clad company!" quoth Goodman Brown.

In truth, they were such. Among them, quivering to-and-fro, between gloom and splendor, appeared faces that would be seen, next day, at the council-board of the province, and others which, Sabbath after Sabbath, looked devoutly heavenward, and benignantly over the crowded pews, from the holiest pulpits in the land. Some affirm that the lady of the governor was there. At least, there were high dames well known to her, and wives of honored husbands, and widows a great multitude, and ancient maidens, all of excellent repute, and fair young girls, who trembled lest their mothers should espy them. Either the sudden gleams of light, flashing over the obscure field, bedazzled Goodman Brown, or he recognized a score of the church members of Salem village, famous for their especial sanctity. Good old Deacon Gookin had arrived, and waited at the skirts of that venerable saint, his reverend pastor. But, irreverently consorting with these grave, reputable, and pious people, these elders of the church, these chaste dames and dewy virgins, there were men of dissolute lives and women of spotted fame, wretches given over to all mean and filthy vice, and suspected even of horrid crimes. It was strange to see, that the good shrank not from the wicked, nor were the sinners abashed by the saints. Scattered, also, among their pale-faced enemies, were the Indian priests, or powwows, who had often scared their native forest with more hideous incantations than any known to English witchcraft.

"But, where is Faith?" thought Goodman Brown; and, as hope came into his heart, he trembled.

Another verse of the hymn arose, a slow and mournful strain, such as the pious love, but joined to words which expressed all that our nature can conceive of sin, and darkly hinted at far more. Unfathomable to mere mortals is the lore of fiends. Verse after verse was sung, and still the chorus of the desert swelled between, like the deepest tone of a mighty organ. And, with the final peal of that dreadful anthem, there came a sound, as if the roaring wind, the rushing streams, the howling beasts, and every other voice of the unconverted wilderness were mingling and according with the voice of guilty man, in homage to the prince of all. The four blazing pines threw up a loftier flame, and obscurely discovered shapes and visages of horror on the smoke-wreaths, above the impious assembly. At the same moment, the fire on the rock shot redly forth, and formed a glowing arch above its base, where now appeared a figure. With reverence be it spoken, the apparition bore no slight similitude, both in garb and manner, to some grave divine of the New England churches.

"Bring forth the converts!" cried a voice, that echoed through the field and rolled into the forest.

At the word, Goodman Brown stepped forth from the shadow of the trees, and approached the congregation, with whom he felt a loathful brotherhood, by the sympathy of all that was wicked in his heart. He could have well-nigh sworn, that the shape of his own dead father beckoned him to advance, looking downward from a smoke-wreath, while a woman, with dim features of despair, threw out her hand to warn him back. Was it his mother? But he had no power to retreat one step, nor to resist, even in thought, when the minister and good old Deacon Gookin seized his arms, and led him to the blazing rock. Thither came also the slender form of a veiled female, led between Goody Cloyse, that pious teacher of the catechism, and Martha Carrier, who had received the devil's promise to be queen of hell. A rampant hag was she! And there stood the proselytes, beneath the canopy of fire.

"Welcome, my children," said the dark figure, "to the communion of your race! Ye have found, thus young, your nature and your destiny. My children, look behind you!"

They turned; and flashing forth, as it were, in a sheet of flame, the fiend-worshippers were seen; the smile of welcome gleamed darkly on every visage.

"There," resumed the sable form, "are all whom ye have reverenced from youth. Ye deemed them holier than yourselves, and shrank from your own sin, contrasting it with their lives of righteousness and prayerful aspirations heavenward. Yet, here are they all, in my worshipping assembly! This night it shall be granted you to know their secret deeds; how hoary-bearded elders of the church have whispered wanton words to the young maids of their households; how many a woman, eager for widow's weeds, has given her husband a drink at bedtime, and let him sleep his last sleep in her bosom; how beardless youths have made haste to inherit their father's wealth; and how fair damsels—blush not, sweet ones!—have dug little graves in the garden, and bidden me, the sole guest, to an infant's funeral. By the sympathy of your human hearts for sin, ye shall scent out all the places—whether in church, bed-chamber, street, field, or forest—where crime has been committed, and shall exult to behold the whole earth one stain of guilt, one mighty blood-spot. Far more than this! It shall be yours to penetrate, in every bosom, the deep mystery of sin, the fountain of all wicked arts, and which inexhaustibly supplies more evil impulses than human power—than my power, at its utmost!—can make manifest in deeds. And now, my children, look upon each other."

They did so; and, by the blaze of the hell-kindled torches, the wretched man beheld his Faith, and the wife her husband, trembling before that unhallowed altar.

"Lo! there ye stand, my children," said the figure, in a deep and solemn tone, almost sad, with its despairing awfulness, as if his once angelic nature could yet mourn for our miserable race. "Depending upon one another's hearts, ye had still hoped that virtue were not all a dream! Now are ye undeceived!—Evil is the nature of mankind. Evil must be your only happiness. Welcome, again, my children, to the communion of your race!"

"Welcome!" repeated the fiend-worshippers, in one cry of despair and triumph.

And there they stood, the only pair, as it seemed, who were yet hesitating on the verge of wickedness, in this dark world. A basin was hollowed, naturally, in the rock. Did it contain water, reddened by the lurid light? or was it blood? or, perchance, a liquid flame? Herein did the Shape of Evil dip his hand, and prepare to lay the mark of baptism upon their foreheads, that they might be partakers of the mystery of sin, more conscious of the secret guilt of others, both in deed and thought, than they could now be of their own. The husband cast one look at his pale wife, and Faith at him. What polluted wretches would the next glance show them to each other, shuddering alike at what they disclosed and what they saw!

"Faith! Faith!" cried the husband. "Look up to Heaven, and resist the Wicked One!"

Whether Faith obeyed, he knew not. Hardly had he spoken, when he found himself amid calm night and solitude, listening to a roar of the wind, which died heavily away through the forest. He staggered against the rock, and felt it chill and damp, while a hanging twig, that had been all on fire, besprinkled his cheek with the coldest dew.

The next morning, young Goodman Brown came slowly into the street of Salem village staring around him like a bewildered man. The good old minister was taking a walk along the grave-yard, to get an appetite for breakfast and meditate his sermon, and bestowed a blessing, as he passed, on Goodman Brown. He shrank from the venerable saint, as if to avoid an anathema. Old Deacon Gookin was at domestic worship, and the holy words of his prayer were heard through the open window. "What God doth the wizard pray to?" quoth Goodman Brown. Goody Cloyse, that excellent old Christian, stood in the early sunshine, at her own lattice, catechising a little girl, who had brought her a pint of morning's milk. Goodman Brown snatched away the child, as from the grasp of the fiend himself. Turning the corner by the meeting-house, he spied the head of Faith, with the pink ribbons, gazing anxiously forth, and bursting into such joy at sight of him that she skipt along the street, and almost kissed her husband before the whole village. But Goodman Brown looked sternly and sadly into her face, and passed on without a greeting.

Had Goodman Brown fallen asleep in the forest, and only dreamed a wild dream of a witch-meeting?

Be it so, if you will. But, alas! it was a dream of evil omen for young Goodman Brown. A stern, a sad, a darkly meditative, a distrustful, if not a desperate man did he become, from the night of that fearful dream. On the Sabbath day, when the congregation were singing a holy psalm, he could not listen, because an anthem of sin rushed loudly upon his ear, and drowned all the blessed strain. When the minister spoke from the pulpit, with power and fervid eloquence, and with his hand on the open Bible, of the sacred truths of our religion, and of saint-like lives and triumphant deaths, and of future bliss or misery unutterable, then did Goodman Brown turn pale, dreading lest the roof should thunder down upon the gray blasphemer and his hearers. Often, awaking suddenly at midnight, he shrank from the bosom of Faith, and at morning or eventide, when the family knelt down at prayer, he scowled, and muttered to himself, and gazed sternly at his wife, and turned away. And when he had lived long, and was borne to his grave, a hoary corpse, followed by Faith, an aged woman, and children and grandchildren, a goodly procession, besides neighbors not a few, they carved no hopeful verse upon his tombstone; for his dying hour was gloom.

## QUESTIONS

1. Though the main action of "Young Goodman Brown" takes place in the woods outside Salem, the story begins and ends inside Salem village. What is gained by organizing the story in this way?
2. In the opening scene, we might particularly notice the introduction of Goodman Brown's wife, Faith. Why does the narrator say she is "aptly named"? How do Faith's talk of her "fears" and Brown's emphasis on the newness of their marriage set the stage for the story that follows?
3. How does the narrator's description of the forest and of Brown's thoughts (pp. 41–42) establish the atmosphere of the story? How would you describe the atmosphere thus created?
4. On pp. 42–46, what sort of argument is going on within young Goodman Brown, or between him and his companion? What people does he encounter

during this time? What significance do these people have for him? What do you notice about the order in which he meets them?

5. On p. 47, the narrator remarks that "the fiend in his own shape is less hideous, than when he rages in the breast of man." Why does he place such a comment at this point in the story? What development of action or characterization does it emphasize?
6. In the scene on pp. 49–50, with what is the fiend tempting Faith and Goodman Brown? What sort of faith is he trying to get them to renounce? With what would he replace it?
7. On p. 51, the narrator enters the story again to raise (and dismiss) the question of whether Brown's experience had been real or only a dream. Why should he raise the question if he does not intend to answer it? What is your reaction to the passage? (Had the notion that Brown's adventures might be a dream already entered your mind? If it had, what clues had put it there?)
8. Another way to read the story, already hinted at by the narrator in the opening scene, is as an **allegory,** a tale that has not only a literal but also a metaphorical meaning. The central figure in an allegory most often represents any or every person, while the action usually presents a struggle between good and evil forces anxious to save or damn the central character. Since the battleground for this struggle is the mind or soul of the disputed character, this type of allegory is called a **psychomachia,** or soul-battle. How would you interpret "Young Goodman Brown" as allegory? If it is a battle, who has won?
9. Is there one reading of the story—either as the tale of an actual happening, as a tale of a dream, or as an allegory—that seems most satisfactory to you? (If so, what reading is it, and why? If not, what is there in the story that keeps you from deciding?) How does the narrator seem to regard the story? How do his attempts to interpret it and the choice of interpretations he forces on you affect your response to the tale?

## ALBERT CAMUS (1913–1960)

# *The Guest*

The schoolmaster was watching the two men climb toward him. One was on horseback, the other on foot. They had not yet tackled the abrupt rise leading to the schoolhouse built on the hillside. They were toiling onward, making slow progress in the snow, among the stones, on the vast expanse of the high, deserted plateau. From time to time the horse stumbled. He could not be heard yet but the breath issuing from his nostrils could be seen. The schoolmaster calculated that it would take them a half hour to get onto the hill. It was cold; he went back into the school to get a sweater.

He crossed the empty, frigid classroom. On the blackboard the four rivers of France, drawn with four different colored chalks, had been flowing toward their estuaries for the past three days. Snow had suddenly fallen in mid-October after eight months of drought without the transition of rain, and the twenty pupils, more or less, who lived in the villages scattered over the plateau had stopped coming. With fair weather they would return. Daru now heated only the single room that was his lodging, adjoining the classroom. One of the windows faced, like the classroom windows, the south. On that side the school was a few kilometers from the point where the plateau began to slope toward the south. In clear weather the purple mass of the mountain range where the gap opened onto the desert could be seen.

Somewhat warmed, Daru returned to the window from which he had first noticed the two men. They were no longer visible. Hence they must have tackled the rise. The sky was not so dark, for the snow had stopped falling during the night. The morning had dawned with a dirty light which had scarcely become brighter as the ceiling of clouds lifted. At two in the afternoon it seemed as if the day were merely beginning. But still this was better than those three days when the thick snow was falling amidst unbroken darkness with little gusts of wind that rattled the double door of the classroom. Then Daru had spent long hours in his room, leaving it only to go to the shed and feed the chickens or get some coal. Fortunately the delivery truck from Tadjid, the nearest village to the north, had brought his supplies two days before the blizzard. It would return in forty-eight hours.

Besides, he had enough to resist a siege, for the little room was cluttered with bags of wheat that the administration had left as a supply to distribute to those of his pupils whose families had suffered from the drought. Actually they had all been victims because they were all poor. Every day Daru would distribute a ration to the children. They had missed it, he knew, during these bad days. Possibly one of the fathers or big brothers would come this afternoon and he could supply them with grain. It was just a matter of carrying them over to the next harvest. Now shiploads of wheat were arriving from France and the worst was over. But it would be hard to forget that poverty, that army of ragged ghosts wandering in the sunlight, the plateaus burned to a cinder month after month, the earth shriveled up little by little, literally scorched, every stone bursting into dust under one's foot. The sheep had died then by thousands, and even a few men, here and there, sometimes without anyone's knowing.

In contrast with such poverty, he who lived almost like a monk, in his remote schoolhouse, had felt like a lord with his whitewashed walls, his narrow couch, his unpainted shelves, his well, and his weekly provisioning with water and food. And suddenly this snow, without warning, without the foretaste of rain. This is the way the region was, cruel to live in, even without men, who didn't help matters either. But Daru had been born here. Everywhere else, he felt exiled.

He went out and stepped forward on the terrace in front of the schoolhouse. The two men were now halfway up the slope. He recognized the horseman to be Balducci, the old gendarme he had known for a long time. Balducci was holding at the end of a rope an Arab walking behind him with hands bound and head lowered. The gendarme waved a greeting to which Daru did not reply, lost as he was in contemplation of the Arab dressed in a faded blue *jellaba,* his feet in sandals but covered with socks of heavy raw wool, his head crowned with a narrow, short *chèche.* Balducci was holding back his horse in order not to hurt the Arab, and the group was advancing slowly.

Within earshot, Balducci shouted, "One hour to do the three kilometers from El Ameur!" Daru did not answer. Short and square in his thick sweater, he watched them climb. Not once had the Arab raised his head. "Hello," said Daru when they got up onto the terrace. "Come in and warm up." Balducci painfully got down from his horse without letting go of the rope. He smiled at the schoolmaster from under his bristling mustache. His little dark eyes, deep-set under a tanned forehead, and his mouth surrounded with wrinkles made him look attentive and studious. Daru took the bridle, led the horse to the shed, and came back to the two men who were now waiting for him in the school. He led them into his room. "I am going to heat up the classroom," he said. "We'll be more comfortable there."

When he entered the room again, Balducci was on the couch. He had undone the rope tying him to the Arab, who had squatted near the stove. His hands still bound, the *chèche* pushed back on his head, the Arab was looking toward the window. At first Daru noticed only his huge lips, fat, smooth, almost Negroid; yet his nose was straight, his eyes dark and full of fever. The *chèche* uncovered an obstinate forehead and, under the weathered skin now rather discolored by the cold, the whole face had a restless and rebellious look. "Go into the other room," said the schoolmaster, "and I'll make you some mint tea." "Thanks," Balducci said. "What a chore! How I long for retirement." And addressing his prisoner in Arabic, he said, "Come on, you." The Arab got up and, slowly, holding his bound wrists in front of him, went into the classroom.

With the tea, Daru brought a chair. But Balducci was already sitting in state at the nearest pupil's desk, and the Arab had squatted against the teacher's platform facing the stove, which stood between the desk and the window. When he held out the glass of tea to the prisoner, Daru hesitated at the sight of his bound hands. "He might perhaps be untied." "Sure," said Balducci. "That was for the trip." He started to get to his feet. But Daru, setting the glass on the floor, had knelt beside the Arab. Without saying anything, the Arab watched him with his feverish eyes. Once his hands were free, he rubbed his swollen wrists against each other, took the glass of tea and sucked up the burning liquid in swift little sips.

"Good," said Daru. "And where are you headed?"

Balducci withdrew his mustache from the tea. "Here, son."

"Odd pupils! And you're spending the night?"

"No. I'm going back to El Ameur. And you will deliver this fellow to Tinguit. He is expected at police headquarters."

Balducci was looking at Daru with a friendly little smile.

"What's this story?" asked the schoolmaster. "Are you pulling my leg?"

"No, son. Those are the orders."

"The orders? I'm not . . ." Daru hesitated, not wanting to hurt the old Corsican. "I mean, that's not my job."

"What! What's the meaning of that? In wartime people do all kinds of jobs."

"Then I'll wait for the declaration of war!"

Balducci nodded. "O.K. But the orders exist and they concern you too. Things are bubbling, it appears. There is talk of a forthcoming revolt. We are mobilized, in a way."

Daru still had his obstinate look.

"Listen, son," Balducci said. "I like you and you've got to understand. There's only a dozen of us at El Ameur to patrol the whole territory of a small department and I must be back in a hurry. He couldn't be kept there. His village was beginning to stir; they wanted to take him back. You must take him to Tinguit tomorrow before the day is over. Twenty kilometers shouldn't faze a husky fellow like you. After that, all will be over. You'll come back to your pupils and your comfortable life."

Behind the wall the horse could be heard snorting and pawing the earth. Daru was looking out the window. Decidedly the weather was clearing and the light was increasing over the snowy plateau. When all the snow was melted, the sun would take over again and once more would burn the fields of stone. For days still, the unchanging sky would shed its dry light on the solitary expanse where nothing had any connection with man.

"After all," he said, turning around toward Balducci, "what did he do?" And, before the gendarme had opened his mouth, he asked, "Does he speak French?"

"No, not a word. We had been looking for him for a month, but they were hiding him. He killed his cousin."

"Is he against us?"

"I don't think so. But you can never be sure."

"Why did he kill?"

"A family squabble, I think. One owed grain to the other, it seems. It's not at all clear. In short, he killed his cousin with a billhook. You know, like a sheep, *kreezk!*"

Balducci made the gesture of drawing a blade across his throat, and the Arab, his attention attracted, watched him with a sort of anxiety. Daru felt a sudden wrath against the man, against all men with their rotten spite, their tireless hates, their blood lust.

But the kettle was singing on the stove. He served Balducci more tea, hesitated, then served the Arab again, who drank avidly a second time. His raised arms made the *jellaba* fall open, and the schoolmaster saw his thin, muscular chest.

"Thanks, son," Balducci said. "And now I'm off."

He got up and went toward the Arab, taking a small rope from his pocket.

"What are you doing?" Daru asked dryly.

Balducci, disconcerted, showed him the rope.

"Don't bother."

The old gendarme hesitated. "It's up to you. Of course, you are armed?"

"I have my shotgun."

"Where?"

"In the trunk."

"You ought to have it near your bed."

"Why? I have nothing to fear."

"You're crazy, son. If there's an uprising, no one is safe; we're all in the same boat."

"I'll defend myself. I'll have time to see them coming."

Balducci began to laugh, then suddenly the mustache covered the white teeth. "You'll have time? O.K. That's just what I was saying. You always have been a little cracked. That's why I like you; my son was like that."

At the same time he took out his revolver and put it on the desk. "Keep it; I don't need two weapons from here to El Ameur."

The revolver shone against the black paint of the table. When the gendarme turned toward him, the schoolmaster caught his smell of leather and horseflesh.

"Listen, Balducci," Daru said suddenly, "all this disgusts me, beginning with your fellow here. But I won't hand him over. Fight, yes, if I have to. But not that."

The old gendarme stood in front of him and looked at him severely.

"You're being a fool," he said slowly. "I don't like it either. You don't get used to putting a rope on a man even after years of it, and you're even ashamed—yes, ashamed. But you can't let them have their way."

"I won't hand him over," Daru said again.

"It's an order, son, and I repeat it."

"That's right. Repeat to them what I've said to you: I won't hand him over."

Balducci made a visible effort to reflect. He looked at the Arab and at Daru. At last he decided.

"No, I won't tell them anything. If you want to drop us, go ahead; I'll not denounce you. I have an order to deliver the prisoner and I'm doing so. And now you'll just sign this paper for me."

"There's no need. I'll not deny that you left him with me."

"Don't be mean with me. I know you'll tell the truth. You're from around these parts and you are a man. But you must sign; that's the rule."

Daru opened his drawer, took out a little square bottle of purple ink, the red wooden penholder with the "sergeant-major" pen he used for models of handwriting, and signed. The gendarme carefully folded the paper and put it into his wallet. Then he moved toward the door.

"I'll see you off," Daru said.

"No," said Balducci. "There's no use being polite. You insulted me."

He looked at the Arab, motionless in the same spot, sniffed peevishly, and turned away toward the door. "Good-by, son," he said. The door slammed behind him. His footsteps were muffled by the snow. The horse stirred on the other side of the wall and several chickens fluttered in fright. A moment later Balducci reappeared outside the window leading the horse by the bridle. He walked toward the little rise without turning around and disappeared from sight with the horse following him.

Daru walked back toward the prisoner, who, without stirring, never took his eyes off him. "Wait," the schoolmaster said in Arabic and went toward the bedroom. As he was going through the door, he had a second thought, went to the desk, took the revolver, and stuck it in his pocket. Then, without looking back, he went into his room.

For some time he lay on his couch watching the sky gradually close over, listening to the silence. It was this silence that had seemed painful to him during the first days here, after the war. He had requested a post in the little town at the base of the foothills separating the upper plateaus from the desert. There rocky walls, green and black to the north, pink and lavender to the south, marked the frontier of eternal summer. He had been named to a post farther north, on the plateau itself. In the beginning, the solitude and the silence had been hard for him on these wastelands peopled only by stones. Occasionally, furrows suggested cultivation, but they had been dug to uncover a certain kind of stone good for building. The only plowing here was to harvest rocks. Elsewhere a thin layer of soil accumulated in the hollows would be scraped out to enrich paltry village gardens. This is the way it was: bare rock covered three quarters of the region. Towns sprang up, flourished, then disappeared; men came by, loved one another or fought bitterly, then died. No one in this desert, neither he nor his guest, mattered. And yet, outside this desert neither of them, Daru knew, could have really lived.

When he got up, no noise came from the classroom. He was amazed at the unmixed joy he derived from the mere thought that the Arab might have fled and that he would be alone with no decision to make. But the prisoner was there. He had merely stretched out between the stove and the desk and he was staring at the ceiling. In that position, his thick lips were particularly noticeable, giving him a pouting look. "Come," said Daru. The Arab got up and followed him. In the bedroom the schoolmaster pointed to a chair near the table under the window. The Arab sat down without ceasing to watch Daru.

"Are you hungry?"

"Yes," the prisoner said.

Daru set the table for two. He took flour and oil, shaped a cake in a frying pan, and lighted the little stove that functioned on bottled gas. While the cake was cooking, he went out to the shed to get cheese, eggs, dates, and condensed milk. When the cake was done he set it on the window sill to cool, heated some condensed milk diluted with water, and beat up the eggs into an omelette. In one of his motions he bumped into the revolver stuck in his right pocket. He set the bowl down, went into the classroom, and put the revolver in his desk drawer. When he came back to the room, night was falling. He put on the light and served the Arab. "Eat," he said. The Arab took a piece of the cake, lifted it eagerly to his mouth, and stopped short.

"And you?" he asked.

"After you. I'll eat too."

The thick lips opened slightly. The Arab hesitated, then bit into the cake determinedly.

The meal over, the Arab looked at the schoolmaster. "Are you the judge?"

"No, I'm simply keeping you until tomorrow."

"Why do you eat with me?"

"I'm hungry."

The Arab fell silent. Daru got up and went out. He brought back a camp cot from the shed and set it up between the table and the stove, at right angles to his own bed. From a large suitcase which, upright in a corner, served as a shelf for papers, he took two blankets and arranged them on the cot. Then he stopped, felt useless, and sat down on his bed. There was nothing more to do or to get ready. He had to look at this man. He looked at him therefore, trying to imagine his face bursting with rage. He couldn't do so. He could see nothing but the dark yet shining eyes and the animal mouth.

"Why did you kill him?" he asked in a voice whose hostile tone surprised him.

The Arab looked away. "He ran away. I ran after him."

He raised his eyes to Daru again and they were full of a sort of woeful interrogation. "Now what will they do to me?"

"Are you afraid?"

The Arab stiffened, turning his eyes away.

"Are you sorry?"

The Arab stared at him openmouthed. Obviously he did not understand. Daru's annoyance was growing. At the same time he felt awkward and self-conscious with his big body wedged between the two beds.

"Lie down there," he said impatiently. "That's your bed."

The Arab didn't move. He cried out, "Tell me!"

The schoolmaster looked at him.

"Is the gendarme coming back tomorrow?"

"I don't know."

"Are you coming with us?"

"I don't know. Why?"

The prisoner got up and stretched out on top of the blankets, his feet toward the window. The light from the electric bulb shone straight into his eyes and he closed them at once.

"Why?" Daru repeated, standing beside the bed.

The Arab opened his eyes under the blinding light and looked at him, trying not to blink. "Come with us," he said.

In the middle of the night, Daru was still not asleep. He had gone to bed after undressing completely; he generally slept naked. But when he suddenly realized that he had nothing on, he wondered. He felt vulnerable and the temptation came to him to put his clothes back on. Then he shrugged his shoulders; after all, he wasn't a child and, if it came to that, he could break his adversary in two. From his bed, he could observe him lying on his back, still motionless, his eyes closed under the harsh light. When Daru turned out the light, the darkness seemed to congeal all of a sudden. Little by little, the night came back to life in the window where the starless sky was stirring gently. The schoolmaster soon made out the body lying at his feet. The Arab was still motionless but his eyes seemed open. A faint wind was prowling about the schoolhouse. Perhaps it would drive away the clouds and the sun would reappear.

During the night the wind increased. The hens fluttered a little and then were silent. The Arab turned over on his side with his back to Daru, who thought he heard him moan. Then he listened for his guest's breathing, which had become heavier and more regular. He listened to that breathing so close to him and mused without being able to go to sleep. In the room where he had been sleeping alone for a year, this presence bothered him. But it bothered him also because it imposed on him a sort of brotherhood he refused to accept in the present circumstances; yet he was familiar with it. Men who share the same rooms, soldiers or prisoners, develop a strange alliance as if, having cast off their armor with their clothing, they fraternized every evening, over and above their differences, in the ancient community of dream and fatigue. But Daru shook himself; he didn't like such musings, and it was essential for him to sleep.

A little later, however, when the Arab stirred slightly, the schoolmaster was still not asleep. When the prisoner made a second move, he stiffened, on the alert. The Arab was lifting himself slowly on his arms with almost the motion of a sleepwalker. Seated upright in bed, he waited motionless without turning his head toward Daru, as if he were listening attentively. Daru did not stir; it had just occurred to him that the revolver was still in the drawer of his desk. It was better to act at once. Yet he continued to observe the prisoner, who, with the same slithery motion, put his feet on the ground, waited again, then stood up slowly. Daru was about to call out to him when the Arab began to walk, in a quite natural but extraordinarily silent way. He was heading toward the door at the end of the room that opened into the shed. He lifted the latch with precaution and went out, pushing the door behind him but without shutting it.

Daru had not stirred. "He is running away," he merely thought. "Good riddance!" Yet he listened attentively. The hens were not fluttering; the guest must be on the plateau. A faint sound of water reached him, and he didn't know what it was until the Arab again stood framed in the doorway, closed the door carefully, and came back to bed without a sound. Then Daru turned his back on him and fell asleep. Still later he seemed, from the depths of his sleep, to hear furtive steps around the schoolhouse. "I'm dreaming! I'm dreaming!" he repeated to himself. And he went on sleeping.

When he awoke, the sky was clear; the loose window let in a cold, pure air. The Arab was asleep, hunched up under the blankets now, his mouth open, utterly relaxed. But when Daru shook him he started dreadfully, staring at Daru with wild eyes as if he had never seen him and with such a frightened expression that the schoolmaster stepped back. "Don't be afraid. It is I. You must eat." The Arab nodded his head and said yes. Calm had returned to his face, but his expression was vacant and listless.

The coffee was ready. They drank it seated together on the cot as they munched their pieces of the cake. Then Daru led the Arab under the shed and showed him the faucet where he washed. He went back into the room, folded the blankets on the cot, made his own bed, and put the room in order. Then he went through the classroom and out onto the terrace. The sun was already rising in the blue sky; a soft, bright light enveloped the deserted plateau. On the ridge the snow was melting in spots. The stones were about to reappear. Crouched on the edge of the plateau, the schoolmaster looked at the deserted expanse. He thought of Balducci. He had hurt him, for he had sent him off as though he didn't want to be associated with him. He could still hear the gendarme's farewell and, without knowing why, he felt strangely empty and vulnerable.

At that moment, from the other side of the schoolhouse, the prisoner coughed. Daru listened to him almost despite himself and then, furious, threw a pebble that whistled through the air before sinking into the snow. That man's stupid crime revolted him, but to hand him over was contrary to honor; just thinking of it made him boil with humiliation. He simultaneously cursed his own people who had sent him this Arab and the Arab who had dared to kill and not managed to get away. Daru got up, walked in a circle on the terrace, waited motionless, and then went back into the schoolhouse.

The Arab, leaning over the cement floor of the shed, was washing his teeth with two fingers. Daru looked at him and said, "Come." He went back into the room ahead of the prisoner. He slipped a hunting jacket on over his sweater and put on walking shoes. Standing, he waited until the Arab had put on his *chèche* and sandals. They went into the classroom, and the schoolmaster pointed to the exit saying, "Go ahead." The fellow didn't budge. "I'm coming," said Daru. The Arab went out. Daru went back into the room and made a package with pieces of rusk, dates, and sugar in it. In the classroom, before going out, he hesitated a second in front of his desk, then crossed the threshold and locked the door. "That's the way," he said. He started toward the east, followed by the prisoner. But a short distance from the schoolhouse he thought he heard a slight sound behind him. He retraced his steps and examined the surroundings of the house; there was no one there. The Arab watched him without seeming to understand. "Come on," said Daru.

They walked for an hour and rested beside a sharp needle of limestone. The snow was melting faster and faster and the sun was drinking up the puddles just as quickly, rapidly cleaning the plateau, which gradually dried and vibrated like the air itself. When they resumed walking, the ground rang under their feet. From time to time a bird rent the space in front of them with a joyful cry. Daru felt a sort of rapture before the vast familiar expanse, now almost entirely yellow under its dome of blue sky. They walked an hour more, descending toward the south. They reached a sort of flattened elevation made up of crumbly rocks. From there on, the plateau sloped down—eastward toward a low plain on which could be made out a few spindly trees, and to the south toward outcroppings of rock that gave the landscape a chaotic look.

Daru surveyed the two directions. Not a man could be seen. He turned toward the Arab, who was looking at him blankly. Daru offered the package to him. "Take it," he said. "There are dates, bread, and sugar. You can hold out for two days. Here are a thousand francs too."

The Arab took the package and the money but kept his full hands at chest level as if he didn't know what to do with what was being given him.

"Now look," the schoolmaster said as he pointed in the direction of the east, "there's the way to Tinguit. You have a two-hour walk. At Tinguit are the administration and the police. They are expecting you."

The Arab looked toward the east, still holding the package and the money against his chest. Daru took his elbow and turned him rather roughly toward the south. At the foot of the elevation on which they stood could be seen a faint path. "That's the trail across the plateau. In a day's walk from here you'll find pasturelands and the first nomads. They'll take you in and shelter you according to their law."

The Arab had now turned toward Daru, and a sort of panic was visible in his expression. "Listen," he said.

Daru shook his head. "No, be quiet. Now I'm leaving you." He turned his back on him, took two long steps in the direction of the school, looked hesitantly at the motionless Arab, and started off again. For a few minutes he heard nothing but his own step resounding on the cold ground, and he did not turn his head. A moment later, however, he turned around. The Arab was still there on the edge of the hill, his arms hanging now, and he was looking at the schoolmaster. Daru felt something rise in his throat. But he swore with impatience, waved vaguely, and started off again. He had already gone a distance when he again stopped and looked. There was no longer anyone on the hill.

Daru hesitated. The sun was now rather high in the sky and beginning to beat down on his head. The schoolmaster retraced his steps, at first somewhat uncertainly, then with decision. When he reached the little hill, he was bathed in sweat. He climbed it as fast as he could and stopped, out of breath, on the top. The rock fields to the south stood out sharply against the blue sky, but on the plain to the east a steamy heat was rising. And in that slight haze, Daru, with heavy heart, made out the Arab walking slowly on the road to prison.

A little later, standing before the window of the classroom, the schoolmaster was watching the clear light bathing the whole surface of the plateau. Behind him on the blackboard, among the winding French rivers, sprawled the clumsily chalked up words he had just read: "You handed over our brother. You will pay for this." Daru looked at the sky, the plateau, and, beyond, the invisible lands stretching all the way to the sea. In this vast landscape he had loved so much, he was alone.

## QUESTIONS

1. How does Camus's narrator introduce us to the setting and main character of his tale?
2. Note especially paragraph two on page 54. Why is it important that we are given this description of Daru's life and feelings now, before the action of the tale begins? How do Daru's feelings for the land affect your feelings for him?
3. How does Daru react to the approach of his visitors? to their arrival? to Balducci's revelation that the Arab is a murderer and that Daru is to deliver him to the police in the next village? Does Daru's refusal of Balducci's demand come as a surprise to you, or does it seem to fit what you've been learning about his character?
4. Notice, too, Balducci's reaction to Daru's refusal. What feelings toward the two men does it inspire in you? What bonds and conflicts between them does it suggest?
5. Reread paragraph five on page 58 and the last paragraph on page 60. What do these passages contribute to your understanding of Daru and his actions?
6. What sort of interaction is taking place between Daru and the Arab in the scenes on pages 59–60 and 63? What does the Arab want from Daru? How is Daru responding?
7. Note the reemphasis on Daru's love for the land at the end of the story. How have Daru's feelings about the land been used to characterize him throughout the story? What are they emphasizing now?
8. How does Daru's isolation now differ from the isolation that was just ending as the story began? To what extent do you feel this new isolation has been forced upon Daru? How much of it seems to be of his own making?

## QUESTIONS FOR FURTHER THOUGHT

1. "Young Goodman Brown" and "The Guest" can both be considered tales in which the action centers upon the hero's refusal to make a commitment, and his subsequent isolation and alienation from his fellow humans. How would you discuss this theme in the two stories? What aspects of action or characterization would you want to emphasize? What comparisons or contrasts would you want to make?
2. As we have already noted, the setting of each of these tales is endowed with symbolic value by its narrator. How would you plan an essay on the function of the setting in either or both of these tales, considering not only the meanings attached to the setting, but also the relation among setting, character, and action?

The next story, "The Open Boat," is based on a shipwreck actually suffered by its author, Stephen Crane. Yet Crane does not tell the tale in his own voice; rather, he tells it through an omniscient narrator. Read the story; then compose and answer your own set of questions to determine the narrator's tone of voice, his major concerns, and his attitudes towards the people and events he tells of. Finally, decide what Crane has gained by his choice of narrator.

## STEPHEN CRANE (1871–1900)

# *The Open Boat*

*A Tale intended to be after the fact. Being the Experience of Four Men from the Sunk Steamer "Commodore"*

### I

None of them knew the color of the sky. Their eyes glanced level, and were fastened upon the waves that swept toward them. These waves were of the hue of slate, save for the tops, which were of foaming white, and all of the men knew the colors of the sea. The horizon narrowed and widened, and dipped and rose, and at all times its edge was jagged with waves that seemed thrust up in points like rocks.

Many a man ought to have a bath-tub larger than the boat which here rode upon the sea. These waves were most wrongfully and barbarously abrupt and tall, and each froth-top was a problem in small boat navigation.

The cook squatted in the bottom and looked with both eyes at the six inches of gunwale which separated him from the ocean. His sleeves were rolled over his fat forearms, and the two flaps of his unbuttoned vest dangled as he bent to bail out the boat. Often he said: "Gawd! That was a narrow clip." As he remarked it he invariably gazed eastward over the broken sea.

The oiler, steering with one of the two oars in the boat, sometimes raised himself suddenly to keep clear of water that swirled in over the stern. It was a thin little oar and it seemed often ready to snap.

The correspondent, pulling at the other oar, watched the waves and wondered why he was there.

The injured captain, lying in the bow, was at this time buried in that profound dejection and indifference which comes, temporarily at least, to even the bravest and most enduring when, willy nilly, the firm fails, the army loses, the ship goes down. The mind of the master of a vessel is rooted deep in the timbers of her, though he command for a day or a decade, and this captain had on him the stern impression of a scene in the grays of dawn of seven turned faces, and later a stump of a top-mast with a white ball on it that slashed to and fro at the waves, went low and lower, and down. Thereafter there was something strange in his voice. Although steady, it was deep with mourning, and of a quality beyond oration or tears.

"Keep 'er a little more south, Billie," said he.

" 'A little more south,' sir," said the oiler in the stern.

A seat in this boat was not unlike a seat upon a bucking broncho, and, by the same token, a broncho is not much smaller. The craft pranced and reared, and plunged like an animal. As each wave came, and she rose for it, she seemed like a horse making at a fence outrageously high. The manner of her scramble over these walls of water is a mystic thing, and, moreover, at the top of them were ordinarily these problems in white water, the foam racing down from the summit of each wave, requiring a new leap, and a leap from the air. Then, after scornfully bumping a crest, she would slide, and race, and splash down a long incline, and arrive bobbing and nodding in front of the next menance.

A singular disadvantage of the sea lies in the fact that after successfully surmounting one wave you discover that there is another behind it just as important and just as nervously anxious to do something effective in the way of swamping boats. In a ten-foot dingey one can get an idea of the resources of the sea in the line of waves that is not probable to the average experience which is never at sea in a dingey. As each slaty wall of water approached, it shut all else from the view of the men in the boat, and it was not difficult to imagine that this particular wave was the final outburst of the ocean, the last effort of the grim water. There was a terrible grace in the move of the waves, and they came in silence, save for the snarling of the crests.

In the wan light, the faces of the men must have been gray. Their eyes must have glinted in strange ways as they gazed steadily astern. Viewed from a balcony, the whole thing would doubtless have been weirdly picturesque. But the men in the boat had no time to see it, and if they had had leisure there were other things to occupy their minds. The sun swung steadily up the sky, and they knew it was broad day because the color of the sea changed from slate to emerald-green, streaked with amber lights, and the foam was like tumbling snow. The process of the breaking day was unknown to them. They were aware only of this effect upon the color of the waves that rolled toward them.

In disjointed sentences the cook and the correspondent argued as to the difference between a life-saving station and a house of refuge. The cook had said: "There's a house of refuge just north of the Mosquito Inlet Light, and as soon as they see us, they'll come off in their boat and pick us up."

"As soon as who see us?" said the correspondent.

"The crew," said the cook.

"Houses of refuge don't have crews," said the correspondent. "As I understand them, they are only places where clothes and grub are stored for the benefit of shipwrecked people. They don't carry crews."

"Oh, yes, they do," said the cook.

"No, they don't," said the correspondent.

"Well, we're not there yet, anyhow," said the oiler, in the stern.

"Well," said the cook, "perhaps it's not a house of refuge that I'm thinking of as being near Mosquito Inlet Light. Perhaps it's a life-saving station."

"We're not there yet," said the oiler, in the stern.

## II

As the boat bounced from the top of each wave, the wind tore through the hair of the hatless men, and as the craft plopped her stern down again the spray slashed past them. The crest of each of these waves was a hill, from the top of which the men surveyed, for a moment, a broad tumultuous expanse, shining and wind-riven. It was probably splendid. It was probably glorious, this play of the free sea, wild with lights of emerald and white and amber.

"Bully good thing it's an on-shore wind," said the cook. "If not, where would we be? Wouldn't have a show."

"That's right," said the correspondent.

The busy oiler nodded his assent.

Then the captain, in the bow, chuckled in a way that expressed humor, contempt, tragedy, all in one. "Do you think we've got much of a show now, boys?" said he.

Whereupon the three were silent, save for a trifle of hemming and hawing. To express any particular optimism at this time they felt to be childish and stupid, but they all doubtless possessed this sense of the situation in their mind. A young man thinks doggedly at such times. On the other hand, the ethics of their condition was decidedly against any open suggestion of hopelessness. So they were silent.

"Oh, well," said the captain, soothing his children, "we'll get ashore all right."

But there was that in his tone which made them think, so the oiler quoth: "Yes! If this wind holds!"

The cook was bailing: "Yes! If we don't catch hell in the surf."

Canton flannel gulls flew near and far. Sometimes they sat down on the sea, near patches of brown seaweed that rolled over the waves with a movement like carpets on a line in a gale. The birds sat comfortably in groups, and they were envied by some in the dingey, for the wrath of the sea was no more to them than it was to a covey of prairie chickens a thousand miles inland. Often they came very close and stared at the men with black bead-like eyes. At these times they were uncanny and sinister in their unblinking scrutiny, and the men hooted angrily at them, telling them to be gone. One came, and evidently decided to alight on the top of the captain's head. The bird flew parallel to the boat and did not circle, but made short sidelong jumps in the air in chicken-fashion. His black eyes were wistfully fixed upon the captain's head. "Ugly brute," said the oiler to the bird. "You look as if you were made with a jack-knife." The cook and the correspondent swore darkly at the creature. The captain naturally wished to knock it away with the end of the heavy painter; but he did not dare do it, because anything resembling an emphatic gesture would have capsized this freighted boat, and so with his open hand, the captain gently and carefully waved the gull away. After it had been discouraged from the pursuit the captain breathed easier on account of his hair, and others breathed easier because the bird struck their minds at this time as being somehow gruesome and ominous.

In the meantime the oiler and the correspondent rowed. And also they rowed.

They sat together in the same seat, and each rowed an oar. Then the oiler took both oars; then the correspondent took both oars; then the oiler; then the correspondent. They rowed and they rowed. The very ticklish part of the business was when the time came for the reclining one in the stern to take his turn at the oars. By the very last star of truth, it is easier to steal eggs from under a hen than it was to change seats in the dingey. First the man in the stern slid his hand along the thwart and moved with care, as if he were of Sèvres. Then the man in the rowing seat slid his hand along the other thwart. It was all done with the most extraordinary care. As the two sidled past each other, the whole party kept watchful eyes on the coming wave, and the captain cried: "Look out now! Steady there!"

The brown mats of seaweed that appeared from time to time were like islands, bits of earth. They were travelling, apparently, neither one way nor the other. They were, to all intents, stationary. They informed the men in the boat that it was making progress slowly toward the land.

The captain, rearing cautiously in the bow, after the dingey soared on a great swell, said that he had seen the lighthouse at Mosquito Inlet. Presently the cook remarked that he had seen it. The correspondent was at the oars then, and for some reason he too wished to look at the lighthouse, but his back was toward the far shore and the waves were important, and for some time he could not seize an opportunity to turn his head. But at last there came a wave more gentle than the others, and when at the crest of it he swiftly scoured the western horizon.

"See it?" said the captain.

"No," said the correspondent slowly. "I didn't see anything."

"Look again," said the captain. He pointed. "It's exactly in that direction."

At the top of another wave, the correspondent did as he was bid, and this time his eyes chanced on a small still thing on the edge of the swaying horizon. It was precisely like the point of a pin. It took an anxious eye to find a lighthouse so tiny.

"Think we'll make it, captain?"

"If this wind holds and the boat don't swamp, we can't do much else," said the captain.

The little boat, lifted by each towering sea, and splashed viciously by the crests, made progress that in the absence of seaweed was not apparent to those in her. She seemed just a wee thing wallowing, miraculously top up, at the mercy of five oceans. Occasionally, a great spread of water, like white flames, swarmed into her.

"Bail her, cook," said the captain serenely.

"All right, captain," said the cheerful cook.

## III

It would be difficult to describe the subtle brotherhood of men that was here established on the seas. No one said that it was so. No one mentioned it. But it dwelt in the boat, and each man felt it warm him. They were a captain, an oiler, a cook, and a correspondent, and they were friends, friends in a more curiously iron-bound degree than may be common. The hurt captain, lying against the water-jar in the bow, spoke always in a low voice and calmly, but he could never command a more ready and swiftly obedient crew than the motley three of the dingey. It was more than a mere recognition of what was best for the common safety. There was surely in it a quality that was personal and heartfelt. And after this devotion to the commander of the boat there was this comradeship that the correspondent, for instance, who had been taught to be cynical of men, knew even at the time was the best experience of his life. But no one said that it was so. No one mentioned it.

"I wish we had a sail," remarked the captain. "We might try my overcoat on the end of an oar and give you two boys a chance to rest." So the cook and the correspondent held the mast and spread wide the overcoat. The oiler steered, and the little boat made good way with her new rig. Sometimes the oiler had to scull sharply to keep a sea from breaking into the boat, but otherwise sailing was a success.

Meanwhile the lighthouse had been growing slowly larger. It had now almost assumed color, and appeared like a little gray shadow on the sky. The man at the oars could not be prevented from turning his head rather often to try for a glimpse of this little gray shadow.

At last, from the top of each wave the men in the tossing boat could see land. Even as the lighthouse was an upright shadow on the sky, this land seemed but a long black shadow on the sea. It certainly was thinner than paper. "We must be about opposite New Smyrna," said the cook, who had coasted this shore often in schooners. "Captain, by the way, I believe they abandoned that life-saving station there about a year ago."

"Did they?" said the captain.

The wind slowly died away. The cook and the correspondent were not now obliged to slave in order to hold high the oar. But the waves continued their old impetuous swooping at the dingey, and the little craft, no longer under way, struggled woundily over them. The oiler or the correspondent took the oars again.

Shipwrecks are apropos of nothing. If men could only train for them and have them occur when the men had reached pink condition, there would be less drowning at sea. Of the four in the dingey none had slept any time worth mentioning for two days and two nights previous to embarking in the dingey, and in the excitement of clambering about the deck of a foundering ship they had also forgotten to eat heartily.

For these reasons, and for others, neither the oiler nor the correspondent was fond of rowing at this time. The correspondent wondered ingenuously how in the name of all that was sane could there be people who thought it amusing to row a boat. It was not an amusement; it was a diabolical punishment, and even a genius of mental aberrations could never conclude that it was anything but a horror to the muscles and a crime against the back. He mentioned to the boat in general how the amusement of rowing struck him, and the weary-faced oiler smiled in full sympathy. Previously to the foundering, by the way, the oiler had worked double-watch in the engine-room of the ship.

"Take her easy, now, boys," said the captain. "Don't spend yourselves. If we have to run a surf you'll need all your strength, because we'll sure have to swim for it. Take your time."

Slowly the land arose from the sea. From a black line it became a line of black and a line of white, trees and sand. Finally, the captain said that he could make out a house on the shore. "That's the house of refuge, sure," said the cook. "They'll see us before long, and come out after us."

The distant lighthouse reared high. "The keeper ought to be able to make us out now, if he's looking through a glass," said the captain. "He'll notify the life-saving people."

"None of those other boats could have got ashore to give word of the wreck," said the oiler, in a low voice. "Else the life-boat would be out hunting us."

Slowly and beautifully the land loomed out of the sea. The wind came again. It had veered from the north-east to the south-east. Finally, a new sound struck the ears of the men in the boat. It was the low thunder of the surf on the shore. "We'll never be able to make the lighthouse now," said the captain. "Swing her head a little more north, Billie."

" 'A little more north,' sir," said the oiler.

Whereupon the little boat turned her nose once more down the wind, and all but the oarsman watched the shore grow. Under the influence of this expansion doubt and direful apprehension was leaving the minds of the men. The management of the boat was still most absorbing, but it could not prevent a quiet cheerfulness. In an hour, perhaps, they would be ashore.

Their backbones had become thoroughly used to balancing in the boat, and they now rode this wild colt of a dingey like circus men. The correspondent thought that he had been drenched to the skin, but happening to feel in the top pocket of his coat, he found therein eight cigars. Four of them were soaked with sea-water; four were perfectly scatheless. After a search, somebody produced three dry matches, and thereupon the four waifs rode in their little boat, and with an assurance of an impending rescue shining in their eyes, puffed at the big cigars and judged well and ill of all men. Everybody took a drink of water.

## IV

"Cook," remarked the captain, "there don't seem to be any signs of life about your house of refuge."

"No," replied the cook. "Funny they don't see us!"

A broad stretch of lowly coast lay before the eyes of the men. It was of low dunes topped with dark vegetation. The roar of the surf was plain, and sometimes they could see the white lip of a wave as it spun up the beach. A tiny house was blocked out black upon the sky. Southward, the slim lighthouse lifted its little gray length.

Tide, wind, and waves were swinging the dingey northward. "Funny they don't see us," said the men.

The surf's roar was here dulled, but its tone was, nevertheless, thunderous and mighty. As the boat swam over the great rollers, the men sat listening to this roar. "We'll swamp sure," said everybody.

It is fair to say here that there was not a life-saving station within twenty miles in either direction, but the men did not know this fact, and in consequence they made dark and opprobrious remarks concerning the eyesight of the nation's life-savers. Four scowling men sat in the dingey and surpassed records in the invention of epithets.

"Funny they don't see us."

The light-heartedness of a former time had completely faded. To their sharpened minds it was easy to conjure pictures of all kinds of incompetency and blindness and, indeed, cowardice. There was the shore of the populous land, and it was bitter and bitter to them that from it came no sign.

"Well," said the captain, ultimately, "I suppose we'll have to make a try for ourselves. If we stay out here too long, we'll none of us have strength left to swim after the boat swamps."

And so the oiler, who was at the oars, turned the boat straight for the shore. There was a sudden tightening of muscles. There was some thinking.

"If we don't all get ashore—" said the captain. "If we don't all get ashore, I suppose you fellows know where to send news of my finish?"

They then briefly exchanged some addresses and admonitions. As for the reflections of the men, there was a great deal of rage in them. Perchance they might be formulated thus: "If I am going to be drowned—if I am going to be drowned—if I am going to be drowned, why, in the name of the seven mad gods who rule the sea, was I allowed to come thus far and contemplate sand and trees? Was I brought here merely to have my nose dragged away as I was about to nibble the sacred cheese of life? It is preposterous. If this old ninny-woman, Fate, cannot do better than this, she should be deprived of the management of men's fortunes. She is an old hen who knows not her intention. If she has decided to drown me, why did she not do it in the beginning and save me all this trouble? The whole affair is absurd. . . . But no, she cannot mean to drown me. She dare not drown me. She cannot drown me. Not after all this work." Afterward the man might have had an impulse to shake his fist at the clouds: "Just you drown me, now, and then hear what I call you!"

The billows that came at this time were more formidable. They seemed always just about to break and roll over the little boat in a turmoil of foam. There was a preparatory and long growl in the speech of them. No mind unused to the sea would have concluded that the dingey could ascend these sheer heights in time. The shore was still afar. The oiler was a wily surfman. "Boys," he said swiftly, "she won't live three minutes more, and we're too far out to swim. Shall I take her to sea again, captain?"

"Yes! Go ahead!" said the captain.

This oiler, by a series of quick miracles, and fast and steady oarsmanship, turned the boat in the middle of the surf and took her safely to sea again.

There was a considerable silence as the boat bumped over the furrowed sea to deeper water. Then somebody in gloom spoke. "Well, anyhow, they must have seen us from the shore by now."

The gulls went in slanting flight up the wind toward the gray desolate east. A squall, marked by dingy clouds, and clouds brick-red, like smoke from a burning building, appeared from the south-east.

"What do you think of those life-saving people? Ain't they peaches?"

"Funny they haven't seen us."

"Maybe they think we're out here for sport! Maybe they think we're fishin'. Maybe they think we're damned fools."

It was a long afternoon. A changed tide tried to force them southward, but wind and wave said northward. Far ahead, where coastline, sea, and sky formed their mighty angle, there were little dots which seemed to indicate a city on the shore.

"St. Augustine?"

The captain shook his head. "Too near Mosquito Inlet."

And the oiler rowed, and then the correspondent rowed. Then the oiler rowed. It was a weary business. The human back can become the seat of more aches and pains than are registered in books for the composite anatomy of a regiment. It is a limited area, but it can become the theater of innumerable muscular conflicts, tangles, wrenches, knots, and other comforts.

"Did you ever like to row, Billie?" asked the correspondent.

"No," said the oiler. "Hang it!"

When one exchanged the rowing-seat for a place in the bottom of the boat, he suffered a bodily depression that caused him to be careless of everything save an obligation to wiggle one finger. There was cold sea-water swashing to and fro in the boat, and he lay in it. His head, pillowed on a thwart, was within an inch of the swirl of a wave crest, and sometimes a particularly obstreperous sea came in-board and drenched him once more. But these matters did not annoy him. It is almost certain that if the boat had capsized he would have tumbled comfortably out upon the ocean as if he felt sure that it was a great soft mattress.

"Look! There's a man on the shore!"

"Where?"

"There! See 'im? See 'im?"

"Yes, sure! He's walking along."

"Now he's stopped. Look! He's facing us!"

"He's waving at us!"

"So he is! By thunder!"

"Ah, now we're all right! Now we're all right! There'll be a boat out here for us in half an hour."

"He's going on. He's running. He's going up to that house there."

The remote beach seemed lower than the sea, and it required a searching glance to discern the little black figure. The captain saw a floating stick and they rowed to it. A bath-towel was by some weird chance in the boat, and tying this on the stick, the captain waved it. The oarsman did not dare turn his head, so he was obliged to ask questions.

"What's he doing now?"

"He's standing still again. He's looking. I think. . . . There he goes again. Toward the house. . . . Now he's stopped again."

"Is he waving at us?"

"No, not now! he was, though."

"Look! There comes another man!"

"He's running."

"Look at him go, would you."

"Why, he's on a bicycle. Now he's met the other man. They're both waving at us. Look!"

"There comes something up the beach."

"What the devil is that thing?"

"Why, it looks like a boat."

"Why, certainly it's a boat."

"No, it's on wheels."

"Yes, so it is. Well, that must be the life-boat. They drag them along shore on a wagon."

"That's the life-boat, sure."

"No, by–, it's–it's an omnibus."

"I tell you it's a life-boat."

"It is not! It's an omnibus. I can see it plain. See? One of these big hotel omnibuses."

"By thunder, you're right. It's an omnibus, sure as fate. What do you suppose they are doing with an omnibus? Maybe they are going around collecting the life-crew, hey?"

"That's it, likely. Look! There's a fellow waving a little black flag. He's standing on the steps of the omnibus. There come those other two fellows. Now they're all talking together. Look at the fellow with the flag. Maybe he ain't waving it."

"That ain't a flag, is it? That's his coat. Why, certainly, that's his coat."

"So it is. It's his coat. He's taken it off and is waving it around his head. But would you look at him swing it."

"Oh, say, there isn't any life-saving station there. That's just a winter resort hotel omnibus that has brought over some of the boarders to see us drown."

"What's that idiot with the coat mean? What's he signaling, anyhow?"

"It looks as if he were trying to tell us to go north. There must be a life-saving station up there."

"No! He thinks we're fishing. Just giving us a merry hand. See? Ah, there, Willie."

"Well, I wish I could make something out of those signals. What do you suppose he means?"

"He don't mean anything. He's just playing."

"Well, if he'd just signal us to try the surf again, or to go to sea and wait, or go north, or go south, or go to hell—there would be some reason in it. But look at him. He just stands there and keeps his coat revolving like a wheel. The ass!"

"There come more people."

"Now there's quite a mob. Look! Isn't that a boat."

"Where? Oh, I see where you mean. No, that's no boat."

"That fellow is still waving his coat."

"He must think we like to see him do that. Why don't he quit it? It don't mean anything."

"I don't know. I think he is trying to make us go north. It must be that there's a life-saving station there somewhere."

"Say, he ain't tired yet. Look at 'im wave."

"Wonder how long he can keep that up. He's been revolving his coat ever since he caught sight of us. He's an idiot. Why aren't they getting men to bring a boat out? A fishing boat—one of those big yawls—could come out here all right. Why don't he do something?"

"Oh, it's all right, now."

"They'll have a boat out here for us in less than no time, now that they've seen us."

A faint yellow tone came into the sky over the low land. The shadows on the sea slowly deepened. The wind bore coldness with it, and the men began to shiver.

"Holy smoke!" said one, allowing his voice to express his impious mood, "if we keep on monkeying out here! If we've got to flounder out here all night!"

"Oh, we'll never have to stay here all night! Don't you worry. They've seen us now, and it won't be long before they'll come chasing out after us."

The shore grew dusky. The man waving a coat blended gradually into this gloom, and it swallowed in the same manner the omnibus and the group of people. The spray, when it dashed uproariously over the side, made the voyagers shrink and swear like men who were being branded.

"I'd like to catch the chump who waved the coat. I feel like soaking him one, just for luck."

"Why? What did he do?"

"Oh, nothing, but then he seemed so damned cheerful."

In the meantime the oiler rowed, and then the correspondent rowed, and then the oiler rowed. Gray-faced and bowed forward, they mechanically, turn by turn, plied the leaden oars. The form of the lighthouse had vanished from the southern horizon, but finally a pale star appeared, just lifting from the sea. The streaked saffron in the west passed before the all-merging darkness, and the sea to the east was black. The land had vanished, and was expressed only by the low and drear thunder of the surf.

"If I am going to be drowned–if I am going to be drowned–if I am going to be drowned, why, in the name of the seven mad gods who rule the sea, was I allowed to come thus far and contemplate sand and trees? Was I brought here merely to have my nose dragged away as I was about to nibble the sacred cheese of life?"

The patient captain, drooped over the water-jar, was sometimes obliged to speak to the oarsman.

"Keep her head up! Keep her head up!"

" 'Keep her head up,' sir." The voices were weary and low.

This was surely a quiet evening. All save the oarsman lay heavily and listlessly in the boat's bottom. As for him, his eyes were just capable of noting the tall black waves that swept forward in a most sinister silence, save for an occasional subdued growl of a crest.

The cook's head was on a thwart, and he looked without interest at the water under his nose. He was deep in other scenes. Finally he spoke. "Billie," he murmured, dreamfully, "what kind of pie do you like best?"

## V

"Pie," said the oiler and the correspondent, agitatedly. "Don't talk about those things, blast you!"

"Well," said the cook, "I was just thinking about ham sandwiches, and–"

A night on the sea in an open boat is a long night. As darkness settled finally, the shine of the light, lifting from the sea in the south, changed to full gold. On the northern horizon a new light appeared, a small bluish gleam on the edge of the waters. These two lights were the furniture of the world. Otherwise there was nothing but waves.

Two men huddled in the stern, and distances were so magnificent in the dingey that the rower was enabled to keep his feet partly warmed by thrusting them under his companions. Their legs indeed extended far under the rowing-seat until they touched the feet of the captain forward. Sometimes, despite the efforts of the tired oarsman, a wave came piling into the boat, an icy wave of the night, and the chilling water soaked them anew. They would twist their bodies for a moment and groan, and sleep the dead sleep once more, while the water in the boat gurgled about them as the craft rocked.

The plan of the oiler and the correspondent was for one to row until he lost the ability, and then arouse the other from his sea-water couch in the bottom of the boat.

The oiler plied the oars until his head drooped forward, and the overpowering sleep blinded him. And he rowed yet afterward. Then he touched a man in the bottom of the boat, and called his name. "Will you spell me for a little while?" he said, meekly.

"Sure, Billie," said the correspondent, awakening and dragging himself to a sitting position. They exchanged places carefully, and the oiler, cuddling down in the sea-water at the cook's side, seemed to go to sleep instantly.

The particular violence of the sea had ceased. The waves came without snarling. The obligation of the man at the oars was to keep the boat headed so that the tilt of the rollers would not capsize her, and to preserve her from filling when the crests rushed past. The black waves were silent and hard to be seen in the darkness. Often one was almost upon the boat before the oarsman was aware.

In a low voice the correspondent addressed the captain. He was not sure that the captain was awake, although this iron man seemed to be always awake. "Captain, shall I keep her making for that light north, sir?"

The same steady voice answered him. "Yes. Keep it about two points off the port bow."

The cook had tied a life-belt around himself in order to get even the warmth which this clumsy cork contrivance could donate, and he seemed almost stove-like when a rower, whose teeth invariably chattered wildly as soon as he ceased his labor, dropped down to sleep.

The correspondent, as he rowed, looked down at the two men sleeping underfoot. The cook's arm was around the oiler's shoulders, and, with their fragmentary clothing and haggard faces, they were the babes of the sea, a grotesque rendering of the old babes in the wood.

Later he must have grown stupid at his work, for suddenly there was a growling of water, and a crest came with a roar and a swash into the boat, and it was a wonder that it did not set the cook afloat in his life-belt. The cook continued to sleep, but the oiler sat up, blinking his eyes and shaking with the new cold.

"Oh, I'm awful sorry, Billie," said the correspondent, contritely.

"That's all right, old boy," said the oiler, and lay down again and was asleep.

Presently it seemed that even the captain dozed, and the correspondent thought that he was the one man afloat on all the oceans. The wind had a voice as it came over the waves, and it was sadder than the end.

There was a long, loud swishing astern of the boat, and a gleaming trail of phosphorescence, like blue flame, was furrowed on the black waters. It might have been made by a monstrous knife.

Then there came a stillness, while the correspondent breathed with the open mouth and looked at the sea.

Suddenly there was another swish and another long flash of bluish light, and this time it was alongside the boat, and might almost have been reached with an oar. The correspondent saw an enormous fin speed like a shadow through the water, hurling the crystalline spray and leaving the long glowing trail.

The correspondent looked over his shoulder at the captain. His face was hidden, and he seemed to be asleep. He looked at the babes of the sea. They certainly were asleep. So, being bereft of sympathy, he leaned a little way to one side and swore softly into the sea.

But the thing did not then leave the vicinity of the boat. Ahead or astern, on one side or the other, at intervals long or short, fled the long sparkling streak, and there was to be heard the whiroo of the dark fin. The speed and power of the thing was greatly to be admired. It cut the water like a gigantic and keen projectile.

The presence of this biding thing did not affect the man with the same horror that it would if he had been a picnicker. He simply looked at the sea dully and swore in an undertone.

Nevertheless, it is true that he did not wish to be alone. He wished one of his companions to awaken by chance and keep him company with it. But the captain hung motionless over the water-jar, and the oiler and the cook in the bottom of the boat were plunged in slumber.

## VI

"If I am going to be drowned—if I am going to be drowned—if I am going to be drowned, why, in the name of the seven mad gods who rule the sea, was I allowed to come thus far and contemplate sand and trees?"

During this dismal night, it may be remarked that a man would conclude that it was really the intention of the seven mad gods to drown him, despite the abominable injustice of it. For it was certainly an abominable injustice to drown a man who had worked so hard, so hard. The man felt it would be a crime most unnatural. Other people had drowned at sea since galleys swarmed with painted sails, but still—

When it occurs to a man that nature does not regard him as important, and that she feels she would not maim the universe by disposing of him, he at first wishes to throw bricks at the temple, and he hates deeply the fact that there are no bricks and no temples. Any visible expression of nature would surely be pelleted with his jeers.

Then, if there be no tangible thing to hoot he feels, perhaps, the desire to confront a personification and indulge in pleas, bowed to one knee, and with hands supplicant, saying: "Yes, but I love myself."

A high cold star on a winter's night is the word he feels that she says to him. Thereafter he knows the pathos of his situation.

The men in the dingey had not discussed these matters, but each had, no doubt, reflected upon them in silence and according to his mind. There was seldom any expression upon their faces save the general one of complete weariness. Speech was devoted to the business of the boat.

To chime the notes of his emotion, a verse mysteriously entered the correspondent's head. He had even forgotten that he had forgotten this verse, but it suddenly was in his mind.

> "A soldier of the Legion lay dying in Algiers,
> There was lack of woman's nursing, there was dearth of woman's tears;
> But a comrade stood beside him, and he took that comrade's hand,
> And he said: 'I shall never see my own, my native land.' "

In his childhood, the correspondent had been made acquainted with the fact that a soldier of the Legion lay dying in Algiers, but he had never regarded the fact as important. Myriads of his school-fellows had informed him of the soldier's plight, but the dinning had naturally ended by making him perfectly indifferent. He had never considered it his affair that a soldier of the Legion lay dying in Algiers, nor had it appeared to him as a matter for sorrow. It was less to him than the breaking of a pencil's point.

Now, however, it quaintly came to him as a human, living thing. It was no longer merely a picture of a few throes in the breast of a poet, meanwhile drinking tea and warming his feet at the grate; it was an actuality—stern, mournful, and fine.

The correspondent plainly saw the soldier. He lay on the sand with his feet out straight and still. While his pale left hand was upon his chest in an attempt to thwart the going of his life, the blood came between his fingers. In the far Algerian distance, a city of low square forms was set against a sky that was faint with the last sunset hues. The correspondent, plying the oars and dreaming of the slow and slower movements of the lips of the soldier, was moved by a profound and perfectly impersonal comprehension. He was sorry for the soldier of the Legion who lay dying in Algiers.

The thing which had followed the boat and waited had evidently grown bored at the delay. There was no longer to be heard the slash of the cut water, and there was no longer the flame of the long trail. The light in the north still glimmered, but it was apparently no nearer to the boat. Sometimes the boom of the surf rang in the correspondent's ears, and he turned the craft seaward then and rowed harder. Southward, someone had evidently built a watch-fire on the beach. It was too low and too far to be seen, but it made a shimmering, roseate reflection upon the bluff back of it, and this could be discerned from the boat. The wind came stronger, and sometimes a wave suddenly raged out like a mountain-cat, and there was to be seen the sheen and sparkle of a broken crest.

The captain, in the bow, moved on his water-jar and sat erect. "Pretty long night," he observed to the correspondent. He looked at the shore. "Those life-saving people take their time."

"Did you see that shark playing around?"

"Yes, I saw him. He was a big fellow, all right."

"Wish I had known you were awake."

Later the correspondent spoke into the bottom of the boat.

"Billie!" There was a slow and gradual disentanglement. "Billie, will you spell me?"

"Sure," said the oiler.

As soon as the correspondent touched the cold comfortable sea-water in the bottom of the boat, and had huddled close to the cook's life-belt he was deep in sleep, despite the fact that his teeth played all the popular airs. This sleep was so good to him that it was but a moment before he heard a voice call his name in a tone that demonstrated the last stages of exhaustion. "Will you spell me?"

"Sure, Billie."

The light in the north had mysteriously vanished, but the correspondent took his course from the wide-awake captain.

Later in the night they took the boat farther out to sea, and the captain directed the cook to take one oar at the stern and keep the boat facing the seas. He was to call out if he should hear the thunder of the surf. This plan enabled the oiler and the correspondent to get respite together. "We'll give those boys a chance to get into shape again," said the captain. They curled down and, after a few preliminary chatterings and trembles, slept once more the dead sleep. Neither knew they had bequeathed to the cook the company of another shark, or perhaps the same shark.

As the boat caroused on the waves, spray occasionally bumped over the side and gave them a fresh soaking, but this had no power to break their repose. The ominous slash of the wind and the water affected them as it would have affected mummies.

"Boys," said the cook, with the notes of every reluctance in his voice, "she's drifted in pretty close. I guess one of you had better take her to sea again." The correspondent, aroused, heard the crash of the toppled crests.

As he was rowing, the captain gave him some whiskey-and-water, and this steadied the chills out of him. "If I ever get ashore and anybody shows me even a photograph of an oar—"

At last there was a short conversation.
"Billie . . . Billie, will you spell me?"
"Sure," said the oiler.

## VII

When the correspondent again opened his eyes, the sea and the sky were each of the gray hue of the dawning. Later, carmine and gold was painted upon the waters. The morning appeared finally, in its splendor, with a sky of pure blue, and the sunlight flamed on the tips of the waves.

On the distant dunes were set many little black cottages, and a tall white windmill reared above them. No man, nor dog, nor bicycle appeared on the beach. The cottages might have formed a deserted village.

The voyagers scanned the shore. A conference was held in the boat. "Well," said the captain, "if no help is coming, we might better try a run through the surf right away. If we stay out here much longer we will be too weak to do anything for ourselves at all." The others silently acquiesced in this reasoning. The boat was headed for the beach. The correspondent wondered if none ever ascended the tall wind-tower, and if then they never looked seaward. This tower was a giant, standing with its back to the plight of the ants. It represented in a degree, to the correspondent, the serenity of nature amid the struggles of the individual—nature in the wind, and nature in the vision of men. She did not seem cruel to him then, nor beneficent, nor treacherous, nor wise. But she was indifferent, flatly indifferent. It is, perhaps, plausible that a man in this situation, impressed with the unconcern of the universe, should see the innumerable flaws of his life, and have them taste wickedly in his mind and wish for another chance. A distinction between right and wrong seems absurdly clear to him, then, in this new ignorance of the grave-edge, and he understands that if he were given another opportunity he would mend his conduct and his words, and be better and brighter during an introduction or at a tea.

"Now, boys," said the captain, "she is going to swamp sure. All we can do is to work her in as far as possible, and then when she swamps, pile out and scramble for the beach. Keep cool now, and don't jump until she swamps sure."

The oiler took the oars. Over his shoulders he scanned the surf. "Captain," he said, "I think I'd better bring her about, and keep her head-on to the seas and back her in."

"All right, Billie," said the captain. "Back her in." The oiler swung the boat then and, seated in the stern, the cook and the correspondent were obliged to look over their shoulders to contemplate the lonely and indifferent shore.

The monstrous in-shore rollers heaved the boat high until the men were again enabled to see the white sheets of water scudding up the slanted beach. "We won't get in very close," said the captain. Each time a man could wrest his attention from the rollers, he turned his glance toward the shore, and in the expression of the eyes during this contemplation there was a singular quality. The correspondent, observing the others, knew that they were not afraid, but the full meaning of their glances was shrouded.

As for himself, he was too tired to grapple fundamentally with the fact. He tried to coerce his mind into thinking of it, but the mind was dominated at this time by the muscles, and the muscles said they did not care. It merely occurred to him that if he should drown it would be a shame.

There were no hurried words, no pallor, no plain agitation. The men simply looked at the shore. "Now, remember to get well clear of the boat when you jump," said the captain.

Seaward the crest of a roller suddenly fell with a thunderous crash, and the long white comber came roaring down upon the boat.

"Steady now," said the captain. The men were silent. They turned their eyes from the shore to the comber and waited. The boat slid up the incline, leaped at the furious top, bounced over it, and swung down the long back of the waves. Some water had been shipped and the cook bailed it out.

But the next crest crashed also. The tumbling, boiling flood of white water caught the boat and whirled it almost perpendicular. Water swarmed in from all sides. The correspondent had his hands on the gunwale at this time, and when the water entered at that place he swiftly withdrew his fingers, as if he objected to wetting them.

The little boat, drunken with this weight of water, reeled and snuggled deeper into the sea.

"Bail her out, cook! Bail her out," said the captain.

"All right, captain," said the cook.

"Now, boys, the next one will do for us, sure," said the oiler. "Mind to jump clear of the boat."

The third wave moved forward, huge, furious, implacable. It fairly swallowed the dingey, and almost simultaneously the men tumbled into the sea. A piece of life-belt had lain in the bottom of the boat, and as the correspondent went overboard he held this to his chest with his left hand.

The January water was icy, and he reflected immediately that it was colder than he had expected to find it off the coast of Florida.

This appeared to his dazed mind as a fact important enough to be noted at the time. The coldness of the water was sad; it was tragic. This fact was somehow so mixed and confused with his opinion of his own situation that it seemed almost a proper reason for tears. The water was cold.

When he came to the surface he was conscious of little but the noisy water. Afterward he saw his companions in the sea. The oiler was ahead in the race. He was swimming strongly and rapidly. Off to the correspondent's left, the cook's great white and corked back bulged out of the water, and in the rear the captain was hanging with his one good hand to the keel of the overturned dingey.

There is a certain immovable quality to a shore, and the correspondent wondered at it amid the confusion of the sea.

It seemed also very attractive, but the correspondent knew that it was a long journey, and he paddled leisurely. The piece of life-preserver lay under him, and sometimes he whirled down the incline of a wave as if he were on a hand-sled.

But finally he arrived at a place in the sea where travel was beset with difficulty. He did not pause swimming to inquire what manner of current had caught him, but there his progress ceased. The shore was set before him like a bit of scenery on a stage, and he looked at it and understood with his eyes each detail of it.

As the cook passed, much farther to the left, the captain was calling to him, "Turn over on your back, cook! Turn over on your back and use the oar."

"All right, sir." The cook turned on his back, and, paddling with an oar, went ahead as if he were a canoe.

Presently the boat also passed to the left of the correspondent with the captain clinging with one hand to the keel. He would have appeared like a man raising himself to look over a board fence, if it were not for the extraordinary gymnastics of the boat. The correspondent marvelled that the captain could still hold to it.

They passed on, nearer to shore—the oiler, the cook, the captain—and following them went the water-jar, bouncing gaily over the seas.

The correspondent remained in the grip of this strange new enemy—a current. The shore, with its white slope of sand and its green bluff, topped with little silent cottages, was spread like a picture before him. It was very near to him then, but he was impressed as one who in a gallery looks at a scene from Brittany or Algiers.

He thought: "I am going to drown? Can it be possible? Can it be possible? Can it be possible?" Perhaps an individual must consider his own death to be the final phenomenon of nature.

But later a wave perhaps whirled him out of this small deadly current, for he found suddenly that he could again make progress toward the shore. Later still, he was aware that the captain, clinging with one hand to the keel of the dingey, had his face turned away from the shore and toward him, and was calling his name. "Come to the boat! Come to the boat!"

In his struggle to reach the captain and the boat, he reflected that when one gets properly wearied, drowning must really be a comfortable arrangement, a cessation of hostilities accompanied by a large degree of relief, and he was glad of it, for the main thing in his mind for some moments had been horror of the temporary agony. He did not wish to be hurt.

Presently he saw a man running along the shore. He was undressing with most remarkable speed. Coat, trousers, shirt, everything flew magically off him.

"Come to the boat," called the captain.

"All right, captain." As the correspondent paddled, he saw the captain let himself down to bottom and leave the boat. Then the correspondent performed his one little marvel of the voyage. A large wave caught him and flung him with ease and supreme speed completely over the boat and far beyond it. It struck him even then as an event in gymnastics, and a true miracle of the sea. An overturned boat in the surf is not a plaything to a swimming man.

The correspondent arrived in water that reached only to his waist, but his condition did not enable him to stand for more than a moment. Each wave knocked him into a heap, and the under-tow pulled at him.

Then he saw the man who had been running and undressing, and undressing and running, come bounding into the water. He dragged ashore the cook, and then waded toward the captain, but the captain waved him away, and sent him to the correspondent. He was naked, naked as a tree in winter, but a halo was about his head, and he shone like a saint. He gave a strong pull, and a long drag, and a bully heave at the correspondent's hand. The correspondent, schooled in the minor formulae, said: "Thanks, old man." But suddenly the man cried: "What's that?" He pointed a swift finger. The correspondent said: "Go."

In the shallows, face downward, lay the oiler. His forehead touched sand that was periodically, between each wave, clear of the sea.

The correspondent did not know all that transpired afterward. When he achieved safe ground he fell, striking the sand with each particular part of his body. It was as if he had dropped from a roof, but the thud was grateful to him.

It seems that instantly the beach was populated with men, with blankets, clothes, and flasks, and women with coffee-pots and all the remedies sacred to their minds. The welcome of the land to the men from the sea was warm and generous, but a still and dripping shape was carried slowly up the beach, and the land's welcome for it could only be the different and sinister hospitality of the grave.

When it came night, the white waves paced to and fro in the moonlight, and the wind brought the sound of the great sea's voice to the men on shore, and they felt that they could then be interpreters.

---

## The Structure of a Story

The ordering of incidents within a story may be spoken of as its **structure.** Traditionally, a story's structure has been said to consist of four basic parts:

1. The **exposition.** The beginning of the story, which introduces the reader to the tale's setting (time and place) and to some or all of its characters.
2. The **conflict.** Every story centers on a conflict of some sort: one person, or group of people, against another; people against nature; an individual against some rule or custom of society. Generally the conflict increases in tension or in complexity until it reaches a climax.
3. The **climax.** The point of greatest tension, at which the turning-point or breaking-point is reached.
4. The **denouement** or **resolution.** The ending, which brings the tale to a close, picking up the pieces of the action and reordering the lives left disordered by the conflict and its climax.

Of these four parts, only numbers two and three, the conflict and the climax, are essential. You don't have to begin with an exposition; your first sentence can show your characters already embroiled in their conflict. You don't have to end with a resolution; you can stop your tale short at its climactic moment, as Shirley Jackson does in "The Lottery." But you must have some sort of conflict in your action; and it must rise to some peak of intensity somewhere between the middle and end of your story.

To familiarize yourself with the notion of structure, analyze the structures of "Young Goodman Brown," "The Guest," and "The Open Boat." Do all four parts appear in each of these stories? What parts of each story would you assign to each section?

---

We round out our selection of stories told by omniscient narrators with "A Worn Path," which follows. Although this story focuses on a single figure, it is told by an **objective narrator.** The last three stories gained much of their impact by studying their characters as they tried to find some meaning or place some interpretation on the world around them and the events in which they were caught up. In contrast, this tale gains much of its effectiveness from its protagonist's willingness to accept things as they are, and from the steadfastness with which she declares herself to be a natural part of the universe in which she lives.

EUDORA WELTY (1909–    )

# A Worn Path

It was December—a bright frozen day in the early morning. Far out in the country there was an old Negro woman with her head tied in a red rag, coming along a path through the pinewoods. Her name was Phoenix Jackson. She was very old and small and she walked slowly in the dark pine shadows, moving a little from side to side in her steps, with the balanced heaviness and lightness of a pendulum in a grandfather clock. She carried a thin, small cane made from an umbrella, and with this she kept tapping the frozen earth in front of her. This made a grave and persistent noise in the still air, that seemed meditative like the chirping of a solitary little bird.

She wore a dark striped dress reaching down to her shoetops, and an equally long apron of bleached sugar sacks, with a full pocket; all neat and tidy, but every time she took a step she might have fallen over her shoe-laces, which dragged from her unlaced shoes. She looked straight ahead. Her eyes were blue with age. Her skin had a pattern all its own of numberless branching wrinkles and as though a whole little tree stood in the middle of her forehead, but a golden color ran underneath, and the two knobs of her cheeks were illuminated by a yellow burning under the dark. Under the red rag her hair came down on her neck in the frailest of ringlets, still black, and with an odor like copper.

Now and then there was a quivering in the thicket. Old Phoenix said, "Out of my way, all you foxes, owls, beetles, jack rabbits, coons, and wild animals! . . . Keep out from under these feet, little bob-whites. . . . Keep the big wild hogs out of my path. Don't let none of those come running my direction. I got a long way." Under her small black-freckled hand her cane, limber as a buggy whip, would switch at the brush as if to rouse up any hiding things.

On she went. The woods were deep and still. The sun made the pine needles almost too bright to look at, up where the wind rocked. The cones dropped as light as feathers. Down in the hollow was the mourning dove—it was not too late for him.

The path ran up a hill. "Seems like there is chains about my feet, time I get this far," she said, in the voice of argument old people keep to use with themselves. "Something always take a hold on his hill—pleads I should stay."

After she got to the top she turned and gave a full, severe look behind her where she had come. "Up through pines," she said at length. "Now down through oaks."

Her eyes opened their widest and she started down gently. But before she got to the bottom of the hill a bush caught her dress.

Her fingers were busy and intent, but her skirts were full and long, so that before she could pull them free in one place they were caught in another. It was not possible to allow the dress to tear. "I in the thorny bush," she said. "Thorns, you doing your appointed work. Never want to let folks pass—no sir. Old eyes thought you was a pretty little green bush."

Finally, trembling all over, she stood free, and after a moment dared to stoop for her cane.

"Sun so high!" she cried, leaning back and looking, while the thick tears went over her eyes. "The time getting all gone here."

At the foot of this hill was a place where a log was laid across the creek.

"Now comes the trial," said Phoenix.

Putting her right foot out, she mounted the log and shut her eyes. Lifting her skirt, levelling her cane fiercely before her, like a festival figure in some parade, she began to march across. Then she opened her eyes and she was safe on the other side.

"I wasn't as old as I thought," she said.

But she sat down to rest. She spread her skirts on the bank around her and folded her hands over her knees. Up above her was a tree in a pearly cloud of mistletoe. She did not dare to close her eyes, and when a little boy brought her a little plate with a slice of marble-cake on it she spoke to him. "That would be acceptable," she said. But when she went to take it there was just her own hand in the air.

So she left that tree, and had to go through a barbed-wire fence. There she had to creep and crawl, spreading her knees and stretching her fingers like a baby trying to climb the steps. But she talked loudly to herself: she could not let her dress be torn now, so late in the day, and she could not pay for having her arm or her leg sawed off if she got caught fast where she was.

At last she was safe through the fence and risen up out in the clearing. Big dead trees, like black men with one arm, were standing in the purple stalks of the withered cotton field. There sat a buzzard.

"Who you watching?"

In the burrow she made her way along.

"Glad this not the season for bulls," she said, looking sideways, "and the good Lord made his snakes to curl up and sleep in the winter. A pleasure I don't see no two-headed snake coming around that tree, where it come once. It took a while to get by him, back in the summer."

She passed through the old cotton and went into a field of dead corn. It whispered and shook, and was taller than her head. "Through the maze now," she said, for there was no path.

Then there was something tall, black, and skinny there, moving before her.

At first she took it for a man. It could have been a man dancing in the field. But she stood still and listened, and it did not make a sound. It was as silent as a ghost.

"Ghost," she said sharply, "who be you the ghost of? For I have heard of nary death close by."

But there was no answer, only the ragged dancing in the wind.

She shut her eyes, reached out her hand, and touched a sleeve. She found a coat and inside that an emptiness, cold as ice.

"You scarecrow," she said. Her face lighted. "I ought to be shut up for good," she said with laughter. "My senses is gone. I too old. I the oldest people I ever know. Dance, old scarecrow," she said, "while I dancing with you."

She kicked her foot over the furrow, and with mouth drawn down shook her head once or twice in a little strutting way. Some husks blew down and whirled in streamers about her skirts.

Then she went on, parting her way from side to side with the cane, through the whispering field. At last she came to the end, to a wagon track, where the silver grass blew between the red ruts. The quail were walking around like pullets, seeming all dainty and unseen.

"Walk pretty," she said. "This the easy place. This the easy going."

She followed the track, swaying through the quiet bare fields, through the little strings of trees silver in their dead leaves, past cabins silver from weather, with the doors and windows boarded shut, all like old women under a spell sitting there. "I walking in their sleep," she said, nodding her head vigorously.

In a ravine she went where a spring was silently flowing through a hollow log. Old Phoenix bent and drank. "Sweetgum makes the water sweet," she said, and drank more. "Nobody knows who made this well, for it was here when I was born."

The track crossed a swampy part where the moss hung as white as lace from every limb. "Sleep on, alligators, and blow your bubbles." Then the track went into the road.

Deep, deep the road went down between the high green-colored banks. Overhead the live-oaks met, and it was as dark as a cave.

A black dog with a lolling tongue came up out of the weeds by the ditch. She was meditating, and not ready, and when he came at her she only hit him a little with her cane. Over she went in the ditch, like a little puff of milk-weed.

Down there, her senses drifted away. A dream visited her, and she reached her hand up, but nothing reached down and gave her a pull.

So she lay there and presently went to talking. "Old woman," she said to herself, "that black dog came up out of the weeds to stall you off, and now there he sitting on his fine tail, smiling at you."

A white man finally came along and found her—a hunter, a young man, with his dog on a chain.

"Well, Granny!" he laughed. "What are you doing there?"

"Lying on my back like a June-bug waiting to be turned over, mister," she said, reaching up her hand.

He lifted her up, gave her a swing in the air, and set her down, "Anything broken, Granny?"

"No sir, them old dead weeds is springy enough," said Phoenix, when she had got her breath. "I thank you for your trouble."

"Where do you live, Granny?" he asked, while the two dogs were growling at each other.

"Away back yonder, sir, behind the ridge. You can't even see it from here."

"On your way home?"

"No, sir, I going to town."

"Why, that's too far! That's as far as I walk when I come out myself, and I get something for my trouble." He patted the stuffed bag he carried, and there hung down a little closed claw. It was one of the bobwhites, with its beak hooked bitterly to show it was dead. "Now you go on home, Granny!"

"I bound to go to town, mister," said Phoenix. "The time come around."

He gave another laugh, filling the whole landscape. "I know you colored people! Wouldn't miss going to town to see Santa Claus!"

But something held Old Phoenix very still. The deep lines in her face went into a fierce and different radiation. Without warning she had seen with her own eyes a flashing nickel fall out of the man's pocket on to the ground.

"How old are you, Granny?" he was saying.

"There is no telling, mister," she said, "no telling."

Then she gave a little cry and clapped her hands, and said, "Git on away from here, dog! Look at that dog!" She laughed as if in admiration. "He ain't scared of nobody. He a big black dog." She whispered, "Sick him!"

"Watch me get rid of that cur," said the man. "Sick him, Pete! Sick him!"

Phoenix heard the dogs fighting and heard the man running and throwing sticks. She even heard a gunshot. But she was slowly bending forward by that time, further and further forward, the lids stretched down over her eyes, as if she were doing this in her sleep. Her chin was lowered almost to her knees. The yellow palm of her hand came out from the fold of her apron. Her fingers slid down and along the ground under the piece of money with the grace and care they would have in lifting an egg from under a sitting hen. Then she slowly straightened up, she stood erect, and the nickel was in her apron pocket. A bird flew by. Her lips moved. "God watching me the whole time. I come to stealing."

The man came back, and his own dog panted about them. "Well, I scared him off that time," he said, and then he laughed and lifted his gun and pointed it at Phoenix.

She stood straight and faced him.

"Doesn't the gun scare you?" he said, still pointing it.

"No, sir, I seen plenty go off closer by, in my day, and for less than what I done," she said, holding utterly still.

He smiled, and shouldered the gun. "Well, Granny," he said, "you must be a hundred years old and scared of nothing. I'd give you a dime if I had any money with me. But you take my advice and stay home, and nothing will happen to you."

"I bound to go on my way, mister," said Phoenix. She inclined her head in the red rag. Then they went in different directions, but she could hear the gun shooting again and again over the hill.

She walked on. The shadows hung from the oak trees to the road like curtains. Then she smelled wood-smoke, and smelled the river, and she saw a steeple and the cabins on their steep steps. Dozens of little black children whirled around her. There ahead was Natchez shining. Bells were ringing. She walked on.

In the paved city it was Christmas time. There were red and green electric lights strung and crisscrossed everywhere, and all turned on in the daytime. Old Phoenix would have been lost if she had not distrusted her eyesight and depended on her feet to know where to take her.

She paused quietly on the sidewalk, where people were passing by. A lady came along in the crowd, carrying an armful of red-, green-, and silver-wrapped presents; she gave off perfume like the red roses in hot summer, and Phoenix stopped her.

"Please, missy, will you lace up my shoe?" She held up her foot.

"What do you want, Grandma?"

"See my shoe," said Phoenix. "Do all right for out in the country, but wouldn't look right to go in a big building."

"Stand still then, Grandma," said the lady. She put her packages down carefully on the sidewalk beside her and laced and tied both shoes tightly.

"Can't lace 'em with a cane," said Phoenix. "Thank you, missy. I doesn't mind asking a nice lady to tie up my shoe when I gets out on the street."

Moving slowly and from side to side, she went into the stone building and into a tower of steps, where she walked up and around and around until her feet knew to stop.

She entered a door, and there she saw nailed up on the wall the document that had been stamped with the gold seal and framed in the gold frame which matched the dream that was hung up in her head.

"Here I be," she said. There was a fixed and ceremonial stiffness over her body.

"A charity case, I suppose," said an attendant who sat at the desk before her.

But Phoenix only looked above her head. There was sweat on her face; the wrinkles shone like a bright net.

"Speak up, Grandma," the woman said. "What's your name? We must have your history, you know. Have you been here before? What seems to be the trouble with you?"

Old Phoenix only gave a twitch to her face as if a fly were bothering her.

"Are you deaf?" cried the attendant.

But then the nurse came in.

"Oh, that's just old Aunt Phoenix," she said. "She doesn't come for herself—she has a little grandson. She makes these trips just as regular as clockwork. She lives away back off the Old Natchez Trace." She bent down. "Well, Aunt Phoenix, why don't you just take a seat? We won't keep you standing after your long trip." She pointed.

The old woman sat down, bolt upright in the chair.

"Now, how is the boy?" asked the nurse.

Old Phoenix did not speak.

"I said, how is the boy?"

But Phoenix only waited and stared straight ahead, her face very solemn and withdrawn into rigidity.

"Is his throat any better?" asked the nurse. "Aunt Phoenix, don't you hear me? Is your grandson's throat any better since the last time you came for the medicine?"

With her hand on her knees, the old woman waited, silent, erect and motionless, just as if she were in armor.

"You mustn't take up our time this way, Aunt Phoenix," the nurse said. "Tell us quickly about your grandson, and get it over. He isn't dead, is he?"

At last there came a flicker and then a flame of comprehension across her face, and she spoke.

"My grandson. It was my memory had left me. There I sat and forgot why I made my long trip."

"Forgot?" The nurse frowned. "After you came so far?"

Then Phoenix was like an old woman begging a dignified forgiveness for waking up frightened in the night. "I never did go to school

—I was too old at the Surrender," she said in a soft voice. "I'm an old woman without an education. It was my memory fail me. My little grandson, he is just the same, and I forgot it in the coming."

"Throat never heals, does it?" said the nurse, speaking in a loud, sure voice to Old Phoenix. By now she had a card with something written on it, a little list. "Yes. Swallowed lye. When was it—January —two—three years ago—"

Phoenix spoke unasked now. "No, missy, he not dead, he just the same. Every little while his throat begin to close up again, and he not able to swallow. He not get his breath. He not able to help himself. So the time come around, and I go on another trip for the soothing-medicine."

"All right. The doctor said as long as you came to get it you could have it," said the nurse. "But it's an obstinate case."

"My little grandson, he sit up there in the house all wrapped up, waiting by himself," Phoenix went on. "We is the only two left in the world. He suffer and it don't seem to put him back at all. He got a sweet look. He going to last. He wear a little patch quilt and peep out, holding his mouth open like a little bird. I remembers so plain now. I not going to forget him again, no, the whole enduring time. I could tell him from all the others in creation."

"All right." The nurse was trying to hush her now. She brought her a bottle of medicine. "Charity," she said, making a check mark in a book.

Old Phoenix held the bottle close to her eyes and then carefully put it into her pocket.

"I thank you," she said.

"It's Christmas time, Grandma," said the attendant. "Could I give you a few pennies out of my purse?"

"Five pennies is a nickel," said Phoenix stiffly.

"Here's a nickel," said the attendant.

Phoenix rose carefully and held out her hand. She received the nickel and then fished the other nickel out of her pocket and laid it beside the new one. She stared at her palm closely, with her head on one side.

Then she gave a tap with her cane on the floor.

"This is what come to me to do," she said. "I going to the store and buy my child a little windmill they sells, made out of paper. He going to find it hard to believe there such a thing in the world. I'll march myself back where he waiting, holding it straight up in this hand."

She lifted her free hand, gave a little nod, turned round, and walked out of the doctor's office. Then her slow step began on the stairs, going down.

QUESTIONS

1. How much of the story takes place with Granny Phoenix as its only character? What happens in this first part of the tale? What effect does it have on you, the reader?
2. Describe Granny's first meeting with another person. What new information do we learn from it?
3. The story's climax comes at the point of the scene in the clinic. Here we finally learn why Granny has made her long journey. What is your reaction to this scene? How have the story and its narrator brought you to feel as you do?

# 3 *The First-Person Narrator*

Omniscient narrators stand somewhat apart from their stories. Having no role in the action themselves, they can interpret its events and characters impartially. Thus, the narrator of "The Open Boat" speaks for all his tale's characters when he opens the story by declaring that "none of them knew the color of the sky" and closes it with, "they felt that they could then be interpreters." Even when an omniscient narrator shows us most of the story through one central character's eyes, as does the narrator of "Young Goodman Brown," he can still give us glimpses into minds and actions that the character cannot see, as when Hawthorne's narrator tells us that Brown's townsmen "carved no hopeful verse upon his tombstone." Moreover, he can still interpret the events he relates from his own point of view, even when his view of the matter conflicts with his central character's: "Had Goodman Brown fallen asleep in the forest . . . ?"

First-person narrators, on the other hand, are participants in their own stories. They are telling us of something that happened to them, and are telling their tale from their own point of view. They cannot see into the minds of the other characters; indeed, they may hardly understand their own actions. In contrast to the total knowledge of the omniscient narrator, the first-person narrator's powers of interpretation may be slight indeed.

As the narrator's knowledge shrinks, the readers' role expands. If we cannot trust the narrator as an omniscient, final authority, then our own wisdom and judgment must come into play. We must weigh the narrator's perceptions against our own and so create our own understanding of the actions and characters within the story.

Often, therefore, first-person narratives are rich in **irony,** with the narrators describing what they think they see and the readers interpreting the descriptions to discover what "really" happened. In these stories the relationship between reader and narrator is completely reversed. Now we are the wise ones, the ones with the fullest perception of what's going on. If we could only speak to these narrators, as they seem to be speaking to us, how much we could tell them!

In other stories, however, first-person narrators retain the full authority of the storyteller. Indeed, if the tales they tell are set far enough in their pasts, the narrators may view themselves as nearly omniscient. They know what they were thinking and feeling when the events took place, so they can take us into their major character's mind; they know how events turned out, so they feel that they can interpret the patterns within them. Moreover, they may feel that they have grown considerably wiser since the time of the actions they are relating and can therefore combine past feelings and present understanding to interpret events and emotions as no one else could.

In either case, and in less extreme cases as well, we often feel closer to first-person narrators than we feel either to omniscient narrators or to the characters they describe. The limitations of human knowledge and insight within which the first-person narrators work, the blend of attempted objectivity and personal involvement their voices convey, and their apparent openness in telling their own stories appeal to our sympathy and our sense of fellowship. In telling us, as they often do, of their dreams and desires, first-person narrators speak eloquently of human aspirations; in confessing (consciously or unconsciously) their shortcomings, they speak no less eloquently of human limitations.

The narrators of "Bartleby the Scrivener" and "The Secret Sharer" are storytellers in the grand tradition. Don't plan to read these stories in haste. Their narrators set a leisurely pace for tales that are rich in detail and in reflection; and they will not be hurried. Melville's narrator, in particular, is conscientious both in telling his story as fully as he can and in admitting the limits of his knowledge; while Conrad's tale echoes the pace and rhythms of the spoken word.

"The Yellow Wall-Paper" and "Really, *Doesn't* Crime Pay?" represent a second tradition in first-person narrative: the creation of a tale in the shape of a journal or diary. Unlike the first two stories, which claim clear descent from the oral tradition of tale-telling, these latter two stories come from a purely written tradition. You must have journals—and hence writing—before you can create a story that pretends to be a group of entries from somebody's journal.

Stories written in this "diary-like" tradition share several interesting features. First, they allow their narrators to ponder and reveal things the narrators would shrink from saying aloud. As the narrator of "The Yellow Wall-Paper" says, "I would not say it to a living soul, of course, but this is dead paper and a great relief to my mind." We, however, do read this "dead paper"; and we thus gain a closeness to the narrator that his or her closest friends might not have.

Second, the diary-like tale assumes that each event within it is chronicled on the day it occurs. It thus makes possible an immediacy which few other types of writing allow.

There is little room for hindsight in this sort of writing, little chance for the narrator to fit events into a pattern. We, as readers, must provide the pattern ourselves, just as we must come to our own understanding of the narrator by observing how her feelings and perceptions change during the course of the narrative. Caught up in the flow of events, the narrator may or may not be able to interpret them. We, standing outside those events, are challenged to do so.

In addition to serving as examples of the diary-like style of fiction, "The Yellow Wall-Paper" and "Really, *Doesn't* Crime Pay?" offer us an unusually fine chance to notice how a story can mirror the society in which it was written. The basic theme of the two tales is nearly identical; but the treatment of that theme, and the details used to point it, reveal clearly the different times in which the two were written. Read each story first for itself. But then, if you read them both, consider how they match and how they differ. The exercise will point out, once again, the uniqueness of each voice that we hear speaking to us from literature.

## HERMAN MELVILLE (1819–1891)

# *Bartleby the Scrivener*

I am a rather elderly man. The nature of my avocations, for the last thirty years, has brought me into more than ordinary contact with what would seem an interesting and somewhat singular set of men, of whom, as yet, nothing, that I know of, has ever been written—I mean, the law-copyists, or scriveners. I have known very many of them, professionally and privately, and, if I pleased, could relate divers histories, at which good-natured gentlemen might smile, and sentimental souls might weep. But I waive the biographies of all other scriveners, for a few passages in the life of Bartleby, who was a scrivener, the strangest I ever saw, or heard of. While, of other law-copyists, I might write the complete life, of Bartleby nothing of that sort can be done. I believe that no materials exist, for a full and satisfactory biography of this man. It is an irreparable loss to literature. Bartleby was one of those beings of whom nothing is ascertainable, except from the original sources, and, in his case, those are very small. What my own astonished eyes saw of Bartleby, *that* is all I know of him, except, indeed, one vague report, which will appear in the sequel.

Ere introducing the scrivener, as he first appeared to me, it is fit I make some mention of myself, my *employés,* my business, my chambers, and general surroundings; because some such description is indispensable to an adequate understanding of the chief character about to be presented. Imprimis: I am a man who, from his youth upwards, has been filled with a profound conviction that the easiest way of life is the best. Hence, though I belong to a profession proverbially energetic and nervous, even to turbulence, at times, yet nothing of that sort have I ever suffered to invade my peace. I am one of those unambitious lawyers who never addresses a jury, or in any way draws down public applause; but, in the cool tranquillity of a snug retreat, do a snug business among rich men's bonds, and mortgages, and title-deeds. All who know me, consider me an eminently *safe* man. The late John Jacob Astor,[1] a personage little given to poetic enthusiasm, had no hesitation in pronouncing my first grand point to be prudence; my next, method. I do not speak it in vanity, but simply record the fact, that I was not unemployed in my profession by the late John Jacob Astor, a name which, I admit, I love to repeat; for it hath a rounded and orbicular sound to it, and rings like unto bullion. I will freely add, that I was not insensible to the late John Jacob Astor's good opinion.

Some time prior to the period at which this little history begins, my avocations had been largely increased. The good old office, now extinct in the State of New York, of a Master in Chancery, had been conferred upon me. It was not a very arduous office, but very pleasantly remunerative. I seldom lose my temper; much more seldom indulge in dangerous indignation at wrongs and outrages; but, I must be permitted to be rash here, and declare, that I consider the sudden and violent abrogation of the office of Master in Chancery, by the new Constitution, as a —— premature act; inasmuch as I had counted upon a life-lease of the profits, whereas I only received those of a few short years. But this is by the way.

My chambers were up stairs, at No. — Wall Street. At one end, they looked upon the white wall of the interior of a spacious sky-light shaft, penetrating the building from top to bottom.

This view might have been considered rather tame than otherwise, deficient in what landscape painters call "life." But, if so, the view from the other end of my chambers offered, at least, a contrast, if nothing more. In that direction, my windows commanded an unobstructed view of a lofty brick wall, black by age and everlasting shade; which wall required no spy-glass to bring out its lurking beauties, but, for the benefit of all near-sighted spectators, was pushed up to within ten feet of my window panes. Owing to the great height of the surrounding buildings, and my chambers being on the second floor, the interval between this wall and mine not a little resembled a huge square cistern.

At the period just preceding the advent of Bartleby, I had two persons as copyists in my employment, and a promising lad as an

[1] *John Jacob Astor* (1763–1848), an American fur trader and financier.

office-boy. First, Turkey; second, Nippers; third, Ginger Nut. These may seem names, the like of which are not usually found in the Directory. In truth, they were nicknames, mutually conferred upon each other by my three clerks, and were deemed expressive of their respective persons or characters. Turkey was a short, pursy Englishman, of about my own age—that is, somewhere not far from sixty. In the morning, one might say, his face was of a fine florid hue, but after twelve o'clock, meridian—his dinner hour—it blazed like a grate full of Christmas coals; and continued blazing—but, as it were, with a gradual wane—till six o'clock, P.M., or thereabouts; after which, I saw no more of the proprietor of the face, which, gaining its meridian with the sun, seemed to set with it, to rise, culminate, and decline the following day, with the like regularity and undiminished glory. There are many singular coincidences I have known in the course of my life, not the least among which was the fact, that, exactly when Turkey displayed his fullest beams from his red and radiant countenance, just then, too, at that critical moment, began the daily period when I considered his business capacities as seriously disturbed for the remainder of the twenty-four hours. Not that he was absolutely idle, or averse to business, then; far from it. The difficulty was, he was apt to be altogether too energetic. There was a strange, inflamed, flurried, flighty recklessness of activity about him. He would be incautious in dipping his pen into his inkstand. All his blots upon my documents were dropped there after twelve o'clock, meridian. Indeed, not only would he be reckless, and sadly given to making blots in the afternoon, but, some days, he went further, and was rather noisy. At such times, too, his face flamed with augmented blazonry, as if cannel coal had been heaped on anthracite. He made an unpleasant racket with his chair; spilled his sand-box; in mending his pens, impatiently split them all to pieces, and threw them on the floor in a sudden passion; stood up, and leaned over his table, boxing his papers about in a most indecorous manner, very sad to behold in an elderly man like him. Nevertheless, as he was in many ways a most valuable person to me, and all the time before twelve o'clock, meridian, was the quickest, steadiest creature, too, accomplishing a great deal of work in a style not easily to be matched—for these reasons, I was willing to overlook his eccentricities, though, indeed, occasionally, I remonstrated with him. I did this very gently, however, because, though the civilest, nay, the blandest and most reverential of men in the morning, yet, in the afternoon, he was disposed, upon provocation, to be slightly rash with his tongue—in fact, insolent. Now, valuing his morning services as I did, and resolved not to lose them—yet, at the same time, made uncomfortable by his inflamed ways after twelve o'clock—and being a man of peace, unwilling by my admonitions to call forth unseemly retorts from him, I took upon me, one Saturday noon (he was always worse on Saturdays) to hint to him, very kindly, that, perhaps, now that he was growing old, it might be well to abridge his labors; in short, he need not come to my chambers after twelve o'clock, but, dinner over, had best go home to his lodgings, and rest himself till tea-time. But no; he insisted upon his afternoon devotions. His countenance became intolerably fervid, as he oratorically assured me—gesticulating with a long ruler at the other end of the room—that if his services in the morning were useful, how indispensable, then, in the afternoon?

"With submission, sir," said Turkey, on this occasion, "I consider myself your right-hand man. In the morning I but marshal and deploy my columns; but in the afternoon I put myself at their head, and gallantly charge the foe, thus"—and he made a violent thrust with the ruler.

"But the blots, Turkey," intimated I.

"True; but, with submission, sir, behold these hairs! I am getting old. Surely, sir, a blot or two of a warm afternoon is not to be severely urged against gray hairs. Old age—even if it blot the page—is honorable. With submission, sir, we *both* are getting old."

This appeal to my fellow-feeling was hardly to be resisted. At all events, I saw that go he would not. So, I made up my mind to let him stay, resolving, nevertheless, to see to it that, during the afternoon, he had to do with my less important papers.

Nippers, the second on my list, was a whiskered, sallow, and, upon the whole, rather piratical-looking young man, of about five and twenty. I always deemed him the victim of two evil powers—ambition and indigestion. The ambition was evinced by a certain impatience of the duties of a mere copyist, an unwarrantable usurpation of strictly professional affairs, such as the original drawing up of legal documents. The indigestion seemed betokened in an occasional nervous testiness and grinning irritability, causing the teeth to audibly grind together over mistakes committed in copying; unnecessary maledictions, hissed, rather than spoken, in the heat of business; and especially by a continual discontent with the height of the table where he worked. Though of a very ingenious mechanical turn, Nippers could never get this table to suit him. He put chips under it, blocks of various sorts, bits of pasteboard, and at last went so far as to attempt an exquisite adjustment, by final pieces of folded blotting-paper. But no invention would answer. If, for the sake of easing his back, he brought the table lid at a sharp angle well up towards his chin, and wrote there like a man using the steep roof of a Dutch house for his desk, then he declared that it stopped the circulation in his arms. If now he lowered the table to his waistbands, and stooped over it in writing, then there was a sore aching in his back. In short, the truth of the matter was, Nippers knew not what he wanted. Or, if he wanted anything, it was to be rid of a scrivener's table altogether. Among the manifestations of his diseased ambition was a fondness he had for receiving visits from certain ambiguous-looking fellows in seedy coats, whom he called his clients. Indeed, I was aware that not only was he, at times, considerable of a ward-politician, but he occasionally did a little business at the Justices' courts, and was not unknown on the steps of the Tombs. I have good reason to believe, however, that one individual who called upon him at my chambers, and who, with a grand air, he insisted was his client, was no other than a dun, and the alleged title-deed, a bill. But, with all his failings, and the annoyances he caused me, Nippers, like his compatriot Turkey, was a very useful man to me; wrote a neat, swift hand; and, when he chose, was not deficient in a gentlemanly sort of deportment. Added to this, he always dressed in a gentlemanly sort of way; and so, incidentally, reflected credit upon my chambers. Whereas, with respect to Turkey, I had much ado to keep him from being a reproach to me. His clothes were apt to look oily, and smell of eating-houses. He wore his pantaloons very loose and baggy in summer. His coats were execrable; his hat not to be handled. But while the hat was a thing of indifference to me, inasmuch as his natural civility and deference, as a dependent Englishman, always led him to doff it the moment he entered the room, yet his coat was another matter. Concerning his coats, I reasoned with him; but with no effect. The truth was, I suppose, that a man with so small an income could not afford to sport such a lustrous face and a lustrous coat at one and the same time. As Nippers once observed, Turkey's money went chiefly for red ink. One winter day, I presented Turkey with a highly respectable-looking coat of my own—a padded gray coat, of a most comfortable warmth, and which buttoned straight up from the knee to the neck. I thought Turkey would appreciate the favor, and abate his rashness and obstreperousness of afternoons. But no; I verily believe that buttoning himself up in so downy and blanket-like a coat had a pernicious effect upon him—upon the same principle that too much oats are bad for horses. In fact, precisely as a rash, restive horse is said to feel his oats, so Turkey felt his coat. It made him insolent. He was a man whom prosperity harmed.

Though, concerning the self-indulgent habits of Turkey, I had my own private surmises, yet, touching Nippers, I was well persuaded that, whatever might be his faults in other respects, he was, at least, a temperate young man. But, indeed, nature herself seemed to have been his vintner, and, at his birth, charged him so thoroughly with an irritable, brandy-like disposition, that all subsequent potations were needless. When I consider how, amid the stillness of my chambers, Nippers would sometimes impatiently rise from his seat, and stooping over his table, spread his arms wide apart, seize the whole desk, and move it, and jerk it, with a grim, grinding motion on the floor, as if the table were a perverse voluntary agent, intent on thwarting and vexing him, I plainly perceive that, for Nippers, brandy-and-water were altogether superfluous.

It was fortunate for me that, owing to its peculiar cause—indigestion—the iritability and consequent nervousness of Nippers were mainly observable in the morning, while in the afternoon he was comparatively mild. So that, Turkey's paroxysms only coming on about twelve o'clock, I never had to do with their eccentricities at one time. Their fits relieved each other, like guards. When Nippers' was on, Turkey's was off; and *vice versa*. This was a good natural arrangement, under the circumstances.

Ginger Nut, the third on my list, was a lad, some twelve years old. His father was a car-man, ambitious of seeing his son on the bench instead of a cart, before he died. So he sent him to my office, as student at law, errand-boy, cleaner and sweeper, at the rate of one dollar a week. He had a little desk to himself, but he did not use it much. Upon inspection, the drawer exhibited a great array of the shells of various sorts of nuts. Indeed, to this quick-witted youth, the whole noble science of the law was contained in a nut-shell. Not the least among the employments of Ginger Nut, as well as one which he discharged with the most alacrity, was his duty as cake and apple purveyor for Turkey and Nippers. Copying law-papers being proverbially a dry, husky sort of business, my two scriveners were fain to moisten their mouths very often with Spitzenbergs, to be had at the numerous stalls nigh the Custom House and Post Office. Also, they sent Ginger Nut very frequently for that peculiar cake—small, flat, round, and very spicy—after which he had been named by them. Of a cold morning, when business was but dull, Turkey would gobble up scores of these cakes, as if they were mere wafers—indeed, they sell them at the rate of six or eight for a penny—the scrape of his pen blending with the crunching of the crisp particles in his mouth. Of all the fiery afternoon blunders and flurried rashnesses of Turkey, was his once moistening a ginger-cake between his lips, and clapping it on to a mortgage, for a seal. I came within an ace of dismissing him then. But he mollified me by making an oriental bow, and saying—

"With submission, sir, it was generous of me to find you in stationery on my own account."

Now my original business—that of a conveyancer and title hunter, and drawer-up of recondite documents of all sorts—was considerably increased by receiving the master's office. There was now great work for scriveners. Not only must I push the clerks already with me, but I must have additional help.

In answer to my advertisement, a motionless young man one morning stood upon my office threshold, the door being open, for it was summer. I can see that figure now—pallidly neat, pitiably respectable, incurably forlorn! It was Bartleby.

After a few words touching his qualifications, I engaged him, glad to have among my corps of copyists a man of so singularly sedate an aspect, which I thought might operate beneficially upon the flighty temper of Turkey, and the fiery one of Nippers.

I should have stated before that ground glass folding-doors divided my premises into two parts, one of which was occupied by my scriveners, the other by myself. According to my humor, I threw open these doors, or closed them. I resolved to assign Bartleby a corner by the folding-doors, but on my side of them, so as to have this quiet man within easy call, in case any trifling thing was to be done. I placed his desk close up to a small side-window in that part of the room, a window which originally had afforded a lateral view of certain grimy backyards and bricks, but which, owing to subsequent erections, commanded at present no view at all, though it gave some light. Within three feet of the panes was a wall, and the light came down from far above, between two lofty buildings, as from a very small opening in a dome. Still further to a satisfactory arrangement, I procured a high green folding screen, which might entirely isolate Bartleby from my sight, though not remove him from my voice. And thus, in a manner, privacy and society were conjoined.

At first, Bartleby did an extraordinary quantity of writing. As if long famishing for something to copy, he seemed to gorge himself on my documents. There was no pause for digestion. He ran a day and night line, copying by sun-light and by candle-light. I should have been quite delighted with his application, had he been cheerfully industrious. But he wrote on silently, palely, mechanically.

It is, of course, an indispensable part of a scrivener's business to verify the accuracy of his copy, word by word. Where there are two or more scriveners in an office, they assist each other in this examination, one reading from the copy, the other holding the original. It is a very dull, wearisome, and lethargic affair. I can readily imagine that, to some sanguine temperaments, it would be altogether intolerable. For example, I cannot credit that the mettlesome poet, Byron, would have contentedly sat down with Bartleby to examine a law document of, say five hundred pages, closely written in a crimpy hand.

Now and then, in the haste of business, it had been my habit to assist in comparing some brief document myself, calling Turkey or Nippers for this purpose. One object I had, in placing Bartleby so handy to me behind the screen, was, to avail myself of his services on such trivial occasions. It was on the third day, I think, of his being with me, and before any necessity had arisen for having his own writing examined, that, being much hurried to complete a small affair I had in hand, I abruptly called to Bartleby. In my haste and natural expectancy of instant compliance, I sat with my head bent over the original on my desk, and my right hand sideways, and somewhat nervously extended with the copy, so that, immediately upon emerging from his retreat, Bartleby might snatch it and proceed to business without the least delay.

In this very attitude did I sit when I called to him, rapidly stating what it was I wanted him to do—namely, to examine a small paper with me. Imagine my surprise, nay, my consternation, when, without moving from his privacy, Bartleby, in a singularly mild, firm voice, replied, "I would prefer not to."

I sat awhile in perfect silence, rallying my stunned faculties. Immediately it occurred to me that my ears had deceived me, or Bartleby had entirely misunderstood my meaning. I repeated my request in the clearest tone I could assume; but in quite as clear a one came the previous reply, "I would prefer not to."

"Prefer not to," echoed I, rising in high excitement, and crossing the room with a stride. "What do you mean? Are you moon-struck? I want you to help me compare this sheet here—take it," and I thrust it towards him.

"I would prefer not to," said he.

I looked at him steadfastly. His face was leanly composed; his gray eye dimly calm. Not a wrinkle of agitation rippled him. Had there been the least uneasiness, anger, impatience or impertinence in his manner; in other words, had there been any thing ordinarily human about him, doubtless I should have violently dismissed him from the premises. But as it was, I should have as soon thought of turning my pale plaster-of-paris bust of Cicero out of doors. I stood gazing at him awhile, as he went on with his own writing, and then reseated myself at my desk. This is very strange, thought I. What had one best do? But my business hurried me. I concluded to forget the matter for the present, reserving it for my future leisure. So calling Nippers from the other room, the paper was speedily examined.

A few days after this, Bartleby concluded four lengthy documents, being quadruplicates of a week's testimony taken before me in my High Court of Chancery. It became necessary to examine them. It was an important suit, and great accuracy was imperative. Having all things arranged, I called Turkey, Nippers, and Ginger Nut, from the next room, meaning to place the four copies in the hands of my four clerks, while I should read from the original. Accordingly, Turkey, Nippers, and Ginger Nut had taken their seats in a row, each with his document in his hand, when I called to Bartleby to join this interesting group.

"Bartleby! quick, I am waiting."

I heard a slow scrape of his chair legs on the uncarpeted floor, and soon he appeared standing at the entrance of his hermitage.

"What is wanted?" said he, mildly.

"The copies, the copies," said I, hurriedly. "We are going to examine them. There"—and I held towards him the fourth quadruplicate.

"I would prefer not to," he said, and gently disappeared behind the screen.

For a few moments I was turned into a pillar of salt, standing at the head of my seated column of clerks. Recovering myself, I advanced towards the screen, and demanded the reason for such extraordinary conduct.

"*Why* do you refuse?"

"I would prefer not to."

With any other man I should have flown outright into a dreadful passion, scorned all further words, and thrust him ignominiously from my presence. But there was something about Bartleby that not only strangely disarmed me, but, in a wonderful manner, touched and disconcerted me. I began to reason with him.

"These are your own copies we are about to examine. It is labor saving to you, because one examination will answer for your four papers. It is common usage. Every copyist is bound to help examine his copy. Is it not so? Will you not speak? Answer!"

"I prefer not to," he replied in a flutelike tone. It seemed to me that, while I had been addressing him, he carefully revolved every statement that I made; fully comprehended the meaning; could not gainsay the irresistible conclusion; but, at the same time, some paramount consideration prevailed with him to reply as he did.

"You are decided, then, not to comply with my request—a request made according to common usage and common sense?"

He briefly gave me to understand, that on that point my judgment was sound. Yes: his decision was irreversible.

It is not seldom the case that, when a man is browbeaten in some unprecedented and violently unreasonable way, he begins to stagger in his own plainest faith. He begins, as it were, vaguely to surmise that, wonderful as it may be, all the justice and all the reason is on the other side. Accordingly, if any disinterested persons are present, he turns to them for some reinforcement of his own faltering mind.

"Turkey," said I, "what do you think of this? Am I not right?"

"With submission, sir," said Turkey, in his blandest tone, "I think that you are."

"Nippers," said I, "what do *you* think of it?"

"I think I should kick him out of the office."

(The reader, of nice perceptions, will here perceive that, it being morning, Turkey's answer is couched in polite and tranquil terms, but Nippers' replies in ill-tempered ones. Or, to repeat a previous sentence, Nippers' ugly mood was on duty, and Turkey's off.)

"Ginger Nut," said I, willing to enlist the smallest suffrage in my behalf, "what do *you* think of it?"

"I think, sir, he's a little *luny*," replied Ginger Nut, with a grin.

"You hear what they say," said I, turning towards the screen, "come forth and do your duty."

But he vouchsafed no reply. I pondered a moment in sore perplexity. But once more business hurried me. I determined again to postpone the consideration of this dilemma to my future leisure. With a little trouble we made out to examine the papers without Bartleby, though at every page or two Turkey deferentially dropped his opinion, that this proceeding was quite out of the common; while Nippers, twitching in his chair with a dyspeptic nervousness, ground out, between his set teeth, occasional hissing maledictions against the stubborn oaf behind the screen. And for his (Nippers') part, this was the first and the last time he would do another man's business without pay.

Meanwhile Bartleby sat in his hermitage, oblivious to everything but his own peculiar business there.

Some days passed, the scrivener being employed upon another lengthy work. His late remarkable conduct led me to regard his ways narrowly. I observed that he never went to dinner; indeed, that he never went anywhere. As yet I had never, of my personal knowledge, known him to be outside of my office. He was a perpetual sentry in the corner. At about eleven o'clock though, in the morning, I noticed that Ginger Nut would advance toward the opening in Bartleby's screen, as if silently beckoned thither by a gesture invisible to me where I sat. The boy would then leave the office, jingling a few pence, and reappear with a handful of ginger-nuts, which he delivered in the hermitage, receiving two of the cakes for his trouble.

He lives, then, on ginger-nuts, thought I; never eats a dinner, properly speaking; he must be a vegetarian, then; but no; he never eats even vegetables, he eats nothing but ginger-nuts. My mind then ran on in reveries concerning the probable effects upon the human constitution of living entirely on ginger-nuts. Ginger-nuts are so called, because they contain ginger as one of their peculiar constituents, and the final flavoring one. Now, what was ginger? A hot, spicy thing. Was Bartleby hot and spicy? Not at all. Ginger, then, had no effect upon Bartleby. Probably he preferred it should have none.

Nothing so aggravates an earnest person as a passive resistance. If the individual so resisted be of a not inhumane temper, and the resisting one perfectly harmless in his passivity, then, in the better moods of the former, he will endeavor charitably to construe to his imagination what proves impossible to be solved by his judgment. Even so, for the most part, I regarded Bartleby and his ways. Poor fellow! thought I, he means no mischief; it is plain he intends no insolence; his aspect sufficiently evinces that his eccentricities are involuntary. He is useful to me. I can get along with him. If I turn him away, the chances are he will fall in with some less-indulgent employer, and then he will be rudely treated, and perhaps driven forth miserably to starve. Yes. Here I can cheaply purchase a delicious self-approval. To befriend Bartleby; to humor him in his strange willfulness, will cost me little or nothing, while I lay up in my soul what will eventually prove a sweet morsel for my conscience. But this mood was not invariable with me. The passiveness of Bartleby sometimes irritated me. I felt strangely goaded on to encounter him in new opposition—to elicit some angry spark from him answerable to my own. But, indeed, I might as well have essayed to strike fire with my knuckles against a bit of Windsor soap. But one afternoon the evil impulse in me mastered me, and the following little scene ensued:

"Bartleby," said I, "when those papers are all copied, I will compare them with you."

"I would prefer not to."

"How? Surely you do not mean to persist in that mulish vagary?"

No answer.

I threw open the folding-doors near by, and, turning upon Turkey and Nippers, exclaimed:

"Bartleby a second time says, he won't examine his papers. What do you think of it, Turkey?"

It was afternoon, be it remembered. Turkey sat glowing like a brass boiler; his bald head steaming; his hands reeling among his blotted papers.

"Think of it?" roared Turkey; "I think I'll just step behind his screen, and black his eyes for him!"

So saying, Turkey rose to his feet and threw his arms into a pugilistic position. He was hurrying away to make good his promise, when I detained him, alarmed at the effect of incautiously rousing Turkey's combativeness after dinner.

"Sit down, Turkey," said I, "and hear what Nippers has to say. What do you think of it, Nippers? Would I not be justified in immediately dismissing Bartleby?"

"Excuse me, that is for you to decide, sir. I think his conduct quite unusual, and, indeed, unjust, as regards Turkey and myself. But it may only be a passing whim."

"Ah," exclaimed I, "you have strangely changed your mind, then—you speak very gently of him now."

"All beer," cried Turkey; "gentleness is effects of beer—Nippers and I dined together to-day. You see how gentle *I* am, sir. Shall I go and black his eyes?"

"You refer to Bartleby, I suppose. No, not to-day, Turkey," I replied; "pray, put up your fists."

I closed the doors, and again advanced towards Bartleby. I felt additional incentives tempting me to my fate. I burned to be rebelled against again. I remember that Bartleby never left the office.

"Bartleby," said I, "Ginger Nut is away; just step around to the Post Office, won't you? (it was but a three minutes' walk), and see if there is anything for me."

"I would prefer not to."

"You *will* not?"

"I *prefer* not."

I staggered to my desk, and sat there in a deep study. My blind inveteracy returned. Was there any other thing in which I could procure myself to be ignominiously repulsed by this lean, penniless wight?—my hired clerk? What added thing is there, prefectly reasonable, that he will be sure to refuse to do?

"Bartleby!"

No answer.

"Bartleby," in a louder tone.

No answer.

"Bartleby," I roared.

Like a very ghost, agreeably to the laws of magical invocation, at the third summons, he appeared at the entrance of his hermitage.

"Go to the next room, and tell Nippers to come to me."

"I prefer not to," he respectfully and slowly said, and mildly disappeared.

"Very good, Bartleby," said I, in a quiet sort of serenely-severe self-possessed tone, intimating the unalterable purpose of some terrible retribution very close at hand. But upon the whole, as it was drawing towards my dinner-hour, I thought it best to put on my hat and walk home for the day, suffering much from perplexity and distress of mind.

Shall I acknowledge it? The conclusion of this whole business was, that it soon became a fixed fact of my chambers, that a pale young scrivener, by the name of Bartleby, had a desk there; that he copied for me at the usual rate of four cents a folio (one hundred words); but he was permanently exempt from examining the work done by him, that duty being transferred to Turkey and Nippers, out of compliment, doubtless, to their superior acuteness; moreover, said Bartleby was never, on any account, to be dispatched on the most trivial errand of any sort; and that even if entreated to take upon him such a matter, it was generally understood that he would "prefer not to"—in other words, that he would refuse point-blank.

As days passed on, I became considerably reconciled to Bartleby. His steadiness, his freedom from all dissipation, his incessant industry (except when he chose to throw himself into a standing revery behind his screen), his great stillness, his unalterableness of demeanor under all circumstances, made him a valuable acquisition. One prime thing was this—*he was always there*—first in the morning, continually through the day, and the last at night. I had a singular confidence in his honesty. I felt my most precious papers perfectly safe in his hands. Sometimes, to be sure, I could not, for the very soul of me, avoid falling into sudden spasmodic passions with him. For it was exceeding difficult to bear in mind all the time those strange peculiarities, privileges, and unheard of exemptions, forming the tacit stipulations on Bartleby's part under which he remained in my office. Now and then, in the eagerness of dispatching pressing business, I would inadvertently summon Bartleby, in a short, rapid tone, to put his finger, say, on the incipient tie of a bit of red tape with which I was about compressing some papers. Of course, from behind the screen the usual answer, "I prefer not to," was sure to come; and then, how could a human creature, with the common infirmities of our nature, refrain from bitterly exclaiming upon such perverseness—such unreasonableness. However, every added repulse of this sort which I received only tended to lessen the probability of my repeating the inadvertence.

Here it must be said, that according to the custom of most legal gentlemen occupying chambers in densely-populated law buildings, there were several keys to my door. One was kept by a woman residing in the attic, which person weekly scrubbed and daily swept and dusted my apartments. Another was kept by Turkey for convenience sake. The third I sometimes carried in my own pocket. The fourth I knew not who had.

Now, one Sunday morning I happened to go to Trinity Church, to hear a celebrated preacher, and finding myself rather early on the ground I thought I would walk around to my chambers for a while. Luckily I had my key with me; but upon applying it to the lock, I found it resisted by something inserted from the inside. Quite surprised, I called out; when to my consternation a key was turned from within; and thrusting his lean visage at me, and holding the door ajar, the apparition of Bartleby appeared, in his shirt sleeves, and otherwise in a strangely tattered deshabille, saying quietly that he was sorry, but he was deeply engaged just then, and—preferred not admitting me at present. In a brief word or two, he moreover added, that perhaps I had better walk around the block two or three times, and by that time he would probably have concluded his affairs.

Now, the utterly unsurmised appearance of Bartleby, tenanting my law-chambers of a Sunday morning, with his cadaverously gentlemanly *nonchalance,* yet withal firm and self-possessed, had such a strange effect upon me, that incontinently I slunk away from my own door, and did as desired. But not without sundry twinges of impotent rebellion against the mild effrontery of this unaccountable scrivener. Indeed, it was his wonderful mildness chiefly, which not only disarmed me, but unmanned me as it were. For I consider that one, for the time, is somehow unmanned when he tranquilly permits his hired clerk to dictate to him, and order him away from his own premises. Furthermore, I was full of uneasiness as to what Bartleby could possibly be doing in my office in his shirt sleeves, and in an otherwise dismantled condition of a Sunday morning. Was anything amiss going on? Nay, that was out of the question. It was not to be thought of for a moment that Bartleby was an immoral person. But what could he be doing there?—copying? Nay again, whatever might be his eccentricities, Bartleby was an eminently decorous person. He would be the last man to sit down to his desk in any state approaching to nudity. Besides, it was Sunday; and there was something about Bartleby that forbade the supposition that he would by any secular occupation violate the proprieties of the day.

Nevertheless, my mind was not pacified; and full of a restless curiosity, at last I returned to the door. Without hindrance I inserted my key, opened it, and entered. Bartleby was not to be seen. I looked round anxiously, peeped behind his screen; but it was very plain that he was gone. Upon more closely examining the place, I surmised that for an indefinite period Bartleby must have ate, dressed, and slept in my office, and that, too, without plate, mirror, or bed. The cushioned seat of a rickety old sofa in one corner bore the faint impression of a lean, reclining form. Rolled away under his desk, I found a blanket; under the empty grate, a blacking box and brush; on a chair, a tin basin, with soap and a ragged towel; in a newspaper a few crumbs of ginger-nuts and a morsel of cheese. Yes, thought I, it is evident enough that Bartleby has been making his home here, keeping bachelor's hall all by himself. Immediately then the thought came sweeping across me, what miserable friendlessness and loneliness are here revealed! His poverty is great; but his solitude, how horrible! Think of it. Of a Sunday, Wall Street is deserted as Petra;[2] and every night of every day it is an emptiness. This building, too, which of week-days hums with industry and life, at nightfall echoes with sheer vacancy, and all through Sunday is forlorn. And here Bartleby makes his home; sole spectator of a solitude which he has seen all populous —a sort of innocent and transformed Marius brooding among the ruins of Carthage!

For the first time in my life a feeling of over-powering stinging

[2] *Petra,* ancient city in Syria.

melancholy seized me. Before, I had never experienced aught but a not unpleasing sadness. The bond of a common humanity now drew me irresistibly to gloom. A fraternal melancholy! For both I and Bartleby were sons of Adam. I remembered the bright silks and sparkling faces I had seen that day, in gala trim, swan-like sailing down the Mississippi of Broadway; and I contrasted them with the pallid copyist, and thought to myself, Ah, happiness courts the light, so we deem the world is gay; but misery hides aloof, so we deem that misery there is none. These sad fancyings—chimeras, doubtless, of a sick and silly brain—led on to other and more special thoughts, concerning the eccentricities of Bartleby. Presentiments of strange discoveries hovered round me. The scrivener's pale form appeared to me laid out, among uncaring strangers, in its shivering winding sheet.

Suddenly I was attracted by Bartleby's closed desk, the key in open sight left in the lock.

I mean no mischief, seek the gratification of no heartless curiosity, thought I; besides, the desk is mine, and its contents, too, so I will make bold to look within. Everything was methodically arranged, the papers smoothly placed. The pigeon holes were deep, and removing the files of documents, I groped into their recesses. Presently I felt something there, and dragged it out. It was an old bandanna handkerchief, heavy and knotted. I opened it, and saw it was a saving's bank.

I now recalled all the quiet mysteries which I had noted in the man. I remembered that he never spoke but to answer; that, though at intervals he had considerable time to himself, yet I had never seen him reading—no, not even a newspaper; that for long periods he would stand looking out, at his pale window behind the screen, upon the dead brick wall; I was quite sure he never visited any refectory or eating house; while his pale face clearly indicated that he never drank beer like Turkey, or tea and coffee even, like other men; that he never went anywhere in particular that I could learn; never went out for a walk, unless, indeed, that was the case at present; that he had declined telling who he was, or whence he came, or whether he had any relatives in the world; that though so thin and pale, he never complained of ill health. And more than all, I remembered a certain unconscious air of pallid—how shall I call it?—of pallid haughtiness, say, or rather an austere reserve about him, which had positively awed me into my tame compliance with his eccentricities, when I had feared to ask him to do the slightest incidental thing for me, even though I might know, from his long-continued motionlessness, that behind his screen he must be standing in one of those dead-wall reveries of his.

Revolving all these things, and coupling them with the recently discovered fact, that he made my office his constant abiding place and home, and not forgetful of his morbid moodiness; revolving all these things, a prudential feeling began to steal over me. My first emotions had been those of pure melancholy and sincerest pity; but just in proportion as the forlornness of Bartleby grew and grew to my imagination, did that same melancholy merge into fear, that pity into repulsion. So true it is, and so terrible, too, that up to a certain point the thought or sight of misery enlists our best affections; but, in certain special cases, beyond that point it does not. They err who would assert that invariably this is owing to the inherent selfishness of the human heart. It rather proceeds from a certain hopelessness of remedying excessive and organic ill. To a sensitive being, pity is not seldom pain. And when at last it is perceived that such pity cannot lead to effectual succor, common sense bids the soul be rid of it. What I saw that morning persuaded me that the scrivener was the victim of inate and incurable disorder. I might give alms to his body; but his body did not pain him; it was his soul that suffered, and his soul I could not reach.

I did not accomplish the purpose of going to Trinity Church that morning. Somehow, the things I had seen disqualified me for the time from church-going. I walked homeward, thinking what I would do with Bartleby. Finally, I resolved upon this—I would put certain calm questions to him the next morning, touching his history, etc., and if he declined to answer them openly and unreservedly (and I supposed he would prefer not), then to give him a twenty dollar bill over and above whatever I might owe him, and tell him his services were no longer required; but that if in any other way I could assist him, I would be happy to do so, especially if he desired to return to his native place, wherever that might be, I would willingly help to defray the expenses. Moreover, if, after reaching home, he found himself at any time in want of aid, a letter from him would be sure of a reply.

The next morning came.

"Bartleby," said I, gently calling to him behind his screen.

No reply.

"Bartleby," said I, in a still gentler tone, "come here; I am not going to ask you to do anything you would prefer not to do—I simply wish to speak to you."

Upon this he noiselessly slid into view.

"Will you tell me, Bartleby, where you were born?"

"I would prefer not to."

"Will you tell me *anything* about yourself?"

"I would prefer not to."

"But what reasonable objection can you have to speak to me? I feel friendly towards you."

He did not look at me while I spoke, but kept his glance fixed upon my bust of Cicero, which, as I then sat, was directly behind me, some six inches above my head.

"What is your answer, Bartleby," said I, after waiting a considerable time for a reply, during which his countenance remained immovable, only there was the faintest conceivable tremor of the white attenuated mouth.

"At present I prefer to give no answer," he said, and retired into his hermitage.

It was rather weak in me I confess, but his manner, on this occasion, nettled me. Not only did there seem to lurk in it a certain calm disdain, but his perverseness seemed ungrateful, considering the undeniable good usage and indulgence he had received from me.

Again I sat ruminating what I should do. Mortified as I was at his behavior, and resolved as I had been to dismiss him when I entered my office, nevertheless I strangely felt something superstitious knocking at my heart, and forbidding me to carry out my purpose, and denouncing me for a villain if I dared to breathe one bitter word against this forlornest of mankind. At last, familiarly drawing my chair behind his screen, I sat down and said: "Bartleby, never mind, then, about revealing your history; but let me entreat you, as a friend, to comply as far as may be with the usages of this office. Say now, you will help to examine papers to-morrow or next day: in short, say now, that in a day or two you will begin to be a little reasonable:—say so, Bartleby."

"At present I would prefer not to be a little reasonable," was his mildly cadaverous reply.

Just then the folding-doors opened, and Nippers approached. He seemed suffering from an unusually bad night's rest, induced by severer indigestion than common. He overheard those final words of Bartleby.

*"Prefer not,* eh?" gritted Nippers—"I'd *prefer* him, if I were you, sir," addressing me—"I'd *prefer* him; I'd give him preferences, the stubborn mule! What is it, sir, pray, that he *prefers* not to do now?"

Bartleby moved not a limb.

"Mr. Nippers," said I, "I'd prefer that you would withdraw for the present."

Somehow, of late, I had got into the way of involuntarily using this word "prefer" upon all sorts of not exactly suitable occasions. And I trembled to think that my contact with the scrivener had already and seriously affected me in a mental way. And what further and deeper aberration might it not yet produce? This apprehension had not been without efficacy in determining me to summary measures.

As Nippers, looking very sour and sulky, was departing, Turkey blandly and deferentially approached.

"With submission, sir," said he, "yesterday I was thinking abut Bartleby here, and I think that if he would but prefer to take a quart of good ale every day, it would do much towards mending him, and enabling him to assist in examining his papers."

"So you have got the word, too," said I, slightly excited.

"With submission, what word, sir," asked Turkey, respectfully crowding himself into the contracted space behind the screen, and by so doing, making me jostle the scrivener. "What word, sir?"

"I would prefer to be left alone here," said Bartleby, as if offended at being mobbed in his privacy.

*"That's* the word, Turkey," said I—*"that's* it."

"Oh, *prefer?* oh yes—queer word. I never use it myself. But, sir, as I was saying, if he would but prefer—"

"Turkey," interrupted I, "you will please withdraw."

"Oh, certainly, sir, if you prefer that I should."

As he opened the folding-door to retire, Nippers at his desk caught a glimpse of me, and asked whether I would prefer to have a certain paper copied on blue paper or white. He did not in the least roguishly accent the word prefer. It was plain that it involuntarily rolled from his tongue. I thought to myself, surely I must get rid of a demented man, who already has in some degree turned the tongues, if not the heads of myself and clerks. But I thought it prudent not to break the dismission at once.

The next day I noticed that Bartleby did nothing but stand at his window in his dead-wall revery. Upon asking him why he did not write, he said that he had decided upon doing no more writing.

"Why, how now? what next?" exclaimed I, "do no more writing?"

"No more."

"And what is the reason?"

"Do you not see the reason for yourself," he indifferently replied.

I looked steadfastly at thim, and perceived that his eyes looked dull and glazed. Instantly it occurred to me, that his unexampled diligence in copying by his dim window for the first few weeks of his stay with me might have temporarily impaired his vision.

I was touched. I said something in condolence with him. I hinted that of course he did wisely in abstaining from writing for a while; and urged him to embrace that opportunity of taking wholesome exercise in the open air. This, however, he did not do. A few days after this, my other clerks being absent, and being in a great hurry to dispatch certain letters by the mail, I thought that, having nothing else earthly to do, Bartleby would surely be less inflexible than usual, and carry these letters to the post-office. But he blankly declined. So, much to my inconvenience, I went myself.

Still added days went by. Whether Bartleby's eyes improved or not, I could not say. To all appearance, I thought they did. But when I asked him if they did, he vouchsafed no answer. At all events, he would do no copying. At last, in reply to my urgings, he informed me that he had permanently given up copying.

"What!" exclaimed I; "suppose your eyes should get entirely well—better than ever before—would you not copy then?"

"I have given up copying," he answered, and slid aside.

He remained as ever, a fixture in my chamber. Nay—if that were possible—he became still more of a fixture than before. What was to be done? He would do nothing in the office; why should he stay there? In plain fact, he had now become a millstone to me, not only useless as a necklace, but afflictive to bear. Yet I was sorry for him. I speak less than truth when I say that, on his own account, he occasioned me uneasiness. If he would but have named a single relative or friend, I would instantly have written, and urged their taking the poor fellow away to some convenient retreat. But he seemed alone, absolutely alone in the universe. A bit of wreck in the mid Atlantic. At length, necessities connected with my business tyrannized over all other considerations. Decently as I could, I told Bartleby that in six days time he must unconditionally leave the office. I warned him to take measures, in the interval, for procuring some other abode. I offered to assist him in this endeavor, if he himself would but take the first step towards a removal. "And when you finally quit me, Bartleby," added I, "I shall see that you go not away entirely unprovided. Six days from this hour, remember."

At the expiration of that period, I peeped behind the screen, and lo! Bartleby was there.

I buttoned up my coat, balanced myself; advanced slowly towards him, touched his shoulder, and said, "The time has come; you must quit this place; I am sorry for you; here is money; but you must go."

"I would prefer not," he replied, with his back still towards me.

"You *must.*"

He remained silent.

Now I had an unbounded confidence in this man's common honesty. He had frequently restored to me sixpences and shillings carelessly dropped upon the floor, for I am apt to be very reckless in such shirt-button affairs. The proceeding, then, which followed will not be deemed extraordinary.

"Bartleby," said I, "I owe you twelve dollars on account; here are thirty-two; the odd twenty are yours—Will you take it?" and I handed the bills towards him.

But he made no motion.

"I will leave them here, then," putting them under a weight on the table. Then taking my hat and cane and going to the door, I tranquilly turned and added—"After you have removed your things from these offices, Bartleby, you will of course lock the door—since every one is now gone for the day but you—and if you please, slip your key underneath the mat, so that I may have it in the morning. I shall not see you again; so good-by to you. If, hereafter, in your new place of abode, I can be of any service to you, do not fail to advise me by letter. Good-by, Bartleby, and fare you well."

But he answered not a word; like the last column of some ruined temple, he remained standing mute and solitary in the middle of the otherwise deserted room.

As I walked home in a pensive mood, my vanity got the better of my pity. I could not but highly plume myself on my masterly management in getting rid of Bartleby. Masterly I call it, and such it must appear to any dispassionate thinker. The beauty of my procedure seemed to consist in its perfect quietness. There was no vulgar bullying, no bravado of any sort, no choleric hectoring, and striding to and fro across the apartment, jerking out vehement commands for Bartleby to bundle himself off with his beggarly traps. Nothing of the kind. Without loudly bidding Bartleby depart—as an inferior genius might have done—I *assumed* the ground that depart he must; and upon that assumption built all I had to say. The more I thought over my procedure, the more I was charmed with it. Nevertheless, next morning, upon awakening, I had my doubts—I had somehow slept off the fumes of vanity. One of the coolest and wisest hours a man has, is just after he awakes in the morning. My procedure seemed as sagacious as ever—but only in theory. How it would prove in practice—there was the rub. It was truly a beautiful thought to have assumed Bartleby's departure; but, after all, that assumption was simply my own, and none of Bartleby's. The great point was, not whether I had assumed that he would quit me, but whether he would prefer so to do. He was more a man of preferences than assumptions.

After breakfast, I walked down town, arguing the probabilities *pro* and *con*. One moment I thought it would prove a miserable failure, and Bartleby would be found all alive at my office as usual; the next moment it seemed certain that I should find his chair empty. And so I kept veering about. At the corner of Broadway and Canal Street, I saw quite an excited group of people standing in earnest conversation.

"I'll take odds he doesn't," said a voice as I passed.

"Doesn't go?—done!" said I, "put up your money."

I was instinctively putting my hand in my pocket to produce my own, when I remembered that this was an election day. The words I had overheard bore no reference to Bartleby, but to the success or nonsuccess of some candidate for the mayoralty. In my intent frame of mind, I had, as it were, imagined that all Broadway shared in my excitement, and were debating the same question with me. I passed on, very thankful that the uproar of the street screened my momentary absent-mindedness.

As I had intended, I was earlier than usual at my office door. I stood listening for a moment. All was still. He must be gone. I tried the knob. The door was locked. Yes, my procedure had worked to a charm; he indeed must be vanished. Yet a certain melancholy mixed with this: I was almost sorry for my brilliant success. I was fumbling under the door mat for the key, which Bartleby was to have left there for me, when accidentally my knee knocked against a panel, producing a summoning sound, and in response a voice came to me from within—"Not yet; I am occupied."

It was Bartleby.

I was thunderstruck. For an instant I stood like the man who, pipe in mouth, was killed one cloudless afternoon long ago in Virginia, by summer lightning; at his own warm open window he was killed, and remained leaning out there upon the dreamy afternoon, till some one touched him, when he fell.

"Not gone!" I murmured at last. But again obeying that wondrous ascendancy which the inscrutable scrivener had over me, and from which ascendancy, for all my chafing, I could not completely escape, I slowly went down stairs and out into the street, and while walking round the block, considered what I should next do in this unheard-of perplexity. Turn the man out by an actual thrusting I could not; to drive him away by calling him hard names would not do; calling in the police was an unpleasant idea; and yet, permit him to enjoy his cadaverous triumph over me—this, too, I could not think of. What was to be done? or, if nothing could be done, was there anything further that I could *assume* in the matter? Yes, as before I had prospectively assumed that Bartleby would depart, so now I might retrospectively assume that departed he was. In the legitimate carrying out of this assumption, I might enter my office in a great hurry, and pretending not to see Bartleby at all, walk straight against him as if he were air. Such a proceeding would in a singular degree have the appearance of a home-thrust. It was hardly possible that Bartleby could withstand such an application of the doctrine of assumptions. But upon second thoughts the success of the plan seemed rather dubious. I resolved to argue the matter over with him again.

"Bartleby," said I, entering the office, with a quietly severe expression, "I am seriously displeased. I am pained, Bartleby. I had thought better of you. I had imagined you of such a gentlemanly organization, that in any delicate dilemma a slight hint would suffice—in short, an assumption. But it appears I am deceived. Why," I added, unaffectedly starting, "you have not even touched that money yet," pointing to it, just where I had left it the evening previous.

He answered nothing.

"Will you, or will you not, quit me?" I now demanded in a sudden passion, advancing close to him.

"I would prefer *not* to quit you," he replied, gently emphasizing the *not.*

"What earthly right have you to stay here? Do you pay any rent? Do you pay my taxes? Or is this property yours?"

He answered nothing.

"Are you ready to go on and write now? Are your eyes recovered? Could you copy a small paper for me this morning? or help examine a few lines? or step round to the post-office? In a word, will you do anything at all, to give a coloring to your refusal to depart the premises?"

He silently retired into his hermitage.

I was now in such a state of nervous resentment that I thought it but prudent to check myself at present from further demonstrations. Bartleby and I were alone. I remembered the tragedy of the unfortunate Adams and the still more unfortunate Colt in the solitary office of the latter; and how poor Colt, being dreadfully incensed by Adams, and imprudently permitting himself to get wildly excited, was at unawares hurried into his fatal act—an act which certainly no man could possibly deplore more than the actor himself. Often it had occurred to me in my ponderings upon the subject, that had that altercation taken place in the public street, or at a private residence, it would not have terminated as it did. It was the circumstance of being alone in a solitary office, up stairs, of a building entirely unhallowed by humanizing domestic associations—an uncarpeted office, doubtless, of a dusty, haggard sort of appearance—this it must have been, which greatly helped to enhance the irritable desperation of the hapless Colt.[3]

But when this old Adam of resentment rose in me and tempted me concerning Bartleby, I grappled him and threw him. How? Why, simply by recalling the divine injunction: "A new commandment give I unto you, that ye love one another." Yes, this it was that saved me. Aside from higher considerations, charity often operates as a vastly wise and prudent principle—a great safeguard to its possessor. Men have committed murder for jealousy's sake, and anger's sake, and hatred's sake, and selfishness' sake, and spiritual pride's sake; but no man, that ever I heard of, ever committed a diabolical murder for

---

[3] *Adams . . . Colt,* a widely publicized murder-case in which John C. Colt killed Samuel Adams, in New York City, in January, 1842.

sweet charity's sake. Mere self-interest, then, if no better motive can be enlisted, should, especially with high-tempered men, prompt all beings to charity and philanthropy. At any rate, upon the occasion in question, I strove to drown my exasperated feelings towards the scrivener by benevolently construing his conduct. Poor fellow, poor fellow! thought I, he don't mean anything; and besides, he has seen hard times, and ought to be indulged.

I endeavored, also, immediately to occupy myself, and at the same time to comfort my despondency. I tried to fancy, that in the course of the morning, at such time as might prove agreeable to him, Bartleby, of his own free accord, would emerge from his hermitage and take up some decided line of march in the direction of the door. But no. Half-past twelve o'clock came; Turkey began to glow in the face, overturn his inkstand, and become generally obstreperous; Nippers abated down into quietude and courtesy; Ginger Nut munched his noon apple; and Bartleby remained standing at his window in one of his profoundest dead-wall reveries. Will it be credited? Ought I to acknowledge it? That afternoon I left the office without saying one further word to him.

Some days now passed, during which, at leisure intervals I looked a little into "Edwards on the Will," and "Priestly on Necessity." Under the circumstances, those books induced a salutary feeling. Gradually I slid into the persuasion that these troubles of mine, touching the scrivener, had been all predestinated from eternity, and Bartleby was billeted upon me for some mysterious purpose of an allwise Providence, which it was not for a mere mortal like me to fathom. Yes, Bartleby, stay there behind your screen, thought I; I shall persecute you no more; you are harmless and noiseless as any of these old chairs; in short, I never feel so private as when I know you are here. At last I see it, I feel it; I penetrate to the predestinated purpose of my life. I am content. Others may have loftier parts to enact; but my mission in this world, Bartleby, is to furnish you with office-room for such period as you may see fit to remain.

I believe that this wise and blessed frame of mind would have continued with me, had it not been for the unsolicited and uncharitable remarks obtruded upon me by my professional friends who visited the rooms. But thus it often is, that the constant friction of illiberal minds wears out at last the best resolves of the more generous. Though to be sure, when I reflected upon it, it was not strange that people entering my office should be struck by the peculiar aspect of the unaccountable Bartleby, and so be tempted to throw out some sinister observations concerning him. Sometimes an attorney, having business with me, and calling at my office, and finding no one but the scrivener there, would undertake to obtain some sort of precise information from him touching my whereabouts;

but without heeding his idle talk, Bartleby would remain standing immovable in the middle of the room. So after contemplating him in that position for a time, the attorney would depart, no wiser than he came.

Also, when a reference was going on, and the room full of lawyers and witnesses, and business driving fast, some deeply-occupied legal gentleman present, seeing Bartleby wholly unemployed, would request him to run round to his (the legal gentleman's) office and fetch some papers for him. Thereupon, Bartleby would tranquilly decline, and yet remain idle as before. Then the lawyer would give a great stare, and turn to me. And what could I say? At last I was made aware that all through the circle of my professional acquaintance, a whisper of wonder was running round, having reference to the strange creature I kept at my office. This worried me very much. And as the idea came upon me of his possibly turning out a long-lived man, and keep occupying my chambers, and denying my authority; and perplexing my visitors; and scandalizing my professional reputation; and casting a general gloom over the premises; keeping soul and body together to the last upon his savings (for doubtless he spent but half a dime a day), and in the end perhaps outlive me, and claim possession of my office by right of his perpetual occupancy: as all these dark anticipations crowded upon me more and more, and my friends continually intruded their relentless remarks upon the apparition in my room; a great change was wrought in me. I resolved to gather all my faculties together, and forever rid me of this intolerable incubus.

Ere revolving any complicated project, however, adapted to this end, I first simply suggested to Bartleby the propriety of his permanent departure. In a calm and serious tone, I commended the idea to his careful and mature consideration. But, having taken three days to meditate upon it, he apprised me, that his original determination remained the same; in short, that he still preferred to abide with me.

What shall I do? I now said to myself, buttoning up my coat to the last button. What shall I do? what ought I to do? what does conscience say I *should* do with this man, or, rather, ghost. Rid myself of him, I must; go, he shall. But how? You will not thrust him, the poor, pale, passive mortal—you will not thrust such a helpless creature out of your door? you will not dishonor yourself by such cruelty? No, I will not, I cannot do that. Rather would I let him live and die here, and then mason up his remains in the wall. What, then, will you do? For all your coaxing, he will not budge. Bribes he leaves under your own paper-weight on your table; in short, it is quite plain that he prefers to cling to you.

Then something severe, something unusual must be done. What! surely you will not have him collared by a constable, and commit his innocent pallor to the common jail? And upon what ground could you procure such a thing to be done?—a vagrant, is he? What! he a vagrant, a wanderer, who refuses to budge? It is because he will *not* be a vagrant, then, that you seek to count him *as* a vagrant. That is too absurd. No visible means of support: there I have him. Wrong again: for indubitably he *does* support himself, and that is the only unanswerable proof that any man can show of his possessing the means so to do. No more, then. Since he will not quit me, I must quit him. I will change my offices; I will move elsewhere, and give him fair notice, that if I find him on my new premises I will then proceed against him as a common trespasser.

Acting accordingly, next day I thus addressed him: "I find these chambers too far from the City Hall; the air is unwholesome. In a word, I propose to remove my offices next week, and shall no longer require your services. I tell you this now, in order that you may seek another place."

He made no reply, and nothing more was said.

On the appointed day I engaged carts and men, proceeded to my chambers, and, having but little furniture, everything was removed in a few hours. Throughout, the scrivener remained standing behind the screen, which I directed to be removed the last thing. It was withdrawn; and, being folded up like a huge folio, left him the motionless occupant of a naked room. I stood in the entry watching him a moment, while something from within me upbraided me.

I re-entered, with my hand in my pocket—and—and my heart in my mouth.

"Good-by, Bartleby; I am going—good-by, and God some way bless you; and take that," slipping something in his hand. But it dropped upon the floor, and then—strange to say—I tore myself from him whom I had so longed to be rid of.

Established in my new quarters, for a day or two I kept the door locked, and started at every footfall in the passages. When I returned to my rooms, after any little absence, I would pause at the threshold for an instant, and attentively listen, ere applying my key. But these fears were needless. Bartleby never came nigh me.

I thought all was going well, when a perturbed-looking stranger visited me, inquiring whether I was the person who had recently occupied rooms at No. — Wall Street.

Full of forebodings, I replied that I was.

"Then, sir," said the stranger, who proved a lawyer, "you are responsible for the man you left there. He refuses to do any copying; he refuses to do anything; he says he prefers not to; and he refuses to quit the premises."

"I am very sorry, sir," said I, with assumed tranquillity, but an inward tremor, "but, really, the man you allude to is nothing to me—he is no relation or apprentice of mine, that you should hold me responsible for him."

"In mercy's name, who is he?"

"I certainly cannot inform you. I know nothing about him. Formerly I employed him as a copyist; but he has done nothing for me now for some time past."

"I shall settle him, then—good morning, sir."

Several days passed, and I heard nothing more; and, though I often felt a charitable prompting to call at the place and see poor Bartleby, yet a certain squeamishness, of I know not what, withheld me.

All is over with him, by this time, thought I, at last, when, through another week, no further intelligence reached me. But, coming to my room the day after, I found several persons waiting at my door in a high state of nervous excitement.

"That's the man—here he comes," cried the foremost one, whom I recognized as the lawyer who had previously called upon me alone.

"You must take him away, sir, at once," cried a portly person among them, advancing upon me, and whom I knew to be the landlord of No. — Wall Street. "These gentlemen, my tenants, cannot stand it any longer; Mr. B——," pointing to the lawyer, "has turned him out of his room, and he now persists in haunting the building generally, sitting upon the banisters of the stairs by day, and sleeping in the entry by night. Everybody is concerned; clients are leaving the offices; some fears are entertained of a mob; something you must do, and that without delay."

Aghast at this torrent, I fell back before it, and would fain have locked myself in my new quarters. In vain I persisted that Bartleby was nothing to me—no more than to any one else. In vain—I was the last person known to have anything to do with him, and they held me to the terrible account. Fearful, then, of being exposed in the papers (as one person present obscurely threatened), I considered the matter, and, at length, said, that if the lawyer would give me a confidential interview with the scrivener, in his (the lawyer's) own room, I would, that afternoon, strive my best to rid them of the nuisance they complained of.

Going up stairs to my old haunt, there was Bartleby silently sitting upon the banister at the landing.

"What are you doing here, Bartleby?" said I.

"Sitting upon the banister," he mildly replied.

I motioned him into the lawyer's room, who then left us.

"Bartleby," said I, "are you aware that you are the cause of great tribulation to me, by persisting in occupying entry after being dismissed from the office?"

No answer.

"Now one of two things must take place. Either you must do something, or something must be done to you. Now what sort of business would you like to engage in? Would you like to re-engage in copying for some one?"

"No; I would prefer not to make any change."

"Would you like a clerkship in a dry-goods store?"

"There is too much confinement about that. No, I would not like a clerkship; but I am not particular."

"Too much confinement," I cried, "why you keep yourself confined all the time!"

"I would prefer not to take a clerkship," he rejoined, as if to settle that little item at once.

"How would a bar-tender's business suit you? There is no trying of the eye-sight in that."

"I would not like it at all; though, as I said before, I am not particular."

His unwonted wordiness inspirited me. I returned to the charge.

"Well, then, would you like to travel through the country collecting bills for the merchants? That would improve your health."

"No, I would prefer to be doing something else."

"How, then, would going as a companion to Europe, to entertain some young gentleman with your conversation—how would that suit you?"

"Not at all. It does not strike me that there is anything definite about that. I like to be stationary. But I am not particular."

"Stationary you shall be, then," I cried, now losing all patience, and, for the first time in all my exasperating connection with him, fairly flying into a passion. "If you do not go away from these premises before night, I shall feel bound—indeed, I *am* bound—*to—to—to* quit the premises myself!" I rather absurdly concluded, knowing not with what possible threat to try to frighten his immobility into compliance. Despairing of all further efforts, I was precipitately leaving him, when a final thought occurred to me—one which had not been wholly unindulged before.

"Bartleby," said I, in the kindest tone I could assume under such exciting circumstances, "will you go home with me now—not to my office, but my dwelling—and remain there till we can conclude upon some convenient arrangement for you at our leisure? Come, let us start now, right away."

"No: at present I would prefer not to make any change at all."

I answered nothing; but, effectually dodging every one by the suddenness and rapidity of my flight, rushed from the building, ran up Wall Street towards Broadway, and, jumping into the first omnibus, was soon removed from pursuit. As soon as tranquillity returned, I distinctly perceived that I had now done all that I possibly could, both in respect to the demands of the landlord and his tenants, and with regard to my own desire and sense of duty, to benefit Bartleby, and shield him from rude persecution. I now strove to be entirely care-free and quiescent; and my conscience justified me in the attempt; though, indeed, it was not so successful as I could have wished. So fearful was I of being again hunted out by the incensed landlord and his exasperated tenants, that, surrendering my business to Nippers, for a few days, I drove about the upper part of the town and through the suburbs, in my rockaway; crossed over to Jersey City and Hoboken, and paid fugitive visits to Manhattanville and Astoria. In fact, I almost lived in my rockaway for the time.

When again I entered my office, lo, a note from the landlord lay upon the desk. I opened it with trembling hands. It informed me that the writer had sent to the police, and had Bartleby removed to the Tombs as a vagrant. Moreover, since I knew more about him than any one else, he wished me to appear at that place, and make a suitable statement of the facts. These tidings had a conflicting effect upon me. At first I was indignant; but, at last, almost approved. The landlord's energetic, summary disposition, had led him to adopt a procedure which I do not think I would have decided upon myself; and yet, as a last resort, under such peculiar circumstances, it seemed the only plan.

As I afterwards learned, the poor scrivener, when told that he must be conducted to the Tombs, offered not the slightest obstacle, but, in his pale, unmoving way, silently acquiesced.

Some of the compassionate and curious bystanders joined the party; and headed by one of the constables arm in arm with Bartleby, the silent procession filed its way through all the noise, and heat, and joy of the roaring thoroughfares at noon.

The same day I received the note, I went to the Tombs, or, to speak more properly, the Halls of Justice. Seeking the right officer, I stated the purpose of my call, and was informed that the individual I described was, indeed, within. I then assured the functionary that Bartleby was a perfectly honest man, and greatly to be compassionated, however unaccountably eccentric. I narrated all I knew, and closed by suggesting the idea of letting him remain in as indulgent confinement as possible, till something less harsh might be done—though, indeed, I hardly knew what. At all events, if nothing else could be decided upon, the almshouse must receive him. I then begged to have an interview.

Being under no disgraceful charge, and quite serene and harmless in all his ways, they had permitted him freely to wander about the prison, and, especially, in the inclosed grass-platted yards thereof. And so I found him there, standing all alone in the quietest of the yards, his face towards a high wall, while all around, from the narrow slits of the jail windows, I thought I saw peering out upon him the eyes of murderers and thieves.

"Bartleby!"

"I know you," he said without looking round—"and I want nothing to say to you."

"It was not I that brought you here, Bartleby," said I, keenly pained at his implied suspicion. "And to you, this should not be so vile a place. Nothing reproachful attaches to you by being here. And see, it is not so sad a place as one might think. Look, there is the sky, and here is the grass."

"I know where I am," he replied, but would say nothing more, and so I left him.

As I entered the corridor again, a broad meat-like man, in an apron, accosted me, and, jerking his thumb over his shoulder, said—"Is that your friend?"

"Yes."

"Does he want to starve? If he does, let him live on the prison fare, that's all."

"Who are you?" asked I, not knowing what to make of such an unofficially speaking person in such a place.

"I am the grub-man. Such gentlemen as have friends here, hire me to provide them with something good to eat."

"Is this so?" said I, turning to the turnkey.

He said it was.

"Well, then," said I, slipping some silver into the grub-man's hands (for so they called him), "I want you to give particular attention to my friend there; let him have the best dinner you can get. And you must be as polite to him as possible."

"Introduce me, will you?" said the grub-man, looking at me with an expression which seemed to say he was all impatience for an opportunity to give a specimen of his breeding.

Thinking it would prove of benefit to the scrivener, I acquiesced; and, asking the grub-man his name, went up with him to Bartleby.

"Bartleby, this is a friend; you will find him very useful to you."

"Your sarvant, sir, your sarvant," said the grub-man, making a low salutation behind his apron. "Hope you find it pleasant here, sir; nice grounds—cool apartments—hope you'll stay with us sometime—try to make it agreeable. What will you have for dinner to-day?"

"I prefer not to dine to-day," said Bartleby, turning away. "It would disagree with me; I am unused to dinners." So saying, he slowly moved to the other side of the inclosure, and took up a position fronting the dead-wall.

"How's this?" said the grub-man, addressing me with a stare of astonishment, "He's odd, ain't he?"

"I think he is a little deranged," said I, sadly.

"Deranged? deranged is it? Well, now, upon my word, I thought that friend of yourn was a gentleman forger; they are always pale and genteel-like, them forgers. I can't help pity 'em—can't help it, sir. Did you know Monroe Edwards?" he added, touchingly, and paused. Then, laying his hand piteously on my shoulder, sighed, "he died of consumption at Sing-Sing. So you weren't acquainted with Monroe?"

"No, I was never socially acquainted with any forgers. But I cannot stop longer. Look to my friend yonder. You will not lose by it. I will see you again."

Some few days after this, I again obtained admission to the Tombs, and went through the corridors in quest of Bartleby; but without finding him.

"I saw him coming from his cell not long ago," said a turnkey, "may be he's gone to loiter in the yards."

So I went in that direction.

"Are you looking for the silent man?" said another turnkey, passing me. "Yonder he lies—sleeping in the yard there. 'Tis not twenty minutes since I saw him lie down."

The yard was entirely quiet. It was not accessible to the common prisoners. The surrounding walls, of amazing thickness, kept off all sounds behind them. The Egyptian character of the masonry weighed upon me with its gloom. But a soft imprisoned turf grew under foot. The heart of the eternal pyramids, it seemed, wherein, by some strange magic, through the clefts, grass-seed, dropped by birds, had sprung.

Strangely huddled at the base of the wall, his knees drawn up, and lying on his side, his head touching the cold stones, I saw the wasted Bartleby. But nothing stirred. I paused; then went close up to him; stooped over, and saw that his dim eyes were open; otherwise he seemed profoundly sleeping. Something prompted me to touch him. I felt his hand, when a tingling shiver ran up my arm and down my spine to my feet.

The round face of the grub-man peered upon me now. "His dinner is ready. Won't he dine to-day, either? Or does he live without dining?"

"Lives without dining," said I, and closed the eyes.

"Eh!—He's asleep, ain't he?"

"With kings and counselors," murmured I.

⌘

There would seem little need for proceeding further in this history. Imagination will readily supply the meagre recital of poor Bartleby's interment. But, ere parting with the reader, let me say, that if this little narrative has sufficiently interested him, to awaken curiosity as to who Bartleby was, and what manner of life he led prior to the present narrator's making his acquaintance, I can only reply, that in such curiosity I fully share, but am wholly unable to gratify it. Yet here I hardly know whether I should divulge one little item of rumor, which came to my ear a few months after the scrivener's decease. Upon what basis it rested, I could never ascertain; and hence, how true it is I cannot now tell. But, inasmuch as this vague report has not been without a certain suggestive interest to me, however sad, it may prove the same with some others; and so I will briefly mention it. The report was this: that Bartleby had been a subordinate clerk in the Dead Letter Office at Washington, from which he had been suddenly removed by a change in the administration. When I think over this rumor, hardly can I express the emotions which seize me. Dead letters! does it not sound like dead men? Conceive a man by nature and misfortune prone to a pallid hopelessness, can any business seem more fitted to heighten it than that of continually handling these dead letters, and assorting them for the flames? For by the cartload they are annually burned. Sometimes from out the folded paper the pale clerk takes a ring—the finger it was meant for, perhaps, moulders in the grave; a bank-note sent in swiftest charity—he whom it would relieve, nor eats nor hungers any more; pardon for those who died despairing; hope for those who died unhoping; good tidings for those who died stifled by unrelieved calamities. On errands of life, these letters speed to death.

Ah, Bartleby! Ah, humanity!

## QUESTIONS

1. The narrator of "Bartleby the Scrivener" begins his narration with the word *I* and ends it with the word *humanity.* We may wonder, therefore, if the events that form the conflict and climax of the story have altered the narrator's vision to allow his attention to shift from himself to others. If so, how did this happen? The following questions may help you develop your answer.
2. We note that the narrator begins his tale by introducing himself. Why does he do so? What does he reveal as his goals? What things does he seem to value most highly?
3. We might ask what tone of voice the narrator is using in this early part of the story. (Paragraph five may be especially helpful here.)
4. We then look at his introduction of his office and of his first staff member, Turkey. How does the lawyer/narrator act toward Turkey? What reasons does he give for acting as he does? Do his actions seem to match his reasons? What impression of the lawyer's character do we receive?
5. We then look at his introductions of Nippers and Ginger Nut, and end our study of the tale's introductory section by asking how the narrator's characterization of his three employees, and our impression of his interactions

with them, prepare the way for the introduction of Bartleby and for the narrator's response to him and to his behavior.

6. Having seen how the narrator prepares the way for the introduction of his main character, we now look at the first episodes involving that character (pp. 105–110). How well does Bartleby fit into our picture of the office? What does this do for our sense of him and of his relationship with his employer?
7. We next ask, what is the turning-point of the story? How does it change the narrator's view of Bartleby? What emotions does it raise in him? What action does it prompt him to take? What are the results of that action?
8. We then examine the story's progress from this turning-point to Bartleby's death. We ask ourselves, what changes are taking place in the tone of the narrative? the actions? the characterizations? We examine our reactions to these changes and developments. Have we been prepared for them? Can we accept them, or do we find them out of character or hard to believe? How do we react to Bartleby's death? Has the death been made to seem inevitable? Does it seem appropriate that the narrator be the one to discover it? How do we feel now about the narrator's relation to Bartleby?
9. At this point, too, we might notice the use of walls to set scenes throughout the story. This will let us glance at the whole story once more and will give us a good key for discussing some of the shifts in tone and atmosphere that occur as the story progresses. It will also let us sum up some of our impressions of Bartleby, since he is the character most closely associated with these walls. What is the effect on us of the combination of walls and Bartleby?
10. Similarly, we might look at mentions of money throughout the story. What character is most closely associated with them? What characterization do we draw from this association?
11. We must look as well at the after-note that ends the story, and ask what it adds to our sense of Bartleby, the narrator, and the story.
12. And then we must sum up our thoughts for ourselves. Has the narrator changed during the story? And, if he has, what do we make of the change?
13. Another way to approach the story would be to look at the effects of keeping Bartleby so sketchily characterized. We might ask how essential this pared-down characterization is to the story; how the narrator's sense of his own lack of knowledge about Bartleby affects him; and how it affects our feelings toward Bartleby, toward the narrator, and toward the relationship that develops between the two men. We might also ask whether the characterization given Bartleby suggests any symbolic values for Bartleby, the narrator, or their relationship; or whether you feel the story is better dealt with as a realistic tale.

## JOSEPH CONRAD (1857–1924)

# *The Secret Sharer*

On my right hand there were lines of fishing stakes resembling a mysterious system of half-submerged bamboo fences, incomprehensible in its division of the domain of tropical fishes, and crazy of aspect as if abandoned forever by some nomad tribe of fishermen now gone to the other end of the ocean; for there was no sign of human habitation as far as the eye could reach. To the left a group of barren islets, suggesting ruins of stone walls, towers, and blockhouses, had its foundations set in a blue sea that itself looked solid, so still and stable did it lie below my feet; even the track of light from the westering sun shone smoothly, without that animated glitter which tells of an imperceptible ripple. And when I turned my head to take a parting glance at the tug which had just left us anchored outside the bar, I saw the straight line of the flat shore joined to the stable sea, edge to edge, with a perfect and unmarked closeness, in one leveled floor half brown, half blue under the enormous dome of the sky. Corresponding in their significance to the islets of the sea, two small clumps of trees, one on each side of the only fault in the impeccable joint, marked the mouth of the river Meinam we had just left on the first preparatory stage of our homeward journey; and, far back on the inland level, a larger and loftier mass, the grove surrounding the great Paknam pagoda, was the only thing on which the eye could rest from the vain task of exploring the monotonous sweep of the horizon. Here and there gleams as of a few scattered pieces of silver marked the windings of the great river; and on the nearest of them, just within the bar, the tug steaming right into the land became lost to my sight, hull and funnel and masts, as though the impassive earth had swallowed her up without an effort, without a tremor. My eye followed the light cloud of her smoke, now here, now there, above the plain, according to the devious curves of the stream, but always fainter and farther away, till I lost it at last behind the miter-shaped hill of the great pagoda. And then I was left alone with my ship, anchored at the head of the Gulf of Siam.

She floated at the starting point of a long journey, very still in an immense stillness, the shadows of her spars flung far to the eastward by the setting sun. At that moment I was alone on her decks. There was not a sound in her—and around us nothing moved, nothing lived, not a canoe on the water, not a bird in the air, not a cloud in the sky. In this breathless pause at the threshold of a long passage we seemed to be measuring our fitness for a long and arduous enterprise, the appointed task of both our existences to be carried out, far from all human eyes, with only sky and sea for spectators and for judges.

There must have been some glare in the air to interfere with one's sight, because it was only just before the sun left us that my roaming eyes made out beyond the highest ridge of the principal islet of the group something which did away with the solemnity of perfect solitude. The tide of darkness flowed on swiftly; and with tropical suddenness a swarm of stars came out above the shadowy earth, while I lingered yet, my hand resting lightly on my ship's rail as if on the shoulder of a trusted friend. But, with all that multitude of celestial bodies staring down at one, the comfort of quiet communion with her was gone for good. And there were also disturbing sounds by this time—voices, footsteps forward; the steward flitted along the main deck, a busily ministering spirit; a hand bell tinkled urgently under the poop deck. . . .

I found my two officers waiting for me near the supper table, in the lighted cuddy. We sat down at once, and as I helped the chief mate, I said:

"Are you aware that there is a ship anchored inside the islands? I saw her mastheads above the ridge as the sun went down."

He raised sharply his simple face, overcharged by a terrible growth of whisker, and emitted his usual ejaculations: "Bless my soul, sir! You don't say so!"

My second mate was a round-cheeked, silent young man, grave beyond his years, I thought; but as our eyes happened to meet I detected a slight quiver on his lips. I looked down at once. It was not my part to encourage sneering on board my ship. It must be said, too, that I knew very little of my officers. In consequence of certain events of no particular significance, except to myself, I had been appointed to the command only a fortnight before. Neither did I know much of the hands forward. All these people had been together for eighteen months or so, and my position was that of the only stranger on board. I mention this because it has some bearing on what is to follow. But what I felt most was my being a stranger to the ship; and if all the truth must be told, I was somewhat of a stranger to myself. The youngest man on board (barring the second mate), and untried as yet by a position of the fullest responsibility, I was willing to take the adequacy of the others for granted. They had simply to be equal to their tasks; but I wondered how far I should turn out faithful to that ideal conception of one's own personality every man sets up for himself secretly.

Meantime the chief mate, with an almost visible effect of collaboration on the part of his round eyes and frightful whiskers, was trying to evolve a theory of the anchored ship. His dominant trait was to take all things into earnest consideration. He was of a painstaking turn of mind. As he used to say, he "liked to account to himself" for practically everything that came in his way, down to a miserable scorpion he had found in his cabin a week before. The why and the wherefore of that scorpion—how it got on board and came to select his room rather than the pantry (which was a dark place and more what a scorpion would be partial to), and how on earth it managed to drown itself in the inkwell of his writing desk—had exercised him infinitely. The ship within the islands was much more easily accounted for; and just as we were about to rise from the table he made his pronouncement. She was, he doubted not, a ship from home lately arrived. Probably she drew too much water to cross the bar except at the top of spring tides. Therefore she went into that natural harbor to wait for a few days in preference to remaining in an open roadstead.

"That's so," confirmed the second mate, suddenly, in his slightly hoarse voice. "She draws over twenty feet. She's the Liverpool ship *Sephora* with a cargo of coal. Hundred and twenty-three days from Cardiff."

We looked at him in surprise.

"The tugboat skipper told me when he came on board for your letters, sir," explained the young man. "He expects to take her up the river the day after tomorrow."

After thus overwhelming us with the extent of his information he slipped out of the cabin. The mate observed regretfully that he "could not account for that young fellow's whims." What prevented him telling us all about it at once, he wanted to know.

I detained him as he was making a move. For the last two days the crew had had plenty of hard work, and the night before they had very little sleep. I felt painfully that I—a stranger—was doing something unusual when I directed him to let all hands turn in without setting an anchor watch. I proposed to keep on deck myself till one o'clock or thereabouts. I would get the second mate to relieve me at that hour.

"He will turn out the cook and the steward at four," I concluded, "and then give you a call. Of course at the slightest sign of any sort of wind we'll have the hands up and make a start at once."

He concealed his astonishment. "Very well, sir." Outside the cuddy he put his head in the second mate's door to inform him of my unheard-of caprice to take a five hours' anchor watch on myself. I heard the other raise his voice incredulously: "What? The captain himself?" Then a few more murmurs, a door closed, then another. A few moments later I went on deck.

My strangeness, which had made me sleepless, had prompted that unconventional arrangement, as if I had expected in those solitary hours of the night to get on terms with the ship of which I knew nothing, manned by men of whom I knew very little more. Fast alongside a wharf, littered like any ship in port with a tangle of unrelated things, invaded by unrelated shore people, I had hardly seen her yet properly. Now, as she lay cleared for sea, the stretch of her main deck seemed to me very fine under the stars. Very fine, very roomy for her size, and very inviting. I descended the poop and paced the waist, my mind picturing to myself the coming passage through the Malay Archipelago, down the Indian Ocean, and up the Atlantic. All its phases were familiar enough to me, every characteristic, all the alternatives which were likely to face me on the high seas—everything! . . . except the novel responsibility of command. But I took heart from the reasonable thought that the ship was like other ships, the men like other men, and that the sea was not likely to keep any special surprises expressly for my discomfiture.

Arrived at that comforting conclusion, I bethought myself of a cigar and went below to get it. All was still down there. Everybody at the after end of the ship was sleeping profoundly. I came out again on the quarter-deck, agreeably at ease in my sleeping suit on that warm breathless night, barefooted, a glowing cigar in my teeth, and, going forward, I was met by the profound silence of the fore end of the ship. Only as I passed the door of the forecastle I heard a deep, quiet, trustful sigh of some sleeper inside. And suddenly I rejoiced in the great security of the sea as compared with the unrest of the land, in my choice of that untempted life presenting no disquieting problems, invested with an elementary moral beauty by the absolute straight-forwardness of its appeal and by the singleness of its purpose.

The reading light in the fore-rigging burned with a clear, untroubled, as if symbolic, flame, confident and bright in the mysterious shades of the night. Passing on my way aft along the other side of the ship, I observed that the rope side-ladder, put over, no doubt, for the master of the tug when he came to fetch away our letters, had not been hauled in as it should have been. I became annoyed at this, for exactitude in small matters is the very soul of discipline. Then I reflected that I had myself peremptorily dismissed my officers from duty, and by my own act had prevented the anchor watch being formally set and things properly attended to. I asked myself whether it was wise ever to interfere with the established routine of duties even from the kindest of motives. My action might have made me appear eccentric. Goodness only knew how that absurdly whiskered mate would "account" for my conduct, and what the whole ship thought of that informality of their new captain. I was vexed with myself.

Not from compunction certainly, but, as it were mechanically, I proceeded to get the ladder in myself. Now a side ladder of that sort is a light affair and comes in easily, yet my vigorous tug, which should have brought it flying on board, merely recoiled upon my body in a totally unexpected jerk. What the devil . . . I was so astounded by the immovableness of that ladder that I remained stock-still, trying to account for it to myself like that imbecile mate of mine. In the end, of course, I put my head over the rail.

The side of the ship made an opaque belt of shadow on the darkling glassy shimmer of the sea. But I saw at once something elongated and pale floating very close to the ladder. Before I could form a guess a faint flash of phosphorescent light, which seemed to issue suddenly from the naked body of a man, flickered in the sleeping water with the elusive, silent play of summer lightning in a night sky. With a gasp I saw revealed to my stare a pair of feet, the long legs, a broad livid back immersed right up to the neck in a greenish cadaverous glow. One hand awash, clutched the bottom rung of the ladder. He was complete but for the head. A headless corpse! The cigar dropped out of my gaping mouth with a tiny plop and a short hiss quite audible in the absolute stillness of all things under heaven. At that I suppose he raised up his face, a dimly pale oval in the shadow of the ship's side. But even then I could only barely make out down there the shape of his blackhaired head. However, it was enough for the horrid, frost-bound sensation which had gripped me about the chest to pass off. The moment of vain exclamations was past, too. I only climbed on the spare spar and leaned over the rail as far as I could, to bring my eyes nearer to that mystery floating alongside.

As he hung by the ladder, like a resting swimmer, the sea lightning played about his limbs at every stir; and he appeared in it ghastly, silvery, fishlike. He remained as mute as a fish, too. He made no motion to get out of the water, either. It was inconceivable that he should not attempt to come on board, and strangely troubling to suspect that perhaps he did not want to. And my first words were prompted by just that troubled incertitude.

"What's the matter?" I asked in my ordinary tone; speaking down to the face upturned exactly under mine.

"Cramp," it answered, no louder. Then slightly anxious, "I say, no need to call anyone."

"I was not going to," I said.

"Are you alone on deck?"

"Yes."

I had somehow the impression that he was on the point of letting go the ladder to swim away beyond my ken—mysterious as he came. But, for the moment, this being appearing as if he had risen from the bottom of the sea (it was certainly the nearest land to the ship) wanted only to know the time. I told him. And he, down there, tentatively:

"I suppose your captain's turned in?"

"I am sure he isn't," I said.

He seemed to struggle with himself, for I heard something like the low, bitter murmur of doubt. "What's the good?" His next words came out with a hesitating effort.

"Look here, my man. Could you call him out quietly?"

I thought the time had come to declare myself.

"*I* am the captain."

I heard a "By Jove!" whispered at the level of the water. The phosphorescence flashed in the swirl of the water all about his limbs, his other hand seized the ladder.

"My name's Leggatt."

The voice was calm and resolute. A good voice. The self-possession of that man had somehow induced a corresponding state in myself. It was very quietly that I remarked:

"You must be a good swimmer."

"Yes. I've been in the water practically since nine o'clock. The question for me now is whether I am to let go this ladder and go on swimming till I sink from exhaustion, or–to come on board here."

I felt this was no mere formula of desperate speech, but a real alternative in the view of a strong soul. I should have gathered from this that he was young; indeed, it is only the young who are ever confronted by such clear issues. But at the time it was pure intuition on my part. A mysterious communication was established already between us two–in the face of that silent, darkened tropical sea. I was young, too; young enough to make no comment. The man in the water began suddenly to climb up the ladder, and I hastened away from the rail to fetch some clothes.

Before entering the cabin I stood still, listening in the lobby at the foot of the stairs. A faint snore came through the closed door of the chief mate's room. The second mate's door was on the hook, but the darkness in there was absolutely soundless. He, too, was young and could sleep like a stone. Remained the steward, but he was not likely to wake up before he was called. I got a sleeping suit out of my room and, coming back on deck, saw the naked man from the sea sitting on the main hatch, glimmering white in the darkness, his elbows on his knees and his head in his hands. In a moment he had concealed his damp body in a sleeping suit of the same gray-stripe pattern as the one I was wearing and followed me like my double on the poop. Together we moved right aft, barefooted, silent.

"What is it?" I asked in a deadened voice, taking the lighted lamp out of the binnacle, and raising it to his face.

"An ugly business."

He had rather regular features; a good mouth; light eyes under somewhat heavy, dark eyebrows; a smooth, square forehead; no growth on his cheeks; a small, brown mustache, and a well-shaped, round chin. His expression was concentrated, meditative, under the inspecting light of the lamp I held up to his face; such as a man thinking hard in solitude might wear. My sleeping suit was just right for his size. A well-knit young fellow of twenty-five at most. He caught his lower lip with the edge of white, even teeth.

"Yes," I said, replacing the lamp in the binnacle. The warm, heavy tropical night closed upon his head again.

"There's a ship over there," he murmured.

"Yes, I know. The *Sephora*. Did you know of us?"

"Hadn't the slightest idea. I am the mate of her—" He paused and corrected himself. "I should say I *was*."

"Aha! Something wrong?"

"Yes. Very wrong indeed. I've killed a man."

"What do you mean? Just now?"

"No, on the passage. Weeks ago. Thirty-nine south. When I say a man—"

"Fit of temper," I suggested, confidently.

The shadowy, dark head, like mine, seemed to nod imperceptibly above the ghostly gray of my sleeping suit. It was, in the night, as though I had been faced by my own reflection in the depths of a somber and immense mirror.

"A pretty thing to have to own up to for a *Conway* boy," murmured my double, distinctly.

"You're a *Conway* boy?"

"I am," he said, as if startled. Then slowly . . . "Perhaps you too—"

It was so; but being a couple of years older I had left before he joined. After a quick interchange of dates a silence fell; and I thought suddenly of my absurd mate with his terrific whiskers and the "Bless my soul—you don't say so" type of intellect. My double gave me an inkling of his thoughts by saying:

"My father's a parson in Norfolk. Do you see me before a judge and jury on that charge? For myself I can't see the necessity. There are fellows that an angel from heaven— And I am not that. He was one of those creatures that are just simmering all the time with a silly sort of wickedness. Miserable devils that have no business to live at all. He wouldn't do his duty and wouldn't let anybody else do theirs. But what's the good of talking! You know well enough the sort of ill-conditioned snarling cur—"

He appealed to me as if our experiences had been as identical as our clothes. And I knew well enough the pestiferous anger of such a character where there are no means of legal repression. And I knew well enough also that my double there was no homicidal ruffian. I did not think of asking him for details, and he told me the story roughly in brusque, disconnected sentences. I needed no more. I saw it all going on as though I were myself inside that other sleeping suit.

"It happened while we were setting a reefed foresail, at dusk. Reefed foresail! You understand the sort of weather. The only sail we had left to keep the ship running; so you may guess what it had been like for days. Anxious sort of job, that. He gave me some of his cursed insolence at the sheet. I tell you I was overdone with this terrific weather that seemed to have no end to it. Terrific, I tell you—and a deep ship. I believe the fellow himself was half crazed with funk. It was no time for gentlemanly reproof, so I turned round and felled him like an ox. He up and at me. We closed just as an awful sea made for the ship. All hands saw it coming and took to the rigging, but I had him by the throat, and went on shaking him like a rat, the men above us yelling, 'Look out! look out!' Then a crash as if the sky had fallen on my head. They say that for over ten minutes hardly anything was to be seen of the ship—just the three masts and a bit of the forecastle head and of the poop all awash driving along in a smother of foam. It was a miracle that they found us, jammed together behind the forebits. It's clear that I meant business, because I was holding him by the throat still when they picked us up. He was black in the face. It was too much for them. It seems they rushed us aft together, gripped as we were, screaming 'Murder!' like a lot of lunatics, and broke into the cuddy. And the ship running for her life, touch and go all the time, any minute her last in a sea fit to turn your hair gray only a-looking at it. I understand that the skipper, too, started raving like the rest of them. The man had been deprived of sleep for more than a week, and to have this sprung on him at the height of a furious gale nearly drove him out of his mind. I wonder they didn't fling me overboard after getting the carcass of their precious shipmate out of my fingers. They had rather a job to separate us, I've been told. A sufficiently fierce story to make an old judge and a respectable jury sit up a bit. The first thing I heard when I came to myself was the maddening howling of that endless gale, and on that the voice of the old man. He was hanging on to my bunk, staring into my face out of his sou'wester.

" 'Mr. Leggatt, you have killed a man. You can act no longer as chief mate of this ship.' "

His care to subdue his voice made it sound monotonous. He rested a hand on the end of the skylight to steady himself with, and all that time did not stir a limb, so far as I could see. "Nice little tale for a quiet tea party," he concluded in the same tone.

One of my hands, too, rested on the end of the skylight; neither did I stir a limb, so far as I knew. We stood less than a foot from each other. It occurred to me that if old "Bless my soul—you don't say so" were to put his head up the companion and catch sight of us, he would think he was seeing double, or imagine himself come upon a scene of weird witchcraft; the strange captain having a quiet confabulation by the wheel with his own gray ghost. I became very much concerned to prevent anything of the sort. I heard the other's soothing undertone.

"My father's a parson in Norfolk," it said. Evidently he had forgotten he had told me this important factor before. Truly a nice little tale.

"You had better slip down into my stateroom now," I said, moving off stealthily. My double followed my movements; our bare feet made no sound; I let him in, closed the door with care, and, after giving a call to the second mate, returned on deck for my relief.

"Not much sign of any wind yet," I remarked when he approached.

"No, sir. Not much," he assented, sleepily, in his hoarse voice, with just enough deference, no more, and barely suppressing a yawn.

"Well, that's all you have to look out for. You have got your orders."

"Yes, sir."

I paced a turn or two on the poop and saw him take up his position face forward with his elbow in the ratlines of the mizen-rigging before I went below. The mate's faint snoring was still going on peacefully. The cuddy lamp was burning over the table on which stood a vase with flowers, a polite attention from the ships' provision merchant—the last flowers we should see for the next three months at the very least. Two bunches of bananas hung from the beam symmetrically, one on each side of the rudder casing. Everything was as before in the ship—except that two of her captain's sleeping suits were simultaneously in use, one motionless in the cuddy, the other keeping very still in the captain's stateroom.

It must be explained here that my cabin had the form of the capital letter L, the door being within the angle and opening into the short part of the letter. A couch was to the left, the bed-place to the right; my writing desk and the chronometers' table faced the door. But anyone opening it, unless he stepped right inside, had no view of what I call the long (or vertical) part of the letter. It contained some lockers surmounted by a book case; and a few clothes, a thick jacket or two, caps, oilskin coat, and such like, hung on hooks. There was at the bottom of that part a door opening into my bathroom, which could be entered also directly from the saloon. But that way was never used.

The mysterious arrival had discovered the advantage of this particular shape. Entering my room, lighted strongly by a big bulkhead lamp swung on gimbals above my writing desk, I did not see him anywhere till he stepped out quietly from behind the coats hung in the recessed part.

"I heard somebody moving about, and went in there at once," he whispered.

I, too, spoke under my breath.

"Nobody is likely to come in here without knocking and getting permission."

He nodded. His face was thin and the sunburn faded, as though he had been ill. And no wonder. He had been, I heard presently, kept under arrest in his cabin for nearly seven weeks. But there was nothing sickly in his eyes or in his expression. He was not a bit like me, really; yet, as we stood leaning over my bed-place, whispering side by side, with our dark heads together and our backs to the door, anybody bold enough to open it stealthily would have been treated to the uncanny sight of a double captain busy talking in whispers with his other self.

"But all this doesn't tell how you came to hang on to our side ladder," I inquired, in the hardly audible murmurs we used, after he had told me something more of the proceedings on board the *Sephora* once the bad weather was over.

"When we sighted Java Head I had had time to think all those matters out several times over. I had six weeks of doing nothing else, and with only an hour or so every evening for a tramp on the quarter-deck."

He whispered, his arms folded on the side of my bed-place, staring through the open port. And I could imagine perfectly the manner of this thinking out—a stubborn if not a steadfast operation; something of which I should have been perfectly incapable.

"I reckoned it would be dark before we closed with the land," he continued, so low that I had to strain my hearing, near as we were to each other, shoulder touching shoulder almost. "So I asked to speak to the old man. He always seemed very sick when he came to see me—as if he could not look me in the face. You know, that foresail saved the ship. She was too deep to have run long under bare poles. And it was I that managed to set it for him. Anyway, he came. When I had him in my cabin—he stood by the door looking at me as if I had the halter around my neck already—I asked him right away to leave my cabin door unlocked at night while the ship was going through Sunda Straits. There would be the Java coast within two or three miles, off Angier Point. I wanted nothing more. I've had a prize for swimming my second year in the *Conway*."

"I can believe it," I breathed out.

"God only knows why they locked me in every night. To see some of their faces you'd have thought they were afraid I'd go about at night strangling people. Am I a murdering brute? Do I look it? By Jove! if I had been he wouldn't have trusted himself like that in my room. You'll say I might have chucked him aside and bolted out, there and then—it was dark already. Well, no. And for the same reason I wouldn't think of trying to smash the door. There would have been a rush to stop me at the noise, and I did not mean to get into a confounded scrimmage. Somebody else might have got killed—for I would not have broken out only to get chucked back, and I did not want any more of that work. He refused, looking more sick than ever. He was afraid of the men, and also of that old second mate of his who had been sailing with him for years—a gray-headed old humbug; and his steward, too, had been with him devil knows how long—seventeen years or more—a dogmatic sort of loafer who hated me like poison, just because I was the chief mate. No chief mate ever made more than one voyage in the *Sephora,* you know. Those two old chaps ran the ship. Devil only knows what the skipper wasn't afraid of (all his nerve went to pieces altogether in that hellish spell of bad weather we had)—of what the law would do to him—of his wife, perhaps. Oh, yes! she's on board. Though I don't think she would have meddled. She would have been only too glad to have me out of the ship in any way. The 'brand of Cain' business, don't you see. That's all right. I was ready enough to go off wandering on the face of the earth—and that was price enough to pay for an Abel of that sort. Anyhow, he wouldn't listen to me. 'This thing must take its course. I represent the law here.' He was shaking like a leaf. 'So you won't?' 'No!' 'Then I hope you will be able to sleep on that,' I said, and turned my back on him. 'I wonder that *you* can,' cries he, and locks the door.

"Well, after that, I couldn't. Not very well. That was three weeks ago. We have had a slow passage through the Java Sea; drifted about Carimata for ten days. When we anchored here they thought, I suppose, it was all right. The nearest land (and that's five miles) is the ship's destination; the consul would soon set about catching me; and there would have been no object in bolting to these islets there. I don't suppose there's a drop of water on them. I don't know how it was, but tonight that steward, after bringing me my supper, went out to let me eat it, and left the door unlocked. And I ate it—all there was, too. After I had finished I strolled out on the quarter-deck. I don't know that I meant to do anything. A breath of fresh air was all I wanted, I believe. Then a sudden temptation came over me.

I kicked off my slippers and was in the water before I had made up my mind fairly. Somebody heard the splash and they raised an awful hullabaloo. 'He's gone! Lower the boats! He's committed suicide! No, he's swimming.' Certainly I was swimming. It's not so easy for a swimmer like me to commit suicide by drowning. I landed on the nearest islet before the boat left the ship's side. I heard them pulling about in the dark, hailing, and so on, but after a bit they gave up. Everything quieted down and the anchorage became as still as death. I sat down on a stone and began to think. I felt certain they would start searching for me at daylight. There was no place to hide on those stony things—and if there had been, what would have been the good? But now I was clear of that ship, I was not going back. So after a while I took off all my clothes, tied them up in a bundle with a stone inside, and dropped them in the deep water on the outer side of that islet. That was suicide enough for me. Let them think what they liked, but I didn't mean to drown myself. I meant to swim till I sank—but that's not the same thing. I struck out for another of these little islands, and it was from that one that I first saw your riding light. Something to swim for. I went on easily, and on the way I came upon a flat rock a foot or two above water. In the daytime, I dare say, you might make it out with a glass from your poop. I scrambled up on it and rested myself for a bit. Then I made another start. That last spell must have been over a mile."

His whisper was getting fainter and fainter, and all the time he stared straight out through the porthole, in which there was not even a star to be seen. I had not interrupted him. There was something that made comment impossible in his narrative, or perhaps in himself; a sort of feeling, a quality, which I can't find a name for. And when he ceased, all I found was a futile whisper: "So you swam for our light?"

"Yes—straight for it. It was something to swim for. I couldn't see any stars low down because the coast was in the way, and I couldn't see the land, either. The water was like glass. One might have been swimming in a confounded thousand-feet deep cistern with no place for scrambling out anywhere; but what I didn't like was the notion of swimming round and round like a crazed bullock before I gave out; and as I didn't mean to go back . . . No. Do you see me being hauled back, stark naked, off one of these little islands by the scruff of the neck and fighting like a wild beast? Somebody would have got killed for certain, and I did not want any of that. So I went on. Then your ladder—"

"Why didn't you hail the ship?" I asked, a little louder.

He touched my shoulder lightly. Lazy footsteps came right over our heads and stopped. The second mate had crossed from the other side of the poop and might have been hanging over the rail, for all we knew.

"He couldn't hear us talking—could he?" My double breathed into my ear, anxiously.

His anxiety was an answer, a sufficient answer, to the question I had put to him. An answer containing all the difficulty of that situation. I closed the porthole quietly, to make sure. A louder word might have been overheard.

"Who's that?" he whispered then.

"My second mate. But I don't know much more of the fellow than you do."

And I told him a little about myself. I had been appointed to take charge while I least expected anything of the sort, not quite a fortnight ago. I didn't know either the ship or the people. Hadn't had the time in port to look about me or size anybody up. And as to the crew, all they knew was that I was appointed to take the ship home. For the rest, I was almost as much of a stranger on board as himself, I said. And at the moment I felt it most acutely. I felt that it would take very little to make me a suspect person in the eyes of the ship's company.

He had turned about meantime; and we, the two strangers in the ship, faced each other in identical attitudes.

"Your ladder—" he murmured, after a silence. "Who'd have thought of finding a ladder hanging over at night in a ship anchored out here! I felt just then a very unpleasant faintness. After the life I've been leading for nine weeks, anybody would have got out of condition. I wasn't capable of swimming round as far as your rudder chains. And, lo and behold! there was a ladder to get hold of. After I gripped it I said to myself, 'What's the good?' When I saw a man's head looking over I thought I would swim away presently and leave him shouting—in whatever language it was. I didn't mind being looked at. I—I liked it. And then you speaking to me so quietly—as if you had expected me—made me hold on a little longer. It had been a confounded lonely time—I don't mean while swimming. I was glad to talk a little to somebody that didn't belong to the *Sephora*. As to asking for the captain, that was a mere impulse. It could have been no use, with all the ship knowing about me and the other people pretty certain to be round here in the morning. I don't know—I wanted to be seen, to talk with somebody, before I went on. I don't know what I would have said. . . . 'Fine night, isn't it?' or something of the sort."

"Do you think they will be round here presently?" I asked with some incredulity.

"Quite likely," he said faintly.

He looked extremely haggard all of a sudden. His head rolled on his shoulders.

"H'm. We shall see then. Meantime get into that bed," I whispered. "Want help? There."

It was a rather high bed-place with a set of drawers underneath. This amazing swimmer really needed the lift I gave him by seizing his leg. He tumbled in, rolled over on his back, and flung one arm across his eyes. And then, with his face nearly hidden, he must have looked exactly as I used to look in that bed. I gazed upon my other self for a while before drawing across carefully the two green serge curtains which ran on a brass rod. I thought for a moment of pinning them together for greater safety, but I sat down on the couch, and once there I felt unwilling to rise and hunt for a pin. I would do it in a moment. I was extremely tired, in a peculiarly intimate way, by the strain of stealthiness, by the effort of whispering and the general secrecy of this excitement. It was three o'clock by now and I had been on my feet since nine, but I was not sleepy; I could not have gone to sleep. I sat there, fagged out, looking at the curtains, trying to clear my mind of the confused sensation of being in two places at once, and greatly bothered by an exasperating knocking in my head. It was a relief to discover suddenly that it was not in my head at all, but on the outside of the door. Before I could collect myself the words "Come in" were out of my mouth, and the steward entered with a tray, bringing in my morning coffee. I had slept, after all, and I was so frightened that I shouted, "This way! I am here, steward," as though he had been miles away. He put down the tray on the table next the couch and only then said, very quietly, "I can see you are here, sir." I felt him give me a keen look, but I dared not meet his eyes just then. He must have wondered why I had drawn the curtains of my bed before going to sleep on the couch. He went out, hooking the door open as usual.

I heard the crew washing decks above me. I knew I would have been told at once if there had been any wind. Calm, I thought, and I was doubly vexed. Indeed, I felt dual more than ever. The steward reappeared suddenly in the doorway. I jumped up from the couch so quickly that he gave a start.

"What do you want here?"

"Close your port, sir—they are washing decks."

"It is closed," I said, reddening.

"Very well, sir." But he did not move from the doorway and returned my stare in an extraordinary, equivocal manner for a time. Then his eyes wavered, all his expression changed, and in a voice unusually gentle, almost coaxingly:

"May I come in to take the empty cup away, sir?"

"Of course!" I turned my back on him while he popped in and

out. Then I unhooked and closed the door and even pushed the bolt. This sort of thing could not go on very long. The cabin was as hot as an oven, too. I took a peep at my double, and discovered that he had not moved, his arm was still over his eyes; but his chest heaved; his hair was wet; his chin glistened with perspiration. I reached over him and opened the port.

"I must show myself on deck," I reflected.

Of course, theoretically, I could do what I liked, with no one to say nay to me within the whole circle of the horizon; but to lock my cabin door and take the key away I did not dare. Directly I put my head out of the companion I saw the group of my two officers, the second mate barefooted, the chief mate in long india-rubber boots, near the break of the poop, and the steward halfway down the poop ladder talking to them eagerly. He happened to catch sight of me and dived, the second ran down on the main deck shouting some order or other, and the chief mate came to meet me, touching his cap.

There was a sort of curiosity in his eye that I did not like. I don't know whether the steward had told them that I was "queer" only, or downright drunk, but I know the man meant to have a good look at me. I watched him coming with a smile which, as he got into point-blank range, took effect and froze on his very whiskers. I did not give him time to open his lips.

"Square the yards by lifts and braces before the hands go to breakfast."

It was the first particular order I had given on board that ship; and I stayed on deck to see it executed, too. I had felt the need of asserting myself without loss of time. That sneering young cub got taken down a peg or two on that occasion, and I also seized the opportunity of having a good look at the face of every foremast man as they filed past me to go to the after braces. At breakfast time, eating nothing myself, I presided with such frigid dignity that the two mates were only too glad to escape from the cabin as soon as decency permitted and all the time the dual working of my mind distracted me almost to the point of insanity. I was constantly watching myself, my secret self, as dependent on my actions as my own personality, sleeping in that bed, behind that door which faced me as I sat at the head of the table. It was very much like being mad, only it was worse because one was aware of it.

I had to shake him for a solid minute, but when at last he opened his eyes it was in the full possession of his senses, with an inquiring look.

"All's well so far," I whispered. "Now you must vanish into the bathroom."

He did so, as noiseless as a ghost, and I then rang for the steward, and facing him boldly, directed him to tidy up my stateroom while

I was having my bath—"and be quick about it." As my tone admitted of no excuses, he said, "Yes, sir," and ran off to fetch his dustpan and brushes. I took a bath and did most of my dressing, splashing, and whistling softly for the steward's edification, while the secret sharer of my life stood drawn up bolt upright in that little space, his face looking very sunken in daylight, his eyelids lowered under the stern, dark line of his eyebrows drawn together by a slight frown.

When I left him there to go back to my room the steward was finishing dusting. I sent for the mate and engaged him in some insignificant conversation. It was, as it were, trifling with the terrific character of his whiskers; but my object was to give him an opportunity for a good look at my cabin. And then I could at last shut, with a clear conscience, the door of my stateroom and get my double back into the recessed part. There was nothing else for it. He had to sit still on a small folding stool, half smothered by the heavy coats hanging there. We listened to the steward going into the bathroom out of the saloon, filling the water bottles there, scrubbing the bath, setting things to rights, whisk, bang, clatter—out again into the saloon—turn the key—click. Such was my scheme for keeping my second self invisible. Nothing better could be contrived under the circumstances. And there we sat; I at my writing desk ready to appear busy with some papers, he behind me, out of sight of the door. It would not have been prudent to talk in daytime; and I could not have stood the excitement of that queer sense of whispering to myself. Now and then, glancing over my shoulder, I saw him far back there, sitting rigidly on the low stool, his bare feet close together, his arms folded, his head hanging on his breast—and perfectly still. Anybody would have taken him for me.

I was fascinated by it myself. Every moment I had to glance over my shoulder. I was looking at him when a voice outside the door said:

"Beg pardon, sir."

"Well!" . . . I kept my eyes on him, and so, when the voice outside the door announced, "There's a ship's boat coming our way, sir," I saw him give a start—the first movement he had made for hours. But he did not raise his bowed head.

"All right. Get the ladder over."

I hesitated. Should I whisper something to him? But what? His immobility seemed to have been never disturbed. What could I tell him he did not know already? . . . Finally I went on deck.

## II

The skipper of the *Sephora* had a thin red whisker all round his face, and the sort of complexion that goes with hair of that color;

also the particular, rather smeary shade of blue in the eyes. He was not exactly a showy figure; his shoulders were high, his stature but middling—one leg slightly more bandy than the other. He shook hands, looking vaguely around. A spiritless tenacity was his main characteristic, I judged. I behaved with a politeness which seemed to disconcert him. Perhaps he was shy. He mumbled to me as if he were ashamed of what he was saying; gave his name (it was something like Archbold—but at this distance of years I hardly am sure), his ship's name, and a few other particulars of that sort, in the manner of a criminal making a reluctant and doleful confession. He had had terrible weather on the passage out—terrible—terrible—wife aboard, too.

By this time we were seated in the cabin and the steward brought in a tray with a bottle and glasses. "Thanks! No." Never took liquor. Would have some water, though. He drank two tumblerfuls. Terrible thirsty work. Ever since daylight had been exploring the islands round his ship.

"What was that for—fun?" I asked, with an appearance of polite interest.

"No!" He sighed. "Painful duty."

As he persisted in his mumbling and I wanted my double to hear every word, I hit upon the notion of informing him that I regretted to say I was hard of hearing.

"Such a young man, too!" he nodded, keeping his smeary blue, unintelligent eyes fastened upon me. What was the cause of it—some disease? he inquired, without the least sympathy and as if he thought that, if so, I'd got no more than I deserved.

"Yes; disease," I admitted in a cheerful tone which seemed to shock him. But my point was gained, because he had to raise his voice to give me his tale. It is not worth while to record that version. It was just over two months since all this had happened, and he had thought so much about it that he seemed completely muddled as to its bearings, but still immensely impressed.

"What would you think of such a thing happening on board your own ship? I've had the *Sephora* for these fifteen years. I am a well-known shipmaster."

He was densely distressed—and perhaps I should have sympathized with him if I had been able to detach my mental vision from the unsuspected sharer of my cabin as though he were my second self. There he was on the other side of the bulkhead, four or five feet from us, no more, as we sat in the saloon. I looked politely at Captain Archbold (if that was his name), but it was the other I saw, in a gray sleeping suit, seated on a low stool, his bare feet close together, his arms folded, and every word said between us falling into the ears of his dark head bowed on his chest.

"I have been at sea now, man and boy, for seven-and-thirty years, and I've never heard of such a thing happening in an English ship. And that it should be my ship. Wife on board, too."

I was hardly listening to him.

"Don't you think," I said, "that the heavy sea which, you told me, came aboard just then might have killed the man? I have seen the sheer weight of a sea kill a man very neatly, by simply breaking his neck."

"Good God!" he uttered, impressively, fixing his smeary blue eyes on me. "The sea! No man killed by the sea ever looked like that." He seemed positively scandalized at my suggestion. And as I gazed at him, certainly not prepared for anything original on his part, he advanced his head close to mine and thrust his tongue out at me so suddenly that I couldn't help starting back.

After scoring over my calmness in this graphic way he nodded wisely. If I had seen the sight, he assured me, I would never forget it as long as I lived. The weather was too bad to give the corpse a proper sea burial. So next day at dawn they took it up on the poop, covering its face with a bit of bunting; he read a short prayer, and then, just as it was, in its oilskins and long boots, they launched it amongst those mountainous seas that seemed ready every moment to swallow up the ship herself and the terrified lives on board of her.

"That reefed foresail saved you," I threw in.

"Under God—it did," he exclaimed fervently. "It was by a special mercy, I firmly believe, that it stood some of those hurricane squalls."

"It was the setting of that sail which—" I began.

"God's own hand in it," he interrupted me. "Nothing less could have done it. I don't mind telling you that I hardly dared give the order. It seemed impossible that we could touch anything without losing it, and then our last hope would have been gone."

The terror of that gale was on him yet. I let him go on for a bit, then said, casually—as if returning to a minor subject:

"You were very anxious to give up your mate to the shore people, I believe?"

He was. To the law. His obscure tenacity on that point had in it something incomprehensible and a little awful; something, as it were, mystical, quite apart from his anxiety that he should not be suspected of "countenancing any doings of that sort." Seven-and-thirty virtuous years at sea, of which over twenty of immaculate command, and the last fifteen in the *Sephora* seemed to have laid him under some pitiless obligation.

"And you know," he went on, groping shamefacedly amongst his feelings, "I did not engage that young fellow. His people had some interest with my owners. I was in a way forced to take him on. He looked very smart, very gentlemanly, and all that. But do you know—

I never liked him, somehow. I am a plain man. You see, he wasn't exactly the sort for the chief mate of a ship like the *Sephora*."

I had become so connected in thoughts and impressions with the secret sharer of my cabin that I felt as if I, personally, were being given to understand that I, too, was not the sort that would have done for the chief mate of a ship like the *Sephora*. I had no doubt of it in my mind.

"Not at all the style of man. You understand," he insisted, superfluously, looking hard at me.

I smiled urbanely. He seemed at a loss for a while.

"I suppose I must report a suicide."

"Beg pardon?"

"Sui-cide! That's what I'll have to write to my owners directly I get in."

"Unless you manage to recover him before tomorrow," I assented, dispassionately . . . "I mean, alive."

He mumbled something which I really did not catch, and I turned my ear to him in a puzzled manner. He fairly bawled:

"The land—I say, the mainland is at least seven miles off my anchorage."

"About that."

My lack of excitement, of curiosity, of surprise, of any sort of pronounced interest, began to arouse his distrust. But except for the felicitous pretense of deafness I had not tried to pretend anything. I had felt utterly incapable of playing the part of ignorance properly, and therefore was afraid to try. It is also certain that he had brought some ready-made suspicions with him, and that he viewed my politeness as a strange and unnatural phenomenon. And yet how else could I have received him? Not heartily! That was impossible for psychological reasons, which, I need not state here. My only object was to keep off his inquiries. Surlily? Yes, but surliness might have provoked a point-blank question. From its novelty to him and from its nature, punctilious courtesy was the manner best calculated to restrain the man. But there was the danger of his breaking through my defense bluntly. I could not, I think, have met him by a direct lie, also for psychological (not moral) reasons. If he had only known how afraid I was of his putting my feeling of identity with the other to the test! But, strangely enough—(I thought of it only afterward)—I believe that he was not a little disconcerted by the reverse side of that weird situation, by something in me that reminded him of the man he was seeking—suggested a mysterious similitude to the young fellow he had distrusted and disliked from the first.

However that might have been, the silence was not very prolonged. He took another oblique step.

"I reckon I had no more than a two-mile pull to your ship. Not a bit more."

"And quite enough, too, in this awful heat," I said.

Another pause full of mistrust followed. Necessity, they say, is mother of invention, but fear, too, is not barren of ingenious suggestions. And I was afraid he would ask me pointblank for news of my other self.

"Nice little saloon, isn't it?" I remarked, as if noticing for the first time the way his eyes roamed from one closed door to the other. "And very well fitted out, too. Here, for instance," I continued, reaching over the back of my seat negligently and flinging the door open, "is my bathroom."

He made an eager movement, but hardly gave it a glance. I got up, shut the door of the bathroom, and invited him to have a look round, as if I were very proud of my accommodation. He had to rise and be shown round, but he went through the business without any raptures whatever.

"And now we'll have a look at my stateroom," I declared, in a voice as loud as I dared to make it, crossing the cabin to the starboard side with purposely heavy steps.

He followed me in and gazed around. My intelligent double had vanished. I played my part.

"Very convenient—isn't it?"

"Very nice. Very com . . ." He didn't finish, and went out brusquely as if to escape from some unrighteous wiles of mine. But it was not to be. I had been too frightened not to feel vengeful; I felt I had him on the run, and I meant to keep him on the run. My polite insistence must have had something menacing in it, because he gave in suddenly. And I did not let him off a single item; mate's room, pantry, storerooms, the very sail locker which was also under the poop—he had to look into them all. When at last I showed him out on the quarter-deck he drew a long, spiritless sigh, and mumbled dismally that he must really be going back to his ship now. I desired my mate, who had joined us, to see to the captain's boat.

The man of whiskers gave a blast on the whistle which he used to wear hanging round his neck, and yelled, "*Sephora* away!" My double down there in my cabin must have heard, and certainly could not feel more relieved than I. Four fellows came running out from somewhere forward and went over the side, while my own men, appearing on deck too, lined the rail. I escorted my visitor to the gangway ceremoniously, and nearly overdid it. He was a tenacious beast. On the very ladder he lingered, and in that unique, guiltily conscientious manner of sticking to the point:

"I say . . . you . . . you don't think that—"

I covered his voice loudly:

"Certainly not . . . I am delighted. Good-by."

I had an idea of what he meant to say, and just saved myself by the privilege of defective hearing. He was too shaken generally to insist, but my mate, close witness of that parting, looked mystified and his face took on a thoughtful cast. As I did not want to appear as if I wished to avoid all communication with my officers, he had the opportunity to address me.

"Seems a very nice man. His boat's crew told our chaps a very extraordinary story, if what I am told by the steward is true. I suppose you had it from the captain, sir?"

"Yes. I had a story from the captain."

"A very horrible affair—isn't it, sir?"

"It is."

"Beats all these tales we hear about murders in Yankee ships."

"I don't think it beats them. I don't think it resembles them in the least."

"Bless my soul—you don't say so! But of course I've no acquaintance whatever with American ships, not I, so I couldn't go against your knowledge. It's horrible enough for me . . . But the queerest part is that those fellows seemed to have some idea the man was hidden aboard here. They had really. Did you ever hear of such a thing?"

"Preposterous—isn't it?"

We were walking to and fro athwart the quarterdeck. No one of the crew forward could be seen (the day was Sunday), and the mate pursued:

"There was some little dispute about it. Our chaps took offense. 'As if we would harbor a thing like that,' they said. 'Wouldn't you like to look for him in our coal hole?' Quite a tiff. But they made it up in the end. I suppose he did drown himself. Don't you, sir?"

"I don't suppose anything."

"You have no doubt in the matter, sir?"

"None whatever."

I left him suddenly. I felt I was producing a bad impression, but with my double down there it was most trying to be on deck. And it was almost as trying to be below. Altogether a nerve-trying situation. But on the whole I felt less torn in two when I was with him. There was no one in the whole ship whom I dared take into my confidence. Since the hands had got to know his story, it would have been impossible to pass him off for anyone else, and an accidental discovery was to be dreaded now more than ever. . . .

The steward being engaged in laying the table for dinner, we could talk only with our eyes when I first went down. Later in the afternoon we had a cautious try at whispering. The Sunday quietness of the ship was against us; the elements, the men were against us—everything was against us in our secret partnership; time itself—for this could not go on forever. The very trust in Providence was, I suppose, denied to his guilt. Shall I confess that this thought cast me down very much? And as to the chapter of accidents which counts for so much in the book of success, I could only hope that it was closed. For what favorable accident could be expected?

"Did you hear everything?" were my first words as soon as we took up our position side by side, leaning over my bed-place.

He had. And the proof of it was his earnest whisper, "The man told you he hardly dared to give the order."

I understood the reference to be to that saving foresail.

"I assure you he never gave the order. He may think he did, but he never gave it. He stood there with me on the break of the poop after the maintopsail blew away, and whimpered about our last hope—positively whimpered about it and nothing else—and the night coming on! To hear one's skipper go on like that in such weather was enough to drive any fellow out of his mind. It worked me up into a sort of desperation. I just took it into my own hands and went away from him, boiling, and—But what's the use telling you? *You* know! . . . Do you think that if I had not been pretty fierce with them I should have got the men to do anything? Not it! The bosun perhaps? Perhaps! It wasn't a heavy sea—it was a sea gone mad! I suppose the end of the world will be something like that; and a man may have the heart to see it coming once and be done with it—but to have to face it day after day—I don't blame anybody. I was precious little better than the rest. Only—I was an officer of that old coal-wagon, anyhow—"

"I quite understand," I conveyed that sincere assurance into his ear. He was out of breath with whispering; I could hear him pant slightly. It was all very simple. The same strung-up force which had given twenty-four men a chance, at least, for their lives, had, in a sort of recoil, crushed an unworthy mutinous existence.

But I had no leisure to weigh the merits of the matter—footsteps in the saloon, a heavy knock. "There's enough wind to get under way with, sir." Here was the call of a new claim upon my thoughts and even upon my feelings.

"Turn the hands up," I cried through the door. "I'll be on deck directly."

I was going out to make the acquaintance of my ship. Before I left the cabin our eyes met—the eyes of the only two strangers on board. I pointed to the recessed part where the little campstool awaited him and laid my finger on my lips. He made a gesture—somewhat vague—a little mysterious, accompanied by a faint smile, as if of regret.

This is not the place to enlarge upon the sensations of a man who feels for the first time a ship move under his feet to his own independent word. In my case they were not unalloyed. I was not wholly alone with my command; for there was that stranger in my cabin. Or rather, I was not completely and wholly with her. Part of me was absent. That mental feeling of being in two places at once affected me physically as if the mood of secrecy had penetrated my very soul. Before an hour had elapsed since the ship had begun to move, having occasion to ask the mate (he stood by my side) to take a compass bearing of the Pagoda, I caught myself reaching up to his ear in whispers. I say I caught myself, but enough had escaped to startle the man. I can't describe it otherwise than by saying that he shied. A grave, preoccupied manner, as though he were in possession of some perplexing intelligence, did not leave him henceforth. A little later I moved away from the rail to look at the compass with such a stealthy gait that the helmsman noticed it—and I could not help noticing the unusual roundness of his eyes. These are trifling instances, though it's to no commander's advantage to be suspected of ludicrous eccentricities. But I was also more seriously affected. There are to a seaman certain words, gestures, that should in given conditions come as naturally, as instinctively as the winking of a menaced eye. A certain order should spring on to his lips without thinking; a certain sign should get itself made, so to speak, without reflection. But all unconscious alertness had abandoned me. I had to make an effort of will to recall myself back (from the cabin) to the conditions of the moment. I felt that I was appearing an irresolute commander to those people who were watching me more or less critically.

And, besides, there were the scares. On the second day out, for instance, coming off the deck in the afternoon (I had straw slippers on my bare feet) I stopped at the open pantry door and spoke to the steward. He was doing something there with his back to me. At the sound of my voice he nearly jumped out of his skin, as the saying is, and incidentally broke a cup.

"What on earth's the matter with you?" I asked, astonished.

He was extremely confused. "Beg pardon, sir. I made sure you were in your cabin."

"You see I wasn't."

"No, sir. I could have sworn I had heard you moving in there not a moment ago. It's most extraordinary . . . very sorry, sir."

I passed on with an inward shudder. I was so identified with my secret double that I did not even mention that fact in those scanty, fearful whispers we exchanged. I suppose he had made some slight noise of some kind or other. It would have been miraculous if he hadn't at one time or another. And yet, haggard as he appeared, he looked always perfectly self-controlled, more than calm—almost invulnerable. On my suggestion he remained almost entirely in the bathroom, which, upon the whole, was the safest place. There could be really no shadow of an excuse for anyone ever wanting to go in there, once the steward had done with it. It was a very tiny place. Sometimes he reclined on the floor, his legs bent, his head sustained on one elbow. At others I would find him on the campstool, sitting in his gray sleeping suit and with his cropped dark hair like a patient, unmoved convict. At night I would smuggle him into my bed-place, and we would whisper together, with the regular footfalls of the officer of the watch passing and repassing over our heads. It was an infinitely miserable time. It was lucky that some tins of fine preserves were stowed in a locker in my stateroom; hard bread I could always get hold of; and so he lived on stewed chicken, paté de foie gras, asparagus, cooked oysters, sardines—on all sorts of abominable sham delicacies out of tins. My early morning coffee he always drank; and it was all I dared do for him in that respect.

Every day there was the horrible maneuvering to go through so that my room and then the bathroom should be done in the usual way. I came to hate the sight of the steward, to abhor the voice of that harmless man. I felt that it was he who would bring on the disaster of discovery. It hung like a sword over our heads.

The fourth day out, I think (we were then working down the east side of the Gulf of Siam, tack for tack, in light winds and smooth water)—the fourth day, I say, of this miserable juggling with the unavoidable, as we sat at our evening meal, that man, whose slightest movement I dreaded, after putting down the dishes ran upon deck busily. This could not be dangerous. Presently he came down again; and then it appeared that he had remembered a coat of mine which I had thrown over a rail to dry after having been wetted in a shower which had passed over the ship in the afternoon. Sitting stolidly at the head of the table I became terrified at the sight of the garment on his arm. Of course he made for my door. There was no time to lose.

"Steward," I thundered. My nerves were so shaken that I could not govern my voice and conceal my agitation. This was the sort of thing that made my terrifically whiskered mate tap his forehead with his forefinger. I had detected him using that gesture while talking on deck with a confidential air to the carpenter. It was too far to hear a word, but I had no doubt that this pantomime could only refer to the strange new captain.

"Yes, sir," the pale-faced steward turned resignedly to me. It was this maddening course of being shouted at, checked without rhyme or reason, arbitrarily chased out of my cabin, suddenly called into it, sent flying out of his pantry on incomprehensible errands, that accounted for the growing wretchedness of his expression.

"Where are you going with that coat?"

"To your room, sir."

"Is there another shower coming?"

"I'm sure I don't know, sir. Shall I go up again and see, sir?"

"No! never mind."

My object was attained, as of course my other self in there would have heard everything that passed. During this interlude my two officers never raised their eyes off their respective plates; but the lip of that confounded cub, the second mate, quivered visibly.

I expected the steward to hook my coat on and come out at once. He was very slow about it; but I dominated my nervousness sufficiently not to shout after him. Suddenly I became aware (it could be heard plainly enough) that the fellow for some reason or other was opening the door of the bathroom. It was the end. The place was literally not big enough to swing a cat in. My voice died in my throat and I went stony all over. I expected to hear a yell of surprise and terror, and made a movement, but had not the strength to get on my legs. Everything remained still. Had my second self taken the poor wretch by the throat? I don't know what I would have done next moment if I had not seen the steward come out of my room, close the door, and then stand quietly by the sideboard.

Saved, I thought. But no! Lost! Gone! He was gone!

I laid my knife and fork down and leaned back in my chair. My head swam. After a while, when sufficiently recovered to speak in a steady voice, I instructed my mate to put the ship round at eight o'clock himself.

"I won't come on deck," I went on. "I think I'll turn in, and unless the wind shifts I don't want to be disturbed before midnight. I feel a bit seedy."

"You did look middling bad a little while ago," the chief mate remarked without showing any great concern.

They both went out, and I stared at the steward clearing the table. There was nothing to be read on that wretched man's face. But why did he avoid my eyes I asked myself. Then I thought I should like to hear the sound of his voice.

"Steward!"

"Sir!" Startled as usual.

"Where did you hang up that coat?"

"In the bathroom, sir." The usual anxious tone. "It's not quite dry yet, sir."

For some time longer I sat in the cuddy. Had my double vanished as he had come? But of his coming there was an explanation, whereas his disappearance would be inexplicable . . . I went slowly into my dark room, shut the door, lighted the lamp, and for a time dared not turn round. When at last I did I saw him standing bolt upright in the narrow recessed part. It would not be true to say I had a shock, but an irresistible doubt of his bodily existence flitted through my mind. Can it be, I asked myself, that he is not visible to other eyes than mine? It was like being haunted. Motionless, with a grave face, he raised his hands slightly at me in a gesture which meant clearly, "Heavens! what a narrow escape!" Narrow indeed. I think I had come creeping quietly as near insanity as any man who has not actually gone over the border. That gesture restrained me, so to speak.

The mate with the terrific whiskers was now putting the ship on the other tack. In the moment of profound silence which follows upon the hands going to their stations I heard on the poop his raised voice: "Hard alee!" and the distant shout of the order repeated on the main-deck. The sails, in that breeze, made but a faint fluttering noise. It ceased. The ship was coming round slowly; I held my breath in the renewed stillness of expectation; one wouldn't have thought that there was a single living soul on her decks. A sudden brisk shout, "Mainsail haul!" broke the spell, and in the noisy cries and rush overhead of the men running away with the main brace we two, down in my cabin, came together in our usual position by the bed-place.

He did not wait for my question. "I heard him fumbling here and just managed to squat myself down in the bath," he whispered to me. "The fellow only opened the door and put his arm in to hang the coat up. All the same–"

"I never thought of that," I whispered back, even more appalled than before at the closeness of the shave, and marvelling at that something unyielding in his character which was carrying him through so finely. There was no agitation in his whisper. Whoever was being driven distracted, it was not he. He was sane. And the proof of his sanity was continued when he took up the whispering again.

"It would never do for me to come to life again."

It was something that a ghost might have said. But what he was alluding to was his old captain's reluctant admission of the theory of suicide. It would obviously serve his turn–if I had understood at all the view which seemed to govern the unalterable purpose of his action.

"You must maroon me as soon as ever you can get amongst these islands off the Cambodje shore," he went on.

"Maroon you! We are not living in a boy's adventure tale," I protested. His scornful whispering took me up.

"We aren't indeed! There's nothing of a boy's tale in this. But there's nothing else for it. I want no more. You don't suppose I am afraid of what can be done to me? Prison or gallows or whatever they may please. But you don't see me coming back to explain such things to an old fellow in a wig and twelve respectable tradesmen, do you? What can they know whether I am guilty or not—or of *what* I am guilty, either? That's my affair. What does the Bible say? 'Driven off the face of the earth.' Very well. I am off the face of the earth now. As I came at night so I shall go."

"Impossible!" I murmured. "You can't."

"Can't? . . . Not naked like a soul on the Day of Judgment. I shall freeze on to this sleeping suit. The Last Day is not yet—and . . . you have understood thoroughly. Didn't you?"

I felt suddenly ashamed of myself. I may say truly that I understood—and my hesitation in letting that man swim away from my ship's side had been a mere sham sentiment, a sort of cowardice.

"It can't be done now till next night," I breathed out. "The ship is on the offshore tack and the wind may fail us."

"As long as I know that you understand," he whispered. "But of course you do. It's a great satisfaction to have got somebody to understand. You seem to have been there on purpose." And in the same whisper, as if we two whenever we talked had to say things to each other which were not fit for the world to hear, he added, "It's very wonderful."

We remained side by side talking in our secret way—but sometimes silent or just exchanging a whispered word or two at long intervals. And as usual he stared through the port. A breath of wind came now and again into our faces. The ship might have been moored in dock, so gently and on an even keel she slipped through the water, that did not murmur even at our passage, shadowy and silent like a phantom sea.

At midnight I went on deck, and to my mate's great surprise put the ship round on the other tack. His terrible whiskers flitted round me in silent criticism. I certainly should not have done it if it had been only a question of getting out of that sleepy gulf as quickly as possible. I believe he told the second mate, who relieved him, that it was a great want of judgment. The other only yawned. That intolerable cub shuffled about so sleepily and lolled against the rails in such a slack, improper fashion that I came down on him sharply.

"Aren't you properly awake yet?"

"Yes, sir! I am awake."

"Well, then, be good enough to hold yourself as if you were. And keep a lookout. If there's any current we'll be closing with some islands before daylight."

The east side of the gulf is fringed with islands, some solitary, others in groups. On the blue background of the high coast they seem to float on silvery patches of calm water, arid and gray, or dark green and rounded like clumps of evergreen bushes, with the larger ones, a mile or two long, showing the outlines of ridges, ribs of gray rock under the dark mantle of matted leafage. Unknown to trade, to travel, almost to geography, the manner of life they harbor is an unsolved secret. There must be villages—settlements of fishermen at least—on the largest of them, and some communication with the world is probably kept up by native craft. But all that forenoon, as we headed for them, fanned along by the faintest of breezes, I saw no sign of man or canoe in the field of the telescope I kept on pointing at the scattered group.

At noon I gave no orders for a change of course, and the mate's whiskers became much concerned and seemed to be offering themselves unduly to my notice. At last I said:

"I am going to stand right in. Quite in—as far as I can take her."

The stare of extreme surprise imparted an air of ferocity also to his eyes, and he looked truly terrific for a moment.

"We're not doing well in the middle of the gulf," I continued, casually. "I am going to look for the land breezes tonight."

"Bless my soul! Do you mean, sir, in the dark amongst the lot of all them islands and reefs and shoals?"

"Well—if there are any regular land breezes at all on this coast one must get close inshore to find them, mustn't one?"

"Bless my soul!" he exclaimed again under his breath. All that afternoon he wore a dreamy, contemplative appearance which in him was a mark of perplexity. After dinner I went into my stateroom as if I meant to take some rest. There we two bent our dark heads over a half-unrolled chart lying on my bed.

"There," I said. "It's got to be Koh-ring. I've been looking at it ever since sunrise. It has got two hills and a low point. It must be inhabited. And on the coast opposite there is what looks like the mouth of a biggish river—with some town, no doubt, not far up. It's the best chance for you that I can see."

"Anything. Koh-ring let it be."

He looked thoughtfully at the chart as if surveying chances and distances from a lofty height—and following with his eyes his own figure wandering on the blank land of Cochin-China, and then passing off that piece of paper clean out of sight into uncharted regions. And it was as if the ship had two captains to plan her course for her. I had been so worried and restless running up and down that I had not had the patience to dress that day, I had remained in my sleeping suit, with straw slippers and a soft floppy hat. The closeness of the heat in the gulf had been most oppressive, and the crew were used to see me wandering in that airy attire.

"She will clear the south point as she heads now," I whispered into his ear. "Goodness only knows when, though, but certainly after dark. I'll edge her in to half a mile, as far as I may be able to judge in the dark—"

"Be careful," he murmured, warningly—and I realized suddenly that all my future, the only future for which I was fit, would perhaps go irretrievably to pieces in any mishap to my first command.

I could not stop a moment longer in the room. I motioned him to get out of sight and made my way on the poop. That unplayful cub had the watch. I walked up and down for a while thinking things out, then beckoned him over.

"Send a couple of hands to open the two quarter-deck ports," I said, mildly.

He actually had the impudence, or else so forgot himself in his wonder at such an incomprehensible order, as to repeat:

"Open the quarter-deck ports! What for, sir?"

"The only reason you need concern yourself about is because I tell you to do so. Have them open wide and fastened properly."

He reddened and went off, but I believe made some jeering remark to the carpenter as to the sensible practice of ventilating a ship's quarter-deck. I know he popped into the mate's cabin to impart the fact to him because the whiskers came on deck, as it were by chance, and stole glances at me from below—for signs of lunacy or drunkenness, I suppose.

A little before supper, feeling more restless than ever, I rejoined, for a moment, my second self. And to find him sitting so quietly was surprising, like something against nature, inhuman.

I developed my plan in a hurried whisper.

"I shall stand in as close as I dare and then put her round. I shall presently find means to smuggle you out of here into the sail locker, which communicates with the lobby. But there is an opening, a sort of square for hauling the sails out which gives straight on the quarter-deck and which is never closed in fine weather, so as to give air to the sails. When the ship's way is deadened in stays and all the hands are aft at the main braces you shall have a clear road to slip out and get overboard through the open quarter-deck port. I've had them both fastened up. Use a rope's end to lower yourself into the water so as to avoid a splash—you know. It could be heard and cause some beastly complication."

He kept silent for a while, then whispered, "I understand."

"I won't be there to see you go," I began with an effort. "The rest . . . I only hope I have understood, too."

"You have. From first to last," and for the first time there seemed to be a faltering, something strained in his whisper. He caught hold of my arm, but the ringing of the supper bell made me start. He didn't, though; he only released his grip.

After supper I didn't come below again till well past eight o'clock. The faint, steady breeze was loaded with dew; and the wet, darkened sails held all there was of propelling power in it. The night, clear and starry, sparkled darkly, and the opaque, lightless patches shifting slowly against the low stars were the drifting islets. On the port bow there was a big one more distant and shadowily imposing by the great space of sky it eclipsed.

On opening the door I had a back view of my very own self looking at a chart. He had come out of the recess and was standing near the table.

"Quite dark enough," I whispered.

He stepped back and leaned against my bed with a level, quiet glance. I sat on the couch. We had nothing to say to each other. Over our heads the officer of the watch moved here and there. Then I heard him move quickly. I knew what that meant. He was making for the companion; and presently his voice was outside my door.

"We are drawing in pretty fast, sir. Lands look rather close."

"Very well," I answered. "I am coming on deck directly."

I waited till he was gone out of the cuddy, then rose. My double moved too. The time had come to exchange our last whispers, for neither of us was ever to hear each other's natural voice.

"Look here!" I opened a drawer and took out three sovereigns. "Take this, anyhow. I've got six and I'd give you the lot, only I must keep a little money to buy some fruit and vegetables for the crew from native boats as we go through Sunda Straits."

He shook his head.

"Take it," I urged him, whispering desperately. "No one can tell what—"

He smiled and slapped meaningly the only pocket of the sleeping jacket. It was not safe, certainly. But I produced a large old silk handkerchief of mine, and tying the three pieces of gold in a corner, pressed it on him. He was touched, I suppose, because he took it at last and tied it quickly round his waist under the jacket, on his bare skin.

Our eyes met; several seconds elapsed, till, our glances still mingled, I extended my hand and turned the lamp out. Then I passed through the cuddy, leaving the door of my room wide open . . . "Steward!"

He was still lingering in the pantry in the greatness of his zeal, giving a rub-up to a plated cruet stand the last thing before going to bed. Being careful not to wake up the mate, whose room was opposite, I spoke in an undertone.

He looked round anxiously. "Sir!"

"Can you get me a little hot water from the galley?"

"I am afraid, sir, the galley fire's been out for some time now."

"Go and see."

He fled up the stairs.

"Now," I whispered, loudly, into the saloon—too loudly, perhaps, but I was afraid I couldn't make a sound. He was by my side in an instant—the double captain slipped past the stairs—through the tiny dark passage . . . a sliding door. We were in the sail locker, scrambling on our knees over the sails. A sudden thought struck me. I saw myself wandering barefooted, bareheaded, the sun beating on my dark poll. I snatched off my floppy hat and tried hurriedly in the dark to ram it on my other self. He dodged and fended off silently. I wonder what he thought had come to me before he understood and suddenly desisted. Our hands met gropingly, lingered united in a steady, motionless clasp for a second . . . No word was breathed by either of us when they separated.

I was standing quietly by the pantry door when the steward returned.

"Sorry, sir. Kettle barely warm. Shall I light the spirit lamp?"

"Never mind."

I came out on deck slowly. It was now a matter of conscience to shave the land as close as possible—for now he must go overboard whenever the ship was put in stays. Must! There could be no going back for him. After a moment I walked over to leeward and my heart flew into my mouth at the nearness of the land on the bow. Under any other circumstances I would not have held on a minute longer. The second mate had followed me anxiously.

I looked on till I felt I could command my voice.

"She will weather," I said then in a quiet tone.

"Are you going to try that, sir?" he stammered out incredulously. I took no notice of him and raised my tone just enough to be heard by the helmsman.

"Keep her good full."

"Good full, sir."

The wind fanned my cheek, the sails slept, the world was silent. The strain of watching the dark loom of the land grow bigger and denser was too much for me. I had shut my eyes—because the ship must go closer. She must! The stillness was intolerable. Were we standing still?

When I opened my eyes the second view started my heart with a thump. The black southern hill of Koh-ring seemed to hang right over the ship like a towering fragment of the everlasting night. On that enormous mass of blackness there was not a gleam to be seen, not a sound to be heard. It was gliding irresistibly toward us and yet seemed already within reach of the hand. I saw the vague figures of the watch grouped in the waist, gazing in awed silence.

"Are you going on, sir?" inquired an unsteady voice at my elbow.

I ignored it. I had to go on.

"Keep her full. Don't check her way. That won't do now," I said warningly.

"I can't see the sails very well," the helmsman answered me, in strange, quavering tones.

Was she close enough? Already she was, I won't say in the shadow of the land, but in the very blackness of it, already swallowed up as it were, gone too close to be recalled, gone from me altogether.

"Give the mate a call," I said to the young man who stood at my elbow as still as death. "And turn all hands up."

My tone had a borrowed loudness reverberated from the height of the land. Several voices cried out together: "We are all on deck, sir."

Then stillness again, with the great shadow gliding closer, towering higher, without a light, without a sound. Such a hush had fallen on the ship that she might have been a bark of the dead floating in slowly under the very gate of Erebus.

"My God! Where are we?"

It was the mate moaning at my elbow. He was thunderstruck, and as it were deprived of the moral support of his whiskers. He clapped his hands and absolutely cried out, "Lost!"

"Be quiet," I said sternly.

He lowered his tone, but I saw the shadowy gesture of his despair. "What are we doing here?"

"Looking for the land wind."

He made as if to tear his hair, and addressed me recklessly.

"She will never get out. You have done it, sir. I knew it'd end in something like this. She will never weather, and you are too close now to stay. She'll drift ashore before she's round. O my God!"

I caught his arm as he was raising it to batter his poor devoted head, and shook it violently.

"She's ashore already," he wailed, trying to tear himself away.

"Is she? . . . Keep good full there!"

"Good full, sir," cried the helmsman in a frightened, thin, child-like voice.

I hadn't let go the mate's arm and went on shaking it. "Ready about, do you hear? You go forward"—shake—"and stop there"—shake—"and hold your noise"—shake—"and see these head sheets properly overhauled"—shake, shake—shake.

And all the time I dared not look toward the land lest my heart should fail me. I released my grip at last and he ran forward as if fleeing for dear life.

I wondered what my double there in the sail locker thought of this commotion. He was able to hear everything—and perhaps he was able to understand why, on my conscience, it had to be thus close—no less. My first order, "Hard alee!" re-echoed ominously under the towering shadow of Koh-ring as if I had shouted in a mountain gorge. And then I watched the land intently. In that smooth water and light wind it was impossible to feel the ship coming-to. No! I could not feel her. And my second self was making now ready to slip out and lower himself overboard. Perhaps he was gone already . . . ?

The great black mass brooding over our very mastheads began to pivot away from the ship's side silently. And now I forgot the secret stranger ready to depart, and remembered only that I was a total stranger to the ship. I did not know her. Would she do it? How was she to be handled?

I swung the mainyard and waited helplessly. She was perhaps stopped, and her very fate hung in the balance, with the black mass of Koh-ring like the gate of the everlasting night towering over her taffrail. What would she do now? Had she way on her yet? I stepped to the side swiftly, and on the shadowy water I could see nothing except a faint phosphorescent flash revealing the glassy smoothness of the sleeping surface. It was impossible to tell—and I had not learned yet the feel of my ship. Was she moving? What I needed was something easily seen, a piece of paper, which I could throw overboard and watch. I had nothing on me. To run down for it I didn't dare. There was no time. All at once my strained, yearning stare distinguished a white object floating within a yard of the ship's side. White on the black water. A phosphorescent flash passed under it. What was that thing? . . . I recognized my own floppy hat. It must have fallen off his head . . . and he didn't bother. Now I had what I wanted—the saving mark for my eyes. But I hardly thought of my other self, now gone from the ship, to be hidden forever from all friendly faces, to be a fugitive and a vagabond on the earth, with no brand of the curse on his sane forehead to stay a slaying hand . . . too proud to explain.

And I watched the hat—the expression of my sudden pity for his mere flesh. It had been meant to save his homeless head from the dangers of the sun. And now—behold—it was saving the ship, by serving me for a mark to help out the ignorance of my strangeness. Ha! It was drifting forward, warning me just in time that the ship had gathered sternway.

"Shift the helm," I said in a low voice to the seaman standing still like a statue.

The man's eyes glistened wildly in the binnacle light as he jumped round to the other side and spun round the wheel.

I walked to the break of the poop. On the overshadowed deck all hands stood by the forebraces waiting for my order. The stars ahead seemed to be gliding from right to left. And all was so still in the world that I heard the quiet remark "She's round," passed in a tone of intense relief between two seamen.

"Let go and haul."

The foreyards ran round with a great noise, amidst cheery cries. And now the frightful whiskers made themselves heard giving various orders. Already the ship was drawing ahead. And I was alone with her. Nothing! no one in the world should stand now between us, throwing a shadow on the way of silent knowledge and mute affection, the perfect communion of a seaman with his first command.

Walking to the taffrail, I was in time to make out, on the very edge of a darkness thrown by a towering black mass like the very gateway of Erebus—yes, I was in time to catch an evanescent glimpse of my white hat left behind to mark the spot where the secret sharer of my cabin and of my thoughts, as though he were my second self, had lowered himself into the water to take his punishment: a free man, a proud swimmer striking out for a new destiny.

## QUESTIONS

"The Secret Sharer" is a complex tale. It can be approached and interpreted in many ways. After the first question, therefore, this set of questions is not sequential. Rather, the questions represent some of the different approaches an essay might take. We suggest, therefore, that you first consider each question to see where an essay based on it might lead and what sort of comments on the story it might provide; and then choose one question (from questions 2 through 4) to write on at length.

1. The responsibility held by the captain of a sailing vessel plays an important part in this story. What are the captain's responsibilities? What authority does he have? (Answer from your own knowledge and from what Conrad's narrator tells you.)
2. What happens to our (and, presumably, the narrator's) normal moral values in this story? Are they adhered to? Discarded? Replaced (and, if so, replaced by what other values)? (Remember to quote specific passages from the story to substantiate your answer.)
3. One frequently useful method for approaching a story is to consider how the author balances his characters. In this story, for instance, one can see the "secret sharer" as a man balanced between the two captains: the one captain representing the "law," the other representing what? (Notice that this second captain finds himself occasionally threatened by a "sentimental pity . . . a sort of cowardice." How does this affect the balance between the two men?)
4. If one concentrates on the hero, one can see him as a man caught between his duty to the ship on the one hand, and his response to the "secret sharer" and his predicament on the other hand. How does he work out his dilemma? Is he ever in danger? If so, of what sort? How successful do you think he is in the end?

## QUESTIONS FOR FURTHER THOUGHT

1. How would you compare the narrative style of "The Secret Sharer" with that of "The Open Boat"? Which do you prefer? Why?
2. "The Secret Sharer" and "The Guest" have at least two things in common: both have as hero a man who suddenly finds himself host to a murderer; and both concern the hero's relation not only to the murderer but also to that part of the natural world (plateau or sea) he has chosen for his own. How do the two stories handle these themes? What comparisons or contrasts can you make between them?

## CHARLOTTE PERKINS GILMAN (1860–1935)

# *The Yellow Wall-Paper*

It is very seldom that mere ordinary people like John and myself secure ancestral halls for the summer.

A colonial mansion, a hereditary estate, I would say a haunted house, and reach the height of romantic felicity—but that would be asking too much of fate!

Still I will proudly declare that there is something queer about it.

Else, why should it be let so cheaply? And why have stood so long untenanted?

John laughs at me, of course, but one expects that in marriage.

John is practical in the extreme. He has no patience with faith, an intense horror of superstition, and he scoffs openly at any talk of things not to be felt and seen and put down in figures.

John is a physician, and *perhaps*—(I would not say it to a living soul, of course, but this is dead paper and a great relief to my mind)—*perhaps* that is one reason I do not get well faster.

You see he does not believe I am sick!

And what can one do?

If a physician of high standing, and one's own husband, assures friends and relatives that there is really nothing the matter with one but temporary nervous depression—a slight hysterical tendency—what is one to do?

My brother is also a physician, and also of high standing, and he says the same thing.

So I take phosphates or phosphites—whichever it is, and tonics, and journeys, and air, and exercise, and am absolutely forbidden to "work" until I am well again.

Personally, I disagree with their ideas.

Personally, I believe that congenial work, with excitement and change, would do me good.

But what is one to do?

I did write for a while in spite of them; but it *does* exhaust me a good deal—having to be so sly about it, or else meet with heavy opposition.

I sometimes fancy that in my condition if I had less opposition and more society and stimulus—but John says the very worst thing I can do is to think about my condition, and I confess it always makes me feel bad.

So I will let it alone and talk about the house.

The most beautiful place! It is quite alone, standing well back from the road, quite three miles from the village. It makes me think of English places that you read about, for there are hedges and walls and gates that lock, and lots of separate little houses for the gardeners and people.

There is a *delicious* garden! I never saw such a garden—large and shady, full of box-bordered paths, and lined with long grape-covered arbors with seats under them.

There were greenhouses, too, but they are all broken now.

There was some legal trouble, I believe, something about the heirs and coheirs; anyhow, the place has been empty for years.

That spoils my ghostliness, I am afraid, but I don't care—there is something strange about the house—I can feel it.

I even said so to John one moonlight evening, but he said what I felt was a *draught,* and shut the window.

I get unreasonably angry with John sometimes. I'm sure I never used to be so sensitive. I think it is due to this nervous condition.

But John says if I feel so, I shall neglect proper self-control; so I take pains to control myself—before him, at least, and that makes me very tired.

I don't like our room a bit. I wanted one downstairs that opened on the piazza and had roses all over the window, and such pretty old-fashioned chintz hangings! but John would not hear of it.

He said there was only one window and not room for two beds, and no near room for him if he took another.

He is very careful and loving, and hardly lets me stir without special direction.

I have a schedule prescription for each hour in the day; he takes all care from me, and so I feel basely ungrateful not to value it more.

He said we came here solely on my account, that I was to have perfect rest and all the air I could get. "Your exercise depends on your strength, my dear," said he, "and your food somewhat on your appetite; but air you can absorb all the time." So we took the nursery at the top of the house.

It is a big, airy room, the whole floor nearly, with windows that look all ways, and air and sunshine galore. It was nursery first and then playroom and gymnasium, I should judge; for the windows are barred for little children, and there are rings and things in the walls.

The paint and paper look as if a boys' school had used it. It is stripped off—the paper—in great patches all around the head of my bed, about as far as I can reach, and in a great place on the other side of the room low down. I never saw a worse paper in my life.

One of those sprawling flamboyant patterns committing every artistic sin.

It is dull enough to confuse the eye in following, pronounced enough to constantly irritate and provoke study, and when you follow the lame uncertain curves for a little distance they suddenly commit suicide—plunge off at outrageous angles, destroy themselves in unheard of contradictions.

The color is repellent, almost revolting; a smouldering unclean yellow, strangely faded by the slow-turning sunlight.

It is a dull yet lurid orange in some places, a sickly sulphur tint in others.

No wonder the children hated it! I should hate it myself if I had to live in this room long.

There comes John, and I must put this away,—he hates to have me write a word.

We have been here two weeks, and I haven't felt like writing before, since that first day.

I am sitting by the window now, up in this atrocious nursery, and there is nothing to hinder my writing as much as I please, save lack of strength.

John is away all day, and even some nights when his cases are serious.

I am glad my case is not serious!

But these nervous troubles are dreadfully depressing.

John does not know how much I really suffer. He knows there is no *reason* to suffer, and that satisfies him.

Of course it is only nervousness. It does weigh on me so not to do my duty in any way!

I meant to be such a help to John, such a real rest and comfort, and here I am a comparative burden already!

Nobody would believe what an effort it is to do what little I am able,—to dress and entertain, and order things.

It is fortunate Mary is so good with the baby. Such a dear baby!

And yet I *cannot* be with him, it makes me so nervous.

I suppose John never was nervous in his life. He laughs at me so about this wall-paper!

At first he meant to repaper the room, but afterwards he said that I was letting it get the better of me, and that nothing was worse for a nervous patient than to give way to such fancies.

He said that after the wall-paper was changed it would be the heavy bedstead, and then the barred windows, and then that gate at the head of the stairs, and so on.

"You know the place is doing you good," he said, "and really, dear, I don't care to renovate the house just for a three months' rental."

"Then do let us go downstairs," I said, "there are such pretty rooms there."

Then he took me in his arms and called me a blessed little goose, and said he would go down to the cellar, if I wished, and have it whitewashed into the bargain.

But he is right enough about the beds and windows and things.

It is an airy and comfortable room as any one need wish, and, of course, I would not be so silly as to make him uncomfortable just for a whim.

I'm really getting quite fond of the big room, all but that horrid paper.

Out of one window I can see the garden, those mysterious deep-shaded arbors, the riotous old-fashioned flowers, and bushes and gnarly trees.

Out of another I get a lovely view of the bay and a little private wharf belonging to the estate. There is a beautiful shaded lane that runs down there from the house. I always fancy I see people walking in these numerous paths and arbors, but John has cautioned me not to give way to fancy in the least. He says that with my imaginative power and habit of story-making, a nervous weakness like mine is sure to lead to all manner of excited fancies, and that I ought to use my will and good sense to check the tendency. So I try.

I think sometimes that if I were only well enough to write a little it would relieve the press of ideas and rest me.

But I find I get pretty tired when I try.

It is so discouraging not to have any advice and companionship about my work. When I get really well, John says we will ask Cousin Henry and Julia down for a long visit; but he says he would as soon put fireworks in my pillow-case as to let me have those stimulating people about now.

I wish I could get well faster.

But I must not think about that. This paper looks to me as if it *knew* what a vicious influence it had!

There is a recurrent spot where the pattern lolls like a broken neck and two bulbous eyes stare at you upside down.

I get positively angry with the impertinence of it and the everlastingness. Up and down and sideways they crawl, and those absurd, unblinking eyes are everywhere. There is one place where two breadths didn't match, and the eyes go all up and down the line, one a little higher than the other.

I never saw so much expression in an inanimate thing before, and we all know how much expression they have! I used to lie awake as a child and get more entertainment and terror out of blank walls and plain furniture than most children could find in a toy-store.

I remember what a kindly wink the knobs of our big, old bureau used to have, and there was one chair that always seemed like a strong friend.

I used to feel that if any of the other things looked too fierce I could always hop into that chair and be safe.

The furniture in this room is no worse than inharmonious, however, for we had to bring it all from downstairs. I suppose when this was used as a playroom they had to take the nursery things out, and no wonder! I never saw such ravages as the children have made here.

The wall-paper, as I said before, is torn off in spots, and it sticketh closer than a brother—they must have had perseverance as well as hatred.

Then the floor is scratched and gouged and splintered, the plaster itself is dug out here and there, and this great heavy bed which is all we found in the room, looks as if it had been through the wars.

But I don't mind it a bit—only the paper.

There comes John's sister. Such a dear girl as she is, and so careful of me! I must not let her find me writing.

She is a perfect and enthusiastic housekeeper, and hopes for no better profession. I verily believe she thinks it is the writing which made me sick!

But I can write when she is out, and see her a long way off from these windows.

There is one that commands the road, a lovely shaded winding road, and one that just looks off over the country. A lovely country, too, full of great elms and velvet meadows.

This wall-paper has a kind of sub-pattern in a different shade, a particularly irritating one, for you can only see it in certain lights, and not clearly then.

But in the places where it isn't faded and where the sun is just so—I can see a strange, provoking, formless sort of figure, that seems to skulk about behind that silly and conspicuous front design.

There's sister on the stairs!

Well, the Fourth of July is over! The people are all gone and I am tired out. John thought it might do me good to see a little company, so we just had mother and Nellie and the children down for a week.

Of course I didn't do a thing. Jennie sees to everything now.

But it tired me all the same.

John says if I don't pick up faster he shall send me to Weir Mitchell in the fall.

But I don't want to go there at all. I had a friend who was in his hands once, and she says he is just like John and my brother, only more so!

Besides, it is such an undertaking to go so far.

I don't feel as if it was worth while to turn my hand over for anything, and I'm getting dreadfully fretful and querulous.

I cry at nothing, and cry most of the time.

Of course I don't when John is here, or anybody else, but when I am alone.

And I am alone a good deal just now. John is kept in town very often by serious cases, and Jennie is good and lets me alone when I want her to.

So I walk a little in the garden or down that lovely lane, sit on the porch under the roses, and lie down up here a good deal.

I'm getting really fond of the room in spite of the wall-paper. Perhaps *because* of the wall-paper.

It dwells in my mind so!

I lie here on this great immovable bed—it is nailed down, I believe—and follow that pattern about by the hour. It is as good as gymnastics, I assure you. I start, we'll say, at the bottom, down in the corner over there where it has not been touched, and I determine for the thousandth time that I *will* follow that pointless pattern to some sort of a conclusion.

I know a little of the principle of design, and I know this thing was not arranged on any laws of radiation, or alternation, or repetition, or symmetry, or anything else that I ever heard of.

It is repeated, of course, by the breadths, but not otherwise.

Looked at in one way each breadth stands alone, the bloated curves and flourishes—a kind of "debased Romanesque" with *delirium tremens*—go waddling up and down in isolated columns of fatuity.

But, on the other hand, they connect diagonally, and the sprawling outlines run off in great slanting waves of optic horror, like a lot of wallowing seaweeds in full chase.

The whole thing goes horizontally, too, at least it seems so, and I exhaust myself in trying to distinguish the order of its going in that direction.

They have used a horizontal breadth for a frieze, and that adds wonderfully to the confusion.

There is one end of the room where it is almost intact, and there, when the crosslights fade and the low sun shines directly upon it, I can almost fancy radiation after all,—the interminable grotesques seem to form around a common centre and rush off in headlong plunges of equal distraction.

It makes me tired to follow it. I will take a nap I guess.

I don't know why I should write this.

I don't want to.

I don't feel able.

And I know John would think it absurd. But I *must* say what I feel and think in some way—it is such a relief!

But the effort is getting to be greater than the relief.

Half the time now I am awfully lazy, and lie down ever so much.

John says I mustn't lose my strength, and has me take cod liver oil and lots of tonics and things, to say nothing of ale and wine and rare meat.

Dear John! He loves me very dearly, and hates to have me sick. I tried to have a real earnest reasonable talk with him the other day, and tell him how I wish he would let me go and make a visit to Cousin Henry and Julia.

But he said I wasn't able to go, nor able to stand it after I got there; and I did not make out a very good case for myself, for I was crying before I had finished.

It is getting to be a great effort for me to think straight. Just this nervous weakness I suppose.

And dear John gathered me up in his arms, and just carried me upstairs and laid me on the bed, and sat by me and read to me till it tired my head.

He said I was his darling and his comfort and all he had, and that I must take care of myself for his sake, and keep well.

He says no one but myself can help me out of it, that I must use my will and self-control and not let any silly fancies run away with me.

There's one comfort, the baby is well and happy, and does not have to occupy this nursery with the horrid wall-paper.

If we had not used it, that blessed child would have! What a fortunate escape! Why, I wouldn't have a child of mine, an impressionable little thing, live in such a room for worlds.

I never thought of it before, but it is lucky that John kept me here after all, I can stand it so much easier than a baby, you see.

Of course I never mention it to them any more—I am too wise,—but I keep watch of it all the same.

There are things in that paper that nobody knows but me, or ever will.

Behind that outside pattern the dim shapes get clearer every day.

It is always the same shape, only very numerous.

And it is like a woman stooping down and creeping about behind that pattern. I don't like it a bit. I wonder—I begin to think—I wish John would take me away from here!

It is so hard to talk with John about my case, because he is so wise, and because he loves me so.

But I tried it last night.

It was moonlight. The moon shines in all around just as the sun does.

I hate to see it sometimes, it creeps so slowly, and always comes in by one window or another.

John was asleep and I hated to waken him, so I kept still and watched the moonlight on that undulating wall-paper till I felt creepy.

The faint figure behind seemed to shake the pattern, just as if she wanted to get out.

I got up softly and went to feel and see if the paper *did* move, and when I came back John was awake.

"What is it, little girl?" he said. "Don't go walking about like that—you'll get cold."

I thought it was a good time to talk, so I told him that I really was not gaining here, and that I wished he would take me away.

"Why darling!" said he, "our lease will be up in three weeks, and I can't see how to leave before.

"The repairs are not done at home, and I cannot possibly leave town just now. Of course if you were in any danger, I could and would, but you really are better, dear, whether you can see it or not. I am a doctor, dear, and I know. You are gaining flesh and color, your appetite is better, I feel really much easier about you."

"I don't weigh a bit more," said I, "nor as much; and my appetite may be better in the evening when you are here, but it is worse in the morning when you are away!"

"Bless her little heart!" said he with a big hug, "she shall be as sick as she pleases! But now let's improve the shining hours by going to sleep, and talk about it in the morning!"

"And you won't go away?" I asked gloomily.

"Why, how can I, dear? It is only three weeks more and then we will take a nice little trip of a few days while Jennie is getting the house ready. Really dear you are better!"

"Better in body perhaps—" I began, and stopped short, for he sat up straight and looked at me with such a stern, reproachful look that I could not say another word.

"My darling," said he, "I beg of you, for my sake and for our child's sake, as well as for your own, that you will never for one instant let that idea enter your mind! There is nothing so dangerous, so fascinating, to a temperament like yours. It is a false and foolish fancy. Can you not trust me as a physician when I tell you so?"

So of course I said no more on that score, and we went to sleep before long. He thought I was asleep first, but I wasn't, and lay there for hours trying to decide whether that front pattern and the back pattern really did move together or separately.

On a pattern like this, by daylight, there is a lack of sequence, a defiance of law, that is a constant irritant to a normal mind.

The color is hideous enough, and unreliable enough, and infuriating enough, but the pattern is torturing.

You think you have mastered it, but just as you get well underway in following, it turns a back-somersault and there you are. It slaps you in the face, knocks you down, and tramples upon you. It is like a bad dream.

The outside pattern is a florid arabesque, reminding one of a fungus. If you can imagine a toadstool in joints, an interminable string of toadstools, budding and sprouting in endless convolutions—why, that is something like it.

That is, sometimes!

There is one marked peculiarity about this paper, a thing nobody seems to notice but myself, and that is that it changes as the light changes.

When the sun shoots in through the east window—I always watch for that first long, straight ray—it changes so quickly that I never can quite believe it.

That is why I watch it always.

By moonlight—the moon shines in all night when there is a moon—I wouldn't know it was the same paper.

At night in any kind of light, in twilight, candle light, lamplight, and worst of all by moonlight, it becomes bars! The outside pattern I mean, and the woman behind it is as plain as can be.

I didn't realize for a long time what the thing was that showed behind, that dim sub-pattern, but now I am quite sure it is a woman.

By daylight she is subdued, quiet. I fancy it is the pattern that keeps her so still. It is so puzzling. It keeps me quiet by the hour.

I lie down ever so much now. John says it is good for me, and to sleep all I can.

Indeed he started the habit by making me lie down for an hour after each meal.

It is a very bad habit I am convinced, for you see I don't sleep.

And that cultivates deceit, for I don't tell them I'm awake—O no!

The fact is I am getting a little afraid of John.

He seems very queer sometimes, and even Jennie has an inexplicable look.

It strikes me occasionally, just as a scientific hypothesis,—that perhaps it is the paper!

I have watched John when he did not know I was looking, and come into the room suddenly on the most innocent excuses, and I've caught him several times *looking at the paper!* And Jennie too. I caught Jennie with her hand on it once.

She didn't know I was in the room, and when I asked her in a quiet, a very quiet voice, with the most restrained manner possible, what she was doing with the paper—she turned around as if she had been caught stealing, and looked quite angry—asked me why I should frighten her so!

Then she said that the paper stained everything it touched, that she had found yellow smooches on all my clothes and John's, and she wished we would be more careful!

Did not that sound innocent? But I know she was studying that pattern, and I am determined that nobody shall find it out but myself!

Life is very much more exciting now than it used to be. You see I have something more to expect, to look forward to, to watch. I really do eat better, and am more quiet than I was.

John is so pleased to see me improve! He laughed a little the other day, and said I seemed to be flourishing in spite of my wall-paper.

I turned it off with a laugh. I had no intention of telling him it was *because* of the wall-paper—he would make fun of me. He might even want to take me away.

I don't want to leave now until I have found it out. There is a week more, and I think that will be enough.

I'm feeling ever so much better! I don't sleep much at night, for it is so interesting to watch developments; but I sleep a good deal in the daytime.

In the daytime it is tiresome and perplexing.

There are always new shoots on the fungus, and new shades of yellow all over it. I cannot keep count of them, though I have tried conscientiously.

It is the strangest yellow, that wall-paper! It makes me think of all the yellow things I ever saw—not beautiful ones like buttercups, but old foul, bad yellow things.

But there is something else about that paper—the smell! I noticed it the moment we came into the room, but with so much air and sun it was not bad. Now we have had a week of fog and rain, and whether the windows are open or not, the smell is here.

It creeps all over the house.

I find it hovering in the dining-room, skulking in the parlor, hiding in the hall, lying in wait for me on the stairs.

It gets into my hair.

Even when I go to ride, if I turn my head suddenly and surprise it—there is that smell!

Such a peculiar odor, too! I have spent hours in trying to analyze it, to find what it smelled like.

It is not bad—at first, and very gentle, but quite the subtlest, most enduring odor I ever met.

In this damp weather it is awful, I wake up in the night and find it hanging over me.

It used to disturb me at first. I thought seriously of burning the house—to reach the smell.

But now I am used to it. The only thing I can think of that it is like is the *color* of the paper! A yellow smell.

There is a very funny mark on this wall, low down, near the mopboard. A streak that runs round the room. It goes behind every piece of furniture, except the bed, a long, straight, even *smooch,* as if it had been rubbed over and over.

I wonder how it was done and who did it, and what they did it for. Round and round and round—round and round and round—it makes me dizzy!

I really have discovered something at last.

Through watching so much at night, when it changes so, I have finally found out.

The front pattern *does* move—and no wonder! The woman behind shakes it!

Sometimes I think there are a great many women behind, and sometimes only one, and she crawls around fast, and her crawling shakes it all over.

Then in the very bright spots she keeps still, and in the very shady spots she just takes hold of the bars and shakes them hard.

And she is all the time trying to climb through. But nobody could climb through that pattern—it strangles so; I think that is why it has so many heads.

They get through, and then the pattern strangles them off and turns them upside down, and makes their eyes white!

If those heads were covered or taken off it would not be half so bad.

I think that woman gets out in the daytime!

And I'll tell you why—privately—I've seen her!

I can see her out of every one of my windows!

It is the same woman, I know, for she is always creeping, and most women do not creep by daylight.

I see her on that long road under the trees, creeping along, and when a carriage comes she hides under the blackberry vines.

I don't blame her a bit. It must be very humiliating to be caught creeping by daylight!

I always lock the door when I creep by daylight. I can't do it at night, for I know John would suspect something at once.

And John is so queer now, that I don't want to irritate him. I wish he would take another room! Besides, I don't want anybody to get that woman out at night but myself.

I often wonder if I could see her out of all the windows at once.

But, turn as fast as I can, I can only see out of one at one time.

And though I always see her, she *may* be able to creep faster than I can turn!

I have watched her sometimes away off in the open country, creeping as fast as a cloud shadow in a high wind.

If only that top pattern could be gotten off from the under one! I mean to try it, little by little.

I have found out another funny thing, but I shan't tell it this time! It does not do to trust people too much.

There are only two more days to get this paper off, and I believe John is beginning to notice. I don't like the look in his eyes.

And I heard him ask Jennie a lot of professional questions about me. She had a very good report to give.

She said I slept a good deal in the daytime.

John knows I don't sleep very well at night, for all I'm so quiet!

He asked me all sorts of questions, too, and pretended to be very loving and kind.

As if I couldn't see through him!

Still, I don't wonder he acts so, sleeping under this paper for three months.

It only interests me, but I feel sure John and Jennie are secretly affected by it.

Hurrah! This is the last day, but it is enough. John is to stay in town over night, and won't be out until this evening.

Jennie wanted to sleep with me—the sly thing! but I told her I should undoubtedly rest better for a night all alone.

That was clever, for really I wasn't alone a bit! As soon as it was moonlight and that poor thing began to crawl and shake the pattern, I got up and ran to help her.

I pulled and she shook, I shook and she pulled, and before morning we had peeled off yards of that paper.

A strip about as high as my head and half around the room.

And then when the sun came and that awful pattern began to laugh at me, I declared I would finish it to-day!

We go away to-morrow, and they are moving all my furniture down again to leave things as they were before.

Jennie looked at the wall in amazement, but I told her merrily that I did it out of pure spite at the vicious thing.

She laughed and said she wouldn't mind doing it herself, but I must not get tired.

How she betrayed herself that time!

But I am here, and no person touches this paper but me,—not *alive!*

She tried to get me out of the room—it was too patent! But I said it was so quiet and empty and clean now that I believed I would lie down again and sleep all I could; and not to wake me even for dinner—I would call when I woke.

So now she is gone, and the servants are gone, and the things are gone, and there is nothing left but that great bedstead nailed down, with the canvas mattress we found on it.

We shall sleep downstairs to-night, and take the boat home to-morrow.

I quite enjoy the room, now it is bare again.

How those children did tear about here!

This bedstead is fairly gnawed!

But I must get to work.

I have locked the door and thrown the key down into the front path.

I don't want to go out, and I don't want to have anybody come in, till John comes.

I want to astonish him.

I've got a rope up here that even Jennie did not find. If that woman does get out, and tries to get away, I can tie her!

But I forgot I could not reach far without anything to stand on!

This bed will *not* move!

I tried to lift and push it until I was lame, and then I got so angry I bit off a little piece at one corner—but it hurt my teeth.

Then I peeled off all the paper I could reach standing on the floor. It sticks horribly and the pattern just enjoys it! All those strangled heads and bulbous eyes and waddling fungus growths just shriek with derision!

I am getting angry enough to do something desperate. To jump out of the window would be admirable exercise, but the bars are too strong even to try.

Besides I wouldn't do it. Of course not. I know well enough that a step like that is improper and might be misconstrued.

I don't like to *look* out of the windows even—there are so many of those creeping women, and they creep so fast.

I wonder if they all come out of that wall-paper as I did?

But I am securely fastened now by my well-hidden rope—you don't get *me* out in the road there!

I suppose I shall have to get back behind the pattern when it comes night, and that is hard!

It is so pleasant to be out in this great room and creep around as I please!

I don't want to go outside. I won't, even if Jennie asks me to.

For outside you have to creep on the ground, and everything is green instead of yellow.

But here I can creep smoothly on the floor, and my shoulder just fits in that long smooch around the wall, so I cannot lose my way.

Why there's John at the door!

It is no use, young man, you can't open it!

How he does call and pound!

Now he's crying for an axe.

It would be a shame to break down that beautiful door!

"John dear!" said I in the gentlest voice, "the key is down by the front steps, under a plantain leaf!"

That silenced him for a few moments.

Then he said—very quietly indeed, "Open the door, my darling!"

"I can't," said I. "The key is down by the front door under a plantain leaf!"

And then I said it again, several times, very gently and slowly, and said it so often that he had to go and see, and he got it of course, and came in. He stopped short by the door.

"What is the matter?" he cried. "For God's sake, what are you doing!"

I kept on creeping just the same, but I looked at him over my shoulder.

"I've got out at last," said I, "in spite of you and Jennie. And I've pulled off most of the paper, so you can't put me back!"

Now why should that man have fainted? But he did, and right across my path by the wall, so that I had to creep over him every time!

## QUESTIONS

1. Obviously, the yellow wall-paper is the central image in the story. One way to analyze the story, therefore, would be to trace the narrator's impressions of the wall-paper throughout the tale. We might ask how large a part the paper plays in her narration of each episode; how her description of the paper itself changes from scene to scene; how she describes the effect the paper has on her; and how those descriptions change. We might also ask how we respond to each change, each new description. How do we use the changing descriptions to interpret the narrator's state of mind? What feelings toward her do we have, and how do they change (or develop) as the story progresses?
2. For a brief paper, you might concentrate on the wall-paper as part of the tale's setting. Notice how the surroundings narrow for the narrator, from her description of the house and its grounds on the first day to her description of her path around the room on the final day. How has this narrowing been accomplished? What does it symbolize?
3. Another approach might be to ask why the wall-paper is in the narrator's room at all? What does her explanation of its presence tell you about her marriage—about her feelings about herself and her husband, and about his feelings about himself and her? How is this theme developed throughout the story? How does it end? (Make sure you take note of the tone of the story's final sentence!)
4. "The Yellow Wall-Paper" is certainly a tale that demands much participation from its readers. The narrator and her husband disagree about her needs and her health; and we feel ourselves called on to decide who is right. The wife also describes herself in solitude (particularly with reference to the wall-paper); and again we must decide how far to believe what she says, or how to reinterpret it. You might write a paper, therefore, discussing the narrative style of the tale, explaining where your sympathies lie at various points and describing the means by which the narrative shifts you from being a listener in the first scene (which is a fairly straightforward description) to being the only person who really understands what is going on in the final scene, the one who could answer the narrator's final question.

## QUESTIONS FOR FURTHER THOUGHT

Unlike the central characters of "The Guest" and "Young Goodman Brown," who seem to have withdrawn from their fellow humans at least partly of their own volition, the narrators of "Bartleby the Scrivener" and "The Yellow Wall-Paper" want to communicate with other people, but are prevented from doing so. What would you say is blocking communication for them? Who or what is to be blamed for the miseries all four characters endure?

## ALICE WALKER (1944–    )

# *Really,* Doesn't *Crime Pay?*

(Myrna)
SEPTEMBER, 1961

page 118

I sit here by the window in a house with a thirty-year mortgage, writing in this notebook, looking down at my Helena Rubenstein hands . . . and why not? Since I am not a serious writer my nails need not be bitten off, my cuticles need not have jagged edges. I can indulge myself—my hands—in Herbessence nail-soak, polish, lotions, and creams. The result is a truly beautiful pair of hands: sweet-smelling, small, and soft. . . .

I lift them from the page where I have written the line "Really, *Doesn't* Crime Pay?" and send them seeking up my shirt front (it is a white and frilly shirt) and smoothly up the column of my throat, where gardenia scent floats beneath my hairline. If I should spread my arms and legs or whirl, just for an instant, the sweet smell of my body would be more than I could bear. But I fit into my new surroundings perfectly; like a jar of cold cream melting on a mirrored vanity shelf.

page 119

"I have a surprise for you," Ruel said, the first time he brought me here. And you know how sick he makes me now when he grins.

"What is it?" I asked, not caring in the least.

And that is how we drove up to the house. Four bedrooms and two toilets and a half.

"Isn't it a beauty?" he said, not touching me, but urging me out of the car with the phony enthusiasm of his voice.

"Yes," I said. It is "a beauty." Like new Southern houses everywhere. The bricks resemble cubes of raw meat; the roof presses down, a field hat made of iron. The windows are narrow, beady eyes; the aluminum glints. The yard is a long undressed wound, the few trees as bereft of foliage as hairpins stuck in a mud cake.

"Yes," I say, "it sure is a beauty." He beams, in his chill and reassured way. I am startled that he doesn't still wear some kind of military uniform. But no. He came home from Korea a hero, and a glutton for sweet smells.

"Here we can forget the past," he says.

page 120

We have moved in and bought new furniture. The place reeks of newness, the green walls turn me bilious. He stands behind me, his hands touching the edges of my hair. I pick up my hairbrush and brush his hands away. I have sweetened my body to such an extent that even he (especially he) may no longer touch it.

I do not want to forget the past; but I say "Yes," like a parrot. "We can forget the past here."

The past of course is Mordecai Rich, the man who, Ruel claims, caused my breakdown. The past is the night I tried to murder Ruel with one of his chain saws.

MAY, 1958

page 2

Mordecai Rich

Mordecai does not believe Ruel Johnson is my husband. "*That* old man," he says, in a mocking, cruel way.

"Ruel is not old," I say. "Looking old is just his way." Just as, I thought, looking young is your way, although you're probably not much younger than Ruel.

Maybe it is just that Mordecai is a vagabond, scribbling down impressions of the South, from no solid place, going to none . . . and Ruel has never left Hancock County, except once, when he gallantly went off to war. He claims travel broadened him, especially his two months of European leave. He married me because although my skin is brown he thinks I look like a Frenchwoman. Sometimes he tells me I look Oriental: Korean or Japanese. I console myself with this thought: My family tends to darken and darken as we get older. One day he may wake up in bed with a complete stranger.

"He works in the store," I say. "He also raises a hundred acres of peanuts." Which is surely success.

"That many," muses Mordecai.

It is not pride that makes me tell him what my husband does, is. It is a way I can tell him about myself.

page 4

Today Mordecai is back. He tells a funny/sad story about a man in town who could not move his wife. "He huffed and puffed," laughed Mordecai, "to no avail." Then one night as he was sneaking up to her bedroom he heard joyous cries. Rushing in he found his wife in the arms of another woman! The wife calmly dressed and began to pack her bags. The husband begged and pleaded. "Anything you want," he promised. "What *do* you want?" he pleaded. The wife began to chuckle and, laughing, left the house with her friend.

Now the husband gets drunk every day and wants an ordinance passed. He cannot say what the ordinance will be against, but that is what he buttonholes people to say: "I want a goddam ordinance passed!" People who know the story make jokes about him. They pity him and give him enough money to keep him drunk.

page 5

I think Mordecai Rich has about as much heart as a dirt-eating toad. Even when he makes me laugh I know that nobody ought to look on other people's confusion with that cold an eye.

"But that's what I am," he says, flipping through the pages of his scribble pad. "A cold eye. An eye looking for Beauty. An eye looking for Truth."

"Why don't you look for other things?" I want to know. "Like neither Truth nor Beauty, but places in people's lives where things have just slipped a good bit off the track."

"That's too vague," said Mordecai, frowning.

"So is Truth," I said. "Not to mention Beauty."

page 10

Ruel wants to know why "the skinny black tramp"—as he calls Mordecai—keeps hanging around. I made the mistake of telling him Mordecai is thinking of using our house as the setting for one of his Southern country stories.

"Mordecai is from the North," I said. "He never saw a wooden house with a toilet in the yard."

"Well maybe he better go back where he from," said Ruel, "and shit the way he's used to."

It's Ruel's pride that is hurt. He's ashamed of this house that seems perfectly adequate to me. One day we'll have a new house, he says, of brick, with a Japanese bath. How should I know why?

page 11

When I told Mordecai what Ruel said he smiled in that snake-eyed way he has and said, "Do *you* mind me hanging around?"

I didn't know what to say. I stammered something. Not because of his question but because he put his hand point-blank on my left nipple. He settled his other hand deep in my hair.

"I am married more thoroughly than a young boy like you could guess," I told him. But I don't expect that to stop him. Especially since the day he found out I wanted to be a writer myself.

It happened this way: I was writing in the grape arbor, on the ledge by the creek that is hidden from the house by trees. He was right in front of me before I could put my notebook away. He snatched it from me and began to read. What is worse, he read aloud. I was embarrassed to death.

*"No wife of mine is going to embarrass me with a lot of foolish, vulgar stuff,"* Mordecai read. (This is Ruel's opinion of my writing.) *Every time he tells me how peculiar I am for wanting to write stories he brings up having a baby or going shopping, as if these things are the same. Just something to occupy my time.*

*"If you have time on your hands," he said today, "why don't you go shopping in that new store in town."*

*I went. I bought six kinds of face cream, two eyebrow pencils, five nightgowns and a longhaired wig. Two contour sticks and a pot of gloss for my lips.*

*And all the while I was grieving over my last story. Outlined—which is as far as I take stories now—but dead in embryo. My hand stilled by cowardice, my heart the heart of a slave.*

page 14

Of course Mordecai wanted to see the story. What did I have to lose?

"Flip over a few pages," I said. "It is the very skeleton of a story, but one that maybe someday I will write."

"The One-Legged Woman," Mordecai began to read aloud, then continued silently.

> The characters are poor dairy farmers. One morning the husband is too hung over to do the milking. His wife does it and when she has finished the cows are frightened by thunder and stampede, trampling her. She is also hooked severely in one leg. Her husband is asleep and does not hear her cry out. Finally she drags herself home and wakes him up. He washes her wounds and begs her to forgive him. He does not go for a doctor because he is afraid the doctor will accuse him of being lazy and a drunk, undeserving of his good wife. He wants the doctor to respect him. The wife, understanding, goes along with this.
>
> However, gangrene sets in and the doctor comes. He lectures the husband and amputates the leg of the wife. The wife lives and tries to forgive her husband for his weakness.

> While she is ill the husband tries to show he loves her, but cannot look at the missing leg. When she is well he finds he can no longer make love to her. The wife, sensing his revulsion, understands her sacrifice was for nothing. She drags herself to the barn and hangs herself.
>
> The husband, ashamed that anyone should know he was married to a one-legged woman, buries her himself and later tells everyone that she is visiting her mother.

While Mordecai was reading the story I looked out over the fields. If he says one good thing about what I've written, I promised myself, I will go to bed with him. (How else could I repay him? All I owned in any supply were my jars of cold cream!) As if he read my mind he sank down on the seat beside me and looked at me strangely.

"*You* think about things like this?" he asked.

He took me in his arms, right there in the grape arbor. "You sure do have a lot of heavy, sexy hair," he said, placing me gently on the ground. After that, a miracle happened. Under Mordecai's fingers my body opened like a flower and carefully bloomed. And it was strange as well as wonderful. For I don't think love had anything to do with this at all.

page 17

After that, Mordecai praised me for my intelligence, my sensitivity, the depth of the work he had seen—and naturally I showed him everything I had: old journals from high school, notebooks I kept hidden under tarpaulin in the barn, stories written on paper bags, on table napkins, even on shelf paper from over the sink. I am amazed—even more amazed than Mordecai—by the amount of stuff I have written. It is over twenty years' worth, and would fill, easily, a small shed.

"You must give these to me," Mordecai said finally, holding three notebooks he selected from the rather messy pile. "I will see if something can't be done with them. You could be another Zora Hurston—" he smiled—"another Simone de Beauvoir!"

Of course I am flattered. "Take it! Take it!" I cry. Already I see myself as he sees me. A famous authoress, miles away from Ruel, miles away from anybody. I am dressed in dungarees, my hands are a mess. I smell of sweat. I glow with happiness.

"How could such pretty brown fingers write such ugly, deep stuff?" Mordecai asks, kissing them.

page 20

For a week we deny each other nothing. If Ruel knows (how could he not know? His sheets are never fresh), he says nothing. I realize now that he never considered Mordecai a threat. Because Mordecai seems to have nothing to offer but his skinny self and his funny talk. I gloat over this knowledge. Now Ruel will find that I am not a womb without a brain that can be bought with Japanese bathtubs and shopping sprees. The moment of my deliverance is at hand!

page 24

Mordecai did not come today. I sit in the arbor writing down those words and my throat begins to close up. I am nearly strangled by my fear.

page 56

I have not noticed anything for weeks. Not Ruel, not the house. Everything whispers to me that Mordecai has forgotten me. Yesterday Ruel told me not to go into town and I said I wouldn't, for I have been hunting Mordecai up and down the streets. People look at me strangely, their glances slide off me in a peculiar way. It is as if they see something on my face that embarrasses them. Does everyone know about Mordecai and me? Does good loving show so soon? . . . But it is not soon. He has been gone already longer than I have known him.

page 61

Ruel tells me I act like my mind's asleep. It is asleep, of course. Nothing will wake it but a letter from Mordecai telling me to pack my bags and fly to New York.

page 65

If I could have read Mordecai's scribble pad I would know exactly what he thought of me. But now I realize he never once offered to show it to me, though he had a chance to read every serious thought I ever had. I'm afraid to know what he thought. I feel crippled, deformed. But if he ever wrote it down, that would make it true.

page 66

Today Ruel brought me in from the grape arbor, out of the rain. I didn't know it was raining. "Old folks like us might catch rheumatism if we don't be careful," he joked. I don't know what he means. I am thirty-two. He is forty. I never felt old before this month.

page 79

Ruel came up to bed last night and actually cried in my arms! He would give anything for a child, he says.

"Do you think we could have one?" he said.

"Sure," I said. "Why not?"

He began to kiss me and carry on about my goodness. I began to laugh. He became very angry, but finished what he started. He really does intend to have a child.

page 80

I must really think of something better to do than kill myself.

page 81

Ruel wants me to see a doctor about speeding up conception of the child.

"Will you go, honey?" he asks, like a beggar.

"Sure," I say. "Why not?"

page 82

Today at the doctor's office the magazine I was reading fell open at a story about a one-legged woman. They had a picture of her, drawn by someone who painted the cows orange and green, and painted the woman white, like a white cracker, with little slit-blue eyes. Not black and heavy like she was in the story I had in mind. But it is still my story, filled out and switched about as things are. The author is said to be Mordecai Rich. They show a little picture of him on a back page. He looks severe and has grown a beard. And underneath his picture there is that same statement he made to me about going around looking for Truth.

They say his next book will be called "The Black Woman's Resistance to Creativity in the Arts."

page 86

Last night while Ruel snored on his side of the bed I washed the prints of his hands off my body. Then I plugged in one of his chain saws and tried to slice off his head. This failed because of the noise. Ruel woke up right in the nick of time.

page 95

The days pass in a haze that is not unpleasant. The doctors and nurses do not take me seriously. They fill me full of drugs and never even bother to lock the door. When I think of Ruel I think of the song the British sing: "Ruel Britannia"! I can even whistle it, or drum it with my fingers.

SEPTEMBER, 1961

page 218

People tell my husband all the time that I do not look crazy. I have been out for almost a year and he is beginning to believe them. Nights, he climbs on me with his slobber and his hope, cursing Mordecai Rich for messing up his life. I wonder if he feels our wills clashing in the dark. Sometimes I see the sparks fly inside my head. It is amazing how normal everything is.

page 223

The house still does not awaken to the pitter-patter of sweet little feet, because I religiously use the Pill. It is the only spot of humor in my entire day, when I am gulping that little yellow tablet and washing it down with soda pop or tea. Ruel spends long hours at the store and in the peanut field. He comes in sweaty, dirty, tired, and I wait for him smelling of Arpège, My Sin, Wind Song, and Jungle Gardenia. The women of the community feel sorry for him, to be married to such a fluff of nothing.

I wait, beautiful and perfect in every limb, cooking supper as if my life depended on it. Lying unresisting on his bed like a drowned body washed to shore. But he is not happy. For he knows now that I intend to do nothing but say yes until he is completely exhausted.

I go to the new shopping mall twice a day now; once in the morning and once in the afternoon, or at night. I buy hats I would not dream of wearing, or even owning. Dresses that are already on their way to Goodwill. Shoes that will go to mold and mildew in the cellar. And I keep the bottles of perfume, the skin softeners, the pots of gloss and eye shadow. I amuse myself painting my own face.

When he is quite, quite tired of me I will tell him how long I've relied on the security of the Pill. When I am quite, quite tired of the sweet, sweet smell of my body and the softness of these Helena Rubenstein hands I will leave him and this house. Leave them forever without once looking back.

## QUESTIONS

1. "Sweet smells" are an important motif in "Really, *Doesn't* Crime Pay?". Discuss the use of this motif. What do the smells mean to each of the characters who care about them? With what are they associated?
2. "Really, *Doesn't* Crime Pay?" is a tale built, in part, on the so-called "eternal triangle" (in this case, one woman and two men). What is it within each participant's personality that creates the dynamics of this particular triangle? How does each one interpret the part that the relationships play in the story's plot?
3. Within "Really, *Doesn't* Crime Pay?" is a second story, "The One-Legged Woman." How does this second story figure in the plot? What does it mean to the narrator? What does it tell us about her? How does she resemble and differ from her one-legged heroine?

## QUESTIONS FOR FURTHER THOUGHT

1. Compare the organization of "The Yellow Wall-Paper" and "Really, *Doesn't* Crime Pay?". Note that each has one feature which distinguishes the story from a genuine day-by-day journal. How do these features add to the stories' impact?
2. How would you characterize the narrators of these two tales? How do they resemble each other? How do they differ?
3. The narrator's relationship with her husband is crucial in these two tales. Discuss the similarities and differences in the relationships and in the way the narrators discuss them and react to them.
4. In each story, one external feature of the narrator's world takes on undue prominence: the wallpaper in the first tale, cosmetics in the second. Discuss how the differing treatment of these motifs in the two tales reflects the different narrative styles.
5. What does each story suggest about the future for its narrator? What might you predict for each?

# *Interlude*

After the somewhat grim pair of tales that closed Chapter 3, here's a more upbeat story. This first-person narrator seems to delight in both the past and the future. In contrast to the carefully laid out tales we've just read, "The Loudest Voice" is informal and conversational in tone and structure. The narrator's speech patterns shift between dialect and standard English; her perspective shifts between that of the woman she is and the child she was at the time of the episode recounted in the story.

The story is notable for its narrator's ability to both comment on and enjoy all that surrounds her. She brings herself and her neighborhood to life with a seemingly careless vividness. Our own role becomes that of audience and friend; the narrator's view of the world (which must necessarily include us) admits of no alternative.

## GRACE PALEY (1922– )

# *The Loudest Voice*

There is a certain place where dumb-waiters boom, doors slam, dishes crash; every window is a mother's mouth bidding the street shut up, go skate somewhere else, come home. My voice is the loudest.

There, my own mother is still as full of breathing as me and the grocer stands up to speak to her. "Mrs. Abramowitz," he says, "people should not be afraid of their children."

"Ah, Mr. Bialik," my mother replies, "if you say to her or her father 'Ssh,' they say, 'In the grave it will be quiet.' "

"From Coney Island to the cemetery," says my papa. "It's the same subway; it's the same fare."

I am right next to the pickle barrel. My pinky is making tiny whirlpools in the brine. I stop a moment to announce: "Campbell's Tomato Soup. Campbell's Vegetable Beef Soup. Campbell's S-c-otch Broth . . ."

"Be quiet," the grocer says, "the labels are coming off."

"Please, Shirley, be a little quiet," my mother begs me.

In that place the whole street groans: Be quiet! Be quiet! but steals from the happy chorus of my inside self not a tittle or a jot.

There, too, but just around the corner, is a red brick building that has been old for many years. Every morning the children stand before it in double lines which must be straight. They are not insulted. They are waiting anyway.

I am usually among them. I am, in fact, the first, since I begin with "A."

One cold morning the monitor tapped me on the shoulder. "Go to Room 409, Shirley Abramowitz," he said. I did as I was told. I went in a hurry up a down staircase to Room 409, which contained sixth-graders. I had to wait at the desk without wiggling until Mr. Hilton, their teacher, had time to speak.

After five minutes he said, "Shirley?"

"What?" I whispered.

He said, "My! My! Shirley Abramowitz! They told me you had a particularly loud, clear voice and read with lots of expression. Could that be true?"

"Oh yes," I whispered.

"In that case, don't be silly; I might very well be your teacher someday. Speak up, speak up."

"Yes," I shouted.

"More like it," he said. "Now, Shirley, can you put a ribbon in your hair or a bobby pin? It's too messy."

"Yes!" I bawled.

"Now, now, calm down." He turned to the class. "Children, not a sound. Open at page 39. Read till 52. When you finish, start again." He looked me over once more. "Now, Shirley, you know, I suppose, that Christmas is coming. We are preparing a beautiful play. Most of the parts have been given out. But I still need a child with a strong voice, lots of stamina. Do you know what stamina is? You do? Smart kid. You know, I heard you read 'The Lord is my shepherd' in Assembly yesterday. I was very impressed. Wonderful delivery. Mrs. Jordan, your teacher, speaks highly of you. Now listen to me, Shirley Abramowitz, if you want to take the part and be in the play repeat after me, 'I swear to work harder than I ever did before.' "

I looked to heaven and said at once, "Oh, I swear." I kissed my pinky and looked at God.

"That is an actor's life, my dear," he explained. "Like a soldier's, never tardy or disobedient to his general, the director. Everything," he said, "absolutely everything will depend on you."

That afternoon, all over the building, children scraped and scrubbed the turkeys and the sheaves of corn off the schoolroom windows. Goodbye Thanksgiving. The next morning a monitor brought red paper and green paper from the office. We made new shapes and hung them on the walls and glued them to the doors.

The teachers became happier and happier. Their heads were ringing like the bells of childhood. My best friend Evie was prone to evil, but she did not get a single demerit for whispering. We learned "Holy Night" without an error. "How wonderful!" said Miss Glacé, the student teacher. "To think that some of you don't even speak the language!" We learned "Deck the Halls" and "Hark! The Herald Angels". . . . They weren't ashamed and we weren't embarrassed.

Oh, but when my mother heard about it all, she said to my father: "Misha, you don't know what's going on there. Cramer is the head of the Tickets Committee."

"Who?" asked my father. "Cramer? Oh yes, an active woman."

"Active? Active has to have a reason. Listen," she said sadly, "I'm surprised to see my neighbors making tra-la-la for Christmas."

My father couldn't think of what to say to that. Then he decided: "You're in America! Clara, you wanted to come here. In Palestine the Arabs would be eating you alive. Europe you had pogroms. Argentina is full of Indians. Here you got Christmas. . . . Some joke, ha?"

"Very funny, Misha. What is becoming of you? If we came to a new country a long time ago to run away from tyrants, and instead we fall into a creeping pogrom, that our children learn a lot of lies, so what's the joke? Ach, Misha, your idealism is going away."

"So is your sense of humor."

"That I never had, but idealism you had a lot of."

"I'm the same Misha Abramovitch, I didn't change an iota. Ask anyone."

"Only ask me," says my mama, may she rest in peace. "I got the answer."

Meanwhile the neighbors had to think of what to say too.

Marty's father said: "You know, he has a very important part, my boy."

"Mine also," said Mr. Sauerfeld.

"Not my boy!" said Mrs. Klieg. "I said to him no. The answer is no. When I say no! I mean no!"

The rabbi's wife said, "It's disgusting!" But no one listened to her. Under the narrow sky of God's great wisdom she wore a strawberry-blond wig.

Every day was noisy and full of experience. I was Right-hand Man. Mr. Hilton said: "How could I get along without you, Shirley?"

He said: "Your mother and father ought to get down on their knees every night and thank God for giving them a child like you."

He also said: "You're absolutely a pleasure to work with, my dear, dear child."

Sometimes he said: "For God's sakes, what did I do with the script? Shirley! Shirley! Find it."

Then I answered quietly: "Here it is, Mr. Hilton."

Once in a while, when he was very tired, he would cry out: "Shirley, I'm just tired of screaming at those kids. Will you tell Ira Pushkov not to come in till Lester points to that star the second time?"

Then I roared: "Ira Pushkov, what's the matter with you? Dope! Mr. Hilton told you five times already, don't come in till Lester points to that star the second time."

"Ach, Clara," my father asked, "what does she do there till six o'clock she can't even put the plates on the table?"

"Christmas," said my mother coldly.

"Ho! Ho!" my father said. "Christmas. What's the harm? After all, history teaches everyone. We learn from reading this is a holiday from pagan times also, candles, lights, even Chanukah. So we learn it's not altogether Christian. So if they think it's a private holiday, they're only ignorant, not patriotic. What belongs to history, belongs to all men. You want to go back to the Middle Ages? Is it better to shave your head with a secondhand razor? Does it hurt Shirley to learn to speak up? It does not. So maybe someday she won't live between the kitchen and the shop. She's not a fool."

I thank you, Papa, for your kindness. It is true about me to this day. I am foolish but I am not a fool.

That night my father kissed me and said with great interest in my career, "Shirley, tomorrow's your big day. Congrats."

"Save it," my mother said. Then she shut all the windows in order to prevent tonsillitis.

In the morning it snowed. On the street corner a tree had been decorated for us by a kind city administration. In order to miss its chilly shadow our neighbors walked three blocks east to buy a loaf of bread. The butcher pulled down black window shades to keep the colored lights from shining on his chickens. Oh, not me. On the way to school, with both hands I tossed it a kiss of tolerance. Poor thing, it was a stranger in Egypt.

I walked straight into the auditorium past the staring children. "Go ahead, Shirley!" said the monitors. Four boys, big for their age, had already started work as propmen and stagehands.

Mr. Hilton was very nervous. He was not even happy. Whatever he started to say ended in a sideward look of sadness. He sat slumped in the middle of the first row and asked me to help Miss Glacé. I did this, although she thought my voice too resonant and said, "Showoff!"

Parents began to arrive long before we were ready. They wanted to make a good impression. From among the yards of drapes I peeked out at the audience. I saw my embarrassed mother.

Ira, Lester, and Meyer were pasted to their beards by Miss Glacé. She almost forgot to thread the star on its wire, but I reminded her. I coughed a few times to clear my throat. Miss Glacé looked around and saw that everyone was in costume and on line waiting to play his part. She whispered, "All right . . ." Then:

Jackie Sauerfeld, the prettiest boy in first grade, parted the curtains with his skinny elbow and in a high voice sang out:

> "Parents dear
> We are here
> To make a Christmas play in time.
> It we give
> In narrative
> And illustrate with pantomime."

He disappeared.

My voice burst immediately from the wings to the great shock of Ira, Lester, and Meyer, who were waiting for it but were surprised all the same.

"I remember, I remember, the house where I was born . . ."

Miss Glacé yanked the curtain open and there it was, the house—an old hayloft, where Celia Kornbluh lay in the straw with Cindy

Lou, her favorite doll. Ira, Lester, and Meyer moved slowly from the wings toward her, sometimes pointing to a moving star and sometimes ahead to Cindy Lou.

It was a long story and it was a sad story. I carefully pronounced all the words about my lonesome childhood, while little Eddie Braunstein wandered upstage and down with his shepherd's stick, looking for sheep. I brought up lonesomeness again, and not being understood at all except by some women everybody hated. Eddie was too small for that and Marty Groff took his place, wearing his father's prayer shawl. I announced twelve friends, and half the boys in the fourth grade gathered round Marty, who stood on an orange crate while my voice harangued. Sorrowful and loud, I declaimed about love and God and Man, but because of the terrible deceit of Abie Stock we came suddenly to a famous moment. Marty, whose remembering tongue I was, waited at the foot of the cross. He stared desperately at the audience. I groaned, "My God, my God why hast thou forsaken me?" The soldiers who were sheiks grabbed poor Marty to pin him up to die, but he wrenched free, turned again to the audience, and spread his arms aloft to show despair and the end. I murmured at the top of my voice, "The rest is silence, but as everyone in this room, in this city—in this world—now knows, I shall have life eternal."

That night Mrs. Kornbluh visited our kitchen for a glass of tea.

"How's the virgin?" asked my father with a look of concern.

"For a man with a daughter, you got a fresh mouth, Abramovitch."

"Here," said my father kindly, "have some lemon, it'll sweeten your disposition."

They debated a little in Yiddish, then fell in a puddle of Russian and Polish. What I understood next was my father, who said, "Still and all, it was certainly a beautiful affair, you have to admit, introducing us to the beliefs of a different culture."

"Well, yes," said Mrs. Kornbluh. "The only thing . . . you know Charlie Turner—that cute boy in Celia's class—a couple others? They got very small parts or no part at all. In very bad taste, it seemed to me. After all, it's their religion."

"Ach," explained my mother, "what could Mr. Hilton do? They got very small voices; after all, why should they holler? The English language they know from the beginning by heart. They're blond like angels. You think it's so important they should get in the play? Christmas . . . the whole piece of goods . . . they own it."

I listened and listened until I couldn't listen any more. Too sleepy, I climbed out of bed and kneeled. I made a little church of my hands and said, "Hear, O Israel . . ." Then I called out in Yiddish, "Please, good night, good night. Ssh." My father said, "Ssh yourself," and slammed the kitchen door.

I was happy. I fell asleep at once. I had prayed for everybody: my talking family, cousins far away, passersby, and all the lonesome Christians. I expected to be heard. My voice was certainly the loudest.

## QUESTIONS

1. What does the narrator's possession of the "loudest voice" mean to the various people around her? What did it mean to her when she was a child, at the time of which the story tells? What does it mean to her now?
2. The central incident of the story turns on an immigrant Jewish child given a leading role in the school Christmas play: her own feelings about the play, the neighborhood adults' feelings about the holiday and its celebration, the child's response to the grownups' debates. How does Paley use this theme? How does she play the child's lack of knowledge off against our fuller knowledge of the situation?
3. Note the shifts between past and present tenses in the story. Note also the places where the narrator's adult voice breaks through. What sense of nearness or distance does this give you? How close do the narrator's childish and adult selves seem to be? What continuity of feelings and ideas do they share?

# CHARACTER STUDY AND SOCIAL COMMENT

# 4 *Looking Inward and Outward*

Fiction is the most flexible of literary forms. A story can focus on two or three characters, as "If Not Higher" and "The Guest" do; or it may include an entire community in its cast of characters, as do "The Lottery" and "Young Goodman Brown." It may keep us distanced from its characters, as "The Lottery" does, or it may take us into their minds, as do "The Secret Sharer" and "Young Goodman Brown." In works that strive for immediate effect, as "The Loudest Voice" does, we may even seem to be watching the character's thoughts form, change, and re-form.

A story may focus exclusively on the events of a few hours, as "The Open Boat" does; it may suggest the years of history that lie behind the few hours it covers, as "The Lottery" does; or its action may cover the events of many years. Fiction writers may place their narrators inside the tale or outside it; they may choose to let all the tale's characters speak freely, or they may allow us to hear only the narrator's voice. They may restrict their narrators to reporting things heard or seen, or they may let them comment, interpret, or moralize freely. In choice of characters, action, and stance, the freedom that fiction gives its writers is immense.

Fiction also offers its writers the full range from realism to fantasy in which to place their stories. "The Open Boat," with its seemingly objective stance and its careful reporting of a common type of event, is an example of realism. "Young Goodman Brown," with its action poised between dream and waking and its use of supernatural characters, is an example of fantasy. These styles, realism and fantasy, may be seen as the two ends of a scale, with other, less extreme styles falling between them. Where on the scale would you place "The Lottery"? "The Secret Sharer"? "If Not Higher"? "Bartleby the Scrivener"?

Fiction, then, is an art form of great flexibility. Largely because of this flexibility, works of fiction have the power to look in two directions at once. They can look into their characters, revealing their minds and feelings to us, exploring their personalities. And they can look out at the society to which the characters belong. Looking inward, they seem to ask, "What sort of people are these?" Looking outward, they seem to ask, "What has made them that way?"

Writers of fiction have long felt that their form's unique ability to deal with the common reality of everyday life made it an ideal vehicle for examining the interaction of individuals with their society. We find that concern reflected in nearly all forms of fiction, from old and traditional tales such as "Bartleby the Scrivener" to some of the most experimental contemporary works. Many Americans in the latter half of the twentieth century are deeply concerned with questions of society's influence and power over the individual and of the individual's own power to shape his or her own personality and future. Contemporary fiction reflects these concerns.

The four stories that follow are all works that engage our concern for some central character or characters, while forcing upon us some realization of or comment on the society in which these characters live. In these stories, as in others we have read, the physical settings often become metaphors for the social settings. The influence of society, and the characters' reactions to it, thus form an important part of each tale.

As you read these stories, therefore, take note of their physical and social settings, and of how these settings are used to define the characters' actions and personalities. Take note, too—as always when dealing with fiction—of the narrators' voices. What tones of voice do you hear in these stories? What attitudes do they convey? How do the narrators blend their stories' dual focus on individual and society into a concern for the fulfillment or happiness of their central characters? What moods do they leave you in at the stories' ends? How do they get you there?

## WILLIAM FAULKNER (1897–1962)

# *A Rose for Emily*

### I

When Miss Emily Grierson died, our whole town went to her funeral: the men through a sort of respectful affection for a fallen monument, the women mostly out of curiosity to see the inside of her house, which no one save an old man-servant—a combined gardener and cook—had seen in at least ten years.

It was a big, squarish frame house that had once been white, decorated with cupolas and spires, and scrolled balconies in the heavily lightsome style of the seventies, set on what had once been our most select street. But garages and cotton gins had encroached and obliterated even the august names of that neighborhood; only Miss Emily's house was left, lifting its stubborn and coquettish decay above the cotton wagons and the gasoline pumps—an eyesore among eyesores. And now Miss Emily had gone to join the representatives of those august names where they lay in the cedar-bemused cemetery among the ranked and anonymous graves of Union and Confederate soldiers who fell at the battle of Jefferson.

Alive, Miss Emily had been a tradition, a duty, and a care; a sort of hereditary obligation upon the town, dating from that day in 1894 when Colonel Sartoris, the mayor—he who fathered the edict that no Negro woman should appear on the street without an apron—remitted her taxes, the dispensation dating from the death of her father on into perpetuity. Not that Miss Emily would have accepted charity. Colonel Sartoris invented an involved tale to the effect that Miss Emily's father had loaned money to the town, which the town, as a matter of business, preferred this way of repaying. Only a man of Colonel Sartoris' generation and thought could have invented it, and only a woman could have believed it.

When the next generation, with its more modern ideas, became mayors and aldermen, this arrangement created some little dissatisfaction. On the first of the year they mailed her a tax notice. February came, and there was no reply. They wrote her a formal letter, asking her to call at the sheriff's office at her convenience. A week later the mayor wrote her himself, offering to call or to send his car for her, and received in reply a note on paper of an archaic shape, in a thin, flowing calligraphy in faded ink, to the effect that she no longer went out at all. The tax notice was also enclosed, without comment.

They called a special meeting of the Board of Aldermen. A deputation waited upon her, knocked at the door through which no visitor had passed since she ceased giving china-painting lessons eight or ten years earlier. They were admitted by the old Negro into a dim hall from which a stairway mounted into still more shadow. It smelled of dust and disuse—a close, dank smell. The Negro led them into the parlor. It was furnished in heavy, leather-covered furniture. When the Negro opened the blinds of one window, they could see that the leather was cracked; and when they sat down, a faint dust rose sluggishly about their thighs, spinning with slow motes in the single sun-ray. On a tarnished gilt easel before the fireplace stood a crayon portrait of Miss Emily's father.

They rose when she entered—a small, fat woman in black, with a thin gold chain descending to her waist and vanishing into her belt, leaning on an ebony cane with a tarnished gold head. Her skeleton was small and spare; perhaps that was why what would have been merely plumpness in another was obesity in her. She looked bloated, like a body long submerged in motionless water, and of that pallid hue. Her eyes, lost in the fatty ridges of her face, looked like two small pieces of coal pressed into a lump of dough as they moved from one face to another while the visitors stated their errand.

She did not ask them to sit. She just stood in the door and listened quietly until the spokesman came to a stumbling halt. Then they could hear the invisible watch ticking at the end of the gold chain.

Her voice was dry and cold. "I have no taxes in Jefferson. Colonel Sartoris explained it to me. Perhaps one of you can gain access to the city records and satisfy yourselves."

"But we have. We are the city authorities, Miss Emily. Didn't you get a notice from the sheriff, signed by him?"

"I received a paper, yes," Miss Emily said. "Perhaps he considers himself the sheriff . . . I have no taxes in Jefferson."

"But there is nothing on the books to show that, you see. We must go by the—"

"See Colonel Sartoris. I have no taxes in Jefferson."

"But Miss Emily—"

"See Colonel Sartoris." (Colonel Sartoris had been dead almost ten years.) "I have no taxes in Jefferson. Tobe!" The Negro appeared. "Show these gentlemen out."

## II

So she vanquished them, horse and foot, just as she had vanquished their fathers thirty years before about the smell. That was two years after her father's death and a short time after her sweetheart—the one we believed would marry her—had deserted her. After her father's death she went out very little; after her sweetheart went away, people hardly saw her at all. A few of the ladies had the temerity to call, but were not received, and the only sign of life about the place was the Negro man—a young man then—going in and out with a market basket.

"Just as if a man—any man—could keep a kitchen properly," the ladies said; so they were not surprised when the smell developed. It was another link between the gross, teeming world and the high and mighty Griersons.

A neighbor, a woman, complained to the mayor, Judge Stevens, eighty years old.

"But what will you have me do about it, madam?" he said.

"Why, send her word to stop it," the woman said. "Isn't there a law?"

"I'm sure that won't be necessary," Judge Stevens said. "It's probably just a snake or a rat that nigger of hers killed in the yard. I'll speak to him about it."

The next day he received two more complaints, one from a man who came in diffident deprecation. "We really must do something about it, Judge. I'd be the last one in the world to bother Miss Emily, but we've got to do something." That night the Board of Aldermen met—three graybeards and one younger man, a member of the rising generation.

"It's simple enough," he said. "Send her word to have her place cleaned up. Give her a certain time do it in, and if she don't . . ."

"Dammit, sir," Judge Stevens said, "will you accuse a lady to her face of smelling bad?"

So the next night, after midnight, four men crossed Miss Emily's lawn and slunk about the house like burglars, sniffing along the base of the brickwork and at the cellar openings while one of them performed a regular sowing motion with his hand out of a sack slung from his shoulder. They broke open the cellar door and sprinkled lime there, and in all the outbuildings. As they recrossed the lawn, a window that had been dark was lighted and Miss Emily sat in it, the light behind her, and her upright torso motionless as that of an idol. They crept quietly across the lawn and into the shadow of the locusts that lined the street. After a week or two the smell went away.

That was when people had begun to feel really sorry for her. People in our town, remembering how old lady Wyatt, her great-aunt, had gone completely crazy at last, believed that the Griersons held themselves a little too high for what they really were. None of the young men were quite good enough for Miss Emily and such. We had long thought of them as a tableau, Miss Emily a slender figure in white in the background, her father a spraddled silhouette in the foregound, his back to her and clutching a horsewhip, the two of them framed by the backflung front door. When she got to be thirty and was still single, we were not pleased exactly, but vindicated; even with insanity in the family she wouldn't have turned down all of her chances if they had really materialized.

When her father died, it got about that the house was all that was left to her; and in a way, people were glad. At last they could pity Miss Emily. Being left alone, and a pauper, she had become humanized. Now she too would know the old thrill and the old despair of a penny more or less.

The day after his death all the ladies prepared to call at the house and offer condolence and aid, as is our custom. Miss Emily met them at the door, dressed as usual and with no trace of grief on her face. She told them that her father was not dead. She did that for three days, with the ministers calling on her, and the doctors, trying to persuade her to let them dispose of the body. Just as they were about to resort to law and force, she broke down, and they buried her father quickly.

We did not say she was crazy then. We believed she had to do that. We remembered all the young men her father had driven away, and we knew that with nothing left, she would have to cling to that which had robbed her, as people will.

## III

She was sick for a long time. When we saw her again, her hair was cut short, making her look like a girl, with a vague resemblance to those angels in colored church windows—sort of tragic and serene.

The town had just let the contracts for paving the sidewalks, and in the summer after her father's death they began the work. The construction company came with niggers and mules and machinery, and a foreman named Homer Barron, a Yankee—a big, dark, ready man, with a big voice and eyes lighter than his face. The little boys would follow in groups to hear him cuss the niggers, and the niggers singing in time to the rise and fall of picks. Pretty soon he knew everybody in town. Whenever you heard a lot of laughing anywhere about the square, Homer Barron would be in the center of the group.

Presently we began to see him and Miss Emily on Sunday afternoons driving in the yellow-wheeled buggy and the matched team of bays from the livery stable.

At first we were glad that Miss Emily would have an interest, because the ladies all said, "Of course a Grierson would not think seriously of a Northerner, a day laborer." But there were still others, older people, who said that even grief could not cause a real lady to forget *noblesse oblige*—without calling it *noblesse oblige*. They just said, "Poor Emily. Her kinsfolk should come to her." She had some kin in Alabama; but years ago her father had fallen out with them over the estate of old Lady Wyatt, the crazy woman, and there was no communication between the two families. They had not even been represented at the funeral.

And as soon as the old people said, "Poor Emily," the whispering began. "Do you suppose it's really so?" they said to one another. "Of course it is. What else could . . ." This behind their hands; rustling of craned silk and satin behind jalousies closed upon the sun of Sunday afternoon as the thin, swift clop-clop-clop of the matched team passed: "Poor Emily."

She carried her head high enough—even when we believed that she was fallen. It was as if she demanded more than ever the recognition of her dignity as the last Grierson; as if it had wanted that touch of earthiness to reaffirm her imperviousness. Like when she bought the rat poison, the arsenic. That was over a year after they had begun to say "Poor Emily," and while the two female cousins were visiting her.

"I want some poison," she said to the druggist. She was over thirty then, still a slight woman, though thinner than usual, with cold, haughty black eyes in a face the flesh of which was strained across the temples and about the eye-sockets as you imagine a lighthouse-keeper's face ought to look. "I want some poison," she said.

"Yes, Miss Emily. What kind? For rats and such? I'd recom—"

"I want the best you have. I don't care what kind."

The druggist named several. "They'll kill anything up to an elephant. But what you want is—"

"Arsenic," Miss Emily said. "Is that a good one?"

"Is . . . arsenic? Yes, ma'am. But what you want—"

"I want arsenic."

The druggist looked down at her. She looked back at him, erect, her face like a strained flag. "Why, of course," the druggist said. "If that's what you want. But the law requires you to tell what you are going to use it for."

Miss Emily just stared at him, her head tilted back in order to look him eye for eye, until he looked away and went and got the arsenic and wrapped it up. The Negro delivery boy brought her the package; the druggist didn't come back. When she opened the package at home there was written on the box, under the skull and bones: "For rats."

## IV

So the next day we all said, "She will kill herself"; and we said it would be the best thing. When she had first begun to be seen with Homer Barron, we had said, "She will marry him." Then we said, "She will persuade him yet," because Homer himself had remarked—he liked men, and it was known that he drank with the younger men in the Elks' Club—that he was not a marrying man. Later we said, "Poor Emily" behind the jalousies as they passed on Sunday afternoon in the glittering buggy, Miss Emily with her head high and Homer Barron with his hat cocked and cigar in his teeth, reins and whip in a yellow glove.

Then some of the ladies began to say that it was a disgrace to the town and a bad example to the young people. The men did not want to interfere, but at last the ladies forced the Baptist minister— Miss Emily's people were Episcopal—to call upon her. He would never divulge what happened during that interview, but he refused to go back again. The next Sunday they again drove about the streets, and the following day the minister's wife wrote to Miss Emily's relations in Alabama.

So she had blood-kin under her roof again and we sat back to watch developments. At first nothing happened. Then we were sure that they were to be married. We learned that Miss Emily had been to the jeweler's and ordered a man's toilet set in silver, with the letters H. B. on each piece. Two days later we learned that she had bought a complete outfit of men's clothing, including a nightshirt, and we said, "They are married." We were really glad. We were glad because the two female cousins were even more Grierson than Miss Emily had ever been.

So we were not surprised when Homer Barron—the streets had been finished some time since—was gone. We were a little disappointed that there was not a public blowing-off, but we believed that he had gone on to prepare for Miss Emily's coming, or to give her a chance to get rid of the cousins. (By that time it was a cabal, and we were all Miss Emily's allies to help circumvent the cousins.) Sure enough, after another week they departed. And, as we had expected all along, within three days Homer Barron was back in town. A neighbor saw the Negro man admit him at the kitchen door at dusk one evening.

And that was the last we saw of Homer Barron. And of Miss Emily for some time. The Negro man went in and out with the market basket, but the front door remained closed. Now and then we would see her at a window for a moment, as the men did that night when they sprinkled the lime, but for almost six months she did not appear on the streets. Then we knew that this was to be expected too; as if that quality of her father which had thwarted her woman's life so many times had been too virulent and too furious to die.

When we next saw Miss Emily, she had grown fat and her hair was turning gray. During the next few years it grew grayer and grayer until it attained an even pepper-and-salt iron-gray, when it ceased turning. Up to the day of her death at seventy-four it was still that vigorous iron-gray, like the hair of an active man.

From that time on her front door remained closed, save for a period of six or seven years, when she was about forty, during which she gave lessons in china-painting. She fitted up a studio in one of the downstairs rooms, where the daughters and granddaughters of Colonel Sartoris' contemporaries were sent to her with the same regularity and in the same spirit that they were sent to church on Sunday with a twenty-five-cent piece for the collection plate. Meanwhile her taxes had been remitted.

Then the newer generation became the backbone and the spirit of the town, and the painting pupils grew up and fell away and did not send their children to her with boxes of color and tedious brushes and pictures cut from the ladies' magazines. The front door closed upon the last one and remained closed for good. When the town got free postal delivery, Miss Emily alone refused to let them fasten the metal numbers above her door and attach a mailbox to it. She would not listen to them.

Daily, monthly, yearly we watched the Negro grow grayer and more stooped, going in and out with the market basket. Each December we sent her a tax notice, which would be returned by the post office a week later, unclaimed. Now and then we would see her in one of the downstairs windows—she had evidently shut up the top floor of the house—like the carven torso of an idol in a niche, looking or not looking at us, we could never tell which. Thus she passed from generation to generation—dear, inescapable, impervious, tranquil, and perverse.

And so she died. Fell ill in the house filled with dust and shadows, with only a doddering Negro man to wait on her. We did not even know she was sick; we had long since given up trying to get any information from the Negro. He talked to no one, probably not even to her, for his voice had grown harsh and rusty, as if from disuse.

She died in one of the downstairs rooms, in a heavy walnut bed with a curtain, her gray head propped on a pillow yellow and moldy with age and lack of sunlight.

## V

The Negro met the first of the ladies at the front door and let them in, with their hushed, sibilant voices and their quick, curious glances, and then he disappeared. He walked right through the house and out the back and was not seen again.

The two female cousins came at once. They held the funeral on the second day, with the town coming to look at Miss Emily beneath a mass of bought flowers, with the crayon face of her father musing profoundly above the bier and the ladies sibilant and macabre; and the very old men—some in their brushed Confederate uniforms—on the porch and the lawn, talking of Miss Emily as if she had been a contemporary of theirs, believing that they had danced with her and courted her perhaps, confusing time with its mathematical progression, as the old do, to whom all the past is not a diminishing road but, instead, a huge meadow which no winter ever quite touches, divided from them now by the narrow bottle-neck of the most recent decade of years.

Already we knew that there was one room in that region above stairs which no one had seen in forty years, and which would have to be forced. They waited until Miss Emily was decently in the ground before they opened it.

The violence of breaking down the door seemed to fill this room with pervading dust. A thin, acrid pall of the tomb seemed to lie everywhere upon this room decked and furnished as for a bridal: upon the valance curtains of faded rose color, upon the rose-shaded lights, upon the dressing table, upon the delicate array of crystal and the man's toilet things backed with tarnished silver, silver so tarnished that the monogram was obscured. Among them lay a collar and tie, as if they had just been removed, which, lifted, left upon the surface a pale crescent in the dust. Upon a chair hung the suit, carefully folded; beneath it the two mute shoes and the discarded socks.

The man himself lay in the bed.

For a long while we just stood there, looking down at the profound and fleshless grin. The body had apparently once lain in the attitude of an embrace, but now the long sleep that outlasts love, that conquers even the grimace of love, had cuckolded him. What was left of him, rotted beneath what was left of the nightshirt, had become inextricable from the bed in which he lay; and upon him and upon the pillow beside him lay that even coating of the patient and biding dust.

Then we noticed that in the second pillow was the indentation of a head. One of us lifted something from it, and leaning forward, that faint and invisible dust dry and acrid in the nostrils, we saw a long strand of iron-gray hair.

### QUESTIONS

1. Part of the effectiveness of "A Rose for Emily" comes from its surprise ending. How effective do you find the ending? Why?
2. How do the narrator and the townsfolk view the young Miss Emily? How does Miss Emily change with time? How does the town? How does the narrator's view of Miss Emily change? How does yours?

## JAMES BALDWIN (1924– )

# *Sonny's Blues*

I read about it in the paper, in the subway, on my way to work. I read it, and I couldn't believe it, and I read it again. Then perhaps I just stared at it, at the newsprint spelling out his name, spelling out the story. I stared at it in the swinging lights of the subway car, and in the faces and bodies of the people, and in my own face, trapped in the darkness which roared outside.

It was not to be believed and I kept telling myself that as I walked from the subway station to the high school. And at the same time I couldn't doubt it. I was scared, scared for Sonny. He became real to me again. A great block of ice got settled in my belly and kept melting there slowly all day long, while I taught my classes algebra. It was a special kind of ice. It kept melting, sending trickles of ice water all up and down my veins, but it never got less. Sometimes it hardened and seemed to expand until I felt my guts were going to come spilling out or that I was going to choke or scream. This would always be at a moment when I was remembering some specific thing Sonny had once said or done.

When he was about as old as the boys in my classes his face had been bright and open, there was a lot of copper in it; and he'd had wonderfully direct brown eyes, and great gentleness and privacy. I wondered what he looked like now. He had been picked up, the evening before, in a raid on an apartment downtown, for peddling and using heroin.

I couldn't believe it: but what I mean by that is that I couldn't find any room for it anywhere inside me. I had kept it outside me for a long time. I hadn't wanted to know. I had had suspicions, but I didn't name them, I kept putting them away. I told myself that Sonny was wild, but he wasn't crazy. And he'd always been a good boy, he hadn't ever turned hard or evil or disrespectful, the way kids can, so quick, so quick, especially in Harlem. I didn't want to believe that I'd ever see my brother going down, coming to nothing, all that light in his face gone out, in the condition I'd already seen so many others. Yet it had happened and here I was, talking about algebra to a lot of boys who might, every one of them for all I knew, be popping off needles every time they went to the head. Maybe it did more for them than algebra could.

I was sure that the first time Sonny had ever had horse, he couldn't have been much older than these boys were now. These boys, now, were living as we'd been living then, they were growing up with a rush and their heads bumped abruptly against the low ceiling of their actual possibilities. They were filled with rage. All they really knew were two darknesses, the darkness of their lives, which was now closing in on them, and the darkness of the movies, which had blinded them to that other darkness, and in which they now, vindictively, dreamed, at once more together than they were at any other time, and more alone.

When the last bell rang, the last class ended, I let out my breath. It seemed I'd been holding it for all that time. My clothes were wet—I may have looked as though I'd been sitting in a steam bath, all dressed up, all afternoon. I sat alone in the classroom a long time. I listened to the boys outside, downstairs, shouting and cursing and laughing. Their laughter struck me for perhaps the first time. It was not the joyous laughter which—God knows why—one associates with children. It was mocking and insular, its intent was to denigrate. It was disenchanted, and in this, also, lay the authority of their curses. Perhaps I was listening to them because I was thinking about my brother and in them I heard my brother. And myself.

One boy was whistling a tune, at once very complicated and very simple, it seemed to be pouring out of him as though he were a bird, and it sounded very cool and moving through all that harsh, bright air, only just holding its own through all those other sounds.

I stood up and walked over to the window and looked down into the courtyard. It was the beginning of the spring and the sap was rising in the boys. A teacher passed through them every now and again, quickly, as though he or she couldn't wait to get out of that courtyard, to get those boys out of their sight and off their minds. I started collecting my stuff. I thought I'd better get home and talk to Isabel.

The courtyard was almost deserted by the time I got downstairs. I saw this boy standing in the shadow of a doorway, looking just like Sonny. I almost called his name. Then I saw that it wasn't Sonny, but somebody we used to know, a boy from around our block. He'd been Sonny's friend. He'd never been mine, having been too young for me, and, anyway, I'd never liked him. And now, even though he was a grown-up man, he still hung around that block, still spent hours on the street corner, was always high and raggy. I used to run into him from time to time and he'd often work around to asking me for a quarter or fifty cents. He always had some real good excuse, too, and I always gave it to him, I don't know why.

But now, abruptly, I hated him. I couldn't stand the way he looked at me, partly like a dog, partly like a cunning child. I wanted to ask him what the hell he was doing in the school courtyard.

He sort of shuffled over to me, and he said, "I see you got the papers. So you already know about it."

"You mean about Sonny? Yes, I already know about it. How come they didn't get you?"

He grinned. It made him repulsive and it also brought to mind what he'd looked like as a kid. "I wasn't there. I stay away from them people."

"Good for you." I offered him a cigarette and I watched him through the smoke. "You come all the way down here just to tell me about Sonny?"

"That's right." He was sort of shaking his head and his eyes looked strange, as though they were about to cross. The bright sun deadened his damp dark brown skin and it made his eyes look yellow and showed up the dirt in his conked hair. He smelled funky. I moved a little away from him and I said, "Well, thanks. But I already know about it and I got to get home."

"I'll walk you a little ways," he said. We started walking. There were a couple of kids still loitering in the courtyard and one of them said good night to me and looked strangely at the boy beside me.

"What're you going to do?" he asked me. "I mean, about Sonny?"

"Look. I haven't seen Sonny for over a year, I'm not sure I'm going to do anything. Anyway, what the hell *can* I do?"

"That's right," he said quickly, "ain't nothing you can do. Can't much help old Sonny no more, I guess."

It was what I was thinking and so it seemed to me he had no right to say it.

"I'm surprised at Sonny, though," he went on—he had a funny way of talking, he looked straight ahead as though he were talking to himself—"I thought Sonny was a smart boy, I thought he was too smart to get hung."

"I guess he thought so too," I said sharply, "and that's how he got hung. And how about you? You're pretty goddamn smart, I bet."

Then he looked directly at me, just for a minute. "I ain't smart," he said. "If I was smart, I'd have reached for a pistol a long time ago."

"Look. Don't tell *me* your sad story, if it was up to me, I'd give you one." Then I felt guilty—guilty, probably, for never having supposed that the poor bastard *had* a story of his own, much less a sad one, and I asked, quickly, "What's going to happen to him now?"

He didn't answer this. He was off by himself some place. "Funny thing," he said, and from his tone we might have been discussing the quickest way to get to Brooklyn, "when I saw the papers this morning, the first thing I asked myself was if I had anything to do with it. I felt sort of responsible."

I began to listen more carefully. The subway station was on the corner, just before us, and I stopped. He stopped, too. We were in front of a bar and he ducked slightly, peering in, but whoever he was looking for didn't seem to be there. The juke box was blasting away with something black and bouncy and I half watched the barmaid as she danced her way from the juke box to her place behind the bar. And I watched her face as she laughingly responded to something someone said to her, still keeping time to the music. When she smiled one saw the little girl, one sensed the doomed, still-struggling woman beneath the battered face of the semi-whore.

"I never *give* Sonny nothing," the boy said finally, "but a long time ago I come to school high and Sonny asked me how it felt." He paused, I couldn't bear to watch him, I watched the barmaid, and I listened to the music which seemed to be causing the pavement to shake. "I told him it felt great." The music stopped, the barmaid paused and watched the juke box until the music began again. "It did."

All this was carrying me some place I didn't want to go. I certainly didn't want to know how it felt. It filled everything, the people, the houses, the music, the dark, quicksilver barmaid, with menace; and this menace was their reality.

"What's going to happen to him now?" I asked again.

"They'll send him away some place and they'll try to cure him." He shook his head. "Maybe he'll even think he's kicked the habit. Then they'll let him loose"—he gestured, throwing his cigarette into the gutter. "That's all."

"What do you mean, that's *all?*"

But I knew what he meant.

"I *mean,* that's *all.*" He turned his head and looked at me, pulling down the corners of his mouth. "Don't you know what I mean?" he asked softly.

"How the hell *would* I know what you mean?" I almost whispered it, I don't know why.

"That's right," he said to the air, "how would *he* know what I mean?" He turned toward me again, patient and calm, and yet I somehow felt him shaking, shaking as though he were going to fall apart. I felt that ice in my guts again, the dread I'd felt all afternoon; and again I watched the barmaid, moving about the bar, washing glasses, and singing. "Listen. They'll let him out and then it'll just start all over again. That's what I mean."

"You mean—they'll let him out. And then he'll just start working his way back in again. You mean he'll never kick the habit. Is that what you mean?"

"That's right," he said, cheerfully. "*You* see what I mean."

"Tell me," I said at last, "why does he want to die? He must want to die, he's killing himself, why does he want to die?"

He looked at me in surprise. He licked his lips. "He don't want to die. He wants to live. Don't nobody want to die, ever."

Then I wanted to ask him—too many things. He could not have answered, or if he had, I could not have borne the answers. I started walking. "Well, I guess it's none of my business."

"It's going to be rough on old Sonny," he said. We reached the subway station. "This is your station?" he asked. I nodded. I took one step down. "Damn!" he said, suddenly. I looked up at him. He grinned again. "Damn if I didn't leave all my money home. You ain't got a dollar on you, have you? Just for a couple of days, is all."

All at once something inside gave and threatened to come pouring out of me. I didn't hate him any more. I felt that in another moment I'd start crying like a child.

"Sure," I said. "Don't sweat." I looked in my wallet and didn't have a dollar, I only had a five. "Here," I said. "That hold you?"

He didn't look at it—he didn't want to look at it. A terrible, closed look came over his face, as though he were keeping the number on the bill a secret from him and me. "Thanks," he said, and now he was dying to see me go. "Don't worry about Sonny. Maybe I'll write him or something."

"Sure," I said. "You do that. So long."

"Be seeing you," he said. I went on down the steps.

And I didn't write Sonny or send him anything for a long time. When I finally did, it was just after my little girl died, he wrote me back a letter which made me feel like a bastard.

Here's what he said:

DEAR BROTHER,

You don't know how much I needed to hear from you. I wanted to write you many a time but I dug how much I must have hurt you and so I didn't write. But now I feel like a man who's been trying to climb up out of some deep, real deep and funky hole and just saw the sun up there, outside. I got to get outside.

I can't tell you much about how I got here. I mean I don't know how to tell you. I guess I was afraid of something or I was trying to escape from something and you know I have never been very strong in the head (smile). I'm glad Mama and Daddy are dead and can't see what's happened to their son and I swear if I'd known what I was doing I would never have hurt you so, you and a lot of other fine people who were nice to me and who believed in me.

I don't want you to think it had anything to do with me being a musician. It's more than that. Or maybe less than that. I can't get anything straight in my head down here and I try not to think about what's going to happen to me when I get outside again. Sometime I think I'm going to flip and *never* get outside and sometime I think I'll come straight back. I tell you one thing, though, I'd rather blow my brains out than go through this again. But that's what they all say, so they tell me. If I tell you when I'm coming to New York and if you could meet me, I sure would appreciate it. Give my love to Isabel and the kids and I was sorry to hear about little Gracie. I wish I could be like Mama and say the Lord's will be done, but I don't know it seems to me that trouble is the one thing that never does get stopped and I don't know what good it does to blame it on the Lord. But maybe it does some good if you believe it.

Your brother,
SONNY

Then I kept in constant touch with him and I sent him whatever I could and I went to meet him when he came back to New York. When I saw him many things I thought I had forgotten came flooding back to me. This was because I had begun, finally, to wonder about Sonny, about the life that Sonny lived inside. This life, whatever it was, had made him older and thinner and it had deepened the distant stillness in which he had always moved. He looked very unlike my baby brother. Yet, when he smiled, when we shook hands, the baby brother I'd never known looked out from the depths of his private life, like an animal waiting to be coaxed into the light.

"How you been keeping?" he asked me.

"All right. And you?"

"Just fine." He was smiling all over his face. "It's good to see you again."

"It's good to see you."

The seven years' difference in our ages lay between us like a chasm: I wondered if these years would ever operate between us as a bridge. I was remembering, and it made it hard to catch my breath, that I had been there when he was born; and I had heard the first words he had ever spoken. When he started to walk, he walked from our mother straight to me. I caught him just before he fell when he took the first steps he ever took in this world.

"How's Isabel?"

"Just fine. She's dying to see you."

"And the boys?"

"They're fine, too. They're anxious to see their uncle."

"Oh, come on. You know they don't remember me."

"Are you kidding? Of course they remember you."

He grinned again. We got into a taxi. We had a lot to say to each other, far too much to know how to begin.

As the taxi began to move, I asked, "You still want to go to India?"

He laughed. "You still remember that. Hell, no. This place is Indian enough for me."

"It used to belong to them," I said.

And he laughed again. "They damn sure knew what they were doing when they got rid of it."

Years ago, when he was around fourteen, he'd been all hipped on the idea of going to India. He read books about people sitting on rocks, naked, in all kinds of weather, but mostly bad, naturally, and walking barefoot through hot coals and arriving at wisdom. I used to say that it sounded to me as though they were getting away from wisdom as fast as they could. I think he sort of looked down on me for that.

"Do you mind," he asked, "if we have the driver drive alongside the park? On the west side—I haven't seen the city in so long."

"Of course not," I said. I was afraid that I might sound as though I were humoring him, but I hoped he wouldn't take it that way.

So we drove along, between the green of the park and the stony, lifeless elegance of hotels and apartment buildings, toward the vivid, killing streets of our childhood. These streets hadn't changed, though housing projects jutted up out of them now like rocks in the middle of a boiling sea. Most of the houses in which we had grown up had vanished, as had the stores from which we had stolen, the basements in which we had first tried sex, the rooftops from which we had hurled tin cans and bricks. But houses exactly like the houses of our past yet dominated the landscape, boys exactly like the boys we once had been found themselves smothering in these houses, came down into the streets for light and air and found themselves encircled by disaster. Some escaped the trap, most didn't. Those who got out always left something of themselves behind, as some animals amputate a leg and leave it in the trap. It might be said, perhaps, that I had escaped, after all, I was a school teacher; or that Sonny had, he hadn't lived in Harlem for years. Yet, as the cab moved uptown through streets which seemed, with a rush, to darken with dark people, and as I covertly studied Sonny's face, it came to me that what we both were seeking through our separate cab windows was that part of ourselves which had been left behind. It's always at the hour of trouble and confrontation that the missing member aches.

We hit 110th Street and started rolling up Lenox Avenue. And I'd known this avenue all my life, but it seemed to me again, as it had seemed on the day I'd first heard about Sonny's trouble, filled with a hidden menance which was its very breath of life.

"We almost there," said Sonny.

"Almost." We were both too nervous to say anything more.

We live in a housing project. It hasn't been up long. A few days after it was up it seemed uninhabitably new, now, of course, it's already run-down. It looks like a parody of the good, clean, faceless life—God knows the people who live in it do their best to make it a parody. The beat-looking grass lying around isn't enough to make their lives green, the hedges will never hold out the streets, and they know it. The big windows fool no one, they aren't big enough to make space out of no space. They don't bother with the windows, they watch the TV screen instead. The playground is most popular with the children who don't play at jacks, or skip rope, or roller skate, or swing, and they can be found in it after dark. We moved in partly because it's not too far from where I teach, and partly for the kids; but it's really just like the houses in which Sonny and I grew up. The same things happen, they'll have the same things to remember. The moment Sonny and I started into the house I had the feeling that I was simply bringing him back into the danger he had almost died trying to escape.

Sonny has never been talkative. So I don't know why I was sure he'd be dying to talk to me when supper was over the first night. Everything went fine, the oldest boy remembered him, and the youngest boy liked him, and Sonny had remembered to bring something for each of them; and Isabel, who is really much nicer than I am, more open and giving, had gone to a lot of trouble about dinner and was genuinely glad to see him. And she's always been able to tease Sonny in a way that I haven't. It was nice to see her face so vivid again and to hear her laugh and watch her make Sonny laugh. She wasn't, or, anyway, she didn't seem to be, at all uneasy or embarrassed. She chatted as though there were no subject which had to be avoided and she got Sonny past his first, faint stiffness. And thank God she was there, for I was filled with that icy dread again. Everything I did seemed awkward to me, and everything I said sounded freighted with hidden meaning. I was trying to remember everything I'd heard about dope addiction and I couldn't help watching Sonny for signs. I wasn't doing it out of malice. I was trying to find out something about my brother. I was dying to hear him tell me he was safe.

"Safe!" my father grunted, whenever Mama suggested trying to move to a neighborhood which might be safer for children. "Safe, hell! Ain't no place safe for kids, nor nobody."

He always went on like this, but he wasn't, ever, really as bad as he sounded, not even on weekends, when he got drunk. As a matter of fact, he was always on the lookout for "something a little better," but he died before he found it. He died suddenly, during a drunken weekend in the middle of the war, when Sonny was fifteen. He and Sonny hadn't ever got on too well. And this was partly because Sonny was the apple of his father's eye. It was because he loved Sonny so much and was frightened for him, that he was always fighting with him. It doesn't do any good to fight with Sonny. Sonny just moves back, inside himself, where he can't be reached. But the principal reason that they never hit it off is that they were so much alike. Daddy was big and rough and loud-talking, just the opposite of Sonny, but they both had—that same privacy.

Mama tried to tell me something about this, just after Daddy died. I was home on leave from the army.

This was the last time I ever saw my mother alive. Just the same, this picture gets all mixed up in my mind with pictures I had of her when she was younger. The way I always see her is the way she used to be on a Sunday afternoon, say, when the old folks were talking after the big Sunday dinner. I always see her wearing pale blue. She'd be sitting on the sofa. And my father would be sitting in the easy chair, not far from her. And the living room would be full of church folks and relatives. There they sit, in chairs all around the living room, and the night is creeping up outside, but nobody knows it yet. You can see the darkness growing against the window-panes and you hear the street noises every now and again, or maybe the jangling beat of a tambourine from one of the churches close by, but it's real quiet in the room. For a moment nobody's talking, but every face looks darkening, like the sky outside. And my mother rocks a little from the waist, and my father's eyes are closed. Everyone is looking at something a child can't see. For a minute they've forgotten the children. Maybe a kid is lying on the rug half asleep. Maybe somebody's got a kid on his lap and is absent-mindedly stroking the kid's head. Maybe there's a kid, quiet and big-eyed, curled up in a big chair in the corner. The silence, the darkness coming, and the darkness in the faces frightens the child obscurely. He hopes that the hand which strokes his forehead will never stop—will never die. He hopes that there will never come a time when the old folks won't be sitting around the living room, talking about where they've come from, and what they've seen, and what's happened to them and their kinfolk.

But something deep and watchful in the child knows that this is bound to end, is already ending. In a moment someone will get up and turn on the light. Then the old folks will remember the children and they won't talk any more that day. And when light fills the room, the child is filled with darkness. He knows that every time this happens he's moved just a little closer to that darkness outside. The darkness outside is what the old folks have been talking about. It's what they've come from. It's what they endure. The child knows that they won't talk any more because if he knows too much about what's happened to *them,* he'll know too much too soon, about what's going to happen to *him.*

The last time I talked to my mother, I remember I was restless. I wanted to get out and see Isabel. We weren't married then and we had a lot to straighten out between us.

There Mama sat, in black, by the window. She was humming an old church song, *Lord, you brought me from a long ways off.* Sonny was out somewhere. Mama kept watching the streets.

"I don't know," she said, "if I'll ever see you again, after you go off from here. But I hope you'll remember the things I tried to teach you."

"Don't talk like that," I said, and smiled. "You'll be here a long time yet."

She smiled, too, but she said nothing. She was quiet for a long time. And I said, "Mama, don't you worry about nothing. I'll be writing all the time, and you be getting the checks. . . ."

"I want to talk to you about your brother," she said, suddenly. "If anything happens to me he ain't going to have nobody to look out for him."

"Mama," I said, "ain't nothing going to happen to you *or* Sonny. Sonny's all right. He's a good boy and he's got good sense."

"It ain't a question of his being a good boy," Mama said, "nor of his having good sense. It ain't only the bad ones, nor yet the dumb ones that gets sucked under." She stopped, looking at me. "Your Daddy once had a brother," she said, and she smiled in a way that made me feel she was in pain. "You didn't never know that, did you?"

"No," I said, "I never knew that," and I watched her face.

"Oh, yes," she said, "your Daddy had a brother." She looked out of the window again. "I know you never saw your Daddy cry. But *I* did—many a time, through all these years."

I asked her, "What happened to his brother? How come nobody's ever talked about him?"

This was the first time I ever saw my mother look old.

"His brother got killed," she said, "when he was just a little younger than you are now. I knew him. He was a fine boy. He was maybe a little full of the devil, but he didn't mean nobody no harm."

Then she stopped and the room was silent, exactly as it had sometimes been on those Sunday afternoons. Mama kept looking out into the streets.

"He used to have a job in the mill," she said, "and, like all young folks, he just liked to perform on Saturday nights. Saturday nights, him and your father would drift around to different places, go to dances and things like that, or just sit around with people they knew, and your father's brother would sing, he had a fine voice, and play along with himself on his guitar. Well, this particular Saturday night, him and your father was coming home from some place, and they were both a little drunk and there was a moon that night, it was bright like day. Your father's brother was feeling kind of good, and he was whistling to himself, and he had his guitar slung over his shoulder. They was coming down a hill and beneath them was a road that turned off from the highway. Well, your father's brother, being always kind of frisky, decided to run down this hill, and he did, with that guitar banging and clanging behind him, and he ran across the road, and he was making water behind a tree. And your father was sort of amused at him and he was still coming down the hill, kind of slow. Then he heard a car motor and that same minute his brother stepped from behind the tree, into the road, in the moonlight. And he started to cross the road. And your father started to run down the hill, he says he don't know why. This car was full of white men. They was all drunk, and when they seen your father's brother they let out a great whoop and holler and they aimed the car straight at him. They was having fun, they just wanted to scare him, the way they do sometimes, you know. But they was drunk. And I guess the boy, being drunk, too, and scared, kind of lost his head. By the time he jumped it was too late. Your father says he heard his brother scream when the car rolled over him, and he heard the wood of that guitar when it give, and he heard them strings go flying, and he heard them white men shouting, and the car kept on a-going and it ain't stopped till this day. And, time your father got down the hill, his brother weren't nothing but blood and pulp."

Tears were gleaming on my mother's face. There wasn't anything I could say.

"He never mentioned it," she said, "because I never let him mention it before you children. Your Daddy was like a crazy man that night and for many a night thereafter. He says he never in his life seen anything as dark as that road after the lights of that car had gone away. Weren't nothing, weren't nobody on that road, just your Daddy and his brother and that busted guitar. Oh, yes. Your Daddy never did really get right again. Till the day he died he weren't sure but that every white man he saw was the man that killed his brother."

She stopped and took out her handkerchief and dried her eyes and looked at me.

"I ain't telling you all this," she said, "to make you scared or bitter or to make you hate nobody. I'm telling you this because you got a brother. And the world ain't changed."

I guess I didn't want to believe this. I guess she saw this in my face. She turned away from me, toward the window again, searching those streets.

"But I praise my Redeemer," she said at last, "that He called your Daddy home before me. I ain't saying it to throw no flowers at myself, but, I declare, it keeps me from feeling too cast down to know I helped your father get safely through this world. Your father always acted like he was the roughest, strongest man on earth. And everybody took him to be like that. But if he hadn't had *me* there—to see his tears!"

She was crying again. Still, I couldn't move. I said, "Lord, Lord, Mama, I didn't know it was like that."

"Oh, honey," she said, "there's a lot that you don't know. But you are going to find it out." She stood up from the window and came over to me. "You got to hold on to your brother," she said, "and don't let him fall, no matter what it looks like is happening to him and no matter how evil you gets with him. You going to be evil with him many a time. But don't you forget what I told you, you hear?"

"I won't forget," I said. "Don't you worry, I won't forget. I won't let nothing happen to Sonny."

My mother smiled as though she were amused at something she saw in my face. Then, "You may not be able to stop nothing from happening. But you got to let him know you's *there*."

Two days later I was married, and then I was gone. And I had a lot of things on my mind and I pretty well forgot my promise to Mama until I got shipped home on a special furlough for her funeral.

And, after the funeral, with just Sonny and me alone in the empty kitchen, I tried to find out something about him.

"What do you want to do?" I asked him.

"I'm going to be a musician," he said.

For he had graduated, in the time I had been away, from dancing to the juke box to finding out who was playing what, and what they were doing with it, and he had bought himself a set of drums.

"You mean, you want to be a drummer?" I somehow had the feeling that being a drummer might be all right for other people but not for my brother Sonny.

"I don't think," he said, looking at me very gravely, "that I'll ever be a good drummer. But I think I can play a piano."

I frowned. I'd never played the role of the older brother quite so seriously before, had scarcely ever, in fact, *asked* Sonny a damn thing. I sensed myself in the presence of something I didn't really know how to handle, didn't understand. So I made my frown a little deeper as I asked: "What kind of musician do you want to be?"

He grinned. "How many kinds do you think there are?"

"Be *serious,*" I said.

He laughed, throwing his head back, and then looked at me. "I *am* serious."

"Well, then, for Christ's sake, stop kidding around and answer a serious question. I mean, do you want to be a concert pianist, you want to play classical music and all that, or—or what?" Long before I finished he was laughing again. "For Christ's *sake,* Sonny!"

He sobered, but with difficulty. "I'm sorry. But you sound so—*scared!*" and he was off again.

"Well, you may think it's funny now, baby, but it's not going to be so funny when you have to make your living at it, let me tell you *that.*" I was furious because I knew he was laughing at me and I didn't know why.

"No," he said, very sober now, and afraid, perhaps, that he'd hurt me, "I don't want to be a classical pianist. That isn't what interests me. I mean"—he paused, looking hard at me, as though his eyes would help me to understand, and then gestured helplessly, as though perhaps his hand would help—"I mean, I'll have a lot of studying to do, and I'll have to study *everything,* but I mean, I want to play *with*—jazz musicians." He stopped. "I want to play jazz," he said.

Well, the word had never before sounded as heavy, as real, as it sounded that afternoon in Sonny's mouth. I just looked at him and I was probably frowning a real frown by this time. I simply couldn't see why on earth he'd want to spend his time hanging around night clubs, clowning around on bandstands, while people pushed each other around a dance floor. It seemed—beneath him, somehow. I had never thought about it before, had never been forced to, but I suppose I had always put jazz musicians in a class with what Daddy called "good-time people."

"Are you *serious?*"

"Hell, *yes,* I'm serious."

He looked more helpless than ever, and annoyed, and deeply hurt.

I suggested, helpfully: "You mean—like Louis Armstrong?"

His face closed as though I'd struck him. "No. I'm not talking about none of that old-time, down home crap."

"Well, look, Sonny, I'm sorry, don't get mad. I just don't altogether get it, that's all. Name somebody—you know, a jazz musician you admire."

"Bird."

"Who?"

"Bird! Charlie Parker! Don't they teach you nothing in the goddamn army?"

I lit a cigarette. I was surprised and then a little amused to discover that I was trembling. "I've been out of touch," I said, "You'll have to be patient with me. Now. Who's this Parker character?"

"He's just one of the greatest jazz musicians alive," said Sonny, sullenly, his hands in his pockets, his back to me. "Maybe *the* greatest," he added, bitterly, "that's probably why *you* never heard of him."

"All right," I said, "I'm ignorant. I'm sorry. I'll go out and buy all the cat's records right away, all right?"

"It don't," said Sonny, with dignity, "make any difference to me. I don't care what you listen to. Don't do me no favors."

I was beginning to realize that I'd never seen him so upset before. With another part of my mind I was thinking that this would probably turn out to be one of those things kids go through and that I shouldn't make it seem important by pushing it too hard. Still, I didn't think it would do any harm to ask: "Doesn't all this take a lot of time? Can you make a living at it?"

He turned back to me and half leaned, half sat, on the kitchen table. "Everything takes time," he said, "and—well, yes, sure, I can make a living at it. But what I don't seem to be able to make you understand is that it's the only thing I want to do."

"Well Sonny," I said, gently, "you know people can't always do exactly what they *want* to do—"

"*No,* I don't know that," said Sonny, surprising me. "I think people *ought* to do what they want to do, what else are they alive for?"

"You getting to be a big boy," I said desperately, "it's time you started thinking about your future."

"I'm thinking about my future," said Sonny, grimly. "I think about it all the time."

I gave up. I decided, if he didn't change his mind, that we could always talk about it later. "In the meantime," I said, "you got to finish school." We had already decided that he'd have to move in with Isabel and her folks. I knew this wasn't the ideal arrangement because Isabel's folks are inclined to be dicty and they hadn't especially wanted Isabel to marry me. But I didn't know what else to do. "And we have to get you fixed up at Isabel's."

There was a long silence. He moved from the kitchen table to the window. "That's a terrible idea. You know it yourself."

"Do you have a *better* idea?"

He just walked up and down the kitchen for a minute. He was as tall as I was. He had started to shave. I suddenly had the feeling that I didn't know him at all.

He stopped at the kitchen table and picked up my cigarettes. Looking at me with a kind of mocking, amused defiance, he put one between his lips. "You mind?"

"You smoking already?"

He lit the cigarette and nodded, watching me through the smoke. "I just wanted to see if I'd have the courage to smoke in front of you." He grinned and blew a great cloud of smoke to the ceiling. "It was easy." He looked at my face. "Come on, now. I bet you was smoking at my age, tell the truth."

I didn't say anything but the truth was on my face, and he laughed. But now there was something very strained in his laugh. "Sure. And I bet that ain't all you was doing."

He was frightening me a little. "Cut the crap," I said. "We already decided that you was going to go and live at Isabel's. Now what's got into you all of a sudden?"

"*You* decided it," he pointed out. "*I* didn't decide nothing." He stopped in front of me, leaning against the stove, arms loosely folded. "Look, brother. I don't want to stay in Harlem no more, I really don't." He was very earnest. He looked at me, then over toward the kitchen window. There was something in his eyes I'd never seen before, some thoughtfulness, some worry all his own. He rubbed the muscle of one arm. "It's time I was getting out of here."

"Where do you want to *go,* Sonny?"

"I want to join the army. Or the navy, I don't care. If I say I'm old enough they'll believe me."

Then I got mad. It was because I was so scared. "You must be crazy. You goddamn fool, what the hell do you want to go and join the *army* for?"

"I just told you. To get out of Harlem."

"Sonny, you haven't even finished *school.* And if you really want to be a musician, how do you expect to study if you're in the *army?*"

He looked at me, trapped, and in anguish. "There's ways. I might be able to work out some kind of deal. Anyway, I'll have the G.I. Bill when I come out."

"*If* you come out." We stared at each other. "Sonny, please. Be reasonable. I know the setup is far from perfect. But we got to do the best we can."

"I ain't learning nothing in school," he said. "Even when I go." He turned away from me and opened the window and threw his cigarette out into the narrow alley. I watched his back. "At least, I ain't learning nothing you'd want me to learn." He slammed the window so hard I thought the glass would fly out, and turned back to me. "And I'm sick of the stink of these garbage cans!"

"Sonny," I said, "I know how you feel. But if you don't finish school now, you're going to be sorry later that you didn't." I grabbed him by the shoulders. "And you only got another year. It ain't so bad. And I'll come back and I swear I'll help you do *whatever* you want to do. Just try to put up with it till I come back. Will you please do that? For me?"

He didn't answer and he wouldn't look at me.

"Sonny. You hear me?"

He pulled away. "I hear you. But you never hear anything *I* say."

I didn't know what to say to that. He looked out of the window and then back at me. "OK," he said, and sighed. "I'll try."

Then I said, trying to cheer him up a little, "They got a piano at Isabel's. You can practice on it."

And as a matter of fact, it did cheer him up for a minute. "That's right," he said to himself. "I forgot that." His face relaxed a little. But the worry, the thoughtfulness, played on it still, the way shadows play on a face which is staring into the fire.

But I thought I'd never hear the end of that piano. At first, Isabel would write me, saying how nice it was that Sonny was so serious about his music and how, as soon as he came in from school, or wherever he had been when he was supposed to be at school, he went straight to that piano and stayed there until suppertime. And, after supper, he went back to that piano and stayed there until everybody went to bed. He was at the piano all day Saturday and all day Sunday. Then he bought a record player and started playing records. He'd play one record over and over again, all day long sometimes, and he'd improvise along with it on the piano. Or he'd play one section of the record, one chord, one change, one progression, then he'd do it on the piano. Then back to the record. Then back to the piano.

Well, I really don't know how they stood it. Isabel finally confessed that it wasn't like living with a person at all, it was like living with sound. And the sound didn't make any sense to her, didn't make any sense to any of them—naturally. They began, in a way, to be afflicted by this presence that was living in their home. It was as though Sonny were some sort of god, or monster. He moved in an atmosphere which wasn't like theirs at all. They fed him and he ate, he washed himself, he walked in and out of their door; he certainly wasn't nasty or unpleasant or rude, Sonny isn't any of those things; but it was as though he were all wrapped up in some cloud, some fire, some vision all his own; and there wasn't any way to reach him.

At the same time, he wasn't really a man yet, he was still a child, and they had to watch out for him in all kinds of ways. They certainly couldn't throw him out. Neither did they dare to make a great scene about that piano because even they dimly sensed, as I sensed, from so many thousands of miles away, that Sonny was at that piano playing for his life.

But he hadn't been going to school. One day a letter came from the school board and Isabel's mother got it—there had, apparently, been other letters but Sonny had torn them up. This day, when Sonny came in, Isabel's mother showed him the letter and asked where he'd been spending his time. And she finally got it out of him that he'd been down in Greenwich Village, with musicians and other characters, in a white girl's apartment. And this scared her and she started to scream at him and what came up, once she began—though she denies it to this day—was what sacrifices they were making to give Sonny a decent home and how little he appreciated it.

Sonny didn't play the piano that day. By evening, Isabel's mother had calmed down but then there was the old man to deal with, and Isabel herself. Isabel says she did her best to be calm but she broke down and started crying. She says she just watched Sonny's face. She could tell, by watching him, what was happening with him. And what was happening was that they penetrated his cloud, they had reached him. Even if their fingers had been a thousand times more gentle than human fingers ever are, he could hardly help feeling that they had stripped him naked and were spitting on that nakedness. For he also had to see that his presence, that music, which was life or death to him, had been torture for them and that they had endured it, not at all for his sake, but only for mine. And Sonny couldn't take that. He can take it a little better today than he could then but he's still not very good at it and, frankly, I don't know anybody who is.

The silence of the next few days must have been louder than the sound of all the music ever played since time began. One morning, before she went to work, Isabel was in his room for something and she suddenly realized that all of his records were gone. And she knew for certain that he was gone. And he was. He went as far as the navy would carry him. He finally sent me a postcard from some place in Greece and that was the first I knew that Sonny was still alive. I didn't see him any more until we were both back in New York and the war had long been over.

He was a man by then, of course, but I wasn't willing to see it. He came by the house from time to time, but we fought almost every time we met. I didn't like the way he carried himself, loose and dreamlike all the time, and I didn't like his friends, and his music seemed to be merely an excuse for the life he led. It sounded just that weird and disordered.

Then we had a fight, a pretty awful fight, and I didn't see him for months. By and by I looked him up, where he was living, in a furnished room in the Village, and I tried to make it up. But there were lots of other people in the room and Sonny just lay on his bed, and he wouldn't come downstairs with me, and he treated these other people as though they were his family and I weren't. So I got mad and then he got mad, and then I told him that he might just as well be dead as live the way he was living. Then he stood up and he told me not to worry about him any more in life, that he *was* dead as far as I was concerned. Then he pushed me to the door and the other people looked on as though nothing were happening, and he slammed the door behind me. I stood in the hallway, staring at the door. I heard somebody laugh in the room and then the tears came to my eyes. I started down the steps, whistling to keep from crying, I kept whistling to myself, *You going to need me, baby, one of these cold, rainy days.*

I read about Sonny's trouble in the spring. Little Grace died in the fall. She was a beautiful little girl. But she only lived a little over two years. She died of polio and she suffered. She had a slight fever for a couple of days, but it didn't seem like anything and we just kept her in bed. And we would certainly have called the doctor, but the fever dropped, she seemed to be all right. So we thought it had just been a cold. Then, one day, she was up, playing, Isabel was in the kitchen fixing lunch for the two boys when they'd come in from school, and she heard Grace fall down in the living room. When you have a lot of children you don't always start running when one of them falls, unless they start screaming or something. And, this time, Grace was quiet. Yet, Isabel says that when she heard that *thump* and then that silence, something happened in her to make her afraid. And she ran to the living room and there was little Grace on the floor, all twisted up and the reason she hadn't screamed was that she couldn't get her breath. And when she did scream, it was the worst sound, Isabel says, that she'd ever heard in all her life, and she still hears it sometimes in her dreams. Isabel will sometimes wake me up with a low, moaning, strangled sound and I have to be quick to awaken her and hold her to me and where Isabel is weeping against me seems a mortal wound.

I think I may have written Sonny the very day that little Grace was buried. I was sitting in the living room in the dark, by myself, and I suddenly thought of Sonny. My trouble made his real.

One Saturday afternoon, when Sonny had been living with us, or, anyway, been in our house, for nearly two weeks, I found myself wandering aimlessly about the living room, drinking from a can of beer, and trying to work up the courage to search Sonny's room. He was out, he was usually out whenever I was home, and Isabel had taken the children to see their grandparents. Suddenly I was standing still in front of the living room window, watching Seventh Avenue. The idea of searching Sonny's room made me still. I scarcely dared to admit to myself what I'd be searching for. I didn't know what I'd do if I found it. Or if I didn't.

On the sidewalk across from me, near the entrance to a barbecue joint, some people were holding an old-fashioned revival meeting. The barbecue cook, wearing a dirty white apron, his conked hair reddish and metallic in the pale sun, and a cigarette between his lips, stood in the doorway, watching them. Kids and older people paused in their errands and stood there, along with some older men and a couple of very tough-looking women who watched everything that happened on the avenue, as though they owned it, or were maybe owned by it. Well, they were watching this, too. The revival was being carried on by three sisters in black, and a brother. All they had were their voices and their Bibles and a tambourine. The brother was testifying and while he testified two of the sisters stood together, seeming to say, Amen, and the third sister walked around with the tambourine outstretched and a couple of people dropped coins into it. Then the brother's testimony ended and the sister who had been taking up the collection dumped the coins into her palm and transferred them to the pocket of her long black robe. Then she raised both hands, striking the tambourine against the air, and then against one hand, and she started to sing. And the two other sisters and the brother joined in.

It was strange, suddenly, to watch, though I had been seeing these street meetings all my life. So, of course, had everybody else down there. Yet, they paused and watched and listened and I stood still at the window. *"Tis the old ship of Zion,"* they sang, and the sister with the tambourine kept a steady, jangling beat, *"It has rescued many a thousand!"* Not a soul under the sound of their voices was hearing this song for the first time, not one of them had been rescued. Nor had they seen much in the way of rescue work being done around them. Neither did they especially believe in the holiness of the three sisters and the brother, they knew too much about them, knew where they lived, and how. The woman with the tambourine, whose voice dominated the air, whose face was bright with joy, was divided by very little from the woman who stood watching her, a cigarette between her heavy, chapped lips, her hair a cuckoo's nest, her face scarred and swollen from many beatings, and her black eyes glittering like coal. Perhaps they both knew this, which was why, when, as rarely, they addressed each other, they addressed each other as Sister. As the singing filled the air the watching, listening faces underwent a change, the eyes focusing on something within; the music seemed to soothe a poison out of them; and time seemed, nearly, to fall away from the sullen, belligerent, battered faces, as though they were fleeing back to their first condition, while dreaming of their last. The barbecue cook half shook his head and smiled, and dropped his cigarette and disappeared into his joint. A man fumbled in his pockets for change and stood holding it in his hand impatiently, as though he had just remembered a pressing appointment further up the avenue. He looked furious. Then I saw Sonny, standing on the edge of the crowd. He was carrying a wide, flat notebook with a green cover, and it made him look, from where I was standing, almost like a schoolboy. The coppery sun brought out the copper in his skin, he was very faintly smiling, standing very still. Then the singing stopped, the tambourine turned into a collection plate again. The furious man dropped in his coins and vanished, so did a couple of the women, and Sonny dropped some change in the plate, looking directly at the woman with a little smile. He started across the avenue, toward the house. He has a slow, loping walk, something like the way Harlem hipsters walk, only he's imposed on this his own halfbeat. I had never really noticed it before.

I stayed at the window, both relieved and apprehensive. As Sonny disappeared from my sight, they began singing again. And they were still singing when his key turned in the lock.

"Hey," he said.

"Hey, yourself. You want some beer?"

"No. Well, maybe." But he came up to the window and stood beside me, looking out. "What a warm voice," he said.

They were singing *If I could only hear my mother pray again!*

"Yes," I said, "and she can sure beat that tambourine."

"But what a terrible song," he said, and laughed. He dropped his notebook on the sofa and disappeared into the kitchen. "Where's Isabel and the kids?"

"I think they went to see their grandparents. You hungry?"

"No." He came back into the living room with his can of beer. "You want to come some place with me tonight?"

I sensed, I don't know how, that I couldn't possibly say No. "Sure. Where?"

He sat down on the sofa and picked up his notebook and started leafing through it. "I'm going to sit in with some fellows in a joint in the Village."

"You mean, you're going to play, tonight?"

"That's right." He took a swallow of his beer and moved back to the window. He gave me a sidelong look. "If you can stand it."

"I'll try," I said.

He smiled to himself and we both watched as the meeting across the way broke up. The three sisters and the brother, heads bowed, were singing *God be with you till we meet again.* The faces around them were very quiet. Then the song ended. The small crowd dispersed. We watched the three women and the lone man walk slowly up the avenue.

"When she was singing before," said Sonny, abruptly, "her voice reminded me for a minute of what heroin feels like sometimes—when it's in your veins. It makes you feel sort of warm and cool at the same time. And distant. And—and sure." He sipped his beer, very deliberately not looking at me. I watched his face. "It makes you feel—in control. Sometimes you've got to have that feeling."

"Do you?" I sat down slowly in the easy chair.

"Sometimes." He went to the sofa and picked up his notebook again. "Some people do."

"In order," I asked, "to play?" And my voice was very ugly, full of contempt and anger.

"Well"—he looked at me with great, troubled eyes, as though, in fact, he hoped his eyes would tell me things he could never otherwise say—"they *think* so. And *if* they think so—!"

"And what do *you* think?" I asked.

He sat on the sofa and put his can of beer on the floor. "I don't know," he said, and I couldn't be sure if he were answering my question or pursuing his thoughts. His face didn't tell me. "It's not so much to *play.* It's to *stand* it, to be able to make it at all. On any level." He frowned and smiled: "In order to keep from shaking to pieces."

"But these friends of yours," I said, "they seem to shake themselves to pieces pretty goddamn fast."

"Maybe." He played with the notebook. And something told me that I should curb my tongue, that Sonny was doing his best to talk, that I should listen. "But of course you only know the ones that've gone to pieces. Some don't—or at least they haven't *yet* and that's just about all *any* of us can say." He paused. "And then there are some who just live, really, in hell, and they know it and they see what's happening and they go right on. I don't know." He sighed, dropped the notebook, folded his arms. "Some guys, you can tell from the way they play, they on something *all* the time. And you can see that, well, it makes something real for them. But of course," he picked up his beer from the floor and sipped it and put the can down again, "they *want* to, too, you've got to see that. Even some of them that say they don't—*some,* not all."

"And what about you?" I asked—I couldn't help it. "What about you? Do *you* want to?"

He stood up and walked to the window and remained silent for a long time. Then he sighed. "Me," he said. Then: "While I was downstairs before, on my way here, listening to that woman sing, it struck me all of a sudden how much suffering she must have had to go through—to sing like that. It's *repulsive* to think you have to suffer that much."

I said: "But there's no way not to suffer—is there, Sonny?"

"I believe not," he said, and smiled, "but that's never stopped anyone from trying." He looked at me. "Has it?" I realized, with this mocking look, that there stood between us, forever, beyond the power of time or forgiveness, the fact that I had held silence—so long!—when he had needed human speech to help him. He turned back to the window. "No, there's no way not to suffer. But you try all kinds of ways to keep from drowning in it, to keep on top of it, and to make it seem—well, like *you*. Like you did something, all right, and now you're suffering for it. You know?" I said nothing. "Well you know," he said, impatiently, "why *do* people suffer? Maybe it's better to do something to give it a reason, *any* reason."

"But we just agreed," I said, "that there's no way not to suffer. Isn't it better, then, just to—take it?"

"But nobody just takes it," Sonny cried, "that's what I'm telling you! *Everybody* tries not to. You're just hung up on the *way* some people try—it's not *your* way!"

The hair on my face began to itch, my face felt wet. "That's not true," I said, "that's not true. I don't give a damn what other people do, I don't even care how they suffer. I just care how *you* suffer." And he looked at me. "Please believe me," I said, "I don't want to see you—die—trying not to suffer."

"I won't," he said, flatly, "die trying not to suffer. At least, not any faster than anybody else."

"But there's no need," I said, trying to laugh, "is there? in killing yourself."

I wanted to say more, but I couldn't. I wanted to talk about will power and how life could be—well, beautiful. I wanted to say that it was all within; but was it? or, rather, wasn't that exactly the trouble? And I wanted to promise that I would never fail him again. But it would all have sounded—empty words and lies.

So I made the promise to myself and prayed that I would keep it.

"It's terrible sometimes, inside," he said, "that's what's the trouble. You walk these streets, black and funky and cold, and there's not really a living ass to talk to, and there's nothing shaking, and there's no way of getting it out—that storm inside. You can't talk it and you can't make love with it, and when you finally try to get with it and play it, you realize *nobody's* listening. So *you've* got to listen. You got to find a way to listen."

And then he walked away from the window and sat on the sofa again, as though all the wind had suddenly been knocked out of him.

"Sometimes you'll do *anything* to play, even cut your mother's throat." He laughed and looked at me. "Or your brother's." Then he sobered. "Or your own." Then: "Don't worry. I'm all right now and I think I'll *be* all right. But I can't forget—where I've been. I don't mean just the physical place I've been, I mean where I've *been*. And *what* I've been."

"What have you been, Sonny?" I asked.

He smiled—but sat sideways on the sofa, his elbow resting on the back, his fingers playing with his mouth and chin, not looking at me. "I've been something I didn't recognize, didn't know I could be. Didn't know anybody could be." He stopped, looking inward, looking helplessly young, looking old. "I'm not talking about it now because I feel *guilty* or anything like that—maybe it would be better if I did, I don't know. Anyway, I can't really talk about it. Not to you, not to anybody," and now he turned and faced me. "Sometimes, you know, and it was actually when I was most *out* of the world, I felt that I was in it, and that I was *with* it, really, and I could play or I didn't really have to *play,* it just came out of me, it was there. And I don't know how I played, thinking about it now, but I know I did awful things, those times, sometimes, to people. Or it wasn't that I *did* anything to them—it was that they weren't real." He picked up the beer can; it was empty; he rolled it between his palms: "And other times—well, I needed a fix, I needed to find a place to lean, I needed to clear a space to *listen*—and I couldn't find it, and I—went crazy, I did terrible things to *me,* I was terrible *for* me." He began pressing the beer can between his hands, I watched the metal begin to give. It glittered, as he played with it, like a knife, and I was afraid he would cut himself, but I said nothing. "Oh well. I can never tell you. I was all by myself at the bottom of something, stinking and sweating and crying and shaking, and I smelled it, you know? *my* stink, and I thought I'd die if I couldn't get away from it and yet, all the same, I knew that everything I was doing was just locking me in with it. And I didn't know," he paused, still flattening the beer can, "I didn't know, I still *don't* know, something kept telling me that maybe it was good to smell your own stink, but I didn't think that *that* was what I'd been trying to do—and—who can stand it?" and he abruptly dropped the ruined beer can, looking at me with a small, still smile, and then rose, walking to the window as though it were the lodestone rock. I watched his face, he watched the avenue. "I couldn't tell you when Mama died—but the reason I wanted to leave Harlem so bad was to get away from drugs. And then, when I ran away, that's what I was running from—really. When I came back, nothing had changed, *I* hadn't changed, I was just—older." And he stopped, drumming with his fingers on the windowpane. The sun had vanished, soon darkness would fall. I watched his face. "It can come again," he said, almost as though speaking to himself. Then he turned to me. "It can come again," he repeated. "I just want you to know that."

"All right," I said, at last. "So it can come again. All right."

He smiled, but the smile was sorrowful. "I had to try to tell you," he said.

"Yes," I said. "I understand that."

"You're my brother," he said, looking straight at me, and not smiling at all.

"Yes," I repeated, "yes. I understand that."

He turned back to the window, looking out. "All that hatred down there," he said, "all that hatred and misery and love. It's a wonder it doesn't blow the avenue apart."

We went to the only night club on a short, dark street, downtown. We squeezed through the narrow, chattering, jam-packed bar to the entrance of the big room, where the bandstand was. And we stood there for a moment, for the lights were very dim in this room and we couldn't see. Then, "Hello, boy," said a voice and an enormous black man, much older than Sonny or myself, erupted out of all that atmospheric lighting and put an arm around Sonny's shoulder. "I been sitting right here," he said, "waiting for you."

He had a big voice, too, and heads in the darkness turned toward us.

Sonny grinned and pulled a little away, and said, "Creole, this is my brother. I told you about him."

Creole shook my hand. "I'm glad to meet you, son," he said, and it was clear that he was glad to meet me *there,* for Sonny's sake. And he smiled, "You got a real musician in *your* family," and he took his arm from Sonny's shoulder and slapped him, lightly, affectionately, with the back of his hand.

"Well. Now I've heard it all," said a voice behind us. This was another musician, and a friend of Sonny's, a coal-black, cheerful-looking man, built close to the ground. He immediately began confiding to me, at the top of his lungs, the most terrible things about Sonny, his teeth gleaming like a lighthouse and his laugh coming up out of him like the beginning of an earthquake. And it turned out that everyone at the bar knew Sonny, or almost everyone; some were musicians, working there, or nearby, or not working, some were simply hangers-on, and some were there to hear Sonny play. I was introduced to all of them and they were all very polite to me. Yet, it was clear that, for them, I was only Sonny's brother. Here, I was in Sonny's world. Or, rather: his kingdom. Here, it was not even a question that his veins bore royal blood.

They were going to play soon and Creole installed me, by myself, at a table in a dark corner. Then I watched them, Creole, and the little black man, and Sonny, and the others, while they horsed around, standing just below the bandstand. The light from the bandstand spilled just a little short of them and, watching them laughing and gesturing and moving about, I had the feeling that they, nevertheless, were being most careful not to step into that circle of light too suddenly: that if they moved into the light too suddenly, without thinking, they would perish in flame. Then, while I watched, one of them, the small, black man, moved into the light and crossed the bandstand and started fooling around with his drums. Then—being funny and being, also, extremely ceremonious—Creole took Sonny by the arm and led him to the piano. A woman's voice called Sonny's name and a few hands started clapping. And Sonny, also being funny and being ceremonious, and so touched, I think, that he could have cried, but neither hiding it nor showing it, riding it like a man, grinned, and put both hands to his heart and bowed from the waist.

Creole then went to the bass fiddle and a lean, very bright-skinned brown man jumped up on the bandstand and picked up his horn. So there they were, and the atmosphere on the bandstand and in the room began to change and tighten. Someone stepped up to the microphone and announced them. Then there were all kinds of murmurs. Some people at the bar shushed others. The waitress ran around, frantically getting in the last orders, guys and chicks got closer to each other, and the lights on the bandstand, on the quartet, turned to a kind of indigo. Then they all looked different there. Creole looked about him for the last time, as though he were making certain that all his chickens were in the coop, and then he—jumped and struck the fiddle. And there they were.

All I know about music is that not many people ever really hear it. And even then, on the rare occasions when something opens within, and the music enters, what we mainly hear, or hear corroborated, are personal private, vanishing evocations. But the man who creates the music is hearing something else, is dealing with the roar rising from the void and imposing order on it as it hits the air. What is evoked in him, then, is of another order, more terrible because it has no words, and triumphant, too, for that same reason. And his triumph, when he triumphs, is ours. I just watched Sonny's face. His face was troubled, he was working hard, but he wasn't with it. And I had the feeling that, in a way, everyone on the bandstand was waiting for him, both waiting for him and pushing him along. But as I began to watch Creole, I realized that it was Creole who held them all back. He had them on a short rein. Up there, keeping the beat with his whole body, wailing on the fiddle, with his eyes half closed, he was listening to everything, but he was listening to Sonny. He was having a dialogue with Sonny. He wanted Sonny to leave the shore line and strike out for the deep water. He was Sonny's witness that deep water and drowning were not the same thing—he had been there, and he knew. And he wanted Sonny to know. He was waiting for Sonny to do the things on the keys which would let Creole know that Sonny was in the water.

And, while Creole listened, Sonny moved, deep within, exactly like someone in torment. I had never before thought of how awful the relationship must be between the musician and his instrument. He has to fill it, this instrument, with the breath of life, his own. He has to make it do what he wants it to do. And a piano is just a piano. It's made out of so much wood and wires and little hammers and big ones, and ivory. While there's only so much you can do with it, the only way to find this out is to try and make it do everything.

And Sonny hadn't been near a piano for over a year. And he wasn't on much better terms with his life, not the life that stretched before him now. He and the piano stammered, started one way, got scared, stopped; started another way, panicked, marked time, started again; then seemed to have found a direction, panicked again, got stuck. And the face I saw on Sonny I'd never seen before. Everything had been burned out of it, and, at the same time, things usually hidden were being burned in, by the fire and fury of the battle which was occurring in him up there.

Yet, watching Creole's face as they neared the end of the first set, I had the feeling that something had happened, something I hadn't heard. Then they finished, there was scattered applause, and then, without an instant's warning, Creole started into something else, it was almost sardonic, it was *Am I Blue*. And, as though he commanded, Sonny began to play. Something began to happen. And Creole let out the reins. The dry, low, black man said something awful on the drums, Creole answered, and the drums talked back. Then the horn insisted, sweet and high, slightly detached perhaps, and Creole listened, commenting now and then, dry, and driving, beautiful and calm and old. Then they all came together again, and Sonny was part of the family again. I could tell this from his face. He seemed to have found, right there beneath his fingers, a damn brand-new piano. It seemed that he couldn't get over it. Then, for awhile, just being happy with Sonny, they seemed to be agreeing with him that brand-new pianos certainly were a gas.

Then Creole stepped forward to remind them that what they were playing was the blues. He hit something in all of them, he hit something in me, myself, and the music tightened and deepened, apprehension began to beat the air. Creole began to tell us what the blues were all about. They were not about anything very new. He and his boys up there were keeping it new, at the risk of ruin, destruction, madness, and death, in order to find new ways to make us listen. For, while the tale of how we suffer, and how we are delighted, and how we may triumph is never new, it always must be heard. There isn't any other tale to tell, it's the only light we've got in all this darkness.

And this tale, according to that face, that body, those strong hands on those strings, has another aspect in every country, and a new depth in every generation. Listen, Creole seemed to be saying, listen. Now these are Sonny's blues. He made the little black man on the drums know it, and the bright, brown man on the horn. Creole wasn't trying any longer to get Sonny in the water. He was wishing him Godspeed. Then he stepped back, very slowly, filling the air with the immense suggestion that Sonny speak for himself.

Then they all gathered around Sonny and Sonny played. Every now and again one of them seemed to say, Amen. Sonny's fingers filled the air with life, his life. But that life contained so many others. And Sonny went all the way back, he really began with the spare, flat statement of the opening phrase of the song. Then he began to make it his. It was very beautiful because it wasn't hurried and it was no longer a lament. I seemed to hear with what burning he had made it his, with what burning we had yet to make it ours, how we could cease lamenting. Freedom lurked around us and I understood, at last, that he could help us to be free if we would listen, that he would never be free until we did. Yet, there was no battle in his face now. I heard what he had gone through, and would continue to go through until he came to rest in earth. He had made it his: that long line, of which we knew only Mama and Daddy. And he was giving it back, as everything must be given back, so that, passing through death, it can live forever. I saw my mother's face again, and felt, for the first time, how the stones of the road she had walked on must have bruised her feet. I saw the moonlit road where my father's brother died. And it brought something else back to me, and carried me past it, I saw my little girl again and felt Isabel's tears again, and I felt my own tears begin to rise. And I was yet aware that this was only a moment, that the world waited outside, as hungry as a tiger, and that trouble stretched above us, longer than the sky.

Then it was over. Creole and Sonny let out their breath, both soaking wet, and grinning. There was a lot of applause and some of it was real. In the dark, the girl came by and I asked her to take drinks to the bandstand. There was a long pause, while they talked up there in the indigo light and after awhile I saw the girl put a Scotch and milk on top of the piano for Sonny. He didn't seem to notice it, but just before they started playing again, he sipped from it and looked toward me, and nodded. Then he put it back on top of the piano. For me, then, as they began to play again, it glowed and shook above my brother's head like the very cup of trembling.

## QUESTIONS

1. Explore the use of music as a metaphor in "Sonny's Blues." How many types of music do you find in the story? What meanings does the narrator give them?
2. The narrator says that he and Sonny, riding through the streets of New York, "both were seeking through our separate cab windows . . . that part of ourselves which had been left behind. It's always at the hour of trouble and confrontation that the missing member aches." What has been amputated? What happens to the lost member during the course of the story?
3. "He wanted Sonny to leave the shore line and strike out for the deep water. He was Sonny's witness that deep water and drowning were not the same thing—he had been there, and he knew." Discuss this metaphor. Notice the word *witness*. It could come from legal terminology but in this story it has a different connotation. Discuss.

## KATHERINE MANSFIELD (1888–1923)

# *Miss Brill*

Although it was so brilliantly fine—the blue sky powdered with gold and great spots of light like white wine splashed over the Jardins Publiques[1]—Miss Brill was glad that she had decided on her fur. The air was motionless, but when you opened your mouth there was just a faint chill, like a chill from a glass of iced water before you sip, and now and again a leaf came drifting—from nowhere, from the sky. Miss Brill put up her hand and touched her fur. Dear little thing! It was nice to feel it again. She had taken it out of its box that afternoon, shaken out the moth powder, given it a good brush, and rubbed the life back into the dim little eyes. "What has been happening to me?" said the sad little eyes. Oh, how sweet it was to see them snap at her again from the red eiderdown! [2] . . . But the nose, which was of some black composition, wasn't at all firm. It must have had a knock, somehow. Never mind—a little dab of black sealing-wax when the time came—when it was absolutely necessary . . . Little rogue! Yes, she really felt like that about it. Little rogue biting its tail just by her left ear. She could have taken it off and laid it on her lap and stroked it. She felt a tingling in her hands and arms, but that came from walking, she supposed. And when she breathed, something light and sad—no, not sad, exactly—something gentle seemed to move in her bosom.

There were a number of people out this afternoon, far more than last Sunday. And the band sounded louder and gayer. That was because the Season had begun. For although the band played all the year round on Sundays, out of season it was never the same. It was like some one playing with only the family to listen; it didn't care how it played if there weren't any strangers present. Wasn't the conductor wearing a new coat, too? She was sure it was new. He scraped with his foot and flapped his arms like a rooster about to crow, and the bandsmen sitting in the green rotunda blew out their cheeks and glared at the music. Now there came a little "flutey" bit—very pretty!

---

1 *Jardins Publiques,* public gardens.
2 *eiderdown,* a quilt stuffed with the down of the eider duck.

—a little chain of bright drops. She was sure it would be repeated. It was; she lifted her head and smiled.

Only two people shared her "special" seat: a fine old man in a velvet coat, his hands clasped over a huge carved walking-stick, and a big old woman, sitting upright, with a roll of knitting on her embroidered apron. They did not speak. This was disappointing, for Miss Brill always looked forward to the conversation. She had become really quite expert, she thought, at listening as though she didn't listen, at sitting in other people's lives just for a minute while they talked round her.

She glanced, sideways, at the old couple. Perhaps they would go soon. Last Sunday, too, hadn't been as interesting as usual. An Englishman and his wife, he wearing a dreadful Panama hat and she button boots. And she'd gone on the whole time about how she ought to wear spectacles; she knew she needed them; but that it was no good getting any; they'd be sure to break and they'd never keep on. And he'd been so patient. He'd suggested everything—gold rims, the kind that curved round your ears, little pads inside the bridge. No, nothing would please her. "They'll always be sliding down my nose!" Miss Brill had wanted to shake her.

The old people sat on the bench, still as statues. Never mind, there was always the crowd to watch. To and fro, in front of the flower beds and the band rotunda, the couples and groups paraded, stopped to talk, to greet, to buy a handful of flowers from the old beggar who had his tray fixed to the railings. Little children ran among them, swooping and laughing; little boys with big white silk bows under their chins, little girls, little French dolls, dressed up in velvet and lace. And sometimes a tiny staggerer came suddenly rocking into the open from under the trees, stopped, stared, as suddenly sat down "flop," until its small high-stepping mother, like a young hen, rushed scolding to its rescue. Other people sat on the benches and green chairs, but they were nearly always the same, Sunday after Sunday, and—Miss Brill had often noticed—there was something funny about nearly all of them. They were odd, silent, nearly all old, and from the way they stared they looked as though they'd just come from dark little rooms or even—even cupboards!

Behind the rotunda the slender trees with yellow leaves down drooping, and through them just a line of sea, and beyond the blue sky with gold-veined clouds.

Tum-tum-tum tiddle-um! tiddle-um! tum tiddley-um tum ta! blew the band.

Two young girls in red came by and two young soldiers in blue met them, and they laughed and paired and went off arm-in-arm. Two peasant women with funny straw hats passed, gravely, leading beautiful smoke-colored donkeys. A cold, pale nun hurried by. A beautiful woman came along and dropped her bunch of violets, and a little boy ran after to hand them to her, and she took them and threw them away as if they'd been poisoned. Dear me! Miss Brill didn't know whether to admire that or not! And now an ermine toque[3] and a gentleman in gray met just in front of her. He was tall, stiff, dignified, and she was wearing the ermine toque she'd bought when her hair was yellow. Now everything, her hair, her face, even her eyes, was the same color as the shabby ermine, and her hand, in its cleaned glove, lifted to dab her lips, was a tiny yellowish paw. Oh, she was so pleased to see him—delighted! She rather thought they were going to meet that afternoon. She described where she'd been—everywhere, here, there, along by the sea. The day was so charming—didn't he agree? And wouldn't he, perhaps? . . . But he shook his head, lighted a cigarette, slowly breathed a great deep puff into her face, and, even while she was still talking and laughing, flicked the match away and walked on. The ermine toque was alone; she smiled more brightly than ever. But even the band seemed to know what she was feeling and played more softly, played tenderly, and the drum beat, "The Brute! The Brute!" over and over. What would she do? What was going to happen now? But as Miss Brill wondered, the ermine toque turned, raised her hand as though she'd seen some one else, much nicer, just over there, and pattered away. And the band changed again and played more quickly, more gayly than ever, and the old couple on Miss Brill's seat got up and marched away, and such a funny old man with long whiskers hobbled along in time to the music and was nearly knocked over by four girls walking abreast.

Oh, how fascinating it was! How she enjoyed it! How she loved sitting here, watching it all! It was like a play. It was exactly like a play. Who could believe the sky at the back wasn't painted? But it wasn't till a little brown dog trotted on solemn and then slowly trotted off, like a little "theater" dog, a little dog that had been drugged, that Miss Brill discovered what it was that made it so exciting. They were all on the stage. They weren't only the audience, not only looking on; they were acting. Even she had a part and came every Sunday. No doubt somebody would have noticed if she hadn't been there; she was a part of the performance after all. How strange she'd never thought of it like that before! And yet it explained why she made such a point of starting from home at just the same time each week—so as not to be late for the performance—and it also explained why she had quite a queer, shy feeling at telling her English pupils how she spent her Sunday afternoons. No wonder! Miss Brill nearly laughed out loud. She was on the stage. She thought of the

---

3 *toque,* a woman's small, round, close-fitting hat—in this case, such a hat made from the white fur of the ermine.

old invalid gentleman to whom she read the newspaper four afternoons a week while he slept in the garden. She had got quite used to the frail head on the cotton pillow, the hollowed eyes, the open mouth and the high pinched nose. If he'd been dead she mightn't have noticed for weeks; she wouldn't have minded. But suddenly he knew he was having the paper read to him by an actress! "An actress!" The old head lifted; two points of light quivered in the old eyes. "An actress—are ye?" And Miss Brill smoothed the newspaper as though it were the manuscript of her part and said gently: "Yes, I have been an actress for a long time."

The band had been having a rest. Now they started again. And what they played was warm, sunny, yet there was just a faint chill—a something, what was it?—not sadness—no, not sadness—a something that made you want to sing. The tune lifted, lifted, the light shone; and it seemed to Miss Brill that in another moment all of them, all the whole company, would begin singing. The young ones, the laughing ones who were moving together, they would begin, and the men's voices, very resolute and brave, would join them. And then she too, she too, and the others on the benches—they would come in with a kind of accompaniment—something low, that scarcely rose or fell, something so beautiful—moving . . . And Miss Brill's eyes filled with tears and she looked smiling at all the other members of the company. Yes, we understand, we understand, she thought—though what they understood she didn't know.

Just at that moment a boy and a girl came and sat down where the old couple had been. They were beautifully dressed; they were in love. The hero and heroine, of course, just arrived from his father's yacht. And still soundlessly singing, still with that trembling smile, Miss Brill prepared to listen.

"No, not now," said the girl. "Not here, I can't."

"But why? Because of that stupid old thing at the end there?" asked the boy. "Why does she come here at all—who wants her? Why doesn't she keep her silly old mug at home?"

"It's her fu-fur which is so funny," giggled the girl. "It's exactly like a fried whiting." [4]

"Ah, be off with you!" said the boy in an angry whisper. Then: "Tell me, ma petite chère—" [5]

"No, not here," said the girl. "Not *yet*."

On her way home she usually bought a slice of honeycake at the baker's. It was her Sunday treat. Sometimes there was an almond in her slice, sometimes not. It made a great difference. If there was an almond it was like carrying home a tiny present—a surprise—some-

---

4 *whiting,* a food fish related to cod.
5 *ma petite chère,* my dear little one.

thing that might very well not have been there. She hurried on the almond Sundays and struck the match for the kettle in quite a dashing way.

But today she passed the baker's by, climbed the stairs, went into the little dark room—her room like a cupboard—and sat down on the red eiderdown. She sat there for a long time. The box that the fur came out of was on the bed. She unclasped the necklet quickly; quickly, without looking, laid it inside. But when she put the lid on she thought she heard something crying.

## QUESTIONS

Katherine Mansfield's style in "Miss Brill" concentrates on details—details seen, heard, and interpreted by her highly observant and imaginative heroine. Note how the story is built and shaped by these details.

1. During the first part of the story, notice how the accumulation of details sets the scene. Note how observation mixes with imagination. For example, how does Miss Brill see or describe her fur piece? The bandmaster? The people on benches? The woman in the ermine toque?
2. The climax of the tale turns on a "discovery" made by Miss Brill, which tries to impose a unity on the scene and its many details. The climax itself, however, builds up in three stages. The first begins with the sentence, "Oh, how fascinating it was!" and ends with the sentence, "Yes, I have been an actress for a long time." The second begins with "The band had been having a rest" and continues through "Yes, we understand, we understand, she thought—though what they understood she didn't know." The third begins with "Just at that moment a boy and girl came" and closes with " 'No, not here,' said the girl. 'Not *yet.*' "
   a. What is the theme of each of these three stages? What part do observation, imagination, and feeling play in each? How fully do you accept each discovery? To what extent do you believe it to be true or feel in sympathy with it?
   b. What progression and/or contrast is created by the three stages? How do you react to it?
3. What does Mansfield do with her heroine after the climax? How does the story finish? Note again the use of details observed and imagined; how does the end tie in with the story's beginning and climax? How effective a means is this for rounding off the story?

## TILLIE OLSEN (1913?- )

# *Tell Me a Riddle*

*"These Things Shall Be"*

### I

For forty-seven years they had been married. How deep back the stubborn, gnarled roots of the quarrel reached, no one could say—but only now, when tending to the needs of others no longer shackled them together, the roots swelled up visible, split the earth between them, and the tearing shook even to the children, long since grown.

Why now, why now? wailed Hannah.

As if when we grew up weren't enough, said Paul.

Poor Ma. Poor Dad. It hurts so for both of them, said Vivi. They never had very much; at least in old age they should be happy.

Knock their heads together, insisted Sammy; tell 'em: you're too old for this kind of thing; no reason not to get along now.

Lennie wrote to Clara: They've lived over so much together; what could possibly tear them apart?

Something tangible enough.

Arthritic hands, and such work as he got, occasional. Poverty all his life, and there was little breath left for running. He could not, could not turn away from this desire: to have the troubling of responsibility, the fretting with money, over and done with; to be free, to be *care*free where success was not measured by accumulation, and there was use for the vitality still in him.

There was a way. They could sell the house, and with the money join his lodge's Haven, cooperative for the aged. Happy communal life, and was he not already an official; had he not helped organize it, raise funds, served as a trustee?

But she—would not consider it.

"What do we need all this for?" he would ask loudly, for her hearing aid was turned down and the vacuum was shrilling. "Five rooms" (pushing the sofa so she could get into the corner) "furniture" (smoothing down the rug) "floors and surfaces to make work. Tell me, why do we need it" And he was glad he could ask in a scream.

"Because I'm use't."

"Because you're use't. This is a reason, Mrs. Word Miser? Used to can get unused!"

"Enough unused I have to get used to already. . . . Not enough words?" turning off the vacuum a moment to hear herself answer. "Because soon enough we'll need only a little closet, no windows, no furniture, nothing to make work, but for worms. Because now I want room. . . . Screech and blow like you're doing, you'll need that closet even sooner. . . . Ha, again!" for the vacuum bag wailed, puffed half up, hung stubbornly limp. "This time fix it so it stays; quick before the phone rings and you get too important-busy."

But while he struggled with the motor, it seethed in him. Why fix it? Why have to bother? And if it can't be fixed, have to wring the mind with how to pay the repair? At the Haven they come in with their own machines to clean your room or your cottage; you fish, or play cards, or make jokes in the sun, not with knotty fingers fight to mend vacuums.

Over the dishes, coaxingly: "For once in your life, to be free, to have everything done for you, like a queen."

"I never liked queens."

"No dishes, no garbage, no towel to sop, no worry what to buy, what to eat."

"And what else would I do with my empty hands? Better to eat at my own table when I want, and to cook and eat how I want."

"In the cottages they buy what you ask, and cook it how you like. *You* are the one who always used to say: better mankind born without mouths and stomachs than always to worry for money to buy, to shop, to fix, to cook, to wash, to clean."

"How cleverly you hid that you heard. I said it then because eighteen hours a day I ran. And you never scraped a carrot or knew a dish towel sops. Now—for you and me—who cares? A herring out of a jar is enough. But when *I* want, and nobody to bother." And she turned off her ear button, so she would not have to hear.

But as *he* had no peace, juggling and rejuggling the money to figure: how will I pay for this now?; prying out the storm windows (there they take care of this); jolting in the streetcar on errands (there I would not have to ride to take care of this or that); fending the patronizing relatives just back from Florida (at the Haven it matters what one is, not what one can afford), he gave *her* no peace.

"Look! In their bulletin. A reading circle. Twice a week it meets."

"Haumm," her answer of not listening.

"A reading circle. Chekhov they read that you like, and Peretz.[1] Cultured people at the Haven that you would enjoy."

---

[1] *Chekhov,* Anton Chekhov (1860–1904), Russian writer; *Peretz,* I. L. Peretz (1852–1915), Polish writer who worked mainly in Yiddish. Works by both appear elsewhere in this book.

"Enjoy!" She tasted the word. "Now, when it pleases you, you find a reading circle for me. And forty years ago when the children were morsels and there was a Circle, did you stay home with them once so I could go? Even once? You trained me well. I do not need others to enjoy. Others!" Her voice trembled. "Because *you* want to be there with others. Already it makes me sick to think of you always around others. Clown, grimacer, floormat, yesman, entertainer, whatever they want of you."

And now it was he who turned on the television loud so he need not hear.

Old scar tissue ruptured and the wounds festered anew. Chekhov indeed. She thought without softness of that young wife, who in the deep night hours while she nursed the current baby, and perhaps held another in her lap, would try to stay awake for the only time there was to read. She would feel again the weather of the outside on his cheek when, coming late from a meeting, he would find her so, and stimulated and ardent, sniffing her skin, coax: "I'll put the baby to bed, and you—put the book away, don't read, don't read."

That had been the most beguiling of all the "don't read, put your book away" her life had been. Chekhov indeed!

"Money?" She shrugged him off. "Could we get poorer than once we were? And in America, who starves?"

But as still he pressed:

"Let me alone about money. Was there ever enough? Seven little ones—for every penny I had to ask—and sometimes, remember, there was nothing. But always *I* had to manage. Now *you* manage. Rub your nose in it good."

But from those years she had had to manage, old humiliations and terrors rose up, lived again, and forced her to relive them. The children's needings; that grocer's face or this merchant's wife she had had to beg credit from when credit was a disgrace; the scenery of the long blocks walked around when she could not pay; school coming, and the desperate going over the old to see what could yet be remade; the soups of meat bones begged "for-the-dog" one winter. . . .

Enough. Now they had no children. Let *him* wrack his head for how they would live. She would not exchange her solitude for anything. *Never again to be forced to move to the rhythms of others.*

For in this solitude she had won to a reconciled peace.

Tranquillity from having the empty house no longer an enemy, for it stayed clean—not as in the days when it was her family, the life in it, that had seemed the enemy: tracking, smudging, littering, dirtying, engaging her in endless defeating battle—and on whom her endless defeat had been spewed.

The few old books, memorized from rereading; the pictures to ponder (the magnifying glass superimposed on her heavy eyeglasses). Or if she wishes, when he is gone, the phonograph, that if she turns up very loud and strains, she can hear: the ordered sounds and the struggling.

Out in the garden, growing things to nurture. Birds to be kept out of the pear tree, and when the pears are heavy and ripe, the old fury of work, for all must be canned, nothing wasted.

And her one social duty (for she will not go to luncheons or meetings) the boxes of old clothes left with her, as with a life-practised eye for finding what is still wearable within the worn (again the magnifying glass superimposed on the heavy glasses) she scans and sorts—this for rag or rummage, that for mending and cleaning, and this for sending away.

*Being able at last to live within, and not move to the rhythms of others,* as life had forced her to: denying; removing; isolating; taking the children one by one; then deafening, half-blinding—and at last, presenting her solitude.

And in it she had won to a reconciled peace.

Now he was violating it with his constant campaigning: *Sell the house and move to the Haven.* (You sit, you sit—there too you could sit like a stone.) He was making of her a battleground where old grievances tore. (Turn on your ear button—I am talking.) And stubbornly she resisted—so that from wheedling, reasoning, manipulation, it was bitterness he now started with.

And it came to where every happening lashed up a quarrel.

"I will sell the house anyway," he flung at her one night. "I am putting it up for sale. There will be a way to make you sign."

The television blared, as always it did on the evenings he stayed home, and as always it reached her only as noise. She did not know if the tumult was in her or outside. Snap! she turned the sound off. "Shadows," she whispered to him, pointing to the screen, "look, it is only shadows." And in a scream: "Did you say that you will sell the house? Look at me, not at that. I am no shadow. You cannot sell without me."

"Leave on the television. I am watching."

"Like Paulie, like Jenny, a four-year-old. Staring at shadows. *You cannot sell the house.*"

"I will. We are going to the Haven. There you would not hear the television when you do not want it. I could sit in the social room and watch. You could lock yourself up to smell your unpleasantness in a room by yourself—for who would want to come near you?"

"No, no selling." A whisper now.

"The television is shadows. Mrs. Enlightened! Mrs. Cultured! A world comes into your house—and it is shadows. People you would never meet in a thousand lifetimes. Wonders. When you were four years old, yes, like Paulie, like Jenny, did you know of Indian dances, alligators, how they use bamboo in Malaya? No, you scratched in your dirt with the chickens and thought Olshana[2] was the world. Yes, Mrs. Unpleasant, I will sell the house, for there better can we be rid of each other than here."

She did not know if the tumult was outside, or in her. Always a ravening inside, a pull to the bed, to lie down, to succumb.

"Have you thought maybe Ma should let a doctor have a look at her?" asked their son Paul after Sunday dinner, regarding his mother crumpled on the couch, instead of, as was her custom, busying herself in Nancy's kitchen.

"Why not the President too?"

"Seriously, Dad. This is the third Sunday she's lain down like that after dinner. Is she that way at home?"

"A regular love affair with the bed. Every time I start to talk to her."

Good protective reaction, observed Nancy to herself. The workings of hos-til-ity.

"Nancy could take her. I just don't like how she looks. Let's have Nancy arrange an appointment."

"You think she'll go?" regarding his wife gloomily. "All right, we have to have doctor bills, we have to have doctor bills." Loudly: "Something hurts you?"

She startled, looked to his lips. He repeated: "Mrs. Take It Easy, something hurts?"

"Nothing. . . . Only you."

"A woman of honey. That's why you're lying down?"

"Soon I'll get up to do the dishes, Nancy."

"Leave them, Mother, I like it better this way."

"Mrs. Take It Easy, Paul says you should start ballet. You should go to see a doctor and ask: how soon can you start ballet?"

"A doctor?" she begged. "Ballet?"

"We were talking, Ma," explained Paul, "you don't seem any too well. It would be a good idea for you to see a doctor for a checkup."

"I get up now to do the kitchen. Doctors are bills and foolishness, my son. I need no doctors."

"At the Haven," he could not resist pointing out, "a doctor is *not* bills. He lives beside you. You start to sneeze, he is there before you open up a Kleenex. You can be sick there for free, all you want."

"Diarrhea of the mouth, is there a doctor to make you dumb?"

"Ma. Promise me you'll go. Nancy will arrange it."

2 *Olshana,* a village in the Soviet Union.

"It's all of a piece when you think of it," said Nancy, "the way she attacks my kitchen, scrubbing under every cup hook, doing the inside of the oven so I can't enjoy Sunday dinner, knowing that half-blind or not, she's going to find every speck of dirt. . . ."

"Don't, Nancy, I've told you–it's the only way she knows to be useful. What did the *doctor* say?"

"A real fatherly lecture. Sixty-nine is young these days. Go out, enjoy life, find interests. Get a new hearing aid, this one is antiquated. Old age is sickness only if one makes it so. Geriatrics, Inc."

"So there was nothing physical."

"Of course there was. How can you live to yourself like she does without there being? Evidence of a kidney disorder, and her blood count is low. He gave her a diet, and she's to come back for follow-up and lab work. . . . But he was clear enough: Number One prescription–start living like a human being. . . . When I think of your dad, who could really play the invalid with that arthritis of his, as active as a teenager, and twice as much fun. . . ."

"You didn't tell me the doctor says your sickness is in you, how you live." He pushed his advantage. "Life and enjoyments you need better than medicine. And this diet, how can you keep it? To weigh each morsel and scrape away each bit of fat, to make this soup, that pudding. There, at the Haven, they have a dietician, they would do it for you."

She is silent.

"You would feel better there, I know it," he says gently. "There there is life and enjoyments all around."

"What is the matter, Mr. Importantbusy, you have no card game or meeting you can go to?"–turning her face to the pillow.

For a while he cut his meetings and going out, fussed over her diet, tried to wheedle her into leaving the house, brought in visitors:

"I should come to a fashion tea. I should sit and look at pretty babies in clothes I cannot buy. This is pleasure?"

"Always you are better than everyone else. The doctor said you should go out. Mrs. Brem comes to you with goodness and you turn her away."

"Because *you* asked her to, she asked me."

"They won't come back. People you need, the doctor said. Your own cousins I asked; they were willing to come and make peace as if nothing had happened. . . ."

"No more crushers of people, pushers, hypocrites, around me. No more in *my* house. You go to them if you like."

"Kind he is to visit. And you, like ice."
"A babbler. All my life around babblers. Enough!"

"She's even worse, Dad? Then let her stew a while," advised Nancy. "You can't let it destroy you; it's a psychological thing, maybe too far gone for any of us to help."

So he let her stew. More and more she lay silent in bed, and sometimes did not even get up to make the meals. No longer was the tongue-lashing inevitable if he left the coffee cup where it did not belong, or forgot to take out the garbage or mislaid the broom. The birds grew bold that summer and for once pocked the pears, undisturbed.

A bellyful of bitterness and every day the same quarrel in a new way and a different old grievance the quarrel forced her to enter and relive. And the new torment: I am not really sick, the doctor said it, then why do I feel so sick?

One night she asked him: "You have a meeting tonight? Do not go. Stay . . . with me."

He had planned to watch "This Is Your Life," but half sick himself from the heavy heat, and sickening therefore the more after the brooks and woods of the Haven, with satisfaction he grated:

"Hah, Mrs. Live Alone And Like It wants company all of a sudden. It doesn't seem so good the time of solitary when she was a girl exile in Siberia. 'Do not go. Stay with me.' A new song for Mrs. Free As A Bird. Yes, I am going out, and while I am gone chew this aloneness good, and think how you keep us both from where if you want people, you do not need to be alone."

"Go, go. All your life you have gone without me."

After him she sobbed curses he had not heard in years, old-country curses from their childhood: Grow, oh shall you grow like an onion, with your head in the ground. Like the hide of a drum shall you be, beaten in life, beaten in death. Oh shall you be like a chandelier, to hang, and to burn. . . .

She was not in their bed when he came back. She lay on the cot on the sun porch. All week she did not speak or come near him; nor did he try to make peace or care for her.

He slept badly, so used to her next to him. After all the years, old harmonies and dependencies deep in their bodies; she curled to him, or he coiled to her, each warmed, warming, turning as the other turned, the nights a long embrace.

It was not the empty bed or the storm that woke him, but a faint singing. *She* was singing. Shaking off the drops of rain, the lightning riving her lifted face, he saw her so; the cot covers on the floor.

"This is a private concert?" he asked. "Come in, you are wet."

"I can breathe now," she answered; "my lungs are rich." Though indeed the sound was hardly a breath.

"Come in, come in." Loosing the bamboo shades. "Look how wet you are." Half helping, half carrying her, still faint-breathing her song.

A Russian love song of fifty years ago.

He had found a buyer, but before he told her, he called together those children who were close enough to come. Paul, of course, Sammy from New Jersey, Hannah from Connecticut, Vivi from Ohio.

With a kindling of energy for her beloved visitors, she arrayed the house, cooked and baked. She was not prepared for the solemn after-dinner conclave, they too probing in and tearing. Her frightened eyes watched from mouth to mouth as each spoke.

His stories were eloquent and funny of her refusal to go back to the doctor; of the scorned invitations; of her stubborn silence or the bile "like a Niagara"; of her contrariness: "If I clean it's no good how I cleaned; if I don't clean, I'm still a master who thinks he has a slave."

(Vinegar he poured on me all his life; I am well marinated; how can I be honey now?)

Deftly he marched in the rightness for moving to the Haven; their money from social security free for visiting the children, not sucked into daily needs and into the house; the activities in the Haven for him; but mostly the Haven for *her:* her health, her need of care, distraction, amusement, friends who shared her interests.

"This does offer an outlet for Dad," said Paul; "he's always been an active person. And economic peace of mind isn't to be sneezed at, either. I could use a little of that myself."

But when they asked: "And you, Ma, how do you feel about it?" could only whisper:

"For him it is good. It is not for me. I can no longer live between people."

"You lived all your life *for* people," Vivi cried.

"Not with." Suffering doubly for the unhappiness on her children's faces.

"You have to find some compromise," Sammy insisted. "Maybe sell the house and buy a trailer. After forty-seven years there's surely some way you can find to live in peace."

"There is no help, my children. Different things we need."

"Then live alone!" He could control himself no longer. "I have a buyer for the house. Half the money for you, half for me. Either alone or with me to the Haven. You think I can live any longer as we are doing now?"

"Ma doesn't have to make a decision this minute, however you feel, Dad," Paul said quickly, "and you wouldn't want her to. Let's let it lay a few months, and then talk some more."

"I think I can work it out to take Mother home with me for a while," Hannah said. "You both look terrible, but especially you, Mother. I'm going to ask Phil to have a look at you."

"Sure," cracked Sammy. "What's the use of a doctor husband if you can't get free service out of him once in a while for the family? And absence might make the heart . . . you know."

"There was something after all," Paul told Nancy in a colorless voice. "That was Hannah's Phil calling. Her gall bladder. . . . Surgery."

"Her *gall* bladder. If that isn't classic. 'Bitter as gall'—talk of psychosom—"

He stepped closer, put his hand over her mouth, and said in the same colorless, plodding voice. "We have to get Dad. They operated at once. The cancer was everywhere, surrounding the liver, everywhere. They did what they could . . . at best she has a year. Dad . . . we have to tell him."

## II

Honest in his weakness when they told him, and that she was not to know. "I'm not an actor. She'll know right away by how I am. Oh that poor woman. I am old too, it will break me into pieces. Oh that poor woman. She will spit on me: 'So my sickness was how I live.' Oh Paulie, how she will be, that poor woman. Only she should not suffer. . . . I can't stand sickness, Paulie, I can't go with you."

But went. And play-acted.

"A grand opening and you did not even wait for me. . . . A good thing Hannah took you with her."

"Fashion teas I needed. They cut out what tore in me; just in my throat something hurts yet. . . . Look! so many flowers, like a funeral. Vivi called, did Hannah tell you? And Lennie from San Francisco, and Clara; and Sammy is coming." Her gnome's face pressed happily into the flowers.

It is impossible to predict in these cases, but once over the immediate effects of the operation, she should have several months of comparative well-being.

*The money, where will come the money?*

Travel with her, Dad. Don't take her home to the old associations. The other children will want to see her.

*The money, where will I wring the money?*

Whatever happens, she is not to know. No, you can't ask her to sign papers to sell the house; nothing to upset her. Borrow instead, then after. . . .

*I had wanted to leave you each a few dollars to make life easier, as other fathers do. There will be nothing left now.* (*Failure! you and your "business is exploitation." Why didn't you make it when it could be made?—Is that what you're thinking, Sammy?*)

Sure she's unreasonable, Dad—but you have to stay with her; if there's to be any happiness in what's left of her life, it depends on you.

*Prop me up, children, think of me, too. Shuffled, chained with her, bitter woman. No Haven, and the little money* going. . . . *How happy she looks, poor creature.*

The look of excitement. The straining to hear everything (the new hearing aid turned full). Why are you so happy, dying woman?

How the petals are, fold on fold, and the gladioli color. The autumn air.

Stranger grandsons, tall above the little gnome grandmother, the little spry grandfather. Paul in a frenzy of picture-taking before going.

She, wandering the great house. Feeling the books; laughing at the maple shoemaker's bench of a hundred years ago used as a table. The ear turned to music.

"Let us go home. See how good I walk now." "One step from the hospital," he answers, "and she wants to fly. Wait till Doctor Phil says."

"Look—the birds too are flying home. Very good Phil is and will not show it, but he is sick of sickness by the time he comes home."

"Mrs. Telepathy, to read minds," he answers; "read mine what it says: when the trunks of medicines become a suitcase, then we will go."

The grandboys, they do not know what to say to us. . . . Hannah, she runs around here, there, when is there time for herself?

Let us go home. Let us go home.

Musing; gentleness—*but for the incidents of the rabbi in the hospital, and of the candles of benediction.*

*Of the rabbi in the hospital:*

Now tell me what happened, Mother.

From the sleep I awoke, Hannah's Phil, and he stands there like a devil in a dream and calls me by name. I cannot hear. I think he prays. Go away, please, I tell him, I am not a believer. Still he stands, while my heart knocks with fright.

You scared *him,* Mother. He thought you were delirious.

Who sent him? Why did he come to me?

It is a custom. The men of God come to visit those of their religion they might help. The hospital makes up the list for them—race, religion—and you are on the Jewish list.

Not for rabbis. At once go and make them change. Tell them to write: Race, human; Religion, none.

*And of the candles of benediction:*

Look how you have upset yourself, Mrs. Excited Over Nothing. Pleasant memories you should leave.

Go in, go back to Hannah and the lights. Two weeks I saw candles and said nothing. But she asked me.

So what was so terrible? She forgets you never did, she asks you to light the Friday candles and say the benediction like Phil's mother when she visits. If the candles give her pleasure, why shouldn't she have the pleasure?

Not for pleasure she does it. For emptiness. Because his family does. Because all around her do.

That is not a good reason too? But you did not hear her. For heritage, she told you. For the boys, from the past they should have tradition.

Superstition! From our ancestors, savages, afraid of the dark, of themselves: mumbo words and magic lights to scare away ghosts.

She told you: how it started does not take away the goodness. For centuries, peace in the house it means.

Swindler! does she look back on the dark centuries? Candles bought instead of bread and stuck into a potato for a candlestick? Religion that stifled and said: in Paradise, woman, you will be the footstool of your husband, and in life—poor chosen Jew—ground under, despised, trembling in cellars. And cremated. And cremated.

This is religion's fault? You think you are still an orator of the 1905 revolution? [3] Where are the pills for quieting? Which are they?

Heritage. How have we come from our savage past, how no longer to be savages—this to teach. To look back and learn what humanizes—this to teach. To smash all ghettos that divide us—

[3] *1905 revolution,* an unsuccessful attempt to establish a democratic government in czarist Russia.

not to go back, not to go back—this to teach. Learned books in the house, will humankind live or die, and she gives to her boys —superstition.

Hannah that is so good to you. Take your pill, Mrs. Excited For Nothing, swallow.

Heritage! But when did I have time to teach? Of Hannah I asked only hands to help.

Swallow.

Otherwise—musing; gentleness.

Not to travel. To go home.

The children want to see you. We have to show them you are as thorny a flower as ever.

Not to travel.

Vivi wants you should see her new baby. She sent the tickets—airplane tickets—a Mrs. Roosevelt[4] she wants to make of you. To Vivi's we have to go.

A new baby. How many warm, seductive babies. She holds him stiffly, *away* from her, so that he wails. And a long shudder begins, and the sweat beads on her forehead.

"Hush, shush," croons the grandfather, lifting him back. "You should forgive your grandmamma, little prince, she has never held a baby before, only seen them in glass cases. Hush, shush."

"You're tired, Ma," says Vivi. "The travel and the noisy dinner. I'll take you to lie down."

(*A long travel from, to, what the feel of a baby evokes.*)

In the airplane, cunningly designed to encase from motion (no wind, no feel of flight), she had sat severely and still, her face turned to the sky through which they cleaved and left no scar.

So this was how it looked, the determining, the crucial sky, and this was how man moved through it, remote above the dwindled earth, the concealed human life. Vulnerable life, that could scar.

There was a steerage ship of memory that shook across a great, circular sea: clustered, ill human beings; and through the thick-stained air, tiny fretting waters in a window round like the airplane's—sun round, moon round. (The round thatched roofs of Olshana.) Eye round—like the smaller window that framed distance the solitary year of exile when only her eyes could travel, and no voice spoke. And the polar winds hurled themselves across snows trackless and

---

[4] *Mrs. Roosevelt,* Eleanor Roosevelt (1884–1962), President Franklin D. Roosevelt's wife, noted for her worldwide travels.

endless and white—like the clouds which had closed together below and hidden the earth.

Now they put a baby in her lap. Do not ask me, she would have liked to beg. Enough the worn face of Vivi, the remembered grandchildren. I cannot, cannot. . . .

*Cannot what?* Unnatural grandmother, not able to make herself embrace a baby.

She lay there in the bed of the two little girls, her new hearing aid turned full, listening to the sound of the children going to sleep, the baby's fretful crying and hushing, the clatter of dishes being washed and put away. They thought she slept. Still she rode on.

It was not that she had not loved her babies, her children. The love—the passion of tending—had risen with the need like a torrent; and like a torrent drowned and immolated all else. But when the need was done—oh the power that was lost in the painful damming back and drying up of what still surged, but had nowhere to go. Only the thin pulsing left that could not quiet, suffering over lives one felt, but could no longer hold nor help.

On that torrent she had borne them to their own lives, and the riverbed was desert long years now. Not there would she dwell, a memoried wraith. Surely that was not all, surely there was more. Still the springs, the springs were in her seeking. Somewhere an older power that beat for life. Somewhere coherence, transport, meaning. If they would but leave her in the air now stilled of clamor, in the reconciled solitude, to journey on.

And they put a baby in her lap. Immediacy to embrace, and the breath of *that* past: warm flesh like this that had claims and nuzzled away all else and with lovely mouths devoured; hot-living like an animal—intensely and now; the turning maze; the long drunkenness; the drowning into needing and being needed. Severely she looked back—and the shudder seized her again, and the sweat. Not that way. Not there, not now could she, not yet. . . .

And all that visit, she could not touch the baby.

"Daddy, is it the . . . sickness she's like that?" asked Vivi. "I was so glad to be having the baby—for her. I told Tim, it'll give her more happiness than anything, being around a baby again. And she hasn't played with him once."

He was not listening. "Aahh little seed of life, little charmer," he crooned, "Hollywood should see you. A heart of ice you would melt. Kick, kick. The future you'll have for a ball. In 2050 still kick. Kick for your grandaddy then."

Attentive with the older children; sat through their performances (command performance; we command you to be the audience); helped

Ann sort autumn leaves to find the best for a school program; listened gravely to Richard tell about his rock collection, while her lips mutely formed the words to remember: *igneous, sedimentary, metamorphic;*[5] looked for missing socks, books, and bus tickets; watched the children whoop after their grandfather who knew how to tickle, chuck, lift, toss, do tricks tell secrets, make jokes, match riddle for riddle. (Tell me a riddle, Grammy. I know no riddles, child.) Scrubbed sills and woodwork and furniture in every room; folded the laundry; straightened drawers; emptied the heaped baskets waiting for ironing (while he or Vivi or Tim nagged: You're supposed to rest here, you've been sick) but to none tended or gave food—and could not touch the baby.

After a week she said: "Let us go home. Today call about the tickets."

"You have important business, Mrs. Inahurry? The President waits to consult with you?" He shouted, for the fear of the future raced in him. "The clothes are still warm from the suitcase, your children cannot show enough how glad they are to see you, and you want home. There is plenty of time for home. We cannot be with the children at home."

"Blind to around you as always: the little ones sleep four in a room because we take their bed. We are two more people in a house with a new baby, and no help."

"Vivi is happy so. The children should have their grandparents a while, she told to me. I should have my mommy and daddy. . . ."

"Babbler and blind. Do you look at her so tired? How she starts to talk and she cries? I am not strong enough yet to help. Let us go home."

(To reconciled solitude.)

*For it seemed to her the crowded noisy house was listening to her, listening* for *her. She could feel it like a great ear pressed under her heart. And everything knocked: quick constant raps: let me in, let me in.*

*How was it that soft reaching tendrils also became blows that knocked?*

C'mon, Grandma, I want to show you. . . .

Tell me a riddle, Grandma. (*I know no riddles.*)

Look, Grammy, he's so dumb he can't even find his hands. (Dody and the baby on a blanket over the fermenting autumn mould.)

---

[5] *igneous . . . metamorphic,* three basic categories of rocks.

I made them—for you. (Ann) (Flat paper dolls with aprons that lifted on scalloped skirts that lifted on flowered pants; hair of yarn and great ringed questioning eyes.)
Watch me, Grandma. (Richard snaking up the tree, hanging exultant, free, with one hand at the top. Below Dody hunching over in pretend-cooking.) (*Climb too, Dody, climb and look.*)
Be my nap bed, Grammy. (The "No!" too late.) Morty's abandoned heaviness, while his fingers ladder up and down her hearing-aid cord to his drowsy chant: eentsiebeentsiespider. (*Children trust.*)
It's to start off your own rock collection, Grandma. That's a trilobite fossil, 200 million years old (millions of years on a boy's mouth) and that one's obsidian, black glass.

*Knocked and knocked.*

Mother, I *told* you the teacher said we had to bring it back all filled out this morning. Didn't you even ask Daddy? Then tell *me* which plan and I'll check it: evacuate or stay in the city or wait for you to come and take me away. (Seeing the look of straining to hear.) It's for Disaster, Grandma. (*Children trust.*)

Vivi in the maze of the long, the lovely drunkenness. The old old noises: baby sounds; screaming of a mother flayed to exasperation; children quarreling; children playing; singing; laughter.

*And Vivi's tears and memories,* spilling so fast, half the words not understood.

She had started remembering out loud deliberately, so her mother would know the past was cherished, still lived in her.

Nursing the baby: My friends marvel, and I tell them, oh it's easy to be such a cow. I remember how beautiful my mother seemed nursing my brother, and the milk just flows. . . . Was that Davy? It must have been Davy. . . .

Lowering a hem: How did you ever . . . when I think how you made everything we wore . . . Tim, just think, seven kids and Mommy sewed everything . . . do I remember you sang while you sewed? That white dress with the red apples on the skirt you fixed over for me, was it Hannah's or Clara's before it was mine?

Washing sweaters: Ma, I'll never forget, one of those days so nice you washed clothes outside; one of the first spring days it must have been. The bubbles just danced while you scrubbed, and we chased after, and you stopped to show us how to blow our own bubbles with green onion stalks . . . you always. . . .

"Strong onion, to still make you cry after so many years," her father said, to turn the tears into laughter.

While Richard bent over his homework: Where is it now, do we still have it, the Book of the Martyrs? It always seemed so, well—exalted, when you'd put it on the round table and we'd all look at it together; there was even a halo from the lamp. The lamp with the beaded fringe you could move up and down; they're in style again, pulley lamps like that, but without the fringe. You know the book I'm talking about, Daddy, the Book of the Martyrs, the first picture was a bust of Spartacus . . . Socrates? I wish there was something like that for the children, Mommy, to give them what you. . . . (And the tears splashed again.)

(What I intended and did not? Stop it, daughter, stop it, leave that time. And he, the hyprocrite, sitting there with tears in his eyes —it was nothing to you then, nothing.)

. . . The time you came to school and I almost died of shame because of your accent and because I knew you knew I was ashamed; how could I? . . . Sammy's harmonica and you danced to it once, yes you did, you and Davy squealing in your arms. . . . That time you bundled us up and walked us down to the railway station to stay the night 'cause it was heated and we didn't have any coal, that winter of the strike, you didn't think I remembered that, did you, Mommy? . . . How you'd call us out to see the sunsets. . . .

Day after day, the spilling memories. Worse now, questions, too. Even the grandchildren: Grandma, in the olden days, when you were little. . . .

It was the afternoons that saved.

While they thought she napped, she would leave the mosaic on the wall (of children's drawings, maps, calendars, pictures, Ann's cardboard dolls with their great ringed questioning eyes) and hunch in the girls' closet on the low shelf where the shoes stood, and the girls' dresses covered.

For that while she would painfully sheathe against the listening house, the tendrils and noises that knocked, and Vivi's spilling memories. Sometimes it helped to braid and unbraid the sashes that dangled, or to trace the pattern on the hoop slips.

Today she had jacks and children under jet trails to forget. Last night, Ann and Dody silhouetted in the window against a sunset of flaming man-made clouds of jet trail, their jacks ball accenting the peaceful noise of dinner being made. Had she told them, yes she had told them of how they played jacks in her village though there was no ball, no jacks. Six stones, round and flat, toss them out, the seventh on the back of the hand, toss, catch and swoop up as many as possible, toss again. . . .

Of stones (repeating Richard) there are three kinds: earth's fire jetting; rock of layered centuries; crucibled new out of the old (*igne-*

*ous, sedimentary, metamorphic*). But there was that other—frozen to black glass, never to transform or hold the fossil memory . . . (let not my seed fall on stone). There was an ancient man who fought to heights a great rock that crashed back down eternally—eternal labor, freedom, labor . . . (stone will perish, but the word remain).[6] And you, David, who with a stone slew, screaming: Lord, take my heart of stone and give me flesh.

*Who* was screaming? Why was she back in the common room of the prison, the sun motes dancing in the shafts of light, and the informer being brought in, a prisoner now, like themselves. And Lisa leaping, yes, Lisa, the gentle and tender, biting at the betrayer's jugular. Screaming and screaming.

No, it is the children screaming. Another of Paul and Sammy's terrible fights?

In Vivi's house. Severely: you are in Vivi's house.

Blows, screams, a call: "Grandma!" For her? Oh please not for her. Hide, hunch behind the dresses deeper. But a trembling little body hurls itself beside her—surprised, smothered laughter, arms surround her neck, tears rub dry on her cheek, and words too soft to understand whisper into her ear (Is this where you hide too, Grammy? It's my secret place, we have a secret now).

And the sweat beads, and the long shudder seizes.

It seemed the great ear pressed inside now, and the knocking. "We have to go home," she told him, "I grow ill here."

"It's your own fault, Mrs. Bodybusy, you do not rest, you do too much." He raged, but the fear was in his eyes. "It was a serious operation, they told you to take care. . . . All right, we will go to where you can rest."

But where? Not home to death, not yet. He had thought to Lennie's, to Clara's; beautiful visits with each of the children. She would have to rest first, be stronger. If they could but go to Florida—it glittered before him, the never-realized promise of Florida. California: of course. (The money, the money, dwindling!) Los Angeles first for sun and rest, then to Lennie's in San Francisco.

He told her the next day. "You saw what Nancy wrote: snow and wind back home, a terrible winter. And look at you—all bones and a swollen belly. I called Phil: he said: 'A prescription, Los Angeles sun and rest.' "

She watched the words on his lips: "You have sold the house," she

---

[6] An allusion to the Greek myth of Sisyphus, a cruel king condemned forever to roll a boulder up a hill in Hades only to have it roll down again each time he neared the top.

cried, "that is why we do not go home. That is why you talk no more of the Haven, why there is money for travel. After the children you will drag me to the Haven."

"The Haven! Who thinks of the Haven any more? Tell her, Vivi, tell Mrs. Suspicious: a prescription, sun and rest, to make you healthy. . . . And how could I sell the house without *you?*"

At the place of farewells and greetings, of winds of coming and winds of going, they say their good-byes.

They look back at her with the eyes of others before them: Richard with her own blue blaze; Ann with the nordic eyes of Tim; Morty's dreaming brown of a great-grandmother he will never know: Dody with the laughing eyes of him who had been her springtide love (who stands beside her now); Vivi's, all tears.

The baby's eyes are closed in sleep.

*Good-bye, my children.*

## III

It is to the back of the great city he brought her, to the dwelling places of the cast-off old. Bounded by two lines of amusement piers to the north and to the south, and between a long straight paving rimmed with black benches facing the sand—sands so wide the ocean is only a far fluting.

In the brief vacation season, some of the boarded stores fronting the sands open, and families, young people and children, may be seen. A little tasselled tram shuttles between the piers, and the lights of roller coasters prink and tweak over those who come to have sensation made in them.

The rest of the year it is abandoned to the old, all else boarded up and still; seemingly empty, except the occasional days and hours when the sun, like a tide, sucks them out of the low rooming houses, casts them onto the benches and sandy rim of the walk—and sweeps them into decaying enclosures once again.

A few newer apartments glint among the low bleached squares. It is in one of these Lennie's Jeannie has arranged their rooms. "Only a few miles north and south people pay hundreds of dollars a month for just this gorgeous air, Grandaddy, just this ocean closeness."

She had been ill on the plane, lay ill for days in the unfamiliar room. Several times the doctor came by—left medicine she would not take. Several times Jeannie drove in the twenty miles from work, still in her Visiting Nurse uniform, the lightness and brightness of her like a healing.

"Who can believe it is winter?" he asked one morning. "Beautiful it is outside like an ad. Come, Mrs. Invalid, come to taste it. You are well enough to sit in here, you are well enough to sit outside. The doctor said it too."

But the benches were encrusted with people, and the sands at the sidewalk's edge. Besides, she had seen the far ruffle of the sea: "there take me," and though she leaned against him, it was she who led.

Plodding and plodding, sitting often to rest, he grumbling. Patting the sand so warm. Once she scooped up a handful, cradling it close to her better eye; peered, and flung it back. And as they came almost to the brink and she could see the glistening wet, she sat down, pulled off her shoes and stockings, left him and began to run. "You'll catch cold," he screamed, but the sand in his shoes weighed him down—he who had always been the agile one—and already the white spray creamed her feet.

He pulled her back, took a handkerchief to wipe off the wet and the sand. "Oh no," she said, "the sun will dry," seized the square and smoothed it flat, dropped on it a mound of sand, knotted the kerchief corners and tied it to a bag—"to look at with the strong glass" (for the first time in years explaining an action of hers)—and lay down with the little bag against her cheek, looking toward the shore that nurtured life as it first crawled toward consciousness the millions of years ago.

He took her one Sunday in the evil-smelling bus, past flat miles of blister houses, to the home of relatives. Oh what is this? she cried as the light began to smoke and the houses to dim and recede. Smog, he said, everyone knows but you. . . . Outside he kept his arms about her, but she walked with hands pushing the heavy air as if to open it, whispered: who has done this? sat down suddenly to vomit at the curb and for a long while refused to rise.

*One's age as seen on the altered face of those known in youth.* Is this they he has come to visit? This Max and Rose, smooth and pleasant, introducing them to polite children, disinterested grandchildren, "the whole family, once a month on Sundays. And why not? We have the room, the help, the food."

Talk of cars, of houses, of success: this son that, that daughter this. And *your* children? Hastily skimped over, the intermarriages, the obscure work—"my doctor son-in-law, Phil"—all he has to offer. She silent in a corner. (Car-sick like a baby, he explains.) Years since he has taken her to visit anyone but the children, and old apprehensions prickle: "no incidents," he silently begs, "no incidents." He itched to tell them. "A very sick woman," significantly, indicating her with his eyes, "a very sick woman." Their restricted faces did not react. "Have you thought maybe she'd do better at Palm Springs?" Rose asked. "Or at least a nicer section of the beach, nicer people, a pool." Not to have to say "money" he said instead: "would she have sand to look at through a magnifying glass?" and went on, detail after detail, the old habit betraying of parading the queerness of her for laughter.

After dinner—the others into the living room in men- or women-clusters, or into the den to watch TV—the four of them alone. She sat close to him, and did not speak. Jokes, stories, people they had known, beginning of reminiscence, Russia fifty-six years ago. Strange words across the Duncan Phyfe[7] table: *hunger; secret meetings; human rights; spies; betrayals; prison; escape*—interrupted by one of the grandchildren: "Commercial's on; any Coke left? Gee, you're missing a real hair-raiser." And then a granddaughter (Max proudly: "look at her, an American queen") drove them home on her way back to U.C.L.A. No incident—except that there had been no incidents.

The first few mornings she had taken with her the magnifying glass, but he would sit only on the benches, so she rested at the foot, where slatted bench shadows fell, and unless she turned her hearing aid down, other voices invaded.

Now on the days when the sun shone and she felt well enough, he took her on the tram to where the benches ranged in oblongs, some with tables for checkers or cards. Again the blanket on the sand in the striped shadows, but she no longer brought the magnifying glass. He played cards, and she lay in the sun and looked towards the waters; or they walked—two blocks down to the scaling hotel, two blocks back—past chili-hamburger stands, open-doored bars, Next -to- New and perpetual rummage sale stores.

Once, out of the aimless walkers, slow and shuffling like themselves, someone ran unevenly towards them, embraced, kissed, wept: "dear friends, old friends." A friend of *hers,* not his: Mrs. Mays who had lived next door to them in Denver when the children were small.

Thirty years are compressed into a dozen sentences; and the present, not even in three. All is told: the children scattered; the husband dead; she lives in a room two blocks up from the sing hall—and points to the domed auditorium jutting before the pier. The leg? phlebitis; the heavy breathing? that, one does not ask. She, too, comes to the benches each day to sit. And tomorrow, tomorrow, are they going to the community sing? Of course he would have heard of it, everybody goes—the big doings they wait for all week. They

[7] *Duncan Phyfe* (1768–1854), a Scottish-American furniture maker renowned for the excellence and elegance of his tables, chairs, and couches.

have never been? She will come to them for dinner tomorrow and they will all go together.

*So it is that she sits in the wind of the singing, among the thousand various faces of age.*

*She had turned off her hearing aid at once they came into the auditorium—as she would have wished to turn off sight.*

*One by one they streamed by and imprinted on her—and though the savage zest of their singing came voicelessly soft and distant, the faces still roared—the faces densened the air—chorded into*

children-chants, mother-croons, singing of the chained
love serenades, Beethoven storms, mad Lucia's scream
drunken joy-songs, keens for the dead, work-singing

> *while from floor to balcony to dome a bare-footed sore-covered little girl threaded the sound-thronged tumult, danced her ecstasy of grimace to flutes that scratched at a cross-roads village wedding*

*Yes, faces became sound, and the sound became faces; and faces and sound became weight—pushed, pressed*

"Air"—her hands claw his.

"Whenever I enjoy myself. . . ." Then he saw the gray sweat on her face. "Here. Up. Help me, Mrs. Mays," and they support her out to where she can gulp the air in sob after sob.

"A doctor, we should get for her a doctor."

"Tch, it's nothing," says Ellen Mays. "I get it all the time. You've missed the tram; come to my place. Fix your hearing aid, honey . . . close . . . tea. My view. See, she *wants* to come. Steady now, that's how." Adding mysteriously: "Remember your advice, easy to keep your head above water, empty things float. Float."

The singing a fading march for them, tall woman with a swollen leg, weaving little man, and the swollen thinness they help between.

The stench in the hall: mildew? decay? "We sit and rest then climb. My gorgeous view. We help each other and here we are."

The stench along into the slab of room. A washstand for a sink, a box with oilcloth tacked around for a cupboard, a three-burner gas plate. Artificial flowers, colorless with dust. Everywhere pictures foaming: wedding, baby, party, vacation, graduation, family pictures. From the narrow couch under a slit of window, sure enough the view: lurching rooftops and a scallop of ocean heaving, preening, twitching under the moon.

"While the water heats. Excuse me . . . down the hall." Ellen Mays has gone.

"You'll live?" he asks mechanically, sat down to feel his fright; tried to pull her alongside.

She pushed him away. "For air," she said; stood clinging to the dresser. Then, in a terrible voice:

After a lifetime of room. Of many rooms.

Shhh.

You remember how she lived. Eight children. And now one room like a coffin.

She pays rent!

Shrinking the life of her   into one room   like a coffin   Rooms and rooms like this   I lie on the quilt and hear them talk

Please, Mrs. Orator-without-Breath.

Once you went for coffee   I walked   I saw   A Balzac[8]   a Chekhov to write it   Rummage   Alone   On scraps

Better old here than in the old country!

On scraps   Yet they sang like   like   Wondrous! *Humankind one has to believe*   So strong   for what? To rot   not grow?

Your poor lungs beg you. They sob between each word.

Singing.   Unused   the life in them.   She   in this poor room with her pictures   Max   You   The children   Everywhere unused the life   And who has meaning?   Century after century still all in us   not   to grow?

Coffins, rummage, plants: sick woman. Oh lay down. We will get for you the doctor.

"And when will it end. Oh, *the end.*" *That* nightmare thought, and this time she writhed, crumpled against him, seized his hand (for a moment again the weight, the soft distant roaring of humanity) and on the strangled-for breath, begged: "Man. . . we'll destroy ourselves?"

And looking for answer—in the helpless pity and fear for her (for *her*) that distorted his face—she understood the last months, and knew that she was dying.

## IV

"Let us go home," she said after several days.

"You are in training for a cross-country run? That is why you do not even walk across the room? Here, like a prescription Phil said,

[8] *Balzac,* Honoré de Balzac (1799–1850), French writer.

till you are stronger from the operation. You want to break doctor's orders?"

She saw the fiction was necessary to him, was silent; then: "At home I will get better. If the doctor here says?"

"And winter? And the visits to Lennie and to Clara? All right," for he saw the tears in her eyes, "I will write Phil, and talk to the doctor."

Days passed. He reported nothing. Jeannie came and took her out for air, past the boarded concessions, the hooded and tented amusement rides, to the end of the pier. They watched the spent waves feeding the new, the gulls in the clouded sky; even up where they sat, the wind-blown sand stung.

She did not ask to go down the crooked steps to the sea.

Back in her bed, while he was gone to the store, she said: "Jeannie, this doctor, he is not one I can ask questions. Ask him for me, can I go home?"

Jeannie looked at her, said quickly: "Of course, poor Granny. You want your own things around you, don't you? I'll call him tonight. . . . Look, I've something to show you," and from her purse unwrapped a large cookie, intricately shaped like a little girl. "Look at the curls—can you hear me well, Granny?—and the darling eyelashes. I just came from a house where they were baking them."

"The dimples, there in the knees," she marveled, holding it to the better light, turning, studying, "like art. Each singly they cut, or a mold?"

"Singly," said Jeannie, "and if it is a child only the mother can make them. Oh Granny, it's the likeness of a real little girl who died yesterday—Rosita. She was three years old. *Pan del Muerto,* the Bread of the Dead. It was the custom in the part of Mexico they came from."

Still she turned and inspected. "Look, the hollow in the throat, the little cross necklace. . . . I think for the mother it is a good thing to be busy with such bread. You know the family?"

Jeannie nodded. "On my rounds. I nursed. . . . Oh Granny, it is like a party; they play songs she liked to dance to. The coffin is lined with pink velvet and she wears a white dress. There are candles. . . ."

"In the house?" Surprised, "They keep her in the house?"

"Yes," said Jeannie, "and it is against the health law. The father said it will be sad to bury her in this country; in Oaxaca[9] they have a feast night with candles each year; everyone picnics on the graves of those they loved until dawn."

---

[9] *Oaxaca,* the name of both a state in Mexico and its capital city.

"Yes, Jeannie, the living must comfort themselves." And closed her eyes.

"You want to sleep, Granny?"

"Yes, tired from the pleasure of you. I may keep the Rosita? There stand it, on the dresser, where I can see; something of my own around me."

In the kitchenette, helping her grandfather unpack the groceries, Jeannie said in her light voice:

"I'm resigning my job, Grandaddy."

"Ah, the lucky young man. Which one is he?"

"Too late. You're spoken for." She made a pyramid of cans, unstacked, and built again.

"Something is wrong with the job?"

"With me. I can't be"—she searched for the word—"What they call professional enough. I let myself feel things. And tomorrow I have to report a family. . . ." The cans clicked again. "It's not that, either. I just don't know what I want to do, maybe go back to school, maybe go to art school. I thought if you went to San Francisco I'd come along and talk it over with Momma and Daddy. But I don't see how you can go. She wants to go home. She asked me to ask the doctor."

The doctor told her himself. "Next week you may travel, when you are a little stronger." But next week there was the fever of an infection, and by the time that was over, she could not leave the bed—a rented hospital bed that stood beside the double bed he slept in alone now.

Outwardly the days repeated themselves. Every other afternoon and evening he went out to his newfound cronies, to talk and play cards. Twice a week, Mrs. Mays came. And the rest of the time, Jeannie was there.

By the sickbed stood Jeannie's FM radio. Often into the room the shapes of music came. She would lie curled on her side, her knees drawn up, intense in listening (Jeannie sketched her so, coiled, convoluted like an ear), then thresh her hand out and abruptly snap the radio mute—still to lie in her attitude of listening, concealing tears.

Once Jeannie brought in a young Marine to visit, a friend from high-school days she had found wandering near the empty pier. Because Jeannie asked him to, gravely, without self-consciousness, he sat himself cross-legged on the floor and performed for them a dance of his native Samoa.

Long after they left, a tiny thrumming sound could be heard

where, in her bed, she strove to repeat the beckon, flight, surrender of his hands, the fluttering footbeats, and his low plaintive calls.

Hannah and Phil sent flowers. To deepen her pleasure, he placed one in her hair. "Like a girl," he said, and brought the hand mirror so she could see. She looked at the pulsing red flower, the yellow skull face; a desolate, excited laugh shuddered from her, and she pushed the mirror away—but let the flower burn.

The week Lennie and Helen came, the fever returned. With it the excited laugh, and incessant words. She, who in her life had spoken but seldom and then only when necessary (never having learned the easy, social uses of words), now in dying, spoke incessantly.

In a half-whisper: "Like Lisa she is, your Jeannie. Have I told you of Lisa who taught me to read? Of the highborn she was, but noble in herself. I was sixteen; they beat me; my father beat me so I would not go to her. It was forbidden, she was a Tolstoyan.[10] At night, past dogs that howled, terrible dogs, my son, in the snows of winter to the road, I to ride in her carriage like a lady, to books. To her, life was holy, knowledge was holy, and she taught me to read. They hung her. Everything that happens one must try to understand why. She killed one who betrayed many. Because of betrayal, betrayed all she lived and believed. In one minute she killed, before my eyes (there is so much blood in a human being, my son), in prison with me. All that happens, one must try to understand.

"The name?" Her lips would work. "The name that was their pole star; the doors of the death houses fixed to open on it; I read of it my year of penal servitude. Thuban!" very excited, "Thuban, in ancient Egypt the pole star. Can you see, look out to see it, Jeannie, if it swings around *our* pole star that seems to *us* not to move.

"Yes, Jeannie, at your age my mother and grandmother had already buried children . . . yes, Jeannie, it is more than oceans between Olshana and you . . . yes, Jeannie, they danced, and for all the bodies they had they might as well be chickens, and indeed, they scratched and flapped their arms and hopped.

"And Andrei Yefimitch, who for twenty years had never known of it and never wanted to know, said as if he wanted to cry: but why my dear friend this malicious laughter?" Telling to herself half-memorized phrases from her few books. "Pain I answer with tears and cries, baseness with indignation, meanness with repulsion . . . for life may be hated or wearied of, but never despised."

---

[10] *Tolstoyan,* a follower of the Russian writer and reformer Leo Tolstoy (1828–1910).

Delirious: "Tell me, my neighbor, Mrs. Mays, the pictures never lived, but what of the flowers? Tell them who ask: no rabbis, no ministers, no priests, no speeches, no ceremonies: ah, false—let the living comfort themselves. Tell Sammy's boy, he who flies, tell him to go to Stuttgart[11] and see where Davy has no grave. And what? . . . And what? where millions have no graves—save air."

In delirium or not, wanting the radio on; not seeming to listen, the words still jetting, wanting the music on. Once, silencing it abruptly as of old, she began to cry, unconcealed tears this time. "You have pain, Granny?" Jeannie asked.

"The music," she said, "still it is there and we do not hear; knocks, and our poor human ears too weak. What else, what else we do not hear?"

Once she knocked his hand aside as he gave her a pill, swept the bottles from her bedside table: "no pills, let me feel what I feel," and laughed as on his hands and knees he groped to pick them up. Nighttimes her hand reached across the bed to hold his.

A constant retching began. Her breath was too faint for sustained speech now, but still the lips moved:

*When no longer necessary    to injure others*
*Pick    pick pick    Blind chicken*
*As a human being    responsibility*

"David!" imperious, "Basin!" and she would vomit, rinse her mouth, the wasted throat working to swallow, and begin the chant again.

She will be better off in the hospital now, the doctor said.

He sent the telegrams to the children, was packing her suitcase, when her hoarse voice startled. She had roused, was pulling herself to sitting.

"Where now?" she asked. "Where now do you drag me?"

"You do not even have to have a baby to go this time," he soothed, looking for the brush to pack. "Remember, after Davy you told me—worthy to have a baby for the pleasure of the ten-day rest in the hospital?"

"Where now? Not home yet?" Her voice mourned. "Where *is* my home?"

He rose to ease her back. "The doctor, the hospital," he started to explain, but deftly, like a snake, she had slithered out of bed and stood swaying, propped behind the night table.

---

11 *Stuttgart,* a city in Germany.

"Coward," she hissed, "runner."

"You stand," he said senselessly.

"To take me there and run. Afraid of a little vomit."

He reached her as she fell. She struggled against him, half slipped from his arms, pulled herself up again.

"Weakling," she taunted, "to leave me there and run. Betrayer. All your life you have run."

He sobbed, telling Jeannie. "A Marilyn Monroe to run for her virtue. Fifty-nine pounds she weighs, the doctor said, and she beats at me like a Dempsey.[12] Betrayer, she cries, and I running like a dog when she calls; day and night, running to her, her vomit, the bedpan. . . ."

"She needs you, Grandaddy," said Jeannie. "Isn't that what they call love? I'll see if she sleeps, and if she does, poor worn-out darling, we'll have a party, you and I: I brought us rum babas."

They did not move her. By her bed now stood the tall hooked pillar that held the solutions—blood and dextrose—to feed her veins. Jeannie moved down the hall to take over the sickroom, her face so radiant, her grandfather asked her once: "you are in love?" (Shameful the joy, the pure overwhelming joy from being with her grandmother; the peace, the serenity that breathed.) "My darling escape," she answered incoherently, "my darling Granny"—as if that explained.

Now one by one the children came, those that were able. Hannah, Paul, Sammy. Too late to ask: and what did you learn with your living, Mother, and what do we need to know?

Clara, the eldest, clenched:

*Pay me back, Mother, pay me back for all you took from me. Those others you crowded into your heart. The hands I needed to be for you, the heaviness, the responsibility.*

*Is this she? Noises the dying make, the crablike hands crawling over the covers. The ethereal singing.*

*She hears that music, that singing from childhood; forgotten sound—not heard since, since. . . . And the hardness breaks like a cry: Where did we lose each other, first mother, singing mother?*

*Annulled: the quarrels, the gibing, the harshness between; the fall into silence and the withdrawal.*

*I do not know you, Mother. Mother, I never knew you.*

---

[12] *Dempsey,* Jack Dempsey, the world heavyweight boxing champion from 1919 to 1926.

Lennie, suffering not alone for her who was dying, but for that in her which never lived (for that which in him might never live). From him too, unspoken words: *good-bye Mother who taught me to mother myself.*

Not Vivi, who must stay with her children; not Davy, but he is already here, having to die again with *her* this time, for the living take their dead with them when they die.

Light she grew, like a bird, and, like a bird, sound bubbled in her throat while the body fluttered in agony. Night and day, asleep or awake (though indeed there was no difference now) the songs and the phrases leaping.

And he, who had once dreaded a long dying (from fear of himself, from horror of the dwindling money) now desired her quick death profoundly, for *her* sake. He no longer went out, except when Jeannie forced him; no longer laughed, except when, in the bright kitchenette, Jeannie coaxed his laughter (and she, who seemed to hear nothing else, would laugh too, conspiratorial wisps of laughter).

Light, like a bird, the fluttering body, the little claw hands, the beaked shadow on her face; and the throat, bubbling, straining.

He tried not to listen, as he tried not to look on the face in which only the forehead remained familiar, but trapped with her the long nights in that little room, the sounds worked themselves into his consciousness, with their punctuation of death swallows, whimpers, gurglings.

*Even in reality* (swallow) *life's lack of it*

*Slaveships   deathtrains   clubs   eeenough*

*The bell   summon what enables*

*78,000 in one minute*[13] (whisper of a scream) *78,000 human beings we'll destroy ourselves?*

"Aah, Mrs. Miserable," he said, as if she could hear, "all your life working, and now in bed you lie, servants to tend, you do not even need to call to be tended, and still you work. Such hard work it is to die? Such hard work?"

The body threshed, her hand clung in his. A melody, ghost-thin, hovered on her lips, and like a guilty ghost, the vision of her bent in listening to it, silencing the record instantly he was near. Now, heedless of his presence, he floated the melody on and on.

"Hid it from me," he complained, "how many times you listened to remember it so?" And tried to think when she had first played it, or first begun to silence her few records when he came near—but

---

[13] 78,000 people were killed in the bombing of Hiroshima.

could reconstruct nothing. There was only this room with its tall hooked pillar and its swarm of sounds.

*No man one except through others*
*Strong with the not yet in the now*
*Dogma dead war dead one country*

"It helps, Mrs. Philosopher, words from books? It helps?" And it seemed to him that for seventy years she had hidden a tape recorder, infinitely microscopic, within her, that it had coiled infinite mile on mile, trapping every song, every melody, every word read, heard, and spoken—and that maliciously she was playing back only what said nothing of him, of the children, of their intimate life together.

"Left us indeed, Mrs. Babbler," he reproached, "you who called others babbler and cunningly saved your words. A lifetime you tended and loved, and now not a word of us, for us. Left us indeed? Left me."

And he took out his solitaire deck, shuffled the cards loudly, slapped them down.

*Lift high banner of reason* (tatter of an orator's voice) *justice freedom light*
*Humankind life worthy capacities*
*Seeks* (blur of shudder) *belong human being*

"Words, words," he accused, "and what human beings did *you* seek around you, Mrs. Live Alone, and what humankind think worthy?"

Though even as he spoke, he remembered she had not always been isolated, had not always wanted to be alone (as he knew there had been a voice before this gossamer one; before the hoarse voice that broke from silence to lash, make incidents, shame him—a girl's voice of eloquence that spoke their holiest dreams). But again he could reconstruct, image, nothing of what had been before, or when, or how, it had changed.

Ace, queen, jack. The pillar shadow fell, so, in two tracks; in the mirror depths glistened a moonlike blob, the empty solution bottle. And it worked in him: *of reason and justice and freedom . . . Dogma dead:* he remembered the full quotation, laughed bitterly. "Hah, good you do not know what you say; good Victor Hugo[14] died and did not see it, his twentieth century."

Deuce, ten, five. Dauntlessly she began a song of their youth of belief:

*These things shall be, a loftier race*
*than e'er the world hath known shall rise*

---

[14] *Victor Hugo* (1802–1885), the French author of Romantic novels, poems, and plays, prophesied the triumph of peace and freedom in the twentieth century.

*with flame of freedom in their souls*
*and light of knowledge in their eyes*

King, four, jack "In the twentieth century, hah!"

*They shall be gentle, brave and strong*
*to spill no drop of blood, but dare*
*all . . .*
*on earth and fire and sea and air*

"To spill no drop of blood, hah! So, cadaver, and you too, cadaver Hugo, 'in the twentieth century ignorance will be dead, dogma will be dead, war will be dead, and for all mankind one country—of fulfilment?' Hah!"

*And every life* (long strangling cough) *shall*
*be a song*

The cards fell from his fingers. Without warning, the bereavement and betrayal he had sheltered—compounded through the years—hidden even from himself—revealed itself,

uncoiled,
released,
*sprung*

and with it the monstrous shapes of what had actually happened in the century.

A ravening hunger or thirst seized him. He groped into the kitchenette, switched on all three lights, piled a tray—"you have finished your night snack, Mrs. Cadaver, now I have mine." And he was shocked at the tears that splashed on the tray.

"Salt tears. For free. I forgot to shake on salt?"

Whispered: "Lost, how much I lost."

Escaped to the grandchildren whose childhoods were childish, who had never hungered, who lived unravaged by disease in warm houses of many rooms, had all the school for which they cared, could walk on any street, stood a head taller than their grandparents, towered above—beautiful skins, straight backs, clear straightforward eyes. "Yes, you in Olshana," he said to the town of sixty years ago, "they would be nobility to you."

And was this not the dream then, come true in ways undreamed? he asked.

*And are there no other children in the world?* he answered, as if in her harsh voice.

*And the flame of freedom, the light of knowledge?*
*And the drop, to spill no drop of blood?*

And he thought that at six Jeannie would get up and it would be his turn to go to her room and sleep, that he could press the buzzer and she would come now; that in the afternoon Ellen Mays was coming, and this time they would play cards and he could marvel at how rouge can stand half an inch on the cheek; that in the evening the doctor would come, and he could beg him to be merciful, to stop the feeding solutions, to let her die.

To let her die, and with her their youth of belief out of which her bright, betrayed words foamed; stained words, that on her working lips came stainless.

Hours yet before Jeannie's turn. He could press the buzzer and wake her to come now; he could take a pill, and with it sleep; he could pour more brandy into his milk glass, though what he had poured was not yet touched.

Instead he went back, checked her pulse, gently tended with his knotty fingers as Jeannie had taught.

She was whimpering; her hand crawled across the covers for his. Compassionately he enfolded it, and with his free hand gathered up the cards again. Still was there thirst or hunger ravening in him.

That world of their youth—dark, ignorant, terrible with hate and disease—how was it that living in it, in the midst of corruption, filth, treachery, degradation, they had not mistrusted man nor themselves; had believed so beautifully, so . . . falsely?

"Aaah, children," he said out loud, "how we believed, how we belonged." And he yearned to package for each of the children, the grandchildren, for everyone, *that joyous certainty, that sense of mattering, of moving and being moved, of being one and indivisible with the great of the past, with all that freed, ennobled.* Package it, stand on corners, in front of stadiums and on crowded beaches, knock on doors, give it as a fabled gift.

"And why not in cereal boxes, in soap packages?" he mocked himself. "Aah. You have taken my senses, cadaver."

Words foamed, died unsounded. Her body writhed; she made kissing motions with her mouth. (Her lips moving as she read, poring over the Book of the Martyrs, the magnifying glass superimposed over the heavy eyeglasses.) *Still she believed?* "Eva!" he whispered. "Still you believed? You lived by it? These Things Shall Be?"

"One pound soup meat," she answered distinctly, "one soup bone."

"My ears heard you. Ellen Mays was witness: 'Humankind . . . one has to believe.' " Imploringly: "Eva!"

"Bread, day-old." She was mumbling. "Please, in a wooden box . . . for kindling. The thread, hah, the thread breaks. Cheap thread" —and a gurgling, enormously loud, began in her throat.

"I ask for stone; she gives me bread—day-old." He pulled his hand away, shouted: "Who wanted questions? Everything you have to wake?" Then dully, "Ah, let me help you turn, poor creature."

Words jumbled, cleared. In a voice of crowded terror:

"Paul, Sammy, don't fight.

"Hannah, have I ten hands?

"How can I give it, Clara, how can I give it if I don't have?"

"You lie," he said sturdily, "there was joy too." Bitterly: "Ah how cheap you speak of us at the last."

As if to rebuke him, as if her voice had no relationship with her flailing body, she sang clearly, beautifully, a school song the children had taught her when they were little; begged:

"Not look   my hair   where they cut. . . ."

(The crown of braids shorn.) And instantly he left the mute old woman poring over the Book of the Martyrs; went past the mother treading at the sewing machine, singing with the children; past the girl in her wrinkled prison dress, hiding her hair with scarred hands, lifting to him her awkward, shamed, imploring eyes of love; and took her in his arms, dear, personal, fleshed, in all the heavy passion he had loved to rouse from her.

"Eva!"

Her little claw hand beat the covers. How much, how much can a man stand? He took up the cards, put them down, circled the beds, walked to the dresser, opened, shut drawers, brushed his hair, moved his hand bit by bit over the mirror to see what of the reflection he could blot out with each move, and felt that at any moment he would die of what was unendurable. Went to press the buzzer to wake Jeannie, looked down, saw on Jeannie's sketch pad the hospital bed, with *her;* the double bed alongside, with him; the tall pillar feeding into her veins, and their hands, his and hers, clasped, feeding each other. And as if he had been instructed he went to his bed, lay down, holding the sketch (as if it could shield against the monstrous shapes of loss, of betrayal, of death) and with his free hand took hers back into his.

So Jeannie found them in the morning.

That last day the agony was perpetual. Time after time it lifted her almost off the bed, so they had to fight to hold her down. He could not endure and left the room; wept as if there never would be tears enough.

Jeannie came to comfort him. In her light voice she said: Grandaddy, Grandaddy don't cry. She is not there, she promised me. On the last day, she said she would go back to when she first heard music, a little girl on the road of the village where she was born. She promised me. It is a festival and they dance, while the flutes so joyous and vibrant tremble in the air. Leave her there, Grandaddy, it is all right. She promised me. Come back, come back and help her poor body to die.

*For two of that generation*
*Seevya and Genya*
*Infinite, dauntless, incorruptible*

*Death deepens the wonder*

QUESTIONS

1. What significance would you assign to the title of this story? What riddles does Olsen suggest that her protagonist wants answered?
2. How does Olsen build the portrait of a life and its concerns in a tale set in its protagonist's final years? What techniques does Olsen use to show you the woman at different stages in her life and the development of her relationships with the people and societies around her?
3. How does the story suggest wider concerns than simply the depiction of an old woman and her relationship with her family? What concerns do you think it addresses? Where do you think the author's sympathies lie?

# AN ANTHOLOGY OF SHORT STORIES

## EDGAR ALLAN POE (1809–1849)

# *The Purloined Letter*

*Nil sapientae odiosius acumine nimio.*

—Seneca[1]

At Paris, just after dark one gusty evening in the autumn of 18—, I was enjoying the twofold luxury of meditation and a meerschaum, in company with my friend C. Auguste Dupin, in his little back library, or book-closet, *au troisième, No. 33, Rue Donôt, Faubourg St. Germain.*[2] For one hour at least we had maintained a profound silence; while each, to any casual observer, might have seemed intently and exclusively occupied with the curling eddies of smoke that oppressed the atmosphere of the chamber. For myself, however, I was mentally discussing certain topics which had formed matter for conversation between us at an earlier period of the evening; I mean the affair of the Rue Morgue, and the mystery attending the murder of Marie Rogêt.[3] I looked upon it, therefore, as something of a coincidence, when the door of our apartment was thrown open and admitted our old acquaintance, Monsieur G——, the Prefect of the Parisian police.

We gave him a hearty welcome; for there was nearly half as much of the entertaining as of the contemptible about the man, and we had not seen him for several years. We had been sitting in the dark, and Dupin now arose for the purpose of lighting a lamp, but sat down again, without doing so, upon G.'s saying that he had called to consult us, or rather to ask the opinion of my friend, about some official business which had occasioned a great deal of trouble.

"If it is any point requiring reflection," observed Dupin, as he forbore to enkindle the wick, "we shall examine it to better purpose in the dark."

"That is another of your odd notions," said the Prefect, who had a fashion of calling every thing "odd" that was beyond his comprehension, and thus lived amid an absolute legion of "oddities."

---

[1] "Nothing is more distasteful to good sense than too much cunning"; Lucius Annaeus Seneca (4 B.C.–65 A.D.), Roman poet and philosopher.

[2] Fashionable quarter of Paris. The "troisième" is literally the third floor, but is equivalent to the fourth floor in North America.

[3] "The Mystery of Marie Rogêt" and "The Murders in the Rue Morgue" are titles of earlier Dupin tales by Poe.

"Very true," said Dupin, as he supplied his visitor with a pipe, and rolled towards him a comfortable chair.

"And what is the difficulty now?" I asked. "Nothing more in the assassination way, I hope?"

"Oh no; nothing of that nature. The fact is, the business is *very* simple indeed, and I make no doubt that we can manage it sufficiently well ourselves; but then I thought Dupin would like to hear the details of it, because it is so excessively *odd.*"

"Simple and odd," said Dupin.

"Why, yes; and not exactly that either. The fact is, we have all been a good deal puzzled because the affair *is* so simple, and yet baffles us altogether."

"Perhaps it is the very simplicity of the thing which puts you at fault," said my friend.

"What nonsense you *do* talk!" replied the Prefect, laughing heartily.

"Perhaps the mystery is a little *too* plain," said Dupin.

"Oh, good heavens! who ever heard of such an idea?"

"A little *too* self-evident."

"Ha! ha! ha!—ha! ha! ha!—ho! ho! ho!"—roared our visitor, profoundly amused, "oh, Dupin, you will be the death of me yet!"

"And what, after all, *is* the matter on hand?" I asked.

"Why, I will tell you," replied the Prefect, as he gave a long, steady, and contemplative puff, and settled himself in his chair. "I will tell you in a few words; but, before I begin, let me caution you that this is an affair demanding the greatest secrecy, and that I should most probably lose the position I now hold, were it known that I confided it to any one."

"Proceed," said I.

"Or not," said Dupin.

"Well, then; I have received personal information, from a very high quarter, that a certain document of the last importance has been purloined from the royal apartments. The individual who purloined it is known; this beyond a doubt; he was seen to take it. It is known, also, that it still remains in his possession."

"How is this known?" asked Dupin.

"It is clearly inferred," replied the Prefect, "from the nature of the document, and from the non-appearance of certain results which would at once arise from its passing *out* of the robber's possession;—that is to say, from his employing it as he must design in the end to employ it."

"Be a little more explicit," I said.

"Well, I may venture so far as to say that the paper gives its holder a certain power in a certain quarter where such power is immensely valuable." The Prefect was fond of the cant of diplomacy.

"Still I do not quite understand," said Dupin.

"No? Well; the disclosure of the document to a third person, who shall be nameless, would bring in question the honour of a personage of most exalted station; and this fact gives the holder of the document an ascendancy over the illustrious personage whose honour and peace are so jeopardized."

"But this ascendancy," I interposed, "would depend upon the robber's knowledge of the loser's knowledge of the robber. Who would dare—"

"The thief," said G., "is the Minister D———, who dares all things, those unbecoming as well as those becoming a man. The method of the theft was not less ingenious than bold. The document in question—a letter, to be frank—had been received by the personage robbed while alone in the royal *boudoir.* During its perusal she was suddenly interrupted by the entrance of the other exalted personage from whom especially it was her wish to conceal it. After a hurried and vain endeavour to thrust it in a drawer, she was forced to place it, open it was, upon a table. The address, however, was uppermost, and, the contents thus unexposed, the letter escaped notice. At this juncture enters the Minister D———. His lynx eye immediately perceives the paper, recognizes the handwriting of the address, observes the confusion of the personage addressed, and fathoms her secret. After some business transactions, hurried through in his ordinary manner, he produces a letter somewhat similar to the one in question, opens it, pretends to read it, and then places it in close juxtaposition to the other. Again he converses, for some fifteen minutes, upon the public affairs. At length, in taking leave, he takes also from the table the letter to which he had no claim. Its rightful owner saw, but, of course, dared not call attention to the act, in the presence of the third personage who stood at her elbow. The minister decamped; leaving his own letter—one of no importance—upon the table."

"Here, then," said Dupin to me, "you have precisely what you demand to make the ascendancy complete—the robber's knowledge of the loser's knowledge of the robber."

"Yes," replied the Prefect; "and the power thus attained has, for some months past, been wielded, for political purposes, to a very dangerous extent. The personage robbed is more thoroughly convinced, every day, of the necessity of reclaiming her letter. But this, of course, cannot be done openly. In fine, driven to despair, she has committed the matter to me."

"Than whom," said Dupin, amid a perfect whirlwind of smoke, "no more sagacious agent could, I suppose, be desired, or even imagined."

"You flatter me," replied the Prefect; "but it is possible that some such opinion may have been entertained."

"It is clear," said I, "as you observe, that the letter is still in the possession of the minister; since it is this possession, and not any employment of the letter, which bestows the power. With the employment the power departs."

"True," said G.; "and upon this conviction I proceeded. My first care was to make thorough search of the minister's hotel;[4] and here my chief embarrassment lay in the necessity of searching without his knowledge. Beyond all things, I have been warned of the danger which would result from giving him reason to suspect our design."

"But," said I, "you are quite *au fait*[5] in these investigations. The Parisian police have done this thing often before."

"O yes; and for this reason I did not despair. The habits of the minister gave me, too, a great advantage. He is frequently absent from home all night. His servants are by no means numerous. They sleep at a distance from their master's apartment, and being chiefly Neapolitans, are readily made drunk. I have keys, as you know, with which I can open any chamber or cabinet in Paris. For three months a night has not passed, during the greater part of which I have not been engaged, personally, in ransacking the D—— Hôtel. My honour is interested, and, to mention a great secret, the reward is enormous. So I did not abandon the search until I had become fully satisfied that the thief is a more astute man than myself. I fancy that I have investigated every nook and corner of the premises in which it is possible that the paper can be concealed."

"But is it not possible," I suggested, "that although the letter may be in the possession of the minister, as it unquestionably is, he may have concealed it elsewhere than upon his own premises?"

"This is barely possible," said Dupin. "The present peculiar condition of affairs at court, and especially of those intrigues in which D—— is known to be involved, would render the instant availability of the document—its susceptibility of being produced at a moment's notice—a point of nearly equal importance with its possession."

"Its susceptibility of being produced?" said I.

"That is to say, of being *destroyed,*" said Dupin.

"True," I observed; "the paper is clearly then upon the premises. As for its being upon the person of the minister, we may consider that as out of the question."

"Entirely," said the Prefect. "He had been twice waylaid, as if by footpads, and his person rigorously searched under my own inspection."

"You might have spared yourself this trouble," said Dupin. "D——, I presume, is not altogether a fool, and, if not, must have anticipated these waylayings, as a matter of course."

"Not *altogether* a fool," said G., "but then he is a poet, which I take to be only one remove from a fool."

---

[4] *hotel,* town house.

[5] *au fait,* adept.

"True," said Dupin, after a long and thoughtful whiff from his meerschaum, "although I have been guilty of certain doggerel myself."

"Suppose you detail," said I, "the particulars of your search."

"Why the fact is, we took our time, and we searched *every where.* I have had long experience in these affairs. I took the entire building, room by room; devoting the nights of a whole week to each. We examined, first, the furniture of each apartment. We opened every possible drawer; and I presume you know that, to a properly trained police agent, such a thing as a *secret* drawer is impossible. Any man is a dolt who permits a 'secret' drawer to escape him in a search of this kind. The thing is *so* plain. There is a certain amount of bulk—of space—to be accounted for in every cabinet. Then we have accurate rules.[6] The fiftieth part of a line could not escape us. After the cabinets we took the chairs. The cushions we probed with the fine long needles you have seen me employ. From the tables we removed the tops."

"Why so?"

"Sometimes the top of a table, or other similarly arranged piece of furniture, is removed by the person wishing to conceal an article; then the leg is excavated, the article deposited within the cavity, and the top replaced. The bottoms and tops of bedposts are employed in the same way."

"But could not the cavity be detected by sounding?" I asked.

"By no means, if, when the article is deposited, a sufficient wadding of cotton be placed around it. Besides, in our case, we were obliged to proceed without noise."

"But you could not have removed—you could not have taken to pieces *all* articles of furniture in which it would have been possible to make a deposit in the manner you mention. A letter may be compressed into a thin spiral roll, not differing much in shape or bulk from a large knitting-needle, and in this form it might be inserted into the rung of a chair, for example. You did not take to pieces all the chairs?"

"Certainly not; but we did better—we examined the rungs of every chair in the hotel, and indeed the jointings of every description of furniture, by the aid of a most powerful microscope.[7] Had there been any traces of recent disturbance we should not have failed to detect it instantly. A single grain of gimlet-dust, for example, would have been as obvious as an apple. Any disorder in the glueing—any unusual gaping in the joints—would have sufficed to insure detection."

"I presume you looked to the mirrors, between the boards and the plates, and you probed the beds and the bed-clothes, as well as the curtains and carpets."

---

[6] *rules,* rulers.

[7] *microscope,* magnifying glass.

"That of course; and when we had absolutely completed every particle of the furniture in this way, then we examined the house itself. We divided its entire surface into compartments, which we numbered, so that none might be missed; then we scrutinized each individual square inch throughout the premises, including the two houses immediately adjoining, with the microscope as before."

"The two houses adjoining!" I exclaimed; "you must have had a great deal of trouble."

"We had; but the reward offered is prodigious."

"You include the *grounds* about the houses?"

"All the grounds are paved with brick. They gave us comparatively little trouble. We examined the moss between the bricks, and found it undisturbed."

"You looked among D———'s papers, of course, and into the books of the library?"

"Certainly; we opened every package and parcel; we not only opened every book, but we turned over every leaf in each volume, not contenting ourselves with a mere shake, according to the fashion of some of our police officers. We also measured the thickness of every book-*cover,* with the most accurate admeasurement, and applied to each the most jealous scrutiny of the microscope. Had any of the bindings been recently meddled with, it would have been utterly impossible that the fact should have escaped observation. Some five or six volumes, just from the hands of the binder, we carefully probed, longitudinally, with the needles."

"You explored the floors beneath the carpets?"

"Beyond doubt. We removed every carpet, and examined the boards with the microscope."

"And the paper on the walls?"

"Yes."

"You looked into the cellars?"

"We did."

"Then," I said, "you have been making a miscalculation, and the letter is *not* upon the premises as you suppose."

"I fear you are right there," said the Prefect. "And now, Dupin, what would you advise me to do?"

"To make a thorough re-search of the premises."

"That is absolutely needless," replied G———. "I am not more sure that I breathe than I am that the letter is not at the Hôtel."

"I have no better advice to give you," said Dupin. "You have, of course, an accurate description of the letter?"

"Oh, yes!"—And here the Prefect, producing a memorandum-book, proceeded to read aloud a minute account of the internal, and especially of the external, appearance of the missing document. Soon after finishing the perusal of this description, he took his departure, more entirely depressed in spirits than I had ever known the good gentleman before.

In about a month afterward he paid us another visit, and found us occupied very nearly as before. He took a pipe and a chair and entered into some ordinary conversation. At length I said;—

"Well, but G———, what of the purloined letter? I presume you have at last made up your mind that there is no such thing as overreaching the Minister?"

"Confound him, say I—yes; I made the re-examination, however, as Dupin suggested—but it was all labour lost, as I knew it would be."

"How much was the reward offered, did you say?" asked Dupin.

"Why, a very great deal—a *very* liberal reward—I don't like to say how much, precisely; but one thing I *will* say, that I wouldn't mind giving my individual check for fifty thousand francs to any one who could obtain me that letter. The fact is, it is becoming of more and more importance every day; and the reward has been lately doubled. If it were trebled, however, I could do no more than I have done."

"Why, yes," said Dupin, drawlingly, between the whiffs of his meerschaum, "I really—think, G———, you have not exerted yourself—to the utmost in this matter. You might—do a little more, I think, eh?"

"How?—in what way?"

"Why—puff, puff,—you might—puff, puff—employ counsel in the matter, eh?—puff, puff, puff. Do you remember the story they tell of Abernethy?"

"No; hang Abernethy!"

"To be sure! hang him and welcome. But, once upon a time, a certain rich miser conceived the design of spunging upon this Abernethy for a medical opinion. Getting up, for this purpose, an ordinary conversation in a private company, he insinuated his case to the physician, as that of an imaginary individual.

" 'We will suppose,' said the miser, 'that his symptoms are such and such; now, doctor, what would *you* have directed him to take?"

" 'Take!' said Abernethy, 'why, take *advice,* to be sure.' "

"But," said the Prefect, a little discomposed, "I am *perfectly* willing to take advice, and to pay for it. I would *really* give fifty thousand francs to any one who would aid me in the matter."

"In that case," replied Dupin, opening a drawer, and producing a check-book, "you may as well fill me up a check for the amount you mentioned. When you have signed it, I will hand you the letter."

I was astounded. The Prefect appeared absolutely thunderstricken. For some minutes he remained speechless and motionless, looking incredulously at my friend with open mouth, and eyes that seemed starting from their sockets; then, apparently recovering himself in some measure, he seized a pen, and after several pauses and vacant stares, finally filled up and signed a check for fifty thousand francs, and handed it across the table to Dupin. The latter examined it carefully and deposited it in his pocket-book; then, unlocking an *escritoire,*[8] took thence a letter and gave it to the Prefect. This functionary grasped it in a perfect agony of joy, opened it with a trembling hand, cast a rapid glance at its contents, and then, scrambling and struggling to the door, rushed at length unceremoniously from the room and from the house, without having uttered a syllable since Dupin had requested him to fill up the check.

When he had gone, my friend entered into some explanations.

"The Parisian police," he said, "are exceedingly able in their way. They are persevering, ingenious, cunning, and thoroughly versed in the knowledge which their duties seem chiefly to demand. Thus, when G——— detailed to us his mode of searching the premises at the Hôtel D———, I felt entire confidence in his having made a satisfactory investigation—so far as his labours extended."

"So far as his labours extended?" said I.

"Yes," said Dupin. "The measures adopted were not only the best of their kind, but carried out to absolute perfection. Had the letter been deposited within the range of their search, these fellows would, beyond a question, have found it."

I merely laughed—but he seemed quite serious in all that he said.

"The measures, then," he continued, "were good in their kind, and well executed; their defect lay in their being inapplicable to the case, and to the man. A certain set of highly ingenious resources are, with the Prefect, a sort of Procrustean bed,[9] to which he forcibly adapts his designs. But he perpetually errs by being too deep or too shallow, for the matter in hand; and many a schoolboy is a better reasoner than he. I knew one about eight years of age, whose success at guessing in the game of 'even and odd' attracted universal admiration. This game is simple, and is played with marbles. One player holds in his hand a number of these toys, and demands of another whether that number is even or odd. If the guess is right, the guesser wins one; if wrong, he loses one. The boy to whom I allude won all the marbles of the school. Of course he had some principle of guessing; and this lay in mere observation and admeasurement of the astuteness of his opponents. For example, an arrant simpleton is his opponent, and, holding up his closed hand, asks: 'Are they even or odd?' Our schoolboy replies, 'Odd,' and loses; but upon the second trial he wins, for he then says to himself, 'The simpleton had them even upon the first trial, and his amount of

---

[8] *escritoire,* a writing table.

[9] In Greek mythology the giant Procrustes tied travelers to an iron bed and made them fit it by either stretching or amputating their limbs.

cunning is just sufficient to make him have them odd upon the second; I will therefore guess odd;'—he guesses odd, and wins. Now, with a simpleton a degree above the first, he would have reasoned thus: 'This fellow finds that in the first instance I guessed odd, and, in the second, he will propose to himself upon the first impulse, a simple variation from even to odd, as did the first simpleton; but then a second thought will suggest that this is too simple a variation, and finally he will decide upon putting it even as before. I will therefore guess even';—he guesses even, and wins. Now this mode of reasoning in the schoolboy, whom his fellows termed 'lucky,'—what, in its last analysis, is it?"

"It is merely," I said, "an identification of the reasoner's intellect with that of his opponent."

"It is," said Dupin; "and, upon inquiring of the boy by what means he effected the *thorough* identification in which his success consisted, I received answer as follows: 'When I wish to find out how wise, or how stupid, or how good, or how wicked is any one, or what are his thoughts at the moment, I fashion the expression on my face, as accurately as possible, in accordance with the expression of his, and then wait to see what thoughts or sentiments arise in my mind or heart, as if to match or correspond with the expression.' This response of the schoolboy lies at the bottom of all the spurious profundity which has been attributed to Rochefoucault, to La Bougive, to Machiavelli, and to Campanella."[10]

"And the identification," I said, "of the reasoner's intellect with that of his opponent, depends, if I understand you aright, upon the accuracy with which the opponent's intellect is admeasured."

"For its practical value it depends upon this," replied Dupin; "and the Prefect and his cohort fail so frequently, first, by default of this identification, and secondly, by ill-admeasurement, or rather through non--admeasurement, of the intellect with which they are engaged. They consider only their *own* ideas of ingenuity; and, in searching for anything hidden, advert only to the modes in which *they* would have hidden it. They are right in this much—that their own ingenuity is a faithful representative of that of *the mass;* but when the cunning of the individual felon is diverse in character from their own, the felon foils them, of course. This always happens when it is above their own, and very usually when it is below. They have no variation of principle in their investigations; at best, when urged by some unusual emergency—by some extraordinary reward—they extend or exaggerate their old modes of *practice,* without touching their principles. What, for example, in this case of D———, has been done to vary the principle of action? What is all this

[10] François, Duc de la Rochefoucauld (1613–1680), French moralist and courtier; La Bougive is probably Jean de la Bruyere (1645–1696); Niccolò Machiavelli (1469–1527), Italian statesman and writer; Tommaso Campanella (1568–1639), Italian philosopher and Dominican monk.

boring, and probing, and sounding, and scrutinizing with the microscope, and dividing the surface of the building into registered square inches—what is it all but an exaggeration *of the application* of one principle or set of principles of search, which are based upon the one set of notions regarding human ingenuity, to which the Prefect, in the long routine of his duty, has been accustomed? Do you not see he has taken it for granted that *all* men proceed to conceal a letter,—not exactly in a gimlet-hole bored in a chair-leg—but, at least, in *some* out-of-the-way hole or corner suggested by the same tenor or thought which would urge a man to secrete a letter in a gimlet-hole bored in a chair-leg? And do you not see also, that such *recherchés*[11] nooks for concealment are adapted only for ordinary occasions, and would be adopted only by ordinary intellects; for, in all cases of concealment, a disposal of the article concealed—a disposal of it in this *recherché* manner—is, in the very first instance, presumable and presumed; and thus its discovery depends, not at all upon the acumen, but altogether upon the mere care, patience, and determination of the seekers; and where the case is of importance—or, what amounts to the same thing in the political eyes, when the reward is of magnitude,—the qualities in question have *never* been known to fail. You will now understand what I meant in suggesting that, had the purloined letter been hidden anywhere within the limits of the Prefect's examination—in other words, had the principle of its concealment been comprehended within the principles of the Prefect—its discovery would have been a matter altogether beyond question. This functionary, however, has been thoroughly mystified; and the remote source of his defeat lies in the supposition that the Minister is a fool, because he has acquired renown as a poet. All fools are poets; this the Prefect *feels;* and he is merely guilty of a *non distributio medii*[12] in thence inferring that all poets are fools.

"But is this really the poet?" I asked. "There are two brothers, I know; and both have attained reputation in letters. The Minister I believe has written learnedly on the Differential Calculus. He is a mathematician, and no poet."

"You are mistaken; I know him well: he is both. As poet *and* mathematician, he would reason well; as mere mathematician, he could not have reasoned at all, and thus would have been at the mercy of the Prefect."

"You surprise me," I said, "by these opinions, which have been contradicted by the voice of the world. You do not mean to set at naught the well-digested idea of centuries. The mathematical reason has long been regarded as *the* reason *par excellence.*"

---

[11] *recherchés,* excessively cunning.

[12] *non distributio medii,* the undistributed middle, an error in logic.

" '*Il y a à parier,*' " replied Dupin, quoting from Chamfort, " '*que toute idée publique, toute convention reçue, est une sottise, car elle a convenu au plus grand nombre.*'[13] The mathematicians, I grant you, have done their best to promulgate the popular error to which you allude, and which is none the less an error for its promulgation as truth. With an art worthy a better cause, for example, they have insinuated the term 'analysis' into application to algebra. The French are the originators of this particular deception; but if a term is of any importance—if words derive any value from applicability—then 'analysis' conveys 'algebra' about as much as, in Latin, '*ambitus*' implies 'ambition,' '*religio*' 'religion,' or '*homines honesti,*' a set of *honourable* men."

"You have a quarrel on hand, I see," said I, "with some of the algebraists of Paris; but proceed."

"I dispute the availability, and thus the value, of that reason which is cultivated in any especial form other than the abstractly logical. I dispute, in particular, the reason educed by mathematical study. The mathematics are the science of form and quantity; mathematical reasoning is merely logic applied to observation upon form and quantity. The great error lies in supposing that even the truths of what is called *pure* algebra, are abstract or general truths. And this error is so egregious that I am confounded at the universality with which it has been received. Mathematical axioms are *not* axioms of general truth. What is true of *relation*—of form and quantity—is often grossly false in regard to morals, for example. In this latter science it is very usually *un*true that the aggregated parts are equal to the whole. In chemistry also the axiom fails. In the consideration of motive it fails; for two motives, each of a given value, have not, necessarily, a value when united, equal to the sum of their values apart. There are numerous other mathematical truths which are only truths within the limits of *relation*. But the mathematician argues from his *finite truths,* through habit, as if they were of an absolutely general applicability—as the world indeed imagines them to be. Bryant, in his very learned 'Mythology,'[14] mentions an analogous source of error, when he says that 'although the Pagan fables are not believed, yet we forget ourselves continually, and make inferences from them as existing realities.' With the algebraists, however, how are Pagans themselves, the 'Pagan fables' *are* believed, and the inferences are made, not so much through lapse of memory as through an unaccountable addling of the brains. In short, I never yet encountered the mere mathematician who could be trusted out of equal roots, or one who did not clandes-

---

[13] "The odds are that every popular idea, every accepted convention is nonsense, because it has suited itself to the majority"; from *Maximes et Pensées* by Sébastian Chamfort (1741–1794).

[14] *A New System, or an Analysis of Antient Mythology,* by Jacob Bryant (1715–1804), an English scholar.

tinely hold it as a point of his faith that $x^2 + px$ was absolutely and unconditionally equal to $q$. Say to one of these gentlemen, by way of experiment, if you please, that you believe occasions may occur where $x^2 + px$ is *not* altogether equal to $q$, and having made him understand what you mean, get out of his reach as speedily as convenient, for, beyond doubt, he will endeavour to knock you down.

"I mean to say," continued Dupin, while I merely laughed at his last observations, "that if the Minister had been no more than a mathematician, the Prefect would have been under no necessity of giving me this check. I knew him, however, as both mathematician and poet, and my measures were adapted to his capacity, with reference to the circumstances by which he was surrounded. I knew him as a courtier, too, and as a bold *intriguant.*[15] Such a man, I considered, could not fail to be aware of the ordinary political modes of action. He could not have failed to anticipate—and events have proved that he did not fail to anticipate—the waylayings to which he was subjected. He must have foreseen, I reflected, the secret investigations of his premises. His frequent absences from home at night, which were hailed by the Prefect as certain aids to his success, I regarded only as *ruses,* to afford opportunity for thorough search to the police, and thus the sooner to impress them with the conviction to which G———, in fact, did finally arrive—the conviction that the letter was not upon the premises. I felt, also, that the whole train of thought, which I was at some pains in detailing to you just now, concerning the invariable principle of political action in searches for articles concealed—I felt that this whole train of thought would necessarily pass through the mind of the Minister. It would imperatively lead him to despise all the ordinary *nooks* of concealment. *He* could not, I reflected, be so weak as not to see that the most intricate and remote recess of his hotel would be as open as his commonest closets to the eyes, to the probes, to the gimlets, and to the microscopes of the Prefect. I saw, in fine, that he would be driven, as a matter of course, to simplicity, if not deliberately induced to it as a matter of choice. You will remember, perhaps, how desperately the Prefect laughed when I suggested, upon our first interview, that it was just possible this mystery troubled him so much on account of its being so *very* self-evident."

"Yes," said I, "I remember his merriment well. I really thought he would have fallen into convulsions."

"The material world," continued Dupin, "abounds with very strict analogies to the immaterial; and thus some color of truth has been given to the rhetorical dogma, that metaphor, or simile, may be made to strengthen an argument as well as to embellish a description. The principle of the *vis inertiae,*[16] for example, seems to be identical in physics

[15] *intriguant,* intriguer.
[16] *vis inertiae,* the power of inertia.

and metaphysics. It is not more true in the former, that a large body is with more difficulty set in motion than a smaller one, and that its subsequent *momentum* is commensurate with this difficulty, than it is, in the latter, that intellects of the vaster capacity, while more forcible, more constant, and more eventful in their movements than those of inferior grade, are yet the less readily moved, and more embarrassed and full of hesitation in the first few steps of their progress. Again: have you ever noticed which of the street signs, over the shop doors, are the most attractive of attention?"

"I have never given the matter a thought," I said.

"There is a game of puzzles," he resumed, "which is played upon a map. One party playing requires another to find a given word—the name of town, river, state, or empire—any word, in short, upon the motley and perplexed surface of the chart. A novice in the game generally seeks to embarrass his opponents by giving them the most minutely lettered names; but the adept selects such words as stretch, in large characters, from one end of the chart to the other. These, like the over-largely lettered signs and placards of the street, escape observation by the dint of being excessively obvious; and here the physical oversight is precisely analogous with the moral inapprehension by which the intellect suffers to pass unnoticed those considerations which are too obtrusively and too palpably self-evident. But this is a point, it appears, somewhat above or beneath the understanding of the Prefect. He never once thought it probable, or possible, that the Minister had deposited the letter immediately beneath the nose of the whole world, by way of best preventing any portion of that world from perceiving it.

"But the more I reflected upon the daring, dashing, and discriminating ingenuity of D———; upon the fact that the document must always have been *at hand,* if he intended to use it to good purpose; and upon the decisive evidence, obtained by the Prefect, that it was not hidden within the limits of that dignitary's ordinary search—the more satisfied I became that, to conceal this letter, The Minister had resorted to the comprehensive and sagacious expedient of not attempting to conceal it at all.

"Full of these ideas, I prepared myself with a pair of green spectacles, and called one fine morning, quite by accident, at the Ministerial hotel. I found D——— at home, yawning, lounging, and dawdling, as usual, and pretending to be in the last extremity of *ennui.* He is, perhaps, the most really energetic human being now alive—but that is only when nobody sees him.

"To be even with him, I complained of my weak eyes, and lamented the necessity of the spectacles, under cover of which I cautiously and thoroughly surveyed the whole apartment, while seemingly intent only upon the conversation of my host.

"I paid especial attention to a large writing-table near which he sat, and upon which lay confusedly, some miscellaneous letters and other papers, with one or two musical instruments and a few books. Here, however, after a long and very deliberate scrutiny, I saw nothing to excite particular suspicion.

"At length my eyes, in going the circuit of the room, fell upon a trumpery filigree card-rack of pasteboard, that hung dangling by a dirty blue ribbon, from a little brass knob just beneath the middle of the mantel-piece. In this rack, which had three or four compartments, were five or six visiting cards and a solitary letter. This last was much soiled and crumpled. It was torn nearly in two, across the middle—as if a design, in the first instance, to tear it entirely up as worthless, had been altered, or stayed, in the second. It had a large black seal, bearing the D——— cipher *very* conspicuously, and was addressed, in a diminutive female hand, to D———, the minister, himself. It was thrust carelessly, and even, as it seemed, contemptuously, into one of the upper divisions of the rack.

"No sooner had I glanced at this letter than I concluded it to be that of which I was in search. To be sure, it was, to all appearance, radically different from the one of which the Prefect had read us so minute a description. Here the seal was large and black, with the D——— cipher; there it was small and red, with the ducal arms of the S——— family. Here, the address, to the Minister, was diminutive and feminine; there the superscription, to a certain royal personage, was markedly bold and decided; the size alone formed a point of correspondence. But, then, the *radicalness* of these differences, which was excessive; the dirt; the soiled and torn condition of the paper, so inconsistent with the *true* methodical habits of D———, and so suggestive of a design to delude the beholder into an idea of the worthlessness of the document; these things, together with the hyperobtrusive situation of this document, full in the view of every visitor, and thus exactly in accordance with the conclusions to which I had previously arrived; these things, I say, were strongly corroborative of suspicion, in one who came with the intention to suspect.

"I protracted my visit as long as possible, and, while I maintained a most animated discussion with the Minister, upon a topic which I knew well had never failed to interest and excite him, I kept my attention really riveted upon the letter. In this examination, I committed to memory its external appearance and arrangement in the rack; and also fell, at length, upon a discovery which set at rest whatever trivial doubt I might have entertained. In scrutinizing the edges of the paper, I observed them to be more *chafed* than seemed necessary. They presented the *broken* appearance which is manifested when a stiff paper, having been once folded and pressed with a folder, is refolded in a reversed direction, in the same creases or edges which had formed the original fold. This discovery was sufficient. It was clear to me that the letter had been turned, as a glove, inside out, re-directed, and re-sealed. I bade the Minister good morning, and took my departure at once, leaving a gold snuff-box upon the table.

"The next morning I called for the snuff-box, when we resumed, quite eagerly, the conversation of the preceding day. While thus engaged, however, a loud report, as if of a pistol, was heard immediately beneath the windows of the hotel, and was succeeded by a series of fearful screams, and the shoutings of a mob. D——— rushed to a casement, threw it open, and looked out. In the meantime I stepped to the card-rack, took the letter, put it in my pocket, and replaced it by a *fac-simile,* (so far as regards externals) which I had carefully prepared at my lodgings; imitating the D——— cipher, very readily, by means of a seal formed of bread.

"The disturbance in the street had been occasioned by the frantic behaviour of a man with a musket. He had fired it among a crowd of women and children. It proved, however, to have been without ball, and the fellow was suffered to go his way as a lunatic or a drunkard. When he had gone, D——— came from the window, whither I had followed him immediately upon securing the object in view. Soon afterward I bade him farewell. The pretended lunatic was a man in my own pay."

"But what purpose had you," I asked, "in replacing the letter by a *fac-simile?* Would it not have been better, at the first visit, to have seized it openly, and departed?"

"D———," replied Dupin, "is a desperate man, and a man of nerve. His hotel, too, is not without attendants devoted to his interests. Had I made the wild attempt you suggest, I might never have left the Ministerial presence alive. The good people of Paris might have heard of me no more. But I had an object apart from these considerations. You know my political prepossessions. In this matter, I act as a partisan of the lady concerned. For eighteen months the Minister has had her in his power. She has now him in hers; since, being unaware that the letter is not in his possession, he will proceed with his exactions as if it was. Thus will he inevitably commit himself, at once, to his political destruction. His downfall, too, will not be more precipitate than awkward. It is all very well to talk about the *facilis descensus Averni;*[17] but in all kinds of climbing, as Catalani[18] said of singing, it is far more easy to get up than to come down. In the present instance I have no sympathy—at least no pity—for him who descends. He is that *monstrum horrendum,*[19] an unprincipled man of genius. I confess, however, that I should like very

[17] "Easy is the descent into hell . . . but to recall thy steps and issue to upper air, this is the task, this the burden"; *Aeneid* 6.126, by Virgil (70–19 B.C.), Roman poet.

[18] Angelica Catalani (1780–1844), Italian singer.

[19] The description of Polyphemus the Cyclops after his one eye had been put out by Ulysses; *Aeneid* 3.658.

well to know the precise character of his thoughts, when, being defied by her whom the Prefect terms 'a certain personage,' he is reduced to opening the letter which I left for him in the card-rack."

"How? did you put any thing particular in it?"

"Why—it did not seem altogether right to leave the interior blank—that would have been insulting. D———, at Vienna once, did me an evil turn, which I told him, quite good-humouredly, that I should remember. So, as I knew he would feel some curiosity in regard to the identity of the person who had outwitted him, I thought it a pity not to give him a clue. He is well acquainted with my MS., and I just copied into the middle of the blank sheet the words—

*———Un dessein si funeste,*
*S'il n'est digne d'Atrée, est digne*
*de Thyeste.*

They are to be found in Crébillon's 'Atrée.' "[20]

---

[20] "So baneful a plot, if not worthy of Atreus, is worthy of Thyestes"; from *Atrée et Thyeste* by Prosper Jolyot de Crébillon (1674–1762).

## ANTON CHEKHOV (1860–1904)

# *Gooseberries*

The sky had been covered with rain-clouds ever since the early morning, it was a still day, cool and dull, one of those misty days when the clouds have long been lowering overhead and you keep thinking it is just going to rain, and the rain holds off. Ivan Ivanich, the veterinary surgeon, and Burkin, the high-school teacher, had walked till they were tired, and the way over the fields seemed endless to them. Far ahead they could just make out the windmill of the village of Mironositskoye, and what looked like a range of low hills at the right extending well beyond the village, and they both knew that this range was really the bank of the river, and that further on were meadows, green willow-trees, country-estates; if they were on top of these hills, they knew they would see the same boundless fields and telegraph-posts, and the train, like a crawling caterpillar in the distance, while in fine weather even the town would be visible. On this still day, when the whole of nature seemed kindly and pensive, Ivan Ivanich and Burkin felt a surge of love for this plain, and thought how vast and beautiful their country was.

"The last time we stayed in Elder Prokofy's hut," said Burkin, "you said you had a story to tell me."

"Yes. I wanted to tell you the story of my brother."

Ivan Ivanich took a deep breath and lighted his pipe as a preliminary to his narrative, but just then the rain came. Five minutes later it was coming down in torrents and nobody could say when it would stop. Ivan Ivanich and Burkin stood still, lost in thought. The dogs, already soaked, stood with drooping tails, gazing at them wistfully.

"We must try and find shelter," said Burkin. "Let's go to Alekhin's. It's quite near."

"Come on, then."

They turned aside and walked straight across the newly reaped field, veering to the right till they came to a road. Very soon poplars, an orchard, and the red roofs of barns came into sight. The surface of a river gleamed, and they had a view of an extensive reach of water, a windmill and a whitewashed bathing-shed. This was Sofyino, where Alekhin lived.

The mill was working, and the noise made by its sails drowned the sound of the rain; the whole dam trembled. Horses, soaking wet, were standing near some carts, their heads drooping, and people were moving about with sacks over their heads and shoulders. It was wet, muddy, bleak, and the water looked cold and sinister. Ivan Ivanich and Burkin were already experiencing the misery of dampness, dirt, physical discomfort, their boots were caked with mud, and when, having passed the mill-dam, they took the upward path to the landowner's barns, they fell silent, as if vexed with one another.

The sound of winnowing[1] came from one of the barns; the door was open, and clouds of dust issued from it. Standing in the doorway was Alekhin himself, a stout man of some forty years, with longish hair, looking more like a professor or an artist than a landed proprietor. He was wearing a white shirt, greatly in need of washing, belted with a piece of string, and long drawers with no trousers over them. His boots, too, were caked with mud and straw. His eyes and nose were ringed with dust. He recognized Ivan Ivanich and Burkin, and seemed glad to see them.

"Go up to the house, gentlemen," he said, smiling. "I'll be with you in a minute."

It was a large two-storey house. Alekhin occupied the ground floor, two rooms with vaulted ceilings and tiny windows, where the stewards had lived formerly. They were poorly furnished, and smelled of rye-bread, cheap vodka, and harness. He hardly ever went into the upstairs rooms, excepting when he had guests. Ivan Ivanich and Burkin were met by a maid-servant, a young woman of such beauty that they stood still involuntarily and exchanged glances.

"You have no idea how glad I am to see you here, dear friends," said Alekhin, overtaking them in the hall. "It's quite a surprise! Pelageya," he said, turning to the maid, "find the gentlemen a change of clothes. And I might as well change, myself. But I must have a wash first, for I don't believe I've had a bath since the spring. Wouldn't you like to go and have a bathe while they get things ready here?"

The beauteous Pelageya, looking very soft and delicate, brought them towels and soap, and Alekhin and his guests set off for the bathing-house.

"Yes, it's a long time since I had a wash," he said, taking off his clothes. "As you see I have a nice bathing-place, my father had it built, but somehow I never seem to get time to wash."

He sat on the step, soaping his long locks and his neck, and all round him the water was brown.

---

[1] *winnowing*, the separation of the chaff, or husks, from grain.

"Yes, you certainly..." remarked Ivan Ivanich, with a significant glance at his host's head.

"It's a long time since I had a wash..." repeated Alekhin, somewhat abashed, and he soaped himself again, and now the water was dark-blue, like ink.

Ivan Ivanich emerged from the shed, splashed noisily into the water, and began swimming beneath the rain, spreading his arms wide, making waves all round him, and the white water-lilies rocked on the waves he made. He swam into the very middle of the river and then dived, a moment later came up at another place and swam further, diving constantly, and trying to touch the bottom. "Ah, my God," he kept exclaiming in his enjoyment. "Ah, my God...." He swam up to the mill, had a little talk with some peasants there and turned back, but when he got to the middle of the river, he floated, holding his face up to the rain. Burkin and Alekhin were dressed and ready to go, but he went on swimming and diving.

"God! God!" he kept exclaiming. "Dear God!"

"Come out!" Burkin shouted to him.

They went back to the house. And only after the lamp was lit in the great drawing-room on the upper floor, and Burkin and Ivan Ivanich, in silk dressing-gowns and warm slippers, were seated in arm-chairs, while Alekhin, washed and combed, paced the room in his new frock-coat, enjoying the warmth, the cleanliness, his dry clothes and comfortable slippers, while the fair Pelageya, smiling benevolently, stepped noiselessly over the carpet with her tray of tea and preserves, did Ivan Ivanich embark upon his yarn, the ancient dames, young ladies, and military gentlemen looking down at them severely from the gilded frames, as if they, too, were listening.

"There were two of us brothers," he began. "Ivan Ivanich (me), and my brother Nikolai Ivanich, two years younger than myself. I went in for learning and became a veterinary surgeon, but Nikolai started working in a government office when he was only nineteen. Our father, Chimsha-Himalaisky, was educated in a school for the sons of private soldiers, but was later promoted to officer's rank, and was made a hereditary nobleman and given a small estate. After his death the estate had to be sold for debts, but at least our childhood was passed in the freedom of the country-side, where we roamed the fields and the woods like peasant children, taking the horses to graze, peeling bark from the trunks of lime-trees, fishing, and all that sort of thing. And anyone who has once in his life fished for perch, or watched the thrushes fly south in the autumn, rising high over the village on clear, cool days, is spoilt for town life, and will long for the country-side for the rest of his days. My brother pined in his government office. The years passed and he sat in the same place every day, writing out the same documents and thinking all the time of the same thing—how to get back to the country. And these longings of his gradually turned into a definite desire, into a dream of purchasing a little estate somewhere on the bank of a river or the shore of a lake.

"He was a meek, good-natured chap, I was fond of him, but could feel no sympathy with the desire to lock oneself up for life in an estate of one's own. They say man only needs six feet of earth. But it is a corpse, and not man, which needs these six feet. And now people are actually saying that it is a good sign for our intellectuals to yearn for the land and try to obtain country-dwellings. And yet these estates are nothing but those same six feet of earth. To escape from the town, from the struggle, from the noise of life, to escape and hide one's head on a country-estate, is not life, but egoism, idleness, it is a sort of renunciation, but renunciation without faith. It is not six feet of earth, not a country-estate, that man needs, but the whole globe, the whole of nature, room to display his qualities and the individual characteristics of his soul.

"My brother Nikolai sat at his office-desk, dreaming of eating soup made from his own cabbages, which would spread a delicious smell all over his own yard, of eating out of doors, on the green grass, of sleeping in the sun, sitting for hours on a bench outside his gate, and gazing at the fields and woods. Books on agriculture, and all those hints printed on calendars were his delight, his favourite spiritual nourishment. He was fond of reading newspapers, too, but all he read in them was advertisements of the sale of so many acres of arable and meadowland, with residence attached, a river, an orchard, a mill, and ponds fed by springs. His head was full of visions of garden paths, flowers, fruit, nesting-boxes, carp-ponds, and all that sort of thing. These visions differed according to the advertisements he came across, but for some reason gooseberry bushes invariably figured in them. He could not picture to himself a single estate or picturesque nook that did not have gooseberry bushes in it.

" 'Country life has its conveniences,' he would say. 'You sit on the verandah, drinking tea, with your own ducks floating on the pond, and everything smells so nice, and . . . and the gooseberries ripen on the bushes.'

"He drew up plans for his estate, and every plan showed the same features: a) the main residence, b) the servant's wing, c) the kitchen-garden, d) gooseberry bushes. He lived thriftily, never ate or drank his fill, dressed anyhow, like a beggar, and saved up all his money in the bank. He became terribly stingy. I could hardly bear to look at him, and whenever I gave him a little money, or sent him a present on some holiday, he put that away, too. Once a man gets an idea into his head, there's no doing anything with him.

"The years passed, he was sent to another gubernia,[2] he was over forty, and was still reading advertisements in the papers, and saving up. At last I heard he had married. All for the same purpose, to buy himself an estate with gooseberry bushes on it, he married an ugly elderly widow, for whom he had not the slightest affection, just because she had some money. After his marriage he went on living as thriftily as ever, half-starving his wife, and putting her money in his own bank account. Her first husband had been a postmaster, and she was used to pies and cordials, but with her second husband she did not even get enough black bread to eat. She began to languish under such a regime, and three years later yielded up her soul to God. Of course my brother did not for a moment consider himself guilty of her death. Money, like vodka, makes a man eccentric. There was a merchant in our town who asked for a plate of honey on his deathbed and ate up all his bank-notes and lottery tickets with the honey, so that no one else should get it. And one day when I was examining a consignment of cattle at a railway station, a drover fell under the engine and his leg was severed from his body. We carried him all bloody into the waiting-room, a terrible sight, and he did nothing but beg us to look for his leg, worrying all the time—there were twenty rubles in the boot, and he was afraid they would be lost."

"You're losing the thread," put in Burkin.

Ivan Ivanich paused for a moment, and went on: "After his wife's death my brother began to look about for an estate. You can search for five years, of course, and in the end make a mistake and buy something quite different from what you dreamed of. My brother Nikolai bought three hundred acres, complete with gentleman's house, servants' quarters, and a park, as well as a mortgage to be paid through an agent, but there were neither an orchard, gooseberry bushes, nor a pond with ducks on it. There was a river, but it was as dark as coffee, owing to the fact that there was a brick-works on one side of the estate, and bone-kilns on the other. Nothing daunted, however, my brother Nikolai Ivanich ordered two dozen gooseberry bushes and settled down as a landed proprietor.

"Last year I paid him a visit. I thought I would go and see how he was getting on there. In his letters my brother gave his address as Chumbaroklova Pustosh or Himalaiskoye. I arrived at Himalaiskoye in the afternoon. It was very hot. Everywhere were ditches, fences, hedges, rows of fir-trees, and it was hard to drive into the yard and find a place to leave one's carriage. As I went a fat ginger-coloured

---

2 *gubernia,* a province.

dog, remarkably like a pig, came out to meet me. It looked as if it would have barked if it were not so lazy. The cook, who was also fat and like a pig, came out of the kitchen, barefoot, and said her master was having his after-dinner rest. I made my way to my brother's room, and found him sitting up in bed, his knees covered by a blanket. He had aged, and grown stout and flabby. His cheeks, nose and lips protruded—I almost expected him to grunt into the blanket.

"We embraced and wept—tears of joy, mingled with melancholy—because we had once been young and were now both grey-haired and approaching the grave. He put on his clothes and went out to show me over his estate.

" 'Well, how are you getting on here?' I asked.

" 'All right, thanks be, I'm enjoying myself.' "

"He was no longer the poor, timid clerk, but a true proprietor, a gentleman. He had settled down, and was entering with zest into country life. He ate a lot, washed in the bath-house, and put on flesh. He had already got into litigation with the village commune, the brick-works and the bone-kilns, and took offence if the peasants failed to call him 'Your Honour.' He went in for religion in a solid, gentlemanly way, and there was nothing casual about his pretentious good works. And what were these good works? He treated all the diseases of the peasants with bicarbonate of soda and castor-oil, and had a special thanksgiving service held on his name-day, after which he provided half a pail of vodka, supposing that this was the right thing to do. Oh, those terrible half pails! Today the fat landlord hauls the peasants before the Zemstvo representative[3] for letting their sheep graze on his land, tomorrow, on the day of rejoicing, he treats them to half a pail of vodka, and they drink and sing and shout hurrah, prostrating themselves before him when they are drunk. Any improvement in his conditions, anything like satiety or idleness, develops the most insolent complacency in a Russian. Nikolai Ivanich, who had been afraid of having an opinion of his own when he was in the government service, was now continually coming out with axioms, in the most ministerial manner: 'Education is essential, but the people are not ready for it yet,' 'corporal punishment is an evil, but in certain cases it is beneficial and indispensable.'

" 'I know the people and I know how to treat them,' he said. 'The people love me. I only have to lift my little finger, and the people will do whatever I want.'

"And all this, mark you, with a wise, indulgent smile. Over and

[3] *Zemstvo representative,* a law-enforcing official of the Zemstvo, the elective council responsible for the local administration of a province.

over again he repeated: 'We the gentry,' or 'speaking as a gentleman,' and seemed to have quite forgotten that our grandfather was a peasant, and our father a common soldier. Our very surname—Chimsha-Himalaisky—in reality so absurd, now seemed to him a resounding, distinguished, and euphonious name.

"But it is of myself, and not of him, that I wish to speak. I should like to describe to you the change which came over me in those few hours I spent on my brother's estate. As we were drinking tea in the evening, the cook brought us a full plate of gooseberries. These were not gooseberries bought for money, they came from his own garden, and were the first fruits of the bushes he had planted. Nikolai Ivanich broke into a laugh and gazed at the gooseberries, in tearful silence for at least five minutes. Speechless with emotion, he popped a single gooseberry into his mouth, darted at me the triumphant glance of a child who has at last gained possession of a longed-for toy, and said:

" 'Delicious!'

"And he ate them greedily, repeating over and over again:

" 'Simply delicious! You try them.' "

"They were hard and sour, but, as Pushkin says: 'The lie which elates us is dearer than a thousand sober truths.' I saw before me a really happy man, one whose dearest wish had come true, who had achieved his aim in life, got what he wanted, and was content with his lot and with himself. There had always been a tinge of melancholy in my conception of human happiness, and now, confronted by a happy man, I was overcome by a feeling of sadness bordering on desperation. This feeling grew strongest of all in the night. A bed was made up for me in the room next to my brother's bedroom, and I could hear him moving about restlessly, every now and then getting up to take a gooseberry from a plate. How many happy, satisfied people there are, after all, I said to myself! What an overwhelming force! Just consider this life—the insolence and idleness of the strong, the ignorance and bestiality of the weak, all around intolerable poverty, cramped dwellings, degeneracy, drunkenness, hypocrisy, lying. . . . And yet peace and order apparently prevail in all those homes and in the streets. Of the fifty thousand inhabitants of a town, not one will be found to cry out, to proclaim his indignation aloud. We see those who go to the market to buy food, who eat in the day-time and sleep at night, who prattle away, marry, grow old, carry their dead to the cemeteries. But we neither hear nor see those who suffer, and the terrible things in life are played out behind the scenes. All is calm and quiet, only statistics, which are dumb, protest: so many have gone mad, so many barrels of drink have been consumed, so many children died of malnutrition. . . . And apparently this is as it should be. Apparently those who are happy can only enjoy themselves because the unhappy bear their burdens in silence, and but for this silence happiness would be impossible. It is a kind of universal hypnosis. There ought to be a man with a hammer behind the door of every happy man, to remind him by his constant knocks that there are unhappy people, and that happy as he himself may be, life will sooner or later show him its claws, catastrophe will overtake him—sickness, poverty, loss—and nobody will see it, just as he now neither sees nor hears the misfortunes of others. But there is no man with a hammer, the happy man goes on living and the petty vicissitudes of life touch him lightly, like the wind in an aspen-tree, and all is well.

"That night I understood that I, too, was happy and content," continued Ivan Ivanich, getting up. "I, too, while out hunting, or at the dinner table, have held forth on the right way to live, to worship, to manage the people. I, too, have declared that without knowledge there can be no light, that education is essential, but that bare literacy is sufficient for the common people. Freedom is a blessing, I have said, one can't get on without it, any more than without air, but we must wait. Yes, that is what I said, and now I ask: In the name of what must we wait?" Here Ivan Ivanich looked angrily at Burkin. "In the name of what must we wait, I ask you. What is there to be considered? Don't be in such a hurry, they tell me, every idea materializes gradually, in its own time. But who are they who say this? What is the proof that it is just? You refer to the natural order of things, to the logic of facts, but according to what order, what logic do I, a living, thinking individual, stand on the edge of a ditch and wait for it to be gradually filled up, or choked with silt, when I might leap across it or build a bridge over it? And again, in the name of what must we wait? Wait, when we have not the strength to live, though live we must and to live we desire!

"I left my brother early the next morning, and ever since I have found town life intolerable. The peace and order weigh on my spirits, and I am afraid to look into windows, because there is now no sadder spectacle for me than a happy family seated around the tea-table. I am old and unfit for the struggle, I am even incapable of feeling hatred. I can only suffer inwardly, and give way to irritation and annoyance, at night my head burns from the rush of thoughts, and I am unable to sleep. . . . Oh, if only I were young!"

Ivan Ivanich began pacing backwards and forwards, repeating:

"If only I were young still!"

Suddenly he went up to Alekhin and began pressing first one of his hands, and then the other.

"Pavel Konstantinich," he said in imploring accents. "Don't *you* fall into apathy, don't *you* let your conscience be lulled to sleep! While you are still young, strong, active, do not be weary of well-doing. There is no such thing as happiness, nor ought there to be, but if there is any sense or purpose in life, this sense and purpose are to be found not in our own happiness, but in something greater and more rational. Do good!"

Ivan Ivanich said all this with a piteous, imploring smile, as if he were asking for something for himself.

Then they all three sat in their armchairs a long way apart from one another, and said nothing. Ivan Ivanich's story satisfied neither Burkin or Alekhin. It was not interesting to listen to the story of a poor clerk who ate gooseberries, when from the walls generals and fine ladies, who seemed to come to life in the dark, were looking down from their gilded frames. It would have been much more interesting to hear about elegant people, lovely women. And the fact that they were sitting in a drawing-room in which everything—the swathed chandeliers, the arm-chairs, the carpet on the floor, proved that the people now looking out of the frames had once moved about here, sat in the chairs, drunk tea, where the fair Pelageya was now going noiselessly to and fro, was better than any story.

Alekhin was desperately sleepy. He had got up early, at three o'clock in the morning, to go about his work on the estate, and could now hardly keep his eyes open. But he would not go to bed, for fear one of his guests would relate something interesting after he was gone. He could not be sure whether what Ivan Ivanich had just told them was wise or just, but his visitors talked of other things besides grain, hay, or tar, of things which had no direct bearing on his daily life, and he liked this, and wanted them to go on. . . .

"Well, time to go to bed," said Burkin, getting up. "Allow me to wish you a good night."

Alekhin said good night and went downstairs to his own room, the visitors remaining on the upper floor. They were allotted a big room for the night, in which were two ancient bedsteads of carved wood, and an ivory crucifix in one corner. There was a pleasant smell of freshly laundered sheets from the wide, cool beds which the fair Pelageya made up for them.

Ivan Ivanich undressed in silence and lay down.

"Lord have mercy on us, sinners," he said, and covered his head with the sheet.

There was a strong smell of stale tobacco from his pipe, which he put on the table, and Burkin lay awake a long time, wondering where the stifling smell came from.

The rain tapped on the window-panes all night.

## JAMES JOYCE (1882–1941)

# *Araby*

North Richmond Street, being blind, was a quiet street except at the hour when the Christian Brothers' School set the boys free. An uninhabited house of two stories stood at the blind end, detached from its neighbours in a square ground. The other houses of the street, conscious of decent lives within them, gazed at one another with brown imperturbable faces.

The former tenant of our house, a priest, had died in the back drawing-room. Air, musty from having been long enclosed, hung in all the rooms, and the waste room behind the kitchen was littered with old useless papers. Among these I found a few paper-covered books, the pages of which were curled and damp: *The Abbot,* by Walter Scott, *The Devout Communicant,* and *The Memoirs of Vidocq.* I liked the last best because its leaves were yellow. The wild garden behind the house contained a central apple tree and a few straggling bushes under one of which I found the late tenant's rusty bicycle pump. He had been a very charitable priest; in his will he had left all his money to institutions and the furniture of his house to his sister.

When the short days of winter came dusk fell before we had well eaten our dinners. When we met in the street the houses had grown sombre. The space of sky above us was the colour of ever-changing violet and towards it the lamps of the street lifted their feeble lanterns. The cold air stung us and we played till our bodies glowed. Our shouts echoed in the silent street. The career of our play brought us through the dark muddy lanes behind the houses where we ran the gauntlet of the rough tribes from the cottages, to the back doors of the dark dripping gardens where odours arose from the ash-pits, to the dark odorous stables where a coachman smoothed and combed the horse or shook music from the buckled harness. When we returned to the street, light from the kitchen windows had filled the areas. If my uncle was seen turning the corner we hid in the shadow until we had seen him safely housed. Or if Mangan's sister came out on the doorstep to call her brother in to his tea we watched her from our shadow peer up and down the street. We waited to see whether she would remain or go in and, if she remained, we left our shadow and walked up to Mangan's steps resignedly. She was waiting for us, her figure defined by the light from the half-opened door. Her brother always teased her before he obeyed and I stood by the railings looking at her. Her dress swung as she moved her body and the soft rope of her hair tossed from side to side.

Every morning I lay on the floor in the front parlour watching her door. The blind was pulled down to within an inch of the sash so that I could not be seen. When she came out on the doorstep my heart leaped. I ran to the hall, seized my books and followed her. I kept her brown figure always in my eye and, when we came near the point at which our ways diverged, I quickened my pace and passed her. This happened morning after morning. I had never spoken to her, except for a few casual words, and yet her name was like a summons to all my foolish blood.

Her image accompanied me even in places the most hostile to romance. On Saturday evenings when my aunt went marketing I had to go to carry some of the parcels. We walked through the flaring streets, jostled by drunken men and bargaining women, amid the curses of labourers, the shrill litanies of shop-boys who stood on guard by the barrels of pigs' cheeks, the nasal chanting of street-singers, who sang a *come-all-you* about O'Donovan Rossa, or a ballad about the troubles in our native land. These noises converged in a single sensation of life for me: I imagined that I bore my chalice safely through a throng of foes. Her name sprang to my lips at moments in strange prayers and praises which I myself did not understand. My eyes were often full of tears (I could not tell why) and at times a flood from my heart seemed to pour itself out into my bosom. I thought little of the future. I did not know whether I would ever speak to her or not or, if I spoke to her, how I could tell her of my confused adoration.. But my body was like a harp and her words and gestures were like fingers running upon the wires.

One evening I went into the back drawing-room in which the priest had died. It was a dark rainy evening and there was no sound in the house. Through one of the broken panes I heard the rain impinge upon the earth, the fine incessant needles of water playing in the sodden beds. Some distant lamp or lighted window gleamed below me. I was thankful that I could see so little. All my senses seemed to desire to veil themselves and, feeling that I was about to slip from them, I pressed the palms of my hands together until they trembled, murmuring: *"O love! O love!"* many times.

At last she spoke to me. When she addressed the first words to me I was so confused that I did not know what to answer. She asked me was I going to *Araby*. I forgot whether I answered yes or no. It would be a splendid bazaar, she said she would love to go.

"And why can't you?" I asked.

While she spoke she turned a silver bracelet round and round her wrist. She could not go, she said, because there would be a retreat that week in her convent. Her brother and two other boys were fighting for their caps and I was alone at the railings. She held one of the spikes, bowing her head towards me. The light from the lamp opposite our door caught the white curve of her neck, lit up her hair that rested there and, falling, lit up the hand upon the railing. It fell over one side of her dress and caught the white border of a petticoat, just visible as she stood at ease.

"It's well for you," she said.

"If I go," I said, "I will bring you something."

What innumerable follies laid waste my waking and sleeping thoughts after the evening! I wished to annihilate the tedious intervening days. I chafed against the work of school. At night in my bedroom and by day in the classroom her image came between me and the page I strove to read. The syllables of the word *Araby* were called to me through the silence in which my soul luxuriated and cast an Eastern enchantment over me. I asked for leave to go to the bazaar on Saturday night. My aunt was surprised and hoped it was not some Freemason affair. I answered few questions in class. I watched my master's face pass from amiability to sternness; he hoped I was not beginning to idle, I could not call my wandering thoughts together. I had hardly any patience with the serious work of life which, now that it stood between me and my desire, seemed to me child's play, ugly monotonous child's play.

On Saturday morning I reminded my uncle that I wished to go to the bazaar in the evening. He was fussing at the hall-stand, looking for the hat brush, and answered me curtly:

"Yes, boy, I know."

As he was in the hall I could not go into the front parlour and lie at the window. I left the house in bad humour and walked slowly towards the school. The air was pitilessly raw and already my heart misgave me.

When I came home to dinner my uncle had not yet been home. Still it was early. I sat staring at the clock for some time and, when its ticking began to irritate me, I left the room. I mounted the staircase and gained the upper part of the house. The high cold empty gloomy rooms liberated me and I went from room to room singing. From the front window I saw my companions playing below in the street. Their cries reached me weakened and indistinct and, leaning my forehead against the cool glass, I looked over at the dark house where she lived. I may have stood there for an hour, seeing nothing but the brown-clad figure cast by my imagination, touched discreetly by the lamplight at the curved neck, at the hand upon the railings and at the border below the dress.

When I came downstairs again I found Mrs. Mercer sitting at the fire. She was an old garrulous woman, a pawnbroker's widow, who collected used stamps for some pious purpose. I had to endure the gossip of the tea-table. The meal was prolonged beyond an hour and still my uncle did not come. Mrs. Mercer stood up to go: she was sorry she couldn't wait any longer, but it was after eight o'clock and she did not like to be out late, as the night air was bad for her. When she had gone I began to walk up and down the room, clenching my fists. My aunt said:

"I'm afraid you may put off your bazaar for this night of Our Lord."

At nine o'clock I heard my uncle's latchkey in the hall-door. I heard him talking to himself and heard the hall-stand rocking when it had received the weight of his overcoat. I could interpret these signs. When he was midway through his dinner I asked him to give me the money to go to the bazaar. He had forgotten.

"The people are in bed and after their first sleep now," he said.

I did not smile. My aunt said to him energetically:

"Can't you give him the money and let him go? You've kept him late enough as it is."

My uncle said he was very sorry he had forgotten. He said he believed in the old saying: "All work and no play makes Jack a dull boy." He asked me where I was going and, when I had told him a second time, he asked me did I know *The Arab's Farewell to his Steed.* When I left the kitchen he was about to recite the opening lines of the piece to my aunt.

I held a florin tightly in my hand as I strode down Buckingham Street towards the station. The sight of the streets thronged with buyers and glaring with gas recalled to me the purpose of my journey. I took my seat in a third-class carriage of a deserted train. After an intolerable delay the train moved out of the station slowly. It crept onward among ruinous houses and over the twinkling river. At Westland Row Station a crowd of people pressed to the carriage doors; but the porters moved them back, saying that it was a special train for the bazaar. I remained alone in the bare carriage. In a few minutes the train drew up beside an improvised wooden platform. I passed out on the road and saw by the lighted dial of a clock that it was ten minutes to ten. In front of me was a large building which displayed the magical name.

I could not find any sixpenny entrance and, fearing that the bazaar would be closed, I passed in quickly through a turnstile, handing a shilling to a weary-looking man. I found myself in a big hall girdled at half its height by a gallery. Nearly all the stalls were closed and the greater part of the hall was in darkness. I recognized a silence like that which pervades a church after a service. I walked into the center of the bazaar timidly. A few people were gathered about the stalls which were still open. Before a curtain, over which the words *Café Chantant* were written in coloured lamps, two men were counting money on a salver. I listened to the fall of the coins.

Remembering with difficulty why I had come I went over to one of the stalls and examined porcelain vases and flowered tea-sets. At the door of the stall a young lady was talking and laughing with two young gentlemen. I remarked their English accents and listened vaguely to their conversation.

"O, I never said such a thing!"

"O, but you did!"

"O, but I didn't!"

"Didn't she say that?"

"Yes. I heard her."

"O, there's a . . . fib!"

Observing me, the young lady came over and asked me did I wish to buy anything. The tone of her voice was not encouraging; she seemed to have spoken to me out of a sense of duty. I looked humbly at the great jars that stood like eastern guards at either side of the dark entrance to the stall and murmured:

"No, thank you."

The young lady changed the position of one of the vases and went back to the two young men. They began to talk of the same subject. Once or twice the young lady glanced at me over her shoulder.

I lingered before her stall, though I knew my stay was useless, to make my interest in her wares seem the more real. Then I turned away slowly and walked down the middle of the bazaar. I allowed the two pennies to fall against the sixpence in my pocket. I heard a voice call from one end of the gallery that the light was out. The upper part of the hall was now completely dark.

Gazing up into the darkness I saw myself as a creature driven and derided by vanity; and my eyes burned with anguish and anger.

## FRANZ KAFKA (1883–1924)

# *The Bucket-Rider*

Coal all spent; the bucket empty, the shovel useless; the stove breathing out cold; the room freezing; the leaves outside the window rigid, covered with rime; the sky a silver shield against anyone who looks for help from it. I must have coal; I cannot freeze to death; behind me is the pitiless stove, before me the pitiless sky, so I must ride out between them and on my journey seek aid from the coal-dealer. But he has already grown deaf to ordinary appeals; I must prove irrefutably to him that I have not a single grain of coal left, and that he means to me the very sun in the firmament. I must approach like a beggar who, with the death-rattle already in his throat, insists on dying on the doorstep, and to whom the grand people's cook accordingly decides to give the dregs of the coffee-pot; just so must the coal-dealer, filled with rage, but acknowledging the command, "Thou shalt not kill," fling a shovelful of coal into my bucket.

My mode of arrival must decide the matter; so I ride off on the bucket. Seated on the bucket, my hands on the handle, the simplest kind of bridle, I propel myself with difficulty down the stairs; but once down below my bucket ascends, superbly, superbly; camels humbly squatting on the ground do not rise with more dignity, shaking themselves under the sticks of their drivers. Through the hard frozen streets we go at a regular canter; often I am upraised as high as the first story of a house; never do I sink as low as the house doors. And at last I float at an extraordinary height above the vaulted cellar of the dealer, whom I see far below crouching over his table, where he is writing; he has opened the door to let out the excessive heat.

"Coal-dealer!" I cry in a voice burned hollow by the frost and muffled in the cloud made by my breath, "please, coal-dealer, give me a little coal. My bucket is so light that I can ride on it. Be kind. When I can I'll pay you."

The dealer puts his hand to his ear. "Do I hear rightly?" He throws the question over his shoulder to his wife. "Do I hear rightly? A customer."

"I hear nothing," says his wife, breathing in and out peacefully while she knits on, her back pleasantly warmed by the heat.

"Oh, yes, you must hear," I cry. "It's me; an old customer; faithful and true; only without means at the moment."

"Wife," says the dealer, "it's some one, it must be; my ears can't have deceived me so much as that; it must be an old, a very old customer, that can move me so deeply."

"What ails you, man?" says his wife, ceasing from her work for a moment and pressing her knitting to her bosom. "It's nobody, the street is empty, all our customers are provided for; we could close down the shop for several days and take a rest."

"But I'm sitting up here on the bucket," I cry, and unfeeling frozen tears dim my eyes, "please look up here, just once; you'll see me directly; I beg you, just a shovelful; and if you give me more it'll make me so happy that I won't know what to do. All the other customers are provided for. Oh, if I could only hear the coal clattering into the bucket!"

"I'm coming," says the coal-dealer, and on his short legs he makes to climb the steps of the cellar, but his wife is already beside him, holds him back by the arm and says: "You stay here; seeing you persist in your fancies I'll go myself. Think of the bad fit of coughing you had during the night. But for a piece of business, even if it's one you've only fancied in your head, you're prepared to forget your wife and child and sacrifice your lungs. I'll go."

"Then be sure to tell him all the kinds of coal we have in stock; I'll shout out the prices after you."

"Right," says his wife, climbing up to the street. Naturally she sees me at once. "Frau Coal-dealer," I cry, "my humblest greetings; just one shovelful of coal; here in my bucket; I'll carry it home myself. One shovelful of the worst you have. I'll pay you in full for it, of course, but not just now, not just now." What a knell-like sound the words "not just now" have, and how bewilderingly they mingle with the evening chimes that fall from the church steeple nearby!

"Well, what does he want?" shouts the dealer. "Nothing," his wife shouts back, "there's nothing here; I see nothing, I hear nothing; only six striking, and now we must shut up the shop. The cold is terrible; tomorrow we'll likely have lots to do again."

She sees nothing and hears nothing; but all the same she loosens her apron-strings and waves her apron to waft me away. She succeeds, unluckily. My bucket has all the virtues of a good steed except powers of resistance, which it has not; it is too light; a woman's apron can make it fly through the air.

"You bad woman!" I shout back, while she, turning into the shop, half-contemptuous, half-reassured, flourishes her fist in the air. "You bad woman! I begged you for a shovelful of the worst coal and you would not give me it." And with that I ascend into the regions of the ice mountains and am lost forever.

## D. H. LAWRENCE (1885–1930)

# *The Rocking-Horse Winner*

There was a woman who was beautiful, who started with all the advantages, yet she had no luck. She married for love, and the love turned to dust. She had bonny children, yet she felt they had been thrust upon her, and she could not love them. They looked at her coldly, as if they were finding fault with her. And hurriedly she felt she must cover up some fault in herself. Yet what it was that she must cover up she never knew. Nevertheless, when her children were present, she always felt the centre of her heart go hard. This troubled her, and in her manner she was all the more gentle and anxious for her children, as if she loved them very much. Only she herself knew that at the centre of her heart was a hard little place that could not feel love, no, not for anybody. Everybody else said of her: "She is such a good mother. She adores her children." Only she herself, and her children themselves, knew it was not so. They read it in each other's eyes.

There were a boy and two little girls. They lived in a pleasant house, with a garden, and they had discreet servants, and felt themselves superior to anyone in the neighbourhood.

Although they lived in style, they felt always an anxiety in the house. There was never enough money. The mother had a small income, and the father had a small income, but not nearly enough for the social position which they had to keep up. The father went into town to some office. But though he had good prospects, these prospects never materialized. There was always the grinding sense of the shortage of money, though the style was always kept up.

At last the mother said: "I will see if I can't make something." But she did not know where to begin. She racked her brains, and tried this thing and the other, but could not find anything successful. The failure made deep lines come into her face. Her children were growing up, they would have to go to school. There must be more money, there must be more money. The father, who was always very handsome and expensive in his tastes, seemed as if he never would be able to do anything worth doing. And the mother, who had a great belief in herself, did not succeed any better, and her tastes were just as expensive.

And so the house came to be haunted by the unspoken phrase: There must be more money! There must be more money! The children could hear it all the time, though nobody said it aloud. They heard it at Christmas, when the expensive and splendid toys filled the nursery. Behind the shining modern rocking horse, behind the smart doll's-house, a voice would start whispering: "There must be more money! There must be more money!" And the children would stop playing, to listen for a moment. They would look into each other's eyes, to see if they had all heard. And each one saw in the eyes of the other two that they too had heard. "There must be more money! There must be more money!"

It came whispering from the springs of the still-swaying rocking horse, and even the horse, bending his wooden, champing head, heard it. The big doll, sitting so pink and smirking in her new pram, could hear it quite plainly, and seemed to be smirking all the more self-consciously because of it. The foolish puppy, too, that took the place of the Teddy bear, he was looking so extraordinarily foolish for no other reason but that he heard the secret whisper all over the house: "There must be more money!"

Yet nobody ever said it aloud. The whisper was everywhere, and therefore no one spoke it. Just as no one ever says: "We are breathing!" in spite of the fact that breath is coming and going all the time.

"Mother," said the boy Paul one day, "why don't we keep a car of our own? Why do we always use uncle's, or else a taxi?"

"Because we're the poor members of the family," said the mother.

"But why are we, mother?"

"Well—I suppose," she said slowly and bitterly, "it's because your father has no luck."

The boy was silent for some time.

"Is luck money, mother?" he asked, rather timidly.

"No, Paul. Not quite. It's what causes you to have money."

"Oh!" said Paul vaguely. "I thought when Uncle Oscar said filthy lucker, it meant money."

"Filthy lucre does mean money," said the mother. "But it's lucre, not luck."

"Oh!" said the boy. "Then what is luck, mother?"

"It's what causes you to have money. If you're lucky you have money. That's why it's better to be born lucky than rich. If you're rich, you may lose your money. But if you're lucky, you will always get more money."

"Oh! Will you? And is father not lucky?"

"Very unlucky, I should say," she said bitterly.

The boy watched her with unsure eyes.

"Why?" he asked.

"I don't know. Nobody ever knows why one person is lucky and another unlucky."

"Don't they? Nobody at all? Does nobody know?"

"Perhaps God. But He never tells."

"He ought to, then. And aren't you lucky either, mother?"

"I can't be, if I married an unlucky husband."

"But by yourself, aren't you?"

"I used to think I was, before I married. Now I think I am very unlucky indeed."

"Why?"

"Well—never mind! Perhaps I'm not really," she said.

The child looked at her, to see if she meant it. But he saw, by the lines of her mouth, that she was only trying to hide something from him.

"Well, anyhow," he said stoutly, "I'm a lucky person."

"Why?" said his mother, with a sudden laugh.

He stared at her. He didn't even know why he had said it.

"God told me," he asserted, brazening it out.

"I hope He did, dear!" she said, again with a laugh, but rather bitter.

"He did, mother!"

"Excellent!" said the mother, using one of her husband's exclamations.

The boy saw she did not believe him; or, rather, that she paid no attention to his assertion. This angered him somewhat, and made him want to compel her attention.

He went off by himself, vaguely, in a childish way, seeking for the clue to "luck." Absorbed, taking no heed of other people, he went about with a sort of stealth, seeking inwardly for luck. He wanted luck, he wanted it, he wanted it. When the two girls were playing dolls in the nursery, he would sit on his big rocking horse, charging madly into space, with a frenzy that made the little girls peer at him uneasily. Wildly the horse careered, the waving dark hair of the boy tossed, his eyes had a strange glare in them. The little girls dared not speak to him.

When he had ridden to the end of his mad little journey, he climbed down and stood in front of his rocking horse, staring fixedly into its lowered face. Its red mouth was slightly open, its big eye was wide and glassy-bright.

"Now!" he would silently command the snorting steed. "Now, take me to where there is luck! Now take me!"

And he would slash the horse on the neck with the little whip he had asked Uncle Oscar for. He knew the horse could take him to where there was luck, if only he forced it. So he would mount again, and start on his furious ride, hoping at last to get there. He knew he could get there.

"You'll break your horse, Paul!" said the nurse.

"He's always riding like that! I wish he'd leave off!" said his elder sister Joan.

But he only glared down on them in silence. Nurse gave him up.

She could make nothing of him. Anyhow he was growing beyond her.

One day his mother and his Uncle Oscar came in when he was on one of his furious rides. He did not speak to them.

"Hallo, you young jockey! Riding a winner?" said his uncle.

"Aren't you growing too big for a rocking horse? You're not a very little boy any longer, you know," said his mother.

But Paul only gave a blue glare from his big, rather close-set eyes. He would speak to nobody when he was in full tilt. His mother watched him with an anxious expression on her face.

At last he suddenly stopped forcing his horse into the mechanical gallop, and slid down.

"Well, I got there!" he announced fiercely, his blue eyes still flaring, and his sturdy long legs straddling apart.

"Where did you get to?" asked his mother.

"Where I wanted to go," he flared back at her.

"That's right, son!" said Uncle Oscar. "Don't you stop till you get there. What's the horse's name?"

"He doesn't have a name," said the boy.

"Gets on without all right?" asked the uncle.

"Well, he has different names. He was called Sansovino last week."

"Sansovino, eh? Won the Ascot. How did you know his name?"

"He always talks about horse races with Bassett," said Joan.

The uncle was delighted to find that his small nephew was posted with all the racing news. Bassett, the young gardener, who had been wounded in the left foot in the war and had got his present job through Oscar Cresswell, whose batman he had been, was a perfect blade of the "turf." He lived in the racing events, and the small boy lived with him.

Oscar Cresswell got it all from Bassett.

"Master Paul comes and asks me, so I can't do more than tell him, sir," said Bassett, his face terribly serious, as if he were speaking of religious matters.

"And does he ever put anything on a horse he fancies?"

"Well—I don't want to give him away—he's a young sport, a fine sport, sir. Would you mind asking him yourself? He sort of takes a pleasure in it, and perhaps he'd feel I was giving him away, sir, if you don't mind."

Bassett was serious as a church.

The uncle went back to his nephew, and took him off for a ride in the car.

"Say, Paul, old man, do you ever put anything on a horse?" the uncle asked.

The boy watched the handsome man closely.

"Why, do you think I oughtn't to?" he parried.

"Not a bit of it! I thought perhaps you might give me a tip for the Lincoln."

The car sped on into the country, going down to Uncle Oscar's place in Hampshire.

"Honour bright?" said the nephew.

"Honour bright, son!" said the uncle.

"Well, then, Daffodil."

"Daffodil! I doubt it, sonny. What about Mirza?"

"I only know the winner," said the boy. "That's Daffodil."

"Daffodil, eh?"

There was a pause. Daffodil was an obscure horse comparatively.

"Uncle!"

"Yes, son?"

"You won't let it go any further, will you? I promised Bassett."

"Bassett be damned, old man! What's he got to do with it?"

"We're partners. We've been partners from the first. Uncle, he lent me my first five shillings, which I lost. I promised him, honour bright, it was only between me and him; only you gave me that ten-shilling note I started winning with, so I thought you were lucky. You won't let it go any further, will you?"

The boy gazed at his uncle from those big, hot, blue eyes, set rather close together. The uncle stirred and laughed uneasily.

"Right you are, son! I'll keep your tip private. Daffodil, eh? How much are you putting on him?"

"All except twenty pounds," said the boy. "I keep that in reserve."

The uncle thought it a good joke.

"You keep twenty pounds in reserve, do you, you young romancer? What are you betting, then?"

"I'm betting three hundred," said the boy gravely. "But it's between you and me, Uncle Oscar! Honour bright?"

The uncle burst into a roar of laughter.

"It's between you and me all right, you young Nat Gould," he said, laughing. "But where's your three hundred?"

"Bassett keeps it for me. We're partners."

"You are, are you! And what is Bassett putting on Daffodil?"

"He won't go quite as high as I do, I expect. Perhaps he'll go a hundred and fifty."

"What, pennies?" laughed the uncle.

"Pounds," said the child, with a surprised look at his uncle. "Bassett keeps a bigger reserve than I do."

Between wonder and amusement Uncle Oscar was silent. He pursued the matter no further, but he determined to take his nephew with him to the Lincoln races.

"Now, son," he said, "I'm putting twenty on Mirza, and I'll put five for you on any horse you fancy. What's your pick?"

"Daffodil, uncle."

"No, not the fiver on Daffodil!"

"I should if it was my own fiver," said the child.

"Good! Good! Right you are! A fiver for me and a fiver for you on Daffodil."

The child had never been to a race meeting before, and his eyes were blue fire. He pursed his mouth tight, and watched. A Frenchman just in front had put his money on Lancelot. Wild with excitement, he flayed his arms up and down, yelling "Lancelot! Lancelot!" in his French accent.

Daffodil came in first, Lancelot second, Mirza third. The child, flushed and with eyes blazing, was curiously serene. His uncle brought him four five-pound notes, four to one.

"What am I to do with these?" he cried, waving them before the boy's eyes.

"I suppose we'll talk to Bassett," said the boy. "I expect I have fifteen hundred now; and twenty in reserve; and this twenty."

His uncle studied him for some moments.

"Look here, son!" he said. "You're not serious about Bassett and that fifteen hundred, are you?"

"Yes, I am. But it's between you and me, uncle. Honour bright!"

"Honour bright all right, son! But I must talk to Bassett."

"If you'd like to be a partner, uncle, with Bassett and me, we could all be partners. Only, you'd have to promise, honour bright, uncle, not to let it go beyond us three. Bassett and I are lucky, and you must be lucky, because it was your ten shillings I started winning with . . ."

Uncle Oscar took both Bassett and Paul into Richmond Park for an afternoon, and there they talked.

"It's like this, you see, sir," Bassett said. "Master Paul would get me talking about racing events, spinning yarns, you know, sir. And he was always keen on knowing if I'd made or if I'd lost. It's about a year since, now, that I put five shillings on Blush of Dawn for him—and we lost. Then the luck turned, with that ten shillings he had from you, that we put on Singhalese. And since that time, it's been pretty steady, all things considering. What do you say, Master Paul?"

"We're all right when we're sure," said Paul. "It's when we're not quite sure that we go down."

"Oh, but we're careful then," said Bassett.

"But when are you sure?" smiled Uncle Oscar.

"It's Master Paul, sir," said Bassett, in a secret, religious voice. "It's as if he had it from heaven. Like Daffodil, now, for the Lincoln. That was as sure as eggs."

"Did you put anything on Daffodil?" asked Oscar Cresswell.

"Yes, sir, I made my bit."

"And my nephew?"

Bassett was obstinately silent, looking at Paul.

"I made twelve hundred, didn't I, Bassett? I told uncle I was putting three hundred on Daffodil."

"That's right," said Bassett, nodding.

"But where's the money?" asked the uncle.

"I keep it safe locked up, sir. Master Paul he can have it any minute he likes to ask for it."

"What, fifteen hundred pounds?"

"And twenty! and forty, that is, with the twenty he made on the course."

"It's amazing!" said the uncle.

"If Master Paul offers you to be partners, sir, I would, if I were you; if you'll excuse me," said Bassett.

Oscar Cresswell thought about it.

"I'll see the money," he said.

They drove home again, and sure enough, Bassett came round to the garden-house with fifteen hundred pounds in notes. The twenty pounds reserve was left with Joe Glee, in the Turf Commission deposit.

"You see, it's all right, uncle, when I'm sure! Then we go strong, for all we're worth. Don't we, Bassett?"

"We do that, Master Paul."

"And when are you sure?" said the uncle, laughing.

"Oh, well, sometimes I'm absolutely sure, like about Daffodil," said the boy; "and sometimes I have an idea; and sometimes I haven't even an idea, have I, Bassett? Then we're careful, because we mostly go down."

"You do, do you! And when you're sure, like about Daffodil, what makes you sure, sonny?"

"Oh, well, I don't know," said the boy uneasily. "I'm sure, you know, uncle; that's all."

"It's as if he had it from heaven, sir," Bassett reiterated.

"I should say so!" said the uncle.

But he became a partner. And when the Leger was coming on, Paul was "sure" about Lively Spark, which was a quite inconsiderable horse. The boy insisted on putting a thousand on the horse, Bassett went for five hundred, and Oscar Cresswell two hundred. Lively Spark came in first, and the betting had been ten to one against him. Paul had made ten thousand.

"You see," he said, "I was absolutely sure of him."

Even Oscar Cresswell had cleared two thousand.

"Look here, son," he said, "this sort of thing makes me nervous."

"It needn't, uncle! Perhaps I shan't be sure again for a long time."

"But what are you going to do with your money?" asked the uncle.

"Of course," said the boy, "I started it for mother. She said she had no luck, because father is unlucky, so I thought if I was lucky, it might stop whispering."

"What might stop whispering?"

"Our house. I hate our house for whispering."

"What does it whisper?"

"Why—why"—the boy fidgeted—"why, I don't know. But it's always short of money, you know, uncle."

"I know it, son, I know it."

"You know people send mother writs, don't you, uncle?"

"I'm afraid I do," said the uncle.

"And then the house whispers, like people laughing at you behind your back. It's awful, that is! I thought if I was lucky . . ."

"You might stop it," added the uncle.

The boy watched him with big blue eyes that had an uncanny cold fire in them, and he said never a word.

"Well, then!" said the uncle. "What are we doing?"

"I shouldn't like mother to know I was lucky," said the boy.

"Why not, son?"

"She'd stop me."

"I don't think she would."

"Oh!"—and the boy writhed in an odd way—"I don't want her to know, uncle."

"All right, son! We'll manage it without her knowing."

They managed it very easily. Paul, at the other's suggestion, handed over five thousand pounds to his uncle, who deposited it with the family lawyer, who was then to inform Paul's mother that a relative had put five thousand pounds into his hands, which sum was to be paid out a thousand pounds at a time, on the mother's birthday, for the next five years.

"So she'll have a birthday present of a thousand pounds for five successive years," said Uncle Oscar. "I hope it won't make it all the harder for her later."

Paul's mother had her birthday in November. The house had been "whispering" worse than ever lately, and, even in spite of his luck, Paul could not bear up against it. He was very anxious to see the effect of the birthday letter, telling his mother about the thousand pounds.

When there were no visitors, Paul now took his meals with his parents, as he was beyond the nursery control. His mother went into town nearly every day. She had discovered that she had an odd knack of sketching furs and dress materials, so she worked secretly in the studio of a friend who was the chief "artist" for the leading drapers. She drew the figures of ladies in furs and ladies in silk and sequins for the newspaper advertisements. This young woman artist earned several thousand pounds a year, but Paul's mother only made several hundreds, and she was again dissatisfied. She so wanted to be first in something, and she did not suceed, even in making sketches for drapery advertisements.

She was down to breakfast on the morning of her birthday. Paul watched her face as she read her letters. He knew the lawyer's letter. As his mother read it, her face hardened and became more expressionless. Then a cold, determined look came on her mouth. She hid the letter under the pile of others, and said not a word about it.

"Didn't you have anything nice in the post for your birthday, mother?" said Paul.

"Quite moderately nice," she said, her voice cold and absent.

She went away to town without saying more.

But in the afternoon Uncle Oscar appeared. He said Paul's mother had had a long interview with the lawyer, asking if the whole five thousand could be advanced at once, as she was in debt.

"What do you think, uncle?" said the boy.

"I leave it to you, son."

"Oh, let her have it, then! We can get some more with the other," said the boy.

"A bird in the hand is worth two in the bush, laddie!" said Uncle Oscar.

"But I'm sure to know for the Grand National; or the Lincolnshire; or else the Derby. I'm sure to know for one of them," said Paul.

So Uncle Oscar signed the agreement, and Paul's mother touched the whole five thousand. Then something very curious happened. The voices in the house suddenly went mad, like a chorus of frogs on a spring evening. There were certain new furnishings, and Paul had a tutor. He was really going to Eton, his father's school, in the following autumn. There were flowers in the winter, and a blossoming of the luxury Paul's mother had been used to. And yet the voices in the house, behind the sprays of mimosa and almond blossom, and from under the piles of iridescent cushions, simply trilled and screamed in a sort of ecstasy: "There must be more money! Oh-h-h, there must be more money. Oh, now, now-w! Now-w-w—there must be more money—more than ever! More than ever!"

It frightened Paul terribly. He studied away at his Latin and Greek with his tutors. But his intense hours were spent with Bassett. The Grand National had gone by: he had not "known," and had lost a hundred pounds. Summer was at hand. He was in agony for the Lincoln. But even for the Lincoln he didn't "know" and he lost fifty pounds. He became wild-eyed and strange, as if something were going to explode in him.

"Let it alone, son! Don't you bother about it!" urged Uncle Oscar. But it was as if the boy couldn't really hear what his uncle was saying.

"I've got to know for the Derby! I've got to know for the Derby!" the child reiterated, his big blue eyes blazing with a sort of madness.

His mother noticed how overwrought he was.

"You'd better go to the seaside. Wouldn't you like to go now to the seaside, instead of waiting? I think you'd better," she said, looking down at him anxiously, her heart curiously heavy because of him.

But the child lifted his uncanny blue eyes.

"I couldn't possibly go before the Derby, mother!" he said. "I couldn't possibly!"

"Why not?" she said, her voice becoming heavy when she was opposed. "Why not? You can still go from the seaside to see the Derby with your Uncle Oscar, if that's what you wish. No need for you to wait here. Besides, I think you care too much about these races. It's a bad sign. My family has been a gambling family, and you won't know till you grow up how much damage it has done. But it has done damage. I shall have to send Bassett away, and ask Uncle Oscar not to talk racing to you, unless you promise to be reasonable about it; go away to the seaside and forget it. You're all nerves!"

"I'll do what you like, mother, so long as you don't send me away till after the Derby," the boy said.

"Send you away from where? Just from this house?"

"Yes," he said, gazing at her.

"Why, you curious child, what makes you care about this house so much, suddenly? I never knew you loved it."

He gazed at her without speaking. He had a secret within a secret, something he had not divulged, even to Bassett or to his Uncle Oscar.

But his mother, after standing undecided and a little bit sullen for some moments, said:

"Very well, then! Don't go to the seaside till after the Derby, if you don't wish it. But promise me you won't let your nerves go to pieces. Promise you won't think so much about horse racing and events, as you call them!"

"Oh, no," said the boy casually. "I won't think much about them, mother. You needn't worry. I wouldn't worry, mother, if I were you."

"If you were me and I were you," said his mother, "I wonder what we should do!"

"But you know you needn't worry, mother, don't you?" the boy repeated.

"I should be awfully glad to know it," she said wearily.

"Oh, well, you can, you know. I mean, you ought to know you needn't worry," he insisted.

"Ought I? Then I'll see about it," she said.

Paul's secret of secrets was his wooden horse, that which had no name. Since he was emancipated from a nurse and a nursery-governess, he had had his rocking horse removed to his own bedroom at the top of the house.

"Surely, you're too big for a rocking horse!" his mother had remonstrated.

"Well, you see, mother, till I can have a real horse, I like to have some sort of animal about," had been his quaint answer.

"Do you feel he keeps you company?" she laughed.

"Oh, yes! He's very good, he always keeps me company, when I'm there," said Paul.

So the horse, rather shabby, stood in an arrested prance in the boy's bedroom.

The Derby was drawing near, and the boy grew more and more tense. He hardly heard what was spoken to him, he was very frail, and his eyes were really uncanny. His mother had sudden seizures of uneasiness about him. Sometimes, for half-an-hour, she would feel a sudden anxiety about him that was almost anguish. She wanted to rush to him at once, and know he was safe.

Two nights before the Derby, she was at a big party in town, when one of her rushes of anxiety about her boy, her first-born, gripped her heart till she could hardly speak. She fought with the feeling, might and main, for she believed in common sense. But it was too strong. She had to leave the dance and go downstairs to telephone to the country. The children's nursery-governess was terribly surprised and startled at being rung up in the night.

"Are the children all right, Miss Wilmot?"

"Oh, yes, they are quite all right."

"Master Paul? Is he all right?"

"He went to bed as right as a trivet. Shall I run up and look at him?"

"No," said Paul's mother reluctantly. "No! Don't trouble. It's all right. Don't sit up. We shall be home fairly soon." She did not want her son's privacy intruded upon.

"Very good," said the governess.

It was about one o'clock when Paul's mother and father drove up to their house. All was still. Paul's mother went to her room and slipped off her white fur coat. She had told her maid not to wait up for her. She heard her husband downstairs, mixing a whisky-and-soda.

And then, because of the strange anxiety at her heart, she stole upstairs to her son's room. Noiselessly she went along the upper corridor. Was there a faint noise? What was it?

She stood, with arrested muscles, outside his door, listening. There was a strange, heavy, and yet not loud noise. Her heart stood still. It was a soundless noise, yet rushing and powerful. Something huge, in violent, hushed motion. What was it? What in God's name was it? She ought to know. She felt that she knew the noise. She knew what it was.

Yet she could not place it. She couldn't say what it was. And on and on it went, like a madness.

Softly, frozen with anxiety and fear, she turned the door handle.

The room was dark. Yet in the space near the window, she heard and saw something plunging to and fro. She gazed in fear and amazement.

Then suddenly she switched on the light, and saw her son, in his green pyjamas, madly surging on the rocking horse. The blaze of light suddenly lit him up, as he urged the wooden horse, and lit her up, as she stood, blonde, in her dress of pale green and crystal, in the doorway.

"Paul!" she cried. "Whatever are you doing?"

"It's Malabar!" he screamed, in a powerful, strange voice. "It's Malabar."

His eyes blazed at her for one strange and senseless second, as he ceased urging his wooden horse. Then he fell with a crash to the ground, and she, all her tormented motherhood flooding upon her, rushed to gather him up.

But he was unconscious, and unconscious he remained, with some brain-fever. He talked and tossed, and his mother sat stonily by his side.

"Malabar! It's Malabar! Bassett, Bassett, I know it! It's Malabar!"

So the child cried, trying to get up and urge the rocking horse that gave him his inspiration.

"What does he mean by Malabar?" asked the heart-frozen mother.

"I don't know," said the father stonily.

"What does he mean by Malabar?" she asked her brother Oscar.

"It's one of the horses running for the Derby," was the answer.

And, in spite of himself, Oscar Cresswell spoke to Bassett, and himself put a thousand on Malabar: at fourteen to one.

The third day of the illness was critical: they were waiting for a change. The boy, with his rather long, curly hair, was tossing ceaselessly on the pillow. He neither slept nor regained consciousness, and his eyes were like blue stones. His mother sat, feeling her heart had gone, turned actually into a stone.

In the evening, Oscar Cresswell did not come, but Bassett sent a message, saying could he come up for one moment, just one moment? Paul's mother was very angry at the intrusion, but on second thought she agreed. The boy was the same. Perhaps Bassett might bring him to consciousness.

The gardener, a shortish fellow with a little brown moustache, and sharp little brown eyes, tiptoed into the room, touched his imaginary cap to Paul's mother, and stole to the bedside, staring with glittering, smallish eyes, at the tossing, dying child.

"Master Paul!" he whispered. "Master Paul! Malabar come in first all right, a clean win. I did as you told me. You've made over seventy thousand pounds, you have; you've got over eighty thousand. Malabar came in all right, Master Paul."

"Malabar! Malabar! Did I say Malabar, mother? Did I say Malabar? Do you think I'm lucky, mother? I knew Malabar, didn't I? Over eighty thousand pounds! I call that lucky, don't you, mother? Over eighty thousand pounds! I knew, didn't I know I knew? Malabar came in all right. If I ride my horse till I'm sure, then I tell you, Bassett, you can go as high as you like. Did you go for all you were worth, Bassett?"

"I went a thousand on it, Master Paul."

"I never told you, mother, that if I can ride my horse, and get there, then I'm absolutely sure—oh, absolutely! Mother, did I ever tell you? I'm lucky."

"No, you never did," said the mother.

But the boy died in the night.

And even as he lay dead, his mother heard her brother's voice saying to her: "My God, Hester, you're eighty-odd thousand to the good and a poor devil of a son to the bad. But, poor devil, poor devil, he's best gone out of a life where he rides his rocking horse to find a winner."

## RING LARDNER (1885–1933)

# *Haircut*

I got another barber that comes over from Carterville and helps me out Saturdays, but the rest of the time I can get along all right alone. You can see for yourself that this ain't no New York City and besides that, the most of the boys works all day and don't have no leisure to drop in here and get themselves prettied up.

You're a newcomer, ain't you? I thought I hadn't seen you round before. I hope you like it good enough to stay. As I say, we ain't no New York City or Chicago, but we have pretty good times. Not as good, though, since Jim Kendall got killed. When he was alive, him and Hod Meyers used to keep this town in an uproar. I bet they was more laughin' done here than any town its size in America.

Jim was comical, and Hod was pretty near a match for him. Since Jim's gone, Hod tries to hold his end up just the same as ever, but it's tough goin' when you ain't got nobody to kind of work with.

They used to be plenty fun in here Saturdays. This place is jam-packed Saturdays, from four o'clock on. Jim and Hod would show up right after their supper, round six o'clock. Jim would set himself down in that big chair, nearest the blue spittoon. Whoever had been settin' in that chair, why they'd get up when Jim come in and give it to him.

You'd of thought it was a reserved seat like they have sometimes in a theayter. Hod would generally always stand or walk up and down, or some Saturdays, of course, he'd be settin' in this chair part of the time, gettin' a haircut.

Well, Jim would set there a w'ile without openin' his mouth only to spit, and then finally he'd say to me, "Whitey,"—my right name, that is, my right first name, is Dick, but everybody round here calls me Whitey—Jim would say, "Whitey, your nose looks like a rosebud tonight. You must of been drinkin' some of your aw de cologne."

So I'd say, "No, Jim, but you look like you'd been drinkin' somethin' of that kind or somethin' worse."

Jim would have to laugh at that, but then he'd speak up and say, "No, I ain't had nothin' to drink, but that ain't sayin' I wouldn't like somethin'. I wouldn't even mind if it was wood alcohol."

Then Hod Meyers would say, "Neither would your wife." That would set everybody to laughin' because Jim and his wife wasn't on very good terms. She'd of divorced him only they wasn't no chance to get alimony and she didn't have no way to take care of herself and the kids. She couldn't never understand Jim. He *was* kind of rough, but a good fella at heart.

Him and Hod had all kinds of sport with Milt Sheppard. I don't suppose you've seen Milt. Well, he's got an Adam's apple that looks more like a mushmelon.[1] So I'd be shavin' Milt and when I'd start to shave down here on his neck, Hod would holler, "Hey, Whitey, wait a minute! Before you cut into it, let's make up a pool and see who can guess closest to the number of seeds."

And Jim would say, "If Milt hadn't of been so hoggish, he'd of ordered a half a cantaloupe instead of a whole one and it might not of stuck in his throat."

All the boys would roar at this and Milt himself would force a smile, though the joke was on him. Jim certainly was a card!

There's his shavin' mug, settin' on the shelf, right next to Charley Vail's. "Charles M. Vail." That's the druggist. He comes in regular for his shave, three times a week. And Jim's is the cup next to Charley's. "James H. Kendall." Jim won't need no shavin' mug no more, but I'll leave it there just the same for old time's sake. Jim certainly was a character!

Years ago, Jim used to travel for a canned goods concern over in Carterville. They sold canned goods. Jim had the whole northern half of the State and was on the road five days out of every week. He'd drop in here Saturdays and tell his experiences for that week. It was rich.

I guess he paid more attention to playin' jokes than makin' sales. Finally the concern let him out and he come right home here and told everybody he'd been fired instead of sayin' he'd resigned like most fellas would of.

It was a Saturday and the shop was full and Jim got up out of that chair and says, "Gentlemen, I got an important announcement to make. I been fired from my job."

Well, they asked him if he was in earnest and he said he was and nobody could think of nothin' to say till Jim finally broke the ice himself. He says, "I been sellin' canned goods and now I'm canned goods myself."

You see, the concern he'd been workin' for was a factory that made canned goods. Over in Carterville. And now Jim said he was canned himself. He was certainly a card!

Jim had a great trick that he used to play w'ile he was travelin'. For instance, he'd be ridin' on a train and they'd come to some little

---

[1] that is, a muskmelon.

town like, well, like, we'll say, like Benton. Jim would look out the train window and read the signs on the stores.

For instance, they'd be a sign, "Henry Smith, Dry Goods." Well, Jim would write down the name and the name of the town and when he got to wherever he was goin' he'd mail back a postal card to Henry Smith at Benton and not sign no name to it, but he'd write on the card, well, somethin' like "Ask your wife about that book agent that spent the afternoon last week," or "Ask your Missus who kept her from gettin' lonesome the last time you was in Carterville." And he'd sign the card, "A Friend."

Of course, he never knew what really come of none of these jokes, but he could picture what *probably* happened and that was enough.

Jim didn't work very steady after he lost his position with the Carterville people. What he did earn, doin' odd jobs round town, why he spent pretty near all of it on gin and his family might of starved if the stores hadn't of carried them along. Jim's wife tried her hand at dressmakin', but they ain't nobody goin' to get rich makin' dresses in this town.

As I say, she'd of divorced Jim, only she seen that she couldn't support herself and the kids and she was always hopin' that some day Jim would cut out his habits and give her more than two or three dollars a week.

They was a time when she would go to whoever he was workin' for and ask them to give her his wages, but after she done this once or twice, he beat her to it by borrowin' most of his pay in advance. He told it all round town, how he had outfoxed his Missus. He certainly was a caution!

But he wasn't satisfied with just outwittin' her. He was sore the way she had acted, tryin' to grab off his pay. And he made up his mind he'd get even. Well, he waited till Evans's Circus was advertised to come to town. Then he told his wife and two kiddies that he was goin' to take them to the circus. The day of the circus, he told them he would get the tickets and meet them outside the entrance to the tent.

Well, he didn't have no intentions of bein' there or buyin' tickets or nothin'. He got full of gin and laid round Wright's poolroom all day. His wife and the kids waited and waited and of course he didn't show up. His wife didn't have a dime with her, or nowhere else, I guess. So she finally had to tell the kids it was all off and they cried like they wasn't never goin' to stop.

Well, it seems, w'ile they was cryin', Doc Stair came along and he asked what was the matter, but Mrs. Kendall was stubborn and wouldn't tell him, but the kids told him and he insisted on takin' them and their mother in the show. Jim found this out afterwards and it was one reason why he had it in for Doc Stair.

Doc Stair come here about a year and a half ago. He's a mighty handsome young fella and his clothes always look like he has them made to order. He goes to Detroit two or three times a year and w'ile he's there he must have a tailor take his measure and then make him a suit to order. They cost pretty near twice as much, but they fit a whole lot better than if you just bought them in a store.

For a w'ile everybody was wonderin' why a young doctor like Doc Stair should come to a town like this where we already got old Doc Gamble and Doc Foote that's both been here for years and all the practice in town was always divided between the two of them.

Then they was a story got round that Doc Stair's gal had throwed him over, a gal up in the Northern Peninsula somewheres, and the reason he come here was to hide himself away and forget it. He said himself that he thought they wasn't nothin' like general practice in a place like ours to fit a man to be a good all round doctor. And that's why he'd came.

Anyways, it wasn't long before he was makin' enough to live on, though they tell me that he never dunned nobody for what they owed him, and the folks here certainly has got the owin' habit, even in my business. If I had all that was comin' to me for just shaves alone, I could go to Carterville and put up at the Mercer for a week and see a different picture every night. For instance, they's old George Purdy—but I guess I shouldn't ought to be gossipin'.

Well, last year, our coroner died, died of the flu. Ken Beatty, that was his name. He was the coroner. So they had to choose another man to be coroner in his place and they picked Doc Stair. He laughed at first and said he didn't want it, but they made him take it. It ain't no job that anybody would fight for and what a man makes out of it in a year would just about buy seeds for their garden. Doc's the kind, though, that can't say no to nothin' if you keep at him long enough.

But I was goin' to tell you about a poor boy we got here in town—Paul Dickson. He fell out of a tree when he was about ten years old. Lit on his head and it done somethin' to him and he ain't never been right. No harm in him, but just silly. Jim Kendall used to call him cuckoo; that's a name Jim had for anybody that was off their head, only he called people's head their bean. That was another of his gags, callin' head bean and callin' crazy people cuckoo. Only poor Paul ain't crazy, but just silly.

You can imagine that Jim used to have all kinds of fun with Paul. He'd send him to the White Front Garage for a left-handed monkey wrench. Of course they ain't no such a thing as a left-handed monkey wrench.

And once we had a kind of a fair here and they was a baseball game between the fats and the leans and before the game started

Jim called Paul over and sent him way down to Schrader's hardware store to get a key for the pitcher's box.

They wasn't nothin' in the way of gags that Jim couldn't think up, when he put his mind to it.

Poor Paul was always kind of suspicious of people, maybe on account of how Jim had kept foolin' him. Paul wouldn't have much to do with anybody only his own mother and Doc Stair and a girl here in town named Julie Gregg. That is, she ain't a girl no more, but pretty near thirty or over.

When Doc first come to town, Paul seemed to feel like here was a real friend and he hung around Doc's office most of the w'ile; the only time he wasn't there was when he'd go home to eat or sleep or when he seen Julie Gregg doin' her shoppin'.

When he looked out Doc's window and seen her, he'd run downstairs and join her and tag along with her to the different stores. The poor boy was crazy about Julie and she always treated him mighty nice and made him feel like he was welcome, though of course it wasn't nothin' but pity on her side.

Doc done all he could to improve Paul's mind and he told me once that he really thought the boy was gettin' better, that they was times when he was as bright and sensible as anybody else.

But I was goin' to tell you about Julie Gregg. Old Man Gregg was in the lumber business, but got to drinkin' and lost the most of his money and when he died, he didn't leave nothin' but the house and just enough insurance for the girl to skimp along on.

Her mother was a kind of a half invalid and didn't hardly ever leave the house. Julie wanted to sell the place and move somewheres else after the old man died, but the mother said she was born here and would die here. It was tough on Julie, as the young people round this town—well, she's too good for them.

She's been away to school and Chicago and New York and different places and they ain't no subject she can't talk on, where you take the rest of the young folks here and you mention anything to them outside of Gloria Swanson or Tommy Meighan and they think you're delirious. Did you see Gloria in Wages of Virtue? You missed somethin'!

Well, Doc Stair hadn't been here more than a week when he come in one day to get shaved and I recognized who he was as he had been pointed out to me, so I told him about my old lady. She's been ailin' for a couple of years and either Doc Gamble or Doc Foote, neither one, seemed to be helpin' her. So he said he would come out and see her, but if she was able to get out herself, it would be better to bring her to his office where he could make a completer examination.

So I took her to his office and w'ile I was waitin' for her in the reception room, in come Julie Gregg. When somebody comes in Doc Stair's office, they's a bell that rings in his inside office so as he can tell they's somebody to see him.

So he left my old lady inside and come out to the front office and that's the first time him and Julie met and I guess it was what they call love at first sight. But it wasn't fifty-fifty. This young fella was the slickest lookin' fella she'd ever seen in this town and she went wild over him. To him she was just a young lady that wanted to see the doctor.

She'd came on about the same business I had. Her mother had been doctorin' for years with Doc Gamble and Doc Foote and without no results. So she'd heard they was a new doc in town and decided to give him a try. He promised to call and see her mother that same day.

I said a minute ago that it was love at first sight on her part. I'm not only judgin' by how she acted afterwards but how she looked at him that first day in his office. I ain't no mind reader, but it was wrote all over her face that she was gone.

Now Jim Kendall, besides bein' a jokesmith and a pretty good drinker, well, Jim was quite a lady-killer. I guess he run pretty wild durin' the time he was on the road for them Carterville people, and besides that, he'd had a couple little affairs of the heart right here in town. As I say, his wife would of divorced him, only she couldn't.

But Jim was like the majority of men, and women, too, I guess. He wanted what he couldn't get. He wanted Julie Gregg and worked his head off tryin' to land her. Only he'd of said bean instead of head.

Well, Jim's habits and his jokes didn't appeal to Julie and of course he was a married man, so he didn't have no more chance than, well, than a rabbit. That's an expression of Jim's himself. When somebody didn't have no chance to get elected or somethin', Jim would always say they didn't have no more chance than a rabbit.

He didn't make no bones about how he felt. Right in here, more than once, in front of the whole crowd, he said he was stuck on Julie and anybody that could get her for him was welcome to his house and his wife and kids included. But she wouldn't have nothin' to do with him; wouldn't even speak to him on the street. He finally seen he wasn't gettin' nowheres with his usual line so he decided to try the rough stuff. He went right up to her house one evenin' and when she opened the door he forced his way in and grabbed her But she broke loose and before he could stop her, she run in the next room and locked the door and phoned to Joe Barnes. Joe's the marshal. Jim could hear who she was phonin' to and he beat it before Joe got there.

Joe was an old friend of Julie's pa. Joe went to Jim the next day and told him what would happen if he ever done it again.

I don't know how the news of this little affair leaked out. Chances is that Joe Barnes told his wife and she told somebody else's wife and they told their husband. Anyways, it did leak out and Hod Meyers had the nerve to kid Jim about it, right here in this shop. Jim didn't deny nothin' and kind of laughed it off and said for us all to wait; that lots of people had tried to make a monkey out of him, but he always got even.

Meanw'ile everybody in town was wise to Julie's bein' wild mad over the Doc. I don't suppose she had any idear how her face changed when him and her was together; of course she couldn't of, or she'd of kept away from him. And she didn't know that we was all noticin' how many times she made excuses to go up to his office or pass it on the other side of the street and look up in his window to see if he was there. I felt sorry for her and so did most other people.

Hod Meyers kept rubbin' it into Jim about how the Doc had cut him out. Jim didn't pay no attention to the kiddin' and you could see he was plannin' one of his jokes.

One trick Jim had was the knack of changin' his voice. He could make you think he was a girl talkin' and he could mimic any man's voice. To show you how good he was along this line, I'll tell you the joke he played on me once.

You know, in most towns of any size, when a man is dead and needs a shave, why the barber that shaves him soaks him five dollars for the job; that is, he don't soak *him,* but whoever ordered the shave. I just charge three dollars because personally I don't mind much shavin' a dead person. They lay a whole lot stiller than live customers. The only thing is that you don't feel like talkin' to them and you get kind of lonesome.

Well, about the coldest day we ever had here, two years ago last winter, the phone rung at the house w'ile I was home to dinner and I answered the phone and it was a woman's voice and she said she was Mrs. John Scott and her husband was dead and would I come out and shave him.

Old John had always been a good customer of mine. But they live seven miles out in the country, on the Streeter road. Still I didn't see how I could say no.

So I said I would be there, but would have to come in a jitney[2]

---

[2] *jitney,* an automobile or a small bus that transports passengers along a set route for a small fare.

and it might cost three or four dollars besides the price of the shave. So she, or the voice, it said that was all right, so I got Frank Abbott to drive me out to the place and when I got there, who should open the door but old John himself! He wasn't no more dead than, well, than a rabbit.

It didn't take no private detective to figure out who had played me this little joke. Nobody could of thought it up but Jim Kendall. He certainly was a card!

I tell you this incident just to show you how he could disguise his voice and make you believe it was somebody else talkin'. I'd of swore it was Mrs. Scott had called me. Anyways, some woman.

Well, Jim waited till he had Doc Stair's voice down pat; then he went after revenge.

He called Julie up on a night when he knew Doc was over in Carterville. She never questioned but what it was Doc's voice. Jim said he must see her that night; he couldn't wait no longer to tell her somethin'. She was all excited and told him to come to the house. But he said he was expectin' an important long distance call and wouldn't she please forget her manners for once and come to his office. He said they couldn't nothin' hurt her and nobody would see her and he just *must* talk to her a little w'ile. Well, poor Julie fell for it.

Doc always keeps a night light in his office, so it looked to Julie like they was somebody there.

Meanw'ile Jim Kendall had went to Wright's poolroom, where they was a whole gang amusin' themselves. The most of them had drank plenty of gin, and they was a rough bunch even when sober. They was always strong for Jim's jokes and when he told them to come with him and see some fun they give up their card games and pool games and followed along.

Doc's office is on the second floor. Right outside his door they's a flight of stairs leadin' to the floor above. Jim and his gang hid in the dark behind these stairs.

Well, Julie come up to Doc's door and rung the bell and they was nothin' doin'. She rung it again and rung it seven or eight times. Then she tried the door and found it locked. Then Jim made some kind of a noise and she heard it and waited a minute, and then she says, "Is that you, Ralph?" Ralph is Doc's first name.

They was no answer and it must of came to her all of a sudden that she'd been bunked. She pretty near fell downstairs and the whole gang after her. They chased her all the way home, hollerin', "Is that you, Ralph?" and "Oh, Ralphie, dear, is that you?" Jim says he couldn't holler it himself, as he was laughin' too hard.

Poor Julie! She didn't show up here on Main Street for a long, long time afterward.

And of course Jim and his gang told everybody in town, everybody but Doc Stair. They was scared to tell him, and he might of never knowed only for Paul Dickson. The poor cuckoo, as Jim called him, he was here in the shop one night when Jim was still gloatin' yet over what he'd done to Julie. And Paul took in as much of it as he could understand and he run to Doc with the story.

It's a cinch Doc went up in the air and swore he'd make Jim suffer. But it was a kind of a delicate thing, because if it got out that he had beat Jim up, Julie was bound to hear of it and then she'd know that Doc knew and of course knowin' that he knew would make it worse for her than ever. He was goin' to do somethin', but it took a lot of figurin'.

Well, it was a couple days later when Jim was here in the shop again, and so was the cuckoo. Jim was goin' duck-shootin' the next day and had came in lookin' for Hod Meyers to go with him. I happened to know that Hod had went over to Carterville and wouldn't be home till the end of the week. So Jim said he hated to go alone and he guessed he would call it off. Then poor Paul spoke up and said if Jim would take him he would go along. Jim thought a w'ile and then he said, well, he guessed a half-wit was better than nothin'.

I suppose he was plottin' to get Paul out in the boat and play some joke on him, like pushin' him in the water. Anyways, he said Paul could go. He asked him had he ever shot a duck and Paul said no, he'd never even had a gun in his hands. So Jim said he could set in the boat and watch him and if he behaved himself, he might lend him his gun for a couple of shots. They made a date to meet in the mornin' and that's the last I seen of Jim alive.

Next mornin', I hadn't been open more than ten minutes when Doc Stair come in. He looked kind of nervous. He asked me had I seen Paul Dickson. I said no, but I knew where he was, out duck-shootin' with Jim Kendall. So Doc says that's what he had heard, and he couldn't understand it because Paul had told him he wouldn't never have no more to do with Jim as long as he lived.

He said Paul had told him about the joke Jim had played on Julie. He said Paul had asked him what he thought of the joke and the Doc had told him that anybody that would do a thing like that ought not to be let live.

I said it had been a kind of a raw thing, but Jim just couldn't resist no kind of a joke, no matter how raw. I said I thought he was all right at heart, but just bubblin' over with mischief. Doc turned and walked out.

At noon he got a phone call from old John Scott. The lake where Jim and Paul had went shootin' is on John's place. Paul had come runnin' up to the house a few minutes before and said they'd been an accident. Jim had shot a few ducks and then give the gun to Paul and told him to try his luck. Paul hadn't never handled a gun and he was nervous. He was shakin' so hard that he couldn't control the gun. He let fire and Jim sunk back in the boat, dead.

Doc Stair, bein' the coroner, jumped in Frank Abbott's flivver[3] and rushed out to Scott's farm. Paul and old John was down on the shore of the lake. Paul had rowed the boat to shore, but they'd left the body in it, waitin' for Doc to come.

Doc examined the body and said they might as well fetch it back to town. They was no use leavin' it there or callin' a jury, as it was a plain case of accidental shootin'.

Personally I wouldn't never leave a person shoot a gun in the same boat I was in unless I was sure they knew somethin' about guns. Jim was a sucker to leave a new beginner have his gun, let alone a half-wit. It probably served Jim right, what he got. But still we miss him round here. He certainly was a card!

Comb it wet or dry?

---

[3] *flivver,* a small, cheap automobile—especially an old one.

## SHERWOOD ANDERSON (1876–1941)

# *I'm a Fool*

It was a hard jolt for me, one of the most bitterest I ever had to face. And it all came about through my own foolishness, too. Even yet sometimes, when I think of it, I want to cry or swear or kick myself. Perhaps, even now, after all this time, there will be a kind of satisfaction in making myself look cheap by telling of it.

It began at three o'clock one October afternoon as I sat in the grand stand at the fall trotting and pacing meet at Sandusky, Ohio.

To tell the truth, I felt a little foolish that I should be sitting in the grand stand at all. During the summer before I had left my home town with Harry Whitehead and, with a nigger named Burt, had taken a job as swipe with one of the two horses Harry was campaigning through the fall race meets that year. Mother cried and my sister Mildred, who wanted to get a job as a schoolteacher in our town that fall, stormed and scolded about the house all during the week before I left. They both thought it something disgraceful that one of our family should take a place as a swipe with race horses. I've an idea Mildred thought my taking the place would stand in the way of her getting the job she'd been working so long for.

But after all I had to work, and there was no other work to be got. A big lumbering fellow of nineteen couldn't just hang around the house and I had got too big to mow people's lawns and sell newspapers. Little chaps who could get next to people's sympathies by their sizes were always getting jobs away from me. There was one fellow who kept saying to everyone who wanted a lawn mowed or a cistern cleaned that he was saving money to work his way through college, and I used to lay awake nights thinking up ways to injure him without being found out. I kept thinking of wagons running over him and bricks falling on his head as he walked along the street. But never mind him.

I got the place with Harry and I liked Burt fine. We got along splendid together. He was a big nigger with a lazy sprawling body and soft, kind eyes, and when it came to a fight he could hit like Jack Johnson. He had Bucephalus, a big black pacing stallion that could do 2.09 or 2.10 if he had to, and I had a little gelding named

Doctor Fritz that never lost a race all fall when Harry wanted him to win.

We set out from home late in July, in a box car with the two horses and after that, until late November, we kept moving along to the race meets and the fairs. It was a peachy time for me, I'll say that. Sometimes now I think that boys who are raised regular in houses, and never have a fine nigger like Burt for best friend, and go to high schools and college, and never steal anything, or get drunk a little, or learn to swear from fellows who know how, or come walking up in front of a grand stand in their shirt sleeves and with dirty horsy pants on when the races are going on and the grand stand is full of people all dressed up—What's the use of talking about it? Such fellows don't know nothing at all. They've never had no opportunity.

But I did. Burt taught me how to rub down a horse and put the bandages on after a race and steam a horse out and a lot of valuable things for any man to know. He could wrap a bandage on a horse's leg so smooth that if it had been the same color you would think it was his skin, and I guess he'd have been a big driver, too, and got to the top like Murphy and Walter Cox and the others if he hadn't been black.

Gee whizz! it was fun. You got to a county-seat town, maybe say on a Saturday or Sunday, and the fair began the next Tuesday and lasted until Friday afternoon. Doctor Fritz would be, say, in the 2.25 trot on Tuesday afternoon and on Thursday afternoon Bucephalus would knock 'em cold in the "free-for-all" pace. It left you a lot of time to hang around and listen to horse talk, and see Burt knock some yap cold that got too gay, and you'd find out about horses and men and pick up a lot of stuff you could use all the rest of your life, if you had some sense and salted down what you heard and felt and saw.

And then at the end of the week when the race meet was over, and Harry had run home to tend up to his livery-stable business, you and Burt hitched the two horses to carts and drove slow and steady across country, to the place for the next meeting, so as to not overheat the horses, etc., etc., you know.

Gee whizz! Gosh amighty! the nice hickory-nut and beechnut and oaks and other kinds of trees along the roads, all brown and red, and the good smells, and Burt singing a song called "Deep River," and the country girls at the windows of houses and everything. You can stick your colleges up your nose for all me. I guess I know where I got my education.

Why, one of those little burgs of towns you came to on the way, say now on a Saturday afternoon, and Burt says, "Let's lay up here." And you did.

And you took the horses to a livery stable and fed them, and you got your good clothes out of a box and put them on.

And the town was full of farmers gaping, because they could see you were racehorse people, and the kids maybe never see a nigger before and was afraid and run away when the two of us walked down their main street.

And that was before prohibition and all that foolishness, and so you went into a saloon, the two of you, and all the yaps come and stood around, and there was always some one pretended he was horsy and knew things and spoke up and began asking questions, and all you did was to lie and lie all you could about what horses you had, and I said I owned them, and then some fellow said, "Will you have a drink of whisky?" and Burt knocked his eye out the way he could say, offhand like, "Oh, well, all right, I'm agreeable to a little nip. I'll split a quart with you." Gee whizz!

But that isn't what I want to tell my story about. We got home late in November and I promised mother I'd quit the race horses for good. There's a lot of things you've got to promise a mother because she don't know any better.

And so, there not being any work in our town any more than when I left there to go to the races, I went off to Sandusky and got a pretty good place taking care of horses for a man who owned a teaming and delivery and storage and coal and real-estate business there. It was a pretty good place with good eats, and a day off each week, and sleeping on a cot in a big barn, and mostly just shoveling in hay and oats to a lot of big good-enough skates of horses that couldn't have trotted a race with a toad. I wasn't dissatisfied and I could send money home.

And then, as I started to tell you, the fall races come to Sandusky and I got the day off and I went. I left the job at noon and had on my good clothes and my new brown derby hat I'd bought the Saturday before, and a stand-up collar.

First of all I went downtown and walked about with the dudes. I've always thought to myself, "Put up a good front," and so I did it. I had forty dollars in my pockets and so I went into the West House, a big hotel, and walked up to the cigar stand. "Give me three twenty-five cent cigars," I said. There was a lot of horsemen and strangers and dressed-up people from other towns standing around in the lobby and in the bar, and I mingled amongst them. In the bar there was a fellow with a cane and a Windsor tie on, that it made me sick to look at him. I like a man to be a man and dressed up, but not to go put on that kind of airs. So I pushed him aside, kind of rough, and had me a drink of whisky. And then he looked at me, as though he thought maybe he'd get gay, but he changed his mind and didn't say anything. And then I had another drink of whisky, just to show him something, and went out and had a hack out to the races, all to myself, and when I got there I bought myself the best seat I could get up in the grand stand, but didn't go in for any of these boxes. That's putting on too many airs.

And so there I was, sitting up in the grand stand as gay as you please and looking down on the swipes coming out with their horses, and with their dirty horsy pants on and the horseblankets swung over their shoulders, same as I had been doing all the year before. I liked one thing about the same as the other, sitting up there and feeling grand and being down there and looking up at the yaps and feeling grander and more important, too.

One thing's about as good as another, if you take it just right. I've often said that.

Well, right in front of me, in the grand stand that day, there was a fellow with a couple of girls and they was about my age. The young fellow was a nice guy, all right. He was the kind maybe that goes to college and then comes to be a lawyer or maybe a newspaper editor or something like that, but he wasn't stuck on himself. There are some of that kind are all right and he was one of the ones.

He had his sister with him and another girl and the sister looked around over his shoulder, accidental at first, not intending to start anything–she wasn't that kind–and her eyes and mine happened to meet.

You know how it is. Gee, she was a peach! She had on a soft dress, kind of a blue stuff and it looked carelessly made, but was well sewed and made and everything. I knew that much. I blushed when she looked right at me and so did she. She was the nicest girl I've ever seen in my life. She wasn't stuck on herself and she could talk proper grammar without being like a schoolteacher or something like that. What I mean is, she was O.K. I think maybe her father was well-to-do, but not rich to make her chesty because she was his daughter, as some are. Maybe he owned a drug store or a dry-goods store in their home town, or something like that. She never told me and I never asked.

My own people are all O.K. too, when you come to that. My grandfather was Welsh and over in the old country, in Wales he was– But never mind that.

The first heat of the first race come off and the young fellow setting there with the two girls left them and went down to make a bet. I knew what he was up to, but he didn't talk big and noisy and let everyone around know he was a sport, as some do. He wasn't that kind. Well, he come back and I heard him tell the two girls what horse he'd bet on, and when the heat trotted they all half got to their feet and acted in the excited, sweaty way people do when they've got money down on a race, and the horse they bet on is up there pretty close at the end, and they think maybe he'll come on with a rush, but he never does because he hasn't got the old juice in him, come right down to it.

And then, pretty soon, the horses came out for the 2.18 pace and there was a horse in it I knew. He was a horse Bob French had in his string but Bob didn't own him. He was a horse owned by a Mr. Mathers down at Marietta, Ohio.

This Mr. Mathers had a lot of money and owned some coal mines or something and he had a swell place out in the country, and he was stuck on race horses, but was a Presbyterian or something, and I think more than likely his wife was one, too, maybe a stiffer one than himself. So he never raced his horses hisself, and the story round the Ohio race tracks was that when one of his horses got ready to go to the races he turned him over to Bob French and pretended to his wife he was sold.

So Bob had the horses and he did pretty much as he pleased and you can't blame Bob, at least, I never did. Sometimes he was out to win and sometimes he wasn't. I never cared much about that when I was swiping a horse. What I did want to know was that my horse had the speed and could go out in front, if you wanted him to.

And, as I'm telling you, there was Bob in this race with one of Mr. Mathers' horses, was named "About Ben Ahem" or something like that, and was fast as a streak. He was a gelding and had a mark of 2.21, but could step in .08 or .09.

Because when Burt and I were out, as I've told you, the year before, there was a nigger Burt knew, worked for Mr. Mathers and we went out there one day when we didn't have no race on at the Marietta Fair and our boss Harry was gone home.

And so everyone was gone to the fair but just this one nigger and he took us all through Mr. Mathers' swell house and he and Burt tapped a bottle of wine Mr. Mathers had hid in his bedroom, back in a closet, without his wife knowing, and he showed us this Ahem horse. Burt was always stuck on being a driver but didn't have much chance to get to the top, being a nigger, and he and the other nigger gulped the whole bottle of wine and Burt got a little lit up.

So the nigger let Burt take this About Ben Ahem and step him a mile in a track Mr. Mathers had all to himself, right there on the farm. And Mr. Mathers had one child, a daughter, kinda sick and not very good looking, and she came home and we had to hustle to get About Ben Ahem stuck back in the barn.

I'm only telling you to get everything straight. At Sandusky, that afternoon I was at the fair, this young fellow with the two girls was fussed, being with the girls and losing his bet. You know how a fellow is that way. One of them was his girl and the other his sister. I had figured that out.

"Gee whizz," I says to myself, "I'm going to give him the dope."

He was mighty nice when I touched him on the shoulder. He and the girls were nice to me right from the start and clear to the end. I'm not blaming them.

And so he leaned back and I give him the dope on About Ben Ahem. "Don't bet a cent on this first heat because he'll go like an oxen hitched to a plow, but when the first heat is over go right down and lay on your pile." That's what I told him.

Well, I never saw a fellow treat any one sweller. There was a fat man sitting beside the little girl, that had looked at me twice by this time, and I at her, and both blushing, and what did he do but have the nerve to turn and ask the fat man to get up and change places with me so I could set with his crowd.

Gee whizz, craps amighty. There I was. What a chump I was to go and get gay up there in the West House bar, and just because that dude was standing there with a cane and that kind of a necktie on, to go and get all balled up and drink that whisky, just to show off.

Of course she would know, me setting right beside her and letting her smell of my breath. I could have kicked myself right down out of that grand stand and all around that race track and made a faster record than most of the skates of horses they had there that year.

Because that girl wasn't any mutt of a girl. What wouldn't I have give right then for a stick of chewing gum to chew, or a lozenger, or some licorice, or most anything. I was glad I had those twenty-five cent cigars in my pocket and right away I give that fellow one and lit one myself. Then that fat man got up and we changed places and there I was, plunked right down beside her.

They introduced themselves and the fellow's best girl, he had with him, was named Miss Elinor Woodbury, and her father was a manufacturer of barrels from a place called Tiffin, Ohio. And the fellow himself was named Wilbur Wessen and his sister was Miss Lucy Wessen.

I suppose it was their having such swell names that got me off my trolley. A fellow, just because he has been a swipe with a race horse, and works taking care of horses for a man in the teaming, delivery, and storage business isn't any better or worse than any one else. I've often thought that, and said it too.

But you know how a fellow is. There's something in that kind of nice clothes, and the kind of nice eyes she had, and the way she had looked at me, awhile before, over her brother's shoulder, and me looking back at her, and both of us blushing.

I couldn't show her up for a boob, could I?

I made a fool of myself, that's what I did. I said my name was Walter Mathers from Marietta, Ohio, and then I told all three of them the smashingest lie you ever heard. What I said was that my father owned the horse About Ben Ahem and that he had let him out to this Bob French for racing purposes, because our family was proud and had never gone into racing that way, in our own name, I mean, and Miss Lucy Wessen's eyes were shining, and I went the whole hog.

I told about our place down at Marietta, and about the big stables and the grand brick house we had on a hill, up above the Ohio River, but I knew enough not to do it in no bragging way. What I did was to start things and then let them drag the rest out of me. I acted just as reluctant to tell as I could. Our family hasn't got any barrel factory, and since I've known us, we've always been pretty poor, but not asking anything of any one at that, and my grandfather, over in Wales—but never mind that.

We set there talking like we had known each other for years and years, and I went and told them that my father had been expecting maybe this Bob French wasn't on the square, and had sent me up to Sandusky on the sly to find out what I could.

And I bluffed it through I had found out all about the 2.18 pace, in which About Ben Ahem was to start.

I said he would lose the first heat by pacing like a lame cow and then he would come back and skin 'em alive after that. And to back up what I said I took thirty dollars out of my pocket and handed it to Mr. Wilbur Wessen and asked him, would he mind, after the first heat, to go down and place it on About Ben Ahem for whatever odds he could get. What I said was that I didn't want Bob French to see me and none of the swipes.

Sure enough the first heat come off and About Ben Ahem went off his stride, up the back stretch, and looked like a wooden horse or a sick one, and come in to be last. Then this Wilbur Wessen went down to the betting place under the grand stand and there I was with the two girls, and when that Miss Woodbury was looking the other way once, Lucy Wessen kinda, with her shoulder you know, kinda touched me. Not just tucking down, I don't mean. You know how a woman can do. They get close, but not getting gay either. You know what they do. Gee whizz.

And then they give me a jolt. What they had done, when I didn't know, was to get together, and they had decided Wilbur Wessen would bet fifty dollars, and the two girls had gone and put in ten dollars each, of their own money, too. I was sick then, but I was sicker later.

About the gelding, About Ben Ahem, and their winning their money, I wasn't worried a lot about that. It came out O.K. Ahem stepped the next three heats like a bushel of spoiled eggs going to market before they could be found out, and Wilbur Wessen had got nine to two for the money. There was something else eating at me.

Because Wilbur come back, after he had bet the money, and after that he spent most of his time talking to that Miss Woodbury, and Lucy Wessen and I was left alone together like on a desert island. Gee, if I'd only been on the square or if there had been any way of getting myself on the square. There ain't any Walter Mathers, like I said to her and them, and there hasn't ever been one, but if there was, I bet I'd go to Marietta, Ohio, and shoot him tomorrow.

There I was, big boob that I am. Pretty soon the race was over, and Wilbur had gone down and collected our money, and we had a hack downtown, and he stood us a swell supper at the West House, and a bottle of champagne beside.

And I was with the girl and she wasn't saying much, and I wasn't saying much either. One thing I know. She wasn't stuck on me because of the lie about my father being rich and all that. There's a way you know . . . Craps amighty. There's a kind of girl you see just once in your life, and if you don't get busy and make hay, then you're gone for good and all, and might as well go jump off a bridge. They give you a look from inside of them somewhere, and it ain't no vamping, and what it means is—you want that girl to be your wife, and you want nice things around her like flowers and swell clothes, and you want her to have the kids you're going to have, and you want good music played and no ragtime. Gee whizz.

There's a place over near Sandusky, across a kind of bay, and it's called Cedar Point. And after we had supper we went over to it in a launch, all by ourselves. Wilbur and Miss Lucy and that Miss Woodbury had to catch a ten o'clock train back to Tiffin, Ohio, because, when you're out with girls like that you can't get careless and miss any trains and stay out all night, like you can with some kinds of Janes.

And Wilbur blowed himself to the launch and it cost him fifteen cold plunks, but I wouldn't never have knew if I hadn't listened. He wasn't no tin horn kind of a sport.

Over at the Cedar Point place, we didn't stay around where there was a gang of common kind of cattle at all.

There was big dance halls and dining places for yaps, and there was a beach you could walk along and get where it was dark, and we went there.

She didn't talk hardly at all and neither did I, and I was thinking how glad I was my mother was all right, and always made us kids learn to eat with a fork at the table, and not swill soup, and not be noisy and rough like a gang you see around a race track that way.

Then Wilbur and his girl went away up the beach and Lucy and I sat down in a dark place, where there was some roots of old trees the water had washed up, and after that the time, till we had to go back in the launch and they had to catch their trains, wasn't nothing at all. It went like winking your eye.

Here's how it was. The place we were setting in was dark, like I said, and there was the roots from that old stump sticking up like arms, and there was a watery smell, and the night was like—as if you could put your hand out and feel it—so warm and soft and dark and sweet like an orange.

I most cried and I most swore and I most jumped up and danced, I was so mad and happy and sad.

When Wilbur come back from being alone with his girl, and she saw him coming, Lucy she says, "We got to go to the train now," and she was most crying too, but she never knew nothing I knew, and she couldn't be so all busted up. And then, before Wilbur and Miss Woodbury got up to where we was, she put her face up and kissed me quick and put her head up against me and she was all quivering and—Gee whizz.

Sometimes I hope I have cancer and die. I guess you know what I mean. We went in the launch across the bay to the train like that, and it was dark, too. She whispered and said it was like she and I could get out of the boat and walk on water, and it sounded foolish, but I knew what she meant.

And then quick we were right at the depot, and there was a big gang of yaps, the kind that goes to the fairs, and crowded and milling around like cattle, and how could I tell her? "It won't be long because you'll write and I'll write to you." That's all she said.

I got a chance like a hay barn afire. A swell chance I got.

And maybe she would write me, down at Marietta that way, and the letter would come back, and stamped on the front of it by the U.S.A. "there ain't any such guy," or something like that, whatever they stamp on a letter that way.

And me trying to pass myself off for a big-bug and a swell—to her, as decent a little body as God ever made. Craps amighty—swell chance I got!

And then the train come in, and she got on it, and Wilbur Wessen, he come and shook hands with me, and that Miss Woodbury was nice too and bowed to me, and I at her, and the train went and I busted out and cried like a kid.

Gee, I could have run after the train and made Dan Patch look like a freight train after a wreck but, socks amighty, what was the use? Did you ever see such a fool?

I'll bet you what—if I had an arm broke right now or a train had run over my foot—I wouldn't go to no doctor at all. I'd go set down and let her hurt and hurt—that's what I'd do.

I'll bet you what—if I hadn't a drunk that booze I'd never been such a boob as to go tell such a lie—that couldn't never be made straight to a lady like her.

I wish I had that fellow right here that had on a Windsor tie and carried a cane. I'd smash him for fair. Gosh darn his eyes. He's a big fool—that's what he is.

And if I'm not another you just go find me one and I'll quit working and be a bum and give him my job. I don't care nothing for working, and earning money, and saving it for no such boob as myself.

## KATHERINE ANNE PORTER (1890–1980)

# *The Jilting of Granny Weatherall*

She flicked her wrist neatly out of Doctor Harry's pudgy careful fingers and pulled the sheet up to her chin. The brat ought to be in knee breeches. Doctoring around the country with spectacles on his nose! "Get along now, take your schoolbooks and go. There's nothing wrong with me."

Doctor Harry spread a warm paw like a cushion on her forehead where the forked green vein danced and made her eyelids twitch. "Now, now, be a good girl, and we'll have you up in no time."

"That's no way to speak to a woman nearly eighty years old just because she's down. I'd have you respect your elders, young man."

"Well, Missy, excuse me." Doctor Harry patted her cheek. "But I've got to warn you, haven't I? You're a marvel, but you must be careful or you're going to be good and sorry."

"Don't tell me what I'm going to be. I'm on my feet now, morally speaking. It's Cornelia. I had to go to bed to get rid of her."

Her bones felt loose, and floated around in her skin, and Doctor Harry floated like a balloon around the foot of the bed. He floated and pulled down his waistcoat and swung his glasses on a cord. "Well, stay where you are, it certainly can't hurt you."

"Get along and doctor your sick," said Granny Weatherall. "Leave a well woman alone. I'll call for you when I want you. . . . Where were you forty years ago when I pulled through milk-leg[1] and double pneumonia? You weren't even born. Don't let Cornelia lead you on," she shouted, because Doctor Harry appeared to float up to the ceiling and out. "I pay my own bills, and I don't throw my money away on nonsense!"

She meant to wave good-by, but it was too much trouble. Her eyes closed of themselves, it was like a dark curtain drawn around the bed. The pillow rose and floated under her, pleasant as a hammock in a light wind. She listened to the leaves rustling outside the window. No, somebody was swishing newspapers: no, Cornelia and Doctor

---

[1] *milk-leg,* a painful swelling of the legs sometimes occurring in women after childbirth.

Harry were whispering together. She leaped broad awake, thinking they whispered in her ear.

"She was never like this, *never* like this!" "Well, what can we expect?" "Yes, eighty years old. . . ."

Well, and what if she was? She still had ears. It was like Cornelia to whisper around doors. She always kept things secret in such a public way. She was always being tactful and kind. Cornelia was dutiful; that was the trouble with her. Dutiful and good: "So good and dutiful," said Granny, "that I'd like to spank her." She saw herself spanking Cornelia and making a fine job of it.

"What'd you say, Mother?"

Granny felt her face tying up in hard knots.

"Can't a body think, I'd like to know?"

"I thought you might want something."

"I do. I want a lot of things. First off, go away and don't whisper."

She lay and drowsed, hoping in her sleep that the children would keep out and let her rest a minute. It had been a long day. Not that she was tired. It was always pleasant to snatch a minute now and then. There was always so much to be done, let me see: tomorrow.

Tomorrow was far away and there was nothing to trouble about. Things were finished somehow when the time came; thank God there was always a little margin over for peace: then a person could spread out the plan of life and tuck in the edges orderly. It was good to have everything clean and folded away, with the hair brushes and tonic bottles sitting straight on the white embroidered linen: the day started without fuss and the pantry shelves laid out with rows of jelly glasses and brown jugs and white stone-china jars with blue whirligigs and words painted on them: coffee, tea, sugar, ginger, cinnamon, allspice: and the bronze clock with the lion on top nicely dusted off. The dust that lion could collect in twenty-four hours! The box in the attic with all those letters tied up, well, she'd have to go through that tomorrow. All those letters—George's letters and John's letters and her letters to them both—lying around for the children to find afterwards made her uneasy. Yes, that would be tomorrow's business. No use to let them know how silly she had been once.

While she was rummaging around she found death in her mind and it felt clammy and unfamiliar. She had spent so much time preparing for death there was no need for bringing it up again. Let it take care of itself now. When she was sixty she had felt very old, finished, and went around making farewell trips to see her children and grandchildren, with a secret in her mind: This is the very last of your mother, children! Then she made her will and came down with a long fever. That was all just a notion like a lot of other things, but it was lucky too, for she had once for all got over the idea of dying for a long time. Now she couldn't be worried. She hoped she had better sense now. Her father had lived to be one hundred and two years old and had drunk a noggin[2] of strong hot toddy[3] on his last birthday. He told the reporters it was his daily habit, and he owed his long life to that. He had made quite a scandal and was very pleased about it. She believed she'd just plague Cornelia a little.

"Cornelia! Cornelia!" No footsteps, but a sudden hand on her cheek. "Bless you, where have you been?"

"Here, mother."

"Well, Cornelia, I want a noggin of hot toddy."

"Are you cold, darling?"

"I'm chilly, Cornelia. Lying in bed stops the circulation. I must have told you that a thousand times."

Well, she could just hear Cornelia telling her husband that Mother was getting a little childish and they'd have to humor her. The thing that most annoyed her was that Cornelia thought she was deaf, dumb, and blind. Little hasty glances and tiny gestures tossed around her and over her head saying, "Don't cross her, let her have her way, she's eighty years old," and she sitting there as if she lived in a thin glass cage. Sometimes Granny almost made up her mind to pack up and move back to her own house where nobody could remind her every minute that she was old. Wait, wait, Cornelia, till your own children whisper behind your back!

In her day she had kept a better house and had got more work done. She wasn't too old yet for Lydia to be driving eighty miles for advice when one of the children jumped the track, and Jimmy still dropped in and talked things over: "Now, Mammy, you've a good business head, I want to know what you think of this? . . ." Old. Cornelia couldn't change the furniture around without asking. Little things, little things! They had been so sweet when they were little. Granny wished the old days were back again with the children young and everything to be done over. It had been a hard pull, but not too much for her. When she thought of all the food she had cooked, and all the clothes she had cut and sewed, and all the gardens she had made—well, the children showed it. There they were, made out of her, and they couldn't get away from that. Sometimes she wanted to see John again and point to them and say, Well, I didn't do so badly, did I? But that would have to wait. That was for tomorrow. She used to think of him as a man, but now all the children were older than their father, and he would be a child beside her if she saw him now. It seemed strange and there was something wrong in the idea. Why, he couldn't possibly recognize her. She had fenced in a hundred

---

[2] *noggin,* a small mug.
[3] *hot toddy,* a drink consisting of brandy or other liquor mixed with hot water, lemon, sugar, and spices.

acres once, digging the post holes herself and clamping the wires with just a Negro boy to help. That changed a woman. John would be looking for a young woman with the peaked Spanish comb in her hair and the painted fan. Digging post holes changed a woman. Riding country roads in the winter when women had their babies was another thing: sitting up nights with sick horses and sick Negroes and sick children and hardly ever losing one. John, I hardly ever lost one of them! John would see that in a minute, that would be something he could understand, she wouldn't have to explain anything!

It made her feel like rolling up her sleeves and putting the whole place to rights again. No matter if Cornelia was determined to be everywhere at once, there were a great many things left undone on this place. She would start tomorrow and do them. It was good to be strong enough for everything, even if all you made melted and changed and slipped under your hands, so that by the time you finished you almost forgot what you were working for. What was it I set out to do? she asked herself intently, but she could not remember. A fog rose over the valley, she saw it marching across the creek swallowing the trees and moving up the hill like an army of ghosts. Soon it would be at the near edge of the orchard, and then it was time to go in and light the lamps. Come in, children, don't stay out in the night air.

Lighting the lamps had been beautiful. The children huddled up to her and breathed like little calves waiting at the bars in the twilight. Their eyes followed the match and watched the flame rise and settle in a blue curve, then they moved away from her. The lamp was lit, they didn't have to be scared and hang on to mother any more. Never, never, never more. God, for all my life I thank Thee. Without Thee, my God, I could never have done it. Hail, Mary, full of grace.

I want you to pick all the fruit this year and see that nothing is wasted. There's always someone who can use it. Don't let good things rot for want of using. You waste life when you waste good food. Don't let things get lost. It's bitter to lose things. Now, don't let me get to thinking, not when I am tired and taking a little nap before supper. . . .

The pillow rose about her shoulders and pressed against her heart and the memory was being squeezed out of it: oh, push down the pillow, somebody: it would smother her if she tried to hold it. Such a fresh breeze blowing and such a green day with no threats in it. But he had not come, just the same. What does a woman do when she has put on the white veil and set out the white cake for a man and he doesn't come? She tried to remember. No, I swear he never harmed me but in that. He never harmed me but in that . . . and what if he did? There was the day, the day, but a whirl of dark smoke rose and covered it, crept up and over into the bright field where everything was planted so carefully in orderly rows. That was hell, she knew hell when she saw it. For sixty years she had prayed against remembering him and against losing her soul in the deep pit of hell, and now the two things were mingled in one and the thought of him was a smoky cloud from hell that moved and crept in her head when she had just got rid of Doctor Harry and was trying to rest a minute. Wounded vanity, Ellen, said a sharp voice in the top of her mind. Don't let your wounded vanity get the upper hand of you. Plenty of girls get jilted. You were jilted, weren't you? Then stand up to it. Her eyelids wavered and let in streamers of blue-gray light like tissue paper over her eyes. She must get up and pull the shades down or she'd never sleep. She was in bed again and the shades were not down. How could that happen? Better turn over, hide from the light, sleeping in the light gave you nightmares. "Mother, how do you feel now?" and a stinging wetness on her forehead. But I don't like having my face washed in cold water!

Hapsy? George? Lydia? Jimmy? No, Cornelia, and her features were swollen and full of little puddles. "They're coming, darling, they'll all be here soon." Go wash your face, child, you look funny.

Instead of obeying, Cornelia knelt down and put her head on the pillow. She seemed to be talking but there was no sound. "Well, are you tongue-tied? Whose birthday is it? Are you going to give a party?"

Cornelia's mouth moved urgently in strange shapes. "Don't do that, you bother me, daughter."

"Oh, no, Mother. Oh, no. . . ."

Nonsense. It was strange about children. They disputed your every word. "No what, Cornelia?"

"Here's Doctor Harry."

"I won't see that boy again. He just left five minutes ago."

"That was this morning, Mother. It's night now. Here's the nurse."

"This is Doctor Harry, Mrs. Weatherall. I never saw you look so young and happy!"

"Ah, I'll never be young again—but I'd be happy if they'd let me lie in peace and get rested."

She thought she spoke up loudly, but no one answered. A warm weight on her forehead, a warm bracelet on her wrist, and a breeze went on whispering, trying to tell her something. A shuffle of leaves in the everlasting hand of God, He blew on them and they danced and rattled. "Mother, don't mind, we're going to give you a little hypodermic." "Look here, daughter, how do ants get in this bed? I saw sugar ants yesterday." Did you send for Hapsy too?

It was Hapsy she really wanted. She had to go a long way back through a great many rooms to find Hapsy standing with a baby on her arm. She seemed to herself to be Hapsy also, and the baby on Hapsy's arm was Hapsy and himself and herself, all at once, and there was no surprise in the meeting. Then Hapsy melted from within and turned flimsy as gray gauze and the baby was a gauzy shadow, and Hapsy came up close and said, "I thought you'd never come," and looked at her very searchingly and said, "You haven't changed a bit!" They leaned forward to kiss, when Cornelia began whispering from a long way off, "Oh, is there anything you want to tell me? Is there anything I can do for you?"

Yes, she had changed her mind after sixty years and she would like to see George. I want you to find George. Find him and be sure to tell him I forgot him. I want him to know I had my husband just the same and my children and my house like any other woman. A good house too and a good husband that I loved and fine children out of him. Better than I hoped for even. Tell him I was given back everything he took away and more. Oh, no, oh, God, no, there was something else besides the house and the man and the children. Oh, surely they were not all? What was it? Something not given back. . . . Her breath crowded down under her ribs and grew into a monstrous frightening shape with cutting edges; it bored up into her head, and the agony was unbelievable: Yes, John, get the Doctor now, no more talk, my time has come.

When this one was born it should be the last. The last. It should have been born first, for it was the one she had truly wanted. Everything came in good time. Nothing left out, left over. She was strong, in three days she would be as well as ever. Better. A woman needed milk in her to have her full health.

"Mother, do you hear me?"

"I've been telling you—"

"Mother, Father Connolly's here."

"I went to Holy Communion only last week. Tell him I'm not so sinful as all that."

"Father just wants to speak to you."

He could speak as much as he pleased. It was like him to drop in and inquire about her soul as if it were a teething baby, and then stay on for a cup of tea and a round of cards and gossip. He always had a funny story of some sort, usually about an Irishman who made his little mistakes and confessed them, and the point lay in some absurd thing he would blurt out in the confessional showing his struggles between native piety and original sin. Granny felt easy about her soul. Cornelia, where are your manners? Give Father Connolly a chair. She had her secret comfortable understanding with a few favorite saints who cleared a straight road to God for her. All as surely signed and sealed as the papers for the new Forty Acres. Forever . . . heirs and assigns forever. Since the day the wedding cake was not cut, but thrown out and wasted. The whole bottom dropped out of the world, and there she was blind and sweating with nothing under her feet and the walls falling away. His hand had caught her under the breast, she had not fallen, there was the freshly polished floor with the green rug on it, just as before. He had cursed like a sailor's parrot and said, "I'll kill him for you." Don't lay a hand on him, for my sake leave something to God. "Now, Ellen, you must believe what I tell you. . . ."

So there was nothing, nothing to worry about any more, except sometimes in the night one of the children screamed in a nightmare, and they both hustled out shaking and hunting for the matches and calling, "There, wait a minute, here we are!" John, get the doctor now, Hapsy's time has come. But there was Hapsy standing by the bed in a white cap. "Cornelia, tell Hapsy to take off her cap. I can't see her plain."

Her eyes opened very wide and the room stood out like a picture she had seen somewhere. Dark colors with the shadows rising towards the ceiling in long angles. The tall black dresser gleamed with nothing on it but John's picture, enlarged from a little one, with John's eyes very black when they should have been blue. You never saw him, so how do you know how he looked? But the man insisted the copy was perfect, it was very rich and handsome. For a picture, yes, but it's not my husband. The table by the bed had a linen cover and a candle and a crucifix. The light was blue from Cornelia's silk lampshades. No sort of light at all, just frippery. You had to live forty years with kerosene lamps to appreciate honest electricity. She felt very strong and she saw Doctor Harry with a rosy nimbus around him.

"You look like a saint, Doctor Harry, and I vow that's as near as you'll ever come to it."

"She's saying something."

"I heard you, Cornelia. What's all this carrying-on?"

"Father Connolly's saying—"

Cornelia's voice staggered and bumped like a cart in a bad road. It rounded corners and turned back again and arrived nowhere. Granny stepped up in the cart very lightly and reached for the reins, but a man sat beside her and she knew him by his hands, driving the cart. She did not look in his face, for she knew without seeing, but looked instead down the road where the trees leaned over and bowed to each other and a thousand birds were singing a Mass. She felt like singing too, but she put her hand in the bosom of her dress and pulled out a rosary, and Father Connolly murmured Latin in a very solemn voice and tickled her feet. My God, will you stop that nonsense? I'm a married woman. What if he did run away and leave me to face the priest by myself? I found another a whole world better. I wouldn't have exchanged my husband for anybody except St. Michael himself, and you may tell him that for me with a thank you in the bargain.

Light flashed on her closed eyelids, and a deep roaring shook her. Cornelia, is that lightning? I hear thunder. There's going to be a storm. Close all the windows. Call the children in. . . . "Mother, here we are, all of us." "Is that you, Hapsy?" "Oh, no, I'm Lydia. We drove as fast as we could." Their faces drifted above her, drifted away. The rosary fell out of her hands and Lydia put it back. Jimmy tried to help, their hands fumbled together, and Granny closed two fingers around Jimmy's thumb. Beads wouldn't do, it must be something alive. She was so amazed her thoughts ran round and round. So, my dear Lord, this is my death and I wasn't even thinking about it. My children have come to see me die. But I can't, it's not time. Oh, I always hated surprises. I wanted to give Cornelia the amethyst set—Cornelia, you're to have the amethyst set, but Hapsy's to wear it when she wants, and, Doctor Harry, do shut up. Nobody sent for you. Oh, my dear Lord, do wait a minute. I meant to do something about the Forty Acres, Jimmy doesn't need it and Lydia will later on, with that worthless husband of hers. I meant to finish the altar cloth and send six bottles of wine to Sister Borgia for her dyspepsia.[4] I want to send six bottles of wine to Sister Borgia, Father Connolly, now don't let me forget.

Cornelia's voice made short turns and tilted over and crashed. "Oh, Mother, oh, Mother, oh, Mother. . . ."

"I'm not going, Cornelia. I'm taken by surprise. I can't go."

You'll see Hapsy again. What about her? "I thought you'd never come." Granny made a long journey outward, looking for Hapsy. What if I don't find her? What then? Her heart sank down and down, there was no bottom to death, she couldn't come to the end of it. The blue light from Cornelia's lampshade drew into a tiny point in the center of her brain, it flickered and winked like an eye, quietly it fluttered and dwindled. Granny lay curled down within herself, amazed and watchful, staring at the point of light that was herself; her body was now only a deeper mass of shadow in an endless darkness and this darkness would curl around the light and swallow it up. God, give a sign!

For the second time there was no sign. Again no bridegroom and the priest in the house. She could not remember any other sorrow because this grief wiped them all away. Oh, no, there's nothing more cruel than this—I'll never forgive it. She stretched herself with a deep breath and blew out the light.

---

[4] *dyspepsia,* indigestion.

## JAMES THURBER (1894–1961)

# *The Secret Life of Walter Mitty*

"We're going through!" The Commander's voice was like thin ice breaking. He wore his full-dress uniform, with the heavily braided white cap pulled down rakishly over one cold gray eye. "We can't make it, sir. It's spoiling for a hurricane, if you ask me." "I'm not asking you, Lieutenant Berg," said the Commander. "Throw on the power lights! Rev her up to 8,500! We're going through!" The pounding of the cylinders increased: ta-pocketa-pocketa-pocketa-*pocketa-pocketa.* The Commander stared at the ice forming on the pilot window. He walked over and twisted a row of complicated dials. "Switch on No. 8 auxiliary!" he shouted. "Switch on No. 8 auxiliary!" repeated Lieutenant Berg. "Full strength in No. 3 turret!" shouted the Commander. "Full strength in No. 3 turret!" The crew, bending to their various tasks in the huge, hurtling eight-engined Navy hydroplane, looked at each other and grinned. "The Old Man'll get us through," they said to one another. "The Old Man ain't afraid of Hell!" . . .

"Not so fast! You're driving too fast!" said Mrs. Mitty. "What are you driving so fast for?"

"Hmm?" said Walter Mitty. He looked at his wife, in the seat beside him, with shocked astonishment. She seemed grossly unfamiliar, like a strange woman who had yelled at him in a crowd. "You were up to fifty-five," she said. "You know I don't like to go more than forty. You were up to fifty-five." Walter Mitty drove on toward Waterbury in silence, the roaring of the SN202 through the worst storm in twenty years of Navy flying fading in the remote, intimate airways of his mind. "You're tensed up again," said Mrs. Mitty. "It's one of your days. I wish you'd let Dr. Renshaw look you over."

Walter Mitty stopped the car in front of the building where his wife went to have her hair done. "Remember to get those overshoes while I'm having my hair done," she said. "I don't need overshoes," said Mitty. She put her mirror back into her bag. "We've been all through that," she said, getting out of the car. "You're not a young man any longer." He raced the engine a little. "Why don't you wear your gloves? Have you lost your gloves?" Walter Mitty reached in a pocket and brought out the gloves. He put them on, but after she had turned and gone into the building and he had driven on to a red light, he took them off again. "Pick it up, brother!" snapped a cop as the light changed, and Mitty hastily pulled on his gloves and lurched ahead. He drove around the streets aimlessly for a time, and then he drove past the hospital on his way to the parking lot.

. . . "It's the millionaire banker, Wellington McMillan," said the pretty nurse. "Yes?" said Walter Mitty, removing his gloves slowly. "Who has the case?" "Dr. Renshaw and Dr. Benbow, but there are two specialists here, Dr. Remington from New York and Dr. Pritchard-Mitford from London. He flew over." A door opened down a long, cool corridor and Dr. Renshaw came out. He looked distraught and haggard. "Hello, Mitty," he said. "We're having the devil's own time with McMillan, the millionaire banker and close personal friend of Roosevelt. Obstreosis of the ductal tract. Tertiary.[1] Wish you'd take a look at him." "Glad to," said Mitty.

In the operating room there were whispered introductions: "Dr. Remington, Dr. Mitty, Dr. Pritchard-Mitford, Dr. Mitty." "I've read your book on streptothricosis," said Pritchard-Mitford, shaking hands. "A brilliant performance, sir." "Thank you," said Walter Mitty. "Didn't know you were in the States, Mitty," grumbled Remington. "Coals to Newcastle, bringing Mitford and me up here for a tertiary." "You are very kind," said Mitty. A huge, complicated machine, connected to the operating table, with many tubes and wires, began at this moment to go pocketa-pocketa-pocketa. "The new anesthetizer is giving way!" shouted an interne. "There is no one in the East who knows how to fix it!" "Quiet, man!" said Mitty, in a low, cool voice. He sprang to the machine, which was now going pocketa-pocketa-queep-pocketa-queep. He began fingering delicately a row of glistening dials. "Give me a fountain pen!" he snapped. Someone handed him a fountain pen. He pulled a faulty piston out of the machine and inserted the pen in its place. "That will hold for ten minutes," he said. "Get on with the operation." A nurse hurried over and whispered to Renshaw, and Mitty saw the man turn pale. "Coreopsis[2] has set in," said Renshaw nervously. "If you would take over, Mitty?" Mitty looked at him and at the craven figure of Benbow, who drank, and at the grave, uncertain faces of the two great specialists. "If you wish," he said. They slipped a white gown on him; he adjusted a mask and drew on thin gloves; nurses handed him shining . .

"Back it up, Mac! Look out for that Buick!" Walter Mitty jammed on the brakes. "Wrong lane, Mac," said the parking-lot attendant, looking at Mitty closely. "Gee. Yeh," muttered Mitty. He began cautiously to back out of the lane marked "Exit Only." "Leave her sit there," said the attendant. "I'll put her away." Mitty got out of the car. "Hey, better leave the key." "Oh," said Mitty, handing the man the ignition key. The attendant vaulted into the car, backed it up with insolent skill, and put it where it belonged.

---

[1] *tertiary,* at the third—advanced—stage of the disease. "Obstreosis" and "streptothricosis" (below) are nonsense words for imaginary diseases.

[2] *coreopsis,* a genus of herb, not a medical condition.

They're so damn cocky, thought Walter Mitty, walking along Main Street; they think they know everything. Once he had tried to take his chains off, outside New Milford, and he had got them wound around the axles. A man had had to come out in a wrecking car and unwind them, a young, grinning garageman. Since then Mrs. Mitty always made him drive to the garage to have the chains taken off. The next time, he thought, I'll wear my right arm in a sling; they won't grin at me then. I'll have my right arm in a sling and they'll see I couldn't possibly take the chains off myself. He kicked at the slush on the sidewalk. "Overshoes," he said to himself, and he began looking for a shoe store.

When he came out into the street again, with the overshoes in a box under his arm, Walter Mitty began to wonder what the other thing was his wife had told him to get. She had told him, twice, before they set out from their house for Waterbury. In a way he hated these weekly trips to town—he was always getting something wrong. Kleenex, he thought, Squibb's, razor blades? No. Toothpaste, toothbrush, bicarbonate, carborundum, initiative and referendum? He gave it up. But she would remember it. "Where's the what's-its-name?" she would ask. "Don't tell me you forgot the what's-its-name." A newsboy went by shouting something about the Waterbury trial.

. . . "Perhaps this will refresh your memory." The District Attorney suddenly thrust a heavy automatic at the quiet figure on the witness stand. "Have you ever seen this before?" Walter Mitty took the gun and examined it expertly. "This is my Webley-Vickers 50.80," he said calmly. An excited buzz ran around the courtroom. The Judge rapped for order. "You are a crack shot with any sort of firearms, I believe?" said the District Attorney, insinuatingly. "Objection!" shouted Mitty's attorney. "We have shown that the defendant could not have fired the shot. We have shown that he wore his right arm in a sling on the night of the fourteenth of July." Walter Mitty raised his hand briefly and the bickering attorneys were stilled. "With any known make of gun," he said evenly, "I could have killed Gregory Fitzhurst at three hundred feet *with my left hand.*" Pandemonium broke loose in the courtroom. A woman's scream rose above the bedlam and suddenly a lovely, dark-haired girl was in Walter Mitty's arms. The District Attorney struck at her savagely. Without rising from his chair, Mitty let the man have it on the point of the chin. "You miserable cur!" . . .

"Puppy biscuit," said Walter Mitty. He stopped walking and the buildings of Waterbury rose up out of the misty courtroom and surrounded him again. A woman who was passing laughed. "He said 'Puppy biscuit,' " she said to her companion. "That man said 'Puppy biscuit' to himself." Walter Mitty hurried on. He went into an A. & P., not the first one he came to but a smaller one farther up the street. "I want some biscuit for small, young dogs," he said to the clerk. "Any special brand, sir?" The greatest pistol shot in the world thought a moment. "It says 'Puppies Bark for It' on the box," said Walter Mitty.

His wife would be through at the hairdresser's in fifteen minutes, Mitty saw in looking at his watch, unless they had trouble drying it; sometimes they had trouble drying it. She didn't like to get to the hotel first; she would want him to be there waiting for her as usual. He found a big leather chair in the lobby, facing a window, and he put the overshoes and the puppy biscuit on the floor beside it. He picked up an old copy of *Liberty*[3] and sank down into the chair. "Can Germany Conquer the World Through the Air?" Walter Mitty looked at the pictures of bombing planes and of ruined streets.

. . . "The cannonading has got the wind up in young Raleigh, sir," said the sergeant. Captain Mitty looked up at him through touseled hair. "Get him to bed," he said wearily. "With the others. I'll fly alone." "But you can't, sir," said the sergeant anxiously. "It takes two men to handle that bomber and the Archies[4] are pounding hell out of the air. Von Richtman's circus[5] is between here and Saulier." "Somebody's got to get that ammunition dump," said Mitty. "I'm going over. Spot of brandy?" He poured a drink for the sergeant and one for himself. War thundered and whined around the dugout[6] and battered at the door. There was a rending of wood and splinters flew through the room. "A bit of a near thing," said Captain Mitty carelessly. "The box barrage[7] is closing in," said the sergeant. "We only live once, Sergeant," said Mitty, with his faint, fleeting smile. "Or do we?" He poured another brandy and tossed it off. "I never see a man could hold his brandy like you, sir," said the sergeant. "Begging your pardon, sir." Captain Mitty stood up and strapped on his huge Webley-Vickers automatic. "It's forty kilometers through hell, sir," said the sergeant. Mitty finished one last brandy. "After all," he said softly, "what isn't?" The pounding of the cannon increased; there was the rat-tat-tatting of machine guns, and from somewhere came the menacing pocketa-pocketa-pocketa of the new flame-throwers. Walter Mitty walked to the door of the dugout humming "Auprès de Ma Blonde."[8] He turned and waved to the sergeant. "Cheerio!" he said. . . .

Something struck his shoulder. "I've been looking all over this hotel for you," said Mrs. Mitty. "Why do you have to hide in this old chair? How did you expect me to find you?" "Things close in," said Walter Mitty vaguely. "What?" Mrs. Mitty said. "Did you get the what's-its-name? The puppy biscuit? What's in that box?" "Overshoes," said Mitty.

---

[3] *Liberty*, popular weekly magazine (1924–1951).

[4] *Archies*, slang for antiaircraft guns.

[5] In World War I the battle groups of fighter squadrons were known as "flying circuses"; the group commanded by Baron Manfred von Richthofen (1892–1918) was the most deadly German flying circus.

[6] *dugout*, sheltered area dug out of the side of a trench.

[7] *box barrage*, an artillery barrage from all four sides.

[8] "Close to My Blonde," French song popular during World War I.

"Couldn't you have put them on in the store?" "I was thinking," said Walter Mitty. "Does it ever occur to you that I am sometimes thinking?" She looked at him. "I'm going to take your temperature when I get you home," she said.

They went out through the revolving doors that made a faintly derisive whistling sound when you pushed them. It was two blocks to the parking lot. At the drugstore on the corner she said, "Wait here for me. I forgot something. I won't be a minute." She was more than a minute. Walter Mitty lighted a cigarette. It began to rain, rain with sleet in it. He stood up against a wall of the drugstore, smoking. . . . He put his shoulders back and his heels together. "To hell with the handkerchief," said Walter Mitty scornfully. He took one last drag on his cigarette and snapped it away. Then, with that faint, fleeting smile playing about his lips, he faced the firing squad; erect and motionless, proud and disdainful, Walter Mitty the Undefeated, inscrutable to the last.

## ERNEST HEMINGWAY (1899–1961)

# *The Snows of Kilimanjaro*

*Kilimanjaro is a snow covered mountain 19,710 feet high, and is said to be the highest mountain in Africa. Its western summit is called the Masai "Ngàje Ngài," the House of God. Close to the western summit there is the dried and frozen carcass of a leopard. No one has explained what the leopard was seeking at that altitude.*

"The marvellous thing is that it's painless," he said. "That's how you know when it starts."

"Is it really?"

"Absolutely. I'm awfully sorry about the odor though. That must bother you."

"Don't! Please don't."

"Look at them," he said. "Now is it sight or is it scent that brings them like that?"

The cot the man lay on was in the wide shade of a mimosa tree and as he looked out past the shade onto the glare of the plain there were three of the big birds squatted obscenely, while in the sky a dozen more sailed, making quick-moving shadows as they passed.

"They've been there since the day the truck broke down," he said. "Today's the first time any have lit on the ground. I watched the way they sailed very carefully at first in case I ever wanted to use them in a story. That's funny now."

"I wish you wouldn't," she said.

"I'm only talking," he said. "It's much easier if I talk. But I don't want to bother you."

"You know it doesn't bother me," she said. "It's that I've gotten so very nervous not being able to do anything. I think we might make it as easy as we can until the plane comes."

"Or until the plane doesn't come."

"Please tell me what I can do. There must be something I can do."

"You can take the leg off and that might stop it, though I doubt it. Or you can shoot me. You're a good shot now. I taught you to shoot didn't I?"

"Please don't talk that way. Couldn't I read to you?"

"Read what?"

"Anything in the book bag that we haven't read."

"I can't listen to it," he said. "Talking is the easiest. We quarrel and that makes the time pass."

"I don't quarrel. I never want to quarrel. Let's not quarrel any more. No matter how nervous we get. Maybe they will be back with another truck today. Maybe the plane will come."

"I don't want to move," the man said. "There is no sense in moving now except to make it easier for you."

"That's cowardly."

"Can't you let a man die as comfortably as he can without calling him names? What's the use of slanging me?"

"You're not going to die."

"Don't be silly. I'm dying now. Ask those bastards." He looked over to where the huge, filthy birds sat, their naked heads sunk in the hunched feathers. A fourth planed down, to run quick-legged and then waddle slowly toward the others.

"They are around every camp. You never notice them. You can't die if you don't give up."

"Where did you read that? You're such a bloody fool."

"You might think about some one else."

"For Christ's sake," he said, "That's been my trade."

He lay then and was quiet for a while and looked across the heat shimmer of the plain to the edge of the bush. There were a few Tommies that showed minute and white against the yellow and, far off, he saw a herd of zebra, white against the green of the bush. This was a pleasant camp under big trees against a hill, with good water, and close by, a nearly dry water hole where sand grouse flighted in the mornings.

"Wouldn't you like me to read?" she asked. She was sitting on a canvas chair beside his cot. "There's a breeze coming up."

"No thanks."

"Maybe the truck will come."

"I don't give a damn about the truck."

"I do."

"You give a damn about so many things that I don't."

"Not so many, Harry."

"What about a drink?"

"It's supposed to be bad for you. It said in Black's to avoid all alcohol. You shouldn't drink."

"Molo!" he shouted.

"Yes Bwana."

"Bring whiskey-soda."

"Yes Bwana."

"You shouldn't," she said. "That's what I mean by giving up. It says it's bad for you. I know it's bad for you."

"No," he said. "It's good for me."

So now it was all over, he thought. So now he would never have a chance to finish it. So this was the way it ended in a bickering over a drink. Since the gangrene started in his right leg he had no pain and with the pain the horror had gone and all he felt now was a great tiredness and anger that this was the end of it. For this, that now was coming, he had very little curiosity. For years it had obsessed him; but now it meant nothing in itself. It was strange how easy being tired enough made it.

Now he would never write the things that he had saved to write until he knew enough to write them well. Well, he would not have to fail at trying to write them either. Maybe you could never write them, and that was why you put them off and delayed the starting. Well he would never know, now.

"I wish we'd never come," the woman said. She was looking at him holding the glass and biting her lip. "You never would have gotten anything like this in Paris. You always said you loved Paris. We could have stayed in Paris or gone anywhere. I'd have gone anywhere. I said I'd go anywhere you wanted. If you wanted to shoot we could have gone shooting in Hungary and been comfortable."

"Your bloody money," he said.

"That's not fair," she said. "It was always yours as much as mine. I left everything and I went wherever you wanted to go and I've done what you wanted to do. But I wish we'd never come here."

"You said you loved it."

"I did when you were all right. But now I hate it. I don't see why that had to happen to your leg. What have we done to have that happen to us?"

"I suppose what I did was to forget to put iodine on it when I first scratched it. Then I didn't pay any attention to it because I never infect. Then, later, when it got bad, it was probably using that weak carbolic solution when the other antiseptics ran out that paralyzed the minute blood vessels and started the gangrene." He looked at her, "What else?"

"I don't mean that."

"If we would have hired a good mechanic instead of a half baked kikuyu driver, he would have checked the oil and never burned out that bearing in the truck."

"I don't mean that."

"If you hadn't left your own people, your goddamned Old Westbury, Saratoga, Palm Beach people to take me on—"

"Why, I loved you. That's not fair. I love you now. I'll always love you. Don't you love me?"

"No," said the man. "I don't think so. I never have."

"Harry, what are you saying? You're out of your head."

"No. I haven't any head to go out of."

"Don't drink that," she said. "Darling, please don't drink that. We have to do everything we can."

"You do it," he said. "I'm tired."

*Now in his mind he saw a railway station at Karagatch and he was standing with his pack and that was the headlight of the Simplon-Orient cutting the dark now and he was leaving Thrace then after the retreat. That was one of the things he had saved to write, with, in the morning at breakfast, looking out the window and seeing snow on the mountains in Bulgaria and Nansen's Secretary asking the old man if it were snow and the old man looking at it and saying, No, that's not snow. It's too early for snow. And the Secretary repeating to the other girls, No, you see. It's not snow and them all saying, It's not snow we were mistaken. But it was the snow all right and he sent them on into it when he evolved exchange of populations. And it was snow they tramped along in until they died that winter.*

*It was snow too that fell all Christmas week that year up in the Gauertal, that year they lived in the woodcutter's house with the big square porcelain stove that filled half the room, and they slept on mattresses filled with beech leaves, the time the deserter came with his feet bloody in the snow. He said the police were right behind him and they gave him woolen socks and held the gendarmes talking until the tracks had drifted over.*

*In Schrunz, on Christmas day, the snow was so bright it hurt your eyes when you looked out from the weinstube and saw every one coming home from church. That was where they walked up the sleigh-smoothed urine-yellowed road along the river with the steep pine hills, skis heavy on the shoulder, and where they ran that great run down the glacier above the Madlener-haus, the snow as smooth to see as cake frosting and as light as powder and he remembered the noiseless rush the speed made as you dropped down like a bird.*

*They were snow-bound a week in the Madlener-haus that time in the blizzard playing cards in the smoke by the lantern light and the stakes were higher all the time as Herr Lent lost more. Finally he lost it all. Everything, the skischule money and all the season's profit and then his capital. He could see him with his long nose, picking up the cards and then opening, "Sans Voir." There was always gambling then. When there was no snow you gambled and when there was too much you gambled. He thought of all the time in his life he had spent gambling.*

*But he had never written a line of that, nor of that cold, bright Christmas day with the mountains showing across the plain that Barker had flown across the lines to bomb the Austrian officers' leave train, machine-gunning them as they scattered and ran. He remem-*

*bered Barker afterwards coming into the mess and starting to tell about it. And how quiet it got and then somebody saying, "You bloody murderous bastard."*

*Those were the same Austrians they killed then that he skied with later. No not the same. Hans, that he skied with all that year, had been in the Kaiser-Jägers and when they went hunting hares together up the little valley above the saw-mill they had talked of the fighting on Pasubio and of the attack on Pertica and Asalone and he had never written a word of that. Nor of Monte Corno, nor the Siete Commum, nor of Arsiedo.*

*How many winters had he lived in the Voralberg and the Arlberg? It was four and then he remembered the man who had the fox to sell when they had walked into Bludenz, that time to buy presents, and the cherry-pit taste of good kirsch, the fast-slipping rush of running powder-snow on crust, singing "Hi! Ho! said Rolly!" as you ran down the last stretch to the steep drop, taking it straight, then running the orchard in three turns and out across the ditch and onto the icy road behind the inn. Knocking your bindings loose, kicking the skis free and leaning them up against the wooden wall of the inn, the lamplight coming from the window, where inside, in the smoky, new-wine smelling warmth, they were playing the accordion.*

"Where did we stay in Paris?" he asked the woman who was sitting by him in a canvas chair, now, in Africa.

"At the Crillon. You know that."

"Why do I know that?"

"That's where we always stayed."

"No. Not always."

"There and at the Pavillion Henri-Quatre in St. Germain. You said you loved it there."

"Love is a dunghill," said Harry. "And I'm the cock that gets on it to crow."

"If you have to go away," she said, "is it absolutely necessary to kill off everything you leave behind? I mean do you have to take away everything? Do you have to kill your horse, and your wife and burn your saddle and your armour?"

"Yes," he said. "Your damned money was my armour. My Swift and my Armour."

"Don't."

"All right. I'll stop that. I don't want to hurt you."

"It's a little bit late now."

"All right then. I'll go on hurting you. It's more amusing. The only thing I ever really liked to do with you I can't do now."

"No, that's not true. You liked to do many things and everything you wanted to do I did."

"Oh, for Christ sake stop bragging, will you?"

He looked at her and saw her crying.

"Listen," he said. "Do you think that it is fun to do this? I don't know why I'm doing it. It's trying to kill to keep yourself alive, I imagine. I was all right when we started talking. I didn't mean to start this, and now I'm crazy as a coot and being as cruel to you as I can be. Don't pay any attention, darling, to what I say. I love you, really. You know I love you. I've never loved any one else the way I love you."

He slipped into the familiar lie he made his bread and butter by.

"You're sweet to me."

"You bitch," he said. "You rich bitch. That's poetry. I'm full of poetry now. Rot and poetry. Rotten poetry."

"Stop it. Harry, why do you have to turn into a devil now?"

"I don't like to leave anything," the man said. "I don't like to leave things behind."

⌘

It was evening now and he had been asleep. The sun was gone behind the hill and there was a shadow all across the plain and the small animals were feeding close to camp; quick dropping heads and switching tails, he watched them keeping well out away from the bush now. The birds no longer waited on the ground. They were all perched heavily in a tree. There were many more of them. His personal boy was sitting by the bed.

"Memsahib's gone to shoot," the boy said. "Does Bwana want?"

"Nothing."

She had gone to kill a piece of meat and, knowing how he liked to watch the game, she had gone well away so she would not disturb this little pocket of the plain that he could see. She was always thoughtful, he thought. On anything she knew about, or had read, or that she had ever heard.

It was not her fault that when he went to her he was already over. How could a woman know that you meant nothing that you said; that you spoke only from habit and to be comfortable? After he no longer meant what he said, his lies were more successful with women than when he had told them the truth.

It was not so much that he lied as that there was no truth to tell. He had had his life and it was over and then he went on living it again with different people and more money, with the best of the same places, and some new ones.

You kept from thinking and it was all marvellous. You were equipped with good insides so that you did not go to pieces that way, the way most of them had, and you made an attitude that you cared nothing for the work you used to do, now that you could no longer do it. But, in yourself, you said that you would write about these people; about the very rich; that you were really not of them but a spy in their country; that you would leave it and write of it and for once it would be written by some one who knew what he was writing of. But he would never do it, because each day of not writing, of comfort, of being that which he despised, dulled his ability and softened his will to work so that, finally, he did no work at all. The people he knew now were all much more comfortable when he did not work. Africa was where he had been happiest in the good time of his life, so he had come out here to start again. They had made this safari with the minimum of comfort. There was no hardship; but there was no luxury and he had thought that he could get back into training that way. That in some way he could work the fat off his soul the way a fighter went into the mountains to work and train in order to burn it out of his body.

She had liked it. She said she loved it. She loved anything that was exciting, that involved a change of scene, where there were new people and where things were pleasant. And he had felt the illusion of returning strength of will to work. Now if this was how it ended, and he knew it was, he must not turn like some snake biting itself because its back was broken. It wasn't this woman's fault. If it had not been she it would have been another. If he lived by a lie he should try to die by it. He heard a shot beyond the hill.

She shot very well this good, this rich bitch, this kindly caretaker and destroyer of his talent. Nonsense. He had destroyed his talent himself. Why should he blame this woman because she kept him well? He had destroyed his talent by not using it, by betrayals of himself and what he believed in, by drinking so much that he blunted the edge of his perceptions, by laziness, by sloth, and by snobbery, by pride and by prejudice, by hook and by crook. What was this? A catalogue of old books? What was his talent anyway? It was a talent all right but instead of using it, he had traded on it. It was never what he had done, but always what he could do. And he had chosen to make his living with something else instead of a pen or a pencil. It was strange, too, wasn't it, that when he fell in love with another woman, that woman should always have more money than the last one? But when he no longer was in love, when he was only lying, as to this woman, now, who had the most money of all, who had all the money there was, who had had a husband and children, who had taken lovers and been dissatisfied with them, and who loved him dearly as a writer, as a man, as a companion and as a proud possession; it was strange that when he did not love her at all and was lying, that he should be able to give her more for her money than when he had really loved.

We must all be cut out for what we do, he thought. However you make your living is where your talent lies. He had sold vitality, in one form or another, all his life and when your affections are not too involved you give much better value for the money. He had found that out but he would never write that, now, either. No, he would not write that, although it was well worth writing.

Now she came in sight, walking across the open toward the camp. She was wearing jodphurs and carrying her rifle. The two boys had a Tommie slung and they were coming along behind her. She was still a good-looking woman, he thought, and she had a pleasant body. She had a great talent and appreciation for the bed, she was not pretty, but he liked her face, she read enormously, liked to ride and shoot and, certainly, she drank too much. Her husband had died when she was still a comparatively young woman and for a while she had devoted herself to her two just-grown children, who did not need her and were embarrassed at having her about, to her stable of horses, to books, and to bottles. She liked to read in the evening before dinner and she drank Scotch and soda while she read. By dinner she was fairly drunk and after a bottle of wine at dinner she was usually drunk enough to sleep.

That was before the lovers. After she had the lovers she did not drink so much because she did not have to be drunk to sleep. But the lovers bored her. She had been married to a man who had never bored her and these people bored her very much.

Then one of her two children was killed in a plane crash and after that was over she did not want the lovers, and drink being no anæsthetic she had to make another life. Suddenly, she had been acutely frightened of being alone. But she wanted some one that she respected with her.

It had begun very simply. She liked what he wrote and she had always envied the life he led. She thought he did exactly what he wanted to. The steps by which she had acquired him and the way in which she had finally fallen in love with him were all part of a regular progression in which she had built herself a new life and he had traded away what remained of his old life.

He had traded it for security, for comfort too, there was no denying that, and for what else? He did not know. She would have bought him anything he wanted. He knew that. She was a damned nice woman too. He would as soon be in bed with her as any one; rather with her, because she was richer, because she was very pleasant and appreciative and because she never made scenes. And now this life that she had built again was coming to a term because he had not used iodine two weeks ago when a thorn had scratched his knee as they moved forward trying to photograph a herd of waterbuck standing, their heads up, peering while their nostrils searched the air, their ears spread wide to hear the first noise that would send them rushing into the bush. They had bolted, too, before he got the picture.

Here she came now.

He turned his head on the cot to look toward her. "Hello," he said.

"I shot a Tommy ram," she told him. "He'll make you good broth and I'll have them mash some potatoes with the Klim. How do you feel?"

"Much better."

"Isn't that lovely? You know I thought perhaps you would. You were sleeping when I left."

"I had a good sleep. Did you walk far?"

"No. Just around behind the hill. I made quite a good shot on the Tommy."

"You shoot marvellously, you know."

"I love it. I've loved Africa. Really. If *you're* all right it's the most fun that I've ever had. You don't know the fun it's been to shoot with you. I've loved the country."

"I love it too."

"Darling, you don't know how marvellous it is to see you feeling better. I couldn't stand it when you felt that way. You won't talk to me like that again, will you? Promise me?"

"No," he said. "I don't remember what I said."

"You don't have to destroy me. Do you? I'm only a middle-aged woman who loves you and wants to do what you want to do. I've been destroyed two or three times already. You wouldn't want to destroy me again, would you?"

"I'd like to destroy you a few times in bed," he said.

"Yes. That's the good destruction. That's the way we're made to be destroyed. The plane will be here tomorrow."

"How do you know?"

"I'm sure. It's bound to come. The boys have the wood all ready and the grass to make the smudge. I went down and looked at it again today. There's plenty of room to land and we have the smudges ready at both ends."

"What makes you think it will come tomorrow?"

"I'm sure it will. It's overdue now. Then, in town, they will fix up your leg and then we will have some good destruction. Not that dreadful talking kind."

"Should we have a drink? The sun is down."

"Do you think you should?"

"I'm having one."

"We'll have one together. *Molo, letti dui whiskey-soda!*" she called.

"You'd better put on your mosquito boots," he told her.

"I'll wait till I bathe . . ."

While it grew dark they drank and just before it was dark and there was no longer enough light to shoot, a hyena crossed the open on his way around the hill.

"That bastard crosses there every night," the man said. "Every night for two weeks."

"He's the one makes the noise at night. I don't mind it. They're a filthy animal though."

Drinking together, with no pain now except the discomfort of lying in the one position, the boys lighting a fire, its shadow jumping on the tents, he could feel the return of acquiescence in this life of pleasant surrender. She *was* very good to him. He had been cruel and unjust in the afternoon. She was a fine woman, marvellous really. And just then it occurred to him that he was going to die.

It came with a rush; not as a rush of water nor of wind; but of a sudden evil-smelling emptiness and the odd thing was that the hyena slipped lightly along the edge of it.

"What is it, Harry?" she asked him.

"Nothing," he said. "You had better move over to the other side. To windward."

"Did Molo change the dressing?"

"Yes. I'm just using the boric now."

"How do you feel?"

"A little wobbly."

"I'm going in to bathe," she said. "I'll be right out. I'll eat with you and then we'll put the cot in."

So, he said to himself, we did well to stop the quarrelling. He had never quarrelled much with this woman, while with the women that he loved he had quarrelled so much they had finally, always, with the corrosion of the quarrelling, killed what they had together. He had loved too much, demanded too much, and he wore it all out.

*He thought about alone in Constantinople that time, having quarrelled in Paris before he had gone out. He had whored the whole time and then, when that was over, and he had failed to kill his loneliness, but only made it worse, he had written her, the first one, the one who left him, a letter telling her how he had never been able to kill it. . . . How when he thought he saw her outside the* Regence *one time it made him go all faint and sick inside, and that he would follow a woman who looked like her in some way, along the Boulevard, afraid to see it was not she, afraid to lose the feeling it gave him. How every one he had slept with had only made him miss her more. How what she had done could never matter since he knew he could not cure himself of loving her. He wrote this letter at the*

*Club, cold sober, and mailed it to New York asking her to write him at the office in Paris. That seemed safe. And that night missing her so much it made him feel hollow sick inside, he wandered up past Taxim's, picked a girl up and took her out to supper. He had gone to a place to dance with her afterward, she danced badly, and left her for a hot Armenian slut, that swung her belly against him so it almost scalded. He took her away from a British gunner subaltern after a row. The gunner asked him outside and they fought in the street on the cobbles in the dark. He'd hit him twice, hard, on the side of the jaw and when he didn't go down he knew he was in for a fight. The gunner hit him in the body, then beside his eye. He swung with his left again and landed and the gunner fell on him and grabbed his coat and tore the sleeve off and he clubbed him twice behind the ear and then smashed him with his right as he pushed him away. When the gunner went down his head hit first and he ran with the girl because they heard the M.P.'s coming. They got into a taxi and drove out to Rimmily Hissa along the Bosphorus, and around, and back in the cool night and went to bed and she felt as over-ripe as she looked but smooth, rose-petal, syrupy, smooth-bellied, big-breasted and needed no pillow under her buttocks, and he left her before she was awake looking blousy enough in the first daylight and turned up at the Pera Palace with a black eye, carrying his coat because one sleeve was missing.*

*That same night he left for Anatolia and he remembered, later on that trip, riding all day through fields of the poppies that they raised for opium and how strange it made you feel, finally, and all the distances seemed wrong, to where they had made the attack with the newly arrived Constantine officers, that did not know a god-damned thing, and the artillery had fired into the troops and the British observer had cried like a child.*

*That was the day he'd first seen dead men wearing white ballet skirts and upturned shoes with pompons on them. The Turks had come steadily and lumpily and he had seen the skirted men running and the officers shooting into them and running themselves and he and the British observer had run too until his lungs ached and his mouth was full of the taste of pennies and they stopped behind some rocks and there were the Turks coming as lumpily as ever. Later he had seen the things that he could never think of and later still he had seen much worse. So when he got back to Paris that time he could not talk about it or stand to have it mentioned. And there in the café as he passed was that American poet with a pile of saucers in front of him and a stupid look on his potato face talking about the Dada movement with a Roumanian who said his name was Tristan Tzara, who always wore a monocle and had a headache, and, back at the apartment with his wife that now he loved again, the quarrel all over, the madness all over, glad to be home, the office sent his mail up to the flat. So then the letter in answer to the one he'd written came in on a platter one morning and when he saw the handwriting he went cold all over and tried to slip the letter underneath another. But his wife said, "Who is that letter from, dear?" and that was the end of the beginning of that.*

*He remembered the good times with them all, and the quarrels. They always picked the finest places to have the quarrels. And why had they always quarrelled when he was feeling best? He had never written any of that because, at first, he never wanted to hurt any one and then it seemed as though there was enough to write without it. But he had always thought that he would write it finally. There was so much to write. He had seen the world change; not just the events; although he had seen many of them and had watched the people, but he had seen the subtler change and he could remember how the people were at different times. He had been in it and he had watched it and it was his duty to write of it; but now he never would.*

"How do you feel?" she said. She had come out from the tent now after her bath.

"All right."

"Could you eat now?" He saw Molo behind her with the folding table and the other boy with the dishes.

"I want to write," he said.

"You ought to take some broth to keep your strength up."

"I'm going to die tonight," he said. "I don't need my strength up."

"Don't be melodramatic, Harry, please," she said.

"Why don't you use your nose? I'm rotted half way up my thigh now. What the hell should I fool with broth for? Molo bring whiskey-soda."

"Please take the broth," she said gently.

"All right."

The broth was too hot. He had to hold it in the cup until it cooled enough to take it and then he just got it down without gagging.

"You're a fine woman," he said. "Don't pay any attention to me."

She looked at him with her well-known, well-loved face from *Spur* and *Town and Country*, only a little the worse for drink, only a little the worse for bed, but *Town and Country* never showed those good breasts and those useful thighs and those lightly small-of-back-caressing hands, and as he looked and saw her well known pleasant smile, he felt death come again. This time there was no rush. It was a puff, as of a wind that makes a candle flicker and the flame go tall.

"They can bring my net out later and hang it from the tree and build the fire up. I'm not going in the tent tonight. It's not worth moving. It's a clear night. There won't be any rain."

So this was how you died, in whispers that you did not hear. Well, there would be no more quarrelling. He could promise that. The one experience that he had never had he was not going to spoil now. He probably would. You spoiled everything. But perhaps he wouldn't.

"You can't take dictation, can you?"

"I never learned," she told him.

"That's all right."

There wasn't time, of course, although it seemed as though it telescoped so that you might put it all into one paragraph if you could get it right.

*There was a log house, chinked white with mortar, on a hill above the lake. There was a bell on a pole by the door to call the people in to meals. Behind the house were fields and behind the fields was the timber. A line of lombardy poplars ran from the house to the dock. Other poplars ran along the point. A road went up to the hills along the edge of the timber and along that road he picked blackberries. Then that log house was burned down and all the guns that had been on deer foot racks above the open fire place were burned and afterwards their barrels, with the lead melted in the magazines, and the stocks burned away, lay out on the heap of ashes that were used to make lye for the big iron soap kettles, and you asked Grandfather if you could have them to play with, and he said, no. You see they were his guns still and he never bought any others. Nor did he hunt any more. The house was rebuilt in the same place out of lumber now and painted white and from its porch you saw the poplars and the lake beyond; but there were never any more guns. The barrels of the guns that had hung on the deer feet on the wall of the log house lay out there on the heap of ashes and no one ever touched them.*

*In the Black Forest, after the war, we rented a trout stream and there were two ways to walk to it. One was down the valley from Triberg and around the valley road in the shade of the trees that bordered the white road, and then up a side road that went up through the hills past many small farms, with the big Schwarzwald houses, until that road crossed the stream. That was where our fishing began.*

*The other way was to climb steeply up to the edge of the woods and then go across the top of the hills through the pine woods, and then out to the edge of a meadow and down across this meadow to the bridge. There were birches along the stream and it was not big, but narrow, clear and fast, with pools where it had cut under the roots of the birches. At the Hotel in Triberg the proprietor had a fine season. It was very pleasant and we were all great friends. The next year came the inflation and the money he had made the year before was not enough to buy supplies to open the hotel and he hanged himself.*

*You could dictate that, but you could not dictate the Place Contrescarpe where the flower sellers dyed their flowers in the street and the dye ran over the paving where the autobus started and the old men and the women, always drunk on wine and bad marc; and the children with their noses running in the cold; the smell of dirty sweat and poverty and drunkenness at the Café des Amateurs and the whores at the Bal Musette they lived above. The Concierge who entertained the trooper of the Garde Republicaine in her loge, his horse-hair-plumed helmet on a chair. The locataire across the hall whose husband was a bicycle racer and her joy that morning at the Cremerie when she had opened L'Auto and seen where he placed third in Paris-Tours, his first big race. She had blushed and laughed and then gone upstairs crying with the yellow sporting paper in her hand. The husband of the woman who ran the Bal Musette drove a taxi and when he, Harry, had to take an early plane the husband knocked upon the door to wake him and they each drank a glass of white wine at the zinc of the bar before they started. He knew his neighbors in that quarter then because they all were poor.*

*Around that Place there were two kinds; the drunkards and the sportifs. The drunkards killed their poverty that way; the sportifs took it out in exercise. They were the descendants of the Communards and it was no struggle for them to know their politics. They knew who had shot their fathers, their relatives, their brothers, and their friends when the Versailles troops came in and took the town after the Commune and executed any one they could catch with calloused hands, or who wore a cap, or carried any other sign he was a working man. And in that poverty, and in that quarter across the street from a Boucherie Chevaline and a wine co-operative he had written the start of all he was to do. There never was another part of Paris that he loved like that, the sprawling trees, the old white plastered houses painted brown below, the long green of the autobus in that round square, the purple flower dye upon the paving, the sudden drop down the hill of the rue Cardinal Lemoine to the River, and the other way the narrow crowded world of the rue Mouffetard. The street that ran up toward the Pantheon and the other that he always took with the bicycle, the only asphalted street in all that quarter, smooth under the tires, with the high narrow houses and the cheap tall hotel where Paul Verlaine had died. There were only two rooms in the apartments where they lived and he had a room on the top floor of that hotel that cost him sixty francs a month where he did his writing, and from it he could see the roofs and chimney pots and all the hills of Paris.*

*From the apartment you could only see the wood and coal man's place. He sold wine too, bad wine. The golden horse's head outside the Boucherie Chevaline where the carcasses hung yellow gold and red in the open window, and the green painted co-operative where they bought their wine; good wine and cheap. The rest was plaster walls and the windows of the neighbors. The neighbors who, at night, when some one lay drunk in the street, moaning and groaning in that typical French* ivresse *that you were propaganded to believe did not exist, would open their windows and then the murmur of talk.*

*"Where is the policeman? When you don't want him the bugger is always there. He's sleeping with some concierge. Get the* Agent.*" Till some one threw a bucket of water from a window and the moaning stopped. "What's that? Water. Ah, that's intelligent." And the windows shutting. Marie, his femme de menage, protesting against the eight-hour day saying, "If a husband works until six he gets only a little drunk on the way home and does not waste too much. If he works only until five he is drunk every night and one has no money. It is the wife of the working man who suffers from this shortening of hours."*

"Wouldn't you like some more broth?" the woman asked him now.

"No, thank you very much. It is awfully good."

"Try just a little."

"I would like a whiskey-soda."

"It's not good for you."

"No. It's bad for me. Cole Porter wrote the words and the music. This knowledge that you're going mad for me."

"You know I like you to drink."

"Oh yes. Only it's bad for me."

When she goes, he thought. I'll have all I want. Not all I want but all there is. Ayee he was tired. Too tired. He was going to sleep a little while. He lay still and death was not there. It must have gone around another street. It went in pairs, on bicycles, and moved absolutely silently on the pavements.

*No, he had never written about Paris. Not the Paris that he cared about. But what about the rest that he had never written?*

*What about the ranch and the silvered gray of the sage brush, the quick, clear water in the irrigation ditches, and the heavy green of the alfalfa. The trail went up into the hills and the cattle in the summer were shy as deer. The bawling and the steady noise and slow moving mass raising a dust as you brought them down in the fall. And behind the mountains, the clear sharpness of the peak in the evening light and, riding down along the trail in the moonlight, bright across the valley. Now he remembered coming down through the timber in the dark holding the horse's tail when you could not see and all the stories that he meant to write.*

*About the half-wit chore boy who was left at the ranch that time and told not to let any one get any hay, and that old bastard from the Forks who had beaten the boy when he had worked for him stopping to get some feed. The boy refusing and the old man saying he would beat him again. The boy got the rifle from the kitchen and shot him when he tried to come into the barn and when they came back to the ranch he'd been dead a week, frozen in the corral, and the dogs had eaten part of him. But what was left you packed on a sled wrapped in a blanket and roped on and you got the boy to help you haul it, and the two of you took it out over the road on skis, and sixty miles down to town to turn the boy over. He having no idea that he would be arrested. Thinking he had done his duty and that you were his friend and he would be rewarded. He'd helped to haul the old man in so everybody could know how bad the old man had been and how he'd tried to steal some feed that didn't belong to him, and when the sheriff put the handcuffs on the boy he couldn't believe it. Then he'd started to cry. That was one story he had saved to write. He knew at least twenty good stories from out there and he had never written one. Why?*

"You tell them why," he said.

"Why what, dear?"

"Why nothing."

She didn't drink so much, now, since she had him. But if he lived he would never write about her, he knew that now. Nor about any of them. The rich were dull and they drank too much, or they played too much backgammon. They were dull and they were repetitious. He remembered poor Julian and his romantic awe of them and how he had started a story once that began, "The very rich are different from you and me." And how some one had said to Julian, Yes, they have more money. But that was not humorous to Julian. He thought they were a special glamourous race and when he found they weren't it wrecked him just as much as any other thing that wrecked him.

He had been contemptuous of those who wrecked. You did not have to like it because you understood it. He could beat anything, he thought, because no thing could hurt him if he did not care.

All right. Now he would not care for death. One thing he had always dreaded was the pain. He could stand pain as well as any man, until it went on too long, and wore him out, but here he had something that had hurt frightfully and just when he had felt it breaking him, the pain had stopped.

*He remembered long ago when Williamson, the bombing officer, had been hit by a stick bomb some one in a German patrol had thrown as he was coming in through the wire that night and, screaming, had begged every one to kill him. He was a fat man, very brave, and a good officer, although addicted to fantastic shows. But that night he was caught in the wire, with a flare lighting him up and his bowels spilled out into the wire, so when they brought him in, alive, they had to cut him loose. Shoot me, Harry. For Christ sake shoot me. They had had an argument one time about our Lord never sending you anything you could not bear and some one's theory had been that meant that at a certain time the pain passed you out automatically. But he had always remembered Williamson, that night. Nothing passed out Williamson until he gave him all his morphine tablets that he had always saved to use himself and then they did not work right away.*

Still this now, that he had, was very easy; and if it was no worse as it went on there was nothing to worry about. Except that he would rather be in better company.

He thought a little about the company that he would like to have.

No, he thought, when everything you do, you do too long, and do too late, you can't expect to find the people still there. The people all are gone. The party's over and you are with your hostess now.

I'm getting as bored with dying as with everything else, he thought.

"It's a bore," he said out loud.

"What is, my dear?"

"Anything you do too bloody long."

He looked at her face between him and the fire. She was leaning back in the chair and the firelight shone on her pleasantly lined face and he could see that she was sleepy. He heard the hyena make a noise just outside the range of the fire.

"I've been writing," he said. "But I got tired."

"Do you think you will be able to sleep?"

"Pretty sure. Why don't you turn in?"

"I like to sit here with you."

"Do you feel anything strange?" he asked her.

"No. Just a little sleepy."

"I do," he said.

He had just felt death come by again.

"You know the only thing I've never lost is curiosity," he said to her.

"You've never lost anything. You're the most complete man I've ever known."

"Christ," he said. "How little a woman knows. What is that? Your intuition?"

Because, just then, death had come and rested its head on the foot of the cot and he could smell its breath.

"Never believe any of that about a scythe and a skull," he told her. "It can be two bicycle policemen as easily, or be a bird. Or it can have a wide snout like a hyena."

It had moved up on him now, but it had no shape any more. It simply occupied space.

"Tell it to go away."

It did not go away but moved a little closer.

"You've got a hell of a breath," he told it. "You stinking bastard."

It moved up closer to him still and now he could not speak to it, and when it saw he could not speak it came a little closer, and now he tried to send it away without speaking, but it moved in on him so its weight was all upon his chest, and while it crouched there and he could not move, or speak, he heard the woman say, "Bwana is asleep now. Take the cot up very gently and carry it into the tent."

He could not speak to tell her to make it go away and it crouched now, heavier, so he could not breathe. And then, while they lifted the cot, suddenly it was all right and the weight went from his chest.

It was morning and had been morning for some time and he heard the plane. It showed very tiny and then made a wide circle and the boys ran out and lit the fires, using kerosene, and piled on grass so there were two big smudges at each end of the level place and the morning breeze blew them toward the camp and the plane circled twice more, low this time, and then glided down and levelled off and landed smoothly and, coming walking toward him, was old Compton in slacks, a tweed jacket and a brown felt hat.

"What's the matter, old cock?" Compton said.

"Bad leg," he told him. "Will you have some breakfast?"

"Thanks. I'll just have some tea. It's the Puss Moth you know. I won't be able to take the Memsahib. There's only room for one. Your lorry is on the way."

Helen had taken Compton aside and was speaking to him. Compton came back more cheery than ever.

"We'll get you right in," he said. "I'll be back for the Mem. Now I'm afraid I'll have to stop at Arusha to refuel. We'd better get going."

"What about the tea?"

"I don't really care about it you know."

The boys had picked up the cot and carried it around the green tents and down along the rock and out onto the plain and along past the smudges that were burning brightly now, the grass all consumed, and the wind fanning the fire, to the little plane. It was difficult getting him in, but once in he lay back in the leather seat, and the leg was stuck straight out to one side of the seat where Compton sat. Compton started the motor and got in. He waved to Helen and to the boys and, as the clatter moved into the old familiar roar, they swung around with Compie watching for wart-hog holes and roared, bumping, along the stretch between the fires and with the last bump rose and he saw them all standing below, waving, and the camp beside the hill, flattening now, and the plain spreading, clumps of trees, and the bush flattening, while the game trails ran now smoothly to the dry waterholes, and there was a new water that he had never known of. The zebra, small rounded backs now, and the wildebeeste, big-headed dots seeming to climb as they moved in long fingers across the plain, now scattering as the shadow came toward them, they were tiny now, and the movement had no gallop, and the plain as far as you could see, gray-yellow now and ahead old Compie's tweed back and the brown felt hat. Then they were over the first hills and the wildebeeste were trailing up them, and then they were over mountains with sudden depths of green-rising forest and the solid bamboo slopes, and then the heavy forest again, sculptured into peaks and hollows until they crossed, and hills sloped down and then another plain, hot now, and purple brown, bumpy with heat and Compie looking back to see how he was riding. Then there were other mountains dark ahead.

And then instead of going on to Arusha they turned left, he evidently figured that they had the gas, and looking down he saw a pink sifting cloud, moving over the ground, and in the air, like the first snow in a blizzard, that comes from nowhere, and he knew the locusts were coming up from the South. Then they began to climb and they were going to the East it seemed, and then it darkened and they were in a storm, the rain so thick it seemed like flying through a waterfall, and then they were out and Compie turned his head and grinned and pointed and there, ahead, all he could see, as wide as all the world, great, high, and unbelievably white in the sun, was the square top of Kilimanjaro. And then he knew that there was where he was going.

Just then the hyena stopped whimpering in the night and started to make a strange, human, almost crying sound. The woman heard it and stirred uneasily. She did not wake. In her dream she was at the house on Long Island and it was the night before her daughter's début. Somehow her father was there and he had been very rude. Then the noise the hyena made was so loud she woke and for a moment she did not know where she was and she was very afraid. Then she took the flashlight and shone it on the other cot that they had carried in after Harry had gone to sleep. She could see his bulk under the mosquito bar but somehow he had gotten his leg out and it hung down alongside the cot. The dressings had all come down and she could not look at it.

"Molo," she called, "Molo! Molo!"

Then she said, "Harry, Harry!" Then her voice rising, "Harry! Please, Oh Harry!"

There was no answer and she could not hear him breathing.

Outside the tent the hyena made the same strange noise that had awakened her. But she did not hear him for the beating of her heart.

## JORGE LUIS BORGES (1899– )

# *The South*

The man who landed in Buenos Aires in 1871 bore the name of Johannes Dahlmann and he was a minister in the Evangelical Church. In 1939, one of his grandchildren, Juan Dahlmann, was secretary of a municipal library on Calle Córdoba, and he considered himself profoundly Argentinian. His maternal grandfather had been that Francisco Flores, of the Second Line-Infantry Division, who had died on the frontier of Buenos Aires, run through with a lance by Indians from Catriel; in the discord inherent between his two lines of descent, Juan Dahlmann (perhaps driven to it by his Germanic blood) chose the line represented by his romantic ancestor, his ancestor of the romantic death. An old sword, a leather frame containing the daguerreotype of a blank-faced man with a beard, the dash and grace of certain music, the familiar strophes of *Martín Fierro,* the passing years, boredom and solitude, all went to foster this voluntary, but never ostentatious nationalism. At the cost of numerous small privations, Dahlmann had managed to save the empty shell of a ranch in the South which had belonged to the Flores family; he continually recalled the image of the balsamic eucalyptus trees and the great rose-colored house which had once been crimson. His duties, perhaps even indolence, kept him in the city. Summer after summer he contented himself with the abstract idea of possession and with the certitude that his ranch was waiting for him on a precise site in the middle of the plain. Late in February, 1939, something happened to him.

Blind to all fault, destiny can be ruthless at one's slightest distraction. Dahlmann had succeeded in acquiring, on that very afternoon, an imperfect copy of Weil's edition of *The Thousand and One Nights.* Avid to examine this find, he did not wait for the elevator but hurried up the stairs. In the obscurity, something brushed by his forehead: a bat, a bird? On the face of the woman who opened the door to him he saw horror engraved, and the hand he wiped across his face came away red with blood. The edge of a recently painted door which someone had forgotten to close had caused this wound. Dahlmann was able to fall asleep, but from the moment he awoke at dawn the savor of all things was atrociously poignant. Fever wasted him and the pictures in *The Thousand and One Nights* served to illustrate nightmares. Friends and relatives paid him visits and, with exaggerated smiles, assured him that they thought he looked fine. Dahlmann listened to them with a kind of feeble stupor and he marveled at their not knowing that he was in hell. A week, eight days passed, and they were like eight centuries. One afternoon, the usual doctor appeared, accompanied by a new doctor, and they carried him off to a sanitarium on the Calle Ecuador, for it was necessary to X-ray him. Dahlmann, in the hackney coach which bore them away, thought that he would, at last, be able to sleep in a room different from his own. He felt happy and communicative. When he arrived at his destination, they undressed him, shaved his head, bound him with metal fastenings to a stretcher; they shone bright lights on him until he was blind and dizzy, auscultated him, and a masked man stuck a needle into his arm. He awoke with a feeling of nausea, covered with a bandage, in a cell with something of a well about it; in the days and nights which followed the operation he came to realize that he had merely been, up until then, in a suburb of hell. Ice in his mouth did not leave the least trace of freshness. During these days Dahlmann hated himself in minute detail: he hated his identity, his bodily necessities, his humiliation, the beard which bristled upon his face. He stoically endured the curative measures, which were painful, but when the surgeon told him he had been on the point of death from septicemia, Dahlmann dissolved in tears of self-pity for his fate. Physical wretchedness and the incessant anticipation of horrible nights had not allowed him time to think of anything so abstract as death. On another day, the surgeon told him he was healing and that, very soon, he would be able to go to his ranch for convalescence. Incredibly enough, the promised day arrived.

Reality favors symmetries and slight anachronisms: Dahlmann had arrived at the sanitarium in a hackney coach and now a hackney coach was to take him to the Constitución station. The first fresh tang of autumn, after the summer's oppressiveness, seemed like a symbol in nature of his rescue and release from fever and death. The city, at seven in the morning, had not lost that air of an old house lent it by the night; the streets seemed like long vestibules, the plazas were like patios. Dahlmann recognized the city with joy on the edge of vertigo: a second before his eyes registered the phenomena themselves, he recalled the corners, the billboards, the modest variety of Buenos Aires. In the yellow light of the new day, all things returned to him.

Every Argentine knows that the South begins at the other side of Rivadavia. Dahlmann was in the habit of saying that this was no mere convention, that whoever crosses this street enters a more ancient and sterner world. From inside the carriage he sought out, among the new buildings, the iron grill window, the brass knocker, the arched door, the entrance way, the intimate patio.

At the railroad station he noted that he still had thirty minutes. He quickly recalled that in a café on the Calle Brazil (a few dozen feet from Yrigoyen's house) there was an enormous cat which allowed itself to be caressed as if it were a disdainful divinity. He entered the café. There was the cat, asleep. He ordered a cup of coffee, slowly stirred the sugar, sipped it (this pleasure had been denied him in the clinic), and thought, as he smoothed the cat's black coat, that this contact was an illusion and that the two beings, man and cat, were as good as separated by a glass, for man lives in time, in succession, while the magical animal lives in the present, in the eternity of the instant.

Along the next to the last platform the train lay waiting. Dahlmann walked through the coaches until he found one almost empty. He arranged his baggage in the network rack. When the train started off, he took down his valise and extracted, after some hesitation, the first volume of *The Thousand and One Nights*. To travel with this book, which was so much a part of the history of his ill-fortune, was a kind of affirmation that his ill-fortune had been annulled; it was a joyous and secret defiance of the frustrated forces of evil.

Along both sides of the train the city dissipated into suburbs; this sight, and then a view of the gardens and villas, delayed the beginning of his reading. The truth was that Dahlmann read very little. The magnetized mountain and the genie who swore to kill his benefactor are—who would deny it?—marvelous, but not so much more than the morning itself and the mere fact of being. The joy of life distracted him from paying attention to Scheherezade and her superfluous miracles. Dahlmann closed his book and allowed himself to live.

Lunch—the bouillon served in shining metal bowls, as in the remote summers of childhood—was one more peaceful and rewarding delight.

*Tomorrow I'll wake up at the ranch,* he thought, and it was as if he was two men at a time: the man who traveled through the autumn day and across the geography of the fatherland, and the other one, locked up in a sanitarium and subject to methodical servitude. He saw unplastered brick houses, long and angled, timelessly watching the trains go by; he saw horsemen along the dirt roads; he saw gullies and lagoons and ranches; he saw great luminous clouds that resembled marble; and all these things were accidental, casual, like dreams of the plain. He also thought he recognized trees and crop fields; but he would not have been able to name them, for his actual knowledge of the countryside was quite inferior to his nostalgic and literary knowledge.

From time to time he slept, and his dreams were animated by the impetus of the train. The intolerable white sun of high noon had already become the yellow sun which precedes nightfall, and it would not be long before it would turn red. The railroad car was now also different; it was not the same as the one which had quit the station siding at Constitución; the plain and the hours had transfigured it. Outside, the moving shadow of the railroad car stretched toward the horizon. The elemental earth was not perturbed either by settlements or other signs of humanity. The country was vast but at the same time intimate and, in some measure, secret. The limitless country sometimes contained only a solitary bull. The solitude was perfect, perhaps hostile, and it might have occurred to Dahlmann that he was traveling into the past and not merely south. He was distracted from these considerations by the railroad inspector who, on reading his ticket, advised him that the train would not let him off at the regular station but at another: an earlier stop, one scarcely known to Dahlmann. (The man added an explanation which Dahlmann did not attempt to understand, and which he hardly heard, for the mechanism of events did not concern him.)

The train laboriously ground to a halt, practically in the middle of the plain. The station lay on the other side of the tracks; it was not much more than a siding and a shed. There was no means of conveyance to be seen, but the station chief supposed that the traveler might secure a vehicle from a general store and inn to be found some ten or twelve blocks away.

Dahlmann accepted the walk as a small adventure. The sun had already disappeared from view, but a final splendor exalted the vivid and silent plain, before the night erased its color. Less to avoid fatigue than to draw out his enjoyment of these sights, Dahlmann walked slowly, breathing in the odor of clover with sumptuous joy.

The general store at one time had been painted a deep scarlet, but the years had tempered this violent color for its own good. Something in its poor architecture recalled a steel engraving, perhaps one from an old edition of *Paul et Virginie*. A number of horses were hitched up to the paling. Once inside, Dahlmann thought he recognized the shopkeeper. Then he realized that he had been deceived by the man's resemblance to one of the male nurses in the sanitarium. When the shopkeeper heard Dahlmann's request, he said he would have the shay made up. In order to add one more event to that day and to kill time, Dahlmann decided to eat at the general store.

Some country louts, to whom Dahlmann did not at first pay any attention, were eating and drinking at one of the tables. On the floor, and hanging on to the bar, squatted an old man, immobile as an object. His years had reduced and polished him as water does a stone or the generations of men do a sentence. He was dark, dried up, diminutive, and seemed outside time, situated in eternity. Dahlmann noted with satisfaction the kerchief, the thick poncho, the long *chiripá,* and the colt boots, and told himself, as he recalled futile discussions with people from the Northern counties or from the province of Entre Rios, that gauchos like this no longer existed outside the South.

Dahlmann sat down next to the window. The darkness began overcoming the plain, but the odor and sound of the earth penetrated the iron bars of the window. The shop owner brought him sardines, followed by some roast meat. Dahlmann washed the meal down with several glasses of red wine. Idling, he relished the tart savor of the wine, and let his gaze, now grown somewhat drowsy, wander over the shop. A kerosene lamp hung from a beam. There were three customers at the other table: two of them appeared to be farm workers; the third man, whose features hinted at Chinese blood, was drinking with his hat on. Of a sudden, Dahlmann felt something brush lightly against his face. Next to the heavy glass of turbid wine, upon one of the stripes in the table cloth, lay a spit ball of breadcrumb. That was all: but someone had thrown it there.

The men at the other table seemed totally cut off from him. Perplexed, Dahlmann decided that nothing had happened, and he opened the volume of *The Thousand and One Nights,* by way of suppressing reality. After a few moments another little ball landed on his table, and now the *peones* laughed outright. Dahlmann said to himself that he was not frightened, but he reasoned that it would be a major blunder if he, a convalescent, were to allow himself to be dragged by strangers into some chaotic quarrel. He determined to leave, and had already gotten to his feet when the owner came up and exhorted him in an alarmed voice:

"*Señor* Dahlmann, don't pay any attention to those lads; they're half high."

Dahlmann was not surprised to learn that the other man, now, knew his name. But he felt that these conciliatory words served only to aggravate the situation. Previous to this moment, the *peones'* provocation was directed against an unknown face, against no one in particular, almost against no one at all. Now it was an attack against him, against his name, and his neighbors knew it. Dahlmann pushed the owner aside, confronted the *peones,* and demanded to know what they wanted of him.

The tough with a Chinese look staggered heavily to his feet. Almost in Juan Dahlmann's face he shouted insults, as if he had been a long way off. His game was to exaggerate his drunkenness, and this extravagance constituted a ferocious mockery. Between curses and obscenities, he threw a long knife into the air, followed it with his eyes, caught and juggled it, and challenged Dahlmann to a knife fight. The owner objected in a tremulous voice, pointing out that Dahlmann was unarmed. At this point, something unforeseeable occurred.

From a corner of the room, the old ecstatic gaucho—in whom Dahlmann saw a summary and cipher of the South (his South)—threw him a naked dagger, which landed at his feet. It was as if the South had resolved that Dahlmann should accept the duel. Dahlmann bent over to pick up the dagger, and felt two things. The first, that this almost instinctive act bound him to fight. The second, that the weapon, in his torpid hand, was no defense at all, but would merely serve to justify his murder. He had once played with a poniard, like all men, but his idea of fencing and knife-play did not go further than the notion that all strokes should be directed upwards, with the cutting edge held inwards. *They would not have allowed such things to happen to me in the sanitarium,* he thought.

"Let's get on our way," said the other man.

They went out and if Dahlmann was without hope, he was also without fear. As he crossed the threshold, he felt that to die in a knife fight, under the open sky, and going forward to the attack, would have been a liberation, a joy, and a festive occasion, on the first night in the sanitarium, when they stuck him with the needle. He felt that if he had been able to choose, then, or to dream his death, this would have been the death he would have chosen or dreamt.

Firmly clutching his knife, which he perhaps would not know how to wield, Dahlmann went out into the plain.

## RICHARD WRIGHT (1908–1960)

# *The Man Who Was Almost a Man*

Dave struck out across the fields, looking homeward through paling light. Whut's the use talkin wid em niggers in the field? Anyhow, his mother was putting supper on the table. Them niggers can't understan nothing. One of these days he was going to get a gun and practice shooting, then they couldn't talk to him as though he were a little boy. He slowed, looking at the ground. Shucks, Ah ain scareda them even ef they are biggern me! Aw, Ah know whut Ahma do. Ahm going by ol Joe's sto n git that Sears Roebuck catlog n look at them guns. Mebbe Ma will lemme buy one when she gits mah pay from ol man Hawkins. Ahma beg her t gimme some money. Ahm ol ernough to hava gun. Ahm seventeen. Almost a man. He strode, feeling his long loose-jointed limbs. Shucks, a man oughta hava little gun aftah he done worked hard all day.

He came in sight of Joe's store. A yellow lantern glowed on the front porch. He mounted steps and went through the screen door, hearing it bang behind him. There was a strong smell of coal oil and mackerel fish. He felt very confident until he saw fat Joe walk in through the rear door, then his courage began to ooze.

"Howdy, Dave! Whutcha want?"

"How yuh, Mistah Joe? Aw, Ah don wanna buy nothing. Ah jus wanted t see ef yuhd lemme look at tha catlog erwhile."

"Sure! You wanna see it here?"

"Nawsuh. Ah wans t take it home wid me. Ah'll bring it back termorrow when Ah come in from the fiels."

"You plannin on buying something?"

"Yessuh."

"Your ma lettin you have your own money now?"

"Shucks. Mistah Joe, Ahm gittin t be a man like anybody else!"

Joe laughed and wiped his greasy white face with a red bandanna.

"Whut you plannin on buyin?"

Dave looked at the floor, scratched his head, scratched his thigh, and smiled. Then he looked up shyly.

"Ah'll tell yuh, Mistah Joe, ef yuh promise yuh won't tell."

"I promise."

"Waal, Ahma buy a gun."

"A gun? Whut you want with a gun?"

"Ah wanna keep it."

"You ain't nothing but a boy. You don't need a gun."

"Aw, lemme have the catlog, Mistah Joe. Ah'll bring it back."

Joe walked through the rear door. Dave was elated. He looked around at barrels of sugar and flour. He heard Joe coming back. He craned his neck to see if he were bringing the book. Yeah, he's got it. Gawddog, he's got it!

"Here, but be sure you bring it back. It's the only one I got."

"Sho, Mistah Joe."

"Say, if you wanna buy a gun, why don't you buy one from me? I gotta gun to sell."

"Will it shoot?"

"Sure it'll shoot."

"Whut kind is it?"

"Oh, it's kinda old . . . a left-hand Wheeler. A pistol. A big one."

"Is it got bullets in it?"

"It's loaded."

"Kin Ah see it?"

"Where's your money?"

"Whut yuh wan fer it?"

"I'll let you have it for two dollars."

"Just two dollahs? Shucks, Ah could buy tha when Ah git mah pay."

"I'll have it here when you want it."

"Awright, suh. Ah be in fer it."

He went through the door, hearing it slam again behind him. Ahma git some money from Ma n buy me a gun! Only two dollahs! He tucked the thick catalogue under his arm and hurried.

"Where yuh been, boy?" His mother held a steaming dish of black-eyed peas.

"Aw, Ma, Ah jus stopped down the road t talk wid the boys."

"Yuh know bettah t keep suppah waitin."

He sat down, resting the catalogue on the edge of the table.

"Yuh git up from there and git to the well n wash yoself! Ah ain feedin no hogs in mah house!"

She grabbed his shoulder and pushed him. He stumbled out of the room, then came back to get the catalogue.

"Whut this?"

"Aw, Ma, it's jusa catlog."

"Who yuh git it from?"

"From Joe, down at the sto."

"Waal, thas good. We kin use it in the outhouse."

"Naw, Ma." He grabbed for it. "Gimme ma catlog, Ma."

She held onto it and glared at him.

"Quit hollerin at me! Whut's wrong wid yuh? Yuh crazy?"

"But Ma, please. It ain mine! It's Joe's! He tol me t bring it back t im termorrow."

She gave up the book. He stumbled down the back steps, hugging the thick book under his arm. When he had splashed water on his face and hands, he groped back to the kitchen and fumbled in a corner for the towel. He bumped into a chair; it clattered to the floor. The catalogue sprawled at his feet. When he had dried his eyes he snatched up the book and held it again under his arm. His mother stood watching him.

"Now, ef yuh gonna act a fool over that ol book, Ah'll take it n burn it up."

"Naw, Ma, please."

"Waal, set down n be still!"

He sat down and drew the oil lamp close. He thumbed page after page, unaware of the food his mother set on the table. His father came in. Then his small brother.

"Whutcha got there, Dave?" his father asked.

"Jusa catlog," he answered, not looking up.

"Yeah, here they is!" His eyes glowed at blue-and-black revolvers. He glanced up, feeling sudden guilt. His father was watching him. He eased the book under the table and rested it on his knees. After the blessing was asked, he ate. He scooped up peas and swallowed fat meat without chewing. Buttermilk helped to wash it down. He did not want to mention money before his father. He would do much better by cornering his mother when she was alone. He looked at his father uneasily out of the edge of his eye.

"Boy, how come yuh don quit foolin wid tha book n eat yo suppah?"

"Yessuh."

"How you n ol man Hawkins gitten erlong?"

"Suh?"

"Can't yuh hear? Why don yuh lissen? Ah ast yu how wuz yuh n ol man Hawkins gittin erlong?"

"Oh, swell, Pa. Ah plows mo lan than anybody over there."

"Waal, yuh oughta keep yo mind on whut yuh doin."

"Yessuh."

He poured his plate full of molasses and sopped it up slowly with a chunk of cornbread. When his father and brother had left the kitchen, he still sat and looked again at the guns in the catalogue, longing to muster courage enough to present his case to his mother. Lawd, ef Ah only had tha pretty one! He could almost feel the slickness of the weapon with his fingers. If he had a gun like that he would polish it and keep it shining so it would never rust. N Ah'd keep it loaded, by Gawd!

"Ma?" His voice was hesitant.

"Hunh?"

"Ol man Hawkins give yuh mah money yit?"

"Yeah, but ain no usa yuh thinking bout throwin nona it erway. Ahm keepin tha money sos yuh kin have cloes t go to school this winter."

He rose and went to her side with the open catalogue in his palms. She was washing dishes, her head bent low over a pan. Shyly he raised the book. When he spoke, his voice was husky, faint.

"Ma, Gawd knows Ah wans one of these."

"One of whut?" she asked, not raising her eyes.

"One of these," he said again, not daring even to point. She glanced up at the page, then at him with wide eyes.

"Nigger, is yuh gone plumb crazy?"

"Aw, Ma–"

"Git outta here! Don yuh talk t me bout no gun! Yuh a fool!"

"Ma, Ah kin buy one fer two dollahs."

"Not ef Ah knows it, yuh ain!"

"But yuh promised me one–"

"Ah don care whut Ah promised! Yuh ain nothing but a boy yit!"

"Ma, ef yuh lemme buy one Ah'll *never* ast yuh fer nothing no mo."

"Ah tol yuh t git outta here! Yuh ain gonna toucha penny of tha money fer no gun! Thas how come Ah has Mistah Hawkins t pay yo wages t me, cause Ah knows yuh ain got no sense."

"But, Ma, we needa gun. Pa ain got no gun. We needa gun in the house. Yuh kin never tell whut might happen."

"Now don yuh try to maka fool outta me, boy! Ef we did hava gun, yuh wouldn't have it!"

He laid the catalogue down and slipped his arm around her waist.

"Aw, Ma, Ah done worked hard alla summer n ain ast yuh fer nothin, is Ah, now?"

"Thas whut yuh spose t do!"

"But Ma, Ah wans a gun. Yuh kin lemme have two dollahs outta mah money. Please, Ma. I kin give it to Pa . . . Please, Ma! Ah loves yuh, Ma."

When she spoke her voice came soft and low.

"Whut yu wan wida gun, Dave? Yuh don need no gun. You'll git in trouble. N ef yo pa jus thought Ah let yuh have money t buy a gun he'd hava fit."

"Ah'll hide it, Ma. It ain but two dollahs."

"Lawd, chil, whut's wrong wid yuh?"

"Ain nothin wrong, Ma. Ahm almos a man now. Ah wans a gun."

"Who gonna sell yuh a gun?"

"Ol Joe at the sto."

"N it don cos but two dollahs?"

"Thas all, Ma. Jus two dollahs. Please, Ma."

She was stacking the plates away; her hands moved slowly, reflectively. Dave kept an anxious silence. Finally, she turned to him.

"Ah'll let yuh git tha gun ef yuh promise me one thing."

"Whut's tha, Ma?"

"Yuh bring it straight back t me, yuh hear? It be fer Pa."

"Yessum! Lemme go now, Ma."

She stooped, turned slightly to one side, raised the hem of her dress, rolled down the top of her stocking, and came up with a slender wad of bills.

"Here," she said. "Lawd knows yuh don need no gun. But yer pa does. Yuh bring it right back t me, yuh hear? Ahma put it up. Now ef yuh don, Ahma have yuh pa lick yuh so hard yuh won fergit it."

"Yessum."

He took the money, ran down the steps, and across the yard.

"Dave! Yuuuuuh Daaaaave!"

He heard, but he was not going to stop now. "Naw, Lawd!"

The first movement he made the following morning was to reach under his pillow for the gun. In the gray light of dawn he held it loosely, feeling a sense of power. Could kill a man with a gun like this. Kill anybody, black or white. And if he were holding his gun in his hand, nobody could run over him; they would have to respect him. It was a big gun, with a long barrel and a heavy handle. He raised and lowered it in his hand, marveling at its weight.

He had not come straight home with it as his mother had asked; instead he had stayed out in the fields, holding the weapon in his hand, aiming it now and then at some imaginary foe. But he had not fired it; he had been afraid that his father might hear. Also he was not sure he knew how to fire it.

To avoid surrendering the pistol he had not come into the house until he knew that they were all asleep. When his mother had tiptoed to his bedside late that night and demanded the gun, he had first played possum; then he had told her that the gun was hidden outdoors, that he would bring it to her in the morning. Now he lay turning it slowly in his hands. He broke it, took out the cartridges, felt them, and then put them back.

He slid out of bed, got a long strip of old flannel from a trunk, wrapped the gun in it, and tied it to his naked thigh while it was still loaded. He did not go in to breakfast. Even though it was not yet daylight, he started for Jim Hawkins' plantation. Just as the sun was rising he reached the barns where the mules and plows were kept.

"Hey! That you, Dave?"

He turned. Jim Hawkins stood eying him suspiciously.

"What're yuh doing here so early?"

"Ah didn't know Ah wuz gittin up so early, Mistah Hawkins. Ah wuz fixin t hitch up ol Jenny n take her t the fiels."

"Good. Since you're so early, how about plowing that stretch down by the woods?"

"Suits me, Mistah Hawkins."

"O.K. Go to it!"

He hitched Jenny to a plow and started across the fields. Hot dog! This was just what he wanted. If he could get down by the woods, he could shoot his gun and nobody would hear. He walked behind the plow, hearing the traces creaking, feeling the gun tied tight to his thigh.

When he reached the woods, he plowed two whole rows before he decided to take out the gun. Finally, he stopped, looked in all directions, then untied the gun and held it in his hand. He turned to the mule and smiled.

"Know whut this is, Jenny? Naw, yuh wouldn know! Yuhs jusa ol mule! Anyhow, this is a gun, n it kin shoot, by Gawd!"

He held the gun at arm's length. Whut t hell, Ahma shoot this thing! He looked at Jenny again.

"Lissen here, Jenny! When Ah pull this ol trigger, Ah don wan yuh t run n acka fool now!"

Jenny stood with head down, her short ears pricked straight. Dave walked off about twenty feet, held the gun far out from him at arm's length, and turned his head. Hell, he told himself, Ah ain afraid. The gun felt loose in his fingers; he waved it wildly for a moment. Then he shut his eyes and tightened his forefinger. Bloom! A report half deafened him and he thought his right hand was torn from his arm. He heard Jenny whinnying and galloping over the field, and he found himself on his knees squeezing his fingers hard between his legs. His hand was numb; he jammed it into his mouth, trying to warm it, trying to stop the pain. The gun lay at his feet. He did not quite know what had happened. He stood up and stared at the gun as though it were a living thing. He gritted his teeth and kicked the gun. Yuh almos broke mah arm! He turned to look for Jenny; she was far over the fields, tossing her head and kicking wildly.

"Hol on there, ol mule!"

When he caught up with her she stood trembling, walling her big white eyes at him. The plow was far away; the traces had broken. Then Dave stopped short, looking, not believing. Jenny was bleeding. Her left side was red and wet with blood. He went closer. Lawd, have mercy! Wondah did Ah shoot this mule? He grabbed for Jenny's mane. She flinched, snorted, whirled, tossing her head.

"Hol on now! Hol on."

Then he saw the hole in Jenny's side, right between the ribs. It was round, wet, red. A crimson stream streaked down the front leg, flowing fast. Good Gawd! Ah wuzn't shootin at tha mule. He felt panic. He knew he had to stop that blood, or Jenny would bleed to death. He had never seen so much blood in all his life. He chased the mule for half a mile, trying to catch her. Finally she stopped, breathing hard, stumpy tail half arched. He caught her mane and led her back to where the plough and gun lay. Then he stooped and grabbed handfuls of damp black earth and tried to plug the bullet hole. Jenny shuddered, whinnied, and broke from him.

"Hol on! Hol on now!"

He tried to plug it again, but blood came anyhow. His fingers were hot and sticky. He rubbed dirt into his palms, trying to dry them. Then again he attempted to plug the bullet hole, but Jenny shied away, kicking her heels high. He stood helpless. He had to do something. He ran at Jenny; she dodged him. He watched a red stream of blood flow down Jenny's leg and form a bright pool at her feet.

"Jenny . . . Jenny," he called weakly.

His lips trembled. She's bleeding t death! He looked in the direction of home, wanting to go back, wanting to get help. But he saw the pistol lying in the damp black clay. He had a queer feeling that if he only did something, this would not be; Jenny would not be there bleeding to death.

When he went to her this time, she did not move. She stood with sleepy, dreamy eyes; and when he touched her she gave a low-pitched whinny and knelt to the ground, her front knees slopping in blood.

"Jenny . . . Jenny . . ." he whispered.

For a long time she held her neck erect; then her head sank, slowly. Her ribs swelled with a mighty heave and she went over.

Dave's stomach felt empty, very empty. He picked up the gun and held it gingerly between his thumb and forefinger. He buried it at the foot of a tree. He took a stick and tried to cover the pool of blood with dirt—but what was the use? There was Jenny lying with her mouth open and her eyes walled and glassy. He could not tell Jim Hawkins he had shot his mule. But he had to tell something. Yeah, Ah'll tell em Jenny started gittin wil n fell on the joint of the plow. . . . But that would hardly happen to a mule. He walked across the field slowly, head down.

It was sunset. Two of Jim Hawkins' men were over near the edge of the woods digging a hole in which to bury Jenny. Dave was surrounded by a knot of people, all of whom were looking down at the dead mule.

"I don't see how in the world it happened," said Jim Hawkins for the tenth time.

The crowd parted and Dave's mother, father, and small brother pushed into the center.

"Where Dave?" his mother called.

"There he is," said Jim Hawkins.

His mother grabbed him.

"Whut happened, Dave? Whut yuh done?"

"Nothin."

"C mon, boy, talk," his father said.

Dave took a deep breath and told the story he knew nobody believed.

"Waal," he drawled. "Ah brung ol Jenny down here sos Ah could do mah plowin. Ah plowed bout two rows, just like yuh see." He stopped and pointed at the long rows of upturned earth. "Then somethin musta been wrong wid ol Jenny. She wouldn ack right a-tall. She started snortin n kickin her heels. Ah tried t hol her, but she pulled erway, rearin n goin in. Then when the point of the plow was stickin up in the air, she swung erroun n twisted herself back on it . . . She stuck herself n started t bleed. N fo Ah could do anything, she wuz dead."

"Did you ever hear of anything like that in all your life?" asked Jim Hawkins.

There were white and black standing in the crowd. They murmured. Dave's mother came close to him and looked hard into his face. "Tell the truth, Dave," she said.

"Looks like a bullet hole to me," said one man.

"Dave, whut yuh do wid the gun?" his mother asked.

The crowd surged in, looking at him. He jammed his hands into his pockets, shook his head slowly from left to right, and backed away. His eyes were wide and painful.

"Did he hava gun?" asked Jim Hawkins.

"By Gawd, Ah tol him tha wuz a gun wound," said a man, slapping his thigh.

His father caught his shoulders and shook him till his teeth rattled. "Tell whut happened, yuh rascal! Tell whut . . ."

Dave looked at Jenny's stiff legs and began to cry.

"Whut yuh do wid tha gun?" his mother asked.

"Whut wuz he doin wida gun?" his father asked.

"Come on and tell the truth," said Hawkins. "Ain't nobody going to hurt you . . ."

His mother crowded close to him.

"Did yuh shoot tha mule, Dave?"

Dave cried, seeing blurred white and black faces.

"Ahh ddinn gggo tt sshooot hher . . . Ah ssswear ffo Gawd Ahh ddin. . . . Ah wuz a-tryin t sssee ef the old gggun would sshoot—"

"Where yuh git the gun from?" his father asked.

"Ah got it from Joe, at the sto."

"Where yuh git the money?"

"Ma give it t me."

"He kept worryin me, Bob. Ah had t. Ah tol im t bring the gun right back t me . . . It was fer yuh, the gun."

"But how yuh happen to shoot that mule?" asked Jim Hawkins.

"Ah wuzn shootin at the mule, Mistah Hawkins. The gun jumped when Ah pulled the trigger . . . N for Ah knowed anythin Jenny was there a-bleedin."

Somebody in the crowd laughed. Jim Hawkins walked close to Dave and looked into his face.

"Well, looks like you have bought a mule, Dave."

"Ah swear to Gawd, Ah didn go t kill the mule, Mistah Hawkins!"

"But you killed her!"

All the crowd was laughing now. They stood on tiptoe and poked heads over one another's shoulders.

"Well, boy, looks like yuh done bought a dead mule! Hahaha!"

"Ain tha ershame."

"Hohohohoho."

Dave stood, head down, twisting his feet in the dirt.

"Well, you needn't worry about it, Bob," said Jim Hawkins to Dave's father. "Just let the boy keep on working and pay me two dollars a month."

"Whut yuh wan fer yo mule, Mistah Hawkins?"

Jim Hawkins screwed up his eyes.

"Fifty dollars."

"Whut yuh do wid tha gun?" Dave's father demanded.

Dave said nothing.

"Yuh wan me t take a tree n beat yuh till yuh talk!"

"Nawsuh!"

"Whut yuh do wid it?"

"Ah throwed it erway."

"Where?"

"Ah . . . Ah throwed it in the creek."

"Waal, c mon home. N firs thing in the mawnin git to tha creek n fin tha gun."

"Yessuh."

"Whut yuh pay fer it?"

"Two dollahs."

"Take tha gun n git yu money back n carry it t Mistah Hawkins, yuh hear? N don fergit Ahma lam you black bottom good fer this! Now march yosef on home, suh!"

Dave turned and walked slowly. He heard people laughing. Dave glared, his eyes welling with tears. Hot anger bubbled in him. Then he swallowed and stumbled on.

That night Dave did not sleep. He was glad that he had gotten out of killing the mule so easily, but he was hurt. Something hot seemed to turn over inside him each time he remembered how they had laughed. He tossed on his bed, feeling his hard pillow. N Pa says he's gonna beat me . . . He remembered other beatings, and his back quivered. Naw, naw. Ah sho don wan im t beat me tha way no mo. Dam em all! Nobody ever gave him anything. All he did was work. They treat me like a mule, n then they beat me. He gritted his teeth. N Ma had t tell on me.

Well, if he had to, he would take old man Hawkins that two dollars. But that meant selling the gun. And he wanted to keep that gun. Fifty dollars for a dead mule.

He turned over, thinking how he had fired the gun. He had an itch to fire it again. Ef other men kin shoota gun, by Gawd, Ah kin! He was still, listening. Mebbe they all sleepin now. The house was still. He heard the soft breathing of his brother. Yes, now! He would go down and get that gun and see if he could fire it! He eased out of bed and slipped into overalls.

The moon was bright. He ran almost all the way to the edge of the woods. He stumbled over the ground, looking for the spot where he had buried the gun. Yeah, here it is. Like a hungry dog scratching for a bone, he pawed it up. He puffed his black cheeks and blew dirt from the trigger and barrel. He broke it and found four cartridges unshot. He looked around; the fields were filled with silence and moonlight. He clutched the gun stiff and hard in his fingers. But, as soon as he wanted to pull the trigger, he shut his eyes and turned his head. Naw, Ah can't shoot wid mah eyes closed n mah head turned. With effort he held his eyes open; then he squeezed. *Blooooom!* He was stiff, not breathing. The gun was still in his hands. Dammit, he'd done it! He fired again. *Blooooom!* He smiled. *Blooooom! Blooooom! Click, click.* There! It was empty. If anybody could shoot a gun, he could. He put the gun into his hip pocket and started across the fields.

When he reached the top of a ridge he stood straight and proud in the moonlight, looking at Jim Hawkins' big white house, feeling the gun sagging in his pocket. Lawd, ef Ah had just one mo bullet Ah'd taka shot at tha house. Ah'd like t scare ol man Hawkins jusa little . . . Jusa enough t let im know Dave Saunders is a man.

To his left the road curved, running to the tracks of the Illinois Central. He jerked his head, listening. From far off came a faint *hoooof-hoooof; hoooof-hoooof; hoooof-hoooof*. . . . He stood rigid. Two dollahs a mont. Les see now . . . Tha means it'll take bout two years. Shucks! Ah'll be dam!

He started down the road, toward the tracks. Yeah, here she comes! He stood beside the track and held himself stiffly. Here she comes, erroun the ben . . . C mon, yuh slow poke! C mon! He had his hand on his gun; something quivered in his stomach. Then the train thundered past, the gray and brown box cars rumbling and clinking. He gripped the gun tightly; then he jerked his hand out of his pocket. Ah betcha Bill wouldn't do it! Ah-betcha . . . The cars slid past, steel grinding upon steel. Ahm ridin yuh ternight, so hep me Gawd! He was hot all over. He hesitated just a moment; then he grabbed, pulled atop of a car, and lay flat. He felt his pocket; the gun was still there. Ahead the long rails were glinting in the moonlight, stretching away, away to somewhere, somewhere where he could be a man . . .

## CARSON McCULLERS (1917–1967)

# *A Tree, A Rock, A Cloud*

It was raining that morning, and still very dark. When the boy reached the streetcar café he had almost finished his route and he went in for a cup of coffee. The place was an all-night café owned by a bitter and stingy man called Leo. After the raw, empty street, the café seemed friendly and bright; along the counter there were a couple of soldiers, three spinners from the cotton mill, and in a corner a man who sat hunched over with his nose and half his face down in a beer mug. The boy wore a helmet such as aviators wear. When he went into the café he unbuckled the chin strap and raised the right flap up over his pink little ear; often as he drank his coffee someone would speak to him in a friendly way. But this morning Leo did not look into his face and none of the men were talking. He paid and was leaving the café when a voice called out to him:

"Son! Hey Son!"

He turned back and the man in the corner was crooking his finger and nodding to him. He had brought his face out of the beer mug and he seemed suddenly very happy. The man was long and pale, with a big nose and faded orange hair.

"Hey Son!"

The boy went toward him. He was an undersized boy of about twelve, with one shoulder drawn higher than the other because of the weight of the paper sack. His face was shallow, freckled, and his eyes were round child eyes.

"Yeah Mister?"

The man laid one hand on the paper boy's shoulders, then grasped the boy's chin and turned his face slowly from one side to the other. The boy shrank back uneasily.

"Say! What's the big idea?"

The boy's voice was shrill; inside the café it was suddenly very quiet.

The man said slowly, "I love you."

All along the counter the men laughed. The boy, who had scowled and sidled away, did not know what to do. He looked over the counter at Leo, and Leo watched him with a weary, brittle jeer. The boy tried to laugh also. But the man was serious and sad.

"I did not mean to tease you, Son," he said. "Sit down and have a beer with me. There is something I have to explain."

Cautiously, out of the corner of his eye, the paper boy questioned the men along the counter to see what he should do. But they had gone back to their beer or their breakfast and did not notice him. Leo put a cup of coffee on the counter and a little jug of cream.

"He is a minor," Leo said.

The paper boy slid himself up onto the stool. His ear beneath the upturned flap of the helmet was very small and red. The man was nodding at him soberly. "It is important," he said. Then he reached in his hip pocket and brought out something which he held up in the palm of his hand for the boy to see.

"Look very carefully," he said.

The boy stared, but there was nothing to look at very carefully. The man held in his big, grimy palm a photograph. It was the face of a woman, but blurred, so that only the hat and the dress she was wearing stood out clearly.

"See?" the man asked.

The boy nodded and the man placed another picture in his palm. The woman was standing on a beach in a bathing suit. The suit made her stomach very big, and that was the main thing you noticed.

"Got a good look?" He leaned over closer and finally asked: "You ever seen her before?"

The boy sat motionless, staring slantwise at the man. "Not so I know of."

"Very well." The man blew on the photographs and put them back into his pocket. "That was my wife."

"Dead?" the boy asked.

Slowly the man shook his head. He pursed his lips as though about to whistle and answered in a long-drawn way: "Nuuu–" he said. "I will explain."

The beer on the counter before the man was in a large brown mug. He did not pick it up to drink. Instead he bent down and, putting his face over the rim, he rested there for a moment. Then with both hands he tilted the mug and sipped.

"Some night you'll go to sleep with your big nose in a mug and drown," said Leo. "Prominent transient drowns in beer. That would be a cute death."

The paper boy tried to signal to Leo. While the man was not looking he screwed up his face and worked his mouth to question soundlessly: "Drunk?" But Leo only raised his eyebrows and turned away to put some pink strips of bacon on the grill. The man pushed the mug away from him, straightened himself, and folded his loose crooked hands on the counter. His face was sad as he looked at the paper boy. He did not blink, but from time to time the lids closed down with delicate gravity over his pale green eyes. It was nearing dawn and the boy shifted the weight of the paper sack.

"I am talking about love," the man said. "With me it is a science."

The boy half slid down from the stool. But the man raised his forefinger, and there was something about him that held the boy and would not let him go away.

"Twelve years ago I married the woman in the photograph. She was my wife for one year, nine months, three days, and two nights. I loved her. Yes. . . ." He tightened his blurred, rambling voice and said again: "I loved her. I thought also that she loved me. I was a railroad engineer. She had all home comforts and luxuries. It never crept into my brain that she was not satisfied. But do you know what happened?"

"Mgneeow!" said Leo.

The man did not take his eyes from the boy's face. "She left me. I came in one night and the house was empty and she was gone. She left me."

"With a fellow?" the boy asked.

Gently the man placed his palm down on the counter. "Why, naturally, Son. A woman does not run off like that alone."

The café was quiet, the soft rain black and endless in the street outside. Leo pressed down the frying bacon with the prongs of his long fork. "So you have been chasing the floozie for eleven years. You frazzled old rascal!"

For the first time the man glanced at Leo. "Please don't be vulgar. Besides, I was not speaking to you." He turned back to the boy and said in a trusting and secretive undertone, "Let's not pay any attention to him. O.K.?"

The paper boy nodded doubtfully.

"It was like this," the man continued. "I am a person who feels many things. All my life one thing after another has impressed me. Moonlight. The leg of a pretty girl. One thing after another. But the point is that when I had enjoyed anything there was a peculiar sensation as though it was laying around loose in me. Nothing seemed to finish itself up or fit in with the other things. Women? I had my portion of them. The same. Afterwards laying around loose in me. I was a man who had never loved."

Very slowly he closed his eyelids, and the gesture was like a curtain drawn at the end of a scene in a play. When he spoke again his voice was excited and the words came fast—the lobes of his large, loose ears seemed to tremble.

"Then I met this woman. I was fifty-one years old and she always said she was thirty. I met her at a filling station and we were married within three days. And do you know what it was like? I just can't tell you. All I had ever felt was gathered together around this woman.

Nothing lay around loose in me any more but was finished up by her."

The man stopped suddenly and stroked his long nose. His voice sank down to a steady and reproachful undertone: "I'm not explaining this right. What happened was this. There were these beautiful feelings and loose little pleasures inside me. And this woman was something like an assembly line for my soul. I run these little pieces of myself through her and I come out complete. Now do you follow me?"

"What was her name?" the boy asked.

"Oh," he said. "I called her Dodo. But that is immaterial."

"Did you try to make her come back?"

The man did not seem to hear. "Under the circumstances you can imagine how I felt when she left me."

Leo took the bacon from the grill and folded two strips of it between a bun. He had a gray face, with slitted eyes, and a pinched nose saddled by faint blue shadows. One of the mill workers signaled for more coffee and Leo poured it. He did not give refills on coffee free. The spinner ate breakfast there every morning, but the better Leo knew his customers the stingier he treated them. He nibbled his own bun as though he grudged it to himself.

"And you never got hold of her again?"

The boy did not know what to think of the man, and his child's face was uncertain with mingled curiosity and doubt. He was new on the paper route; it was still strange to him to be out in the town in the black, queer early morning.

"Yes," the man said. "I took a number of steps to get her back. I went around trying to locate her. I went to Tulsa where she had folks. And to Mobile. I went to every town she had ever mentioned to me, and I hunted down every man she had formerly been connected with. Tulsa, Atlanta, Chicago, Cheehaw, Memphis. . . . For the better part of two years I chased around the country trying to lay hold of her."

"But the pair of them had vanished from the face of the earth!" said Leo.

"Don't listen to him," the man said confidentially. "And also just forget those two years. They are not important. What matters is that around the third year a curious thing begun to happen to me."

"What?" the boy asked.

The man leaned down and tilted his mug to take a sip of beer. But as he hovered over the mug his nostrils fluttered slightly; he sniffed the staleness of the beer and did not drink. "Love is a curious thing to begin with. At first I thought only of getting her back. It was a kind of mania. But then as time went on I tried to remember her. But do you know what happened?"

"No," the boy said.

"When I laid myself down on a bed and tried to think about her my mind became a blank. I couldn't see her. I would take out her pictures and look. No good. Nothing doing. A blank. Can you imagine it?"

"Say Mac!" Leo called down the counter. "Can you imagine this bozo's mind a blank?"

Slowly, as though fanning away flies, the man waved his hand. His green eyes were concentrated and fixed on the shallow little face of the paper boy.

"But a sudden piece of glass on a sidewalk. Or a nickel tune in a music box. A shadow on a wall at night. And I would remember. It might happen in a street and I would cry or bang my head against a lamppost. You follow me?"

"A piece of glass . . ." the boy said.

"Anything. I would walk around and I had no power of how and when to remember her. You think you can put up a kind of shield. But remembering don't come to a man face forward—it corners around sideways. I was at the mercy of everything I saw and heard. Suddenly instead of me combing the countryside to find her she began to chase me around in my very soul. *She* chasing *me,* mind you! and in my soul."

The boy asked finally: "What part of the country were you in then?"

"Ooh," the man groaned, "I was a sick mortal. It was like smallpox. I confess, Son, that I boozed. I fornicated. I committed any sin that suddenly appealed to me. I am loath to confess it but I will do so. When I recall that period it is all curdled in my mind, it was so terrible."

The man leaned his head down and tapped his forehead on the counter. For a few seconds he stayed bowed over in this position, the back of his stringy neck covered with orange furze, his hands with their long warped fingers held palm to palm in an attitude of prayer. Then the man straightened himself; he was smiling and suddenly his face was bright and tremulous and old.

"It was in the fifth year that it happened," he said. "And with it I started my science."

Leo's mouth jerked with a pale, quick grin. "Well none of we boys are getting any younger," he said. Then with sudden anger he balled up a dishcloth he was holding and threw it down hard on the floor. "You draggle-tailed old Romeo!"

"What happened?" the boy asked.

The old man's voice was high and clear: "Peace," he answered.

"Huh?"

"It is hard to explain scientifically, Son," he said. "I guess the logical explanation is that she and I had fleed around from each other for so long that finally we just got tangled up together and lay down and quit. Peace. A queer and beautiful blankness. It was spring in Portland and the rain came every afternoon. All evening I just stayed there on my bed in the dark. And that is how the science come to me."

The windows in the streetcar were pale blue with light. The two soldiers paid for their beers and opened the door—one of the soldiers combed his hair and wiped off his muddy puttees before they went outside. The three mill workers bent silently over their breakfasts. Leo's clock was ticking on the wall.

"It is this. And listen carefully. I meditated on love and reasoned it out. I realized what is wrong with us. Men fall in love for the first time. And what do they fall in love with?"

The boy's soft mouth was partly open and he did not answer.

"A woman," the old man said. "Without science, with nothing to go by, they undertake the most dangerous and sacred experience in God's earth. They fall in love with a woman. Is that correct, Son?"

"Yeah," the boy said faintly.

"They start at the wrong end of love. They begin at the climax. Can you wonder it is so miserable? Do you know how men should love?"

The old man reached over and grasped the boy by the collar of his leather jacket. He gave him a gentle shake and his green eyes gazed down unblinking and grave.

"Son, do you know how love should be begun?"

The boy sat small and listening and still. Slowly he shook his head. The old man leaned closer and whispered:

"A tree. A rock. A cloud."

It was still raining outside in the street: a mild, gray, endless rain. The mill whistle blew for the six o'clock shift and the three spinners paid and went away. There was no one in the café but Leo, the old man, and the little paper boy.

"The weather was like this in Portland," he said. "At the time my science was begun. I meditated and I started very cautious. I would pick up something from the street and take it home with me. I bought a goldfish and I concentrated on the goldfish and I loved it. I graduated from one thing to another. Day by day I was getting this technique. On the road from Portland to San Diego——"

"Aw shut up!" screamed Leo suddenly. "Shut up! Shut up!"

The old man still held the collar of the boy's jacket; he was trembling and his face was earnest and bright and wild. "For six years now I have gone around by myself and built up my science. And now I am a master. Son, I can love anything. No longer do I have to think about it even. I see a street full of people and a beautiful light comes in me. I watch a bird in the sky. Or I meet a traveler on the road. Everything, Son. And anybody. All strangers and all loved! Do you realize what a science like mine can mean?"

The boy held himself stiffly, his hands curled tight around the counter edge. Finally he asked: "Did you ever really find that lady?"

"What? What say, Son?"

"I mean," the boy asked timidly. "Have you fallen in love with a woman again?"

The old man loosened his grasp on the boy's collar. He turned away and for the first time his green eyes had a vague and scattered look. He lifted his mug from the counter, drank down the yellow beer. His head was shaking slowly from side to side. Then finally he answered: "No, Son. You see that is the last step in my science. I go cautious. And I am not quite ready yet."

"Well!" said Leo. "Well well well!"

The old man stood in the open doorway. "Remember," he said. Framed there in the gray damp light of the early morning he looked shrunken and seedy and frail. But his smile was bright. "Remember I love you," he said with a last nod. And the door closed quietly behind him.

The boy did not speak for a long time. He pulled down the bangs on his forehead and slid his grimy little forefinger around the rim of his empty cup. Then without looking at Leo he finally asked:

"Was he drunk?"

"No," said Leo shortly.

The boy raised his clear voice higher. "Then was he a dope fiend?"

"No."

The boy looked up at Leo, and his flat little face was desperate, his voice urgent and shrill. "Was he crazy? Do you think he was a lunatic?" The paper boy's voice dropped suddenly with doubt. "Leo? Or not?"

But Leo would not answer him. Leo had run a night café for fourteen years, and he held himself to be a critic of craziness. There were the town characters and also the transients who roamed in from the night. He knew the manias of all of them. But he did not want to satisfy the questions of the waiting child. He tightened his pale face and was silent.

So the boy pulled down the right flap of his helmet and as he turned to leave he made the only comment that seemed safe to him, the only remark that could not be laughed down and despised:

"He sure has done a lot of traveling."

## FLANNERY O'CONNOR (1925–1964)

# *A Good Man Is Hard to Find*

The grandmother didn't want to go to Florida. She wanted to visit some of her connections in east Tennessee and she was seizing at every chance to change Bailey's mind. Bailey was the son she lived with, her only boy. He was sitting on the edge of his chair at the table, bent over the orange sports section of the *Journal.* "Now look here, Bailey," she said, "see here, read this," and she stood with one hand on her thin hip and the other rattling the newspaper at his bald head. "Here this fellow that calls himself The Misfit is aloose from the Federal Pen and headed toward Florida and you read here what it says he did to these people. Just you read it. I wouldn't take my children in any direction with a criminal like that aloose in it. I couldn't answer to my conscience if I did."

Bailey didn't look up from his reading so she wheeled around then and faced the children's mother, a young woman in slacks, whose face was as broad and innocent as a cabbage and was tied round with a green head-kerchief that had two points on the top like rabbit's ears. She was sitting on the sofa, feeding the baby his apricots out of a jar. "The children have been to Florida before," the old lady said. "You all ought to take them somewhere else for a change so they would see different parts of the world and be broad. They never have been to east Tennessee."

The children's mother didn't seem to hear her but the eight-year-old boy, John Wesley, a stocky child with glasses, said, "If you don't want to go to Florida, why dontcha stay at home?" He and the little girl, June Star, were reading the funny papers on the floor.

"She wouldn't stay at home to be queen for a day," June Star said without raising her yellow head.

"Yes and what would you do if this fellow, The Misfit, caught you?" the grandmother asked.

"I'd smack his face," John Wesley said.

"She wouldn't stay at home for a million bucks," June Star said. "Afraid she'd miss something. She has to go everywhere we go."

"All right, Miss," the grandmother said. "Just remember that the next time you want me to curl your hair."

June Star said her hair was naturally curly.

The next morning the grandmother was the first one in the car, ready to go. She had her big black valise that looked like the head of a hippopotamus in one corner, and underneath it she was hiding a basket with Pitty Sing, the cat, in it. She didn't intend for the cat to be left alone in the house for three days because he would miss her too much and she was afraid he might brush against one of the gas burners and accidentally asphyxiate himself. Her son, Bailey, didn't like to arrive at a motel with a cat.

She sat in the middle of the back seat with John Wesley and June Star on either side of her. Bailey and the children's mother and the baby sat in the front and they left Atlanta at eight forty-five with the mileage on the car at 55890. The grandmother wrote this down because she thought it would be interesting to say how many miles they had been when they got back. It took them twenty minutes to reach the outskirts of the city.

The old lady settled herself comfortably, removing her white cotton gloves and putting them up with her purse on the shelf in front of the back window. The children's mother still had on slacks and still had her head tied up in a green kerchief, but the grandmother had on a navy blue straw sailor hat with a bunch of white violets on the brim and a navy blue dress with a small white dot in the print. Her collar and cuffs were white organdy trimmed with lace and at her neckline she had pinned a purple spray of cloth violets containing a sachet. In case of an accident, anyone seeing her dead on the highway would know at once that she was a lady.

She said she thought it was going to be a good day for driving, neither too hot nor too cold, and she cautioned Bailey that the speed limit was fifty-five miles an hour and that the patrolmen hid themselves behind billboards and small clumps of trees and sped out after you before you had a chance to slow down. She pointed out interesting details of the scenery: Stone Mountain; the blue granite that in some places came up to both sides of the highway; the brilliant red clay banks slightly streaked with purple; and the various crops that made rows of green lace-work on the ground. The trees were full of silver-white sunlight and the meanest of them sparkled. The children were reading comic magazines and their mother had gone back to sleep.

"Let's go through Georgia fast so we won't have to look at it much," John Wesley said.

"If I were a little boy," said the grandmother, "I wouldn't talk about my native state that way. Tennessee has the mountains and Georgia has the hills."

"Tennessee is just a hillbilly dumping ground," John Wesley said, "and Georgia is a lousy state too."

"You said it," June Star said.

"In my time," said the grandmother, folding her thin veined fingers, "children were more respectful of their native states and their parents and everything else. People did right then. Oh look at the cute little pickaninny!" she said and pointed to a Negro child standing in the door of a shack. "Wouldn't that make a picture, now?" she asked and they all turned and looked at the little Negro out of the back window. He waved.

"He didn't have any britches on," June said.

"He probably didn't have any," the grandmother explained. "Little niggers in the country don't have things like we do. If I could paint, I'd paint that picture," she said.

The children exchanged comic books.

The grandmother offered to hold the baby and the children's mother passed him over the front seat to her. She set him on her knee and bounced him and told him about the things they were passing. She rolled her eyes and screwed up her mouth and stuck her leathery thin face into his smooth bland one. Occasionally he gave her a faraway smile. They passed a large cotton field with five or six graves fenced in the middle of it, like a small island. "Look at the graveyard!" the grandmother said, pointing it out. "That was the old family burying ground. That belonged to the plantation."

"Where's the plantation?" John Wesley asked.

"Gone With the Wind," said the grandmother. "Ha. Ha."

When the children finished all the comic books they had brought, they opened the lunch and ate it. The grandmother ate a peanut butter sandwich and an olive and would not let the children throw the box and the paper napkins out the window. When there was nothing else to do they played a game by choosing a cloud and making the other two guess what shape it suggested. John Wesley took one the shape of a cow and June Star guessed a cow and John Wesley said, no, an automobile, and June Star said he didn't play fair, and they began to slap each other over the grandmother.

The grandmother said she would tell them a story if they would keep quiet. When she told a story, she rolled her eyes and waved her head and was very dramatic. She said once when she was a maiden lady she had been courted by a Mr. Edgar Atkins Teagarden from Jasper, Georgia. She said he was a very good-looking man and a gentleman and that he brought her a watermelon every Saturday afternoon with his initials cut in it, E. A. T. Well, one Saturday, she said, Mr. Teagarden brought the watermelon and there was nobody at home and he left it on the front porch and returned in his buggy to Jasper, but she never got the watermelon, she said, because a nigger boy ate it when he saw the initials, E. A. T.! This story tickled John Wesley's funny bone and he giggled and giggled but June Star didn't think it was any good. She said she wouldn't marry a man that just brought her a watermelon on Saturday. The grandmother said she would have done well to marry Mr. Teagarden because he was a gentleman and had bought Coca-Cola stock when it first came out and that he had died only a few years ago, a very wealthy man.

They stopped at The Tower for barbecued sandwiches. The Tower was a part stucco and part wood filling station and dance hall set in a clearing outside of Timothy. A fat man named Red Sammy Butts ran it and there were signs stuck here and there on the building and for miles up and down the highway saying, TRY RED SAMMY'S FAMOUS BARBECUE. NONE LIKE FAMOUS RED SAMMY'S! RED SAM! THE FAT BOY WITH THE HAPPY LAUGH. A VETERAN! SAMMY'S YOUR MAN!

Red Sammy was lying on the bare ground outside The Tower with his head under a truck while a gray monkey about a foot high, chained to a small chinaberry tree, chattered nearby. The monkey sprang back into the tree and got on the highest limb as soon as he saw the children jump out of the car and run toward him.

Inside, The Tower was a long dark room with a counter at one end and tables at the other and dancing space in the middle. They all sat down at a broad table next to the nickelodeon and Red Sam's wife, a tall burnt-brown woman with hair and eyes lighter than her skin, came and took their order. The children's mother put a dime in the machine and played "The Tennessee Waltz," and the grandmother said that tune always made her want to dance. She asked Bailey if he would like to dance but he only glared at her. He didn't have a naturally sunny disposition like she did and trips made him nervous. The grandmother's brown eyes were very bright. She swayed her head from side to side and pretended she was dancing in her chair. June Star said play something she could tap to so the children's mother put in another dime and played a fast number and June Star stepped out onto the dance floor and did her tap routine.

"Ain't she cute?" Red Sam's wife said, leaning over the counter. "Would you like to come be my little girl?"

"No I certainly wouldn't," June Star said. "I wouldn't live in a broken-down place like this for a million bucks!" and she ran back to the table.

"Ain't she cute?" the woman repeated, stretching her mouth politely.

"Aren't you ashamed?" hissed the grandmother.

Red Sam came in and told his wife to quit lounging on the counter and hurry with these people's order. His khaki trousers reached just to his hip bones and his stomach hung over them like a sack of meal swaying under his shirt. He came over and sat down at a table nearby and let out a combination sigh and yodel. "You can't win," he said. "You can't win," and he wiped his sweating red face off with a gray handkerchief. "These days you don't know who to trust," he said. "Ain't that the truth?"

"People are certainly not nice like they used to be," said the grandmother.

"Two fellers come in here last week," Red Sammy said, "driving a Chrysler. It was a old beat-up car but it was a good one and these boys looked all right to me. Said they worked at the mill and you know I let them fellers charge the gas they bought? Now why did I do that?"

"Because you're a good man!" the grandmother said at once.

"Yes'm, I suppose so," Red Sam said as if he were struck with the answer.

His wife brought the orders, carrying the five plates all at once without a tray, two in each hand and one balanced on her arm. "It isn't a soul in this green world of God's that you can trust," she said. "And I don't count anybody out of that, not nobody," she repeated, looking at Red Sammy.

"Did you read about that criminal, The Misfit, that's escaped?" asked the grandmother.

"I wouldn't be a bit surprised if he didn't attact this place right here," said the woman. "If he hears about it being here, I wouldn't be none surprised to see him. If he hears it's two cent in the cash register, I wouldn't be a tall surprised if he . . ."

"That'll do," Red Sam said. "Go bring these people their Co'Colas," and the woman went off to get the rest of the order.

"A good man is hard to find," Red Sammy said. "Everything is getting terrible. I remember the day you could go off and leave your screen door unlatched. Not no more."

He and the grandmother discussed better times. The old lady said that in her opinion Europe was entirely to blame for the way things were now. She said the way Europe acted you would think we were made of money and Red Sam said it was no use talking about it, she was exactly right. The children ran outside into the white sunlight and looked at the monkey in the lacy chinaberry tree. He was busy catching fleas on himself and biting each one carefully between his teeth as if it were a delicacy.

They drove off again into the hot afternoon. The grandmother took cat naps and woke up every few minutes with her own snoring. Outside of Toombsboro she woke up and recalled an old plantation that she had visited in this neighborhood once when she was a young lady. She said the house had six white columns across the front and that there was an avenue of oaks leading up to it and two little wooden trellis arbors on either side in front where you sat down with your suitor after a stroll in the garden. She recalled exactly which road to turn off to get to it. She knew that Bailey would not be willing to lose any time looking at an old house, but the more she talked about it, the more she wanted to see it once again and find out if the little twin arbors were still standing. "There was a secret panel in this house," she said craftily, not telling the truth but wishing that she were, "and the story went that all the family silver was hidden in it when Sherman came through but it was never found . . ."

"Hey!" John Wesley said. "Let's go see it! We'll find it! We'll poke all the woodwork and find it! Who lives there? Where do you turn off at? Hey Pop, can't we turn off there?"

"We never have seen a house with a secret panel!" June Star shrieked. "Let's go to the house with the secret panel! Hey, Pop, can't we go see the house with the secret panel!"

"It's not far from here, I know," the grandmother said. "It wouldn't take over twenty minutes."

Bailey was looking straight ahead. His jaw was as rigid as a horseshoe. "No," he said.

The children began to yell and scream that they wanted to see the house with the secret panel. John Wesley kicked the back of the front seat and June Star hung over her mother's shoulder and whined desperately into her ear that they never had any fun even on their vacation, and that they could never do what THEY wanted to do. The baby began to scream and John Wesley kicked the back of the seat so hard that his father could feel the blows in his kidney.

"All right!" he shouted, and drew the car to a stop at the side of the road. "Will you all shut up? Will you all just shut up for one second? If you don't shut up, we won't go anywhere."

"It would be very educational for them," the grandmother murmured.

"All right," Bailey said, "but get this: this is the only time we're going to stop for anything like this. This is the one and only time."

"The dirt road that you have to turn down is about a mile back," the grandmother directed. "I marked it when we passed."

"A dirt road," Bailey groaned.

After they had turned around and were headed toward the dirt road, the grandmother recalled other points about the house, the beautiful glass over the front doorway and the candle-lamp in the hall. John Wesley said that the secret panel was probably in the fireplace.

"You can't go inside this house," Bailey said. "You don't know who lives there."

"While you all talk to the people in front, I'll run around behind and get in a window," John Wesley suggested.

"We'll all stay in the car," his mother said.

They turned onto the dirt road and the car raced roughly along in a swirl of pink dust. The grandmother recalled the times when there were no paved roads and thirty miles was a day's journey. The dirt road was hilly and there were sudden washes in it and sharp curves on dangerous embankments. All at once they would be on a hill, looking down over the blue tops of trees for miles around, then the next minute, they would be in a red depression with the dust-coated trees looking down on them.

"This place had better turn up in a minute," Bailey said, "or I'm going to turn around."

The road looked as if no one had traveled on it in months.

"It's not much farther," the grandmother said and just as she said it, a horrible thought came to her. The thought was so embarrassing that she turned red in the face and her eyes dilated and her feet jumped up, upsetting her valise in the corner. The instant the valise moved, the newspaper top she had over the basket under it rose with a snarl and Pitty Sing, the cat, sprang onto Bailey's shoulder.

The children were thrown to the floor and their mother, clutching the baby, was thrown out the door onto the ground, the old lady was thrown into the front seat. The car turned over once and landed right-side-up in a gulch on the side of the road. Bailey remained in the driver's seat with the cat—gray-striped with a broad white face and an orange nose—clinging to his neck like a caterpillar.

As soon as the children saw they could move their arms and legs, they scrambled out of the car, shouting. "We've had an ACCIDENT!" The grandmother was curled up under the dashboard, hoping she was injured so that Bailey's wrath would not come down on her all at once. The horrible thought she had had before the accident was that the house she had remembered so vividly was not in Georgia but in Tennessee.

Bailey removed the cat from his neck with both hands and flung it out the window against the side of a pine tree. Then he got out of the car and started looking for the children's mother. She was sitting against the side of the red gutted ditch, holding the screaming baby, but she only had a cut down her face and a broken shoulder. "We've had an ACCIDENT!" the children screamed in a frenzy of delight.

"But nobody's killed," June Star said with disappointment as the grandmother limped out of the car, her hat still pinned to her head but the broken front brim standing up at a jaunty angle and the violet spray hanging off the side. They all sat down in the ditch, except the children, to recover from the shock. They were all shaking.

"Maybe a car will come along," said the children's mother hoarsely.

"I believe I have injured an organ," said the grandmother, pressing her side, but no one answered her. Bailey's teeth were clattering.

He had on a yellow sport shirt with bright blue parrots designed in it and his face was as yellow as the shirt. The grandmother decided that she would not mention that the house was in Tennessee.

The road was about ten feet above and they could see only the tops of the trees on the other side of it. Behind the ditch they were sitting in there were more woods, tall and dark and deep. In a few minutes they saw a car some distance away on top of a hill, coming slowly as if the occupants were watching them. The grandmother stood up and waved both arms dramatically to attract their attention. The car continued to come on slowly, disappeared around a bend and appeared again, moving even slower, on top of the hill they had gone over. It was a big black battered hearse-like automobile. There were three men in it.

It came to a stop just over them and for some minutes, the driver looked down with a steady expressionless gaze to where they were sitting, and didn't speak. Then he turned his head and muttered something to the other two and they got out. One was a fat boy in black trousers and a red sweat shirt with a silver stallion embossed on the front of it. He moved around on the right side of them and stood staring, his mouth partly open in a kind of loose grin. The other had on khaki pants and a blue striped coat and a gray hat pulled down very low, hiding most of his face. He came around slowly on the left side. Neither spoke.

The driver got out of the car and stood by the side of it, looking down at them. He was an older man than the other two. His hair was just beginning to gray and he wore silver-rimmed spectacles that gave him a scholarly look. He had a long creased face and didn't have on any shirt or undershirt. He had on blue jeans that were too tight for him and was holding a black hat and a gun. The two boys also had guns.

"We've had an ACCIDENT!" the children screamed.

The grandmother had the peculiar feeling that the bespectacled man was someone she knew. His face was as familiar to her as if she had known him all her life but she could not recall who he was. He moved away from the car and began to come down the embankment, placing his feet carefully so that he wouldn't slip. He had on tan and white shoes and no socks, and his ankles were red and thin. "Good afternoon," he said. "I see you all had you a little spill."

"We turned over twice!" said the grandmother.

"Oncet," he corrected. "We seen it happen. Try their car and see will it run, Hiram," he said quietly to the boy with the gray hat.

"What you got that gun for?" John Wesley asked. "Whatcha gonna do with that gun?"

"Lady," the man said to the children's mother, "would you mind calling them children to sit down by you? Children make me nervous. I want all you all to sit down right together there where you're at."

"What are you telling us what to do for?" June Star asked.

Behind them the line of woods gaped like a dark open mouth. "Come here," said their mother.

"Look here now," Bailey began suddenly, "we're in a predicament! We're in . . ."

The grandmother shrieked. She scrambled to her feet and stood staring. "You're The Misfit!" she said. "I recognized you at once."

"Yes'm," the man said, smiling slightly as if he were pleased in spite of himself to be known, "but it would have been better for all of you, lady, if you hadn't of reckernized me."

Bailey turned his head sharply and said something to his mother that shocked even the children. The old lady began to cry and The Misfit reddened.

"Lady," he said, "don't you get upset. Sometimes a man says things he don't mean. I don't reckon he meant to talk to you thataway."

"You wouldn't shoot a lady, would you?" the grandmother said and removed a clean handkerchief from her cuff and began to slap at her eyes with it.

The Misfit pointed the toe of his shoe into the ground and made a little hole and then covered it up again. "I would hate to have to," he said.

"Listen," the grandmother almost screamed, "I know you're a good man. You don't look a bit like you have common blood. I know you must come from nice people!"

"Yes mam," he said, "finest people in the world." When he smiled he showed a row of strong white teeth. "God never made a finer woman than my mother and my daddy's heart was pure gold," he said. The boy with the red sweat shirt had come around behind them and was standing with his gun at his hip. The Misfit squatted down on the ground. "Watch them children, Bobby Lee," he said. "You know they make me nervous." He looked at the six of them huddled together in front of him and he seemed to be embarrassed as if he couldn't think of anything to say. "Ain't a cloud in the sky," he remarked, looking up at it. "Don't see no sun but don't see no cloud neither."

"Yes, it's a beautiful day," said the grandmother. "Listen," she said, "you shouldn't call yourself The Misfit because I know you're a good man at heart. I can just look at you and tell."

"Hush!" Bailey yelled. "Hush! Everybody shut up and let me handle this!" He was squatting in the position of a runner about to sprint forward but he didn't move.

"I pre-chate that, lady," The Misfit said and drew a little circle in the ground with the butt of his gun.

"It'll take a half a hour to fix this here car," Hiram called, looking over the raised hood of it.

"Well, first you and Bobby Lee get him and that little boy to step over yonder with you," The Misfit said, pointing to Bailey and John Wesley. "The boys want to ask you something," he said to Bailey. "Would you mind stepping back in them woods there with them?"

"Listen," Bailey began, "we're in a terrible predicament. Nobody realizes what this is," and his voice cracked. His eyes were as blue and intense as the parrots in his shirt and he remained perfectly still.

The grandmother reached up to adjust her hat brim as if she were going to the woods with him but it came off in her hand. She stood staring at it and after a second she let it fall on the ground. Hiram pulled Bailey up by the arm as if he were assisting an old man. John Wesley caught hold of his father's hand and Bobby Lee followed. They went off toward the woods and just as they reached the dark edge, Bailey turned and supporting himself against a gray naked pine trunk, he shouted, "I'll be back in a minute, Mamma, wait on me!"

"Come back this instant!" his mother shrilled but they all disappeared into the woods.

"Bailey Boy!" the grandmother called in a tragic voice but she found she was looking at The Misfit squatting on the ground in front of her. "I just know you're a good man," she said desperately. "You're not a bit common!"

"Nome, I ain't a good man," The Misfit said after a second as if he had considered her statement carefully, "but I ain't the worst in the world neither. My daddy said I was different breed of dog from my brothers and sisters. 'You know,' Daddy said, 'it's some that can live their whole life out without asking about it and it's others has to know why it is, and this boy is one of the latters. He's going to be into everything!' " He put on his black hat and looked up suddenly and then away deep into the woods as if he were embarrassed again. "I'm sorry I don't have on a shirt before you ladies," he said, hunching his shoulders slightly. "We buried our clothes that we had on when we escaped and we're just making do until we can get better. We borrowed these from some folks we met," he explained.

"That's perfectly all right," the grandmother said. "Maybe Bailey has an extra shirt in his suitcase."

"I'll look and see terrectly," The Misfit said.

"Where are they taking him?" the children's mother screamed.

"Daddy was a card himself," the Misfit said. "You couldn't put anything over on him. He never got in trouble with the Authorities though. Just had the knack of handling them."

"You could be honest too if you'd only try," said the grandmother. "Think how wonderful it would be to settle down and live a comfortable life and not have to think about somebody chasing you all the time."

The Misfit kept scratching in the ground with the butt of his gun as if he were thinking about it. "Yes'm, somebody is always after you," he murmured.

The grandmother noticed how thin his shoulder blades were just behind his hat because she was standing up looking down on him. "Do you ever pray?" she asked.

He shook his head. All she saw was the black hat wiggle between his shoulder blades. "Nome," he said.

There was a pistol shot from the woods, followed closely by another. Then silence. The old lady's head jerked around. She could hear the wind move through the tree tops like a long satisfied insuck of breath. "Bailey Boy!" she called.

"I was a gospel singer for a while," The Misfit said. "I been most everything. Been in the arm service, both land and sea, at home and abroad, been twict married, been an undertaker, been with the railroads, plowed Mother Earth, been in a tornado, seen a man burnt alive oncet," and he looked up at the children's mother and the little girl who were sitting close together, their faces white and their eyes glassy; "I even seen a woman flogged," he said.

"Pray, pray," the grandmother began, "pray, pray . . ."

"I never was a bad boy that I remember of," The Misfit said in an almost dreamy voice, "but somewheres along the line I done something wrong and got sent to the penitentiary. I was buried alive," and he looked up and held her attention to him by a steady stare.

"That's when you should have started to pray," she said. "What did you do to get sent to the penitentiary that first time?"

"Turn to the right, it was a wall," The Misfit said, looking up again at the cloudless sky. "Turn to the left, it was a wall. Look up it was a ceiling, look down it was a floor. I forgot what I done, lady. I set there and set there, trying to remember what it was I done and I ain't recalled it to this day. Oncet in a while, I would think it was coming to me, but it never come."

"Maybe they put you in by mistake," the old lady said vaguely.

"Nome," he said. "It wasn't no mistake. They had the papers on me."

"You must have stolen something," she said.

The Misfit sneered slightly. "Nobody had nothing I wanted," he said. "It was a head-doctor at the penitentiary said what I had done was kill my daddy but I know that for a lie. My daddy died in nineteen ought nineteen of the epidemic flu and I never had a thing to do with it. He was buried in the Mount Hopewell Baptist churchyard and you can go there and see for yourself."

"If you would pray," the old lady said, "Jesus would help you."

"That's right," The Misfit said.

"Well then, why don't you pray?" she asked trembling with delight suddenly.

"I don't want no hep," he said. "I'm doing all right by myself."

Bobby Lee and Hiram came ambling back from the woods. Bobby Lee was dragging a yellow shirt with bright blue parrots in it.

"Throw me that shirt, Bobby Lee," The Misfit said. The shirt came flying at him and landed on his shoulder and he put it on. The grandmother couldn't name what the shirt reminded her of. "No, lady," The Misfit said while he was buttoning it up. "I found out the crime don't matter. You can do one thing or you can do another, kill a man or take a tire off his car, because sooner or later you're going to forget what it was you done and just be punished for it."

The children's mother had begun to make heaving noises as if she couldn't get her breath. "Lady," he asked, "would you and that little girl like to step off yonder with Bobby Lee and Hiram and join your husband?"

"Yes, thank you," the mother said faintly. Her left arm dangled helplessly and she was holding the baby, who had gone to sleep, in the other. "Hep that lady up, Hiram," The Misfit said as she struggled to climb out of the ditch, "and Bobby Lee, you hold onto that little girl's hand."

"I don't want to hold hands with him," June Star said. "He reminds me of a pig."

The fat boy blushed and laughed and caught her by the arm and pulled her off into the woods after Hiram and her mother.

Alone with The Misfit, the grandmother found that she had lost her voice. There was not a cloud in the sky nor any sun. There was nothing around her but woods. She wanted to tell him that he must pray. She opened and closed her mouth several times before anything came out. Finally she found herself saying, "Jesus, Jesus," meaning Jesus will help you, but the way she was saying it, it sounded as if she might be cursing.

"Yes'm," The Misfit said as if he agreed. "Jesus thown everything off balance. It was the same case with Him as with me except He hadn't committed any crime and they could prove I had committed one because they had the papers on me. Of course," he said, "they never shown me any papers. That's why I sign myself now. I said long ago, you get you a signature and sign everything you do and keep a copy of it. Then you'll know what you done and you can hold up the crime to the punishment and see do they match and in the end you'll have something to prove you ain't been treated right. I call myself The Misfit," he said, "because I can't make what all I done wrong fit what all I gone through in punishment."

There was a piercing scream from the woods, followed closely by a pistol report. "Does it seem right to you, lady, that one is punished a heap and another ain't punished at all?"

"Jesus!" the old lady cried. "You've got good blood! I know you wouldn't shoot a lady! I know you come from nice people! Pray! Jesus, you ought not to shoot a lady. I'll give you all the money I've got!"

"Lady," The Misfit said, looking beyond her far into the woods, "there never was a body that give the undertaker a tip."

There were two more pistol reports and the grandmother raised her head like a parched old turkey hen crying for water and called, "Bailey Boy, Bailey Boy!" as if her heart would break.

"Jesus was the only One that ever raised the dead," The Misfit continued, "and He shouldn't have done it. He thown everything off balance. If He did what He said, then it's nothing for you to do but thow away everything and follow Him, and if He didn't, then it's nothing for you to do but enjoy the few minutes you got left the best way you can—by killing somebody or burning down his house or doing some other meanness to him. No pleasure but meanness," he said and his voice had become almost a snarl.

"Maybe He didn't raise the dead," the old lady mumbled, not knowing what she was saying and feeling so dizzy that she sank down in the ditch with her legs twisted under her.

"I wasn't there so I can't say He didn't," The Misfit said. "I wisht I had of been there," he said, hitting the ground with his fist. "It ain't right I wasn't there because if I had of been there I would of known. Listen lady," he said in a high voice, "if I had of been there I would of known and I wouldn't be like I am now." His voice seemed about to crack and the grandmother's head cleared for an instant. She saw the man's face twisted close to her own as if he were going to cry and she murmured, "Why you're one of my babies. You're one of my own children!" She reached out and touched him on the shoulder. The Misfit sprang back as if a snake had bitten him and shot her three times through the chest. Then he put his gun down on the ground and took off his glasses and began to clean them.

Hiram and Bobby Lee returned from the woods and stood over the ditch, looking down at the grandmother who half sat and half lay in a puddle of blood with her legs crossed under her like a child's and her face smiling up at the cloudless sky.

Without his glasses, The Misfit's eyes were red-rimmed and pale and defenseless-looking. "Take her off and thow her where you thown the others," he said, picking up the cat that was rubbing itself against his leg.

"She was a talker, wasn't she?" Bobby Lee said, sliding down the ditch with a yodel.

"She would of been a good woman," The Misfit said, "if it had been somebody there to shoot her every minute of her life."

"Some fun!" Bobby Lee said.

"Shut up, Bobby Lee," The Misfit said. "It's no real pleasure in life."

## DONALD BARTHELME (1931– )

# *The Balloon*

The balloon, beginning at a point on Fourteenth Street, the exact location of which I cannot reveal, expanded northward all one night, while people were sleeping, until it reached the Park. There, I stopped it; at dawn the northernmost edges lay over the Plaza; the free-hanging motion was frivolous and gentle. But experiencing a faint irritation at stopping, even to protect the trees, and seeing no reason the balloon should not be allowed to expand upward, over the parts of the city it was already covering, into the "air space" to be found there, I asked the engineers to see to it. This expansion took place throughout the morning, soft imperceptible sighing of gas through the valves. The balloon then covered forty-five blocks north-south and an irregular area east-west, as many as six crosstown blocks on either side of the Avenue in some places. That was the situation, then.

But it is wrong to speak of "situations," implying sets of circumstances leading to some resolution, some escape of tension; there were no situations, simply the balloon hanging there—muted heavy grays and browns for the most part, contrasting with walnut and soft yellows. A deliberate lack of finish, enhanced by skillful installation, gave the surface a rough, forgotten quality; sliding weights on the inside, carefully adjusted, anchored the great, vari-shaped mass at a number of points. Now we have had a flood of original ideas in all media, works of singular beauty as well as significant milestones in the history of inflation, but at that moment there was only *this balloon,* concrete particular, hanging there.

There were reactions. Some people found the balloon "interesting." As a response this seemed inadequate to the immensity of the balloon, the suddenness of its appearance over the city; on the other hand, in the absence of hysteria or other societally-induced anxiety, it must be judged a calm, "mature" one. There was a certain amount of initial argumentation about the "meaning" of the balloon; this subsided, because we have learned not to insist on meanings, and they are rarely even looked for now, except in cases involving the simplest, safest phenomena. It was agreed that since the meaning of the balloon could never be known absolutely, extended discussion was pointless, or at least less purposeful than the activities of those who, for example, hung green and blue paper lanterns from the warm gray underside, in certain streets, or seized the occasion to write messages on the surface, announcing their availability for the performance of unnatural acts, or the availability of acquaintances.

Daring children jumped, especially at those points where the balloon hovered close to a building, so that the gap between balloon and building was a matter of a few inches, or points where the balloon actually made contact, exerting an ever-so-slight pressure against the side of a building, so that balloon and building seemed a unity. The upper surface was so structured that a "landscape" was presented, small valleys as well as slight knolls, or mounds; once atop the balloon, a stroll was possible, or even a trip, from one place to another. There was pleasure in being able to run down an incline, then up the opposing slope, both gently graded, or in making a leap from one side to the other. Bouncing was possible, because of the pneumaticity of the surface, and even falling, if that was your wish. That all these varied motions, as well as others, were within one's possibilities, in experiencing the "up" side of the balloon, was extremely exciting for children, accustomed to the city's flat, hard skin. But the purpose of the balloon was not to amuse children.

Too, the number of people, children and adults, who took advantage of the opportunities described was not so large as it might have been: a certain timidity, lack of trust in the balloon, was seen. There was, furthermore, some hostility. Because we had hidden the pumps, which fed helium to the interior, and because the surface was so vast that the authorities could not determine the point of entry—that is, the point at which the gas was injected—a degree of frustration was evidenced by those city officers into whose province such manifestations normally fell. The apparent purposelessness of the balloon was vexing (as was the fact that it was "there" at all). Had we painted, in great letters, "LABORATORY TESTS PROVE" OR "18% MORE EFFECTIVE" on the sides of the balloon, this difficulty would have been circumvented. But I could not bear to do so. On the whole, these officers were remarkably tolerant, considering the dimensions of the anomaly, this tolerance being the result of, first, secret tests conducted by night that convinced them that little or nothing could be done in the way of removing or destroying the balloon, and, secondly, a public warmth that arose (not uncolored by touches of the aforementioned hostility) toward the balloon, from ordinary citizens.

As a single balloon must stand for a lifetime of thinking about balloons, so each citizen expressed, in the attitude he chose, a complex of attitudes. One man might consider that the balloon had to do with the notion *sullied,* as in the sentence *The big balloon sullied the otherwise clear and radiant Manhattan sky.* That is, the balloon was, in this man's view, an imposture, something inferior to the sky that had formerly been there, something interposed between the people and their "sky." But in fact it was January, the sky was dark and ugly; it was not a sky you could look up into, lying on your back in the street, with pleasure, unless pleasure, for you, proceeded from having been threatened, from having been misused. And the underside of the balloon was a pleasure to look up into, we had seen to that, muted grays and browns for the most part, contrasted with walnut and soft, forgotten yellows. And so, while this man was thinking *sullied,* still there was an admixture of pleasurable cognition in his thinking, struggling with the original perception.

Another man, on the other hand, might view the balloon as if it were part of a system of unanticipated rewards, as when one's employer walks in and says, "Here, Henry, take this package of money I have wrapped for you, because we have been doing so well in the business here, and I admire the way you bruise the tulips, without which bruising your department would not be a success, or at least not the success that it is." For this man the balloon might be a brilliantly heroic "muscle and pluck" experience, even if an experience poorly understood.

Another man might say, "Without the example of ———, it is doubtful that ——— would exist today in its present form," and find many to agree with him, or to argue with him. Ideas of "bloat" and "float" were introduced, as well as concepts of dream and responsibility. Others engaged in remarkably detailed fantasies having to do with a wish either to lose themselves in the balloon, or to engorge it. The private character of these wishes, of their origins, deeply buried and unknown, was such that they were not much spoken of; yet there is evidence that they were widespread. It was also argued that what was important was what you felt when you stood under the balloon; some people claimed that they felt sheltered, warmed, as never before, while enemies of the balloon felt, or reported feeling, constrained, a "heavy" feeling.

Critical opinion was divided:

"monstrous pourings"

"harp"

XXXXXXX "certain contrasts with darker portions"

"inner joy"

"large, square corners"

"conservative eclecticism that has so far governed modern balloon design"

:::::: "abnormal vigor"

"warm, soft, lazy passages"

"Has unity been sacrificed for a sprawling quality?"

*"Quelle catastrophe!"*

"munching"

People began, in a curious way, to locate themselves in relation to aspects of the balloon: "I'll be at that place where it dips down into Forty-seventh Street almost to the sidewalk, near the Alamo Chile House," or, "Why don't we go stand on top, and take the air, and maybe walk about a bit, where it forms a tight, curving line with the façade of the Gallery of Modern Art—" Marginal intersections offered entrances within a given time duration, as well as "warm, soft, lazy passages" in which . . . But it is wrong to speak of "marginal intersections," each intersection was crucial, none could be ignored (as if, walking there, you might not find someone capable of turning your attention, in a flash, from old exercises to new exercises, risks and escalations). Each intersection was crucial, meeting of balloon and building, meeting of balloon and man, meeting of balloon and balloon.

It was suggested that what was admired about the balloon was finally this: that it was not limited, or defined. Sometimes a bulge, blister, or sub-section would carry all the way east to the river on its own initiative, in the manner of an army's movements on a map, as seen in a headquarters remote from the fighting. Then that part would be, as it were, thrown back again, or would withdraw into new dispositions; the next morning, that part would have made another sortie, or disappeared altogether. This ability of the balloon to shift its shape, to change, was very pleasing, especially to people whose lives were rather rigidly patterned, persons to whom change, although desired, was not available. The balloon, for the twenty-two days of its existence, offered the possibility, in its randomness, of mislocation of the self, in contradistinction to the grid of precise, rectangular pathways under our feet. The amount of specialized training currently needed, and the consequent desirability of long-term commitments, has been occasioned by the steadily growing importance of complex machinery, in virtually all kinds of operations; as this tendency increases, more and more people will turn, in bewildered inadequacy, to solutions for which the balloon may stand as a prototype, or "rough draft."

I met you under the balloon, on the occasion of your return from Norway; you asked if it was mine; I said it was. The balloon, I said, is a spontaneous autobiographical disclosure, having to do with the unease I felt at your absence, and with sexual deprivation, but now that your visit to Bergen has been terminated, it is no longer necessary or appropriate. Removal of the balloon was easy; trailer trucks carried away the depleted fabric, which is now stored in West Virginia, awaiting some other time of unhappiness, sometime, perhaps, when we are angry with one another.

## JOHN CHEEVER (1912–1982)

# *The Swimmer*

It was one of those midsummer Sundays when everyone sits around saying, "I *drank* too much last night." You might have heard it whispered by the parishioners leaving church, heard it from the lips of the priest himself, struggling with his cassock in the *vestiarium*, heard it from the golf links and the tennis courts, heard it from the wildlife preserve where the leader of the Audubon group was suffering from a terrible hangover. "I *drank* too much," said Donald Westerhazy. "We all *drank* too much," said Lucinda Merrill. "It must have been the wine," said Helen Westerhazy. "I *drank* too much of that claret."

This was at the edge of the Westerhazys' pool. The pool, fed by an artesian well with a high iron content, was a pale shade of green. It was a fine day. In the west there was a massive stand of cumulus cloud so like a city seen from a distance—from the bow of an approaching ship—that it might have had a name. Lisbon. Hackensack. The sun was hot. Neddy Merrill sat by the green water, one hand in it, one around a glass of gin. He was a slender man—he seemed to have the especial slenderness of youth—and while he was far from young he had slid down his banister that morning and given the bronze backside of Aphrodite on the hall table a smack, as he jogged toward the smell of coffee in his dining room. He might have been compared to a summer's day, particularly the last hours of one, and while he lacked a tennis racket or a sail bag the impression was definitely one of youth, sport, and clement weather. He had been swimming and now he was breathing deeply, stertorously as if he could gulp into his lungs the components of that moment, the heat of the sun, the intenseness of his pleasure. It all seemed to flow into his chest. His own house stood in Bullet Park, eight miles to the south, where his four beautiful daughters would have had their lunch and might be playing tennis. Then it occurred to him that by taking a dogleg to the southwest he could reach his home by water.

His life was not confining and the delight he took in this observation could not explained by its suggestion of escape. He seemed to see, with a cartographer's eye, that string of swimming pools, that quasi-subterranean stream that curved across the county. He had made a discovery, a contribution to modern geography; he would name the stream Lucinda after his wife. He was not a practical joker nor was he a fool but he was determinedly original and had a vague and modest idea of himself as a legendary figure. The day was beautiful and it seemed to him that a long swim might enlarge and celebrate its beauty.

He took off a sweater that was hung over his shoulders and dove in. He had an inexplicable contempt for men who did not hurl themselves into pools. He swam a choppy crawl, breathing either with every stroke or every fourth stroke and counting somewhere well in the back of his mind the one-two one-two of a flutter kick. It was not a serviceable stroke for long distances but the domestication of swimming had saddled the sport with some customs and in his part of the world a crawl was customary. To be embraced and sustained by the light green water was less a pleasure, it seemed, than the resumption of a natural condition, and he would have liked to swim without trunks, but this was not possible, considering his project. He hoisted himself up on the far curb—he never used the ladder—and started across the lawn. When Lucinda asked where he was going he said he was going to swim home.

The only map and charts he had to go by were remembered or imaginary but these were clear enough. First there were the Grahams, the Hammers, the Lears, the Howlands, and the Crosscups. He would cross Ditmar Street to the Bunkers and come, after a short portage, to the Levys, the Welchers, and the public pool in Lancaster. Then there were the Hallorans, the Sachses, the Biswangers, Shirley Adams, the Gilmartins, and the Clydes. The day was lovely, and that he lived in a world so generously supplied with water seemed like a clemency, a beneficence. His heart was high and he ran across the grass. Making his way home by an uncommon route gave him the feeling that he was a pilgrim, an explorer, a man with a destiny, and he knew that he would find friends all along the way; friends would line the banks of the Lucinda River.

He went through a hedge that separated the Westerhazys' land from the Grahams', walked under some flowering apple trees, passed the shed that housed their pump and filter, and came out at the Grahams' pool. "Why, Neddy," Mrs. Graham said, "what a marvelous surprise. I've been trying to get you on the phone all morning. Here, let me get you a drink. " He saw then, like any explorer, that the hospitable customs and traditions of the natives would have to be handled with diplomacy if he was ever going to reach his destination. He did not want to mystify or seem rude to the Grahams nor did he have the time to linger there. He swam the length of their pool and joined them in the sun and was rescued, a few minutes later, by the arrival of two carloads of friends from Connecticut. During the uproarious reunions he was able to slip away. He went down by the front of the Grahams' house, stepped over a thorny hedge, and crossed a vacant lot to the Hammers'. Mrs. Hammer, looking up from her roses, saw him swim by although she wasn't quite sure who it was. The Lears heard him splashing past the open windows of their living room. The Howlands and the Crosscups were away. After leaving the Howlands' he crossed Ditmar Street and started for the Bunkers', where he could hear, even at that distance, the noise of a party.

The water refracted the sound of voices and laughter and seemed to suspend it in midair. The Bunkers' pool was on a rise and he climbed some stairs to a terrace where twenty-five or thirty men and women were drinking. The only person in the water was Rusty Towers, who floated there on a rubber raft. Oh, how bonny and lush were the banks of the Lucinda River! Prosperous men and women gathered by the sapphire-colored waters while caterer's men in white coats passed them cold gin. Overhead a red de Haviland trainer was circling around and around and around in the sky with something like the glee of a child in a swing. Ned felt a passing affection for the scene, a tenderness for the gathering, as if it was something he might touch. In the distance he heard thunder. As soon as Enid Bunker saw him she began to scream: "Oh, look who's here! What a marvelous surprise! When Lucinda said that you couldn't come I thought I'd *die*." She made her way to him through the crowd, and when they had finished kissing she led him to the bar, a progress that was slowed by the fact that he stopped to kiss eight or ten other women and shake the hands of as many men. A smiling bartender he had seen at a hundred parties gave him a gin and tonic and he stood by the bar for a moment, anxious not to get stuck in any conversation that would delay his voyage. When he seemed about to be surrounded he dove in and swam close to the side to avoid colliding with Rusty's raft. At the far end of the pool he bypassed the Tomlinsons with a broad smile and jogged up the garden path. The gravel cut his feet but this was the only unpleasantness. The party was confined to the pool, and as he went toward the house he heard the brilliant, watery sound of voices fade, heard the noise of a radio from the Bunkers' kitchen, where someone was listening to a ball game. Sunday afternoon. He made his way through the parked cars and down the grassy border of their driveway to Alewives Lane. He did not want to be seen on the road in his bathing trunks but there was no traffic and he made the short distance to the Levy's driveway, marked with a PRIVATE PROPERTY sign and a green tube for *The New York Times*. All the doors and windows of the big house were open but there were no signs of life; not even a dog barked. He went around the side of the house to the pool and saw that the Levys had only recently left. Glasses and bottles and dishes of nuts were on a table at the deep end, where there was a bathhouse or gazebo, hung with Japanese lanterns. After swimming the pool he got himself a glass and poured a drink. It was his fourth or fifth drink and he had swum nearly half the length of the Lucinda River. He felt tired, clean, and pleased at that moment to be alone; pleased with everything.

It would storm. The stand of cumulus cloud—that city—had risen and darkened, and while he sat there he heard the percussiveness of thunder again. The de Haviland trainer was still circling overhead and it seemed to Ned that he could almost hear the pilot laugh with pleasure in the afternoon; but when there was another peal of thunder he took off for home. A train whistle blew and he wondered what time it had gotten to be. Four? Five? He thought of the provincial station at that hour, where a waiter, his tuxedo concealed by a raincoat, a dwarf with some flowers wrapped in newspaper, and a woman who had been crying would be waiting for the local. It was suddenly growing dark; it was that moment when the pinheaded birds seem to organize their song into some acute and knowledgeable recognition of the storm's approach. Then there was a fine noise of rushing water from the crown of an oak at his back, as if a spigot there had been turned. Then the noise of fountains came from the crowns of all the tall trees. Why did he love storms, what was the meaning of his excitement when the door sprang open and the rain wind fled rudely up the stairs, why had the simple task of shutting the windows of an old house seemed fitting and urgent, why did the first watery notes of a storm wind have for him the unmistakable sound of good news, cheer, glad tidings? Then there was an explosion, a smell of cordite, and rain lashed the Japanese lanterns that Mrs. Levy had bought in Kyoto the year before last, or was it the year before that?

He stayed in the Levys' gazebo until the storm had passed. The rain had cooled the air and he shivered. The force of the wind had stripped a maple of its red and yellow leaves and scattered them over the grass and the water. Since it was midsummer the tree must be blighted, and yet he felt a peculiar sadness at this sign of autumn. He braced his shoulders, emptied his glass, and started for the Welchers' pool. This meant crossing the Lindleys' riding ring and he was surprised to find it overgrown with grass and all the jumps dismantled. He wondered if the Lindleys had sold their horses or gone away for the summer and put them out to board. He seemed to remember having heard something about the Lindleys and their horses but the memory was unclear. On he went, barefoot through the wet grass, to the Welchers', where he found their pool was dry.

This breach in his chain of water disappointed him absurdly, and he felt like some explorer who seeks a torrential headwater and finds a dead stream. He was disappointed and mystified. It was common enough to go away for the summer but no one ever drained his pool. The Welchers had definitely gone away. The pool furniture was folded, stacked, and covered with a tarpaulin. The bathhouse was locked. All the windows of the house were shut, and when he went around to the driveway in front he saw a FOR SALE sign nailed to a tree. When had he last heard from the Welchers—when, that is, had he and Lucinda last regretted an invitation to dine with them? It seemed only a week or so ago. Was his memory failing or had he so disciplined it in the repression of unpleasant facts that he had damaged his sense of the truth? Then in the distance he heard the sound of a tennis game. This cheered him, cleared away all his apprehensions and let him regard the overcast sky and the cold air with indifference. This was the day that Neddy Merrill swam across the county. That was the day! He started off then for his most difficult portage.

Had you gone for a Sunday afternoon ride that day you might have seen him, close to naked, standing on the shoulders of Route 424, waiting for a chance to cross. You might have wondered if he was the victim of foul play, had his car broken down, or was he merely a fool. Standing barefoot in the deposits of the highway—beer cans, rags, and blowout patches—exposed to all kinds of ridicule, he seemed pitiful. He had known when he started that this was a part of his journey—it had been on his maps—but confronted with the lines of traffic, worming through the summery light, he found himself unprepared. He was laughed at, jeered at, a beer can was thrown at him, and he had no dignity or humor to bring to the situation. He could have gone back, back to the Westerhazys', where Lucinda would still be sitting in the sun. He had signed nothing, vowed nothing, pledged nothing, not even to himself. Why, believing as he did, that all human obduracy was susceptible to common sense, was he unable to turn back? Why was he determined to complete his journey even if it meant putting his life in danger? At what point had this prank, this joke, this piece of horseplay become serious? He could not go back, he could not even recall with any clearness the green water at the Westerhazys', the sense of inhaling the day's components, the friendly and relaxed voices saying that they had *drunk* too much. In the space of an hour, more or less, he had covered a distance that made his return impossible.

An old man, tooling down the highway at fifteen miles an hour, let him get to the middle of the road, where there was a grass divider. Here he was exposed to the ridicule of the northbound traffic, but after ten or fifteen minutes he was able to cross. From here he had a only a short walk to the Recreation Center at the edge of the village of Lancaster, where there were some handball courts and a public pool.

The effect of the water on voices, the illusion of brilliance and suspense, was the same here as it had been at the Bunkers' but the sounds here were louder, harsher, and more shrill, and as soon as he entered the crowded enclosure he was confronted with regimentation. "ALL SWIMMERS MUST TAKE A SHOWER BEFORE USING THE POOL. ALL SWIMMERS MUST USE THE FOOTBATH. ALL SWIMMERS MUST WEAR THEIR IDENTIFICATION DISKS." He took a shower, washed his feet in a cloudy and bitter solution, and made his way to the edge of the water. It stank of chlorine and looked to him like a sink. A pair of lifeguards in a pair of towers blew police whistles at what seemed to be regular intervals and abused the swimmers through a public address system. Neddy remembered the sapphire water at the Bunkers' with longing and thought that he might contaminate himself—damage his own prosperousness and charm—by swimming in this murk, but he reminded himself that he was an explorer, a pilgrim, and that this was merely a stagnant bend in the Lucinda River. He dove, scowling with distaste, into the chlorine and had to swim with his head above water to avoid collisions, but even so he was bumped into, splashed, and jostled. When he got to the shallow end both lifeguards were shouting at him: "Hey, you, you without the identification disk, get outa the water." He did, but they had no way of pursuing him and he went through the reek of suntan oil and chlorine out through the hurricane fence and passed the handball courts. By crossing the road he entered the wooded part of the Halloran estate. The woods were not cleared and the footing was treacherous and difficult until he reached the lawn and the clipped beech hedge that encircled their pool.

The Hallorans were friends, an elderly couple of enormous wealth who seemed to bask in the suspicion that they might be Communists. They were zealous reformers but they were not Communists, and yet when they were accused, as they sometimes were, of subversion, it seemed to gratify and excite them. Their beech hedge was yellow and he guessed this had been blighted like the Levys' maple. He called hullo, hullo, to warn the Hallorans of his approach, to palliate his invasion of their privacy. The Hallorans, for reasons that had never been explained to him, did not wear bathing suits. No explanations were in order, really. Their nakedness was a detail in their uncompromising zeal for reform and he stepped politely out of his trunks before he went through the opening in the hedge.

Mrs. Halloran, a stout woman with white hair and a serene face, was reading the *Times*. Mr. Halloran was taking beech leaves out of the water with a scoop. They seemed not surprised or displeased to see him. Their pool was perhaps the oldest in the country, a fieldstone rectangle, fed by a brook. It had no filter or pump and its waters were the opaque gold of the stream.

"I'm swimming across the county," Ned said.

"Why, I didn't know one could," exclaimed Mrs. Halloran.

"Well, I've made it from the Westerhazys'," Ned said. "That must be about four miles."

He felt his trunks at the deep end, walked to the shallow end, and swam this stretch. As he was pulling himself out of the water he heard Mrs. Halloran say, "We've been *terribly* sorry to hear about all your misfortunes, Neddy."

"My misfortunes?" Ned asked. "I don't know what you mean."

"Why, we heard that you'd sold the house and that your poor children . . ."

"I don't recall having sold the house," Ned said, "and the girls are at home."

"Yes," Mrs. Halloran sighed. "Yes . . ." Her voice filled the air with an unseasonable melancholy and Ned spoke briskly. "Thank you for the swim."

"Well, have a nice trip," said Mrs. Halloran.

Beyond the hedge he pulled on his trunks and fastened them. They were loose and he wondered if, during the space of an afternoon, he could have lost some weight. He was cold and he was tired and the naked Hallorans and their dark water had depressed him. The swim was too much for his strength but how could he have guessed this, sliding down the banister that morning and sitting in the Westerhazys' sun? His arms were lame. His legs felt rubbery and ached at the joints. The worst of it was the cold in his bones and the feeling that he might never be warm again. Leaves were falling down around him and he smelled wood smoke on the wind. Who would be burning wood at this time of year?

He needed a drink. Whiskey would warm him, pick him up, carry him through the last of his journey, refresh his feeling that it was original and valorous to swim across the county. Channel swimmers took brandy. He needed a stimulant. He crossed the lawn in front of the Hallorans' house and went down a little path to where they had built a house for their only daughter, Helen, and her husband, Eric Sachs. The Sachses' pool was small and he found Helen and her husband there.

"Oh, *Neddy,*" Helen said. "Did you lunch at Mother's?"

"Not *really,*" Ned said. "I *did* stop to see your parents." This seemed to be explanation enough. "I'm terribly sorry to break in on you like this but I've taken a chill and I wonder if you'd give me a drink."

"Why, I'd *love* to," Helen said, "but there hasn't been anything in this house to drink since Eric's operation. That was three years ago."

Was he losing his memory, had his gift for concealing painful facts let him forget that he had sold his house, that his children were in trouble, and that his friend had been ill? His eyes slipped from Eric's face to his abdomen, where he saw three pale, sutured scars, two of them at least a foot long. Gone was his navel, and what, Neddy thought, would the roving hand, bed-checking one's gifts at 3 A.M., make of a belly with no navel, no link to birth, this breach in the succession?

"I'm sure you can get a drink at the Biswangers'," Helen said. "They're having an enormous do. You can hear it from here. Listen!"

She raised her head and from across the road, the lawns, the gardens, the woods, the fields, he heard again the brilliant noise of voices over water. "Well, I'll get wet," he said, still feeling that he had no freedom of choice about his means of travel. He dove into the Sachses' cold water and, gasping, close to drowning, made his way from one end of the pool to the other. "Lucinda and I want *terribly* to see you," he said over his shoulder, his face set toward the Biswangers'. "We're sorry it's been so long and we'll call you *very* soon."

He crossed some fields to the Biswangers' and the sounds of revelry there. They would be honored to give him a drink, they would be happy to give him a drink. The Biswangers invited him and Lucinda for dinner four times a year, six weeks in advance. They were always rebuffed and yet they continued to send out their invitations, unwilling to comprehend the rigid and undemocratic realities of their society. They were the sort of people who discussed the price of things at cocktails, exchanged market tips during dinner, and after dinner told dirty stories to mixed company. They did not belong to Neddy's set—they were not even on Lucinda's Christmas-card list. He went toward their pool with feelings of indifference, charity, and some unease, since it seemed to be getting dark and these were the longest days of the year. The party when he joined it was noisy and large. Grace Biswanger was the kind of hostess who asked the optometrist, the veterinarian, the real-estate dealer, and the dentist. No one was swimming and the twilight, reflected on the water of the pool, had a wintry gleam. There was a bar and he started for this. When Grace Biswanger saw him she came toward him, not affectionately as he had every right to expect, but bellicosely.

"Why, this party has everything," she said loudly, "including a gate crasher."

She could not deal him a social blow—there was no question about this and he did not flinch. "As a gate crasher," he asked politely, "do I rate a drink?"

"Suit yourself," she said. "You don't seem to pay much attention to invitations."

She turned her back on him and joined some guests, and he went to the bar and ordered a whiskey. The bartender served him but he served him rudely. His was a world in which the caterer's men kept the social score, and to be rebuffed by a part-time barkeep meant that he had suffered some loss of social esteem. Or perhaps the man was new and uninformed. Then he heard Grace at his back say: "They went for broke overnight—nothing but income—and he showed up drunk one Sunday and asked us to loan him five thousand dollars. . . ." She was always talking about money. It was worse than eating your peas off a knife. He dove into the pool, swam its length and went away.

The next pool on his list, the last but two, belonged to his old mistress, Shirley Adams. If he had suffered any injuries at the Biswangers' they would be cured here. Love—sexual roughhouse in fact—was the supreme elixir, the pain killer, the brightly colored pill that would put the spring back into his step, the joy of life in his heart. They had had an affair last week, last month, last year. He couldn't remember. It was he who had broken it off, his was the upper hand, and he stepped through the gate of the wall that surrounded her pool with nothing so considered as self-confidence. It seemed in a way to be his pool, as the lover, particularly the illicit lover, enjoys the possessions of his mistress with an authority unknown to holy matrimony. She was there, her hair the color of brass, but her figure, at the edge of the lighted, cerulean water, excited in him no profound memories. It had been, he thought, a lighthearted affair, although she had wept when he broke it off. She seemed confused to see him and he wondered if she was still wounded. Would she, God forbid, weep again?

"What do you want?" she asked.

"I'm swimming across the county."

"Good Christ. Will you ever grow up?"

"What's the matter?"

"If you've come here for money," she said, "I won't give you another cent."

"You could give me a drink."

"I could but I won't. I'm not alone."

"Well, I'm on my way."

He dove in and swam the pool, but when he tried to haul himself up onto the curb he found that the strength in his arms and shoulders had gone, and he paddled to the ladder and climbed out. Looking over his shoulder he saw, in the lighted bathhouse, a young man. Going out onto the dark lawn he smelled chrysanthemums or marigolds—some stubborn autumnal fragrance—on the night air, strong as gas. Looking overhead he saw that the stars had come out, but why should he seem to see Andromeda, Cepheus, and Cassiopeia? What had become of the constellations of midsummer? He began to cry.

It was probably the first time in his adult life that he had ever cried, certainly the first time in his life that he had ever felt so miserable, cold, tired, and bewildered. He could not understand the rudeness of the caterer's barkeep or the rudeness of a mistress who had come to him on her knees and showered his trousers with tears. He had swum too long, he had been immersed too long, and his nose and his throat were sore from the water. What he needed then was a drink, some company, and some clean, dry clothes, and while he could have cut directly across the road to his house he went on to the Gilmartins' pool. Here, for the first time in his life, he did not dive but went down the steps into the icy water and swam a hobbled sidestroke that he might have learned as a youth. He staggered with fatigue on his way to the Clydes' and paddled the length of their pool, stopping again and again with his hand on the curb to rest. He climbed up the ladder and wondered if he had the strength to get home. He had done what he wanted, he had swum the county, but he was so stupefied with exhaustion that his triumph seemed vague. Stooped, holding on to the gateposts for support, he turned up the driveway of his own house.

The place was dark. Was it so late that they had all gone to bed? Had Lucinda stayed at the Westerhazys' for supper? Had the girls joined her there or gone someplace else? Hadn't they agreed, as they usually did on Sunday, to regret all their inviations and stay at home? He tried the garage doors to see what cars were in but the doors were locked and rust came off the handles onto his hands. Going toward the house, he saw that the force of the thunderstorm had knocked one of the rain gutters loose. It hung down over the front door like an umbrella rib, but it could be fixed in the morning. The house was locked, and he thought that the stupid cook or the stupid maid must have locked the place up until he remembered that it had been some time since they had employed a maid or a cook. He shouted, pounded on the door, tried to force it with his shoulder, and then, looking in at the windows, saw that the place was empty.

# POETRY

# 1 *Reading Poetry*

Poetry may well be the oldest of all literary forms. Certainly, a great deal of the oldest literature of which we have written records is in verse. Yet today poetry is often regarded as the most sophisticated or difficult of literary forms. What has happened to cause the change? Why should something that seems so difficult to us today have seemed so natural to our ancestors? There are, I suspect, two answers to these questions. The first deals with music; the second with memory.

Poetry is musical, or at least rhythmic, speech. It is also usually a harmonious speech, employing words whose sounds echo each other or blend well. It may even be set to music, to be chanted or sung rather than simply spoken.

Because of its musical nature, poetry is easily remembered. Everyone knows how much easier it is to memorize the words to a song than to memorize even a few paragraphs from a newspaper or textbook. Poetry can thus serve as an aid to memory. If you must remember something, and have no written notes to help you, you can make a song of what you need to remember, and your chances of keeping it in your head will improve.

In almost any society, the desire to keep records, remember events, or tell stories precedes the invention of writing. Poetry, being pleasant and memorable, is then the natural first form for histories and tales. Once the art of writing develops, however, poetry is no longer essential. But it is still pleasing and has by now a tradition of use behind it. Prose takes over for record keeping and for transmitting technical information, but poetry keeps its hold on certain important affairs. Songs are still written to celebrate victories and loves, to mourn deaths, and to worship.

The printing of books, which gave so many people access to written words, has been one factor in the promotion of prose in our society. The invention of radio and television—whose announcers universally speak in the blandest, least musical cadences possible—has been another factor. After the age of nursery rhymes, most of us live in a world where the cadences of poetry are no longer part of our everyday life. Moreover, we live in a society where so many written and spoken words bombard us that we learn to skim through them quickly for whatever information they carry. We take no time to look for the beauty of words or for rhythm—neither of which is very likely to be there anyway.

Poetry, however, cannot be read rapidly. Newspapers can be, and, in fact, are meant to be. Fiction can be. And, again, some of it is meant for the quick, careless reader, though most good fiction improves with slow, thoughtful reading. Drama, in general, must be read more slowly, if we are to catch the sound of the individual speeches. But poetry must be read most slowly of all. It requires not only that we read it silently at the same pace that we would read it aloud, but also that we pause after we read it, to think about it for a few moments at least, to savor the mood the poem has created before we go on to something else.

It is no wonder, then, that poetry sometimes seems strange or difficult. Almost every other influence in our environment is telling us, "Hurry up! Grab the central fact or idea I'm selling and run!" Poetry is saying, "Slow down! Enjoy the music; let yourself become part of the emotion. I have many suggestions to make. Take time to let them unfold for you." In today's rush of prepackaged ideas, the stubborn individualism and refusal to be hurried that poetry represents are indeed unusual.

But anything that lets us think for ourselves, that offers us a chance to find our own feelings, ideas, and emotions, is worth pursuing. And poetry certainly encourages this kind of thinking and reflection. Moreover, once we agree to slow down enough to savor a poem completely, we discover that poetry is very similar to the literature we've been enjoying all along. Like fiction and drama, poetry tells us of people, of what it means to them and to us to be human. And, like the other forms of literature, it relays this information through the sound of human voices.

So closely related are poetry, fiction, and drama, in fact, that it is sometimes hard to tell which is which. Some poetic dramas seem better suited for reading than for performance. Should they be classed as poetry or as plays? Similarly, there are narratives that tell a complete story in verse. Should they be considered fiction as well as poetry? Or shall we simply ignore the classifications and enjoy each work for what we like best in it, whether that be a supposedly "poetic" quality, such as rhythm, or a supposedly "fictional" or "dramatic" one, such as plot, characterization, or dramatic irony?

We must, then, read poetry with the same close attention we give to all our readings in this course. Poetry, too, demands these basic questions:

1. Who is speaking?
2. What kind of person is he or she? In what mood? Thinking what thoughts? Feeling what emotions?
3. Of whom or what is he or she speaking?
4. How is this person or object being described?
5. What attitudes are being projected?
6. Are we led to share the attitudes and emotions in sympathy, or to rebel against them with feelings of anger or irony?

But, since poetry is both the most structured and the most subjective of literary forms, we may also ask questions about its forms and its sounds, to learn how they contribute to the poem's effect on us. In doing this, we may get some sense of what qualities we want to consider poetic.

Because poetry is a genre of great variety, it cannot be easily defined. Only by reading a variety of poems can we create our knowledge of poetry, enhance our enjoyment of it, and gain a sense of what it has to offer us.

Let us begin, therefore, by reading some traditional ballads. Ballads are tales told in song. Traditional ballads (or folk ballads) are songs that have been passed from one singer to another, not by having been written down but by having been sung, heard, and resung.* Ballads are thus very like folk tales in their mode of creation and in their sense of the audience. So we may expect that the voices within the ballads will be like the voices of those archetypal storytellers we first met when reading fiction. And yet ballads are sung. Their creators are singers, not speakers. How, then, will these tales sung in verse differ from tales told in prose? How will their stories be told? What will we hear that we have not heard before?

Read the ballads, and then decide what you think are the characteristics of ballads and how you think they differ from tales told in prose. To clarify your thinking, you may want to consider how the tales sung by these ballads would be told if they were written as stories, or how some story would be changed if it were turned into a ballad. You might even try your hand at writing a ballad yourself.

---

* This oral tradition accounts for the number of variations ballads possess. A singer may repeat a ballad just as he or she first heard it; or he or she may change the ballad slightly, either on purpose or accidentally. A third singer then learns this new version, and either preserves or changes it. Thus a ballad of any great age may exist in many versions, each being sung by a different group of singers.

ANONYMOUS

**Get Up and Bar the Door**

It fell about the Martinmas[1] time,
And a gay time it was then,
When our good wife got puddings[2] to make,
And she's boild them in the pan.

5 The wind sae cauld blew south and north,
And blew into the floor;
Quoth our goodman to our goodwife,
"Gae out and bar the door."

"My hands is in my hussyfskap,[3]
10 Goodman, as ye may see;
An it shoud nae be barrd this hundred year,
It's no be barrd for me."

They made a paction tween them twa,
They made it firm and sure,
15 That the first word whaeer shoud speak,
Shoud rise and bar the door.

Then by there came two gentlemen,
At twelve oclock at night,
And they could neither see house nor hall,
20 Nor coal nor candle-light.

"Now whether is this a rich man's house,
Or whether is it a poor?"
But neer a word wad ane o them speak,
For barring of the door.

25 And first they ate the white puddings,
And then they ate the black;
Tho muckle[4] thought the goodwife to hersel,
Yet neer a word she spake.

Then said the one unto the other,
30 "Here, man, tak ye my knife;

---

[1] November 11.
[2] Sausages.
[3] Household chores.
[4] Much.

Do ye tak aff the auld man's beard,
  And I'll kiss the goodwife."

"But there's nae water in the house,
  And what shall we do than?"
35 "What ails ye at the pudding-broo,
  That boils into the pan?"

O up then started our goodman,
  An angry man was he:
"Will ye kiss my wife before my een,
40  And scad me wi pudding-bree?"

Then up and started our goodwife,
  Gied three skips on the floor:
"Goodman, you've spoken the foremost word,
  Get up and bar the door."

## Lord Randal

"O where ha you been, Lord Randal, my son?
And where ha you been, my handsome young man?"
"I ha been at the greenwood; mother, mak my bed soon,
For I'm wearied wi hunting, and fain wad lie down."

5 "An wha met ye there, Lord Randal, my son?
An wha met you there, my handsome young man?"
"O I met wi my true-love; mother, mak my bed soon,
For I'm wearied wi hunting, and fain wad lie down."

"And what did she give you, Lord Randal, my son?
10 And what did she give you, my handsome young man?"
"Eels fried in a pan; mother, mak my bed soon,
For I'm wearied wi huntin, and fain wad lie down."

"And wha gat your leavins, Lord Randal, my son?
And wha gat your leavins, my handsome young man?"
15 "My hawks and my hounds; mother, mak my bed soon,
For I'm wearied wi hunting, and fain wad lie down."

"And what becam of them, Lord Randal, my son?
And what becam of them, my handsome young man?"
"They stretched their legs out and died; mother, mak my bed soon,
20 For I'm wearied wi huntin, and fain wad lie down."

"O I fear you are poisoned, Lord Randal, my son!
I fear you are poisoned, my handsome young man!"
"O yes, I am poisoned: mother, mak my bed soon,
For I'm sick at the heart, and I fain wad lie down."

25 "What d'ye leave to your mother, Lord Randal, my son?
What d'ye leave to your mother, my handsome young man?"
"Four and twenty milk kye;[1] mother, mak my bed soon,
For I'm sick at the heart, and I fain wad lie down."

"What d'ye leave to your sister, Lord Randal, my son?
30 What d'ye leave to your sister, my handsome young man?"
"My gold and my silver; mother, mak my bed soon,
For I'm sick at the heart, an I fain wad lie down."

"What d'ye leave to your brother, Lord Randal, my son?
What d'ye leave to your brother, my handsome young man?"
35 "My houses and my lands; mother, mak my bed soon,
For I'm sick at the heart, and I fain wad lie down."

"What d'ye leave to your true-love, Lord Randal, my son?
What d'ye leave to your true-love, my handsome young man?"
"I leave her hell and fire; mother, mak my bed soon,
40 For I'm sick at the heart, and I fain wad lie down."

## Sir Patrick Spens

The king sits in Dumferling town,
  Drinking the blude-reid wine:
"O whar will I get guid sailor,
  To sail this ship of mine?"

5 Up and spak an eldern knicht,
  Sat at the king's richt knee:
"Sir Patrick Spens is the best sailor
  That sails upon the sea."

The king has written a braid letter
10 And signed it wi' his hand,
And sent it to Sir Patrick Spens,
  Was walking on the sand.

---

[1] Kine = cows.

The first line that Sir Patrick read,
A loud lauch[1] lauched he;
15 The next line that Sir Patrick read,
The tear blinded his ee.[2]

"O wha is this has done this deed,
This ill deed done to me,
To send me out this time o' the year,
20 To sail upon the sea?

"Mak haste, mak haste, my mirry men all,
Our guid ship sails the morn."
"O say na sae, my master dear,
For I fear a deadly storm.

25 "Late, late yestre'en I saw the new moon
Wi' the auld moon in hir arm,
And I fear, I fear, my dear master,
That we will come to harm."

O our Scots nobles were richt laith[3]
30 To weet[4] their cork-heeled shoon,[5]
But lang or[6] a' the play were played
Their hats they swam aboon.[7]

O lang, lang may their ladies sit,
Wi' their fans into their hand,
35 Or ere they see Sir Patrick Spens
Come sailing to the land.

O lang, lang may the ladies stand
Wi' their gold kems[8] in their hair,
Waiting for their ain dear lords,
40 For they'll see them na mair.

---

[1] Laugh.
[2] Eye.
[3] Loath.
[4] Wet.
[5] Shoes.
[6] Before.
[7] Above.
[8] Combs.

Half o'er, half o'er to Aberdour[9]
It's fifty fadom[10] deep,
And there lies guid Sir Patrick Spens
Wi' the Scots lords at his feet.

## The Cherry-Tree Carol

Joseph was an old man,
and an old man was he,
When he wedded Mary,
in the land of Galilee.

5 Joseph and Mary walked
through an orchard good,
Where was cherries and berries,
so red as any blood.

Joseph and Mary walked
10 through an orchard green,
Where was berries and cherries,
as thick as might be seen.

O then bespoke Mary,
so meek and so mild:
15 "Pluck me one cherry, Joseph,
for I am with child."

O then bespoke Joseph:
with words most unkind:
"Let him pluck thee a cherry
20 that brought thee with child."

O then bespoke the babe,
within his mother's womb:
"Bow down then the tallest tree,
for my mother to have some."

25 Then bowed down the highest tree
unto his mother's hand;
Then she cried, "See, Joseph,
I have cherries at command."

---

[9] Halfway back to Aberdour, on the Firth of Forth.
[10] Fathoms.

O then bespoke Joseph:
30 "I have done Mary wrong;
But cheer up, my dearest,
and be not cast down."

Then Mary plucked a cherry,
as red as the blood,
35 Then Mary went home
with her heavy load.

Then Mary took her babe,
and sat him on her knee,
Saying, "My dear son, tell me
40 what this world will be."

"O I shall be as dead, mother,
as the stones in the wall;
O the stones in the streets, mother,
shall mourn for me all.

45 "Upon Easter-day, mother,
my uprising shall be;
O the sun and the moon, mother,
shall both rise with me."

DUDLEY RANDALL (1914– )

## Ballad of Birmingham

*(On the bombing of a church in Birmingham, Alabama, 1963)*

"Mother dear, may I go downtown
Instead of out to play,
And march the streets of Birmingham
In a Freedom March today?"

5 "No, baby, no, you may not go,
For the dogs are fierce and wild,
And clubs and hoses, guns and jails
Aren't good for a little child."

"But, mother, I won't be alone,
10 Other children will go with me,
And march the streets of Birmingham
To make our country free."

"No, baby, no, you may not go,
For I fear those guns will fire.
15 But you may go to church instead
And sing in the children's choir."

She has combed and brushed her night-dark hair.
And bathed rose petal sweet,
And drawn white gloves on her small brown hands,
20 And white shoes on her feet.

The mother smiled to know her child
Was in the sacred place,
But that smile was the last smile
To come upon her face.

25 For when she heard the explosion,
Her eyes grew wet and wild.
She raced through the streets of Birmingham
Calling for her child.

She clawed through bits of glass and brick,
30 Then lifted out a shoe.
"O, here's the shoe my baby wore,
But, baby, where are you?"

QUESTIONS

Although "Ballad of Birmingham" was written by a twentieth-century poet, both its form and its content qualify it as a true ballad in the folk tradition. Discuss the various elements in the poem that make this so. What special power or perspective does Randall give to his telling of this historical incident by putting it in ballad form?

# ELEMENTS OF POETRY

# 2 *Repetition and Rhythm*

Two elements prominent in ballads are **repetition** and **rhythm.** Sometimes single words or phrases are repeated for emphasis, as in "Lord Randal": "O where ha you been. . . . And where ha you been." Sometimes one or more lines appear in every verse as a refrain: "Mother, mak my bed soon,/For I'm wearied wi hunting, and fain wad lie down." In each case, the repetition emphasizes both the content and the rhythm of the ballad, calling our attention to the meter (that is, to the rhythmic pattern of each line) or to the grouping of lines into stanzas.

Of the three ballads printed in the previous chapter, "Lord Randal" is easily the most repetitive. In fact, it is built on a technique known as **incremental repetition.** At least half of each line is repeated from stanza to stanza, and the pattern of question and answer never varies. Yet the changes that occur reveal and develop the dying lord's story.

Repetition is important not only in ballads, but in lyric poetry in general. It is most pronounced in songs, as in the next example. But it appears frequently (and often quite subtly) in spoken lyrics as well. Let us look at some poems in which repetition plays an important role, and let us see what effects are being gained by it.

## WILLIAM SHAKESPEARE (1564–1616)

### It Was a Lover and His Lass

It was a lover and his lass,
With a hey, and a ho, and hey nonino,
That o'er the green corn-field did pass
In the spring time, the only pretty ring time,
5 When birds do sing, hey ding a ding, ding:
Sweet lovers love the spring.

Between the acres of the rye,
With a hey, and a ho, and a hey nonino,
These pretty country folk would lie,
10 In the spring time, the only pretty ring time,
When birds do sing, hey ding a ding, ding:
Sweet lovers love the spring.

This carol they began that hour,
With a hey, and a ho, and a hey nonino,
15 How that a life was but a flower
In the spring time, the only pretty ring time,
When birds do sing, hey ding a ding, ding:
Sweet lovers love the spring.

And therefore take the present time,
20 With a hey, and a ho, and a hey nonino,
For love is crownèd with the prime
In the spring time, the only pretty ring time,
When birds do sing, hey ding a ding, ding:
Sweet lovers love the spring.

QUESTIONS

1. How would you characterize this song? What is its mood?
2. How does the refrain help set the mood of the song?
3. What other repetitions of sounds do you find in the poem? What do they contribute? (Note: Two important categories here are **rhyme**—the use of words that end with the same sound, like **rye** and **lie**—and **alliteration,** the use of words that begin with the same sound, like **lover** and **lass; hey, ho,** and **hey.**)
4. Discuss the progression of thought and feeling from the first stanza to the final one. What sense of completeness does the progression impart to Shakespeare's song?

THOMAS HARDY (1840–1928)

**The Ruined Maid**

"O 'Melia, my dear, this does everything crown!
Who could have supposed I should meet you in Town?
And whence such fair garments, such prosperi-ty?"—
"O didn't you know I'd been ruined?" said she.

5 —"You left us in tatters, without shoes or socks,
Tired of digging potatoes, and spudding up docks;[1]
And now you've gay bracelets and bright feathers three!"—
"Yes: that's how we dress when we're ruined," said she.

—"At home in the barton[2] you said 'thee' and 'thou,'
10 And 'thik oon,' and 'theäs oon,' and 't'other'; but now
Your talking quite fits 'ee for high compa-ny!"—
"Some polish is gained with one's ruin," said she.

—"Your hands were like paws then, your face blue and bleak
But now I'm bewitched by your delicate cheek,
15 And your little gloves fit as on any la-dy!"—
"We never do work when we're ruined," said she.

—"You used to call home-life a hag-ridden dream,
And you'd sigh, and you'd sock; but at present you seem
To know not of megrims[3] or melancho-ly!"—
20 "True. One's pretty lively when ruined," said she.

—"I wish I had feathers, a fine sweeping gown,
And a delicate face, and could strut about Town!"—
"My dear—a raw country girl, such as you be,
Cannot quite expect that. You ain't ruined," said she.

QUESTIONS

1. How does Hardy use question and answer to characterize the two women?
2. What balance exists here between the two sides of the dialogue? What is the effect of the repetitions in the final line of each stanza?
3. What sort of tone or consciousness would you expect to find in a poem about a "ruined maid" that is absent from this poem? What effect does this have on the tone of the poem and on the characterization of the speakers? On the poet's apparent attitude toward them?

[1] Digging up weeds.
[2] Farmyard.
[3] Low spirits.

## WILLIAM BLAKE (1757–1827)

### *From* Songs of Innocence

### The Lamb

Little Lamb, who made thee?
Dost thou know who made thee?
Gave thee life & bid thee feed,
By the stream & o'er the mead;
5 Gave thee clothing of delight,
Softest clothing wooly bright;
Gave thee such a tender voice,
Making all the vales rejoice!
Little Lamb who made thee?
10 Dost thou know who made thee?

Little Lamb I'll tell thee,
Little Lamb I'll tell thee!
He is callèd by thy name,
For he calls himself a Lamb:
15 He is meek & he is mild,
He became a little child:
I a child & thou a lamb,
We are callèd by his name.
Little Lamb God bless thee.
20 Little Lamb God bless thee.

### *From* Songs of Experience

### The Tyger

Tyger! Tyger! burning bright
In the forests of the night,
What immortal hand or eye
Could frame thy fearful symmetry?

5 In what distant deeps or skies
Burnt the fire of thine eyes?
On what wings dare he aspire?
What the hand, dare seize the fire?

And what shoulder, & what art,
10 Could twist the sinews of thy heart?
And when thy heart began to beat,
What dread hand? & what dread feet?

What the hammer? what the chain?
In what furnace was thy brain?
15 What the anvil? what dread grasp
Dare its deadly terrors clasp?

When the stars threw down their spears,
And water'd heaven with their tears,
Did he smile his work to see?
20 Did he who made the Lamb make thee?

Tyger! Tyger! burning bright
In the forests of the night,
What immortal hand or eye
Dare frame thy fearful symmetry?

QUESTIONS

If you were to write an essay on "The Lamb" and "The Tyger," you might start with the following question:

1. Both "The Lamb" and "The Tyger" are essentially religious poems. Yet they seem to describe two different aspects of religious feeling. How would you characterize each aspect? How does the first fit the conception of "innocence," the second of "experience"? How are the animals, and the feelings they represent, characterized within the poem?

To develop the answer, you could then look at the following aspects of each poem:

2. "The Lamb" and "The Tyger" have almost the same rhythm, being based on a seven-syllable line with the odd-numbered syllables accented: Ty-ger! Ty-ger! burn-ing bright. But "The Lamb" varies this meter in places, while "The Tyger" holds to it firmly throughout. Look at the rhythm and repetitions carefully in each poem, and then explain how they reinforce each other. Why is the effect so different for each poem?
3. "The Lamb" and "The Tyger" both make use of repeated questions. How does their use in "The Lamb" differ from their use in "The Tyger"? How do these differences help create the contrasting tones of the two poems?
4. What images are connected with the lamb? With the tiger? How are they related? How contrasted?
5. What attitude does the speaker seem to have toward each animal? With what evidence would you support your answer to this question?

The next two poems show what can happen to the ballad form in the hands of highly sophisticated poets who are concerned less with relating incidents than with conveying emotion and demonstrating the various effects that can be gained by a concentration on the sounds and rhythms of words. We may note that these poems provide freer and more self-consciously artistic variations on balladic themes than do any we have previously read. In contrast to folk ballads or to modern ballads that adhere closely to the folk tradition, such as Randall's "Ballad of Birmingham," these freer adaptations of the ballad form are known as **literary ballads.** We will read one nineteenth-century and one twentieth-century example.

EDGAR ALLAN POE (1809–1849)

**Annabel Lee**

It was many and many a year ago,
In a kingdom by the sea,
That a maiden there lived whom you may know
By the name of Annabel Lee;—
5 And this maiden she lived with no other thought
Than to love and be loved by me.

*She* was a child and *I* was a child,
In this kingdom by the sea,
But we loved with a love that was more than love—
10 I and my Annabel Lee—
With a love that the wingèd seraphs of Heaven
Coveted her and me.

And this was the reason that, long ago,
In this kingdom by the sea,
15 A wind blew out of a cloud by night
Chilling my Annabel Lee;
So that her highborn kinsmen came
And bore her away from me,
To shut her up in a sepulchre
20 In this kingdom by the sea.

The angels, not half so happy in Heaven,
Went envying her and me—
Yes!—that was the reason (as all men know,
In this kingdom by the sea)
25 That the wind came out of the cloud chilling
And killing my Annabel Lee.

But our love it was stronger by far than the love
Of those who were older than we—
Of many far wiser than we—

30 And neither the angels in Heaven above,
Nor the demons down under the sea,
Can ever dissever my soul from the soul
Of the beautiful Annabel Lee:—

For the moon never beams without bringing me dreams
35 Of the beautiful Annabel Lee;
And the stars never rise but I see the bright eyes
Of the beautiful Annabel Lee;
And so, all the night-tide, I lie down by the side
Of my darling, my darling, my life and my bride,
40 In her sepulchre there by the sea—
In her tomb by the side of the sea.

QUESTIONS

1. What elements in "Annabel Lee" come from the ballad tradition? What elements have been added or altered? In developing your answer, consider the basic use of rhythm and rhyme, repetition, refrain, alliteration, vocabulary, and so on.
2. Consider the story told by the poem, and the emotions it evokes. Is the story one that fits well into the ballad form? Again, what elements harmonize well with the ballad tradition? Which suggest a more sophisticated speaker and audience?

E. E. CUMMINGS (1894–1963)

## All in green went my love riding

All in green went my love riding
on a great horse of gold
into the silver dawn.

four lean hounds crouched low and smiling
5 the merry deer ran before.

Fleeter be they than dappled dreams
the swift sweet deer
the red rare deer.

Four red roebuck[1] at a white water
10 the cruel bugle sang before.

[1] Male roe deer.

Horn at hip went my love riding
riding the echo down
into the silver dawn.

four lean hounds crouched low and smiling
15 the level meadows ran before.

Softer be they than slippered sleep
the lean lithe deer
the fleet flown deer.

Four fleet does at a gold valley
20 the famished arrow sang before.

Bow at belt went my love riding
riding the mountain down
into the silver dawn.

four lean hounds crouched low and smiling
25 the sheer peaks ran before.

Paler be they than daunting death
the sleek slim deer
the tall tense deer.

Four tall stags at a green mountain
30 the lucky hunter sang before.

All in green went my love riding
on a great horse of gold
into the silver dawn.

four lean hounds crouched low and smiling
35 my heart fell dead before.

QUESTIONS

1. Incremental repetition is used in this modern poem for an almost balladlike effect. But how would you describe the way stanzas are linked in this poem?
2. What effects would you say the poem achieves? How would you distinguish between its effects and those of traditional ballads?

# 3 *Compression and Verse Forms*

To write a short story based on the tale told in "Lord Randal" or "Get Up and Bar the Door" would require at least one thousand words. (That would be roughly the length of "If Not Higher"—quite a short story, as stories go.) These two ballads, however, have less than five hundred words each, including refrains and repetitions. And even though the ballads are much shorter than a very short story, they seem long and loosely constructed when they are compared with such tightly written lyrics as "The Tyger."

Verse, then, is a highly compressed form. Eliminating inessentials—the name of Lord Randal's sweetheart, the reason she killed him—it takes us directly to the heart of a situation, to the one or two moments most highly charged with emotion. In the case of "Lord Randal," this technique reduces the ballad to a single moment, that in which mother and son discover that the son has been poisoned. In the case of "Get Up and Bar the Door," it produces a ballad centering on two episodes: the one that begins the quarrel and the one that ends it.

Time becomes flexible in these ballads, as one memorable moment is juxtaposed with the next, ignoring all that may have gone between: "Then by there came two gentlemen,/At twelve oclock at night." We can imagine that the lateness of the hour would have made the silent house seem even stranger than it was to the "gentlemen," and we may also suspect that quite a few hours must have passed since the feuding couple made their pact. But all the singer gives us is the crucial hour—"twelve"—and the number of intruders. The time between incidents is not important. The conflict between the couple is.

Similarly, "The Cherry-Tree Carol" moves with almost no consciousness of elapsed time from the wedding of Joseph and Mary to the scene in the orchard to a final scene between Mary and her infant son. In each case, a simple "then" defines the sequence, whether the incidents follow each other instantly, as in "then bespoke the babe," "then bowed down the highest tree," and "O then bespoke Joseph," or whether a gap of several months is indicated: "Then Mary took her babe." The passage of time, which affects everyone, is of no concern to the singer. The unique situation of parents confronted with their child's divinity engrosses all the attention, linking together the unusual circumstances of Joseph's marriage, the miracle in the orchard, and Christ's prophecy of his death and resurrection. "The Cherry-Tree Carol" assumes that its hearers are all familiar with the story of Christ's birth and death; it therefore feels free to concentrate on those aspects of the legend that bear on its central theme, leaving us to place them in chronological time if we wish.

Every literary form is somewhat selective in its choice of times and episodes, and in the amount of attention it gives to each. "If Not Higher," for example, tells its tale of a conflict between two types of religion by focusing on two men and spending half of its narration following the two through a single hour of a morning. Similarly, *Oedipus Rex*'s tale of the fall of a king (which you will find in the drama section of this anthology) focuses on the last day of his reign, a day of crisis and steadily mounting emotion. But neither drama nor fiction can match the intense selectivity, the rigorous paring-down, of poetry.

Poetic form demands **compression.** A line of eight or ten syllables, a stanza of two, four, or six lines will not allow any wasted words. The poet must pare away all the needless background and inessential details in order to fit the essential ones into those brief stanzas.

Yet this strictness of form also helps the hearer to accept the compression it produces. We would not accept so few details as "Lord Randal" gives us in a prose account of his death. Nor could the information given in "The Lamb" or "The Tyger" stand alone as prose. Ballad and lyric alike need the cadence of their verse—the rhyme, the rhythm, the rounded-off pattern formed by the stanzas—to give our ear and mind the sense of completeness and satisfaction that allows us to enjoy the brief, tightly focused statements their poetry makes.

Compression, then, is another technique that allows the material presented and the form of its presentation to reinforce each other, providing for the reader not only a satisfying unity, but also one that seems notably poetic. Let us now examine that technique in action by looking at a few types of poetry that have compression as their most notable feature, beginning with the oldest of these forms, the **epigram.**

Epigrams may be serious or humorous, flattering or insulting. But they are usually descriptive of a person, animal, or object; and they are invariably brief. Probably the most popular type today is the **satiric epigram,** a form that can be described as a description with a sting. Here is an example:

COUNTEE CULLEN (1903–1946)

**For a Lady I Know**

She even thinks that up in heaven
Her class lies late and snores,
While poor black cherubs rise at seven
To do celestial chores.

QUESTIONS

1. What single fact do the four lines of this poem tell us about the "Lady" who is their subject?
2. What further facts do they suggest about her?
3. How do words like *her class* and *poor black cherubs* characterize the lady and the attitudes that the poet suggests she holds?
4. What do words like *snores* and *celestial chores* do for the poem? What do they suggest about the poet's attitude?

Not all brief poems with a punch are epigrams, however. The following poem has a sting of its own and is as highly compressed in technique as any poem you will see. Yet its structure is not that of the epigram. How would you define it?

GWENDOLYN BROOKS (1915–     )

**We Real Cool**

*The Pool Players.*
*Seven at the Golden Shovel.*

We real cool. We
Left school. We

5 Lurk late. We
Strike straight. We

Sing sin. We
Thin gin. We

Jazz June. We
10 Die soon.

QUESTIONS

1. What does the subtitle tell us about the speakers of the poem?
2. How do the speakers characterize themselves?
3. Discuss the use of repetition in the poem.
4. Note also the breaks in the pattern. Why has Brooks placed the word *We* at the end of each line rather than letting it come at the beginning as it does in the first line? Is the word *We* stressed more heavily, less heavily, or just as heavily at the end of the line as it would be at the beginning? What happens to the verbs? Does placing them at the beginning of the line give them any extra stress? What happens to the length of the last line? What effect does it produce?
5. What does Brooks seem to be saying in this poem about the "Seven" or about people like them? How does the form of her poem express or emphasize her feelings?

In contrast with these two very brief poems, here is a slightly longer poem. Like the other two, it is thought-provoking. But while Cullen's and Brooks's speakers merely make their statements, leaving us to gather the implications for ourselves, the next speaker argues with us quite directly.

WILLIAM WORDSWORTH (1770–1850)

**The World Is Too Much with Us**

The world is too much with us; late and soon,
Getting and spending, we lay waste our powers:
Little we see in Nature that is ours;
We have given our hearts away, a sordid boon!
5 This Sea that bares her bosom to the moon;
The winds that will be howling at all hours,
And are up-gathered now like sleeping flowers;
For this, for everything, we are out of tune;
It moves us not.—Great God! I'd rather be
10 A Pagan suckled in a creed outworn;
So might I, standing on this pleasant lea,

Have glimpses that would make me less forlorn;
Have sight of Proteus rising from the sea;
Or hear old Triton blow his wreathèd horn.[1]

QUESTIONS

1. What is the argument of this poem?
2. How does Wordsworth's invocation of Triton and Proteus fit in with the argument of the poem?
3. What words or images in the poem do you find most striking? How do they support the poem's argument?
4. Note the poem's movement from "us" and "we" in the first lines to "I" at the end. At what line does the change take place? How is it marked or signaled? What changes of tone of voice and of mood go with it? What change of imagery?
5. What qualities in the poem make it suitable as a study in compression? Alternatively, if you disagree with this classification, why do you challenge the poem's placement in this chapter?

Another extremely brief form, which was introduced to English and American poetry in the twentieth century, is the **imagist** poem. Imagist poetry grew out of an interest in Oriental poetry, especially in the brief, seventeen-syllable form known as **haiku.** (The poems by Pound that follow are sometimes called haiku.) As the word *imagist* implies, this poetry focuses on a single sensory image—a sight, sound, or feeling—and presents it in as brief and vivid a form as the writer can manage. Read the following four poems, and then ask what image each poem starts from and what further images it uses to reinforce the first one. How are the images combined? How would you contrast the form and effect of these poems with the form and effect of the epigrams you have just read, or with the effect and form of Blake's lyrics?

EZRA POUND (1885–1972) - most well known imagist

**In a Station of the Metro**

The apparition of these faces in the crowd;
Petals on a wet, black bough.

---

[1] In Greek mythology Proteus was a prophetic sea god who, when seized, changed shape to try to escape prophesying. Triton, the son of the sea god Poseidon, played a trumpet made of a conch shell.

## AMY LOWELL (1874–1925)

### Wind and Silver

Greatly shining,
The Autumn moon floats in the thin sky;
And the fish-ponds shake their backs and flash their
dragon scales
As she passes over them.

## DENISE LEVERTOV (1923– )

### Six Variations (part iii)

Shlup, shlup, the dog
as it laps up
water
makes intelligent
5 music, resting
now and then to take breath in irregular
measure.

## H. D. (HILDA DOOLITTLE) (1886–1961)

### Heat

O wind, rend open the heat,
cut apart the heat,
rend it to tatters.

Fruit cannot drop
5 through this thick air—
fruit cannot fall into heat
that presses up and blunts
the points of pears
and rounds the grapes.

10 Cut the heat—
plough through it,
turning it on either side
of your path.

Here is one more poem by Pound, who was one of the founders of imagist poetry. What does this poem do with imagist techniques? How does it differ from the preceding poems?

### L'Art 1910

Green arsenic smeared on an egg-white cloth,
Crushed strawberries! Come, let us feast our eyes.

A slightly longer descriptive poem is William Carlos Williams's "The Dance," in which the crowding of as many words and images as possible into eight lines is in contrast with the spareness of imagist poetry. The form seems almost too limited for the magnitude of the sounds and motions "The Dance" attempts to contain.

## WILLIAM CARLOS WILLIAMS (1883–1963)

### The Dance

In Breughel's[1] great picture, The Kermess,[2]
the dancers go round, they go round and
around, the squeal and the blare and the
tweedle of bagpipes, a bugle and fiddles
5 tipping their bellies (round as the thick-
sided glasses whose wash they impound)
their hips and their bellies off balance
to turn them. Kicking and rolling about
the Fair Grounds, swinging their butts, those
10 shanks must be sound to bear up under such
rollicking measures, prance as they dance
in Breughel's picture, The Kermess.

QUESTIONS

1. Although you might expect a poem describing a painting to concentrate on color or form, Williams's poem concentrates at least as heavily on motion and sound. What words or phrases describe the sounds of the scene? Which describe shapes or forms? Which describe motion? What sorts of music and dancers does Williams seem to be portraying with these terms?
2. How do the poem's rhythm and shape support the sense of sound and motion? Note particularly the large number of heavily stressed monosyllables. What effect do they provide? How have sentence structure and grammar been reshaped to contribute to the sensation of noise and speed?
3. Note the plays on words within the poem: "bellies" for both fiddles and dancers, legs called "sound" in a poem much concerned with musical

[1] Peter Breughel, or Brueghel (1525?–1569), a Flemish painter.
[2] A kermess is a carnival or fair.

sounds. How does such wordplay help unify the scene? Note also the use of repetition: how does it help shape the poem?

4. If you are able to find a print of *The Kermess,* decide how well you think Williams has caught the spirit of the painting. What aspects of the poem stand out for you as being particularly apt?

Finally, we should look at some poems by Emily Dickinson. No study of compression in poetry would be complete without a consideration of the work of this American poet, who was far ahead of her time in the concentration and spareness of her verse. Description and argument blend in Dickinson's poetry into a remarkable unity of vision and idea. Notice, in the following two poems, how images of light and motion bridge the gap between the physical and spiritual worlds and between our own physical and spiritual responses to these worlds.

EMILY DICKINSON (1830–1886)

**There's a Certain Slant of Light (#258)**

There's a certain Slant of light,
Winter Afternoons—
That oppresses, like the Heft
Of Cathedral Tunes—

5 Heavenly Hurt, it gives us—
We can find no scar,
But internal difference,
Where the Meanings, are—

None may teach it—Any—
10 'Tis the Seal Despair—
An imperial affliction
Sent us of the Air—

When it comes, the Landscape listens—
Shadows—hold their breath—
15 When it goes, 'tis like the Distance
On the look of Death—

**Tell All the Truth but Tell It Slant (#1129)**

Tell all the Truth but tell it slant—
Success in Circuit lies

Too bright for our infirm Delight
The Truth's superb surprise
5 As Lightning to the Children eased
With explanation kind
The Truth must dazzle gradually
Or every man be blind—

## QUESTIONS

1. Give examples of images of light and motion in these poems. How are the two types of images connected?
2. Give examples of lines or phrases that you think are particularly good examples of compression. How is Dickinson creating this effect? For what purpose is she using it?
3. What does being human seem to mean in these poems? What aspects of our nature are being emphasized? (Note that we as readers are definitely included in these descriptions of what being human entails. How are we brought into them?)

# 4 *Word Choice: Meanings and Suggestions*

## Common Phrases and New Meanings

Our study of ballads gave us insight into the use of repetition and selectivity in poetry, and thus into poetry's balance of narrative and rhythmic patterns. We saw that poetry is based on the combination of satisfying sounds and sharply focused content. And we saw how the pattern of sounds and words created by the skillful use of rhythm, repetition, and word-sound can be used to heighten the effect of compression or to set a mood.

But ballads could not tell us a great deal about word choice in poetry. For ballads, like other oral poetry, tend to rely on a shared vocabulary of predictable phrases and stock epithets. Hearing ballads, we recognize in them traditional terms, pairings, and comparisons: "my true-love," "my hawks and my hounds," "the sun and the moon," "as red as the blood," and "as dead as the stones." We are not meant to linger on any of them, or on any particular line. Rather, we let each recognized phrase add its bit to mood or situation, while we reserve our main attention for the pattern made by the story as it unfolds.

In written poetry, on the other hand, word choice is all-important. The play on words by which Shakespeare blends spring, songs, and rings to create an atmosphere (p. 440); the indelicate verb *snores* with which Cullen mocks his "lady's" pretensions to gentility (p. 449); and even the archaic spelling "tyger," which gives Blake's beast its first hint of strangeness and mystery, all testify to the power of the well-chosen word. The words themselves are not unusual ones; but they surprise us when they appear, nonetheless. They call on us to pay attention and reward us for our attention by bringing their overtones of meaning and suggestion into the poem, enriching our enjoyment and understanding.

The language of poetry, then, is not necessarily composed of strange, unusual, or uniquely "poetic" words. More often, poetry gains its effects through unexpected juxtapositions of common words, bringing new meaning into the ordinary. Look, for instance, at this poem by Emily Dickinson, and consider how the poet gives significance to the simplest language.

**The Bustle in a House (#1078)**

The Bustle in a House
The Morning after Death
Is solemnest of industries
Enacted upon Earth—

5 The Sweeping up the Heart
And putting Love away
We shall not want to use again
Until Eternity.

The language of the first stanza is almost like prose. A few extra words, and it would be a simple prose statement: The bustle that takes place in a house, the day after someone who lived there has died, represents one of the most solemn tasks on earth. (The word *industries* may seem a bit strange in this context. At the time this poem was written, however, it was used to denote any sort of labor, just as the word *industrious* does today.)

In the second stanza, however, we notice a change. Here the poet is amplifying her first statement. She is explaining that the "bustle" is caused by the housecleaning that takes place between a death and the funeral, and that it is "solemn" because the workers must reconcile themselves to the loss of a loved one. In fact, the workers are coming to grips with their emotions even as they do the chores.

She does not, however, resort to wordy explanations. Rather, she combines housework and emotions in a tightly compressed pair of images. The verbs of the second stanza speak of housecleaning matters; the nouns, of love. It is not dust that is swept up, but "the heart"; not blankets to be put away, but "love." The combination conveys the sense of loss. "The sweeping up the heart," in particular, suggests that the heart is broken, is in pieces; and the thought of a broken heart, in turn, suggests grief.

But the poet also says that the grief and loss are not permanent. "Love" is not thrown away, but rather "put away" to be used again on a future occasion. "Until eternity": the phrase suggests a fearfully long wait, but insists, nonetheless, that the waiting will end. "Eternity" thus balances "earth," tempering the present sense of loss with faith in restoration. And in that balance the poem ends and rests.

Here is another poem by Dickinson that is notable for its unusual use of words. How would you analyze it?

EMILY DICKINSON (1830–1886)

**Because I Could Not Stop for Death (#712)**

Because I could not stop for Death—
He kindly stopped for me—
The Carriage held but just Ourselves—
And Immortality.

5 We slowly drove—He knew no haste
And I had put away
My labor and my leisure too,
For His Civility—

We passed the School, where Children strove
10 At Recess—in the Ring—
We passed the Fields of Gazing Grain—
We passed the Setting Sun—

Or rather—He passed Us—
The Dews drew quivering and chill—
15 For only Gossamer, my Gown—
My Tippet[1]—only Tulle[2]—

We paused before a House that seemed
A Swelling of the Ground—
The Roof was scarcely visible—
20 The Cornice—in the Ground—

[1] A shoulder cape.
[2] A stiff, sheer fabric.

Since then—'tis Centuries—and yet
Feels shorter than the Day
I first surmised the Horses' Heads
Were toward Eternity—

### Suggestion and Interpretation

The language of Blake's "The Tyger" is stranger and more complex than Dickinson's. The description of the tiger as "Burning bright/In the forests of the night" links notions of burning passion, glowing cat-eyes, dark trees, and forests of stars to create, from words that literally are near nonsense, a beast half earthly and half unearthly, combining in his "fearful symmetry" brutal ferocity and supernatural beauty.

"The Tyger" again brings us to realize that word choice in poetry often means choosing words that can carry many meanings at once and then combining those words for the greatest power of suggestion. Blake's tiger is more than mere animal. The striking images and the strong sense of awe that pervade the poem insist that the tiger stands for something special in its questioner's eyes. But they will not tell us specifically what that something is. In this the language of the poem is poetic—it moves always toward greater suggestiveness, never toward a narrowing of meaning. As a result, the tiger symbolizes many things for many people, with all readers bringing their own experiences to this "Song of Experience" and coming away with their own visions of what the tiger can mean for them.

Sound, sense, and suggestion all blend in poetry. Words gain new relevance, new connections. They carry several meanings, suggest several more, and join with other words to suggest yet further meanings. Word choice, the craft of selecting and joining words to enrich their power to communicate, is one of the basic skills of the poet's craft.

Since the rhythms of the following two poems are smoother than those of "The Bustle in the House," and their rhymes are more satisfyingly matched, they have a more traditional sound. Yet their use of language resembles that in Dickinson's poem in that their words and syntax, basically simple and straightforward, are highlighted by a few unexpected words or images. Discuss what you think the highlights in these poems are, and how you think they function.

## WILLIAM WORDSWORTH (1770–1850)

### She Dwelt Among the Untrodden Ways

She dwelt among the untrodden ways
  Beside the springs of Dove.

A Maid whom there were none to praise
And very few to love;

5 A violet by a mossy stone
Half hidden from the eye!
—Fair as a star, when only one
Is shining in the sky.

She lived unknown, and few could know
10 When Lucy ceased to be;
But she is in her grave, and, oh,
The difference to me!

ROBERT HERRICK (1591–1674)

**Upon Julia's Clothes**

Whenas in silks my Julia goes,
Then, then, methinks, how sweetly flows
The liquefaction of her clothes.

Next, when I cast mine eyes and see
5 The brave vibration each way free,
O how that glittering taketh me!

Again, the following poem presents a straightforward statement. But here the language is slightly richer, the play on words is more pronounced, and the words take on more resonance of meaning. Discuss the poem and its language. How does the choice of words give the poem more impact than its main statement, "Many friends of mine have died," would have?

A. E. HOUSMAN (1859–1936)

**With Rue My Heart Is Laden**

With rue my heart is laden
For golden friends I had,
For many a rose-lipt maiden
And many a lightfoot lad.

5 By brooks too broad for leaping
The lightfoot boys are laid;
The rose-lipt girls are sleeping
In fields where roses fade.

QUESTIONS

1. What repetitions do you find in the poem? How does the second stanza develop the images begun in the first stanza?
2. How does the word *golden* in line 2 fit into the mood and imagery?
3. Note the heavy use of "r" and "l" sounds. What effect does the alliteration of these sounds produce? What other examples of alliteration can you find in the poem? How would you summarize your view of Housman's choice of words for sound and sense?

The next poem uses a number of straightforward statements to create a debate on the importance of love. Note how the longer lines and more formal construction of this poem set off the total simplicity of its language. But note, too, the movement from the detachment and objectivity of the opening to the restrained intensity of the final line.

EDNA ST. VINCENT MILLAY (1892–1950)

**Love Is Not All: It Is Not Meat nor Drink**

Love is not all: it is not meat nor drink
Nor slumber nor a roof against the rain;
Nor yet a floating spar to men that sink
And rise and sink and rise and sink again;
5 Love can not fill the thickened lung with breath,
Nor clean the blood, nor set the fractured bone;
Yet many a man is making friends with death
Even as I speak, for lack of love alone.
It well may be that in a difficult hour,
10 Pinned down by pain and moaning for release,
Or nagged by want past resolution's power,
I might be driven to sell your love for peace,
Or trade the memory of this night for food.
It well may be. I do not think I would.

QUESTIONS

1. How does the argument in this poem progress?
   a. What is being said in the lines 1–4? In lines 5–6?
   b. What shift occurs in lines 7–8?
   c. What shift occurs in lines 9–13? What is being discussed now?
   d. What happens in line 14?
2. List the verbs in the poem. What progressions, repetitions, and changes do you find in the verbs that support and emphasize the movement of the debate?
3. What words suggest time? Where are they located in the poem? What is their function? Note especially the phrase, "Even as I speak," in line 8. How is that pivotal, in terms of the poem's structure, its sense of time and person?

4. How many sentences does the poem contain? How long (in terms of lines of verse) is each one?
5. How many words does the poem contain? How many of them are monosyllables? Do you notice any lines that consist wholly of monosyllables?
6. Putting all the above facts together—and adding any others you think important—what effect would you say Millay was trying to produce? How successful do you think she was?

The next two poems are written in **free verse,** a verse form invented in the early twentieth century. Free verse is marked by uneven line lengths and often by the absence of rhyme, as well. Note how these poems mix repetition and compression to create their very different effects.

CARL SANDBURG (1878–1967)

**Cool Tombs**

When Abraham Lincoln was shoveled into the tombs, he forgot the
copperheads and the assassin . . . in the dust, in the cool tombs.
And Ulysses Grant lost all thought of con men and Wall Street, cash
and collateral turned ashes . . . in the dust, in the cool tombs.
5 Pocahontas' body, lovely as a poplar, sweet as a red haw in November
or a pawpaw in May, did she wonder? does she remember? . . . in
the dust, in the cool tombs?
Take any streetful of people buying clothes and groceries, cheering a
hero or throwing confetti and blowing tin horns . . . tell me if the
10 lovers are losers . . . tell me if any get more than the lovers . . . in
the dust . . . in the cool tombs.

QUESTIONS

1. What images are associated with each person? Why have they been chosen? What do they suggest?
2. Is there a message to the poem? If so, what is it? How does the poem travel from its opening statements to its final suggestions?
3. How would you describe the sound of this poem? The rhythm? How do sound and rhythm fit the meaning of the poem? How do they create its mood?

EZRA POUND (1885–1972)

**These Fought in Any Case**[1]

These fought in any case,
and some believing,
pro domo,[2] in any case . . .

[1] Section IV from "E. P. Ode pour L'Election de Son Sépulcre" ("E. P. Ode on the Selection of His Tomb").
[2] "For homeland."

Some quick to arm,
5 some for adventure,
some from fear of weakness,
some from fear of censure,
some for love of slaughter, in imagination,
learning later . . .
10 some in fear, learning love of slaughter;

Died some, pro patria,
non "dulce" non "et decor"[3] . . .
walked eye-deep in hell
believing in old men's lies, then unbelieving
15 came home, home to a lie,
home to many deceits,
home to old lies and new infamy;
usury age-old and age-thick
and liars in public places.

20 Daring as never before, wastage as never before.
Young blood and high blood,
fair cheeks, and fine bodies;

fortitude as never before

frankness as never before,
25 disillusions as never told in the old days,
hysterias, trench confessions,
laughter out of dead bellies.

QUESTIONS

1. How would you describe the tone of voice in this poem? What do the repetitions contribute to it? The word choice? (Be sure you give examples to prove your assertions.)
2. What attitude does the poem suggest towards the soldiers of which it speaks? Is the attitude simple or complex? How is it suggested?
3. What of the poem's attitude to war in general?
4. An **ode** is a poem of irregular form. How does Pound use irregularity of form to reinforce the suggestions his poem makes?
5. Although "Cool Tombs" and "These Fought in Any Case" are both written in free verse and make heavy use of repetition, the **tone** and **pace** of the two poems are completely different. Why?

[3] An ironic allusion to the famous line of Horace: "Dulce et decorum est pro patria mori" ("It is sweet and fitting to die for one's country").

The words in this next poem deserve special notice. Their underlying tone and syntax are more casual and friendly than any we have met so far. And yet Cummings has taken enormous liberties with words and syntax alike, even to the point of inventing new words and positioning each word individually on the page. To what new responses does the resulting poem seem to invite you?

E. E. CUMMINGS (1894–1963)

**in Just-**

in Just-
spring          when the world is mud-
luscious the little
lame balloonman

5 whistles          far          and wee

and eddieandbill come
running from marbles and
piracies and it's
spring

10 when the world is puddle-wonderful

the queer
old balloonman whistles
far          and          wee
and bettyandisbel come dancing

15 from hop-scotch and jump-rope and

it's
spring
and
          the

20                     goat-footed

balloonMan          whistles
far
and
wee

## QUESTIONS

1. In analyzing this poem, we may begin with its wordplay. How do compound words such as *mud-luscious* and *puddle-wonderful* affect the sound and meaning of the lines in which they occur? How many meanings does the word *wee* have, and what is the effect of using it? The balloon-man is described through incremental repetition, beginning as "lame" and ending as "goat-footed." Why goat-footed?
2. We may then note two unusual rhythmic devices: the breaking of lines in the middle of words or phrases, and the spacing out or running together of words. And we may ask how these affect the sound and mood of the poem, and our sense of the scene it describes.
3. Then we may put this play with words and rhythms together with the poem's use of names and detail, and ask how Cummings creates and enhances his description. What does the intent of the poem seem to be? What message does it seem to carry? How do the sound and word choices create the tone and the message?

# THE SPEAKER IN THE POEM

# 5 *The Speaker's Voice*

We have said that ballads, being traditional, oral poetry, rely on common words and images rather than on the unique images of written poetry. We may now make one final distinction by remarking that this stylization of ballads leaves these songs lacking uniquely memorable voices. A deserted lover in one ballad, for instance, sounds much like a deserted lover in any other ballad. They will speak at least some of the same words in the same tones and rhythms. This is not the case in written poetry, where we would take the appearance of a lover who sounds like any other lover as the sign of a second-rate poem. If we read twenty lyrics about love—or even twenty lyrics about lost love—we expect to hear twenty different voices.

This reflection brings us to one of the basic paradoxes of poetry. Because of its use of rhythm and sound patterns, the language of poetry may be the farthest of all literary languages from everyday speech. Yet the voices within poems are the most intimate of literary voices, speaking to us most vividly and directly and conveying to us most openly the speakers' deepest and most immediate emotions. No other form of literature demands so much care and craft in its writing as poetry; yet no other form can seem to present the spontaneous flow of emotion as convincingly as poetry can.

Because poetry can so thoroughly convince us that in responding to it we are sharing a genuine, strongly felt emotion, it can attract our strongest

response. Subjectively, this is good; it repı
should do. Objectively, however, poetry's seem
ical danger that we may mistake the voice wit
of the poet. The further danger then arises that
single poem, slipping from the critically accep
'Tyger' presents the tiger as a beautiful but ter
unacceptable, "As 'The Tyger' shows, Blake was a

We cannot fall into this error so easily in drama ... the number of characters and the abundance of circu... detail continually warn us of the distance between author and ...ork. Poetry, however, often has but one voice in a poem. The voice often speaks in the first person: "Oh, how that glittering taketh me!" And the intensity of emotion that is felt only in the climatic scenes of fiction and drama may illuminate an entire lyric. This combination of single voice, first person, and unflagging intensity of emotion often obliterates the distance between the poet and speaker. If the speaker then gives us the slightest hint that he or she may represent the poet, we become all too willing to make the identification.

But we must not make the identification so simply. We can speak of a poet's voice—can compare Blake's voice to Dickinson's, for example. But when we do this we must compare all the voices from at least a dozen of Blake's poems to all the voices from an equal number of Dickinson's. We can then speak either of a range of voices that seems typical of each poet or of some specific characteristics that remain constant through all their individual voices. Moreover, we may equally well make comparisons between voices belonging to a single poet—comparing the voices of Blake's early poems to those of his later poems, for instance—which we could not do if the voice in each poem were the poet's only voice.

To further emphasize this distance between speaker and poet, we may look again at poems such as "We Real Cool" and "Sir Patrick Spens." They seem to speak to us as directly and to be as immediately felt as any other poems, but we know no author for "Sir Patrick Spens" and are sure that Gwendolyn Brooks is not seven adolescents in a pool hall.

The poem is the poet's vision, nothing more. Its speakers may be inside the action (as in "Upon Julia's Clothes") or outside it (as in "The Cherry-Tree Carol"). They may have elements of the poet's own situation or emotions in them, or they may not. But they are speakers and not writers; they are the poet's creations and not the poet's self.

For discussing speakers who do seem to mirror their poets, we have the useful critical term **persona.** The speakers of "The Lamb" and "The Tyger," of "There's a Certain Slant of Light," and of "Upon Julia's Clothes" may be called their poets' personae. Personae represent one aspect of their poet's personality or experience, isolated from the rest of the

amatized, and re-created through art. Poets—like all human
e complex and changeable. Personae are simpler: fixed, change-
nd slightly exaggerated. Unlike their makers, who must respond to
e many demands of the everyday world in which they live, personae exist only within their poems and respond only to the thoughts and sensations that gave the poems birth.

Here, for the further study of speakers in poetry, are four groups of poems. The first three groups employ speakers who might well be spoken of as personae; the fourth has speakers who cannot. Be aware, as you read these poems, of sound and language and total effect. But pay most attention to the characterization of the speakers and to the varying voices with which they speak.

## THEODORE ROETHKE (1908–1963)

### My Papa's Waltz

The whiskey on your breath
Could make a small boy dizzy;
But I hung on like death:
Such waltzing was not easy.

5 We romped until the pans
Slid from the kitchen shelf;
My mother's countenance
Could not unfrown itself.

The hand that held my wrist
10 Was battered on one knuckle;
At every step you missed
My right ear scraped a buckle.

You beat time on my head
With a palm caked hard by dirt,
15 Then waltzed me off to bed
Still clinging to your shirt.

### I Knew a Woman

I knew a woman, lovely in her bones,
When small birds sighed, she would sigh back at them;
Ah, when she moved, she moved more ways than one:
The shapes a bright container can contain!
5 Of her choice virtues only gods should speak,

Or English poets who grew up on Greek
(I'd have them sing in chorus, cheek to cheek).

How well her wishes went! She stroked my chin,
She taught me Turn, and Counter-turn, and Stand;[1]
10 She taught me Touch, that undulant white skin;
I nibbled meekly from her proffered hand;
She was the sickle; I, poor I, the rake,
Coming behind her for her pretty sake
(But what prodigious mowing we did make).

15 Love likes a gander, and adores a goose:
Her full lips pursed, the errant note to seize;
She played it quick, she played it light and loose;
My eyes, they dazzled at her flowing knees;
Her several parts could keep a pure repose,
20 Or one hip quiver with a mobile nose
(She moved in circles, and those circles moved).

Let seed be grass, and grass turn into hay:
I'm martyr to a motion not my own;
What's freedom for? To know eternity.
25 I swear she cast a shadow white as stone.
But who would count eternity in days?
These old bones live to learn her wanton ways:
(I measure time by how a body sways).

QUESTIONS

1. What is the subject of each of these poems? What is the emotional state of the speaker?
2. How does the language of the two poems compare? What sort of images does each use? How does the language match the subject and mood in each?
3. How would you characterize the speaker of each poem? What would you have to say to move from a characterization of the speakers to a characterization of the poet?

ROBERT FROST (1908–1963)

**Two Tramps in Mud Time**

Out of the mud two strangers came
And caught me splitting wood in the yard.

---

[1] Terms for the three parts of a Pindaric ode.

And one of them put me off my aim
By hailing cheerily "Hit them hard!"
5 I knew pretty well why he dropped behind
And let the other go on a way.
I knew pretty well what he had in mind:
He wanted to take my job for pay.

Good blocks of oak it was I split,
10 As large around as the chopping block;
And every piece I squarely hit
Fell splinterless as a cloven rock.
The blows that a life of self-control
Spares to strike for the common good,
15 That day, giving a loose to my soul,
I spent on the unimportant wood.

The sun was warm but the wind was chill.
You know how it is with an April day
When the sun is out and the wind is still,
20 You're one month on in the middle of May.
But if you so much as dare to speak,
A cloud comes over the sunlit arch,
A wind comes off a frozen peak,
And you're two months back in the middle of March.

25 A bluebird comes tenderly up to alight
And turns to the wind to unruffle a plume,
His song so pitched as not to excite
A single flower as yet to bloom.
It is snowing a flake: and he half knew
30 Winter was only playing possum.
Except in color he isn't blue,
But he wouldn't advise a thing to blossom.

The water for which we may have to look
In summertime with a witching wand,
35 In every wheelrut's now a brook,
In every print of a hoof a pond.
Be glad of water, but don't forget
The lurking frost in the earth beneath
That will steal forth after the sun is set
40 And show on the water its crystal teeth.

The time when most I loved my task
These two must make me love it more

By coming with what they came to ask.
You'd think I never had felt before
45 The weight of an ax-head poised aloft,
The grip on earth of outspread feet,
The life of muscles rocking soft
And smooth and moist in vernal heat.

Out of the woods two hulking tramps
50 (From sleeping God knows where last night,
But not long since in the lumber camps).
They thought all chopping was theirs of right.
Men of the woods and lumberjacks,
They judged me by their appropriate tool.
55 Except as a fellow handled an ax
They had no way of knowing a fool.

Nothing on either side was said.
They knew they had but to stay their stay
And all their logic would fill my head:
60 As that I had no right to play
With what was another man's work for gain.
My right might be love but theirs was need.
And where the two exist in twain
Theirs was the better right—agreed.

65 But yield who will to their separation,
My object in living is to unite
My avocation and my vocation
As my two eyes make one in sight.
Only where love and need are one,
70 And the work is play for mortal stakes,
Is the deed ever really done
For Heaven and the future's sakes.

**Provide, Provide**

The witch that came (the withered hag)
To wash the steps with pail and rag
Was once the beauty Abishag,

The picture pride of Hollywood.
5 Too many fall from great and good
For you to doubt the likelihood.

Die early and avoid the fate.
Or if predestined to die late,
Make up your mind to die in state.

10 Make the whole stock exchange your own!
If need be occupy a throne,
Where nobody can call *you* crone.

Some have relied on what they knew,
Others on being simply true.
15 What worked for them might work for you.

No memory of having starred
Atones for later disregard
Or keeps the end from being hard.

Better to go down dignified
20 With boughten friendship at your side
Than none at all. Provide, provide!

QUESTIONS

Each of these two poems starts with an incident and ends with a moral drawn from the incident.

1. To what extent do incident and moral affect the speaker in each poem? To what extent does he seem to hope they'll affect his audience?
2. How much of each poem does Frost spend describing the incident that supposedly triggered the poem? How much on generalizations and lessons? What is the effect of this balance on your sense of each poem?
3. How would you describe the speaker's tone (or tones) of voice in each poem?
4. What uses of language do you find notable in each poem?
5. How would you describe the overall tone and philosophy of each poem? Do both seem capable of forming parts of one person's philosophy? What effect does their diversity have on your sense of Frost as a poet?

ANONYMOUS—MIDDLE ENGLISH LYRIC

**Western Wind**

Western wind, when will thou blow,
  The small rain down can rain?
Christ, if my love were in my arms
  And I in my bed again.

## SIR THOMAS WYATT (1503–1542)

### To a Lady to Answer Directly with Yea or Nay

Madame, withouten many words,
Once I am sure you will or no;
And if you will, then leave your boords[1]
And use your wit, and shew[2] it so,
5 For with a beck[3] you shall me call.
And if of one that burns alway
Ye have pity or ruth[4] at all,
Answer him fair[5] with yea or nay.
If it be yea, I shall be fain;[6]
10 If it be nay, friends as before.
You shall another man obtain,
And I mine own, and yours no more.

## SIR JOHN SUCKLING (1609–1642)

### The Constant Lover

Out upon it! I have loved
  Three whole days together;
And am like to love three more,
  If it prove fair weather!

5 Time shall moult away his wings,
  Ere he shall discover
In the whole wide world again
  Such a constant lover.

But the spite on't is, no praise
10   Is due at all to me:
Love with me had made no stays,
  Had it any been but she.

---

[1] Jokes.
[2] Show.
[3] Gesture.
[4] Compassion.
[5] Clearly, honestly.
[6] Glad, delighted.

Had it any been but she,
  And that very face,
15 There had been at least ere this
  A dozen dozen in her place!

QUESTIONS

These three poems are spoken by three different lovers. How would you compare and contrast them?

1. To whom does each speak?
2. In what situation does each find himself? What is his reaction to the situation? What emotions and/or thoughts does he express?
3. How do the form and language of each poem, together with the emotion and situation represented, create your picture of each of these lovers?

THOMAS HARDY (1840–1928)

**The Man He Killed**

"Had he and I but met
  By some old ancient inn,
We should have sat us down to wet
  Right many a nipperkin![1]

5 "But ranged as infantry,
  And staring face to face,
I shot at him as he at me,
  And killed him in his place.

"I shot him dead because—
10 Because he was my foe,
Just so: my foe of course he was;
  That's clear enough; although

"He thought he'd 'list, perhaps,
  Off-hand like—just as I—
15 Was out of work—had sold his traps—
  No other reason why.

"Yes; quaint and curious war is!
  You shoot a fellow down

[1] About a half-pint.

You'd treat if met where any bar is,
20 Or help to half-a-crown."

WILLIAM BUTLER YEATS (1865–1939)

**An Irish Airman Foresees His Death**[1]

I know that I shall meet my fate
Somewhere among the clouds above;
Those that I fight I do not hate,
Those that I guard I do not love;
5 My country is Kiltartan Cross,[2]
My countrymen Kiltartan's poor,
No likely end could bring them loss
Or leave them happier than before.
Nor law, nor duty bade me fight,
10 Nor public men, nor cheering crowds,
A lonely impulse of delight
Drove to this tumult in the clouds;
I balanced all, brought all to mind,
The years to come seemed waste of breath,
15 A waste of breath the years behind
In balance with this life, this death.

QUESTIONS

1. What theme is common to these two poems?
2. How would you compare the two speakers?
3. How would you characterize the tone of each poem? The language? (Note the use of repetition. What effect does it produce in Hardy's poem? In Yeats's? How does it help characterize each speaker?)
4. How does the difference in character and mood of the two speakers contribute to the difference in overall effect of the two poems? (What reaction does each poet seem to want from you? What message—if any—does his poem seem to carry?)

The final poem in this chapter represents a form known as **dramatic monologue.** After you have read the poem, answer the following questions:

[1] Major Robert Gregory, son of Yeats's friend and patroness Lady Augusta Gregory, was killed in action in 1918.
[2] Kiltartan is an Irish village near Coole Park, the estate of the Gregorys.

1. Who is the speaker?
2. To whom is he speaking? On what occasion?
3. What does the speaker tell you about his own character? How does he do so?
4. What do you think happened to the "last duchess"?
5. If you were the person being addressed, how would you feel at the end of the monologue?

ROBERT BROWNING (1812–1889)

**My Last Duchess**

*Ferrara*

That's my last duchess painted on the wall,
Looking as if she were alive. I call
That piece a wonder, now: Frà Pandolf's[1] hands
Worked busily a day, and there she stands.
5 Will't please you sit and look at her? I said
"Frà Pandolf" by design, for never read
Strangers like you that pictured countenance,
The depth and passion of its earnest glance,
But to myself they turned (since none puts by
10 The curtain I have drawn for you, but I)
And seemed as they would ask me, if they durst,
How such a glance came there; so, not the first
Are you to turn and ask thus. Sir, 'twas not
Her husband's presence only, called that spot
15 Of joy into the Duchess' cheek: perhaps
Frà Pandolf chanced to say "Her mantle laps
"Over my lady's wrist too much," or "Paint
"Must never hope to reproduce the faint
"Half-flush that dies along her throat": such stuff
20 Was courtesy, she thought, and cause enough
For calling up that spot of joy. She had
A heart—how shall I say?—too soon made glad,
Too easily impressed; she liked whate'er
She looked on, and her looks went everywhere.
25 Sir, 'twas all one! My favor at her breast,
The dropping of the daylight in the West,

[1] A fictitious artist, as is Claus of Innsbruck in the last line.

The bough of cherries some officious fool
Broke in the orchard for her, the white mule
She rode with round the terrace—all and each
30 Would draw from her alike the approving speech,
Or blush, at least. She thanked men—good! but thanked
Somehow—I know not how—as if she ranked
My gift of a nine-hundred-years-old name
With anybody's gift. Who'd stoop to blame
35 This sort of trifling? Even had you skill
In speech—which I have not—to make your will
Quite clear to such an one, and say, "Just this
"Or that in you disgusts me; here you miss,
"Or there exceed the mark"—and if she let
40 Herself be lessoned so, nor plainly set
Her wits to yours, forsooth, and made excuse,
—E'en then would be some stooping; and I choose
Never to stoop. Oh sir, she smiled, no doubt,
Whene'er I passed her; but who passed without
45 Much the same smile? This grew; I gave commands;
Then all smiles stopped together. There she stands
As if alive. Will 't please you rise? We'll meet
The company below, then. I repeat,
The Count your master's known munificence
50 Is ample warrant that no just pretense
Of mine for dowry will be disallowed;
Though his fair daughter's self, as I avowed
At starting, is my object. Nay, we'll go
Together down, sir. Notice Neptune, though,
55 Taming a sea-horse, thought a rarity,
Which Claus of Innsbruck cast in bronze for me!

if she would listen or had some intellect

The duke had a high opinion of himself

He killed her or had her put away

Duke is
pretentous
jealous
"all man"
greedy
arrogant
pompous

The duchess is
naive
flirtatous
simple
appreciative

theme - how one person can control & destroy another

# 6 The Speaker's Vision

Like other writers, poets find their visions in three basic sources: the world around them, their own experiences, and their inner vision of what is or might be. The speakers of their poems, who are charged with communicating these visions, may therefore be observers, recording scenes and experiences for our mutual pleasure and insight; or they may be visionaries, recasting real or imagined scenes to produce a new vision for our sharing.

We can see the distinction clearly enough in poems we have already read. For instance, we have already seen two types of reporters at work. The speakers in "Get Up and Bar the Door" and "The Cherry-Tree Carol" are most obviously reporters; they simply tell us what occurred and let us draw our own conclusions about it. The speakers of "We Real Cool" and "For a Lady I Know" are also reporters but are less obviously so, because we sense that the poets are not as objective as their speakers. The speakers provide no interpretation and show no emotion. But the poets' attitudes come through, nonetheless. Indeed, much of the effectiveness of these poems comes from the disparity between the speakers' objectivity and the poets' concern, a disparity felt by the reader as irony. But that is a subject we will speak of more thoroughly in the next chapter.

We can also recall poems in which the speaker was primarily a visionary. Dickinson's poems come to mind here, and Blake's. "The Lamb" and "The Tyger" are far more concerned with the religious visions the animals arouse in Blake's speakers than they are with the animals themselves; and "Tell All

the Truth" is pure vision, having no objective scene
as its starting point. Another visionary is the spea
Fought in Any Case," who draws on visions of so
soldiers that we soon lose all sense of individuals i
vision of the war itself.

These, then, are poems that mark the two extr
stance: the objective extreme and the visionary ext
come those poems (probably typical of the majority o
speaker is reporter and interpreter both. These poem ...ance what is seen and what is felt, allowing neither to overwhelm the other. Their speakers report on what is happening while explaining or suggesting its implications. Thus, "There's a Certain Slant of Light" conveys its atmospheric sensation most vividly by interpreting its spiritual overtones. And poems such as "in Just-," and "I Knew a Woman" blend recollection and response so perfectly that it's hard to say where one stops and the other begins. Through the speaker's emotional response, the vision is made real for us; reporter, responder, and interpreter are one.

The poems we shall look at in this chapter blend objective and visionary stances, observation and interpretation. Take careful note of the speaker's character and stance within each poem. Before you answer any of the questions, make sure you know what sort of person is speaking, to what the speaker is responding, and how much of the speaker's response is to things outside himself or herself and how much to inner visions or emotions.

The common factor in the first two poems is memory. Read each poem, and then discuss:

1. The details by which the memories are presented.
2. The comparisons and contrasts created between the memories and the speaker's present circumstances or emotional state.
3. Any sense of movement through time the poem may create, and the way in which it creates it.
4. What we are told in the poem's conclusion, and what sense of the speaker's feelings or attitudes the conclusion gives us.

D. H. LAWRENCE (1885–1930)

**Piano**

Softly, in the dusk, a woman is singing to me;
Taking me back down the vista of years, till I see
A child sitting under the piano, in the boom of the tingling strings
And pressing the small, poised feet of a mother who smiles as she
  sings.

ite of myself, the insidious mastery of song
trays me back, till the heart of me weeps to belong
To the old Sunday evenings at home, with winter outside
And hymns in the cozy parlor, the tinkling piano our guide.

So now it is vain for the singer to burst into clamor
10 With the great black piano appassionato. The glamour
Of childish days is upon me, my manhood is cast
Down in the flood of remembrance, I weep like a child for the past.

ROBERT FROST (1874–1963)

## Birches

When I see birches bend to left and right
Across the lines of straighter darker trees,
I like to think some boy's been swinging them.
But swinging doesn't bend them down to stay
5 As ice-storms do. Often you must have seen them
Loaded with ice a sunny winter morning
After a rain. They click upon themselves
As the breeze rises, and turn many-colored
As the stir cracks and crazes their enamel.
10 Soon the sun's warmth makes them shed crystal shells
Shattering and avalanching on the snowcrust—
Such heaps of broken glass to sweep away
You'd think the inner dome of heaven had fallen.
They are dragged to the withered bracken by the load,
15 And they seem not to break; though once they are bowed
So low for long, they never right themselves:
You may see their trunks arching in the woods
Years afterwards, trailing their leaves on the ground
Like girls on hands and knees that throw their hair
20 Before them over their heads to dry in the sun.
But I was going to say when Truth broke in
With all her matter of fact about the ice-storm,
I should prefer to have some boy bend them
As he went out and in to fetch the cows—
25 Some boy too far from town to learn baseball,
Whose only play was what he found himself,
Summer or winter, and could play alone.
One by one he subdued his father's trees
By riding them down over and over again
30 Until he took the stiffness out of them,

And not one but hung limp, not one was left
For him to conquer. He learned all there was
To learn about not launching out too soon
And so not carrying the tree away
35 Clear to the ground. He always kept his poise
To the top branches, climbing carefully
With the same pains you use to fill a cup
Up to the brim, and even above the brim.
Then he flung outward, feet first, with a swish,
40 Kicking his way down through the air to the ground.
So was I once myself a swinger of birches.
And so I dream of going back to be.
It's when I'm weary of considerations,
And life is too much like a pathless wood
45 Where your face burns and tickles with the cobwebs
Broken across it, and one eye is weeping
From a twig's having lashed across it open.
I'd like to get away from earth awhile
And then come back to it and begin over.
50 May no fate willfully misunderstand me
And half grant what I wish and snatch me away
Not to return. Earth's the right place for love:
I don't know where it's likely to go better.
I'd like to go by climbing a birch tree,
55 And climb black branches up a snow-white trunk
*Toward* heaven, till the tree could bear no more,
But dipped its top and set me down again.
That would be good both going and coming back.
One could do worse than be a swinger of birches.

The next three poems all concern ongoing relationships between the speakers and the natural and social worlds around them. In each case, the speaker's reaction to the "natural" world is linked with and contrasted to a more problematical relationship with the "social" world and with the speaker's place—as poet, lover, family member, citizen—within that world. Notice, in each of these three poems, how the two relationships illuminate each other, and how they ultimately fuse to create the vision presented by the poem.

## SIR PHILIP SIDNEY (1554–1586)

### *From* **Astrophil and Stella**

### Sonnet 31

With how sad steps, O moon, thou climb'st the skies!
  How silently, and with how wan a face!
  What! may it be that even in heavenly place
  That busy archer his sharp arrows tries?
5 Sure, if that long-with-love-acquainted eyes
  Can judge of love, thou feel'st a lover's case;
  I read it in thy looks—thy languished grace
  To me, that feel the like, thy state descries.
Then, even of fellowship, O moon, tell me,
10  Is constant love deemed there but want of wit?
  Are beauties there as proud as here they be?
Do they above love to be loved, and yet
  Those lovers scorn whom that love doth possess?
  Do they call virtue there ungratefulness?

QUESTIONS

1. The technique of having the speaker seem to address someone or something within a poem is called **apostrophe.** What use is Sidney making of apostrophe in this poem?
2. What features of the moon's appearance does the speaker note? What interpretation does he put on them? Why?
3. Who is "that busy archer"? What overtones does his mention lend to the poem?
4. Why does the speaker claim "fellowship" with the moon? What do his questions to her tell you of his own state?
5. How would you describe the tone of the poem? How seriously does the speaker seem to take his interpretation of the moon's condition? What seems to be his attitude toward his own state?

## JOHN KEATS (1795–1821)

### When I Have Fears

When I have fears that I may cease to be
  Before my pen has gleaned my teeming brain,
Before high-piled books, in charactery,[1]

[1] Characters, writing.

Hold like rich garners the full ripened grain;
5 When I behold, upon the night's starred face,
Huge cloudy symbols of a high romance,
And think that I may never live to trace
Their shadows, with the magic hand of chance;
And when I feel, fair creature of an hour,
10 That I shall never look upon thee more,
Never have relish in the faery power
Of unreflecting love;—then on the shore
Of the wide world I stand alone, and think
Till love and fame to nothingness do sink.

QUESTIONS

1. Since the whole poem is one sentence, its syntax gets a bit complicated. Let's start, therefore, by examining it clause by clause, beginning with the three "when" clauses that make up the first eleven-and-a-half lines of the poem: What are the first four lines concerned with? The second four? The third? How are the three tied together? (Who is the "fair creature of an hour"? Why might the speaker call her so at this point in the poem?)
2. What overtones do words like *rich, romance, magic* and *faery* give to the poem? What contrast do they suggest between the poet's wishes and his sense of reality?
3. Then look at the final clause of the sentence—the last two-and-a-half lines. What action does it show the speaker taking? How explicit are his feelings made? What are you left to fill in?

NIKKI GIOVANNI (1943– )

**The Beep Beep Poem**

I should write a poem
but there's almost nothing
that hasn't been said
and said and said
5 beautifully, ugly, blandly
excitingly
stay in school
make love not war
death to all tyrants
10 where have all the flowers gone
and don't they understand at kent state
the troopers will shoot . . . again

i could write a poem
because i love walking
15 in the rain
and the solace of my naked
body in a tub of warm water
cleanliness may not be next
to godliness but it sure feels
20 good

i wrote a poem
for my father but it was so constant
i burned it up
he hates change
25 and i'm baffled by sameness

i composed a ditty
about encore american and worldwide news
but the editorial board
said no one would understand it
30 as if people have to be tricked
into sensitivity
though of course they do

i love to drive my car
hours on end
35 along back country roads
i love to stop for cider and apples and acorn squash
three for a dollar
i love my CB when the truckers talk
and the hum of the diesel in my ear
40 i love the aloneness of the road
when I ascend descending curves
the power within my toe delights me
and i fling my spirit down the highway
i love the way i feel
45 when i pass the moon and i holler to the stars
i'm coming through

Beep Beep

QUESTIONS

1. The earlier poems in this chapter were each tightly focussed on a single memory or emotion. "The Beep Beep Poem" is much looser in construction,

each stanza presenting a separate topic. When interpreting this poem, therefore, it may be useful to go through the following sequence of steps:

a. Look at each stanza separately. Consider: the topic of each stanza; the speaker's tone of voice and attitude; and any notable uses of language (wordplay, repetition, imagery, etc.) within the stanza.
b. Then consider the progression from stanza to stanza throughout the poem. (Note, for example, the opening verbs of each stanza. What progression do they suggest? How is that progression carried out?)
c. Finally, put together your answers to items (a) and (b), along with any overall impressions you may want to add to them, to describe your interpretation of the poem.

2. There is a certain paradox in the fact that all poems that touch on their speakers' frustration as poets unable to write as freely or as well as they would like to are, nonetheless, completed and successful poems—and thus are signs that their poets have, at least for the moment, triumphed in some way over their frustration, even while acknowledging it.

   In how many ways does "The Beep Beep Poem" suggest frustration? Triumph? How do the two blend to create the "vision" of the poem?

So far, the poems in this chapter have all had realistic settings; that is, they have all been based on scenes, incidents, or persons that have or could have occurred in the poet's own life. Poetry is not limited to the real world, however, for either its settings or its characters. The next poem portrays a wholly imaginary landscape, speaker, and incident. Its emotions and resonances, however, are as fully "human" as those of any poem we have read so far. Read the poem, and then consider how Browning uses imagination and fantasy to illuminate a human dilemma.

ROBERT BROWNING (1812–1889)

## Childe Roland to the Dark Tower Came[1]

1

My first thought was, he lied in every word,
  That hoary cripple, with malicious eye
  Askance to watch the working of his lie
On mine, and mouth scarce able to afford
5 Suppression of the glee, that pursed and scored
  Its edge, at one more victim gained thereby.

[1] In Shakespeare's *King Lear,* II. iv, Edgar, Gloucester's son, disguised as a madman, meets Lear in the midst of a storm; at the end of the scene, Edgar sings: "Child Rowland to the dark tower came;/His word was still, 'Fie, foh, and fum,/I smell the blood of a British man.' " (*Childe:* medieval title applied to a youth awaiting knighthood.)

2

What else should he be set for, with his staff?
What, save to waylay with his lies, ensnare
All travelers who might find him posted there,
10 And ask the road? I guessed what skull-like laugh
Would break, what crutch 'gin write my epitaph
For pastime in the dusty thoroughfare,

3

If at his counsel I should turn aside
Into that ominous tract which, all agree,
15 Hides the Dark Tower. Yet acquiescingly
I did turn as he pointed: neither pride
Nor hope rekindling at the end descried,
So much as gladness that some end might be.

4

For, what with my whole world-wide wandering,
20 What with my search drawn out through years, my hope
Dwindled into a ghost not fit to cope
With that obstreperous joy success would bring,—
I hardly tried now to rebuke the spring
My heart made, finding failure in its scope.

5

25 As when a sick man very near to death
Seems dead indeed, and feels begin and end
The tears, and takes the farewell of each friend,
And hears one bid the other go, draw breath
Freelier outside, ("since all is o'er," he saith,
30 "And the blow fallen no grieving can amend;")

6

While some discuss if near the other graves
Be room enough for this, and when a day
Suits best for carrying the corpse away,
With care about the banners, scarves and staves:
35 And still the man hears all, and only craves
He may not shame such tender love and stay.

7

Thus, I had so long suffered in this quest,
Heard failure prophesied so oft, been writ
So many times among "The Band"—to wit,
40 The knights who to the Dark Tower's search addressed
Their steps—that just to fail as they, seemed best,
And all the doubt was now—should I be fit?

8

So, quiet as despair, I turned from him,
That hateful cripple, out of his highway
45 Into the path he pointed. All the day
Had been a dreary one at best, and dim
Was settling to its close, yet shot one grim
Red leer to see the plain catch its estray.[2]

9

For mark! no sooner was I fairly found
50 Pledged to the plain, after a pace or two,
Than, pausing to throw backward a last view
O'er the safe road, 'twas gone; gray plain all round:
Nothing but plain to the horizon's bound.
I might go on; naught else remained to do.

10

55 So, on I went. I think I never saw
Such starved ignoble nature; nothing throve:
For flowers—as well expect a cedar grove!
But cockle, spurge,[3] according to their law
Might propagate their kind, with none to awe,
60 You'd think: a burr had been a treasure trove.

11

No! penury, inertness and grimace,
In some strange sort, were the land's portion. "See
Or shut your eyes," said Nature peevishly,
"It nothing skills:[4] I cannot help my case:

---

[2] A stray or unclaimed domestic animal.
[3] Cockle here is a weed that grows in wheatfields; spurge, a plant with minute flowers.
[4] Avails.

65 'Tis the Last Judgment's fire must cure this place,
Calcine[5] its clods and set my prisoners free."

12

If there pushed any ragged thistle-stalk
Above its mates, the head was chopped; the bents[6]
Were jealous else. What made those holes and rents
70 In the dock's[7] harsh swarth[8] leaves, bruised as to balk
All hope of greenness? 'tis a brute must walk
Pashing[9] their life out, with a brute's intents.

13

As for the grass, it grew as scant as hair
In leprosy; thin dry blades pricked the mud
75 Which underneath looked kneaded up with blood.
One stiff blind horse, his every bone a-stare,
Stood stupefied, however he came there:
Thrust out past service from the devil's stud!

14

Alive? he might be dead for aught I know,
80 With that red gaunt and colloped[10] neck a-strain,
And shut eyes underneath the rusty mane;
Seldom went such grotesqueness with such woe;
I never saw a brute I hated so;
He must be wicked to deserve such pain.

15

85 I shut my eyes and turned them on my heart.
As a man calls for wine before he fights,
I asked one draught of earlier, happier sights,
Ere fitly I could hope to play my part.
Think first, fight afterwards—the soldier's art:
90 One taste of the old time sets all to rights.

---

[5] Burn to powder.
[6] Reeds, rushes.
[7] Coarse weedy plant.
[8] Dark.
[9] Crushing.
[10] Chafed, ridged.

16

Not it! I fancied Cuthbert's reddening face
  Beneath its garniture of curly gold,
  Dear fellow, till I almost felt him fold
An arm in mine to fix me to the place,
95 That way he used. Alas, one night's disgrace!
  Out went my heart's new fire and left it cold.

17

Giles then, the soul of honor—there he stands
  Frank as ten years ago when knighted first.
  What honest man should dare (he said) he durst.
100 Good—but the scene shifts—faugh! what hangman hands
Pin to his breast a parchment? His own bands
  Read it. Poor traitor, spit upon and curst!

18

Better this present than a past like that;
  Back therefore to my darkening path again!
105 No sound, no sight as far as eye could strain.
Will the night send a howlet[11] or a bat?
I asked: when something on the dismal flat
  Came to arrest my thoughts and change their train.

19

A sudden little river crossed my path
110 As unexpected as a serpent comes.
  No sluggish tide congenial to the glooms;
This, as it frothed by, might have been a bath
For the fiend's glowing hoof—to see the wrath
  Of its black eddy bespate[12] with flakes and spumes.

20

115 So petty yet so spiteful! All along,
  Low scrubby alders kneeled down over it;
  Drenched willows flung them headlong in a fit
Of mute despair, a suicidal throng:

[11] Owl.
[12] Spattered.

The river which had done them all the wrong,
120 Whate'er that was, rolled by, deterred no whit.

21

Which, while I forded,—good saints, how I feared
To set my foot upon a dead man's cheek,
Each step, or feel the spear I thrust to seek
For hollows, tangled in his hair or beard!
125 —It may have been a water-rat I speared,
But, ugh! it sounded like a baby's shriek.

22

Glad was I when I reached the other bank.
Now for a better country. Vain presage!
Who were the strugglers, what war did they wage,
130 Whose savage trample thus could pad the dank
Soil to a plash?[13] Toads in a poisoned tank,
Or wild cats in a red-hot iron cage—

23

The fight must so have seemed in that fell cirque.[14]
What penned them there, with all the plain to choose?
135 No footprint leading to that horrid mews.[15]
None out of it. Mad brewage set to work
Their brains, no doubt, like galley-slaves the Turk
Pits for his pastime, Christians against Jews.

24

And more than that—a furlong on—why, there!
140 What bad use was that engine[16] for, that wheel,
Or brake,[17] not wheel—that harrow fit to reel
Men's bodies out like silk? with all the air
Of Tophet's[18] tool, on earth left unaware,
Or brought to sharpen its rusty teeth of steel.

---

[13] Puddle.
[14] Rounded hollow encircled by heights.
[15] Stabling area.
[16] Mechanical contrivance.
[17] Here in the sense of a tool for breaking up flax or hemp, to separate the fiber.
[18] Hell's.

25

145 Then came a bit of stubbed ground, once a wood,
Next a marsh, it would seem, and now mere earth
Desperate and done with; (so a fool finds mirth,
Makes a thing and then mars it, till his mood
Changes and off he goes!) within a rood[19]—
150 Bog, clay and rubble, sand and stark black dearth.

26

Now blotches rankling,[20] colored gay and grim,
Now patches where some leanness of the soil's
Broke into moss or substances like boils;
Then came some palsied oak, a cleft in him
155 Like a distorted mouth that splits its rim
Gaping at death, and dies while it recoils.

27

And just as far as ever from the end!
Nought in the distance but the evening, nought
To point my footstep further! At the thought,
160 A great black bird, Apollyon's[21] bosom-friend,
Sailed past, nor beat his wide wing dragon-penned[22]
That brushed my cap—perchance the guide I sought.

28

For, looking up, aware I somehow grew,
'Spite of the dusk, the plain had given place
165 All round to mountains—with such name to grace
Mere ugly heights and heaps now stolen in view.
How thus they had surprised me,—solve it, you!
How to get from them was no clearer case.

29

Yet half I seemed to recognize some trick
170 Of mischief happened to me, God knows when—

---

[19] Linear measure, varying locally from six to eight yards.
[20] Festering.
[21] ". . . The angel of the bottomless pit, whose name in the Hebrew tongue is Abaddon, but in the Greek tongue . . . Apollyon." Revelation ix.11.
[22] With pinions like a dragon's.

In a bad dream perhaps. Here ended, then,
Progress this way. When, in the very nick
Of giving up, one time more, came a click
As when a trap shuts—you're inside the den!

30

175 Burningly it came on me all at once,
This was the place! those two hills on the right,
Crouched like two bulls locked horn in horn in fight;
While to the left, a tall scalped mountain . . . Dunce,
Dotard, a-dozing at the very nonce,[23]
180 After a life spent training for the sight!

31

What in the midst lay but the Tower itself?
The round squat turret, blind as the fool's heart,
Built of brown stone, without a counterpart
In the whole world. The tempest's mocking elf
185 Points to the shipman thus the unseen shelf
He strikes on, only when the timbers start.

32

Not see? because of night perhaps?—why, day
Came back again for that! before it left,
The dying sunset kindled through a cleft:
190 The hills, like giants at a hunting, lay,
Chin upon hand, to see the game at bay,—
"Now stab and end the creature—to the heft!"[24]

33

Not hear? when noise was everywhere! it tolled
Increasing like a bell. Names in my ears
195 Of all the lost adventurers my peers,—
How such a one was strong, and such was bold,
And such was fortunate, yet each of old
Lost, lost! one moment knelled the woe of years.

---

[23] Moment.
[24] Handle of dagger or knife.

34

There they stood, ranged along the hillsides, met
200 To view the last of me, a living frame
For one more picture! in a sheet of flame
I saw them and I knew them all. And yet
Dauntless the slug-horn[25] to my lips I set,
And blew. *"Childe Roland to the Dark Tower came."*

---

[25] Rough trumpet made from the horn of an ox or cow.

# 7 Beyond the Speaker: The Double Vision of Irony

Irony exists whenever we say one thing and mean the opposite. "An exam? What fun!" is an ironic statement. More generally, irony exists whenever we feel a disparity between what someone says or thinks and what we know to be the truth. Irony can be intentional or unintentional, depending on whether the speaker means the statement to be ironic or not. A student who says, "A test today? What fun!" is almost certainly indulging in deliberate irony: he or she neither thinks of the test as fun nor expects others to think of it in that manner.

Suppose, however, that we are fellow students; suppose that you know (but I don't) that an English test has been scheduled for today; and suppose that I now say something like, "Boy, am I tired! I think I'll sleep through English class today!" This is unintentional irony. I am seriously planning to sleep. You know, however, that I will *not* be sleeping through English class. Instead, I will be cudgeling my tired brain, trying to pass an unexpected exam. In this case, it is your perception (as audience) that creates the irony. You know (as I, the innocent speaker, cannot know) how far from reality my words and expectations are.

The emotions of irony arise from our perceptions of a conflict between intent or ideal and reality. The technique of irony consists of creating a parallel disparity in words, by creating an opposition between the apparent meaning of the words and their ironic significance. Always there is some hint of pain in irony, some overtone of pity or anger. And always the emotion is a shared one: shared between reader and speaker if the irony is intentional, shared between reader and writer if it is not.

In responding to irony, then, we are aligning ourselves with someone whose perceptions we share, having been invited—as one right-thinking person by another—to share both the ironist's view of the subject and the emotions of scorn or pity or rage that go with it. Always, therefore, there will be some hint of argument (implicit or explicit) in an ironic poem. And always, the use of irony will produce some distancing of effect, as we stand back and judge the presented disparity.

Beyond these basic facts, however, we will see that irony is a technique that allows many variations of meaning, tone, and effect. As with most definitions, when we have defined a poem as ironic, we have only begun to talk about its construction, its meaning, and its power to touch us.

As you read the poems that follow, decide:

1. What disparity is being highlighted?
2. What ideals or beliefs that you hold are being appealed to? Is the appeal explicit or implicit?
3. Is the speaker conscious or unconscious of the irony of his or her speech?
4. If there is more than one voice in the poem, how are they contrasted? What part does the contrast play in your sense of the poem's irony?
5. What range of feelings does the poem suggest?

Then discuss each poem more fully, making whatever points you think are most helpful in deciding what role the irony plays in your appreciation of the poem as a whole.

ADRIENNE RICH (1929– )

**Aunt Jennifer's Tigers**

Aunt Jennifer's tigers prance across a screen,
Bright topaz denizens of a world of green.
They do not fear the men beneath the tree;
They pace in sleek chivalric certainty.

5 Aunt Jennifer's fingers fluttering through her wool
Find even the ivory needle hard to pull.
The massive weight of Uncle's wedding band
Sits heavily upon Aunt Jennifer's hand.

When Aunt is dead, her terrified hands will lie
10 Still ringed with ordeals she was mastered by.
The tigers in the panel that she made
Will go on prancing, proud and unafraid.

## ARTHUR HUGH CLOUGH (1819–1861)

### The Latest Decalogue

Thou shalt have one God only; who
Would be at the expense of two?
No graven images may be
Worshiped, except the currency:
5 Swear not at all; for for thy curse
Thine enemy is none the worse:
At church on Sunday to attend
Will serve to keep the world thy friend:
Honour thy parents; that is, all
10 From whom advancement may befall:
Thou shalt not kill; but need'st not strive
Officiously to keep alive:
Do not adultery commit;
Advantage rarely comes of it:
15 Thou shalt not steal; an empty feat,
When it's so lucrative to cheat:
Bear not false witness; let the lie
Have time on its own wings to fly:
Thou shalt not covet; but tradition
20 Approves all forms of competition.

The sum of all is, thou shalt love,
If any body, God above:
At any rate shall never labour
*More* than thyself to love thy neighbour.

## A. E. HOUSMAN (1859–1936)

### *From* A Shropshire Lad

### When I Was One-and-Twenty

When I was one-and-twenty
  I heard a wise man say,
"Give crowns and pounds and guineas
  But not your heart away;

5 Give pearls away and rubies
  But keep your fancy free."
But I was one-and-twenty,
  No use to talk to me.

When I was one-and-twenty
10 I heard him say again,

"The heart out of the bosom
Was never given in vain;

'Tis paid with sighs a plenty
And sold for endless rue."
15 And I am two-and-twenty,
And oh, 'tis true, 'tis true.

WILLIAM BUTLER YEATS (1865–1939)

**The Folly of Being Comforted**

One that is ever kind said yesterday:
"Your well-belovèd's hair has threads of gray,
And little shadows come about her eyes;
Time can but make it easier to be wise
5 Though now it seem impossible, and so
All that you need is patience."
Heart cries, "No,
I have not a crumb of comfort, not a grain.
Time can but make her beauty over again:
Because of that great nobleness of hers
10 The fire that stirs about her, when she stirs,
Burns but more clearly. O she had not these ways
When all the wild summer was in her gaze."

O heart! O heart! if she'd but turn her head,
You'd know the folly of being comforted.

PERCY BYSSHE SHELLEY (1792–1822)

**Ozymandias**

I met a traveler from an antique land
Who said: Two vast and trunkless legs of stone
Stand in the desert . . . Near them, on the sand,
Half sunk, a shattered visage lies, whose frown,
5 And wrinkled lip, and sneer of cold command,
Tell that its sculptor well those passions read
Which yet survive, stamped on these lifeless things,
The hand that mocked them, and the heart that fed:
And on the pedestal these words appear:
10 "My name is Ozymandias, king of kings:
Look on my works, ye Mighty, and despair!"
Nothing beside remains. Round the decay
Of that colossal wreck, boundless and bare
The lone and level sands stretch far away.

## W. H. AUDEN (1907–1973)

### The Unknown Citizen

*(To JS/07/M/378*
*This Marble Monument*
*Is Erected by the State)*

He was found by the Bureau of Statistics to be
One against whom there was no official complaint,
And all the reports on his conduct agree
That, in the modern sense of an old-fashioned word, he was
a saint,
5 For in everything he did he served the Greater Community.
Except for the War till the day he retired
He worked in a factory and never got fired,
But satisfied his employers, Fudge Motors Inc.
Yet he wasn't a scab or odd in his views,
10 For his Union reports that he paid his dues,
(Our report on his Union shows it was sound)
And our Social Psychology workers found
That he was popular with his mates and liked a drink.
The Press are convinced that he bought a paper every day
15 And that his reactions to advertisements were normal in every
way.
Policies taken out in his name prove that he was fully insured,
And his Health-card shows he was once in hospital but left it
cured.
Both Producers Research and High-Grade Living declare
He was fully sensible to the advantages of the Instalment Plan
20 And had everything necessary to the Modern Man,
A phonograph, a radio, a car, and a frigidaire.
Our researchers into Public Opinion are content
That he held the proper opinions for the time of year;
When there was peace, he was for peace; when there was war, he
went.
25 He was married and added five children to the population,
Which our Eugenist says was the right number for a parent of his
generation,
And our teachers report that he never interfered with their
education.
Was he free? Was he happy? The question is absurd:
Had anything been wrong, we should certainly have heard.

# IMAGERY

# 8 Similes, Metaphors, and Personification

The three basic elements of any poem are the vision it embodies, the speaker who gives voice to the vision, and the language that creates voice and vision alike. (By stretching the terminology a bit, we could call them the three V's: voice, vision, and vocabulary.) In the preceding chapters, we examined the ways in which the language of a poem—its vocabulary, its connotations, its sounds—created and characterized the poem's speaker. Now it is time to look at the ways in which the language creates the vision.

Vision in literature always implies a shared vision. Originating in the writer's mind, the vision is first translated into words and then re-created in our minds, to be felt by us as it was felt by its writer. When we come to the end of a poem, therefore, the feeling we experience is likely to be a blend of recognition and surprise. We will have seen something familiar —perhaps even something of ourselves—as we have never seen it before.

There are two ways in which poets can go about creating this feeling. The first is to word their vision so precisely that we feel we are seeing things with a new closeness and clearness. This is the method chosen by Levertov in "Six Variations (part iii)" and Lawrence in "Piano."

The second method relies on figures of speech or on unexpected comparisons to lead us into making connections we may not have made before. This is Pound's method in "In a Station of the Metro," where human "faces in the crowd" are seen as "petals on a wet black bough," beauty and impersonality mingling. It is Dickinson's method, too, when she describes her "certain slant of light" as being one that "oppresses, like the weight/Of cathedral tunes."

This trick of mingling appeals to different senses in a single image—of describing a sound in terms of color, or a sight in terms of sound or feel—is called **synaesthesia.** Rather than trying to define a type of light in terms of its appearance, Dickinson compares it to a sound. But she speaks of both in terms of weight that presses down physically or spiritually. The word *cathedral,* meanwhile, not only defines the solemn, religious music that parallels the "slant of light," but also prepares us for the image of "heavenly hurt" introduced in the next line. Thus the poem weaves its pattern of imagery.

We have, then, already met poems that make use of both the literal and the figurative styles of imagery. To make sure the contrast is clear, however, let's look at two poems on one subject and see how the language works in each.

WALT WHITMAN (1819–1892)

## The Dalliance of the Eagles

Skirting the river road, (my forenoon walk, my rest,)
Skyward in air a sudden muffled sound, the dalliance of the eagles,
The rushing amorous contact high in space together,
The clinching interlocking claws, a living, fierce, gyrating wheel,
5 Four beating wings, two beaks, a swirling mass tight grappling,
In tumbling turning clustering loops, straight downward falling,
Till o'er the river pois'd, the twain yet one, a moment's lull,
A motionless still balance in the air, then parting, talons loosing,
Upward again on slow-firm pinions slanting, their separate diverse
flight,
10 She hers, he his, pursuing.

ALFRED, LORD TENNYSON (1809–1892)

## The Eagle

He clasps the crag with crooked hands;
Close to the sun in lonely lands,
Ringed with the azure world, he stands.

The wrinkled sea beneath him crawls;
5 He watches from his mountain walls,
And like a thunderbolt he falls.

Obviously, these are very dissimilar poems. One, talking of a single eagle that remains unmoving throughout most of the poem, creates an atmosphere of space and solitude. The other, speaking of two eagles, seems a constant rush of motion. In part, it is the sound of the words the poets have chosen that creates these different atmospheres. Tennyson's words, lines, and sentences are all short, and the stop at the end of each line is strongly marked. Whitman uses longer lines, with less pronounced breaks between them; and his sentences are so involved and complex that they keep the reader's mind and voice in almost constant motion as dizzying as that of the eagles themselves. Yet the basic difference in the way these eagles are shown to us lies not in their motion or motionlessness, but rather in the imagery in which they are described.

If we go through each poem, noting carefully each descriptive term used, we will discover a marked contrast. Whitman relies heavily on adjectives, particularly on participles (adjectives formed from verbs). *Clinching, interlocking, living, gyrating, beating, swirling, grappling, tumbling, turning, clustering, falling*—from these comes the poem's sense of action, as well as much of its power of description. The poet's stance is primarily that of the observer. Taking a walk, he has been startled first by the "sudden muffled sound" and then by the sight of the eagles; and he describes sight and sound alike as carefully and vividly as he can:

> The clinching interlocking claws, a living, fierce, gyrating
>   wheel,
> Four beating wings, two beaks, a swirling mass tight
>   grappling,
> In tumbling turning clustering loops, straight downward
>   falling.

Tennyson's fragment, too, is pure description. But its phrasing and its imagery come as much from the poet's imagination as from his powers of observation. Where Whitman uses no words that could not, in sober prose, be applied to an eagle, Tennyson uses almost none that could. His eagle is presented largely in terms that compare it to other things: an old man, grown crooked with age; an explorer in "lonely lands"; a thunderbolt. By calling our attention to these other things, he draws on our feelings about them (respect, for instance, or awe) and uses those feelings to influence our feelings about the eagle itself. Thus, instead of a bird's "clinching . . . claws," Tennyson's eagle has "crooked hands." He "stands"—which, to some readers, may sound more human than birdlike—and "watches," as men and birds both do. Later, he "falls"—an ambiguous verb. The landscape in which he is pictured is similarly humanized. The lands are "lonely," the sea is "wrinkled" and "crawls." There is exaggeration (or **hyperbole**) as well. The eagle's perch is "close to the sun"; the sky against which he is seen is an entire "azure world"; the eagle falls "like a thunderbolt." High and remote, yet somehow in his very remoteness human, Tennyson's eagle presents a striking image of a being in lofty isolation.

By linking disparate things, by forcing us to think of one thing in terms of another, poets make us see those things in new ways, creating new images, calling forth unexpected emotions, fostering new insights. With homely and familiar images, they bring strange things closer to us, while with exotic images they cast new light on everyday things. Abstract ideas are given vivid life by concrete images, while more abstract imagery suggests new significance for particular items or experiences. Poets can speak of their subjects in the most precise, closely fitting words they can find; or they can seek out unexpected startling terms that will call our own imaginations and creative impulses into play. Since it is so largely this choice of how language will be handled in any given poem that determines our sense of that poem, our first or final reaction to it—the totally different feelings that Whitman's torrent of precisely denotative adjectives and Tennyson's careful balance of connotations of humanity, space, and isolation provoke—it will be worth our while to examine some of the techniques that poets use in the creation of imagery. Let us look, therefore, at some of the commoner forms of imagery found in poetry. Since comparisons are often the result of figurative speech, we will start with figures that are forms of comparison: the explicit comparisons, the simile and the metaphor; and the implicit ones, implied metaphor and personification.

## Simile

A **simile** is a comparison and is always stated as such. You will always find *like, as, so,* or some such word of comparison within it. Usually, the things it compares resemble each other in only one or two ways, differing in all other respects. An eagle and a thunderbolt are not really much alike; yet the fact that both go from the sky to the ground can allow Tennyson to declare that "like a thunderbolt he falls." In the differences between the two lies the simile's power. The fact that a thunderbolt is so much swifter, so much more powerful and dangerous than the eagle, lends a sense of speed and power and danger to the eagle's fall. A simile may be as brief as the traditional "red as blood," or it may be considerably more complicated, as in this example from "Tell All the Truth":

> As Lightning to the Children eased
> With explanation kind
> The Truth must dazzle gradually
> Or every man be blind—

Notice the use of similes in the following poem.

LANGSTON HUGHES (1902–1967)

## Harlem

What happens to a dream deferred?

Does it dry up
like a raisin in the sun?
Or fester like a sore—
5 And then run?
Does it stink like rotten meat?
Or crust and sugar over—
like a syrupy sweet?

Maybe it just sags
10 like a heavy load.

*Or does it explode?*

QUESTIONS

1. What relationship do the various similes have to each other and to the subject of the poem, as defined by the title and first line?
2. What has been done with the last simile? Why?

## Metaphor and Implied Metaphor

Like similes, **metaphors** are direct comparisons of one object with another. In metaphors, however, the fusion between the two objects is more complete, for metaphor uses no "as" or "like" to separate the two things being compared. Instead, a metaphor simply declares that *A* "is" *B;* one element of the comparison becomes, for the moment at least, the other.

Some metaphors go even farther and omit the "is." They simply talk about *A* as if it were *B,* using terms appropriate to *B.* They may not even name *B* at all but rather let us guess what it is from the words being used. In this case, the metaphor becomes an **implied metaphor.**

Since a simile merely says that *A* is "like" *B,* it needs to find only one point or moment of similarity between two otherwise dissimilar objects in order to achieve its effect. (For example, the cherry that is "red as the blood" resembles blood in no other way.) Metaphors, in contrast, tend to make more detailed claims for closer likenesses between the subjects of their comparisons. Notice, for instance, how many points of similarity are suggested by the metaphors in the next two poems. Ask yourself, in each case, what points of comparison the metaphor makes openly or explicitly and what further points of comparison it suggests to you.

## JOHN KEATS (1795–1821)

### On First Looking into Chapman's Homer

Much have I travelled in the realms of gold,
  And many goodly states and kingdoms seen;
  Round many western islands have I been
Which bards in fealty to Apollo hold.
5 Oft of one wide expanse had I been told
  That deep-browed Homer ruled as his demesne;
  Yet did I never breathe its pure serene
Till I heard Chapman speak out loud and bold:
Then felt I like some watcher of the skies
10 When a new planet swims into his ken;
Or like stout Cortez when with eagle eyes
  He stared at the Pacific—and all his men
Looked at each other with a wild surmise—
  Silent, upon a peak in Darien.

QUESTIONS

1. The vocabulary in the first eight lines of this poem is taken mostly from the Middle Ages and its system of feudalism: *realms* for *kingdoms,* for example; *bards* for *poets; fealty* for the system under which a nobleman would rule part of a country, being himself ruled by a king or a greater nobleman; and *demesne* for the nobleman's domain, the part of the country he ruled. (*Oft* for *often, serene* for *air,* and *ken* for *knowledge* are also old words that are no longer in daily use.) Apollo, on the other hand, comes from classical mythology, and is the god of poets. (He's also the god of the sun, but that doesn't particularly enter into this poem.) Homer is an ancient Greek poet and Chapman a sixteenth-century English poet who translated Homer's *Iliad* into English verse. The question therefore arises: why should Keats use the language of the Middle Ages and the metaphor of traveling to talk about his joy in reading poetry and the great delight he felt when his discovery of Chapman's translation let him feel that he was really hearing Homer for the first time?
2. When Keats does discover Chapman's translation, two new similes occur to him that support the traveler metaphor. What is the first (ll. 9–10)? What sort of progression has been made: how does the new identity the poet feels resemble his earlier identity as traveler? How is it different? What sort of feelings go with each identity? (Note the phrase "a new planet"; why *new?*)
3. In lines 11–14, the second simile is set out. Whom does Keats feel like now? What kinds of feelings go with this third identity? How do they form a climax for the poem? (It was really Balboa, and not Cortez, who was the first European to see the Pacific Ocean. Does this make any difference to your enjoyment of the poem?)

CARL SANDBURG (1878–1967)

**Fog**

The fog comes
on little cat feet.
It sits looking
over harbor and city
5 on silent haunches
and then moves on.

## Personification

Implied metaphors, being more compact and requiring the reader to share in their creation slightly more than regular metaphors do, are frequent in poetry. But one type appears so frequently that it has a name of its own. This is **personification,** the trick of talking about some non-human thing as if it were human. We saw personification used in Blake's "When the stars threw down their spears" and in the "crooked hands" of Tennyson's "Eagle."

The poems in the rest of this chapter are notable for their figures of speech. They can thus serve both as exercises in identifying metaphors, similes, and implied metaphors, and as poems illustrating how these figures of speech can help create tone and meaning in poetry. Read each of the poems through at least once. Then go through the poem and note the figures of speech you find in it. Identify each one: is it a simile, a metaphor, an implied metaphor, a personification? Decide what elements make up the comparison: what is being compared to what? And jot down your ideas on why the poet might have wanted his or her readers to think about that comparison.

When you have done this, read the poem through once more. Then look again at the figures of speech you have found. Decide how each relates to the subject of the poem, and how each contributes to your sense of the speaker's feelings toward that subject. Decide, too, how many subjects of comparison there are. Is each subject compared to one other thing, or is one subject compared to several things?

If one subject is compared to one other thing, is that comparison developed at any length? If it is, what does its development lend your sense of the poem and its progression?

If one subject is compared to more than one other thing, or if several subjects of comparison exist, how are the different images fitted together? Are unrelated images juxtaposed for you to fit into some total picture; or does the speaker suggest some relationship of similarity or contrast between them? How does the pattern thus created of related or juxtaposed images help create your sense of the speaker's vision, of the poem's meaning or movement?

Finally, read the poem through once again to see whether you are satisfied with the conclusions you have come to, or whether you think there are other things that should be said about the poem or its imagery.

This may sound like a very complicated procedure. But the method of reading through, looking closely, and reading through again allows you to give attention to details of technique without losing your grip on the poem as a whole. When dealing with relatively simple poems, it's a handy practice. When dealing with more complex poetry, it's essential.

ROBERT BURNS (1759–1796)

**A Red, Red Rose**

O my luve's like a red, red rose,
  That's newly sprung in June;
O my luve's like the melodie
  That's sweetly played in tune.

5 As fair art thou, my bonnie lass,
  So deep in luve am I;
And I will luve thee still, my dear,
  Till a' the seas gang[1] dry.

Till a' the seas gang dry, my dear,
10 And the rocks melt wi' the sun:
O I will love thee still, my dear,
  While the sands o' life shall run.

And fare thee weel, my only luve,
  And fare thee weel awhile!
15 And I will come again, my luve,
  Though it were ten thousand mile.

EMILY DICKINSON (1830–1886)

**I Like to See It Lap the Miles (#585)**

I like to see it lap the Miles—
And lick the Valleys up—
And stop to feed itself at Tanks—
And then—prodigious step

1 Go.

5 Around a Pile of Mountains—
And supercilious peer
In Shanties—by the sides of Roads—
And then a Quarry pare

To fit its sides
10 And crawl between
Complaining all the while
In horrid—hooting stanza—
Then chase itself down Hill—

And neigh like Boanerges[1]—
15 Then—prompter than a Star
Stop—docile and omnipotent
At its own stable door—

NIKKI GIOVANNI (1943– )

**Woman**

she wanted to be a blade
of grass amid the fields
but he wouldn't agree
to be the dandelion

5 she wanted to be a robin singing
through the leaves
but he refused to be
her tree

she spun herself into a web
10 and looking for a place to rest
turned to him
but he stood straight
declining to be her corner

she tried to be a book
15 but he wouldn't read

she turned herself into a bulb
but he wouldn't let her grow

[1] Jesus' name for his apostles John and James; also used to refer to a loud-voiced preacher or speaker.

she decided to become  
a woman  
20 and though he still refused  
to be a man  
she decided it was all  
right

## SEAMUS HEANEY (1939– )

### Docker

There, in the corner, staring at his drink.  
The cap juts like a gantry's crossbeam,  
Cowling plated forehead and sledgehead jaw.  
Speech is clamped in the lips' vice.

5 That fist would drop a hammer on a Catholic—  
Oh yes, that kind of thing could start again;  
The only Roman collar he tolerates  
Smiles all round his sleek pint of porter.[1]

Mosaic imperatives bang home like rivets;  
10 God is a foreman with certain definite views  
Who orders life in shifts of work and leisure.  
A factory horn will blare the Resurrection.

He sits, strong and blunt as a Celtic cross,  
Clearly used to silence and an armchair:  
15 Tonight the wife and children will be quiet  
At slammed door and smoker's cough in the hall.

## WILLIAM WORDSWORTH (1770–1850)

### Composed upon Westminster Bridge, September 3, 1802

Earth has not anything to show more fair:  
Dull would he be of soul who could pass by  
A sight so touching in its majesty;  
This City now doth, like a garment, wear  
5 The beauty of the morning; silent, bare,  
Ships, towers, domes, theaters, and temples lie  
Open unto the fields, and to the sky;  
All bright and glittering in the smokeless air.  
Never did sun more beautifully steep

[1] Short for porter's beer—a dark beer resembling light stout.

10 In his first splendor, valley, rock, or hill;
Ne'er saw I, never felt, a calm so deep!
The river glideth at his own sweet will:
Dear God! the very houses seem asleep;
And all that mighty heart is lying still!

SYLVIA PLATH (1932–1963)

**Morning Song**

Love set you going like a fat gold watch.
The midwife slapped your footsoles, and your bald cry
Took its place among the elements.

Our voices echo, magnifying your arrival. New statue.
5 In a drafty museum, your nakedness
Shadows our safety. We stand round blankly as walls.

I'm no more your mother
Than the cloud that distils a mirror to reflect its own slow
Effacement at the wind's hand.

10 All night your moth-breath
Flickers among the flat pink roses. I wake to listen:
A far sea moves in my ear.

One cry, and I stumble from bed, cow-heavy and floral
In my Victorian nightgown.
15 Your mouth opens clean as a cat's. The window square

Whitens and swallows its dull stars. And now you try
Your handful of notes;
The clear vowels rise like balloons.

Most metaphors and similes have a certain timelessness to them. Wordsworth's vision of London asleep and Hughes's picture of energy turning angry in Harlem are both visions of something real and, therefore, enduring. In the following poem, however, the metaphorical vision is transitory and illusory. Nonetheless, it illuminates the speaker's view of the world. Note the movement of the imagery from metaphorical to literal within the poem. Consider how it expresses and develops the statement made by the poem's title. (Note particularly the "difficult balance" in the last line. What meanings does that phrase have here at the end of the poem?) Then discuss how the metaphor's statement and development create both the specific picture of the waking man and the wider vision that fills the speaker's mind.

## RICHARD WILBUR (1921– )

### Love Calls Us to the Things of This World

The eyes open to a cry of pulleys,
And spirited from sleep, the astounded soul
Hangs for a moment bodiless and simple
As false dawn.
5 Outside the open window
The morning air is all awash with angels.

Some are in bed-sheets, some are in blouses,
Some are in smocks: but truly there they are.
Now they are rising together in calm swells
10 Of halcyon feeling, filling whatever they wear
With the deep joy of their impersonal breathing;

Now they are flying in place, conveying
The terrible speed of their omnipresence, moving
And staying like white water; and now of a sudden
15 They swoon down into so rapt a quiet
That nobody seems to be there.
The soul shrinks

From all that it is about to remember,
From the punctual rape of every blessèd day,
20 And cries,
"Oh, let there be nothing on earth but laundry,
Nothing but rosy hands in the rising steam
And clear dances done in the sight of heaven."

Yet, as the sun acknowledges
25 With a warm look the world's hunks and colors,
The soul descends once more in bitter love
To accept the waking body, saying now
In a changed voice as the man yawns and rises,

"Bring them down from their ruddy gallows;
30 Let there be clean linen for the backs of thieves;
Let lovers go fresh and sweet to be undone,
And the heaviest nuns walk in a pure floating
Of dark habits,
keeping their difficult balance."

# 9 Symbol and Allegory

Similes and metaphors make their comparisons quickly and explicitly. They occupy a line or two; and then they are set, ready for further development, but equally ready to be superseded by another simile or metaphor. How the poet uses them, or how many are used within a poem, is up to the poet. The range of possibilities is wide.

Symbol and allegory, however, tend to dominate the poems in which they are used. Moreover, they usually stand alone: one symbol or allegory is usually the most any given poem can support.

Similes and metaphors are used to make us look more attentively at the poem's subject: at the beauty of an evening or early morning scene, at laundry on a clothesline, at a newborn child. They appeal directly to our senses: "cow-heavy," "clean as a cat's," "the clear vowels rise like balloons." Often, they illuminate some larger question: "What happens to a dream deferred?" What are some of the feelings a new mother might have toward her child and her own motherhood? But they illuminate the larger question by keeping our attention on the things they describe: the rotten meat and the early-morning cries.

Symbols and allegories, on the other hand, urge us to look beyond the literal significance of the poem's statements or action. "Birches," for instance, goes beyond a simple description of trees to express a freedom of spirit that the birch trees symbolize for the speaker. "The Tyger" does not call our attention to tigers so much as to the awesome qualities suggested by the tiger's fierce beauty and to the godlike powers involved in the beast's creation. If we wish, in fact, "The Tyger" can take us even further, to the question of the existence of evil, as symbolized by the tiger's murderous nature. How far we wish to pursue the questionings begun by the poem is up to us.

When we meet with imagery that seems to be calling to us to look beyond the immediate event and its emotional ramifications, we may suspect we are dealing with symbol or allegory. But how are we to distinguish which we are dealing with?

An **allegory** always tells of an action. The events of that action should make sense literally but make more profound sense through a second, allegorical, interpretation. Usually that second interpretation will have a spiritual or a psychological significance; for allegories are particularly good at using physical actions to describe the workings of the human mind and spirit. "Young Goodman Brown," we recall, was an allegory of this type. On the literal level, it described a young man's encounter with witchcraft (or his dream of witchcraft). On the allegorical level, it described the process by which a person (who can be anyone, male or female) loses faith in human goodness.

In allegory, then, we are given a story that presents a one-to-one correspondence between some physical action (most often an encounter of some kind) and some second action (usually psychological or spiritual), with each step in the literal tale corresponding to a parallel step on the allegorical level. **Symbolism** may likewise present us with a tale or an action. But it may equally well present us with a description of some unchanging being or object. And it is more likely to suggest several possible interpretations than it is to insist on a single one.

In "Ozymandias," for instance, the whole tale of the power and fall of the king is symbolic. But the most striking symbol within it is the broken statue with its vainly boastful inscription. (For many of us, it's the sight of that statue that leaps to mind when anyone says "Ozymandias." The full tale tends to come as an afterthought.)

And how do we explain the tale's symbolism? Does the king's fall symbolize the fall of the proud (which would give the poem a moral interpretation), the fall of tyranny (which would give it a political one), or merely the inevitable destruction by time of human lives and civilizations? May we not, in fact, read overtones of all three types of meaning into the traveler's tale? Certainly the tyrant, with his "sneer of cold command," seems unpleasant enough for us to rejoice in his overthrow. But the sculptor, he with "the hand that mocked" the sneer, is dead as well; and even his longer-enduring work is half destroyed. How do we feel about that? The picture the sonnet paints is straightforward enough; its tone and message are somewhat more complicated.

Some symbols are conventional; and these will suggest a single interpretation. "The Lamb," relying on the traditional association of the lamb as Christ, is an example of conventional symbolism in poetry. Alternatively, the poet may invent a symbol and provide its interpretation as well. In general, however, symbols in poetry ask the reader to interpret them. The interaction between poet and reader thus admits the greatest possible freedom of suggestion and response.

As you read the following poems, decide whether you think them better interpreted symbolically or allegorically. How would you discuss the poem's language, imagery, and progression to support your interpretation?

GEORGE HERBERT (1593–1633)

**Love (III)**

Love bade me welcome; yet my soul drew back,
Guilty of dust and sin.
But quick-eyed Love, observing me grow slack
From my first entrance in,
5 Drew nearer to me, sweetly questioning
If I lacked anything.

"A guest," I answered, "worthy to be here."
Love said, "You shall be he."
"I, the unkind, ungrateful? Ah my dear,
10 I cannot look on Thee."
Love took my hand, and smiling, did reply,
"Who made the eyes but I?"

"Truth, Lord, but I have marred them; let my shame
Go where it doth deserve."
15 "And know you not," says Love, "who bore the blame?"
"My dear, then I will serve."
"You must sit down," says Love, "and taste my meat."
So I did sit and eat.

WILLIAM BLAKE (1757–1827)

*From* **Songs of Experience**

**The Sick Rose**

O Rose, thou art sick.
The invisible worm
That flies in the night
In the howling storm

5 Has found out thy bed
Of crimson joy,
And his dark secret love
Does thy life destroy.

## RALPH WALDO EMERSON (1803–1882)

### Days

Daughters of Time, the hypocritic Days,
Muffled and dumb like barefoot dervishes,
And marching single in an endless file,
Bring diadems and fagots in their hands.
5 To each they offer gifts after his will,
Bread, kingdoms, stars, and sky that holds them all.
I, in my pleached garden, watched the pomp,
Forgot my morning wishes, hastily
Took a few herbs and apples, and the Day
10 Turned and departed silent. I, too late,
Under her solemn fillet saw the scorn.

## AMY LOWELL (1874–1925)

### Patterns

I walk down the garden paths,
And all the daffodils
Are blowing, and the bright blue squills.
I walk down the patterned garden paths
5 In my stiff, brocaded gown.
With my powdered hair and jewelled fan,
I too am a rare
Pattern. As I wander down
The garden paths.

10 My dress is richly figured,
And the train
Makes a pink and silver stain
On the gravel, and the thrift
Of the borders.
15 Just a plate of current fashion,
Tripping by in high-heeled, ribboned shoes.

Not a softness anywhere about me,
Only whalebone and brocade.
And I sink on a seat in the shade
20 Of a lime tree. For my passion
Wars against the stiff brocade.
The daffodils and squills
Flutter in the breeze
As they please.
25 And I weep;
For the lime-tree is in blossom
And one small flower has dropped upon my bosom.

And the plashing of waterdrops
In the marble fountain
30 Comes down the garden paths.
The dripping never stops.
Underneath my stiffened gown
Is the softness of a woman bathing in a marble basin,
A basin in the midst of hedges grown
35 So thick, she cannot see her lover hiding,
But she guesses he is near,
And the sliding of the water
Seems the stroking of a dear
Hand upon her.
40 What is Summer in a fine brocaded gown!
I should like to see it lying in a heap upon the ground.
All the pink and silver crumpled up on the ground.

I would be the pink and silver as I ran along the paths,
And he would stumble after,
45 Bewildered by my laughter.
I should see the sun flashing from his sword-hilt and the
buckles on his shoes.
I would choose
To lead him in a maze along the patterned paths,
A bright and laughing maze for my heavy-booted lover.
50 Till he caught me in the shade,
And the buttons of his waistcoat bruised my body as he
clasped me,
Aching, melting, unafraid.
With the shadows of the leaves and the sundrops,
And the plopping of the waterdrops,
55 All about us in the open afternoon—
I am very like to swoon

With the weight of this brocade,
For the sun sifts through the shade.

Underneath the fallen blossom
60 In my bosom,
Is a letter I have hid.
It was brought to me this morning by a rider from the
Duke.
'Madam, we regret to inform you that Lord Hartwell
Died in action Thursday se'nnight.'
65 As I read it in the white, morning sunlight,
The letters squirmed like snakes.
'Any answer, Madam,' said my footman.
'No,' I told him.
'See that the messenger takes some refreshment.
70 No, no answer.'
And I walked into the garden,
Up and down the patterned paths,
In my stiff, correct brocade.
The blue and yellow flowers stood up proudly in the sun,
75 Each one.
I stood upright too,
Held rigid to the pattern
By the stiffness of my gown.
Up and down I walked,
80 Up and down.

In a month he would have been my husband.
In a month, here, underneath this lime,
We would have broke the pattern;
He for me, and I for him,
85 He as Colonel, I as Lady,
On this shady seat.
He had a whim
That sunlight carried blessing.
And I answered, 'It shall be as you have said.'
90 Now he is dead.

In Summer and in Winter I shall walk
Up and down
The patterned garden paths
In my stiff, brocaded gown.
95 The squills and daffodils

Will give place to pillared roses, and to asters, and to snow.
I shall go
Up and down,
In my gown.
100 Gorgeously arrayed,
Boned and stayed.
And the softness of my body will be guarded from embrace
By each button, hook, and lace.
For the man who should loose me is dead,
105 Fighting with the Duke in Flanders,
In a pattern called a war.
Christ! What are patterns for?

ALLEN GINSBERG (1926– )

**In back of the real**

railroad yard in San Jose
I wandered desolate
in front of a tank factory
and sat on a bench
5 near the switchman's shack.

A flower lay on the hay on
the asphalt highway
—the dread hay flower
I thought—It had a
10 brittle black stem and
corolla of yellowish dirty
spikes like Jesus' inchlong
crown, and a soiled
dry center cotton tuft
15 like a used shaving brush
that's been lying under
the garage for a year.

Yellow, yellow flower, and
flower of industry,
20 tough spikey ugly flower,
flower nonetheless,
with the form of the great yellow
Rose in your brain!
This is the flower of the World.

## JOHN KEATS (1795–1821)

### Ode on a Grecian Urn

1

Thou still unravished bride of quietness,
Thou foster-child of silence and slow time,
Sylvan historian, who canst thus express
A flowery tale more sweetly than our rhyme:
5 What leaf-fringed legend haunts about thy shape
Of deities or mortals, or of both,
In Tempe or the dales of Arcady?[1]
What men or gods are these? What maidens loath?
What mad pursuit? What struggle to escape?
10 What pipes and timbrels? What wild ecstasy?

2

Heard melodies are sweet, but those unheard
Are sweeter; therefore, ye soft pipes, play on;
Not to the sensual ear, but, more endeared,
Pipe to the spirit ditties of no tone:
15 Fair youth, beneath the trees, thou canst not leave
Thy song, nor ever can those trees be bare;
Bold Lover, never, never canst thou kiss,
Though winning near the goal—yet, do not grieve;
She cannot fade, though thou hast not thy bliss,
20 Forever wilt thou love, and she be fair!

3

Ah, happy, happy boughs! that cannot shed
Your leaves, nor ever bid the Spring adieu;
And, happy melodist, unweariѐd,
Forever piping songs forever new;
25 More happy love! more happy, happy love!
Forever warm and still to be enjoyed,
Forever panting, and forever young;
All breathing human passion far above,
That leaves a heart high-sorrowful and cloyed,
30 A burning forehead, and a parching tongue.

[1] The vale of Tempe and Arcady (Arcadia) in Greece are symbolic of pastoral beauty.

4

Who are these coming to the sacrifice?
To what green altar, O mysterious priest,
Lead'st thou that heifer lowing at the skies,
And all her silken flanks with garlands dressed?
35 What little town by river or sea shore,
Or mountain-built with peaceful citadel,
Is emptied of this folk, this pious morn?
And, little town, thy streets for evermore
Will silent be; and not a soul to tell
40 Why thou art desolate, can e'er return.

5

O Attic[2] shape! Fair attitude! with brede[3]
Of marble men and maidens overwrought,
With forest branches and the trodden weed;
Thou, silent form, dost tease us out of thought
45 As doth eternity: Cold Pastoral!
When old age shall this generation waste,
Thou shalt remain, in midst of other woe
Than ours, a friend to man, to whom thou say'st,
"Beauty is truth, truth beauty,—that is all
50 Ye know on earth, and all ye need to know."

WILLIAM BUTLER YEATS (1865–1939)

**The Circus Animals' Desertion**

1

I sought a theme and sought for it in vain,
I sought it daily for six weeks or so.
Maybe at last, being but a broken man,
I must be satisfied with my heart, although
5 Winter and summer till old age began
My circus animals were all on show,
Those stilted boys, that burnished chariot,
Lion and woman and the Lord knows what.

---

[2] Grecian, especially Athenian.
[3] Embroidery.

2

What can I but enumerate old themes?
10 First that sea-rider Oisin[1] led by the nose
Through three enchanted islands, allegorical dreams,
Vain gaiety, vain battle, vain repose,
Themes of the embittered heart, or so it seems,
That might adorn old songs or courtly shows;
15 But what cared I that set him on to ride,
I, starved for the bosom of his faery bride?

And then a counter-truth filled out its play,
*The Countess Cathleen*[2] was the name I gave it;
She, pity-crazed, had given her soul away,
20 But masterful Heaven had intervened to save it.
I thought my dear must her own soul destroy,
So did fanaticism and hate enslave it,
And this brought forth a dream and soon enough
This dream itself had all my thought and love.

25 And when the Fool and Blind Man stole the bread
Cuchulain[3] fought the ungovernable sea;
Heart-mysteries there, and yet when all is said
It was the dream itself enchanted me:
Character isolated by a deed
30 To engross the present and dominate memory.
Players and painted stage took all my love,
And not those things that they were emblems of.

3

Those masterful images because complete
Grew in pure mind, but out of what began?

---

[1] In Irish legend, Oisin was a bard who married a fairy and travelled throughout fairyland with her. *The Wanderings of Oisin and Other Poems,* published in 1889, was Yeats' first volume of verse.

[2] Yeats' first published play, written in 1891 and inspired in part by Yeats' love for Maud Gonne and his concern over the intensity of her involvement in political activism. Cathleen, a figure from Irish folk tale, sold her soul to the devil to save the lives and souls of her tenants during a famine.

[3] Various poems throughout Yeats' career mention Cuchulain, a legendary Irish king who became for Yeats a symbol of Ireland's heroic past. "Cuchulain's Fight with the Sea" appeared in 1893. ("The Circus Animals' Desertion" itself was written in the 1930's.)

35 A mound of refuse or the sweeping of a street,
Old kettles, old bottles, and a broken can,
Old iron, old bones, old rags, that raving slut
Who keeps the till. Now that my ladder's gone,
I must lie down where all the ladders start,
40 In the foul rag-and-bone shop of the heart.

ROBERT HAYDEN (1913–1980)

**Those Winter Sundays**

Sundays too my father got up early
and put his clothes on in the blueblack cold,
then with cracked hands that ached
from labor in the weekday weather made
5 banked fires blaze. No one ever thanked him.

I'd wake and hear the cold splintering, breaking.
When the rooms were warm, he'd call,
and slowly I would rise and dress,
fearing the chronic angers of that house,

10 Speaking indifferently to him,
who had driven out the cold
and polished my good shoes as well.
What did I know, what did I know
of love's austere and lonely offices?

# 10 *Conceits and Allusions*

Metaphors and similes, because of their instant appeal, are usually the first types of figurative speech to catch our attention. Symbols and allegories, which develop as their poems progress, require more preparation from us if we are to enjoy them fully. They offer themselves only to those who are willing not only to read closely and well, but also to go beyond the poem's literal meaning into a realm of wider suggestion. Conceits and allusions may be brief or extensive in scope; but they are the most demanding figures of all, requiring extreme alertness and some outside knowledge in order to be unraveled.

## Conceits

A **conceit** could be defined as an outrageous metaphor, but a more traditional definition is a comparison between two highly dissimilar objects. Conceits are often developed at some length, revealing and weighing point after point of comparison or contrast between their two objects. In love poetry, they often grow out of Renaissance traditions that depict the man as a warrior and the woman as a walled town; he attacks, she defends herself or surrenders. Or the man might be a hunter and the woman a wild animal. Or she might be the warrior, wounding him with sharp looks or sharper words. Or, if she were kinder, she might be a treasure mine or a goddess of love. (The list could go on and on.) Some

Renaissance poets take the conceits seriously; others play with them, making use of the surprise that can come from turning an expected cliché upside down.

With the metaphysical poets of the seventeenth century, the unexpected becomes a key ingredient in the conceit. The metaphysical poets used conceits not only in love poetry, but in religious poetry as well, thereby creating for both types of poetry conceits of unparalleled complexity and ingenuity. Physics, astronomy, navigation—any science, any intellectual endeavor—might yield a conceit that viewed the soul's progress and passions as parallels to the workings of the universe it inhabited. The resulting poetry tends to be remarkably tough intellectually (you read this poetry *very* slowly the first few times), but also remarkably free, self-assured, and optimistic in its visions.

Here is an example of conceits in metaphysical poetry. Note that there are two main clusters of imagery in the poem. The first turns on maps and voyages, the second on the image of Christ as "the second Adam." And note also that the two are connected by the concept of the soul's journey to salvation as an annihilation of time and space and by the physical image of the sick man, flat on his back in bed and sweating heavily with fever.

JOHN DONNE (1572–1631)

**Hymn to God My God, in My Sickness**

Since I am coming to that holy room,
Where, with thy choir of Saints for evermore,
I shall be made thy music; as I come
I tune the instrument here at the door,
5 And what I must do then, think now before.

Whilst my physicians by their love are grown
Cosmographers, and I their map, who lie
Flat on this bed, that by them may be shown
That this is my Southwest discovery
10 *Per fretum febris,*[1] by these straits to die,

I joy, that in these straits, I see my west;[2]
For, though their currents yield return to none,
What shall my west hurt me? As west and east
In all flat maps (and I am one) are one,
15 So death doth touch the Resurrection.

[1] Through the straits of fever.
[2] My death.

Is the Pacific Sea my home? Or are
The eastern riches? Is Jerusalem?
Anyan,[3] and Magellan, and Gibraltàr,
All straits, and none but straits, are ways to them,
20 Whether where Japhet dwelt, or Cham, or Shem.[4]

We think that Paradise and Calvary,
Christ's Cross, and Adam's tree, stood in one place;
Look Lord, and find both Adams met in me;
As the first Adam's sweat surrounds my face,
25 May the last Adam's blood my soul embrace.

So, in his purple wrapped receive me, Lord,
By these his thorns give me his other crown;
And as to others' souls I preached thy word,
Be this my text, my sermon to mine own,
30 Therefore that he may raise, the Lord throws down.

## Allusions

Conceits ask that we bring some knowledge to our reading if we are to understand their implications. For example, we must understand the distortions of space involved in making a flat map represent a round world if we are to understand Donne's hymn. An **allusion** likewise asks us to bring some knowledge to our reading. For an allusion may be defined as a reference to some work of art or literature, or to some well-known person, event, or story. If we do not catch the reference, then we will miss the point of the allusion.

Here is a frequently anthologized Middle English poem that celebrates spring. Following that poem is a "celebration" of winter by a twentieth-century poet who, knowing of the earlier poem's popularity, felt free to burlesque it. Note that Pound's poem can stand on its own, and that it makes no direct reference to the lyric to which it alludes. But note also how much more effective its irascible tone becomes when set off in its reader's mind against the cheerfulness of its medieval model.

[3] Modern Annam, then thought of as a strait between Asia and America.
[4] Sons of Noah, said to have settled Europe, Asia, and Africa after the flood.

## ANONYMOUS—MIDDLE ENGLISH LYRIC

### Sumer Is Icumen In[1]

Sumer is icumen in,
  Lhude sing cuccu!
Groweth sed and bloweth med
  And springth the wude nu.
5    Sing cuccu!

Awe bleteth after lomb,
  Lhouth after calve cu,
Bulluc sterteth, bucke verteth;
  Murie sing cuccu!
10    Cuccu! cuccu!
Wel sings thu cuccu.
Ne swik thu naver nu!

Sing cuccu nu, Sing cuccu!
Sing cuccu, Sing cuccu nu!

## EZRA POUND (1885–1972)

### Ancient Music

Winter is icumen in,
Lhude sing Goddamm,
Raineth drop and staineth slop,
And how the wind doth ramm!
5        Sing : Goddamm.
Skiddeth bus and sloppeth us,
An ague hath my ham.
Freezeth river, turneth liver,
        Damn you, sing : Goddamm.

---

[1] *Translation:*
Spring has come in,
  Loudly sing cuckoo!
Grows seed and blooms mead
  And springs the wood now.
    Sing cuckoo!

Ewe bleats after lamb,
  Lows after calf the cow,
Bullock starts, buck farts;
  Merrily sing cuckoo!
    Cuckoo! cuckoo!
Well sing thou cuckoo.
Cease thou never now!

Sing cuckoo now etc.

10 Goddamm, Goddamm, 'tis why I am, Goddamm,
So 'gainst the winter's balm.
Sing goddamm, damm, sing Goddamm,
Sing goddamm, sing goddam, DAMM.

Discuss how the speakers of the following three poems use conceits or allusions to praise the women they love and to enlarge on the benefits of love. (You will want to concentrate on the poems' imagery; but note also the use of apostrophe, or direct address, and the different tones and logical progressions within each poem. Use the questions that follow each poem to help you.)

EDMUND SPENSER (1552?–1599)

*From* **Amoretti**

**Sonnet 15**

Ye tradefull Merchants, that with weary toyle,
Do seeke most pretious things to make your gain,
And both the Indias of their treasure spoile,
What needeth you to seeke so farre in vaine?
5 For loe, my Love doth in her selfe containe
All this worlds riches that may farre be found:
If saphyres, loe her eies be saphyres plaine;
If rubies, loe hir lips be rubies sound;
If pearles, hir teeth be pearles both pure and round;
10 If yvorie, her forhead yvory weene;
If gold, her locks are finest gold on ground;
If silver, her faire hands are silver sheene:
But that which fairest is but few behold:—
Her mind, adornd with vertues manifold.

QUESTIONS

1. To whom is the poet speaking in the opening four lines (and, by implication, in the rest of the poem as well)? Why should he select this audience? How do the merchants differ from the poet? What do the words *weary* and *in vain* suggest about them or their activities?
2. What similarities do you find among the successive metaphors that occupy lines 7–12?
3. How does the conclusion continue the theme of treasure? How does it alter it? (Note especially the phrase "adorned with virtues manifold.") What new questions does the conclusion raise about the usefulness of the merchants' search for precious things?

## WILLIAM SHAKESPEARE (1564–1616)

### Sonnet 18

Shall I compare thee to a summer's day?
Thou art more lovely and more temperate:
Rough winds do shake the darling buds of May,
And summer's lease hath all too short a date:
5 Sometime too hot the eye of heaven shines,
And often is his gold complexion dimmed;
And every fair from fair sometime declines,
By chance or nature's changing course untrimmed:
But thy eternal summer shall not fade
10 Nor lose possession of that fair thou ow'st,[1]
Nor shall Death brag thou wand'rest in his shade,
When in eternal lines to time thou grow'st.
So long as men can breathe or eyes can see,
So long lives this, and this gives life to thee.

QUESTIONS

This sonnet, too, starts with a question relating to physical qualities—beauty and temperature—and ends up dealing with intangible ones. By what contrasts and what train of logic does it achieve this progression? (Note in particular the "summer's day" of line 1, "the eye of heaven" in line 5, and "eternal summer" in line 9. These phrases mark the starting points of three stages in the argument, with the last two lines marking the final stage. And be warned that "fair" has three meanings. It's a noun meaning "a lovely thing," an adjective meaning "lovely", and a noun meaning "beauty.")

## JOHN DONNE (1572–1631)

### The Sun Rising

Busy old fool, unruly sun,
Why dost thou thus
Through windows and through curtains call on us?
Must to thy motions lovers' seasons run?
5 Saucy, pedantic wretch, go chide
Late schoolboys and sour 'prentices,
Go tell court huntsmen that the king will ride,
Call country ants to harvest offices.
Love, all alike, no season knows nor clime,
10 Nor hours, days, months, which are the rags of time.

---

[1] Ownest.

Thy beams, so reverend and strong
Why shouldst thou think?
I could eclipse and cloud them with a wink,
But that I would not lose her sight so long.
15 If her eyes have not blinded thine,
Look, and tomorrow late tell me
Whether both th' Indias of spice and mine
Be where thou left'st them, or lie here with me;
Ask for those kings whom thou saw'st yesterday,
20 And thou shalt hear: All here in one bed lay.

She's all states, and all princes I;
Nothing else is.
Princes do but play us; compared to this,
All honor's mimic, all wealth alchemy.
25 Thou, sun, art half as happy as we,
In that the world's contracted thus;
Thine age asks ease, and since thy duties be
To warm the world, that's done in warming us.
Shine here to us, and thou art everywhere;
30 This bed thy center is, these walls thy sphere.

### QUESTIONS

1. This poem falls into the category of **aubades**, or "dawn songs." What dramatic value does this placement in time give it?
2. Note that here again earthly riches are first equated with the woman's beauty and then devalued by it, and that time is forced to yield to timelessness. How does Donne's treatment of these conceits differ from those of Shakespeare and Spenser?
3. In general, how would you compare this love poem with those two earlier ones?

The next three poems are spoken by discontented lovers. What could you say about the ways in which they use conceits or allusions to describe their predicaments or to convince themselves or their hearers that some change should be made?

## SIR PHILIP SIDNEY (1554–1586)

*From* **Astrophil and Stella**

### Leave Me, O Love

Leave me, O Love, which reachest but to dust,
And thou, my mind, aspire to higher things.

Grow rich in that which never taketh rust.
Whatever fades but fading pleasure brings.

5 Draw in thy beams and humble all thy might
To that sweet yoke where lasting freedoms be,
Which breaks the clouds and opens forth the light
That doth both shine and give us sight to see.

O take fast hold; let that light be thy guide
10 In this small course which birth draws out to death,
And think how evil becometh him to slide
Who seeketh heaven and comes of heavenly breath.
  Then farewell, world! Thy uttermost I see!
  Eternal Love, maintain thy life in me.

## ANDREW MARVELL (1621–1678)

### To His Coy Mistress

Had we but world enough, and time,
This coyness, lady, were no crime.
We would sit down, and think which way
To walk, and pass our long love's day.
5 Thou by the Indian Ganges' side
Shouldst rubies find; I by the tide
Of Humber would complain. I would
Love you ten years before the Flood,
And you should, if you please, refuse
10 Till the conversion of the Jews.
My vegetable love should grow
Vaster than empires, and more slow;
An hundred years should go to praise
Thine eyes and on thy forehead gaze,
15 Two hundred to adore each breast,
But thirty thousand to the rest:
An age at least to every part,
And the last age should show your heart.
For, lady, you deserve this state,
20 Nor would I love at lower rate.
  But at my back I always hear
Time's wingèd chariot hurrying near;
And yonder all before us lie
Deserts of vast eternity.
25 Thy beauty shall no more be found,
Nor in thy marble vault shall sound

My echoing song; then worms shall try
That long preserved virginity,
And your quaint honor turn to dust,
30 And into ashes all my lust.
The grave's a fine and private place,
But none, I think, do there embrace.
Now, therefore, while the youthful hue
Sits on thy skin like morning dew,
35 And while thy willing soul transpires
At every pore with instant fires,
Now let us sport us while we may,
And now, like amorous birds of prey,
Rather at once our time devour
40 Than languish in his slow-chapped power.
Let us roll all our strength and all
Our sweetness up into one ball,
And tear our pleasures with rough strife
Thorough the iron gates of life.
45 Thus, though we cannot make our sun
Stand still, yet we will make him run.

ROBERT GRAVES (1895–1985)

**Down, Wanton, Down!**

Down, wanton, down! Have you no shame
That at the whisper of Love's name,
Or Beauty's, presto! up you raise
Your angry head and stand at gaze?

5 Poor bombard-captain, sworn to reach
The ravelin and effect a breach—
Indifferent what you storm or why,
So be that in the breach you die!

Love may be blind, but Love at least
10 Knows what is man and what mere beast;
Or Beauty wayward, but requires
More delicacy from her squires.

Tell me, my witless, whose one boast
Could be your staunchness at the post,
15 When were you made a man of parts
To think fine and profess the arts?

Will many-gifted Beauty come
Bowing to your bald rule of thumb,
Or Love swear loyalty to your crown?
20 Be gone, have done! Down, wanton, down!

Although it is the work of a twentieth-century poet, "Down, Wanton, Down!" contains conceits that are very much in the fashion of the seventeenth century. Graves chooses one central comparison and then elaborates it and varies it throughout the poem. (The theme of love and the use of the word *wanton* to describe an overeager lover are also well within the seventeenth-century tradition.) In the next poem, the twentieth-century poet Marianne Moore adapts the use of conceits to her own equally playful and thoughtful but more kaleidoscopic style. What theme do the conceits in "The Mind Is an Enchanting Thing" combine to create? How do they do so? How are such disparate images fitted together?

MARIANNE MOORE (1887–1972)

### The Mind Is an Enchanting Thing

is an enchanted thing
like the glaze on a
katydid-wing
subdivided by sun
5 till the nettings are legion.
Like Gieseking[1] playing Scarlatti;[2]

like the apteryx-awl[3]
as a beak, or the
kiwi's rain-shawl
10 of haired feathers, the mind
feeling its way as though blind,
walks along with its eyes on the ground.

It has memory's ear
that can hear without

---

[1] Walter Gieseking (1895–1956), eminent German pianist.
[2] Domenico Scarlatti (1685–1757), Italian composer of brilliant keyboard sonatas.
[3] A flightless bird with a long, slender beak resembling the shape of an awl.

15 having to hear.
Like the gyroscope's fall,
truly unequivocal
because trued by regnant certainty,

it is a power of
20 strong enchantment. It
is like the dove-
neck animated by
sun; it is memory's eye;
it's conscientious inconsistency.

25 It tears off the veil; tears
the temptation, the
mist the heart wears,
from its eyes,—if the heart
has a face; it takes apart
30 dejection. It's fire in the dove-neck's

iridescence; in the
inconsistencies
of Scarlatti.
Unconfusion submits
35 its confusion to proof; it's
not a Herod's oath[4] that cannot change.

---

[4] See Matthew 2 : 1–16.

# 11 *Patterns of Imagery*

So far, we have spoken of different figures of speech in isolation. In practice, however, the various figures are almost always found in combination with each other. "Days," for instance, is an allegory. But the various gifts the Days carry are symbolic; and the phrase "morning wishes" is metaphorical. Moreover, just as form and meaning reinforce each other, so a poem's figures of speech reinforce each other to create the poem's overall patterns of meaning and imagery. When we discuss a poem, we may start by discussing some particularly striking aspect; and that may mean a particular use of imagery. But eventually we will want to talk of the complete poem; and that will mean talking of the patterns it contains.

The poems in the last chapter were heavily patterned. The Renaissance poems tended to be static, stating a position and then elaborating on it. The metaphysical poems showed more movement, following the speaker's mind through the ramifications of an idea or situation. The poems in this chapter will also display carefully worked-out patterns of imagery. And, as most of them are somewhat longer poems, the patterns will be even more complex. But these poems will also show a freer and more passionate movement, for they come either from the Romantic poetry of the nineteenth century or from twentieth-century poetry that was influenced by that movement. In the more melodious rhythms and harmonies of these poems, we find a vivid sense of immediacy, of unfolding memories or emotions, of minds and spirits caught up in vision and experience. Flowing sound and richly suggestive imagery create the sense of intense experience that was a trademark of the Romantic movement and that still provides some overtones of meaning to the common use of the word *romantic*.

As you read the following poems, be prepared for shifts of emotion as much as for shifts of thought. Note how these more modern poets create scenes, moods, and speakers through sound and imagery.

PERCY BYSSHE SHELLEY (1792–1822)

## Ode to the West Wind

1

O wild West Wind, thou breath of Autumn's being,
Thou, from whose unseen presence the leaves dead
Are driven, like ghosts from an enchanter fleeing,

Yellow, and black, and pale, and hectic red,
5 Pestilence-stricken multitudes: O thou,
Who chariotest to their dark wintry bed

The wingèd seeds, where they lie cold and low,
Each like a corpse within its grave, until
Thine azure sister of the Spring shall blow

10 Her clarion o'er the dreaming earth, and fill
(Driving sweet buds like flocks to feed in air)
With living hues and odors plain and hill:

Wild Spirit, which art moving everywhere;
Destroyer and preserver; hear, oh, hear!

2

15 Thou on whose stream, mid the steep sky's commotion,
Loose clouds like earth's decaying leaves are shed,
Shook from the tangled boughs of Heaven and Ocean,

Angels of rain and lightning: there are spread
On the blue surface of thine aery surge,
20 Like the bright hair uplifted from the head

Of some fierce Maenad,[1] even from the dim verge
Of the horizon to the zenith's height,
The locks of the approaching storm. Thou dirge

Of the dying year, to which this closing night
25 Will be the dome of a vast sepulcher,
Vaulted with all thy congregated might

Of vapors, from whose solid atmosphere
Black rain, and fire, and hail will burst: oh, hear!

3

Thou who didst waken from his summer dreams
30 The blue Mediterranean, where he lay,
Lulled by the coil of his crystàlline streams,

Beside a pumice isle in Baiae's[2] bay,
And saw in sleep old palaces and towers
Quivering within the wave's intenser day,

35 All overgrown with azure moss and flowers
So sweet, the sense faints picturing them! Thou
For whose path the Atlantic's level powers

Cleave themselves into chasms, while far below
The sea-blooms and the oozy woods which wear
40 The sapless foliage of the ocean, know

Thy voice, and suddenly grow gray with fear,
And tremble and despoil themselves: oh, hear!

4

If I were a dead leaf thou mightest bear;
If I were a swift cloud to fly with thee;
45 A wave to pant beneath thy power, and share

The impulse of thy strength, only less free
Than thou, O uncontrollable! If even
I were as in my boyhood, and could be

The comrade of thy wanderings over Heaven,
50 As then, when to outstrip thy skiey speed
Scarce seemed a vision; I would ne'er have striven

[1] A female attendant of Dionysus.
[2] Ancient Roman resort whose submerged ruins can be seen north of Naples.

As thus with thee in prayer in my sore need.
Oh, lift me as a wave, a leaf, a cloud!
I fall upon the thorns of life! I bleed!

55 A heavy weight of hours has chained and bowed
One too like thee: tameless, and swift, and proud.

5

Make me thy lyre, even as the forest is:
What if my leaves are falling like its own!
The tumult of thy mighty harmonies

60 Will take from both a deep, autumnal tone,
Sweet though in sadness. Be thou, Spirit fierce,
My spirit! Be thou me, impetuous one!

Drive my dead thoughts over the universe
Like withered leaves to quicken a new birth!
65 And, by the incantation of this verse,

Scatter, as from an unextinguished hearth
Ashes and sparks, my words among mankind!
Be through my lips to unawakened earth

The trumpet of a prophecy! O Wind,
70 If Winter comes, can Spring be far behind?

## JOHN KEATS (1795–1821)

### Ode to a Nightingale

I

My heart aches, and a drowsy numbness pains
My sense, as though of hemlock I had drunk,
Or emptied some dull opiate to the drains
One minute past, and Lethe-wards[1] had sunk:
5 'Tis not through envy of thy happy lot,
But being too happy in thine happiness—
That thou, light-wingèd Dryad of the trees,
In some melodious plot
Of beechen green, and shadows numberless,
10 Singest of summer in full-throated ease.

---

[1] Towards the river Lethe, in the underworld.

2

O, for a draught of vintage! that hath been
Cooled a long age in the deep-delvèd earth,
Tasting of Flora[2] and the country green,
Dance, and Provençal song, and sunburnt mirth!
15 O for a beaker full of the warm South,
Full of the true, the blushful Hippocrene,[3]
With beaded bubbles winking at the brim,
And purple-stainèd mouth;
That I might drink, and leave the world unseen,
20 And with thee fade away into the forest dim:

3

Fade far away, dissolve, and quite forget
What thou among the leaves hast never known,
The weariness, the fever, and the fret
Here, where men sit and hear each other groan;
25 Where palsy shakes a few, sad, last gray hairs,
Where youth grows pale, and spectre-thin, and dies,
Where but to think is to be full of sorrow
And leaden-eyed despairs,
Where Beauty cannot keep her lustrous eyes,
30 Or new Love pine at them beyond tomorrow.

4

Away! away! for I will fly to thee,
Not charioted by Bacchus and his pards,[4]
But on the viewless wings of Poesy,
Though the dull brain perplexes and retards:
35 Already with thee! tender is the night,
And haply the Queen-Moon is on her throne,
Clustered around by all her starry Fays;
But here there is no light,
Save what from heaven is with the breezes blown
40 Through verdurous glooms and winding mossy ways.

5

I cannot see what flowers are at my feet,
Nor what soft incense hangs upon the boughs,

---

[2] Goddess of flowers.
[3] Fountain of the Muses on Mt. Helicon.
[4] Leopards drawing the chariot of Bacchus, god of wine.

But, in embalmèd darkness, guess each sweet
Wherewith the seasonable month endows
45 The grass, the thicket, and the fruit-tree wild;
White hawthorn, and the pastoral eglantine;
Fast fading violets covered up in leaves;
And mid-May's eldest child,
The coming musk-rose, full of dewy wine,
50 The murmurous haunt of flies on summer eves.

6

Darkling[5] I listen; and for many a time
I have been half in love with easeful Death,
Called him soft names in many a musèd rhyme,
To take into the air my quiet breath;
55 Now more than ever seems it rich to die,
To cease upon the midnight with no pain,
While thou art pouring forth thy soul abroad
In such an ecstasy!
Still wouldst thou sing, and I have ears in vain—
60 To thy high requiem become a sod.

7

Thou wast not born for death, immortal Bird!
No hungry generations tread thee down;
The voice I hear this passing night was heard
In ancient days by emperor and clown:
65 Perhaps the selfsame song that found a path
Through the sad heart of Ruth, when, sick for home,
She stood in tears amid the alien corn:
The same that oft-times hath
Charmed magic casements, opening on the foam
70 Of perilous seas, in faery lands forlorn.

8

Forlorn! the very word is like a bell
To toll me back from thee to my sole self!
Adieu! the fancy cannot cheat so well
As she is famed to do, deceiving elf.

---

[5] In the darkness.

75 Adieu! adieu! thy plaintive anthem fades
   Past the near meadows, over the still stream,
      Up the hill side; and now 'tis buried deep
         In the next valley-glades:
   Was it a vision, or a waking dream?
      Fled is that music:—Do I wake or sleep?

MATTHEW ARNOLD (1822–1888)

**Dover Beach**

The sea is calm tonight.
The tide is full, the moon lies fair
Upon the straits;—on the French coast the light
Gleams and is gone; the cliffs of England stand,
5 Glimmering and vast, out in the tranquil bay.
Come to the window, sweet is the night-air!
Only, from the long line of spray
Where the sea meets the moon-blanched land,
Listen! you hear the grating roar
10 Of pebbles which the waves draw back, and fling,
At their return, up the high strand,
Begin, and cease, and then again begin,
With tremulous cadence slow, and bring
The eternal note of sadness in.

15 Sophocles long ago
Heard it on the Aegean, and it brought
Into his mind the turbid ebb and flow
Of human misery; we
Find also in the sound a thought,
20 Hearing it by this distant northern sea.

The Sea of Faith
Was once, too, at the full, and round earth's shore
Lay like the folds of a bright girdle furled.
But now I only hear
25 Its melancholy, long, withdrawing roar,
Retreating, to the breath
Of the night-wind, down the vast edges drear
And naked shingles of the world.

Ah, love, let us be true
30 To one another! for the world, which seems

To lie before us like a land of dreams,
So various, so beautiful, so new,
Hath really neither joy, nor love, nor light,
Nor certitude, nor peace, nor help for pain;
35 And we are here as on a darkling plain
Swept with confused alarms of struggle and flight,
Where ignorant armies clash by night.

## WILLIAM BUTLER YEATS (1865–1939)

### Sailing to Byzantium

1

That is no country for old men. The young
In one another's arms, birds in the trees
—Those dying generations—at their song,
The salmon-falls, the mackerel-crowded seas,
5 Fish, flesh, or fowl, commend all summer long
Whatever is begotten, born, and dies.
Caught in that sensual music all neglect
Monuments of unageing intellect.

2

An aged man is but a paltry thing,
10 A tattered coat upon a stick, unless
Soul clap its hands and sing, and louder sing
For every tatter in its mortal dress,
Nor is there singing school but studying
Monuments of its own magnificence;
15 And therefore I have sailed the seas and come
To the holy city of Byzantium.

3

O sages standing in God's holy fire
As in the gold mosaic of a wall,
Come from the holy fire, perne in a gyre,
20 And be the singing-masters of my soul.
Consume my heart away; sick with desire
And fastened to a dying animal
It knows not what it is; and gather me
Into the artifice of eternity.

4

25 Once out of nature I shall never take
My bodily form from any natural thing,
But such a form as Grecian goldsmiths make
Of hammered gold and gold enamelling
To keep a drowsy Emperor awake;
30 Or set upon a golden bough to sing
To lords and ladies of Byzantium
Of what is past, or passing, or to come.

DYLAN THOMAS (1914–1953)

**Fern Hill**

Now as I was young and easy under the apple boughs
About the lilting house and happy as the grass was green,
The night above the dingle starry,
Time let me hail and climb
5 Golden in the heydays of his eyes,
And honored among wagons I was prince of the apple towns
And once below a time I lordly had the trees and leaves
Trail with daisies and barley
Down the rivers of the windfall light.

10 And as I was green and carefree, famous among the barns
About the happy yard and singing as the farm was home,
In the sun that is young once only,
Time let me play and be
Golden in the mercy of his means,
15 And green and golden I was huntsman and herdsman, the calves
Sang to my horn, the foxes on the hills barked clear and cold,
And the sabbath rang slowly
In the pebbles of the holy streams.

All the sun long it was running, it was lovely, the hay
20 Fields high as the house, the tunes from the chimneys, it was air
And playing, lovely and watery
And fire green as grass.
And nightly under the simple stars
As I rode to sleep the owls were bearing the farm away,
25 All the moon long I heard, blessed among stables, the night-jars
Flying with the ricks, and the horses
Flashing into the dark.

And then to awake, and the farm, like a wanderer white<br>
With the dew, come back, the cock on his shoulder: it was all<br>
30         Shining, it was Adam and maiden,<br>
                The sky gathered again<br>
        And the sun grew round that very day.<br>
So it must have been after the birth of the simple light<br>
In the first, spinning place, the spellbound horses walking warm<br>
35         Out of the whinnying green stable<br>
                On to the fields of praise.

And honored among foxes and pheasants by the gay house<br>
Under the new made clouds and happy as the heart was long,<br>
        In the sun born over and over,<br>
40                 I ran my heedless ways,<br>
        My wishes raced through the house high hay<br>
And nothing I cared, at my sky blue trades, that time allows<br>
In all his tuneful turning so few and such morning songs<br>
        Before the children green and golden<br>
45                 Follow him out of grace,

Nothing I cared, in the lamb white days, that time would take me<br>
Up to the swallow thronged loft by the shadow of my hand,<br>
        In the moon that is always rising,<br>
                Nor that riding to sleep<br>
50         I should hear him fly with the high fields<br>
And wake to the farm forever fled from the childless land.<br>
Oh as I was young and easy in the mercy of his means,<br>
                Time held me green and dying<br>
        Though I sang in my chains like the sea.

# SOUND

# 12 *Meter and Its Variations*

Sound in poetry is a function of two elements: the rhythm of a poem's lines, and the sounds of its words. Throughout our study of poetry, we have been aware of the important part sound and rhythm play in establishing our sense of a poem. But we have been more concerned with recognizing how the sounds of a given poem reinforce its ideas or emotions than with classifying the sounds themselves; and so we have not paused to build up a vocabulary of technical terms for meter and versification. Now it is time to learn that vocabulary, so that we may supplement our discussions of character and language in poetry with more detailed comments on the techniques of sound that reinforce them. Since rhythm is perhaps the most basic element of sound in a poem, and meter the most basic element of rhythm, we will start with meter.

**Meter** is the term used to describe the underlying rhythm of a poem, based on the number and the placement of stressed syllables in each line. In most poetry, these **stresses** will fall into a pattern and the pattern will have a particular name: **iambic pentameter,** for instance, to name one of the most common. When we learn to **scan** a poem, therefore, to find out the rhythm or meter in which it is written, these stresses and their patterns are what we will be looking at.

What do we mean by a **stress** or a **stressed syllable?** We mean that the word or syllable involved is one to which our voice will give greater emphasis than to its neighbors. Every word of more than one syllable in English has one accented, or stressed, syllable and one or more unaccented or unstressed ones. Thus, in the word *human* we stress the first syllable: *hú - man;* while in the word *humane* we stress the second: *hu - máne.* When we speak a sentence, these natural accents, or stresses, will be heard. Usually they will be joined by a second type of stress, one used for emphasis. If I say, "Is she coming?," for instance, and leave the strongest stress on the first syllable of *coming* ("Is she *coming?*"), there will be nothing startling in the sentence. If, however, I move the accent to the word *is* ("*Is* she coming?"), I sound doubtful or surprised that she'd come; while if I accent the word *she* (" Is *she* coming?") the stressed word suggests that "she" is the last person I would have expected (or perhaps wanted) to come. The emphasis may fall in an expected or an unexpected place. But it is sure to fall somewhere, for English is a heavily accented language; it sounds neither normal nor natural without the contrast of its stressed and unstressed syllables.

The number of stresses in a line of poetry, therefore, is the number of syllables on which our voice naturally tends to put a stronger emphasis. The emphasis must be natural; it must come either from the sound of the words themselves or from the meaning and emphasis of the lines. Thus, we must be able to find the meter by reading naturally; we should not distort either the sense or the natural rhythm of the lines to make them fit some preconceived meter.

So basic is this matter of stresses, in fact, that line lengths receive their names according to the number of stressed syllables they contain. One simply counts up the stressed syllables, translates the resulting number into Greek, and adds the word *meter* to finish out the term, as follows:

1. **Dimeter:** two stresses per line

   Díe soón

2. **Trimeter:** three stresses

   Dóst thou knów who máde thee?

3. **Tetrameter:** four stresses

   Tell áll the trúth but téll it slánt

4. **Pentameter:** five stresses:

   Leáve me, O Lóve, which reáches bút to dúst

5. **Hexameter:** six stresses (also known as an **alexandrine**)

   Which, like a wóunded snáke, drágs its slow léngth alóng

By counting the number of stresses per line, we thus discover the skeleton of a poem's rhythm. The question then becomes how those stresses are linked. In **accentual poetry,** they are linked by **alliteration** or **assonance.** There will be (usually) four stressed syllables per line; and two or three of them will start with the same sound or contain the same vowel. Here is an example, from a poem you will meet again at the chapter's end:

> Bítter breást-cares have Í abíded,
> Knówn on my kéel many a cáre's hóld,
> And díre seá-súrge, and there I oft spént
> Nárrow níghtwatch nígh the ship's héad
> While she tóssed close to clíffs. Cóldly afflicted,
> My féet wére by fróst benúmbed.

The first line is marked by the alliteration of *bitter* and *breast* and the assonance of *I* and *abided.* The second is similarly linked by the alliteration of the *k* sound in *keel* and *care* and the assonance of the *o* sound in *known* and *hold.* But the other lines are all marked by the alliteration of one sound each: *s* in the third line, *n* in the fourth, *c* in the fifth, and *f* in the sixth. This is the patterning of Old English poetry, a patterning used for several hundred years before the Norman Conquest brought French influences and rhymed verse to England. Since that time, accentual poetry has been relatively rare. One nineteenth-century poet, Gerard Manley Hopkins, however, worked out an accentual style of his own, which he called **sprung rhythm.** His style reflects the Old English influence in its irregular placement of stresses and its marked use of alliteration and assonance.

Most English and American verse is **accentual syllabic.** This means that its rhythm depends not only on the number of stressed syllables, but also on the total number of syllables per line, and on the placement of the stresses within that totality. Tetrameter lines, for instance, vary in length from the four stressed syllables of "We real cool. We," to the eight syllables, half of them stressed, of "Tell all the truth but tell it slant," to the eleven or twelve syllables (every third syllable stressed) of "You left us in tatters, without shoes or socks,/Tired of digging potatoes and spudding up docks."

To define its various combinations of stressed and unstressed syllables, therefore, accentual-syllabic meters divide each line of poetry into **feet,** a **foot** consisting of one stressed syllable with its attendant unstressed syllables. Each type of foot—that is, each pattern of syllables—is given a name. An unstressed syllable followed by a stressed one, for instance (*the wórd*) is an **iamb;** two unstressed syllables followed by a stressed one (*that she heárd*) make an **anapest.** The meter of the poem thus consists of the *name of the foot* most frequently found in the poem joined to the basic *line length.* "There's a certain slant of light" thus becomes **iambic trimeter,** despite the fact that not all its feet are iambs and not all its lines have three feet.

With this background in mind, let us chart the types of feet most commonly found in English poetry. One of the most common **duple meters** is the **iambic,** which has two syllables, the second stressed.

Tell áll | the trúth | but téll | it slańt

The **trochaic** has two syllables, the first stressed.

Dóst thou | knów who | máde thee?

One of the two most common **triple meters** is the **anapestic:** with three syllables, the last stressed.

And thére | was my Ró- | land to béar | the whole weíght

The **dactylic** has three syllables, the first stressed.

Táking me | báck down the | vísta of | yéars, till I | sée

One should also know the **spondee,** a two-syllable foot with both syllables accented. The spondee is used only to lend particular emphasis or variety to poetry written in other meters; there is no "spondaic meter." The **amphibrach** is a three-syllable foot with the accent on the middle syllable. Unlike the spondee, the amphibrach can be used as a sustained meter; but it's not an easy meter to work with and isn't often used for an entire poem. The **monosyllabic foot** has one syllable, accented; Gwendolyn Brooks's "We Real Cool" is an example of this foot in action. The **paeon** is a four-syllable foot. It may be called first paeon, second paeon, third paeon, or fourth paeon, depending on whether the accented syllable comes first, second, third, or fourth. There may also be a secondary accent within the foot. Traditional ballads are often written in paeonic meters.

Meter, then, will create the basic rhythm of a poem, setting up a pattern to be repeated or varied with each line. Seldom does the pattern remain perfectly regular, for to hold too closely to a meter in spoken verse is to risk monotony and boredom.

How does a poet avoid monotony? By shifting stresses, so that a poem written in iambic meter will have some feet that are trochees and some that are spondees. By adding syllables, so that an iambic line will contain an occasional dactyl or anapest. By dropping syllables, substituting a pause for the expected sound, or laying greater stress on the remaining syllables, as when a spondee is substituted for an anapest.

More importantly, poets vary their meters by making the sense of the poem, and the cadence of the speaker's voice, move in counterpoint to the rhythm.

The sea is calm tonight.
The tide is full, the moon lies fair
Upon the straits;—on the French coast the light
Gleams and is gone; the cliffs of England stand,
Glimmering and vast, out in the tranquil bay.

The first statement fits the first line perfectly. But the next overlaps the second line, so that your voice cannot stop on "fair" but must continue with "Upon the straits." A pause, then, and the thought continues through that line and half of the next; then pauses more briefly, finishes the line with a slight pause, and comes to rest at the end of the fifth line. Because your voice stops at the end of them, the first and fifth lines are called **end-stopped lines.** Because the movement of thought and phrase forces your voice to continue past their ends, the second, third, and fourth lines are called **run-on lines.** Both end-stopped and run-on lines may contain internal pauses. We find one such pause after "full" in the second line, one after "straits" in the third," one after "gone" in the fourth, and one after "vast" in the fifth. These pauses are called **cesuras;** and their use and placement are vital in breaking the rhythms of poetry to create the sound of a speaking voice.

In contrast to "Dover Beach" (which you might want to reread in its entirety, to notice how flexible the lines are throughout), recall Blake's poems "The Lamb" and "The Tyger." Notice that many of their lines are end-stopped and that the regularity of the rhythm, with its procession of end-stopped lines and repeated questions, gives these poems almost the sound of incantations, sounds far removed from the wistful accents of Arnold's speaker. But notice, too, that even here, although each phrase is strongly separated from its fellows and heavily accented, the length of the phrases still varies, and cesuras and occasional run-on lines are still found:

> What the hammer? what the chain?
> In what furnace was thy brain?
> What the anvil? what dread grasp
> Dare its deadly terrors clasp?

We may notice, too, that Blake restricts himself to seven-syllable lines in "The Tyger," and to a patterned alternation between trimeter and tetrameter lines in "The Lamb," while Arnold varies his line lengths in "Dover Beach," the lines growing longer as the speaker warms to his topic. And, finally, we notice that all the lines quoted from Blake and Arnold end with stressed syllables. Your voice rises slightly to the stress at the end of these lines, and they are therefore said to have a **rising rhythm.** In contrast, lines that end on unstressed syllables—"O wild West Wind, thou breath of Autumn's being"—are said to have a **falling rhythm.** It's a small thing, but it can create subtle variations in tone.

These, then, are the basic meters of accentual-syllabic verse and the most common devices used to lend them variety. You will no doubt find many other devices at work as you continue your study of poetry. And you will also find that in much modern verse, such as that of Whitman and Cummings, the rules of accentual-syllabic verse have been replaced by the uncharted techniques and devices of **free verse.** Pauses and phrasings in free verse tend to be visual devices as well as rhythmic ones; line lengths and stress placement vary at the poet's will. Sounds are still being shaped with care, but the writers of free verse are being equally careful to avoid setting up rules to which critics can then bind them. In free verse, as in all verse, ultimately the total effect is the sole criterion.

Here are a modern translation of an Old English poem and a brief example of Hopkins's sprung rhythm. How would you compare and contrast the two types of verse?

ANONYMOUS (Eighth Century)

**The Seafarer (modern version by Ezra Pound)**

May I for my own self song's truth reckon,
Journey's jargon, how I in harsh days
Hardship endured oft.
Bitter breast-cares have I abided,
5 Known on my keel many a care's hold,
And dire sea-surge, and there I oft spent
Narrow nightwatch nigh the ship's head
While she tossed close to cliffs. Coldly afflicted,
My feet were by frost benumbed.
10 Chill its chains are; chafing signs
Hew my heart round and hunger begot.
Mere-weary mood. Lest man know not
That he on dry land loveliest liveth,
List how I, care-wretched, on ice-cold sea,
15 Weathered the winter, wretched outcast
Deprived of my kinsmen;
Hung with hard ice-flakes, where hail-scur flew,
There I heard naught save the harsh sea
And ice-cold wave, at whiles the swan cries,
20 Did for my games the gannet's clamor,
Sea-fowls' loudness was for me laughter,
The mews' singing all my mead-drink.
Storms, on the stone-cliffs beaten, fell on the stern
In icy feathers; full oft the eagle screamed
25 With spray on his pinion.
Not any protector
May make merry man faring needy.
This he little believes, who aye in winsome life
Abides 'mid burghers some heavy business,
Wealthy and wine-flushed, how I weary oft

30 Must bide above brine.
Neareth nightshade, snoweth from north,
Frost froze the land, hail fell on earth then,
Corn of the coldest. Nathless there knocketh now
The heart's thought that I on high streams
35 The salt-wavy tumult traverse alone.
Moaneth alway my mind's lust
That I fare forth, that I afar hence
Seek out a foreign fastness.
For this there's no mood-lofty man over earth's midst,
40 Not though he be given his good, but will have in his youth greed;
Nor his deed to the daring, nor his king to the faithful
But shall have his sorrow for sea-fare
Whatever his lord will.
He hath not heart for harping, nor in ring-having
45 Nor winsomeness to wife, nor world's delight
Nor any whit else save the wave's slash,
Yet longing comes upon him to fare forth on the water.
Bosque taketh blossom, cometh beauty of berries,
Fields to fairness, land fares brisker,
50 All this admonisheth man eager of mood,
The heart turns to travel so that he then thinks
On flood-ways to be far departing.
Cuckoo calleth with gloomy crying,
He singeth summerward, bodeth sorrow,
55 The bitter heart's blood. Burgher knows not—
He the prosperous man—what some perform
Where wandering them widest draweth.
So that but now my heart burst from my breastlock,
My mood 'mid the mere-flood,
60 Over the whale's acre, would wander wide.
On earth's shelter cometh oft to me,
Eager and ready, the crying lone-flyer,
Whets for the whale-path the heart irresistibly,
O'er tracks of ocean; seeing that anyhow
65 My lord deems to me this dead life
On loan and on land, I believe not
That any earth-weal eternal standeth
Save there be somewhat calamitous
That, ere a man's tide go, turn it to twain.
70 Disease or oldness or sword-hate
Beats out the breath from doom-gripped body.
And for this, every earl whatever, for those speaking after—
Laud of the living, boasteth some last word,

That he will work ere he pass onward,
75 Frame on the fair earth 'gainst foes his malice,
Daring ado, . . .
So that all men shall honor him after
And his laud beyond them remain 'mid the English,
Aye, for ever a lasting life's-blast,
80 Delight 'mid the doughty.
Days little durable,
And all arrogance of earthen riches,
There come now no kings nor Caesars
Nor gold-giving lords like those gone.
Howe'er in mirth most magnified,
85 Whoe'er lived in life most lordliest,
Drear all this excellence, delights undurable!
Waneth the watch, but the world holdeth.
Tomb hideth trouble. The blade is layed low.
Earthly glory ageth and seareth.
90 No man at all going the earth's gait,
But age fares against him, his face paleth,
Grey-haired he groaneth, knows gone companions,
Lordly men, are to earth o'ergiven,
Nor may he then the flesh-cover, whose life ceaseth,
95 Nor eat the sweet nor feel the sorry,
Nor stir hand nor think in mid heart,
And though he strew the grave with gold,
His born brothers, their buried bodies
Be an unlikely treasure hoard.

QUESTIONS

Notice the movement of the speaker's mood and thought. How does he characterize himself? What response does he seek from his audience?

## GERARD MANLEY HOPKINS (1844–1889)

### Pied Beauty

Glory be to God for dappled things—
For skies of couple-colour as a brindled cow;
For rose-moles all in stipple upon trout that swim;
Fresh-firecoal chestnut-falls; finches wings;
5 Landscape plotted and pieced—fold, fallow, and plough;
And áll trádes, their gear and tackle and trim.

All things, counter, original, spare, strange;
  Whatever is fickle, freckled (who knows how?)
    With swift, slow; sweet, sour; adazzle, dim;
10 He fathers-forth whose beauty is past change:
                    Praise him.

QUESTIONS

1. How do the examples of dappled things given in lines 2–4 differ from those in lines 5 and 6? How do those in the first stanza (lines 2–6) differ from those in the second stanza (lines 7–9)? What has Hopkins expanded the notion of "dappled things" to include?
2. What holds all these examples and images together? Is there any unity to them; anything single or unchanging behind them? If so, what is it? How and where in the poem is it expressed? How important is it to the speaker's vision of "pied beauty"?

Now read these two examples of accentual-syllable verse. Note the metrical techniques that make the first sound like a song. The second is like the voice of a man arguing with himself.

ALFRED, LORD TENNYSON (1809–1892)

## The Splendor Falls on Castle Walls

The splendor falls on castle walls
  And snowy summits old in story:
The long light shakes across the lakes,
  And the wild cataract leaps in glory.
5 Blow, bugle, blow, set the wild echoes flying,
Blow, bugle; answer, echoes, dying, dying, dying.

O hark, O hear! how thin and clear,
  And thinner, clearer, farther going!
O sweet and far from cliff and scar
10   The horns of Elfland faintly blowing!
Blow, let us hear the purple glens replying:
Blow, bugle; answer, echoes, dying, dying, dying.

O love, they die in yon rich sky,
  They faint on hill or field or river;
15 Our echoes roll from soul to soul,
  And grow for ever and for ever.
Blow, bugle, blow, set the wild echoes flying,
And answer, echoes, answer, dying, dying, dying.

QUESTIONS

1. What is the meter of the main part of the poem? What is the meter of the refrain? What has been achieved by combining the two?
2. What does Tennyson mean by the phrase "our echoes" (line 15)? How do these echoes differ from the other "echoes" of which the poem speaks?
3. Fairyland and fairy things are usually pictured in literature as being immortal and unchanging, in contrast to human affairs, which are transitory. Why does Tennyson reverse that contrast in this poem?
4. How do sound and imagery combine in this poem to reinforce the speaker's message?

## GEORGE HERBERT (1593–1633)

### The Collar[1]

I struck the board[2] and cried, "No more!
I will abroad!
What, shall I ever sigh and pine?
My lines and life are free: free as the road,
5 Loose as the wind, as large as store.
Shall I be still in suit?[3]
Have I no harvest but a thorn
To let me blood, and not restore
What I have lost with cordial[4] fruit?
10 Sure there was wine
Before my sighs did dry it; there was corn
Before my tears did drown it.
Is the year only lost to me?
Have I no bays[5] to crown it,
15 No flowers, no garlands gay? all blasted?
All wasted?
Not so, my heart; but there is fruit,
And thou hast hands.
Recover all thy sigh-blown age
20 On double pleasures. Leave thy cold dispute
Of what is fit and not. Forsake thy cage,
Thy rope of sands,

[1] The iron band encircling the neck of a prisoner or slave; also perhaps a pun on "choler" as "rebellious anger."
[2] Dining table.
[3] Always petitioning.
[4] Restorative.
[5] Laurels.

Which petty thoughts have made and made to thee
Good cable, to enforce and draw,
25 And be thy law,
While thou didst wink and wouldst not see.
Away! take heed!
I will abroad!
Call in thy death's-head there! Tie up thy fears!
30 He that forbears
To suit and serve his need,
Deserves his load."
But as I raved, and grew more fierce and wild
At every word,
35 Methought I heard one calling, "Child!"
And I replied, "My Lord."

QUESTIONS

Discuss how the movement of sound in "The Collar" helps create the sound of the speaker arguing with himself. (Note the addition of a second voice near the end of the poem. How do the speech of this second voice and the speaker's response to it bring the poem to its resolution?)

Finally, here are two examples of iambic pentameter by two masters of that meter. Note that even the use of the identical meter does not give these poems identical sounds. The rhythm of Shakespeare's sonnet, for all its basic regularity, is flexible and almost conversational; the rhythm of Milton's poem is as firm and regular as the marble tomb he uses as his poem's chief conceit. Read the two poems and then answer the following questions:

1. How does each poet handle his meter? How are phrasing and sentence structure fitted to the pentameter? How is the progression of the speaker's thought emphasized?
2. How does each poem's rhythm enhance or emphasize its imagery? Give examples.

WILLIAM SHAKESPEARE (1564–1616)

**Sonnet 29**

When, in disgrace with Fortune and men's eyes,
I all alone beweep my outcast state,
And trouble deaf heaven with my bootless cries,

And look upon myself and curse my fate,
5 Wishing me like to one more rich in hope,
Featured like him, like him with friends possessed,
Desiring this man's art, and that man's scope,
With what I most enjoy contented least;
Yet in these thoughts myself almost depising,
10 Haply I think on thee, and then my state,
Like to the lark at break of day arising
From sullen earth, sings hymns at heaven's gate;
For thy sweet love remembered such wealth brings
That then I scorn to change my state with kings.

## JOHN MILTON (1608–1674)

### On Shakespeare

What needs my Shakespeare for his honored bones
The labor of an age in pilèd stones?
Or that his hallowed reliques should be hid
Under a star-ypointing[1] pyramid?
5 Dear son of memory, great heir of fame,
What need'st thou such weak witness of thy name?
Thou in our wonder and astonishment
Has built thyself a livelong monument.
For whilst, to the shame of slow-endeavoring art,
10 Thy easy numbers flow, and that each heart
Hath from the leaves of thy unvalued[2] book
Those Delphic[3] lines with deep impression took,
Then thou, our fancy of itself bereaving,
Dost make us marble with too much conceiving,[4]
15 And so sepùlchred in such pomp dost lie
That kings for such a tomb would wish to die.

QUESTIONS

Look back at the poems you have read in this book. Select several that you especially like. Analyze the meter in each, and consider the techniques by which it is varied. Then discuss how these metrical techniques enhance your enjoyment of each poem.

---

[1] Milton added the "y" for the sake of rhythm.
[2] Invaluable.
[3] Inspired—as by the oracle at Delphi.
[4] Thinking.

# 13 *Rhyme Schemes and Verse Forms*

Although rhyme is not found in all poetry written in English, it has been so important in the history of English and American verse that we often first divide poetry into two categories–rhymed and unrhymed–and then divide further from there. Accepting that categorization for the moment, we will note that unrhymed poems tend to fall into one of three major divisions: accentual verse, which has existed from Old English times and which we met in "The Seafarer" and "Pied Beauty"; blank verse (unrhymed iambic pentameter), a sixteenth-century invention of which Hamlet's soliloquies are classic examples; or free verse, sometimes called by the French name **vers libre,** a modern (and not always unrhymed) form that we met in the works of such diverse poets as Whitman, Cummings, Pound, and Levertov.

## Rhymed Verse

Rhymed verse is harder to classify. There are so many ways of combining rhymed lines! Still, one can distinguish between those forms of rhymed verse that have a fixed total length (such as the **limerick,** with five lines; the **sonnet,** with fourteen; and the **villanelle,** with nineteen) and those that do not. Rhymed verse with no fixed length is usually composed of **stanzas.** Each stanza usually has a fixed length; but the number of stanzas, and hence the length of the poem as a whole, remain variable.

Underlying both types of rhymed verse, however, stand the basic combinations of rhyme. These embrace two-, three-, and four-line patterns, called the couplet, triplet, terza rima, and the quatrain. The **couplet** has two consecutive lines that rhyme:

> So long as men can breathe or eyes can see,
> So long lives this, and this gives life to thee.

The **tercet** or **triplet** has three lines that rhyme:

> He clasps the crag with crooked hands;
> Close to the sun in lonely lands,
> Ringed with the azure world, he stands.

The **terza rima** also has three lines, but only the first and last rhyme. When terza rima stanzas are linked together, the middle line of one stanza rhymes with the first and third lines of the stanza that follows.

> O wild West Wind, thou breath of Autumn's being,
> Thou, from whose unseen presence the leaves dead
> Are driven, like ghosts from an enchanter fleeing,
>
> Yellow, and black, and pale, and hectic red,
> Pestilence-stricken multitudes: O thou
> Who chariotest to their dark wintry bed

The **quatrain** has four lines joined by any one of the following rhyme schemes:

1. Second and fourth lines rhyming (*abcb*):

   When I was one-and-twenty
     I heard a wise man say,
   "Give crowns and pounds and guineas
     But not your heart away;

2. First and third, second and fourth lines rhyming (*abab*):

   She even thinks that up in heaven
   Her class lies late and snores,
   While poor black cherubs rise at seven
   To do celestial chores.

3. First and fourth, second and third lines rhyming (*abba*):

   Earth hath not anything to show more fair!
   Dull would he be of soul who could pass by
   A sight so touching in its majesty.
   The city now doth, like a garment, wear

4. First and second, third and fourth lines rhyming (*aabb*):

 "O 'Melia, my dear, this does everything crown!
 Who could have supposed I should meet you in Town?
 And whence such fair garments, such prosperi-ty?"—
 "O didn't you know I'd been ruined?" said she.

Any of these patterns can stand alone as a stanza. Or, patterns may be added to or combined to produce more complicated stanzas, such as the **rime royale** in which the following poem is written. Notice, in this poem, not only the stanzaic pattern, but also the change of tone and of tense in each stanza. What progression of argument and emotion occurs in this poem? What is its effect?

SIR THOMAS WYATT (1503–1542)

**They Flee from Me**

They flee from me that sometime did me seek
With naked foot stalking in my chamber.
I have seen them gentle, tame, and meek
That now are wild and do not remember
5 That sometime they put themselves in danger
To take bread at my hand; and now they range
Busily seeking with a continual change.

Thankèd be Fortune, it hath been otherwise
Twenty times better; but once in special,
10 In thin array after a pleasant guise,
When her loose gown from her shoulders did fall,
And she me caught in her arms long and small;
And therewithall sweetly did me kiss,
And softly said, "Dear heart, how like you this?"

15 It was no dream; I lay broad waking.
But all is turned thorough my gentleness
Into a strange fashion of forsaking;
And I have leave to go of her goodness,
And she also to use newfangleness.
20 But since that I so kindely am served,
I fain would know what she hath deserved.

## Limericks and Villanelles

Let us now look at two rhymed forms of fixed length: the limerick and the villanelle. (We will consider a third fixed-length form, the sonnet, in the next chapter.)

Limericks have five lines. The rhyme scheme is *aabba,* with all *a* lines having three feet, and all *b* lines two feet. The meter is usually anapestic.

Limericks are humorous verse, frequently employing puns, off-color humor, or deliberately tortured rhymes or rhythms. As one anonymous writer and critic remarks,

> The limerick packs laughs anatomical,
> Into space that is quite economical.
> But the good ones I've seen
> So seldom are clean,
> And the clean ones so seldom are comical.

More serious, but equally tightly controlled in form, is the **villanelle.** Entire lines, as well as rhyme sounds, are repeated in the villanelle to make up its prescribed pattern. Here is one of the finest twentieth-century villanelles. Analyze its form and discuss what the poet has done with it.

DYLAN THOMAS (1914–1953)

### Do Not Go Gentle into That Good Night

Do not go gentle into that good night,
Old age should burn and rave at close of day;
Rage, rage against the dying of the light.

Though wise men at their end know dark is right,
5 Because their words had forked no lightning they
Do not go gentle into that good night.

Good men, the last wave by, crying how bright
Their frail deeds might have danced in a green bay,
Rage, rage against the dying of the light.

10 Wild men who caught and sang the sun in flight,
And learn, too late, they grieved it on its way,
Do not go gentle into that good night.

Grave men, near death, who see with blinding sight
Blind eyes could blaze like meteors and be gay,
15 Rage, rage against the dying of the light.

And you, my father, there on the sad height,
Curse, bless, me now with your fierce tears, I pray.
Do not go gentle into that good night.
Rage, rage against the dying of the light.

## Ballades, Ballads, and Odes

Three forms without fixed length are the **ballade, ballad,** and **ode.**

The **ballade** was popular during the Middle Ages. It uses seven- or eight-line stanzas, usually in groups of three. Each stanza ends with the same line, the **refrain.** The ballade itself ends with a shorter stanza, the **envoy** or **envoi.** The envoy is addressed directly to the person for whom the ballade is being written. It, too, ends with the refrain.

Here is a nineteenth-century translation of a medieval French ballade. Note how the envoy provides both a personal note and a conclusion to a catalog that might otherwise have no logical ending.

DANTE GABRIEL ROSSETTI (1828–1882)

**The Ballad of Dead Ladies**[1]

*François Villon, 1450*

Tell me now in what hidden way is
  Lady Flora[2] the lovely Roman?
Where's Hipparchia,[3] and where is Thaïs,[4]
  Neither of them the fairer woman?
5  Where is Echo, beheld of no man,
Only heard on river and mere,—
  She whose beauty was more than human? . . .
But where are the snows of yester-year?

Where's Héloïse, the learned nun,
10  For whose sake Abeillard, I ween,

[1] This is a translation of the "Ballade des Dames de Temps Jadis" by François Villon (b. 1431).
[2] A famous Roman courtesan.
[3] A Greek courtesan.
[4] An Athenian courtesan.

Lost manhood and put priesthood on?[5]
(From Love he won such dule and teen!)
And where, I pray you, is the Queen[6]
Who willed that Buridan should steer
15 Sewed in a sack's mouth down the Seine? . . .
But where are the snows of yester-year?

White Queen Blanche, like a queen of lilies,[7]
With a voice like any mermaiden,—
Bertha Broadfoot, Beatrice, Alice,[8]
20 And Ermengarde the lady of Maine,[9]—
And that good Joan[10] whom Englishmen
At Rouen doomed and burned her there,—
Mother of God, where are they then? . . .
But where are the snows of yester-year?

25 Nay, never ask this week, fair lord,
Where they are gone, nor yet this year,
Except with this for an overword,—
But where are the snows of yester-year?

In contrast to the tightly defined ballade, the term **ballad** (without the final **e**) may be used for any poem that is, or can be, sung, and that has regular stanzas. Usually, the poems we refer to as ballads have four-line stanzas. Frequently, like the ballade, they make use of repeated lines or refrains. Note, in this next poem, how thoroughly and skillfully William Morris uses the battle cry he has chosen for his refrain, hammering it home at the end of each short stanza until it almost takes on the sound of the speaker's own pulse pounding in his temples.

---

[5] Héloïse, the beautiful niece of a church official, fell in love with her teacher, the famous philosopher Abelard (1079–1142). They eloped, and the uncle was so incensed that he caused Abelard to be set upon and emasculated. As a result Abelard became a monk and Héloïse a nun, and the reward of their love was sorrow and pain.

[6] Queen Margaret of Burgundy who used to have her lovers, among whom was the scholar Buridan, sewn in sacks and thrown into the Seine.

[7] Perhaps Blanche of Castile, or perhaps a figment of Villon's imagination.

[8] Bertha Broadfoot, in epic accounts is the mother of Charlemagne. The identity of Beatrice and Alice is uncertain.

[9] The countess of Anjou in France.

[10] Joan of Arc.

WILLIAM MORRIS (1834–1896)

**The Gillyflower of Gold**

A golden gillyflower today
I wore upon my helm alway,
And won the prize of this tourney.
*Hah! hah! la belle jaune giroflée.*[1]

5 However well Sir Giles might sit,
His sun was weak to wither it;
Lord Miles's blood was dew on it.
*Hah! hah! la belle jaune giroflée.*

Although my spear in splinters flew,
10 From John's steel-coat, my eye was true;
I wheeled about, and cried for you,
*Hah! hah! la belle jaune giroflée.*

Yea, do not doubt my heart was good,
Though my sword flew like rotten wood,
15 To shout, although I scarcely stood,
*Hah! hah! la belle jaune giroflée.*

My hand was steady too, to take,
My ax from round my neck, and break
John's steel-coat up for my love's sake.
20 *Hah! hah! la belle jaune giroflée*—

When I stood in my tent again,
Arming afresh, I felt a pain
Take hold of me, I was so fain—
*Hah! hah! la belle jaune giroflée*—

25 To hear *Honneur aux fils des preux!*[2]
Right in my ears again, and shew
The gillyflower blossomed new.
*Hah! hah! la belle jaune giroflée.*

The Sieur Guillaume against me came,
30 His tabard[3] bore three points of flame

---

[1] The beautiful yellow gillyflower.
[2] Honor to the sons of valiant knights!
[3] A kind of cloak or mantle worn by knights.

From a red heart; with little blame[4]—
*Hah! hah! la belle jaune giroflée—*

Our tough spears crackled up like straw;
He was the first to turn and draw
35 His sword, that had nor speck nor flaw;
*Hah! hah! la belle jaune giroflée.*

But I felt weaker than a maid,
And my brain, dizzied and afraid,
Within my helm a fierce tune played,
40 *Hah! hah! la belle jaune giroflée,*

Until I thought of your dear head,
Bowed to the gillyflower bed,
The yellow flowers stained with red;
*Hah! hah! la belle jaune giroflée.*

45 Crash! how the swords met—*giroflée!*
The fierce tune in my helm would play,
*La belle! la belle! jaune giroflée!*
*Hah! hah! la belle jaune giroflée.*

Once more the great swords met again;
50 "*La belle! la belle!*" but who fell then?
Le Sieur Guillaume, who struck down ten;
*Hah! hah! la belle jaune giroflée.*

And as with mazed and unarmed face
Toward my own crown and the Queen's place,
55 They led me at a gentle pace—
*Hah! hah! la belle jaune giroflée—*

I almost saw your quiet head
Bowed o'er the gillyflower bed,
The yellow flowers stained with red.
60 *Hah! hah! la belle jaune giroflée.*

[4] Damage.

Among the rhymed poetic forms, the **ode** is unique in leaving both the rhyme scheme and the length of each individual line to the poet's discretion. The one constant feature of odes in English poetry, in fact, is their elevated tone. In Keats's "Ode on a Grecian Urn" and "Ode to a Nightingale," and in Shelley's "Ode to the West Wind," we saw three different stanzaic patterns. Look back at these odes now (on pages 518, 536, and 534) and define their patterns. Note, too, that in each case the stanzaic form is constant throughout the ode. For this reason, these are sometimes called **Horatian odes.**

To conclude this chapter, we will read one further ode, this one of the type called the **irregular ode.** This particular ode, written by the early Romantic poet William Wordsworth, makes skillful use of rhyme and rhythm both. Yet, for all its careful contrivance, it maintains a remarkable freshness of tone, in keeping with its subject of early joys and maturer delights. Because it is an irregular ode, the stanzas in this poem vary among themselves, changing shape to follow the motions of the poet's mind. The basic meter remains iambic throughout, but line lengths and rhyme schemes shift constantly. The result is an unusual blend of patterning and fluidity that sometimes mutes its tone to a thoughtful expression of philosophy and sometimes rises to a hymn of joyful praise.

The ode deals with the relations between the human soul, nature, and immortality. In it, Wordsworth suggests not only that we know immortality after death, but that we know it before birth as well: "trailing clouds of glory do we come, / From God, who is our home." The ode thus celebrates the heavenlike joy the young child sees in the natural world; and it laments the dulling of that joy that occurs when the child, responding to the novelty of his mundane existence, turns his mind more fully upon earthly things. Yet the final tone is not sorrow but a greater joy, as Wordsworth passes beyond mourning this early loss into celebrating the fully human joys and loves that are the gift of the mature soul.

As you read the ode, pay careful attention to the way Wordsworth develops this train of thought, and notice how the sound and shape of the stanzas convey the changing emotions the speaker feels.

## WILLIAM WORDSWORTH (1770–1850)

### Ode

Intimations of Immortality from Recollections
of Early Childhood

*The Child is father of the Man;*
*And I could wish my days to be*
*Bound each to each by natural piety.*

1

There was a time when meadow, grove, and stream,
The earth, and every common sight,
To me did seem
Apparelled in celestial light,
5 The glory and the freshness of a dream.
It is not now as it hath been of yore;—
Turn wheresoe'er I may,
By night or day,
The things which I have seen I now can see no more.

2

10 The Rainbow comes and goes,
And lovely is the Rose,
The Moon doth with delight
Look round her when the heavens are bare;
Waters on a starry night
15 Are beautiful and fair;
The sunshine is a glorious birth;
But yet I know, where'er I go,
That there hath past away a glory from the earth.

3

Now, while the birds thus sing a joyous song,
20 And while the young lambs bound
As to the tabor's sound,
To me alone there came a thought of grief:
A timely utterance gave that thought relief,
And I again am strong:
25 The cataracts blow their trumpets from the steep;
No more shall grief of mine the season wrong;
I hear the Echoes through the mountains throng,
The Winds come to me from the fields of sleep,
And all the earth is gay;
30 Land and sea
Give themselves up to jollity,
And with the heart of May
Doth every Beast keep holiday;—
Thou Child of Joy,
35 Shout round me, let me hear thy shouts, thou happy Shepherd-boy!

4

Ye blessèd Creatures, I have heard the call
Ye to each other make; I see
The heavens laugh with you in your jubilee;
My heart is at your festival,
40 My head hath its coronal,
The fulness of your bliss, I feel—I feel it all.
Oh evil day! if I were sullen
While Earth herself is adorning,
This sweet May-morning,
45 And the Children are culling
On every side,
In a thousand valleys far and wide,
Fresh flowers; while the sun shines warm,
And the Babe leaps up on his Mother's arm:—
50 I hear, I hear, with joy I hear!
—But there's a Tree, of many, one,
A single Field which I have looked upon,
Both of them speak of something that is gone:
The Pansy at my feet
55 Doth the same tale repeat:
Whither is fled the visionary gleam?
Where is it now, the glory and the dream?

5

Our birth is but a sleep and a forgetting:
The Soul that rises with us, our life's Star,
60 Hath had elsewhere its setting,
And cometh from afar:
Not in entire forgetfulness,
And not in utter nakedness,
But trailing clouds of glory do we come
65 From God, who is our home:
Heaven lies about us in our infancy!
Shades of the prison-house begin to close
Upon the growing Boy,
But He
70 Beholds the light, and whence it flows,
He sees it in his joy;
The Youth, who daily farther from the east
Must travel, still is Nature's Priest,
And by the vision splendid

75 Is on his way attended;
At length the Man perceives it die away,
And fade into the light of common day.

6

Earth fills her lap with pleasures of her own;
Yearnings she hath in her own natural kind,
80 And, even with something of a Mother's mind,
And no unworthy aim,
The homely Nurse doth all she can
To make her Foster-child, her Inmate Man,
Forget the glories he hath known,
85 And that imperial palace whence he came.

7

Behold the Child among his new-born blisses,
A six years' Darling of a pigmy size!
See, where 'mid work of his own hand he lies,
Fretted by sallies of his mother's kisses,
90 With light upon him from his father's eyes!
See, at his feet, some little plan or chart,
Some fragment from his dream of human life,
Shaped by himself with newly-learnèd art;
A wedding or a festival,
95 A mourning or a funeral;
And this hath now his heart,
And unto this he frames his song:
Then will he fit his tongue
To dialogues of business, love, or strife;
100 But it will not be long
Ere this be thrown aside,
And with new joy and pride
The little Actor cons another part;
Filling from time to time his "humorous stage"
105 With all the Persons, down to palsied Age,
That Life brings with her in her equipage;
As if his whole vocation
Were endless imitation.

8

Thou, whose exterior semblance doth belie
110 Thy Soul's immensity;

Thou best Philosopher, who yet dost keep
Thy heritage, thou Eye among the blind,
That, deaf and silent, read'st the eternal deep,
Haunted for ever by the eternal mind,—
115 Mighty Prophet! Seer blest!
On whom those truths do rest,
Which we are toiling all our lives to find,
In darkness lost, the darkness of the grave;
Thou, over whom thy Immortality
120 Broods like the Day, a Master o'er a Slave,
A Presence which is not to be put by;
Thou little Child, yet glorious in the might
Of heaven-born freedom on thy being's height,
Why with such earnest pains dost thou provoke
125 The years to bring the inevitable yoke,
Thus blindly with thy blessedness at strife?
Full soon thy Soul shall have her earthly freight,
And custom lie upon thee with a weight,
Heavy as frost, and deep almost as life!

9

130 O joy! that in our embers
Is something that doth live,
That nature yet remembers
What was so fugitive!
The thought of our past years in me doth breed
135 Perpetual benediction: not indeed
For that which is most worthy to be blest;
Delight and liberty, the simple creed
Of Childhood, whether busy or at rest,
With new-fledged hope still fluttering in his breast:—
140 Not for these I raise
The song of thanks and praise;
But for those obstinate questionings
Of sense and outward things,
Falling from us, vanishings;
145 Blank misgivings of a Creature
Moving about in worlds not realised,
High instincts before which our mortal Nature
Did tremble like a guilty Thing surprised:
But for those first affections,
150 Those shadowy recollections,
Which, be they what they may,
Are yet the fountain-light of all our day,

Are yet a master-light of all our seeing;
Uphold us, cherish, and have power to make
155 Our noisy years seem moments in the being
Of the eternal Silence: truths that wake,
To perish never:
Which neither listlessness, nor mad endeavor,
Nor Man nor Boy,
160 Nor all that is at enmity with joy,
Can utterly abolish or destroy!
Hence in a season of calm weather
Though inland far we be,
Our Souls have sight of that immortal sea
165 Which brought us hither,
Can in a moment travel thither,
And see the Children sport upon the shore,
And hear the mighty waters rolling evermore.

10

Then sing, ye Birds, sing, sing a joyous song!
170 And let the young Lambs bound
As to the tabor's sound!
We in thought will join your throng,
Ye that pipe and ye that play,
Ye that through your hearts to-day
175 Feel the gladness of the May!
What though the radiance which was once so bright
Be now for ever taken from my sight,
Though nothing can bring back the hour
Of splendor in the grass, of glory in the flower;
180 We will grieve not, rather find
Strength in what remains behind;
In the primal sympathy
Which having been must ever be;
In the soothing thoughts that spring
185 Out of human suffering;
In the faith that looks through death,
In years that bring the philosophic mind.

11

And O, ye Fountains, Meadows, Hills, and Groves,
Forebode not any severing of our loves!
190 Yet in my heart of hearts I feel your might;

I only have relinquished one delight
To live beneath your more habitual sway.
I love the Brooks which down their channels fret,
Even more than when I tripped lightly as they;
195 The innocent brightness of a new-born Day
Is lovely yet;
The Clouds that gather round the setting sun
Do take a sober coloring from an eye
That hath kept watch o'er man's mortality;
200 Another race hath been, and other palms are won.
Thanks to the human heart by which we live,
Thanks to its tenderness, its joys, and fears,
To me the meanest flower that blows can give
Thoughts that do often lie too deep for tears.

# 14 *The Sonnet*

Without a doubt, the most popular of the defined forms in English and American poetry is the **sonnet.** Sonnets are always fourteen lines long. Traditionally, they are divided into two main forms. The **Petrarchan sonnet** consists of an octet, rhymed *abba abba,* and a sestet, rhymed either *cdcdcd* or *cdecde;* and the **Shakespearean sonnet,** with three quatrains, usually rhymes *abab cdcd efef,* and a couplet at the end, *gg*. Less standard rhyme forms do, of course, exist. Notice, for example, the rhyme scheme in Cummings's "the Cambridge ladies who live in furnished souls," at the end of this chapter.

Of the two traditional forms, the Shakespearean usually seems the more emphatic. Because no sound needs to be used more than twice, it is also slightly easier to write. It was the favored form during the Renaissance. The Petrarchan sonnet, on the other hand, tends to have a somewhat smoother flow and often seems more graceful. It was therefore preferred by the Romantic poets of the nineteenth century.

The sonnet came into English as a love poem: we have read love sonnets by Shakespeare, Sidney, and Spenser. But the sonnet has proved capable of handling almost any subject and of expressing many moods and tones. Look back, for example, at "Ozymandias" (p. 497) and "Composed upon Westminster Bridge" (p. 508). And look, too, at the following examples of what can be done with the sonnet form.

WILLIAM SHAKESPEARE (1564–1616)

## Sonnet 116

Let me not to the marriage of true minds
Admit impediments. Love is not love
Which alters when it alteration finds,
Or bends with the remover to remove.
5 O no! it is an ever-fixèd mark
That looks on tempests and is never shaken;
It is the star to every wand'ring bark,
Whose worth's unknown, although his height be taken.
Love's not Time's fool, though rosy lips and cheeks
10 Within his bending sickle's compass come.
Love alters not with his brief hours and weeks,
But bears it out even to the edge of doom.
If this be error, and upon me proved,
I never writ, nor no man ever loved.

JOHN DONNE (1572–1631)

## Sonnet 10

Death, be not proud, though some have callèd thee
Mighty and dreadful, for thou art not so;
For those whom thou think'st thou dost overthrow
Die not, poor Death, nor yet canst thou kill me.
5 From rest and sleep, which but thy pictures be,
Much pleasure; then from thee much more must flow;
And soonest our best men with thee do go,
Rest of their bones and souls' delivery.
Thou'rt slave to fate, chance, kings, and desperate men,
10 And dost with poison, war, and sickness dwell;
And poppy or charms can make us sleep as well
And better than thy stroke. Why swell'st thou then?
One short sleep past, we wake eternally,
And Death shall be no more: Death, thou shalt die.

JOHN MILTON (1608–1674)

## On His Blindness

When I consider how my light is spent,
Ere half my days, in this dark world and wide,
And that one talent which is death to hide

Lodged with me useless, though my soul more bent
5 To serve therewith my Maker, and present
My true account, lest he returning chide,
"Doth God exact day labor, light denied?"
I fondly ask; but Patience, to prevent
That murmur, soon replies: "God doth not need
10 Either man's work or his own gifts; who best
Bear his mild yoke, they serve him best. His state
Is kingly: thousands at his bidding speed
And post o'er land and ocean without rest.
They also serve who only stand and wait."

## GERARD MANLEY HOPKINS (1844–1899)

### (Carrion Comfort[1])

Not, I'll not, carrion comfort, Despair, not feast on thee;
Not untwist—slack they may be—these last strands of man
In me ór, most weary, cry *I can no more*. I can;
Can something, hope, wish day come, not choose not to be.

5 But ah, but O thou terrible, why wouldst thou rude on me
Thy wring-world right foot rock? lay a lionlimb against me? scan
With darksome devouring eyes my bruisèd bones? and fan,
O in turns of tempest, me heaped there; me frantic to avoid thee and
flee?

Why? That my chaff might fly; my grain lie, sheer and clear.
10 Nay in all that toil, that coil, since (seems) I kissed the rod,
Hand rather, my heart lo! lapped strength, stole joy, would laugh,
chéer.
Cheer whom though? the hero whose heaven-handling flung me, fóot
tród
Me? or me that fought him? O which one? is it each one? That
night, that year
Of now done darkness I wretch lay wrestling with (my God!) my
God.

[1] The title was added by Robert Bridges.

ROBERT FROST (1874–1963)

## Design

I found a dimpled spider, fat and white,
On a white heal-all, holding up a moth
Like a white piece of rigid satin cloth—
Assorted characters of death and blight
5 Mixed ready to begin the morning right,
Like the ingredients of a witches' broth—
A snow-drop spider, a flower like a froth,
And dead wings carried like a paper kite.

What had that flower to do with being white,
10 The wayside blue and innocent heal-all?
What brought the kindred spider to that height,
Then steered the white moth thither in the night?
What but design of darkness to appall?—
If design govern in a thing so small.

EDNA ST. VINCENT MILLAY (1892–1950)

## What Lips My Lips Have Kissed, and Where, and Why

What lips my lips have kissed, and where, and why,
I have forgotten, and what arms have lain
Under my head till morning; but the rain
Is full of ghosts tonight, that tap and sigh
5 Upon the glass and listen for reply,
And in my heart there stirs a quiet pain
For unremembered lads that not again
Will turn to me at midnight with a cry.
Thus in the winter stands the lonely tree,
10 Nor knows what birds have vanished one by one,
Yet knows its boughs more silent than before:
I cannot say what loves have come and gone,
I only know that summer sang in me
A little while, that in me sings no more.

## WILFRED OWEN (1893–1918)

### Anthem for Doomed Youth

What passing-bells for these who die as cattle?
  Only the monstrous anger of the guns.
  Only the stuttering rifles' rapid rattle
Can patter out their hasty orisons.
5 No mockeries now for them; no prayers nor bells,
  Nor any voice of mourning save the choirs—
The shrill, demented choirs of wailing shells;
  And bugles calling for them from sad shires.

What candles may be held to speed them all?
10  Not in the hands of boys, but in their eyes
Shall shine the holy glimmers of good-byes.
  The pallor of girls' brows shall be their pall;
Their flowers the tenderness of patient minds,
And each slow dusk a drawing-down of blinds.

## E. E. CUMMINGS (1894–1963)

### the Cambridge ladies who live in furnished souls

the Cambridge ladies who live in furnished souls
are unbeautiful and have comfortable minds
(also, with the church's protestant blessings,
daughters, unscented shapeless spirited)
5 they believe in Christ and Longfellow, both dead,
are invariably interested in so many things—
at the present writing one still finds
delighted fingers knitting for the is it Poles?
perhaps. While permanent faces coyly bandy
10 scandal of Mrs. N and Professor D
. . . . the Cambridge ladies do not care, above
Cambridge if sometimes in its box of
sky lavender and cornerless, the
moon rattles like a fragment of angry candy

# AN ANTHOLOGY OF POEMS

CHRISTOPHER MARLOWE (1564–1593)

**The Passionate Shepherd to His Love**

Come live with me, and be my love,
And we will all the pleasures prove
That hills and valleys, dales and fields,
Woods, or steepy mountain yields.

5 And we will sit upon the rocks,
Seeing the shepherds feed their flocks,
By shallow rivers, to whose falls
Melodious birds sings madrigals.

And I will make thee beds of roses
10 And a thousand fragrant posies.
A cap of flowers, and a kirtle
Embroidered all with leaves of myrtle;

A gown made of the finest wool,
Which from our pretty lambs we pull,
15 Fair linèd slippers, for the cold,
With buckles of the purest gold;

A belt of straw and ivy-buds
With coral clasps and amber studs.
And if these pleasures may thee move,
20 Come live with me, and be my love.

The shepherds' swains shall dance and sing
For thy delight each May morning.
If these delights thy mind may move,
Then live with me, and be my love.

## SIR WALTER RALEGH (1552?–1618)

### The Nymph's Reply to the Shepherd

If all the world and love were young,
And truth in every shepherd's tongue,
These pretty pleasures might me move
To live with thee and be thy love.

5 Time drives the flocks from field to fold
When rivers rage and rocks grow cold,
And Philomel becometh dumb;
The rest complains of cares to come.

The flowers do fade, and wanton fields
10 To wayward winter reckoning yields;
A honey tongue, a heart of gall,
Is fancy's spring, but sorrow's fall.

Thy gowns, thy shoes, thy beds of roses,
Thy cap, thy kirtle, and thy posies
15 Soon break, soon wither, soon forgotten—
In folly ripe, in reason rotten.

Thy belt of straw and ivy buds,
Thy coral clasps and amber studs,
All these in me no means can move
20 To come to thee and be thy love.

But could youth last and love still breed,
Had joys no date nor age no need,
Then these delights my mind might move
To live with thee and be thy love.

## WILLIAM SHAKESPEARE (1564–1616)

### Sonnet 55

Not marble nor the gilded monuments
Of princes shall outlive this powerful rime;
But you shall shine more bright in these contents
Than unswept stone, besmeared with sluttish time.
5 When wasteful war shall statues overturn,
And broils root out the work of masonry,

Nor Mars his sword nor war's quick fire shall burn
The living record of your memory.
'Gainst death and all oblivious enmity
10 Shall you pace forth; your praise shall still find room
Even in the eyes of all posterity
That wear this world out to the ending doom.
So, till the Judgment that yourself arise,
You live in this, and dwell in lovers' eyes.

## JOHN DONNE (1572–1631)

### Sonnet 7

At the round earth's imagined corners, blow
Your trumpets, angels, and arise, arise
From death, you numberless infinities
Of souls, and to your scattered bodies go;
5 All whom the flood did, and fire shall o'erthrow;
All whom war, dearth, age, agues, tyrannies,
Despair, law, chance, hath slain, and you whose eyes
Shall behold God, and never taste death's woe.
But let them sleep, Lord, and me mourn a space,
10 For if above all these my sins abound,
'Tis late to ask abundance of thy grace
When we are there; here on this lowly ground
Teach me how to repent; for that's as good
As if thou hadst sealed my pardon with thy blood.

## ROBERT HERRICK (1591–1674)

### The Night-Piece, to Julia

Her eyes the glowworm lend thee;
The shooting stars attend thee;
And the elves also,
Whose little eyes glow
5 Like the sparks of fire, befriend thee.

No will-o'-the-wisp mislight thee;
Nor snake or slowworm bite thee;
But on, on thy way,
Not making a stay,
10 Since ghost there's none to affright thee.

Let not the dark thee cumber;
What though the moon does slumber?
  The stars of the night
  Will lend thee their light,
15 Like tapers clear without number.

Then, Julia, let me woo thee,
Thus, thus to come unto me;
  And when I shall meet
  Thy silvery feet,
20 My soul I'll pour into thee.

ALEXANDER POPE (1688–1744)

**Ode on Solitude**

Happy the man whose wish and care
  A few paternal acres bound,
Content to breathe his native air,
        In his own ground.

5 Whose herds with milk, whose fields with bread,
  Whose flocks supply him with attire,
Whose trees in summer yield him shade,
        In winter fire.

Blest, who can unconcernedly find
10  Hours, days, and years slide soft away,
In health of body, peace of mind,
        Quiet by day,

Sound sleep by night; study and ease,
  Together mixed; sweet recreation;
15 And innocence, which most does please
        With meditation.

Thus let me live, unseen, unknown;
  Thus unlamented let me die;
Steal from the world, and not a stone
20      Tell where I lie.

## WILLIAM BLAKE (1757–1827)

### London

I wander thro' each charter'd street,
Near where the charter'd Thames does flow,
And mark in every face I meet
Marks of weakness, marks of woe.

5 In every cry of every Man,
In every Infant's cry of fear,
In every voice, in every ban,
The mind-forg'd manacles I hear.

How the Chimney-sweeper's cry
10 Every blackning Church appalls;
And the hapless Soldier's sigh
Runs in blood down Palace walls.

But most thro' midnight streets I hear
How the youthful Harlot's curse
15 Blasts the new-born Infant's tear,
And blights with plagues the Marriage hearse.

## SAMUEL TAYLOR COLERIDGE (1772–1834)

### Kubla Khan

In Xanadu did Kubla Kahn
A stately pleasure-dome decree:
Where Alph, the sacred river, ran
Through caverns measureless to man
5 Down to a sunless sea.
So twice five miles of fertile ground
With walls and towers were girdled round:
And there were gardens bright with sinuous rills,
Where blossomed many an incense-bearing tree;
10 And here were forests ancient as the hills,
Enfolding sunny spots of greenery.

But oh! that deep romantic chasm which slanted
Down the green hill athwart a cedarn cover!
A savage place! as holy and enchanted
15 As e'er beneath a waning moon was haunted
By woman wailing for her demon-lover!

And from this chasm, with ceaseless turmoil seething,
As if this earth in thick pants were breathing,
A mighty fountain momently was forced:
20 Amid whose swift half-intermitted burst
Huge fragments vaulted like rebounding hail,
Or chaffy grain beneath the thresher's flail:
And 'mid these dancing rocks at once and ever
It flung up momently the sacred river.
25 Five miles meandering with a mazy motion
Through wood and dale the sacred river ran,
Then reached the caverns measureless to man,

And sank in tumult to a lifeless ocean:
And 'mid this tumult Kubla heard from far
30 Ancestral voices prophesying war!

The shadow of the dome of pleasure
Floated midway on the waves;
Where was heard the mingled measure
From the fountain and the caves.

35 It was a miracle of rare device,
A sunny pleasure-dome with caves of ice!

A damsel with a dulcimer
In a vision once I saw:
It was an Abyssinian maid,
40 And on her dulcimer she played,
Singing of Mount Abora.
Could I revive within me
Her symphony and song,
To such a deep delight 'twould win me,

45 That with music loud and long,
I would build that dome in air,
That sunny dome! those caves of ice!
And all who heard should see them there,
And all should cry, Beware! Beware!
50 His flashing eyes, his floating hair!
Weave a circle round him thrice,
And close your eyes with holy dread,
For he on honey-dew hath fed,
And drunk the milk of Paradise.

## ALFRED, LORD TENNYSON (1809–1892)

### Ulysses

It little profits that an idle king,
By this still hearth, among these barren crags,
Matched with an aged wife, I mete and dole
Unequal laws unto a savage race,
5 That hoard, and sleep, and feed, and know not me.
I cannot rest from travel; I will drink
Life to the lees. All times I have enjoyed
Greatly, have suffered greatly, both with those
That loved me, and alone; on shore, and when
10 Through scudding drifts the rainy Hyades[1]
Vexed the dim sea: I am become a name;
For always roaming with a hungry heart
Much have I seen and known—cities of men
And manners, climates, councils, governments,
15 Myself not least, but honored of them all;
And drunk delight of battle with my peers,
Far on the ringing plains of windy Troy.
I am a part of all that I have met;
Yet all experience is an arch wherethrough
20 Gleams that untraveled world whose margin fades
For ever and for ever when I move.
How dull it is to pause, to make an end,
To rust unburnished, not to shine in use!
As though to breathe were life! Life piled on life
25 Were all too little, and of one to me
Little remains; but every hour is saved
From that eternal silence, something more,
A bringer of new things; and vile it were
For some three suns to store and hoard myself,
30 And this gray spirit yearning in desire
To follow knowledge like a sinking star,
Beyond the utmost bound of human thought.

This is my son, mine own Telemachus,
To whom I leave the scepter and the isle—
35 Well-loved of me, discerning to fulfil
This labor, by slow prudence to make mild
A rugged people, and through soft degrees

---

[1] A group of stars in the constellation Taurus, whose rise with the sun heralded the spring rains.

Subdue them to the useful and the good.
Most blameless is he, centered in the sphere
40 Of common duties, decent not to fail
In offices of tenderness, and pay
Meet adoration to my household gods,
When I am gone. He works his work, I mine.

There lies the port; the vessel puffs her sail;
45 There gloom the dark, broad seas. My mariners,
Souls that have toiled, and wrought, and thought with me—
That ever with a frolic welcome took
The thunder and the sunshine, and opposed
Free hearts, free foreheads—you and I are old;
50 Old age hath yet his honor and his toil.
Death closes all; but something ere the end,
Some work of noble note, may yet be done,
Not unbecoming men that strove with Gods.
The lights begin to twinkle from the rocks:
55 The long day wanes: the slow moon climbs: the deep
Moans round with many voices. Come, my friends,
'Tis not too late to seek a newer world.
Push off, and sitting well in order smite
The sounding furrows; for my purpose holds
60 To sail beyond the sunset, and the baths
Of all the western stars, until I die.
It may be that the gulfs will wash us down;
It may be we shall touch the Happy Isles,
And see the great Achilles, whom we knew.
65 Though much is taken, much abides; and though
We are not now that strength which in old days
Moved earth and heaven, that which we are, we are;
One equal temper of heroic hearts,
Made weak by time and fate, but strong in will
70 To strive, to seek, to find, and not to yield.

ROBERT BROWNING (1812–1889)

**The Bishop Orders His Tomb at Saint Praxed's Church**

*Rome, 15—*

Vanity, saith the preacher, vanity!
Draw round my bed: is Anselm keeping back?

Nephews[1]—sons mine . . . ah God, I know not! Well—
She, men would have to be your mother once,
5 Old Gandolf envied me, so fair she was!
What's done is done, and she is dead beside,
Dead long ago, and I am Bishop since,
And as she died so must we die ourselves,
And thence ye may perceive the world's a dream.
10 Life, how and what is it? As here I lie
In this state-chamber, dying by degrees,
Hours and long hours in the dead night, I ask
"Do I live, am I dead?" Peace, peace seems all.
Saint Praxed's ever was the church for peace;
15 And so, about this tomb of mine. I fought
With tooth and nail to save my niche, ye know:
—Old Gandolf cozened me, despite my care;
Shrewd was that snatch from out the corner South
He graced his carrion with, God curse the same!
20 Yet still my niche is not so cramped but thence
One sees the pulpit o' the epistle side,[2]
And somewhat of the choir, those silent seats,
And up into the aery dome where live
The angels, and a sunbeam's sure to lurk:
25 And I shall fill my slab of basalt there,
And 'neath my tabernacle take my rest,
With those nine columns round me, two and two,
The odd one at my feet where Anselm stands:
Peach-blossom marble all, the rare, the ripe
30 As fresh-poured red wine of a mighty pulse.
—Old Gandolf with his paltry onion-stone,
Put me where I may look at him! True peach,
Rosy and flawless: how I earned the prize!
Draw close: that conflagration of my church
35 —What then? So much was saved if aught were missed!
My sons, ye would not be my death? Go dig
The white-grape vineyard where the oil-press stood,
Drop water gently till the surface sink,
And if ye find . . . Ah God, I know not, I! . . .
40 Bedded in store of rotten fig-leaves soft,
And corded up in a tight olive-frail,
Some lump, ah God, of *lapis lazuli*,

---

[1] Euphemism for illegitimate sons.
[2] The right-hand side, as one faces the altar.

Big as a Jew's head cut off at the nape,
Blue as a vein o'er the Madonna's breast . . .
45 Sons, all have I bequeathed you, villas, all,
That brave Frascati villa with its bath,
So, let the blue lump poise between my knees,
Like God the Father's globe on both his hands
Ye worship in the Jesu Church so gay,
50 For Gandolf shall not choose but see and burst!
Swift as a weaver's shuttle fleet our years:
Man goeth to the grave, and where is he?
Did I say basalt for my slab, sons? Black—
'Twas ever antique-black I meant! How else
55 Shall ye contrast my frieze to come beneath?
The bas-relief in bronze ye promised me,
Those Pans and Nymphs ye wot of, and perchance
Some tripod,[3] thyrsus,[4] with a vase or so,
The Saviour at his sermon on the mount,
60 Saint Praxed in a glory, and one Pan
Ready to twitch the Nymph's last garment off,
And Moses with the tables . . . but I know
Ye mark me not! What do they whisper thee,
Child of my bowels, Anselm? Ah, ye hope
65 To revel down my villas while I gasp
Bricked o'er with beggar's moldy travertine
Which Gandolf from his tomb-top chuckles at!
Nay, boys, ye love me—all of jasper, then!
'Tis jasper ye stand pledged to, lest I grieve
70 My bath must needs be left behind, alas!
One block, pure green as a pistachio nut,
There's plenty jasper somewhere in the world—
And have I not Saint Praxed's ear to pray
Horses for ye, and brown Greek manuscripts,
75 And mistresses with great smooth marbly limbs?
—That's if ye carve my epitaph aright,
Choice Latin, picked phrase, Tully's[5] every word,
No gaudy ware like Gandolf's second line—
Tully, my masters? Ulpian[6] serves his need!
80 And then how I shall lie through centuries,
And hear the blessed mutter of the mass,
And see God made and eaten all day long,

---

[3] Three-legged stool used by the oracle at Delphi.
[4] Staff carried by Dionysus and his followers.
[5] Marcus Tullius Cicero, master of Latin prose style.
[6] Domitius Ulpianus, third century Roman jurist, noted for bad prose.

And feel the steady candle-flame, and taste
Good strong thick stupefying incense-smoke!
85 For as I lie here, hours of the dead night,
Dying in state and by such slow degrees,
I fold my arms as if they clasped a crook,
And stretch my feet forth straight as stone can point,
And let the bedclothes, for a mortcloth, drop
90 Into great laps and folds of sculptor's-work:
And as yon tapers dwindle, and strange thoughts
Grow, with a certain humming in my ears,
About the life before I lived this life,
And this life too, popes, cardinals, and priests,
95 Saint Praxed at his sermon on the mount,[7]
Your tall pale mother with her talking eyes,
And new-found agate urns as fresh as day,
And marble's language, Latin pure, discreet
—Aha, ELUCESCEBAT[8] quoth our friend?
100 No Tully, said I, Ulpian at the best!
Evil and brief hath been my pilgrimage.
All *lapis,* all, sons! Else I give the Pope
My villas! Will ye ever eat my heart?
Ever your eyes were as a lizard's quick,
105 They glitter like your mother's for my soul,
Or ye would heighten my impoverished frieze,
Piece out its starved design, and fill my vase
With grapes, and add a vizor and a Term,[9]
And to the tripod you would tie a lynx
110 That in his struggle throws the thyrsus down,
To comfort me on my entablature
Whereon I am to lie till I must ask
"Do I live, am I dead?" There, leave me, there!
For ye have stabbed me with ingratitude
115 To death—ye wish it—God, ye wish it! Stone—
Gritstone, a-crumble! Clammy squares which sweat
As if the corpse they keep were oozing through—
And no more *lapis* to delight the world!
Well go! I bless ye. Fewer tapers there,
120 But in a row: and, going, turn your backs
—Aye, like departing altar-ministrants,
And leave me in my church, the church for peace,

---

[7] The bishop's failing mind attributes the Sermon on the Mount to Saint Praxed (a woman) instead of Christ.
[8] "He was illustrious," an example of Ulpian Latin.
[9] A mask and bust on a pedestal.

That I may watch at leisure if he leers—
Old Gandolf, at me, from his onion-stone,
125 As still he envied me, so fair she was!

ROBERT BROWNING (1812–1889)

**Home-Thoughts, from Abroad**

1

Oh, to be in England
Now that April's there,
And whoever wakes in England
Sees, some morning, unaware,
5 That the lowest boughs and the brushwood sheaf
Round the elm-tree bole are in tiny leaf,
While the chaffinch sings on the orchard bough
In England—now!

2

And after April, when May follows,
10 And the whitethroat builds, and all the swallows!
Hark, where my blossomed pear-tree in the hedge
Leans to the field and scatters on the clover
Blossoms and dewdrops—at the bent spray's edge—
That's the wise thrush; he sings each song twice over,
15 Lest you should think he never could recapture
The first fine careless rapture!
And though the fields look rough with hoary dew,
All will be gay when noontide wakes anew
The buttercups, the little children's dower
20 —Far brighter than this gaudy melon-flower!

WALT WHITMAN (1819–1892)

**Out of the Cradle Endlessly Rocking**

Out of the cradle endlessly rocking,
Out of the mocking-bird's throat, the musical shuttle,
Out of the Ninth-month midnight,
Over the sterile sands and the fields beyond, where the child leaving
his bed wander'd alone, bareheaded, barefoot,

5 Down from the shower'd halo,
Up from the mystic play of shadows twining and twisting as if they were alive,
Out from the patches of briers and blackberries,
From the memories of the bird that chanted to me,
From your memories sad brother, from the fitful risings and fallings I heard,
10 From under that yellow half-moon late-risen and swollen as if with tears,
From those beginning notes of yearning and love there in the mist,
From the thousand responses of my heart never to cease,
From the myriad thence-arous'd words,
From the word stronger and more delicious than any,
15 From such as now they start the scene revisiting,
As a flock, twittering, rising, or overhead passing,
Borne hither, ere all eludes me, hurriedly,
A man, yet by these tears a little boy again,
Throwing myself on the sand, confronting the waves,
20 I, chanter of pains and joys, uniter of here and hereafter,
Taking all hints to use them, but swiftly leaping beyond them,
A reminiscence sing.

Once Paumanok,[1]
When the lilac-scent was in the air and Fifth-month grass was growing,
25 Up this seashore in some briers,
Two feather'd guests from Alabama, two together,
And their nest, and four light-green eggs spotted with brown,
And every day the he-bird to and fro near at hand,
And every day the she-bird crouch'd on her nest, silent, with bright eyes,
30 And every day I, a curious boy, never too close, never disturbing them,
Cautiously peering, absorbing, translating.

*Shine! shine! shine!*
*Pour down your warmth, great sun!*
*While we bask, we two together.*

35 *Two together!*
*Winds blow south, or winds blow north,*

[1] The Indian name for Long Island.

*Day come white, or night come black,*
*Home, or rivers and mountains from home,*
*Singing all time, minding no time,*
40 *While we two keep together.*

Till of a sudden,
May-be kill'd unknown to her mate,
One forenoon, the she-bird crouch'd not on the nest,
Nor return'd that afternoon, nor the next,
45 Nor ever appear'd again.

And thenceforward all summer in the sound of the sea,
And at night under the full of the moon in calmer weather,
Over the hoarse surging of the sea,
Or flitting from brier to brier by day,
50 I saw, I heard at intervals the remaining one, the he-bird,
The solitary guest from Alabama.

*Blow! blow! blow!*
*Blow up sea-winds along Paumanok's shore;*
*I wait and I wait till you blow my mate to me.*

55 Yes, when the stars glisten'd,
All night long on the prong of a moss-scallop'd stake,
Down almost amid the slapping waves,
Sat the lone singer wonderful causing tears.

He call'd on his mate,
60 He pour'd forth the meanings which I of all men know.

Yes my brother I know,
The rest might not, but I have treasur'd every note,
For more than once dimly down to the beach gliding,
Silent, avoiding the moonbeams, blending myself with the shadows,
65 Recalling now the obscure shapes, the echoes, the sounds and sights
after their sorts,
The white arms out in the breakers tirelessly tossing,
I, with bare feet, a child, the wind wafting my hair,
Listen'd long and long.

Listen'd to keep, to sing, now translating the notes,
70 Following you my brother.

*Soothe! soothe! soothe!*
*Close on its wave soothes the wave behind,*

*And again another behind embracing and lapping, every one close,*
*But my love soothes not me, not me.*

75 *Low hangs the moon, it rose late,*
*It is lagging—O I think it is heavy with love, with love.*

*O madly the sea pushes upon the land,*
*With love, with love.*

*O night! do I not see my love fluttering out among the breakers?*
80 *What is that little black thing I see there in the white?*

*Loud! loud! loud!*
*Loud I call to you, my love!*
*High and clear I shoot my voice over the waves,*
*Surely you must know who is here, is here,*
85 *You must know who I am, my love.*

*Low-hanging moon!*
*What is that dusky spot in your brown yellow?*
*O it is the shape, the shape of my mate!*
*O moon do not keep her from me any longer.*

90 *Land! land! O land!*
*Whichever way I turn, O I think you could give me my mate back again if you only would,*
*For I am almost sure I see her dimly whichever way I look.*

*O rising stars!*
*Perhaps the one I want so much will rise, will rise with some of you.*

95 *O throat! O trembling throat!*
*Sound clearer through the atmosphere!*
*Pierce the woods, the earth,*
*Somewhere listening to catch you must be the one I want.*

*Shake out carols!*
100 *Solitary here, the night's carols!*
*Carols of lonesome love! death's carols!*
*Carols under that lagging, yellow, waning moon!*
*O under that moon where she droops almost down into the sea!*
*O reckless despairing carols.*

105 *But soft! sink low!*
*Soft! let me just murmur,*

*And do you wait a moment you husky-nois'd sea,*
*For somewhere I believe I heard my mate responding to me,*
*So faint, I must be still, be still to listen,*
110 *But not altogether still, for then she might not come immediately to me.*

*Hither my love!*
*Here I am! here!*
*With this just-sustain'd note I announce myself to you,*
*This gentle call is for you my love, for you.*

115 *Do not be decoy'd elsewhere,*
*That is the whistle of the wind, it is not my voice,*
*That is the fluttering, the fluttering of the spray,*
*Those are the shadows of leaves.*

*O darkness! O in vain!*
120 *O I am very sick and sorrowful.*

*O brown halo in the sky near the moon, drooping upon the sea!*
*O troubled reflection in the sea!*
*O throat! O throbbing heart!*
*And I singing uselessly, uselessly all the night.*

125 *O past! O happy life! O songs of joy!*
*In the air, in the woods, over fields,*
*Loved! loved! loved! loved! loved!*
*But my mate no more, no more with me!*
*We two together no more.*

130 The aria sinking,
All else continuing, the stars shining,
The winds blowing, the notes of the bird continuous echoing,
With angry moans the fierce old mother incessantly moaning,
On the sands of Paumanok's shore gray and rustling,
135 The yellow half-moon enlarged, sagging down, drooping, the face of the sea almost touching,
The boy ecstatic, with his bare feet the waves, with his hair the atmosphere dallying,
The love in the heart long pent, now loose, now at last tumultuously bursting,
The aria's meaning, the ears, the soul, swiftly depositing,
The strange tears down the cheeks coursing,
140 The colloquy there, the trio, each uttering,

The undertone, the savage old mother incessantly crying,
To the boy's soul's questions sullenly timing, some drown'd secret hissing,
To the outsetting bard.

Demon or bird! (said the boy's soul,)
145 Is it indeed toward your mate you sing? or is it really to me?
For I, that was a child, my tongue's use sleeping, now I have heard you,
Now in a moment I know what I am for, I awake,
And already a thousand singers, a thousand songs, clearer, louder and more sorrowful than yours,
A thousand warbling echoes have started to life within me, never to die.

150 O you singer solitary, singing by yourself, projecting me,
O solitary me listening, never more shall I cease perpetuating you,
Never more shall I escape, never more the reverberations,
Never more the cries of unsatisfied love be absent from me,
Never again leave me to be the peaceful child I was before what there in the night,
155 By the sea under the yellow and sagging moon,
The messenger there arous'd, the fire, the sweet hell within,
The unknown want, the destiny of me.

O give me the clew! (it lurks in the night here somewhere,)
O if I am to have so much, let me have more!

160 A word then, (for I will conquer it,)
The word final, superior to all,
Subtle, sent up—what is it?—I listen;
Are you whispering it, and have been all the time, you sea-waves?
Is that it from your liquid rims and wet sands?

165 Whereto answering, the sea,
Delaying not, hurrying not,
Whisper'd me through the night, and very plainly before daybreak,
Lisp'd to me the low and delicious word death,
And again death, death, death, death,
170 Hissing melodious, neither like the bird nor like my arous'd child's heart,
But edging near as privately for me rustling at my feet,
Creeping thence steadily up to my ears and laving me softly all over,
Death, death, death, death, death.

Which I do not forget,
175 But fuse the song of my dusky demon and brother,
That he sang to me in the moonlight on Paumanok's gray beach,
With the thousand responsive songs at random,
My own songs awaked from that hour,
And with them the key, the word up from the waves,
180 The word of the sweetest song and all songs,
That strong and delicious word which, creeping to my feet,
(Or like some old crone rocking the cradle, swathed in sweet garments, bending aside,)
The sea whisper'd me.

EMILY DICKINSON (1830–1886)

## The Poets Light but Lamps (#883)

The Poets light but Lamps—
Themselves—go out—
The Wicks they stimulate—
If vital Light

5 Inhere as do the Suns—
Each Age a Lens
Disseminating their
Circumference—

A. E. HOUSMAN (1859–1936)

## "Terence, This Is Stupid Stuff . . ."

"Terence, this is stupid stuff:
You eat your victuals fast enough;
There can't be much amiss, 'tis clear,
To see the rate you drink your beer.
5 But oh, good Lord, the verse you make,
It gives a chap the belly-ache.
The cow, the old cow, she is dead;
It sleeps well, the hornèd head:
We poor lads, 'tis our turn now
10 To hear such tunes as killed the cow.
Pretty friendship 'tis to rhyme
Your friends to death before their time
Moping melancholy mad:
Come, pipe a tune to dance to, lad."

15 Why, if 'tis dancing you would be,
There's brisker pipes than poetry.
Say, for what were hop-yards meant,
Or why was Burton built on Trent?[1]
Oh many a peer of England brews
20 Livelier liquor than the Muse,
And malt does more than Milton can
To justify God's ways to man.
Ale, man, ale's the stuff to drink
For fellows whom it hurts to think:
25 Look into the pewter pot
To see the world as the world's not.
And faith, 'tis pleasant till 'tis past:
The mischief is that 'twill not last.
Oh I have been to Ludlow fair
30 And left my necktie God knows where,
And carried half-way home, or near,
Pints and quarts of Ludlow beer:
Then the world seemed none so bad,
And I myself a sterling lad;
35 And down in lovely muck I've lain,
Happy till I woke again.
Then I saw the morning sky:
Heigho, the tale was all a lie;
The world, it was the old world yet,
40 I was I, my things were wet,
And nothing now remained to do
But begin the game anew.

Therefore, since the world has still
Much good, but much less good than ill,
45 And while the sun and moon endure
Luck's a chance, but trouble's sure,
I'd face it as a wise man would,
And train for ill and not for good.
'Tis true, the stuff I bring for sale
50 Is not so brisk a brew as ale:
Out of a stem that scored the hand
I wrung it in a weary land.
But take it: if the smack is sour,
The better for the embittered hour;

---

[1] A town noted for its breweries.

55 It should do good to heart and head
When your soul is in my soul's stead;
And I will friend you, if I may,
In the dark and cloudy day.

There was a king reigned in the East:
60 There, when kings will sit to feast,
They get their fill before they think
With poisoned meat and poisoned drink.
He gathered all that springs to birth
From the many-venomed earth;
65 First a little, thence to more,
He sampled all her killing store;
And easy, smiling, seasoned sound,
Sate the king when healths went round.
They put arsenic in his meat
70 And stared aghast to watch him eat;
They poured strychnine in his cup
And shook to see him drink it up:
They shook, they stared as white's their shirt:
Them it was their poison hurt.
75 —I tell the tale that I heard told.
Mithridates,[2] he died old.

A. E. HOUSMAN (1859–1936)

## To an Athlete Dying Young

The time you won your town the race
We chaired you through the market-place;
Man and boy stood cheering by,
And home we brought you shoulder-high.

5 To-day, the road all runners come,
Shoulder-high we bring you home,
And set you at your threshold down,
Townsman of a stiller town.

Smart lad, to slip betimes away
10 From fields where glory does not stay
And early though the laurel grows
It withers quicker than the rose.

---

[2] King of Pontus in the first century B.C., who made himself immune to certain poisons by taking them frequently in small doses.

Eyes the shady night has shut
Cannot see the record cut,
15 And silence sounds no worse than cheers
After earth has stopped the ears:

Now you will not swell the rout
Of lads that wore their honors out,
Runners whom renown outran
20 And the name died before the man.

So set, before its echoes fade,
The fleet foot on the sill of shade,
And hold to the low lintel up
The still-defended challenge-cup.

25 And round that early-laurelled head
Will flock to gaze the strengthless dead,
And find unwithered on its curls
The garland briefer than a girl's.

## EDWIN ARLINGTON ROBINSON (1869–1935)

### Mr. Flood's Party

Old Eben Flood, climbing alone one night
Over the hill between the town below
And the forsaken upland hermitage
That held as much as he should ever know
5 On earth again of home, paused warily.
The road was his with not a native near;
And Eben, having leisure, said aloud,
For no man else in Tilbury Town to hear:

"Well, Mr. Flood, we have the harvest moon
10 Again, and we may not have many more;
The bird is on the wing, the poet says,[1]
And you and I have said it here before.
Drink to the bird." He raised up to the light
The jug that he had gone so far to fill,
15 And answered huskily: "Well, Mr. Flood,
Since you propose it, I believe I will."

---

[1] A reference to stanza 7 of *The Rubáiyát of Omar Khayyám.*

Alone, as if enduring to the end
A valiant armor of scarred hopes outworn,
He stood there in the middle of the road
20 Like Roland's ghost winding a silent horn.[2]
Below him, in the town among the trees,
Where friends of other days had honored him,
A phantom salutation of the dead
Rang thinly till old Eben's eyes were dim.

25 Then, as a mother lays her sleeping child
Down tenderly, fearing it may awake,
He set the jug down slowly at his feet
With trembling care, knowing that most things break;
And only when assured that on firm earth
30 It stood, as the uncertain lives of men
Assuredly did not, he paced away,
And with his hand extended paused again:

"Well, Mr. Flood, we have not met like this
In a long time; and many a change has come
35 To both of us, I fear, since last it was
We had a drop together. Welcome home!"
Convivially returning with himself,
Again he raised the jug up to the light;
And with an acquiescent quaver said:
40 "Well, Mr. Flood, if you insist, I might.

"Only a very little, Mr. Flood—
For auld lang syne. No more, sir; that will do."
So, for the time, apparently it did,
And Eben evidently thought so too;
45 For soon amid the silver loneliness
Of night he lifted up his voice and sang,
Secure, with only two moons listening,
Until the whole harmonious landscape rang—

"For auld lang syne." The weary throat gave out,
50 The last word wavered; and the song being done,
He raised again the jug regretfully

---

[2] In the medieval *Song of Roland,* the hero refuses to blow his horn for help at the Battle of Roncevaux and loses his life.

And shook his head, and was again alone.
There was not much that was ahead of him,
And there was nothing in the town below—
55 Where strangers would have shut the many doors
That many friends had opened long ago.

## JAMES WELDON JOHNSON (1871–1938)

### O Black and Unknown Bards

O black and unknown bards of long ago,
How came your lips to touch the sacred fire?
How, in your darkness, did you come to know
The power and beauty of the minstrel's lyre?
5 Who first from midst his bonds lifted his eyes?
Who first from out the still watch, lone and long,
Feeling the ancient faith of prophets rise
Within his dark-kept soul, burst into song?

Heart of what slave poured out such melody
10 As "Steal away to Jesus"? On its strains
His spirit must have nightly floated free,
Though still about his hands he felt his chains.
Who heard great "Jordan roll"? Whose starward eye
Saw chariot "swing low"? And who was he
15 That breathed that comforting, melodic sigh,
"Nobody knows de trouble I see"?

What merely living clod, what captive thing,
Could up toward God through all its darkness grope,
And find within its deadened heart to sing
20 These songs of sorrow, love and faith, and hope?
How did it catch that subtle undertone,
That note in music heard not with the ears?
How sound the elusive reed so seldom blown,
Which stirs the soul or melts the heart to tears?

25 Not that great German master[1] in his dream
Of harmonies that thundered amongst the stars
At the creation, ever heard a theme
Nobler than "Go down, Moses." Mark its bars,

---

[1] Beethoven.

How like a mighty trumpet-call they stir
30 The blood. Such are the notes that men have sung
Going to valorous deeds; such tones there were
That helped make history when Time was young.

There is a wide, wide wonder in it all,
That from degraded rest and servile toil
35 The fiery spirit of the seer should call
These simple children of the sun and soil.

O black slave singers, gone, forgot, unfamed,
You—you alone, of all the long, long line
Of those who've sung untaught, unknown, unnamed,
40 Have stretched out upward, seeking the divine.

You sang not deeds of heroes or of kings;
No chant of bloody war, no exulting paean
Of arms-won triumphs; but your humble strings
You touched in chord with music empyrean.
45 You sang far better than you knew; the songs
That for your listeners' hungry hearts sufficed
Still live—but more than this to you belongs:
You sang a race from wood and stone to Christ.

## ROBERT FROST (1874–1963)

### "Out, Out—" [1]

The buzz-saw snarled and rattled in the yard
And made dust and dropped stove-length sticks of wood,
Sweet-scented stuff when the breeze drew across it.
And from there those that lifted eyes could count
5 Five mountain ranges one behind the other
Under the sunset far into Vermont.
And the saw snarled and rattled, snarled and rattled,
As it ran light, or had to bear a load.
And nothing happened: day was all but done.
10 Call it a day, I wish they might have said
To please the boy by giving him the half hour
That a boy counts so much when saved from work.
His sister stood beside them in her apron

[1] An allusion to *Macbeth,* Act 5, Scene 5.

To tell them "Supper." At the word, the saw,
15 As if to prove saws knew what supper meant,
Leaped out at the boy's hand, or seemed to leap—
He must have given the hand. However it was,
Neither refused the meeting. But the hand!
The boy's first outcry was a rueful laugh,
20 As he swung toward them holding up the hand
Half in appeal, but half as if to keep
The life from spilling. Then the boy saw all—
Since he was old enough to know, big boy
Doing a man's work, though a child at heart—
25 He saw all spoiled. "Don't let him cut my hand off—
The doctor, when he comes. Don't let him, sister!"

So. But the hand was gone already.
The doctor put him in the dark of ether.
He lay and puffed his lips out with his breath.
30 And then—the watcher at his pulse took fright.
No one believed. They listened at his heart.
Little—less—nothing!—and that ended it.
No more to build on there. And they, since they
Were not the one dead, turned to their affairs.

## WALLACE STEVENS (1879–1955)

### Thirteen Ways of Looking at a Blackbird

I

Among twenty snowy mountains,
The only moving thing
Was the eye of the blackbird.

II

I was of three minds,
5 Like a tree
In which there are three blackbirds.

III

The blackbird whirled in the autumn winds.
It was a small part of the pantomime.

IV

A man and a woman
10 Are one.
A man and a woman and a blackbird
Are one.

V

I do not know which to prefer,
The beauty of inflections,
15 Or the beauty of innuendoes,
The blackbird whistling
Or just after.

VI

Icicles filled the long window
With barbaric glass.
20 The shadow of the blackbird
Crossed it, to and fro.
The mood
Traced in the shadow
An indecipherable cause.

VII

25 O thin men of Haddam,[1]
Why do you imagine golden birds?
Do you not see how the blackbird
Walks around the feet
Of the women about you?

VIII

30 I know noble accents
And lucid, inescapable rhythms;
But I know, too,
That the blackbird is involved
In what I know.

IX

35 When the blackbird flew out of sight,
It marked the edge
Of one of many circles.

---

[1] A town in Connecticut; Stevens liked its name.

X

At the sight of blackbirds
Flying in a green light,
40 Even the bawds of euphony
Would cry out sharply.

XI

He rode over Connecticut
In a glass coach.
Once, a fear pierced him,
45 In that he mistook
The shadow of his equipage
For blackbirds.

XII

The river is moving.
The blackbird must be flying.

XIII

50 It was evening all afternoon.
It was snowing
And it was going to snow.
The blackbird sat
In the cedar-limbs.

## ROBINSON JEFFERS (1887–1962)

### Love the Wild Swan

"I hate my verses, every line, every word.
Oh pale and brittle pencils ever to try
One grass-blade's curve, or the throat of one bird
That clings to twig, ruffled against white sky.
5 Oh cracked and twilight mirrors ever to catch
One color, one glinting flash, of the splendor of things.
Unlucky hunter, Oh bullets of wax,
The lion beauty, the wild-swan wings, the storm of the wings."
—This wild swan of a world is no hunter's game.
10 Better bullets than yours would miss the white breast,
Better mirrors than yours would crack in the flame.
Does it matter whether you hate your . . . self? At least
Love your eyes that can see, your mind that can
Hear the music, the thunder of the wings. Love the wild swan.

## MARIANNE MOORE (1887–1972)

### Poetry

I, too, dislike it: there are things that are important beyond all this
fiddle.
Reading it, however, with a perfect contempt for it, one discovers
in
it after all, a place for the genuine.
Hands that can grasp, eyes
5 that can dilate, hair that can rise
if it must, there things are important not because a

high-sounding interpretation can be put upon them but because they
are
useful. When they become so derivative as to become unintelligble,
the same thing may be said for all of us, that we
10 do not admire what
we cannot understand: the bat
holding on upside down or in quest of something to

eat, elephants pushing, a wild horse taking a roll, a tireless wolf
under
a tree, the immovable critic twitching his skin like a horse that
feels a flea, the base-
15 ball fan, the statistician—
nor is it valid
to discriminate against "business documents and

school-books";[1] all these phenomena are important. One must make
a distinction
however: when dragged into prominence by half poets, the result
is not poetry,
20 nor till the poets among us can be
"literalists of
the imagination" [2]—above
insolence and triviality and can present

for inspection, "imaginary gardens with real toads in them," shall we
have
25 it. In the meantime, if you demand on the one hand,

---

[1] Moore's note cites the Diary of Tolstoy: "poetry is everything with the exception of business documents and school books."
[2] From Yeats, *Ideas of Good and Evil.*

the raw material of poetry in
  all its rawness and
  that which is on the other hand
    genuine, you are interested in poetry.

## JOHN CROWE RANSOM (1888–1974)

### Bells for John Whiteside's Daughter

There was such speed in her little body,
And such lightness in her footfall,
It is no wonder her brown study
Astonishes us all.

5 Her wars were bruited in our high window.
We looked among orchard trees and beyond
Where she took arms against her shadow,
Or harried unto the pond

The lazy geese, like a snow cloud
10 Dripping their snow on the green grass,
Tricking and stopping, sleepy and proud,
Who cried in goose, Alas,

For the tireless heart within the little
Lady with rod that made them rise
15 From their noon apple-dreams and scuttle
Goose-fashion under the skies!

But now go the bells, and we are ready,
In one house we are sternly stopped
To say we are vexed at her brown study,
20 Lying so primly propped.

## T. S. ELIOT (1888–1965)

### The Love Song of J. Alfred Prufrock

*S'io credesse che mia risposta fosse*
*A persona che mai tornasse al mondo,*
*Questa fiamma staria senza piu scosse.*
*Ma perciocche giammai di questo fondo*

*Non torno vivo alcun, s'i'odo il vero,*
*Senza tema d'infamia ti rispondo.*[1]

Let us go then, you and I,
When the evening is spread out against the sky
Like a patient etherized upon a table;
Let us go, through certain half-deserted streets,
5 The muttering retreats
Of restless nights in one-night cheap hotels
And sawdust restaurants with oyster-shells:
Streets that follow like a tedious argument
Of insidious intent
10 To lead you to an overwhelming question . . .

Oh, do not ask, "What is it?"
Let us go and make our visit.

In the room the women come and go
Talking of Michelangelo.

15 The yellow fog that rubs its back upon the window-panes
The yellow smoke that rubs its muzzle on the window-panes
Licked its tongue into the corners of the evening,
Lingered upon the pools that stand in drains,
Let fall upon its back the soot that falls from chimneys,
20 Slipped by the terrace, made a sudden leap,
And seeing that it was a soft October night,
Curled once about the house, and fell asleep.

And indeed there will be time
For the yellow smoke that slides along the street,
25 Rubbing its back upon the window-panes;
There will be time, there will be time
To prepare a face to meet the faces that you meet;
There will be time to murder and create,
And time for all the works and days of hands
30 That lift and drop a question on your plate;
Time for you and time for me,

---

1 "If I thought that my response were given to one who would ever return to the world, this flame would move no more. But since never from this depth has man returned alive, if what I hear is true, without fear of infamy I answer thee." In Dante's *Inferno* these words are addressed to the poet by the spirit of Guido da Montefeltro.

And time yet for a hundred indecisions,
And for a hundred visions and revisions,
Before the taking of a toast and tea.

35 In the room the women come and go
Talking of Michelangelo.

And indeed there will be time
To wonder, "Do I dare?" and, "Do I dare?"
Time to turn back and descend the stair,
40 With a bald spot in the middle of my hair—
[They will say: "How his hair is growing thin!"]
My morning coat, my collar mounting firmly to the chin,
My necktie rich and modest, but asserted by a simple pin—
[They will say: "But how his arms and legs are thin!"]
45 Do I dare
Disturb the universe?
In a minute there is time
For decisions and revisions which a minute will reverse.

For I have known them all already, known them all:
50 Have known the evenings, mornings, afternoons,
I have measured out my life with coffee spoons;
I know the voices dying with a dying fall
Beneath the music from a farther room.
So how should I presume?

55 And I have known the eyes already, known them all—
The eyes that fix you in a formulated phrase,
And when I am formulated, sprawling on a pin,
When I am pinned and wriggling on the wall,
Then how should I begin
60 To spit out all the butt-ends of my days and ways?
And how should I presume?

And I have known the arms already, known them all—
Arms that are braceleted and white and bare
[But in the lamplight, downed with light brown hair!]
65 Is it perfume from a dress
That makes me so digress?
Arms that lie along a table, or wrap about a shawl.
And should I then presume?
And how should I begin?

. . . . .

70 Shall I say, I have gone at dusk through narrow streets
And watched the smoke that rises from the pipes
Of lonely men in shirt-sleeves, leaning out of windows? . . .

I should have been a pair of ragged claws
Scuttling across the floors of silent seas.

. . . . .

75 And the afternoon, the evening, sleeps so peacefully!
Smoothed by long fingers,
Asleep . . . tired . . . or it malingers,
Stretched on the floor, here beside you and me.
Should I, after tea and cakes and ices,
80 Have the strength to force the moment to its crisis?
But though I have wept and fasted, wept and prayed,
Though I have seen my head [grown slightly bald] brought in upon a
platter,
I am no prophet—and here's no great matter;
I have seen the moment of my greatness flicker,
85 And I have seen the eternal Footman hold my coat, and snicker,
And in short, I was afraid.

And would it have been worth it, after all,
After the cups, the marmalade, the tea,
Among the porcelain, among some talk of you and me,
90 Would it have been worth while,
To have bitten off the matter with a smile,
To have squeezed the universe into a ball
To roll it toward some overwhelming question,

To say: "I am Lazarus, come from the dead,
95 Come back to tell you all, I shall tell you all"—
If one, settling a pillow by her head,
Should say: "That is not what I meant at all.
That is not it, at all."

And would it have been worth it, after all,
100 Would it have been worth while,
After the sunsets and the dooryards and the sprinkled streets,
After the novels, after the teacups, after the skirts that trail along the
floor—
And this, and so much more?—
It is impossible to say just what I mean!
105 But as if a magic lantern threw the nerves in patterns on a screen:
Would it have been worth while
If one, settling a pillow or throwing off a shawl,
And turning toward the window, should say:

"That is not it at all,
110 That is not what I meant, at all."

. . . . . .

No! I am not Prince Hamlet, nor was meant to be;
Am an attendant lord, one that will do
To swell a progress, start a scene or two,
Advise the prince; no doubt, an easy tool,
115 Deferential, glad to be of use,
Politic, cautious, and meticulous;
Full of high sentence, but a bit obtuse;
At times, indeed, almost ridiculous—
Almost, at times, the Fool.

120 I grow old . . . I grow old . . .
I shall wear the bottoms of my trousers rolled.

Shall I part my hair behind? Do I dare to eat a peach?
I shall wear white flannel trousers, and walk upon the beach.
I have heard the mermaids singing, each to each.

125 I do not think that they will sing to me.

I have seen them riding seaward on the waves
Combing the white hair of the waves blown back
When the wind blows the water white and black.

We have lingered in the chambers of the sea
130 By sea-girls wreathed with seaweed red and brown
Till human voices wake us, and we drown.

## ARCHIBALD MacLEISH (1892–1982)

### Ars Poetica

A poem should be palpable and mute
As a globed fruit,

Dumb
As old medallions to the thumb,

5 Silent as the sleeve-worn stone
Of casement ledges where the moss has grown—

A poem should be wordless
As the flight of birds.

A poem should be motionless in time
10 As the moon climbs,

Leaving, as the moon releases
Twig by twig the night-entangled trees,

Leaving, as the moon behind the winter leaves
Memory by memory the mind—

15 A poem should be motionless in time
As the moon climbs.

A poem should be equal to:
Not true.

For all the history of grief
20 An empty doorway and a maple leaf.

For love
The leaning grasses and two lights above the sea—

A poem should not mean
But be.

DOROTHY PARKER (1893–1967)

**Résumé**

Razors pain you;
Rivers are damp;
Acids stain you;
And drugs cause cramp.
5 Guns aren't lawful;
Nooses give;
Gas smells awful;
You might as well live.

E. E. CUMMINGS (1894–1963)

**"next to of course god america i**

"next to of course god america i
love you land of the pilgrims' and so forth oh
say can you see by the dawn's early my

country 'tis of centuries come and go
5 and are no more what of it we should worry
in every language even deafanddumb
thy sons acclaim your glorious name by gorry
by jingo by gee by gosh by gum
why talk of beauty what could be more beaut-
10 iful than these heroic happy dead
who rushed like lions to the roaring slaughter
they did not stop to think they died instead
then shall the voice of liberty be mute?"

He spoke. And drank rapidly a glass of water

## W. H. AUDEN (1907–1973)

### Musée des Beaux Arts[1]

About suffering they were never wrong,
The Old Masters: how well they understood
Its human position; how it takes place
While someone else is eating or opening a window or just walking
dully along;
5 How, when the aged are reverently, passionately waiting
For the miraculous birth, there always must be
Children who did not specially want it to happen, skating
On a pond at the edge of the wood:
They never forgot
10 That even the dreadful martyrdom must run its course
Anyhow in a corner, some untidy spot
Where the dogs go on with their doggy life and the torturer's horse
Scratches its innocent behind on a tree.

In Brueghel's *Icarus,*[2] for instance: how everything turns away
15 Quite leisurely from the disaster; the plowman may
Have heard the splash, the forsaken cry,
But for him it was not an important failure; the sun shone
As it had to on the white legs disappearing into the green
Water; and the expensive delicate ship that must have seen

---

[1] The Museum of Fine Arts in Brussels, where Brueghel's *Landscape with the Fall of Icarus* hangs.

[2] In Greek mythology Icarus falls into the sea and drowns when he flies too close to the sun on his wings of wax. In Brueghel's painting Icarus is an insignificant part of the picture.

20 Something amazing, a boy falling out of the sky,
Had somewhere to get to and sailed calmly on.

## DYLAN THOMAS (1914–1953)

### In My Craft or Sullen Art

In my craft or sullen art
Exercised in the still night
When only the moon rages
And the lovers lie abed
5 With all their griefs in their arms,
I labor by singing light
Not for ambition or bread
Or the strut and trade of charms
On the ivory stages
10 But for the common wages
Of their most secret heart.

Not for the proud man apart
From the raging moon I write
On these spindrift pages
15 Nor for the towering dead
With their nightingales and psalms
But for the lovers, their arms
Round the griefs of the ages,
Who pay no praise or wages
20 Nor heed my craft or art.

## GWENDOLYN BROOKS (1917–

### The Bean Eaters

They eat beans mostly, this old yellow pair.
Dinner is a casual affair.
Plain chipware on a plain and creaking wood,
Tin flatware.

5 Two who are Mostly Good.
Two who have lived their day,
But keep on putting on their clothes
And putting things away.

And remembering . . .
10 Remembering, with twinklings and twinges,
As they lean over the beans in their rented back room that is full of beads and receipts and dolls and clothes, tobacco crumbs, vases and fringes.

## ROBERT LOWELL (1917–1977)

### For the Union Dead

*"Relinquunt Omnia Servare Rem Publican."*[1]

The old South Boston Aquarium stands
in a Sahara of snow now. Its broken windows are boarded.
The bronze weathervane cod has lost half its scales.
The airy tanks are dry.

5 Once my nose crawled like a snail on the glass;
my hand tingled
to burst the bubbles
drifting from the noses of the cowed, compliant fish.

My hand draws back. I often sigh still
10 for the dark downward and vegetating kingdom
of the fish and reptile. One morning last March,
I pressed against the new barbed and galvanized

fence on the Boston Common. Behind their cage,
yellow dinosaur steamshovels were grunting
15 as they cropped up tons of mush and grass
to gouge their underworld garage.

Parking spaces luxuriate like civic
sandpiles in the heart of Boston.
A girdle of orange, Puritan-pumpkin colored girders
20 braces the tingling Statehouse,

shaking over the excavations, as it faces Colonel Shaw
and his bell-cheeked Negro infantry
on St. Gaudens' shaking Civil War relief,
propped by a plank splint against the garage's earthquake.

---

[1] "They gave up all to serve the republic."

25 Two months after marching through Boston,
half the regiment was dead;
at the dedication,
William James could almost hear the bronze Negroes breathe.

Their monument sticks like a fishbone
30 in the city's throat.
Its Colonel is as lean
as a compass-needle.

He has an angry wrenlike vigilance,
a greyhound's gentle tautness;
35 he seems to wince at pleasure,
and suffocate for privacy.

He is out of bounds now. He rejoices in man's lovely,
peculiar power to choose life and die—
when he leads his black soldiers to death,
40 he cannot bend his back.

On a thousand small town New England greens,
the old white churches hold their air
of sparse, sincere rebellion; frayed flags
quilt the graveyards of the Grand Army of the Republic.

45 The stone statues of the abstract Union Soldier
grow slimmer and younger each year—
wasp-waisted, they doze over muskets
and muse through their sideburns . . .

Shaw's father wanted no monument
50 except the ditch,
where his son's body was thrown
and lost with his "niggers."

The ditch is nearer.
There are no statues for the last war here;
55 on Boylston Street, a commercial photograph
shows Hiroshima boiling

over a Mosler Safe, the "Rock of Ages"
that survived the blast. Space is nearer.
When I crouch to my television set,
60 the drained faces of Negro school-children rise like balloons.

Colonel Shaw
is riding on his bubble,
he waits
for the blessèd break.

65 The Aquarium is gone. Everywhere,
giant finned cars nose forward like fish;
a savage servility
slides by on grease.

## LAWRENCE FERLINGHETTI (1919– )

### The pennycandystore beyond the El

The pennycandystore beyond the El
is where I first
                    fell in love
                                    with unreality
5 Jellybeans glowed in the semi-gloom
of that september afternoon
A cat upon the counter moved among
                                          the licorice sticks
                      and tootsie rolls
10          and Oh Boy Gum

Outside the leaves were falling as they died

A wind had blown away the sun
A girl ran in
Her hair was rainy
15 Her breasts were breathless in the little room

Outside the leaves were falling
                              and they cried
                                                  Too soon! too soon!

## RICHARD WILBUR (1921– )

### Place Pigalle

Now homing tradesmen scatter through the streets
Toward suppers, thinking on improved conditions,
While evening, with a million simple fissions,
Takes up its warehouse watches, storefront beats,
5 By nursery windows its assigned positions.

Now at the corners of the Place Pigalle
Bright bars explode against the dark's embraces;
The soldiers come, the boys with ancient faces.
Seeking their ancient friends, who stroll and loll
10 Amid the glares and glass: electric graces.

The puppies are asleep, and snore the hounds;
But here wry hares, the soldier and the whore,
Mark off their refuge with a gaudy door,
Brazen at bay, and boldly out of bounds:
15 The puppies dream, the hounds superbly snore.

Ionized innocence: this pair reclines,
She on the table, he in a tilting chair,
With Arden ease; her eyes as pale as air
Travel his priestgoat face; his hand's thick tines
20 Touch the gold whorls of her Corinthian hair.

"Girl, if I love thee not, then let me die;
Do I not scorn to change my state with kings?
Your muchtouched flesh, incalculable, which wrings
Me so, now shall I gently seize in my
25 Desperate soldier's hands which kill all things."

ALLEN GINSBERG (1926– )

**A Supermarket in California**

What thoughts I have of you tonight, Walt Whitman, for I walked down the sidestreets under the trees with a headache self-conscious looking at the full moon.

In my hungry fatigue, and shopping for images, I went into the neon fruit supermarket, dreaming of your enumerations!

What peaches and what penumbras! Whole families shopping at night! Aisles full of husbands! Wives in the avocados, babies in the tomatoes!—and you, Garcia Lorca,[1] what were you doing down by the watermelons?

I saw you, Walt Whitman, childless, lonely old grubber, poking among the meats in the refrigerator and eyeing the grocery boys.

---

[1] Federico García Lorca (1899–1936), Spanish poet and playwright. He was murdered at the start of the Spanish Civil War; his works were suppressed by the Franco government.

5 I heard you asking questions of each: Who killed the pork chops? What price bananas? Are you my Angel?

I wandered in and out of the brilliant stacks of cans following you, and followed in my imagination by the store detective.

We strode down the open corridors together in our solitary fancy tasting artichokes, possessing every frozen delicacy, and never passing the cashier.

Where are we going, Walt Whitman? The doors close in an hour. Which way does your beard point tonight?

(I touch your book and dream of our odyssey in the supermarket and feel absurd.)

10 Will we walk all night through solitary streets? The trees add shade to shade, lights out in the houses, we'll both be lonely.

Will we stroll dreaming of the lost America of love past blue automobiles in driveways, home to our silent cottage?

Ah, dear father, graybeard, lonely old courage-teacher, what America did you have when Charon quit poling his ferry and you got out on a smoking bank and stood watching the boat disappear on the black waters of Lethe?[2]

## ANNE SEXTON (1928–1974)

### Her Kind

I have gone out, a possessed witch,
haunting the black air, braver at night;
dreaming evil, I have done my hitch
over the plain houses, light by light:
5 lonely thing, twelve-fingered, out of mind.
A woman like that is not a woman, quite.
I have been her kind.

I have found the warm caves in the woods,
filled them with skillets, carvings, shelves,
10 closets, silks, innumerable goods;
fixed the suppers for the worms and the elves:
whining, rearranging the disaligned.
A woman like that is misunderstood.
I have been her kind.

---

[2] Charon, in Greek myth, ferried the shades of the dead to Hades across Lethe, River of Forgetfulness.

15 I have ridden in your cart, driver,
waved my nude arms at villages going by,
learning the last bright routes, survivor
where your flames still bite my thigh
and my ribs crack where your wheels wind.
20 A woman like that is not ashamed to die.
I have been her kind.

## TED HUGHES (1930– )

### Pike

Pike, three inches long, perfect
Pike in all parts, green tigering the gold.
Killers from the egg: the malevolent aged grin.
They dance on the surface among the flies.

5 Or move, stunned by their own grandeur,
Over a bed of emerald, silhouette
Of submarine delicacy and horror.
A hundred feet long in their world.

In ponds, under the heat-struck lily pads—
10 Gloom of their stillness:
Logged on last year's black leaves, watching upwards.
Or hung in an amber cavern of weeds

The jaw's hooked clamp and fangs
Not to be changed at this date;
15 A life subdued to its instrument;
The gills kneading quietly, and the pectorals.

Three we kept behind glass,
Jungled in weed: three inches, four,
And four and a half: fed fry to them—
20 Suddenly there were two. Finally one

With a sag belly and the grin it was born with.
And indeed they spare nobody.
Two, six pounds each, over two feet long,
High and dry and dead in the willow-herb—

25 One jammed past its gills down the other's gullet:
The outside eye stared: as a vice locks—
The same iron in this eye
Though its film shrank in death.

A pond I fished, fifty yards across,
30 Whose lilies and muscular tench
Had outlasted every visible stone
Of the monastery that planted them—

Stilled legendary depth:
It was as deep as England. It held
35 Pike too immense to stir, so immense and old
That past nightfall I dared not cast

But silently cast and fished
With the hair frozen on my head
For what might move, for what eye might move.
40 The still splashes on the dark pond,

Owls hushing the floating woods
Frail on my ear against the dream
Darkness beneath night's darkness had freed,
That rose slowly towards me, watching.

## SYLVIA PLATH (1932–1963)

### Metaphors

I'm a riddle in nine syllables,
An elephant, a ponderous house,
A melon strolling on two tendrils.
O red fruit, ivory, fine timbers!
5 This loaf's big with its yeasty rising.
Money's new-minted in this fat purse.
I'm a means, a stage, a cow in calf.
I've eaten a bag of green apples,
Boarded the train there's no getting off.

## AMIRI BARAKA (LeROI JONES) (1934– )

### W.W.

Back home the black women are all beautiful,
and the white ones fall back, cutoff from 1000
years stacked booty, and Charles of the Ritz
where jooshladies turn into billy burke in blueglass
5 kicks. With wings, and jingly bew-teeful things.
The black women in Newark are fine. Even with all that grease

in their heads. I mean even the ones where the wigs
slide around, and they coming at you 75 degrees off course.
I could talk to them. Bring them around. To something.
10 Some kind of quick course, on the sidewalk, like Hey baby
why don't you take that thing off yo' haid. You look like
Miss Muffet in a runaway ugly machine. I mean. Like that.

# DRAMA

# 1 *Reading Drama*

Analyzing Greek drama around 330 B.C., the philosopher Aristotle found each play to be composed of six parts: plot, character, thought, diction, spectacle, and music. Of these, he considered the plot—the putting together of diverse happenings to create a complete and unified action—to be the most important. Without plot, he says, there can be no play; for the chief purpose of drama is the acting-out of an action.

Characters come next in importance for Aristotle. Thought—by which he seems to mean not only the ideas expressed by the various speakers, but also their use of speech to sway the emotions of the audience—comes third. Diction, the choice of words, is fourth. Music and scenery, being pleasant and often impressive, but not essential, come last.

With the exception of music and spectacle, which apply only to plays in performance, Aristotle's categories are essentially the same categories we've been using in discussing fiction. The further we read in Aristotle, the more similarities we find: Aristotle warns would-be authors that their plots, to be complete, must have a natural beginning, middle, and end; that they must provide scope for their heroes to pass from happiness to unhappiness, or from unhappiness to happiness; and that they must be unified, containing nothing that could be taken away without leaving the drama incomplete.

In addition, Aristotle points out that the most important moments in the plot are those concerned with **reversals** and **recognition.** A reversal occurs when an action that is expected to have one result produces the opposite result instead. A recognition occurs when a character suddenly "recognizes" some fact or person, thus moving from a state of ignorance to a state of knowledge. In the best plays, the two events are joined and form the turning point of the play: the hero suddenly learns something of great personal importance, either by being informed of some facts by another character or by coming to a realization or insight himself. In either case, the result of the hero's enlightenment is a reversal, changing the course of the play's action and of the hero's life (from happiness to unhappiness or vice versa).

In discussing characterization Aristotle reminds us that all characters must be people basically like ourselves, though some may be better and some worse. And again, he insists that consistency and probability are the two most important standards of judgment. The writer must make sure that the characters' actions are consistent with their natures, and that their natures remain consistent throughout the drama.

If we have not already discussed all of these ideas, at least we have no difficulty in applying them to the fiction we've read. To discuss consistency of character, for instance, we could look at any number of characters—at Daru in "The Guest," so consistently unable to link himself to his fellow humans, or at the narrator of "Bartleby the Scrivener," with his deep and basically kindly desire for tranquility in human relations and his persistent and misplaced faith in money as a means of attaining that tranquility. These are consistently drawn characters. Given their natures and situations created by their authors, they have no chance of escaping their fate.*

The basic elements of drama, then, are the same as those of fiction. It is the method of presentation that differs.

Fiction is the telling of tales. Its roots go back to the archetypal figure of the storyteller, rehearsing old legends and inventing new marvels for the listeners who surround him. The importance of voice in fiction, therefore, can hardly be overemphasized. One use of voice is evident in the many tales in which the narrative voice is that of the storyteller: tales such as those by Faulkner, Hemingway, Wright, and O'Connor. Another use can be seen in works such as Barthelme's that begin in a storytelling voice but then move beyond that voice to more direct (if occasionally less coherent) appeals to the reader, asking the reader to join the narrator in considering what speech, writing, or storytelling implies.

---

* Two other Aristotelian concepts are illustrated here as well. One is the movement from happiness to unhappiness: both characters are happier when their tales begin than when they end. The second concept is that of inevitability, discussed on p. 5.

As fiction has become a more silent experience, writers seem to have attached increasing importance to the question of what voice would speak through their works. Listening to stories is still enjoyable. Any good story can be read aloud and be enjoyed the better for it. But our society seems to feel that listening to tales is a pleasure most proper for children and for those who cannot read to themselves. For most of us, therefore, fiction is something read silently and alone. It involves one book, one writer, one reader. We discuss stories in company, but we tend to read them in solitude.

Drama—in performance, at least—is wholly different. It is not written for one voice, but for many. It depends not on storytellers but on actors, men and women who impersonate their tale's characters not only in voice, but also in motion, gesture, and appearance, making them live for our eyes as well as our ears. Moreover, it is written for many viewers, for only in the midst of an audience can we appreciate fully the magic of drama. Laughing alone at a joke in print is enjoyable; being one laughing person among a hundred people can be hilarious.

Actors know this well. They know how fully they must bring their characters alive for their audience. They know, too, how dependent they are on the audience's response if they are to perform well. Many actors have declared that the best performances are those during which the emotions portrayed on stage are caught and sent back by the audience until audience and actors alike are caught up in the atmosphere they have created between them, and the illusion of the play becomes more real than the realities of the world outside. Similarly, many have said that acting in films, where no audience is present to reflect the emotional impact of the scene, is a more difficult and less enjoyable form of acting than acting on the stage. Playgoers and filmgoers, in their turn, agree that the experience of attending a live performance has an electric quality not to be found in viewing a film.

The fervor with which most of us discuss a really good play or film we've just seen, as opposed to the milder delight with which we discuss a really good book, testifies to the power of drama to move and delight us. A knowledge of the origins of drama, about which we shall speak in the next chapter, may help explain the intensity of our response. Within this course, however, we are readers rather than viewers of drama. And so the very power of drama in performance is likely to raise questions for us. "Here we are," we say, "with no stage, no actors—nothing but a playscript in front of us. What can we expect from this experience?"

Reading drama is certainly different from reading fiction. Drama gives us no narrator to describe scenes and characters, to comment on the significance of the action, to tie scenes together, or to provide a unifying viewpoint. Instead, drama gives us several characters, distinguished in the text only by their names, talking mostly to each other instead of to us, intent on their own affairs, entering and leaving the scene in bewildering succession.

If we were watching a play, we would recognize the characters by their appearance, mannerisms, and voices. Knowing the characters, we would then find it easy to follow the action. When we read a play, however, we must do without these visual clues. Or, rather, we must supply them for ourselves. We must use the text as the play's director would, judging from its words and from the actions they describe how the play would look and sound on stage.

Reading plays, in fact, gives our imagination free rein. How would I stage this scene? What sort of actor would I want for this role? What kind of stage setting would I use? Or, what kind of camera work would I use in a film? Which would be my long shots, which my close-ups? What emotions would my filming be trying to capture?

Most of all, perhaps, you will think of the various characters as they are revealed in the text. What characteristics will each one exhibit? How will they carry themselves on stage? What tones of voice will they use in their speeches? How will they act toward each other?* The more clearly you can visualize the play's action and characters, the more readily the text will come alive for you.

Don't be afraid to experiment in your thinking. Actors, directors, and scene designers all allow themselves some freedom of interpretation when they put on a play. You can read for days about famous actors who have played Hamlet, each applying a very personal interpretation to emphasize one aspect or another of the prince's complex personality. Why should not we, as readers, enjoy the same freedom to visualize the play, interpreting and fitting together its parts to develop our vision of its conflicts and its meanings?

The text of a play will supply us with plenty of help. Since drama does depend so largely on the art of the actor, dramatists must create characters who can carry the play by their speeches and actions. Everything the actors (and readers) need must be contained in the speeches and stage directions. Here are some of the things we can look for.

We can look for characters who, like first-person narrators in fiction, reveal in their speech information about their habits, personalities, and thinking—information they do not always know they are giving us. We can expect to be wiser than most of these characters because we have the ability to stand apart from the action in which they participate, to see it fully or judge it objectively.

We can look for patterns in characterization. We can look for characters who support each other and characters who oppose each other. We can expect to see strong characters opposed to weak ones, inflexible characters opposed to reasonable ones, good characters opposed to evil ones.

---

* A handy device for keeping track of a play's characters, in fact, is to "cast" the play for yourself with actors you'd enjoy watching in it. Then you can follow those actors through each scene, imagining how they would interpret the roles.

There is always conflict in a play, just as there is in fiction; and the conflict is generally between people. Fiction writers such as Crane can deal with the conflict between people and nature. Dramatists, accustomed to thinking in terms of human actors, and finding it difficult, for instance, to bring an ocean on stage to act as antagonist, generally restrict themselves to conflicts among human beings.

The speeches of the actors, therefore, set down in the play's text, will describe the play's characters for us, develop the action and conflict of the play, and contain the play's themes. The conflict between the ideas expressed in speeches will often be basic to the conflict of the play. Thus, in *Oedipus Rex,* much of the play's conflict centers around the question of whether it is wise or foolish for Oedipus to seek the truth about Laios' murder. And in *Hamlet,* the conflict between Hamlet and Claudius over who shall rule Denmark becomes almost secondary to the mental conflicts between Hamlet and other characters (and within Hamlet himself) on the moral and practical issues arising from the political conflict.

Patterns of speech, characterization, and thought, then, are as important in drama as they are in fiction. Patterns of language and of imagery, too, are important. Some plays, such as *A Doll's House* and *Death of a Salesman,* try to imitate everyday speech patterns in their language. Others shift those patterns. *The Importance of Being Earnest,* while keeping a fairly close semblance of natural speech rhythms and vocabulary, permits its characters a greater fluency of speech and aptness of comic rejoinder than ordinary conversation would show. Still other plays, such as *Hamlet* or *Oedipus Rex,* use the full power of poetry in their speeches. Dialogue in these plays can move in a few lines from the accents of everyday speech to those of extreme poetic passion, as the playwrights draw from the rhythms of poetry a capacity for dignity and grandeur and openness of expression that the limits of everyday speech deny them.

Patterns of imagery, too, can be used to great effect in these poetic plays. But imagery, as we have seen already in our work with fiction, is not restricted to poetry. Certainly, *Hamlet* is the richest in imagery of the nine plays presented here. But all make some use of imagery, from the imagery of physical and mental blindness in *Oedipus Rex* to *Death of a Salesman's* contrasted images of congested city and open country and its almost symbolic use of stockings as a visual image.

Reading drama, therefore, can offer an intensification of the pleasure provided by reading fiction. More richly patterned in action, language, and characterization than most short stories, allowing its readers more scope for interpretation and for the visual imagination, drama offers us a chance to be actors, director, and audience in one.

As a prologue to our study of drama, here is a very brief play by the late-nineteenth-century Swedish writer August Strindberg. When you've finished this play, you may feel that there's remarkably little plot to it; but you'll have to agree that Strindberg seems to have accepted the importance of recognition and reversal as key elements in the drama!

## AUGUST STRINDBERG (1849–1912)

# *The Stronger*

CHARACTERS

MRS. X., *an actress, married*
MISS Y., *an actress, unmarried*
A WAITRESS

SCENE. *The corner of a ladies' cafe. Two little iron tables, a red velvet sofa, several chairs. Enter* MRS. X., *dressed in winter clothes, carrying a Japanese basket on her arm.*

MISS Y. *sits with a half-empty beer bottle before her, reading an illustrated paper, which she changes later for another.*

MRS. X. Good afternoon, Amelia. You're sitting here alone on Christmas eve like a poor bachelor!

MISS Y. (*Looks up, nods, and resumes her reading.*)

MRS. X. Do you know it really hurts me to see you like this, alone, in a café, and on Christmas eve, too. It makes me feel as I did one time when I saw a bridal party in a Paris restaurant, and the bride sat reading a comic paper, while the groom played billiards with the witnesses. Huh, thought I, with such a beginning, what will follow, and what will be the end? He played billiards on his wedding eve! (MISS Y. *starts to speak*) And she read a comic paper, you mean? Well, they are not altogether the same thing.

(A WAITRESS *enters, places a cup of chocolate before* MRS. X. *and goes out.*)

MRS. X. You know what, Amelia! I believe you would have done better to have kept him! Do you remember, I was the first to say "Forgive him?" Do you remember that? You would be married now and have a home. Remember that Christmas when you went out to visit your fiancé's parents in the country? How you gloried in the happiness of home life and really longed to quit the theatre forever? Yes, Amelia dear, home is the best of all—next to the theatre—and as for children—well, you don't understand that.

MISS Y. (*Looks up scornfully.*)

(MRS. X. *sips a few spoonfuls out of the cup, then opens her basket and shows Christmas presents.*)

MRS. X. Now you shall see what I bought for my piggywigs. [*Takes up a doll*] Look at this! This is for Lisa, ha! Do you see how she can roll her eyes and turn her head, eh? And here is Maja's popgun.

(*Loads it and shoots at* MISS Y.)

MISS Y. (*Makes a startled gesture.*)

MRS. X. Did I frighten you? Do you think I would like to shoot you, eh? On my soul, if I don't think you did! If you wanted to shoot *me* it wouldn't be so surprising, because I stood in your way —and I know you can never forget that—although I was absolutely innocent. You still believe I intrigued and got you out of the Stora theatre, but I didn't. I didn't do that, although you think so. Well, it doesn't make any difference what I say to you. You still believe I did it. (*Takes up a pair of embroidered slippers*) And these are for my better half. I embroidered them myself—I can't bear tulips, but he wants tulips on everything.

MISS Y. (*Looks up ironically and curiously.*)

MRS. X. (*putting a hand in each slipper*) See what little feet Bob has! What? And you should see what a splendid stride he has! You've never seen him in slippers! (MISS Y. *laughs aloud.*) Look! (*She makes the slippers walk on the table.* MISS Y. *laughs loudly.*) And when he is grumpy he stamps like this with his foot. "What! damn those servants who can never learn to make coffee. Oh, now those creatures haven't trimmed the lamp wick properly!" And then there are draughts on the floor and his feet are cold. "Ugh, how cold it is; the stupid idiots can never keep the fire going." (*She rubs the slippers together, one sole over the other.*)

MISS Y. (*Shrieks with laughter.*)

MRS. X. And then he comes home and has to hunt for his slippers which Marie has stuck under the chiffonier—oh, but it's sinful to sit here and make fun of one's husband this way when he is kind and a good little man. You ought to have had such a husband, Amelia. What are you laughing at? What? What? And you see he's true to me. Yes, I'm sure of that, because he told me himself—what are you laughing at?—that when I was touring in Norway that brazen Frederika came and wanted to seduce him! Can you fancy anything so infamous? (*pause*) I'd have torn her eyes out if she had come to see him when I was at home. (*pause*) It was lucky that Bob told me about it himself and that it didn't reach me through gossip. (*pause*) But would you believe it, Frederika wasn't the only one! I don't know why, but the women are crazy about my husband. They must think he has influence about getting them theatrical engagements, because he is connected with the government. Perhaps you were after him yourself. I didn't use to trust you any too much. But now I know he never bothered his head about you, and you always seemed to have a grudge against him someway.

(*Pause. They look at each other in a puzzled way.*)

MRS. X. Come and see us this evening, Amelia, and show us that you're not put out with us—not put out with me at any rate. I don't know, but I think it would be uncomfortable to have you for an enemy. Perhaps it's because I stood in your way (*more slowly*) or—I really—don't know why—in particular.

(*Pause.* MISS Y. *stares at* MRS. X. *curiously.*)

MRS. X. (*thoughtfully*) Our acquaintance has been so queer. When I saw you for the first time I was afraid of you, so afraid that I didn't dare let you out of my sight; no matter when or where, I always found myself near you—I didn't dare have you for an enemy, so I became your friend. But there was always discord when you came to our house, because I saw that my husband couldn't endure you, and the whole thing seemed as awry to me as an ill-fitting gown—and I did all I could to make him friendly toward you, but with no success until you became engaged. Then came a violent friendship between you, so that it looked all at once as though you both dared show your real feelings only when you were secure—and then—how was it later? I didn't get jealous—strange to say! And I remember at the christening, when you acted as godmother, I made him kiss you—he did so, and you became so confused—as it were; I didn't notice it then—didn't think about it later, either—have never thought about it until—now! (*Rises suddenly.*) Why are you silent? You haven't said a word this whole time, but you have let me go on talking! You have sat there, and your eyes have reeled out of me all these thoughts which lay like raw silk in its cocoon—thoughts—suspicious thoughts, perhaps. Let me see—why did you break your engagement? Why do you never come to our house any more? Why won't you come to see us tonight?

(MISS Y. *appears as if about to speak.*)

MRS. X. Hush, you needn't speak—I understand it all! It was because—and because—and because! Yes, yes! Now all the accounts balance. That's it. Fie, I won't sit at the same table with you. (*Moves her things to another table.*) That's the reason I had to embroider tulips—which I hate—on his slippers, because you are fond of tulips; that's why (*throws slippers on the floor*) we go to Lake Mälarn in the summer, because you don't like salt water; that's why my boy is named Eskil—because it's your father's name; that's why I wear your colors, read your authors, eat your favorite dishes, drink your drinks—chocolate, for instance; that's why—oh—my God—it's terrible, when I think about it; it's terrible. Everything, everything came from you to me, even your passions. Your soul crept into mine, like a worm into an apple, ate and ate, bored and bored, until nothing was left but the rind and a little black dust within. I wanted to get away from you, but I couldn't; you lay like a snake and charmed me with your black eyes; I felt that when I lifted my wings they only dragged me down; I lay in the water with bound feet, and the stronger I strove to keep up the deeper I worked myself down, down, until I sank to the bottom, where you lay like a giant crab to clutch me in your claws—and there I am lying now.

I hate you, hate you, hate you! And you only sit there silent—silent and indifferent; indifferent whether it's new moon or waning moon, Christmas or New Year's, whether others are happy or unhappy; without power to hate or to love; as quiet as a stork by a rat hole—you couldn't scent your prey and capture it, but you could lie in wait for it! You sit here in your corner of the café—did you know it's called "The Rat Trap" for you?—and read the papers to see if misfortune hasn't befallen someone, to see if someone hasn't been given notice at the theatre, perhaps; you sit here and calculate about your next victim and reckon on your chances of recompense like a pilot in a shipwreck. Poor Amelia, I pity you, nevertheless, because I know you are unhappy, unhappy like one who has been wounded, and angry because you are wounded. I can't be angry with you, no matter how much I want to be—because you come out the weaker one. Yes, all that with Bob doesn't trouble me. What is that to me, after all? And what difference does it make whether I learned to drink chocolate from you or some one else. (*Sips a spoonful from her cup*) Besides, chocolate is very healthful. And if you taught me how to dress—tant mieux!—that has only made me more attractive to my husband; so you lost and I won there. Well, judging by certain signs, I believe you have already lost him; and you certainly intended that I should leave him—do as you did with your fiancé and regret as you now regret; but, you see, I don't do that—we mustn't be too exacting. And why should I take only what no else wants?

Perhaps, take it all in all, I am at this moment the stronger one. You received nothing from me, but you gave me much. And now I seem like a thief since you have awakened and find I possess what is your loss. How could it be otherwise when everything is worthless and sterile in your hands? You can never keep a man's love with your tulips and your passions—but I can keep it. You can't learn how to live from your authors, as I have learned. You have no little Eskil to cherish, even if your father's name was Eskil. And why are you always silent, silent, silent? I thought that was strength, but perhaps it is because you have nothing to say! Because you never think about anything! (*Rises and picks up slippers.*) Now I'm going home—and take the tulips with me—*your* tulips! You are unable to learn from another; you can't bend—therefore, you broke like a dry stalk. But I won't break! Thank you, Amelia, for all your good lessons. Thanks for teaching my husband how to love. Now I'm going home to love him. (*Goes.*)

## QUESTIONS

1. What is the "recognition" in this play? The "reversal"? How would you describe the progress of the speaker's state of mind during the play?
2. Like "I'm a Fool" and "My Last Duchess," *The Stronger* is a dramatic monologue.
   a. How does your experience of reading this dramatic monologue differ from your experience of reading "I'm a Fool"? "My Last Duchess"?
   b. How do you think the experience of seeing *The Stronger* played on the stage, or of hearing "I'm a Fool" and "My Last Duchess" read aloud, would be different from the experience of reading them?
   c. How might you go about turning "I'm a Fool" or "My Last Duchess" into a monologue to be acted? How would you stage the piece? Would you want to alter the text in any way to make it easier to stage?
3. a. Think back over other short stories you have read. Which ones could be easily turned into plays? Which ones not? In each case, what would be the major reasons behind your decision?
   b. Choose one story you think would make a good play, and decide what you'd have to do to make a play of it. What actors would your play need? How would you stage it? Would any rewriting be required? You might even try acting out a scene or so, to see what effect your dramatization would have on the story.

# 2 *Greek Tragedy*

Western drama is often said to have originated in ancient Greece. Certainly its two most outstanding forms, tragedy and comedy, began there.

About the beginnings of this drama, little is known, for few records have survived. We do know, however, that it began at festivals honoring Dionysus, or Bacchus, a god who was supposed to have taught men to cultivate grapes and make wine. Song and dance were the means by which this god was worshipped. At early festivals, choruses of fifty men dressed in tattered garments with wine-smeared faces or disguised as Dionysus' mythical companions, the satyrs, sang hymns praising the god's deeds while they half-danced, half-mimed his exploits. Eventually one man stepped out of the chorus and engaged his fellows in dialogue. Later still, the soloist began impersonating the god, thus dramatizing the events of which he was singing.

Sometime during this process, the content of the songs also shifted. Some still pertained to Dionysus, but some dealt with other, human, heroes. Although worshippers were reportedly shocked at the first introduction of the new tales, asking, "What has this to do with Dionysus?", the novelty soon became the rule. By 530 B.C., the performances were being called tragedies and were competing in Athens for an annual prize.

In the next hundred years, tragedy reached what Aristotle considered its full form. A second actor was added, and then a third. Episodes of dialogue among the actors, with the chorus occasionally joining in, became as important as the choric songs and dances with which they alternated. Painted backdrops, stage machinery, and special effects were introduced.

For all its developments, however, Greek drama remained a religious event. Plays were performed only at Dionysus' festivals; actors were considered his servants. Performances took place three times a year: twice at Athens, once at various rural festivals. The older of the Athenian festivals, the *Lenaea,* became the festival for comedy; but the *City Dionysia,* which drew visitors from all over Greece, was the festival for tragedy.

For this festival, three playwrights were chosen by Athenian authorities. Each was given a chorus and actors, who were paid and costumed by some rich citizen as a public service; each was allotted one day of the festival on which to perform. The performance would consist of three tragedies (sometimes on the same subject, sometimes not), followed by a satyr play, an obscene or satiric parody of some legendary event. At the end of the three days of playing, a jury of ten citizens, chosen by lot, judged the plays and awarded the prizes.* Any Athenian was welcome to attend these plays, which were held in a natural amphitheater that seated some 30,000 people. Since the theater was reported to be crowded at every performance, we may assume that virtually everybody who could attend, did.

All in all, drama in ancient Athens seems to have been regarded almost as a public possession. Looked on with a mixture of religious devotion, civic pride, and open enjoyment, it maintained a great and general popularity that seems to have declined only with the decline of Athens itself. And still the plays remained influential, both in themselves and in the theory of drama that Aristotle's comments on them provided. First the Romans copied them. Then, some 1500 years later, Renaissance playwrights took ideas from both Greek and Roman drama. We will discuss that development in the next chapter.

## Tragedy and Comedy

Greek drama segregated its forms carefully. Tragedy dealt with the noble, the heroic, the sacrificial. In performance, three tragedies would be followed by a satyr play, which turned heroic figures into tricksters or clowns and often mocked the very legends that had supplied the day's

---

* Sophocles, the author of *Oedipus Rex,* held the all-time record of eighteen first prizes and is said never to have won less than second prize. Yet *Oedipus Rex* itself, which was praised by Aristotle and is still considered one of the finest of Greek tragedies, won only second prize when it was first produced.

tragedies. Comedy had its own festival, in which it could deal with the more practical aspirations of everyday people—good food, warm beds, and peaceful households and cities. The heroes of comedy battle such unheroic opponents as thieves, con men, unreasonable parents, and crooked politicians. Often, they must resort to trickery to outwit these unsavory sorts, who may very well be tricksters themselves. A happy ending is guaranteed.

## *Oedipus Rex* and *Antigonê*

*Oedipus Rex* is, in many ways, the embodiment of Greek tragedy. It deals with a somewhat idealized, larger-than-life hero, a man caught in a dilemma between his ideals and his personal safety and fighting his way towards a terrifying knowledge. "Ah," cries the Shepherd in one climactic scene, "I am on the brink of dreadful speech." "And I of dreadful hearing," replies Oedipus. "Yet I must hear." This insistence on following through in a search, an action, the pursuit of an ideal has always attracted readers, perhaps because we all know how difficult that sort of courage is to sustain. It is the one force that is constant in tragedy.

The sad or terrible ending, incidentally, is not essential to tragedy. Some Greek tragedies end happily, in a reconciliation of their opposed forces, new knowledge having created new peace. The essentials of tragedy are the protagonist's own insistence on action or enlightenment and the ability of the play, however it ends, to arouse a sympathetic "fear and pity" (Aristotle's terms) in the audience as they watch the working-out of the hero's quest. *Oedipus Rex,* which begins on p. 637, clearly has these essentials.

*Oedipus Rex* gains much of its power from the unwavering intensity of its focus on the central character. But this focus, though not uncommon in tragedy, is also not essential to it. Many Greek tragedies have more than one central character. *The Trojan Women,* for example, has as heroines all the famous women who were caught up in the sack of Troy. *Antigonê,* which follows *Oedipus Rex* in this chapter, concentrates not so much on a single character as on the clash of wills between two characters. One of these characters is Kreon, Oedipus' uncle, now the ruler of Thebes; the other is Antigonê, Oedipus' daughter.

The action of *Antigonê* takes place some years after that of *Oedipus Rex.* In the time between the two plays, Oedipus' two sons have quarreled. In fact, just before *Antigonê* opens, one of the brothers (Polyneicês) has gathered a group of supporters and has attacked both his brother (Eteoclês) and the city of Thebes itself. In the battle, the two brothers have killed each other. Kreon, now ruling Thebes, has ordered a hero's funeral for Eteoclês, the defender of Thebes, but has refused burial to Polyneicês, Thebes's attacker. Antigonê's response to this proclamation, and Kreon's reaction to her response, form the action of the tragedy.

Throughout the play, Kreon's concern is for public welfare and order; he speaks most frequently as the voice of public authority, the defender of the public good. Antigonê's concern is for piety and for family ties. She speaks most often from her own conscience, as a private person. When she does speak of public matters, it is generally to contrast social law with divine law. Between these two forces of public and private good lies the play's tension. This is a play in which *thought,* Aristotle's third element of tragedy, is predominant. Yet, as with *Oedipus,* it is the strong-willed, dedicated nature of the antagonists that makes the play a true tragedy, not merely an argument. The issues involved are still argued; their expression here in tragedy is unique.

## SOPHOCLES (496–406 B.C.)

# *Oedipus Rex*

An English version by Dudley Fitts and Robert Fitzgerald

CHARACTERS

OEDIPUS, *King of Thebes, supposed son of Polybos and Meropê, King and Queen of Corinth*
IOKASTÊ, *wife of Oedipus and widow of the late King Laïos*
KREON, *brother of Iokastê, a prince of Thebes*
TEIRESIAS, *a blind seer who serves Apollo*
PRIEST
MESSENGER, *from Corinth*
SHEPHERD, *former servant of Laïos*
SECOND MESSENGER, *from the palace*
CHORUS OF THEBAN ELDERS
CHORAGOS, *leader of the Chorus*
ANTIGONÊ *and* ISMENÊ, *young daughters of Oedipus and Iokastê. They appear in the Exodos but do not speak.*
SUPPLIANTS, GUARDS, SERVANTS

THE SCENE. *Before the palace of* OEDIPUS, *King of Thebes. A central door and two lateral doors open onto a platform which runs the length of the façade. On the platform, right and left, are altars; and three steps lead down into the* orchestra *or chorus-ground. At the beginning of the action these steps are crowded by suppliants who have brought branches and chaplets of olive leaves and who sit in various attitudes of despair.* OEDIPUS *enters.*

## PROLOGUE

OEDIPUS My children, generations of the living
In the line of Kadmos,[1] nursed at his ancient hearth:
Why have you strewn yourselves before these altars
5 In supplication, with your boughs and garlands?

[1] *Kadmos* founder of Thebes

The breath of incense rises from the city
With a sound of prayer and lamentation.
Children,
I would not have you speak through messengers,
5 And therefore I have come myself to hear you—
I, Oedipus, who bear the famous name.
(*To a* PRIEST) You, there, since you are eldest in the company,
Speak for them all, tell me what preys upon you,
Whether you come in dread, or crave some blessing:
10 Tell me, and never doubt that I will help you
In every way I can; I should be heartless
Were I not moved to find you suppliant here.

PRIEST Great Oedipus, O powerful king of Thebes!
You see how all the ages of our people
15 Cling to your altar steps: here are boys
Who can barely stand alone, and here are priests
By weight of age, as I am a priest of God,
And young men chosen from those yet unmarried;
As for the others, all that multitude,
20 They wait with olive chaplets in the squares,
At the two shrines of Pallas, and where Apollo
Speaks in the glowing embers.
Your own eyes
Must tell you: Thebes is tossed on a murdering sea
25 And can not lift her head from the death surge.
A rust consumes the buds and fruits of the earth;
The herds are sick; children die unborn,
And labor is vain. The god of plague and pyre
Raids like detestable lightning through the city,
30 And all the house of Kadmos is laid waste,
All emptied, and all darkened: Death alone
Battens upon the misery of Thebes.

You are not one of the immortal gods, we know;
Yet we have come to you to make our prayer
35 As to the man surest in mortal ways
And wisest in the ways of God. You saved us
From the Sphinx, that flinty singer, and the tribute
We paid to her so long; yet you were never
Better informed than we, nor could we teach you:
40 A god's touch, it seems, enabled you to help us.

Therefore, O mighty power, we turn to you:
Find us our safety, find us a remedy,

Whether by counsel of the gods or of men.
A king of wisdom tested in the past
Can act in a time of troubles, and act well.
Noblest of men, restore
5 Life to your city! Think how all men call you
Liberator for your boldness long ago;
Ah, when your years of kingship are remembered,
Let them not say *We rose, but later fell*—
Keep the State from going down in the storm!
10 Once, years ago, with happy augury,
You brought us fortune; be the same again!
No man questions your power to rule the land:
But rule over men, not over a dead city!
Ships are only hulls, high walls are nothing,
15 When no life moves in the empty passageways.

OEDIPUS Poor children! You may be sure I know
All that you longed for in your coming here.
I know that you are deathly sick; and yet,
Sick as you are, not one is as sick as I.
20 Each of you suffers in himself alone
His anguish, not another's; but my spirit
Groans for the city, for myself, for you.

I was not sleeping, you are not waking me.
No, I have been in tears for a long while
25 And in my restless thought walked many ways.
In all my search I found one remedy,
And I have adopted it: I have sent Kreon,
Son of Menoikeus, brother of the queen,
To Delphi, Apollo's place of revelation,
30 To learn there, if he can,
What act or pledge of mine may save the city.
I have counted the days, and now, this very day,
I am troubled, for he has overstayed his time.
What is he doing? He has been gone too long.
35 Yet whenever he comes back, I should do ill
Not to take any action the god orders.

PRIEST It is a timely promise. At this instant
They tell me Kreon is here.

OEDIPUS O Lord Apollo!
40 May his news be fair as his face is radiant!

PRIEST Good news, I gather! he is crowned with bay,
The chaplet is thick with berries.

OEDIPUS We shall soon know;
He is near enough to hear us now.

(*Enter* KREON.)

O prince:
5 Brother: son of Menoikeus:
What answer do you bring us from the god?
KREON A strong one. I can tell you, great afflictions
Will turn out well, if they are taken well.
OEDIPUS What was the oracle? These vague words
10 Leave me still hanging between hope and fear.
KREON Is it your pleasure to hear me with all these
Gathered around us? I am prepared to speak,
But should we not go in?
OEDIPUS Speak to them all,
15 It is for them I suffer, more than for myself.
KREON Then I will tell you what I heard at Delphi.
In plain words
The god commands us to expel from the land of Thebes
An old defilement we are sheltering.
20 It is a deathly thing, beyond cure;
We must not let it feed upon us longer.
OEDIPUS What defilement? How shall we rid ourselves of it?
KREON By exile or death, blood for blood. It was
Murder that brought the plague-wind on the city.
25 OEDIPUS Murder of whom? Surely the god has named him?
KREON My lord: Laïos once ruled this land,
Before you came to govern us.
OEDIPUS I know;
I learned of him from others; I never saw him.
30 KREON He was murdered; and Apollo commands us now
To take revenge upon whoever killed him.
OEDIPUS Upon whom? Where are they? Where shall we find a clue
To solve that crime, after so many years?
KREON Here in this land, he said. Search reveals
35 Things that escape an inattentive man.
OEDIPUS Tell me: Was Laïos murdered in his house,
Or in the fields, or in some foreign country?
KREON He said he planned to make a pilgrimage.
He did not come home again.
40 OEDIPUS And was there no one,
No witness, no companion, to tell what happened?
KREON They were all killed but one, and he got away

So frightened that he could remember one thing only.
OEDIPUS What was the one thing? One may be the key
To everything, if we resolve to use it.
KREON He said that a band of highwaymen attacked them,
5 Outnumbered them, and overwhelmed the king.
OEDIPUS Strange, that a highwayman should be so daring—
Unless some faction here bribed him to do it.
KREON We thought of that. But after Laïos' death
New troubles arose and we had no avenger.
10 OEDIPUS What troubles could prevent your hunting down the killers?
KREON The riddling Sphinx's song
Made us deaf to all mysteries but her own.
OEDIPUS Then once more I must bring what is dark to light.
15 It is most fitting that Apollo shows,
As you do, this compunction for the dead.
You shall see how I stand by you, as I should,
Avenging this country and the god as well,
And not as though it were for some distant friend,
20 But for my own sake, to be rid of evil.
Whoever killed King Laïos might—who knows?—
Lay violent hands even on me—and soon.
I act for the murdered king in my own interest.

Come, then, my children: leave the altar steps,
25 Lift up your olive boughs!
One of you go
And summon the people of Kadmos to gather here.
I will do all that I can; you may tell them that.

(*Exit a* PAGE.)

30 So, with the help of God,
We shall be saved—or else indeed we are lost.
PRIEST Let us rise, children. It was for this we came,
And now the king has promised it.
Phoibos[1] has sent us an oracle; may he descend
35 Himself to save us and drive out the plague.

(*Exeunt* OEDIPUS *and* KREON *into the palace by the central door. The* PRIEST *and the* SUPPLIANTS *disperse R and L. After a short pause the* CHORUS *enters the* orchestra.)

[1] *Phoibos* Apollo

## PARODOS [1]

### Strophe 1

CHORUS What is God singing in his profound
Delphi of gold and shadow?
5 What oracle for Thebes, the sunwhipped city?
Fear unjoints me, the roots of my heart tremble.
Now I remember, O Healer, your power, and wonder:
Will you send doom like a sudden cloud, or weave it
Like nightfall of the past?
10 Speak to me, tell me, O
Child of golden Hope, immortal Voice.

### Antistrophe 1

Let me pray to Athenê, the immortal daughter of Zeus,
And to Artemis her sister
15 Who keeps her famous throne in the market ring,
And to Apollo, archer from distant heaven—
O gods, descend! Like three streams leap against
The fires of our grief, the fires of darkness;
Be swift to bring us rest!
20 As in the old time from the brilliant house
Of air you stepped to save us, come again!

### Strophe 2

Now our afflictions have no end,
Now all our stricken host lies down
25 And no man fights off death with his mind;
The noble plowland bears no grain,
And groaning mothers can not bear—
See, how our lives like birds take wing,

---

[1] *Párodos* the song or ode chanted by the chorus on its entry. It is accompanied by dancing and music played on a flute. The chorus in this play represents elders of the city of Thebes. Chorus members remain on stage (on a level lower than the principal actors) for the remainder of the play. The choral odes and dances serve to separate one scene from another (there was no curtain in Greek theater) as well as to comment on the action, reinforce the emotion, and interpret the situation. The chorus also performs dance movements during certain portions of the scenes themselves. *Strophe* and *antistrophe* are terms denoting the movement and counter-movement of the chorus from one side of its playing area to the other. When the chorus participates in dialogue with the other characters, its lines are spoken by the Choragos, its leader.

Like sparks that fly when a fire soars,
To the shore of the god of evening.

**Antistrophe 2**

The plague burns on, it is pitiless,
5 Though pallid children laden with death
Lie unwept in the stony ways,
And old gray women by every path
Flock to the strand about the altars
There to strike their breasts and cry
10 Worship of Phoibos in wailing prayers:
Be kind, God's golden child!

**Strophe 3**

There are no swords in this attack by fire,
No shields, but we are ringed with cries.
15 Send the besieger plunging from our homes
Into the vast sea-room of the Atlantic
Or into the waves that foam eastward of Thrace—
For the day ravages what the night spares—
Destroy our enemy, lord of the thunder!
20 Let him be riven by lightning from heaven!

**Antistrophe 3**

Phoibos Apollo, stretch the sun's bowstring,
That golden cord, until it sing for us,
Flashing arrows in heaven!
25 Artemis, Huntress,
Race with flaring lights upon our mountains!
O scarlet god, O golden-banded brow,
O Theban Bacchos in a storm of Maenads,

(*Enter* OEDIPUS, *C.*)

30 Whirl upon Death, that all the Undying hate!
Come with blinding torches, come in joy!

SCENE I

OEDIPUS Is this your prayer? It may be answered. Come,
Listen to me, act as the crisis demands,
35 And you shall have relief from all these evils.

Until now I was a stranger to this tale,
As I had been a stranger to the crime.

Could I track down the murderer without a clue?
But now, friends,
As one who became a citizen after the murder,
I make this proclamation to all Thebans:
5 If any man knows by whose hand Laïos, son of Labdakos,
Met his death, I direct that man to tell me everything,
No matter what he fears for having so long withheld it.
Let it stand as promised that no further trouble
Will come to him, but he may leave the land in safety.

10 Moreover: If anyone knows the murderer to be foreign,
Let him not keep silent: he shall have his reward from me.
However, if he does conceal it; if any man
Fearing for his friend or for himself disobeys this edict,
Hear what I propose to do:

15 I solemnly forbid the people of this country,
Where power and throne are mine, ever to receive that man
Or speak to him, no matter who he is, or let him
Join in sacrifice, lustration, or in prayer.
I decree that he be driven from every house,
20 Being, as he is, corruption itself to us: the Delphic
Voice of Apollo has pronounced this revelation.
Thus I associate myself with the oracle
And take the side of the murdered king.

As for the criminal, I pray to God—
25 Whether it be a lurking thief, or one of a number—
I pray that that man's life be consumed in evil and wretchedness.
And as for me, this curse applies no less
If it should turn out that the culprit is my guest here,
Sharing my hearth.
30 You have heard the penalty.
I lay it on you now to attend to this
For my sake, for Apollo's, for the sick
Sterile city that heaven has abandoned.
Suppose the oracle had given you no command:
35 Should this defilement go uncleansed for ever?
You should have found the murderer: your king,
A noble king, had been destroyed!
Now I,
Having the power that he held before me,
40 Having his bed, begetting children there
Upon his wife, as he would have, had he lived—
Their son would have been my children's brother,

If Laïos had had luck in fatherhood!
(And now his bad fortune has struck him down)—
I say I take the son's part, just as though
I were his son, to press the fight for him
5 And see it won! I'll find the hand that brought
Death to Labdakos' and Polydoros' child,
Heir of Kadmos' and Agenor's line.[1]
And as for those who fail me,
May the gods deny them the fruit of the earth,
10 Fruit of the womb, and may they rot utterly!
Let them be wretched as we are wretched, and worse!

For you, for loyal Thebans, and for all
Who find my actions right, I pray the favor
Of justice, and of all the immortal gods.

15 CHORAGOS Since I am under oath, my lord, I swear
I did not do the murder, I can not name
The murderer. Phoibos ordained the search;
Why did he not say who the culprit was?
OEDIPUS An honest question. But no man in the world
20 Can make the gods do more than the gods will.
CHORAGOS There is an alternative, I think—
OEDIPUS Tell me.
Any or all, you must not fail to tell me.
CHORAGOS A lord clairvoyant to the lord Apollo,
25 As we all know, is the skilled Teiresias.
One might learn much about this from him, Oedipus.
OEDIPUS I am not wasting time:
Kreon spoke of this, and I have sent for him—
Twice, in fact; it is strange that he is not here.
30 CHORAGOS The other matter—that old report—seems useless.
OEDIPUS What was that? I am interested in all reports.
CHORAGOS The king was said to have been killed by highwaymen.
OEDIPUS I know. But we have no witnesses to that.
CHORAGOS If the killer can feel a particle of dread,
35 Your curse will bring him out of hiding!
OEDIPUS No.
The man who dared that act will fear no curse.

(*Enter the blind seer* TEIRESIAS, *led by a* PAGE.)

CHORAGOS But there is one man who may detect the criminal.

[1] *Labdakos, Polydoros, Kadmos,* and *Agenor* father, grandfather, great-grandfather, and great-great-grandfather of Laïos

This is Teiresias, this is the holy prophet
In whom, alone of all men, truth was born.

OEDIPUS Teiresias: seer: student of mysteries,
Of all that's taught and all that no man tells,
5 Secrets of Heaven and secrets of the earth:
Blind though you are, you know the city lies
Sick with plague; and from this plague, my lord,
We find that you alone can guard or save us.

Possibly you did not hear the messengers?
10 Apollo, when we sent to him,
Sent us back word that this great pestilence
Would lift, but only if we established clearly
The identity of those who murdered Laïos.
They must be killed or exiled.
15 Can you use
Birdflight[1] or any art of divination
To purify yourself, and Thebes, and me
From this contagion? We are in your hands.
There is no fairer duty
20 Than that of helping others in distress.

TEIRESIAS How dreadful knowledge of the truth can be
When there's no help in truth! I knew this well,
But did not act on it: else I should not have come.

OEDIPUS What is troubling you? Why are your eyes so cold?

25 TEIRESIAS Let me go home. Bear your own fate, and I'll
Bear mine. It is better so: trust what I say.

OEDIPUS What you say is ungracious and unhelpful
To your native country. Do not refuse to speak.

TEIRESIAS When it comes to speech, your own is neither temperate
30 Nor opportune. I wish to be more prudent.

OEDIPUS In God's name, we all beg you—

TEIRESIAS You are all ignorant.
No; I will never tell you what I know.
Now it is my misery; then, it would be yours.

35 OEDIPUS What! You do know something, and will not tell us?
You would betray us all and wreck the State?

TEIRESIAS I do not intend to torture myself, or you.
Why persist in asking? You will not persuade me.

OEDIPUS What a wicked old man you are! You'd try a stone's
40 Patience! Out with it! Have you no feeling at all?

---

[1] *Birdflight* Prophets predicted the future or divined the unknown by observing the flight of birds.

TEIRESIAS You call me unfeeling. If you could only see
The nature of your own feelings . . .

OEDIPUS Why,
Who would not feel as I do? Who could endure
5 Your arrogance toward the city?

TEIRESIAS What does it matter?
Whether I speak or not, it is bound to come.

OEDIPUS Then, if "it" is bound to come, you are bound to tell me.

TEIRESIAS No, I will not go on. Rage as you please.

10 OEDIPUS Rage? Why not!
And I'll tell you what I think:
You planned it, you had it done, you all but
Killed him with your own hands: if you had eyes,
I'd say the crime was yours, and yours alone.

15 TEIRESIAS So? I charge you, then,
Abide by the proclamation you have made:
From this day forth
Never speak again to these men or to me;
You yourself are the pollution of this country.

20 OEDIPUS You dare say that! Can you possibly think you have
Some way of going free, after such insolence?

TEIRESIAS I have gone free. It is the truth sustains me.

OEDIPUS Who taught you shamelessness? It was not your craft.

TEIRESIAS You did. You made me speak. I did not want to.

25 OEDIPUS Speak what? Let me hear it again more clearly.

TEIRESIAS Was it not clear before? Are you tempting me?

OEDIPUS I did not understand it. Say it again.

TEIRESIAS I say that you are the murderer whom you seek.

OEDIPUS Now twice you have spat out infamy. You'll pay for it!

30 TEIRESIAS Would you care for more? Do you wish to be
really angry?

OEDIPUS Say what you will. Whatever you say is worthless.

TEIRESIAS I say you live in hideous shame with those
Most dear to you. You can not see the evil.

35 OEDIPUS Can you go on babbling like this for ever?

TEIRESIAS I can, if there is power in truth.

OEDIPUS There is:
But not for you, not for you,
You sightless, witless, senseless, mad old man!

40 TEIRESIAS You are the madman. There is no one here
Who will not curse you soon, as you curse me.

OEDIPUS You child of total night! I would not touch you;
Neither would any man who sees the sun.

TEIRESIAS True: it is not from you my fate will come.

That lies within Apollo's competence,
As it is his concern.

OEDIPUS Tell me, who made
These fine discoveries? Kreon? or someone else?

5 TEIRESIAS Kreon is no threat. You weave your own doom.

OEDIPUS Wealth, power, craft of statesmanship!
Kingly position, everywhere admired!
What savage envy is stored up against these,
If Kreon, whom I trusted, Kreon my friend,
10 For this great office which the city once
Put in my hands unsought—if for this power
Kreon desires in secret to destroy me!

He has bought this decrepit fortune-teller, this
Collector of dirty pennies, this prophet fraud—
15 Why, he is no more clairvoyant than I am!
Tell us:
Has your mystic mummery ever approached the truth?
When that hellcat the Sphinx was performing here,
What help were you to these people?
Her magic was not for the first man who came along:
20 It demanded a real exorcist. Your birds—
What good were they? or the gods, for the matter of that?
But I came by,
Oedipus, the simple man, who knows nothing—
I thought it out for myself, no birds helped me!
25 And this is the man you think you can destroy,
That you may be close to Kreon when he's king!
Well, you and your friend Kreon, it seems to me,
Will suffer most. If you were not an old man,
You would have paid already for your plot.

30 CHORAGOS We can not see that his words or yours
Have been spoken except in anger, Oedipus,
And of anger we have no need. How to accomplish
The god's will best: that is what most concerns us.

TEIRESIAS You are a king. But where argument's concerned
35 I am your man, as much a king as you.
I am not your servant, but Apollo's.
I have no need of Kreon or Kreon's name.

Listen to me. You mock my blindness, do you?
But I say that you, with both your eyes, are blind:
40 You can not see the wretchedness of your life,
Nor in whose house you live, no, nor with whom.
Who are your father and mother? Can you tell me?

You do not even know the blind wrongs
That you have done them, on earth and in the world below.
But the double lash of your parents' curse will whip you
Out of this land some day, with only night
5 Upon your precious eyes.
Your cries then—where will they not be heard?
What fastness of Kithairon[1] will not echo them?
And that bridal-descant of yours—you'll know it then,
The song they sang when you came here to Thebes
10 And found your misguided berthing.
All this, and more, that you can not guess at now,
Will bring you to yourself among your children.

Be angry, then. Curse Kreon. Curse my words.
I tell you, no man that walks upon the earth
15 Shall be rooted out more horribly than you.

OEDIPUS Am I to bear this from him?—Damnation
Take you! Out of this place! Out of my sight!

TEIRESIAS I would not have come at all if you had not asked me.

OEDIPUS Could I have told that you'd talk nonsense, that
20 You'd come here to make a fool of yourself, and of me?

TEIRESIAS A fool? Your parents thought me sane enough.

OEDIPUS My parents again!—Wait: who were my parents?

TEIRESIAS This day will give you a father, and break your heart.

OEDIPUS Your infantile riddles! Your damned abracadabra!

25 TEIRESIAS You were a great man once at solving riddles.

OEDIPUS Mock me with that if you like; you will find it true.

TEIRESIAS It was true enough. It brought about your ruin.

OEDIPUS But if it saved this town?

TEIRESIAS (*to the* PAGE) Boy, give me your hand.

30 OEDIPUS Yes, boy; lead him away.
—While you are here
We can do nothing. Go; leave us in peace.

TEIRESIAS I will go when I have said what I have to say.
How can you hurt me? And I tell you again:
35 The man you have been looking for all this time,
The damned man, the murderer of Laïos,
That man is in Thebes. To your mind he is foreign-born,
But it will soon be shown that he is a Theban,
A revelation that will fail to please.
40 A blind man,

[1] *Kithairon* the mountain where Oedipus was taken to be exposed as an infant

Who has his eyes now; a penniless man, who is rich now;
And he will go tapping the strange earth with his staff.
To the children with whom he lives now he will be
Brother and father—the very same; to her
5 Who bore him, son and husband—the very same
Who came to his father's bed, wet with his father's blood.

Enough. Go think that over.
If later you find error in what I have said,
You may say that I have no skill in prophecy.

10 (*Exit* TEIRESIAS, *led by his* PAGE. OEDIPUS *goes into the palace.*)

## ODE I

### Strophe 1

CHORUS The Delphic stone of prophecies
Remembers ancient regicide
15 And a still bloody hand.
That killer's hour of flight has come.
He must be stronger than riderless
Coursers of untiring wind,
For the son[1] of Zeus armed with his father's thunder
20 Leaps in lightning after him;
And the Furies hold his track, the sad Furies.

### Antistrophe 1

Holy Parnassos'[2] peak of snow
Flashes and blinds that secret man,
25 That all shall hunt him down:
Though he may roam the forest shade
Like a bull gone wild from pasture
To rage through glooms of stone.
Doom comes down on him; flight will not avail him;
30 For the world's heart calls him desolate,
And the immortal voices follow, for ever follow.

### Strophe 2

But now a wilder thing is heard
From the old man skilled at hearing Fate in the wing-beat
35 of a bird.

---

1 *son* Apollo
2 *Parnassos* mountain sacred to Apollo

Bewildered as a blown bird, my soul hovers and can not find
Foothold in this debate, or any reason or rest of mind.
But no man ever brought—none can bring
Proof of strife between Thebes' royal house,
5 Labdakos' line, and the son of Polybos;
And never until now has any man brought word
Of Laïos' dark death staining Oedipus the King.

**Antistrophe 2**

Divine Zeus and Apollo hold
10 Perfect intelligence alone of all tales ever told;
And well though this diviner works, he works in his own night;
No man can judge that rough unknown or trust in second sight,
For wisdom changes hands among the wise.
Shall I believe my great lord criminal
15 At a raging word that a blind old man let fall?
I saw him, when the carrion woman[1] faced him of old,
Prove his heroic mind. These evil words are lies.

SCENE II

KREON Men of Thebes:
20 I am told that heavy accusations
Have been brought against me by King Oedipus.

I am not the kind of man to bear this tamely.

If in these present difficulties
He holds me accountable for any harm to him
25 Through anything I have said or done—why, then,
I do not value life in this dishonor.
It is not as though this rumor touched upon
Some private indiscretion. The matter is grave.
The fact is that I am being called disloyal
30 To the State, to my fellow citizens, to my friends.
CHORAGOS He may have spoken in anger, not from his mind.
KREON But did you not hear him say I was the one
Who seduced the old prophet into lying?
CHORAGOS The thing was said; I do not know how seriously.
35 KREON But you were watching him! Were his eyes steady?
Did he look like a man in his right mind?
CHORAGOS I do not know.

---

[1] *woman* the Sphinx

I can not judge the behavior of great men.
But here is the king himself.

(*Enter* OEDIPUS.)

OEDIPUS So you dared come back.
5 Why? How brazen of you to come to my house,
You murderer!
Do you think I do not know
That you plotted to kill me, plotted to steal my throne?
Tell me, in God's name: am I coward, a fool,
10 That you should dream you could accomplish this?
A fool who could not see your slippery game?
A coward, not to fight back when I saw it?
You are the fool, Kreon, are you not? hoping
Without support or friends to get a throne?
15 Thrones may be won or bought: you could do neither.
KREON Now listen to me. You have talked; let me talk, too.
You can not judge unless you know the facts.
OEDIPUS You speak well: there is one fact; but I find it hard
To learn from the deadliest enemy I have.
20 KREON That above all I must dispute with you.
OEDIPUS That above all I will not hear you deny.
KREON If you think there is anything good in being stubborn
Against all reason, then I say you are wrong.
OEDIPUS If you think a man can sin against his own kind
25 And not be punished for it, I say you are mad.
KREON I agree. But tell me: What have I done to you?
OEDIPUS You advised me to send for that wizard, did you not?
KREON I did. I should do it again.
OEDIPUS Very well. Now tell me:
30 How long has it been since Laïos—
KREON What of Laïos?
OEDIPUS Since he vanished in that onset by the road?
KREON It was long ago, a long time.
OEDIPUS And this prophet,
35 Was he practicing here then?
KREON He was; and with honor, as now.
OEDIPUS Did he speak of me at that time?
KREON He never did,
At least, not when I was present.
40 OEDIPUS But . . . the enquiry?
I suppose you held one?
KREON We did, but we learned nothing.

OEDIPUS Why did the prophet not speak against me then?
KREON I do not know; and I am the kind of man
Who holds his tongue when he has no facts to go on.
OEDIPUS There's one fact that you know, and you could tell it.
5 KREON What fact is that? If I know it, you shall have it.
OEDIPUS If he were not involved with you, he could not say
That it was I who murdered Laïos.
KREON If he says that, you are the one that knows it!—
But now it is my turn to question you.
10 OEDIPUS Put your questions. I am no murderer.
KREON First, then: You married my sister?
OEDIPUS I married your sister.
KREON And you rule the kingdom equally with her?
OEDIPUS Everything that she wants she has from me.
15 KREON And I am the third, equal to both of you?
OEDIPUS That is why I call you a bad friend.
KREON No. Reason it out, as I have done.
Think of this first: Would any sane man prefer
Power, with all a king's anxieties,
20 To that same power and the grace of sleep?
Certainly not I.
I have never longed for the king's power—only his rights.
Would any wise man differ from me in this?
As matters stand, I have my way in everything
25 With your consent, and no responsibilities.
If I were king, I should be a slave to policy.

How could I desire a scepter more
Than what is now mine—untroubled influence?
No, I have not gone mad; I need no honors,
30 Except those with the perquisites I have now.
I am welcome everywhere; every man salutes me,
And those who want your favor seek my ear,
Since I know how to manage what they ask.
Should I exchange this ease for that anxiety?
35 Besides, no sober mind is treasonable.
I hate anarchy
And never would deal with any man who likes it.
Test what I have said. Go to the priestess
At Delphi, ask if I quoted her correctly.
40 And as for this other thing: if I am found
Guilty of treason with Teiresias,
Then sentence me to death. You have my word

It is a sentence I should cast my vote for—
But not without evidence!
You do wrong
When you take good men for bad, bad men for good.
5 A true friend thrown aside—why, life itself
Is not more precious!
In time you will know this well:
For time, and time alone, will show the just man,
Though scoundrels are discovered in a day.
10 CHORAGOS This is well said, and a prudent man would ponder it.
Judgments too quickly formed are dangerous.
OEDIPUS But is he not quick in his duplicity?
And shall I not be quick to parry him?
Would you have me stand still, hold my peace, and let
15 This man win everything, through my inaction?
KREON And you want—what is it, then? To banish me?
OEDIPUS No, not exile. It is your death I want,
So that all the world may see what treason means.
KREON You will persist, then? You will not believe me?
20 OEDIPUS How can I believe you?
KREON Then you are a fool.
OEDIPUS To save myself?
KREON In justice, think of me.
OEDIPUS You are evil incarnate.
25 KREON But suppose that you are wrong?
OEDIPUS Still I must rule.
KREON But not if you rule badly.
OEDIPUS O city, city!
KREON It is my city, too!
30 CHORAGOS Now, my lords, be still. I see the queen,
Iokastê, coming from her palace chambers;
And it is time she came, for the sake of you both.
This dreadful quarrel can be resolved through her.

(*Enter* IOKASTÊ.)

35 IOKASTÊ Poor foolish men, what wicked din is this?
With Thebes sick to death, is it not shameful
That you should rake some private quarrel up?
(*To* OEDIPUS) Come into the house.
—And you, Kreon, go now:
40 Let us have no more of this tumult over nothing.
KREON Nothing? No, sister: what your husband plans for me
Is one of two great evils: exile or death.

OEDIPUS He is right.
Why, woman I have caught him squarely
Plotting against my life.
KREON No! Let me die
5 Accurst if ever I have wished you harm!
IOKASTÊ Ah, believe it, Oedipus!
In the name of the gods, respect this oath of his
For my sake, for the sake of these people here!

**Strophe 1**

10 CHORAGOS Open your mind to her, my lord. Be ruled by her, I beg you!
OEDIPUS What would you have me do?
CHORAGOS Respect Kreon's word. He has never spoken like a fool,
And now he has sworn an oath.
15 OEDIPUS You know what you ask?
CHORAGOS I do.
OEDIPUS Speak on, then.
CHORAGOS A friend so sworn should not be baited so,
In blind malice, and without final proof.
20 OEDIPUS You are aware, I hope, that what you say
Means death for me, or exile at the least.

**Strophe 2**

CHORAGOS No, I swear by Helios, first in Heaven!
May I die friendless and accurst,
25 The worst of deaths, if ever I meant that!
It is the withering fields
That hurt my sick heart:
Must we bear all these ills,
And now your bad blood as well?
30 OEDIPUS Then let him go. And let me die, if I must,
Or be driven by him in shame from the land of Thebes.
It is your unhappiness, and not his talk,
That touches me.
As for him—
35 Wherever he goes, hatred will follow him.
KREON Ugly in yielding, as you were ugly in rage!
Natures like yours chiefly torment themselves.
OEDIPUS Can you not go? Can you not leave me?
KREON I can.
40 You do not know me; but the city knows me,
And in its eyes I am just, if not in yours.

(*Exit* KREON.)

### Antistrophe 1

CHORAGOS Lady Iokastê, did you not ask the King to go to
his chambers?

5 IOKASTÊ First tell me what has happened.

CHORAGOS There was suspicion without evidence; yet it rankled
As even false charges will.

IOKASTÊ On both sides?

CHORAGOS On both.

10 IOKASTÊ But what was said?

CHORAGOS. Oh let it rest, let it be done with!
Have we not suffered enough?

OEDIPUS You see to what your decency has brought you:
You have made difficulties where my heart saw none.

### 15 Antistrophe 2

CHORAGOS Oedipus, it is not once only I have told you—
You must know I should count myself unwise
To the point of madness, should I now forsake you—
You, under whose hand,
20 In the storm of another time,
Our dear land sailed out free.
But now stand fast at the helm!

IOKASTÊ In God's name, Oedipus, inform your wife as well:
Why are you so set in this hard anger?

25 OEDIPUS I will tell you, for none of these men deserves
My confidence as you do. It is Kreon's work,
His treachery, his plotting against me.

IOKASTÊ Go on, if you can make this clear to me.

OEDIPUS He charges me with the murder of Laïos.

30 IOKASTÊ Has he some knowledge? Or does he speak from hearsay?

OEDIPUS He would not commit himself to such a charge,
But he has brought in that damnable soothsayer
To tell his story.

IOKASTÊ Set your mind at rest.
35 If it is a question of soothsayers, I tell you
That you will find no man whose craft gives knowledge
Of the unknowable.
Here is my proof:
An oracle was reported to Laïos once
40 (I will not say from Phoibos himself, but from
His appointed ministers, at any rate)

That his doom would be death at the hands of his own son—
His son, born of his flesh and of mine!

Now, you remember the story: Laïos was killed
By marauding strangers where three highways meet;
5 But his child had not been three days in this world
Before the king had pierced the baby's ankles
And left him to die on a lonely mountainside.

Thus, Apollo never caused that child
To kill his father, and it was not Laïos' fate
10 To die at the hands of his son, as he had feared.
This is what prophets and prophecies are worth!
Have no dread of them.
It is God himself
Who can show us what he wills, in his own way.

15 OEDIPUS How strange a shadowy memory crossed my mind,
Just now while you were speaking; it chilled my heart.

IOKASTÊ What do you mean? What memory do you speak of?

OEDIPUS If I understand you, Laïos was killed
At a place where three roads meet.

20 IOKASTÊ So it was said;
We have no later story.

OEDIPUS Where did it happen?

IOKASTÊ Phokis, it is called: at a place where the Theban Way
Divides into the roads toward Delphi and Daulia.

25 OEDIPUS When?

IOKASTÊ We had the news not long before you came
And proved the right to your succession here.

OEDIPUS Ah, what net has God been weaving for me?

IOKASTÊ Oedipus! Why does this trouble you?

30 OEDIPUS Do not ask me yet.
First, tell me how Laïos looked, and tell me
How old he was.

IOKASTÊ He was tall, his hair just touched
With white; his form was not unlike your own.

35 OEDIPUS I think that I myself may be accurst
By my own ignorant edict.

IOKASTÊ You speak strangely.
It makes me tremble to look at you, my king.

OEDIPUS I am not sure that the blind man can not see.
40 But I should know better if you were to tell me—

IOKASTÊ Anything—though I dread to hear you ask it.

OEDIPUS Was the king lightly escorted, or did he ride
With a large company, as a ruler should?
IOKASTÊ There were five men with him in all: one was a herald.
And a single chariot, which he was driving.
5 OEDIPUS Alas, that makes it plain enough!
But who—
Who told you how it happened?
IOKASTÊ A household servant,
The only one to escape.
10 OEDIPUS And is he still
A servant of ours?
IOKASTÊ No; for when he came back at last
And found you enthroned in the place of the dead king,
He came to me, touched my hand with his, and begged
15 That I would send him away to the frontier district
Where only the shepherds go—
As far away from the city as I could send him.
I granted his prayer; for although the man was a slave,
He had earned more than this favor at my hands.
20 OEDIPUS Can he be called back quickly?
IOKASTÊ Easily.
But why?
OEDIPUS I have taken too much upon myself
Without enquiry; therefore I wish to consult him.
25 IOKASTÊ Then he shall come.
But am I not one also
To whom you might confide these fears of yours?
OEDIPUS That is your right; it will not be denied you,
Now least of all; for I have reached a pitch
30 Of wild foreboding. Is there anyone
To whom I should sooner speak?

Polybos of Corinth is my father.
My mother is a Dorian: Meropê.
I grew up chief among the men of Corinth
35 Until a strange thing happened—
Not worth my passion, it may be, but strange.
At a feast, a drunken man maundering in his cups
Cries out that I am not my father's son! [1]

---

[1] *not my father's son* Oedipus perhaps interprets this as an allegation that he is a bastard, the son of Meropê but not of Polybos. The implication, at any rate, is that he is not of royal birth, not the legitimate heir to the throne of Corinth.

I contained myself that night, though I felt anger
And a sinking heart. The next day I visited
My father and mother, and questioned them. They stormed,
Calling it all the slanderous rant of a fool;
5 And this relieved me. Yet the suspicion
Remained always aching in my mind;
I knew there was talk; I could not rest;
And finally, saying nothing to my parents,
I went to the shrine at Delphi.

10 The god dismissed my question without reply;
He spoke of other things.
Some were clear,
Full of wretchedness, dreadful, unbearable:
As, that I should lie with my own mother, breed
15 Children from whom all men would turn their eyes;
And that I should be my father's murderer.

I heard all this, and fled. And from that day
Corinth to me was only in the stars
Descending in that quarter of the sky,
20 As I wandered farther and farther on my way
To a land where I should never see the evil
Sung by the oracle. And I came to this country
Where, so you say, King Laïos was killed.

I will tell you all that happened there, my lady.

25 There were three highways
Coming together at a place I passed;
And there a herald came towards me, and a chariot
Drawn by horses, with a man such as you describe
Seated in it. The groom leading the horses
30 Forced me off the road at his lord's command;
But as this charioteer lurched over towards me
I struck him in my rage. The old man saw me
And brought his double goad down upon my head
As I came abreast.
35 He was paid back, and more!
Swinging my club in this right hand I knocked him
Out of his car, and he rolled on the ground.
I killed him.

I killed them all.
40 Now if that stranger and Laïos were—kin,
Where is a man more miserable than I?
More hated by the gods? Citizen and alien alike

Must never shelter me or speak to me—
I must be shunned by all.
And I myself
Pronounced this malediction upon myself!

5 Think of it: I have touched you with these hands,
These hands that killed your husband. What defilement!

Am I all evil, then? It must be so,
Since I must flee from Thebes, yet never again
See my own countrymen, my own country,
10 For fear of joining my mother in marriage
And killing Polybos, my father.
Ah,
If I was created so, born to this fate,
Who could deny the savagery of God?

15 O holy majesty of heavenly powers!
May I never see that day! Never!
Rather let me vanish from the race of men
Than know the abomination destined me!

CHORAGOS We too, my lord, have felt dismay at this.
20 But there is hope: you have yet to hear the shepherd.

OEDIPUS Indeed, I fear no other hope is left me.

IOKASTÊ What do you hope from him when he comes?

OEDIPUS This much:
If his account of the murder tallies with yours,
25 Then I am cleared.

IOKASTÊ What was it that I said
Of such importance?

OEDIPUS Why, "marauders," you said,
Killed the king, according to this man's story.
30 If he maintains that still, if there were several,
Clearly the guilt is not mine: I was alone.
But if he says one man, singlehanded, did it,
Then the evidence all points to me.

IOKASTÊ You may be sure that he said there were several;
35 And can he call back that story now? He can not.
The whole city heard it as plainly as I.
But suppose he alters some detail of it:
He can not ever show that Laïos' death
Fulfilled the oracle: for Apollo said
40 My child was doomed to kill him; and my child—
Poor baby!—it was my child that died first.

No. From now on, where oracles are concerned,
I would not waste a second thought on any.
OEDIPUS You may be right.
But come: let someone go
5 For the shepherd at once. This matter must be settled.
IOKASTÊ I will send for him.
I would not wish to cross you in anything,
And surely not in this.—Let us go in.

(*Exeunt into the palace.*)

10 ODE II

**Strophe 1**

CHORUS Let me be reverent in the ways of right,
Lowly the paths I journey on;
Let all my words and actions keep
15 The laws of the pure universe
From highest Heaven handed down.
For Heaven is their bright nurse,
Those generations of the realms of light;
Ah, never of mortal kind were they begot,
20 Nor are they slaves of memory, lost in sleep:
Their Father is greater than Time, and ages not.

**Antistrophe 1**

The tyrant is a child of Pride
Who drinks from his great sickening cup
25 Recklessness and vanity,
Until from his high crest headlong
He plummets to the dust of hope.
That strong man is not strong.
But let no fair ambition be denied;
30 May God protect the wrestler for the State
In government, in comely policy,
Who will fear God, and on His ordinance wait.

**Strophe 2**

Haughtiness and the high hand of disdain
35 Tempt and outrage God's holy law;
And any mortal who dares hold
No immortal Power in awe
Will be caught up in a net of pain:

The price for which his levity is sold.
Let each man take due earnings, then,
And keep his hands from holy things,
And from blasphemy stand apart—
5 Else the crackling blast of heaven
Blows on his head, and on his desperate heart.
Though fools will honor impious men,
In their cities no tragic poet sings.

**Antistrophe 2**

10 Shall we lose faith in Delphi's obscurities,
We who have heard the world's core
Discredited, and the sacred wood
Of Zeus at Elis praised no more?
The deeds and the strange prophecies
15 Must make a pattern yet to be understood.
Zeus, if indeed you are lord of all,
Throned in light over night and day,
Mirror this in your endless mind:
Our masters call the oracle
20 Words on the wind, and the Delphic vision blind!
Their hearts no longer know Apollo,
And reverence for the gods has died away.

## SCENE III

(*Enter* IOKASTÊ.)

25 IOKASTÊ Princes of Thebes, it has occurred to me
To visit the altars of the gods, bearing
These branches as a suppliant, and this incense.
Our king is not himself: his noble soul
Is overwrought with fantasies of dread,
30 Else he would consider
The new prophecies in the light of the old.
He will listen to any voice that speaks disaster,
And my advice goes for nothing.

(*She approaches the altar, R.*)

35 To you, then, Apollo,
Lycéan lord, since you are nearest, I turn in prayer.
Receive these offerings, and grant us deliverance
From defilement. Our hearts are heavy with fear

When we see our leader distracted, as helpless sailors
Are terrified by the confusion of their helmsman.

(*Enter* MESSENGER.)

MESSENGER Friends, no doubt you can direct me:
5 Where shall I find the house of Oedipus,
Or, better still, where is the king himself?
CHORAGOS It is this very place, stranger; he is inside.
This is his wife and mother of his children.
MESSENGER I wish her happiness in a happy house,
10 Blest in all the fulfillment of her marriage.
IOKASTÊ I wish as much for you: your courtesy
Deserves a like good fortune. But now, tell me:
Why have you come? What have you to say to us?
MESSENGER Good news, my lady, for your house and your husband.
15 IOKASTÊ What news? Who sent you here?
MESSENGER I am from Corinth.
The news I bring ought to mean joy for you,
Though it may be you will find some grief in it.
IOKASTÊ What is it? How can it touch us in both ways?
20 MESSENGER The word is that the people of the Isthmus
Intend to call Oedipus to be their king.
IOKASTÊ But old King Polybos—is he not reigning still?
MESSENGER No. Death holds him in his sepulchre.
IOKASTÊ What are you saying? Polybos is dead?
25 MESSENGER If I am not telling the truth, may I die myself.
IOKASTÊ (*to a* MAIDSERVANT) Go in, go quickly; tell this to your master.

O riddlers of God's will, where are you now!
This was the man whom Oedipus, long ago,
30 Feared so, fled so, in dread of destroying him—
But it was another fate by which he died.

(*Enter* OEDIPUS, *C.*)

OEDIPUS Dearest Iokastê, why have you sent for me?
IOKASTÊ Listen to what this man says, and then tell me
35 What has become of the solemn prophecies.
OEDIPUS Who is this man? What is his news for me?
IOKASTÊ He has come from Corinth to announce your father's death!
OEDIPUS Is it true, stranger? Tell me in your own words.
40 MESSENGER I can not say it more clearly: the king is dead.

OEDIPUS Was it by treason? Or by an attack of illness?
MESSENGER A little thing brings old men to their rest.
OEDIPUS It was sickness, then?
MESSENGER Yes, and his many years.
5 OEDIPUS Ah!
Why should a man respect the Pythian hearth,[1] or
Give heed to the birds that jangle above his head?
They prophesied that I should kill Polybos,
Kill my own father; but he is dead and buried,
10 And I am here—I never touched him, never,
Unless he died of grief for my departure,
And thus, in a sense, through me. No. Polybos
Has packed the oracles off with him underground.
They are empty words.
15 IOKASTÊ Had I not told you so?
OEDIPUS You had; it was my faint heart that betrayed me.
IOKASTÊ From now on never think of those things again.
OEDIPUS And yet—must I not fear my mother's bed?
IOKASTÊ Why should anyone in this world be afraid,
20 Since Fate rules us and nothing can be foreseen?
A man should live only for the present day.

Have no more fear of sleeping with your mother:
How many men, in dreams, have lain with their mothers!
No reasonable man is troubled by such things.
25 OEDIPUS That is true; only—
If only my mother were not still alive!
But she is alive. I can not help my dread.
IOKASTÊ Yet this news of your father's death is wonderful.
OEDIPUS Wonderful. But I fear the living woman.
30 MESSENGER Tell me, who is this woman that you fear?
OEDIPUS It is Meropê, man; the wife of King Polybos.
MESSENGER Meropê? Why should you be afraid of her?
OEDIPUS An oracle of the gods, a dreadful saying.
MESSENGER Can you tell me about it or are you sworn to silence?
35 OEDIPUS I can tell you, and I will.
Apollo said through his prophet that I was the man
Who should marry his own mother, shed his father's blood
With his own hands. And so, for all these years
I have kept clear of Corinth, and no harm has come—
40 Though it would have been sweet to see my parents again.

---

[1] *Pythian hearth* Delphi

MESSENGER And is this the fear that drove you out of Corinth?
OEDIPUS Would you have me kill my father?
MESSENGER As for that
You must be reassured by the news I gave you.
5 OEDIPUS If you could reassure me, I would reward you.
MESSENGER I had that in mind, I will confess: I thought
I could count on you when you returned to Corinth.
OEDIPUS No: I will never go near my parents again.
MESSENGER Ah, son, you still do not know what you are doing—
10 OEDIPUS What do you mean? In the name of God tell me!
MESSENGER —if these are your reasons for not going home.
OEDIPUS I tell you, I fear the oracle may come true.
MESSENGER And guilt may come upon you through your parents?
OEDIPUS That is the dread that is always in my heart.
15 MESSENGER Can you not see that all your fears are groundless?
OEDIPUS Groundless? Am I not my parents' son?
MESSENGER Polybos was not your father.
OEDIPUS Not my father?
MESSENGER No more your father than the man speaking to you.
20 OEDIPUS But you are nothing to me!
MESSENGER Neither was he.
OEDIPUS Then why did he call me son?
MESSENGER I will tell you:
Long ago he had you from my hands, as a gift.
25 OEDIPUS Then how could he love me so, if I was not his?
MESSENGER He had no children, and his heart turned to you.
OEDIPUS What of you? Did you buy me? Did you find me by chance?
MESSENGER I came upon you in the woody vales of Kithairon.
30 OEDIPUS And what were you doing there?
MESSENGER Tending my flocks.
OEDIPUS A wandering shepherd?
MESSENGER But your savior, son, that day.
OEDIPUS From what did you save me?
35 MESSENGER Your ankles should tell you that.
OEDIPUS Ah, stranger, why do you speak of that childhood pain?
MESSENGER I pulled the skewer that pinned your feet together.
OEDIPUS I have had the mark as long as I can remember.
MESSENGER That was why you were given the name you bear.
40 OEDIPUS God! Was it my father or my mother who did it?
Tell me!
MESSENGER I do not know. The man who gave you to me
Can tell you better than I.
OEDIPUS It was not you that found me, but another?

MESSENGER It was another shepherd gave you to me.
OEDIPUS Who was he? Can you tell me who he was?
MESSENGER I think he was said to be one of Laïos' people.
OEDIPUS You mean the Laïos who was king here years ago?
5 MESSENGER Yes; King Laïos; and the man was one of his herdsmen.
OEDIPUS Is he still alive? Can I see him?
MESSENGER These men here
Know best about such things.
10 OEDIPUS Does anyone here
Know this shepherd that he is talking about?
Have you seen him in the fields, or in the town?
If you have, tell me. It is time things were made plain.
CHORAGOS I think the man he means is that same shepherd
15 You have already asked to see. Iokastê perhaps
Could tell you something.
OEDIPUS Do you know anything
About him, Lady? Is he the man we have summoned?
Is that the man this shepherd means?
20 IOKASTÊ Why think of him?
Forget this herdsman. Forget it all.
This talk is a waste of time.
OEDIPUS How can you say that,
When the clues to my true birth are in my hands?
25 IOKASTÊ For God's love, let us have no more questioning!
Is your life nothing to you?
My own is pain enough for me to bear.
OEDIPUS You need not worry. Suppose my mother a slave,
And born of slaves: no baseness can touch you.
30 IOKASTÊ Listen to me, I beg you: do not do this thing!
OEDIPUS I will not listen; the truth must be made known.
IOKASTÊ Everything that I say is for your own good!
OEDIPUS My own good
Snaps my patience, then! I want none of it.
35 IOKASTÊ You are fatally wrong! May you never learn who you are!
OEDIPUS Go, one of you, and bring the shepherd here.
Let us leave this woman to brag of her royal name.
IOKASTÊ Ah, miserable!
That is the only word I have for you now.
40 That is the only word I can ever have.

(*Exit into the palace.*)

CHORAGOS Why has she left us, Oedipus? Why has she gone

In such a passion of sorrow? I fear this silence:
Something dreadful may come of it.

OEDIPUS Let it come!
However base my birth, I must know about it.
5 The Queen, like a woman, is perhaps ashamed
To think of my low origin. But I
Am a child of Luck; I can not be dishonered.
Luck is my mother; the passing months, my brothers,
Have seen me rich and poor.
10 If this is so,
How could I wish that I were someone else?
How could I not be glad to know my birth?

## ODE III

### Strophe

15 CHORUS If ever the coming time were known
To my heart's pondering,
Kithairon, now by Heaven I see the torches
At the festival of the next full moon,
And see the dance, and hear the choir sing
20 A grace to your gentle shade:
Mountain where Oedipus was found,
O mountain guard of a noble race!
May the god [1] who heals us lend his aid,
And let that glory come to pass
25 For our king's cradling-ground.

### Antistrophe

Of the nymphs that flower beyond the years,
Who bore you,[2] royal child,
To Pan of the hills or the timberline Apollo,
30 Cold in delight where the upland clears,
Or Hermês for whom Kyllenê's heights are piled?
Or flushed as evening cloud,
Great Dionysos, roamer of mountains,
He—was it he who found you there,

---

[1] *god* Apollo

[2] *Who bore you* The chorus is suggesting that perhaps Oedipus is the son of one of the immortal nymphs and of a god—Pan, Apollo, Hermes, or Dionysos. The "sweet god-ravisher" (below) is the presumed mother.

And caught you up in his own proud
Arms from the sweet god-ravisher
Who laughed by the Muses' fountains?

## SCENE IV

5 OEDIPUS Sirs: though I do not know the man,
I think I see him coming, this shepherd we want:
He is old, like our friend here, and the men
Bringing him seem to be servants of my house.
But you can tell, if you have ever seen him.

10 (*Enter* SHEPHERD *escorted by* SERVANTS.)

CHORAGOS I know him, he was Laïos' man. You can trust him.
OEDIPUS Tell me first, you from Corinth: is this the shepherd
We were discussing?
MESSENGER This is the very man.
15 OEDIPUS (*to* SHEPHERD) Come here. No, look at me. You must answer
Everything I ask.—You belonged to Laïos?
SHEPHERD Yes: born his slave, brought up in his house.
OEDIPUS Tell me: what kind of work did you do for him?
20 SHEPHERD I was a shepherd of his, most of my life.
OEDIPUS Where mainly did you go for pasturage?
SHEPHERD Sometimes Kithairon, sometimes the hills near-by.
OEDIPUS Do you remember ever seeing this man out there?
SHEPHERD What would he be doing there? This man?
25 OEDIPUS This man standing here. Have you ever seen him before?
SHEPHERD No. At least, not to my recollection.
MESSENGER And that is not strange, my lord. But I'll refresh
His memory: he must remember when we two
Spent three whole seasons together, March to September,
30 On Kithairon or thereabouts. He had two flocks;
I had one. Each autumn I'd drive mine home
And he would go back with his to Laïos' sheepfold.—
Is this not true, just as I have described it?
SHEPHERD True, yes; but it was all so long ago.
35 MESSENGER Well, then: do you remember, back in those days,
That you gave me a baby boy to bring up as my own?
SHEPHERD What if I did? What are you trying to say?
MESSENGER King Oedipus was once that little child.
SHEPHERD Damn you, hold your tongue!
40 OEDIPUS No more of that!
It is your tongue needs watching, not this man's.

SHEPHERD My king, my master, what is it I have done wrong?
OEDIPUS You have not answered his question about the boy.
SHEPHERD He does not know . . . He is only making trouble . . .
OEDIPUS Come, speak plainly, or it will go hard with you.
5 SHEPHERD In God's name, do not torture an old man!
OEDIPUS Come here, one of you; bind his arms behind him.
SHEPHERD Unhappy king! What more do you wish to learn?
OEDIPUS Did you give this man the child he speaks of?
SHEPHERD I did.
10 And I would to God I had died that very day.
OEDIPUS You will die now unless you speak the truth.
SHEPHERD Yet if I speak the truth, I am worse than dead.
OEDIPUS (*to* ATTENDANT) He intends to draw it out, apparently—
SHEPHERD No! I have told you already that I gave him the boy.
15 OEDIPUS Where did you get him? From your house? From somewhere else?
SHEPHERD Not from mine, no. A man gave him to me.
OEDIPUS Is that man here? Whose house did he belong to?
SHEPHERD For God's love, my king, do not ask me any more!
20 OEDIPUS You are a dead man if I have to ask you again.
SHEPHERD Then . . . Then the child was from the palace of Laïos.
OEDIPUS A slave child? or a child of his own line?
SHEPHERD Ah, I am on the brink of dreadful speech!
OEDIPUS And I of dreadful hearing. Yet I must hear.
25 SHEPHERD If you must be told, then . . .
They said it was Laïos' child;
But it is your wife who can tell you about that.
OEDIPUS My wife!—Did she give it to you?
SHEPHERD My lord, she did.
30 OEDIPUS Do you know why?
SHEPHERD I was told to get rid of it.
OEDIPUS Oh heartless mother!
SHEPHERD But in dread of prophecies . . .
OEDIPUS Tell me.
35 SHEPHERD It was said that the boy would kill his own father.
OEDIPUS Then why did you give him over to this old man?
SHEPHERD I pitied the baby, my king,
And I thought that this man would take him far away
To his own country.
40 He saved him—but for what a fate!
For if you are what this man says you are,
No man living is more wretched than Oedipus.
OEDIPUS Ah God!
It was true!

All the prophecies!
—Now,
O Light, may I look on you for the last time!
I, Oedipus,
5 Oedipus, damned in his birth, in his marriage damned,
Damned in the blood he shed with his own hand!

(*He rushes into the palace.*)

## ODE IV

### Strophe 1

10 CHORUS Alas for the seed of men.
What measure shall I give these generations
That breathe on the void and are void
And exist and do not exist?
Who bears more weight of joy
15 Than mass of sunlight shifting in images,
Or who shall make his thought stay on
That down time drifts away?
Your splendor is all fallen.
O naked brow of wrath and tears,
20 O change of Oedipus!
I who saw your days call no man blest—
Your great days like ghosts gone.

### Antistrophe 1

That mind was a strong bow.
25 Deep, how deep you drew it then, hard archer,
At a dim fearful range,
And brought dear glory down!
You overcame the stranger[1]—
The virgin with her hooking lion claws—
30 And though death sang, stood like a tower
To make pale Thebes take heart.
Fortress against our sorrow!
True king, giver of laws,
Majestic Oedipus!
35 No prince in Thebes had ever such renown,
No prince won such grace of power.

---

[1] *stranger* the Sphinx

**Strophe 2**

And now of all men ever known
Most pitiful is this man's story:
His fortunes are most changed, his state
5 Fallen to a low slave's
Ground under bitter fate.
O Oedipus, most royal one!
The great door[1] that expelled you to the light
Gave at night—ah, gave night to your glory:
10 As to the father, to the fathering son.
All understood too late.
How could that queen whom Laïos won,
The garden that he harrowed at his height,
Be silent when that act was done?

15 **Antistrophe 2**

But all eyes fail before time's eye,
All actions come to justice there.
Though never willed, though far down the deep past,
Your bed, your dread sirings,
20 Are brought to book at last.
Child by Laïos doomed to die,
Then doomed to lose that fortunate little death,
Would God you never took breath in this air
That with my wailing lips I take to cry:
25 For I weep the world's outcast.
I was blind, and now I can tell why:
Asleep, for you had given ease of breath
To Thebes, while the false years went by.

EXODOS [2]

30 (*Enter, from the palace,* SECOND MESSENGER.)

SECOND MESSENGER Elders of Thebes, most honored in this land,
What horrors are yours to see and hear, what weight
Of sorrow to be endured, if, true to your birth,
You venerate the line of Labdakos!
35 I think neither Istros nor Phasis, those great rivers,
Could purify this place of all the evil

---

[1] *door* Iokastê's womb
[2] *Exodos* final scene

It shelters now, or soon must bring to light—
Evil not done unconsciously, but willed.

The greatest griefs are those we cause ourselves.
CHORAGOS Surely, friend, we have grief enough already;
5 What new sorrow do you mean?
SECOND MESSENGER The queen is dead.
CHORAGOS O miserable queen! But at whose hand?
SECOND MESSENGER Her own.
The full horror of what happened you can not know,
10 For you did not see it; but I, who did, will tell you
As clearly as I can how she met her death.

When she had left us,
In passionate silence, passing through the court,
She ran to her apartment in the house,
15 Her hair clutched by the fingers of both hands.
She closed the doors behind her; then, by that bed
Where long ago the fatal son was conceived—
That son who should bring about his father's death—
We heard her call upon Laïos, dead so many years,
20 And heard her wail for the double fruit of her marriage,
A husband by her husband, children by her child.

Exactly how she died I do not know:
For Oedipus burst in moaning and would not let us
Keep vigil to the end: it was by him
25 As he stormed about the room that our eyes were caught.
From one to another of us he went, begging a sword,
Hunting the wife who was not his wife, the mother
Whose womb had carried his own children and himself.
I do not know: it was none of us aided him,
30 But surely one of the gods was in control!
For with a dreadful cry
He hurled his weight, as though wrenched out of himself,
At the twin doors: the bolts gave, and he rushed in.
And there we saw her hanging, her body swaying
35 From the cruel cord she had noosed about her neck.
A great sob broke from him, heartbreaking to hear,
As he loosed the rope and lowered her to the ground.

I would blot out from my mind what happened next!
For the king ripped from her gown the golden brooches
40 That were her ornament, and raised them, and plunged
them down

Straight into his own eyeballs, crying, "No more,
No more shall you look on the misery about me,
The horrors of my own doing! Too long you have known
The faces of those whom I should never have seen,
5 Too long been blind to those for whom I was searching!
From this hour, go in darkness!" And as he spoke,
He struck at his eyes—not once, but many times;
And the blood spattered his beard,
Bursting from his ruined sockets like red hail.

10 So from the unhappiness of two this evil has sprung,
A curse on the man and woman alike. The old
Happiness of the house of Labdakos
Was happiness enough: where is it today?
It is all wailing and ruin, disgrace, death—all
15 The misery of mankind that has a name—
And it is wholly and for ever theirs.

CHORAGOS Is he in agony still? Is there no rest for him?

SECOND MESSENGER He is calling for someone to open the doors wide
20 So that all the children of Kadmos may look upon
His father's murderer, his mother's—no,
I can not say it!
And then he will leave Thebes,
Self-exiled, in order that the curse
25 Which he himself pronounced may depart from the house.
He is weak, and there is none to lead him,
So terrible is his suffering.
But you will see:
Look, the doors are opening; in a moment
30 You will see a thing that would crush a heart of stone.

(*The central door is opened;* OEDIPUS, *blinded, is led in.*)

CHORAGOS Dreadful indeed for men to see.
Never have my own eyes
Looked on a sight so full of fear.

35 Oedipus!
What madness came upon you, what daemon
Leaped on your life with heavier
Punishment than a mortal man can bear?
No: I can not even
40 Look at you, poor ruined one.
And I would speak, question, ponder,

If I were able. No.
You make me shudder.
OEDIPUS God. God.
Is there a sorrow greater?
5 Where shall I find harbor in this world?
My voice is hurled far on a dark wind.
What has God done to me?
CHORAGOS Too terrible to think of, or to see.

**Strophe 1**

10 OEDIPUS O cloud of night,
Never to be turned away: night coming on,
I can not tell how: night like a shroud!
My fair winds brought me here.
O God. Again
15 The pain of the spikes where I had sight,
The flooding pain
Of memory, never to be gouged out.
CHORAGOS This is not strange.
You suffer it all twice over, remorse in pain,
20 Pain in remorse.

**Antistrophe 1**

OEDIPUS Ah dear friend
Are you faithful even yet, you alone?
Are you still standing near me, will you stay here,
25 Patient, to care for the blind?
The blind man!
Yet even blind I know who it is attends me,
By the voice's tone—
Though my new darkness hide the comforter.
30 CHORAGOS Oh fearful act!
What god was it drove you to rake black
Night across your eyes?

**Strophe 2**

OEDIPUS Apollo. Apollo. Dear
35 Children, the god was Apollo.
He brought my sick, sick fate upon me.
But the blinding hand was my own!
How could I bear to see
When all my sight was horror everywhere?
40 CHORAGOS Everywhere; that is true.

OEDIPUS And now what is left?
Images? Love? A greeting even,
Sweet to the senses? Is there anything?
Ah, no, friends: lead me away.
5 Lead me away from Thebes.
Lead the great wreck
And hell of Oedipus, whom the gods hate.
CHORAGOS Your misery, you are not blind to that.
Would God you had never found it out!

10 **Antistrophe 2**

OEDIPUS Death take the man who unbound
My feet on that hillside
And delivered me from death to life! What life?
If only I had died,
15 This weight of monstrous doom
Could not have dragged me and my darlings down.
CHORAGOS I would have wished the same.
OEDIPUS Oh never to have come here
With my father's blood upon me! Never
20 To have been the man they call his mother's husband!
Oh accurst! Oh child of evil,
To have entered that wretched bed—
the selfsame one!
More primal than sin itself, this fell to me.
25 CHORAGOS I do not know what words to offer you.
You were better dead than alive and blind.

OEDIPUS Do not counsel me any more. This punishment
That I have laid upon myself is just.
If I had eyes,
30 I do not know how I could bear the sight
Of my father, when I came to the house of Death,
Or my mother: for I have sinned against them both
So vilely that I could not make my peace
By strangling my own life.
35 Or do you think my children,
Born as they were born, would be sweet to my eyes?
Ah never, never! Nor this town with its high walls,
Nor the holy images of the gods.
For I,
40 Thrice miserable!—Oedipus, noblest of all the line
Of Kadmos, have condemned myself to enjoy

These things no more, by my own malediction
Expelling that man whom the gods declared
To be a defilement in the house of Laïos.
After exposing the rankness of my own guilt,
5 How could I look men frankly in the eyes?
No, I swear it,
If I could have stifled my hearing at its source,
I would have done it and made all this body
A tight cell of misery, blank to light and sound:
10 So I should have been safe in my dark mind
Beyond external evil.
Ah Kithairon!
Why did you shelter me? When I was cast upon you,
Why did I not die? Then I should never
15 Have shown the world my execrable birth.

Ah Polybos! Corinth, city that I believed
The ancient seat of my ancestors: how fair
I seemed, your child! And all the while this evil
Was cancerous within me!
20 For I am sick
In my own being, sick in my origin.

O three roads, dark ravine, woodland and way
Where three roads met: you, drinking my father's blood,
My own blood, spilled by my own hand: can you remember
25 The unspeakable things I did there, and the things
I went on from there to do?
O marriage, marriage!
That act that engendered me, and again the act
Performed by the son in the same bed—
30 Ah, the net
Of incest, mingling fathers, brothers, sons,
With brides, wives, mothers: the last evil
That can be known by men: no tongue can say
How evil!
35 No. For the love of God, conceal me
Somewhere far from Thebes; or kill me; or hurl me
Into the sea, away from men's eyes for ever.

Come, lead me. You need not fear to touch me.
Of all men, I alone can bear this guilt.

40 (*Enter* KREON.)

CHORAGOS Kreon is here now. As to what you ask,
He may decide the course to take. He only
Is left to protect the city in your place.
OEDIPUS Alas, how can I speak to him? What right have I
5 To beg his courtesy whom I have deeply wronged?
KREON I have not come to mock you, Oedipus,
Or to reproach you, either. (*To* ATTENDANTS)
—You, standing there:
If you have lost all respect for man's dignity,
10 At least respect the flame of Lord Helios:
Do not allow this pollution to show itself
Openly here, an affront to the earth
And Heaven's rain and the light of day. No, take him
Into the house as quickly as you can.
15 For it is proper
That only the close kindred see his grief.
OEDIPUS I pray you in God's name, since your courtesy
Ignores my dark expectation, visiting
With mercy this man of all men most execrable:
20 Give me what I ask—for your good, not for mine.
KREON And what is it that you turn to me begging for?
OEDIPUS Drive me out of this country as quickly as may be
To a place where no human voice can ever greet me.
KREON I should have done that before now—only,
25 God's will had not been wholly revealed to me.
OEDIPUS But his command is plain: the parricide
Must be destroyed. I am that evil man.
KREON That is the sense of it, yes; but as things are,
We had best discover clearly what is to be done.
30 OEDIPUS You would learn more about a man like me?
KREON You are ready now to listen to the god.
OEDIPUS I will listen. But it is to you
That I must turn for help. I beg you, hear me.

The woman in there—
35 Give her whatever funeral you think proper:
She is your sister.
—But let me go, Kreon!
Let me purge my father's Thebes of the pollution
Of my living here, and go out to the wild hills,
40 To Kithairon, that has won such fame with me,
The tomb my mother and father appointed for me,
And let me die there, as they willed I should.

And yet I know
Death will not ever come to me through sickness
Or in any natural way: I have been preserved
For some unthinkable fate. But let that be.

5 As for my sons, you need not care for them.
They are men, they will find some way to live.
But my poor daughters, who have shared my table,
Who never before have been parted from their father—
Take care of them, Kreon; do this for me.

10 And will you let me touch them with my hands
A last time, and let us weep together?
Be kind, my lord,
Great prince, be kind!
Could I but touch them,
15 They would be mine again, as when I had my eyes.

(*Enter* ANTIGONÊ *and* ISMENÊ, *attended.*)

Ah, God!
Is it my dearest children I hear weeping?
Has Kreon pitied me and sent my daughters?
20 KREON Yes, Oedipus: I knew that they were dear to you
In the old days, and know you must love them still.
OEDIPUS May God bless you for this—and be a friendlier
Guardian to you than he has been to me!

Children, where are you?
25 Come quickly to my hands: they are your brother's—
Hands that have brought your father's once clear eyes
To this way of seeing—
Ah dearest ones,
I had neither sight nor knowledge then, your father
30 By the woman who was the source of his own life!
And I weep for you—having no strength to see you—,
I weep for you when I think of the bitterness
That men will visit upon you all your lives.
What homes, what festivals can you attend
35 Without being forced to depart again in tears?
And when you come to marriageable age,
Where is the man, my daughters, who would dare
Risk the bane that lies on all my children?
Is there any evil wanting? Your father killed
40 His father; sowed the womb of her who bore him;
Engendered you at the fount of his own existence!

That is what they will say of you.
Then, whom
Can you ever marry? There are no bridegrooms for you,
And your lives must wither away in sterile dreaming.

5 O Kreon, son of Menoikeus!
You are the only father my daughters have,
Since we, their parents, are both of us gone for ever.
They are your own blood: you will not let them
Fall into beggary and loneliness;
10 You will keep them from the miseries that are mine!
Take pity on them; see, they are only children,
Friendless except for you. Promise me this,
Great prince, and give me your hand in token of it.

(KREON *clasps his right hand.*)

15 Children:
I could say much, if you could understand me,
But as it is, I have only this prayer for you:
Live where you can, be as happy as you can—
Happier, please God, than God has made your father.
20 KREON Enough. You have wept enough. Now go within.
OEDIPUS I must; but it is hard.
KREON Time eases all things.
OEDIPUS You know my mind, then?
KREON Say what you desire.
25 OEDIPUS Send me from Thebes!
KREON God grant that I may!
OEDIPUS But since God hates me . . .
KREON No, he will grant your wish.
OEDIPUS You promise?
30 KREON I can not speak beyond my knowledge.
OEDIPUS Then lead me in.
KREON Come now, and leave your children.
OEDIPUS No! Do not take them from me!
KREON Think no longer
35 That you are in command here, but rather think
How, when you were, you served your own destruction.

(*Exeunt into the house all but the* CHORUS; *the* CHORAGOS *chants directly to the audience.*)

CHORAGOS Men of Thebes: look upon Oedipus.

40 This is the king who solved the famous riddle
And towered up, most powerful of men.

No mortal eyes but looked on him with envy,
Yet in the end ruin swept over him.

Let every man in mankind's frailty
Consider his last day; and let none
5 Presume on his good fortune until he find
Life, at his death, a memory without pain.

## QUESTIONS

According to Aristotle, tragedies such as *Oedipus Rex* succeed by arousing pity and fear in their audiences—pity for the suffering the plays' heroes endure, fear that we might sometime face similar agonies. How does *Oedipus Rex* call forth these feelings? In thinking out your answer, you might want to consider the following.

1. What sort of person do you think Oedipus is? What are his strengths and weaknesses? How is he different from the other characters in the play?
2. What sorts of tensions are built up (for Oedipus, for the other characters, and for the audience) by the gradual unfolding of the truth about Laïos' murder and Oedipus' history?
3. How does your knowledge of the story of Oedipus, and hence your knowledge of how the play will end, affect your reaction to such scenes as those with Teiresias and the shepherds?
4. How are the images of sight and blindness used throughout the play?

# SOPHOCLES (496–406 B.C.)

## *Antigonê*

An English version by Dudley Fitts and Robert Fitzgerald

CHARACTERS

ANTIGONÊ
ISMENÊ
EURYDICÊ
KREON
HAIMON
TEIRESIAS
A SENTRY
A MESSENGER
CHORUS

SCENE. *Before the palace of* KREON, *King of Thebes. A central double door, and two lateral doors. A platform extends the length of the façade, and from this platform three steps lead down into the "orchestra," or chorus-ground.*

TIME. *Dawn of the day after the repulse of the Argive army from the assault on Thebes.*

### PROLOGUE

(ANTIGONÊ *and* ISMENÊ *enter from the central door of the palace.*)

ANTIGONÊ Ismenê, dear sister,
You would think that we had already suffered enough
5 For the curse on Oedipus.
I cannot imagine any grief
That you and I have not gone through. And now—
Have they told you of the new decree of our King Kreon?
ISMENÊ I have heard nothing: I know
10 That two sisters lost two brothers, a double death
In a single hour; and I know that the Argive army
Fled in the night; but beyond this, nothing.

ANTIGONÊ I thought so. And that is why I wanted you
To come out here with me. There is something we must do.
ISMENÊ Why do you speak so strangely?
ANTIGONÊ Listen, Ismenê:
5 Kreon buried our brother Eteoclês
With military honors, gave him a soldier's funeral,
And it was right that he should; but Polyneicês,
Who fought as bravely and died as miserably,—
They say that Kreon has sworn
10 No one shall bury him, no one mourn for him,
But his body must lie in the fields, a sweet treasure
For carrion birds to find as they search for food.
That is what they say, and our good Kreon is coming here
To announce it publicly; and the penalty—
15 Stoning to death in the public square!
There it is,
And now you can prove what you are:
A true sister, or a traitor to your family.
ISMENÊ Antigonê, you are mad! What could I possibly do?
20 ANTIGONÊ You must decide whether you will help me or not.
ISMENÊ I do not understand you. Help you in what?
ANTIGONÊ Ismenê, I am going to bury him. Will you come?
ISMENÊ Bury him! You have just said the new law forbids it.
ANTIGONÊ He is my brother. And he is your brother, too.
25 ISMENÊ But think of the danger! Think what Kreon will do!
ANTIGONÊ Kreon is not strong enough to stand in my way.
ISMENÊ Ah sister!
Oedipus died, everyone hating him
For what his own search brought to light, his eyes
30 Ripped out by his own hand; and Iokastê died,
His mother and wife at once: she twisted the cords
That strangled her life; and our two brothers died,
Each killed by the other's sword. And we are left:
But oh, Antigonê,
35 Think how much more terrible than these
Our own death would be if we should go against Kreon
And do what he has forbidden! We are only women,
We cannot fight with men, Antigonê!
The law is strong, we must give in to the law
40 In this thing, and in worse. I beg the Dead
To forgive me, but I am helpless: I must yield
To those in authority. And I think it is dangerous business
To be always meddling.
ANTIGONÊ If that is what you think,
45 I should not want you, even if you asked to come.

You have made your choice, you can be what you want to be.
But I will bury him; and if I must die,
I say that this crime is holy: I shall lie down
With him in death, and I shall be as dear
5 To him as he to me.
It is the dead,
Not the living, who make the longest demands:
We die for ever . . .
You may do as you like,
10 Since apparently the laws of the gods mean nothing to you.

ISMENÊ They mean a great deal to me; but I have no strength
To break laws that were made for the public good.

ANTIGONÊ That must be your excuse, I suppose. But as for me,
I will bury the brother I love.

15 ISMENÊ Antigonê,
I am so afraid for you!

ANTIGONÊ You need not be:
You have yourself to consider, after all.

ISMENÊ But no one must hear of this, you must tell no one!
20 I will keep it a secret, I promise!

ANTIGONÊ O tell it! Tell everyone!
Think how they'll hate you when it all comes out
If they learn that you knew about it all the time!

ISMENÊ So fiery! You should be cold with fear.

25 ANTIGONÊ Perhaps. But I am doing only what I must.

ISMENÊ But can you do it? I say that you cannot.

ANTIGONÊ Very well: when my strength gives out,
I shall do no more.

ISMENÊ Impossible things should not be tried at all.

30 ANTIGONÊ Go away, Ismenê:
I shall be hating you soon, and the dead will too,
For your words are hateful. Leave me my foolish plan:
I am not afraid of the danger; if it means death,
It will not be the worst of deaths—death without honor.

35 ISMENÊ Go then, if you feel that you must.
You are unwise,
But a loyal friend indeed to those who love you.

(*Exit into the palace.* ANTIGONÊ *goes off, left. Enter the* CHORUS.)

## PÁRODOS

40 **Strophe 1**

CHORUS Now the long blade of the sun, lying
Level east to west, touches with glory

Thebes of the Seven Gates. Open, unlidded
Eye of golden day! O marching light
Across the eddy and rush of Dircê's stream,[1]
Striking the white shields of the enemy
5 Thrown headlong backward from the blaze of morning!
CHORAGOS[2] Polyneicês their commander
Roused them with windy phrases,
He the wild eagle screaming
Insults above our land,
10 His wings their shields of snow,
His crest their marshalled helms.

**Antistrophe 1**

CHORUS Against our seven gates in a yawning ring
The famished spears came onward in the night;
15 But before his jaws were sated with our blood,
Or pinefire took the garland of our towers,
He was thrown back; and as he turned, great Thebes—
No tender victim for his noisy power—
Rose like a dragon behind him, shouting war.
20 CHORAGOS For God hates utterly
The bray of bragging tongues;
And when he beheld their smiling,
Their swagger of golden helms,
The frown of his thunder blasted
25 Their first man from our walls.

**Strophe 2**

CHORUS We heard his shout of triumph high in the air
Turn to a scream; far out in a flaming arc
He fell with his windy torch, and the earth struck him.
30 And others storming in fury no less than his
Found shock of death in the dusty joy of battle.
CHORAGOS Seven captains at seven gates
Yielded their clanging arms to the god
That bends the battle-line and breaks it.
35 These two only, brothers in blood,
Face to face in matchless rage,
Mirroring each the other's death,
Clashed in long combat.

---

1 *Dircês stream* a stream to the west of Thebes
2 *Choragos* the leader of the Chorus

**Antistrophe 2**

CHORUS But now in the beautiful morning of victory
Let Thebes of the many chariots sing for joy!
With hearts for dancing we'll take leave of war:
5 Our temples shall be sweet with hymns of praise,
And the long nights shall echo with our chorus.

## SCENE I

CHORAGOS But now at last our new King is coming:
Kreon of Thebes, Menoikeus' son.
10 In this auspicious dawn of his rein
What are the new complexities
That shifting Fate has woven for him?
What is his counsel? Why has he summoned
The old men to hear him?

15 (*Enter* KREON *from the palace, center. He addresses the* CHORUS *from the top step.*)

KREON Gentlemen: I have the honor to inform you that our Ship of State, which recent storms have threatened to destroy, has come safely to harbor at last, guided by the merciful wisdom of Heaven. 20 I have summoned you here this morning because I know that I can depend upon you: your devotion to King Laïos was absolute; you never hesitated in your duty to our late ruler Oedipus; and when Oedipus died, your loyalty was transferred to his children. Unfortunately, as you know, his two sons, the princes Eteoclês 25 and Polyneicês, have killed each other in battle; and I, as the next in blood, have succeeded to the full power of the throne.

I am aware, of course, that no Ruler can expect complete loyalty from his subjects until he has been tested in office. Nevertheless, I say to you at the very outset that I have nothing but 30 contempt for the kind of Governor who is afraid, for whatever reason, to follow the course that he knows is best for the State; and as for the man who sets private friendship above the public welfare,—I have no use for him, either. I call God to witness that if I saw my country headed for ruin, I should not be afraid 35 to speak out plainly; and I need hardly remind you that I would never have any dealings with an enemy of the people. No one values friendship more highly than I; but we must remember that friends made at the risk of wrecking our Ship are not real friends at all.

40 These are my principles, at any rate, and that is why I have made the following decision concerning the sons of Oedipus:

Eteoclês, who died as a man should die, fighting for his country, is to be buried with full military honors, with all the ceremony that is usual when the greatest heroes die; but his brother Polyneicês, who broke his exile to come back with fire and sword against his native city and the shrines of his fathers' gods, whose one idea was to spill the blood of his blood and sell his own people into slavery—Polyneicês, I say, is to have no burial: no man is to touch him or say the least prayer for him; he shall lie on the plain, unburied; and the birds and the scavenging dogs can do with him whatever they like. 10

This is my command, and you can see the wisdom behind it. As long as I am King, no traitor is going to be honored with the loyal man. But whoever shows by word and deed that he is on the side of the State,—he shall have my respect while he is living and my reverence when he is dead. 15

CHORAGOS If that is your will, Kreon son of Menoikeus,
You have the right to enforce it: we are yours.

KREON That is my will. Take care that you do your part.

CHORAGOS We are old men: let the younger ones carry it out.

KREON I do not mean that: the sentries have been appointed. 20

CHORAGOS Then what is it that you would have us do?

KREON You will give no support to whoever breaks this law.

CHORAGOS Only a crazy man is in love with death!

KREON And death it is; yet money talks, and the wisest
Have sometimes been known to count a few coins too many. 25

(*Enter* SENTRY *from left.*)

SENTRY I'll not say that I'm out of breath from running, King, because every time I stopped to think about what I have to tell you, I felt like going back. And all the time a voice kept saying, "You fool, don't you know you're walking straight into trouble?"; and then another voice: "Yes, but if you let somebody else get the news to Kreon first, it will be even worse than that for you!" But good sense won out, at least I hope it was good sense, and here I am with a story that makes no sense at all; but I'll tell it anyhow, because, as they say, what's going to happen's going to happen and— 30 35

KREON Come to the point. What have you to say?

SENTRY I did not do it. I did not see who did it. You must not punish me for what someone else has done.

KREON A comprehensive defense! More effective, perhaps, 40
If I knew its purpose. Come: what is it?

SENTRY A dreadful thing . . . I don't know how to put it—

KREON Out with it!

SENTRY Well, then;
The dead man—
Polyneicês—

(*Pause. The* SENTRY *is overcome, fumbles for words.* KREON *waits impassively.*)

out there—
someone,—
New dust on the slimy flesh!

(*Pause. No sign from* KREON.)

Someone has given it burial that way, and
Gone . . .

(*Long pause.* KREON *finally speaks with deadly control.*)

KREON And the man who dared do this?
SENTRY I swear I
Do not know! You must believe me!
Listen:
The ground was dry, not a sign of digging, no,
Not a wheeltrack in the dust, no trace of anyone.
It was when they relieved us this morning: and one of them,
The corporal, pointed to it.
There it was,
The strangest—
Look:
The body, just mounded over with light dust: you see?
Not buried really, but as if they'd covered it
Just enough for the ghost's peace. And no sign
Of dogs or any wild animal that had been there.

And then what a scene there was! Every man of us
Accusing the other: we all proved the other man did it,
We all had proof that we could not have done it.
We were ready to take hot iron in our hands,
Walk through fire, swear by all the gods,
*It was not I!*
*I do not know who it was, but it was not I!*

(KREON's *rage has been mounting steadily, but the* SENTRY *is too intent upon his story to notice it.*)

And then, when this came to nothing, someone said
A thing that silenced us and made us stare
Down at the ground: you had to be told the news,
And one of us had to do it! We threw the dice,

And the bad luck fell to me. So here I am,
No happier to be here than you are to have me:
Nobody likes the man who brings bad news.

CHORAGOS I have been wondering, King: can it be that the gods
5 have done this?

KREON (*furiously*) Stop!
Must you doddering wrecks
Go out of your heads entirely? "The gods"!
Intolerable!
10 The gods favor this corpse? Why? How had he served them?
Tried to loot their temples, burn their images,
Yes, and the whole State, and its laws with it!
Is it your senile opinion that the gods love to honor bad men?
A pious thought!—
15 No, from the very beginning
There have been those who have whispered together,
Stiff-necked anarchists, putting their heads together,
Scheming against me in alleys. These are the men,
And they have bribed my own guard to do this thing.
20 (*Sententiously.*) Money!
There's nothing in the world so demoralizing as money.
Down go your cities,
Homes gone, men gone, honest hearts corrupted,
Crookedness of all kinds, and all for money!
25 (*To* SENTRY.) But you—!
I swear by God and by the throne of God,
The man who has done this thing shall pay for it!
Find that man, bring him here to me, or your death
Will be the least of your problems: I'll string you up
30 Alive, and there will be certain ways to make you
Discover your employer before you die;
And the process may teach you a lesson you seem to have
missed:
The dearest profit is sometimes all too dear:
35 That depends on the source. Do you understand me?
A fortune won is often misfortune.

SENTRY King, may I speak?

KREON Your very voice distresses me.

SENTRY Are you sure that it is my voice, and not your conscience?

40 KREON By God, he wants to analyze me now!

SENTRY It is not what I say, but what has been done, that hurts
you.

KREON You talk too much.

SENTRY Maybe; but I've done nothing.

45 KREON Sold your soul for some silver: that's all you've done.

SENTRY How dreadful it is when the right judge judges wrong!
KREON Your figures of speech
May entertain you now; but unless you bring me the man,
You will get little profit from them in the end.

5 (*Exit* KREON *into the palace.*)

SENTRY "Bring me the man"—!
I'd like nothing better than bringing him the man!
But bring him or not, you have seen the last of me here.
At any rate, I am safe!

10 (*Exit* SENTRY.)

## ODE I

### Strophe 1

CHORUS Numberless are the world's wonders, but none
More wonderful than man; the stormgray sea
15 Yields to his prows, the huge crests bear him high;
Earth, holy and inexhaustible, is graven
With shining furrows where his plows have gone
Year after year, the timeless labor of stallions.

### Antistrophe 1

20 The lightboned birds and beasts that cling to cover,
The lithe fish lighting their reaches of dim water,
All are taken, tamed in the net of his mind;
The lion on the hill, the wild horse windy-maned,
Resign to him; and his blunt yoke has broken
25 The sultry shoulders of the mountain bull.

### Strophe 2

Words also, and thought as rapid as air,
He fashions to his good use; statecraft is his,
And his the skill that deflects the arrows of snow,
30 The spears of winter rain: from every wind
He has made himself secure—from all but one:
In the late wind of death he cannot stand.

### Antistrophe 2

O clear intelligence, force beyond all measure!
35 O fate of man, working both good and evil!
When the laws are kept, how proudly his city stands!
When the laws are broken, what of his city then?
Never may the anárchic man find rest at my hearth,
Never be it said that my thoughts are his thoughts.

## SCENE II

(*Reenter* SENTRY *leading* ANTIGONÊ.)

CHORAGOS What does this mean? Surely this captive woman
Is the Princess, Antigonê. Why should she be taken?
5 SENTRY Here is the one who did it! We caught her
In the very act of burying him.—Where is Kreon?
CHORAGOS Just coming from the house.

(*Enter* KREON, *center*.)

KREON What has happened?
10 Why have you come back so soon?
SENTRY (*expansively*) O King,
A man should never be too sure of anything:
I would have sworn
That you'd not see me here again: your anger
15 Frightened me so, and the things you threatened me with;
But how could I tell then
That I'd be able to solve the case so soon?
No dice-throwing this time: I was only too glad to come!
Here is this woman. She is the guilty one:
20 We found her trying to bury him.
Take her, then; question her; judge her as you will.
I am through with the whole thing now, and glad of it.
KREON But this is Antigonê! Why have you brought her here?
SENTRY She was burying him, I tell you!
25 KREON (*severely*) Is this the truth?
SENTRY I saw her with my own eyes. Can I say more?
KREON The details: come, tell me quickly!
SENTRY It was like this:
After those terrible threats of yours, King,
30 We went back and brushed the dust away from the body.
The flesh was soft by now, and stinking,
So we sat on a hill to windward and kept guard.
No napping this time! We kept each other awake.
But nothing happened until the white round sun
35 Whirled in the center of the round sky over us:
Then, suddenly,
A storm of dust roared up from the earth, and the sky
Went out, the plain vanished with all its trees
In the stinging dark. We closed our eyes and endured it.
40 The whirlwind lasted a long time, but it passed;
And then we looked, and there was Antigonê!
I have seen
A mother bird come back to a stripped nest, heard

Her crying bitterly a broken note or two
For the young ones stolen. Just so, when this girl
Found the bare corpse, and all her love's work wasted,
She wept, and cried on heaven to damn the hands
5 That had done this thing.
And then she brought more dust
And sprinkled wine three times for her brother's ghost.

We ran and took her at once. She was not afraid,
Not even when we charged her with what she had done.
10 She denied nothing.
And this was a comfort to me,
And some uneasiness: for it is a good thing
To escape from death, but it is no great pleasure
To bring death to a friend.
15 Yet I always say
There is nothing so comfortable as your own safe skin!

KREON (*slowly, dangerously*) And you, Antigonê,
You with your head hanging,—do you confess this thing?

ANTIGONÊ I do. I deny nothing.

20 KREON (*to* SENTRY) You may go.

(*Exit* SENTRY.)

(*To* ANTIGONÊ.) Tell me, tell me briefly:
Had you heard my proclamation touching this matter?

ANTIGONÊ It was public. Could I help hearing it?

25 KREON And yet you dared defy the law.

ANTIGONÊ I dared.
It was not God's proclamation. That final Justice
That rules the world below makes no such laws.

Your edict, King, was strong,
30 But all your strength is weakness itself against
The immortal unrecorded laws of God.
They are not merely now: they were, and shall be,
Operative for ever, beyond man utterly.

I knew I must die, even without your decree:
35 I am only mortal. And if I must die
Now, before it is my time to die,
Surely this is no hardship: can anyone
Living, as I live, with evil all about me,
Think Death less than a friend? This death of mine
40 Is of no importance; but if I had left my brother
Lying in death unburied, I should have suffered.

Now I do not.
You smile at me. Ah Kreon,
Think me a fool, if you like; but it may well be
That a fool convicts me of folly.

5 CHORAGOS Like father, like daughter: both headstrong, deaf to reason!
She has never learned to yield:

KREON She has much to learn.
The inflexible heart breaks first, the toughest iron
10 Cracks first, and the wildest horses bend their necks
At the pull of the smallest curb.
Pride? In a slave?
This girl is guilty of a double insolence,
Breaking the given laws and boasting of it.
15 Who is the man here,
She or I, if this crime goes unpunished?
Sister's child, or more than sister's child,
Or closer yet in blood—she and her sister
Win bitter death for this!
20 (*To* SERVANTS.) Go, some of you,
Arrest Ismenê. I accuse her equally.
Bring her: you will find her sniffling in the house there.

Her mind's a traitor: crimes kept in the dark
Cry for light, and the guardian brain shudders;
25 But how much worse than this
Is brazen boasting of barefaced anarchy!

ANTIGONÊ Kreon, what more do you want than my death?

KREON Nothing.
That gives me everything.

30 ANTIGONÊ Then I beg you: kill me.
This talking is a great weariness: your words
Are distasteful to me, and I am sure that mine
Seem so to you. And yet they should not seem so:
I should have praise and honor for what I have done.
35 All these men here would praise me
Were their lips not frozen shut with fear of you.
(*Bitterly.*) Ah the good fortune of kings,
Licensed to say and do whatever they please!

KREON You are alone here in that opinion.

40 ANTIGONÊ No, they are with me. But they keep their tongues in leash.

KREON Maybe. But you are guilty, and they are not.

ANTIGONÊ There is no guilt in reverence for the dead.

KREON But Eteoclês—was he not your brother too?

ANTIGONÊ My brother too.
KREON And you insult his memory?
ANTIGONÊ (*softly*) The dead man would not say that I insult it.
KREON He would: for you honor a traitor as much as him.
5 ANTIGONÊ His own brother, traitor or not, and equal in blood.
KREON He made war on his country. Eteoclês defended it.
ANTIGONÊ Nevertheless, there are honors due all the dead.
KREON But not the same for the wicked as for the just.
ANTIGONÊ Ah Kreon, Kreon,
10 Which of us can say what the gods hold wicked?
KREON An enemy is an enemy, even dead.
ANTIGONÊ It is my nature to join in love, not hate.
KREON (*finally losing patience*) Go join them then; if you must have your love,
15 Find it in hell!
CHORAGOS But see, Ismenê comes:

(*Enter* ISMENÊ, *guarded.*)

Those tears are sisterly, the cloud
That shadows her eyes rains down gentle sorrow.
20 KREON You too, Ismenê,
Snake in my ordered house, sucking my blood
Stealthily—and all the time I never knew
That these two sisters were aiming at my throne!
Ismenê
25 Do you confess your share in this crime, or deny it?
Answer me.
ISMENÊ Yes, if she will let me say so. I am guilty.
ANTIGONÊ (*coldly*) No, Ismenê. You have no right to say so.
You would not help me, and I will not have you help me.
30 ISMENÊ But now I know what you meant; and I am here
To join you, to take my share of punishment.
ANTIGONÊ The dead man and the gods who rule the dead
Know whose act this was. Words are not friends.
ISMENÊ Do you refuse me, Antigonê? I want to die with you:
35 I too have a duty that I must discharge to the dead.
ANTIGONÊ You shall not lessen my death by sharing it.
ISMENÊ What do I care for life when you are dead?
ANTIGONÊ Ask Kreon. You're always hanging on his opinions.
ISMENÊ You are laughing at me. Why, Antigonê?
40 ANTIGONÊ It's a joyless laughter, Ismenê.
ISMENÊ But can I do nothing?
ANTIGONÊ Yes. Save yourself. I shall not envy you.
There are those who will praise you; I shall have honor, too.
ISMENÊ But we are equally guilty!

ANTIGONÊ No more, Ismenê.
You are alive, but I belong to Death.
KREON (*to the* CHORUS) Gentlemen, I beg you to observe these girls:
5 One has just now lost her mind; the other,
It seems, has never had a mind at all.
ISMENÊ Grief teaches the steadiest minds to waver, King.
KREON Yours certainly did, when you assumed guilt with the guilty!
ISMENÊ But how could I go on living without her?
10 KREON You are.
She is already dead.
ISMENÊ But your own son's bride!
KREON There are places enough for him to push his plow.
I want no wicked women for my sons!
15 ISMENÊ O dearest Haimon, how your father wrongs you!
KREON I've had enough of your childish talk of marriage!
CHORAGOS Do you really intend to steal this girl from your son?
KREON No; Death will do that for me.
CHORAGOS Then she must die?
20 KREON (*ironically*) You dazzle me.
—But enough of this talk!
(*To* GUARDS.) You, there, take them away and guard them well:
For they are but women, and even brave men run
When they see Death coming.

25 (*Exeunt* ISMENÊ, ANTIGONÊ, *and* GUARDS.)

## ODE II

### Strophe 1

CHORUS Fortunate is the man who has never tasted God's vengeance!
30 Where once the anger of heaven has struck, that house is shaken
For ever: damnation rises behind each child
Like a wave cresting out of the black northeast,
When the long darkness under sea roars up
35 And bursts drumming death upon the windwhipped sand.

### Antistrophe 1

I have seen this gathering sorrow from time long past
Loom upon Oedipus' children: generation from generation
Takes the compulsive rage of the enemy god.
40 So lately this last flower of Oedipus' line

Drank the sunlight; but now a passionate word
And a handful of dust have closed up all its beauty.

**Strophe 2**

What mortal arrogance
5 Transcends the wrath of Zeus?
Sleep cannot lull him nor the effortless long months
Of the timeless gods: but he is young for ever,
And his house is the shining day of high Olympos.
All that is and shall be,
10 And all the past, is his.
No pride on earth is free of the curse of heaven.

**Antistrophe 2**

The straying dreams of men
May bring them ghosts of joy:
15 But as they drowse, the waking embers burn them;
Or they walk with fixed eyes, as blind men walk.
But the ancient wisdom speaks for our own time:
*Fate works most for woe*
*With Folly's fairest show.*
20 Man's little pleasure is the spring of sorrow.

## SCENE III

CHORAGOS But here is Haimon, King, the last of all your sons.
Is it grief for Antigonê that brings him here,
And bitterness at being robbed of his bride?

25 (*Enter* HAIMON.)

KREON We shall soon see, and no need of diviners.
—Son,
You have heard my final judgment on that girl:
Have you come here hating me, or have you come
30 With deference and with love, whatever I do?
HAIMON I am your son, father. You are my guide.
You make things clear for me, and I obey you.
No marriage means more to me than your continuing
wisdom.
35 KREON Good. That is the way to behave: subordinate
Everything else, my son, to your father's will.
This is what a man prays for, that he may get
Sons attentive and dutiful in his house,
Each one hating his father's enemies,
40 Honoring his father's friends. But if his sons

Fail him, if they turn out unprofitably,
What has he fathered but trouble for himself
And amusement for the malicious?
So you are right
5 Not to lose your head over this woman.
Your pleasure with her would soon grow cold, Haimon,
And then you'd have a hellcat in bed and elsewhere.
Let her find her husband in Hell!
Of all the people in this city, only she
10 Has had contempt for my law and broken it.

Do you want me to show myself weak before the people?
Or to break my sworn word? No, and I will not.
The woman dies.
I suppose she'll plead "family ties." Well, let her.
15 If I permit my own family to rebel,
How shall I earn the world's obedience?
Show me the man who keeps his house in hand,
He's fit for public authority.
I'll have no dealings
20 With lawbreakers, critics of the government:
Whoever is chosen to govern should be obeyed—
Must be obeyed, in all things, great and small,
Just and unjust! O Haimon,
The man who knows how to obey, and that man only,
25 Knows how to give commands when the time comes.
You can depend on him, no matter how fast
The spears come: he's a good soldier, he'll stick it out.

Anarchy, anarchy! Show me a greater evil!
This is why cities tumble and the great houses rain down,
30 This is what scatters armies!
No, no: good lives are made so by discipline.
We keep the laws then, and the lawmakers,
And no woman shall seduce us. If we must lose,
Let's lose to a man, at least! Is a woman stronger than we?
35 CHORAGOS Unless time has rusted my wits,
What you say, King, is said with point and dignity.
HAIMON (*boyishly earnest*) Father:
Reason is God's crowning gift to man, and you are right
To warn me against losing mine. I cannot say—
40 I hope that I shall never want to say!—that you
Have reasoned badly. Yet there are other men
Who can reason, too; and their opinions might be helpful.
You are not in a position to know everything

That people say or do, or what they feel:
Your temper terrifies—everyone
Will tell you only what you like to hear.
But I, at any rate, can listen; and I have heard them
5 Muttering and whispering in the dark about this girl.
They say no woman has ever, so unreasonably,
Died so shameful a death for a generous act:
"She covered her brother's body. Is this indecent?
She kept him from dogs and vultures. Is this a crime?
10 Death?—She should have all the honor that we can give her!"

This is the way they talk out there in the city.

You must believe me:
Nothing is closer to me than your happiness.
What could be closer? Must not any son
15 Value his father's fortune as his father does his?
I beg you, do not be unchangeable:
Do not believe that you alone can be right.
The man who thinks that,
The man who maintains that only he has the power
20 To reason correctly, the gift to speak, the soul—
A man like that, when you know him, turns out empty.

It is not reason never to yield to reason!

In flood time you can see how some trees bend,
And because they bend, even their twigs are safe,
25 While stubborn trees are torn up, roots and all.
And the same thing happens in sailing:
Make your sheet fast, never slacken,—and over you go,
Head over heels and under: and there's your voyage.
Forget you are angry! Let yourself be moved!
30 I know I am young; but please let me say this:
The ideal condition
Would be, I admit, that men should be right by instinct;
But since we are all too likely to go astray,
The reasonable thing is to learn from those who can teach.
35 CHORAGOS You will do well to listen to him, King,
If what he says is sensible. And you, Haimon,
Must listen to your father.—Both speak well.
KREON You consider it right for a man of my years
and experience
40 To go to school to a boy?

HAIMON It is not right
If I am wrong. But if I am young, and right,
What does my age matter?
KREON You think it right to stand up for an anarchist?
5 HAIMON Not at all. I pay no respect to criminals.
KREON Then she is not a criminal?
HAIMON The City would deny it, to a man.
KREON And the City proposes to teach me how to rule?
HAIMON Ah. Who is it that's talking like a boy now?
10 KREON My voice is the one voice giving orders in this City!
HAIMON It is no City if it takes orders from one voice.
KREON The State is the King!
HAIMON Yes, if the State is a desert.

*Pause.*

15 KREON This boy, it seems, has sold out to a woman.
HAIMON If you are a woman: my concern is only for you.
KREON So? Your "concern"! In a public brawl with your father!
HAIMON How about you, in a public brawl with justice?
20 KREON With justice, when all that I do is within my rights?
HAIMON You have no right to trample on God's right.
KREON (*completely out of control*) Fool, adolescent fool! Taken in by a woman!
HAIMON You'll never see me taken in by anything vile.
25 KREON Every word you say is for her!
HAIMON (*quietly, darkly*) And for you.
And for me. And for the gods under the earth.
KREON You'll never marry her while she lives.
HAIMON Then she must die.—But her death will cause another.
30 KREON Another?
Have you lost your senses? Is this an open threat?
HAIMON There is no threat in speaking to emptiness.
KREON I swear you'll regret this superior tone of yours!
You are the empty one!
35 HAIMON If you were not my father,
I'd say you were perverse.
KREON You girlstruck fool, don't play at words with me!
HAIMON I am sorry. You prefer silence.
KREON Now, by God—!
40 I swear, by all the gods in heaven above us,
You'll watch it, I swear you shall!
(*To the* SERVANTS.) Bring her out!
Bring the woman out! Let her die before his eyes!
Here, this instant, with her bridegroom beside her!

HAIMON Not here, no; she will not die here, King.
And you will never see my face again.
Go on raving as long as you've a friend to endure you.

(*Exit* HAIMON.)

5 CHORAGOS Gone, gone.
Kreon, a young man in a rage is dangerous!
KREON Let him do, or dream to do, more than a man can.
He shall not save these girls from death.
CHORAGOS These girls?
10 You have sentenced them both?
KREON No, you are right.
I will not kill the one whose hands are clean.
CHORAGOS But Antigonê?
KREON (*somberly*) I will carry her far away
15 Out there in the wilderness, and lock her
Living in a vault of stone. She shall have food,
As the custom is, to absolve the State of her death.
And there let her pray to the gods of hell:
They are her only gods:
20 Perhaps they will show her an escape from death,
Or she may learn,
though late,
That piety shown the dead is pity in vain.

(*Exit* KREON.)

25 ODE III

**Strophe**

CHORUS Love, unconquerable
Waster of rich men, keeper
Of warm lights and all-night vigil
30 In the soft face of a girl:
Sea-wanderer, forest-visitor!
Even the pure Immortals cannot escape you,
And mortal man, in his one day's dusk,
Trembles before your glory.

35 **Antistrophe**

Surely you swerve upon ruin
The just man's consenting heart,
As here you have made bright anger
Strike between father and son—

And none has conquered but Love!
A girl's glance working the will of heaven:
Pleasure to her alone who mocks us,
Merciless Aphroditê.[1]

5 SCENE IV

CHORAGOS (*as* ANTIGONÊ *enters guarded*) But I can no longer stand in awe of this,
Nor, seeing what I see, keep back my tears.
Here is Antigonê, passing to that chamber
10 Where all find sleep at last.

**Strophe 1**

ANTIGONÊ Look upon me, friends, and pity me
Turning back at the night's edge to say
Good-by to the sun that shines for me no longer;
15 Now sleepy Death
Summons me down to Acheron,[2] that cold shore:
There is no bridesong there, nor any music.
CHORUS Yet not unpraised, not without a kind of honor,
You walk at last into the underworld;
20 Untouched by sickness, broken by no sword.
What woman has ever found your way to death?

**Antistrophe 1**

ANTIGONÊ How often I have heard the story of Niobê,[3]
25 Tantalos' wretched daughter, how the stone
Clung fast about her, ivy-close: and they say
The rain falls endlessly
And sifting soft snow; her tears are never done.
I feel the loneliness of her death in mine.
30 CHORUS But she was born of heaven, and you
Are woman, woman-born. If her death is yours,
A mortal woman's, is this not for you
Glory in our world and in the world beyond?

---

[1] *Aphroditê* goddess of love
[2] *Acheron* a river in the underworld
[3] *Niobê* Niobê, the daughter of Tantalos, was turned into a stone on Mount Sipylus while bemoaning the destruction of her many children by Leto, the mother of Apollo.

### Strophe 2

ANTIGONÊ You laugh at me. Ah, friends, friends,
Can you not wait until I am dead? O Thebes,
O men many-charioted, in love with Fortune,
5 Dear springs of Dircê, sacred Theban grove,
Be witnesses for me, denied all pity,
Unjustly judged! and think a word of love
For her whose path turns
Under dark earth, where there are no more tears.
10 CHORUS You have passed beyond human daring and come at last
Into a place of stone where Justice sits.
I cannot tell
What shape of your father's guilt appears in this.

### Antistrophe 2

15 ANTIGONÊ You have touched it at last:
that bridal bed
Unspeakable, horror of son and mother mingling:
Their crime, infection of all our family!
O Oedipus, father and brother!
20 Your marriage strikes from the grave to murder mine.
I have been a stranger here in my own land:
All my life
The blasphemy of my birth has followed me.
CHORUS Reverence is a virtue, but strength
25 Lives in established law: that must prevail.
You have made your choice,
Your death is the doing of your conscious hand.

### Epode

ANTIGONÊ Then let me go, since all your words are bitter,
30 And the very light of the sun is cold to me.
Lead me to my vigil, where I must have
Neither love nor lamentation; no song, but silence.

(KREON *interrupts impatiently.*)

KREON If dirges and planned lamentations could put off death,
35 Men would be singing for ever.
(*To the* SERVANTS) Take her, go!
You know your orders: take her to the vault
And leave her alone there. And if she lives or dies,
That's her affair, not ours: our hands are clean.

40 ANTIGONÊ O tomb, vaulted bride-bed in eternal rock,
Soon I shall be with my own again

Where Persephonê[1] welcomes the thin ghosts
underground:
And I shall see my father again, and you, mother,
And dearest Polyneicês—
5 dearest indeed
To me, since it was my hand
That washed him clean and poured the ritual wine:
And my reward is death before my time!

And yet, as men's hearts know, I have done no wrong,
10 I have not sinned before God. Or if I have,
I shall know the truth in death. But if the guilt
Lies upon Kreon who judged me, then, I pray,
May his punishment equal my own.

CHORAGOS O passionate heart,
15 Unyielding, tormented still by the same winds!

KREON Her guards shall have good cause to regret their delaying.

ANTIGONÊ Ah! That voice is like the voice of death!

KREON I can give you no reason to think you are mistaken.

ANTIGONÊ Thebes, and you my fathers' gods,
20 And rulers of Thebes, you see me now, the last
Unhappy daughter of a line of kings,
Your kings, led away to death. You will remember
What things I suffer, and at what men's hands,
Because I would not transgress the laws of heaven.
25 (*To the* GUARDS, *simply.*) Come: let us wait no longer.

(*Exit* ANTIGONÊ, *left, guarded.*)

## ODE IV

### Strophe 1

CHORUS All Danaê's[2] beauty was locked away
30 In a brazen cell where the sunlight could not come:
A small room still as any grave, enclosed her.
Yet she was a princess too,
And Zeus in a rain of gold poured love upon her.
O child, child,
35 No power in wealth or war

---

[1] *Persephonê* queen of the underworld

[2] *Danaê* the mother of Perseus by Zeus, who visited her during her imprisonment in the form of a golden rain

Or tough sea-blackened ships
Can prevail against untiring Destiny!

**Antistrophe 1**

And Dryas' son[1] also, that furious king,
5 Bore the god's prisoning anger for his pride:
Sealed up by Dionysos in deaf stone,
His madness died among echoes.
So at the last he learned what dreadful power
His tongue had mocked:
10 For he had profaned the revels,
And fired the wrath of the nine
Implacable Sisters[2] that love the sound of the flute.

**Strophe 2**

And old men tell a half-remembered tale
15 Of horror where a dark ledge splits the sea
And a double surf beats on the gráy shóres:
How a king's new woman,[3] sick
With hatred for the queen he had imprisoned,
Ripped out his two sons' eyes with her bloody hands
20 While grinning Arês[4] watched the shuttle plunge
Four times: four blind wounds crying for revenge.

**Antistrophe 2**

Crying, tears and blood mingled.—Piteously born,
Those sons whose mother was of heavenly birth!
25 Her father was the god of the North Wind
And she was cradled by gales,
She raced with young colts on the glittering hills
And walked untrammeled in the open light:
But in her marriage deathless Fate found means
30 To build a tomb like yours for all her joy.

## SCENE V

(*Enter blind* TEIRESIAS, *led by a boy. The opening speeches of* TEIRESIAS *should be in singsong contrast to the realistic lines of* KREON.)

TEIRESIAS This is the way the blind man comes, Princes, Princes,
35 Lock-step, two heads lit by the eyes of one.

---

[1] *Dryas' son* Lycurgus, king of Thrace
[2] *Sisters* the Muses
[3] *king's new woman* Eidothea, King Phineus' second wife, blinded her stepsons.
[4] *Arês* god of war

KREON What new thing have you to tell us, old Teiresias?
TEIRESIAS I have much to tell you: listen to the prophet, Kreon.
KREON I am not aware that I have ever failed to listen.
TEIRESIAS Then you have done wisely, King, and ruled well.
5 KREON I admit my debt to you. But what have you to say?
TEIRESIAS This, Kreon: you stand once more on the edge of fate.
KREON What do you mean? Your words are a kind of dread.
TEIRESIAS Listen, Kreon:
I was sitting in my chair of augury, at the place
10 Where the birds gather about me. They were all a-chatter,
As is their habit, when suddenly I heard
A strange note in their jangling, a scream, a
Whirring fury; I knew that they were fighting,
Tearing each other, dying
15 In a whirlwind of wings clashing. And I was afraid.
I began the rites of burnt-offering at the altar,
But Hephaistos[1] failed me: instead of bright flame,
There was only the sputtering slime of the fat thigh-flesh
Melting: the entrails dissolved in gray smoke,
20 The bare bone burst from the welter. And no blaze!

This was a sign from heaven. My boy described it,
Seeing for me as I see for others.

I tell you, Kreon, you yourself have brought
This new calamity upon us. Our hearths and altars
25 Are stained with the corruption of dogs and carrion birds
That glut themselves on the corpse of Oedipus' son.
The gods are deaf when we pray to them, their fire
Recoils from our offering, their birds of omen
Have no cry of comfort, for they are gorged
30 With the thick blood of the dead.
O my son,
These are no trifles! Think: all men make mistakes,
But a good man yields when he knows his course is wrong,
And repairs the evil. The only crime is pride.

35 Give in to the dead man, then: do not fight with a corpse—
What glory is it to kill a man who is dead?
Think, I beg you:

---

[1] *Hephaistos* god of fire

It is for your own good that I speak as I do.
You should be able to yield for your own good.

KREON It seems that prophets have made me their especial province.
5 All my life long
I have been a kind of butt for the dull arrows
Of doddering fortune-tellers!
No, Teiresias:
If your birds—if the great eagles of God himself
10 Should carry him stinking bit by bit to heaven,
I would not yield. I am not afraid of pollution:
No man can defile the gods.
Do what you will,
Go into business, make money, speculate
15 In India gold or that synthetic gold from Sardis,
Get rich otherwise than by my consent to bury him.
Teiresias, it is a sorry thing when a wise man
Sells his wisdom, lets out his words for hire!

TEIRESIAS Ah Kreon! Is there no man left in the world—

20 KREON To do what?—Come, let's have the aphorism!

TEIRESIAS No man who knows that wisdom outweighs any wealth?

KREON As surely as bribes are baser than any baseness.

TEIRESIAS You are sick, Kreon! You are deathly sick!

KREON As you say: it is not my place to challenge a prophet.

25 TEIRESIAS Yet you have said my prophecy is for sale.

KREON The generation of prophets has always loved gold.

TEIRESIAS The generation of kings has always loved brass.

KREON You forget yourself! You are speaking to your King.

TEIRESIAS I know it. You are a king because of me.

30 KREON You have a certain skill; but you have sold out.

TEIRESIAS King, you will drive me to words that—

KREON Say them, say them!
Only remember: I will not pay you for them.

TEIRESIAS No, you will find them too costly,

35 KREON No doubt. Speak:
Whatever you say, you will not change my will.

TEIRESIAS Then take this, and take it to heart!
The time is not far off when you shall pay back
Corpse for corpse, flesh of your own flesh.
40 You have thrust the child of this world into living night,
You have kept from the gods below the child that is theirs:
The one in a grave before her death, the other,
Dead, denied the grave. This is your crime:
And the Furies and the dark gods of Hell
45 Are swift with terrible punishment for you.

Do you want to buy me now, Kreon?

Not many days,
And your house will be full of men and women weeping,
And curses will be hurled at you from far
5 Cities grieving for sons unburied, left to rot
Before the walls of Thebes.

These are my arrows, Kreon: they are all for you.

(*To* BOY.) But come, child: lead me home.
Let him waste his fine anger upon younger men.
10 Maybe he will learn at last
To control a wiser tongue in a better head.

(*Exit* TEIRESIAS.)

CHORAGOS The old man has gone, King, but his words
Remain to plague us. I am old, too,
15 But I cannot remember that he was ever false.
KREON That is true. . . . It troubles me.
Oh it is hard to give in! but it is worse
To risk everything for stubborn pride.
CHORAGOS Kreon: take my advice.
20 KREON What shall I do?
CHORAGOS Go quickly: free Antigonê from her vault
And build a tomb for the body of Polyneicês.
KREON You would have me do this!
CHORAGOS Kreon, yes!
25 And it must be done at once: God moves
Swiftly to cancel the folly of stubborn men.
KREON It is hard to deny the heart! But I
Will do it: I will not fight with destiny.
CHORAGOS You must go yourself, you cannot leave it to others.
30 KREON I will go.
—Bring axes, servants:
Come with me to the tomb. I buried her, I
Will set her free.
Oh quickly!
35 My mind misgives—
The laws of the gods are mighty, and a man must serve them
To the last day of his life!

(*Exit* KREON.)

## PAEAN[1]

### Strophe 1

CHORAGOS God of many names
CHORUS O Iacchos[2]
5 son
of Kadmeian Sémelê[3]
O born of the Thunder!
Guardian of the West
Regent
10 of Eleusis' plain
O Prince of maenad Thebes
and the Dragon Field by rippling Ismenós:[4]

### Antistrophe 1

CHORAGOS God of many names
15 CHORUS the flame of torches
flares on our hills
the nymphs of Iacchos
dance at the spring of Castalia:[5]
from the vine-close mountain
20 come ah come in ivy:
*Evohé evohé!* sings through the streets of Thebes

### Strophe 2

CHORAGOS God of many names
CHORUS Iacchos of Thebes
25 heavenly Child
of Sémelê bride of the Thunderer!
The shadow of plague is upon us:
come
with clement feet
30 oh come from Parnasos
down the long slopes
across the lamenting water

### Antistrophe 2

CHORAGOS Iô Fire! Chorister of the throbbing stars!
35 O purest among the voices of the night!
Thou son of God, blaze for us!

---

[1] *Paean* a hymn of praise
[2] *Iacchos* another name for Dionysos (Bacchus)
[3] *Sémelê* the daughter of Kadmos, the founder of Thebes
[4] *Ismenós* a river east of Thebes. The ancestors of the Theban nobility sprang from dragon's teeth sown by the Ismenós.
[5] *Castalia* a spring on Mount Parnasos

CHORUS Come with choric rapture of circling Maenads[1]
Who cry *Iô Iacche!*
*God of many names!*

## EXODOS

5 (*Enter* MESSENGER *from left.*)

MESSENGER Men of the line of Kadmos, you who live
Near Amphion's citadel,[2]
I cannot say
Of any condition of human life "This is fixed,
10 This is clearly good, or bad." Fate raises up,
And Fate casts down the happy and unhappy alike:
No man can foretell his Fate.
Take the case of Kreon:
Kreon was happy once, as I count happiness:
15 Victorious in battle, sole governor of the land,
Fortunate father of children nobly born.
And now it has all gone from him! Who can say
That a man is still alive when his life's joy fails?
He is a walking dead man. Grant him rich,
20 Let him live like a king in his great house:
If his pleasure is gone, I would not give
So much as the shadow of smoke for all he owns.
CHORAGOS Your words hint at sorrow: what is your news for us?
MESSENGER They are dead. The living are guilty of their death.
25 CHORAGOS Who is guilty? Who is dead? Speak!
MESSENGER Haimon.
Haimon is dead; and the hand that killed him
Is his own hand.
CHORAGOS His father's? or his own?
30 MESSENGER His own, driven mad by the murder his father had done.
CHORAGOS Teiresias, Teiresias, how clearly you saw it all!
MESSENGER This is my news: you must draw what conclusions you can from it.
35 CHORAGOS But look: Eurydicê, our Queen:
Has she overheard us?

(*Enter* EURYDICÊ *from the palace, center.*)

---

[1] *Maenads* the worshippers of Dionysos
[2] *Amphion's citadel* Amphion used the music of his magic lyre to lure stones to form a wall around Thebes.

EURYDICÊ I have heard something, friends:
As I was unlocking the gate of Pallas'[1] shrine,
For I needed her help today, I heard a voice
Telling of some new sorrow. And I fainted
5 There at the temple all my maidens about me.
But speak again: whatever it is, I can bear it:
Grief and I are no strangers.

MESSENGER Dearest Lady,
I will tell you plainly all that I have seen.
10 I shall not try to comfort you: what is the use,
Since comfort could lie only in what is not true?
The truth is always best.
I went with Kreon
To the outer plain where Polyneicês was lying,
15 No friend to pity him, his body shredded by dogs.
We made our prayers in that place to Hecatê
And Pluto,[2] that they would be merciful. And we bathed
The corpse with holy water, and we brought
Fresh-broken branches to burn what was left of it,
20 And upon the urn we heaped up a towering barrow
Of the earth of his own land.
When we were done, we ran
To the vault where Antigonê lay on her couch of stone.
One of the servants had gone ahead,
25 And while he was yet far off he heard a voice
Grieving within the chamber, and he came back
And told Kreon. And as the King went closer,
The air was full of wailing, the words lost,
And he begged us to make all haste. "Am I a prophet?"
30 He said, weeping, "And must I walk this road,
The saddest of all that I have gone before?
My son's voice calls me on. Oh quickly, quickly!
Look through the crevice there, and tell me
If it is Haimon, or some deception of the gods!"

35 We obeyed; and in the cavern's farthest corner
We saw her lying:
She had made a noose of her fine linen veil
And hanged herself. Haimon lay beside her,
His arms about her waist, lamenting her,

---

[1] *Pallas* Pallas Athena, the goddess of wisdom
[2] *Hecatê . . . Pluto* the ruling deities of the underworld

His love lost under ground, crying out
That his father had stolen her away from him.

When Kreon saw him the tears rushed to his eyes
And he called to him: "What have you done, child?
5 Speak to me.
What are you thinking that makes your eyes so strange?
O my son, my son, I come to you on my knees!"
But Haimon spat in his face. He said not a word,
Staring—
10 And suddenly drew his sword
And lunged. Kreon shrank back, the blade missed; and the boy,
Desperate against himself, drove it half its length
Into his own side, and fell. And as he died
15 He gathered Antigonê close in his arms again,
Choking, his blood bright red on her white cheek.
And now he lies dead with the dead, and she is his
At last, his bride in the house of the dead.

(*Exit* EURYDICÊ *into the palace.*)

20 CHORAGOS She has left us without a word. What can this mean?
MESSENGER It troubles me, too; yet she knows what is best,
Her grief is too great for public lamentation,
And doubtless she has gone to her chamber to weep
For her dead son, leading her maidens in his dirge.

25 (*Pause.*)

CHORAGOS It may be so: but I fear this deep silence.
MESSENGER I will see what she is doing. I will go in.

(*Exit* MESSENGER *into the palace. Enter* KREON *with attendants, bearing* HAIMON'S *body.*)

30 CHORAGOS But here is the king himself: oh look at him,
Bearing his own damnation in his arms.
KREON Nothing you say can touch me any more.
My own blind heart has brought me
From darkness to final darkness. Here you see
35 The father murdering, the murdered son—
And all my civic wisdom!

Haimon my son, so young, so young to die,
I was the fool, not you; and you died for me.
CHORAGOS That is the truth; but you were late in learning it.

KREON This truth is hard to bear. Surely a god
Has crushed me beneath the hugest weight of heaven,
And driven me headlong a barbaric way
To trample out the thing I held most dear.

5 The pains that men will take to come to pain!

(*Enter* MESSENGER *from the palace.*)

MESSENGER The burden you carry in your hands is heavy,
But it is not all: you will find more in your house.
KREON What burden worse than this shall I find there?
10 MESSENGER The Queen is dead.
KREON O port of death, deaf world,
Is there no pity for me? And you, Angel of evil,
I was dead, and your words are death again.
Is it true, boy? Can it be true?
15 Is my wife dead? Has death bred death?
MESSENGER You can see for yourself.

(*The doors are opened and the body of* EURYDICÊ *is disclosed within.*)

KREON Oh pity!
All true, all true, and more than I can bear!
20 O my wife, my son!
MESSENGER She stood before the altar, and her heart
Welcomed the knife her own hand guided,
And a great cry burst from her lips for Megareus[1] dead,
And for Haimon dead, her sons; and her last breath
25 Was a curse for their father, the murderer of her sons.
And she fell, and the dark flowed in through her closing eyes.
KREON O God, I am sick with fear.
Are there no swords here? Has no one a blow for me?
MESSENGER Her curse is upon you for the deaths of both.
30 KREON It is right that it should be. I alone am guilty.
I know it, and I say it. Lead me in,
Quickly, friends.
I have neither life nor substance. Lead me in.
CHORAGOS You are right, if there can be right in so much wrong.
35 The briefest way is best in a world of sorrow.
KREON Let it come,
Let death come quickly, and be kind to me.
I would not ever see the sun again.
CHORAGOS All that will come when it will; but we, meanwhile,

---

[1] *Megareus* Megareus, brother of Haimon, had died in the assault on Thebes.

Have much to do. Leave the future to itself.

KREON All my heart was in that prayer!

CHORAGOS Then do not pray any more: the sky is deaf.

KREON Lead me away. I have been rash and foolish.

5 I have killed my son and my wife.

I look for comfort; my comfort lies here dead.

Whatever my hands have touched has come to nothing.

Fate has brought all my pride to a thought of dust.

(*As* KREON *is being led into the house, the* CHORAGOS *advances and*

10 *speaks directly to the audience.*)

CHORAGOS There is no happiness where there is no wisdom;

No wisdom but in submission to the gods.

Big words are always punished,

And proud men in old age learn to be wise.

## QUESTIONS

1. One might argue that in *Antigonê* each of the major characters undergoes his or her own moment of "recognition" and subsequent reversal of fortune. For instance, one can say that the play opens on Antigonê's recognition of Kreon's edict—both because she has just learned of the edict and because she here expresses her realization of how she must react to it and of what retaliation her reaction is likely to draw.
   a. Arguing along these lines, identify the scenes, events, and speeches that mark Kreon's recognition. What reversal would you say follows from it?
   b. Would you also want to argue for recognitions for Haimon, Eurydicê, and Ismenê? If so, where would you place them, and what reversals would you say follow them?
   c. Write an essay that (1) discusses each of these recognitions and their significance to the characters involved, and (2) demonstrates how the placement and cumulative effect of these several recognitions and reversals give the play its shape and dramatic impact. (Remember that you must define the structure and movement of the play as you see it, to ensure that you and your reader are working from the same basic understanding.)
2. How would you balance the claims of "thought" and "character" as the more important element in *Antigonê*? (In other words, is it the questions argued or the character and fate of the debaters that you feel provide the strongest source of the play's appeal?) Would either element alone suffice? Why or why not?
3. Antigonê and Kreon are, of course, the major antagonists in *Antigonê*. But each has another opponent as well. Ismenê argues against Antigonê's actions, and Haimon argues against Kreon. What do the presence and actions of these two characters add to the play?

# 3 *Hamlet and Elizabethan Tragedy*

## Origins of English Drama

English drama can be traced back to two origins, one in tenth-century England and one in ancient Greece. The two beginnings differed greatly in style and content but did have one important thing in common: both formed parts of religious rituals.

## Medieval Drama

Drama in medieval Europe seems to have begun as part of the Easter services. At some appropriate point during the Mass or the matins service, one or two men would unobtrusively position themselves near the altar or near some representation of a tomb. There, they would be approached by three other men, whose heads were covered to look like women and who moved slowly, as if seeking something. Singing in the Latin of the church service, the "angel" at the tomb would question the "women," "Whom seek you in the tomb, O followers of Christ?" The women would then sing the answer of the three Mary's, "Jesus of Nazareth, who was crucified, O heavenly one." The angel then would sing again, "He is not here; he is risen, just as he foretold. Go, announce that he is risen from the tomb."

The dramatization might stop there, or it might continue with the showing of the empty tomb to the women, their song of joy, and the spreading of the good news to the disciples. In either case, the culmination of the drama would mark a return to the service itself with the singing of the Mass's *Ressurexi* ("I have risen") or the matins' final *Te deum, laudamus* ("We praise thee, Lord").

One medieval manuscript in particular emphasizes the closeness of the connection. It describes the singers of the *Te Deum* as rejoicing with the three women at Christ's triumph over death and commands that all the church bells be rung together as soon as the hymn of praise has begun. Drama and service thus celebrate the same event. The joy expressed by the women at the news of the resurrection is the same joy felt by the worshippers in the congregation.

Latin drama continued to develop within the church services. Manuscripts still survive, not only of Easter and Christmas plays but of plays dealing with prophets and saints as well. They show the plays growing longer and more elaborate than the early one just described, but they still emphasize the close ties between the plays and the services at which they are performed. Thus, one Christmas pageant of the shepherds calls for many boys dressed as angels to sit in the roof of the church and sing in loud voices the angels' song, "Glory to God." But it also directs that, at the end of the pageant, the shepherds must return into the choir and there act as choir leaders for the Mass that follows.

By the fourteenth century, however, drama had also moved outside the church. There it was spoken almost wholly in the vernacular, though some bits of Latin, and a good deal of singing, remained. The plays were acted by laymen (including some professional actors) rather than by clerics, and they were developing modes of performance that might encompass up to three days of playing and involve most of the citizens of the towns where they were performed.

These were the Corpus Christi plays, also known as the "cycle plays" or the "mystery plays." Performed in celebration of Corpus Christi day, they comprised a series of pageants beginning with the creation of the world, proceeding through the history of the Old and New Testaments, and ending with the Last Judgment. Each pageant was performed on its own movable stage—its "pageant wagon." Mounted on four or six wheels, two stories high, the wagons provided facilities for some surprisingly complex stage effects and allowed each pageant to be presented several times at several different locations. One after another, the pageants would move through a town, usually stopping at three or four prearranged places to repeat their performances, so that everyone in town might see all of the twenty to fifty plays that made up the cycle.

The presentation of these cycles was undertaken by the towns themselves, with the town authorities ordering the performances. But the individual pageants were produced by the local trade and craft guilds. Ordinarily each guild would present one pageant, but sometimes several small guilds would team up to perform a single pageant or share the cost of a wagon that each could use. It is easy to imagine the competition this could produce, with each guild trying to outdo the next. But the plays were still religious in subject and import. They often spoke directly to the audience and always emphasized how the events they depicted pertained to each viewer's salvation.

## Early English Dramatic Forms

As we suggested in the last chapter, Greek drama carefully labeled and segregated its forms. Tragedy dealt with noble persons and heroic actions. Comedy dealt with everyday affairs.

Medieval drama did not so carefully distinguish its forms. It had one central sacrificial subject: the death of Christ for the salvation of mankind. This sacrifice was always treated seriously; neither Christ nor Mary were ever burlesqued. But the world that Christ entered at his birth was the world of thin clothes and bad weather, of thieves and tricksters and con men, with the Devil himself, the arch-trickster, as Christ's opponent. It was, in short, the world of comedy. A drama that dealt with the history of man's fall and salvation would thus have to be both comic and tragic. There would be no way of separating the two.

Nor would medieval writers have wanted to separate them. Medieval art always seems to have preferred inclusiveness to exclusiveness. The great Gothic cathedrals themselves, with their profusion of sculpture and stained glass, would give their most prominent and most beautiful art to scenes of Christ, the Virgin, and the saints. But less prominent carvings would be likely to show small boys stealing apples, or people quarreling; while, in other places, comically or frighteningly grotesque demons would round out the portrayals.

A Corpus Christi cycle, therefore, would contain both serious and humorous elements. Some plays would be wholly serious; others would mix the serious with the comic. "The Sacrifice of Isaac," for instance, was always serious. The dilemma of the father, the emotions of the son as he realized what was happening, combined to produce plays that could virtually be described as tragedies with happy endings. "Noah's Flood," on the other hand, was usually given a comic treatment. (What would you do if your husband suddenly started building a giant boat in your front yard?) In some of the plays, Noah's wife thinks her husband has gone crazy. In others, she joins in the building until it is time to get on board, then rebels against leaving the world she knows and loves. In either case, a physical fight ensues before Noah can get her on board, and Noah's prophecies of doom are mixed with his complaints about marriage. Crucifixion plays, meanwhile, generally mixed the solemnity of the highest sacrifice with a certain amount of low comedy centering on the executioners. There was no thought of separating the two. Both were parts of the same event.

In this way, seeking to mirror life and to emphasize its mixture of noble and ignoble, sacred and mundane, the medieval drama provided Elizabethan playwrights a heritage of flexible, all-inclusive drama, capable at its best of seeing both sides of a subject at once, always insistent that both must be recognized. By mixing this heritage with the more single-minded Greek tragic tradition, Elizabethan dramatists produced a tragic form of their own as rich and compelling as any that has existed.

In this chapter, we shall study one of the most highly praised and frequently acted Elizabethan tragedies—William Shakespeare's *Hamlet.*

## *Hamlet* and *Oedipus Rex*

In many ways, *Hamlet* is similar to *Oedipus Rex*. Both were written at times when tragedy was just coming to its full maturity in their playwrights' cultures. Both were written by the most influential playwrights of their time. Both helped set the shape of tragedy for their own period's drama and for the drama of future ages.

Both plays have heroes who dominate the action, catching the audience's attention early in the play and holding their attention and their sympathy throughout. (Hamlet, in fact, can even address the audience in soliloquies and "asides" that no one on stage is meant to hear.) Princely in nature and position, both men seem born to rule. The heroes are somewhat alike in their situations, as well. Both must avenge their father's murder and thus remove a pollution from their land. To do so, however, they must first find out who the murderer is; and they must pursue their search among people who want the truth to remain hidden.

Here, however, the situations diverge. Oedipus' companions want to conceal the truth for Oedipus' own sake. Hamlet's opponent, Claudius, wants the truth to remain hidden because he is the murderer. The element of active, willed evil, which is absent from *Oedipus Rex,* is thus present in *Hamlet*. Hamlet must not only destroy his father's murderer; he must do so before the murderer destroys him.

*Hamlet,* as we suggested earlier, is a play derived from both Greek and medieval drama. From Greek tragedy, it has taken the tragic hero—dominant, strong-willed, determined to accomplish his desires. From Greek tragedy also it has taken a certain elevation of tone and insistence on the dignity of human beings. From medieval drama, it has taken the medieval desire for inclusiveness and the medieval love of significant detail. *Hamlet* is much longer than *Oedipus Rex*. It has more characters, a more complex plot, and a generous amount of comedy.

Let us look at each of these elements in turn. Regarding characters, we notice that Oedipus is unique, but that Hamlet sees himself reflected in two other characters: first in Fortinbras, another son of a warrior king whose father has died and whose uncle has seized the throne, leaving him practically powerless; and later in Laertes, another son determined to avenge himself on his father's murderer. The deeds of Laertes and Fortinbras contrast with and comment on the actions of Hamlet himself, thus enriching our view of Hamlet and his dilemma. At the same time, the actions of the three men intertwine to create three of the play's major themes: fathers and sons, honor, and thought versus action.

Regarding plot, we can be sure that the affairs of three families will create a more complex plot than the affairs of one family. Thus critics sometimes speak of the Fortinbras "overplot" (which is mostly concerned with war and kingship) and the Laertes "underplot" (concerned with private family relationships, while discussing how these two "subplots" complement the "main plot" (which deals with Hamlet's familial and princely concerns). But the English inclusiveness goes even beyond this, adding also a love story between Hamlet and Laertes' sister, Ophelia, a study of true versus false friendship in the persons of Horatio and Rosencrantz and Guildenstern, and a few comments on the contemporary theater by a troupe of strolling players. There are also glimpses of three purely comic characters: two gravediggers and one intolerably affected courtier. Again, all these themes and characters are interwoven to illuminate Hamlet's character and dilemma. (The gravediggers, for instance, who seem at first wildly irrelevant, ultimately serve to bring Hamlet to a new understanding of mortality, an understanding that is crucial to his ability to face his own death.)

In *Hamlet* comedy is not separate from tragedy. Rather, it is used as a means to create a fuller awareness of tragedy. Hamlet himself is a master of comic wordplay. His first speech turns on a pun; and puns and bitter quips mark his speech to Claudius and his courtiers throughout the play. Many of these quips are spoken under the guise of pretended madness; and here the audience shares secrets with Hamlet. We know he is not really mad. But those on stage think he is. (The exception is Claudius, who suspects that Hamlet is not mad but who cannot reveal Hamlet's sanity without revealing his own crimes.) Pretending madness, therefore, Hamlet makes speeches that sound like nonsense to the courtiers but that we recognize as referring to his father's murder and his recognition of treachery in those around him. We are thus let into Hamlet's secrets and feelings as no single character in the play is let into them. Hamlet's use of jesting speech thus becomes not merely a weapon in his fight against Claudius, but also a means of winning the sympathetic partnership of the audience. In comic speech and tragic soliloquy alike, Hamlet reveals himself to us. By the play's end, we know Hamlet as we know few other stage characters.

Adding to our sense of knowledge is the fact that Hamlet is a complex and changing character. In this he differs markedly from Oedipus, whose character remains firm and fixed until it changes so drastically in his final scene. The essentially fixed character is typical of Greek drama, which seems to have been more interested in the clash of character against character (or of character against fate) than it was in the changes within or the development of a single character. It is far less typical of Elizabethan tragedy.

This emphasis on Hamlet's developing character is an indication of the influence of medieval Christian drama, with its concern for salvation and the dangers and triumphs of the soul. English drama was secular drama by Shakespeare's time, being performed regularly by professional troupes for paying audiences. Concern for the soul, however, remained one of its major concerns. When Elizabethan dramatists wrote tragedies, therefore, they tended to make the hero's inner concerns—his passions, his temptations, his spiritual triumphs or defeats—the central focus of their plays. Even the ghost in *Hamlet,* coming to call for revenge, warns Hamlet to "taint not thy mind, nor let thy soul contrive/Against thy mother aught." Hamlet must avenge his father and free Denmark from the polluting rule of Claudius; but he must do so in a manner that will imperil neither his own nor his mother's salvation.

When the play opens, Hamlet is a bitter man. So far from being at peace with himself or his surroundings is he that he seems to have little chance of fulfilling the ghost's demands. So close does he come to flinging away his own soul in pursuit of Claudius, in fact, that some critics have refused to believe that Hamlet's speeches in Act III, Scene 3, mean what they say. In fact, they mean exactly what they say. Hamlet in this scene is on the brink of disaster.

In the next scene, the "closet scene," the unexpected happens. Hamlet is caught in the wrong, realizes it, and begins the painful process of returning from his bitterness and hatreds to a reconciliation with himself, his mother, and humanity in general. Throughout the rest of the play, we watch Hamlet's speeches on human nature become gentler, his attitude more compassionate; we hear a new acceptance of his fate, a new trust in providence, revealed. By the play's end, when Hamlet gets his one chance at Claudius, he is fully ready for the task and its consequences. And so the play ends in mingled triumph and loss: a loss to Denmark and to us in the death of Hamlet, a joy that Hamlet has nobly achieved his purpose.

One final word must be said about the language of *Hamlet,* which is like the language of no other play we will read in this book. Seeking some meter in English that would match the beauty and dignity of the meters in which classical tragedy had been written, the sixteenth century dramatists had created **blank verse.** Blank verse does not rhyme. It usually has ten syllables to a line (though lines may be shorter or longer by a few syllables), and the second, fourth, sixth, eighth, and tenth syllables are generally accented more strongly than the rest. This meter was easily spoken. It was dignified and flexible. And it could slip neatly into prose (for comic scenes) or into rhymed couplets to mark a scene's end.

Blank verse was fairly new when Shakespeare began writing. In some of his early plays, it still sounds stiff and awkward. By the time he wrote

*Hamlet,* however, Shakespeare was entering into a mastery of blank verse that no one has ever surpassed. The rhythms and imagery of Hamlet's language warn us of every change in his moods, from pretended madness to honest friendship to bitter passion. By the modulation of Hamlet's language, as well as by his actions, Shakespeare shows us the battle within Hamlet's soul.

If you can see *Hamlet*—live or on film—or if you can hear recordings of it, do so. If not, read as much of it aloud as you can. For readers unfamiliar with Shakespearean language, *Hamlet* is not an easy play to read. Nearly every word of it counts; so every word must be attended to. But the play is well worth the effort it takes, for it is truly one of the finest plays of all time.

## WILLIAM SHAKESPEARE (1564–1616)

# *Hamlet*

CHARACTERS

CLAUDIUS, *King of Denmark*
HAMLET, *son to the late, and nephew to the present, King*
POLONIUS, *Lord Chamberlain*
HORATIO, *friend to Hamlet*
LAERTES, *son to Polonius*
VOLTEMAND
CORNELIUS
ROSENCRANTZ
GUILDENSTERN
OSRIC
A GENTLEMAN } *courtiers*
A PRIEST
MARCELLUS
BERNARDO } *officers*
FRANCISCO, *a soldier*
REYNALDO, *servant to Polonius*
PLAYERS
TWO CLOWNS, *gravediggers*
FORTINBRAS, *Prince of Norway*
A NORWEGIAN CAPTAIN
ENGLISH AMBASSADORS
GERTRUDE, *Queen of Denmark, mother to Hamlet*
OPHELIA, *daughter to Polonius*
GHOST OF HAMLET'S FATHER
LORDS, LADIES, OFFICERS, SOLDIERS, SAILORS, MESSENGERS, ATTENDANTS

## ACT I

### Scene I

*Elsinore Castle: a sentry-post*

(*Enter* BERNARDO *and* FRANCISCO, *two sentinels*)

5 BERNARDO Who's there?
FRANCISCO Nay, answer me. Stand and unfold yourself.
BERNARDO Long live the king!
FRANCISCO Bernardo?
BERNARDO He.
10 FRANCISCO You come most carefully upon your hour.
BERNARDO 'Tis now struck twelve. Get thee to bed, Francisco.
FRANCISCO For this relief much thanks. 'Tis bitter cold,
And I am sick at heart.
BERNARDO Have you had quiet guard?
15 FRANCISCO Not a mouse stirring.
BERNARDO Well, good night.
If you do meet Horatio and Marcellus,
The rivals[1] of my watch, bid them make haste.

(*Enter* HORATIO *and* MARCELLUS)

20 FRANCISCO I think I hear them. Stand, ho! Who is there?
HORATIO Friends to this ground.
MARCELLUS And liegemen to the Dane.[2]
FRANCISCO Give you good night.
MARCELLUS O, farewell, honest soldier.
25 Who hath relieved you?
FRANCISCO Bernardo hath my place.
Give you good night.

(*Exit* FRANCISCO)

MARCELLUS Holla, Bernardo!
30 BERNARDO Say—
What, is Horatio there?
HORATIO A piece of him.
BERNARDO Welcome, Horatio. Welcome, good Marcellus.
HORATIO What, has this thing appeared again to-night?
35 BERNARDO I have seen nothing.
MARCELLUS Horatio says 'tis but our fantasy,
And will not let belief take hold of him

---

[1] *rivals* sharers [2] *Dane* King of Denmark

Touching this dreaded sight twice seen of us.
Therefore I have entreated him along
With us to watch the minutes of this night,
That, if again this apparition come,
5 He may approve[3] our eyes and speak to it.

HORATIO Tush, tush, 'twill not appear.

BERNARDO Sit down awhile,
And let us once again assail your ears,
That are so fortified against our story,
10 What we two nights have seen.

HORATIO Well, sit we down,
And let us hear Bernardo speak of this.

BERNARDO Last night of all,
When yond same star that's westward from the pole[4]
15 Had made his course t' illume that part of heaven
Where now it burns, Marcellus and myself,
The bell then beating one—

(*Enter* GHOST)

MARCELLUS Peace, break thee off. Look where it comes again.

20 BERNARDO In the same figure like the king that's dead.

MARCELLUS Thou art a scholar; speak to it, Horatio.

BERNARDO Looks 'a not like the king? Mark it, Horatio.

HORATIO Most like. It harrows me with fear and wonder.

BERNARDO It would be spoke to.

25 MARCELLUS Speak to it, Horatio.

HORATIO What art thou that usurp'st this time of night
Together with that fair and warlike form
In which the majesty of buried Denmark[5]
Did sometimes[6] march? By heaven I charge thee, speak.

30 MARCELLUS It is offended.

BERNARDO See, it stalks away.

HORATIO Stay. Speak, speak. I charge thee, speak.

(*Exit* GHOST)

MARCELLUS 'Tis gone and will not answer.

35 BERNARDO How now, Horatio? You tremble and look pale.
Is not this something more than fantasy?
What think you on't?

HORATIO Before my God, I might not this believe

---

[3] *approve* confirm [4] *pole* polestar [5] *buried Denmark* the buried King of Denmark [6] *sometimes* formerly

Without the sensible and true avouch
Of mine own eyes.

MARCELLUS Is it not like the king?

HORATIO As thou art to thyself.
5 Such was the very armor he had on
When he th' ambitious Norway[7] combated.
So frowned he once when, in an angry parle,[8]
He smote the sledded Polacks on the ice.
'Tis strange.

10 MARCELLUS Thus twice before, and jump[9] at this dead hour,
With martial stalk hath he gone by our watch.

HORATIO In what particular thought to work I know not;
But, in the gross and scope[10] of my opinion,
This bodes some strange eruption to our state.

15 MARCELLUS Good now, sit down, and tell me he that knows,
Why this same strict and most observant watch
So nightly toils the subject[11] of the land,
And why such daily cast of brazen cannon
And foreign mart[12] for implements of war,
20 Why such impress[13] of shipwrights, whose sore task
Does not divide the Sunday from the week.
What might be toward [14] that this sweaty haste
Doth make the night joint-laborer with the day?
Who is't that can inform me?

25 HORATIO That can I.
At least the whisper goes so. Our last king,
Whose image even but now appeared to us,
Was as you know by Fortinbras of Norway,
Thereto pricked on by a most emulate[15] pride,
30 Dared to the combat; in which our valiant Hamlet
(For so this side of our known world esteemed him)
Did slay this Fortinbras; who, by a sealed compact
Well ratified by law and heraldry,[16]
Did forfeit, with his life, all those his lands
35 Which he stood seized [17] of to the conqueror;
Against the which a moiety competent[18]
Was gagèd [19] by our king, which had returned
To the inheritance of Fortinbras

---

[7] *Norway* King of Norway [8] *parle* parley [9] *jump* just, exactly [10] *gross and scope* gross scope, general view [11] *toils* makes toil; *subject* subjects [12] *mart* trading [13] *impress* conscription [14] *toward* in preparation [15] *emulate* jealously rivalling [16] *law and heraldry* law of heralds regulating combat [17] *seized* possessed [18] *moiety competent* sufficient portion [19] *gagèd* engaged, staked

Had he been vanquisher, as, by the same comart[20]
And carriage[21] of the article designed,
His fell to Hamlet. Now, sir, young Fortinbras,
Of unimprovèd [22] mettle hot and full,
5 Hath in the skirts of Norway here and there
Sharked [23] up a list of lawless resolutes[24]
For food and diet to some enterprise
That hath a stomach[25] in't; which is no other,
As it doth well appear unto our state,
10 But to recover of us by strong hand
And terms compulsatory those foresaid lands
So by his father lost; and this, I take it,
Is the main motive of our preparations,
The source of this our watch, and the chief head [26]
15 Of this posthaste and romage[27] in the land.

BERNARDO I think it be no other but e'en so.
Well may it sort[28] that this portentous figure
Comes armèd through our watch so like the king
That was and is the question of these wars.

20 HORATIO A mote[29] it is to trouble the mind's eye.
In the most high and palmy state of Rome,
A little ere the mightiest Julius fell,
The graves stood tenantless and the sheeted [30] dead
Did squeak and gibber in the Roman streets;
25 As stars with trains of fire and dews of blood,
Disasters[31] in the sun; and the moist star[32]
Upon whose influence Neptune's empire stands
Was sick almost to doomsday with eclipse.
And even the like precurse[33] of feared events,
30 As harbingers[34] preceding still [35] the fates
And prologue to the omen[36] coming on,
Have heaven and earth together demonstrated
Unto our climatures[37] and countrymen.

(*Enter* GHOST)

35 But soft, behold, lo where it comes again!

---

[20] *comart* joint bargain [21] *carriage* purport [22] *unimprovèd* unused [23] *Sharked* snatched indiscriminately as the shark takes prey [24] *resolutes* desperadoes [25] *stomach* show of venturesomeness [26] *head* fountainhead, source [27] *romage* intense activity [28] *sort* suit [29] *mote* speck of dust [30] *sheeted* in shrouds [31] *Disasters* ominous signs [32] *moist star* moon [33] *precurse* foreshadowing [34] *harbingers* forerunners [35] *still* constantly [36] *omen* calamity [37] *climatures* regions

I'll cross it,[38] though it blast me.—Stay, illusion.

(*He spreads his arms*)

If thou hast any sound or use of voice,
Speak to me.
5 If there be any good thing to be done
That may to thee do ease and grace to me,
Speak to me.
If thou art privy to thy country's fate,
Which happily[39] foreknowing may avoid,
10 O, speak!
Or if thou hast uphoarded in thy life
Extorted treasure in the womb of earth,
For which, they say, you spirits oft walk in death,

(*The cock crows*)

15 Speak of it. Stay and speak. Stop it, Marcellus.
MARCELLUS Shall I strike at it with my partisan?[40]
HORATIO Do, if it will not stand.
BERNARDO 'Tis here.
HORATIO 'Tis here.

20 (*Exit* GHOST)

MARCELLUS 'Tis gone.
We do it wrong, being so majestical,
To offer it the show of violence,
For it is as the air invulnerable,
25 And our vain blows malicious mockery.
BERNARDO It was about to speak when the cock crew.
HORATIO And then it started, like a guilty thing
Upon a fearful summons. I have heard
The cock, that is the trumpet to the morn,
30 Doth with his lofty and shrill-sounding throat
Awake the god of day, and at his warning,
Whether in sea or fire, in earth or air,
Th' extravagant[41] and erring[42] spirit hies
To his confine; and of the truth herein
35 This present object made probation.[43]

---

38 *cross it* cross its path 39 *happily* haply, perchance 40 *partisan* pike 41 *extravagant* wandering beyond bounds 42 *erring* wandering 43 *probation* proof

MARCELLUS It faded on the crowing of the cock.
Some say that ever 'gainst[44] that season comes
Wherein our Saviour's birth is celebrated,
This bird of dawning singeth all night long,
5 And then, they say, no spirit dare stir abroad,
The nights are wholesome, then no planets strike,[45]
No fairy takes,[46] nor witch hath power to charm.
So hallowed and so gracious is that time.

HORATIO So have I heard and do in part believe it.
10 But look, the morn in russet mantle clad
Walks o'er the dew of yon high eastward hill.
Break we our watch up, and by my advice
Let us impart what we have seen to-night
Unto young Hamlet, for upon my life
15 This spirit, dumb to us, will speak to him.
Do you consent we shall acquaint him with it,
As needful in our loves, fitting our duty?

MARCELLUS Let's do't, I pray, and I this morning know
Where we shall find him most conveniently.

20 *(Exeunt)*

## Act I, Scene II

*Elsinore Castle: a room of state*

*Flourish. Enter* CLAUDIUS, *King of Denmark,* GERTRUDE *the Queen,* COUNCILLORS, POLONIUS *and his son* LAERTES, HAMLET, *cum aliis*[1] [*including*
25 VOLTEMAND *and* CORNELIUS]

KING Though yet of Hamlet our dear brother's death
The memory be green, and that it us befitted
To bear our hearts in grief, and our whole kingdom
To be contracted in one brow of woe,
30 Yet so far hath discretion fought with nature
That we with wisest sorrow think on him
Together with remembrance of ourselves.
Therefore our sometime sister, now our queen,
Th' imperial jointress[2] to this warlike state,
35 Have we, as 'twere with a defeated joy,
With an auspicious and a dropping eye,

---

[44] *'gainst* just before [45] *strike* work evil by influence [46] *takes* bewitches
[1] *cum aliis* with others [2] *jointress* a woman who has a jointure, or joint tenancy of an estate

With mirth in funeral and with dirge in marriage,
In equal scale weighing delight and dole,
Taken to wife. Nor have we herein barred [3]
Your better wisdoms, which have freely gone
5 With this affair along. For all, our thanks.
Now follows, that you know, young Fortinbras,
Holding a weak supposal of our worth,
Or thinking by our late dear brother's death
Our state to be disjoint and out of frame,
10 Colleaguèd [4] with this dream of his advantage,
He hath not failed to pester us with message
Importing the surrender of those lands
Lost by his father, with all bands of law,
To our most valiant brother. So much for him.
15 Now for ourself and for this time of meeting.
Thus much the business is: we have here writ
To Norway, uncle of young Fortinbras—
Who, impotent and bedrid, scarcely hears
Of this his nephew's purpose—to suppress
20 His further gait[5] herein, in that the levies,
The lists, and full proportions[6] are all made
Out of his subject; and we here dispatch
You, good Cornelius, and you, Voltemand,
For bearers of this greeting to old Norway,
25 Giving to you no further personal power
To business with the king, more than the scope
Of these delated [7] articles allow.
Farewell, and let your haste commend your duty.

CORNELIUS, VOLTEMAND In that, and all things, will we show our
30 duty.

KING We doubt it nothing. Heartily farewell.

(*Exeunt* VOLTEMAND *and* CORNELIUS)

And now, Laertes, what's the news with you?
You told us of some suit. What is't, Laertes?
35 You cannot speak of reason to the Dane[8]
And lose your voice.[9] What wouldst thou beg, Laertes,
That shall not be my offer, not thy asking?
The head is not more native[10] to the heart,

---

[3] *barred* excluded [4] *Colleaguèd* united [5] *gait* going [6] *proportions* amounts of forces and supplies [7] *delated* detailed [8] *Dane* King of Denmark [9] *lose your voice* speak in vain [10] *native* joined by nature

The hand more instrumental [11] to the mouth,
Than is the throne of Denmark to thy father.
What wouldst thou have, Laertes?

LAERTES My dread lord,
5 Your leave and favor to return to France,
From whence though willingly I came to Denmark
To show my duty in your coronation,
Yet now I must confess, that duty done,
My thoughts and wishes bend again toward France
10 And bow them to your gracious leave and pardon.

KING Have you your father's leave? What says Polonius?

POLONIUS He hath, my lord, wrung from me my slow leave
By laborsome petition, and at last
Upon his will I sealed my hard consent.
15 I do beseech you give him leave to go.

KING Take thy fair hour, Laertes. Time be thine,
And thy best graces spend it at thy will.
But now, my cousin[12] Hamlet, and my son—

HAMLET (*aside*) A little more than kin,[13] and less than kind! [14]

20 KING How is it that the clouds still hang on you?

HAMLET Not so, my lord. I am too much in the sun.[15]

QUEEN Good Hamlet, cast thy nighted color off,
And let thine eye look like a friend on Denmark.
Do not for ever with thy vailèd [16] lids
25 Seek for thy noble father in the dust.
Thou know'st 'tis common. All that lives must die,
Passing through nature to eternity.

HAMLET Ay, madam, it is common.

QUEEN If it be,
30 Why seems it so particular with thee?

HAMLET Seems, madam? Nay, it is. I know not "seems."
'Tis not alone my inky cloak, good mother,
Nor customary suits of solemn black,
Nor windy suspiration of forced breath,
35 No, nor the fruitful [17] river in the eye,
Nor the dejected havior of the visage,
Together with all forms, moods, shapes of grief,

---

[11] *instrumental* serviceable [12] *cousin* kinsman more distant than parent, child, brother, or sister [13] *kin* related as nephew [14] *kind* kindly in feeling, as by kind, or nature, a son would be to his father [15] *sun* sunshine of the king's undesired favor (with the punning additional meaning of "place of a son") [16] *vailèd* downcast [17] *fruitful* copious

That can denote me truly. These indeed seem,
For they are actions that a man might play,
But I have that within which passeth show—
These but the trappings and the suits of woe.

5 KING 'Tis sweet and commendable in your nature, Hamlet,
To give these mourning duties to your father,
But you must know your father lost a father,
That father lost, lost his, and the survivor bound
In filial obligation for some term
10 To do obsequious[18] sorrow. But to persever[19]
In obstinate condolement is a course
Of impious stubbornness. 'Tis unmanly grief.
It shows a will most incorrect to heaven,
A heart unfortified, a mind impatient,
15 An understanding simple and unschooled.
For what we know must be and is as common
As any the most vulgar thing to sense,
Why should we in our peevish opposition
Take it to heart? Fie, 'tis a fault to heaven,
20 A fault against the dead, a fault to nature,
To reason most absurd, whose common theme
Is death of fathers, and who still hath cried,
From the first corse till he that died to-day,
"This must be so." We pray you throw to earth
25 This unprevailing woe, and think of us
As a father, for let the world take note
You are the most immediate to our throne,
And with no less nobility of love
Than that which dearest father bears his son
30 Do I impart toward you. For your intent
In going back to school in Wittenberg,
It is most retrograde[20] to our desire,
And we beseech you, bend you to remain
Here in the cheer and comfort of our eye,
35 Our chiefest courtier, cousin, and our son.

QUEEN Let not thy mother lose her prayers, Hamlet.
I pray thee stay with us, go not to Wittenberg.

HAMLET I shall in all my best obey you, madam.

KING Why, 'tis a loving and a fair reply.
40 Be as ourself in Denmark. Madam, come.

---

[18] *obsequious* proper to obsequies or funerals [19] *persever* persevere (accented on the second syllable, as always in Shakespeare) [20] *retrograde* contrary

This gentle and unforced accord of Hamlet
Sits smiling to my heart, in grace whereof
No jocund health that Denmark drinks to-day
But the great cannon to the clouds shall tell,
5 And the king's rouse[21] the heaven shall bruit[22] again,
Respeaking earthly thunder. Come away.

(*Flourish. Exeunt all but* HAMLET)

HAMLET O that this too too sullied flesh would melt,
Thaw, and resolve itself into a dew,
10 Or that the Everlasting had not fixed
His canon[23] gainst self-slaughter. O God, God,
How weary, stale, flat, and unprofitable
Seem to me all the uses of this world!
Fie on't, ah, fie, 'tis an unweeded garden
15 That grows to seed. Things rank and gross in nature
Possess it merely.[24] That it should come to this,
But two months dead, nay, not so much, not two,
So excellent a king, that was to this
Hyperion[25] to a satyr, so loving to my mother
20 That he might not beteem[26] the winds of heaven
Visit her face too roughly. Heaven and earth,
Must I remember? Why, she would hang on him
As if increase of appetite had grown
By what it fed on, and yet within a month—
25 Let me not think on't; frailty, thy name is woman—
A little month, or ere those shoes were old
With which she followed my poor father's body
Like Niobe,[27] all tears, why she, even she—
O God, a beast that wants discourse[28] of reason
30 Would have mourned longer—married with my uncle,
My father's brother, but no more like my father
Than I to Hercules. Within a month,
Ere yet the salt of most unrighteous tears
Had left the flushing in her gallèd [29] eyes,
35 She married. O, most wicked speed, to post
With such dexterity to incestuous sheets!

---

[21] *rouse* toast drunk in wine [22] *bruit* echo [23] *canon* law [24] *merely* completely [25] *Hyperion* the sun god [26] *beteem* allow [27] *Niobe* the proud mother who boasted of having more children than Leto and was punished when they were slain by Apollo and Artemis, children of Leto; the grieving Niobe was changed by Zeus into a stone, which continually dropped tears [28] *discourse* logical power or process [29] *gallèd* irritated

It is not nor it cannot come to good.
But break my heart, for I must hold my tongue.

(*Enter* HORATIO, MARCELLUS, *and* BERNARDO)

HORATIO Hail to your lordship!
5 HAMLET I am glad to see you well.
Horatio—or I do forget myself.
HORATIO The same, my lord, and your poor servant ever.
HAMLET Sir, my good friend, I'll change[30] that name with you.
And what make[31] you from Wittenberg, Horatio?
10 Marcellus?
MARCELLUS My good lord!
HAMLET I am very glad to see you. (*to* BERNARDO) Good even, sir.
But what, in faith, make you from Wittenberg?
HORATIO A truant disposition, good my lord.
15 HAMLET I would not hear your enemy say so,
Nor shall you do my ear that violence
To make it truster of your own report
Against yourself. I know you are no truant.
But what is your affair in Elsinore?
20 We'll teach you to drink deep ere you depart.
HORATIO My lord, I came to see your father's funeral.
HAMLET I prithee do not mock me, fellow student.
I think it was to see my mother's wedding.
HORATIO Indeed, my lord, it followed hard upon.
25 HAMLET Thrift, thrift, Horatio. The funeral baked meats
Did coldly furnish forth the marriage tables.
Would I had met my dearest[32] foe in heaven
Or ever I had seen that day, Horatio!
My father—methinks I see my father.
30 HORATIO Where, my lord?
HAMLET In my mind's eye, Horatio.
HORATIO I saw him once. 'A was a goodly king.
HAMLET 'A was a man, take him for all in all,
I shall not look upon his like again.
35 HORATIO My lord, I think I saw him yesternight.
HAMLET Saw? who?
HORATIO My lord, the king your father.
HAMLET The king my father?
HORATIO Season your admiration[33] for a while

[30] *change* exchange [31] *make* do [32] *dearest* direst, bitterest [33] *Season your admiration* control your wonder

With an attent ear till I may deliver
Upon the witness of these gentlemen
This marvel to you.
HAMLET For God's love let me hear!
5 HORATIO Two nights together had these gentlemen,
Marcellus and Bernardo, on their watch
In the dead waste and middle of the night
Been thus encountered. A figure like your father,
Armèd at point[34] exactly, cap-a-pe,[35]
10 Appears before them and with solemn march
Goes slow and stately by them. Thrice he walked
By their oppressed and fear-surprisèd eyes
Within his truncheon's[36] length, whilst they, distilled
Almost to jelly with the act of fear,
15 Stand dumb and speak not to him. This to me
In dreadful secrecy impart they did,
And I with them the third night kept the watch,
Where, as they had delivered, both in time,
Form of the thing, each word made true and good,
20 The apparition comes. I knew your father.
These hands are not more like.
HAMLET But where was this?
MARCELLUS My lord, upon the platform where we watched.
HAMLET Did you not speak to it?
25 HORATIO My lord, I did,
But answer made it none. Yet once methought
It lifted up it[37] head and did address
Itself to motion like as it would speak.
But even then the morning cock crew loud,
30 And at the sound it shrunk in haste away
And vanished from our sight.
HAMLET 'Tis very strange.
HORATIO As I do live, my honored lord, 'tis true,
And we did think it writ down in our duty
35 To let you know of it.
HAMLET Indeed, indeed, sirs, but this troubles me.
Hold you the watch to-night?
ALL We do, my lord.
HAMLET Armed, say you?
40 ALL Armed, my lord.

---

[34] *at point* completely [35] *cap-a pe* from head to foot [36] *truncheon* military commander's baton [37] *it* its

HAMLET From top to toe?

ALL My lord, from head to foot.

HAMLET Then saw you not his face?

HORATIO O, yes, my lord. He wore his beaver[38] up.

5 HAMLET What, looked he frowningly?

HORATIO A countenance more in sorrow than in anger.

HAMLET Pale or red?

HORATIO Nay, very pale.

HAMLET And fixed his eyes upon you?

10 HORATIO Most constantly.

HAMLET I would I had been there.

HORATIO It would have much amazed you.

HAMLET Very like, very like. Stayed it long?

HORATIO While one with moderate haste might tell [39] a hundred.

15 BOTH Longer, longer.

HORATIO Not when I saw't.

HAMLET His beard was grizzled,[40] no?

HORATIO It was as I have seen it in his life,
A sable silvered.[41]

20 HAMLET I will watch to-night.
Perchance 'twill walk again.

HORATIO I warr'nt it will.

HAMLET If it assume my noble father's person,
I'll speak to it though hell itself should gape
25 And bid me hold my peace. I pray you all,
If you have hitherto concealed this sight,
Let it be tenable[42] in your silence still,
And whatsomever else shall hap to-night,
Give it an understanding but no tongue.
30 I will requite your loves. So fare you well.
Upon the platform, 'twixt eleven and twelve
I'll visit you.

ALL Our duty to your honor.

HAMLET Your loves, as mine to you. Farewell.

35 (*Exeunt all but* HAMLET)

My father's spirit—in arms? All is not well.
I doubt[43] some foul play. Would the night were come!

---

[38] *beaver* visor or movable faceguard of the helmet [39] *tell* count [40] *grizzled* grey [41] *sable silvered* black mixed with white [42] *tenable* held firmly [43] *doubt* suspect, fear

Till then sit still, my soul. Foul deeds will rise,
Though all the earth o'erwhelm them, to men's eyes.

(*Exit*)

## Act I, Scene III

5 *Elsinore Castle: the chambers of* POLONIUS

(*Enter* LAERTES *and* OPHELIA, *his sister*)

LAERTES My necessaries are embarked. Farewell.
And, sister, as the winds give benefit
And convoy[1] is assistant, do not sleep,
10 But let me hear from you.
OPHELIA Do you doubt that?
LAERTES For Hamlet, and the trifling of his favor,
Hold it a fashion and a toy in blood,
A violet in the youth of primy[2] nature,
15 Forward, not permanent, sweet, not lasting,
The perfume and suppliance[3] of a minute,
No more.
OPHELIA No more but so?
LAERTES Think it no more.
20 For nature crescent[4] does not grow alone
In thews and bulk, but as this temple[5] waxes
The inward service of the mind and soul
Grows wide withal. Perhaps he loves you now,
And now no soil nor cautel[6] doth besmirch
25 The virtue of his will,[7] but you must fear,
His greatness weighed,[8] his will is not his own.
(For he himself is subject to his birth.)
He may not, as unvalued persons do,
Carve for himself, for on his choice depends
30 The safety and health of this whole state,
And therefore must his choice be circumscribed
Unto the voice and yielding[9] of that body
Whereof he is the head. Then if he says he loves you,
It fits your wisdom so far to believe it
35 As he in his particular act and place

---

[1] *convoy* means of transport [2] *primy* of the springtime [3] *perfume and suppliance* filling sweetness [4] *crescent* growing [5] *this temple* the body [6] *cautel* deceit [7] *will* desire [8] *greatness weighed* high position considered [9] *yielding* assent

May give his saying deed, which is no further
Than the main voice of Denmark goes withal.
Then weigh what loss your honor may sustain
If with too credent[10] ear you list his songs,
5 Or lose your heart, or your chaste treasure open
To his unmastered importunity.
Fear it, Ophelia, fear it, my dear sister,
And keep you in the rear of your affection,[11]
Out of the shot and danger of desire.
10 The chariest maid is prodigal enough
If she unmask her beauty to the moon.
Virtue itself scapes not calumnious strokes.
The canker[12] galls[13] the infants of the spring
Too oft before their buttons[14] be disclosed,
15 And in the morn and liquid dew of youth
Contagious blastments[15] are most imminent.
Be wary then; best safety lies in fear.
Youth to itself rebels, though none else near.

OPHELIA I shall the effect of this good lesson keep
20 As watchman to my heart, but, good my brother,
Do not as some ungracious pastors do,
Show me the steep and thorny way to heaven,
Whiles like a puffed and reckless libertine
Himself the primrose path of dalliance treads
25 And recks[16] not his own rede.[17]

(*Enter* POLONIUS)

LAERTES O, fear me not.
I stay too long. But here my father comes.
A double blessing is a double grace;
30 Occasion smiles upon a second leave.

POLONIUS Yet here, Laertes? Aboard, aboard, for shame!
The wind sits in the shoulder of your sail,
And you are stayed for. There—my blessing with thee,
And these few precepts in thy memory
35 Look thou character.[18] Give thy thoughts no tongue,
Nor any unproportioned[19] thought his act.

---

[10] *credent* credulous [11] *affection* feelings, which rashly lead forward into dangers [12] *canker* rose worm [13] *galls* injures [14] *buttons* buds [15] *blastments* blights [16] *recks* regards [17] *rede* counsel [18] *character* inscribe [19] *unproportioned* unadjusted to what is right

Be thou familiar, but by no means vulgar.
Those friends thou hast, and their adoption tried,
Grapple them unto thy soul with hoops of steel,
But do not dull thy palm with entertainment
5 Of each new-hatched, unfledged courage.[20] Beware
Of entrance to a quarrel; but being in,
Bear't that th' opposèd may beware of thee.
Give every man thine ear, but few thy voice;
Take each man's censure,[21] but reserve thy judgment.
10 Costly thy habit as thy purse can buy,
But not expressed in fancy; rich, not gaudy,
For the apparel oft proclaims the man,
And they in France of the best rank and station
Are of a most select and generous chief [22] in that.
15 Neither a borrower nor a lender be,
For loan oft loses both itself and friend,
And borrowing dulleth edge of husbandry.[23]
This above all, to thine own self be true,
And it must follow as the night the day
20 Thou canst not then be false to any man.
Farewell. My blessing season[24] this in thee!

LAERTES Most humbly do I take my leave, my lord.

POLONIUS The time invites you. Go, your servants tend.[25]

LAERTES Farewell, Ophelia, and remember well
25 What I have said to you.

OPHELIA 'Tis in my memory locked,
And you yourself shall keep the key of it.

LAERTES Farewell.

(*Exit* LAERTES)

30 POLONIUS What is't, Ophelia, he hath said to you?

OPHELIA So please you, something touching the Lord Hamlet.

POLONIUS Marry,[26] well bethought.
'Tis told me he hath very oft of late
Given private time to you, and you yourself
35 Have of your audience been most free and bounteous.
If it be so—as so 'tis put on me,
And that in way of caution—I must tell you

---

[20] *courage* man of spirit, young blood [21] *censure* judgment [22] *chief* eminence [23] *husbandry* thriftiness [24] *season* ripen and make fruitful [25] *tend* wait [26] *Marry* by Mary

You do not understand yourself so clearly
As it behooves my daughter and your honor.
What is between you? Give me up the truth.

OPHELIA He hath, my lord, of late made many tenders[27]
5 Of his affection to me.

POLONIUS Affection? Pooh! You speak like a green girl,
Unsifted [28] in such perilous circumstance.
Do you believe his tenders, as you call them?

OPHELIA I do not know, my lord, what I should think.

10 POLONIUS Marry, I will teach you. Think yourself a baby
That you have ta'en these tenders[29] for true pay
Which are not sterling. Tender yourself more dearly,
Or (not to crack the wind of [30] the poor phrase,
Running it thus) you'll tender me a fool.

15 OPHELIA My lord, he hath importuned me with love
In honorable fashion.

POLONIUS Ay, fashion you may call it. Go to, go to.[31]

OPHELIA And hath given countenance to his speech, my lord,
With almost all the holy vows of heaven.

20 POLONIUS Ay, springes[32] to catch woodcocks.[33] I do know,
When the blood burns, how prodigal the soul
Lends the tongue vows. These blazes, daughter,
Giving more light than heat, extinct in both
Even in their promise, as it is a-making,
25 You must not take for fire. From this time
Be something scanter of your maiden presence.
Set your entreatments[34] at a higher rate
Than a command to parley.[35] For Lord Hamlet,
Believe so much in him that he is young,
30 And with a larger tether may he walk
Than may be given you. In few, Ophelia,
Do not believe his vows, for they are brokers,[36]
Not of that dye which their investments[37] show,

---

[27] *tenders* offers [28] *Unsifted* untested [29] *tenders . . . Tender . . . tender* offers . . . hold in regard . . . present (a word play going through three meanings, the last use of the word yielding further complexity with its valid implications that she will show herself to him as a fool, will show him to the world as a fool, and may go so far as to present him with a baby, which would be a fool because "fool" was an Elizabethan term of endearment especially applicable to an infant as a "little innocent") [30] *crack . . . of* make wheeze like a horse driven too hard [31] *Go to* go away, go on (expressing impatience) [32] *springes* snares [33] *woodcocks* birds believed foolish [34] *entreatments* military negotiations for surrender [35] *parley* confer with a besieger [36] *brokers* middlemen, panders [37] *investments* clothes

But mere implorators of unholy suits,
Breathing like sanctified and pious bawds,
The better to beguile. This is for all:
I would not, in plain terms, from this time forth
5 Have you so slander[38] any moment[39] leisure
As to give words or talk with the Lord Hamlet.
Look to't, I charge you. Come your ways.

OPHELIA I shall obey, my lord.

(*Exeunt*)

## 10 Act I, Scene IV

*The sentry-post*

(*Enter* HAMLET, HORATIO, *and* MARCELLUS)

HAMLET The air bites shrewdly[1]; it is very cold.
HORATIO It is a nipping and an eager[2] air.
15 HAMLET What hour now?
HORATIO I think it lacks of twelve.
MARCELLUS No, it is struck.
HORATIO Indeed? I heard it not. It then draws near the season
Wherein the spirit held his wont to walk.

20 (*A flourish of trumpets, and two pieces goes off*)

What does this mean, my lord?
HAMLET The king doth wake to-night and takes his rouse,[3]
Keeps wassail, and the swaggering upspring[4] reels,
And as he drains his draughts of Rhenish[5] down
25 The kettledrum and trumpet thus bray out
The triumph[6] of his pledge.
HORATIO Is it a custom?
HAMLET Ay, marry, is't,
But to my mind, though I am native here
30 And to the manner born, it is a custom
More honored in the breach than the observance.[7]
This heavy-headed revel east and west
Makes us traduced and taxed of [8] other nations.
They clepe[9] us drunkards and with swinish phrase

---

[38] *slander* use disgracefully [39] *moment* momentary
[1] *shrewdly* wickedly [2] *eager* sharp [3] *rouse* carousal [4] *upspring* a German dance [5] *Rhenish* Rhine wine [6] *triumph* achievement, feat (in downing a cup of wine at one draught) [7] *More . . . observance* better broken than observed [8] *taxed of* censured by [9] *clepe* call

Soil our addition,[10] and indeed it takes
From our achievements, though performed at height,
The pith and marrow of our attribute.[11]
So oft it chances in particular men
5 That (for some vicious mole[12] of nature in them,
As in their birth, wherein they are not guilty,
Since nature cannot choose his[13] origin)
By the o'ergrowth of some complexion,[14]
Oft breaking down the pales[15] and forts of reason,
10 Or by some habit that too much o'erleavens[16]
The form of plausive[17] manners—that (these men
Carrying, I say, the stamp of one defect,
Being nature's livery,[18] or fortune's star)[19]
Their virtues else, be they as pure as grace,
15 As infinite as man may undergo,
Shall in the general censure take corruption
From that particular fault. The dram of evil
Doth all the noble substance of a doubt,
To his own scandal.

20 (*Enter* GHOST)

HORATIO Look, my lord, it comes.
HAMLET Angels and ministers of grace defend us!
Be thou a spirit of health[20] or goblin[21] damned,
Bring with thee airs from heaven or blasts from hell,
25 Be thy intents wicked or charitable,
Thou com'st in such a questionable shape
That I will speak to thee. I'll call thee Hamlet,
King, father, royal Dane. O, answer me!
Let me not burst in ignorance, but tell
30 Why thy canonized[22] bones, hearsèd in death,
Have burst their cerements,[23] why the sepulchre
Wherein we saw thee quietly interred
Hath oped his ponderous and marble jaws
To cast thee up again. What may this mean

---

[10] *addition* reputation, title added as a distinction [11] *attribute* reputation, what is attributed [12] *mole* blemish, flaw [13] *his* its [14] *complexion* part of the make-up, combination of humors [15] *pales* barriers, fences [16] *o'erleavens* works change throughout, as yeast ferments dough [17] *plausive* pleasing [18] *livery* characteristic equipment or provision [19] *star* make-up as formed by stellar influence [20] *of health* sound, good [21] *goblin* fiend [22] *canonized* buried with the established rites of the Church [23] *cerements* waxed grave-cloths

That thou, dead corse, again in complete steel,
Revisits thus the glimpses of the moon,
Making night hideous, and we fools of nature[24]
So horridly to shake our disposition
5 With thoughts beyond the reaches of our souls?
Say, why is this? wherefore? what should we do?

(GHOST *beckons*)

HORATIO It beckons you to go away with it,
As if it some impartment did desire
10 To you alone.
MARCELLUS Look with what courteous action
It waves you to a more removèd ground.
But do not go with it.
HORATIO No, by no means.
15 HAMLET It will not speak. Then will I follow it.
HORATIO Do not, my lord.
HAMLET Why, what should be the fear?
I do not set my life at a pin's fee,
And for my soul, what can it do to that,
20 Being a thing immortal as itself?
It waves me forth again. I'll follow it.
HORATIO What if it tempt you toward the flood, my lord,
Or to the dreadful summit of the cliff
That beetles[25] o'er his base into the sea,
25 And there assume some other horrible form,
Which might deprive[26] your sovereignty of reason[27]
And draw you into madness? Think of it.
The very place puts toys[28] of desperation,
Without more motive, into every brain
30 That looks so many fathoms to the sea
And hears it roar beneath.
HAMLET It waves me still.
Go on. I'll follow thee.
MARCELLUS You shall not go, my lord.
35 HAMLET Hold off your hands.
HORATIO Be ruled. You shall not go.
HAMLET My fate cries out
And makes each petty artere[29] in this body

---

[24] *fools of nature* men made conscious of natural limitations by a supernatural manifestation [25] *beetles* juts out [26] *deprive* take away [27] *sovereignty of reason* state of being ruled by reason [28] *toys* fancies [29] *artere* artery

As hardy as the Nemean lion's[30] nerve.[31]
Still am I called. Unhand me, gentlemen.
By heaven, I'll make a ghost of him that lets[32] me!
I say, away! Go on. I'll follow thee.

5 (*Exit* GHOST, *and* HAMLET)

HORATIO He waxes desperate with imagination.
MARCELLUS Let's follow. 'Tis not fit thus to obey him.
HORATIO Have after. To what issue will this come?
MARCELLUS Something is rotten in the state of Denmark.
10 HORATIO Heaven will direct it.
MARCELLUS Nay, let's follow him.

(*Exeunt*)

## Act I, Scene V

*Another part of the fortifications*

15 (*Enter* GHOST *and* HAMLET)

HAMLET Whither wilt thou lead me? Speak. I'll go no further.
GHOST Mark me.
HAMLET I will.
GHOST My hour is almost come,
20 When I to sulph'rous and tormenting flames[1]
Must render up myself.
HAMLET Alas, poor ghost!
GHOST Pity me not, but lend thy serious hearing
To what I shall unfold.
25 HAMLET Speak. I am bound to hear.
GHOST So art thou to revenge, when thou shalt hear.
HAMLET What?
GHOST I am thy father's spirit,
Doomed for a certain term to walk the night,
30 And for the day confined to fast[2] in fires,
Till the foul crimes done in my days of nature
Are burnt and purged away. But that I am forbid
To tell the secrets of my prison house,
I could a tale unfold whose lightest word
35 Would harrow up thy soul, freeze thy young blood,

---

[30] *Nemean lion* a lion slain by Hercules in the performance of one of his twelve labors [31] *nerve* sinew [32] *lets* hinders
[1] *flames* sufferings in purgatory (not hell) [2] *fast* do penance

Make thy two eyes like stars start from their spheres,[3]
Thy knotted and combinèd locks to part,
And each particular hair to stand an[4] end
Like quills upon the fretful porpentine.[5]
5 But this eternal blazon[6] must not be
To ears of flesh and blood. List, list, O, list!
If thou didst ever thy dear father love—

HAMLET O God!

GHOST Revenge his foul and most unnatural murder.

10 HAMLET Murder?

GHOST Murder most foul, as in the best it is,
But this most foul, strange, and unnatural.

HAMLET Haste me to know't, that I, with wings as swift
As meditation[7] or the thoughts of love,
15 May sweep to my revenge.

GHOST I find thee apt,
And duller shouldst thou be than the fat weed
That roots itself in ease on Lethe[8] wharf,
Wouldst thou not stir in this. Now, Hamlet, hear.
20 'Tis given out that, sleeping in my orchard,
A serpent stung me. So the whole ear of Denmark
Is by a forgèd process[9] of my death
Rankly abused. But know, thou noble youth,
The serpent that did sting thy father's life
25 Now wears his crown.

HAMLET O my prophetic soul!
My uncle?

GHOST Ay, that incestuous, that adulterate[10] beast,
With witchcraft of his wit, with traitorous gifts—
30 O wicked wit and gifts, that have the power
So to seduce!—won to this shameful lust
The will of my most seeming-virtuous queen.
O Hamlet, what a falling-off was there,
From me, whose love was of that dignity
35 That it went hand in hand even with the vow
I made to her in marriage, and to decline

---

[3] *spheres* transparent revolving shells in each of which, according to the Ptolemaic astronomy, a planet or other heavenly body was placed [4] *an* on [5] *porpentine* porcupine [6] *eternal blazon* revelation of eternity [7] *meditation* thought [8] *Lethe* the river in Hades which brings forgetfulness of past life to a spirit who drinks of it [9] *forgèd process* falsified official report [10] *adulterate* adulterous

Upon a wretch whose natural gifts were poor
To those of mine!
But virtue, as it never will be moved,
Though lewdness court it in a shape of heaven,[11]
5 So lust, though to a radiant angel linked,
Will sate itself in a celestial bed
And prey on garbage.
But soft, methinks I scent the morning air.
Brief let me be. Sleeping within my orchard,
10 My custom always of the afternoon,
Upon my secure[12] hour thy uncle stole
With juice of cursed hebona[13] in a vial,
And in the porches of my ears did pour
The leperous distilment, whose effect
15 Holds such an enmity with blood of man
That swift as quicksilver it courses through
The natural gates and alleys of the body,
And with a sudden vigor it doth posset[14]
And curd, like eager[15] droppings into milk,
20 The thin and wholesome blood. So did it mine,
And a most instant tetter[16] barked [17] about
Most lazar-like[18] with vile and loathsome crust
All my smooth body.
Thus was I sleeping by a brother's hand
25 Of life, of crown, of queen at once dispatched,
Cut off even in the blossoms of my sin,
Unhouseled,[19] disappointed,[20] unaneled,[21]
No reck'ning made, but sent to my account
With all my imperfections on my head.
30 O, horrible! O, horrible! most horrible!
If thou hast nature in thee, bear it not.
Let not the royal bed of Denmark be
A couch for luxury[22] and damnèd incest.
But howsomever thou pursues this act,
35 Taint not thy mind, nor let thy soul contrive
Against thy mother aught. Leave her to heaven
And to those thorns that in her bosom lodge

---

[11] *shape of heaven* angelic disguise [12] *secure* carefree, unsuspecting [13] *hebona* some poisonous plant [14] *posset* curdle [15] *eager* sour [16] *tetter* eruption [17] *barked* covered as with a bark [18] *lazar-like* leper-like [19] *Unhouseled* without the Sacrament [20] *disappointed* unprepared spiritually [21] *unaneled* without extreme unction [22] *luxury* lust

To prick and sting her. Fare thee well at once.
The glowworm shows the matin[23] to be near
And gins to pale his uneffectual fire.
Adieu, adieu, adieu. Remember me.

5 (*Exit*)

HAMLET O all you host of heaven! O earth! What else?
And shall I couple hell? O fie! Hold, hold, my heart,
And you, my sinews, grow not instant old,
But bear me stiffly up. Remember thee?
10 Ay, thou poor ghost, while memory holds a seat
In this distracted globe.[24] Remember thee?
Yea, from the table[25] of my memory
I'll wipe away all trivial fond records,
All saws[26] of books, all forms,[27] all pressures[28] past
15 That youth and observation copied there,
And thy commandment all alone shall live
Within the book and volume of my brain,
Unmixed with baser matter. Yes, by heaven!
O most pernicious woman!
20 O villain, villain, smiling, damnèd villain!
My tables—meet it is I set it down
That one may smile, and smile, and be a villain.
At least I am sure it may be so in Denmark.

(*Writes*)

25 So, uncle, there you are. Now to my word:
It is "Adieu, adieu, remember me."
I have sworn't.

(*Enter* HORATIO *and* MARCELLUS)

HORATIO My lord, my lord!
30 MARCELLUS Lord Hamlet!
HORATIO Heavens secure him!
HAMLET So be it!
MARCELLUS Illo, ho, ho,[29] my lord!
HAMLET Hillo, ho, ho, boy! Come, bird, come.
35 MARCELLUS How is't, my noble lord?
HORATIO What news, my lord?

---

[23] *matin* morning [24] *globe* head [25] *table* writing tablet, record book [26] *saws* wise sayings [27] *forms* mental images, concepts [28] *pressures* impressions [29] *Illo, ho, ho* cry of the falconer to summon his hawk

HAMLET O, wonderful!
HORATIO Good my lord, tell it.
HAMLET No, you will reveal it.
HORATIO Not I, my lord, by heaven.
5 MARCELLUS Nor I, my lord.
HAMLET How say you then? Would heart of man once think it?
But you'll be secret?
BOTH Ay, by heaven, my lord.
HAMLET There's never a villain dwelling in all Denmark
10 But he's an arrant knave.
HORATIO There needs no ghost, my lord, come from the grave
To tell us this.
HAMLET Why, right, you are in the right,
And so, without more circumstance[30] at all,
15 I hold it fit that we shake hands and part:
You, as your business and desires shall point you,
For every man hath business and desire
Such as it is, and for my own poor part,
Look you, I'll go pray.
20 HORATIO These are but wild and whirling words, my lord.
HAMLET I am sorry they offend you, heartily;
Yes, faith, heartily.
HORATIO There's no offense, my lord.
HAMLET Yes, by Saint Patrick, but there is, Horatio,
25 And much offense too. Touching this vision here,
It is an honest[31] ghost, that let me tell you.
For your desire to know what is between us,
O'ermaster't as you may. And now, good friends,
As you are friends, scholars, and soldiers,
30 Give me one poor request.
HORATIO What is't, my lord? We will.
HAMLET Never make known what you have seen to-night.
BOTH My lord, we will not.
HAMLET Nay, but swear't.
35 HORATIO In faith,
My lord, not I.
MARCELLUS Nor I, my lord—in faith.
HAMLET Upon my sword.[32]
MARCELLUS We have sworn, my lord, already.

---

30 *circumstance* ceremony 31 *honest* genuine (not a disguised demon)
32 *sword* i.e. upon the cross formed by the sword hilt

HAMLET Indeed, upon my sword, indeed.

(GHOST *cries under the stage*)

GHOST Swear.

HAMLET Ha, ha, boy, say'st thou so? Art thou there, truepenny? [33]
5 Come on. You hear this fellow in the cellarage.
Consent to swear.

HORATIO Propose the oath, my lord.

HAMLET Never to speak of this that you have seen,
Swear by my sword.

10 GHOST (*beneath*) Swear.

HAMLET Hic et ubique? [34] Then we'll shift our ground.
Come hither, gentlemen,
And lay your hands again upon my sword.
Swear by my sword
15 Never to speak of this that you have heard.

GHOST (*beneath*) Swear by his sword.

HAMLET Well said, old mole! Canst work i' th' earth so fast?
A worthy pioner! [35] Once more remove, good friends.

HORATIO O day and night, but this is wondrous strange!

20 HAMLET And therefore as a stranger give it welcome.
There are more things in heaven and earth, Horatio,
Than are dreamt of in your philosophy.[36]
But come:
Here as before, never, so help you mercy,
25 How strange or odd some'er I bear myself
(As I perchance hereafter shall think meet
To put an antic[37] disposition on),
That you, at such times seeing me, never shall,
With arms encumb'red [38] thus, or this head-shake,
30 Or by pronouncing of some doubtful phrase,
As "Well, well, we know," or "We could, an if [39] we would,"
Or "If we list to speak," or "There be, an if they might,"
Or such ambiguous giving out, to note
That you know aught of me—this do swear,
35 So grace and mercy at your most need help you.

GHOST (*beneath*) Swear.

(*They swear*)

---

[33] *truepenny* honest old fellow [34] *Hic et ubique* here and everywhere [35] *pioner* pioneer, miner [36] *your philosophy* this philosophy one hears about [37] *antic* grotesque, mad [38] *encumb'red* folded [39] *an if* if

HAMLET Rest, rest, perturbèd spirit! So, gentlemen,
With all my love I do commend [40] me to you,
And what so poor a man as Hamlet is
May do t' express his love and friending to you,
5 God willing, shall not lack. Let us go in together,
And still [41] your fingers on your lips, I pray.
The time is out of joint. O cursèd spite
That ever I was born to set it right!
Nay, come, let's go together.

10 (*Exeunt*)

## ACT II

### Scene I

*The chambers of* POLONIUS

(*Enter old* POLONIUS, *with his man* [REYNALDO])

15 POLONIUS Give him this money and these notes, Reynaldo.
REYNALDO I will, my lord.
POLONIUS You shall do marvellous wisely, good Reynaldo,
Before you visit him, to make inquire
Of his behavior.
20 REYNALDO My lord, I did intend it.
POLONIUS Marry, well said, very well said. Look you, sir,
Enquire me first what Danskers[1] are in Paris,
And how, and who, what means,[2] and where they keep,[3]
What company, at what expense; and finding
25 By this encompassment[4] and drift of question
That they do know my son, come you more nearer
Than your particular demands[5] will touch it.
Take you as 'twere some distant knowledge of him,
As thus, "I know his father and his friends,
30 And in part him"—do you mark this, Reynaldo?
REYNALDO Ay, very well, my lord.
POLONIUS "And in part him, but," you may say, "not well,
But if't be he I mean, he's very wild
Addicted so and so." And there put on him
35 What forgeries[6] you please; marry, none so rank

---

40 *commend* entrust 41 *still* always
1 *Danskers* Danes 2 *what means* what their wealth 3 *keep* dwell 4 *encompassment* circling about 5 *particular demands* definite questions 6 *forgeries* invented wrongdoings

As may dishonor him—take heed of that—
But, sir, such wanton, wild, and usual slips
As are companions noted and most known
To youth and liberty.

5 REYNALDO As gaming, my lord.

POLONIUS Ay, or drinking, fencing, swearing, quarrelling,
Drabbing.[7] You may go so far.

REYNALDO My lord, that would dishonor him.

POLONIUS Faith, no, as you may season[8] it in the charge.
10 You must not put another scandal on him,
That he is open to incontinency.[9]
That's not my meaning. But breathe his faults so quaintly[10]
That they may seem the taints of liberty,
The flash and outbreak of a fiery mind,
15 A savageness in unreclaimèd [11] blood,
Of general assault.[12]

REYNALDO But, my good lord—

POLONIUS Wherefore should you do this?

REYNALDO Ay, my lord,
20 I would know that.

POLONIUS Marry, sir, here's my drift,
And I believe it is a fetch of warrant.[13]
You laying these slight sullies on my son
As 'twere a thing a little soiled i' th' working,
25 Mark you,
Your party in converse, him you would sound,
Having ever[14] seen in the prenominate[15] crimes
The youth you breathe of guilty, be assured
He closes with you[16] in this consequence:[17]
30 "Good sir," or so, or "friend," or "gentleman"—
According to the phrase or the addition[18]
Of man and country—

REYNALDO Very good, my lord.

POLONIUS And then, sir, does 'a this—'a does—
35 What was I about to say? By the mass, I was about to say something! Where did I leave?

---

[7] *Drabbing* whoring [8] *season* soften [9] *incontinency* extreme sensuality [10] *quaintly* expertly, gracefully [11] *unreclaimèd* untamed [12] *Of general assault* assailing all young men [13] *fetch of warrant* allowable trick [14] *Having ever* if he has ever [15] *prenominate* aforementioned [16] *closes with you* follows your lead to a conclusion [17] *consequence* following way [18] *addition* title

REYNALDO At "closes in the consequence," at "friend or so," and "gentleman."

POLONIUS At "closes in the consequence"—Ay, marry!
He closes thus: "I know the gentleman;
5 I saw him yesterday, or t' other day,
Or then, or then, with such or such, and, as you say,
There was 'a gaming, there o'ertook[19] in's rouse,[20]
There falling[21] out at tennis"; or perchance,
"I saw him enter such a house of sale,"
10 Videlicet,[22] a brothel, or so forth.
See you now—
Your bait of falsehood takes this carp of truth,
And thus do we of wisdom and of reach,[23]
With windlasses[24] and with assays of bias,[25]
15 By indirections find directions[26] out.
So, by my former lecture and advice,
Shall you my son. You have me, have you not?

REYNALDO My lord, I have.

POLONIUS God bye ye,[27] fare ye well.

20 REYNALDO Good my lord.

POLONIUS Observe his inclination in yourself.

REYNALDO I shall, my lord.

POLONIUS And let him ply his music.

REYNALDO Well, my lord.

25 POLONIUS Farewell.

(*Exit* REYNALDO)

(*Enter* OPHELIA)

How now, Ophelia, what's the matter?

OPHELIA O my lord, my lord, I have been so affrighted!

30 POLONIUS With what, i' th' name of God?

OPHELIA My lord, as I was sewing in my closet,[28]
Lord Hamlet, with his doublet[29] all unbraced,[30]
No hat upon his head, his stockings fouled,
Ungartered, and down-gyvèd [31] to his ankle,
35 Pale as his shirt, his knees knocking each other,

---

[19] *o'ertook* overcome with drunkenness [20] *rouse* carousal [21] *falling out* quarrelling [22] *Videlicet* namely [23] *reach* far-reaching comprehension [24] *windlasses* roundabout courses [25] *assays of bias* devious attacks [26] *directions* ways of procedure [27] *God bye ye* God be with you, good-bye [28] *closet* private living-room [29] *doublet* jacket [30] *unbraced* unlaced [31] *down-gyvèd* fallen down like gyves or fetters on a prisoner's legs

And with a look so piteous in purport
As if he had been loosèd out of hell
To speak of horrors—he comes before me.
POLONIUS Mad for thy love?
5 OPHELIA My lord, I do not know,
But truly I do fear it.
POLONIUS What said he?
OPHELIA He took me by the wrist and held me hard.
Then goes he to the length of all his arm,
10 And with his other hand thus o'er his brow
He falls to such perusal of my face
As 'a would draw it. Long stayed he so.
At last, a little shaking of mine arm
And thrice his head thus waving up and down,
15 He raised a sigh so piteous and profound
As it did seem to shatter all his bulk
And end his being. That done, he lets me go,
And with his head over his shoulder turned
He seemed to find his way without his eyes,
20 For out o' doors he went without their helps
And to the last bended their light on me.
POLONIUS Come, go with me. I will go seek the king.
This is the very ecstasy[32] of love,
Whose violent property[33] fordoes[34] itself
25 And leads the will to desperate undertakings
As oft as any passion under heaven
That does afflict our natures. I am sorry.
What, have you given him any hard words of late?
OPHELIA No, my good lord; but as you did command
30 I did repel his letters and denied
His access to me.
POLONIUS That hath made him mad.
I am sorry that with better heed and judgment
I had not quoted [35] him. I feared he did but trifle
35 And meant to wrack thee; but beshrew[36] my jealousy.
By heaven, it is as proper to our age
To cast beyond ourselves[37] in our opinions
As it is common for the younger sort
To lack discretion. Come, go we to the king.

---

[32] *ecstasy* madness [33] *property* quality [34] *fordoes* destroys [35] *quoted* observed [36] *beshrew* curse [37] *cast beyond ourselves* find by calculation more significance in something than we ought to

This must be known, which, being kept close,[38] might move[39]
More grief to hide than hate to utter love.[40]
Come.

(*Exeunt*)

5 **Act II, Scene II**

*A chamber in the castle*

(*Flourish. Enter* KING *and* QUEEN, ROSENCRANTZ, *and* GUILDENSTERN [*with others*])

KING Welcome, dear Rosencrantz and Guildenstern.
10 Moreover that[1] we much did long to see you,
The need we have to use you did provoke
Our hasty sending. Something have you heard
Of Hamlet's transformation—so call it,
Sith[2] nor th' exterior nor the inward man
15 Resembles that it was. What it should be,
More than his father's death, that thus hath put him
So much from th' understanding of himself,
I cannot dream of. I entreat you both
That, being of so young days brought up with him,
20 And sith so neighbored to his youth and havior,[3]
That you vouchsafe your rest here in our court
Some little time, so by your companies
To draw him on to pleasures, and to gather
So much as from occasion you may glean,
25 Whether aught to us unknown afflicts him thus,
That opened [4] lies within our remedy.
QUEEN Good gentlemen, he hath much talked of you,
And sure I am two men there are not living
To whom he more adheres.[5] If it will please you
30 To show us so much gentry[6] and good will
As to expend your time with us awhile
For the supply and profit of our hope,
Your visitation shall receive such thanks
As fits a king's remembrance.

---

[38] *close* secret [39] *move* cause [40] *to hide . . . love* by such hiding of love than there would be hate moved by a revelation of it (a violently condensed putting of the case which is a triumph of special statement for Polonius) [1] *Moreover that* besides the fact that [2] *Sith* since [3] *youth and havior* youthful ways of life [4] *opened* revealed [5] *more adheres* is more attached [6] *gentry* courtesy

ROSENCRANTZ Both your majesties
Might, by the sovereign power you have of us,
Put your dread pleasures more into command
Than to entreaty.

5 GUILDENSTERN But we both obey,
And here give up ourselves in the full bent[7]
To lay our service freely at your feet,
To be commanded.

KING Thanks, Rosencrantz and gentle Guildenstern.

10 QUEEN Thanks, Guildenstern and gentle Rosencrantz.
And I beseech you instantly to visit
My too much changèd son.—Go, some of you,
And bring these gentlemen where Hamlet is.

GUILDENSTERN Heavens make our presence and our practices
15 Pleasant and helpful to him!

QUEEN Ay, amen!

(*Exeunt* ROSENCRANTZ *and* GUILDENSTERN [*with some* ATTENDANTS])

(*Enter* POLONIUS)

POLONIUS Th' ambassadors from Norway, my good lord,
20 Are joyfully returned.

KING Thou still[8] hast been the father of good news.

POLONIUS Have I, my lord? Assure you, my good liege,
I hold my duty as I hold my soul,
Both to my God and to my gracious king,
25 And I do think—or else this brain of mine
Hunts not the trail of policy so sure
As it hath used to do—that I have found
The very cause of Hamlet's lunacy.

KING O, speak of that! That do I long to hear.

30 POLONIUS Give first admittance to th' ambassadors.
My news shall be the fruit[9] to that great feast.

KING Thyself do grace[10] to them and bring them in.

(*Exit* POLONIUS)

He tells me, my dear Gertrude, he hath found
35 The head and source of all your son's distemper.

QUEEN I doubt[11] it is no other but the main,
His father's death and our o'erhasty marriage.

---

[7] *in the full bent* at the limit of bending (of a bow), to full capacity [8] *still* always [9] *fruit* dessert [10] *grace* honor [11] *doubt* suspect

KING Well, we shall sift him.

(*Enter* AMBASSADORS [VOLTEMAND *and* CORNELIUS, *with* POLONIUS])

Welcome, my good friends.
Say, Voltemand, what from our brother Norway?
5 VOLTEMAND Most fair return of greetings and desires.
Upon our first,[12] he sent out to suppress
His nephew's levies, which to him appeared
To be a preparation 'gainst the Polack,
But better looked into, he truly found
10 It was against your highness, whereat grieved,
That so his sickness, age, and impotence
Was falsely borne in hand,[13] sends out arrests
On Fortinbras; which he in brief obeys,
Receives rebuke from Norway, and in fine[14]
15 Makes vow before his uncle never more
To give th' assay[15] of arms against your majesty.
Whereon old Norway, overcome with joy,
Gives him threescore thousand crowns in annual fee
And his commission to employ those soldiers,
20 So levied as before, against the Polack,
With an entreaty, herein further shown,

(*Gives a paper*)

That it might please you to give quiet pass
Through your dominions for this enterprise,
25 On such regards[16] of safety and allowance
As therein are set down.
KING It likes us well;
And at our more considered time[17] we'll read,
Answer, and think upon this business.
30 Meantime we thank you for your well-took labor.
Go to your rest; at night we'll feast together.
Most welcome home!

(*Exeunt* AMBASSADORS)

POLONIUS This business is well ended.
35 My liege and madam, to expostulate[18]
What majesty should be, what duty is,

[12] *our first* our first words about the matter [13] *borne in hand* deceived [14] *in fine* in the end [15] *assay* trial [16] *regards* terms [17] *considered time* convenient time for consideration [18] *expostulate* discuss

Why day is day, night night, and time is time,
Were nothing but to waste night, day, and time.
Therefore, since brevity is the soul of wit,[19]
And tediousness the limbs and outward flourishes,
5 I will be brief. Your noble son is mad.
Mad call I it, for, to define true madness,
What is't but to be nothing else but mad?
But let that go.

QUEEN More matter, with less art.

10 POLONIUS Madam, I swear I use no art at all.
That he is mad, 'tis true: 'tis true 'tis pity,
And pity 'tis 'tis true—a foolish figure.[20]
But farewell it, for I will use no art.
Mad let us grant him then, and now remains
15 That we find out the cause of this effect—
Or rather say, the cause of this defect,
For this effect defective comes by cause.
Thus it remains, and the remainder thus.
Perpend.[21]
20 I have a daughter (have while she is mine),
Who in her duty and obedience, mark,
Hath given me this. Now gather, and surmise.

(*Reads the letter*)

"To the celestial, and my soul's idol, the most beautified
25 Ophelia,"—
That's an ill phrase, a vile phrase; "beautified" is a vile phrase.
But you shall hear. Thus:

(*Reads*)

"In her excellent white bosom, these, &c."

30 QUEEN Came this from Hamlet to her?

POLONIUS Good madam, stay awhile. I will be faithful.

(*Reads*)

"Doubt thou the stars are fire;
Doubt that the sun doth move;
35 Doubt[22] truth to be a liar;
But never doubt I love.

O dear Ophelia, I am ill at these numbers.[23] I have not art to

---

[19] *wit* understanding [20] *figure* figure in rhetoric [21] *Perpend* ponder
[22] *Doubt* suspect [23] *numbers* verses

reckon my groans, but that I love thee best, O most best, believe it. Adieu.

Thine evermore, most dear lady,
whilst this machine[24] is to[25] him, Hamlet."

5 This in obedience hath my daughter shown me,
And more above[26] hath his solicitings,
As they fell out by time, by means, and place,
All given to mine ear.

KING But how hath she
10 Received his love?

POLONIUS What do you think of me?

KING As of a man faithful and honorable.

POLONIUS I would fain prove so. But what might you think,
When I had seen this hot love on the wing
15 (As I perceived it, I must tell you that,
Before my daughter told me), what might you,
Or my dear majesty your queen here, think,
If I had played the desk or table book,[27]
Or given my heart a winking,[28] mute and dumb,
20 Or looked upon this love with idle sight?
What might you think? No, I went round [29] to work
And my young mistress thus I did bespeak:
"Lord Hamlet is a prince, out of thy star.[30]
This must not be." And then I prescripts[31] gave her,
25 That she should lock herself from his resort,
Admit no messengers, receive no tokens.
Which done, she took the fruits of my advice,
And he, repellèd, a short tale to make,
Fell into a sadness, then into a fast,
30 Thence to a watch,[32] thence into a weakness,
Thence to a lightness,[33] and, by this declension,
Into the madness wherein now he raves,
And all we mourn for.

KING Do you think 'tis this?

35 QUEEN It may be, very like.

POLONIUS Hath there been such a time—I would fain know that—

---

[24] *machine* body [25] *to* attached to [26] *above* besides [27] *desk or table book* i.e. silent receiver [28] *winking* closing of the eyes [29] *round* roundly, plainly [30] *star* condition determined by stellar influence [31] *prescripts* instructions [32] *watch* sleepless state [33] *lightness* lightheadedness

That I have positively said " 'Tis so,"
When it proved otherwise?

KING Not that I know.

POLONIUS (*pointing to his head and shoulder*)
5 Take this from this, if this be otherwise.
If circumstances lead me, I will find
Where truth is hid, though it were hid indeed
Within the center.[34]

KING How may we try it further?

10 POLONIUS You know sometimes he walks four hours together
Here in the lobby.

QUEEN So he does indeed.

POLONIUS At such a time I'll loose my daughter to him.
Be you and I behind an arras[35] then.
15 Mark the encounter. If he love her not,
And be not from his reason fallen thereon,[36]
Let me be no assistant for a state
But keep a farm and carters.

KING We will try it.

20 (*Enter* HAMLET [*reading on a book*])

QUEEN But look where sadly the poor wretch comes reading.

POLONIUS Away, I do beseech you both, away.

(*Exit* KING *and* QUEEN [*with* ATTENDANTS])

I'll board [37] him presently.[38] O, give me leave.
25 How does my good Lord Hamlet?

HAMLET Well, God-a-mercy.[39]

POLONIUS Do you know me, my lord?

HAMLET Excellent well. You are a fishmonger.[40]

POLONIUS Not I, my lord.

30 HAMLET Then I would you were so honest a man.

POLONIUS Honest, my lord?

HAMLET Ay, sir. To be honest, as this world goes, is to be one man picked out of ten thousand.

POLONIUS That's very true, my lord.

---

[34] *center* center of the earth and also of the Ptolemaic universe [35] *arras* hanging tapestry [36] *thereon* on that account [37] *board* accost [38] *presently* at once [39] *God-a-mercy* thank you (literally, "God have mercy!") [40] *fishmonger* seller of harlots, procurer (a cant term used here with a glance at the fishing Polonius is doing when he offers Ophelia as bait)

HAMLET For if the sun breed maggots in a dead dog, being a good kissing carrion[41]—Have you a daughter?

POLONIUS I have, my lord.

HAMLET Let her not walk i' th' sun. Conception is a blessing, but as your daughter may conceive, friend, look to't.

POLONIUS (*aside*) How say you by that? Still harping on my daughter. Yet he knew me not at first. 'A said I was a fishmonger. 'A is far gone, far gone. And truly in my youth I suffered much extremity for love, very near this. I'll speak to him again.—What do you read, my lord?

HAMLET Words, words, words.

POLONIUS What is the matter, my lord?

HAMLET Between who? [42]

POLONIUS I mean the matter that you read, my lord.

HAMLET Slanders, sir, for the satirical rogue says here that old men have grey beards, that their faces are wrinkled, their eyes purging thick amber and plum-tree gum, and that they have a plentiful lack of wit, together with most weak hams. All which, sir, though I most powerfully and potently believe, yet I hold it not honesty to have it thus set down, for you yourself, sir, should be old as I am if, like a crab, you could go backward.

POLONIUS (*aside*) Though this be madness, yet there is method in't. —Will you walk out of the air, my lord?

HAMLET Into my grave?

POLONIUS Indeed, that's out of the air. (*aside*) How pregnant[43] sometimes his replies are! a happiness[44] that often madness hits on, which reason and sanity could not so prosperously be delivered of. I will leave him and suddenly contrive the means of meeting between him and my daughter.—My honorable lord, I will most humbly take my leave of you.

HAMLET You cannot, sir, take from me anything that I will more willingly part withal [45]—except my life, except my life, except my life.

(*Enter* GUILDENSTERN *and* ROSENCRANTZ)

POLONIUS Fare you well, my lord.

HAMLET These tedious old fools!

POLONIUS You go to seek the Lord Hamlet. There he is.

---

[41] *good kissing carrion* good bit of flesh for kissing [42] *Between who* matter for a quarrel between what persons (Hamlet's willful misunderstanding) [43] *pregnant* full of meaning [44] *happiness* aptness of expression [45] *withal* with

ROSENCRANTZ (*to* POLONIUS) God save you, sir!

(*Exit* POLONIUS)

GUILDENSTERN My honored lord!
ROSENCRANTZ My most dear lord!
5 HAMLET My excellent good friends! How dost thou, Guildenstern? Ah, Rosencrantz! Good lads, how do ye both?
ROSENCRANTZ As the indifferent[46] children of the earth.
GUILDENSTERN Happy in that we are not over-happy. On Fortune's cap we are not the very button.
10 HAMLET Nor the soles of her shoe?
ROSENCRANTZ Neither, my lord.
HAMLET Then you live about her waist, or in the middle of her favors?
GUILDENSTERN Faith, her privates[47] we.
15 HAMLET In the secret parts of Fortune? O, most true! she is a strumpet. What news?
ROSENCRANTZ None, my lord, but that the world's grown honest.
HAMLET Then is doomsday near. But your news is not true. (Let me question more in particular.) What have you, my good friends,
20 deserved at the hands of Fortune that she sends you to prison hither?
GUILDENSTERN Prison, my lord?
HAMLET Denmark 's a prison.
ROSENCRANTZ Then is the world one.
25 HAMLET A goodly one; in which there are many confines,[48] wards,[49] and dungeons, Denmark being one o' th' worst.
ROSENCRANTZ We think not so, my lord.
HAMLET Why, then 'tis none to you, for there is nothing either good or bad but thinking makes it so. To me it is a prison.
30 ROSENCRANTZ Why, then your ambition makes it one. 'Tis too narrow for your mind.
HAMLET O God, I could be hounded in a nutshell and count myself a king of infinite space, were it not that I have bad dreams.
GUILDENSTERN Which dreams indeed are ambition, for the very
35 substance of the ambitious is merely the shadow of a dream.
HAMLET A dream itself is but a shadow.
ROSENCRANTZ Truly, and I hold ambition of so airy and light a quality that it is but a shadow's shadow.

---

[46] *indifferent* average [47] *privates* ordinary men in private, not public, life (with obvious play upon the sexual term "private parts") [48] *confines* places of imprisonment [49] *wards* cells

HAMLET Then are our beggars bodies,[50] and our monarchs and outstretched[51] heroes the beggars' shadows. Shall we to th' court? for, by my fay,[52] I cannot reason.

BOTH We'll wait upon[53] you.

5 HAMLET No such matter. I will not sort you with the rest of my servants, for, to speak to you like an honest man, I am most dreadfully attended. But in the beaten way of friendship, what make[54] you at Elsinore?

ROSENCRANTZ To visit you, my lord; no other occasion.

10 HAMLET Beggar that I am, I am even poor in thanks, but I thank you; and sure, dear friends, my thanks are too dear a halfpenny.[55] Were you not sent for? Is it your own inclining? Is it a free visitation? Come, come, deal justly with me. Come, come. Nay, speak.

GUILDENSTERN What should we say, my lord?

15 HAMLET Why, anything—but to th' purpose. You were sent for, and there is a kind of confession in your looks, which your modesties have not craft enough to color. I know the good king and queen have sent for you.

ROSENCRANTZ To what end, my lord?

20 HAMLET That you must teach me. But let me conjure you by the rights of our fellowship, by the consonancy[56] of our youth, by the obligation of our ever-preserved love, and by what more dear a better proposer[57] can charge you withal,[58] be even[59] and direct with me whether you were sent for or no.

25 ROSENCRANTZ (*aside to* GUILDENSTERN) What say you?

HAMLET (*aside*) Nay then, I have an eye of you.—If you love me, hold not off.

GUILDENSTERN My lord, we were sent for.

HAMLET I will tell you why. So shall my anticipation prevent[60]

30 your discovery,[61] and your secrecy to the king and queen moult no feather.[62] I have of late—but wherefore I know not—lost all my mirth, forgone all custom of exercises; and indeed, it goes so heavily with my disposition that this goodly frame the earth seems to me a sterile promontory; this most excellent canopy, the air, look

35 you, this brave o'erhanging firmament,[63] this majestical roof

---

[50] *bodies* solid substances, not shadows (because beggars lack ambition) [51] *outstretched* elongated as shadows (with a corollary implication of far-reaching with respect to the ambitions that make both heroes and monarchs into shadows) [52] *fay* faith [53] *wait upon* attend [54] *make* do [55] *a halfpenny* at a halfpenny [56] *consonancy* accord (in sameness of age) [57] *proposer* propounder [58] *withal* with [59] *even* straight [60] *prevent* forestall [61] *discovery* disclosure [62] *moult no feather* be left whole [63] *firmament* sky

fretted[64] with golden fire—why, it appeareth nothing to me but a foul and pestilent congregation of vapors. What a piece of work is a man, how noble in reason, how infinite in faculties; in form and moving how express[65] and admirable, in action how like an
5 angel, in apprehension how like a god: the beauty of the world, the paragon of animals! And yet to me what is this quintessence[66] of dust? Man delights not me—nor woman neither, though by your smiling you seem to say so.

ROSENCRANTZ My lord, there was no such stuff in my thoughts.

10 HAMLET Why did ye laugh then, when I said "Man delights not me"?

ROSENCRANTZ To think, my lord, if you delight not in man, what lenten[67] entertainment the players shall receive from you. We coted[68] them on the way, and hither are they coming to offer you
15 service.

HAMLET He that plays the king shall be welcome—his majesty shall have tribute of me—, the adventurous knight shall use his foil and target,[69] the lover shall not sigh gratis, the humorous man[70] shall end his part in peace, the clown shall make those laugh whose
20 lungs are tickle o' th' sere,[71] and the lady shall say her mind freely, or the blank verse shall halt[72] for't. What players are they?

ROSENCRANTZ Even those you were wont to take such delight in, the tragedians of the city.

HAMLET How chances it they travel? Their residence,[73] both in
25 reputation and profit, was better both ways.

ROSENCRANTZ I think their inhibition[74] comes by the means of the late innovation.[75]

HAMLET Do they hold the same estimation they did when I was in the city? Are they so followed?

30 ROSENCRANTZ No indeed, are they not.

HAMLET How comes it? Do they grow rusty?

ROSENCRANTZ Nay, their endeavor keeps in the wonted pace, but there is, sir, an eyrie[76] of children, little eyases,[77] that cry out on

---

[64] *fretted* decorated with fretwork [65] *express* well framed [66] *quintessence* fifth or last and finest essence (an alchemical term) [67] *lenten* scanty [68] *coted* overtook [69] *foil and target* sword and shield [70] *humorous man* eccentric character dominated by one of the humours [71] *tickle o' th' sere* hair-triggered for the discharge of laughter ("sere": part of a gunlock) [72] *halt* go lame [73] *residence* residing at the capital [74] *inhibition* impediment to acting in residence (formal prohibition?) [75] *innovation* new fashion of having companies of boy actors play on the "private" stage (?), political upheaval (?) [76] *eyrie* nest [77] *eyases* nestling hawks

the top of question[78] and are most tyranically clapped for't. These are now the fashion, and so berattle[79] the common stages[80] (so they call them) that many wearing rapiers are afraid of goose-quills[81] and dare scarce come thither.

5 HAMLET What, are they children? Who maintains 'em? How are they escoted? [82] Will they pursue the quality[83] no longer than they can sing? [84] Will they not say afterwards, if they should grow themselves to common players (as it is most like, if their means are no better), their writers do them wrong to make them exclaim

10 against their own succession?

ROSENCRANTZ Faith, there has been much to do on both sides, and the nation holds it no sin to tarre[85] them to controversy. There was, for a while, no money bid for argument[86] unless the poet and the player went to cuffs in the question.

15 HAMLET Is't possible?

GUILDENSTERN O, there has been much throwing about of brains.

HAMLET Do the boys carry it away?

ROSENCRANTZ Ay, that they do, my lord—Hercules and his load [87] too.

20 HAMLET It is not very strange, for my uncle is King of Denmark, and those that would make mows[88] at him while my father lived give twenty, forty, fifty, a hundred ducats apiece for his picture in little. 'Sblood,[89] there is something in this more than natural, if philosophy could find it out.

25 *A flourish*

GUILDENSTERN There are the players.

HAMLET Gentlemen, you are welcome to Elsinore. Your hands, come then. Th' appurtenance of welcome is fashion and ceremony. Let me comply with you in this garb,[90] lest my extent[91] to

30 the players (which I tell you must show fairly outwards) should more appear like entertainment than yours. You are welcome. But my uncle-father and aunt-mother are deceived.

---

[78] *on the top of question* above others on matter of dispute [79] *berattle* berate [80] *common stages* "public" theatres of the "common" players, who were organized in companies mainly composed of adult actors (allusion being made to the "War of the Theatres" in Shakespeare's London) [81] *goosequills* pens (of satirists who made out that the London public stage showed low taste) [82] *escoted* supported [83] *quality* profession of acting [84] *sing* i.e. with unchanged voices [85] *tarre* incite [86] *argument* matter of a play [87] *load* i.e. the whole word (with a topical reference to the sign of the Globe Theatre, a representation of Hercules bearing the world on his shoulders) [88] *mows* grimaces [89] *'Sblood* by God's blood [90] *garb* fashion [91] *extent* showing of welcome

GUILDENSTERN In what, my dear lord?

HAMLET I am but mad north-north-west. When the wind is southerly I know a hawk from a handsaw.[92]

(*Enter* POLONIUS)

5 POLONIUS Well be with you, gentlemen.

HAMLET Hark you, Guildenstern—and you too—at each ear a hearer. That great baby you see there is not yet out of his swaddling clouts.[93]

ROSENCRANTZ Happily[94] he is the second time come to them, for 10 they say an old man is twice a child.

HAMLET I will prophesy he comes to tell me of the players. Mark it.—You say right, sir; a Monday morning, 'twas then indeed.

POLONIUS My lord, I have news to tell you.

HAMLET My lord, I have news to tell you. When Roscius[95] was an 15 actor in Rome—

POLONIUS The actors are come hither, my lord.

HAMLET Buzz, buzz.

POLONIUS Upon my honor—

HAMLET Then came each actor on his ass—

20 POLONIUS The best actors in the world, either for tragedy, comedy, history, pastoral, pastoral-comical, historical-pastoral, tragical-historical, tragical-comical-historical-pastoral; scene individable,[96] or poem unlimited.[97] Seneca[98] cannot be too heavy, nor Plautus[99] too light. For the law of writ[100] and the liberty,[101] these are the 25 only men.

HAMLET O Jephthah,[102] judge of Israel, what a treasure hadst thou!

POLONIUS What treasure had he, my lord?

HAMLET Why,

30 "One fair daughter, and no more,
The which he lovèd passing[103] well."

---

[92] *hawk* mattock or pickaxe (also called "hack"; here used apparently with a play on "hawk": a bird); *handsaw* carpenter's tool (apparently with a play on some corrupt form of "hernshaw"; heron, a bird often hunted with the hawk) [93] *clouts* clothes [94] *Happily* haply, perhaps [95] *Roscius* the greatest of Roman comic actors [96] *scene individable* drama observing the unities [97] *poem unlimited* drama not observing the unities [98] *Seneca* Roman writer of tragedies [99] *Plautus* Roman writer of comedies [100] *law of writ* orthodoxy determined by critical rules of the drama [101] *liberty* freedom from such orthodoxy [102] *Jephthah* the compelled sacrificer of a dearly beloved daughter (Judges xi) [103] *passing* surpassingly (verses are from a ballad on Jephthah)

POLONIUS (*aside*) Still on my daughter.
HAMLET Am I not i' th' right, old Jephthah?
POLONIUS If you call me Jephthah, my lord, I have a daughter that I love passing well.
5 HAMLET Nay, that follows not.
POLONIUS What follows then, my lord?
HAMLET Why,
"As by lot, God wot,"
and then, you know,
10 "It came to pass, as most like it was."
The first row[104] of the pious chanson[105] will show you more, for look where my abridgment[106] comes.

(*Enter the* PLAYERS)

You are welcome, masters, welcome, all.—I am glad to see thee
15 well.—Welcome, good friends.—O, old friend, why, thy face is valanced [107] since I saw thee last. Com'st thou to beard me in Denmark?—What, my young lady[108] and mistress? By'r Lady, your ladyship is nearer to heaven than when I saw you last by the altitude of a chopine.[109] Pray God your voice, like a piece of un-
20 current[110] gold, be not cracked within the ring.[111]—Masters, you are all welcome. We'll e'en to't like French falconers, fly at anything we see. We'll have a speech straight. Come, give us a taste of your quality. Come, a passionate speech.
PLAYER What speech, my good lord?
25 HAMLET I heard thee speak me a speech once, but it was never acted, or if it was, not above once, for the play, I remember, pleased not the million; 'twas caviary[112] to the general,[113] but it was (as I received it, and others, whose judgments in such matters cried in the top of [114] mine) an excellent play, well digested in the
30 scenes, set down with as much modesty as cunning. I remember one said there were no sallets[115] in the lines to make the matter savory, nor no matter in the phrase that might indict the author of affectation, but called it an honest method, as wholesome as sweet, and by very much more handsome than fine. One speech

---

[104] *row* stanza [105] *chanson* song [106] *my abridgment* that which shortens my talk [107] *valanced* fringed (with a beard) [108] *young lady* boy who plays women's parts [109] *chopine* women's thick-soled shoe [110] *uncurrent* not legal tender [111] *within the ring* from the edge through the line circling the design on the coin (with a play on "ring": a sound) [112] *caviary* caviare [113] *general* multitude [114] *in the top of* more authoritatively than [115] *sallets* salads, highly seasoned passages

in't I chiefly loved. 'Twas Aeneas' tale to Dido, and thereabout of it especially where he speaks of Priam's[116] slaughter. If it live in your memory, begin at this line—let me see, let me see:
"The rugged Pyrrhus, like th' Hyrcanian beast[117]—"
5 'Tis not so; it begins with Pyrrhus:
"The rugged Pyrrhus, he whose sable[118] arms,
Black as his purpose, did the night resemble
When he lay couchèd in the ominous[119] horse,[120]
Hath now this dread and black complexion smeared
10 With heraldry more dismal.[121] Head to foot
Now is he total gules,[122] horridly tricked[123]
With blood of fathers, mothers, daughters, sons,
Baked and impasted with the parching[124] streets,
That lend a tyrannous and a damnèd light
15 To their lord's murder. Roasted in wrath and fire,
And thus o'ersizèd[125] with coagulate[126] gore,
With eyes like carbuncles, the hellish Pyrrhus
Old grandsire Priam seeks."
So, proceed you.

20 POLONIUS Fore God, my lord, well spoken, with good accent and good discretion.

PLAYER "Anon he finds him,
Striking too short at Greeks. His antique sword,
Rebellious to his arms, lies where it falls,
25 Repugnant to command. Unequal matched,
Pyrrhus at Priam drives, in rage strikes wide,
But with the whiff and wind of his fell[127] sword
Th' unnervèd father falls. Then senseless[128] Ilium,
Seeming to feel this blow, with flaming top
30 Stoops to his[129] base, and with a hideous crash
Takes prisoner Pyrrhus' ear. For lo! his sword,
Which was declining on the milky head
Of reverend Priam, seemed i' th' air to stick.
So as a painted[130] tyrant Pyrrhus stood,

---

116 *Priam's slaughter* i.e. at the fall of Troy (Aeneid II, 506 ff.) 117 *Hyrcanian beast* tiger 118 *sable* black 119 *ominous* fateful 120 *horse* the wooden horse by which the Greeks gained entrance to Troy 121 *dismal* ill-omened 122 *gules* red (heraldic term) 123 *tricked* decorated in color (heraldic term) 124 *parching* i.e. because Troy was burning 125 *o'ersizèd* covered as with size, a glutinous material used for filling pores of plaster, etc. 126 *coagulate* clotted 127 *fell* cruel 128 *senseless* without feeling 129 *his* its 130 *painted* pictured

And like a neutral to his will and matter[131]
Did nothing.
But as we often see, against[132] some storm,
A silence in the heavens, the rack[133] stand still,
5 The bold winds speechless, and the orb below
As hush as death, anon the dreadful thunder
Doth rend the region,[134] so after Pyrrhus' pause,
Arousèd vengeance sets him new awork,
And never did the Cyclops' [135] hammers fall
10 On Mars' armor, forged for proof eterne,[136]
With less remorse than Pyrrhus' bleeding sword
Now falls on Priam.
Out, out, thou strumpet Fortune! All you gods,
In general synod take away her power,
15 Break all the spokes and fellies[137] from her wheel,
And bowl the round nave[138] down the hill of heaven,
As low as to the fiends."

POLONIUS This is too long.

HAMLET It shall to the barber's, with your beard.—Prithee say on.
20 He's for a jig[139] or a tale of bawdry, or he sleeps. Say on; come to Hecuba.

PLAYER "But who (ah woe!) had seen the mobled [140] queen—"

HAMLET "The mobled queen"?

POLONIUS That's good. "Mobled queen" is good.

25 PLAYER "Run barefoot up and down, threat'ning the flames
With bisson rheum;[141] a clout[142] upon that head
Where late the diadem stood, and for a robe,
About her lank and all o'erteemèd [143] loins,
A blanket in the alarm of fear caught up—
30 Who this had seen, with tongue in venom steeped
'Gainst Fortune's state[144] would treason have pronounced.
But if the gods themselves did see her then,
When she saw Pyrrhus make malicious sport
In mincing with his sword her husband's limbs,
35 The instant burst of clamor that she made

---

[131] *will and matter* purpose and its realization (between which he stands motionless) [132] *against* just before [133] *rack* clouds [134] *region* sky [135] *Cyclops* giant workmen who made armor in the smithy of Vulcan [136] *proof eterne* eternal protection [137] *fellies* segments of the rim [138] *nave* hub [139] *jig* short comic piece with singing and dancing often presented after a play [140] *mobled* muffled [141] *bisson rheum* blinding tears [142] *clout* cloth [143] *o'erteemèd* overproductive of children [144] *state* government of worldly events

(Unless things mortal move them not at all)
Would have made milch[145] the burning eyes[146] of heaven
And passion in the gods."

POLONIUS Look, whe'r[147] he has not turned his color, and has tears
5 in's eyes. Prithee no more.

HAMLET 'Tis well. I'll have thee speak out the rest of this soon.—
Good my lord, will you see the players well bestowed?[148] Do you
hear? Let them be well used, for they are the abstract and brief
chronicles of the time. After your death you were better have a
10 bad epitaph than their ill report while you live.

POLONIUS My lord, I will use them according to their desert.

HAMLET God's bodkin,[149] man, much better! Use every man after
his desert, and who shall scape whipping? Use them after your
own honor and dignity. The less they deserve, the more merit is
15 in your bounty. Take them in.

POLONIUS Come, sirs.

HAMLET Follow him, friends. We'll hear a play tomorrow. (*aside to* PLAYER) Dost thou hear me, old friend? Can you play "The
Murder of Gonzago"?

20 PLAYER Ay, my lord.

HAMLET We'll ha't to-morrow night. You could for a need study a
speech of some dozen or sixteen lines which I would set down and
insert in't, could you not?

PLAYER Ay, my lord.

25 HAMLET Very well. Follow that lord, and look you mock him not.
—My good friends, I'll leave you till night. You are welcome to
Elsinore.

(*Exeunt* POLONIUS *and* PLAYERS)

ROSENCRANTZ Good my lord.

30 (*Exeunt* ROSENCRANTZ *and* GUILDENSTERN)

HAMLET Ay, so, God bye to you.—Now I am alone.
O, what a rogue and peasant slave am I!
Is it not monstrous that this player here,
But in a fiction, in a dream of passion,
35 Could force his soul so to his own conceit[150]
That from her working all his visage wanned,
Tears in his eyes, distraction in his aspect.

---

145 *milch* tearful (milk-giving) 146 *eyes* i.e. stars 147 *whe'r* whether 148 *bestowed* lodged 149 *God's bodkin* by God's little body 150 *conceit* conception, idea

A broken voice, and his whole function[151] suiting
With forms to his conceit? And all for nothing,
For Hecuba!
What's Hecuba to him, or he to Hecuba,
5 That he should weep for her? What would he do
Had he the motive and the cue for passion
That I have? He would drown the stage with tears
And cleave the general ear with horrid speech,
Make mad the guilty and appal the free,
10 Confound the ignorant, and amaze indeed
The very faculties of eyes and ears.
Yet I,
A dull and muddy-mettled [152] rascal, peak[153]
Like John-a-dreams,[154] unpregnant[155] of my cause,
15 And can say nothing. No, not for a king,
Upon whose property and most dear life
A damned defeat was made. Am I a coward?
Who calls me villain? breaks my pate across?
Plucks off my beard and blows it in my face?
20 Tweaks me by the nose? gives me the lie i' th' throat
As deep as to the lungs? Who does me this?
Ha, 'swounds,[156] I should take it, for it cannot be
But I am pigeon-livered [157] and lack gall
To make oppression bitter, or ere this
25 I should ha' fatted all the region kites[158]
With this slave's offal.[159] Bloody, bawdy villain!
Remorseless, treacherous, lecherous, kindless[160] villain!
O, vengeance!
Why, what an ass am I! This is most brave,
30 That I, the son of a dear father murdered,
Prompted to my revenge by heaven and hell,
Must like a whore unpack my heart with words
And fall a-cursing like a very drab,
A stallion! [161] Fie upon't, foh! About, my brains.
35 Hum—
I have heard that guilty creatures sitting at a play
Have by the very cunning of the scene

---

151 *function* action of bodily powers 152 *muddy-mettled* dull-spirited 153 *peak* mope 154 *John-a-dreams* a sleepy dawdler 155 *unpregnant* barren of realization 156 *'swounds* by God's wounds 157 *pigeon-livered* of dove-like gentleness 158 *region kites* kites of the air 159 *offal* guts 160 *kindless* unnatural 161 *stallion* prostitute (male or female)

Been struck so to the soul that presently[162]
They have proclaimed their malefactions.
For murder, though it have no tongue, will speak
With most miraculous organ. I'll have these players
5 Play something like the murder of my father
Before mine uncle. I'll observe his looks.
I'll tent[163] him to the quick. If 'a do blench,[164]
I know my course. The spirit that I have seen
May be a devil, and the devil hath power
10 T' assume a pleasing shape, yea, and perhaps
Out of my weakness and my melancholy,
As he is very potent with such spirits,
Abuses[165] me to damn me. I'll have grounds
More relative[166] than this. The play 's the thing
15 Wherein I'll catch the conscience of the king.
(*Exit*)

## ACT III

### Scene I

*A chamber in the castle*

20 (*Enter* KING, QUEEN, POLONIUS, OPHELIA, ROSENCRANTZ, GUILDENSTERN, LORDS)

KING And can you by no drift of conference[1]
Get from him why he puts on this confusion,
Grating so harshly all his days of quiet
25 With turbulent and dangerous lunacy?
ROSENCRANTZ He does confess he feels himself distracted,
But from what cause 'a will by no means speak.
GUILDENSTERN Nor do we find him forward to be sounded,
But with a crafty madness keeps aloof
30 When we would bring him on to some confession
Of his true state.
QUEEN Did he receive you well?
ROSENCRANTZ Most like a gentleman.
GUILDENSTERN But with much forcing of his disposition.
35 ROSENCRANTZ Niggard of question, but of our demands
Most free in his reply.

---

[162] *presently* immediately [163] *tent* probe [164] *blench* flinch [165] *Abuses* deludes [166] *relative* pertinent
[1] *drift of conference* direction of conversation

QUEEN Did you assay[2] him
To any pastime?
ROSENCRANTZ Madam, it so fell out that certain players
We o'erraught[3] on the way. Of these we told him,
5 And there did seem in him a kind of joy
To hear of it. They are here about the court,
And, as I think, they have already order
This night to play before him.
POLONIUS 'Tis most true,
10 And he beseeched me to entreat your majesties
To hear and see the matter.
KING With all my heart, and it doth much content me
To hear him so inclined.
Good gentlemen, give him a further edge[4]
15 And drive his purpose into these delights.
ROSENCRANTZ We shall, my lord.

(*Exeunt* ROSENCRANTZ *and* GUILDENSTERN)

KING Sweet Gertrude, leave us too,
For we have closely[5] sent for Hamlet hither,
20 That he, as 'twere by accident, may here
Affront[6] Ophelia.
Her father and myself (lawful espials[7])
Will so bestow ourselves that, seeing unseen,
We may of their encounter frankly judge
25 And gather by him, as he is behaved,
If't be th' affliction of his love or no
That thus he suffers for.
QUEEN I shall obey you.—
And for your part, Ophelia, I do wish
30 That your good beauties be the happy cause
Of Hamlet's wildness. So shall I hope your virtues
Will bring him to his wonted way again,
To both your honors.
OPHELIA Madam, I wish it may.

35 (*Exit* QUEEN)

POLONIUS Ophelia, walk you here.—Gracious, so please you,
We will bestow ourselves.—

---

[2] *assay* try to win [3] *o'erraught* overtook [4] *edge* keenness of desire [5] *closely* privately [6] *Affront* come face to face with [7] *espials* spies

(*To* OPHELIA)

Read on this book,

That show of such an exercise[8] may color[9]
Your loneliness. We are oft to blame in this,
5 'Tis too much proved, that with devotion's visage
And pious action we do sugar o'er
The devil himself.

KING (*aside*) O, 'tis too true.
How smart a lash that speech doth give my conscience!
10 The harlot's cheek, beautied with plast'ring art,
Is not more ugly to[10] the thing that helps it
Than is my deed to my most painted word.
O heavy burthen!

POLONIUS I hear him coming. Let's withdraw, my lord.

15 (*Exeunt* KING *and* POLONIUS)

(*Enter* HAMLET)

HAMLET To be, or not to be—that is the question:
Whether 'tis nobler in the mind to suffer
The slings and arrows of outrageous fortune
20 Or to take arms against a sea of troubles
And by opposing end them. To die, to sleep—
No more—and by a sleep to say we end
The heartache, and the thousand natural shocks
That flesh is heir to. 'Tis a consummation
25 Devoutly to be wished. To die, to sleep—
To sleep—perchance to dream: ay, there's the rub,[11]
For in that sleep of death what dreams may come
When we have shuffled off [12] this mortal coil,[13]
Must give us pause. There's the respect[14]
30 That makes calamity of so long life.[15]
For who would bear the whips and scorns of time,
Th' oppressor's wrong, the proud man's contumely
The pangs of despised love, the law's delay,
The insolence of office, and the spurns
35 That patient merit of th' unworthy takes,
When he himself might his quietus[16] make

---

[8] *exercise* religious exercise (the book being obviously one of devotion) [9] *color* give an appearance of naturalness to [10] *to* compared to [11] *rub* obstacle (literally, obstruction encountered by a bowler's ball) [12] *shuffled off* cast off as an encumbrance [13] *coil* to-do, turmoil [14] *respect* consideration [15] *of so long life* so long-lived [16] *quietus* settlement (literally, release from debt)

With a bare bodkin?[17] Who would fardels[18] bear,
To grunt and sweat under a weary life,
But that the dread of something after death,
The undiscovered country, from whose bourn[19]
5 No traveller returns, puzzles the will,
And makes us rather bear those ills we have
Than fly to others that we know not of?
Thus conscience does make cowards of us all,
And thus the native hue of resolution
10 Is sicklied o'er with the pale cast of thought,
And enterprises of great pitch[20] and moment
With this regard[21] their currents turn awry
And lose the name of action.—Soft you now,
The fair Ophelia!—Nymph, in thy orisons[22]
15 Be all my sins remembered.

OPHELIA Good my lord,
How does your honor for this many a day?

HAMLET I humbly thank you, well, well, well.

OPHELIA My lord, I have remembrances of yours
20 That I have longèd long to re-deliver.
I pray you, now receive them.

HAMLET No, not I,
I never gave you aught.

OPHELIA My honored lord, you know right well you did,
25 And with them words of so sweet breath composed
As made the things more rich. Their perfume lost,
Take these again, for to the noble mind
Rich gifts wax poor when givers prove unkind.
There, my lord.

30 HAMLET Ha, ha! Are you honest?[23]

OPHELIA My lord?

HAMLET Are you fair?

OPHELIA What means your lordship?

HAMLET That if you be honest and fair, your honesty should admit
35 no discourse to your beauty.

OPHELIA Could beauty, my lord, have better commerce[24] than with honesty?

HAMLET Ay, truly; for the power of beauty will sooner transform

---

[17] *bodkin* dagger [18] *fardels* burdens [19] *bourn* confine, region [20] *pitch* height (of a soaring falcon's flight) [21] *regard* consideration [22] *orisons* prayers (because of the book of devotion she reads) [23] *honest* chaste [24] *commerce* intercourse

honesty from what it is to a bawd than the force of honesty can translate beauty into his likeness. This was sometime a paradox,[25] but now the time gives it proof. I did love you once.

OPHELIA Indeed, my lord, you made me believe so.

5 HAMLET You should not have believed me, for virtue cannot so inoculate[26] our old stock but we shall relish[27] of it. I loved you not.

OPHELIA I was the more deceived.

HAMLET Get thee to a nunnery. Why wouldst thou be a breeder

10 of sinners? I am myself indifferent honest,[28] but yet I could accuse me of such things that it were better my mother had not borne me: I am very proud, revengeful, ambitious, with more offenses at my beck than I have thoughts to put them in, imagination to give them shape, or time to act them in. What should

15 such fellows as I do crawling between earth and heaven? We are arrant knaves all; believe none of us. Go thy ways to a nunnery. Where's your father?

OPHELIA At home, my lord.

HAMLET Let the doors be shut upon him, that he may play the

20 fool nowhere but in's own house. Farewell.

OPHELIA O, help him, you sweet heavens!

HAMLET If thou dost marry, I'll give thee this plague for thy dowry: be thou as chaste as ice, as pure as snow, thou shalt not escape calumny. Get thee to a nunnery. Go, farewell. Or if thou

25 wilt needs marry, marry a fool, for wise men know well enough what monsters[29] you make of them. To a nunnery, go, and quickly too. Farewell.

OPHELIA O heavenly powers, restore him!

HAMLET I have heard of your paintings too, well enough. God

30 hath given you one face, and you make yourselves another. You jig, you amble, and you lisp; you nickname God's creatures and make your wantonness[30] your ignorance.[31] Go to, I'll no more on't; it hath made me mad. I say we will have no more marriage. Those that are married already—all but one—shall live. The rest

35 shall keep as they are. To a nunnery, go.

(*Exit*)

OPHELIA O, what a noble mind is here o'erthrown!

---

[25] *paradox* idea contrary to common opinion [26] *inoculate* graft [27] *relish* have a flavor (because of original sin) [28] *indifferent honest* moderately respectable [29] *monsters* i.e. unnatural combinations of wisdom and uxorious folly [30] *wantonness* affectation [31] *your ignorance* a matter for which you offer the excuse that you don't know any better

The courtier's, soldier's, scholar's, eye, tongue, sword,
Th' expectancy and rose[32] of the fair state,
The glass[33] of fashion and the mould of form,
Th' observed of all observers, quite, quite down!
5 And I, of ladies most deject and wretched,
That sucked the honey of his music vows,
Now see that noble and most sovereign reason
Like sweet bells jangled, out of time and harsh,
That unmatched form and feature of blown youth
10 Blasted with ecstasy.[34] O, woe is me
T' have seen what I have seen, see what I see!

(*Enter* KING *and* POLONIUS)

KING Love? his affections[35] do not that way tend,
Nor what he spake, though it lacked form a little,
15 Was not like madness. There's something in his soul
O'er which his melancholy sits on brood,
And I do doubt[36] the hatch and the disclose
Will be some danger; which for to prevent,
I have in quick determination
20 Thus set it down: he shall with speed to England
For the demand of our neglected tribute.
Haply the seas, and countries different,
With variable objects, shall expel
This something-settled [37] matter in his heart,
25 Whereon his brains still beating puts him thus
From fashion of himself. What think you on't?
POLONIUS It shall do well. But yet do I believe
The origin and commencement of his grief
Sprung from neglected love.—How now, Ophelia?
30 You need not tell us what Lord Hamlet said.
We heard it all.—My lord, do as you please,
But if you hold it fit, after the play
Let his queen mother all alone entreat him
To show his grief. Let her be round [38] with him,
35 And I'll be placed, so please you, in the ear
Of all their conference. If she find him not,
To England send him, or confine him where
Your wisdom best shall think.

---

[32] *expectancy and rose* fair hope [33] *glass* mirror [34] *ecstasy* madness [35] *affections* emotions [36] *doubt* fear [37] *something-settled* somewhat settled [38] *round* plain-spoken

KING It shall be so.
Madness in great ones must not unwatched go.

(*Exeunt*)

## Act III, Scene II

5 *The hall of the castle*

(*Enter* HAMLET *and three of the* PLAYERS)

HAMLET Speak the speech, I pray you, as I pronounced it to you, trippingly[1] on the tongue. But if you mouth it, as many of our players do, I had as lief the town crier spoke my lines. Nor do
10 not saw the air too much with your hand, thus, but use all gently, for in the very torrent, tempest, and (as I may say) whirlwind of your passion, you must acquire and beget a temperance that may give it smoothness. O, it offends me to the soul to hear a robustious[2] periwig-pated [3] fellow tear a passion to tatters, to very rags,
15 to split the ears of the groundlings,[4] who for the most part are capable of nothing but inexplicable dumb shows[5] and noise. I would have such a fellow whipped for o'erdoing Termagant.[6] It out-herods Herod.[7] Pray you avoid it.

PLAYER I warrant your honor.

20 HAMLET Be not too tame neither, but let your own discretion be your tutor. Suit the action to the word, the word to the action, with this special observance, that you o'erstep not the modesty of nature. For anything so overdone is from[8] the purpose of playing, whose end, both at the first and now, was and is, to hold, as
25 'twere, the mirror up to nature, to show virtue her own feature, scorn her own image, and the very age and body of the time his form and pressure.[9] Now this overdone, or come tardy off,[10] though it make the unskillful laugh, cannot but make the judicious grieve, the censure of the which one[11] must in your allow-
30 ance o'erweigh a whole theatre of others. O, there be players that I have seen play, and heard others praise, and that highly (not to

---

[1] *trippingly* easily [2] *robustious* boisterous [3] *periwig-pated* wig-wearing (after the custom of actors) [4] *groundlings* spectators who paid least and stood on the ground in the pit or yard of the theatre [5] *dumb shows* brief actions without words, forecasting dramatic matter to follow (the play presented later in this scene giving an old-fashioned example) [6] *Termagant* a Saracen "god" in medieval romance and drama [7] *Herod* the raging tyrant of old Biblical plays [8] *from* apart from [9] *pressure* impressed or printed character [10] *come tardy off* brought off slowly and badly [11] *the censure of the which one* the judgment of even one of whom

speak it profanely), that neither having th' accent of Christians, nor the gait of Christian, pagan, nor man, have so strutted and bellowed that I have thought some of Nature's journeymen[12] had made men, and not made them well, they imitated humanity so
5 abominably.

PLAYER I hope we have reformed that indifferently[13] with us, sir.

HAMLET O, reform it altogether! And let those that play your clowns speak no more than is set down for them, for there be of them[14] that will themselves laugh, to set on some quantity of
10 barren spectators to laugh too, though in the mean time some necessary question of the play be then to be considered. That's villainous and shows a most pitiful ambition in the fool that uses it. Go make you ready.

(*Exeunt* PLAYERS)

15 (*Enter* POLONIUS, GUILDENSTERN, *and* ROSENCRANTZ)

How now, my lord? Will the king hear this piece of work?

POLONIUS And the queen too, and that presently.[15]

HAMLET Bid the players make haste.

(*Exit* POLONIUS)

20 Will you two help to hasten them?

ROSENCRANTZ Ay, my lord.

(*Exeunt they two*)

HAMLET What, ho, Horatio!

(*Enter* HORATIO)

25 HORATIO Here, sweet lord, at your service.

HAMLET Horatio, thou art e'en as just a man
As e'er my conversation coped withal.[16]

HORATIO O, my dear lord—

HAMLET Nay, do not think I flatter.
30 For what advancement may I hope from thee,
That no revenue hast but thy good spirits
To feed and clothe thee? Why should the poor be flattered?
No, let the candied tongue lick absurd pomp,
And crook the pregnant[17] hinges of the knee

---

12 *journeymen* workmen not yet masters of their trade 13 *indifferently* fairly well 14 *of them* some of them 15 *presently* at once 16 *conversation coped withal* intercourse with men encountered 17 *pregnant* quick to move

Where thrift[18] may follow fawning. Dost thou hear?
Since my dear soul was mistress of her choice
And could of men distinguish her election,
S' hath sealed [19] thee for herself, for thou hast been
5 As one in suff'ring all that suffers nothing,
A man that Fortune's buffets and rewards
Hast ta'en with equal thanks; and blest are those
Whose blood [20] and judgment are so well commeddled [21]
That they are not a pipe for Fortune's finger
10 To sound what stop she please. Give me that man
That is not passion's slave, and I will wear him
In my heart's core, ay, in my heart of heart,
As I do thee. Something too much of this—
There is a play to-night before the king.
15 One scene of it comes near the circumstance
Which I have told thee, of my father's death.
I prithee, when thou seest that act afoot,
Even with the very comment of thy soul [22]
Observe my uncle. If his occulted [23] guilt
20 Do not itself unkennel in one speech,
It is a damnèd ghost[24] that we have seen,
And my imaginations are as foul
As Vulcan's stithy.[25] Give him heedful note,
For I mine eyes will rivet to his face,
25 And after we will both our judgments join
In censure of [26] his seeming.

HORATIO Well, my lord.
If 'a steal aught the while this play is playing,
And scape detecting, I will pay the theft.

30 (*Enter* TRUMPETS *and* KETTLEDRUMS, KING, QUEEN, POLONIUS, OPHELIA, [ROSENCRANTZ, GUILDENSTERN, *and other* LORDS *attendant*])

HAMLET They are coming to the play. I must be idle.[27]
Get you a place.

KING How fares our cousin[28] Hamlet?

35 HAMLET Excellent, i' faith, of the chameleon's dish.[29] I eat the air, promise-crammed. You cannot feed capons so.

---

[18] *thrift* profit [19] *sealed* marked [20] *blood* passion [21] *commeddled* mixed together [22] *the very . . . soul* thy deepest sagacity [23] *occulted* hidden [24] *damnèd ghost* evil spirit, devil [25] *stithy* smithy [26] *censure of* sentence upon [27] *be idle* be foolish, act the madman [28] *cousin* nephew [29] *chameleon's dish* i.e. air (which was believed the chameleon's food; Hamlet willfully takes *fares* in the sense of "feeds")

KING I have nothing with this answer, Hamlet. These words are not mine.[30]

HAMLET No, nor mine now. (*to Polonius*) My lord, you played once i' th' university, you say?

5 POLONIUS That did I, my lord, and was accounted a good actor.

HAMLET What did you enact?

POLONIUS I did enact Julius Caesar. I was killed i' th' Capitol; Brutus killed me.

HAMLET It was a brute part of him to kill so capital a calf there.
10 Be the players ready?

ROSENCRANTZ Ay, my lord. They stay upon your patience.[31]

QUEEN Come hither, my dear Hamlet, sit by me.

HAMLET No, good mother. Here's metal more attractive.

POLONIUS (*to the King*) O ho! do you mark that?

15 HAMLET Lady, shall I lie in your lap?

*He lies at* OPHELIA'S *feet*

OPHELIA No, my lord.

HAMLET I mean, my head upon your lap?

OPHELIA Ay, my lord.

20 HAMLET Do you think I meant country matters? [32]

OPHELIA I think nothing, my lord.

HAMLET That's a fair thought to lie between maids' legs.

OPHELIA What is, my lord?

HAMLET Nothing.

25 OPHELIA You are merry, my lord.

HAMLET Who, I?

OPHELIA Ay, my lord.

HAMLET O God, your only jig-maker! [33] What should a man do but be merry? For look you how cheerfully my mother looks, and
30 my father died within's two hours.

OPHELIA Nay, 'tis twice two months, my lord.

HAMLET So long? Nay then, let the devil wear black, for I'll have a suit of sables.[34] O heavens! die two months ago, and not forgotten yet? Then there's hope a great man's memory may out-
35 live his life half a year. But, by'r Lady, 'a must build churches then, or else shall 'a suffer not thinking on, with the hobby-

---

[30] *not mine* not for me as the asker of my question [31] *stay upon your patience* await your indulgence [32] *country matters* rustic goings-on, barnyard mating (with a play upon a sexual term) [33] *jig-maker* writer of jigs [34] *sables* black furs (luxurious garb, not for mourning)

horse,[35] whose epitaph is "For O, for O, the hobby-horse is forgot!"

*The trumpets sound. Dumb show follows:*
*Enter a* KING *and a* QUEEN [*very lovingly*], *the* QUEEN *embracing him, and*
5 *he her.* [*She kneels; and makes show of protestation unto him.*] *He takes her up, and declines his head upon her neck. He lies him down upon a bank of flowers. She, seeing him asleep, leaves him. Anon come in another man: takes off his crown, kisses it, pours poison in the sleeper's ears, and leaves him. The* QUEEN *returns, finds the* KING *dead, makes passionate*
10 *action. The poisoner, with some three or four, come in again, seem to condole with her. The dead body is carried away. The poisoner woos the* QUEEN *with gifts; she seems harsh awhile, but in the end accepts love.*

(*Exeunt*)

OPHELIA What means this, my lord?
15 HAMLET Marry, this is miching mallecho;[36] it means mischief.
OPHELIA Belike this show imports the argument of the play.

(*Enter* PROLOGUE)

HAMLET We shall know by this fellow. The players cannot keep counsel; they'll tell all.
20 OPHELIA Will 'a tell us what this show meant?
HAMLET Ay, or any show that you'll show him. Be not you ashamed to show, he'll not shame to tell you what it means.
OPHELIA You are naught, you are naught.[37] I'll mark the play.
PROLOGUE For us and for our tragedy,
25 Here stooping to your clemency,
We beg your hearing patiently.

(*Exit*)

HAMLET Is this a prologue, or the posy[38] of a ring?[39]
OPHELIA 'Tis brief, my lord.
30 HAMLET As woman's love.

(*Enter* [*two* PLAYERS *as*] KING *and* QUEEN)

[P.] KING Full thirty times hath Phoebus' cart[40] gone round
Neptune's salt wash and Tellus'[41] orbèd ground,
And thirty dozen moons with borrowed[42] sheen

---

[35] *hobby-horse* traditional figure strapped round the waist of a performer in May games and morris dances [36] *miching mallecho* sneaking iniquity [37] *naught* indecent [38] *posy* brief motto in rhyme ("poesy") [39] *ring* finger ring [40] *Phoebus' cart* the sun's chariot [41] *Tellus* Roman goddess of the earth [42] *borrowed* i.e. taken from the sun

About the world have times twelve thirties been,
Since love our hearts, and Hymen[43] did our hands,
Unite commutual [44] in most sacred bands.
[P.] QUEEN So many journeys may the sun and moon
5 Make us again count o'er ere love be done!
But woe is me, you are so sick of late,
So far from cheer and from your former state,
That I distrust you.[45] Yet, though I distrust,
Discomfort you, my lord, it nothing must.
10 For women fear too much, even as they love,
And women's fear and love hold quantity,[46]
In neither aught, or in extremity.
Now what my love is, proof hath made you know,
And as my love is sized, my fear is so.
15 Where love is great, the littlest doubts are fear;
Where little fears grow great, great love grows there.
[P.] KING Faith, I must leave thee, love, and shortly too;
My operant powers[47] their functions leave to do.
And thou shalt live in this fair world behind,
20 Honored, beloved, and haply one as kind
For husband shalt thou—
[P.] QUEEN O, confound the rest!
Such love must needs be treason in my breast.
In second husband let me be accurst!
25 None wed the second but who killed the first.
HAMLET (*aside*) That's wormwood.[48]
[P.] QUEEN The instances[49] that second marriage move
Are base respects of thrift, but none of love.
A second time I kill my husband dead
30 When second husband kisses me in bed.
[P.] KING I do believe you think what now you speak,
But what we do determine oft we break.
Purpose is but the slave to[50] memory,
Of violent birth, but poor validity,[51]
35 Which now like fruit unripe sticks on the tree,
But fall unshaken when they mellow be.
Most necessary 'tis that we forget
To pay ourselves what to ourselves is debt.

---

[43] *Hymen* Greek god of marriage [44] *commutual* mutually [45] *distrust you* fear for you [46] *quantity* proportion [47] *operant powers* active bodily forces [48] *wormwood* a bitter herb [49] *instances* motives [50] *slave to* i.e. dependent upon for life [51] *validity* strength

What to ourselves in passion we propose,
The passion ending, doth the purpose lose.
The violence of either grief or joy
Their own enactures[52] with themselves destroy.
5 Where joy most revels, grief doth most lament;
Grief joys, joy grieves, on slender accident.
This world is not for aye, nor 'tis not strange
That even our loves should with our fortunes change,
For 'tis a question left us yet to prove,
10 Whether love lead fortune, or else fortune love.
The great man down, you mark his favorite flies,
The poor advanced makes friends of enemies;
And hitherto doth love on fortune tend,
For who not needs shall never lack a friend,
15 And who in want a hollow friend doth try,
Directly seasons him[53] his enemy.
But, orderly to end where I begun,
Our wills and fates do so contrary run
That our devices still[54] are overthrown;
20 Our thoughts are ours, their ends none of our own.
So think thou wilt no second husband wed,
But die thy thoughts when thy first lord is dead.

[P.] QUEEN Nor earth to me give food, nor heaven light,
Sport and repose lock from me day and night,
25 To desperation turn my trust and hope,
An anchor's[55] cheer in prison be my scope,
Each opposite that blanks[56] the face of joy
Meet what I would have well, and it destroy,
Both here and hence[57] pursue me lasting strife,
30 If, once a widow, ever I be wife!

HAMLET If she should break it now!

[P.] KING 'Tis deeply sworn. Sweet, leave me here awhile.
My spirits grow dull, and fain I would beguile
The tedious day with sleep.

35 [P.] QUEEN Sleep rock thy brain,

(*He sleeps*)

And never come mischance between us twain!

(*Exit*)

---

[52] *enactures* fulfillments [53] *seasons him* ripens him into [54] *still* always [55] *anchor's* hermit's [56] *blanks* blanches, makes pale [57] *hence* in the next world.

HAMLET Madam, how like you this play?

QUEEN The lady doth protest too much, methinks.

HAMLET O, but she'll keep her word.

KING Have you heard the argument?[58] Is there no offense in't?

5 HAMLET No, no, they do but jest, poison in jest; no offense i' th' world.

KING What do you call the play?

HAMLET "The Mousetrap." Marry, how? Tropically.[59] This play is the image of a murder done in Vienna. Gonzago is the duke's
10 name; his wife, Baptista. You shall see anon. 'Tis a knavish piece of work, but what o' that? Your majesty, and we that have free[60] souls, it touches us not. Let the galled[61] jade[62] winch;[63] our withers[64] are unwrung.

(*Enter* LUCIANUS)

15 This is one Lucianus, nephew to the king.

OPHELIA You are as good as a chorus,[65] my lord.

HAMLET I could interpret between you and your love, if I could see the puppets[66] dallying.

OPHELIA You are keen, my lord, you are keen.

20 HAMLET It would cost you a groaning to take off my edge.

OPHELIA Still better, and worse.

HAMLET So you must take your husbands.—Begin, murderer. Leave thy damnable faces and begin. Come, the croaking raven doth bellow for revenge.

25 LUCIANUS Thoughts black, hands apt, drugs fit, and time agreeing,
Confederate season,[67] else no creature seeing,
Thou mixture rank, of midnight weeds collected,
With Hecate's[68] ban[69] thrice blasted, thrice infected,
Thy natural magic and dire property
30 On wholesome life usurps immediately.

(*Pours the poison in his ears*)

HAMLET 'A poisons him i' th' garden for his estate. His name's Gonzago. The story is extant, and written in very choice Italian. You shall see anon how the murderer gets the love of Gonzago's
35 wife.

---

[58] *argument* plot summary [59] *Tropically* in the way of a trope or figure (with a play on "trapically") [60] *free* guiltless [61] *galled* sore-backed [62] *jade* horse [63] *winch* wince [64] *withers* shoulders [65] *chorus* one in a play who explains the action [66] *puppets* i.e. you and your lover as in a puppet show [67] *Confederate season* the occasion being my ally [68] *Hecate* goddess of witchcraft and black magic [69] *ban* curse

OPHELIA The king rises.
HAMLET What, frighted with false fire? [70]
QUEEN How fares my lord?
POLONIUS Give o'er the play.
5 KING Give me some light. Away!
POLONIUS Lights, lights, lights!

(*Exeunt all but* HAMLET *and* HORATIO)

HAMLET Why, let the strucken deer go weep,
The hart ungallèd play.
10 For some must watch, while some must sleep;
Thus runs the world away.
Would not this, sir, and a forest of feathers[71]—if the rest of my fortunes turn Turk[72] with me—with two Provincial roses[73] on my razed [74] shoes, get me a fellowship in a cry[75] of players, sir?
15 HORATIO Half a share.
HAMLET A whole one, I.
For thou dost know, O Damon dear,
This realm dismantled was
Of Jove himself; and now reigns here
20 A very, very—peacock.
HORATIO You might have rhymed.
HAMLET O good Horatio, I'll take the ghost's word for a thousand pound. Didst perceive?
HORATIO Very well, my lord.
25 HAMLET Upon the talk of the poisoning?
HORATIO I did very well note him.
HAMLET Aha! Come, some music! Come, the recorders! [76]
For if the king like not the comedy,
Why then, belike he likes it not, perdy.[77]
30 Come, some music!

(*Enter* ROSENCRANTZ *and* GUILDENSTERN)

GUILDENSTERN Good my lord, vouchsafe me a word with you.
HAMLET Sir, a whole history.
GUILDENSTERN The king, sir—
35 HAMLET Ay, sir, what of him?

---

[70] *false fire* a firing of a gun charged with powder but no shot, a blank-discharge [71] *feathers* plumes for actors' costumes [72] *turn Turk* turn renegade, like a Christian turning Mohammedan [73] *Provincial roses* ribbon rosettes [74] *razed* decorated with cut patterns [75] *cry* pack [76] *recorders* musical instruments of the flute class [77] *perdy* by God ("*par dieu*")

GUILDENSTERN Is in his retirement marvellous distempered.[78]

HAMLET With drink, sir?

GUILDENSTERN No, my lord, with choler.[79]

HAMLET Your wisdom should show itself more richer to signify this
5 to the doctor, for for me to put him to his purgation would perhaps plunge him into more choler.

GUILDENSTERN Good my lord, put your discourse into some frame,[80] and start not so wildly from my affair.

HAMLET I am tame, sir; pronounce.

10 GUILDENSTERN The queen, your mother, in most great affliction of spirit hath sent me to you.

HAMLET You are welcome.

GUILDENSTERN Nay, good my lord, this courtesy is not of the right breed. If it shall please you to make me a wholesome answer, I
15 will do your mother's commandment. If not, your pardon and my return shall be the end of my business.

HAMLET Sir, I cannot.

ROSENCRANTZ What, my lord?

HAMLET Make you a wholesome answer; my wit's diseased. But,
20 sir, such answer as I can make, you shall command, or rather, as you say, my mother. Therefore no more, but to the matter. My mother, you say—

ROSENCRANTZ Then thus she says: your behavior hath struck her into amazement and admiration.[81]

25 HAMLET O wonderful son, that can so stonish a mother! But is there no sequel at the heels of this mother's admiration? Impart.

ROSENCRANTZ She desires to speak with you in her closet[82] ere you go to bed.

HAMLET We shall obey, were she ten times our mother. Have you
30 any further trade with us?

ROSENCRANTZ My lord, you once did love me.

HAMLET And do still, by these pickers and stealers.[83]

ROSENCRANTZ Good my lord, what is your cause of distemper? You do surely bar the door upon your own liberty, if you deny
35 your griefs to your friend.

HAMLET Sir, I lack advancement.

ROSENCRANTZ How can that be, when you have the voice of the king himself for your succession in Denmark?

---

[78] *distempered* out of temper, vexed (twisted by Hamlet into "deranged") [79] *choler* anger (twisted by Hamlet into "biliousness") [80] *frame* logical order [81] *admiration* wonder [82] *closet* private room [83] *pickers and stealers* i.e. hands

HAMLET Ay, sir, but "while the grass grows" [84] the proverb is something musty.

(*Enter the* PLAYER *with recorders*)

O, the recorders. Let me see one. To withdraw[85] with you—why
5 do you go about to recover the wind [86] of me, as if you would drive me into a toil? [87]

GUILDENSTERN O my lord, if my duty be too bold, my love is too unmannerly.[88]

HAMLET I do not well understand that. Will you play upon this
10 pipe?

GUILDENSTERN My lord, I cannot.

HAMLET I pray you.

GUILDENSTERN Believe me, I cannot.

HAMLET I do beseech you.

15 GUILDENSTERN I know no touch of it, my lord.

HAMLET It is as easy as lying. Govern these ventages[89] with your fingers and thumb, give it breath with your mouth, and it will discourse most eloquent music. Look you, these are the stops.

GUILDENSTERN But these cannot I command to any utt'rance of
20 harmony. I have not the skill.

HAMLET Why, look you now, how unworthy a thing you make of me! You would play upon me, you would seem to know my stops, you would pluck out the heart of my mystery, you would sound me from my lowest note to the top of my compass; and there is
25 much music, excellent voice, in this little organ, yet cannot you make it speak. 'Sblood, do you think I am easier to be played on than a pipe? Call me what instrument you will, though you can fret[90] me, you cannot play upon me.

(*Enter* POLONIUS)

30 God bless you, sir!

POLONIUS My lord, the queen would speak with you, and presently.[91]

HAMLET Do you see yonder cloud that's almost in shape of a camel?

35 POLONIUS By th' mass and 'tis, like a camel indeed.

---

[84] *while the grass grows* (a proverb, ending: "the horse starves") [85] *withdraw* step aside [86] *recover the wind* come up to windward like a hunter [87] *toil* snare [88] *is too unmannerly* leads me beyond the restraint of good manners [89] *ventages* holes, vents [90] *fret* irritate (with a play on the fret-fingering of certain stringed musical instruments) [91] *presently* at once

HAMLET Methinks it is like a weasel.
POLONIUS It is backed like a weasel.
HAMLET Or like a whale.
POLONIUS Very like a whale.
5 HAMLET Then I will come to my mother by and by.[92] (*aside*) They fool me to the top of my bent.—I will come by and by.
POLONIUS I will say so.

(*Exit*)

HAMLET "By and by" is easily said. Leave me, friends.

10 (*Exeunt all but* HAMLET)

'Tis now the very witching time of night,
When churchyards yawn, and hell itself breathes out
Contagion to this world. Now could I drink hot blood
And do such bitter business as the day
15 Would quake to look on. Soft, now to my mother.
O heart, lose not thy nature; let not ever
The soul of Nero[93] enter this firm bosom.
Let me be cruel, not unnatural;
I will speak daggers to her, but use none.
20 My tongue and soul in this be hypocrites:
How in my words somever she be shent,[94]
To give them seals[95] never, my soul, consent!

(*Exit*)

## Act III, Scene III

25 *A chamber in the castle*

(*Enter* KING, ROSENCRANTZ, *and* GUILDENSTERN)

KING I like him not, nor stands it safe with us
To let his madness range. Therefore prepare you.
I your commission will forthwith dispatch,
30 And he to England shall along with you.
The terms[1] of our estate[2] may not endure
Hazard so near's as doth hourly grow
Out of his brows.[3]

---

[92] *by and by* immediately [93] *Nero* murderer of his mother [94] *shent* reproved
[95] *seals* authentications in actions
[1] *terms* circumstances [2] *estate* royal position [3] *brows* effronteries (apparently with an implication of knitted brows)

GUILDENSTERN We will ourselves provide.
Most holy and religious fear it is
To keep those many many bodies safe
That live and feed upon your majesty.
5 ROSENCRANTZ The single and peculiar[4] life is bound
With all the strength and armor of the mind
To keep itself from noyance,[5] but much more
That spirit upon whose weal depends and rests
The lives of many. The cess[6] of majesty
10 Dies not alone, but like a gulf [7]doth draw
What's near it with it; or 'tis a massy wheel
Fixed on the summit of the highest mount,
To whose huge spokes ten thousand lesser things
Are mortised and adjoined, which when it falls,
15 Each small annexment, petty consequence,
Attends[8] the boist'rous ruin. Never alone
Did the king sigh, but with a general groan.
KING Arm[9] you, I pray you, to this speedy voyage,
For we will fetters put upon this fear,
20 Which now goes too free-footed.
ROSENCRANTZ We will haste us.

(*Exeunt* GENTLEMEN)

(*Enter* POLONIUS)

POLONIUS My lord, he's going to his mother's closet.
25 Behind the arras I'll convey myself
To hear the process.[10] I'll warrant she'll tax him home,[11]
And, as you said, and wisely was it said,
'Tis meet that some more audience than a mother,
Since nature makes them partial, should o'erhear
30 The speech, of vantage.[12] Fare you well, my liege.
I'll call upon you ere you go to bed
And tell you what I know.
KING Thanks, dear my lord.

(*Exit* POLONIUS)

35 O, my offense is rank, it smells to heaven;
It hath the primal eldest curse[13] upon't,

[4] *peculiar* individual [5] *noyance* harm [6] *cess* cessation, decease [7] *gulf* whirlpool [8] *Attends* joins in (like a royal attendant) [9] *Arm* prepare [10] *process* proceedings [11] *tax him home* thrust home in reprimanding him [13] *of vantage* from an advantageous position [13] *primal eldest curse* that of Cain, who also murdered a brother

A brother's murder. Pray can I not,
Though inclination be as sharp as will.
My stronger guilt defeats my strong intent,
And like a man to double business bound
5 I stand in pause where I shall first begin,
And both neglect. What if this cursèd hand
Were thicker than itself with brother's blood,
Is there not rain enough in the sweet heavens
To wash it white as snow? Whereto serves mercy
10 But to confront the visage of offense? [14]
And what's in prayer but this twofold force,
To be forestallèd ere we come to fall,
Or pardoned being down? Then I'll look up.
My fault is past. But, O, what form of prayer
15 Can serve my turn? "Forgive me my foul murder"?
That cannot be, since I am still possessed
Of those effects[15] for which I did the murder,
My crown, mine own ambition, and my queen.
May one be pardoned and retain th' offense?
20 In the corrupted currents of this world
Offense's gilded [16] hand may shove by justice,
And oft 'tis seen the wicked prize itself
Buys out the law. But 'tis not so above.
There is no shuffling;[17] there the action[18] lies
25 In his true nature, and we ourselves compelled,
Even to the teeth and forehead [19] of our faults,
To give in evidence. What then? What rests?
Try what repentance can. What can it not?
Yet what can it when one cannot repent?
30 O wretched state! O bosom black as death!
O limèd [20] soul, that struggling to be free
Art more engaged! [21] Help, angels! Make assay.[22]
Bow, stubborn knees, and, heart with strings of steel,
Be soft as sinews of the new-born babe.
35 All may be well.

*He kneels*

(*Enter* HAMLET)

---

[14] *offense* sin [15] *effects* things acquired [16] *gilded* gold-laden [17] *shuffling* sharp practice, double-dealing [18] *action* legal proceeding (in heaven's court) [19] *teeth and forehead* face-to-face recognition [20] *limèd* caught in birdlime, a gluey material spread as a bird-snare [21] *engaged* embedded [22] *assay* an attempt

HAMLET Now might I do it pat,[23] now 'a is a-praying,
And now I'll do't. And so 'a goes to heaven,
And so am I revenged. That would be scanned.
A villain kills my father, and for that
5 I, his sole son, do this same villain send
To heaven.
Why, this is hire and salary, not revenge.
'A took my father grossly,[24] full of bread,[25]
With all his crimes broad blown,[26] as flush[27] as May;
10 And how his audit[28] stands, who knows save heaven?
But in our circumstance and course of thought,
'Tis heavy with him; and am I then revenged,
To take him in the purging of his soul,
When he is fit and seasoned for his passage?
15 No.
Up, sword, and know thou a more horrid hent.[29]
When he is drunk asleep, or in his rage,
Or in th' incestuous pleasure of his bed,
At game a-swearing, or about some act
20 That has no relish[30] of salvation in't—
Then trip him, that his heels may kick at heaven,
And that his soul may be as damned and black
As hell, whereto it goes. My mother stays.
This physic but prolongs thy sickly days.

25 (*Exit*)

KING (*rises*) My words fly up, my thoughts remain below.
Words without thoughts never to heaven go.

(*Exit*)

## Act III, Scene IV

30 *The private chamber of the* QUEEN

(*Enter* [QUEEN] GERTRUDE *and* POLONIUS)

POLONIUS 'A will come straight. Look you lay[1] home to him.
Tell him his pranks have been too broad[2] to bear with,
And that your grace hath screened and stood between

---

[23] *pat* opportunely [24] *grossly* in a state of gross unpreparedness [25] *bread* i.e. worldly sense gratification [26] *broad blown* fully blossomed [27] *flush* vigorous [28] *audit* account [29] *more horrid hent* grasping by me on a more horrid occasion [30] *relish* flavor

[1] *lay* thrust [2] *broad* unrestrained

Much heat and him. I'll silence me even here.
Pray you be round [3] with him.
[HAMLET (*within*) Mother, mother, mother!]
QUEEN I'll warrant you; fear me not. Withdraw; I hear him
5 coming.

(POLONIUS *hides behind the arras*)

(*Enter* HAMLET)

HAMLET Now, mother, what's the matter?
QUEEN Hamlet, thou hast thy father much offended.
10 HAMLET Mother, you have my father much offended.
QUEEN Come, come, you answer with an idle[4] tongue.
HAMLET Go, go, you question with a wicked tongue.
QUEEN Why, how now, Hamlet?
HAMLET What's the matter now?
15 QUEEN Have you forgot me?
HAMLET No, by the rood,[5] not so!
You are the queen, your husband's brother's wife,
And (would it were not so) you are my mother.
QUEEN Nay, then I'll set those to you that can speak.
20 HAMLET Come, come, and sit you down. You shall not budge.
You go not till I set you up a glass
Where you may see the inmost part of you.
QUEEN What wilt thou do? Thou wilt not murder me?
Help, ho!
25 POLONIUS (*behind*) What, ho! help!
HAMLET (*draws*) How now? a rat? Dead for a ducat, dead!

(*Makes a pass through the arras and kills* POLONIUS)

POLONIUS (*behind*) O, I am slain!
QUEEN O me, what hast thou done?
30 HAMLET Nay, I know not. Is it the king?
QUEEN O, what a rash and bloody deed is this!
HAMLET A bloody deed—almost as bad, good mother,
As kill a king, and marry with his brother.
QUEEN As kill a king?
35 HAMLET Ay, lady, it was my word.

(*Lifts up the arras and sees* POLONIUS)

Thou wretched, rash, intruding fool, farewell!

---

[3] *round* plain-spoken [4] *idle* foolish [5] *rood* cross

I took thee for thy better. Take thy fortune.
Thou find'st to be too busy is some danger.—
Leave wringing of your hands. Peace, sit you down
And let me wring your heart, for so I shall
5 If it be made of penetrable stuff,
If damnèd custom[6] have not brazed [7] it so
That it is proof [8] and bulwark against sense.[9]

QUEEN What have I done that thou dar'st wag thy tongue
In noise so rude against me?

10 HAMLET Such an act
That blurs the grace and blush of modesty,
Calls virtue hypocrite, takes off the rose
From the fair forehead of an innocent love,
And sets a blister[10] there, makes marriage vows
15 As false as dicers' oaths. O, such a deed
As from the body of contraction[11] plucks
The very soul, and sweet religion[12] makes
A rhapsody of words! Heaven's face does glow,
And this solidity and compound mass,[13]
20 With heated visage, as against[14] the doom,[15]
Is thought-sick at the act.

QUEEN Ay me, what act,
That roars so loud and thunders in the index? [16]

HAMLET Look here upon this picture, and on this,
25 The counterfeit presentment[17] of two brothers.
See what a grace was seated on this brow:
Hyperion's[18] curls, the front[19] of Jove himself,
An eye like Mars, to threaten and command,
A station[20] like the herald Mercury
30 New lighted on a heaven-kissing hill—
A combination and a form indeed
Where every god did seem to set his seal
To give the world assurance of a man.
This was your husband. Look you now what follows.
35 Here is your husband, like a mildewed ear
Blasting his wholesome brother. Have you eyes?

---

[6] *custom* habit [7] *brazed* hardened like brass [8] *proof* armor [9] *sense* feeling [10] *blister* brand (of degradation) [11] *contraction* the marriage contract [12] *religion* i.e. sacred marriage vows [13] *compound mass* the earth as compounded of the four elements [14] *against* in expectation of [15] *doom* Day of Judgment [16] *index* table of contents preceding the body of a book [17] *counterfeit presentment* portrayed representation [18] *Hyperion* the sun god [19] *front* forehead [20] *station* attitude in standing

Could you on this fair mountain leave to feed,
And batten[21] on this moor? Ha! have you eyes?
You cannot call it love, for at your age
The heyday[22] in the blood is tame, it's humble,
5 And waits upon[23] the judgment, and what judgment
Would step from this to this? Sense[24] sure you have,
Else could you not have motion,[25] but sure that sense
Is apoplexed,[26] for madness would not err,
Nor sense to ecstasy[27] was ne'er so thralled
10 But it reserved some quantity of choice
To serve in such a difference. What devil was't
That thus hath cozened[28] you at hoodman-blind?[29]
Eyes without feeling, feeling without sight,
Ears without hands or eyes, smelling sans[30] all,
15 Or but a sickly part of one true sense
Could not so mope.[31]
O shame, where is thy blush? Rebellious hell,
If thou canst mutine[32] in a matron's bones,
To flaming youth let virtue be as wax
20 And melt in her own fire. Proclaim no shame
When the compulsive[33] ardor gives the charge,[34]
Since frost itself as actively doth burn,
And reason panders will.[35]

QUEEN O Hamlet, speak no more.
25 Thou turn'st mine eyes into my very soul,
And there I see such black and grainèd[36] spots
As will not leave their tinct.[37]

HAMLET Nay, but to live
In the rank sweat of an enseamèd[38] bed,
30 Stewed in corruption, honeying and making love
Over the nasty sty—

QUEEN O, speak to me no more.
These words like daggers enter in mine ears.
No more, sweet Hamlet.

35 HAMLET A murderer and a villain,
A slave that is not twentieth part the tithe[39]

---

[21] *batten* feed greedily [22] *heyday* excitement of passion [23] *waits upon* yields to [24] *Sense* feeling [25] *motion* desire, impulse [26] *apoplexed* paralyzed [27] *ecstasy* madness [28] *cozened* cheated [29] *hoodman-blind* blindman's buff [30] *sans* without [31] *mope* be stupid [32] *mutine* mutiny [33] *compulsive* compelling [34] *gives the charge* delivers the attack [35] *panders will* acts as procurer for desire [36] *grainèd* dyed in grain [37] *tinct* color [38] *enseamèd* grease-laden [39] *tithe* tenth part

Of your precedent lord, a vice[40] of kings,
A cutpurse[41] of the empire and the rule,
That from a shelf the precious diadem stole
And put it in his pocket—

5 QUEEN No more.

(*Enter* [*the*] GHOST [*in his nightgown*[42]])

HAMLET A king of shreds and patches—
Save me and hover o'er me with your wings,
You heavenly guards? What would your gracious figure?

10 QUEEN Alas, he's mad.

HAMLET Do you not come your tardy son to chide,
That, lapsed in time and passion,[43] lets go by
Th' important acting of your dread command?
O, say!

15 GHOST Do not forget. This visitation
Is but to whet thy almost blunted purpose.
But look, amazement on thy mother sits.
O, step between her and her fighting soul!
Conceit[44] in weakest bodies strongest works.
20 Speak to her, Hamlet.

HAMLET How is it with you, lady?

QUEEN Alas, how is't with you,
That you do bend your eye on vacancy,
And with th' incorporal [45] air do hold discourse?
25 Forth at your eyes your spirits wildly peep,
And as the sleeping soldiers in th' alarm
Your bedded hairs like life in excrements[46]
Start up and stand an[47] end. O gentle son,
Upon the heat and flame of thy distemper[48]
30 Sprinkle cool patience. Whereon do you look?

HAMLET On him, on him! Look you, how pale he glares!
His form and cause conjoined, preaching to stones,
Would make them capable.[49]—Do not look upon me,
Lest with his piteous action you convert
35 My stern effects.[50] Then what I have to do
Will want true color—tears perchance for blood.

---

[40] *vice* clownish rogue (like the Vice of the morality plays) [41] *cutpurse* skulking thief [42] *nightgown* dressing gown [43] *lapsed . . . passion* having let the moment slip and passion cool [44] *Conceit* imagination [45] *incorporal* bodiless [46] *excrements* outgrowths [47] *an* on [48] *distemper* mental disorder [49] *capable* susceptible [50] *effects* manifestations of emotion and purpose

QUEEN To whom do you speak this?
HAMLET Do you see nothing there?
QUEEN Nothing at all; yet all that is I see.
HAMLET Nor did you nothing hear?
5 QUEEN No, nothing but ourselves.
HAMLET Why, look you there! Look how it steals away!
My father, in his habit as he lived!
Look where he goes even now out at the portal!

(*Exit* GHOST)

10 QUEEN This is the very coinage of your brain.
This bodiless creation ecstasy[51]
Is very cunning in.
HAMLET Ecstasy?
My pulse as yours doth temperately keep time
15 And makes as healthful music. It is not madness
That I have uttered. Bring me to the test,
And I the matter will reword, which madness
Would gambol [52] from. Mother, for love of grace,
Lay not that flattering unction[53] to your soul,
20 That not your trespass but my madness speaks.
It will but skin and film the ulcerous place
Whiles rank corruption, mining[54] all within,
Infects unseen. Confess yourself to heaven,
Repent what's past, avoid what is to come,
25 And do not spread the compost[55] on the weeds
To make them ranker. Forgive me this my virtue.
For in the fatness[56] of these pursy[57] times
Virtue itself of vice must pardon beg,
Yea, curb[58] and woo for leave to do him good.
30 QUEEN O Hamlet, thou hast cleft my heart in twain.
HAMLET O, throw away the worser part of it,
And live the purer with the other half.
Good night—but go not to my uncle's bed.
Assume a virtue, if you have it not.
35 That monster custom, who all sense doth eat,
Of habits devil, is angel yet in this,
That to the use of actions fair and good

---

[51] *ecstasy* madness [52] *gambol* shy (like a startled horse) [53] *unction* ointment [54] *mining* undermining [55] *compost* fertilizing mixture [56] *fatness* gross slackness [57] *pursy* corpulent [58] *curb* bow to

He likewise gives a frock or livery[59]
That aptly is put on. Refrain to-night,
And that shall lend a kind of easiness
To the next abstinence; the next more easy;
5 For use[60] almost can change the stamp[61] of nature,
And either [. . .] [62] the devil, or throw him out
With wondrous potency. Once more, good night,
And when you are desirous to be blest,
I'll blessing beg of you.—For this same lord,
10 I do repent; but heaven hath pleased it so,
To punish me with this, and this with me,
That I must be their scourge and minister.
I will bestow[63] him and will answer well
The death I gave him. So again, good night.
15 I must be cruel only to be kind.
Thus bad begins, and worse remains behind.[64]
One word more, good lady.

QUEEN What shall I do?

HAMLET Not this, by no means, that I bid you do:
20 Let the bloat[65] king tempt you again to bed,
Pinch wanton on your cheek, call you his mouse,
And let him, for a pair of reechy[66] kisses,
Or paddling in your neck with his damned fingers,
Make you to ravel all this matter out,[67]
25 That I essentially am not in madness,
But mad in craft. 'Twere good you let him know,
For who that's but a queen, fair, sober, wise,
Would from a paddock,[68] from a bat, a gib,[69]
Such dear concernings[70] hide? Who would do so?
30 No, in despite of sense and secrecy,
Unpeg the basket on the house's top,
Let the birds fly, and like the famous ape,[71]
To try conclusions,[72] in the basket creep
And break your own neck down.

35 QUEEN Be thou assured, if words be made of breath,
And breath of life, I have no life to breathe

---

[59] *livery* characteristic dress (accompanying the suggestion of "garb" in *habits*) [60] *use* habit [61] *stamp* impression, form [62] A word is apparently omitted here [63] *bestow* stow, hide [64] *behind* to come [65] *bloat* bloated with sense gratification [66] *reechy* filthy [67] *ravel . . . out* disentangle [68] *paddock* toad [69] *gib* tomcat [70] *dear concernings* matters of great personal significance [71] *famous ape* (one in a story now unknown) [72] *conclusions* experiments

What thou hast said to me.

HAMLET I must to England; you know that?

QUEEN Alack,

I had forgot. 'Tis so concluded on.

5 HAMLET There's letters sealed, and my two schoolfellows,
Whom I will trust as I will adders fanged,
They bear the mandate;[73] they must sweep my way
And marshal me to knavery. Let it work.
For 'tis the sport to have the enginer[74]
10 Hoist[75] with his own petar,[76] and 't shall go hard
But I will delve one yard below their mines
And blow them at the moon. O, 'tis most sweet
When in one line two crafts directly meet.
This man shall set me packing.[77]
15 I'll lug the guts into the neighbor room.
Mother, good night. Indeed, this counsellor
Is now most still, most secret, and most grave,
Who was in life a foolish prating knave.
Come, sir, to draw toward an end with you.
20 Good night, mother.

(*Exit the* QUEEN. *Then exit* HAMLET, *tugging in* POLONIUS)

## ACT IV

### Scene I

*A chamber in the castle*

25 (*Enter* KING *and* QUEEN, *with* ROSENCRANTZ *and* GUILDENSTERN)

KING There's matter in these sighs. These profound heaves
You must translate; 'tis fit we understand them.
Where is your son?

QUEEN Bestow this place on us a little while.

30 (*Exeunt* ROSENCRANTZ *and* GUILDENSTERN)

Ah, mine own lord, what have I seen to-night!

KING What, Gertrude? How does Hamlet?

---

73 *mandate* order 74 *enginer* engineer, constructor of military engines or works 75 *Hoist* blown up 76 *petar* petard, bomb or mine 77 *packing* travelling in a hurry (with a play upon his "packing" or shouldering of Polonius' body and also upon his "packing" in the sense of "plotting" or "contriving")

QUEEN Mad as the sea and wind when both contend
Which is the mightier. In his lawless fit,
Behind the arras hearing something stir,
Whips out his rapier, cries, "A rat, a rat!"
5 And in this brainish apprehension[1] kills
The unseen good old man.

KING O heavy deed!
It had been so with us, had we been there.
His liberty is full of threats to all,
10 To you yourself, to us, to every one.
Alas, how shall this bloody deed be answered?
It will be laid to us, whose providence[2]
Should have kept short, restrained, and out of haunt[3]
This mad young man. But so much was our love
15 We would not understand what was most fit,
But, like the owner of a foul disease,
To keep it from divulging,[4] let it feed
Even on the pith of life. Where is he gone?

QUEEN To draw apart the body he hath killed;
20 O'er whom his very madness, like some ore[5]
Among a mineral[6] of metals base,
Shows itself pure. 'A weeps for what is done.

KING O Gertrude, come away!
The sun no sooner shall the mountains touch
25 But we will ship him hence, and this vile deed
We must with all our majesty and skill
Both countenance and excuse. Ho, Guildenstern!

(*Enter* ROSENCRANTZ *and* GUILDENSTERN)

Friends both, go join you with some further aid.
30 Hamlet in madness hath Polonius slain,
And from his mother's closet hath he dragged him.
Go seek him out; speak fair, and bring the body
Into the chapel. I pray you haste in this.

(*Exeunt* ROSENCRANTZ *and* GUILDENSTERN)

35 Come, Gertrude, we'll call up our wisest friends
And let them know both what we mean to do
And what's untimely done [. . .] [7]

---

[1] *brainish apprehension* headstrong conception [2] *providence* foresight [3] *haunt* association with others [4] *divulging* becoming known [5] *ore* vein of gold [6] *mineral* mine [7] Incomplete line; Capell suggests "So, haply, slander"

Whose whisper o'er the world's diameter,
As level[8] as the cannon to his blank[9]
Transports his poisoned shot, may miss our name
And hit the woundless air. O, come away!
5 My soul is full of discord and dismay.

(*Exeunt*)

## Act IV, Scene II

*A passage in the castle*

(*Enter* HAMLET)

10 HAMLET Safely stowed.
GENTLEMEN (*within*) Hamlet! Lord Hamlet!
HAMLET But soft, what noise? Who calls on Hamlet? O, here they come.

(*Enter* ROSENCRANTZ, GUILDENSTERN, *and others*)

15 ROSENCRANTZ What have you done, my lord, with the dead body?
HAMLET Compounded it with dust, whereto 'tis kin.
ROSENCRANTZ Tell us where 'tis, that we may take it thence
And bear it to the chapel.
HAMLET Do not believe it.
20 ROSENCRANTZ Believe what?
HAMLET That I can keep your counsel and not mine own. Besides, to be demanded of a sponge, what replication[1] should be made by the son of a king?
ROSENCRANTZ Take you me for a sponge, my lord?
25 HAMLET Ay, sir, that soaks up the king's countenance,[2] his rewards, his authorities. But such officers do the king best service in the end. He keeps them, like an ape, in the corner of his jaw, first mouthed, to be last swallowed. When he needs what you have gleaned, it is but squeezing you and, sponge, you shall be dry
30 again.
ROSENCRANTZ I understand you not, my lord.
HAMLET I am glad of it. A knavish speech sleeps in[3] a foolish ear.
ROSENCRANTZ My lord, you must tell us where the body is and go with us to the king.
35 HAMLET The body is with the king, but the king is not with the body. The king is a thing—

[8] *As level* with as direct aim [9] *blank* mark, central white spot on a target
[1] *replication* reply [2] *countenance* favor [3] *sleeps in* means nothing to

GUILDENSTERN A thing, my lord?
HAMLET Of nothing.[4] Bring me to him. Hide fox, and all after.[5]

(*Exeunt*)

## Act IV, Scene III

5 *A chamber in the castle*

(*Enter* KING, *and two or three*)

KING I have sent to seek him and to find the body.
How dangerous is it that this man goes loose!
Yet must not we put the strong law on him;
10 He's loved of the distracted [1] multitude,
Who like not in their judgment, but their eyes,
And where 'tis so, th' offender's scourge[2] is weighed,
But never the offense. To bear all smooth and even,
This sudden sending him away must seem
15 Deliberate pause.[3] Diseases desperate grown
By desperate appliance are relieved,
Or not at all.

(*Enter* ROSENCRANTZ, GUILDENSTERN, *and all the rest*)

How now? What hath befallen?
20 ROSENCRANTZ Where the dead body is bestowed, my lord,
We cannot get from him.
KING But where is he?
ROSENCRANTZ Without, my lord; guarded, to know your pleasure.
KING Bring him before us.
25 ROSENCRANTZ Ho! Bring in the lord.

(*They enter* [*with* HAMLET])

KING Now, Hamlet, where's Polonius?
HAMLET At supper.
KING At supper? Where?
30 HAMLET Not where he eats, but where 'a is eaten. A certain convocation of politic worms[4] are e'en at him. Your worm is your

---

[4] *Of nothing* (cf. Prayer Book, Psalm cxliv, 4, "Man is like a thing of naught: his time passeth away like a shadow") [5] *Hide . . . after* (apparently well-known words from some game of hide-and-seek)
[1] *distracted* confused [2] *scourge* punishment [3] *Deliberate pause* something done with much deliberation [4] *politic worms* political and craftily scheming worms (such as Polonius might well attract)

only emperor for diet.[5] We fat all creatures else to fat us, and we fat ourselves for maggots. Your fat king and your lean beggar is but variable service[6]—two dishes, but to one table. That's the end.

KING Alas, alas!

5 HAMLET A man may fish with the worm that hath eat of a king, and eat of the fish that hath fed of that worm.

KING What dost thou mean by this?

HAMLET Nothing but to show you how a king may go a progress[7] through the guts of a beggar.

10 KING Where is Polonius?

HAMLET In heaven. Send thither to see. If your messenger find him not there, seek him i' th' other place yourself. But if indeed you find him not within this month, you shall nose him as you go up the stairs into the lobby.

15 KING (*to* ATTENDANTS) Go seek him there.

HAMLET 'A will stay till you come.

(*Exeunt* ATTENDANTS)

KING Hamlet, this deed, for thine especial safety,
Which we do tender[8] as we dearly[9] grieve
20 For that which thou hast done, must send thee hence
With fiery quickness. Therefore prepare thyself.
The bark is ready and the wind at help,
Th' associates tend,[10] and everything is bent[11]
For England.

25 HAMLET For England?

KING Ay, Hamlet.

HAMLET Good.

KING So is it, if thou knew'st our purposes.

HAMLET I see a cherub[12] that sees them. But come, for England!
30 Farewell, dear mother.

KING Thy loving father, Hamlet.

HAMLET My mother—father and mother is man and wife, man and wife is one flesh, and so, my mother. Come, for England!

(*Exit*)

---

[5] *diet* food and drink (perhaps with a play upon a famous "convocation," the Diet of Worms opened by the Emperor Charles V on January 28, 1521, before which Luther appeared) [6] *variable service* different servings of one food [7] *progress* royal journey of state [8] *tender* hold dear [9] *dearly* intensely [10] *tend* wait [11] *bent* set in readiness (like a bent bow) [12] *cherub* one of the cherubim (angels with a distinctive quality of knowledge)

KING Follow him at foot;[13] tempt him with speed aboard.
Delay it not; I'll have him hence to-night.
Away! for everything is sealed and done
That else leans on[14] th' affair. Pray you make haste.

5 (*Exeunt all but the* KING)

And, England,[15] if my love thou hold'st at aught—
As my great power thereof may give thee sense,
Since yet thy cicatrice looks raw and red
After the Danish sword, and thy free awe[16]
10 Pays homage to us—thou mayst not coldly set[17]
Our sovereign process,[18] which imports at full
By letters congruing[19] to that effect
The present[20] death of Hamlet. Do it, England,
For like the hectic[21] in my blood he rages,
15 And thou must cure me. Till I know 'tis done,
Howe'er my haps,[22] my joys were ne'er begun.

(*Exit*)

## Act IV, Scene IV

*A coastal highway*

20 (*Enter* FORTINBRAS *with his* ARMY *over the stage*)

FORTINBRAS Go, captain, from me greet the Danish king.
Tell him that by his license Fortinbras
Craves the conveyance[1] of a promised march
Over his kingdom. You know the rendezvous.
25 If that his majesty would aught with us,
We shall express our duty in his eye;[2]
And let him know so.

CAPTAIN I will do't, my lord.

FORTINBRAS Go softly[3] on.

30 (*Exeunt all but the* CAPTAIN)

(*Enter* HAMLET, ROSENCRANTZ, GUILDENSTERN, *and others*)

HAMLET Good sir, whose powers[4] are these?

---

[13] *at foot* at heel, close [14] *leans on* is connected with [15] *England* King of England [16] *free awe* voluntary show of respect [17] *set* esteem [18] *process* formal command [19] *congruing* agreeing [20] *present* instant [21] *hectic* a continuous fever [22] *haps* fortunes

[1] *conveyance* escort [2] *eye* presence [3] *softly* slowly [4] *powers* forces

CAPTAIN They are of Norway, sir.
HAMLET How purposed, sir, I pray you?
CAPTAIN Against some part of Poland.
HAMLET Who commands them, sir?
5 CAPTAIN The nephew to old Norway, Fortinbras.
HAMLET Goes it against the main[5] of Poland, sir,
Or for some frontier?
CAPTAIN Truly to speak, and with no addition,[6]
We go to gain a little patch of ground
10 That hath in it no profit but the name.
To pay[7] five ducats, five, I would not farm it,
Nor will it yield to Norway or the Pole
A ranker[8] rate, should it be sold in fee.[9]
HAMLET Why, then the Polack never will defend it.
15 CAPTAIN Yes, it is already garrisoned.
HAMLET Two thousand souls and twenty thousand ducats
Will not debate the question of this straw.
This is th' imposthume[10] of much wealth and peace,
That inward breaks, and shows no cause without
20 Why the man dies. I humbly thank you, sir.
CAPTAIN God bye you, sir.

(*Exit*)

ROSENCRANTZ Will't please you go, my lord?
HAMLET I'll be with you straight. Go a little before.

25 (*Exeunt all but* HAMLET)

How all occasions do inform[11] against me
And spur my dull revenge! What is a man,
If his chief good and market of [12] his time
Be but to sleep and feed? A beast, no more.
30 Sure he that made us with such large discourse,[13]
Looking before and after, gave us not
That capability and godlike reason
To fust[14] in us unused. Now, whether it be
Bestial oblivion,[15] or some craven scruple
35 Of thinking too precisely on th' event—[16]

---

5 *main* main body 6 *addition* exaggeration 7 *To pay* i.e. for a yearly rental of 8 *ranker* more abundant 9 *in fee* outright 10 *imposthume* abscess 11 *inform* take shape 12 *market of* compensation for 13 *discourse* power of thought 14 *fust* grow mouldy 15 *oblivion* forgetfulness 16 *event* outcome

A thought which, quartered, hath but one part wisdom
And ever three parts coward—I do not know
Why yet I live to say, "This thing 's to do,"
Sith I have cause, and will, and strength, and means
5 To do't. Examples gross[17] as earth exhort me.
Witness this army of such mass and charge,[18]
Led by a delicate and tender prince,
Whose spirit, with divine ambition puffed,
Makes mouths[19] at the invisible event,
10 Exposing what is mortal and unsure
To all that fortune, death, and danger dare,
Even for an eggshell. Rightly to be great
Is not to stir without great argument,
But greatly to find quarrel in a straw[20]
15 When honor 's at the stake. How stand I then,
That have a father killed, a mother stained,
Excitements of my reason and my blood,
And let all sleep, while to my shame I see
The imminent death of twenty thousand men
20 That for a fantasy[21] and trick[22] of fame
Go to their graves like beds, fight for a plot
Whereon the numbers cannot try the cause,[23]
Which is not tomb enough and continent[24]
To hide the slain? O, from this time forth,
25 My thoughts be bloody, or be nothing worth!

(*Exit*)

## Act IV, Scene V

*A chamber in the castle*

(*Enter* HORATIO, [QUEEN] GERTRUDE, *and a* GENTLEMAN)

30 QUEEN I will not speak with her.
GENTLEMAN She is importunate, indeed distract.[1]
Her mood will needs be pitied.
QUEEN What would she have?
GENTLEMAN She speaks much of her father, says she hears

---

[17] *gross* large and evident [18] *charge* expense [19] *Makes mouths* makes faces scornfully [20] *greatly . . . straw* to recognize the great argument even in some small matter [21] *fantasy* fanciful image [22] *trick* toy [23] *try the cause* find space in which to settle the issue by battle [24] *continent* receptacle
[1] *distract* insane

There's tricks[2] i' th' world, and hems, and beats her heart,
Spurns enviously[3] at straws,[4] speaks things in doubt
That carry but half sense. Her speech is nothing,
Yet the unshapèd use[5] of it doth move
5 The hearers to collection;[6] they aim[7] at it,
And botch[8] the words up fit to their own thoughts,
Which, as her winks and nods and gestures yield them,
Indeed would make one think there might be thought,
Though nothing sure, yet much unhappily.

10 HORATIO 'Twere good she were spoken with, for she may strew
Dangerous conjectures in ill-breeding minds.

QUEEN Let her come in.

(*Exit* GENTLEMAN)

(*Aside*)

15 To my sick soul (as sin's true nature is)
Each toy[9] seems prologue to some great amiss.[10]
So full of artless[11] jealousy[12] is guilt
It spills[13] itself in fearing to be spilt.

(*Enter* OPHELIA [*distracted*])

20 OPHELIA Where is the beauteous majesty of Denmark?

QUEEN How now, Ophelia?

OPHELIA (*She sings.*)

How should I your true-love know
From another one?
25 By his cockle hat[14] and staff
And his sandal shoon.[15]

QUEEN Alas, sweet lady, what imports this song?

OPHELIA Say you? Nay, pray you mark.

**Song**

30 He is dead and gone, lady,
He is dead and gone;
At his head a grass-green turf,
At his heels a stone.

O, ho!

---

[2] *tricks* deceits [3] *Spurns enviously* kicks spitefully, takes offense [4] *straws* trifles [5] *unshapèd use* disordered manner [6] *collection* attempts at shaping meaning [7] *aim* guess [8] *botch* patch [9] *toy* trifle [10] *amiss* calamity [11] *artless* unskillfully managed [12] *jealousy* suspicion [13] *spills* destroys [14] *cockle hat* hat bearing a cockle shell, worn by a pilgrim who had been to the shrine of St James of Compostela [15] *shoon* shoes

QUEEN Nay, but Ophelia—
OPHELIA Pray you mark.
(*Sings*) White his shroud as the mountain snow—

(*Enter* KING)

5 QUEEN Alas, look here, my lord.
OPHELIA

**Song**

Larded [16] all with sweet flowers;
Which bewept to the grave did not go
10 With true-love showers.

KING How do you, pretty lady?
OPHELIA Well, God dild [17] you! They say the owl [18] was a baker's daughter. Lord, we know what we are, but know not what we may be. God be at your table!
15 KING Conceit[19] upon her father.
OPHELIA Pray let's have no words of this, but when they ask you what it means, say you this:

**Song**

To-morrow is Saint Valentine's day.
20 All in the morning betime,[20]
And I a maid at your window,
To be your Valentine.
Then up he rose and donned his clo'es
And dupped [21] the chamber door,
25 Let in the maid, that out a maid
Never departed more.

KING Pretty Ophelia!
OPHELIA Indeed, la, without an oath, I'll make an end on't:
(*Sings*) By Gis[22] and by Saint Charity,
30 Alack, and fie for shame!
Young men will do't if they come to't.
By Cock,[23] they are to blame.
Quoth she, "Before you tumbled me,
You promised me to wed."

---

[16] *Larded* garnished [17] *dild* yield, repay [18] *the owl* an owl into which, according to a folk-tale, a baker's daughter was transformed because of her failure to show whole-hearted generosity when Christ asked for bread in the baker's shop [19] *Conceit* thought [20] *betime* early [21] *dupped* opened [22] *Gis* Jesus [23] *Cock* God (with a perversion of the name not uncommon in oaths)

He answers:
"So would I 'a' done, by yonder sun,
And thou hadst not come to my bed."

KING How long hath she been thus?

5 OPHELIA I hope all will be well. We must be patient, but I cannot choose but weep to think they would lay him i' th' cold ground. My brother shall know of it; and so I thank you for your good counsel. Come, my coach! Good night, ladies, good night. Sweet ladies, good night, good night.

10 (*Exit*)

KING Follow her close; give her good watch, I pray you.

(*Exit* HORATIO)

O, this is the poison of deep grief; it springs
All from her father's death—and now behold!
15 O Gertrude, Gertrude,
When sorrows come, they come not single spies,
But in battalions: first, her father slain;
Next, your son gone, and he most violent author
Of his own just remove; the people muddied,[24]
20 Thick and unwholesome in their thoughts and whispers
For good Polonius' death, and we have done but greenly[25]
In hugger-mugger[26] to inter him; poor Ophelia
Divided from herself and her fair judgment,
Without the which we are pictures or mere beasts;
25 Last, and as much containing as all these,
Her brother is in secret come from France,
Feeds on his wonder, keeps himself in clouds,[27]
And wants[28] not buzzers[29] to infect his ear
With pestilent speeches of his father's death,
30 Wherein necessity, of matter beggared,[30]
Will nothing stick[31] our person to arraign[32]
In ear and ear. O my dear Gertrude, this,
Like to a murd'ring piece,[33] in many places
Gives me superfluous death.

35 *A noise within*

---

[24] *muddied* stirred up and confused [25] *greenly* foolishly [26] *hugger-mugger* secrecy and disorder [27] *clouds* obscurity [28] *wants* lacks [29] *buzzers* whispering tale-bearers [30] *of matter beggared* unprovided with facts [31] *nothing stick* in no way hesitate [32] *arraign* accuse [33] *murd'ring piece* cannon loaded with shot meant to scatter

(*Enter a* MESSENGER)

QUEEN Alack, what noise is this?
KING Attend, where are my Switzers?[34] Let them guard the door.
What is the matter?
5 MESSENGER Save yourself, my lord.
The ocean, overpeering of[35] his list,[36]
Eats not the flats with more impiteous[37] haste
Than young Laertes, in a riotous head,[38]
O'erbears your officers. The rabble call him lord,
10 And, as the world were now but to begin,
Antiquity forgot, custom not known,
The ratifiers and props of every word,[39]
They cry, "Choose we! Laertes shall be king!"
Caps, hands, and tongues applaud it to the clouds,
15 "Laertes shall be king! Laertes king!"

*A noise within*

QUEEN How cheerfully on the false trail they cry!
O, this is counter,[40] you false Danish dogs!
KING The doors are broke.

20 (*Enter* LAERTES *with others*)

LAERTES Where is this king?—Sirs, stand you all without.
ALL No, let's come in.
LAERTES I pray you give me leave.
ALL We will, we will.
25 LAERTES I thank you. Keep the door.

(*Exeunt his* FOLLOWERS)

O thou vile king,
Give me my father.
QUEEN Calmly, good Laertes.
30 LAERTES That drop of blood that's calm proclaims me bastard,
Cries cuckold to my father, brands the harlot
Even here between the chaste unsmirchèd brows
Of my true mother.
KING What is the cause, Laertes,
35 That thy rebellion looks so giant-like?
Let him go, Gertrude. Do not fear[41] our person.

---

[34] *Switzers* hired Swiss guards [35] *overpeering of* rising to look over and pass beyond [36] *list* boundary [37] *impiteous* pitiless [38] *head* armed force [39] *word* promise [40] *counter* hunting backward on the trail [41] *fear* fear for

There's such divinity doth hedge a king
That treason can but peep to[42] what it would,
Acts little of his will. Tell me, Laertes,
Why thou art thus incensed. Let him go, Gertrude.
5 Speak, man.

LAERTES Where is my father?

KING Dead.

QUEEN But not by him.

KING Let him demand his fill.

10 LAERTES How came he dead? I'll not be juggled with.
To hell allegiance, vows to the blackest devil,
Conscience and grace to the profoundest pit!
I dare damnation. To this point I stand,
That both the worlds[43] I give to negligence,[44]
15 Let come what comes, only I'll be revenged
Most throughly[45] for my father.

KING Who shall stay you?

LAERTES My will, not all the world's.
And for my means, I'll husband them so well
20 They shall go far with little.

KING Good Laertes,
If you desire to know the certainty
Of your dear father, is't writ in your revenge
That swoopstake[46] you will draw both friend and foe,
25 Winner and loser?

LAERTES None but his enemies.

KING Will you know them then?

LAERTES To his good friends thus wide I'll ope my arms
And like the kind life-rend'ring[47] pelican
30 Repast them with my blood.

KING Why, now you speak
Like a good child and a true gentleman.
That I am guiltless of your father's death,
And am most sensibly[48] in grief for it,
35 It shall as level [49] to your judgment 'pear
As day does to your eye.

*A noise within:* "Let her come in!"

---

[42] *peep to* i.e. through the barrier [43] *both the worlds* whatever may result in this world or the next [44] *give to negligence* disregard [45] *throughly* thoroughly [46] *swoopstake* sweepstake, taking all stakes on the gambling table [47] *life-rend'ring* life-yielding (because the mother pelican supposedly took blood from her breast with her bill to feed her young) [48] *sensibly* feelingly [49] *level* plain

LAERTES How now? What noise is that?

(*Enter* OPHELIA)

O heat, dry up my brains; tears seven times salt
Burn out the sense and virtue of mine eye!
5 By heaven, thy madness shall be paid by weight
Till our scale turn the beam.[50] O rose of May,
Dear maid, kind sister, sweet Ophelia!
O heavens, is't possible a young maid's wits
Should be as mortal as an old man's life?
10 Nature is fine[51] in love, and where 'tis fine,
It sends some precious instance[52] of itself
After the thing it loves.

OPHELIA

**Song**

15 They bore him barefaced on the bier
Hey non nony, nony, hey nony
And in his grave rained many a tear—
Fare you well, my dove!

LAERTES Hadst thou thy wits, and didst persuade revenge,
20 It could not move thus.

OPHELIA You must sing "A-down a-down, and you call him a-down-a." O, how the wheel[53] becomes it! It is the false steward, that stole his master's daughter.

LAERTES This nothing 's more than matter.[54]

25 OPHELIA There's rosemary, that's for remembrance. Pray you, love, remember. And there is pansies, that's for thoughts.

LAERTES A document[55] in madness, thoughts and remembrance fitted.

OPHELIA There's fennel[56] for you, and columbines.[57] There's rue[58]
30 for you, and here's some for me. We may call it herb of grace o' Sundays. O, you must wear your rue with a difference. There's a daisy.[59] I would give you some violets,[60] but they withered all when my father died. They say 'a made a good end.
(*Sings*) For bonny sweet Robin is all my joy.

35 LAERTES Thought and affliction, passion, hell itself,
She turns to favor[61] and to prettiness.

---

[50] *beam* bar of a balance [51] *fine* refined to purity [52] *instance* token [53] *wheel* burden, refrain [54] *more than matter* more meaningful than sane speech [55] *document* lesson [56] *fennel* symbol of flattery [57] *columbines* symbol of thanklessness [58] *rue* symbol of repentance [59] *daisy* symbol of dissembling [60] *violets* symbol of faithfulness [61] *favor* charm

OPHELIA

**Song**

And will 'a not come again?
And will 'a not come again?
5 No, no, he is dead;
Go to thy deathbed;
He never will come again.
His beard was as white as snow,
All flaxen was his poll.[62]
10 He is gone, he is gone,
And we cast away moan.
God 'a' mercy on his soul!
And of [63] all Christian souls, I pray God. God bye you.

(*Exit*)

15 LAERTES Do you see this, O God?
KING Laertes, I must commune with your grief,
Or you deny me right. Go but apart,
Make choice of whom your wisest friends you will,
And they shall hear and judge 'twixt you and me.
20 If by direct or by collateral [64] hand
They find us touched,[65] we will our kingdom give,
Our crown, our life, and all that we call ours,
To you in satisfaction; but if not,
Be you content to lend your patience to us,
25 And we shall jointly labor with your soul
To give it due content.
LAERTES Let this be so.
His means of death, his obscure funeral—
No trophy,[66] sword, nor hatchment[67] o'er his bones,
30 No noble rite nor formal ostentation[68]—
Cry to be heard, as 'twere from heaven to earth,
That[69] I must call't in question.
KING So you shall;
And where th' offense is, let the great axe fall.
35 I pray you go with me.

(*Exeunt*)

---

[62] *poll* head [63] *of* on [64] *collateral* indirect [65] *touched* i.e. with the crime
[66] *trophy* memorial [67] *hatchment* coat of arms [68] *ostentation* ceremony
[69] *That* so that

## Act IV, Scene VI

*A chamber in the castle*

(*Enter* HORATIO *and others*)

HORATIO What are they that would speak with me?
5 GENTLEMAN Seafaring men, sir. They say they have letters for you.
HORATIO Let them come in.

(*Exit* ATTENDANT)

I do not know from what part of the world
I should be greeted, if not from Lord Hamlet.

10 (*Enter* SAILORS)

SAILOR God bless you, sir.
HORATIO Let him bless thee too.
SAILOR 'A shall, sir, an't please him. There's a letter for you, sir—it came from th' ambassador that was bound for England—if
15 your name be Horatio, as I am let to know it is.
HORATIO (*reads the letter*) "Horatio, when thou shalt have overlooked [1] this, give these fellows some means[2] to the king. They have letters for him. Ere we were two days old at sea, a pirate of very warlike appointment[3] gave us chase. Finding ourselves too
20 slow of sail, we put on a compelled valor, and in the grapple I boarded them. On the instant they got clear of our ship; so I alone became their prisoner. They have dealt with me like thieves of mercy,[4] but they knew what they did: I am to do a good turn for them. Let the king have the letters I have sent, and repair
25 thou to me with as much speed as thou wouldest fly death. I have words to speak in thine ear will make thee dumb; yet are they much too light for the bore[5] of the matter. These good fellows will bring thee where I am. Rosencrantz and Guildenstern hold their course for England. Of them I have much to tell thee.
30 Farewell.

He that thou knowest thine, Hamlet."

Come, I will give you way for these your letters,
And do't the speedier that you may direct me
To him from whom you brought them.

35 (*Exeunt*)

---

[1] *overlooked* surveyed, scanned [2] *means* i.e. of access [3] *appointment* equipment [4] *thieves of mercy* merciful thieves [5] *bore* caliber (as of a gun)

## Act IV, Scene VII

*A chamber in the castle*

(*Enter* KING *and* LAERTES)

KING Now must your conscience my acquittance seal,
5 And you must put me in your heart for friend,
Sith you have heard, and with a knowing ear,
That he which hath your noble father slain
Pursued my life.

LAERTES It well appears. But tell me
10 Why you proceeded not against these feats[1]
So crimeful and so capital[2] in nature,
As by your safety, wisdom, all things else,
You mainly[3] were stirred up.

KING O, for two special reasons,
15 Which may to you perhaps seem much unsinewed,
But yet to me they're strong. The queen his mother
Lives almost by his looks, and for myself—
My virtue or my plague, be it either which—
She is so conjunctive[4] to my life and soul
20 That, as the star moves not but in his sphere,
I could not but by her. The other motive
Why to a public count[5] I might not go
Is the great love the general gender[6] bear him,
Who, dipping all his faults in their affection,
25 Would, like the spring that turneth wood to stone,
Convert his gyves[7] to graces; so that my arrows,
Too slightly timbered for so loud a wind,
Would have reverted to my bow again,
And not where I had aimed them.

30 LAERTES And so have I a noble father lost,
A sister driven into desp'rate terms,[8]
Whose worth, if praises may go back again,[9]
Stood challenger on mount[10] of all the age
For her perfections. But my revenge will come.

35 KING Break not your sleeps for that. You must not think
That we are made of stuff so flat and dull
That we can let our beard be shook with danger,

---

[1] *feats* deeds [2] *capital* punishable by death [3] *mainly* powerfully [4] *conjunctive* closely united [5] *count* trial, accounting [6] *general gender* common people [7] *gyves* fetters [8] *terms* circumstances [9] *back again* i.e. to her better circumstances [10] *on mount* on a height

And think it pastime. You shortly shall hear more.
I loved your father, and we love ourself,
And that, I hope, will teach you to imagine—

(*Enter a* MESSENGER *with letters*)

5 How now? What news?

MESSENGER Letters, my lord, from Hamlet:
These to your majesty, this to the queen.

KING From Hamlet? Who brought them?

MESSENGER Sailors, my lord, they say; I saw them not.
10 They were given me by Claudio; he received them
Of him that brought them.

KING Laertes, you shall hear them.—
Leave us.

(*Exit* MESSENGER)

15 (*Reads*) "High and mighty, you shall know I am set naked [11] on your kingdom. To-morrow shall I beg leave to see your kingly eyes; when I shall (first asking your pardon thereunto) recount the occasion of my sudden and more strange return. Hamlet."
What should this mean? Are all the rest come back?
20 Or is it some abuse,[12] and no such thing?

LAERTES Know you the hand?

KING 'Tis Hamlet's character.[13] "Naked"!
And in a postscript here, he says "alone."
Can you devise[14] me?

25 LAERTES I am lost in it, my lord. But let him come.
It warms the very sickness in my heart
That I shall live and tell him to his teeth,
"Thus diddest thou."

KING If it be so, Laertes,
30 (As how should it be so? how otherwise?)
Will you be ruled by me?

LAERTES Ay, my lord,
So you will not o'errule me to a peace.

KING To thine own peace. If he be now returned,
35 As checking at[15] his voyage, and that he means
No more to undertake it, I will work him

---

[11] *naked* destitute [12] *abuse* imposture [13] *character* handwriting [14] *devise* explain to [15] *checking at* turning aside from (like a falcon turning from its quarry for other prey)

To an exploit now ripe in my device,
Under the which he shall not choose but fall;
And for his death no wind of blame shall breathe,
But even his mother shall uncharge the practice[16]
5 And call it accident.

LAERTES My lord, I will be ruled;
The rather if you could devise it so
That I might be the organ.[17]

KING It falls right.
10 You have been talked of since your travel much,
And that in Hamlet's hearing, for a quality
Wherein they say you shine. Your sum of parts
Did not together pluck such envy from him
As did that one, and that, in my regard,
15 Of the unworthiest siege.[18]

LAERTES What part is that, my lord?

KING A very riband[19] in the cap of youth,
Yet needful too, for youth no less becomes
The light and careless livery[20] that it wears
20 Than settled age his sables[21] and his weeds,[22]
Importing health[23] and graveness. Two months since
Here was a gentleman of Normandy.
I have seen myself, and served against, the French,
And they can well[24] on horseback, but this gallant
25 Had witchcraft in't. He grew unto his seat,
And to such wondrous doing brought his horse
As had he been incorpsed[25] and demi-natured[26]
With the brave beast. So far he topped[27] my thought[28]
That I, in forgery[29] of shapes and tricks,
30 Come short of what he did.

LAERTES A Norman was't?

KING A Norman.

LAERTES Upon my life, Lamord.

KING The very same.

35 LAERTES I know him well. He is the brooch[30] indeed

---

[16] *uncharge the practice* acquit the stratagem of being a plot [17] *organ* instrument [18] *siege* seat, rank [19] *riband* decoration [20] *livery* distinctive attire [21] *sables* dignified robes richly furred with sable [22] *weeds* distinctive garments [23] *health* welfare, prosperity [24] *can well* can perform well [25] *incorpsed* made one body [26] *demi-natured* made sharer of nature half and half (as man shares with horse in the centaur) [27] *topped* excelled [28] *thought* imagination of possibilities [29] *forgery* invention [30] *brooch* ornament

And gem of all the nation.
KING He made confession[31] of you,
And gave you such a masterly report
For art and exercise in your defense,
5 And for your rapier most especial,
That he cried out 'twould be a sight indeed
If one could match you. The scrimers[32] of their nation
He swore had neither motion, guard, nor eye,
If you opposed them. Sir, this report of his
10 Did Hamlet so envenom with his envy
That he could nothing do but wish and beg
Your sudden coming o'er to play with you.
Now, out of this—
LAERTES What out of this, my lord?
15 KING Laertes, was your father dear to you?
Or are you like the painting of a sorrow,
A face without a heart?
LAERTES Why ask you this?
KING Not that I think you did not love your father,
20 But that I know love is begun by time,
And that I see, in passages of proof,[33]
Time qualifies[34] the spark and fire of it.
There lives within the very flame of love
A kind of wick or snuff[35] that will abate it,
25 And nothing is at a like goodness still,[36]
For goodness, growing to a plurisy,[37]
Dies in his own too-much. That we would do
We should do when we would, for this "would" changes,
And hath abatements and delays as many
30 As there are tongues, are hands, are accidents,
And then this "should" is like a spendthrift sigh,
That hurts[38] by easing. But to the quick[39] o' th' ulcer—
Hamlet comes back; what would you undertake
To show yourself your father's son in deed
35 More than in words?
LAERTES To cut his throat i' th' church!

---

[31] *made confession* admitted the rival accomplishments [32] *scrimers* fencers [33] *passages of proof* incidents of experience [34] *qualifies* weakens [35] *snuff* unconsumed portion of the burned wick [36] *still* always [37] *plurisy* excess [38] *hurts* i.e. shortens life by drawing blood from the heart (as was believed) [39] *quick* sensitive flesh

KING No place indeed should murder sanctuarize;[40]
Revenge should have no bounds. But, good Laertes,
Will you do this? Keep close within your chamber.
Hamlet returned shall know you are come home.
5 We'll put on[41] those shall praise your excellence
And set a double varnish on the fame
The Frenchman gave you, bring you in fine[42] together
And wager on your heads. He, being remiss,[43]
Most generous, and free from all contriving,
10 Will not peruse[44] the foils, so that with ease,
Or with a little shuffling, you may choose
A sword unbated,[45] and, in a pass of practice,[46]
Requite him for your father.

LAERTES I will do't,
15 And for that purpose I'll anoint my sword.
I bought an unction[47] of a mountebank,[48]
So mortal that, but dip a knife in it,
Where it draws blood no cataplasm[49] so rare,
Collected from all simples[50] that have virtue
20 Under the moon, can save the thing from death
That is but scratched withal.[51] I'll touch my point
With this contagion, that, if I gall[52] him slightly,
It may be death.

KING Let's further think of this,
25 Weigh what convenience both of time and means
May fit us to our shape.[53] If this should fail,
And that our drift[54] look[55] through our bad performance,
'Twere better not assayed. Therefore this project
Should have a back or second, that might hold
30 If this did blast in proof.[56] Soft, let me see.
We'll make a solemn wager on your cunnings—
I ha't!
When in your motion you are hot and dry—
As make your bouts more violent to that end—
35 And that he calls for drink, I'll have preferred[57] him
A chalice for the nonce,[58] whereon but sipping,

---

[40] *sanctuarize* protect from punishment, give sanctuary to [41] *put on* instigate [42] *in fine* finally [43] *remiss* negligent [44] *peruse* scan [45] *unbated* not blunted [46] *pass of practice* thrust made effective by trickery [47] *unction* ointment [48] *mountebank* quack-doctor [49] *cataplasm* poultice [50] *simples* herbs [51] *withal* with it [52] *gall* scratch [53] *shape* plan [54] *drift* intention [55] *look* show [56] *blast in proof* burst during trial (like a faulty cannon) [57] *preferred* offered [58] *nonce* occasion

If he by chance escape your venomed stuck,[59]
Our purpose may hold there.—But stay, what noise?

(*Enter* QUEEN)

QUEEN One woe doth tread upon another's heel,
5 So fast they follow. Your sister 's drowned, Laertes.
LAERTES Drowned! O, where?
QUEEN There is a willow grows askant[60] the brook,
That shows his hoar[61] leaves in the glassy stream.
Therewith fantastic garlands did she make
10 Of crowflowers, nettles, daisies, and long purples,
That liberal [62] shepherds give a grosser name,
But our cold maids do dead men's fingers call them.
There on the pendent boughs her crownet[63] weeds
Clamb'ring to hang, an envious sliver broke,
15 When down her weedy trophies and herself
Fell in the weeping brook. Her clothes spread wide,
And mermaid-like awhile they bore her up,
Which time she chanted snatches of old lauds,[64]
As one incapable of [65] her own distress,
20 Or like a creature native and indued [66]
Unto that element. But long it could not be
Till that her garments, heavy with their drink,
Pulled the poor wretch from her melodious lay
To muddy death.
25 LAERTES Alas, then she is drowned?
QUEEN Drowned, drowned.
LAERTES Too much of water hast thou, poor Ophelia,
And therefore I forbid my tears; but yet
It is our trick;[67] nature her custom holds,
30 Let shame say what it will. When these are gone,
The woman[68] will be out. Adieu, my lord.
I have a speech o' fire, that fain would blaze
But that this folly drowns it.

(*Exit*)

35 KING Let's follow, Gertrude.
How much I had to do to calm his rage!

---

59 *stuck* thrust 60 *askant* alongside 61 *hoar* grey 62 *liberal* free-spoken, licentious 63 *crownet* coronet 64 *lauds* hymns 65 *incapable of* insensible to 66 *indued* endowed 67 *trick* way (i.e. to shed tears when sorrowful) 68 *woman* unmanly part of nature.

Now fear I this will give it start again;
Therefore let's follow.

(*Exeunt*)

## ACT V

5 **Scene I**

*A churchyard*

(*Enter two* CLOWNS[1])

CLOWN Is she to be buried in Christian burial[2] when she willfully seeks her own salvation?

10 OTHER I tell thee she is. Therefore make her grave straight.[3] The crowner[4] hath sate on her, and finds it Christian burial.

CLOWN How can that be, unless she drowned herself in her own defense?

OTHER Why, 'tis found so.

15 CLOWN It must be *se offendendo*;[5] it cannot be else. For here lies the point: if I drown myself wittingly, it argues an act, and an act hath three branches—it is to act, to do, and to perform. Argal,[6] she drowned herself wittingly.

OTHER Nay, but hear you, Goodman Delver.[7]

20 CLOWN Give me leave. Here lies the water—good. Here stands the man—good. If the man go to this water and drown himself, it is, will he nill he,[8] he goes, mark you that. But if the water come to him and drown him, he drowns not himself. Argal, he that is not guilty of his own death shortens not his own life.

25 OTHER But is this law?

CLOWN Ay marry, is't—crowner's quest[9] law.

OTHER Will you ha' the truth on't? If this had not been a gentlewoman, she should have been buried out o' Christian burial.

CLOWN Why, there thou say'st.[10] And the more pity that great folk
30 should have count'nance[11] in this world to drown or hang themselves more than their even-Christen.[12] Come, my spade. There

---

[1] *Clowns* rustics [2] *in Christian burial* in consecrated ground with the prescribed service of the Church (a burial denied to suicides) [3] *straight* straightway, at once [4] *crowner* coroner [5] *se offendendo* a clownish transformation of *"se defendendo,"* "in self-defense" [6] *Argal* for *"ergo,"* "therefore" [7] *Delver* Digger [8] *will he nill he* willy-nilly [9] *quest* inquest [10] *thou say'st* you have it right [11] *count'nance* privilege [12] *even-Christen* fellow Christian

is no ancient gentlemen but gard'ners, ditchers, and grave-makers. They hold up Adam's profession.

OTHER Was he a gentleman?

CLOWN 'A was the first that ever bore arms.

5 OTHER Why, he had none.[13]

CLOWN What, art a heathen? How dost thou understand the Scripture? The Scripture says Adam digged. Could he dig without arms? I'll put another question to thee. If thou answerest me not to the purpose, confess thyself—

10 OTHER Go to.

CLOWN What is he that builds stronger than either the mason, the shipwright, or the carpenter?

OTHER The gallows-maker, for that frame outlives a thousand tenants.

15 CLOWN I like thy wit well, in good faith. The gallows does well. But how does it well? It does well to those that do ill. Now thou dost ill to say the gallows is built stronger than the church. Argal, the gallows may do well to thee. To't again, come.

OTHER Who builds stronger than a mason, a shipwright, or a car-
20 penter?

CLOWN Ay, tell me that, and unyoke.[14]

OTHER Marry, now I can tell.

CLOWN To't.

OTHER Mass,[15] I cannot tell.

25 CLOWN Cudgel thy brains no more about it, for your dull ass will not mend his pace with beating. And when you are asked this question next, say "a grave-maker." The houses he makes last till doomsday. Go, get thee in, and fetch me a stoup[16] of liquor.

(*Exit* OTHER CLOWN)

30 (*Enter* HAMLET *and* HORATIO [*as* CLOWN *digs and sings*])

**Song**

In youth when I did love, did love,
  Methought it was very sweet
To contract—O—the time for—a—my behove,[17]
35   O, methought there—a—was nothing—a—meet.

HAMLET Has this fellow no feeling of his business, that 'a sings at grave-making?

---

[13] *had none* i.e. had no gentleman's coat of arms [14] *unyoke* i.e. unharness your powers of thought after a good day's work [15] *Mass* by the Mass [16] *stoup* large mug [17] *behove* behoof, benefit

HORATIO Custom hath made it in him a property[18] of easiness.[19]

HAMLET 'Tis e'en so. The hand of little employment hath the daintier sense.[20]

CLOWN

5 **Song**

But age with his stealing steps
Hath clawed me in his clutch,
And hath shipped me intil[21] the land,
As if I had never been such.

10 (*Throws up a skull*)

HAMLET That skull had a tongue in it, and could sing once. How the knave jowls[22] it to the ground, as if 'twere Cain's jawbone, that did the first murder! This might be the pate of a politician,[23] which this ass now o'erreaches;[24] one that would circumvent 15 God, might it not?

HORATIO It might, my lord.

HAMLET Or of a courtier, which could say "Good morrow, sweet lord! How dost thou, sweet lord?" This might be my Lord Such-a-one, that praised my Lord Such-a-one's horse when 'a meant to 20 beg it, might it not?

HORATIO Ay, my lord.

HAMLET Why, e'en so, and now my Lady Worm's, chapless,[25] and knocked about the mazzard[26] with a sexton's spade. Here's fine revolution, an we had the trick to see't. Did these bones cost no 25 more the breeding but to play at loggets[27] with 'em? Mine ache to think on't.

CLOWN

**Song**

30 A pickaxe and a spade, a spade,
For and[28] a shrouding sheet;
O, a pit of clay for to be made
For such a guest is meet.

(*Throws up another skull*)

---

[18] *property* peculiarity [19] *easiness* easy acceptability [20] *daintier sense* more delicate feeling (because the hand is less calloused) [21] *intil* into [22] *jowls* hurls [23] *politician* crafty schemer [24] *o'erreaches* gets the better of (with a play upon the literal meaning) [25] *chapless* lacking the lower chap or jaw [26] *mazzard* head [27] *loggets* small pieces of wood thrown in a game [28] *For and* and

HAMLET There's another. Why may not that be the skull of a lawyer? Where be his quiddities[29] now, his quillities,[30] his cases, his tenures,[31] and his tricks? Why does he suffer this mad knave now to knock him about the sconce[32] with a dirty shovel, and will not
5 tell him of his action of battery? Hum! This fellow might be in's time a great buyer of land, with his statutes, his recognizances,[33] his fines,[34] his double vouchers,[35] his recoveries. Is this the fine[36] of his fines, and the recovery of his recoveries, to have his fine pate full of fine dirt? Will his vouchers vouch him no more of his
10 purchases, and double ones too, than the length and breadth of a pair of indentures?[37] The very conveyances[38] of his lands will scarcely lie in this box, and must th' inheritor himself have no more, ha?

HORATIO Not a jot more, my lord.

15 HAMLET Is not parchment made of sheepskins?

HORATIO Ay, my lord, and of calveskins too.

HAMLET They are sheep and calves which seek out assurance in that. I will speak to this fellow. Whose grave 's this, sirrah?

CLOWN Mine, sir.

20 (*Sings*) O, a pit of clay for to be made
For such a guest is meet.

HAMLET I think it be thine indeed, for thou liest in't.

CLOWN You lie out on't, sir, and therefore 'tis not yours. For my part, I do not lie in't, yet it is mine.

25 HAMLET Thou dost lie in't, to be in't and say it is thine. 'Tis for the dead, not for the quick;[39] therefore thou liest.

CLOWN 'Tis a quick lie, sir; 'twill away again from me to you.

HAMLET What man dost thou dig it for?

CLOWN For no man, sir.

30 HAMLET What woman then?

CLOWN For none neither.

HAMLET Who is to be buried in't?

CLOWN One that was a woman, sir; but, rest her soul, she's dead.

HAMLET How absolute[40] the knave is! We must speak by the

---

[29] *quiddities* subtleties (from scholastic "*quidditas*," meaning the distinctive nature of anything) [30] *quillities* nice distinctions [31] *tenures* holdings of property [32] *sconce* head [33] *statutes, recognizances* legal documents or bonds acknowledging debt [34] *fines, recoveries* modes of converting estate tail into fee simple [35] *vouchers* persons vouched or called on to warrant a title [36] *fine* end (introducing a word play involving four meanings of "fine") [37] *pair of indentures* deed or legal agreement in duplicate [38] *conveyances* deeds [39] *quick* living [40] *absolute* positive

card,[41] or equivocation[42] will undo us. By the Lord, Horatio, this three years I have taken note of it, the age is grown so picked [43] that the toe of the peasant comes so near the heel of the courtier he galls[44] his kibe.[45]—How long hast thou been a grave-maker?

5 CLOWN Of all the days i' th' year, I came to't that day that our last king Hamlet overcame Fortinbras.

HAMLET How long is that since?

CLOWN Cannot you tell that? Every fool can tell that. It was the very day that young Hamlet was born—he that is mad, and sent 10 into England.

HAMLET Ay, marry, why was he sent into England?

CLOWN Why, because 'a was mad. 'A shall recover his wits there; or, if'a do not, 'tis no great matter there.

HAMLET Why?

15 CLOWN 'Twill not be seen in him there. There the men are as mad as he.

HAMLET How came he mad?

CLOWN Very strangely, they say.

HAMLET How strangely?

20 CLOWN Faith, e'en with losing his wits.

HAMLET Upon what ground?

CLOWN Why, here in Denmark. I have been sexton here, man and boy, thirty years.

HAMLET How long will a man lie i' th' earth ere he rot?

25 CLOWN Faith, if'a be not rotten before 'a die (as we have many pocky[46] corses now-a-days that will scarce hold the laying in), 'a will last you some eight year or nine year. A tanner will last you nine year.

HAMLET Why he more than another?

30 CLOWN Why, sir, his hide is so tanned with his trade that 'a will keep out water a great while, and your water is a sore decayer of your whoreson dead body. Here's a skull now hath lien you i' th' earth three-and-twenty years.

HAMLET Whose was it?

35 CLOWN A whoreson mad fellow's it was. Whose do you think it was?

HAMLET Nay, I know not.

---

[41] *by the card* by the card on which the points of the mariner's compass are marked, absolutely to the point [42] *equivocation* ambiguity [43] *picked* refined, spruce [44] *galls* chafes [45] *kibe* chilblain [46] *pocky* rotten (literally, corrupted by pox, or syphilis)

CLOWN A pestilence on him for a mad rogue! 'A poured a flagon of Rhenish[47] on my head once. This same skull, sir, was—sir—Yorick's skull, the king's jester.

HAMLET This?

5 CLOWN E'en that.

HAMLET Let me see. (*Takes the skull.*) Alas, poor Yorick! I knew him, Horatio, a fellow of infinite jest, of most excellent fancy. He hath borne me on his back a thousand times. And now how abhorred in my imagination it is! My gorge rises at it. Here hung 10 those lips that I have kissed I know not how oft. Where be your gibes now? Your gambols, your songs, your flashes of merriment that were wont to set the table on a roar? Not one now to mock your own grinning? Quite chapfall'n?[48] Now get you to my lady's chamber, and tell her, let her paint an inch thick, to this favor[49] 15 she must come. Make her laugh at that. Prithee, Horatio, tell me one thing.

HORATIO What's that, my lord?

HAMLET Dost thou think Alexander looked o' this fashion i' th' earth?

20 HORATIO E'en so.

HAMLET And smelt so? Pah!

(*Puts down the skull*)

HORATIO E'en so, my lord.

HAMLET To what base uses we may return, Horatio! Why may 25 not imagination trace the noble dust of Alexander till 'a find it stopping a bunghole?

HORATIO 'Twere to consider too curiously,[50] to consider so.

HAMLET No, faith, not a jot, but to follow him thither with modesty[51] enough, and likelihood to lead it; as thus: Alexander died, 30 Alexander was buried, Alexander returneth to dust; the dust is earth; of earth we make loam; and why of that loam whereto he was converted might they not stop a beer barrel?

Imperious[52] Caesar, dead and turned to clay,
Might stop a hole to keep the wind away.
35 O, that that earth which kept the world in awe
Should patch a wall t' expel the winter's flaw![53]

---

[47] *Rhenish* Rhine wine [48] *chapfall'n* lacking the lower chap, or jaw (with a play on the sense "down in the mouth," "dejected") [49] *favor* countenance, aspect [50] *curiously* minutely [51] *modesty* moderation [52] *Imperious* imperial [53] *flaw* gust of wind

But soft, but soft awhile! Here comes the king—

(*Enter* KING, QUEEN, LAERTES, *and the* CORSE [*with* LORDS *attendant and a* DOCTOR OF DIVINITY *as* PRIEST])

The queen, the courtiers. Who is this they follow?
5 And with such maimèd rites? This doth betoken
The corse they follow did with desp'rate hand
Fordo[54] it[55] own life. 'Twas of some estate.[56]
Couch[57] we awhile, and mark.

(*Retires with* HORATIO)

10 LAERTES What ceremony else?
HAMLET That is Laertes,
A very noble youth. Mark.
LAERTES What ceremony else?
DOCTOR Her obsequies have been as far enlarged
15 As we have warranty. Her death was doubtful,
And, but that great command o'ersways the order,
She should in ground unsanctified have lodged
Till the last trumpet. For charitable prayers,
Shards,[58] flints, and pebbles should be thrown on her.
20 Yet here she is allowed her virgin crants,[59]
Her maiden strewments,[60] and the bringing home[61]
Of bell and burial.
LAERTES Must there no more be done?
DOCTOR No more be done.
25 We should profane the service of the dead
To sing a requiem and such rest to her
As to peace-parted souls.
LAERTES Lay her i' th' earth,
And from her fair and unpolluted flesh
30 May violets spring! I tell thee, churlish priest,
A minist'ring angel shall my sister be
When thou liest howling.
HAMLET What, the fair Ophelia?
QUEEN Sweets to the sweet! Farewell.

35 (*Scatters flowers*)

I hoped thou shouldst have been my Hamlet's wife.

---

[54] *Fordo* destroy [55] *it* its [56] *estate* rank [57] *Couch* hide [58] *Shards* broken pieces of pottery [59] *crants* garland [60] *strewments* strewings of the grave with flowers [61] *bringing home* laying to rest

I thought thy bride-bed to have decked, sweet maid,
And not have strewed thy grave.

LAERTES O, treble woe
Fall ten times treble on that cursèd head
5 Whose wicked deed thy most ingenious[62] sense
Deprived thee of! Hold off the earth awhile,
Till I have caught her once more in mine arms.

(*Leaps in the grave*)

Now pile your dust upon the quick and dead
10 Till of this flat a mountain you have made
T' o'ertop old Pelion[63] or the skyish head
Of blue Olympus.

HAMLET (*coming forward*) What is he whose grief
Bears such an emphasis? whose phrase of sorrow
15 Conjures[64] the wand'ring stars,[65] and makes them stand
Like wonder-wounded hearers? This is I,
Hamlet the Dane.

(*Leaps in after* LAERTES)

LAERTES The devil take thy soul!

20 (*Grapples with him*)

HAMLET Thou pray'st not well.
I prithee take thy fingers from my throat,
For, though I am not splenitive[66] and rash,
Yet have I in me something dangerous,
25 Which let thy wisdom fear. Hold off thy hand.

KING Pluck them asunder.

QUEEN Hamlet, Hamlet!

ALL Gentlemen!

HORATIO Good my lord, be quiet.

30 (ATTENDANTS *part them, and they come out of the grave*)

HAMLET Why, I will fight with him upon this theme
Until my eyelids will no longer wag.

QUEEN O my son, what theme?

---

[62] *most ingenious* of quickest apprehension [63] *Pelion* a mountain in Thessaly, like Olympus and also Ossa (the allusion being to the war in which the Titans fought the gods and attempted to heap Ossa and Olympus on Pelion, or Pelion and Ossa on Olympus, in order to scale heaven) [64] *Conjures* charms, puts a spell upon [65] *wand'ring stars* planets [66] *splenitive* of fiery temper (the spleen being considered the seat of anger)

HAMLET I loved Ophelia. Forty thousand brothers
Could not with all their quantity of love
Make up my sum. What wilt thou do for her?
KING O, he is mad, Laertes.
5 QUEEN For love of God, forbear him.
HAMLET 'Swounds, show me what thou't do.
Woo't [67] weep? woo't fight? woo't fast? woo't tear thyself?
Woo't drink up esill? [68] eat a crocodile?
I'll do't. Dost thou come here to whine?
10 To outface me with leaping in her grave?
Be buried quick[69] with her, and so will I.
And if thou prate of mountains, let them throw
Millions of acres on us, till our ground,
Singeing his pate against the burning zone,
15 Make Ossa like a wart! Nay, an thou'lt mouth,
I'll rant as well as thou.
QUEEN This is mere[70] madness;
And thus a while the fit will work on him.
Anon, as patient as the female dove
20 When that her golden couplets[71] are disclosed,[72]
His silence will sit drooping.
HAMLET Hear you, sir.
What is the reason that you use me thus?
I loved you ever. But it is no matter.
25 Let Hercules himself do what he may,
The cat will mew, and dog will have his day.
KING I pray thee, good Horatio, wait upon him.

(*Exit* HAMLET *and* HORATIO)

(*To* LAERTES)

30 Strengthen your patience in[73] our last night's speech.
We'll put the matter to the present push.[74]
Good Gertrude, set some watch over your son.—
This grave shall have a living monument.
An hour of quiet shortly shall we see;
35 Till then in patience our proceeding be.

(*Exeunt*)

---

[67] *Woo't* wilt (thou) [68] *esill* vinegar [69] *quick* alive [70] *mere* absolute
[71] *couplets* pair of fledglings [72] *disclosed* hatched [73] *in* by calling to mind
[74] *present push* immediate trial

## Act V, Scene II

*The hall of the castle*

(*Enter* HAMLET *and* HORATIO)

HAMLET So much for this, sir; now shall you see the other.
5 You do remember all the circumstance?
HORATIO Remember it, my lord!
HAMLET Sir, in my heart there was a kind of fighting
That would not let me sleep. Methought I lay
Worse than the mutines[1] in the bilboes.[2] Rashly,
10 And praised be rashness for it—let us know,
Our indiscretion sometime serves us well
When our deep plots do pall,[3] and that should learn us
There's a divinity that shapes our ends,
Rough-hew[4] them how we will—
15 HORATIO That is most certain.
HAMLET Up from my cabin,
My sea-gown scarfed about me, in the dark
Groped I to find out them, had my desire,
Fingered [5] their packet, and in fine[6] withdrew
20 To mine own room again, making so bold,
My fears forgetting manners, to unseal
Their grand commission; where I found, Horatio—
Ah, royal knavery!—an exact command,
Larded [7] with many several sorts of reasons,
25 Importing[8] Denmark's health, and England's too,
With, ho! such bugs[9] and goblins in my life,[10]
That on the supervise,[11] no leisure bated,[12]
No, not to stay the grinding of the axe,
My head should be struck off.
30 HORATIO Is't possible?
HAMLET Here's the commission; read it at more leisure.
But wilt thou hear me how I did proceed?
HORATIO I beseech you.
HAMLET Being thus benetted round with villainies,
35 Or[13] I could make a prologue to my brains,
They had begun the play. I sat me down,

---

[1] *mutines* mutineers [2] *bilboes* fetters [3] *pall* fail [4] *Rough-hew* shape roughly in trial form [5] *Fingered* filched [6] *in fine* finally [7] *Larded* enriched [8] *Importing* relating to [9] *bugs* bugbears [10] *in my life* to be encountered as dangers if I should be allowed to live [11] *supervise* perusal [12] *bated* deducted, allowed [13] *Or* ere

Devised a new commission, wrote it fair.
I once did hold it, as our statists[14] do,
A baseness to write fair,[15] and labored much
How to forget that learning, but, sir, now
5 It did me yeoman's service.[16] Wilt thou know
Th' effect[17] of what I wrote?

HORATIO Ay, good my lord.

HAMLET An earnest conjuration from the king,
As England was his faithful tributary,
10 As love between them like the palm might flourish,
As peace should still her wheaten garland [18] wear
And stand a comma[19] 'tween their amities,
And many such-like as's of great charge,[20]
That on the view and knowing of these contents,
15 Without debatement further, more or less,
He should the bearers put to sudden death,
Not shriving time[21] allowed.

HORATIO How was this sealed?

HAMLET Why, even in that was heaven ordinant.[22]
20 I had my father's signet in my purse,
Which was the model [23] of that Danish seal,
Folded the writ up in the form of th' other,
Subscribed it, gave't th' impression,[24] placed it safely,
The changeling never known. Now, the next day
25 Was our sea-fight, and what to this was sequent[25]
Thou know'st already.

HORATIO So Guildenstern and Rosencrantz go to't.

HAMLET Why, man, they did make love to this employment.
They are not near my conscience; their defeat
30 Does by their own insinuation[26] grow.
'Tis dangerous when the baser nature comes
Between the pass[27] and fell [28] incensèd points
Of mighty opposites.

---

[14] *statists* statesmen [15] *fair* with professional clarity (like a clerk or a scrivener, not like a gentleman) [16] *yeoman's service* stout service such as yeomen footsoldiers gave as archers [17] *effect* purport [18] *wheaten garland* adornment of fruitful agriculture [19] *comma* connective (because it indicates continuity of thought in a sentence) [20] *charge* burden (with a double meaning to fit a play that makes *as's* into "asses" [21] *shriving time* time for confession and absolution [22] *ordinant* controlling [23] *model* counterpart [24] *impression* i.e. of the signet [25] *sequent* subsequent [26] *insinuation* intrusion [27] *pass* thrust [28] *fell* fierce

HORATIO Why, what a king is this!
HAMLET Does it not, think thee, stand [29] me now upon—
He that hath killed my king, and whored my mother,
Popped in between th' election[30] and my hopes,
5 Thrown out his angle[31] for my proper[32] life,
And with such coz'nage[33]—is't not perfect conscience
To quit[34] him with this arm? And is't not to be damned
To let this canker[35] of our nature come
In further evil?
10 HORATIO It must be shortly known to him from England
What is the issue of the business there.
HAMLET It will be short; the interim is mine,
And a man's life 's no more than to say "one."
But I am very sorry, good Horatio,
15 That to Laertes I forgot myself,
For by the image of my cause I see
The portraiture of his. I'll court his favors.
But sure the bravery[36] of his grief did put me
Into a tow'ring passion.
20 HORATIO Peace, who comes here?

(*Enter* OSRIC, *a courtier*)

OSRIC Your lordship is right welcome back to Denmark.
HAMLET I humbly thank you, sir. (*aside to* HORATIO) Dost know this waterfly?
25 HORATIO (*aside to* HAMLET) No, my good lord.
HAMLET (*aside to* HORATIO) Thy state is the more gracious, for 'tis a vice to know him. He hath much land, and fertile. Let a beast be lord of beasts, and his crib shall stand at the king's mess.[37] 'Tis a chough,[38] but, as I say, spacious in the possession
30 of dirt.
OSRIC Sweet lord, if your lordship were at leisure, I should impart a thing to you from his majesty.
HAMLET I will receive it, sir, with all diligence of spirit. Put your bonnet to his right use. 'Tis for the head.
35 OSRIC I thank your lordship, it is very hot.
HAMLET No, believe me, 'tis very cold; the wind is northerly.
OSRIC It is indifferent[39] cold, my lord, indeed.

---

[29] *stand* rest incumbent [30] *election* i.e. to the kingship (the Danish kingship being elective) [31] *angle* fishing line [32] *proper* own [33] *coz'nage* cozenage, trickery [34] *quit* repay [35] *canker* cancer, ulcer [36] *bravery* ostentatious display [37] *mess* table [38] *chough* jackdaw, chatterer [39] *indifferent* somewhat

HAMLET But yet methinks it is very sultry and hot for my complexion.[40]

OSRIC Exceedingly, my lord; it is very sultry, as 'twere—I cannot tell how. But, my lord, his majesty bade me signify to you that
5 'a has laid a great wager on your head. Sir, this is the matter—

HAMLET I beseech you remember.[41]

(HAMLET *moves him to put on his hat*)

OSRIC Nay, good my lord; for mine ease,[42] in good faith. Sir, here is newly come to court Laertes—believe me, an absolute gentle-
10 man, full of most excellent differences,[43] of very soft society[44] and great showing.[45] Indeed, to speak feelingly[46] of him, he is the card[47] or calendar[48] of gentry,[49] for you shall find in him the continent[50] of what part a gentleman would see.

HAMLET Sir, his definement[51] suffers no perdition[52] in you, though,
15 I know, to divide him inventorially would dozy[53] th' arithmetic of memory, and yet but yaw[54] neither[55] in respect of[56] his quick sail. But, in the verity of extolment, I take him to be a soul of great article,[57] and his infusion[58] of such dearth[59] and rareness as, to make true diction of him, his semblable[60] is his mirror, and
20 who else would trace[61] him, his umbrage,[62] nothing more.

OSRIC Your lordship speaks most infallibly of him.

HAMLET The concernancy,[63] sir? Why do we wrap the gentleman in our more rawer[64] breath?

OSRIC Sir?

25 HORATIO Is't not possible to understand in another tongue? You will to't,[65] sir, really.

HAMLET What imports the nomination[66] of this gentleman?

OSRIC Of Laertes?

---

[40] *complexion* temperament [41] *remember* i.e. remember you have done all that courtesy demands [42] *for mine ease* i.e. I keep my hat off just for comfort (a conventional polite phrase) [43] *differences* differentiating characteristics, special qualities [44] *soft society* gentle manners [45] *great showing* noble appearance [46] *feelingly* appropriately [47] *card* map [48] *calendar* guide [49] *gentry* gentlemanliness [50] *continent* all-containing embodiment (with an implication of geographical continent to go with *card*) [51] *definement* definition [52] *perdition* loss [53] *dozy* dizzy, stagger [54] *yaw* hold to a course unsteadily like a ship that steers wild [55] *neither* for all that [56] *in respect of* in comparison with [57] *article* scope, importance [58] *infusion* essence [59] *dearth* scarcity [60] *semblable* likeness (i.e. only true likeness) [61] *trace* follow [62] *umbrage* shadow [63] *concernancy* relevance [64] *rawer breath* cruder speech [65] *to't* i.e. get to an understanding [66] *nomination* mention

HORATIO (*aside to* HAMLET) His purse is empty already. All's golden words are spent.

HAMLET Of him, sir.

OSRIC I know you are not ignorant—

5 HAMLET I would you did, sir; yet, in faith, if you did, it would not much approve me.[67] Well, sir?

OSRIC You are not ignorant of what excellence Laertes is—

HAMLET I dare not confess that, lest I should compare[68] with him in excellence; but to know a man well were to know himself.

10 OSRIC I mean, sir, for his weapon; but in the imputation laid on him by them, in his meed [69] he's unfellowed.

HAMLET What's his weapon?

OSRIC Rapier and dagger.

HAMLET That's two of his weapons—but well.

15 OSRIC The king, sir, hath wagered with him six Barbary horses, against the which he has impawned,[70] as I take it, six French rapiers and poniards, with their assigns,[71] as girdle, hangers,[72] and so. Three of the carriages, in faith, are very dear to fancy,[73] very responsive[74] to the hilts, most delicate carriages, and of very 20 liberal conceit.[75]

HAMLET What call you the carriages?

HORATIO (*aside to* HAMLET) I knew you must be edified by the margent[76] ere you had done.

OSRIC The carriages, sir, are the hangers.

25 HAMLET The phrase would be more germane to the matter if we could carry a cannon by our sides. I would it might be hangers till then. But on! Six Barbary horses against six French swords, their assigns, and three liberal-conceited carriages—that's the French bet against the Danish. Why is this all impawned, as you 30 call it?

OSRIC The king, sir, hath laid, sir, that in a dozen passes between yourself and him he shall not exceed you three hits; he hath laid on twelve for nine, and it would come to immediate trial if your lordship would vouchsafe the answer.

35 HAMLET How if I answer no?

OSRIC I mean, my lord, the opposition of your person in trial.

---

[67] *approve me* be to my credit [68] *compare* compete [69] *meed* worth [70] *impawned* staked [71] *assigns* appurtenances [72] *hangers* straps by which the sword hangs from the belt [73] *dear to fancy* finely designed [74] *responsive* corresponding closely [75] *liberal conceit* tasteful design, refined conception [76] *margent* margin (i.e. explanatory notes there printed)

HAMLET Sir, I will walk here in the hall. If it please his majesty, it is the breathing time[77] of day with me. Let the foils be brought, the gentleman willing, and the king hold his purpose, I will win for him an[78] I can; if not, I will gain nothing but my shame and
5 the odd hits.

OSRIC Shall I redeliver you e'en so?

HAMLET To this effect, sir, after what flourish your nature will.

OSRIC I commend my duty to your lordship.

HAMLET Your, yours. (*Exit* OSRIC) He does well to commend it
10 himself; there are no tongues else for's turn.

HORATIO This lapwing[79] runs away with the shell on his head.

HAMLET 'A did comply,[80] sir, with his dug[81] before 'a sucked it. Thus has he, and many more of the same bevy[82] that I know the drossy[83] age dotes on, only got the tune of the time and, out of
15 an habit of encounter, a kind of yeasty collection, which carries them through and through the most fanned and winnowed[84] opinions; and do but blow them to their trial, the bubbles are out.

(*Enter a* LORD)

20 LORD My lord, his majesty commended him to you by young Osric, who brings back to him that you attend him in the hall. He sends to know if your pleasure hold to play with Laertes, or that you will take longer time.

HAMLET I am constant to my purposes; they follow the king's
25 pleasure. If his fitness speaks, mine is ready; now or whensoever, provided I be so able as now.

LORD The king and queen and all are coming down.

HAMLET In happy time.[85]

LORD The queen desires you to use some gentle entertainment[86] to
30 Laertes before you fall to play.

HAMLET She well instructs me.

(*Exit* LORD)

HORATIO You will lose this wager, my lord.

HAMLET I do not think so. Since he went into France I have been
35 in continual practice. I shall win at the odds. But thou wouldst not think how ill all's here about my heart. But it is no matter.

---

[77] *breathing time* exercise hour [78] *an* if [79] *lapwing* a bird reputed to be so precocious as to run as soon as hatched [80] *comply* observe formalities of courtesy [81] *dug* mother's nipple [82] *bevy* company [83] *drossy* frivolous [84] *fanned and winnowed* select and refined [85] *In happy time* I am happy (a polite response) [86] *entertainment* words of reception or greeting

HORATIO Nay, good my lord—

HAMLET It is but foolery, but it is such a kind of gaingiving[87] as would perhaps trouble a woman.

HORATIO If your mind dislike anything, obey it. I will forestall
5 their repair hither and say you are not fit.

HAMLET Not a whit, we defy augury. There is special providence in the fall of a sparrow. If it be now, 'tis not to come; if it be not to come, it will be now; if it be not now, yet it will come. The readiness is all.[88] Since no man of aught he leaves knows,
10 what is't to leave betimes? Let be.

*A table prepared. Enter* TRUMPETS, DRUMS, *and* OFFICERS *with cushions;* KING, QUEEN, OSRIC, *and all the* STATE, *with foils, daggers, and stoups of wine borne in; and* LAERTES

KING Come, Hamlet, come, and take this hand from me.

15 (*The* KING *puts* LAERTES' *hand into* HAMLET'S)

HAMLET Give me your pardon, sir. I have done you wrong,
But pardon't, as you are a gentleman.
This presence[89] knows, and you must needs have heard,
How I am punished with a sore distraction.
20 What I have done
That might your nature, honor, and exception[90]
Roughly awake, I here proclaim was madness.
Was't Hamlet wronged Laertes? Never Hamlet.
If Hamlet from himself be ta'en away,
25 And when he's not himself does wrong Laertes,
Then Hamlet does it not, Hamlet denies it.
Who does it then? His madness. If't be so,
Hamlet is of the faction[91] that is wronged;
His madness is poor Hamlet's enemy.
30 Sir, in this audience,
Let my disclaiming from a purposed evil
Free me so far in your most generous thoughts
That I have shot my arrow o'er the house
And hurt my brother.

35 LAERTES I am satisfied in nature,[92]
Whose motive in this case should stir me most
To my revenge. But in my terms of honor[93]

---

[87] *gaingiving* misgiving [88] *all* all that matters [89] *presence* assembly [90] *exception* disapproval [91] *faction* body of persons taking a side in a contention [92] *nature* natural feeling as a person [93] *terms of honor* position as a man of honor

I stand aloof, and will no reconcilement
Till by some elder masters of known honor
I have a voice[94] and precedent of peace
To keep my name ungored.[95] But till that time
5 I do receive your offered love like love,
And will not wrong it.

HAMLET I embrace it freely,
And will this brother's wager frankly play.
Give us the foils. Come on.

10 LAERTES Come, one for me.

HAMLET I'll be your foil,[96] Laertes. In mine ignorance
Your skill shall, like a star i' th' darkest night,
Stick fiery off[97] indeed.

LAERTES You mock me, sir.

15 HAMLET No, by this hand.

KING Give them the foils, young Osric. Cousin Hamlet,
You know the wager?

HAMLET Very well, my lord.
Your grace has laid the odds o' the' weaker side.

20 KING I do not fear it, I have seen you both;
But since he is bettered, we have therefore odds.

LAERTES This is too heavy; let me see another.

HAMLET This likes me well. These foils have all a length?

*Prepare to play*

25 OSRIC Ay, my good lord.

KING Set me the stoups of wine upon that table.
If Hamlet give the first or second hit,
Or quit[98] in answer of the third exchange,
Let all the battlements their ordnance fire.
30 The king shall drink to Hamlet's better breath,
And in the cup an union[99] shall he throw
Richer than that which four successive kings
In Denmark's crown have worn. Give me the cups,
And let the kettle[100] to the trumpet speak,
35 The trumpet to the cannoneer without,
The cannons to the heavens, the heaven to earth,

---

[94] *voice* authoritative statement [95] *ungored* uninjured [96] *foil* setting that displays a jewel advantageously (with a play upon the meaning "weapon") [97] *Stick fiery off* show in brilliant relief [98] *quit* repay by a hit [99] *union* pearl [100] *kettle* kettledrum

"Now the king drinks to Hamlet." Come, begin.

*Trumpets the while*

And you, the judges, bear a wary eye.

HAMLET Come on, sir.

5 LAERTES Come, my lord.

*They play*

HAMLET One.

LAERTES No.

HAMLET Judgment?

10 OSRIC A hit, a very palpable hit.

DRUM, TRUMPETS, *and* SHOT. *Flourish; a piece goes off*

LAERTES Well, again.

KING Stay, give me drink. Hamlet, this pearl is thine.
Here's to thy health. Give him the cup.

15 HAMLET I'll play this bout first; set it by awhile.
Come. (*They play*) Another hit. What say you?

LAERTES A touch, a touch; I do confess't.

KING Our son shall win.

QUEEN He's fat,[101] and scant of breath.

20 Here, Hamlet, take my napkin,[102] rub thy brows.
The queen carouses[103] to thy fortune, Hamlet.

HAMLET Good madam!

KING Gertrude, do not drink.

QUEEN I will, my lord; I pray you pardon me.

25 *Drinks*

KING (*aside*) It is the poisoned cup; it is too late.

HAMLET I dare not drink yet, madam—by and by.

QUEEN Come, let me wipe thy face.

LAERTES My lord, I'll hit him now.

30 KING I do not think't.

LAERTES (*aside*) And yet it is almost against my conscience.

HAMLET Come for the third, Laertes. You but dally.
I pray you pass with your best violence;
I am afeard you make a wanton[104] of me.

---

[101] *fat* not physically fit, out of training [102] *napkin* handkerchief [103] *carouses* drinks a toast [104] *wanton* pampered child

LAERTES Say you so? Come on.

*They play*

OSRIC Nothing neither way.
LAERTES Have at you now!

5 *In scuffling they change rapiers, and both are wounded with the poisoned weapon*

KING Part them. They are incensed.
HAMLET Nay, come—again!

*The* QUEEN *falls*

10 OSRIC Look to the queen there, ho!
HORATIO They bleed on both sides. How is it, my lord?
OSRIC How is't, Laertes?
LAERTES Why, as a woodcock[105] to mine own springe,[106] Osric.
I am justly killed with mine own treachery.
15 HAMLET How does the queen?
KING She sounds[107] to see them bleed.
QUEEN No, no, the drink, the drink! O my dear Hamlet!
The drink, the drink! I am poisoned.

*Dies*

20 HAMLET O villainy! Ho! let the door be locked.
Treachery! Seek it out.

LAERTES *falls*

LAERTES It is here, Hamlet. Hamlet, thou art slain;
No med'cine in the world can do thee good.
25 In thee there is not half an hour's life.
The treacherous instrument is in thy hand,
Unbated [108] and envenomed. The foul practice[109]
Hath turned itself on me. Lo, here I lie,
Never to rise again. Thy mother 's poisoned.
30 I can no more. The king, the king 's to blame.
HAMLET The point envenomed too?
Then venom, to thy work.

*Hurts the* KING

ALL Treason! treason!

---

[105] *woodcock* a bird reputed to be stupid and easily trapped [106] *springe* trap
[107] *sounds* swoons [108] *Unbated* unblunted [109] *practice* stratagem

KING O, yet defend me, friends. I am but hurt.
HAMLET Here, thou incestuous, murd'rous, damnèd Dane,
Drink off this potion. Is thy union here?
Follow my mother.

5 KING *dies*

LAERTES He is justly served.
It is a poison tempered [110] by himself.
Exchange forgiveness with me, noble Hamlet.
Mine and my father's death come not upon thee,
10 Nor thine on me!

*Dies*

HAMLET Heaven make thee free of it! I follow thee.
I am dead, Horatio. Wretched queen, adieu!
You that look pale and tremble at this chance,
15 That are but mutes[111] or audience to this act,
Had I but time—as this fell sergeant,[112] Death,
Is strict in his arrest—O, I could tell you—
But let it be. Horatio, I am dead;
Thou livest; report me and my cause aright
20 To the unsatisfied.
HORATIO Never believe it.
I am more an antique Roman than a Dane.
Here's yet some liquor left.
HAMLET As th' art a man,
25 Give me the cup. Let go. By heaven, I'll ha't!
O God, Horatio, what a wounded name,
Things standing thus unknown, shall live behind me!
If thou didst ever hold me in thy heart,
Absent thee from felicity awhile,
30 And in this harsh world draw thy breath in pain,
To tell my story.

*A march afar off*

What warlike noise is this?
OSRIC Young Fortinbras, with conquest come from Poland,
35 To the ambassadors of England gives
This warlike volley.
HAMLET O, I die, Horatio!

---

[110] *tempered* mixed [111] *mutes* actors in a play who speak no lines [112] *sergeant* sheriff's officer

The potent poison quite o'ercrows[113] my spirit.
I cannot live to hear the news from England,
But I do prophesy th' election[114] lights
On Fortinbras. He has my dying voice.[115]
5 So tell him, with th' occurrents,[116] more and less,
Which have solicited [117]—the rest is silence.

*Dies*

HORATIO Now cracks a noble heart. Good night, sweet prince,
And flights of angels sing thee to thy rest!

10 *March within*

Why does the drum come hither?

(*Enter* FORTINBRAS, *with the* AMBASSADORS [*and with his train of* DRUM, COLORS, *and* ATTENDANTS])

FORTINBRAS Where is this sight?
15 HORATIO What is it you would see?
If aught of woe or wonder, cease your search.
FORTINBRAS This quarry[118] cries on[119] havoc.[120] O proud Death,
What feast is toward [121] in thine eternal cell
That thou so many princes at a shot
20 So bloodily hast struck?
AMBASSADOR The sight is dismal;
And our affairs from England come too late.
The ears are senseless that should give us hearing
To tell him his commandment is fulfilled,
25 That Rosencrantz and Guildenstern are dead.
Where should we have our thanks?
HORATIO Not from his mouth,
Had it th' ability of life to thank you.
He never gave commandment for their death.
30 But since, so jump[122] upon this bloody question,
You from the Polack wars, and you from England,
Are here arrived, give order that these bodies
High on a stage[123] be placèd to the view,

---

[113] *o'ercrows* triumphs over (like a victor in a cockfight) [114] *election* i.e. to the throne [115] *voice* vote [116] *occurrents* occurrences [117] *solicited* incited, provoked [118] *quarry* pile of dead (literally, of dead deer gathered after the hunt) [119] *cries on* proclaims loudly [120] *havoc* indiscriminate killing and destruction such as would follow the order "havoc," or "pillage," given to an army [121] *toward* forthcoming [122] *jump* precisely [123] *stage* platform

And let me speak to th' yet unknowing world
How these things came about. So shall you hear
Of carnal, bloody, and unnatural acts,
Of accidental judgments,[124] casual [125] slaughters,
5 Of deaths put on[126] by cunning and forced cause,
And, in this upshot, purposes mistook
Fall'n on th' inventors' heads. All this can I
Truly deliver.

FORTINBRAS Let us haste to hear it,
10 And call the noblest to the audience.
For me, with sorrow I embrace my fortune.
I have some rights of memory[127] in this kingdom,
Which now to claim my vantage[128] doth invite me.

HORATIO Of that I shall have also cause to speak,
15 And from his mouth whose voice will draw on more.[129]
But let this same be presently[130] performed,
Even while men's minds are wild, lest more mischance
On[131] plots and errors happen.

FORTINBRAS Let four captains
20 Bear Hamlet like a soldier to the stage,
For he was likely, had he been put on,[132]
To have proved most royal; and for his passage[133]
The soldiers' music and the rites of war
Speak loudly for him.
25 Take up the bodies. Such a sight as this
Becomes the field, but here shows much amiss.
Go, bid the soldiers shoot.

(*Exeunt* [*marching; after the which a peal of ordinance are shot off*])

---

124 *judgments* retributions 125 *casual* not humanly planned (reinforcing *accidental*) 126 *put on* instigated 127 *of memory* traditional and kept in mind 128 *vantage* advantageous opportunity 129 *more* i.e. more voices, or votes, for the kingship 130 *presently* immediately 131 *On* on the basis of 132 *put on* set to perform in office 133 *passage* death

## QUESTIONS

1. The climax in *Hamlet* extends over several scenes. Which ones do you think they are?
2. What states does Hamlet pass through within these scenes?
3. How do his actions after the climax contrast with his actions before it?
4. What changes in Hamlet's outlook, or in your reaction to him, begin during these climactic scenes and develop during the latter part of the play?
5. Choose some topic that shows how the climax functions as a turning point in *Hamlet* and develop it as fully as possible, making use of specific examples not only from the climactic scenes but from earlier and later scenes as well.

# 4 *Realistic Drama*

Our study of *Hamlet* brought us from the early Greek drama to the first great age of professional drama in England. In this chapter we move on to another period of notable theatrical growth and development throughout Europe and America—the late nineteenth and early twentieth centuries—the age of **realism.** From this period, we present two full-length plays—Ibsen's *A Doll's House* and Wilde's *The Importance of Being Earnest*—and three one-act plays—Chekhov's *The Marriage Proposal,* Synge's *Riders to the Sea,* and Glaspell's *Trifles.*

A look at the authors represented in this chapter tells us that realism is an international style: it is represented here by Norwegian, English, Russian, Irish, and American playwrights. A somewhat longer look at the scene descriptions that open each play tells us that realism was a style of production as well as a literary style. Note how carefully these sets are put together to imitate actual rooms, such as those the characters, if they were real, would inhabit.

Look, for instance, at the opening of *A Doll's House* on page 845. Not only does Ibsen carefully list the placement of the four doors and the furniture used in the action; he even details the "copperplate etchings on the walls" and the "deluxe editions" that are to fill the "small bookcase."

Note, too, that Ibsen speaks of the "rear wall," "left wall," and "right wall" of the room. To most of us, this seems quite natural. Of course a room has four walls. Of course three of them are shown onstage and the fourth is imagined to be at the front of the stage. Of course characters enter and exit through doors in these walls; how else does one enter or leave a room? In fact, however, this form of stage setting, known as the "box set," was a new form of stage setting. The box set was far more realistic than the older "wings"; but it was more cumbersome as well, requiring long intermissions between acts to allow for scene changes. Thus, it may have helped to promote the popularity, not only of realistic drama, but also of the one-act play, which is often set in one scene and thus requires no change of scenery.

Realism in production, then, meant sets and costumes as like those of everyday life as possible. In playwriting, it meant plots, characters, and language drawn from everyday life, as well. (Comedy, as usual, retained the right of exaggeration in all these areas.)

In addition, realism implied a new approach to drama. The realistic play hoped to make two impacts on its audience. First, of course, it sought to make the audience sympathize with the plight of its characters. But it also strove to raise in the minds of its audience questions as to the rightness of some aspect of social order, and the desire to change what the dramatist perceived as evil or wrong.

From these goals came a new form of play known as the **realistic drama:** a serious play, usually on a domestic or semi-domestic theme, featuring middle-class (or sometimes lower-class) characters, a contemporary setting, and a plot that questions some aspect or dictate of society.

Take, for example, *A Doll's House* by Henrik Ibsen, a Norwegian playwright who was one of the earliest and most admired of the realists. We see in *A Doll's House,* one of Ibsen's most popular plays, the mixture of elements described above. The scene is unrelievedly domestic. Money and marriage (normally the concerns of comedy) are both major concerns in this play. Yet the movement within the play is more like that of tragedy, being, in general, "from happiness to unhappiness." Comedy usually ends in the making of a marriage. *A Doll's House* details the breakup of one. In line with the domesticity of the scene, we notice a new concern with detail: the clothes Nora wears, the ornaments she puts on her Christmas tree, the macaroons she eats or does not eat all reflect her struggle for self-identity. We see, too, her concern with upbringing: what effect has Nora's father had on her? What effect is she having on her own children? Finally, we observe how the domestic nature of the realistic drama heightens the disparity between what the play's main characters perceive and feel and what is perceived of them by those around them. The onlookers in *Oedipus Rex* and *Antigonê* recognize the magnitude of the struggles they are watching. The onlookers in *A Doll's House* see only a peaceful, prosperous, well-ordered household.

Today, *A Doll's House* is most frequently read as a complaint against the undervaluation and suppression of women. But strong arguments can be made for the theory that Ibsen is showing men and women as equal victims of society's insistence on "respectability." Notice, as you read this play, how the characters are grouped in this regard, how each sins and is sinned against. Consider, too, the ending, which is of a type impossible for both tragedy and comedy. What effect does it have on your response to the play?

## Comedy and Realism

Comedy was a favorite form in the nineteenth century, both before and during the age of realism. For one thing, ninteenth-century theater was very strongly oriented toward the middle class; and comedy has always been very much at home in dealing with middle-class characters and dilemmas. For another thing, comedy deals with people as social beings; and so, too, did the nineteenth century most often consider them.

Comedy, indeed, has always been a preeminently social form of drama. Tragedy looks at its heroes when they are becoming involved in dilemmas that will separate them from their fellows or from the normal concerns of society. (Thus, Oedipus dooms himself to blindness and exile, while Hamlet accepts death as the price for freeing Denmark from Claudius.) Comedy, in contrast, studies people within society. Its concerns are most often those of everyday life; its problems are the problems involved in dealing with the people and customs of contemporary society. If the typical end of tragedy is death, with its total separation from the affairs of the world, the typical ending of comedy is marriage, with its commitment to worldly affairs. No matter how hard comic characters may struggle to escape the bonds of society—no matter what unusual methods they may use to outwit other characters or to solve some particular conflict between society's dictates and their own desires—at the play's end they return to the very society they've been fighting. The conflict has been solved, the goal or the marriage won; and society promises to go on exactly as it did before.

Seldom is this game of struggle and surrender more clearly played out than in Oscar Wilde's *The Importance of Being Earnest.* The lovers in this comedy belong to Society with a capital S—a carefully defined world admitting only those who can claim proper birth, breeding, and behavior. Lady Bracknell epitomizes the protocols of this world and seeks to govern (that is, to manipulate the lovers) in its name. The young men, Jack and Algernon, try to manipulate the rules of social behavior, escaping their responsibilities whenever possible; the young women, Cecily and Gwendolyn, manipulate social rules and individuals alike in order to attain their desires. And the entire comedy of maneuver and counter-maneuver is accompanied by Algernon's relentess commentary on social pretense and psychological realities.

In contrast to the light-hearted (and perhaps somewhat cold-blooded) tone of Wilde's comedy, with its epigrammatic language and its characters' tendency to watch themselves posture, to turn themselves into actors of scripts they and their fellow characters have written, Chekhov's *The Marriage Proposal* is almost farcically intense, peopled by characters who have not the slightest ability to view either themselves or any of their actions objectively.

There is no external obstacle to the lovers' happiness in this play. The man wishes to propose, the woman and her father are both delighted at the match. Yet the entire play is based on the struggle to get the proposal uttered and accepted. The language is thoroughly realistic; there is probably not one quotably funny line in the play. The characters show little or no development during the play. They are all exaggerations of the folks next door; in fact, they all exaggerate the same characteristics. Within these chosen limits, however, Chekhov creates a play that is decidedly and constantly funny. It is broad comedy. There is little or no subtlety here, and the speeches and gestures beg for an expansive, almost exaggerated acting style. The appeal thus created is so strong that it carries remarkably well into the written script; it is almost impossible to read *A Marriage Proposal* without considering how it might sound and look on the stage.

## Realism and Tragedy

Tragedy did not fare well during the nineteenth century, for several reasons. First, tragedy took kings and princes for its heroes, not members of the middle class. Second, it tended to insist that these kings and princes speak poetry, a speech form not well suited to discussion of everyday matters. Third, tragedy traditionally portrayed its heroes as people who have power over their societies: Oedipus, Hamlet, and Claudius are directly responsible for the physical and moral health of Thebes and of Denmark. And this characteristic of tragedy did not fit well with the trend of nineteenth-century drama to depict people as beings shaped by the society in which they had been born and reared. The thrust towards realism was thus antithetical to the grand tragedies of the classic and Renaissance styles; and attempts by nineteenth-century playwrights to reproduce some of that grandeur were generally failures.

Once realism was firmly established, however, the twentieth century could try variations on its theme; and some of these variations recreated tragedy as a newly effective form. Some of these new tragedies were written in poetry, but most were in prose—though in some few cases, such as Synge's *Riders to the Sea,* the prose is so artfully handled that it almost becomes poetry.

Many critics consider *Riders to the Sea* to be one of the finest one-act tragedies ever written. Its characters and setting reveal its relationship to realism. Its protagonist, an old peasant woman, performs no heroic deeds; her actions have little effect on the world around her. Indeed, she is as powerless and as circumscribed as any realistic heroine. Yet she has her epiphany, nonetheless, and stands as recipient and bearer of tragic insight.

Glaspell's *Trifles* is an even more emphatic blend of the realistic and tragic. It achieves this by presenting two sets of characters: five realistic ones, who carry all the speech and action of the play; and two tragic ones, who never appear onstage but whose actions form the focus of concern for the other five. When the play begins, the tragic roles have already been played out:

the antagonist has been murdered, and the protagonist is in jail, charged with the crime. The play thus functions largely as a detective story, as its five characters puzzle out the possible whys and wherefores of the murder, sifting through the extremely realistic "trifles" of everyday rural life in search of the answers. Almost like the two halves of a Greek chorus, these three men and two women seek to understand, in practical terms, the forces that have moved the protagonist into her current fearful isolation and led to her husband's death. The successive discoveries that unveil the mystery, and the tensions within and between the characters as their search progresses, create the power and movement of the play. The working-out of the realistic "puzzle" thus exposes the finality and inevitability of the tragic situation. For the women in the play, the result becomes a new dilemma. For the audience, equally faced with a blend of intellectual challenge and emotional demand, there is a similar demand for judgment: how do we judge all seven characters, the five onstage and the two off?

The layering of action and reaction in this play, the mixture of judgment and sympathy asked first of Mrs. Hale and Mrs. Peters and then of us, produces a play well worth seeing and reading. (It's also a good play to read aloud, or to act out.) In addition, the types of questions this play asks and the complexity of response that they demand illustrate one of the major trends (one might almost say, philosophies) of twentieth-century American literature—a style and complexity that we'll meet again in *Death of a Salesman.*

# HENRIK IBSEN (1828–1906)

## *A Doll's House*

A new translation by Otto Reinert

CHARACTERS

TORVALD HELMER, *a lawyer*
NORA, *his wife*
DR. RANK
MRS. LINDE
KROGSTAD
THE HELMERS' THREE SMALL CHILDREN
ANNE-MARIE, *the children's nurse*
A HOUSEMAID
A PORTER

SCENE. *The Helmers' living room.*

## ACT I

*A pleasant, tastefully but not expensively furnished, living room. A door on the rear wall, right, leads to the front hall, another door, left, to* HELMER'S *study. Between the two doors a piano. A third door in the middle of the left wall; further front a window. Near the window a round table and a small couch. Towards the rear of the right wall a fourth door; further front a tile stove with a rocking chair and a couple of armchairs in front of it. Between the stove and the door a small table. Copperplate etchings on the walls. A whatnot with porcelain figurines and other small objects. A small bookcase with de luxe editions. A rug on the floor; fire in the stove. Winter day.*

*The doorbell rings, then the sound of the front door opening.* NORA, *dressed for outdoors, enters, humming cheerfully. She carries several packages, which she puts down on the table, right. She leaves the door to the front hall open; there a* PORTER *is seen holding a Christmas tree and a basket. He gives them to the* MAID *who has let them in.*

NORA Be sure to hide the Christmas tree, Helene. The children mustn't see it before tonight when we've trimmed it. (*Opens her purse; to the* PORTER.) How much?

PORTER Fifty ore.

NORA Here's a crown. No, keep the change. (*The* PORTER *thanks her, leaves.* NORA *closes the door. She keeps laughing quietly to herself as she takes off her coat, etc. She takes a bag of macaroons from her pocket and eats a couple. She walks cautiously over to the door to the study and listens.*) Yes, he's home. (*Resumes her humming, walks over to the table, right.*)

HELMER (*in his study*) Is that my little lark twittering out there?

NORA (*opening some packages*) That's right.

HELMER My squirrel bustling about?

NORA Yes.

HELMER When did squirrel come home?

NORA Just now. (*Puts the bag of macaroons back in her pocket, wipes her mouth.*) Come out here, Torvald. I want to show you what I've bought.

HELMER I'm busy! (*After a little while he opens the door and looks in, pen in hand.*) Bought, eh? All that? So little wastrel has been throwing money around again?

NORA Oh but Torvald, this Christmas we can be a little extravagant, can't we? It's the first Christmas we don't have to scrimp.

HELMER I don't know about that. We certainly don't have money to waste.

NORA Yes, Torvald, we do. A little, anyway. Just a tiny little bit? Now that you're going to get that big salary and make lots and lots of money.

HELMER Starting at New Year's, yes. But payday isn't till the end of the quarter.

NORA That doesn't matter. We can always borrow.

HELMER Nora! (*Goes over to her and playfully pulls her ear.*) There you go being irresponsible again. Suppose I borrowed a thousand crowns today and you spent it all for Christmas and on New Year's Eve a tile hit me in the head and laid me out cold.

NORA (*putting her hand over his mouth*) I won't have you say such horrid things.

HELMER But suppose it happened. Then what?

NORA If it did, I wouldn't care whether we owed money or not.

HELMER But what about the people I had borrowed from?

NORA Who cares about them! They are strangers.

HELMER Nora, Nora, you *are* a woman! No, really! You know how I feel about that. No debts! A home in debt isn't a free home, and if it isn't free it isn't beautiful. We've managed nicely so far, you and I, and that's the way we'll go on. It won't be for much longer.

NORA (*walks over toward the stove*) All right, Torvald. Whatever you say.

HELMER (*follows her*) Come, come, my little songbird mustn't droop her wings. What's this? Can't have a pouty squirrel in the house, you know. (*Takes out his wallet.*) Nora, what do you think I have here?

NORA (*turns around quickly*) Money!

HELMER Here. (*Gives her some bills.*) Don't you think I know Christmas is expensive?

NORA (*counting*) Ten—twenty—thirty—forty. Thank you, thank you, Torvald. This helps a lot.

HELMER I certainly hope so.

NORA It does, it does. But I want to show you what I got. It was cheap, too. Look. New clothes for Ivar. And a sword. And a horse and trumpet for Bob. And a doll and a little bed for Emmy. It isn't any good, but it wouldn't last, anyway. And here's some dress material and scarves for the maids. I feel bad about old Anne-Marie, though. She really should be getting much more.

HELMER And what's in here?

NORA (*cries*) Not till tonight!

HELMER I see. But now what does my little prodigal have in mind for herself?

NORA Oh, nothing. I really don't care.

HELMER Of course you do. Tell me what you'd like. Within reason.

NORA Oh, I don't know. Really, I don't. The only thing—

HELMER Well?

NORA (*fiddling with his buttons, without looking at him*) If you really want to give me something, you might—you could—

HELMER All right, let's have it.

NORA (*quickly*) Some money, Torvald. Just as much as you think you can spare. Then I'll buy myself something one of these days.

HELMER No, really Nora—

NORA Oh yes, please, Torvald. Please? I'll wrap the money in pretty gold paper and hang it on the tree. Won't that be nice?

HELMER What's the name for little birds that are always spending money?

NORA Wastrels, I know. But please let's do it my way, Torvald. Then I'll have time to decide what I need most. Now that's sensible, isn't it?

HELMER (*smiling*) Oh, very sensible. That is, if you really bought yourself something you could use. But it all disappears in the household expenses or you buy things you don't need. And then you come back to me for more.

NORA Oh, but Torvald—

HELMER That's the truth, dear little Nora, and you know it. (*Puts his arm around her.*) My wastrel is a little sweetheart, but she *does* go through an awful lot of money awfully fast. You've no idea how expensive it is for a man to keep a wastrel.

NORA That's not fair, Torvald. I really save all I can.

HELMER (*laughs*) Oh, I believe that. All you can. Meaning, exactly nothing!

NORA (*hums, smiles mysteriously*) You don't know all the things we songbirds and squirrels need money for, Torvald.

HELMER You know, you're funny. Just like your father. You're always looking for ways to get money, but as soon as you do it runs through your fingers and you can never say what you spent it for. Well, I guess I'll just have to take you the way you are. It's in your blood. Yes, that sort of thing is hereditary, Nora.

NORA In that case, I wish I had inherited many of Daddy's qualities.

HELMER And I don't want you any different from just what you are—my own sweet little songbird. Hey!—I think I just noticed something. Aren't you looking—what's the word?—a little—sly—?

NORA I am?

HELMER You definitely are. Look at me.

NORA (*looks at him*) Well?

HELMER (*wagging a finger*) Little sweet-tooth hasn't by any chance been on a rampage today, has she?

NORA Of course not. Whatever makes you think that?

HELMER A little detour by the pastryshop maybe?

NORA No, I assure you, Torvald—

HELMER Nibbled a little jam?

NORA Certainly not!

HELMER Munched a macaroon or two?

NORA No, really, Torvald, I honestly—

HELMER All right. Of course I was only joking.

NORA (*walks toward the table, right*) You know I wouldn't do anything to displease you.

HELMER I know. And I have your promise. (*Over to her.*) All right, keep your little Christmas secrets to yourself, Nora darling. They'll all come out tonight, I suppose, when we light the tree.

NORA Did you remember to invite Rank?

HELMER No, but there's no need to. He knows he'll have dinner with us. Anyway, I'll see him later this morning. I'll ask him then. I did order some good wine. Oh Nora, you've no idea how much I'm looking forward to tonight!

NORA Me, too. And the children Torvald! They'll have such a good time!

HELMER You know, it *is* nice to have a good, safe job and a comfortable income. Feels good just thinking about it. Don't you agree?

NORA Oh, it's wonderful!

HELMER Remember last Christmas? For three whole weeks you shut yourself up every evening till long after midnight making ornaments for the Christmas tree and I don't know what else. Some big surprise for all of us, anyway. I'll be damned if I've ever been so bored in my whole life!

NORA I wasn't bored at all!

HELMER (*smiling*) But you've got to admit you didn't have much to show for it in the end.

NORA Oh, don't tease me again about that! Could I help it that the cat got in and tore up everything?

HELMER Of course you couldn't, my poor little Nora. You just wanted to please the rest of us, and that's the important thing. But I *am* glad the hard times are behind us. Aren't you?

NORA Oh yes. I think it's just wonderful.

HELMER This year, I won't be bored and lonely. And you won't have to strain your dear eyes and your delicate little hands—

NORA (*claps her hands*) No I won't, will I Torvald? Oh, how wonderful, how lovely, to hear you say that! (*Puts her arm under his.*) Let me tell you how I think we should arrange things, Torvald. Soon as Christmas is over—(*The doorbell rings.*) Someone's at the door. (*Straightens things up a bit.*) A caller, I suppose. Bother!

HELMER Remember, I'm not home for visitors.

THE MAID (*in the door to the front hall*) Ma'am, there's a lady here—

NORA All right. Ask her to come in.

THE MAID (*to* HELMER) And the Doctor just arrived.

HELMER Is he in the study?

THE MAID Yes, sir.

(HELMER *exits into his study.* THE MAID *shows* MRS. LINDE *in and closes the door behind her as she leaves.* MRS. LINDE *is in travel dress.*)

MRS. LINDE (*timid and a little hesitant*) Good morning, Nora.

NORA (*uncertainly*) Good morning.

MRS. LINDE I don't believe you know who I am.

NORA No—I'm not sure—Though I know I should—Of course! Kristine! It's you!

MRS. LINDE Yes, it's me.

NORA And I didn't even recognize you! I had no idea (*In a lower voice.*) You've changed, Kristine.

MRS. LINDE I'm sure I have. It's been nine or ten long years.

NORA Has it really been that long? Yes, you're right. I've been so happy these last eight years. And now you're here. Such a long trip in the middle of winter. How brave!

MRS. LINDE I got in on the steamer this morning.

NORA To have some fun over the holidays, of course. That's lovely. For we are going to have fun. But take off your coat! You aren't cold, are you? (*Helps her.*) There, now! Let's sit down here by the fire and just relax and talk. No, you sit there. I want the rocking chair. (*Takes her hands.*) And now you've got your old face back. It was just for a minute, right at first—Though you are a little more pale, Kristine. And maybe a little thinner.

MRS. LINDE And much, much older, Nora.

NORA Maybe a little older. Just a teeny-weeny bit, not much. (*Interrupts herself, serious.*) Oh, but how thoughtless of me, chatting away like this! Sweet, good Kristine, can you forgive me?

MRS. LINDE Forgive you what, Nora?

NORA (*in a low voice*) You poor dear, you lost your husband, didn't you?

MRS. LINDE Three years ago, yes.

NORA I know. I saw it in the paper. Oh please believe me, Kristine. I really meant to write you, but I never got around to it. Something was always coming up.

MRS. LINDE Of course, Nora. I understand.

NORA No, that wasn't very nice of me. You poor thing, all you must have been through. And he didn't leave you much, either, did he?

MRS. LINDE No.

NORA And no children?

MRS. LINDE No.

NORA Nothing at all, in other words?

MRS. LINDE Not so much as a sense of loss—a grief to live on—

NORA (*incredulous*) But Kristine, how can that *be*?

MRS. LINDE (*with a sad smile, strokes* NORA'*s hair*) That's the way it sometimes is, Nora.

NORA All alone. How awful for you. I have three darling children. You can't see them right now, though; they're out with their nurse. But now you must tell me everything—

MRS. LINDE No, no; I'd rather listen to you.

NORA No, you begin. Today I won't be selfish. Today I'll think only of you. Except there's one thing I've just got to tell you first. Something marvelous that's happened to us just these last few days. You haven't heard, have you?

MRS. LINDE No; tell me.

NORA Just think. My husband's been made manager of the Mutual Bank.

MRS. LINDE Your husband—! Oh, I'm so glad!

NORA Yes, isn't that great? You see, private law practice is so uncertain, especially when you won't have anything to do with cases that aren't—you know—quite nice. And of course Torvald won't do that and I quite agree with him. Oh, you've no idea how delighted we are! He takes over at New Year's, and he'll be getting a big salary and all sorts of extras. From now on we'll be able to live in quite a different way—exactly as we like. Oh, Kristine! I feel so carefree and happy! It's lovely to have lots and lots of money and not have to worry about a thing! Don't you agree?

MRS. LINDE It would be nice to have enough at any rate.

NORA No, I don't mean just enough. I mean lots and lots!

MRS. LINDE (*smiles*) Nora, Nora, when are you going to be sensible? In school you spent a great deal of money.

NORA (*quietly laughing*) Yes, and Torvald says I still do. (*Raises her finger at* MRS. LINDE.) But "Nora, Nora" isn't so crazy as you all think. Believe me, we've had nothing to be extravagant with. We've both had to work.

MRS. LINDE You too?

NORA Yes. Oh, it's been little things, mostly—sewing, crocheting, embroidery—that sort of thing. (*Casually.*) And other things too. You know, of course, that Torvald left government service when we got married? There was no chance of promotion in his department, and of course he had to make more money than he had been making. So for the first few years he worked altogether too hard. He had to take jobs on the side and work night and day. It turned out to be too much for him. He became seriously ill. The doctors told him he needed to go south.

MRS. LINDE That's right; you spent a year in Italy, didn't you?

NORA Yes, we did. But you won't believe how hard it was to get away. Ivar had just been born. But of course we had to go. Oh, it was a wonderful trip. And it saved Torvald's life. But it took a lot of money, Kristine.

MRS. LINDE I'm sure it did.

NORA Twelve hundred specie dollars. Four thousand eight hundred crowns. That's a lot of money.

MRS. LINDE Yes. So it's lucky you have it when something like that happens.

NORA Well, actually we got the money from Daddy.

MRS. LINDE I see. That was about the time your father died, I believe.

NORA Yes, just about then. And I couldn't even go and take care of him. I was expecting little Ivar any day. And I had poor Torvald to look after, desperately sick and all. My dear, good Daddy! I never saw him again, Kristine. That's the saddest thing that's happened to me since I got married.

MRS. LINDE I know you were very fond of him. But then you went to Italy?

NORA Yes, for now we had the money, and the doctors urged us to go. So we left about a month later.

MRS. LINDE And when you came back your husband was well again?

NORA Healthy as a horse!

MRS. LINDE But—the doctor?

NORA What do you mean?

MRS. LINDE I thought the maid said it was the doctor, that gentleman who came the same time I did.

NORA Oh, that's Dr. Rank. He doesn't come as a doctor. He's our closest friend. He looks in at least once every day. No, Torvald hasn't been sick once since then. And the children are strong and healthy, too, and so am I. (*Jumps up and claps her hands.*) Oh God, Kristine! Isn't it wonderful to be alive and happy! Isn't it just lovely!—But now I'm being mean again, talking only about myself and my things. (*Sits down on a footstool close to* MRS. LINDE *and puts her arm on her lap.*) Please don't be angry with me! Tell me, is it really true that you didn't care for your husband? Then why did you marry him?

MRS. LINDE Mother was still alive then, but she was bedridden and helpless. And I had my two younger brothers to look after. I didn't think I had the right to turn him down.

NORA No, I suppose not. So he had money then?

MRS. LINDE He was quite well off, I think. But it was an uncertain business, Nora. When he died, the whole thing collapsed and there was nothing left.

NORA And then—?

MRS. LINDE Well, I had to manage as best I could. With a little store and a little school and anything else I could think of. The last three years have been one long work day for me, Nora, without any rest. But now it's over. My poor mother doesn't need me any more. She's passed away. And the boys are on their own too. They've both got jobs and support themselves.

NORA What a relief for you—

MRS. LINDE No, not relief. Just a great emptiness. Nobody to live for any more. (*Gets up restlessly.*) That's why I couldn't stand it any longer in that little hole. Here in town it has to be easier to find something to keep me busy and occupy my thoughts. With a little luck I should be able to find a permanent job, something in an office—

NORA Oh but Kristine, that's exhausting work, and you look worn out already. It would be much better for you to go to a resort.

MRS. LINDE (*walks over to the window*) I don't have a Daddy who can give me the money, Nora.

NORA (*getting up*) Oh, don't be angry with me.

MRS. LINDE (*over to her*) Dear Nora, don't *you* be angry with *me*. That's the worst thing about my kind of situation: you become so bitter. You've nobody to work for, and yet you have to look out for yourself, somehow. You've got to keep on living, and so you become selfish. Do you know—when you told me about your husband's new position I was delighted not so much for your sake as for my own.

NORA Why was that? Oh, I see. You think maybe Torvald can give you a job?

MRS. LINDE That's what I had in mind.

NORA And he will too, Kristine. Just leave it to me. I'll be ever so subtle about it. I'll think of something nice to tell him, something he'll like. Oh I so much want to help you.

MRS. LINDE That's very good of you, Nora—making an effort like that for me. Especially since you've known so little trouble and hardship in your own life.

NORA I—?—have known so little—?

MRS. LINDE (*smiling*) Oh well, a little sewing or whatever it was. You're still a child, Nora.

NORA (*with a toss of her head, walks away*) You shouldn't sound so superior.

MRS. LINDE I shouldn't?

NORA You're just like all the others. None of you think I'm good for anything really serious.

MRS. LINDE Well, now—

NORA That I've never been through anything difficult.

MRS. LINDE But Nora! You just told me all your troubles!

NORA That's nothing! (*Lowers her voice.*) I haven't told you about *it*.

MRS. LINDE It? What's that? What do you mean?

NORA You patronize me, Kristine, and that's not fair. You're proud that you worked so long and so hard for your mother.

MRS. LINDE I don't think I patronize anyone. But it *is* true that I'm both proud and happy that I could make mother's last years comparatively easy.

NORA And you're proud of all you did for your brothers.

MRS. LINDE I think I have the right to be.

NORA And so do I. But now I want to tell you something, Kristine. I have something to be proud and happy about too.

MRS. LINDE I don't doubt that for a moment. But what exactly do you mean?

NORA Not so loud! Torvald mustn't hear—not for anything in the world. Nobody must know about this, Kristine. Nobody but you.

MRS. LINDE But what is it?

NORA Come here. (*Pulls her down on the couch beside her.*) You see, I *do* have something to be proud and happy about. I've saved Torvald's life.

MRS. LINDE Saved—? How do you mean—"saved"?

NORA I told you about our trip to Italy. Torvald would have died if he hadn't gone.

MRS. LINDE I understand that. And so your father gave you the money you needed.

NORA (*smiles*) Yes, that's what Torvald and all the others think. But—

MRS. LINDE But what?

NORA Daddy didn't give us a penny. *I* raised that money.

MRS. LINDE *You* did? That whole big amount?

NORA Twelve hundred specie dollars. Four thousand eight hundred crowns. *Now* what do you say?

MRS. LINDE But Nora, how could you? Did you win in the state lottery?

NORA (*contemptuously*) State lottery! (*Snorts.*) What is so great about that?

MRS. LINDE Where did it come from then?

NORA (*humming and smiling, enjoying her secret*) Hmmm. Tra-la-la-la-la!

MRS. LINDE You certainly couldn't have borrowed it.

NORA Oh? And why not?

MRS. LINDE A wife can't borrow money without her husband's consent.

NORA (*with a toss of her head*) Oh, I don't know—take a wife with a little bit of a head for business—a wife who knows how to manage things—

MRS. LINDE But Nora, I don't understand at all—

NORA You don't have to. I didn't say I borrowed the money, did I? I could have gotten it some other way. (*Leans back.*) An admirer may have given it to me. When you're as tolerably good-looking as I am—

MRS. LINDE Oh, you're crazy.

NORA I think you're dying from curiosity, Kristine.

MRS. LINDE I'm beginning to think you've done something very foolish, Nora.

NORA (*sits up*) Is it foolish to save your husband's life?

MRS. LINDE I say it's foolish to act behind his back.

NORA But don't you see: he couldn't be told! You're missing the whole point, Kristine. We couldn't even let him know how seriously ill he was. The doctors came to *me* and told me his life was in danger, that nothing could save him but a stay in the south. Don't you think I tried to work on him? I told him how lovely it would be if I could go abroad like other young wives. I cried and begged. I said he'd better remember what condition I was in, that he had to be nice to me and do what I wanted. I even hinted he could borrow the money. But that almost made him angry with me. He told me I was being irresponsible and that it was his duty as my husband not to give in to my moods and whims—I think that's what he called it. All right, I said to myself, you've got to be saved somehow, and so I found a way—

MRS. LINDE And your husband never learned from your father that the money didn't come from him?

NORA Never. Daddy died that same week. I thought of telling him all about it and ask him not to say anything. But since he was so sick—It turned out I didn't have to—

MRS. LINDE And you've never told your husband?

NORA Of course not! Good heavens, how could I? He, with his strict principles! Besides, you know how men are. Torvald would find it embarrassing and humiliating to learn that he owed me anything. It would upset our whole relationship. Our happy, beautiful home would no longer be what it is.

MRS. LINDE Aren't you ever going to tell him?

NORA (*reflectively, half smiling*) Yes—one day, maybe. Many, many years from now, when I'm no longer young and pretty. Don't laugh! I mean when Torvald no longer feels about me the way he does now, when he no longer thinks it's fun when I dance for him and put on costumes and recite for him. Then it will be good to have something in reserve—(*Interrupts herself.*) Oh, I'm just being silly! That day will never come.—Well, now, Kristine, what do you think of my great secret? Don't you think I'm good for something too?—By the way, you wouldn't believe all the worry I've had because of it. It's been very hard to meet my obligations on schedule. You see, in business there's something called quarterly interest and something called installments on the principal, and those are terribly hard to come up with. I've had to save a little here and a little there, whenever I could. I couldn't use much of the housekeeping money, for Torvald has to eat well.

And I couldn't use what I got for clothes for the children. They have to look nice, and I didn't think it would be right to spend less than I got—the sweet little things!

MRS. LINDE Poor Nora! So you had to take it from your own allowance!

NORA Yes, of course. After all, it was my affair. Every time Torvald gave me money for a new dress and things like that, I never used more than half of it. I always bought the cheapest, simplest things for myself. Thank God, everything looks good on me, so Torvald never noticed. But it was hard many times, Kristine, for it's fun to have pretty clothes. Don't you think?

MRS. LINDE Certainly.

NORA Anyway, I had other ways of making money too. Last winter I was lucky enough to get some copying work. So I locked the door and sat up writing every night till quite late. God! I often got so tired—! But it was great fun, too, working and making money. It was almost like being a man.

MRS. LINDE But how much have you been able to pay off this way?

NORA I couldn't tell you exactly. You see, it's very difficult to keep track of business like that. All I know is I have been paying off as much as I've been able to scrape together. Many times I just didn't know what to do. (*Smiles.*) Then I used to imagine a rich old gentleman had fallen in love with me—

MRS. LINDE What! What old gentleman?

NORA Phooey! And now he was dead and they were reading his will, and there it said in big letters, "All my money is to be paid in cash immediately to the charming Mrs. Nora Helmer."

MRS. LINDE But dearest Nora—who *was* this old gentleman?

NORA For heaven's sake, Kristine, don't you see? There *was* no old gentleman. He was just somebody I made up when I couldn't think of any way to raise the money. But never mind him. The old bore can be anyone he likes to for all I care. I have no use for him or his last will, for now I don't have a single worry in the world. (*Jumps up.*) Dear God, what a lovely thought this is! To be able to play and have fun with the children, to have everything nice and pretty in the house, just the way Torvald likes it! Not a care! And soon spring will be here, and the air will be blue and high. Maybe we can travel again. Maybe I'll see the ocean again! Oh, yes, yes!—it's wonderful to be alive and happy!

*The doorbell rings.*

MRS. LINDE (*getting up*) There's the doorbell. Maybe I better be going.

NORA No, please stay. I'm sure it's just someone for Torvald—

THE MAID (*in the hall door*) Excuse me, ma'am. There's a gentleman here who'd like to see Mr. Helmer.

NORA You mean the bank manager.

THE MAID Sorry, ma'am; the bank manager. But I didn't know—since the Doctor is with him—

NORA Who is the gentleman?

KROGSTAD (*appearing in the door*) It's just me, Mrs. Helmer.

MRS. LINDE *starts, looks, turns away toward the window.*

NORA (*takes a step toward him, tense, in a low voice*) You? What do you want? What do you want with my husband?

KROGSTAD Bank business—in a way. I have a small job in the Mutual, and I understand your husband is going to be our new boss—

NORA So it's just—

KROGSTAD Just routine business, ma'am. Nothing else.

NORA All right. In that case, why don't you go through the door to the office.

*Dismisses him casually as she closes the door. Walks over to the stove and tends the fire.*

MRS. LINDE Nora—who was that man?

NORA His name's Krogstad. He's a lawyer.

MRS. LINDE So it *was* him.

NORA Do you know him?

MRS. LINDE I used to—many years ago. For a while he clerked in our part of the country.

NORA Right. He did.

MRS. LINDE He has changed a great deal.

NORA I believe he had a very unhappy marriage.

MRS. LINDE And now he's a widower, isn't he?

NORA With many children. There now; it's burning nicely again. (*Closes the stove and moves the rocking chair a little to the side.*)

MRS. LINDE They say he's into all sorts of business.

NORA Really? Maybe so. I wouldn't know. But let's not think about business. It's such a bore.

DR. RANK (*appears in the door to* HELMER*'s study.*) No. I don't want to be in the way. I'd rather talk to your wife a bit. (*Closes the door and notices* MRS. LINDE.) Oh, I beg your pardon. I believe I'm in the way here too.

NORA No, not at all. (*Introduces them.*) Dr. Rank. Mrs. Linde.

RANK Aha. A name often heard in this house. I believe I passed you on the stairs coming up.

MRS. LINDE Yes. I'm afraid I climb stairs very slowly. They aren't good for me.

RANK I see. A slight case of inner decay, perhaps?
MRS. LINDE Overwork, rather.
RANK Oh, is that all? And now you've come to town to relax at all the parties?
MRS. LINDE I have come to look for a job.
RANK A proven cure for overwork, I take it?
MRS. LINDE One has to live, Doctor.
RANK Yes, that seems to be the common opinion.
NORA Come on, Dr. Rank—you want to live just as much as the rest of us.
RANK Of course I do. Miserable as I am, I prefer to go on being tortured as long as possible. All my patients feel the same way. And that's true of the moral invalids too. Helmer is talking with a specimen right this minute.
MRS. LINDE (*in a low voice*) Ah!
NORA What do you mean?
RANK Oh, this lawyer, Krogstad. You don't know him. The roots of his character are decayed. But even he began by saying something about having *to live*—as if it were a matter of the highest importance.
NORA Oh? What did he want with Torvald?
RANK I don't really know. All I heard was something about the bank.
NORA I didn't know that Krog—that this Krogstad had anything to do with the Mutual Bank.
RANK Yes, he seems to have some kind of job there. (*To* MRS. LINDE.) I don't know if you are familiar in your part of the country with the kind of person who is always running around trying to sniff out cases of moral decrepitude and as soon as he finds one puts the individual under observation in some excellent position or other. All the healthy ones are left out in the cold.
MRS. LINDE I should think it's the sick who need looking after the most.
RANK (*shrugs his shoulders*) There we are. That's the attitude that turns society into a hospital.

(NORA, *absorbed in her own thoughts, suddenly starts giggling and clapping her hands.*)

RANK What's so funny about that? Do you even know what society is?
NORA What do I care about your stupid society! I laughed at something entirely different—something terribly amusing. Tell me, Dr. Rank—all the employees in the Mutual Bank, from now on they'll all be dependent on Torvald, right?

RANK Is that what you find so enormously amusing?

NORA (*smiles and hums*) That's my business, that's my business! (*Walks around.*) Yes, I do think it's fun that we—that Torvald is going to have so much influence on so many people's lives. (*Brings out the bag of macaroons.*) Have a macaroon, Dr. Rank.

RANK Well, well—macaroons. I thought they were banned around here.

NORA Yes, but these were some that Kristine gave me.

MRS. LINDE What! I?

NORA That's all right. Don't look so scared. You couldn't know that Torvald won't let me have them. He's afraid they'll ruin my teeth. But who cares! Just once in a while—! Right, Dr. Rank? Have one! (*Puts a macaroon into his mouth.*) You too, Kristine. And one for me. A very small one. Or at most two. (*Walks around again.*) Yes, I really feel very, very happy. Now there's just one thing I'm dying to do.

RANK Oh, And what's that?

NORA Something I'm dying to say so Torvald could hear.

RANK And why can't you?

NORA I don't dare to, for it's not nice.

MRS. LINDE Not nice?

RANK In that case, I guess you'd better not. But surely to the two of us—? What is it you'd like to say for Helmer to hear?

NORA I want to say, "Goddammit!"

RANK Are you out of your mind!

MRS. LINDE For heaven's sake, Nora!

RANK Say it. Here he comes.

NORA (*hiding the macaroons*). Shhh!

(HELMER *enters from his study, carrying his hat and overcoat.*)

NORA (*going to him*) Well, dear, did you get rid of him?

HELMER Yes, he just left.

NORA Torvald, I want you to meet Kristine. She's just come to town.

HELMER Kristine—? I'm sorry; I don't think—

NORA Mrs. Linde, Torvald dear. Mrs. Kristine Linde.

HELMER Ah, yes. A childhood friend of my wife's, I suppose.

MRS. LINDE Yes, we've known each other for a long time.

NORA Just think; she has come all this way just to see you.

HELMER I'm not sure I understand—

MRS. LINDE Well, not really—

NORA You see, Kristine is an absolutely fantastic secretary, and she would so much like to work for a competent executive and learn more than she knows already—

HELMER Very sensible, I'm sure, Mrs. Linde.

NORA So when she heard about your appointment—there was a wire—she came here as fast as she could. How about it, Torvald? Couldn't you do something for Kristine? For my sake. Please?

HELMER Quite possibly. I take it you're a widow, Mrs. Linde?

MRS. LINDE Yes.

HELMER And you've had office experience?

MRS. LINDE Some—yes.

HELMER In that case I think it's quite likely that I'll be able to find you a position.

NORA (*claps her hands*) I knew it! I knew it!

HELMER You've arrived at a most opportune time, Mrs. Linde.

MRS. LINDE Oh, how can I ever thank you—

HELMER Not at all, not at all. (*Puts his coat on.*) But today you'll have to excuse me—

RANK Wait a minute; I'll come with you. (*Gets his fur coat from the front hall, warms it by the stove.*)

NORA Don't be long, Torvald.

HELMER An hour or so; no more.

NORA Are you leaving, too, Kristine?

MRS. LINDE (*putting on her things*) Yes, I'd better go and find a place to stay.

HELMER Good. Then we'll be going the same way.

NORA (*helping her*) I'm sorry this place is so small, but I don't think we very well could—

MRS. LINDE Of course! Don't be silly, Nora. Goodbye, and thank you for everything.

NORA Goodbye. We'll see you soon. You'll be back this evening, of course. And you too, Dr. Rank; right? If you feel well enough? Of course you will. Just wrap yourself up.

(*General small talk as all exit into the hall. Children's voices are heard on the stairs.*)

NORA There they are! There they are! (*She runs and opens the door. The nurse* ANNE-MARIE *enters with the children.*)

NORA Come in! Come in! (*Bends over and kisses them.*) Oh, you sweet, sweet darlings! Look at them, Kristine! Aren't they beautiful?

RANK No standing around in the draft!

HELMER Come along, Mrs. Linde. This place isn't fit for anyone but mothers right now.

(DR. RANK, HELMER, *and* MRS. LINDE *go down the stairs. The* NURSE *enters the living room with the children.* NORA *follows, closing the door behind her.*)

NORA My, how nice you all look! Such red cheeks! Like apples and roses. (*The children all talk at the same time.*) You've had so much fun? I bet you have. Oh, isn't that nice! You pulled both Emmy and Bob on your sleigh? Both at the same time? That's very good, Ivar. Oh, let me hold her for a minute, Anne-Marie. My sweet little doll baby! (*Takes the smallest of the children from the* NURSE *and dances with her.*) Yes, yes, of course; Mama'll dance with you too, Bob. What? You threw snowballs? Oh, I wish I'd been there! No, no; *I* want to take their clothes off, Anne-Marie. Please let me; I think it's so much fun. You go on in. You look frozen. There's hot coffee on the stove.

(*The* NURSE *exits into the room to the left.* NORA *takes the children's wraps off and throws them all around. They all keep telling her things at the same time.*)

NORA Oh, really? A big dog ran after you? But it didn't bite you. Of course not. Dogs don't bite sweet little doll babies. Don't peek at the packages, Ivar! What's in them? Wouldn't you like to know! No, no; that's something terrible! Play? You want to play? What do you want to play? Okay, let's play hide-and-seek. Bob hides first. You want *me* to? All right. I'll go first.

(*Laughing and shouting,* NORA *and the children play in the living room and in the adjacent room, right. Finally,* NORA *hides herself under the table; the children rush in, look for her, can't find her. They hear her low giggle, run to the table, lift the rug that covers it, see her. General hilarity. She crawls out, pretends to scare them. New delight. In the meantime there has been a knock on the door between the living room and the front hall, but nobody has noticed. Now the door is opened halfway;* KROGSTAD *appears. He waits a little. The play goes on.*)

KROGSTAD Pardon me, Mrs. Helmer—

NORA (*with a muted cry turns around, jumps up*) Ah! What do you want?

KROGSTAD I'm sorry. The front door was open. Somebody must have forgotten to close it—

NORA (*standing up*) My husband isn't here, Mr. Krogstad.

KROGSTAD I know.

NORA So what do you want?

KROGSTAD I'd like a word with you.

NORA With—? (*To the children.*) Go in to Anne-Marie. What? No, the strange man won't do anything bad to Mama. When he's gone we'll play some more.

(*She takes the children into the room to the left and closes the door.*)

NORA (*tense, troubled*) You want to speak with me?

KROGSTAD Yes I do.

NORA Today—? It isn't the first of the month yet.

KROGSTAD No, it's Christmas Eve. It's up to you what kind of holiday you'll have.

NORA What do you want? I can't possibly—

KROGSTAD Let's not talk about that just yet. There's something else. You do have a few minutes, don't you?

NORA Yes. Yes, of course. That is,—

KROGSTAD Good. I was sitting in Olsen's restaurant when I saw your husband go by.

NORA Yes—?

KROGSTAD —with a lady.

NORA What of it?

KROGSTAD May I be so free as to ask: wasn't that lady Mrs. Linde?

NORA Yes.

KROGSTAD Just arrived in town?

NORA Yes, today.

KROGSTAD She's a good friend of yours, I understand?

NORA Yes, she is. But I fail to see—

KROGSTAD I used to know her myself.

NORA I know that.

KROGSTAD So you know about that. I thought as much. In that case, let me ask you a simple question. Is Mrs. Linde going to be employed in the bank?

NORA What makes you think you have the right to cross-examine me like this, Mr. Krogstad—you, one of my husband's employees? But since you ask, I'll tell you. Yes, Mrs. Linde is going to be working in the bank. And it was I who recommended her, Mr. Krogstad. Now you know.

KROGSTAD So I was right.

NORA (*walks up and down*) After all, one does have a little influence, you know. Just because you're a woman, it doesn't mean that—Really, Mr. Krogstad, people in a subordinate position should be careful not to offend someone who—oh well—

KROGSTAD —has influence?

NORA Exactly.

KROGSTAD (*changing his tone*) Mrs. Helmer, I must ask you to be good enough to use your influence on my behalf.

NORA What do you mean?

KROGSTAD I want you to make sure that I am going to keep my subordinate position in the bank.

NORA I don't understand. Who is going to take your position away from you?

KROGSTAD There's no point in playing ignorant with me, Mrs. Helmer. I can very well appreciate that your friend would find it unpleasant to run into me. So now I know who I can thank for my dismissal.

NORA But I assure you—

KROGSTAD Never mind. Just want to say you still have time. I advise you to use your influence to prevent it.

NORA But Mr. Krogstad, I don't have any influence—none at all.

KROGSTAD No? I thought you just said—

NORA Of course I didn't mean it that way. I! Whatever makes you think that I have any influence of that kind on my husband?

KROGSTAD I went to law school with your husband. I have no reason to think that the bank manager is less susceptible than other husbands.

NORA If you're going to insult my husband, I'll ask you to leave.

KROGSTAD You're brave, Mrs. Helmer.

NORA I'm not afraid of you any more. After New Year's I'll be out of this thing with you.

KROGSTAD (*more controlled*) Listen, Mrs. Helmer. If necessary I'll fight as for my life to keep my little job in the bank.

NORA So it seems.

KROGSTAD It isn't just the money; that's really the smallest part of it. There is something else—Well, I guess I might as well tell you. It's like this. I'm sure you know, like everybody else, that some years ago I committed—an impropriety.

NORA I believe I've heard it mentioned.

KROGSTAD The case never came to court, but from that moment all doors were closed to me. So I took up the kind of business you know about. I had to do something, and I think I can say about myself that I have not been among the worst. But now I want to get out of all that. My sons are growing up. For their sake I must get back as much of my good name as I can. This job in the bank was like the first rung on the ladder. And now your husband wants to kick me down and leave me back in the mud again.

NORA But I swear to you, Mr. Krogstad; it's not at all in my power to help you.

KROGSTAD That's because you don't want to. But I have the means to force you.

NORA You don't mean you're going to tell my husband I owe you money?

KROGSTAD And if I did?

NORA That would be a mean thing to do. (*Almost crying.*) That secret, which is my joy and my pride—for him to learn about it in such a coarse and ugly manner—to learn it from *you*—! It would be terribly unpleasant for me.

KROGSTAD Just unpleasant?

NORA (*heatedly*) But go ahead! Do it! It will be worse for you than for me. When my husband realizes what a bad person you are, you'll be sure to lose your job.

KROGSTAD I asked you if it was just domestic unpleasantness you were afraid of?

NORA When my husband finds out, of course he'll pay off the loan, and then we won't have anything more to do with you.

KROGSTAD (*stepping closer*) Listen, Mrs. Helmer—either you have a very bad memory, or you don't know much about business. I think I had better straighten you out on a few things.

NORA What do you mean?

KROGSTAD When your husband was ill, you came to me to borrow twelve hundred dollars.

NORA I knew nobody else.

KROGSTAD I promised to get you the money—

NORA And you did.

KROGSTAD I promised to get you the money on certain conditions. At the time you were so anxious about your husband's health and so set on getting him away that I doubt very much that you paid much attention to the details of our transaction. That's why I remind you of them now. Anyway, I promised to get you the money if you would sign an I.O.U., which I drafted.

NORA And which I signed.

KROGSTAD Good. But below your signature I added a few lines, making your father security for the loan. Your father was supposed to put his signature to those lines.

NORA Supposed to—? He did.

KROGSTAD I had left the date blank. That is, your father was to date his own signature. You recall that, don't you, Mrs. Helmer?

NORA I guess so—

KROGSTAD I gave the note to you. You were to mail it to your father. Am I correct?

NORA Yes.

KROGSTAD And of course you did so right away, for no more than five or six days later you brought the paper back to me, signed by your father. Then I paid you the money.

NORA Well? And haven't I been keeping up with the payments?

KROGSTAD Fairly well, yes. But to get back to what we were talking about—those were difficult days for you, weren't they, Mrs. Helmer?

NORA Yes, they were.

KROGSTAD Your father was quite ill, I believe.

NORA He was dying.

KROGSTAD And died shortly afterwards?

NORA That's right.

KROGSTAD Tell me, Mrs. Helmer; do you happen to remember the date of your father's death? I mean the exact day of the month?

NORA Daddy died on September 29.

KROGSTAD Quite correct. I have ascertained that fact. That's why there is something peculiar about this (*takes out a piece of paper*), which I can't account for.

NORA Peculiar? How? I don't understand—

KROGSTAD It seems very peculiar, Mrs. Helmer, that your father signed this promissory note three days after his death.

NORA How so? I don't see what—

KROGSTAD Your father died on September 29. Now look. He has dated his signature October 2. Isn't that odd?

(NORA *remains silent.*)

KROGSTAD Can you explain it?

(NORA *is still silent.*)

KROGSTAD I also find it striking that the date and the month and the year are not in your father's handwriting but in a hand I think I recognize. Well, that might be explained. Your father may have forgotten to date his signature and somebody else may have done it here, guessing at the date before he had learned of your father's death. That's all right. It's only the signature itself that matters. And that is genuine, isn't it, Mrs. Helmer? Your father *did* put his name to this note?

NORA (*after a brief silence tosses her head back and looks defiantly at him*) No, he didn't. *I* wrote Daddy's name.

KROGSTAD Mrs. Helmer—do you realize what a dangerous admission you just made?

NORA Why? You'll get your money soon.

KROGSTAD Let me ask you something. Why didn't you mail this note to your father?

NORA Because it was impossible. Daddy was sick—you know that. If I had asked him to sign it, I would have had to tell him what the money was for. But I couldn't tell him, as sick as he was, that my husband's life was in danger. That was impossible. Surely you can see that.

KROGSTAD Then it would have been better for you if you had given up your trip abroad.

NORA No, that was impossible! That trip was to save my husband's life. I couldn't give it up.

KROGSTAD But didn't you realize that what you did amounted to fraud against me?

NORA I couldn't let that make any difference. I didn't care about you at all. I hated the way you made all those difficulties for me, even though you knew the danger my husband was in. I thought you were cold and unfeeling.

KROGSTAD Mrs. Helmer, obviously you have no clear idea of what you have done. Let me tell you that what I did that time was no more and no worse. And it ruined my name and reputation.

NORA You! Are you trying to tell me that you did something brave once in order to save your wife's life?

KROGSTAD The law doesn't ask about motives.

NORA Then it's a bad law.

KROGSTAD Bad or not—if I produce this note in court you'll be judged according to the law.

NORA I refuse to believe you. A daughter shouldn't have the right to spare her dying old father worry and anxiety? A wife shouldn't have the right to save her husband's life? I don't know the laws very well, but I'm sure that somewhere they make allowance for cases like that. And you, a lawyer, don't know that? I think you must be a bad lawyer, Mr. Krogstad.

KROGSTAD That may be. But business—the kind of business you and I have with one another—don't you think I know something about that? Very well. Do what you like. But let me tell you this: if I'm going to be kicked out again, you'll keep me company. (*He bows and exits through the front hall.*)

NORA (*pauses thoughtfully; then, with a defiant toss of her head*) Oh, nonsense! Trying to scare me like that! I'm not all that silly. (*Starts picking up the children's clothes; soon stops.*) But—? No! That's impossible! I did it for love!

THE CHILDREN (*in the door to the left*) Mama, the strange man just left. We saw him.

NORA Yes, yes; I know. But don't tell anybody about the strange man. Do you hear? Not even Daddy.

THE CHILDREN We won't. But now you'll play with us again, won't you, Mama?

NORA No, not right now.

THE CHILDREN But Mama—you promised.

NORA I know, but I can't just now. Go to your own room. I've so much to do. Be nice now, my little darlings. Do as I say. (*She nudges them gently into the other room and closes the door. She sits down on the couch, picks up a piece of embroidery, makes a few stitches, then stops.*) No! (*Throws the embroidery down, goes to the hall door and calls out.*) Helene! Bring the Christmas tree in here, please! (*Goes to the table, left, opens the drawer, halts.*) No—that's impossible!

THE MAID (*with the Christmas tree*) Where do you want it, ma'am?

NORA There. The middle of the floor.

THE MAID You want anything else?

NORA No, thanks. I have everything I need. (THE MAID *goes out.* NORA *starts trimming the tree.*) I want candles—and flowers—That awful man! Oh, nonsense! There's nothing wrong. This will be a lovely tree. I'll do everything you want me to, Torvald. I'll sing for you—dance for you—

(*Helmer, a bundle of papers under his arm, enters from outside.*)

NORA Ah—you're back already?

HELMER Yes. Has anybody been here?

NORA Here? No.

HELMER That's funny. I saw Krogstad leaving just now.

NORA Oh? Oh yes, that's right. Krogstad was here for just a moment.

HELMER I can tell from your face that he came to ask you to put in a word for him.

NORA Yes.

HELMER And it was supposed to be your own idea, wasn't it? You were not to tell me he'd been here. He asked you that too, didn't he?

NORA Yes, Torvald, but—

HELMER Nora, Nora, how could you! Talk to a man like that and make him promises! And lying to me about it afterwards—!

NORA Lying—?

HELMER Didn't you say nobody had been here? (*Shakes his finger at her.*) My little songbird must never do that again. Songbirds are supposed to have clean beaks to chirp with—no false notes. (*Puts his arms around her waist.*) Isn't that so? Of course it is. (*Lets her go.*) And that's enough about that. (*Sits down in front of the fireplace.*) Ah, it's nice and warm in here. (*Begins to leaf through his papers.*)

NORA (*busy with the tree; after a brief pause*) Torvald.

HELMER Yes.

NORA I'm looking forward so much to the Stenborgs' costume party day after tomorrow.

HELMER And I can't wait to find out what you're going to surprise me with.

NORA Oh, that silly idea!

HELMER Oh?

NORA I can't think of anything. It all seems so foolish and pointless.

HELMER Ah, my little Nora admits that?

NORA (*behind his chair, her arms on the back of the chair*) Are you very busy, Torvald?

HELMER Well—

NORA What are all those papers?

HELMER Bank business.

NORA Already?

HELMER I've asked the board to give me the authority to make certain changes in organization and personnel. That's what I'll be doing over the holidays. I want it all settled before New Year's.

NORA So that's why this poor Krogstad—

HELMER Hm.

NORA (*leisurely playing with the hair on his neck*) If you weren't so busy, Torvald, I'd ask you for a great big favor.

HELMER Let's hear it, anyway.

NORA I don't know anyone with better taste than you, and I want so much to look nice at the party. Couldn't you sort of take charge of me, Torvald, and decide what I'll wear—Help me with my costume?

HELMER Aha! Little Lady Obstinate is looking for someone to rescue her?

NORA Yes, Torvald. I won't get anywhere without your help.

HELMER All right. I'll think about it. We'll come up with something.

NORA Oh, you *are* nice! (*Goes back to the Christmas tree. A pause.*) Those red flowers look so pretty.—Tell me, was it really all that bad what this Krogstad fellow did?

HELMER He forged signatures. Do you have any idea what that means?

NORA Couldn't it have been because he felt he had to?

HELMER Yes, or like so many others he may simply have been thoughtless. I'm not so heartless as to condemn a man absolutely because of a single imprudent act.

NORA Of course not, Torvald!

HELMER People like him can redeem themselves morally by openly confessing their crime and taking their punishment.

NORA Punishment—?

HELMER But that was not the way Krogstad chose. He got out of it with tricks and evasions. That's what has corrupted him.

NORA So you think that if—?

HELMER Can't you imagine how a guilty person like that has to lie and fake and dissemble wherever he goes—putting on a mask before everybody he's close to, even his own wife and children. It's this thing with the children that's the worst part of it, Nora.

NORA Why is that?

HELMER Because when a man lives inside such a circle of stinking lies he brings infection into his own home and contaminates his whole family. With every breath of air his children inhale the germs of something ugly.

NORA (*moving closer behind him*) Are you so sure of that?

HELMER Of course I am. I have seen enough examples of that in my work. Nearly all young criminals have had mothers who lied.

NORA Why mothers—particularly?

HELMER Most often mothers. But of course fathers tend to have the same influence. Every lawyer knows that. And yet, for years this Krogstad has been poisoning his own children in an atmosphere of lies and deceit. That's why I call him a lost soul morally. (*Reaches out for her hands.*) And that's why my sweet little Nora must promise me never to take his side again. Let's shake on that.—What? What's this? Give me your hand. There! Now that's settled. I assure you, I would find it impossible to work in the same room with that man. I feel literally sick when I'm around people like that.

NORA (*withdraws her hand and goes to the other side of the Christmas tree*) It's so hot in here. And I have so much to do.

HELMER (*gets up and collects his papers*) Yes, and I really should try to get some of this reading done before dinner. I must think about your costume too. And maybe just possibly I'll have something to wrap in gilt paper and hang on the Christmas tree. (*Puts his hand on her head.*) Oh my adorable little songbird! (*Enters his study and closes the door.*)

NORA (*after a pause, in a low voice*) It's all a lot of nonsense. It's not that way at all. It's impossible. It has to be impossible.

THE NURSE (*in the door, left*) The little ones are asking ever so nicely if they can't come in and be with their mama.

NORA No, no no! Don't let them in here! You stay with them, Anne-Marie.

THE NURSE If you say so, ma'am. (*Closes the door.*)

NORA (*pale with terror*) Corrupt my little children—! Poison my home—? (*Brief pause; she lifts her head.*) That's not true. Never. Never in a million years.

## ACT II

*The same room. The Christmas tree is in the corner by the piano, stripped, shabby-looking, with burnt-down candles.* NORA'S *outside clothes are on the couch.* NORA *is alone. She walks around restlessly. She stops by the couch and picks up her coat.*

NORA (*drops the coat again*) There's somebody now! (*Goes to the door, listens.*) No. Nobody. Of course not—not on Christmas. And not tomorrow either.[1]—But perhaps—(*Opens the door and looks.*) No, nothing in the mailbox. All empty. (*Comes forward.*) How silly I am! Of course he isn't serious. Nothing like that could happen. After all, I have three small children.

(*The* NURSE *enters from the room, left, carrying a big carton.*)

THE NURSE Well, at last I found it—the box with your costume.

NORA Thanks. Just put it on the table.

NURSE (*does so*) But it's all a big mess, I'm afraid.

NORA Oh, I wish I could tear the whole thing to little pieces!

NURSE Heavens! It's not as bad as all that. It can be fixed all right. All it takes is a little patience.

NORA I'll go over and get Mrs. Linde to help me.

NURSE Going out again? In this awful weather? You'll catch a cold.

NORA That might not be such a bad thing. How are the children?

NURSE The poor little dears are playing with their presents, but—

NORA Do they keep asking for me?

NURSE Well, you know, they're used to being with their mamma.

NORA I know. But Anne-Marie, from now on I can't be with them as much as before.

NURSE Oh well. Little children get used to everything.

NORA You think so? Do you think they'll forget their mamma if I were gone altogether?

NURSE Goodness me—gone altogether?

NORA Listen, Anne-Marie—something I've wondered about. How could you bring yourself to leave your child with strangers?

NURSE But I had to, if I were to nurse you.

NORA Yes, but how could you *want* to?

NURSE When I could get such a nice place? When something like that happens to a poor young girl, she'd better be grateful for whatever she gets. For *he* didn't do a thing for me—the louse!

NORA But your daughter has forgotten all about you, hasn't she?

NURSE Oh no! Not at all! She wrote to me both when she was confirmed and when she got married.

NORA (*putting her arms around her neck*) You dear old thing—you were a good mother to me when I was little.

NURSE Poor little Nora had no one else, you know.

NORA And if my little ones didn't, I know you'd—oh, I'm be-

---

[1] In Norway both December 25 and 26 are legal holidays.

ing silly! (*Opens the carton.*) Go in to them, please. I really should—. Tomorrow you'll see how pretty I'll be.

NURSE I know. There won't be anybody at that party half as pretty as you, ma'am. (*Goes out, left.*)

NORA (*begins to take clothes out of the carton; in a moment she throws it all down*) If only I dared to go out. If only I knew nobody would come. That nothing would happen while I was gone.—How silly! Nobody'll come. Just don't think about it. Brush the muff. Beautiful gloves. Beautiful gloves. Forget it. Forget it. One, two, three, four, five, six—(*Cries out.*) There they are! (*Moves toward the door, stops irresolutely.*)

(MRS. LINDE *enters from the hall. She has already taken off her coat.*)

NORA Oh, it's you, Kristine. There's no one else out there, is there? I'm so glad you're here.

MRS. LINDE They told me you'd asked for me.

NORA I just happened to walk by. I need your help with something—badly. Let's sit here on the couch. Look. Torvald and I are going to a costume party tomorrow night—at Consul Stenborg's upstairs—and Torvald wants me to go as a Neapolitan fisher girl and dance the tarantella. I learned it when we were on Capri.

MRS. LINDE Well, well! So you'll be putting on a whole show?

NORA Yes. Torvald thinks I should. Look, here's the costume. Torvald had it made for me while we were there. But it's all so torn and everything. I just don't know—

MRS. LINDE Oh, that can be fixed. It's not that much. The trimmings have come loose in a few places. Do you have needle and thread? Ah, here we are. All set.

NORA I really appreciate it, Kristine.

MRS. LINDE (*sewing*). So you'll be in disguise tomorrow night, eh? You know—I may come by for just a moment, just to look at you. —Oh dear. I haven't even thanked you for the nice evening last night.

NORA (*gets up, moves around*). Oh, I don't know. I don't think last night was as nice as it usually is.—You should have come to town a little earlier, Kristine.—Yes, Torvald knows how to make it nice and pretty around here.

MRS. LINDE You too, I should think. After all, you're your father's daughter. By the way, is Dr. Rank always as depressed as he was last night?

NORA No, last night was unusual. He's a very sick man, you know —very sick. Poor Rank, his spine is rotting away. Tuberculosis, I think. You see, his father was a nasty old man with mistresses and all that sort of thing. Rank has been sickly ever since he was a little boy.

MRS. LINDE (*dropping her sewing to her lap*) But dearest, Nora, where have you learned about things like that?

NORA (*still walking about*) Oh, you know—with three children you sometimes get to talk with—other wives. Some of them know quite a bit about medicine. So you pick up a few things.

MRS. LINDE (*resumes her sewing; after a brief pause*) Does Dr. Rank come here every day?

NORA Every single day. He's Torvald's oldest and best friend, after all. And my friend too, for that matter. He's part of the family, almost.

MRS. LINDE But tell me, is he quite sincere? I mean, isn't he the kind of man who likes to say nice things to people?

NORA No, not at all. Rather the opposite, in fact. What makes you say that?

MRS. LINDE When you introduced us yesterday, he told me he'd often heard my name mentioned in this house. But later on it was quite obvious that your husband really had no idea who I was. So how could Dr. Rank—?

NORA You're right, Kristine, but I can explain that. You see, Torvald loves me so very much that he wants me all to himself. That's what he says. When we were first married he got almost jealous when I as much as mentioned anybody from back home that I was fond of. So of course I soon stopped doing that. But with Dr. Rank I often talk about home. You see, he likes to listen to me.

MRS. LINDE Look here, Nora. In many ways you're still a child. After all, I'm quite a bit older than you and have had more experience. I want to give you a piece of advice. I think you should get out of this thing with Dr. Rank.

NORA Get out of what thing?

MRS. LINDE Several things in fact, if you want my opinion. Yesterday you said something about a rich admirer who was going to give you money—

NORA One who doesn't exist, unfortunately. What of it?

MRS. LINDE Does Dr. Rank have money?

NORA Yes, he does.

MRS. LINDE And no dependents?

NORA No. But—?

MRS. LINDE And he comes here every day?

NORA Yes, I told you that already.

MRS. LINDE But how can that sensitive man be so tactless?

NORA I haven't the slightest idea what you're talking about.

MRS. LINDE Don't play games with me, Nora. Don't you think I know who you borrowed the twelve hundred dollars from?

NORA Are you out of your mind! The very idea—! A friend of both of us who sees us every day—! What a dreadfully uncomfortable position that would be!

MRS. LINDE So it really isn't Dr. Rank?

NORA Most certainly not! I would never have dreamed of asking him—not for a moment. Anyway, he didn't have any money then. He inherited it afterwards.

MRS. LINDE Well, I still think it may have been lucky for you, Nora dear.

NORA The idea! It would never have occurred to me to ask Dr. Rank—. Though I'm sure that if I *did* ask him—

MRS. LINDE But of course you wouldn't.

NORA Of course not. I can't imagine that that would ever be necessary. But I am quite sure that if I told Dr. Rank—

MRS. LINDE Behind your husband's back?

NORA I must get out of—this other thing. That's also behind his back. I *must* get out of it.

MRS. LINDE That's what I told you yesterday. But—

NORA (*walking up and down*) A man manages these things so much better than a woman—

MRS. LINDE One's husband, yes.

NORA Silly, silly! (*Stops.*) When you've paid off all you owe, you get your I.O.U. back; right?

MRS. LINDE Yes, of course.

NORA And you can tear it into a hundred thousand little pieces and burn it—that dirty, filthy, paper!

MRS. LINDE (*looks hard at her, puts down her sewing, rises slowly*) Nora—you're hiding something from me.

NORA Can you tell?

MRS. LINDE Something's happened to you, Nora, since yesterday morning. What is it?

NORA (*going to her*) Kristine! (*Listens.*) Shhh. Torvald just came back. Listen. Why don't you go in to the children for a while. Torvald can't stand having sewing around. Get Anne-Marie to help you.

MRS. LINDE (*gathers some of the sewing things together*) All right, but I'm not leaving here till you and I have talked.

(*She goes out left, as* HELMER *enters from the front hall.*)

NORA (*towards him*) I have been waiting and waiting for you, Torvald.

HELMER Was that the dressmaker?

NORA No, it was Kristine. She's helping me with my costume. Oh Torvald, just wait till you see how nice I'll look!

HELMER I told you. Pretty good idea I had, wasn't it?

NORA Lovely! And wasn't it nice of me to go along with it?

HELMER (*his hands under her chin*) Nice? To do what your husband tells you? All right, you little rascal; I know you didn't mean it that way. But don't let me interrupt you. I suppose you want to try it on.

NORA And you'll be working?

HELMER Yes. (*Shows her a pile of papers.*) Look. I've been down to the bank. (*Is about to enter his study.*)

NORA Torvald.

HELMER (*halts*) Yes?

NORA What if your little squirrel asked you ever so nicely—

HELMER For what?

NORA Would you do it?

HELMER Depends on what it is.

NORA Squirrel would run around and do all sorts of fun tricks if you'd be nice and agreeable.

HELMER All right. What is it?

NORA Lark would chirp and twitter in all the rooms, up and down—

HELMER So what? Lark does that anyway.

NORA I'll be your elfmaid and dance for you in the moonlight, Torvald.

HELMER Nora, don't tell me it's the same thing you mentioned this morning?

NORA (*closer to him*) Yes, Torvald. I beg you!

HELMER You really have the nerve to bring that up again?

NORA Yes. You've just got to do as I say. You *must* let Krogstad keep his job.

HELMER My dear Nora. It's his job I intend to give to Mrs. Linde.

NORA I know. And that's ever so nice of you. But can't you just fire somebody else?

HELMER This is incredible! You just don't give up do you? Because you make some foolish promise, *I* am supposed to—!

NORA That's not the reason, Torvald. It's for your own sake. That man writes for the worst newspapers. You've said so yourself. There's no telling what he may do to you. I'm scared to death of him.

HELMER Ah, I understand. You're afraid because of what happened before.

NORA What do you mean?

HELMER You're thinking of your father, of course.

NORA Yes. Yes, you're right. Remember the awful things they wrote about Daddy in the newspapers. I really think they might have forced him to resign if the ministry hadn't sent you to look into the charges and if you hadn't been so helpful and understanding.

HELMER My dear little Nora, there is a world of difference between your father and me. Your father's official conduct was not above reproach. Mine is, and I intend for it to remain that way as long as I hold my position.

NORA Oh, but you don't know what vicious people like that may think of. Oh, Torvald! Now all of us could be so happy together here in our own home, peaceful and carefree. Such a good life, Torvald, for you and me and the children! That's why I implore you—

HELMER And it's exactly because you plead for him that you make it impossible for me to keep him. It's already common knowledge in the bank that I intend to let Krogstad go. If it gets out that the new manager has changed his mind because of his wife—

NORA Yes? What then?

HELMER No, of course, that wouldn't matter at all as long as little Mrs. Pighead here got her way! Do you want me to make myself look ridiculous before my whole staff—make people think I can be swayed by just anybody—by outsiders? Believe me, I would soon enough find out what the consequences would be! Besides, there's another thing that makes it absolutely impossible for Krogstad to stay on in the bank now that I'm in charge.

NORA What's that?

HELMER I suppose in a pinch I could overlook his moral shortcomings—

NORA Yes, you could; couldn't you, Torvald?

HELMER And I understand he's quite a good worker, too. But we've known each other for a long time. It's one of those imprudent relationships you get into when you're young that embarrass you for the rest of your life. I guess I might as well be frank with you: he and I are on a first name basis. And that tactless fellow never hides the fact even when other people are around. Rather, he seems to think it entitles him to be familiar with me. Every chance he gets he comes out with his damn "Torvald, Torvald." I'm telling you, I find it most awkward. He would make my position in the bank intolerable.

NORA You don't really mean any of this, Torvald.

HELMER Oh? I don't? And why not?

NORA No, for it's all so petty.

HELMER What! Petty? You think I'm being petty!

NORA No, I *don't* think you are petty, Torvald dear. That's exactly why I—

HELMER Never mind. You think my reasons are petty, so it follows that I must be petty too. Petty! Indeed! By God, I'll put an end to this right now! (*Opens the door to the front hall and calls out.*) Helene!

NORA What are you doing?

HELMER (*searching among his papers*) Making a decision. (THE MAID *enters.*) Here. Take this letter. Go out with it right away. Find somebody to deliver it. But quick. The address is on the envelope. Wait. Here's money.

THE MAID Very good sir. (*She takes the letter and goes out.*)

HELMER (*collecting his papers*) There now, little Mrs. Obstinate!

NORA (*breathless*) Torvald—what was that letter?

HELMER Krogstad's dismissal.

NORA Call it back, Torvald! There's still time! Oh Torvald, please —call it back! For my sake, for your own sake, for the sake of the children! Listen to me, Torvald! Do it! You don't know what you're doing to all of us!

HELMER Too late.

NORA Yes. Too late.

HELMER Dear Nora, I forgive you this fear you're in, although it really is an insult to me. Yes, it is! It's an insult to think that I am scared of a shabby scrivener's revenge. But I forgive you, for it's such a beautiful proof how much you love me. (*Takes her in his arms.*) And that's the way it should be, my sweet darling. Whatever happens, you'll see that when things get really rough I have both strength and courage. You'll find out that I am man enough to shoulder the whole burden.

NORA (*terrified*) What do you mean by that?

HELMER All of it, I tell you—

NORA (*composed*) You'll never have to do that.

HELMER Good. Then we'll share the burden, Nora—like husband and wife, the way it ought to be. (*Caresses her.*) Now are you satisfied? There, there, there. Not that look in your eyes—like a frightened dove. It's all your own foolish imagination.—Why don't you practice the tarantella—and your tambourine, too. I'll be in the inner office and close both doors, so I won't hear you. You can make as much noise as you like. (*Turning in the doorway.*) And when Rank comes, tell him where to find me. (*He nods to her, enters his study carrying his papers, and closes the door.*)

NORA (*transfixed by terror, whispers*) He would do it. He'll do it. He'll do it in spite of the whole world.—No, this mustn't happen.

Anything rather than that! There must be a way—! (*The doorbell rings.*) Dr. Rank! Anything rather than that! Anything—anything at all!

(*She passes her hand over her face, pulls herself together, and opens the door to the hall.* DR. RANK *is out there, hanging up his coat. Darkness begins to fall during the following scene.*)

NORA Hello there, Dr. Rank. I recognized your ringing. Don't go in to Torvald yet. I think he's busy.

RANK And you?

NORA (*as he enters and she closes the door behind him*) You know I always have time for you.

RANK Thanks. I'll make use of that as long as I can.

NORA What do you mean by that—As long as you can?

RANK Does that frighten you?

NORA Well, it's a funny expression. As if something was going to happen.

RANK Something is going to happen that I've long been expecting. But I admit I hadn't thought it would come quite so soon.

NORA (*seizes his arm*) What is it you've found out? Dr. Rank—tell me!

RANK (*sits down by the stove*) I'm going downhill fast. There's nothing to do about that.

NORA (*with audible relief*) So it's *you*—

RANK Who else? No point in lying to myself. I'm in worse shape than any of my other patients, Mrs. Helmer. These last few days I've been making up my inner status. Bankrupt. Chances are that within a month I'll be rotting up in the cemetery.

NORA Shame on you! Talking that horrid way!

RANK The thing itself is horrid—damn horrid. The worst of it, though, is all that other horror that comes first. There is only one more test I need to make. After that I'll have a pretty good idea when I'll start coming apart. There is something I want to say to you. Helmer's refined nature can't stand anything hideous. I don't want him in my sick room.

NORA Oh, but Dr. Rank—

RANK I don't want him there. Under no circumstances. I'll close my door to him. As soon as I have full certainty that the worst is about to begin I'll give you my card with a black cross on it. Then you'll know the last horror of destruction has started.

NORA Today you're really quite impossible. And I had hoped you'd be in a particularly good mood.

RANK With death on my hands? Paying for someone else's sins? Is there justice in that? And yet there isn't a single family that isn't ruled by the same law of ruthless retribution, in one way or another.

NORA (*puts her hands over her ears*) Poppycock! Be fun! Be fun!

RANK Well, yes. You may just as well laugh at the whole thing. My poor, innocent spine is suffering from my father's frolics as a young lieutenant.

NORA (*over by the table, left*) Right. He was addicted to asparagus and goose liver paté, wasn't he?

RANK And truffles.

NORA Of course. Truffles. And oysters too, I think.

RANK And oysters. Obviously.

NORA And all the port and champagne that go with it. It's really too bad that goodies like that ruin your backbone.

RANK Particularly an unfortunate backbone that never enjoyed any of it.

NORA Ah yes, that's the saddest part of it all.

RANK (*looks searchingly at her*) Hm—

NORA (*after a brief pause*) Why did you smile just then?

RANK No, it was you that laughed.

NORA No, it was you that smiled, Dr. Rank!

RANK (*gets up*) You're more of a mischief-maker than I thought.

NORA I feel in the mood for mischief today.

RANK So it seems.

NORA (*with both her hands on his shoulders*) Dear, dear Dr. Rank, don't you go and die and leave Torvald and me.

RANK Oh, you won't miss me for very long. Those who go away are soon forgotten.

NORA (*with an anxious look*) Do you believe that?

RANK You'll make new friends, and then—

NORA Who'll make new friends?

RANK Both you and Helmer, once I'm gone. You yourself seem to have made a good start already. What was this Mrs. Linde doing here last night?

NORA Aha—Don't tell me you're jealous of poor Kristine?

RANK Yes, I am. She'll be my successor in this house. As soon as I have made my excuses, that woman is likely to—

NORA Shh—not so loud. She's in there.

RANK Today too? There you are!

NORA She's mending my costume. My God, you really *are* unreasonable. (*Sits down on the couch*). Now be nice, Dr. Rank. Tomorrow you'll see how beautifully I'll dance, and then you are to pretend I'm dancing just for you—and for Torvald too, of course. (*Takes several items out of the carton.*) Sit down, Dr. Rank; I want to show you something.

RANK (*sitting down*) What?

NORA Look.

RANK Silk stockings.

NORA Flesh-colored. Aren't they lovely? Now it's getting dark in here, but tomorrow—No, no. You only get to see the foot. Oh well, you might as well see all of it.

RANK Hmm.

NORA Why do you look so critical? Don't you think they'll fit?

RANK That's something I can't possibly have a reasoned opinion about.

NORA (*looks at him for a moment*) Shame on you. (*Slaps his ear lightly with the stocking.*) That's what you get. (*Puts the things back in the carton.*)

RANK And what other treasures are you going to show me?

NORA Nothing at all, because you're naughty. (*She hums a little and rummages in the carton.*)

RANK (*after a brief silence*) When I sit here like this, talking confidently with you, I can't imagine—I can't possibly imagine what would have become of me if I hadn't had you and Helmer.

NORA (*smiles*) Well, yes—I do believe you like being with us.

RANK (*in a lower voice, lost in thought*) And then to have to go away from it all—

NORA Nonsense. You are not going anywhere.

RANK (*as before*) —and not to leave behind as much as a poor little token of gratitude, hardly a brief memory of someone missed, nothing but a vacant place that anyone can fill.

NORA And what if I were to ask you—? No—

RANK Ask me what?

NORA For a great proof of your friendship—

RANK Yes, yes—?

NORA No, I mean— for an enormous favor—

RANK Would you really for once make me as happy as all that?

NORA But you don't even know what it is.

RANK Well, then; tell me.

NORA Oh, but I can't, Dr. Rank. It's altogether too much to ask— It's advice and help and a favor—

RANK So much the better. I can't even begin to guess what it is you have in mind. So for heaven's sake tell me! Don't you trust me?

NORA Yes, I trust you more than anyone else I know. You are my best and most faithful friend. I know that. So I will tell you. All right, Dr. Rank. There is something you can help me prevent. You know how much Torvald loves me—beyond all words. Never for a moment would he hesitate to give his life for me.

RANK (*leaning over to her*) Nora—do you really think he's the only one—?

NORA (*with a slight start*) Who—?

RANK —would gladly give his life for you.

NORA (*heavily*) I see.

RANK I have sworn an oath to myself to tell you before I go. I'll never find a better occasion.—All right, Nora; now you know. And now you also know that you can confide in me more than in anyone else.

NORA (*gets up; in a calm, steady voice*) Let me get by.

RANK (*makes room for her but remains seated*) Nora—

NORA (*in the door to the front hall*) Helene, bring the lamp in here, please. (*Walks over to the stove.*) Oh, dear Dr. Rank. That really wasn't very nice of you.

RANK (*gets up*) That I have loved you as much as anybody—was that not nice?

NORA No; not that. But that you told me. There was no need for that.

RANK What do you mean? Have you known—?

(THE MAID *enters with the lamp, puts it on the table, and goes out.*)

RANK Nora—Mrs. Helmer—I'm asking you: did you know?

NORA Oh, how can I tell what I knew and didn't know! I really can't say—But that you could be so awkward, Dr. Rank! Just when everything was so comfortable.

RANK Well, anyway, now you know that I'm at your service with my life and soul. And now you must speak.

NORA (*looks at him*) After what just happened?

RANK I beg of you—let me know what it is.

NORA There is nothing I can tell you now.

RANK Yes, yes. You mustn't punish me this way. Please let me do for you whatever anyone *can* do.

NORA Now there is nothing you can do. Besides, I don't think I really need any help, anyway. It's probably just my imagination. Of course that's all it is. I'm sure of it! (*Sits down in the rocking chair, looks at him, smiles.*) Well, well, well, Dr. Rank! What a fine gentleman you turned out to be! Aren't you ashamed of yourself, now that we have light?

RANK No, not really. But perhaps I ought to leave—and not come back?

NORA Don't be silly; of course not! You'll come here exactly as you have been doing. You know perfectly well that Torvald can't do without you.

RANK Yes, but what about you?

NORA Oh, I always think it's perfectly delightful when you come.

RANK That's the very thing that misled me. You are a riddle to me. It has often seemed to me that you'd just as soon be with me as with Helmer.

NORA Well, you see, there are people you love, and then there are other people you'd almost rather be with.

RANK Yes, there is something in that.

NORA When I lived at home with Daddy, of course I loved him most. But I always thought it was so much fun to sneak off down to the maids' room, for they never gave me good advice and they always talked about such fun things.

RANK Aha! So it's *their* place I have taken.

NORA (*jumps up and goes over to him*) Oh dear, kind Dr. Rank, you know very well I didn't mean it that way. Can't you see that with Torvald it is the way it used to be with Daddy?

(THE MAID *enters from the front hall.*)

THE MAID Ma'am! (*Whispers to her and gives her a caller's card.*)

NORA (*glances at the card*) Ah! (*Puts it in her pocket*).

RANK Anything wrong?

NORA No, no; not at all. It's nothing—just my new costume—

RANK But your costume is lying right there!

NORA Oh yes, that one. But this is another one. I ordered it. Torvald mustn't know—

RANK Aha. So that's the great secret.

NORA That's it. Why don't you go in to him, please. He's in the inner office. And keep him there for a while—

RANK Don't worry. He won't get away. (*Enters* HELMER'S *study.*)

NORA (*to* THE MAID) You say he's waiting in the kitchen?

THE MAID Yes. He came up the back stairs.

NORA But didn't you tell him there was somebody with me?

THE MAID Yes, but he wouldn't listen.

NORA He won't leave?

THE MAID No, not till he's had a word with you, ma'am.

NORA All right. But try not to make any noise. And, Helene—don't tell anyone he's here. It's supposed to be a surprise for my husband.

THE MAID I understand, ma'am—(*She leaves.*)

NORA The terrible is happening. It's happening, after all. No, no, no. It can't happen. It won't happen. (*She bolts the study door.*)

(THE MAID *opens the front hall door for* KROGSTAD *and closes the door behind him. He wears a fur coat for traveling, boots, and a fur hat.*)

NORA (*toward him*) Keep your voice down. My husband's home.

KROGSTAD That's all right.

NORA What do you want?

KROGSTAD To find out something.

NORA Be quick, then. What is it?

KROGSTAD I expect you know I've been fired.

NORA I couldn't prevent it, Mr. Krogstad. I fought for you as long and as hard as I could but it didn't do any good.

KROGSTAD Your husband doesn't love you any more than that? He knows what I can do to you, and yet he runs the risk—

NORA Surely you didn't think I'd tell him?

KROGSTAD No, I really didn't. It wouldn't be like Torvald Helmer to show that kind of guts—

NORA Mr. Krogstad, I insist that you show respect for my husband.

KROGSTAD By all means. All due respect. But since you're so anxious to keep this a secret, may I assume that you are a little better informed than yesterday about exactly what you have done?

NORA Better than *you* could ever teach me.

KROGSTAD Of course. Such a bad lawyer as I am—

NORA What do you want of me?

KROGSTAD I just wanted to find out how you are, Mrs. Helmer. I've been thinking about you all day. You see, even a bill collector, a pen pusher, a—anyway, someone like me—even he has a little of what they call a heart.

NORA Then show it. Think of my little children.

KROGSTAD Have you and your husband thought of mine? Never mind. All I want to tell you is that you don't need to take this business too seriously. I have no intention of bringing charges right away.

NORA Oh no, you wouldn't; would you? I knew you wouldn't.

KROGSTAD The whole thing can be settled quite amiably. Nobody else needs to know anything. It will be between the three of us.

NORA My husband must never find out about this.

KROGSTAD How are you going to prevent that? Maybe you can pay me the balance on the loan?

NORA No, not right now.

KROGSTAD Or do you have a way of raising the money one of these next few days?

NORA None I intend to make use of.

KROGSTAD It wouldn't do you any good, anyway. Even if you had the cash in your hand right this minute, I wouldn't give you your note back. It wouldn't make any difference *how* much money you offered me.

NORA Then you'll have to tell me what you plan to use the note *for*.

KROGSTAD Just keep it; that's all. Have it on hand, so to speak. I won't say a word to anybody else. So if you've been thinking about doing something desperate—

NORA I have.

KROGSTAD —like leaving house and home—

NORA I have!

KROGSTAD —or even something worse—

NORA How did you know?

KROGSTAD —then: don't.

NORA How did you know I was thinking of *that*?

KROGSTAD Most of us do, right at first. I did, too, but when it came down to it I didn't have the courage—

NORA (*tonelessly*) Nor do I.

KROGSTAD (*relieved*) See what I mean? I thought so. You don't either.

NORA I don't. I don't.

KROGSTAD Besides, it would be very silly of you. Once that first domestic blowup is behind you—. Here in my pocket is a letter for your husband.

NORA Telling him everything?

KROGSTAD As delicately as possible.

NORA (*quickly*) He mustn't get that letter. Tear it up. I'll get you the money somehow.

KROGSTAD Excuse me, Mrs. Helmer, I thought I just told you—

NORA I'm not talking about the money I owe you. Just let me know how much money you want from my husband, and I'll get it for you.

KROGSTAD I want no money from your husband.

NORA Then, what *do* you want?

KROGSTAD I'll tell you, Mrs. Helmer. I want to rehabilitate myself; I want to get up in the world; and your husband is going to help me. For a year and a half I haven't done anything disreputable. All that time I have been struggling with the most miserable circumstances. I was content to work my way up step by step. Now I've been kicked out, and I'm no longer satisfied just getting my old job back. I want more than that; I want to get to the top. I'm being quite serious. I want the bank to take me back but in a higher position. I want your husband to create a new job for me—

NORA He'll never do that!

KROGSTAD He will. I know him. He won't dare not to. And once I'm back inside and he and I are working together, you'll see! Within a year I'll be the manager's right hand. It will be Nils

Krogstad and not Torvald Helmer who'll be running the Mutual Bank!

NORA You'll never see that happen!

KROGSTAD Are you thinking of—?

NORA Now I *do* have the courage.

KROGSTAD You can't scare me. A fine, spoiled lady like you—

NORA You'll see, you'll see!

KROGSTAD Under the ice, perhaps? Down into that cold, black water? Then spring comes, and you float up again—hideous, can't be identified, hair all gone—

NORA You don't frighten me.

KROGSTAD Nor you me. One doesn't do that sort of thing, Mrs. Helmer. Besides, what good would it do? He'd still be in my power.

NORA Afterwards? When I'm no longer—?

KROGSTAD Aren't you forgetting that your reputation would be in my hands?

(NORA *stares at him, speechless.*)

KROGSTAD All right; now I've told you what to expect. So don't do anything foolish. When Helmer gets my letter I expect to hear from him. And don't you forget that it's your husband himself who forces me to use such means again. That I'll never forgive him. Goodbye, Mrs. Helmer. (*Goes out through the hall.*)

NORA (*at the door, opens it a little, listens*) He's going. And no letter. Of course not! That would be impossible. (*Opens the door more.*) What's he doing? He's still there. Doesn't go down. Having second thoughts—? Will he—?

(*The sound of a letter dropping into the mailbox. Then* KROGSTAD'*s steps are heard going down the stairs, gradually dying away.*)

NORA (*with a muted cry runs forward to the table by the couch; brief pause*) In the mailbox. (*Tiptoes back to the door to the front hall.*) There it is. Torvald, Torvald—now we're lost!

MRS. LINDE (*enters from the left, carrying* NORA'*s Capri costume*) There now. I think it's all fixed. Why don't we try it on you—

NORA (*in a low, hoarse voice*) Kristine, come here.

MRS. LINDE What's wrong with you? You look quite beside yourself.

NORA Come over here. Do you see that letter? There, look—through the glass in the mailbox.

MRS. LINDE Yes, yes; I see it.

NORA That letter is from Krogstad.

MRS. LINDE Nora—it was Krogstad who lent you the money!

NORA Yes, and now Torvald will find out about it.

MRS. LINDE Oh believe me, Nora. That's the best thing for both of you.

NORA There's more to it than you know. I forged a signature—

MRS. LINDE Oh my God—!

NORA I just want to tell you this, Kristine, that you must be my witness.

MRS. LINDE Witness? How? Witness to what?

NORA If I lose my mind—and that could very well happen—

MRS. LINDE Nora!

NORA —or if something were to happen to me—something that made it impossible for me to be here—

MRS. LINDE Nora, Nora! You're not yourself!

NORA —and if someone were to take all the blame, assume the whole responsibility—Do you understand—?

MRS. LINDE Yes, yes; but how can you think—!

NORA Then you are to witness that that's not so, Kristine. I am not beside myself. I am perfectly rational, and what I'm telling you is that nobody else has known about this. I've done it all by myself, the whole thing. Just remember that.

MRS. LINDE I will. But I don't understand any of it.

NORA Oh, how could you! For it's the wonderful that's about to happen.

MRS. LINDE The wonderful?

NORA Yes, the wonderful. But it's so terrible, Kristine. It mustn't happen for anything in the whole world!

MRS. LINDE I'm going over to talk to Krogstad right now.

NORA No, don't. Don't go to him. He'll do something bad to you.

MRS. LINDE There was a time when he would have done anything for me.

NORA He!

MRS. LINDE Where does he live?

NORA Oh, I don't know—Yes, wait a minute—(*Reaches into her pocket.*) here's his card.—But the letter, the letter—!

HELMER (*in his study, knocks on the door*) Nora!

NORA (*cries out in fear*) Oh, what is it? What do you want?

HELMER That's all right. Nothing to be scared about. We're not coming in. For one thing, you've bolted the door, you know. Are you modeling your costume?

NORA Yes, yes; I am. I'm going to be so pretty, Torvald.

MRS. LINDE (*having looked at the card*) He lives just around the corner.

NORA Yes, but it's no use. Nothing can save us now. The letter is in the mailbox.

MRS. LINDE And your husband has the key?

NORA Yes. He always keeps it with him.

MRS. LINDE Krogstad must ask for his letter back, unread. He's got to think up some pretext or other—

NORA But this is just the time of day when Torvald—

MRS. LINDE Delay him. Go in to him: I'll be back as soon as I can. (*She hurries out through the hall door.*)

NORA (*walks over to* HELMER'*s door, opens it, and peeks in*) Torvald.

HELMER (*still offstage*) Well, well! So now one's allowed in one's own living room again. Come on, Rank. Now we'll see—(*In the doorway.*) But what's this?

NORA What, Torvald dear?

HELMER Rank prepared me for a splendid metamorphosis.

RANK (*in the doorway*) That's how I understood it. Evidently I was mistaken.

NORA Nobody gets to admire me in my costume before tomorrow.

HELMER But, dearest Nora—you look all done in. Have you been practicing too hard?

NORA No, I haven't practiced at all.

HELMER But you'll have to, you know.

NORA I know it, Torvald. I simply must. But I can't do a thing unless you help me. I have forgotten everything.

HELMER Oh it will all come back. We'll work on it.

NORA Oh yes, please, Torvald. You just have to help me. Promise? I am so nervous. That big party—. You mustn't do anything else tonight. Not a bit of business. Don't even touch a pen. Will you promise, Torvald?

HELMER I promise. Tonight I'll be entirely at your service—you helpless little thing.—Just a moment, though. First I want to— (*Goes to the door to the front hall.*)

NORA What are you doing out there?

HELMER Just looking to see if there's any mail.

NORA No, no! Don't, Torvald!

HELMER Why not?

NORA Torvald, I beg you. There is no mail.

HELMER Let me just look, anyway. (*Is about to go out.*)

(NORA *by the piano, plays the first bars of the tarantella dance.*)

HELMER (*halts at the door*) Aha!

NORA I won't be able to dance tomorrow if I don't get to practice with you.

HELMER (*goes to her*) Are you really all that scared, Nora dear?

NORA Yes, so terribly scared. Let's try it right now. There's still time before we eat. Oh please, sit down and play for me, Torvald. Teach me, coach me, the way you always do.

HELMER Of course I will, my darling, if that's what you want. (*Sits down at the piano.*)

(NORA *takes the tambourine out of the carton, as well as a long, many-colored shawl. She quickly drapes the shawl around herself, then leaps into the middle of the floor.*)

NORA Play for me! I want to dance!

(HELMER *plays and* NORA *dances.* DR. RANK *stands by the piano behind* HELMER *and watches.*)

HELMER (*playing*) Slow down, slow down!

NORA Can't!

HELMER Not so violent, Nora!

NORA It has to be this way.

HELMER (*stops playing*) No, no. This won't do at all.

NORA (*laughing, swinging her tambourine*) What did I tell you?

RANK Why don't you let me play?

HELMER (*getting up*) Good idea. Then I can direct her better.

(RANK *sits down at the piano and starts playing.* NORA *dances more and more wildly.* HELMER *stands over by the stove, repeatedly correcting her. She doesn't seem to hear. Her hair comes loose and falls down over her shoulders. She doesn't notice but keeps on dancing.* MRS. LINDE *enters.*)

MRS. LINDE (*stops by the door, dumbfounded*) Ah—!

NORA (*dancing*) We're having such fun, Kristine!

HELMER My dearest Nora, you're dancing as if it were a matter of life and death!

NORA It is! It is!

HELMER Rank, stop. This is sheer madness. Stop, I say!

(RANK *stops playing;* NORA *suddenly stops dancing.*)

HELMER (*goes over to her*) If I hadn't seen it I wouldn't have believed it. You've forgotten every single thing I ever taught you.

NORA (*tosses away the tambourine*) See? I told you.

HELMER Well! You certainly need coaching.

NORA Didn't I tell you I did? Now you've seen for yourself. I'll need your help till the very minute we're leaving for the party. Will you promise, Torvald?

HELMER You can count on it.

NORA You're not to think of anything except me—not tonight and not tomorrow. You're not to read any letters—not to look in the mailbox—

HELMER Ah, I see. You're still afraid of that man.

NORA Yes—yes, that too.

HELMER Nora, I can tell from looking at you. There's a letter from him out there.

NORA I don't know. I think so. But you're not to read it now. I don't want anything ugly to come between us before it's all over.

RANK (*to* HELMER *in a low voice*) Better not argue with her.

HELMER (*throws his arm around her*) The child shall have her way. But tomorrow night, when you've done your dance—

NORA Then you'll be free.

THE MAID (*in the door, right*) Dinner can be served any time, ma'am.

NORA We want champagne, Helene.

THE MAID Very good, ma'am. (*Goes out.*)

HELMER Aha! Having a party, eh?

NORA Champagne from now till sunrise! (*Calls out.*) And some macaroons, Helene. Lots!—just this once.

HELMER (*taking her hands*) There, there—I don't like this wild—frenzy—Be my own sweet little lark again, the way you always are.

NORA Oh, I will. But you go on in. You too, Dr. Rank. Kristine, please help me put up my hair.

RANK (*in a low voice to* HELMER *as they go out*) You don't think she is—you know—expecting—?

HELMER Oh no. Nothing like that. It's just this childish fear I was telling you about. (*They go out, right.*)

NORA Well?

MRS. LINDE Left town.

NORA I saw it in your face.

MRS. LINDE He'll be back tomorrow night. I left him a note.

NORA You shouldn't have. I don't want you to try to stop anything. You see, it's a kind of ecstasy, too, this waiting for the wonderful.

MRS. LINDE But what is it you're waiting *for*?

NORA You wouldn't understand. Why don't you go in to the others. I'll be there in a minute.

(MRS. LINDE *enters the dining room, right.*)

NORA (*stands still for a little while, as if collecting herself; she looks at her watch*) Five o'clock. Seven hours till midnight. Twenty-four more hours till next midnight. Then the tarantella is over. Twenty-four plus seven—thirty-one more hours to live.

HELMER (*in the door, right*) What's happening to my little lark?

NORA (*to him, with open arms*) Here's your lark!

## ACT III

*The same room. The table by the couch and the chairs around it have been moved to the middle of the floor. A lighted lamp is on the table. The door to the front hall is open. Dance music is heard from upstairs.*

MRS. LINDE *is seated by the table, idly leafing through the pages of a book. She tries to read but seems unable to concentrate. Once or twice she turns her head in the direction of the door, anxiously listening.*)

MRS. LINDE (*looks at her watch*) Not yet. It's almost too late. If only he hasn't—(*Listens again.*) Ah! There he is. (*She goes to the hall and opens the front door carefully. Quiet footsteps on the stairs. She whispers.*) Come in. There's nobody here.

KROGSTAD (*in the door*) I found your note when I got home. What's this all about?

MRS. LINDE I've got to talk to you.

KROGSTAD Oh? And it has to be here?

MRS. LINDE It couldn't be at my place. My room doesn't have a separate entrance. Come in. We're quite alone. The maid is asleep and the Helmers are at a party upstairs.

KROGSTAD (*entering*) Really? The Helmers are dancing tonight, are they?

MRS. LINDE And why not?

KROGSTAD You're right. Why not, indeed.

MRS. LINDE All right, Krogstad. Let's talk, you and I.

KROGSTAD I didn't know we had anything to talk about.

MRS. LINDE We have much to talk about.

KROGSTAD I didn't think so.

MRS. LINDE No, because you've never really understood me.

KROGSTAD What was there to understand? What happened was perfectly commonplace. A heartless woman jilts a man when she gets a more attractive offer.

MRS. LINDE Do you think I'm all that heartless? And do you think it was easy for me to break with you?

KROGSTAD No?

MRS. LINDE You really thought it was?

KROGSTAD If it wasn't, why did you write the way you did that time?

MRS. LINDE What else could I do? If I had to make a break, I also had the duty to destroy whatever feelings you had for me.

KROGSTAD (*clenching his hands*) So that's the way it was. And you did—*that*—just for money!

MRS. LINDE Don't forget I had a helpless mother and two small brothers. We couldn't wait for you, Krogstad. You know yourself how uncertain your prospects were then.

KROGSTAD All right. But you still didn't have the right to throw me over for somebody else.

MRS. LINDE I don't know. I have asked myself that question many times. Did I have that right?

KROGSTAD (*in a lower voice*) When I lost you I lost my footing. Look at me now. A shipwrecked man on a raft.

MRS. LINDE Rescue may be near.

KROGSTAD It *was* near. Then you came between.

MRS. LINDE I didn't know that, Krogstad. Only today did I find out it's your job I'm taking over in the bank.

KROGSTAD I believe you when you say so. But now that you *do* know, aren't you going to step aside?

MRS. LINDE No, for it wouldn't do you any good.

KROGSTAD Whether it would or not—*I* would do it.

MRS. LINDE I have learned common sense. Life and hard necessity have taught me that.

KROGSTAD And life has taught me not to believe in pretty speeches.

MRS. LINDE Then life has taught you a very sensible thing. But you do believe in actions, don't you?

KROGSTAD How do you mean?

MRS. LINDE You referred to yourself just now as a shipwrecked man.

KROGSTAD It seems to me I had every reason to do so.

MRS. LINDE And I am a shipwrecked woman. No one to grieve for, no one to care for.

KROGSTAD You made your choice.

MRS. LINDE I had no other choice that time.

KROGSTAD Let's say you didn't. What then?

MRS. LINDE Krogstad, how would it be if we two shipwrecked people got together?

KROGSTAD What's this!

MRS. LINDE Two on one wreck are better off than each on his own.

KROGSTAD Kristine!

MRS. LINDE Why do you think I came to town?

KROGSTAD Surely not because of me?

MRS. LINDE If I'm going to live at all I must work. All my life, for as long as I can remember, I have worked. That's been my one and only pleasure. But now that I'm all alone in the world I feel nothing but this terrible emptiness and desolation. There is no joy in working just for yourself. Krogstad—give me someone and something to work for.

KROGSTAD I don't believe this. Only hysterical females go in for that kind of high-minded self-sacrifice.

MRS. LINDE Did you ever know me to be hysterical?

KROGSTAD You really could do this? Listen—do you know about my past? All of it?

MRS. LINDE Yes, I do.

KROGSTAD Do you also know what people think of me around here?

MRS. LINDE A little while ago you sounded as if you thought that together with me you might have become a different person.

KROGSTAD I'm sure of it.

MRS. LINDE Couldn't that still be?

KROGSTAD Kristine—do you know what you are doing? Yes, I see you do. And you think you have the courage—?

MRS. LINDE I need someone to be a mother to, and your children need a mother. You and I need one another. Nils, I believe in you—in the real you. Together with you I dare to do anything.

KROGSTAD (*seizes her hands*) Thanks, thanks, Kristine—Now I know I'll raise myself in the eyes of others—Ah, but I forget—!

MRS. LINDE (*listening*) Shh!—there's the tarantella. You must go; hurry!

KROGSTAD Why? What is it?

MRS. LINDE Do you hear what they're playing up there? When that dance is over they'll be down.

KROGSTAD All right. I'm leaving. The whole thing is pointless, anyway. Of course you don't know what I'm doing to the Helmers.

MRS. LINDE Yes, Krogstad; I do know.

KROGSTAD Still, you're brave enough—?

MRS. LINDE I very well understand to what extremes despair can drive a man like you.

KROGSTAD If only it could be undone!

MRS. LINDE It could, for your letter is still out there in the mailbox.

KROGSTAD Are you sure?

MRS. LINDE Quite sure. But—

KROGSTAD (*looks searchingly at her*) Maybe I'm beginning to understand. You want to save your friend at any cost. Be honest with me. That's it, isn't it?

MRS. LINDE Krogstad, you may sell yourself once for somebody else's sake, but you don't do it twice.

KROGSTAD I'll demand my letter back.

MRS. LINDE No, no.

KROGSTAD Yes, of course. I'll wait here till Helmer comes down. Then I'll ask him for my letter. I'll tell him it's just about my dismissal—that he shouldn't read it.

MRS. LINDE No, Krogstad. You are not to ask for that letter back.

KROGSTAD But tell me—wasn't that the real reason you wanted to meet me here?

MRS. LINDE At first it was, because I was so frightened. But that was yesterday. Since then I have seen the most incredible things going on in this house. Helmer must learn the whole truth. This miserable secret must come out in the open; those two must come to a full understanding. They simply can't continue with all this concealment and evasion.

KROGSTAD All right; if you want to take that chance. But there is one thing I *can* do, and I'll do that right now.

MRS. LINDE (*listening*) But hurry! Go! The dance is over. We aren't safe another minute.

KROGSTAD I'll be waiting for you downstairs.

MRS. LINDE Yes, do. You must see me home.

KROGSTAD I've never been so happy in my whole life. (*He leaves through the front door. The door between the living room and the front hall remains open.*)

MRS. LINDE (*straightens up the room a little and gets her things ready*) What a change! Oh yes!—what a change! People to work for—to live for—a home to bring happiness to. I can't wait to get to work—! If only they'd come soon—(*Listens.*) Ah, there they are. Get my coat on—(*Puts on her coat and hat.*)

(HELMER'*s and* NORA'*s voices are heard outside. A key is turned in the lock, and* HELMER *almost forces* NORA *into the hall. She is dressed in her Italian costume, with a big black shawl over her shoulders. He is in evening dress under an open black cloak.*)

NORA (*in the door, still resisting*) No, no, no! I don't want to! I want to go back upstairs. I don't want to leave so early.

HELMER But dearest Nora—

NORA Oh please, Torvald—please! I'm asking you as nicely as I can—just another hour!

HELMER Not another minute, sweet. You know we agreed. There now. Get inside. You'll catch a cold out here. (*She still resists, but he guides her gently into the room.*)

MRS. LINDE Good evening.

NORA Kristine!

HELMER Ah, Mrs. Linde. Still here?

MRS. LINDE I know. I really should apologize, but I so much wanted to see Nora in her costume.

NORA You've been waiting up for me?

MRS. LINDE Yes, unfortunately I didn't get here in time. You were already upstairs, but I just didn't feel like leaving till I had seen you.

HELMER (*removing* NORA'*s shawl*) Yes, do take a good look at her, Mrs. Linde. I think I may say she's worth looking at. Isn't she lovely?

MRS. LINDE She certainly is—

HELMER Isn't she a miracle of loveliness, though? That was the general opinion at the party, too. But dreadfully obstinate—that she is, the sweet little thing. What can we do about that? Will you believe it—I practically had to use force to get her away.

NORA Oh Torvald, you're going to be sorry you didn't give me even half an hour more.

HELMER See what I mean, Mrs. Linde? She dances the tarantella—she is a tremendous success—quite deservedly so, though perhaps her performance was a little too natural—I mean, more than could be reconciled with the rules of art. But all right! The point is: she's a success, a tremendous success. So should I let her stay after that? Weaken the effect? Of course not. So I take my lovely little Capri girl—I might say, my capricious little Capri girl—under my arm—a quick turn around the room—a graceful bow in all directions, and—as they say in the novels—the beautiful apparition is gone. A finale should always be done for effect, Mrs. Linde, but there doesn't seem to be any way of getting that into Nora's head. Poooh—! It's hot in here. (*Throws his cloak down on a chair and opens the door to his room.*) Why, it's dark in here! Of course. Excuse me—(*Goes inside and lights a couple of candles.*)

NORA (*in a hurried, breathless whisper*) Well?

MRS. LINDE (*in a low voice*) I have talked to him.

NORA And—?

MRS. LINDE Nora—you've got to tell your husband everything.

NORA (*no expression in her voice*) I knew it.

MRS. LINDE You have nothing to fear from Krogstad. But you must speak.

NORA I'll say nothing.

MRS. LINDE Then the letter will.

NORA Thank you, Kristine. Now I know what I have to do. Shh!

HELMER (*returning*) Well, Mrs. Linde, have you looked your fill?

MRS. LINDE Yes. And now I'll say goodnight.

HELMER So soon? Is that your knitting?

MRS. LINDE (*takes it*) Yes, thank you. I almost forgot.

HELMER So you knit, do you?

MRS. LINDE Oh yes.

HELMER You know—you ought to take up embroidery instead.

MRS. LINDE Oh? Why?

HELMER Because it's so much more beautiful. Look. You hold the embroidery so—in your left hand. Then with your right you move the needle—like this—in an easy, elongated arc—you see?

MRS. LINDE Maybe you're right—

HELMER Knitting, on the other hand, can never be anything but ugly. Look here: arms pressed close to the sides—the needles going up and down—there's something Chinese about it somehow—. That really was an excellent champagne they served us tonight.

MRS. LINDE Well, goodnight! Nora. And don't be obstinate any more.

HELMER Well said, Mrs. Linde!

MRS. LINDE Goodnight, sir.

HELMER (*sees her to the front door*) Goodnight, goodnight. I hope you'll get home all right? I'd be very glad to—but of course you don't have far to walk, do you? Goodnight, goodnight. (*She leaves. He closes the door behind her and returns to the living room.*) There! At last we got rid of her. She really is an incredible bore, that woman.

NORA Aren't you very tired, Torvald?

HELMER No, not in the least.

NORA Not sleepy either?

HELMER Not at all. Quite the opposite. I feel enormously—animated. How about you? Yes, you do look tired and sleepy.

NORA Yes, I am very tired. Soon I'll be asleep.

HELMER What did I tell you? I was right, wasn't I? Good thing I didn't let you stay any longer.

NORA Everything you do is right.

HELMER (*kissing her forehead*) Now my little lark is talking like a human being. But did you notice what splended spirits Rank was in tonight?

NORA Was he? I didn't notice. I didn't get to talk with him.

HELMER Nor did I—hardly. But I haven't seen him in such a good mood for a long time. (*Looks at her, comes closer to her.*) Ah! It does feel good to be back in our own home again, to be quite alone with you—my young, lovely, ravishing woman!

NORA Don't look at me like that, Torvald!

HELMER Am I not to look at my most precious possession? All that loveliness that is mine, nobody's but mine, all of it mine.

NORA (*walks to the other side of the table*) I won't have you talk to me like that tonight.

HELMER (*follows her*) The Tarantella is still in your blood. I can tell. That only makes you all the more alluring. Listen! The guests are beginning to leave. (*Softly.*) Nora—soon the whole house will be quiet.

NORA Yes, I hope so.

HELMER Yes, don't you, my darling? Do you know—when I'm at a party with you, like tonight—do you know why I hardly ever talk to you, why I keep away from you, only look at you once in a while—a few stolen glances—do you know why I do that? It's because I pretend that you are my secret love, my young, secret bride-to-be, and nobody has the slightest suspicion that there is anything between us.

NORA Yes, I know. All your thoughts are with me.

HELMER Then when we're leaving and I lay your shawl around your delicate young shoulders—around that wonderful curve of your neck—then I imagine you're my young bride, that we're coming away from the wedding, that I am taking you to my home for the first time—that I am alone with you for the first time—quite alone with you, you young, trembling beauty! I have desired you all evening—there hasn't been a longing in me that hasn't been for you. When you were dancing the tarantella, chasing, inviting—my blood was on fire; I couldn't stand it any longer—that's why I brought you down so early—

NORA Leave me now, Torvald. Please! I don't want all this.

HELMER What do you mean? You're only playing your little teasing bird game with me; aren't you, Nora? Don't want to? I'm your husband, aren't I?

(*There is a knock on the front door.*)

NORA (*with a start*) Did you hear that—?

HELMER (*on his way to the hall*) Who is it?

RANK (*outside*) It's me. May I come in for a moment?

HELMER (*in a low voice, annoyed*) Oh, what does he want now? (*Aloud.*) Just a minute. (*Opens the door.*) Well! How good of you not to pass by our door.

RANK I thought I heard your voice, so I felt like saying hello. (*Looks around.*) Ah yes—this dear, familiar room. What a cozy, comfortable place you have here, you two.

HELMER Looked to me as if you were quite comfortable upstairs too.

RANK I certainly was. Why not? Why not enjoy all you can in this world? As much as you can for as long as you can, anyway. Excellent wine.

HELMER The champagne, particularly.

RANK You noticed that too? Incredible how much I managed to put away.

NORA Torvald drank a lot of champagne tonight, too.

RANK Did he?

NORA Yes, he did, and then he's always so much fun afterwards.

RANK Well, why not have some fun in the evening after a well spent day?

HELMER Well spent? I'm afraid I can't claim that.

RANK (*slapping him lightly on the shoulder*) But you see, I can!
NORA Dr. Rank, I believe you must have been conducting a scientific test today.
RANK Exactly.
HELMER What do you know—little Nora talking about scientific tests!
NORA May I congratulate you on the result?
RANK You may indeed.
NORA It was a good one?
RANK The best possible for both doctor and patient—certainty.
NORA (*a quick query*) Certainty?
RANK Absolute certainty. So why shouldn't I have myself an enjoyable evening afterwards?
NORA I quite agree with you, Dr. Rank. You should.
HELMER And so do I. If only you don't pay for it tomorrow.
RANK Oh well—you get nothing for nothing in this world.
NORA Dr. Rank—you are fond of costume parties, aren't you?
RANK Yes, particularly when there is a reasonable number of amusing disguises.
NORA Listen—what are the two of us going to be the next time?
HELMER You frivolous little thing! Already thinking about the next party!
RANK You and I? That's easy. You'll be Fortune's Child.
HELMER Yes, but what is a fitting costume for that?
RANK Let your wife appear just the way she always is.
HELMER Beautiful. Very good indeed. But how about yourself? Don't you know what you'll go as?
RANK Yes, my friend. I know precisely what I'll be.
HELMER Yes?
RANK At the next masquerade I'll be invisible.
HELMER That's a funny idea.
RANK There's a certain black hat—you've heard about the hat that makes you invisible, haven't you? You put that on, and nobody can see you.
HELMER (*suppressing a smile*) I guess that's right.
RANK But I'm forgetting what I came for. Helmer, give me a cigar—one of your dark Havanas.
HELMER With the greatest pleasure. (*Offers him his case.*)
RANK (*takes one and cuts off the tip*) Thanks.
NORA (*striking a match*) Let me give you a light.
RANK Thanks. (*She holds the match; he lights his cigar.*) And now goodbye!
HELMER Goodbye, goodbye, my friend.
NORA Sleep well, Dr. Rank.

RANK I thank you.
NORA Wish me the same.
RANK You? Well, if you really want me to—. Sleep well. And thanks for the light. (*He nods to both of them and goes out.*)
HELMER (*in a low voice*) He had had quite a bit to drink.
NORA (*absently*) Maybe so.

(HELMER *takes out his keys and goes out into the hall.*)

NORA Torvald—what are you doing out there?
HELMER Emptying the mailbox. It is quite full. There wouldn't be room for the newspapers in the morning—
NORA Are you going to work tonight?
HELMER You know very well I won't.—Say! What's this? Somebody's been at the lock.
NORA The lock—?
HELMER Yes. Why, I wonder. I hate to think that any of the maids—. Here's a broken hairpin. It's one of yours. Nora.
NORA (*quickly*) Then it must be one of the children.
HELMER You better make damn sure they stop that. Hm, hm.—There! I got it open, finally. (*Gathers up the mail, calls out to the kitchen.*) Helene?—Oh Helene—turn out the light here in the hall, will you? (*He comes back into the living room and closes the door.*) Look how it's been piling up. (*Shows her the bundle of letters. Starts leafing through it.*) What's this?
NORA (*by the window*) The letter! Oh no, no, Torvald!
HELMER Two calling cards—from Rank.
NORA From Dr. Rank?
HELMER (*looking at them*) "Doctor medicinae Rank." They were on top. He must have put them there when he left just now.
NORA Anything written on them?
HELMER A black cross above the name. What a macabre idea. Like announcing his own death.
NORA That's what it is.
HELMER Hm? You know about this? Has he said anything to you?
NORA That card means he has said goodbye to us. He'll lock himself up to die.
HELMER My poor friend. I knew of course he wouldn't be with me very long. But so soon—. And hiding himself away like a wounded animal—
NORA When it has to be, it's better it happens without words. Don't you think so, Torvald?
HELMER (*walking up and down*) He'd grown so close to us. I find it hard to think of him as gone. With his suffering and loneliness he was like a clouded background for our happy sunshine.

Well, it may be better this way. For him, at any rate. (*Stops.*) And perhaps for us, too, Nora. For now we have nobody but each other. (*Embraces her.*) Oh you—my beloved wife! I feel I just can't hold you close enough. Do you know, Nora—many times I have wished some great danger threatened you, so I could risk my life and blood and everything—everything, for your sake.

NORA (*frees herself and says in a strong and firm voice*) I think you should go and read your letters now, Torvald.

HELMER No, no—not tonight. I want to be with you, my darling.

NORA With the thought of your dying friend—?

HELMER You are right. This has shaken both of us. Something not beautiful has come between us. Thoughts of death and dissolution. We must try to get over it—out of it. Till then—we'll each go to our own room.

NORA (*her arms around his neck*) Torvald—goodnight! Goodnight!

HELMER (*kisses her forehead*) Goodnight, my little songbird. Sleep well, Nora. Now I'll read my letters. (*He goes into his room, carrying the mail. Closes the door.*)

NORA (*her eyes desperate, her hands groping, finds Helmer's black cloak and throws it around her; she whispers, quickly, brokenly, hoarsely*) Never see him again. Never. Never. Never. (*Puts her shawl over her head.*) And never see the children again, either. Never; never.—The black, icy water—fathomless—this—! If only it was all over.—Now he has it. Now he's reading it. No, no; not yet. Torvald—goodbye—you—the children—

(*She is about to hurry through the hall, when* HELMER *flings open the door to his room and stands there with an open letter in his hand.*)

HELMER Nora!

NORA (*cries out*) Ah—!

HELMER What is it? You know what's in this letter?

NORA Yes, I do! Let me go! Let me out!

HELMER (*holds her back*). Where do you think you're going?

NORA (*trying to tear herself loose from him*) I won't let you save me, Torvald!

HELMER (*tumbles back*). True! Is it true what he writes? Oh my God! No, no—this can't possibly be true.

NORA It is true. I have loved you more than anything else in the whole world.

HELMER Oh, don't give me any silly excuses.

NORA (*taking a step towards him*) ·Torvald—!

HELMER You wretch! What have you done!

NORA Let me go. You are not to sacrifice yourself for me. You are not to take the blame.

HELMER No more playacting. (*Locks the door to the front hall.*) You'll stay here and answer me. Do you understand what you have done? Answer me! Do you understand?

NORA (*gazes steadily at him with an increasingly frozen expression*) Yes. Now I'm beginning to understand.

HELMER (*walking up and down*) What a dreadful awakening. All these years—all these eight years—she, my pride and my joy—a hypocrite, a liar—oh worse! worse!—a criminal! Oh, the bottomless ugliness in all this! Damn! Damn! Damn!

(NORA, *silent, keeps gazing at him.*)

HELMER (*stops in front of her*) I ought to have guessed that something like this would happen. I should have expected it. All your father's loose principles—Silence! You have inherited every one of your father's loose principles. No religion, no morals, no sense of duty—. Now I am being punished for my leniency with him. I did it for your sake, and this is how you pay me back.

NORA Yes. This is how.

HELMER You have ruined all my happiness. My whole future—that's what you have destroyed. Oh, it's terrible to think about. I am at the mercy of an unscrupulous man. He can do with me whatever he likes, demand anything of me, command me and dispose of me just as he pleases—I dare not say a word! To go down so miserably, to be destroyed—all because of an irresponsible woman!

NORA When I am gone from the world, you'll be free.

HELMER No noble gestures, please. Your father was always full of such phrases too. What good would it do me if you were gone from the world, as you put it? Not the slightest good at all. He could still make the whole thing public, and if he did, people would be likely to think I had been your accomplice. They might even think it was my idea—that it was I who urged you to do it! And for all this I have you to thank—you, whom I've borne on my hands through all the years of our marriage. *Now* do you understand what you've done to me?

NORA (*with cold calm*) Yes.

HELMER I just can't get it into my head that this is happening; it's all so incredible. But we have to come to terms with it somehow. Take your shawl off. Take it off, I say! I have to satisfy him one way or another. The whole affair must be kept quiet at whatever cost.—And as far as you and I are concerned, nothing must seem to have changed. I'm talking about appearances, of course. You'll go on living here; that goes without saying. But I won't let you bring up the children; I dare not trust you with them. —Oh! Having to say this to one I have loved so much, and whom I still—! But all that is past. It's not a question of happiness any more but of hanging on to what can be salvaged—pieces, appearances—(*The doorbell rings.*)

HELMER (*jumps*) What's that? So late. Is the worst—? Has he—! Hide, Nora! Say you're sick.

NORA *doesn't move.* HELMER *opens the door to the hall.*

THE MAID (*half dressed, out in the hall*) A letter for your wife, sir.

HELMER Give it to me. (*Takes the letter and closes the door.*) Yes, it's from him. But I won't let you have it. I'll read it myself.

NORA Yes—you read it.

HELMER (*by the lamp*) I hardly dare. Perhaps we're lost, both you and I. No; I've got to know. (*Tears the letter open, glances through it, looks at an enclosure; a cry of joy.*) Nora!

(NORA *looks at him with a question in her eyes.*)

HELMER Nora!—No, I must read it again.—Yes, yes; it is so! I'm saved! Nora, I'm saved!

NORA And I?

HELMER You too, of course; we're both saved, both you and I. Look! He's returning your note. He writes that he's sorry, he regrets, a happy turn in his life—oh, it doesn't matter what he writes. We're saved, Nora! Nobody can do anything to you now. Oh Nora, Nora—. No, I want to get rid of this disgusting thing first. Let me see—(*Looks at the signature.*) No, I don't want to see it. I don't want it to be more than a bad dream, the whole thing. (*Tears up the note and both letters, throws the pieces in the stove, and watches them burn.*) There! Now it's gone.—He wrote that ever since Christmas Eve—. Good God, Nora, these must have been three terrible days for you.

NORA I have fought a hard fight these last three days.

HELMER And been in agony and seen no other way out than—. No, we won't think of all that ugliness. We'll just rejoice and tell ourselves it's over, it's all over! Oh, listen to me, Nora. You don't seem to understand. It's over. What *is* it? Why do you look like that—that frozen expression on your face? Oh my poor little Nora, don't you think I know what it is? You can't make yourself believe that I have forgiven you. But I have, Nora; I swear to you, I have forgiven you for everything. Of course I know that what you did was for love of me.

NORA That is true.

HELMER You have loved me the way a wife ought to love her husband. You just didn't have the wisdom to judge the means. But do you think I love you any less because you don't know how to act on your own? Of course not. Just lean on me. I'll advise you; I'll guide you. I wouldn't be a man if I didn't find you twice as attractive because of your womanly helplessness. You mustn't pay any attention to the hard words I said to you right at first. It was just that first shock when I thought everything was collapsing all around me. I have forgiven you, Nora. I swear to you—I really have forgiven you.

NORA I thank you for your forgiveness. (*She goes out through the door, right.*)

HELMER No, stay—(*Looks into the room she entered.*) What are you doing in there?

NORA (*within*) Getting out of my costume.

HELMER (*by the open door*) Good, good. Try to calm down and compose yourself, my poor little frightened songbird. Rest safely; I have broad wings to cover you with. (*Walks around near the door.*) What a nice and cozy home we have, Nora. Here's shelter for you. Here I'll keep you safe like a hunted dove I have rescued from the hawk's talons. Believe me: I'll know how to quiet your beating heart. It will happen by and by, Nora; you'll see. Why, tomorrow you'll look at all this in quite a different light. And soon everything will be just the way it was before. I won't need to keep reassuring you that I have forgiven you; you'll feel it yourself. Did you really think I could have abandoned you, or even reproached you? Oh, you don't know a real man's heart, Nora. There is something unspeakably sweet and satisfactory for a man to know deep in himself that he has forgiven his wife—forgiven her in all the fullness of his honest heart. You see, that way she becomes his very own all over again—in a double sense, you might say. He has, so to speak, given her a second birth; it is as if she had become his wife and his child, both. From now on that's what you'll be to me, you lost and helpless creature. Don't worry about a thing, Nora. Only be frank with me, and I'll be your will and your conscience.—What's this? You're not in bed? You've changed your dress—!

NORA (*in an everyday dress*) Yes, Torvald. I have changed my dress.

HELMER But why—now—this late—?

NORA I'm not going to sleep tonight.

HELMER But my dear Nora—

NORA (*looks at her watch*) It isn't all that late. Sit down here with me, Torvald. You and I have much to talk about. (*Sits down at the table.*)

HELMER Nora—what is this all about? That rigid face—

NORA Sit down. This will take a while. I have much to say to you.

HELMER (*sits down, facing her across the table*) You worry me, Nora. I don't understand you.

NORA No, that's just it. You don't understand me. And I have never understood you—not till tonight. No, don't interrupt me. Just listen to what I have to say.—This is a settling of accounts, Torvald.

HELMER What do you mean by that?

NORA (*after a brief silence*) Doesn't one thing strike you, now that we are sitting together like this?

HELMER What would that be?

NORA We have been married for eight years. Doesn't it occur to you that this is the first time that you and I, husband and wife, are having a serious talk?

HELMER Well—serious—. What do you mean by that?

NORA For eight whole years—longer, in fact—ever since we first met, we have never talked seriously to each other about a single serious thing.

HELMER You mean I should forever have been telling you about worries you couldn't have helped me with anyway?

NORA I am not talking about worries. I'm saying we have never tried seriously to get to the bottom of anything together.

HELMER But dearest Nora, I hardly think that would have been something *you*—

NORA That's the whole point. You have never understood me. Great wrong has been done to me, Torvald. First by Daddy and then by you.

HELMER What! By us two? We who have loved you more deeply than anyone else?

NORA (*shakes her head*) You never loved me—neither Daddy nor you. You only thought it was fun to be in love with me.

HELMER But, Nora—what an expression to use!

NORA That's the way it has been, Torvald. When I was home with Daddy, he told me all his opinions, and so they became my opinions too. If I disagreed with him I kept it to myself, for he wouldn't have liked that. He called me his little doll baby, and he played with me the way I played with my dolls. Then I came to your house—

HELMER What a way to talk about our marriage!

NORA (*imperturbably*) I mean that I passed from Daddy's hands into yours. You arranged everything according to your taste, and so I came to share it—or I pretended to; I'm not sure which. I think it was a little of both, now one and now the other. When I look back on it now, it seems to me I've been living here like a pauper—just a hand-to-mouth kind of existence. I have earned my keep by doing tricks for you, Torvald. But that's the way you wanted it. You have great sins against me to answer for, Daddy and you. It's your fault that nothing has become of me.

HELMER Nora, you're being both unreasonable and ungrateful. Haven't you been happy here?

NORA No, never. I thought I was, but I wasn't.

HELMER Not—not happy!

NORA No; just having fun. And you have always been very good to me. But our home has never been more than a playroom. I have been your doll wife here, just the way I used to be Daddy's doll child. And the children have been my dolls. I thought it was fun when you played with me, just as they thought it was fun when I played with them. That's been our marriage, Torvald.

HELMER There is something in what you are saying—exaggerated and hysterical though it is. But from now on things will be different. Playtime is over; it's time for growing up.

NORA Whose growing up—mine or the children's?

HELMER Both yours and the children's, Nora darling.

NORA Oh Torvald, you're not the man to bring me up to be the right kind of wife for you.

HELMER How can you say that?

NORA And I—? What qualifications do I have for bringing up the children?

HELMER Nora!

NORA You said so yourself a minute ago—that you didn't dare to trust me with them.

HELMER In the first flush of anger, yes. Surely, you're not going to count that.

NORA But you were quite right. I am *not* qualified. Something else has to come first. Somehow I have to grow up myself. And you are not the man to help me do that. That's a job I have to do by myself. And that's why I'm leaving you.

HELMER (*jumps up*) What did you say!

NORA I have to be by myself if I am to find out about myself and about all the other things too. So I can't stay here with you any longer.

HELMER Nora, Nora!

NORA I'm leaving now. I'm sure Kristine will put me up for tonight.

HELMER You're out of your mind! I won't let you! I forbid you!

NORA You can't forbid me anything any more; it won't do any good. I'm taking my own things with me. I won't accept anything from you, either now or later.

HELMER But this is madness!

NORA Tomorrow I'm going home—I mean back to my old home town. It will be easier for me to find some kind of job there.

HELMER Oh, you blind, inexperienced creature—!

NORA I must see to it that I get experience, Torvald.

HELMER Leaving your home, your husband, your children! Not a thought of what people will say!

NORA I can't worry about that. All I know is that I have to leave.

HELMER Oh, this is shocking! Betraying your most sacred duties like this!

NORA And what do you consider my most sacred duties?

HELMER Do I need to tell you that? They are your duties to your husband and your children.

NORA I have other duties equally sacred.

HELMER You do not. What duties would they be?

NORA My duties to myself.

HELMER You are a wife and a mother before you are anything else.

NORA I don't believe that any more. I believe I am first of all a human being, just as much as you—or at any rate that I must try to become one. Oh, I know very well that most people agree with you, Torvald, and that it says something like that in all the books. But what people say and what the books say is no longer enough for me. I have to think about these things myself and see if I can't find the answers.

HELMER You mean to tell me you don't know what your proper place in your own home is? Don't you have a reliable guide in such matters? Don't you have religion?

NORA Oh but Torvald—I don't really know what religion is.

HELMER What are you saying!

NORA All I know is what the Reverend Hansen told me when he prepared me for confirmation. He said that religion was *this* and it was *that*. When I get by myself, away from here, I'll have to look into that, too. I have to decide if what the Reverend Hansen said was right, or anyway if it is right for *me*.

HELMER Oh, this is unheard of in a young woman! If religion can't guide you, let me appeal to your conscience. For surely you have moral feelings? Or—answer me—maybe you don't?

NORA Well, you see, Torvald, I don't really know what to say. I just don't know. I am confused about these things. All I know is that my ideas are quite different from yours. I have just found out that the laws are different from what I thought they were, but in no way can I get it into my head that those laws are right. A woman shouldn't have the right to spare her dying old father or save her husband's life! I just can't believe that.

HELMER You speak like a child. You don't understand the society you live in.

NORA No, I don't. But I want to find out about it. I have to make up my mind who is right, society or I.

HELMER You are sick, Nora; you have a fever. I really don't think you are in your right mind.

NORA I have never felt so clearheaded and sure of myself as I do tonight.

HELMER And clearheaded and sure of yourself you're leaving your husband and children?

NORA Yes.

HELMER Then there is only one possible explanation.

NORA What?

HELMER You don't love me any more.

NORA No, that's just it.

HELMER Nora! Can you say that?

NORA I am sorry, Torvald, for you have always been so good to me. But I can't help it. I don't love you any more.

HELMER (*with forced composure*) And this too is a clear and sure conviction?

NORA Completely clear and sure. That's why I don't want to stay here any more.

HELMER And are you ready to explain to me how I came to forfeit your love?

NORA Certainly I am. It was tonight, when the wonderful didn't happen. That was when I realized you were not the man I thought you were.

HELMER You have to explain. I don't understand.

NORA I have waited patiently for eight years, for I wasn't such a fool that I thought the wonderful is something that happens any old day. Then this—thing—came crashing in on me, and then there wasn't a doubt in my mind that now—now comes the wonderful. When Krogstad's letter was in that mailbox, never for a moment did it even occur to me that you would submit to his conditions. I was so absolutely certain that you would say to him: make the whole thing public—tell everybody. And when that had happened—

HELMER Yes, then what? When I had surrendered my wife to shame and disgrace—!

NORA When that had happened, I was absolutely certain that you would stand up and take the blame and say, "I'm the guilty one."

HELMER Nora!

NORA You mean I never would have accepted such a sacrifice from you? Of course not. But what would my protests have counted against yours. *That* was the wonderful I was hoping for in terror. And to prevent that I was going to kill myself.

HELMER I'd gladly work nights and days for you, Nora—endure sorrow and want for your sake. But nobody sacrifices his *honor* for his love.

NORA A hundred thousand women have done so.

HELMER Oh, you think and talk like a silly child.

NORA All right. But you don't think and talk like the man I can live with. When you had gotten over your fright—not because of what threatened *me* but because of the risk to *you*—and the whole danger was past, then you acted as if nothing at all had happened. Once again I was your little songbird, your doll, just as before, only now you had to handle her even more carefully, because she was so frail and weak. (*Rises.*) Torvald—that moment I realized that I had been living here for eight years with a stranger and had borne him three children—Oh, I can't stand thinking about it! I feel like tearing myself to pieces!

HELMER (*heavily*) I see it, I see it. An abyss has opened up between us.—Oh but Nora—surely it can be filled?

NORA The way I am now I am no wife for you.

HELMER I have it in me to change.

NORA Perhaps—if your doll is taken from you.

HELMER To part—to part from you! No, no, Nora! I can't grasp that thought!

NORA (*goes out, right*) All the more reason why it has to be. (*She returns with her outdoor clothes and a small bag, which she sets down on the chair by the table.*)

HELMER Nora, Nora! Not now! Wait till tomorrow.

NORA (*putting on her coat*) I can't spend the night in a stranger's rooms.

HELMER But couldn't we live here together like brother and sister—?

NORA (*tying on her hat*) You know very well that wouldn't last long—. (*Wraps her shawl around her.*) Goodbye, Torvald. I don't want to see the children. I know I leave them in better hands than mine. The way I am now I can't be anything to them.

HELMER But some day, Nora—some day—?

NORA How can I tell? I have no idea what's going to become of me.

HELMER But you're still my wife, both as you are now and as you will be.

NORA Listen, Torvald—when a wife leaves her husband's house, the way I am doing now, I have heard he has no more legal responsibilities for her. At any rate, I now release you from all responsibility. You are not to feel yourself obliged to me for anything, and I have no obligations to you. There has to be full freedom on both sides. Here is your ring back. Now give me mine.

HELMER Even this?

NORA Even this.

HELMER Here it is.

NORA There. So now it's over. I'm putting the keys here. The maids know everything about the house—better than I. Tomorrow, after I'm gone, Kristine will come over and pack my things from home. I want them sent after me.

HELMER Over! It's all over! Nora, will you never think of me?

NORA I'm sure I'll often think of you and the children and this house.

HELMER May I write to you, Nora?

NORA No—never. I won't have that.

HELMER But send you things—? You must let me.

NORA Nothing, nothing.

HELMER —help you, when you need help—?

NORA I told you, no; I won't have it. I'll accept nothing from strangers.

HELMER Nora—can I never again be more to you than a stranger?

NORA (*picks up her bag*) Oh Torvald—then the most wonderful of all would have to happen—

HELMER Tell me what that would be—!

NORA For that to happen, both you and I would have to change so that—Oh Torvald, I no longer believe in the wonderful.

HELMER But I *will* believe. Tell me! Change, so that—?

NORA So that our living together would become a true marriage. Goodbye. (*She goes out through the hall.*)

HELMER (*sinks down on a chair near the door and covers his face with his hands*) Nora! Nora! (*Looks around him and gets up.*) All empty. She's gone. (*With sudden hope.*) The most wonderful—?!

(*From downstairs comes the sound of a heavy door slamming shut.*)

## QUESTIONS

1. The action of *A Doll's House* centers on the development and the alterations of the relationships among Nora, Helmer, Krogstad, and Mrs. Linde. How does Ibsen portray these characters? How do their relationships illuminate their personalities and their actions? How do they emphasize the themes and social comments of the play?
2. Both Nora and Antigonê are women who place moral principles above legal values. What happens to each character in consequence, in terms of her play's plot? Other characters' reactions to her action? Her view of their reaction, and of herself?
3. Discuss the play's ending. Do you find it successful? What is its effect? What do you think is "the most wonderful of all"?

## OSCAR WILDE (1854–1900)

# *The Importance of Being Earnest*

CHARACTERS

JOHN WORTHING, J.P.
ALGERNON MONCRIEFF
REV. CANON CHASUBLE, D.D.
MERRIMAN, *butler*
LANE, *manservant*
LADY BRACKNELL
HON. GWENDOLEN FAIRFAX
CECILY CARDEW
MISS PRISM, *governess*

THE SCENES OF THE PLAY

ACT I. *Algernon Moncrieff's Flat in Half-Moon Street, W.*
ACT II. *The Garden at the Manor House, Woolton.*
ACT III. *Drawing-Room of the Manor House, Woolton.*

TIME—*The Present.*
PLACE—*London.*

## ACT I

SCENE. *Morning-room in* ALGERNON'S *flat in Half-Moon Street. The room is luxuriously and artistically furnished. The sound of a piano is heard in the adjoining room.*

(LANE *is arranging afternoon tea on the table, and after the music has ceased,* ALGERNON *enters.*)

ALGERNON Did you hear what I was playing, Lane?
LANE I didn't think it polite to listen, sir.
ALGERNON I'm sorry for that, for your sake. I don't play accurately—any one can play accurately—but I play with wonderful expression. As far as the piano is concerned, sentiment is my forte. I keep science for Life.
LANE Yes, sir.

ALGERNON And, speaking of the science of Life, have you got the cucumber sandwiches cut for Lady Bracknell?

LANE Yes, sir. (*Hands them on a salver.*)

ALGERNON (*inspects them, takes two, and sits down on the sofa*) Oh! . . . by the way, Lane, I see from your book that on Thursday night, when Lord Shoreman and Mr. Worthing were dining with me, eight bottles of champagne are entered as having been consumed.

LANE Yes, sir; eight bottles and a pint.

ALGERNON Why is it that at a bachelor's establishment the servants invariably drink the champagne? I ask merely for information.

LANE I attribute it to the superior quality of the wine, sir. I have often observed that in married households the champagne is rarely of a first-rate brand.

ALGERNON Good Heavens! Is marriage so demoralizing as that?

LANE I believe it *is* a very pleasant state, sir. I have had very little experience of it myself up to the present. I have only been married once. That was in consequence of a misunderstanding between myself and a young woman.

ALGERNON (*languidly*) I don't know that I am much interested in your family life, Lane.

LANE No, sir; it is not a very interesting subject. I never think of it myself.

ALGERNON Very natural, I am sure. That will do, Lane, thank you.

LANE Thank you, sir. (LANE *goes out.*)

ALGERNON Lane's views on marriage seem somewhat lax. Really, if the lower orders don't set us a good example, what on earth is the use of them? They seem, as a class, to have absolutely no sense of moral responsibility.

*Enter* LANE.

LANE Mr. Ernest Worthing.

*Enter* JACK. LANE *goes out.*

ALGERNON How are you, my dear Ernest? What brings you up to town?

JACK Oh, pleasure, pleasure! What else should bring one anywhere? Eating as usual, I see, Algy!

ALGERNON (*stiffly*) I believe it is customary in good society to take some slight refreshment at five o'clock. Where have you been since last Thursday?

JACK (*sitting down on the sofa*) In the country.

ALGERNON What on earth do you do there?

JACK (*pulling off his gloves*) When one is in town one amuses oneself. When one is in the country one amuses other people. It is excessively boring.

ALGERNON And who are the people you amuse?

JACK (*airily*) Oh, neighbors, neighbors.

ALGERNON Got nice neighbors in your part of Shropshire?

JACK Perfectly horrid! Never speak to one of them.

ALGERNON How immensely you must amuse them! (*Goes over and takes sandwich.*) By the way, Shropshire is your county, is it not?

JACK Eh? Shropshire? Yes, of course. Hallo! Why all these cups? Why cucumber sandwiches? Why such reckless extravagance in one so young? Who is coming to tea?

ALGERNON Oh! merely Aunt Augusta and Gwendolen.

JACK How perfectly delightful!

ALGERNON Yes, that is all very well; but I am afraid Aunt Augusta won't quite approve of your being here.

JACK May I ask why?

ALGERNON My dear fellow, the way you flirt with Gwendolen is perfectly disgraceful. It is almost as bad as the way Gwendolen flirts with you.

JACK I am in love with Gwendolen. I have come up to town expressly to propose to her.

ALGERNON I thought you had come up for pleasure? . . . I call that business.

JACK How utterly unromantic you are!

ALGERNON I really don't see anything romantic in proposing. It is very romantic to be in love. But there is nothing romantic about a definite proposal. Why, one may be accepted. One usually is, I believe. Then the excitement is all over. The very essence of romance is uncertainty. If ever I get married, I'll certainly try to forget the fact.

JACK I have no doubt about that, dear Algy. The Divorce Court was specially invented for people whose memories are so curiously constituted.

ALGERNON Oh! there is no use speculating on that subject. Divorces are made in Heaven—(JACK *puts out his hand to take a sandwich.* ALGERNON *at once interferes.*) Please don't touch the cucumber sandwiches. They are ordered specially for Aunt Augusta. (*Takes one and eats it.*)

JACK Well, you have been eating them all the time.

ALGERNON That is quite a different matter. She is my aunt. (*Takes plate from below.*) Have some bread and butter. The bread and butter is for Gwendolen. Gwendolen is devoted to bread and butter.

JACK (*advancing to table and helping himself*) And very good bread and butter it is, too.

ALGERNON Well, my dear fellow, you need not eat as if you were going to eat it all. You behave as if you were married to her already. You are not married to her already, and I don't think you ever will be.

JACK Why on earth do you say that?

ALGERNON Well, in the first place girls never marry the men they flirt with. Girls don't think it right.

JACK Oh, that is nonsense!

ALGERNON It isn't. It is a great truth. It accounts for the extraordinary number of bachelors that one sees all over the place. In the second place, I don't give my consent.

JACK Your consent!

ALGERNON My dear fellow, Gwendolen is my first cousin. And before I allow you to marry her, you will have to clear up the whole question of Cecily. (*Rings bell.*)

JACK Cecily! What on earth do you mean? What do you mean, Algy, by Cecily? I don't know any one of the name of Cecily.

*Enter* LANE.

ALGERNON Bring me that cigarette case Mr. Worthing left in the smoking-room the last time he dined here.

LANE Yes, sir. (LANE *goes out.*)

JACK Do you mean to say you have had my cigarette case all this time? I wish to goodness you had let me know. I have been writing frantic letters to Scotland Yard about it. I was very nearly offering a large reward.

ALGERNON Well, I wish you would offer one. I happen to be more than usually hard up.

JACK There is no good offering a large reward now that the thing is found.

*Enter* LANE *with the cigarette case on a salver.* ALGERNON *takes it at once.* LANE *goes out.*

ALGERNON I think that is rather mean of you, Ernest, I must say. (*Opens case and examines it.*) However, it makes no matter, for, now that I look at the inscription, I find that the thing isn't yours after all.

JACK Of course it's mine. (*Moving to him.*) You have seen me with it a hundred times, and you have no right whatsoever to read what is written inside. It is a very ungentlemanly thing to read a private cigarette case.

ALGERNON Oh! it is absurd to have a hard-and-fast rule about what one should read and what one shouldn't. More than half of modern culture depends on what one shouldn't read.

JACK I am quite aware of the fact, and I don't propose to discuss modern culture. It isn't the sort of thing one should talk of in private. I simply want my cigarette case back.

ALGERNON Yes; but this isn't your cigarette case. This cigarette case is a present from some one of the name of Cecily, and you said you didn't know any one of that name.

JACK Well, if you want to know, Cecily happens to be my aunt.

ALGERNON Your aunt!

JACK Yes. Charming old lady she is, too. Lives at Tunbridge Wells. Just give it back to me, Algy.

ALGERNON (*retreating to back of sofa*) But why does she call herself little Cecily if she is your aunt and lives at Tunbridge Wells? (*Reading.*) "From little Cecily with her fondest love."

JACK (*moving to sofa and kneeling upon it*) My dear fellow, what on earth is there in that? Some aunts are tall, some aunts are not tall. That is a matter that surely an aunt may be allowed to decide for herself. You seem to think that every aunt should be exactly like your aunt! That is absurd! For Heaven's sake give me back my cigarette case. (*Follows* ALGERNON *round the room.*)

ALGERNON Yes. But why does your aunt call you her uncle? "From little Cecily, with her fondest love to her dear Uncle Jack." There is no objection, I admit, to an aunt being a small aunt, but why an aunt, no matter what her size may be, should call her own nephew her uncle, I can't quite make out. Besides, your name isn't Jack at all; it is Ernest.

JACK It isn't Ernest; it's Jack.

ALGERNON You have always told me it was Ernest. I have introduced you to every one as Ernest. You answer to the name of Ernest. You look as if your name was Ernest. You are the most earnest looking person I ever saw in my life. It is perfectly absurd your saying that your name isn't Ernest. It's on your cards. Here is one of them. (*Taking it from case.*) "Mr. Ernest Worthing, B 4, The Albany." I'll keep this as a proof your name is Ernest if ever you attempt to deny it to me, or to Gwendolen, or to any one else. (*Puts the card in his pocket.*)

JACK Well, my name is Ernest in town and Jack in the country, and the cigarette case was given to me in the country.

ALGERNON Yes, but that does not account for the fact that your small Aunt Cecily, who lives at Tunbridge Wells, calls you her dear uncle. Come, old boy, you had much better have the thing out at once.

JACK My dear Algy, you talk exactly as if you were a dentist. It is very vulgar to talk like a dentist when one isn't a dentist. It produces a false impression.

ALGERNON Well, that is exactly what dentists always do. Now, go on! Tell me the whole thing, I may mention that I have always suspected you of being a confirmed and secret Bunburyist; and I am quite sure of it now.

JACK Bunburyist? What on earth do you mean by a Bunburyist?

ALGERNON I'll reveal to you the meaning of that incomparable expression as soon as you are kind enough to inform me why you are Ernest in town and Jack in the country.

JACK Well, produce my cigarette case first.

ALGERNON Here it is. (*Hands cigarette case.*) Now produce your explanation, and pray make it improbable. (*Sits on sofa.*)

JACK My dear fellow, there is nothing improbable about my explanation at all. In fact it's perfectly ordinary. Old Mr. Thomas Cardew, who adopted me when I was a little boy, made me in his will guardian to his grand-daughter, Miss Cecily Cardew. Cecily, who addresses me as her uncle from motives of respect that you could not possibly appreciate, lives at my place in the country under the charge of her admirable governess, Miss Prism.

ALGERNON Where is that place in the country, by the way?

JACK That is nothing to you, dear boy. You are not going to be invited. . . . I may tell you candidly that the place is not in Shropshire.

ALGERNON I suspected that, my dear fellow! I have Bunburyed all over Shropshire on two separate occasions. Now, go on. Why are you Ernest in town and Jack in the country?

JACK My dear Algy, I don't know whether you will be able to understand my real motives. You are hardly serious enough. When one is placed in the position of guardian, one has to adopt a very high moral tone on all subjects. It's one's duty to do so. And as a high moral tone can hardly be said to conduce very much to either one's health or one's happiness, in order to get up to town I have always pretended to have a younger brother of the name of Ernest, who lives in the Albany, and gets into the most dreadful scrapes. That, my dear Algy, is the whole truth pure and simple.

ALGERNON The truth is rarely pure and never simple. Modern life would be very tedious if it were either, and modern literature a complete impossibility!

JACK That wouldn't be at all a bad thing.

ALGERNON Literary criticism is not your forte, my dear fellow. Don't try it. You should leave that to people who haven't been at a University. They do it so well in the daily papers. What you really are is a Bunburyist. I was quite right in saying you were a Bunburyist. You are one of the most advanced Bunburyists I know.

JACK What on earth do you mean?

ALGERNON You have invented a very useful younger brother called Ernest, in order that you may be able to come up to town as often as you like. I have invented an invaluable permanent invalid called Bunbury, in order that I may be able to go down into the country whenever I choose. Bunbury is perfectly invaluable. If it wasn't for Bunbury's extraordinary bad health, for instance, I wouldn't be able to dine with you at Willis's to-night, for I have been really engaged to Aunt Augusta for more than a week.

JACK I haven't asked you to dine with me anywhere tonight.

ALGERNON I know. You are absolutely careless about sending out invitations. It is very foolish of you. Nothing annoys people so much as not receiving invitations.

JACK You had much better dine with your Aunt Augusta.

ALGERNON I haven't the smallest intention of doing anything of the kind. To begin with, I dined there on Monday, and once a week is quite enough to dine with one's own relatives. In the second place, whenever I do dine there I am always treated as a member of the family, and sent down with either no woman at all, or two. In the third place, I know perfectly well whom she will place me next to, tonight. She will place me next Mary Farquhar, who always flirts with her own husband across the dinner-table. That is not very pleasant. Indeed, it is not even decent . . . and that sort of thing is enormously on the increase. The amount of women in London who flirt with their own husbands is perfectly scandalous. It looks so bad. It is simply washing one's clean linen in public. Besides, now that I know you to be a confirmed Bunburyist I naturally want to talk to you about Bunburying. I want to tell you the rules.

JACK I'm not a Bunburyist at all. If Gwendolen accepts me, I am going to kill my brother, indeed I think I'll kill him in any case. Cecily is a little too much interested in him. It is rather a bore. So I am going to get rid of Ernest. And I strongly advise you to do the same with Mr. —— with your invalid friend who has the absurd name.

ALGERNON Nothing will induce me to part with Bunbury, and if you ever get married, which seems to me extremely problematic, you will be very glad to know Bunbury. A man who marries without knowing Bunbury has a very tedious time of it.

JACK That is nonsense. If I marry a charming girl like Gwendolen, and she is the only girl I ever saw in my life that I would marry, I certainly won't want to know Bunbury.

ALGERNON Then your wife will. You don't seem to realize, that in married life three is company and two is none.

JACK (*sententiously*) That, my dear young friend, is the theory that the corrupt French Drama has been propounding for the last fifty years.

ALGERNON Yes; and that the happy English home has proved in half the time.

JACK For heaven's sake, don't try to be cynical. It's perfectly easy to be cynical.

ALGERNON My dear fellow, it isn't easy to be anything now-a-days. There's such a lot of beastly competition about. (*The sound of an electric bell is heard.*) Ah! that must be Aunt Augusta. Only relatives, or creditors, ever ring in that Wagnerian manner. Now, if I get her out of the way for ten minutes, so that you can have an opportunity for proposing to Gwendolen, may I dine with you to-night at Willis's?

JACK I suppose so, if you want to.

ALGERNON Yes, but you must be serious about it. I have people who are not serious about meals. It is so shallow of them.

*Enter* LANE.

LANE Lady Bracknell and Miss Fairfax. (ALGERNON *goes forward to meet them. Enter* LADY BRACKNELL *and* GWENDOLEN.)

LADY BRACKNELL Good afternoon, dear Algernon, I hope you are behaving very well.

ALGERNON I'm feeling very well, Aunt Augusta.

LADY BRACKNELL That's not quite the same thing. In fact the two things rarely go together. (*Sees* JACK *and bows to him with icy coldness.*)

ALGERNON (*to* GWENDOLEN) Dear me, you are smart!

GWENDOLEN I am always smart! Aren't I, Mr. Worthing?

JACK You're quite perfect, Miss Fairfax.

GWENDOLEN Oh! I hope I am not that. It would leave no room for developments, and I intend to develop in many directions. (GWENDOLEN *and* JACK *sit down together in the corner.*)

LADY BRACKNELL I'm sorry if we are a little late, Algernon, but I was obliged to call on dear Lady Harbury. Hadn't been there since her poor husband's death. I never saw a woman so altered; she looks quite twenty years younger. And now I'll have a cup of tea, and one of those nice cucumber sandwiches you promised me.

ALGERNON Certainly, Aunt Augusta. (*Goes over to tea-table.*)

LADY BRACKNELL Won't you come and sit here, Gwendolen?

GWENDOLEN Thanks, mamma, I'm quite comfortable where I am.

ALGERNON (*picking up empty plate in horror*) Good heavens! Lane! Why are there no cucumber sandwiches? I ordered them specially.

LANE (*gravely*) There were no cucumbers in the market this morning, sir. I went down twice.

ALGERNON No cucumbers!

LANE No, sir. Not even for ready money.

ALGERNON That will do, Lane, thank you.

LANE Thank you, sir. (*Goes out.*)

ALGERNON I am greatly distressed, Aunt Augusta, about there being no cucumbers, not even for ready money.

LADY BRACKNELL It really makes no matter, Algernon. I had some crumpets with Lady Harbury, who seems to me to be living entirely for pleasure now.

ALGERNON I hear her hair has turned quite gold from grief.

LADY BRACKNELL It certainly has changed its color. From what cause I, of course, cannot say. (ALGERNON *crosses and hands tea.*) Thank you. I've quite a treat for you to-night, Algernon. I am going to send you down with Mary Farquhar. She is such a nice woman, and so attentive to her husband. It's delightful to watch them.

ALGERNON I am afraid, Aunt Augusta, I shall have to give up the pleasure of dining with you to-night after all.

LADY BRACKNELL (*frowning*) I hope not, Algernon. It would put my table completely out. Your uncle would have to dine upstairs. Fortunately he is accustomed to that.

ALGERNON It is a great bore, and, I need hardly say, a terrible disappointment to me, but the fact is I have just had a telegram to say that my poor friend Bunbury is very ill again. (*Exchanges glances with* JACK.) They seem to think I should be with him.

LADY BRACKNELL It is very strange. This Mr. Bunbury seems to suffer from curiously bad health.

ALGERNON Yes; poor Bunbury is a dreadful invalid.

LADY BRACKNELL Well, I must say, Algernon, that I think it is high time that Mr. Bunbury made up his mind whether he was going to live or to die. This shilly-shallying with the question is absurd. Nor do I in any way approve of the modern sympathy with invalids. I consider it morbid. Illness of any kind is hardly a thing to be encouraged in others. Health is the primary duty of life. I am always telling that to your poor uncle, but he never seems to take much notice . . . as far as any improvement in his ailments goes. I should be much obliged if you would ask Mr. Bunbury, from me, to be kind enough not to have a relapse on Saturday, for I rely on you to arrange my music for me. It is my last reception and one wants something that will encourage conversation, particularly at the end of the season when every one has practically said whatever they had to say, which, in most cases, was probably not much.

ALGERNON I'll speak to Bunbury, Aunt Augusta, if he is still conscious, and I think I can promise you he'll be all right by Saturday. Of course the music is a great difficulty. You see, if one plays good music, people don't listen, and if one plays bad music, people don't talk. But I'll run over the program I've drawn out, if you will kindly come into the next room for a moment.

LADY BRACKNELL Thank you, Algernon. It is very thoughtful of you. (*Rising, and following* ALGERNON.) I'm sure the program will be delightful, after a few expurgations. French songs I cannot possibly allow. People always seem to think that they are improper, and either look shocked, which is vulgar, or laugh, which is worse. But German sounds a thoroughly respectable language, and indeed, I believe is so. Gwendolen, you will accompany me.

GWENDOLEN Certainly, mamma. (LADY BRACKNELL *and* ALGERNON *go into the music-room;* GWENDOLEN *remains behind.*)

JACK Charming day it has been, Miss Fairfax.

GWENDOLEN Pray don't talk to me about the weather, Mr. Worthing. Whenever people talk to me about the weather, I always feel quite certain that they mean something else. And that makes me so nervous.

JACK I do mean something else.

GWENDOLEN I thought so. In fact, I am never wrong.

JACK And I would like to be allowed to take advantage of Lady Bracknell's temporary absence . . .

GWENDOLEN I would certainly advise you to do so. Mamma has a way of coming back suddenly into a room that I have often had to speak to her about.

JACK (*nervously*) Miss Fairfax, ever since I met you I have admired you more than any girl . . . I have ever met since . . . I met you.

GWENDOLEN Yes, I am quite aware of the fact. And I often wish that in public, at any rate, you had been more demonstrative. For me you have always had an irresistible fascination. Even before I met you I was far from indifferent to you. (JACK *looks at her in amazement.*) We live, as I hope you know, Mr. Worthing, in an age of ideals. The fact is constantly mentioned in the more expensive monthly magazines, and has reached the provincial pulpits I am told: and my ideal has always been to love some one of the name of Ernest. There is something in that name that inspires absolute confidence. The moment Algernon first mentioned to me that he had a friend called Ernest, I knew I was destined to love you.

JACK You really love me, Gwendolen?

GWENDOLEN Passionately!

JACK Darling! You don't know how happy you've made me.

GWENDOLEN My own Ernest!

JACK But you don't really mean to say that you couldn't love me if my name wasn't Ernest?

GWENDOLEN But your name is Ernest.

JACK Yes, I know it is. But supposing it was something else? Do you mean to say you couldn't love me then?

GWENDOLEN (*glibly*) Ah! that is clearly a metaphysical speculation, and like most metaphysical speculations has very little reference at all to the actual facts of real life, as we know them.

JACK Personally, darling, to speak quite candidly, I don't much care about the name of Ernest . . . I don't think that name suits me at all.

GWENDOLEN It suits you perfectly. It is a divine name. It has a music of its own. It produces vibrations.

JACK Well, really, Gwendolen, I must say that I think there are lots of other much nicer names. I think, Jack, for instance, a charming name.

GWENDOLEN Jack? . . . No, there is very little music in the name Jack, if any at all, indeed. It does not thrill. It produces absolutely no vibrations. . . . I have known several Jacks, and they all, without exception, were more than usually plain. Besides, Jack is a notorious domesticity for John! And I pity any woman who is married to a man called John. She would probably never be allowed to know the entrancing pleasure of a single moment's solitude. The only really safe name is Ernest.

JACK Gwendolen, I must get christened at once—I mean we must get married at once. There is no time to be lost.

GWENDOLEN Married, Mr. Worthing?

JACK (*astounded*) Well . . . surely. You know that I love you, and you led me to believe, Miss Fairfax, that you were not absolutely indifferent to me.

GWENDOLEN I adore you. But you haven't proposed to me yet. Nothing has been said at all about marriage. The subject has not even been touched on.

JACK Well . . . may I propose to you now?

GWENDOLEN I think it would be an admirable opportunity. And to spare you any possible disappointment, Mr. Worthing, I think it only fair to tell you quite frankly beforehand that I am fully determined to accept you.

JACK Gwendolen!

GWENDOLEN Yes, Mr. Worthing, what have you got to say to me?

JACK You know what I have got to say to you.

GWENDOLEN Yes, but you don't say it.

JACK Gwendolen, will you marry me? (*Goes on his knees.*)

GWENDOLEN Of course I will, darling. How long you have been about it! I am afraid you have had very little experience in how to propose.

JACK My own one, I have never loved any one in the world but you.

GWENDOLEN Yes, but men often propose for practice. I know my brother Gerald does. All my girl-friends tell me so. What wonderfully blue eyes you have, Ernest! They are quite, quite blue. I hope you will always look at me just like that, especially when there are other people present.

*Enter* LADY BRACKNELL.

LADY BRACKNELL Mr. Worthing! Rise, sir, from this semi-recumbent posture. It is most indecorous.

GWENDOLEN Mamma! (*He tries to rise; she restrains him.*) I must beg you to retire. This is no place for you. Besides, Mr. Worthing has not quite finished yet.

LADY BRACKNELL Finished what, may I ask?

GWENDOLEN I am engaged to Mr. Worthing, mamma. (*They rise together.*)

LADY BRACKNELL Pardon me, you are not engaged to any one. When you do become engaged to some one, I, or your father, should his health permit him, will inform you of the fact. An engagement should come on a young girl as a surprise, pleasant or unpleasant, as the case may be. It is hardly a matter that she could be allowed to arrange for herself. . . . And now I have a few questions to put to you, Mr. Worthing. While I am making these inquiries, you, Gwendolen, will wait for me below in the carriage.

GWENDOLEN (*reproachfully*) Mamma!

LADY BRACKNELL In the carriage, Gwendolen! (GWENDOLEN *goes to the door. She and* JACK *blow kisses to each other behind* LADY BRACKNELL'S *back.* LADY BRACKNELL *looks vaguely about as if she could not understand what the noise was. Finally turns round.*) Gwendolen, the carriage!

GWENDOLEN Yes, mamma. (*Goes out, looking back at* JACK.)

LADY BRACKNELL (*sitting down*) You can take a seat, Mr. Worthing. (*Looks in her pocket for note-book and pencil.*)

JACK Thank you, Lady Bracknell, I prefer standing.

LADY BRACKNELL (*pencil and note-book in hand*) I feel bound to tell you that you are not down on my list of eligible young men, although I have the same list as the dear Duchess of Bolton has. We work together, in fact. However, I am quite ready to enter your name, should your answers be what a really affectionate mother requires. Do you smoke?

JACK Well, yes, I must admit I smoke.

LADY BRACKNELL I am glad to hear it. A man should always have an occupation of some kind. There are far too many idle men in London as it is. How old are you?

JACK Twenty-nine.

LADY BRACKNELL A very good age to be married at. I have always been of the opinion that a man who desires to get married should know either everything or nothing. Which do you know?

JACK (*after some hesitation*) I know nothing, Lady Bracknell.

LADY BRACKNELL I am pleased to hear it. I do not approve of anything that tampers with natural ignorance. Ignorance is like a delicate exotic fruit; touch it and the bloom is gone. The whole theory of modern education is radically unsound. Fortunately in England, at any rate, education produces no effect whatsoever. If it did, it would prove a serious danger to the upper classes, and probably lead to acts of violence in Grosvenor Square. What is your income?

JACK Between seven and eight thousand a year.

LADY BRACKNELL (*makes a note in her book*) In land, or in investments?

JACK In investments, chiefly.

LADY BRACKNELL That is satisfactory. What between the duties expected of one during one's life-time, and the duties exacted from one after one's death, land has ceased to be either a profit or a pleasure. It gives one position, and prevents one from keeping it up. That's all that can be said about land.

JACK I have a country house with some land, of course, attached to it, about fifteen hundred acres, I believe; but I don't depend on that for my real income. In fact, as far as I can make out, the poachers are the only people who make anything out of it.

LADY BRACKNELL A country house! How many bedrooms? Well, that point can be cleared up afterwards. You have a town house, I hope? A girl with a simple, unspoiled nature, like Gwendolen, could hardly be expected to reside in the country.

JACK Well, I own a house in Belgrave Square, but it is let by the year to Lady Bloxham. Of course, I can get it back whenever I like, at six months' notice.

LADY BRACKNELL Lady Bloxham? I don't know her.

JACK Oh, she goes about very little. She is a lady considerably advanced in years.

LADY BRACKNELL Ah, now-a-days that is no guarantee of respectability of character. What number in Belgrave Square?

JACK 149.

LADY BRACKNELL (*shaking her head*) The unfashionable side. I thought there was something. However, that could easily be altered.

JACK Do you mean the fashion, or the side?

LADY BRACKNELL (*sternly*) Both, if necessary, I presume. What are your politics?

JACK Well, I am afraid I really have none. I am a Liberal Unionist.

LADY BRACKNELL Oh, they count as Tories. They dine with us. Or come in the evening, at any rate. Now to minor matters. Are your parents living?

JACK I have lost both my parents.

LADY BRACKNELL Both? . . . That seems like carelessness. Who was your father? He was evidently a man of some wealth. Was he born in what the Radical papers call the purple of commerce, or did he rise from the ranks of the aristocracy?

JACK I am afraid I really don't know. The fact is, Lady Bracknell, I said I had lost my parents. It would be nearer the truth to say that my parents seem to have lost me . . . I don't actually know who I am by birth. I was . . . well, I was found.

LADY BRACKNELL Found!

JACK The late Mr. Thomas Cardew, an old gentleman of a very charitable and kindly disposition, found me, and gave me the name of Worthing, because he happened to have a first-class ticket for Worthing in his pocket at the time. Worthing is a place in Sussex. It is a seaside resort.

LADY BRACKNELL Where did the charitable gentleman who had a first-class ticket for this seaside resort find you?

JACK (*gravely*) In a hand-bag.

LADY BRACKNELL A hand-bag?

JACK (*very seriously*) Yes, Lady Bracknell. I was in a hand-bag—a somewhat large, black leather hand-bag, with handles to it—an ordinary hand-bag in fact.

LADY BRACKNELL In what locality did this Mr. James, or Thomas, Cardew come across this ordinary hand-bag?

JACK In the cloak-room at Victoria Station. It was given to him in mistake for his own.

LADY BRACKNELL The cloak-room at Victoria Station?

JACK Yes. The Brighton line.

LADY BRACKNELL The line is immaterial. Mr. Worthing, I confess I feel somewhat bewildered by what you have just told me. To be born, or at any rate bred, in a handbag, whether it had handles or not, seems to me to display a contempt for the ordinary decencies of family life that remind one of the worst excesses of the French Revolution. And I presume you know what that unfortunate movement led to? As for the particular locality in which the hand-bag was found, a cloak-room at a railway station might serve to conceal a social indiscretion—has probably, indeed, been used for that purpose before now—but it could hardly be regarded as an assured basis for a recognized position in good society.

JACK May I ask you then what you would advise me to do? I need hardly say I would do anything in the world to ensure Gwendolen's happiness.

LADY BRACKNELL I would strongly advise you, Mr. Worthing, to try and acquire some relations as soon as possible, and to make a definite effort to produce at any rate one parent, of either sex, before the season is quite over.

JACK Well, I don't see how I could possibly manage to do that. I can produce the hand-bag at any moment. It is in my dressing-room at home. I really think that should satisfy you, Lady Bracknell.

LADY BRACKNELL Me, sir! What has it to do with me? You can hardly imagine that I and Lord Bracknell would dream of allowing our only daughter—a girl brought up with the utmost care—to marry into a cloak-room, and form an alliance with a parcel? Good morning, Mr. Worthing! (LADY BRACKNELL *sweeps out in majestic indignation.*)

JACK Good morning! (ALGERNON, *from the other room, strikes up the Wedding March.* JACK *looks perfectly furious, and goes to the door.*) For goodness' sake don't play that ghastly tune, Algy! How idiotic you are! (*The music stops, and* ALGERNON *enters cheerily.*)

ALGERNON Didn't it go off all right, old boy? You don't mean to say Gwendolen refused you? I know it is a way she has. She is always refusing people. I think it is most ill-natured of her.

JACK Oh, Gwendolen is as right as a trivet. As far as she is concerned, we are engaged. Her mother is perfectly unbearable. Never met such a Gorgon . . . I don't really know what a Gorgon is like, but I am quite sure that Lady Bracknell is one. In any case, she is a monster, without being a myth, which is rather unfair. . . . I beg your pardon, Algy, I suppose I shouldn't talk about your own aunt in that way before you.

ALGERNON My dear boy, I love hearing my relations abused. It is the only thing that makes me put up with them at all. Relations are simply a tedious pack of people, who haven't got the remotest knowledge of how to live, nor the smallest instinct about when to die.

JACK Oh, that is nonsense!

ALGERNON It isn't!

JACK Well, I won't argue about the matter. You always want to argue about things.

ALGERNON That is exactly what things were originally made for.

JACK Upon my word, if I thought that, I'd shoot myself . . . (*A pause.*) You don't think there is any chance of Gwendolen becoming like her mother in about a hundred and fifty years, do you, Algy?

ALGERNON All women become like their mothers. That is their tragedy. No man does. That's his.

JACK Is that clever?

ALGERNON It is perfectly phrased! and quite as true as any observation in civilized life should be.

JACK I am sick to death of cleverness. Everybody is clever now-a-days. You can't go anywhere without meeting clever people. The thing has become an absolute public nuisance. I wish to goodness we had a few fools left.

ALGERNON We have.

JACK I should extremely like to meet them. What do they talk about?

ALGERNON The fools? Oh! about the clever people, of course.

JACK What fools!

ALGERNON By the way, did you tell Gwendolen the truth about your being Ernest in town, and Jack in the country?

JACK (*in a very patronizing manner*) My dear fellow, the truth isn't quite the sort of thing one tells to a nice, sweet, refined girl. What extraordinary ideas you have about the way to behave to a woman!

ALGERNON The only way to behave to a woman is to make love to her, if she is pretty, and to some one else if she is plain.

JACK Oh, that is nonsense.

ALGERNON What about your brother? What about the profligate Ernest?

JACK Oh, before the end of the week I shall have got rid of him. I'll say he died in Paris of apoplexy. Lots of people die of apoplexy, quite suddenly, don't they?

ALGERNON Yes, but it's hereditary, my dear fellow. It's a sort of thing that runs in families. You had much better say a severe chill.

JACK You are sure a severe chill isn't hereditary, or anything of that kind?

ALGERNON Of course it isn't!

JACK Very well, then. My poor brother Ernest is carried off suddenly in Paris, by a severe chill. That gets rid of him.

ALGERNON But I thought you said that . . . Miss Cardew was a little too much interested in your poor brother Ernest? Won't she feel his loss a good deal?

JACK Oh, that is all right. Cecily is not a silly, romantic girl, I am glad to say. She has got a capital appetite, goes for long walks, and pays no attention at all to her lessons.

ALGERNON I would rather like to see Cecily.

JACK I will take very good care you never do. She is excessively pretty, and she is only just eighteen.

ALGERNON Have you told Gwendolen yet that you have an excessively pretty ward who is only just eighteen?

JACK Oh, one doesn't blurt these things out to people. Cecily and Gwendolen are perfectly certain to be extremely great friends. I'll bet you anything you like that half an hour after they have met, they will be calling each other sister.

ALGERNON Women only do that when they have called each other a lot of other things first. Now, my dear boy, if we want to get a good table at Willis's, we really must go and dress. Do you know it is nearly seven?

JACK (*irritably*) Oh! it always is nearly seven.

ALGERNON Well, I'm hungry.

JACK I never knew you when you weren't. . . .

ALGERNON What shall we do after dinner? Go to a theater?

JACK Oh, no! I loathe listening.

ALGERNON Well, let us go to the Club?

JACK Oh, no! I hate talking.

ALGERNON Well, we might trot round to the Empire at ten?

JACK Oh, no! I can't bear looking at things. It is so silly.

ALGERNON Well, what shall we do?

JACK Nothing!

ALGERNON It is awfully hard work doing nothing. However, I don't mind hard work where there is no definite object of any kind.

*Enter* LANE.

LANE Miss Fairfax.

*Enter* GWENDOLEN. LANE *goes out.*

ALGERNON Gwendolen, upon my word!

GWENDOLEN Algy, kindly turn your back. I have something very particular to say to Mr. Worthing.

ALGERNON Really, Gwendolen, I don't think I can allow this at all.

GWENDOLEN Algy, you always adopt a strictly immoral attitude towards life. You are not quite old enough to do that. (ALGERNON *retires to the fireplace.*)

JACK My own darling!

GWENDOLEN Ernest, we may never be married. From the expression on mamma's face I fear we never shall. Few parents now-a-days pay any regard to what their children say to them. The old-fashioned respect for the young is fast dying out. Whatever influence I ever had over mamma, I lost at the age of three. But although she may prevent us from becoming man and wife, and I may marry some one else, and marry often, nothing that she can possibly do can alter my eternal devotion to you.

JACK Dear Gwendolen.

GWENDOLEN The story of your romantic origin, as related to me by mamma, with unpleasing comments, has naturally stirred the deeper fibers of my nature. Your Christian name has an irresistible fascination. The simplicity of your character makes you exquisitely incomprehensible to me. Your town address at the Albany I have. What is your address in the country?

JACK The Manor House, Woolton, Hertfordshire. (ALGERNON, *who has been carefully listening, smiles to himself, and writes the address on his shirt-cuff. Then picks up the Railway Guide.*)

GWENDOLEN There is a good postal service, I suppose? It may be necessary to do something desperate. That, of course, will require serious consideration. I will communicate with you daily.

JACK My own one!

GWENDOLEN How long do you remain in town?

JACK Till Monday.

GWENDOLEN Good! Algy, you may turn round now.

ALGERNON Thanks, I've turned round already.

GWENDOLEN You may also ring the bell.

JACK You will let me see you to your carriage, my own darling?

GWENDOLEN Certainly.

JACK (*to* LANE, *who now enters*) I will see Miss Fairfax out.

LANE Yes, sir. (JACK *and* GWENDOLEN *go off.* LANE *presents several letters on a salver to* ALGERNON. *It is to be surmised that they are bills, as* ALGERNON, *after looking at the envelopes, tears them up.*)

ALGERNON A glass of sherry, Lane.

LANE Yes, sir.

ALGERNON To-morrow, Lane. I'm going Bunburying.

LANE Yes, sir.

ALGERNON I shall probably not be back till Monday. You can put up my dress clothes, my smoking jacket, and all the Bunbury suits . . .

LANE Yes, sir. (*Handing sherry.*)

ALGERNON I hope to-morrow will be a fine day, Lane.

LANE It never is, sir.

ALGERNON Lane, you're a perfect pessimist.

LANE I do my best to give satisfaction, sir.

*Enter* JACK. LANE *goes off.*

JACK There's a sensible, intellectual girl! the only girl I ever cared for in my life. (ALGERNON *is laughing immoderately.*) What on earth are you so amused at?

ALGERNON Oh, I'm a little anxious about poor Bunbury, that's all.

JACK If you don't take care, your friend Bunbury will get you into a serious scrape some day.

ALGERNON I love scrapes. They are the only things that are never serious.

JACK Oh, that's nonsense, Algy. You never talk anything but nonsense.

ALGERNON Nobody ever does. (JACK *looks indignantly at him, and leaves the room.* ALGERNON *lights a cigarette, reads his shirt-cuff and smiles.*)

*Curtain*

## ACT II

SCENE *Garden at the Manor House. A flight of gray stone steps leads up to the house. The garden, an old-fashioned one, full of roses. Time of year, July. Basket chairs, and a table covered with books, are set under a large yew tree.*

(MISS PRISM *discovered seated at the table.* CECILY *is at the back watering flowers.*)

MISS PRISM (*calling*) Cecily, Cecily! Surely such a utilitarian occupation as the watering of flowers is rather Moulton's duty than yours? Especially at a moment when intellectual pleasures await you. Your German grammar is on the table. Pray open it at page fifteen. We will repeat yesterday's lesson.

CECILY (*coming over very slowly*) But I don't like German. It isn't at all a becoming language. I know perfectly well that I look quite plain after my German lesson.

MISS PRISM Child, you know how anxious your guardian is that you should improve yourself in every way. He laid particular stress on your German, as he was leaving for town yesterday. Indeed, he always lays stress on your German when he is leaving for town.

CECILY Dear Uncle Jack is so very serious! Sometimes he is so serious that I think he cannot be quite well.

MISS PRISM (*drawing herself up*) Your guardian enjoys the best of health, and his gravity of demeanor is especially to be commended in one so comparatively young as he is. I know no one who has a higher sense of duty and responsibility.

CECILY I suppose that is why he often looks a little bored when we three are together.

MISS PRISM Cecily! I am surprised at you. Mr. Worthing has many troubles in his life. Idle merriment and triviality would be out of place in his conversation. You must remember his constant anxiety about that unfortunate young man, his brother.

CECILY I wish Uncle Jack would allow that unfortunate young man, his brother, to come down here sometimes. We might have a good influence over him, Miss Prism. I am sure you certainly would. You know German, and geology, and things of that kind influence a man very much. (CECILY *begins to write in her diary.*)

MISS PRISM (*shaking her head*) I do not think that even I could produce any effect on a character that, according to his own brother's admission, is irretrievably weak and vacillating. Indeed, I am not sure that I would desire to reclaim him. I am not in favor of this modern mania for turning bad people into good people at a moment's notice. As a man sows so let him reap. You must put away your diary, Cecily. I really don't see why you should keep a diary at all.

CECILY I keep a diary in order to enter the wonderful secrets of my life. If I didn't write them down I should probably forget all about them.

MISS PRISM Memory, my dear Cecily, is the diary that we all carry about with us.

CECILY Yes, but it usually chronicles the things that have never happened, and couldn't possibly have happened. I believe that Memory is responsible for nearly all the three-volume novels that Mudie sends us.

MISS PRISM Do not speak slightingly of the three-volume novel, Cecily. I wrote one myself in earlier days.

CECILY Did you really, Miss Prism? How wonderfully clever you are! I hope it did not end happily? I don't like novels that end happily. They depress me so much.

MISS PRISM The good ended happily, and the bad unhappily. That is what Fiction means.

CECILY I suppose so. But it seems very unfair. And was your novel ever published?

MISS PRISM Alas! no. The manuscript unfortunately was abandoned. I use the word in the sense of lost or mislaid. To your work, child, these speculations are profitless.

CECILY (*smiling*) But I see dear Dr. Chasuble coming up through the garden.

MISS PRISM (*rising and advancing*) Dr. Chasuble! This is indeed a pleasure.

*Enter* CANON CHASUBLE.

CHASUBLE And how are we this morning? Miss Prism, you are, I trust, well?

CECILY Miss Prism has just been complaining of a slight headache. I think it would do her so much good to have a short stroll with you in the park, Dr. Chasuble.

MISS PRISM Cecily, I have not mentioned anything about a headache.

CECILY No, dear Miss Prism, I know that, but I felt instinctively that you had a headache. Indeed I was thinking about that, and not about my German lesson, when the Rector came in.

CHASUBLE I hope, Cecily, you are not inattentive.

CECILY Oh, I am afraid I am.

CHASUBLE That is strange. Were I fortunate enough to be Miss Prism's pupil, I would hang upon her lips. (MISS PRISM *glares.*) I spoke metaphorically.—My metaphor was drawn from bees. Ahem! Mr. Worthing, I suppose, has not returned from town yet?

MISS PRISM We do not expect him till Monday afternoon.

CHASUBLE Ah, yes, he usually likes to spend his Sunday in London. He is not one of those whose sole aim is enjoyment, as, by all accounts, that unfortunate young man, his brother, seems to be. But I must not disturb Egeria and her pupil any longer.

MISS PRISM Egeria? My name is Laetitia, Doctor.

CHASUBLE (*bowing*) A classical allusion merely, drawn from the Pagan authors. I shall see you both no doubt at Evensong.

MISS PRISM I think, dear Doctor, I will have a stroll with you. I find I have a headache after all, and a walk might do it good.

CHASUBLE With pleasure, Miss Prism, with pleasure. We might go as far as the schools and back.

MISS PRISM That would be delightful. Cecily, you will read your Political Economy in my absence. The chapter on the Fall of the Rupee you may omit. It is somewhat too sensational. Even these metallic problems have their melodramatic side. (*Goes down the garden with* DR. CHASUBLE.)

CECILY (*picks up books and throws them back on table*) Horrid Political Economy! Horrid Geography! Horrid, horrid German!

*Enter* MERRIMAN *with a card on a salver.*

MERRIMAN Mr. Ernest Worthing has just driven over from the station. He has brought his luggage with him.

CECILY (*takes the card and reads it*) "Mr. Ernest Worthing, B4, The Albany, W." Uncle Jack's brother! Did you tell him Mr. Worthing was in town?

MERRIMAN Yes, Miss. He seemed very much disappointed. I mentioned that you and Miss Prism were in the garden. He said he was anxious to speak to you privately for a moment.

CECILY Ask Mr. Ernest Worthing to come here. I suppose you had better talk to the housekeeper about a room for him.

MERRIMAN Yes, Miss. (MERRIMAN *goes off.*)

CECILY I have never met any really wicked person before. I feel rather frightened. I am so afraid he will look just like every one else.

*Enter* ALGERNON, *very gay and debonair.*

He does!

ALGERNON (*raising his hat*) You are my little cousin Cecily, I'm sure.

CECILY You are under some strange mistake. I am not little. In fact, I am more than usually tall for my age. (ALGERNON *is rather taken aback.*) But I am your cousin Cecily. You, I see from your card, are Uncle Jack's brother, my cousin Ernest, my wicked cousin Ernest.

ALGERNON Oh! I am not really wicked at all, cousin Cecily. You mustn't think that I am wicked.

CECILY If you are not, then you have certainly been deceiving us all in a very inexcusable manner. I hope you have not been leading a double life, pretending to be wicked and being really good all the time. That would be hypocrisy.

ALGERNON (*looks at her in amazement*) Oh! of course I have been rather reckless.

CECILY I am glad to hear it.

ALGERNON In fact, now you mention the subject, I have been very bad in my own small way.

CECILY I don't think you should be so proud of that, though I am sure it must have been very pleasant.

ALGERNON It is much pleasanter being here with you.

CECILY I can't understand how you are here at all. Uncle Jack won't be back till Monday afternoon.

ALGERNON That is a great disappointment. I am obliged to go up by the first train on Monday morning. I have a business appointment that I am anxious . . . to miss.

CECILY Couldn't you miss it anywhere but in London?

ALGERNON No; the appointment is in London.

CECILY Well, I know, of course, how important it is not to keep a business engagement, if one wants to retain any sense of the beauty of life, but still I think you had better wait till Uncle Jack arrives. I know he wants to speak to you about your emigrating.

ALGERNON About my what?

CECILY Your emigrating. He has gone up to buy your outfit.

ALGERNON I certainly wouldn't let Jack buy my outfit. He has no taste in neckties at all.

CECILY I don't think you will require neckties. Uncle Jack is sending you to Australia.

ALGERNON Australia! I'd sooner die.

CECILY Well, he said at dinner on Wednesday night, that you would have to choose between this world, the next world, and Australia.

ALGERNON Oh, well! The accounts I have received of Australia and the next world, are not particularly encouraging. This world is good enough for me, cousin Cecily.

CECILY Yes, but are you good enough for it?

ALGERNON I'm afraid I'm not that. That is why I want you to reform me. You might make that your mission, if you don't mind, cousin Cecily.

CECILY I'm afraid I've not time, this afternoon.

ALGERNON Well, would you mind my reforming myself this afternoon?

CECILY That is rather Quixotic of you. But I think you should try.

ALGERNON I will. I feel better already.

CECILY You are looking a little worse.

ALGERNON That is because I am hungry.

CECILY How thoughtless of me. I should have remembered that when one is going to lead an entirely new life, one requires regular and wholesome meals. Won't you come in?

ALGERNON Thank you. Might I have a button-hole first? I never have any appetite unless I have a button-hole first.

CECILY A Maréchal Niel? (*Picks up scissors.*)

ALGERNON No, I'd sooner have a pink rose.

CECILY Why? (*Cuts a flower.*)

ALGERNON Because you are like a pink rose, cousin Cecily.

CECILY I don't think it can be right for you to talk to me like that. Miss Prism never says such things to me.

ALGERNON Then Miss Prism is a short-sighted old lady. (CECILY *puts the rose in his button-hole.*) You are the prettiest girl I ever saw.

CECILY Miss Prism says that all good looks are a snare.

ALGERNON They are a snare that every sensible man would like to be caught in.

CECILY Oh! I don't think I would care to catch a sensible man. I shouldn't know what to talk to him about. (*They pass into the house.* MISS PRISM *and* DR. CHASUBLE *return.*)

MISS PRISM You are too much alone, dear Dr. Chasuble. You should get married. A misanthrope I can understand—a womanthrope, never!

CHASUBLE (*with a scholar's shudder*) Believe me, I do not deserve so neologistic a phrase. The precept as well as the practice of the Primitive Church was distinctly against matrimony.

MISS PRISM (*sententiously*) That is obviously the reason why the Primitive Church has not lasted up to the present day. And you do not seem to realize, dear Doctor, that by persistently remaining single, a man converts himself into a permanent public temptation. Men should be careful; this very celibacy leads weaker vessels astray.

CHASUBLE But is a man not equally attractive when married?

MISS PRISM No married man is ever attractive except to his wife.

CHASUBLE And often, I've been told, not even to her.

MISS PRISM That depends on the intellectual sympathies of the woman. Maturity can always be depended on. Ripeness can be trusted. Young women are green. (DR. CHASUBLE *starts.*) I spoke horticulturally. My metaphor was drawn from fruits. But where is Cecily?

CHASUBLE Perhaps she followed us to the schools.

*Enter* JACK *slowly from the back of the garden. He is dressed in the deepest mourning, with crape hatband and black gloves.*

MISS PRISM Mr. Worthing!

CHASUBLE Mr. Worthing?

MISS PRISM This is indeed a surprise. We did not look for you till Monday afternoon.

JACK (*shakes* MISS PRISM's *hand in a tragic manner*) I have returned sooner than I expected. Dr. Chasuble, I hope you are well?

CHASUBLE Dear Mr. Worthing, I trust this garb of woe does not betoken some terrible calamity?

JACK My brother.

MISS PRISM More shameful debts and extravagance?

CHASUBLE Still leading his life of pleasure?

JACK (*shaking his head*) Dead!

CHASUBLE Your brother Ernest dead?

JACK Quite dead.

MISS PRISM What a lesson for him! I trust he will profit by it.

CHASUBLE Mr. Worthing, I offer you my sincere condolence. You have at least the consolation of knowing that you were always the most generous and forgiving of brothers.

JACK Poor Ernest! He had many faults, but it is a sad, sad blow.

CHASUBLE Very sad indeed. Were you with him at the end?

JACK No. He died abroad; in Paris, in fact. I had a telegram last night from the manager of the Grand Hotel.

CHASUBLE Was the cause of death mentioned?

JACK A severe chill, it seems.

MISS PRISM As a man sows, so shall he reap.

CHASUBLE (*raising his hand*) Charity, dear Miss Prism, charity! None of us are perfect. I myself am peculiarly susceptible to draughts. Will the interment take place here?

JACK No. He seems to have expressed a desire to be buried in Paris.

CHASUBLE In Paris! (*Shakes his head.*) I fear that hardly points to any very serious state of mind at the last. You would no doubt wish me to make some slight allusion to this tragic domestic affliction next Sunday. (JACK *presses his hand convulsively.*) My sermon on the meaning of the manna in the wilderness can be adapted to almost any occasion, joyful, or, as in the present case, distressing. (*All sigh.*) I have preached it at harvest celebrations, christenings, confirmations, on days of humiliation and festal days. The last time I delivered it was in the Cathedral, as a charity sermon on behalf of the Society for the Prevention of Discontentment among the Upper Orders. The Bishop, who was present, was much struck by some of the analogies I drew.

JACK Ah, that reminds me, you mentioned christenings I think, Dr. Chasuble? I suppose you know how to christen all right? (DR. CHASUBLE *looks astounded.*) I mean, of course, you are continually christening, aren't you?

MISS PRISM It is, I regret to say, one of the Rector's most constant duties in this parish. I have often spoken to the poorer classes on the subject. But they don't seem to know what thrift is.

CHASUBLE But is there any particular infant in whom you are interested, Mr. Worthing? Your brother was, I believe, unmarried, was he not?

JACK Oh, yes.

MISS PRISM (*bitterly*) People who live entirely for pleasure usually are.

JACK But it is not for any child, dear Doctor. I am very fond of children. No! the fact is, I would like to be christened myself, this afternoon, if you have nothing better to do.

CHASUBLE But surely, Mr. Worthing, you have been christened already?

JACK I don't remember anything about it.

CHASUBLE But have you any grave doubts on the subject?

JACK I certainly intend to have. Of course, I don't know if the thing would bother you in any way, or if you think I am a little too old now.

CHASUBLE Not at all. The sprinkling, and, indeed, the immersion of adults is a perfectly canonical practice.

JACK Immersion!

CHASUBLE You need have no apprehensions. Sprinkling is all that is necessary, or indeed I think advisable. Our weather is so changeable. At what hour would you wish the ceremony performed?

JACK Oh, I might trot around about five if that would suit you.

CHASUBLE Perfectly, perfectly! In fact I have two similar ceremonies to perform at that time. A case of twins that occurred recently in one of the outlying cottages on your own estate. Poor Jenkins the carter, a most hard-working man.

JACK Oh! I don't see much fun in being christened along with other babies. It would be childish. Would half-past five do?

CHASUBLE Admirably! Admirably! (*Takes out watch.*) And now, dear Mr. Worthing, I will not intrude any longer into a house of sorrow. I would merely beg you not to be too much bowed down by grief. What seem to us bitter trials at the moment are often blessings in disguise.

MISS PRISM This seems to me a blessing of an extremely obvious kind.

*Enter* CECILY *from the house.*

CECILY Uncle Jack! Oh, I am pleased to see you back. But what horrid clothes you have on! Do go and change them.

MISS PRISM Cecily!

CHASUBLE My child! my child! (CECILY *goes towards* JACK; *he kisses her brow in a melancholy manner.*)

CECILY What is the matter, Uncle Jack? Do look happy! You look as if you had a toothache and I have such a surprise for you. Who do you think is in the dining-room? Your brother!

JACK Who?

CECILY Your brother Ernest. He arrived about half an hour ago.

JACK What nonsense! I haven't got a brother.

CECILY Oh, don't say that. However badly he may have behaved to you in the past he is still your brother. You couldn't be so heartless as to disown him. I'll tell him to come out. And you will shake hands with him, won't you, Uncle Jack? (*Runs back into the house.*)

CHASUBLE These are very joyful tidings.

MISS PRISM After we had all been resigned to his loss, his sudden return seems to me peculiarly distressing.

JACK My brother is in the dining-room? I don't know what it all means. I think it is perfectly absurd.

*Enter* ALGERNON *and* CECILY *hand in hand. They come slowly up to* JACK.

JACK Good heavens! (*Motions* ALGERNON *away.*)

ALGERNON Brother John, I have come down from town to tell you that I am very sorry for all the trouble I have given you, and that I intend to lead a better life in the future. (JACK *glares at him and does not take his hand.*)

CECILY Uncle Jack, you are not going to refuse your own brother's hand?

JACK Nothing will induce me to take his hand. I think his coming down here disgraceful. He knows perfectly well why.

CECILY Uncle Jack, do be nice. There is some good in every one. Ernest has just been telling me about his poor invalid friend, Mr. Bunbury, whom he goes to visit so often. And surely there must be much good in one who is kind to an invalid, and leaves the pleasures of London to sit by a bed of pain.

JACK Oh, he has been talking about Bunbury, has he?

CECILY Yes, he has told me all about poor Mr. Bunbury, and his terrible state of health.

JACK Bunbury! Well, I won't have him talk to you about Bunbury or about anything else. It is enough to drive one perfectly frantic.

ALGERNON Of course I admit that the faults were all on my side. But I must say that I think that Brother John's coldness to me is peculiarly painful. I expected a more enthusiastic welcome, especially considering it is the first time I have come here.

CECILY Uncle Jack, if you don't shake hands with Ernest I will never forgive you.

JACK Never forgive me?

CECILY Never, never, never!

JACK Well, this is the last time I shall ever do it. (*Shakes hands with* ALGERNON *and glares.*)

CHASUBLE It's pleasant, is it not, to see so perfect a reconciliation? I think we might leave the two brothers together.

MISS PRISM Cecily, you will come with us.

CECILY Certainly, Miss Prism. My little task of reconciliation is over.

CHASUBLE You have done a beautiful action to-day, dear child.

MISS PRISM We must not be premature in our judgments.

CECILY I feel very happy. (*They all go off.*)

JACK You young scoundrel, Algy, you must get out of this place as soon as possible. I don't allow any Bunburying here.

*Enter* MERRIMAN.

MERRIMAN I have put Mr. Ernest's things in the room next to yours, sir. I suppose that is all right?

JACK What?

MERRIMAN Mr. Ernest's luggage, sir. I have unpacked it and put it in the room next to your own.

JACK His luggage?

MERRIMAN Yes, sir. Three portmanteaus, a dressing-case, two hat-boxes, and a large luncheon-basket.

ALGERNON I am afraid I can't stay more than a week this time.

JACK Merriman, order the dog-cart at once. Mr. Ernest has been suddenly called back to town.

MERRIMAN Yes, sir. (*Goes back into the house.*)

ALGERNON What a fearful liar you are, Jack. I have not been called back to town at all.

JACK Yes, you have.

ALGERNON I haven't heard any one call me.

JACK Your duty as a gentleman calls you back.

ALGERNON My duty as a gentleman has never interfered with my pleasures in the smallest degree.

JACK I can quite understand that.

ALGERNON Well, Cecily is a darling.

JACK You are not to talk of Miss Cardew like that. I don't like it.

ALGERNON Well, I don't like your clothes. You look perfectly ridiculous in them. Why on earth don't you go up and change? It is perfectly childish to be in deep mourning for a man who is actually staying for a whole week with you in your house as a guest. I call it grotesque.

JACK You are certainly not staying with me for a whole week as a guest or anything else. You have got to leave . . . by the four-five train.

ALGERNON I certainly won't leave you so long as you are in mourning. It would be most unfriendly. If I were in mourning you would stay with me, I suppose. I should think it very unkind if you didn't.

JACK Well, will you go if I change my clothes?

ALGERNON Yes, if you are not too long. I never saw anybody take so long to dress, and with such little result.

JACK Well, at any rate, that is better than being always over-dressed as you are.

ALGERNON If I am occasionally a little over-dressed, I make up for it by being always immensely over-educated.

JACK Your vanity is ridiculous, your conduct an outrage, and your presence in my garden utterly absurd. However, you have got to catch the four-five, and I hope you will have a pleasant journey back to town. This Bunburying, as you call it, has not been a great success for you. (*Goes into the house.*)

ALGERNON I think it has been a great success. I'm in love with Cecily, and that is everything. (*Enter* CECILY *at the back of the garden. She picks up the can and begins to water the flowers.*) But I must see her before I go, and make arrangements for another Bunbury. Ah, there she is.

CECILY Oh, I merely came back to water the roses. I thought you were with Uncle Jack.

ALGERNON He's gone to order the dog-cart for me.

CECILY Oh, is he going to take you for a nice drive?

ALGERNON He's going to send me away.

CECILY Then have we got to part?

ALGERNON I am afraid so. It's a very painful parting.

CECILY It is always painful to part from people whom one has known for a very brief space of time. The absence of old friends one can endure with equanimity. But even a momentary separation from any one to whom one has just been introduced is almost unbearable.

ALGERNON Thank you.

*Enter* MERRIMAN.

MERRIMAN The dog-cart is at the door, sir. (ALGERNON *looks appealingly at* CECILY.)

CECILY It can wait, Merriman . . . for . . . five minutes.

MERRIMAN Yes, miss.

*Exit* MERRIMAN.

ALGERNON I hope, Cecily, I shall not offend you if I state quite frankly and openly that you seem to me to be in every way the visible personification of absolute perfection.

CECILY I think your frankness does you great credit, Ernest. If you will allow me I will copy your remarks into my diary. (*Goes over to table and begins writing in diary.*)

ALGERNON Do you really keep a diary? I'd give anything to look at it. May I?

CECILY Oh, no. (*Puts her hand over it.*) You see it is simply a very young girl's record of her own thoughts and impressions, and consequently meant for publication. When it appears in volume form I hope you will order a copy. But pray, Ernest, don't stop. I delight in taking down from dictation. I have reached "absolute perfection." You can go on. I am quite ready for more.

ALGERNON (*somewhat taken aback*) Ahem! Ahem!

CECILY Oh, don't cough, Ernest. When one is dictating one should speak fluently and not cough. Besides, I don't know how to spell a cough. (*Writes as* ALGERNON *speaks.*)

ALGERNON (*speaking very rapidly*) Cecily, ever since I first looked upon your wonderful and incomparable beauty, I have dared to love you wildly, passionately, devotedly, hopelessly.

CECILY I don't think that you should tell me that you love me wildly, passionately, devotedly, hopelessly. Hopelessly doesn't seem to make much sense, does it?

ALGERNON Cecily!

*Enter* MERRIMAN.

MERRIMAN The dog-cart is waiting, sir.

ALGERNON Tell it to come round next week, at the same hour.

MERRIMAN (*looks at* CECILY, *who makes no sign*) Yes, sir.

MERRIMAN *retires.*

CECILY Uncle Jack would be very much annoyed if he knew you were staying on till next week, at the same hour.

ALGERNON Oh, I don't care about Jack. I don't care for anybody in the whole world but you. I love you, Cecily. You will marry me, won't you?

CECILY You silly you! Of course. Why, we have been engaged for the last three months.

ALGERNON For the last three months?

CECILY Yes, it will be exactly three months on Thursday.

ALGERNON But how did we become engaged?

CECILY Well, ever since dear Uncle Jack first confessed to us that he had a younger brother who was very wicked and bad, you of course have formed the chief topic of conversation between myself and Miss Prism. And of course a man who is much talked about is always very attractive. One feels there must be something in him after all. I daresay it was foolish of me, but I fell in love with you, Ernest.

ALGERNON Darling! And when was the engagement actually settled?

CECILY On the 4th of February last. Worn out by your entire ignorance of my existence, I determined to end the matter one way or the other, and after a long struggle with myself I accepted you under this dear old tree here. The next day I bought this little ring in your name, and this is the little bangle with the true lovers' knot I promised you always to wear.

ALGERNON Did I give you this? It's very pretty, isn't it?

CECILY Yes, you've wonderfully good taste, Ernest. It's the excuse I've always given for your leading such a bad life. And this is the box in which I keep all your dear letters. (*Kneels at table, opens box, and produces letters tied up with blue ribbon.*)

ALGERNON My letters! but my own sweet Cecily, I have never written you any letters.

CECILY You need hardly remind me of that, Ernest. I remember only too well that I was forced to write your letters for you. I wrote always three times a week, and sometimes oftener.

ALGERNON Oh, do let me read them, Cecily?

CECILY Oh, I couldn't possibly. They would make you far too conceited. (*Replaces box.*) The three you wrote me after I had broken off the engagement are so beautiful, and so badly spelled, that even now I can hardly read them without crying a little.

ALGERNON But was our engagement ever broken off?

CECILY Of course it was. On the 22nd of last March. You can see the entry if you like. (*Shows diary.*) "To-day I broke off my engagement with Ernest. I feel it is better to do so. The weather still continues charming."

ALGERNON But why on earth did you break it off? What had I done? I had done nothing at all. Cecily, I am very much hurt indeed to hear you broke it off. Particularly when the weather was so charming.

CECILY It would hardly have been a really serious engagement if it hadn't been broken off at least once. But I forgave you before the week was out.

ALGERNON (*crossing to her, and kneeling*) What a perfect angel you are, Cecily.

CECILY You dear romantic boy. (*He kisses her, she puts her fingers through his hair.*) I hope your hair curls naturally, does it?

ALGERNON Yes, darling, with a little help from others.

CECILY I am so glad.

ALGERNON You'll never break off our engagement again, Cecily?

CECILY I don't think I could break it off now that I have actually met you. Besides, of course, there is the question of your name.

ALGERNON Yes, of course. (*Nervously.*)

CECILY You must not laugh at me, darling, but it had always been a girlish dream of mine to love some one whose name was Ernest. (ALGERNON *rises,* CECILY *also.*) There is something in that name that seems to inspire absolute confidence. I pity any poor married woman whose husband is not called Ernest.

ALGERNON But, my dear child, do you mean to say you could not love me if I had some other name?

CECILY But what name?

ALGERNON Oh, any name you like—Algernon, for instance. . . .

CECILY But I don't like the name of Algernon.

ALGERNON Well, my own dear, sweet, loving little darling, I really can't see why you should object to the name of Algernon. It is not at all a bad name. In fact, it is rather an aristocratic name. Half of the chaps who get into the Bankruptcy Court are called Algernon. But seriously, Cecily . . . (*moving to her*) . . . if my name was Algy, couldn't you love me?

CECILY (*rising*) I might respect you, Ernest, I might admire your character, but I fear that I should not be able to give you my undivided attention.

ALGERNON Ahem! Cecily! (*Picking up hat.*) Your Rector here is, I suppose, thoroughly experienced in the practice of all the rites and ceremonials of the church?

CECILY Oh, yes. Dr. Chasuble is a most learned man. He has never written a single book, so you can imagine how much he knows.

ALGERNON I must see him at once on a most important christening—I mean on most important business.

CECILY Oh!

ALGERNON I sha'n't be away more than half an hour.

CECILY Considering that we have been engaged since February the 14th, and that I only met you to-day for the first time, I think it is rather hard that you should leave me for so long a period as half an hour. Couldn't you make it twenty minutes?

ALGERNON I'll be back in no time. (*Kisses her and rushes down the garden.*)

CECILY What an impetuous boy he is. I like his hair so much. I must enter his proposal in my diary.

*Enter* MERRIMAN.

MERRIMAN A Miss Fairfax has just called to see Mr. Worthing. On very important business, Miss Fairfax states.

CECILY Isn't Mr. Worthing in his library?

MERRIMAN Mr. Worthing went over in the direction of the Rectory some time ago.

CECILY Pray ask the lady to come out here; Mr. Worthing is sure to be back soon. And you can bring tea.

MERRIMAN Yes, miss. (*Goes out.*)

CECILY Miss Fairfax! I suppose one of the many good elderly women who are associated with Uncle Jack in some of his philanthropic work in London. I don't quite like women who are interested in philanthropic work. I think it is so forward of them.

*Enter* MERRIMAN.

MERRIMAN Miss Fairfax.

*Enter* GWENDOLEN. *Exit* MERRIMAN.

CECILY (*advancing to meet her*) Pray let me introduce myself to you. My name is Cecily Cardew.

GWENDOLEN Cecily Cardew? (*Moving to her and shaking hands.*) What a very sweet name! Something tells me that we are going to be great friends. I like you already more than I can say. My first impressions of people are never wrong.

CECILY How nice of you to like me so much after we have known each other such a comparatively short time. Pray sit down.

GWENDOLEN (*still standing up*) I may call you Cecily, may I not?

CECILY With pleasure!

GWENDOLEN And you will always call me Gwendolen, won't you?

CECILY If you wish.

GWENDOLEN Then that is all quite settled, is it not?

CECILY I hope so. (*A pause; they both sit down together.*)

GWENDOLEN Perhaps this might be a favorable opportunity for my mentioning who I am. My father is Lord Bracknell. You have never heard of papa, I suppose?

CECILY I don't think so.

GWENDOLEN Outside the family circle, papa, I am glad to say, is entirely unknown. I think that is quite as it should be. The home seems to me to be the proper sphere for the man. And certainly once a man begins to neglect his domestic duties he becomes painfully effeminate, does he not? And I don't like that. It makes men so very attractive. Cecily, mamma, whose views on education are remarkably strict, has brought me up to be extremely short-sighted; it is part of her system; so do you mind my looking at you through my glasses?

CECILY Oh, not at all, Gwendolen. I am very fond of being looked at.

GWENDOLEN (*after examining* CECILY *carefully through a lorgnette*) You are here on a short visit, I suppose.

CECILY Oh, no, I live here.

GWENDOLEN (*severely*) Really? Your mother, no doubt, or some female relative of advanced years, resides here also?

CECILY Oh, no. I have no mother, nor, in fact, any relations.

GWENDOLEN Indeed?

CECILY My dear guardian, with the assistance of Miss Prism, has the arduous task of looking after me.

GWENDOLEN Your guardian?

CECILY Yes, I am Mr. Worthing's ward.

GWENDOLEN Oh! It is strange he never mentioned to me that he had a ward. How secretive of him! He grows more interesting hourly. I am not sure, however, that the news inspires me with feelings of unmixed delight. (*Rising and going to her.*) I am very fond of you, Cecily; I have liked you ever since I met you. But I am bound to state that now that I know that you are Mr. Worthing's ward, I cannot help expressing a wish you were—well, just a little older than you seem to be—and not quite so very alluring in appearance. In fact, if I may speak candidly—

CECILY Pray do! I think that whenever one has anything unpleasant to say, one should always be quite candid.

GWENDOLEN Well, to speak with perfect candor, Cecily, I wish that you were fully forty-two, and more than usually plain for your age. Ernest has a strong upright nature. He is the very soul of truth and honor.

Disloyalty would be as impossible to him as deception. But even men of the noblest possible moral character are extremely susceptible to the influence of the physical charms of others. Modern, no less than Ancient History, supplies us with many most painful examples of what I refer to. If it were not so, indeed, History would be quite unreadable.

CECILY I beg your pardon, Gwendolen, did you say Ernest?

GWENDOLEN Yes.

CECILY Oh, but it is not Mr. Ernest Worthing who is my guardian. It is his brother—his elder brother.

GWENDOLEN (*sitting down again*) Ernest never mentioned to me that he had a brother.

CECILY I am sorry to say they have not been on good terms for a long time.

GWENDOLEN Ah! that accounts for it. And now that I think of it I have never heard any man mention his brother. The subject seems distasteful to most men. Cecily, you have lifted a load from my mind. I was growing almost anxious. It would have been terrible if any cloud had come across a friendship like ours, would it not? Of course you are quite, quite sure that it is not Mr. Ernest Worthing who is your guardian?

CECILY Quite sure. (*A pause.*) In fact, I am going to be his.

GWENDOLEN (*enquiringly*) I beg your pardon?

CECILY (*rather shy and confidingly*) Dearest Gwendolen, there is no reason why I should make a secret of it to you. Our little county newspaper is sure to chronicle the fact next week. Mr. Ernest Worthing and I are engaged to be married.

GWENDOLEN (*quite politely, rising*) My darling Cecily, I think there must be some slight error. Mr. Ernest Worthing is engaged to me. The announcement will appear in the *Morning Post* on Saturday at the latest.

CECILY (*very politely, rising*) I am afraid you must be under some misconception. Ernest proposed to me exactly ten minutes ago. (*Shows diary.*)

GWENDOLEN (*examines diary through her lorgnette carefully*) It is certainly very curious, for he asked me to be his wife yesterday afternoon at 5:30. If you would care to verify the incident, pray do so. (*Produces diary of her own.*) I never travel without my diary. One should always have something sensational to read in the train. I am so sorry, dear Cecily, if it is any disappointment to you, but I'm afraid *I* have the prior claim.

CECILY It would distress me more than I can tell you, dear Gwendolen, if it caused you any mental or physical anguish, but I feel bound to point out that since Ernest proposed to you he clearly has changed his mind.

GWENDOLEN (*meditatively*) If the poor fellow has been entrapped into any foolish promise I shall consider it my duty to rescue him at once, and with a firm hand.

CECILY (*thoughtfully and sadly*) Whatever unfortunate entanglement my dear boy may have got into, I will never reproach him with it after we are married.

GWENDOLEN Do you allude to me, Miss Cardew, as an entanglement? You are presumptuous. On an occasion of this kind it becomes more than a moral duty to speak one's mind. It becomes a pleasure.

CECILY Do you suggest, Miss Fairfax, that I entrapped Ernest into an engagement? How dare you? This is no time for wearing the shallow mask of manners. When I see a spade I call it a spade.

GWENDOLEN (*satirically*) I am glad to say that I have never seen a spade. It is obvious that our social spheres have been widely different.

*Enter* MERRIMAN, *followed by the footman. He carries a salver, table-cloth, and plate-stand.* CECILY *is about to retort. The presence of the servants exercises a restraining influence, under which both girls chafe.*

MERRIMAN Shall I lay tea here as usual, miss?

CECILY (*sternly, in a calm voice*) Yes, as usual. (MERRIMAN *begins to clear and lay cloth. A long pause.* CECILY *and* GWENDOLEN *glare at each other.*)

GWENDOLEN Are there many interesting walks in the vicinity, Miss Cardew?

CECILY Oh, yes, a great many. From the top of one of the hills quite close one can see five counties.

GWENDOLEN Five counties! I don't think I should like that. I hate crowds.

CECILY (*sweetly*) I suppose that is why you live in town? (GWENDOLYN *bites her lip, and beats her foot nervously with her parasol.*)

GWENDOLEN (*looking round*) Quite a well-kept garden this is, Miss Cardew.

CECILY So glad you like it, Miss Fairfax.

GWENDOLEN I had no idea there were any flowers in the country.

CECILY Oh, flowers are as common here, Miss Fairfax, as people are in London.

GWENDOLEN Personally I cannot understand how anybody manages to exist in the country, if anybody who is anybody does. The country always bores me to death.

CECILY Ah! This is what the newspapers call agricultural depression, is it not? I believe the aristocracy are suffering very much from it just at present. It is almost an epidemic amongst them, I have been told. May I offer you some tea, Miss Fairfax?

GWENDOLEN (*with elaborate politeness*) Thank you. (*Aside.*) Detestable girl! But I require tea!

CECILY (*sweetly*) Sugar?

GWENDOLEN (*superciliously*) No, thank you. Sugar is not fashionable any more. (CECILY *looks angrily at her, takes up the tongs and puts four lumps of sugar into the cup.*)

CECILY (*severely*) Cake or bread and butter?

GWENDOLEN (*in a bored manner*) Bread and butter, please. Cake is rarely seen at the best houses now-a-days.

CECILY (*cuts a very large slice of cake, and puts it on the tray*). Hand that to Miss Fairfax. (MERRIMAN *does so, and goes out with footman.* GWENDOLEN *drinks the tea and makes a grimace. Puts down cup at once, reaches out her hand to the bread and butter, looks at it, and finds it is cake. Rises in indignation.*)

GWENDOLEN You have filled my tea with lumps of sugar, and though I asked most distinctly for bread and butter, you have given me cake. I am known for the gentleness of my disposition, and the extraordinary sweetness of my nature, but I warn you, Miss Cardew, you may go too far.

CECILY (*rising*) To save my poor, innocent, trusting boy from the machinations of any other girl there are no lengths to which I would not go.

GWENDOLEN From the moment I saw you I distrusted you. I felt that you were false and deceitful. I am never deceived in such matters. My first impressions of people are invariably right.

CECILY It seems to me, Miss Fairfax, that I am trespassing on your valuable time. No doubt you have many other calls of a similar character to make in the neighborhood.

*Enter* JACK.

GWENDOLEN (*catching sight of him*) Ernest! My own Ernest!

JACK Gwendolen! Darling! (*Offers to kiss her.*)

GWENDOLEN (*drawing back*) A moment! May I ask if you are engaged to be married to this young lady? (*Points to* CECILY.)

JACK (*laughing*) To dear little Cecily! Of course not! What could have put such an idea into your pretty little head?

GWENDOLEN Thank you. You may. (*Offers her cheek.*)

CECILY (*very sweetly*) I knew there must be some misunderstanding, Miss Fairfax. The gentleman whose arm is at present around your waist is my dear guardian, Mr. John Worthing.

GWENDOLEN I beg your pardon?

CECILY This is Uncle Jack.

GWENDOLEN (*receding*) Jack! Oh!

*Enter* ALGERNON.

CECILY Here is Ernest.

ALGERNON (*goes straight over to* CECILY *without noticing any one else*) My own love! (*Offers to kiss her.*)

CECILY (*drawing back*) A moment, Ernest! May I ask you—are you engaged to be married to this young lady?

ALGERNON (*looking round*) To what young lady? Good heavens! Gwendolen!

CECILY Yes, to good heavens, Gwendolen, I mean to Gwendolen.

ALGERNON (*laughing*) Of course not! What could have put such an idea into your pretty little head?

CECILY Thank you. (*Presenting her cheek to be kissed.*) You may. (ALGERNON *kisses her.*)

GWENDOLEN I felt there was some slight error, Miss Cardew. The gentleman who is now embracing you is my cousin, Mr. Algernon Moncrieff.

CECILY (*breaking away from* ALGERNON) Algernon Moncrieff! Oh! (*The two girls move towards each other and put their arms round each other's waists as if for protection.*)

CECILY Are you called Algernon?

ALGERNON I cannot deny it.

CECILY Oh!

GWENDOLEN Is your name really John?

JACK (*standing rather proudly*) I could deny it if I liked. I could deny anything if I liked. But my name certainly is John. It has been John for years.

CECILY (*to* GWENDOLEN) A gross deception has been practiced on both of us.

GWENDOLEN My poor wounded Cecily!

CECILY My sweet, wronged Gwendolen!

GWENDOLEN (*slowly and seriously*) You will call me sister, will you not? (*They embrace.* JACK *and* ALGERNON *groan and walk up and down.*)

CECILY (*rather brightly*) There is just one question I would like to be allowed to ask my guardian.

GWENDOLEN An admirable idea! Mr. Worthing, there is just one question I would like to be permitted to put to you. Where is your brother Ernest? We are both engaged to be married to your brother Ernest, so it is a matter of some importance to us to know where your brother Ernest is at present.

JACK (*slowly and hesitatingly*) Gwendolen—Cecily—it is very painful for me to be forced to speak the truth. It is the first time in my life that I have ever been reduced to such a painful position, and I am really quite inexperienced in doing anything of the kind. However I will tell you quite frankly that I have no brother Ernest. I have no brother at all. I never had a brother in my life, and I certainly have not the smallest intention of ever having one in the future.

CECILY (*surprised*) No brother at all?

JACK (*cheerily*) None!

GWENDOLEN (*severely*) Had you never a brother of any kind?

JACK (*pleasantly*) Never. Not even of any kind.

GWENDOLEN I am afraid it is quite clear, Cecily, that neither of us is engaged to be married to any one.

CECILY It is not a very pleasant position for a young girl suddenly to find herself in. Is it?

GWENDOLEN Let us go into the house. They will hardly venture to come after us there.

CECILY No, men are so cowardly, aren't they? (*They retire into the house with scornful looks.*)

JACK This ghastly state of things is what you call Bunburying, I suppose?

ALGERNON Yes, and a perfectly wonderful Bunbury it is. The most wonderful Bunbury I have ever had in my life.

JACK Well, you've no right whatsoever to Bunbury here.

ALGERNON That is absurd. One has a right to Bunbury anywhere one chooses. Every serious Bunburyist knows that.

JACK Serious Bunburyist! Good heavens!

ALGERNON Well, one must be serious about something, if one wants to have any amusement in life. I happen to be serious about Bunburying. What on earth you are serious about I haven't got the remotest idea. About everything, I should fancy. You have such an absolutely trivial nature.

JACK Well, the only small satisfaction I have in the whole of this wretched business is that your friend Bunbury is quite exploded. You won't be able to run down to the country quite so often as you used to do, dear Algy. And a very good thing, too.

ALGERNON Your brother is a little off color, isn't he, dear Jack? You won't be able to disappear to London quite so frequently as your wicked custom was. And not a bad thing, either.

JACK As for your conduct towards Miss Cardew, I must say that your taking in a sweet, simple, innocent girl like that is quite inexcusable. To say nothing of the fact that she is my ward.

ALGERNON I can see no possible defense at all for your deceiving a brilliant, clever, thoroughly experienced young lady like Miss Fairfax. To say nothing of the fact that she is my cousin.

JACK I wanted to be engaged to Gwendolen, that is all. I love her.

ALGERNON Well, I simply wanted to be engaged to Cecily. I adore her.

JACK There is certainly no chance of your marrying Miss Cardew.

ALGERNON I don't think there is much likelihood, Jack, of you and Miss Fairfax being united.

JACK Well, that is no business of yours.

ALGERNON If it was my business, I wouldn't talk about it. (*Begins to eat muffins.*) It is very vulgar to talk about one's business. Only people like stock-brokers do that, and then merely at dinner parties.

JACK How you can sit there, calmly eating muffins, when we are in this horrible trouble, I can't make out. You seem to me to be perfectly heartless.

ALGERNON Well, I can't eat muffins in an agitated manner. The butter would probably get on my cuffs. One should always eat muffins quite calmly. It is the only way to eat them.

JACK I say it's perfectly heartless your eating muffins at all, under the circumstances.

ALGERNON When I am in trouble, eating is the only thing that consoles me. Indeed, when I am in really great trouble, as any one who knows me intimately will tell you, I refuse everything except food and drink. At the present moment I am eating muffins because I am unhappy. Besides, I am particularly fond of muffins. (*Rising.*)

JACK (*rising*) Well, that is no reason why you should eat them all in that greedy way. (*Takes muffins from* ALGERNON.)

ALGERNON (*offering tea-cake*) I wish you would have tea-cake instead. I don't like tea-cake.

JACK Good heavens! I suppose a man may eat his own muffins in his own garden.

ALGERNON But you have just said it was perfectly heartless to eat muffins.

JACK I said it was perfectly heartless of you, under the circumstances. That is a very different thing.

ALGERNON That may be. But the muffins are the same. (*He seizes the muffin-dish from* JACK.)

JACK Algy, I wish to goodness you would go.

ALGERNON You can't possibly ask me to go without having some dinner. It's absurd. I never go without my dinner. No one ever does, except vegetarians, and people like that. Besides I have just made arrangements with Dr. Chasuble to be christened at a quarter to six under the name of Ernest.

JACK My dear fellow, the sooner you give up that nonsense the better. I made arrangements this morning with Dr. Chasuble to be christened myself at 5:30, and I naturally will take the name of Ernest. Gwendolen would wish it. We can't both be christened Ernest. It's absurd. Besides, I have a perfect right to be christened if I like. There is no evidence at all that I ever have been christened by anybody. I should think it extremely probable I never was, and so does Dr. Chasuble. It is entirely different in your case. You have been christened already.

ALGERNON Yes, but I have not been christened for years.

JACK Yes, but you have been christened. That is the important thing.

ALGERNON Quite so. So I know my constitution can stand it. If you are not quite sure about your ever having been christened, I must say I think it rather dangerous your venturing on it now. It might make you very unwell. You can hardly have forgotten that some one very closely connected with you was very nearly carried off this week in Paris by a severe chill.

JACK Yes, but you said yourself that a severe chill was not hereditary.

ALGERNON It usedn't to be, I know—but I daresay it is now. Science is always making wonderful improvements in things.

JACK (*picking up the muffin-dish*) Oh, that is nonsense, you are always talking nonsense.

ALGERNON Jack, you are at the muffins again! I wish you wouldn't. There are only two left. (*Takes them.*) I told you I was particularly fond of muffins.

JACK But I hate tea-cake.

ALGERNON Why on earth then do you allow tea-cake to be served up for your guests? What ideas you have of hospitality!

JACK Algernon! I have already told you to go. I don't want you here. Why don't you go?

ALGERNON I haven't quite finished my tea yet, and there is still one muffin left. (JACK *groans, and sinks into a chair.* ALGERNON *still continues eating.*)

*Curtain*

## ACT III

SCENE *Morning-room at the Manor House.* GWENDOLEN *and* CECILY *are at the window, looking out into the garden.*

GWENDOLEN The fact that they did not follow us at once into the house, as any one else would have done, seems to me to show that they have some sense of shame left.

CECILY They have been eating muffins. That looks like repentance.

GWENDOLEN (*after a pause*) They don't seem to notice us at all. Couldn't you cough?

GWENDOLEN They're looking at us. What effrontery!

CECILY They're approaching. That's very forward of them.

GWENDOLEN Let us preserve a dignified silence.

CECILY Certainly. It's the only thing to do now.

*Enter* JACK, *followed by* ALGERNON. *They whistle some dreadful popular air from a British opera.*

GWENDOLEN This dignified silence seems to produce an unpleasant effect.

CECILY A most distasteful one.

GWENDOLEN But we will not be the first to speak.

CECILY Certainly not.

GWENDOLEN Mr. Worthing, I have something very particular to ask you. Much depends on your reply.

CECILY Gwendolen, your common sense is invaluable. Mr. Moncrieff, kindly answer me the following question. Why did you pretend to be my guardian's brother?

ALGERNON In order that I might have an opportunity of meeting you.

CECILY (*to* GWENDOLEN) That certainly seems a satisfactory explanation, does it not?

GWENDOLEN Yes, dear, if you can believe him.

CECILY I don't. But that does not affect the wonderful beauty of his answer.

GWENDOLEN True. In matters of grave importance, style, not sincerity, is the vital thing. Mr. Worthing, what explanation can you offer to me for pretending to have a brother? Was it in order that you might have an opportunity of coming up to town to see me as often as possible?

JACK Can you doubt it, Miss Fairfax?

GWENDOLEN I have the gravest doubts upon the subject. But I intend to crush them. This is not the moment for German skepticism. (*Moving to* CECILY.) Their explanations appear to be quite satisfactory, especially Mr. Worthing's. That seems to me to have the stamp of truth upon it.

CECILY I am more than content with what Mr. Moncrieff said. His voice alone inspires one with absolute credulity.

GWENDOLEN Then you think we should forgive them?

CECILY Yes. I mean no.

GWENDOLEN True! I had forgotten. There are principles at stake that one cannot surrender. Which of us should tell them? The task is not a pleasant one.

CECILY Could we not both speak at the same time?

GWENDOLEN An excellent idea! I nearly always speak at the same time as other people. Will you take the time from me?

CECILY Certainly. (GWENDOLEN *beats time with uplifted finger.*)

GWENDOLEN *and* CECILY (*speaking together*) Your Christian names are still an insuperable barrier. That is all!

JACK and ALGERNON (*speaking together*) Our Christian names! Is that all? But we are going to be christened this afternoon.

GWENDOLEN (*to* JACK) For my sake you are prepared to do this terrible thing?

JACK I am.

CECILY (*to* ALGERNON) To please me you are ready to face this fearful ordeal?

ALGERNON I am!

GWENDOLEN How absurd to talk of the equality of the sexes! Where questions of self-sacrifice are concerned, men are infinitely beyond us.

JACK We are. (*Clasps hands with* ALGERNON.)

CECILY They have moments of physical courage of which we women know absolutely nothing.

GWENDOLEN (*to* JACK) Darling!

ALGERNON (*to* CECILY) Darling! (*They fall into each other's arms.*)

*Enter* MERRIMAN. *When he enters he coughs loudly, seeing the situation.*

MERRIMAN Ahem! Ahem! Lady Bracknell!
JACK Good heavens!

*Enter* LADY BRACKNELL. *The couples separate in alarm. Exit* MERRIMAN.

LADY BRACKNELL Gwendolen! What does this mean?
GWENDOLEN Merely that I am engaged to be married to Mr. Worthing, mamma.
LADY BRACKNELL Come here. Sit down. Sit down immediately. Hesitation of any kind is a sign of mental decay in the young, of physical weakness in the old. (*Turns to* JACK.) Apprised, sir, of my daughter's sudden flight by her trusty maid, whose confidence I purchased by means of a small coin, I followed her at once by a luggage train. Her unhappy father is, I am glad to say, under the impression that she is attending a more than usually lengthy lecture by the University Extension Scheme on the Influence of a Permanent Income on Thought. I do not propose to undeceive him. Indeed I have never undeceived him on any question. I would consider it wrong. But of course you will clearly understand that all communication between yourself and my daughter must cease immediately from this moment. On this point, as indeed on all points, I am firm.
JACK I am engaged to be married to Gwendolen, Lady Bracknell!
LADY BRACKNELL You are nothing of the kind, sir. And now, as regards Algernon! . . . Algernon!
ALGERNON Yes, Aunt Augusta.
LADY BRACKNELL May I ask if it is in this house that your invalid friend Mr. Bunbury resides?
ALGERNON (*stammering*) Oh, no! Bunbury doesn't live here. Bunbury is somewhere else at present. In fact, Bunbury is dead.
LADY BRACKNELL Dead! When did Mr. Bunbury die? His death must have been extremely sudden.
ALGERNON (*airily*) Oh, I killed Bunbury this afternoon. I mean poor Bunbury died this afternoon.
LADY BRACKNELL What did he die of?
ALGERNON Bunbury? Oh, he was quite exploded.
LADY BRACKNELL Exploded! Was he the victim of a revolutionary outrage? I was not aware that Mr. Bunbury was interested in social legislation. If so, he is well punished for his morbidity.
ALGERNON My dear Aunt Augusta, I mean he was found out! The doctors found out that Bunbury could not live, that is what I mean—so Bunbury died.
LADY BRACKNELL He seems to have had great confidence in the opinion of his physicians. I am glad, however, that he made up his mind at

the last to some definite course of action, and acted under proper medical advice. And now that we have finally got rid of this Mr. Bunbury, may I ask, Mr. Worthing, who is that young person whose hand my nephew Algernon is now holding in what seems to me a peculiarly unnecessary manner?

JACK That lady is Miss Cecily Cardew, my ward. (LADY BRACKNELL *bows coldly to* CECILY.)

ALGERNON I am engaged to be married to Cecily, Aunt Augusta.

LADY BRACKNELL I beg your pardon?

CECILY Mr. Moncrieff and I are engaged to be married, Lady Bracknell.

LADY BRACKNELL (*with a shiver, crossing to the sofa and sitting down*) I do not know whether there is anything peculiarly exciting in the air of this particular part of Hertfordshire, but the number of engagements that go on seems to me considerably above the proper average that statistics have laid down for our guidance. I think some preliminary enquiry on my part would not be out of place. Mr. Worthing, is Miss Cardew at all connected with any of the larger railway stations in London? I merely desire information. Until yesterday I had no idea that there were any families or persons whose origin was a Terminus. (JACK *looks perfectly furious, but restrains himself.*)

JACK (*in a clear, cold voice*) Miss Cardew is the granddaughter of the late Mr. Thomas Cardew of 149, Belgrave Square, S.W.; Gervase Park, Dorking, Surrey; and the Sporran, Fifeshire, N.B.

LADY BRACKNELL That sounds not unsatisfactory. Three addresses always inspire confidence, even in tradesmen. But what proof have I of their authenticity?

JACK I have carefully preserved the Court Guides of the period. They are open to your inspection, Lady Bracknell.

LADY BRACKNELL (*grimly*) I have known strange errors in that publication.

JACK Miss Cardew's family solicitors are Messrs. Markby, Markby, and Markby.

LADY BRACKNELL Markby, Markby, and Markby? A firm of the very highest position in their profession. Indeed I am told that one of the Mr. Markbys is occasionally to be seen at dinner parties. So far I am satisfied.

JACK (*very irritably*) How extremely kind of you, Lady Bracknell! I have also in my possession, you will pleased to hear, certificates of Miss Cardew's birth, baptism, whooping cough, registration, vaccination, confirmation, and the measles; both the German and the English variety.

LADY BRACKNELL Ah! A life crowded with incident, I see; though perhaps somewhat too exciting for a young girl. I am not myself in favor of premature experiences. (*Rises, looks at her watch.*) Gwendolen! the time approaches for our departure. We have not a moment to lose. As a matter of form, Mr. Worthing, I had better ask you if Miss Cardew has any little fortune?

JACK Oh, about a hundred and thirty thousand pounds in the Funds. That is all. Goodby, Lady Bracknell. So pleased to have seen you.

LADY BRACKNELL (*sitting down again*) A moment, Mr. Worthing. A hundred and thirty thousand pounds! And in the Funds! Miss Cardew seems to me a most attractive young lady, now that I look at her. Few girls of the present day have any really solid qualities, any of the qualities that last, and improve with time. We live, I regret to say, in an age of surfaces. (*To* CECILY.) Come over here, dear. (CECILY *goes across.*) Pretty child! your dress is sadly simple, and your hair seems almost as Nature might have left it. But we can soon alter all that. A thoroughly experienced French maid produces a really marvelous result in a very brief space of time. I remember recommending one to young Lady Lancing, and after three months her own husband did not know her.

JACK (*aside*) And after six months nobody knew her.

LADY BRACKNELL (*glares at* JACK *for a few moments, then bends, with a practiced smile, to* CECILY) Kindly turn round, sweet child. (CECILY *turns completely round.*) No, the side view is what I want. (CECILY *presents her profile.*) Yes, quite as I expected. There are distinct social possibilities in your profile. The two weak points in our age are its want of principle and its want of profile. The chin a little higher, dear. Style largely depends on the way the chin is worn. They are worn very high, just at present. Algernon!

ALGERNON Yes, Aunt Augusta!

LADY BRACKNELL There are distinct social possibilities in Miss Cardew's profile.

ALGERNON Cecily is the sweetest, dearest, prettiest girl in the whole world. And I don't care twopence about social possibilities.

LADY BRACKNELL Never speak disrespectfully of society, Algernon. Only people who can't get into it do that. (*To* CECILY.) Dear child, of course you know that Algernon has nothing but his debts to depend upon. But I do not approve of mercenary marriages. When I married Lord Bracknell I had no fortune of any kind. But I never dreamed for a moment of allowing that to stand in my way. Well, I suppose I must give my consent.

ALGERNON Thank you, Aunt Augusta.

LADY BRACKNELL Cecily, you may kiss me!

CECILY (*kisses her*) Thank you, Lady Bracknell.

LADY BRACKNELL You may address me as Aunt Augusta for the future.

CECILY Thank you, Aunt Augusta.

LADY BRACKNELL The marriage, I think, had better take place quite soon.

ALGERNON Thank you, Aunt Augusta.

CECILY Thank you, Aunt Augusta.

LADY BRACKNELL To speak frankly, I am not in favor of long engagements. They give people the opportunity of finding out each other's character before marriage, which I think is never advisable.

JACK I beg your pardon for interrupting you, Lady Bracknell, but this engagement is quite out of the question. I am Miss Cardew's guardian, and she cannot marry without my consent until she comes of age. That consent I absolutely decline to give.

LADY BRACKNELL Upon what grounds, may I ask? Algernon is an extremely, I may almost say an ostentatiously, eligible young man. He has nothing, but he looks everything. What more can one desire?

JACK It pains me very much to have to speak frankly to you, Lady Bracknell, about your nephew, but the fact is that I do not approve at all of his moral character. I suspect him of being untruthful. (ALGERNON *and* CECILY *look at him in indignant amazement.*)

LADY BRACKNELL Untruthful! My nephew Algernon? Impossible! He is an Oxonian.

JACK I fear there can be no possible doubt about the matter. This afternoon, during my temporary absence in London on an important question of romance, he obtained admission to my house by means of the false pretense of being my brother. Under an assumed name he drank, I've just been informed by my butler, an entire pint bottle of my Perrier-Jouet, Brut, '89; a wine I was specially reserving for myself. Continuing his disgraceful deception, he succeeded in the course of the afternoon in alienating the affections of my only ward. He subsequently stayed to tea, and devoured every single muffin. And what makes his conduct all the more heartless is, that he was perfectly well aware from the first that I have no brother, that I never had a brother, and that I don't intend to have a brother, not even of any kind. I distinctly told him so myself yesterday afternoon.

LADY BRACKNELL Ahem! Mr. Worthing, after careful consideration I have decided entirely to overlook my nephew's conduct to you.

JACK That is very generous of you, Lady Bracknell. My own decision, however, is unalterable. I decline to give my consent.

LADY BRACKNELL (*to* CECILY) Come here, sweet child. (CECILY *goes over.*) How old are you, dear?

CECILY Well, I am really only eighteen, but I always admit to twenty when I go to evening parties.

LADY BRACKNELL You are perfectly right in making some slight alteration. Indeed, no woman should ever be quite accurate about her age. It looks so calculating. . . . (*In meditative manner.*) Eighteen, but admitting to twenty at evening parties. Well, it will not be very long before you are of age and free from the restraints of tutelage. So I don't think your guardian's consent is, after all, a matter of any importance.

JACK Pray excuse me, Lady Bracknell, for interrupting you again, but it is only fair to tell you that according to the terms of her grandfather's will Miss Cardew does not come legally of age till she is thirty-five.

LADY BRACKNELL That does not seem to me to be a grave objection. Thirty-five is a very attractive age. London society is full of women of the very highest birth who have, of their own free choice, remained thirty-five for years. Lady Dumbleton is an instance in point. To my own knowledge she has been thirty-five ever since she arrived at the age of forty, which was many years ago now. I see no reason why our dear Cecily should not be even still more attractive at the age you mention than she is at present. There will be a large accumulation of property.

CECILY Algy, could you wait for me till I was thirty-five?

ALGERNON Of course I could, Cecily. You know I could.

CECILY Yes, I felt it instinctively, but I couldn't wait all that time. I hate waiting even five minutes for anybody. It always makes me rather cross. I am not punctual myself, I know, but I do like punctuality in others, and waiting, even to be married, is quite out of the question.

ALGERNON Then what is to be done, Cecily?

CECILY I don't know, Mr. Moncrieff.

LADY BRACKNELL My dear Mr. Worthing, as Miss Cardew states positively that she cannot wait till she is thirty-five—a remark which I am bound to say seems to me to show a somewhat impatient nature—I would beg of you to reconsider your decision.

JACK But, my dear Lady Bracknell, the matter is entirely in your own hands. The moment you consent to my marriage with Gwendolen, I will most gladly allow your nephew to form an alliance with my ward.

LADY BRACKNELL (*rising and drawing herself up*) You must be quite aware that what you propose is out of the question.

JACK Then a passionate celibacy is all that any of us can look forward to.

LADY BRACKNELL That is not the destiny I propose for Gwendolen. Algernon, of course, can choose for himself. (*Pulls out her watch.*) Come, dear (GWENDOLEN *rises*), we have already missed five, if not six, trains. To miss any more might expose us to comment on the platform.

*Enter* DR. CHASUBLE.

CHASUBLE Everything is quite ready for the christenings.

LADY BRACKNELL The christenings, sir! Is not that somewhat premature?

CHASUBLE (*looking rather puzzled, and pointing to* JACK *and* ALGERNON) Both these gentlemen have expressed a desire for immediate baptism.

LADY BRACKNELL At their age? The idea is grotesque and irreligious! Algernon, I forbid you to be baptized. I will not hear of such excesses. Lord Bracknell would be highly displeased if he learned that that was the way in which you wasted your time and money.

CHASUBLE Am I to understand then that there are to be no christenings at all this afternoon?

JACK I don't think that, as things are now, it would be of much practical value to either of us, Dr. Chasuble.

CHASUBLE I am grieved to hear such sentiments from you, Mr. Worthing. They savor of the heretical views of the Anabaptists, views that I have completely refuted in four of my unpublished sermons. However, as your present mood seems to be one peculiarly secular, I will return to the church at once. Indeed, I have just been informed by the pewopener that for the last hour and a half Miss Prism has been waiting for me in the vestry.

LADY BRACKNELL (*starting*) Miss Prism! Did I hear you mention a Miss Prism?

CHASUBLE Yes, Lady Bracknell. I am on my way to join her.

LADY BRACKNELL Pray allow me to detain you for a moment. This matter may prove to be one of vital importance to Lord Bracknell and myself. Is this Miss Prism a female of repellent aspect, remotely connected with education?

CHASUBLE (*somewhat indignantly*) She is the most cultivated of ladies, and the very picture of respectability.

LADY BRACKNELL It is obviously the same person. May I ask what position she holds in your household?

CHASUBLE (*severely*) I am a celibate, madam.

JACK (*interposing*) Miss Prism, Lady Bracknell, has been for the last three years Miss Cardew's esteemed governess and valued companion.

LADY BRACKNELL In spite of what I hear of her, I must see her at once. Let her be sent for.

CHASUBLE (*looking off*) She approaches; she is nigh.

*Enter* MISS PRISM *hurriedly.*

MISS PRISM I was told you expected me in the vestry, dear Canon. I have been waiting for you there for an hour and three-quarters. (*Catches sight of* LADY BRACKNELL, *who has fixed her with a stony glare.* MISS PRISM *grows pale and quails. She looks anxiously round as if desirous to escape.*)

LADY BRACKNELL (*in a severe, judicial voice*) Prism! (MISS PRISM *bows her head in shame.*) Come here, Prism! (MISS PRISM *approaches in a humble manner.*) Prism! Where is that baby? (*General consternation. The Canon starts back in horror.* ALGERNON *and* JACK *pretend to be anxious to shield* CECILY *and* GWENDOLEN *from hearing the details of a terrible public scandal.*) Twenty-eight years ago, Prism, you left Lord Bracknell's house, Number 104, Upper Grosvenor Street, in charge of a perambulator that contained a baby, of the male sex. You never returned. A few weeks later, through the elaborate investigations of the Metropolitan police, the perambulator was discovered at midnight, standing by itself in a remote corner of Bayswater. It contained the manuscript of a three-volume novel of more than usually revolting sentimentality. (MISS PRISM *starts in involuntary indignation.*) But the baby was not there! (*Every one looks at* MISS PRISM.) Prism, where is that baby? (*A pause.*)

MISS PRISM Lady Bracknell, I admit with shame that I do not know. I only wish I did. The plain facts of the case are these. On the morning of the day you mention, a day that is forever branded on my memory, I prepared as usual to take the baby out in its perambulator. I had also with me a somewhat old but capacious hand-bag in which I had intended to place the manuscript of a work of fiction that I had written during my few unoccupied hours. In a moment of mental abstraction, for which I never can forgive myself, I deposited the manuscript in the bassinet, and placed the baby in the hand-bag.

JACK (*who has been listening attentively*) But where did you deposit the hand-bag?

MISS PRISM Do not ask me, Mr. Worthing.

JACK Miss Prism, this is a matter of no small importance to me. I insist on knowing where you deposited the hand-bag that contained that infant.

MISS PRISM I left it in the cloak-room of one of the larger railway stations in London.

JACK What railway station?

MISS PRISM (*quite crushed*) Victoria. The Brighton line. (*Sinks into a chair.*)

JACK I must retire to my room for a moment. Gwendolen, wait here for me.

GWENDOLEN If you are not too long, I will wait here for you all my life.

*Exit* JACK *in great excitement.*

CHASUBLE What do you think this means, Lady Bracknell?

LADY BRACKNELL I dare not even suspect, Dr. Chasuble. I need hardly tell you that in families of high position strange coincidences are not supposed to occur. They are hardly considered the thing. (*Noises heard overhead as if some one was throwing trunks about. Everybody looks up.*)

CECILY Uncle Jack seems strangely agitated.

CHASUBLE Your guardian has a very emotional nature.

LADY BRACKNELL This noise is extremely unpleasant. It sounds as if he was having an argument. I dislike arguments of any kind. They are always vulgar, and often convincing.

CHASUBLE (*looking up*) It has stopped now. (*The noise is redoubled.*)

LADY BRACKNELL I wish he would arrive at some conclusion.

GWENDOLEN This suspense is terrible. I hope it will last.

*Enter* JACK *with a hand-bag of black leather in his hand.*

JACK (*rushing over to* MISS PRISM) Is this the hand-bag, Miss Prism? Examine it carefully before you speak. The happiness of more than one life depends on your answer.

MISS PRISM (*calmly*) It seems to be mine. Yes, here is the injury it received through the upsetting of a Gower Street omnibus in younger and happier days. Here is the stain on the lining caused by the explosion of a temperance beverage, an incident that occurred at Leamington. And here, on the lock, are my initials. I had forgotten that in an extravagant mood I had had them placed there. The bag is undoubtedly mine. I am delighted to have it so unexpectedly restored to me. It has been a great inconvenience being without it all these years.

JACK (*in a pathetic voice*) Miss Prism, more is restored to you than this hand-bag. I was the baby you placed in it.

MISS PRISM (*amazed*) You?

JACK (*embracing her*) Yes . . . mother!

MISS PRISM (*recoiling in indignant astonishment*) Mr. Worthing! I am unmarried!

JACK Unmarried! I do not deny that is a serious blow. But after all, who has the right to cast a stone against one who has suffered? Cannot repentance wipe out an act of folly? Why should there be one law for men and another for women? Mother, I forgive you. (*Tries to embrace her again.*)

MISS PRISM (*still more indignant*) Mr. Worthing, there is some error. (*Pointing to* LADY BRACKNELL.) There is the lady who can tell you who you really are.

JACK (*after a pause*) Lady Bracknell, I hate to seem inquisitive, but would you kindly inform me who I am?

LADY BRACKNELL I am afraid that the news I have to give you will not altogether please you. You are the son of my poor sister, Mrs. Moncrieff, and consequently Algernon's elder brother.

JACK Algy's elder brother! Then I have a brother after all. I knew I had a brother! I always said I had a brother! Cecily,—how could you have ever doubted that I had a brother? (*Seizes hold of* ALGERNON.) Dr. Chasuble, my unfortunate brother. Miss Prism, my unfortunate brother. Gwendolen, my unfortunate brother. Algy, you young scoundrel, you will have to treat me with more respect in the future. You have never behaved to me like a brother in all your life.

ALGERNON Well, not till to-day, old boy, I admit. I did my best, however, though I was out of practice. (*Shakes hands.*)

GWENDOLEN (*to* JACK) My own! but what own are you? What is your Christian name, now that you have become some one else?

JACK Good heavens! . . . I had quite forgotten that point. Your decision on the subject of my name is irrevocable, I suppose?

GWENDOLEN I never change, except in my affections.

CECILY What a noble nature you have, Gwendolen!

JACK Then the question had better be cleared up at once. Aunt Augusta, a moment. At the time when Miss Prism left me in the handbag, had I been christened already?

LADY BRACKNELL Every luxury that money could buy, including christening, had been lavished on you by your fond and doting parents.

JACK Then I was christened! That is settled. Now, what name was I given? Let me know the worst.

LADY BRACKNELL Being the eldest son you were naturally christened after your father.

JACK (*irritably*) Yes, but what was my father's Christian name?

LADY BRACKNELL (*meditatively*) I cannot at the present moment recall what the General's Christian name was. But I have no doubt he had one. He was eccentric, I admit. But only in later years. And that was the result of the Indian climate, and marriage, and indigestion, and other things of that kind.

JACK Algy! Can't you recollect what our father's Christian name was?

ALGERNON My dear boy, we were never even on speaking terms. He died before I was a year old.

JACK His name would appear in the Army Lists of the period, I suppose, Aunt Augusta?

LADY BRACKNELL The General was essentially a man of peace, except in his domestic life. But I have no doubt his name would appear in any military directory.

JACK The Army Lists of the last forty years are here. These delightful records should have been my constant study. (*Rushes to bookcase and tears the books out.*) M. Generals . . . Mallam, Maxbohm, Magley, what ghastly names they have—Markby, Migsby, Mobbs, Moncrieff! Lieutenant 1840, Captain, Lieutenant-Colonel, Colonel, General 1869, Christian names, Ernest John. (*Puts book very quietly down and speaks quite calmly.*) I always told you, Gwendolen, my name was Ernest, didn't I? Well, it is Ernest after all. I mean it naturally is Ernest.

LADY BRACKNELL Yes, I remember that the General was called Ernest. I knew I had some particular reason for disliking the name.

GWENDOLEN Ernest! My own Ernest! I felt from the first that you could have no other name!

JACK Gwendolen, it is a terrible thing for a man to find out suddenly that all his life he has been speaking nothing but the truth. Can you forgive me?

GWENDOLEN I can. For I feel that you are sure to change.

JACK My own one!

CHASUBLE (*to* MISS PRISM) Laetitia! (*Embraces her.*)

MISS PRISM (*enthusiastically*) Frederick! At last!

ALGERNON Cecily! (*Embraces her.*) At last!

JACK Gwendolen! (*Embraces her.*) At last!

LADY BRACKNELL My nephew, you seem to be displaying signs of triviality.

JACK On the contrary, Aunt Augusta, I've now realized for the first time in my life the vital Importance of Being Earnest.

*Tableau*

*Curtain*

QUESTIONS

1. This comedy has been called one of the wittiest plays in the English language. What might you say about the play, or what lines from it might you quote, in support of this statement?
2. Compare and contrast the town and country milieus depicted in *The Importance of Being Earnest.* Why might Wilde have used both in the play?
3. It's hard not to notice the amount of eating and drinking that occurs in this play. Discuss how Wilde uses this to support particular themes and characterizations.
4. Do you think a production of *The Importance of Being Earnest* would be a success at your school? Why or why not?

## ANTON CHEKHOV (1860–1904)

# *A Marriage Proposal*

An English version by Hilmar Baukhage and Barrett H. Clark

CHARACTERS

STEPAN STEPANOVITCH TSCHUBUKOV, *a country farmer*
NATALIA STEPANOVNA, *his daughter (aged 25)*
IVAN VASSILIYITCH LOMOV, *Tschubukov's neighbor*

SCENE: *Reception room in* TSCHUBUKOV'S *country home, Russia*

TIME: *The present.*

SCENE: *The reception room in* TSCHUBUKOV'S *home.* TSCHUBUKOV *discovered as the curtain rises.*

(*Enter* LOMOV, *wearing a dress-suit.*)

TSCHUB (*going toward him and greeting him*) Who is this I see? My dear fellow! Ivan Vassiliyitch! I'm so glad to see you! (*Shakes hands.*) But this is a surprise! How are you?

LOMOV Thank you! And how are you?

TSCHUB Oh, so-so, my friend. Please sit down. It isn't right to forget one's neighbor. But tell me; why all this ceremony? Dress clothes, white gloves and all? Are you on your way to some engagement, my good fellow?

LOMOV No, I have no engagement except with you, Stepan Stepanovich.

TSCHUB But why in evening clothes, my friend? This isn't New Year's!

LOMOV You see, it's simply this, that—(*Composing himself.*) I have come to you, Stepan Stepanovitch, to trouble you with a request. It is not the first time I have had the honor of turning to you for assistance, and you have always, that is—I beg your pardon, I am a bit excited! I'll take a drink of water first, dear Stepan Stepanovitch. (*He drinks.*)

TSCHUB (*aside*) He's come to borrow money! I won't give him any! (To LOMOV.) What is it, then, dear Lomov?

LOMOV You see—dear—Stepanovitch, pardon me, Stepan—Stepan—dearvitch—I mean—I am terribly nervous, as you will be so good as to see—! What I mean to say—you are the only one who can help me, though I don't deserve it, and—and I have no right whatever to make this request of you.

TSCHUB Oh, don't beat about the bush, my dear fellow. Tell me!

LOMOV Immediately—in a moment. Here it is, then: I have come to ask for the hand of your daughter, Natalia Stepanovna.

TSCHUB (*joyfully*) Angel! Ivan Vassiliyitch! Say that once again! I didn't quite hear it!

LOMOV I have the honor to beg——

TSCHUB (*interrupting*) My dear, dear man! I am so happy that everything is so—everything! (*Embraces and kisses him.*) I have wanted this to happen for so long. It has been my dearest wish! (*He represses a tear.*) And I have always loved you, my dear fellow, as my own son! May God give you His blessings and His grace and—I always wanted it to happen. But why am I standing here like a blockhead? I am completely dumbfounded with pleasure, completely dumbfounded. My whole being—I'll call Natalia——

LOMOV Dear Stepan Stepanovitch, what do you think? May I hope for Natalia Stepanovna's acceptance?

TSCHUB Really! A fine boy like you—and you think she won't accept on the minute? Lovesick as a cat and all that—! (*He goes out, right.*)

LOMOV I'm cold. My whole body is trembling as though I was going to take my examination! But the chief thing is to settle matters! If a person meditates too much, or hesitates, or talks about it, waits for an ideal or for true love, he never gets it. Brrr! It's cold! Natalia is an excellent housekeeper, not at all bad-looking, well educated—what more could I ask? I'm so excited my ears are roaring! (*He drinks water.*) And not to marry, that won't do! In the first place, I'm thirty-five—a critical age, you might say. In the second place, I must live a well-regulated life. I have a weak heart, continual palpitation, and I am very sensitive and always getting excited. My lips begin to tremble and the pulse in my right temple throbs terribly. But the worst of all is sleep! I hardly lie down and begin to doze before something in my left side begins to pull and tug, and something begins to hammer in my left shoulder—and in my head, too! I jump up like a madman, walk about a little, lie down again, but the moment I fall asleep I have a terrible cramp in the side. And so it is all night long!

(*Enter* NATALIA STEPANOVNA.)

NATALIA Ah! It's you. Papa said to go in: there was a dealer in there who'd come to buy something. Good afternoon, Ivan Vassiliyitch.

LOMOV Good day, my dear Natalia Stepanovna.

NATALIA You must pardon me for wearing my apron and this old dress: we are working to-day. Why haven't you come to see us oftener? You've not been here for so long! Sit down. (*They sit down.*) Won't you have something to eat?

LOMOV Thank you, I have just had lunch.

NATALIA Smoke, do, there are the matches. To-day it is beautiful and only yesterday it rained so hard that the workmen couldn't do a stroke of work. How many bricks have you cut? Think of it! I was so anxious that I had the whole field mowed, and now I'm sorry I did it, because I'm afraid the hay will rot. It would have been better if I had waited. But what on earth is this? You are in evening clothes! The latest cut! Are you on your way to a ball? And you seem to be looking better, too—really. Why are you dressed up so gorgeously?

LOMOV (*excited*) You see, my dear Natalia Stepanovna—it's simply this: I have decided to ask you to listen to me—of course it will be a surprise, and indeed you'll be angry, but I—(*Aside.*) How fearfully cold it is!

NATALIA What is it? (*A pause.*) Well?

LOMOV I'll try to be brief. My dear Natalia Stepanovna, as you know, for many years, since my childhood, I have had the honor to know your family. My poor aunt and her husband, from whom, as you know, I inherited the estate, always had the greatest respect for your father and your poor mother. The Lomovs and the Tschubukovs have been for decades on the friendliest, indeed the closest, terms with each other, and furthermore my property, as you know, adjoins your own. If you will be so good as to remember, my meadows touch your birch woods.

NATALIA Pardon the interruption. You said "my meadows"—but are they yours?

LOMOV Yes, they belong to me.

NATALIA What nonsense! The meadows belong to us—not to you!

LOMOV No, to me! Now, my dear Natalia Stepanovna!

NATALIA Well, that is certainly news to me. How do they belong to you?

LOMOV How? I am speaking of the meadows lying between your birch woods and my brick-earth.

NATALIA Yes, exactly. They belong to us.

LOMOV No, you are mistaken, my dear Natalia Stepanovna, they belong to me.

NATALIA Try to remember exactly, Ivan Vassiliyitch. Is it so long ago that you inherited them?

LOMOV Long ago! As far back as I can remember they have always belonged to us.

NATALIA But that isn't true! You'll pardon my saying so.

LOMOV It is all a matter of record, my dear Natalia Stepanovna. It is true that at one time the title to the meadows was disputed, but now everyone knows they belong to me. There is no room for discussion. Be so good as to listen: my aunt's grandmother put these meadows, free from all costs, into the hands of your father's grandfather's peasants for a certain time while they were making bricks for my grandmother. These people used the meadows free of cost for about forty years, living there as they would on their own property. Later, however, when——

NATALIA There's not a word of truth in that! My grandfather, and my great-grandfather, too, knew that their estate reached back to the swamp, so that the meadows belong to us. What further discussion can there be? I can't understand it. It is really most annoying.

LOMOV I'll show you the papers, Natalia Stepanovna.

NATALIA No, either you are joking, or trying to lead me into a discussion. That's not at all nice! We have owned this property for nearly three hundred years, and now all at once we hear that it doesn't belong to us. Ivan Vassiliyitch, you will pardon me, but I really can't believe my ears. So far as I am concerned, the meadows are worth very little. In all they don't contain more than five acres and they are worth only a few hundred roubles, say three hundred, but the injustice of the thing is what affects me. Say what you will, I can't bear injustice.

LOMOV Only listen until I have finished, please! The peasants of your respected father's grandfather, as I have already had the honor to tell you, baked bricks for my grandmother. My aunt's grandmother wished to do them a favor——

NATALIA Grandfather! Grandmother! Aunt! I know nothing about them. All I know is that the meadows belong to us, and that ends the matter.

LOMOV No, they belong to me!

NATALIA And if you keep on explaining it for two days, and put on five suits of evening clothes, the meadows are still ours, ours, ours! I don't want to take your property, but I refuse to give up what belongs to us!

LOMOV Natalia Stepanovna, I don't need the meadows, I am only concerned with the principle. If you are agreeable, I beg of you, accept them as a gift from me!

NATALIA But I can give them to you, because they belong to me!

That is very peculiar, Ivan Vassiliyitch! Until now we have considered you as a good neighbor and a good friend; only last year we lent you our threshing machine so that we couldn't thresh until November, and now you treat us like thieves! You offer to give me my own land. Excuse me, but neighbors don't treat each other that way. In my opinion, it's a very low trick—to speak frankly——

LOMOV According to you I'm a usurper, then, am I? My dear lady, I have never appropriated other people's property, and I shall permit no one to accuse me of such a thing! (*He goes quickly to the bottle and drinks water.*) The meadows are mine!

NATALIA That's not the truth! They are mine!

LOMOV Mine!

NATALIA Eh? I'll prove it to you! This afternoon I'll send my reapers into the meadows.

LOMOV W—h—a—t?

NATALIA My reapers will be there to-day!

LOMOV And I'll chase them off!

NATALIA If you dare!

LOMOV The meadows are mine, you understand? Mine!

NATALIA Really, you needn't scream so! If you want to scream and snort and rage you may do it at home, but here please keep yourself within the limits of common decency.

LOMOV My dear lady, it it weren't that I were suffering from palpitation of the heart and hammering of the arteries in my temples, I would deal with you very differently! (*In a loud voice.*) The meadows belong to me!

NATALIA Us!

LOMOV Me! (*Enter* TSCHUBUKOV, *right.*)

TSCHUB What's going on here? What is he yelling about?

NATALIA Papa, please tell this gentleman to whom the meadows belong, to us or to him?

TSCHUB (*to* LOMOV) My dear fellow, the meadows are ours.

LOMOV But, merciful heavens, Stepan Stepanovitch, how do you make that out? You at least might be reasonable. My aunt's grandmother gave the use of the meadows free of cost to your grandfather's peasants; the peasants lived on the land for forty years and used it as their own, but later when——

TSCHUB Permit me, my dear friend. You forget that your grandmother's peasants never paid, because there had been a lawsuit over the meadows, and everyone knows that the meadows belong to us. You haven't looked at the map.

LOMOV I'll prove to you that they belong to me!

TSCHUB Don't try to prove it, my dear fellow.

LOMOV I will!

TSCHUB My good fellow, what are you shrieking about? You can't prove anything by yelling, you know. I don't ask for anything that belongs to you, nor do I intend to give up anything of my own. Why should I? If it has gone so far, my dear man, that you really intend to claim the meadows, I'd rather give them to the peasants than you, and I certainly shall!

LOMOV I can't believe it! By what right can you give away property that doesn't belong to you?

TSCHUB Really, you must allow me to decide what I am to do with my own land! I'm not accustomed, young man, to have people address me in that tone of voice. I, young man, am twice your age, and I beg you to address me respectfully.

LOMOV No! No! You think I'm a fool! You're making fun of me! You call my property yours and then expect me to stand quietly by and talk to you like a human being. That isn't the way a good neighbor behaves, Stepan Stepanovitch! You are no neighbor, you're no better than a landgrabber. That's what you are!

TSCHUB Wh—at? What did he say?

NATALIA Papa, send the reapers into the meadows this minute!

TSCHUB (*to* LOMOV) What was that you said, sir?

NATALIA The meadows belong to us and I won't give them up! I won't give them up! I won't give them up!

LOMOV We'll see about that! I'll prove in court that they belong to me.

TSCHUB In court! You may sue in court, sir, if you like! Oh, I know you, you are only waiting to find an excuse to go to law! You're an intriguer, that's what you are! Your whole family were always looking for quarrels. The whole lot!

LOMOV Kindly refrain from insulting my family. The entire race of Lomov has always been honorable! And never has one been brought to trial for embezzlement, as your dear uncle was!

TSCHUB And the whole Lomov family were insane!

NATALIA Every one of them!

TSCHUB Your grandmother was a dipsomaniac, and the younger aunt, Nastasia Michailovna, ran off with an architect.

LOMOV And your mother limped. (*He puts his hand over his heart.*) Oh, my side pains! My temples are bursting! Lord in Heaven! Water!

TSCHUB And your dear father was a gambler—and a glutton!

NATALIA And your aunt was a gossip like few others!

LOMOV And you are an intriguer. Oh, my heart! And it's an open secret that you cheated at the elections—my eyes are blurred! Where is my hat?

NATALIA Oh, how low! Liar! Disgusting thing!

LOMOV Where's the hat—? My heart! Where shall I go? Where is the door—? Oh—it seems—as though I were dying! I can't—my legs won't hold me—(*Goes to the door.*)

TSCHUB (*following him*) May you never darken my door again!

NATALIA Bring your suit to court! We'll see! (LOMOV *staggers out, center.*)

TSCHUB (*angrily*) The devil!

NATALIA Such a good-for-nothing! And then they talk about being good neighbors!

TSCHUB Loafer! Scarecrow! Monster!

NATALIA A swindler like that takes over a piece of property that doesn't belong to him and then dares to argue about it!

TSCHUB And to think that this fool dares to make a proposal of marriage!

NATALIA What? A proposal of marriage?

TSCHUB Why, yes! He came here to make you a proposal of marriage!

NATALIA Why didn't you tell me that before?

TSCHUB That's why he had on his evening clothes! The poor fool!

NATALIA Proposal for me? Oh! (*Falls into an armchair and groans.*) Bring him back! Bring him back!

TSCHUB Bring whom back?

NATALIA Faster, faster, I'm sinking! Bring him back! (*She becomes hysterical.*)

TSCHUB What is it? What's wrong with you? (*His hands to his head.*) I'm cursed with bad luck! I'll shoot myself! I'll hang myself!

NATALIA I'm dying! Bring him back!

TSCHUB Bah! In a minute! Don't bawl! (*He rushes out, center.*)

NATALIA (*groaning*) What have they done to me? Bring him back! Bring him back!

TSCHUB (*comes running in*) He's coming at once! The devil take him! Ugh! Talk to him yourself, I can't.

NATALIA (*groaning*) Bring him back!

TSCHUB He's coming, I tell you! "Oh, Lord! What a task it is to be the father of a grown daughter!" I'll cut my throat! I really will cut my throat! We've argued with the fellow, insulted him, and now we've thrown him out!—and you did it all, you!

NATALIA No, you! You haven't any manners, you are brutal! If it weren't for you, he wouldn't have gone!

TSCHUB Oh, yes, I'm to blame! If I shoot or hang myself, remember *you'll* be to blame. You forced me to it! You! (LOMOV *appears in the doorway.*) There, talk to him yourself! (*He goes out.*)

LOMOV Terrible palpitation!—My leg is lamed! My side hurts me——

NATALIA Pardon us, we were angry, Ivan Vassiliyitch. I remember now—the meadows really belong to you.

LOMOV My heart is beating terribly! My meadows—my eyelids tremble—(*They sit down.*) We were wrong. It was only the principle of the thing—the property isn't worth much to me, but the principle is worth a great deal.

NATALIA Exactly, the principle! Let us talk about something else.

LOMOV Because I have proofs that my aunt's grandmother had, with the peasants of your good father——

NATALIA Enough, enough. (*Aside.*) I don't know how to begin. (*To* LOMOV.) Are you going hunting soon?

LOMOV Yes, heath-cock shooting, respected Natalia Stepanovna. I expect to begin after the harvest. Oh, did you hear? My dog, Ugadi, you know him—limps!

NATALIA What a shame! How did that happen?

LOMOV I don't know. Perhaps it's a dislocation, or maybe he was bitten by some other dog. (*He sighs.*) The best dog I ever had—to say nothing of his price! I paid Mironov a hundred and twenty-five roubles for him.

NATALIA That was too much to pay, Ivan Vassiliyitch.

LOMOV In my opinion it was very cheap. A wonderful dog!

NATALIA Papa paid eighty-five roubles for his Otkatai, and Otkatai is much better than your Ugadi.

LOMOV Really? Otkatai is better than Ugadi? What an idea! (*He laughs.*) Otkatai better than Ugadi!

NATALIA Of course he is better. It is true Otkatai is still young; he isn't full-grown yet, but in the pack or on the leash with two or three, there is no better than he, even——

LOMOV I really beg your pardon, Natalia Stepanovna, but you quite overlooked the fact that he has a short lower jaw, and a dog with a short lower jaw can't snap.

NATALIA Short lower jaw? That's the first time I ever heard that!

LOMOV I assure you, his lower jaw is shorter than the upper.

NATALIA Have you measured it?

LOMOV I have measured it. He is good at running, though.

NATALIA In the first place, our Otkatai is pure-bred, a full-blooded son of Sapragavas and Stameskis, and as for your mongrel, nobody could ever figure out his pedigree; he's old and ugly, and as skinny as an old hag.

LOMOV Old, certainly! I wouldn't take five of your Otkatais for him! Ugadi is a dog and Otkatai is—it is laughable to argue about it! Dogs like your Otkatai can be found by the dozens at any dog dealer's, a whole pound-full!

NATALIA Ivan Vassiliyitch, you are very contrary to-day. First our meadows belong to you and then Ugadi is better than Otkatai. I don't like it when a person doesn't say what he really thinks. You know perfectly well that Otkatai is a hundred times better than your silly Ugadi. What makes you keep on saying he isn't?

LOMOV I can see, Natalia Stepanovna, that you consider me either a blindman or a fool. But at least you may as well admit that Otkatai has a short lower jaw!

NATALIA It isn't so!

LOMOV Yes, a short lower jaw!

NATALIA (*loudly*) It's not so!

LOMOV What makes you scream, my dear lady?

NATALIA What makes you talk such nonsense? It's disgusting! It is high time that Ugadi was shot, and yet you compare him with Otkatai!

LOMOV Pardon me, but I can't carry on this argument any longer. I have palpitation of the heart!

NATALIA I have always noticed that the hunters who do the most talking know the least about hunting.

LOMOV My dear lady, I beg of you to be still. My heart is bursting! (*He shouts.*) Be still!

NATALIA I won't be still until you admit that Otkatai is better! (*Enter* TSCHUBUKOV.)

TSCHUB Well, has it begun again?

NATALIA Papa, say frankly, on your honor, which dog is better: Otkatai or Ugadi?

LOMOV Stepan Stepanovitch, I beg of you, just answer this: has your dog a short lower jaw or not? Yes or no?

TSCHUB And what if he has? Is it of such importance? There is no better dog in the whole country.

LOMOV My Ugadi is better. Tell the truth, now!

TSCHUB Don't get so excited, my dear fellow! Permit me. Your Ugadi certainly has his good points. He is from a good breed, has a good stride, strong haunches, and so forth. But the dog, if you really want to know it, has two faults; he is old and he has a short lower jaw.

LOMOV Pardon me, I have palpitation of the heart!—Let us keep to facts—just remember in Maruskins's meadows, my Ugadi kept ear to ear with the Count Rasvachai and your dog.

TSCHUB He was behind, because the Count struck him with his whip.

LOMOV Quite right. All the other dogs were on the fox's scent, but Otkatai found it necessary to bite a sheep.

TSCHUB That isn't so!—I am sensitive about that and beg you to stop this argument. He struck him because everybody looks on a strange dog of good blood with envy. Even you, sir, aren't free from the sin. No sooner do you find a dog better than Ugadi than you begin to—this, that—his, mine—and so forth! I remember distinctly.

LOMOV I remember something, too!

TSCHUB (*mimicking him*) I remember something, too! What do you remember?

LOMOV Palpitation! My leg is lame—I can't——

NATALIA Palpitation! What kind of hunter are you? You ought to stay in the kitchen by the stove and wrestle with the potato peelings, and not go fox-hunting! Palpitation!

TSCHUB And what kind of hunter are you? A man with your diseases ought to stay at home and not jolt around in the saddle. If you were a hunter—! But you only ride round in order to find out about other people's dogs, and make trouble for everyone. I am sensitive! Let's drop the subject. Besides, you're no hunter.

LOMOV You only ride around to flatter the Count!—My heart! You intriguer! Swindler!

TSCHUB And what of it? (*Shouting.*) Be still!

LOMOV Intriguer!

TSCHUB Baby! Puppy! Walking drug-store!

LOMOV Old rat! Jesuit! Oh, I know you!

TSCHUB Be still! Or I'll shoot you—with my worst gun, like a partridge! Fool! Loafer!

LOMOV Everyone knows that—oh, my heart!—that your poor late wife beat you. My leg—my temples—Heavens—I'm dying—I——

TSCHUB And your housekeeper wears the trousers in your house!

LOMOV Here—here—there—there—my heart has burst! My shoulder is torn apart. Where is my shoulder? I'm dying! (*He falls into a chair.*) The doctor! (*Faints.*)

TSCHUB Baby! Half-baked clam! Fool!

NATALIA Nice sort of hunter you are! You can't even sit on a horse. (*To* TSCHUB.) Papa, what's the matter with him? (*She screams.*) Ivan Vassiliyitch! He is dead!

LOMOV I'm ill! I can't breathe! Air!

NATALIA He is dead! (*She shakes* LOMOV *in the chair.*) Ivan Vassiliyitch! What have we done! He is dead! (*She sinks into a chair.*) The doctor—doctor! (*She goes into hysterics.*)

TSCHUB Ahh! What is it? What's the matter with you?

NATALIA (*groaning*) He's dead!—Dead!

TSCHUB Who is dead? Who? (*Looking at* LOMOV.) Yes, he is dead! Good God! Water! The doctor! (*Holding the glass to* LOMOV's *lips.*) Drink! No, he won't drink! He's dead! What a terrible situation! Why didn't I shoot myself? Why have I never cut my throat? What am I waiting for now? Only give me a knife! Give me a pistol! (LOMOV *moves.*) He's coming to! Drink some water—there!

LOMOV Sparks! Mists! Where am I?

TSCHUB Get married! Quick, and then go to the devil. She's willing! (*He joins the hands of* LOMOV *and* NATALIA.) She's agreed! Only leave me in peace!

LOMOV Wh—what? (*Getting up.*) Whom?

TSCHUB She's willing! Well? Kiss each other and—the devil take you both!

NATALIA (*groans*) He lives! Yes, yes, I'm willing!

TSCHUB Kiss each other!

LOMOV Eh? Whom? (NATALIA *and* LOMOV *kiss.*) Very nice—! Pardon me, but what is this for? Oh, yes, I understand! My heart—sparks—I am happy, Natalia Stepanovna. (*He kisses her hand.*) My leg is lame!

NATALIA I'm happy, too!

TSCHUB Ahh! A load off my shoulders! Ahh!

NATALIA And now at least you'll admit that Ugadi is worse than Otkatai!

LOMOV Better!

NATALIA Worse!

TSCHUB Now the domestic joys have begun.—Champagne!

LOMOV Better!

NATALIA Worse, worse, worse!

TSCHUB (*trying to drown them out*) Champagne, champagne!

*Curtain*

(Copies of this play, in individual paper-covered acting editions, are available from Samuel French, Inc., 25 W. 45th St., New York, N.Y. 10036, or 7623 Sunset Blvd., Hollywood, Calif. 90046; or, in Canada, Samuel French (Canada) Ltd., 80 Richmond St. East, Toronto M5C 1P1, Canada.)

## QUESTIONS

1. Most people would not care to have the hero or the heroine of *A Marriage Proposal* as friends; yet most people enjoy watching or reading the play. Why might this be so? What would this suggest concerning the appeal of comedy in general?
2. Get together with two other people and read the play aloud. Have fun with it. Of all the pieces this book contains, *A Marriage Proposal* is perhaps the one that least begs to be taken seriously and most begs to be enjoyed.

## JOHN MILLINGTON SYNGE (1871–1909)

# *Riders to the Sea*

*A Play in One Act*

CHARACTERS

MAURYA, *an old woman*
BARTLEY, *her son*
CATHLEEN, *her daughter*
NORA, *a younger daughter*
MEN *and* WOMEN

SCENE: *An Island off the West of Ireland.*

*Cottage kitchen, with nets, oil-skins, spinning-wheel, some new boards standing by the wall, etc.* CATHLEEN, *a girl of about twenty, finishes kneading cake, and puts it down in the pot-oven by the fire; then wipes her hands, and begins to spin at the wheel.* NORA, *a young girl, puts her head in at the door.*

NORA (*in a low voice*) Where is she?

CATHLEEN She's lying down, God help her, and may be sleeping, if she's able.

NORA *comes in softly, and takes a bundle from under her shawl.*

CATHLEEN (*spinning the wheel rapidly*) What is it you have?

NORA The young priest is after bringing them. It's a shirt and a plain stocking were got off a drowned man in Donegal.

CATHLEEN *stops her wheel with a sudden movement, and leans out to listen.*

NORA We're to find out if it's Michael's they are, some time herself will be down looking by the sea.

CATHLEEN How would they be Michael's, Nora? How would he go the length of that way to the far north?

NORA The young priest says he's known the like of it. "If it's Michael's they are," says he, "you can tell herself he's got a clean burial by the grace of God, and if they're not his, let no one say a word about them, for she'll be getting her death," says he, "with crying and lamenting."

*The door which* NORA *half-closed is blown open by a gust of wind.*

CATHLEEN (*looking out anxiously*) Did you ask him would he stop Bartley going this day with the horses to the Galway fair?

NORA "I won't stop him," says he, "but let you not be afraid. Herself does be saying prayers half through the night, and the Almighty God won't leave her destitute," says he, "with no son living."

CATHLEEN Is the sea bad by the white rocks, Nora?

NORA Middling bad, God help us. There's a great roaring in the west, and it's worse it'll be getting when the tide's turned to the wind.

*She goes over to the table with the bundle.*

Shall I open it now?

CATHLEEN Maybe she'd wake up on us, and come in before we'd done. (*Coming to the table.*) It's a long time we'll be, and the two of us crying.

NORA (*goes to the inner door and listens*) She's moving about on the bed. She'll be coming in a minute.

CATHLEEN Give me the ladder, and I'll put them up in the turf-loft, the way she won't know of them at all, and maybe when the tide turns she'll be going down to see would he be floating from the east.

*They put the ladder against the gable of the chimney;* CATHLEEN *goes up a few steps and hides the bundle in the turf-loft.* MAURYA *comes from the inner room.*

MAURYA (*looking up at* CATHLEEN *and speaking querulously*) Isn't it turf enough you have for this day and evening?

CATHLEEN There's a cake baking at the fire for a short space (*throwing down the turf*) and Bartley will want it when the tide turns if he goes to Connemara.

NORA *picks up the turf and puts it round the pot-oven.*

MAURYA (*sitting down on a stool at the fire*) He won't go this day with the wind rising from the south and west. He won't go this day, for the young priest will stop him surely.

NORA He'll not stop him, mother, and I heard Eamon Simon and Stephen Pheety and Colum Shawn saying he would go.

MAURYA Where is he itself?

NORA He went down to see would there be another boat sailing in the week, and I'm thinking it won't be long till he's here now, for the tide's turning at the green head, and the hooker's[1] tacking from the east.

CATHLEEN I hear some one passing the big stones.

NORA (*looking out*) He's coming now, and he in a hurry.

BARTLEY (*comes in and looks round the room. Speaking sadly and quietly*) Where is the bit of new rope, Cathleen, was bought in Connemara?

CATHLEEN (*coming down*) Give it to him, Nora; it's on a nail by the white boards. I hunt it up this morning, for the pig with the black feet was eating it.

---

[1] *hooker* a single-masted fishing boat.

NORA (*giving him a rope*) Is that it, Bartley?

MAURYA You'd do right to leave that rope, Bartley, hanging by the boards. (BARTLEY *takes the rope.*) It will be wanting in this place, I'm telling you, if Michael is washed up tomorrow morning, or the next morning, or any morning in the week, for it's a deep grave we'll make him by the grace of God.

BARTLEY (*beginning to work with the rope*) I've no halter the way I can ride down on the mare, and I must go now quickly. This is the one boat going for two weeks or beyond it, and the fair will be a good fair for horses I heard them saying below.

MAURYA It's a hard thing they'll be saying below if the body is washed up and there's no man in it to make the coffin, and I after giving a big price for the finest white boards you'd find in Connemara.

*She looks round at the boards.*

BARTLEY How would it be washed up, and we after looking each day for nine days, and a strong wind blowing a while back from the west and south?

MAURYA If it wasn't found itself, that wind is raising the sea, and there was a star up against the moon, and it rising in the night. If it was a hundred horses, or a thousand horses you had itself, what is the price of a thousand horses against a son where there is one son only?

BARTLEY (*working at the halter, to* CATHLEEN) Let you go down each day, and see the sheep aren't jumping in on the rye, and if the jobber comes you can sell the pig with the black feet if there is a good price going.

MAURYA How would the like of her get a good price for a pig?

BARTLEY (*to* CATHLEEN) If the west wind holds with the last bit of the moon let you and Nora get up weed enough for another cock for the kelp.[2] It's hard set we'll be from this day with no one in it but one man to work.

MAURYA It's hard set we'll be surely the day you're drown'd with the rest. What way will I live and the girls with me, and I an old woman looking for the grave?

BARTLEY *lays down the halter, takes off his old coat, and puts on a newer one of the same flannel.*

BARTLEY (*to* NORA) Is she coming to the pier?

NORA (*looking out*) She's passing the green head and letting fall her sails.

BARTLEY (*getting his purse and tobacco*) I'll have half an hour to go down, and you'll see me coming again in two days, or in three days, or maybe in four days if the wind is bad.

---

[2] *kelp* seaweed (used for manure).

MAURYA (*turning round to the fire, and putting her shawl over her head*) Isn't it a hard and cruel man won't hear a word from an old woman, and she holding him from the sea?

CATHLEEN It's the life of a young man to be going on the sea, and who would listen to an old woman with one thing and she saying it over?

BARTLEY (*taking the halter*) I must go now quickly. I'll ride down on the red mare, and the gray pony'll run behind me. . . . The blessing of God on you.

*He goes out.*

MAURYA (*crying out as he is in the door*) He's gone now, God spare us, and we'll not see him again. He's gone now, and when the black night is falling I'll have no son left me in the world.

CATHLEEN Why wouldn't you give him your blessing and he looking round in the door? Isn't it sorrow enough is on every one in this house without your sending him out with an unlucky word behind him, and a hard word in his ear?

MAURYA *takes up the tongs and begins raking the fire aimlessly without looking round.*

NORA (*turning towards her*) You're taking away the turf from the cake.

CATHLEEN (*crying out*) The Son of God forgive us, Nora, we're after forgetting his bit of bread.

*She comes over to the fire.*

NORA And it's destroyed he'll be going till dark night, and he after eating nothing since the sun went up.

CATHLEEN (*turning the cake out of the oven*) It's destroyed he'll be, surely. There's no sense left on any person in a house where an old woman will be talking for ever.

MAURYA *sways herself on her stool.*

CATHLEEN (*cutting off some of the bread and rolling it in a cloth; to Maurya*) Let you go down now to the spring well and give him this and he passing. You'll see him then and the dark word will be broken, and you can say "God speed you," the way he'll be easy in his mind.

MAURYA (*taking the bread*) Will I be in it as soon as himself?

CATHLEEN If you go now quickly.

MAURYA (*standing up unsteadily*) It's hard set I am to walk.

CATHLEEN (*looking at her anxiously*) Give her the stick, Nora, or maybe she'll slip on the big stones.

NORA What stick?

CATHLEEN The stick Michael brought from Connemara.

MAURYA (*taking a stick* NORA *gives her*) In the big world the old people do be leaving things after them for their sons and children, but in this place it is the young men do be leaving things behind for them that do be old.

*She goes out slowly.* NORA *goes over to the ladder.*

CATHLEEN Wait, Nora, maybe she'd turn back quickly. She's that sorry, God help her, you wouldn't know the thing she'd do.

NORA Is she gone around by the bush?

CATHLEEN (*looking out*) She's gone now. Throw it down quickly, for the Lord knows when she'll be out of it again.

NORA (*getting the bundle from the loft*) The young priest said he'd be passing to-morrow, and we might go down and speak to him below if it's Michael's they are surely.

CATHLEEN (*taking the bundle*) Did he say what way they were found?

NORA (*coming down*) "There were two men," says he, "and they rowing round with poteen[3] before the cocks crowed, and the oar of one of them caught the body, and they passing the black cliffs of the north."

CATHLEEN (*trying to open the bundle*) Give me a knife, Nora, the string's perished with the salt water, and there's a black knot on it you wouldn't loosen in a week.

NORA (*giving her a knife*) I've heard tell it was a long way to Donegal.

CATHLEEN (*cutting the string*) It is surely. There was a man in here a while ago—the man sold us that knife—and he said if you set off walking from the rock beyond, it would be seven days you'd be in Donegal.

NORA And what time would a man take, and he floating?

CATHLEEN *opens the bundle and takes out a bit of a stocking. They look at them eagerly.*

CATHLEEN (*in a low voice*) The Lord spare us, Nora! isn't it a queer hard thing to say if it's his they are surely?

NORA I'll get his shirt off the hook the way we can put the one flannel on the other. (*She looks through some clothes hanging in the corner.*) It's not with them, Cathleen, and where will it be?

CATHLEEN I'm thinking Bartley put it on him in the morning, for his own shirt was heavy with the salt in it. (*Pointing to the corner.*) There's a bit of a sleeve was of the same stuff. Give me that and it will do.

NORA *brings it to her and they compare the flannel.*

CATHLEEN It's the same stuff, Nora; but if it is itself aren't there great rolls of it in the shops of Galway, and isn't it many another man may have a shirt of it as well as Michael himself?

---

[3] *poteen* illegal whiskey.

NORA (*who has taken up the stocking and counted the stitches, crying out*) It's Michael, Cathleen, it's Michael; God spare his soul, and what will herself say when she hears this story, and Bartley on the sea?

CATHLEEN (*taking the stocking*) It's a plain stocking.

NORA It's the second one of the third pair I knitted, and I put up three score stitches, and I dropped four of them.

CATHLEEN (*counts the stitches*) It's that number is in it. (*Crying out.*) Ah, Nora, isn't it a bitter thing to think of him floating that way to the far north, and no one to keen[4] him but the black hags that do be flying on the sea?

NORA (*swinging herself round, and throwing out her arms on the clothes*) And isn't it a pitiful thing when there is nothing left of a man who was a great rower and fisher, but a bit of an old shirt and a plain stocking?

CATHLEEN (*after an instant*) Tell me is herself coming, Nora? I hear a little sound on the path.

NORA (*looking out*) She is, Cathleen. She's coming up to the door.

CATHLEEN Put these things away before she'll come in. Maybe it's easier she'll be after giving her blessing to Bartley, and we won't let on we've heard anything the time he's on the sea.

NORA (*helping* CATHLEEN *to close the bundle*) We'll put them here in the corner.

*They put them into a hole in the chimney corner.* CATHLEEN *goes back to the spinning-wheel.*

NORA Will she see it was crying I was?

CATHLEEN Keep your back to the door the way the light'll not be on you.

NORA *sits down at the chimney corner, with her back to the door.* MAURYA *comes in very slowly, without looking at the girls, and goes over to her stool at the other side of the fire. The cloth with the bread is still in her hand. The girls look at each other, and* NORA *points to the bundle of bread.*

CATHLEEN (*after spinning for a moment*) You didn't give him his bit of bread?

MAURYA *begins to keen softly, without turning round.*

CATHLEEN Did you see him riding down?

MAURYA *goes on keening.*

CATHLEEN (*a little impatiently*) God forgive you; isn't it a better thing to raise your voice and tell what you seen, than to be making lamentation for a thing that's done? Did you see Bartley, I'm saying to you.

MAURYA (*with a weak voice*) My heart's broken from this day.

---

[4] *keen* lament.

CATHLEEN (*as before*) Did you see Bartley?

MAURYA I seen the fearfulest thing.

CATHLEEN (*leaves her wheel and looks out*) God forgive you; he's riding the mare now over the green head, and the gray pony behind him.

MAURYA (*starts, so that her shawl falls back from her head and shows her white tossed hair. With a frightened voice*) The gray pony behind him.

CATHLEEN (*coming to the fire*) What is it ails you, at all?

MAURYA (*speaking very slowly*) I've seen the fearfulest thing any person has seen, since the day Bride Dara seen the dead man with the child in his arms.

CATHLEEN AND NORA Uah.

*They crouch down in front of the old woman at the fire.*

NORA Tell us what it is you seen.

MAURYA I went down to the spring well, and I stood there saying a prayer to myself. Then Bartley came along, and he riding on the red mare with the gray pony behind him. (*She puts up her hands, as if to hide something from her eyes.*) The Son of God spare us, Nora!

CATHLEEN What is it you seen?

MAURYA I seen Michael himself.

CATHLEEN (*speaking softly*) You did not, mother; it wasn't Michael you seen, for his body is after being found in the far north, and he's got a clean burial by the grace of God.

MAURYA (*a little defiantly*) I'm after seeing him this day, and he riding and galloping. Bartley came first on the red mare; and I tried to say "God speed you," but something choked the words in my throat. He went by quickly; and "the blessing of God on you," says he, and I could say nothing. I looked up then, and I crying, at the gray pony, and there was Michael upon it—with fine clothes on him, and new shoes on his feet.

CATHLEEN (*begins to keen*) It's destroyed we are from this day. It's destroyed, surely.

NORA Didn't the young priest say the Almighty God wouldn't leave her destitute with no son living?

MAURYA (*in a low voice, but clearly*) It's little the like of him knows of the sea. . . . Bartley will be lost now, and let you call in Eamon and make me a good coffin out of the white boards, for I won't live after them. I've had a husband, and a husband's father, and six sons in this house—six fine men, though it was a hard birth I had with every one of them and they coming to the world—and some of them were found and some of them were not found, but they're gone now the lot of them. . . . There were Stephen, and Shawn, were lost in the great wind, and found after in the Bay of Gregory of the Golden Mouth, and carried up the two of them, on the one plank, and in by that door.

*She pauses for a moment, the girls start as if they heard something through the door that is half open behind them.*

NORA (*in a whisper*) Did you hear that, Cathleen? Did you hear a noise in the northeast?

CATHLEEN (*in a whisper*) There's some one after crying out by the seashore.

MAURYA (*continues without hearing anything*) There was Sheamus and his father, and his own father again, were lost in a dark night, and not a stick or sign was seen of them when the sun went up. There was Patch after was drowned out of a curagh[5] that turned over. I was sitting here with Bartley, and he a baby, lying on my two knees, and I seen two women, and three women, and four women coming in, and they crossing themselves, and not saying a word. I looked out then, and there were men coming after them, and they holding a thing in the half of a red sail, and water dripping out of it—it was a dry day, Nora—and leaving a track to the door.

*She pauses again with her hand stretched out towards the door. It opens softly and old women begin to come in, crossing themselves on the threshold, and kneeling down in front of the stage with red petticoats over their heads.*

MAURYA (*half in a dream, to* CATHLEEN) Is it Patch, or Michael, or what is it at all?

CATHLEEN Michael is after being found in the far north, and when he is found there how could he be here in this place?

MAURYA There does be a power of young men floating round in the sea, and what way would they know if it was Michael they had, or another man like him, for when a man is nine days in the sea, and the wind blowing, it's hard set his own mother would be to say what man was it.

CATHLEEN It's Michael, God spare him, for they're after sending us a bit of his clothes from the far north.

*She reaches out and hands* MAURYA *the clothes that belonged to Michael.* MAURYA *stands up slowly and takes them in her hand.* NORA *looks out.*

NORA They're carrying a thing among them and there's water dripping out of it and leaving a track by the big stones.

CATHLEEN (*in a whisper to the women who have come in*) Is it Bartley it is?

ONE OF THE WOMEN It is surely, God rest his soul.

*Two younger women come in and pull out the table. Then men carry in the body of* BARTLEY, *laid on a plank, with a bit of sail over it, and lay it on the table.*

CATHLEEN (*to the women, as they are doing so*) What way was he drowned?

---

[5] *curagh* unstable vessel of tarred canvas on a wood frame; canoe.

ONE OF THE WOMEN The gray pony knocked him into the sea, and he was washed out where there is a great surf on the white rocks.

MAURYA *has gone over and knelt down at the head of the table. The women are keening softly and swaying themselves with a slow movement.* CATHLEEN *and* NORA *kneel at the other end of the table. The men kneel near the door.*

MAURYA (*raising her head and speaking as if she did not see the people around her*) They're all gone now, and there isn't anything more the sea can do to me. . . . I'll have no call now to be up crying and praying when the wind breaks from the south, and you can hear the surf is in the east, and the surf is in the west, making a great stir with the two noises, and they hitting one on the other. I'll have no call now to be going down and getting Holy Water in the dark nights after Samhain,[6] and I won't care what way the sea is when the other women will be keening. (*To* NORA.) Give me the Holy Water, Nora, there's a small sup still on the dresser.

NORA *gives it to her.*

MAURYA (*drops Michael's clothes across* BARTLEY'*s feet, and sprinkles the Holy Water over him*) It isn't that I haven't prayed for you, Bartley, to the Almighty God. It isn't that I haven't said prayers in the dark night till you wouldn't know what I'd be saying; but it's a great rest I'll have now, and it's time surely. It's a great rest I'll have now, and great sleeping in the long nights after Samhain, if it's only a bit of wet flour we do have to eat, and maybe a fish that would be stinking.

*She kneels down again, crossing herself, and saying prayers under her breath.*

CATHLEEN (*to an old man*) Maybe yourself and Eamon would make a coffin when the sun rises. We have fine white boards herself bought, God help her, thinking Michael would be found, and I have a new cake you can eat while you'll be working.

THE OLD MAN (*looking at the boards*) Are there nails with them?

CATHLEEN There are not, Colum; we didn't think of the nails.

ANOTHER MAN It's a great wonder she wouldn't think of the nails, and all the coffins she's seen made already.

CATHLEEN It's getting old she is, and broken.

MAURYA *stands up again very slowly and spreads out the pieces of Michael's clothes beside the body, sprinkling them with the last of the Holy Water.*

NORA (*in a whisper to* CATHLEEN) She's quiet now and easy; but the day Michael was drowned you could hear her crying out from this to the spring well. It's fonder she was of Michael, and would any one have thought that?

---

[6]*Samhain* November 1, All Saints' Day.

CATHLEEN (*slowly and clearly*) An old woman will be soon tired with anything she will do, and isn't it nine days herself is after crying and keening, and making great sorrow in the house?

MAURYA (*puts the empty cup mouth downwards on the table, and lays her hands together on* BARTLEY'S *feet*) They're all together this time, and the end is come. May the Almighty God have mercy on Bartley's soul, and on Michael's soul, and on the souls of Sheamus and Patch, and Stephen and Shawn (*bending her head*); and may He have mercy on my soul, Nora, and on the soul of every one is left living in the world.

*She pauses, and the keen rises a little more loudly from the women, then sinks away.*

MAURYA (*continuing*) Michael has a clean burial in the far north, by the grace of the Almighty God. Bartley will have a fine coffin out of the white boards, and a deep grave surely. What more can we want than that? No man at all can be living for ever, and we must be satisfied.

*She kneels down again and the curtain falls slowly.*

## QUESTIONS

1. In tragedy, the protagonist generally acts, suffers, and learns. The suffering is clear in this play; but what about the acting and learning?
   a. Does the protagonist act, or react? What are the effects of her actions?
   b. What does she learn? How is she different at the play's end than at the beginning?
2. What is the effect of a tragedy in which the protagonist is essentially "acted upon" rather than active? Support your thesis by references to *Riders to the Sea* (and to other tragedies that fit this not-very-common pattern, if you know any).
3. Discuss the language of the play. How does it support both the realistic and tragic aspects of the drama?

## SUSAN GLASPELL (1882–1948)

# *Trifles*

CHARACTERS

SHERIFF PETERS
MRS. PETERS
HALE
MRS. HALE
COUNTY ATTORNEY HENDERSON

SCENE. *The kitchen in the now abandoned farmhouse of John Wright, a gloomy kitchen, and left without having been put in order—the walls covered with a faded wall paper. Down right is a door leading to the parlor. On the right wall above this door is a built-in kitchen cupboard with shelves in the upper portion and drawers below. In the rear wall at right, up two steps is a door opening onto stairs leading to the second floor. In the rear wall at left is a door to the shed and from there to the outside. Between these two doors is an old-fashioned black iron stove. Running along the left wall from the shed door is an old iron sink and sink shelf, in which is set a hand pump. Downstage of the sink is an uncurtained window. Near the window is an old wooden rocker. Center stage is an unpainted wooden kitchen table with straight chairs on either side. There is a small chair down right. Unwashed pans under the sink, a loaf of bread outside the breadbox, a dish towel on the table—other signs of incompleted work. At the rear the shed door opens and the* SHERIFF *comes in followed by the* COUNTY ATTORNEY *and* HALE. *The* SHERIFF *and* HALE *are men in middle life, the* COUNTY ATTORNEY *is a young man; all are much bundled up and go at once to the stove. They are followed by the two women—the* SHERIFF'S *wife,* MRS. PETERS, *first; she is a slight wiry woman, a thin nervous face.* MRS. HALE *is larger and would ordinarily be called more comfortable looking, but she is disturbed now and looks fearfully about as she enters. The women have come in slowly, and stand close together near the door.*

COUNTY ATTORNEY (*at stove rubbing his hands*) This feels good. Come up to the fire, ladies.

MRS. PETERS (*after taking a step forward*) I'm not—cold.

SHERIFF (*unbuttoning his overcoat and stepping away from the stove to right of table as if to mark the beginning of official business*) Now, Mr. Hale, before we move things about, you explain to Mr. Henderson just what you saw when you came here yesterday morning.

COUNTY ATTORNEY (*crossing down to left of the table*) By the way, has anything been moved? Are things just as you left them yesterday?

SHERIFF (*looking about*) It's just about the same. When it dropped below zero last night I thought I'd better send Frank out this morning to make a fire for us—(*sits right of center table*) no use getting pneumonia with a big case on, but I told him not to touch anything except the stove—and you know Frank.

COUNTY ATTORNEY Somebody should have been left here yesterday.

SHERIFF Oh—yesterday. When I had to send Frank to Morris Center for that man who went crazy—I want you to know I had my hands full yesterday. I knew you could get back from Omaha by today and as long as I went over everything here myself——

COUNTY ATTORNEY Well, Mr. Hale, tell just what happened when you came here yesterday morning.

HALE (*crossing down to above table*) Harry and I had started to town with a load of potatoes. We came along the road from my place and as I got here I said, "I'm going to see if I can't get John Wright to go in with me on a party telephone." I spoke to Wright about it once before and he put me off, saying folks talked too much anyway, and all he asked was peace and quiet—I guess you know about how much he talked himself; but I thought maybe if I went to the house and talked about it before his wife, though I said to Harry that I didn't know as what his wife wanted made much difference to John——

COUNTY ATTORNEY Let's talk about that later, Mr. Hale. I do want to talk about that, but tell now just what happened when you got to the house.

HALE I didn't hear or see anything; I knocked at the door, and still it was all quiet inside. I knew they must be up, it was past eight o'clock. So I knocked again, and I thought I heard somebody say, "Come in." I wasn't sure, I'm not sure yet, but I opened the door—this door (*indicating the door by which the two women are still standing*) and there in that rocker—(*pointing to it*) sat Mrs. Wright. (*They all look at the rocker down left.*)

COUNTY ATTORNEY What—was she doing?

HALE She was rockin' back and forth. She had her apron in her hand and was kind of—pleating it.

COUNTY ATTORNEY And how did she—look?

HALE Well, she looked queer.

COUNTY ATTORNEY How do you mean—queer?

HALE Well, as if she didn't know what she was going to do next. And kind of done up.

COUNTY ATTORNEY (*takes out notebook and pencil and sits left of center table*) How did she seem to feel about your coming?

HALE Why, I don't think she minded—one way or other. She didn't pay much attention. I said, "How do, Mrs. Wright, it's cold, ain't it?" And she said, "Is it?"—and went on kind of pleating at her apron. Well, I was surprised; she didn't ask me to come up to the stove, or to set down, but just sat there, not even looking at me, so I said, "I want to see John." And then she—laughed. I guess you would call it a laugh. I thought of Harry and the team outside, so I said a little sharp: "Can't I see John?" "No," she says, kind o' dull like. "Ain't he home?" says I. "Yes," says she, "he's home." "Then why can't I see him?" I asked her, out of patience. " 'Cause he's dead," says she. "*Dead?*" says I. She just nodded her head, not getting a bit excited, but rockin' back and forth. "Why—where is he?" says I, not knowing what to say. She just pointed upstairs—like that. (*Himself pointing to the room above.*) I started for the stairs, with the idea of going up there. I walked from there to here—then I says, "Why, what did he die of?" "He died of a rope round his neck," says she, and just went on pleatin' at her apron. Well, I went out and called Harry. I thought I might—need help. We went upstairs and there he was lyin'——

COUNTY ATTORNEY I think I'd rather have you go into that upstairs, where you can point it all out. Just go on now with the rest of the story.

HALE Well, my first thought was to get that rope off. It looked . . . (*stops, his face twitches*) . . . but Harry, he went up to him, and he said, "No, he's dead all right, and we'd better not touch anything." So we went back downstairs. She was still sitting that same way. "Has anybody been notified?" I asked. "No," says she, unconcerned. "Who did this, Mrs. Wright?" said Harry. He said it business-like—and she stopped pleatin' of her apron. "I don't know," she says. "You don't *know*?" says Harry. "No," says she. "Weren't you sleepin' in the bed with him?" says Harry. "Yes," says she, "but I was on the inside." "Somebody slipped a rope round his neck and strangled him and you didn't wake up?" says Harry. "I didn't wake up," she said after him. We must 'a' looked as if we didn't see how that could be, for after a minute she said, "I sleep sound." Harry was going to ask her more questions but I said maybe we ought to let her tell her story first to the coroner, or the sheriff, so Harry went fast as he could to Rivers' place, where there's a telephone.

COUNTY ATTORNEY And what did Mrs. Wright do when she knew that you had gone for the coroner?

HALE She moved from the rocker to that chair over there (*pointing to a small chair in the down right corner*) and just sat there with her hands held together and looking down. I got a feeling that I ought to make some conversation, so I said I had come in to see if John wanted to put in a telephone, and at that she started to laugh, and then she stopped and looked at me—scared. (*The* COUNTY ATTORNEY, *who has had his notebook out, makes a note.*) I dunno, maybe it wasn't scared. I wouldn't like to say it was. Soon Harry got back, and then Dr. Lloyd came and you, Mr. Peters, and so I guess that's all I know that you don't.

COUNTY ATTORNEY (*rising and looking around*) I guess we'll go upstairs first—and then out to the barn and around there. (*To the* SHERIFF.) You're convinced that there was nothing important here—nothing that would point to any motive?

SHERIFF Nothing here but kitchen things. (*The* COUNTY ATTORNEY, *after again looking around the kitchen, opens the door of a cupboard closet in right wall. He brings a small chair from right—gets on it and looks on a shelf. Pulls his hand away, sticky.*)

COUNTY ATTORNEY Here's a nice mess. (*The women draw nearer up center.*)

MRS. PETERS (*to the other woman*) Oh, her fruit; it did freeze. (*To the Lawyer.*) She worried about that when it turned so cold. She said the fire'd go out and her jars would break.

SHERIFF (*rises*) Well, can you beat the woman! Held for murder and worryin' about her preserves.

COUNTY ATTORNEY (*getting down from chair*) I guess before we're through she may have something more serious than preserves to worry about. (*Crosses down right center.*)

HALE Well, women are used to worrying over trifles. (*The two women move a little closer together.*)

COUNTY ATTORNEY (*with the gallantry of a young politician*) And yet, for all their worries, what would we do without the ladies? (*The women do not unbend. He goes below the center table to the sink, takes a dipperful of water from the pail and pouring it into a basin, washes his hands. While he is doing this the* SHERIFF *and* HALE *cross to cupboard, which they inspect. The* COUNTY ATTORNEY *starts to wipe his hands on the roller towel, turns it for a cleaner place.*) Dirty towels! (*Kicks his foot against the pans under the sink.*) Not much of a housekeeper, would you say, ladies?

MRS. HALE (*stiffly*) There's a great deal of work to be done on a farm.

COUNTY ATTORNEY To be sure. And yet (*with a little bow to her*) I know there are some Dickson County farmhouses which do not have such roller towels. (*He gives it a pull to expose its full length again.*)

MRS. HALE Those towels get dirty awful quick. Men's hands aren't always as clean as they might be.

COUNTY ATTORNEY Ah, loyal to your sex, I see. But you and Mrs. Wright were neighbors. I suppose you were friends, too.

MRS. HALE (*shaking her head*) I've not seen much of her of late years. I've not been in this house—it's more than a year.

COUNTY ATTORNEY (*crossing to women up center*) And why was that? You didn't like her?

MRS. HALE I liked her all well enough. Farmers' wives have their hands full, Mr. Henderson. And then——

COUNTY ATTORNEY Yes ——?

MRS. HALE (*looking about*) It never seemed a very cheerful place.

COUNTY ATTORNEY No—it's not cheerful. I shouldn't say she had the homemaking instinct.

MRS. HALE Well, I don't know as Wright had, either.

COUNTY ATTORNEY You mean that they didn't get on very well?

MRS. HALE No, I don't mean anything. But I don't think a place'd be any cheerfuller for John Wright's being in it.

COUNTY ATTORNEY I'd like to talk more of that a little later. I want to get the lay of things upstairs now. (*He goes past the women to up right where steps lead to a stair door.*)

SHERIFF I suppose anything Mrs. Peters does'll be all right. She was to take in some clothes for her, you know, and a few little things. We left in such a hurry yesterday.

COUNTY ATTORNEY Yes, but I would like to see what you take, Mrs. Peters, and keep an eye out for anything that might be of use to us.

MRS. PETERS Yes, Mr. Henderson. (*The men leave by up right door to stairs. The women listen to the men's steps on the stairs, then look about the kitchen.*)

MRS. HALE (*crossing left to sink*) I'd hate to have men coming into my kitchen, snooping around and criticizing. (*She arranges the pans under sink which the* LAWYER *had shoved out of place.*)

MRS. PETERS Of course it's no more than their duty. (*Crosses to cupboard up right.*)

MRS. HALE Duty's all right, but I guess that deputy sheriff that came out to make the fire might have got a little of this on. (*Gives the roller towel a pull.*) Wish I'd thought of that sooner. Seems mean to talk about her for not having things slicked up when she had to come away in such a hurry. (*Crosses right to* MRS. PETERS *at cupboard.*)

MRS. PETERS (*who has been looking through cupboard, lifts one end of towel that covers a pan*) She had bread set. (*Stands still.*)

MRS. HALE (*eyes fixed on a loaf of bread beside the breadbox, which is on a low shelf of the cupboard.*) She was going to put this in there. (*Picks up loaf, then abruptly drops it. In a manner of returning to familiar things.*) It's a shame about her fruit. I wonder if it's all gone. (*Gets up on the chair and looks.*) I think there's some here that's all right, Mrs. Peters. Yes—here; (*holding it toward the window*) this is cherries, too. (*Looking again.*) I declare I believe that's the only one. (*Gets down, jar in her hand. Goes to the sink and wipes it off on the outside.*) She'll feel awful bad after all her hard work in the hot weather. I remember the afternoon I put up my cherries last summer. (*She puts the jar on the big kitchen table, center of the room. With a sigh, is about to sit down in the rocking chair. Before she is seated realizes what chair it is; with a slow look at it, steps back. The chair which she has touched rocks back and forth.* MRS. PETERS *moves to center table and they both watch the chair rock for a moment or two.*)

MRS. PETERS (*shaking off the mood which the empty rocking chair has evoked. Now in a businesslike manner she speaks.*) Well I must get those things from the front room closet. (*She goes to the door at the right but, after looking into the other room, steps back.*) You coming with me, Mrs. Hale? You could help me carry them. (*They go in the other room; reappear,* MRS. PETERS *carrying a dress, petticoat and skirt,* MRS. HALE *following with a pair of shoes.*) My, it's cold in there. (*She puts the clothes on the big table, and hurries to the stove.*)

MRS. HALE (*right of center table examining the skirt*) Wright was close. I think maybe that's why she kept so much to herself. She didn't even belong to the Ladies' Aid. I suppose she felt she couldn't do her part, and then you don't enjoy things when you feel shabby. I heard she used to wear pretty clothes and be lively, when she was Minnie Foster, one of the town girls singing in the choir. But that—oh, that was thirty years ago. This all you want to take in?

MRS. PETERS She said she wanted an apron. Funny thing to want, for there isn't much to get you dirty in jail, goodness knows. But I suppose just to make her feel more natural. (*Crosses to cupboard.*) She said they was in the top drawer in this cupboard. Yes, here. And then her little shawl that always hung behind the door. (*Opens stair door and looks.*) Yes, here it is. (*Quickly shuts door leading upstairs.*)

MRS. HALE (*abruptly moving toward her*) Mrs. Peters?

MRS. PETERS Yes, Mrs. Hale? (*At up right door.*)

MRS. HALE Do you think she did it?

MRS. PETERS (*in a frightened voice*) Oh, I don't know.

MRS. HALE Well, I don't think she did. Asking for an apron and her little shawl. Worrying about her fruit.

MRS. PETERS (*starts to speak, glances up, where footsteps are heard in the room above. In a low voice*) Mr. Peters says it looks bad for her. Mr. Henderson is awful sarcastic in a speech and he'll make fun of her sayin' she didn't wake up.

MRS. HALE Well, I guess John Wright didn't wake when they was slipping that rope under his neck.

MRS. PETERS (*crossing slowly to table and placing shawl and apron on table with other clothing*) No, it's strange. It must have been done awful crafty and still. They say it was such a—funny way to kill a man, rigging it all up like that.

MRS. HALE (*crossing to left of* MRS. PETERS *at table*) That's just what Mr. Hale said. There was a gun in the house. He says that's what he can't understand.

MRS. PETERS Mr. Henderson said coming out that what was needed for the case was a motive; something to show anger, or—sudden feeling.

MRS. HALE (*who is standing by the table*) Well, I don't see any signs of anger around here. (*She puts her hand on the dish towel which lies on the table, stands looking down at table, one-half of which is clean, the other half messy.*) It's wiped to here. (*Makes a move as if to finish work, then turns and looks at loaf of bread outside the breadbox. Drops towel. In that voice of coming back to familiar things.*) Wonder how they are finding things upstairs. (*Crossing below table to down right.*) I hope she had it a little more red-up up there. You know, it seems kind of *sneaking*. Locking her up in town and then coming out here and trying to get her own house to turn against her!

MRS. PETERS But, Mrs. Hale, the law is the law.

MRS. HALE I s'pose 'tis. (*Unbuttoning her coat.*) Better loosen up your things, Mrs. Peters. You won't feel them when you go out. (MRS.

PETERS *takes off her fur tippet, goes to hang it on chair back left of table, stands looking at the work basket on floor near down left window.*)

MRS. PETERS She was piecing a quilt. (*She brings the large sewing basket to the center table and they look at the bright pieces,* MRS. HALE *above the table and* MRS. PETERS *left of it.*)

MRS. HALE It's a log cabin pattern. Pretty, isn't it? I wonder if she was goin' to quilt it or just knot it? (*Footsteps have been heard coming down the stairs. The* SHERIFF *enters followed by* HALE *and the* COUNTY ATTORNEY.)

SHERIFF They wonder if she was going to quilt it or just knot it! (*The men laugh, the women look abashed.*)

COUNTY ATTORNEY (*rubbing his hands over the stove*) Frank's fire didn't do much up there, did it? Well, let's go out to the barn and get that cleared up. (*The men go outside by up left door.*)

MRS. HALE (*resentfully*) I don't know as there's anything so strange, our takin' up our time with little things while we're waiting for them to get the evidence. (*She sits in chair right of table smoothing out a block with decision.*) I don't see as it's anything to laugh about.

MRS. PETERS (*apologetically*) Of course they've got awful important things on their minds. (*Pulls up a chair and joins* MRS. HALE *at the left of the table.*)

MRS. HALE (*examining another block*) Mrs. Peters, look at this one. Here, this is the one she was working on, and look at the sewing! All the rest of it has been so nice and even. And look at this! It's all over the place! Why, it looks as if she didn't know what she was about! (*After she has said this they look at each other, then start to glance back at the door. After an instant* MRS. HALE *has pulled at a knot and ripped the sewing.*)

MRS. PETERS Oh, what are you doing, Mrs. Hale?

MRS. HALE (*mildly*) Just pulling out a stitch or two that's not sewed very good. (*Threading a needle.*) Bad sewing always made me fidgety.

MRS. PETERS (*with a glance at door, nervously*) I don't think we ought to touch things.

MRS. HALE I'll just finish up this end. (*Suddenly stopping and leaning forward.*) Mrs. Peters?

MRS. PETERS Yes, Mrs. Hale?

MRS. HALE What do you suppose she was so nervous about?

MRS. PETERS Oh—I don't know. I don't know as she was nervous. I sometimes sew awful queer when I'm just tired. (MRS. HALE *starts to say something, looks at* MRS. PETERS, *then goes on sewing.*) Well, I must get these things wrapped up. They may be through sooner than we think. (*Putting apron and other things together.*) I wonder where I can find a piece of paper, and string. (*Rises.*)

MRS. HALE In that cupboard, maybe.

MRS. PETERS (*crosses right looking in cupboard*) Why, here's a bird-cage. (*Holds it up.*) Did she have a bird, Mrs. Hale?

MRS. HALE Why, I don't know whether she did or not—I've not been here for so long. There was a man around last year selling canaries cheap, but I don't know as she took one; maybe she did. She used to sing real pretty herself.

MRS. PETERS (*glancing around*) Seems funny to think of a bird here. But she must have had one, or why would she have a cage? I wonder what happened to it?

MRS. HALE I s'pose maybe the cat got it.

MRS. PETERS No, she didn't have a cat. She's got that feeling some people have about cats—being afraid of them. My cat got in her room and she was real upset and asked me to take it out.

MRS. HALE My sister Bessie was like that. Queer, ain't it?

MRS. PETERS (*examining the cage*) Why, look at this door. It's broke. One hinge is pulled apart. (*Takes a step down to* MRS. HALE*'s right.*)

MRS. HALE (*looking too*) Looks as if someone must have been rough with it.

MRS. PETERS Why, yes. (*She brings the cage forward and puts it on the table.*)

MRS. HALE (*glancing toward up left door*) I wish if they're going to find any evidence they'd be about it. I don't like this place.

MRS. PETERS But I'm awful glad you came with me, Mrs. Hale. It would be lonesome for me sitting here alone.

MRS. HALE It would, wouldn't it? (*Dropping her sewing.*) But I tell you what I do wish, Mrs. Peters. I wish I had come over sometimes when *she* was here. I—(*looking around the room*)—wish I had.

MRS. PETERS But of course you were awful busy, Mrs. Hale—your house and your children.

MRS. HALE (*rises and crosses left*) I could've come. I stayed away because it weren't cheerful—and that's why I ought to have come. I—(*looking out left window*)—I've never liked this place. Maybe because it's down in a hollow and you don't see the road. I dunno what it is, but it's a lonesome place and always was. I wish I had come over to see Minnie Foster sometimes. I can see now—(*Shakes her head.*)

MRS. PETERS (*left of table and above it*) Well, you mustn't reproach yourself, Mrs. Hale. Somehow we just don't see how it is with other folks until—something turns up.

MRS. HALE Not having children makes less work—but it makes a quiet house, and Wright out to work all day, and no company when he did come in. (*Turning from window.*) Did you know John Wright, Mrs. Peters?

MRS. PETERS Not to know him; I've seen him in town. They say he was a good man.

MRS. HALE Yes—good; he didn't drink, and kept his word as well as most, I guess, and paid his debts. But he was a hard man, Mrs. Peters. Just to pass the time of day with him——(*Shivers.*) Like a raw wind that gets to the bone. (*Pauses, her eye falling on the cage.*) I should think she would 'a' wanted a bird. But what do you suppose went with it?

MRS. PETERS I don't know, unless it got sick and died. (*She reaches over and swings the broken door, swings it again, both women watch it.*)

MRS. HALE You weren't raised round here, were you? (MRS. PETERS *shakes her head.*) You didn't know—her?

MRS. PETERS Not till they brought her yesterday.

MRS. HALE She—come to think of it, she was kind of like a bird herself—real sweet and pretty, but kind of timid and—fluttery. How—she—did—change. (*Silence: then as if struck by a happy thought and relieved to get back to everyday things. Crosses right above* MRS. PETERS *to cupboard, replaces small chair used to stand on to its original place down right.*) Tell you what, Mrs. Peters, why don't you take the quilt in with you? It might take up her mind.

MRS. PETERS Why, I think that's a real nice idea, Mrs. Hale. There couldn't possibly be any objection to it could there? Now, just what would I take? I wonder if her patches are in here—and her things. (*They look in the sewing basket.*)

MRS. HALE (*crosses to right of table*) Here's some red. I expect this has got sewing things in it. (*Brings out a fancy box.*) What a pretty box. Looks like something somebody would give you. Maybe her scissors are in here. (*Opens box. Suddenly puts her hand to her nose.*) Why——(MRS. PETERS *bends nearer, then turns her face away.*) There's something wrapped up in this piece of silk.

MRS. PETERS Why, this isn't her scissors.

MRS. HALE (*lifting the silk*) Oh, Mrs. Peters—it's——(MRS. PETERS *bends closer.*)

MRS. PETERS It's the bird.

MRS. HALE But, Mrs. Peters—look at it! Its neck! Look at its neck! It's all—other side *to.*

MRS. PETERS Somebody—wrung—its—neck. (*Their eyes meet. A look of growing comprehension, of horror. Steps are heard outside.* MRS. HALE *slips box under quilt pieces, and sinks into her chair. Enter* SHERIFF *and* COUNTY ATTORNEY. MRS. PETERS *steps down left and stands looking out of window.*)

COUNTY ATTORNEY (*as one turning from serious things to little pleasantries*) Well, ladies, have you decided whether she was going to quilt it or knot it? (*Crosses to center above table.*)

MRS. PETERS We think she was going to—knot it. (SHERIFF *crosses to right of stove, lifts stove lid and glances at fire, then stands warming hands at stove.*)

COUNTY ATTORNEY Well, that's interesting, I'm sure. (*Seeing the birdcage.*) Has the bird flown?

MRS. HALE (*putting more quilt pieces over the box*) We think the—cat got it.

COUNTY ATTORNEY (*preoccupied*) Is there a cat? (MRS. HALE *glances in a quick covert way at* MRS. PETERS.)

MRS. PETERS Well, not *now.* They're superstitious, you know. They leave.

COUNTY ATTORNEY (*to* SHERIFF PETERS, *continuing an interrupted conversation*) No sign at all of anyone having come from the outside. Their own rope. Now let's go up again and go over it piece by piece. (*They start upstairs.*) It would have to have been someone who knew just the—— (MRS. PETERS *sits down left of table. The two women sit there not looking at one another, but as if peering into something and at the same time holding back. When they talk now it is in the manner of feeling their way over strange ground, as if afraid of what they are saying, but as if they cannot help saying it.*)

MRS. HALE She liked the bird. She was going to bury it in that pretty box.

MRS. PETERS (*in a whisper*) When I was a girl—my kitten—there was a boy took a hatchet, and before my eyes—and before I could get there—— (*Covers her face an instant.*) If they hadn't held me back I would have—(*catches herself, looks upstairs where steps are heard, falters weakly*)—hurt him.

MRS. HALE (*with a slow look around her*) I wonder how it would seem never to have had any children around. (*Pause.*) No, Wright wouldn't like the bird—a thing that sang. She used to sing. He killed that, too.

MRS. PETERS (*moving uneasily*) We don't know who killed the bird.

MRS. HALE I knew John Wright.

MRS. PETERS It was an awful thing was done in this house that night, Mrs. Hale. Killing a man while he slept, slipping a rope around his neck that choked the life out of him.

MRS. HALE His neck. Choked the life out of him. (*Her hand goes out and rests on the bird-cage.*)

MRS. PETERS (*with rising voice*) We don't know who killed him. We don't *know*.

MRS. HALE (*her own feeling not interrupted*) If there'd been years and years of nothing, then a bird to sing to you, it would be awful—still, after the bird was still.

MRS. PETERS (*something within her speaking*) I know what stillness is. When we homesteaded in Dakota, and my first baby died—after he was two years old, and me with no other then——

MRS. HALE (*moving*) How soon do you suppose they'll be through looking for the evidence?

MRS. PETERS I know what stillness is. (*Pulling herself back.*) The law has got to punish crime, Mrs. Hale.

MRS. HALE (*not as if answering that*) I wish you'd seen Minnie Foster when she wore a white dress with blue ribbons and stood up there in the choir and sang. (*A look around the room.*) Oh, I *wish* I'd come over here once in a while! That was a crime! That was a crime! Who's going to punish that?

MRS. PETERS (*looking upstairs*) We mustn't—take on.

MRS. HALE I might have known she needed help! I know how things can be—for women. I tell you, it's queer, Mrs. Peters. We live close together and we live far apart. We all go through the same things—it's all just a different kind of the same thing. (*Brushes her eyes, noticing the jar of fruit, reaches out for it.*) If I was you I wouldn't tell her her fruit was gone. Tell her it *ain't*. Tell her it's all right. Take this in to prove it to her. She—she may never know whether it was broke or not.

MRS. PETERS (*takes the jar, looks about for something to wrap it in; takes petticoat from the clothes brought from the other room, very nervously begins winding this around the jar. In a false voice*) My, it's a good thing the men couldn't hear us. Wouldn't they just laugh! Getting all stirred up over a little thing like a—dead canary. As if that could have anything to do with—with—wouldn't they *laugh!* (*The men are heard coming downstairs.*)

MRS. HALE (*under her breath*) Maybe they would—maybe they wouldn't.

COUNTY ATTORNEY No, Peters, it's all perfectly clear except a reason for doing it. But you know juries when it comes to women. If there was some definite thing. (*Crosses slowly to above table.* SHERIFF *crosses down right.* MRS. HALE *and* MRS. PETERS *remain seated at either side of table.*) Something to show—something to make a story about—a thing that would connect up with this strange way of doing it——(*The women's eyes meet for an instant. Enter* HALE *from outer door.*)

HALE (*remaining by door*) Well, I've got the team around. Pretty cold out there.

COUNTY ATTORNEY I'm going to stay awhile by myself. (*To the* SHERIFF.) You can send Frank out for me, can't you? I want to go over everything. I'm not satisfied that we can't do better.

SHERIFF Do you want to see what Mrs. Peters is going to take in? (*The* LAWYER *picks up the apron, laughs.*)

COUNTY ATTORNEY Oh, I guess they're not very dangerous things the ladies have picked out. (*Moves a few things about, disturbing the quilt pieces which cover the box. Steps back.*) No, Mrs. Peters doesn't need supervising. For that matter a sheriff's wife is married to the law. Ever think of it that way, Mrs. Peters?

MRS. PETERS Not—just that way.

SHERIFF (*chuckling*) Married to the law. (*Moves to down right door to the other room.*) I just want you to come in here a minute, George. We ought to take a look at these windows.

COUNTY ATTORNEY (*scoffingly*) Oh, windows!

SHERIFF We'll be right out, Mr. Hale. (HALE *goes outside. The* SHERIFF *follows the* COUNTY ATTORNEY *into the room. Then* MRS. HALE *rises, hands tight together, looking intensely at* MRS. PETERS, *whose eyes make a slow turn, finally meeting* MRS. HALE'*s. A moment* MRS. HALE *holds her, then her own eyes point the way to where the box is concealed. Suddenly* MRS. PETERS *throws back quilt pieces and tries to put the box in the bag she is carrying. It is too big. She opens box, starts to take bird out, cannot touch it, goes to pieces, stands there helpless. Sound of a knob turning in the other room.* MRS. HALE *snatches the box and puts it in the pocket of her big coat. Enter* COUNTY ATTORNEY *and* SHERIFF, *who remains down right.*)

COUNTY ATTORNEY (*crosses to up left door facetiously*) Well, Henry, at least we found out that she was not going to quilt it. She was going to—what is it you call it, ladies?

MRS. HALE (*standing center below table facing front, her hand against her pocket*) We call it—knot it, Mr. Henderson.

*Curtain*

## QUESTIONS

1. What does *Trifles* say about men? about women? about the ways in which they act toward each other? In how many different ways does Glaspell touch on this theme? (Notice the speech patterns of the men and the women. How do they differ? What themes and concerns do you hear from each?)
2. Discuss the use of "trifles" in the play.
3. Discuss the characterization of Mrs. Hale and Mrs. Peters. How are they contrasted in the early part of the play? What happens to them during the course of the play?
4. With which of the characters in this play do your sympathies lie? Why? To what extent do you approve of their actions?

# 5 *Contemporary Drama*

Our final readings in drama bring our study up to the middle of the twentieth century. They include two plays: one a tragedy, Arthur Miller's *Death of a Salesman,* and the other a comedy, Eugène Ionesco's *The Gap.*

In *Death of a Salesman,* Miller has blended many of the practices of the nineteenth-century realistic drama with those of classical Greek and Shakespearean tragedies to create a modern tragedy, a tragedy of the common man. The blend is made possible by the deliberate setting aside of one of Aristotle's rules, which says that tragic heroes must be people we can look up to. We cannot look up to Willy Loman. Hamlet and Oedipus were both seekers of truth. Willy is afraid of the truth, because if he should realize and admit the truth, he would admit his failures as husband, father, and salesman. And failure, by Willy's standards, is as great a crime as incest is by Oedipus'.

Miller has said that "the tragic feeling is evoked in us when we are in the presence of a character who is ready to lay down his life, if need be, to secure one thing—his sense of personal dignity." In this sense, Willy is certainly tragic; and the fact that the vision of dignity for which he kills himself is seen by many to be a false one (including, within the play, Willy's son Biff, who bitterly protests his father's choice of sham dignity over true) merely makes the tragedy the more fearful. Can we be sure that our own values are truer?

Early tragedy, dealing with outstanding individuals, spoke of how those individuals could shape the society around them. The character of the man who rules Thebes or Denmark is seen as important to the health of those countries—and Hamlet is judged, in his play, as both man and prince. But twentieth-century drama, like its immediate predecessor realistic drama, and like twentieth-century fiction, deals with heroes and heroines who have no power to alter society. Instead, these people are at society's mercy for much of their own character. Indeed, even their sense of their own worth is formed not so much from self-knowledge as from the dictates of their society.

In its emphasis of society's effects on the individual and of parents' influence on their children, *Death of a Salesman* embodies many of the concerns of nineteenth-century drama and contemporary fiction. Biff and Willy are not judged for what they can or cannot contribute to society. Rather, society is judged for what it has contributed to creating Willy—and, through him, Biff. Money, normally the province of fiction or comedy, is a major subject in *Death of a Salesman.* And where money is a subject, society (which determines who shall have money, and why) is aways an issue.

In form, too, *Death of a Salesman* is notably a product of the twentieth century. The language is that of everyday speech. The stage setting and costumes suggest average people. Within this frame of simple realism, however, Willy's imaginings are given life. The realities of the mind are made visible, superimposed on the realities of the world; and the audience, as so often happens in twentieth-century art, is given the task of sorting the two out.

Willy is a man on the brink of madness. He hears and sees things that are not there: scenes from the past, words from an absent brother. But whenever he hears or sees them, we hear or see them as well. One minute we see Biff as a thirty-four-year-old man, the next as a high school student; for Willy can no longer keep the past and the present apart. Intolerant of a present that contains no promises of good things to come, his mind shifts between the remembered past and an imaginary future; and his viewers must shift with him.

Watching past and present, reality and fantasy intertwine, we piece together Willy's past and his values. He could not state them so clearly as his uncontrollable mind acts them out. The soul-searching that Willy's conscious mind rejects, his unconscious mind insists on. We witness the insistence and rejection both, and so are led to our understanding of the man and his tragedy.

The comedy we will read is Ionesco's *The Gap.* Again, self-knowledge is in question; again, the issue of how a revelation in self-knowledge will affect the hero is paramount. Again too, the theme of an individual's true worth, as contrasted with society's belief of his worth, is raised. But Ionesco is a highly innovative playwright. He experiments with various mixtures of realism and fantasy, in revolt against the nineteenth century's emphasis on undiluted realism. And so we see not only an individual set against society, but our own sense of contemporary society set against the comedy's distortions of that society.

Like Wilde's comedy, Ionesco's comedy concerns itself with the essential absurdity of certain social assumptions and pretenses. In *The Importance of Being Earnest,* however, the attack is expressed primarily in speeches that are so clever and light-hearted as to rob the attack of a large part of its force: these pretenses may be very silly, the play seems to say, but they do provide some delightful fun. In contrast, Ionesco's speech is not witty; nor does his comedy contain any suggestion that its characters are enjoying their situation. The speech is as plain and abrupt as that of any realistic drama; it, and the action, depart from realism only to become absurd. Indeed, as *The Gap* unfolds, the social mores depicted, and the characters' dependence on them, become almost nightmarish in their intensification of particular social absurdities.

Twentieth-century drama is thus most notable for its experimental blends of realism and fantasy, its striving for a deeper truthfulness than realism alone can convey. Further experimentation along this line is being made; for ours is a period when fantasy and its relationship to psychological truth are much in use among writers and other artists. The final point to be made, therefore, is that drama, like any other art form, is never static. Its most enduring appeal—whether within one play or within a century of plays—lies in our expectation of looking around the next corner, wondering what is coming next.

# ARTHUR MILLER (1915–  )

## *Death of a Salesman*

*Certain Private Conversations in Two Acts and a Requiem*

CHARACTERS

| | |
|---|---|
| WILLY LOMAN | UNCLE BEN |
| LINDA | HOWARD WAGNER |
| BIFF | JENNY |
| HAPPY | STANLEY |
| BERNARD | MISS FORSYTHE |
| THE WOMAN | LETTA |
| CHARLEY | |

*The action takes place in* WILLY LOMAN'S *house and yard and in various places he visits in the New York and Boston of today. Throughout the play, in the stage directions, left and right mean stage left and stage right.*

## ACT ONE

### An Overture

*A melody is heard, played upon a flute. It is small and fine, telling of grass and trees and the horizon. The curtain rises.*

*Before us is the Salesman's house. We are aware of towering, angular shapes behind it, surrounding it on all sides. Only the blue light of the sky falls upon the house and forestage; the surrounding area shows an angry glow of orange. As more light appears, we see a solid vault of apartment houses around the small, fragile-seeming home. An air of the dream clings to the place, a dream rising out of reality. The kitchen at center seems actual enough, for there is a kitchen table with three chairs, and a refrig-*

*erator. But no other fixtures are seen. At the back of the kitchen there is a draped entrance, which leads to the living room. To the right of the kitchen, on a level raised two feet, is a bedroom furnished only with a brass bedstead and a straight chair. On a shelf over the bed a silver athletic trophy stands. A window opens onto the apartment house at the side.*

*Behind the kitchen, on a level raised six and a half feet, is the boys' bedroom, at present barely visible. Two beds are dimly seen, and at the back of the room a dormer window. (This bedroom is above the unseen living room.) At the left a stairway curves up to it from the kitchen.*

*The entire setting is wholly or, in some places, partially transparent. The roof-line of the house is one-dimensional; under and over it we see the apartment buildings. Before the house lies an apron, curving beyond the forestage into the orchestra. This forward area serves as the back yard as well as the locale of all* WILLY'S *imaginings and of his city scenes. Whenever the action is in the present the actors observe the imaginary wall-lines, entering the house only through its door at the left. But in the scenes of the past these boundaries are broken, and characters enter or leave a room by stepping "through" a wall onto the forestage.*

*From the right,* WILLY LOMAN, *the Salesman, enters, carrying two large sample cases. The flute plays on. He hears but is not aware of it. He is past sixty years of age, dressed quietly. Even as he crosses the stage to the doorway of the house, his exhaustion is apparent. He unlocks the door, comes into the kitchen, and thankfully lets his burden down, feeling the soreness of his palms. A word-sigh escapes his lips—it might be "Oh, boy, oh, boy." He closes the door, then carries his cases out into the living room, through the draped kitchen doorway.*

LINDA, *his wife, has stirred in her bed at the right. She gets out and puts on a robe, listening. Most often jovial, she has developed an iron repression of her exceptions to* WILLY'S *behavior—she more than loves him, she admires him, as though his mercurial nature, his temper, his massive dreams and little cruelties, served her only as sharp reminders of the turbulent longings within him, longings which she shares but lacks the temperament to utter and follow to their end.*

LINDA (*hearing* WILLY *outside the bedroom, calls with some trepidation*) Willy!

WILLY It's all right. I came back.

LINDA Why? What happened? (*Slight pause*) Did something happen, Willy?

WILLY No, nothing happened.

LINDA You didn't smash the car, did you?

WILLY (*with casual irritation*) I said nothing happened. Didn't you hear me?

LINDA Don't you feel well?

WILLY I'm tired to the death. (*The flute has faded away. He sits on the bed beside her, a little numb*) I couldn't make it. I just couldn't make it, Linda.

LINDA (*very carefully, delicately*) Where were you all day? You look terrible.

WILLY I got as far as a little above Yonkers. I stopped for a cup of coffee. Maybe it was the coffee.

LINDA What?

WILLY (*after a pause*) I suddenly couldn't drive any more. The car kept going off onto the shoulder, y'know?

LINDA (*helpfully*) Oh. Maybe it was the steering again. I don't think Angelo knows the Studebaker.

WILLY No, it's me, it's me. Suddenly I realize I'm goin' sixty miles an hour and I don't remember the last five minutes. I'm—I can't seem to—keep my mind to it.

LINDA Maybe it's your glasses. You never went for your new glasses.

WILLY No, I see everything. I came back ten miles an hour. It took me nearly four hours from Yonkers.

LINDA (*resigned*) Well, you'll just have to take a rest, Willy, you can't continue this way.

WILLY I just got back from Florida.

LINDA But you didn't rest your mind. Your mind is overactive, and the mind is what counts, dear.

WILLY I'll start out in the morning. Maybe I'll feel better in the morning. (*She is taking off his shoes*) These goddam arch supports are killing me.

LINDA Take an aspirin. Should I get you an aspirin? It'll soothe you.

WILLY (*with wonder*) I was driving along, you understand? And I was fine. I was even observing the scenery. You can imagine, me looking at scenery, on the road every week of my life. But it's so beautiful up there, Linda, the trees are so thick, and the sun is warm. I opened the windshield and just let the warm air bathe over me. And then all of a sudden I'm goin' off the road! I'm tellin' ya, I absolutely forgot I was driving. If I'd've gone the other way over the white line I might've killed somebody. So I went on again—and five minutes later I'm dreamin' again, and I nearly—(*He presses two fingers against his eyes*) I have such thoughts, I have such strange thoughts.

LINDA Willy, dear. Talk to them again. There's no reason why you can't work in New York.

WILLY They don't need me in New York. I'm the New England man. I'm vital in New England.

LINDA But you're sixty years old. They can't expect you to keep traveling every week.

WILLY I'll have to send a wire to Portland. I'm supposed to see

Brown and Morrison tomorrow morning at ten o'clock to show the line. Goddammit, I could sell them! (*He starts putting on his jacket*)

LINDA (*taking the jacket from him*) Why don't you go down to the place tomorrow and tell Howard you've simply got to work in New York? You're too accommodating, dear.

WILLY If old man Wagner was alive I'd a been in charge of New York now! That man was a prince, he was a masterful man. But that boy of his, that Howard, he don't appreciate. When I went north the first time, the Wagner Company didn't know where New England was!

LINDA Why don't you tell those things to Howard, dear?

WILLY (*encouraged*) I will, I definitely will. Is there any cheese?

LINDA I'll make you a sandwich.

WILLY No, go to sleep. I'll take some milk. I'll be up right away. The boys in?

LINDA They're sleeping. Happy took Biff on a date tonight.

WILLY (*interested*) That so?

LINDA It was so nice to see them shaving together, one behind the other, in the bathroom. And going out together. You notice? The whole house smells of shaving lotion.

WILLY Figure it out. Work a lifetime to pay off a house. You finally own it, and there's nobody to live in it.

LINDA Well, dear, life is a casting off. It's always that way.

WILLY No, no, some people—some people accomplish something. Did Biff say anything after I went this morning?

LINDA You shouldn't have criticized him, Willy, especially after he just got off the train. You mustn't lose your temper with him.

WILLY When the hell did I lose my temper? I simply asked him if he was making any money. Is that a criticism?

LINDA But, dear, how could he make any money?

WILLY (*worried and angered*) There's such an undercurrent in him. He became a moody man. Did he apologize when I left this morning?

LINDA He was crestfallen, Willy. You know how he admires you. I think if he finds himself, then you'll both be happier and not fight any more.

WILLY How can he find himself on a farm? Is that a life? A farmhand? In the beginning, when he was young, I thought, well, a young man, it's good for him to tramp around, take a lot of different jobs. But it's more than ten years now and he has yet to make thirty-five dollars a week!

LINDA He's finding himself, Willy.

WILLY Not finding yourself at the age of thirty-four is a disgrace!

LINDA Shh!

WILLY The trouble is he's lazy, goddammit!

LINDA Willy, please!

WILLY Biff is a lazy bum!

LINDA They're sleeping. Get something to eat. Go on down.

WILLY Why did he come home? I would like to know what brought him home.

LINDA I don't know. I think he's still lost, Willy. I think he's very lost.

WILLY Biff Loman is lost. In the greatest country in the world a young man with such—personal attractiveness, gets lost. And such a hard worker. There's one thing about Biff—he's not lazy.

LINDA Never.

WILLY (*with pity and resolve*) I'll see him in the morning; I'll have a nice talk with him. I'll get him a job selling. He could be big in no time. My God! Remember how they used to follow him around in high school? When he smiled at one of them their faces lit up. When he walked down the street . . . (*He loses himself in reminiscences*)

LINDA (*trying to bring him out of it*) Willy, dear, I got a new kind of American-type cheese today. It's whipped.

WILLY Why do you get American when I like Swiss?

LINDA I just thought you'd like a change—

WILLY I don't want a change! I want Swiss cheese. Why am I always being contradicted?

LINDA (*with a covering laugh*) I thought it would be a surprise.

WILLY Why don't you open a window in here, for God's sake?

LINDA (*with infinite patience*) They're all open, dear.

WILLY The way they boxed us in here. Bricks and windows, windows and bricks.

LINDA We should've bought the land next door.

WILLY The street is lined with cars. There's not a breath of fresh air in the neighborhood. The grass don't grow any more, you can't raise a carrot in the back yard. They should've had a law against apartment houses. Remember those two beautiful elm trees out there? When I and Biff hung the swing between them?

LINDA Yeah, like being a million miles from the city.

WILLY They should've arrested the builder for cutting those down. They massacred the neighborhood. (*Lost*) More and more I think of those days, Linda. This time of year it was lilac and wisteria. And then the peonies would come out, and the daffodils. What fragrance in this room!

LINDA Well, after all, people had to move somewhere.

WILLY No, there's more people now.

LINDA I don't think there's more people. I think—

WILLY There's more people! That's what's ruining this country! Population is getting out of control. The competition is maddening! Smell the stink from that apartment house! And another one on the other side . . . How can they whip cheese?

*On* WILLY's *last line,* BIFF *and* HAPPY *raise themselves up in their beds, listening.*

LINDA Go down, try it. And be quiet.

WILLY (*turning to* LINDA, *guiltily*) You're not worried about me, are you, sweetheart?

BIFF What's the matter?

HAPPY Listen!

LINDA You've got too much on the ball to worry about.

WILLY You're my foundation and my support, Linda.

LINDA Just try to relax, dear. You make mountains out of molehills.

WILLY I won't fight with him any more. If he wants to go back to Texas, let him go.

LINDA He'll find his way.

WILLY Sure. Certain men just don't get started till later in life. Like Thomas Edison, I think. Or B. F. Goodrich. One of them was deaf. (*He starts for the bedroom doorway*) I'll put my money on Biff.

LINDA And Willy—if it's warm Sunday we'll drive in the country. And we'll open the windshield, and take lunch.

WILLY No, the windshields don't open on the new cars.

LINDA But you opened it today.

WILLY Me? I didn't. (*He stops*) Now isn't that peculiar! Isn't that a remarkable—(*He breaks off in amazement and fright as the flute is heard distantly*)

LINDA What, darling?

WILLY That is the most remarkable thing.

LINDA What, dear?

WILLY I was thinking of the Chevvy. (*Slight pause*) Nineteen twenty-eight . . . when I had that red Chevvy—(*Breaks off*) That funny? I coulda sworn I was driving that Chevvy today.

LINDA Well, that's nothing. Something must've reminded you.

WILLY Remarkable. Ts. Remember those days? The way Biff used to simonize that car? The dealer refused to believe there was eighty thousand miles on it. (*He shakes his head*) Heh! (*To* LINDA) Close your eyes, I'll be right up. (*He walks out of the bedroom*)

HAPPY (*to* BIFF) Jesus, maybe he smashed up the car again!

LINDA (*calling after* WILLY) Be careful on the stairs, dear! The cheese is on the middle shelf! (*She turns, goes over to the bed, takes his jacket, and goes out of the bedroom*)

*Light has risen on the boys' room. Unseen,* WILLY *is heard talking to himself, "Eighty thousand miles," and a little laugh.* BIFF *gets out of bed, comes downstage a bit, and stands attentively.* BIFF *is two years older than his brother* HAPPY, *well built, but in these days bears a worn air and seems less self-assured. He has succeeded less, and his dreams are stronger and less acceptable than* HAPPY'S. HAPPY *is tall, powerfully made. Sexuality is like a visible color on him, or a scent that many women have discovered. He, like his brother, is lost, but in a different way, for he has never allowed himself to turn his face toward defeat and is thus more confused and hard-skinned, although seemingly more content.*

HAPPY (*getting out of bed*) He's going to get his license taken away if he keeps that up. I'm getting nervous about him, y'know, Biff?

BIFF His eyes are going.

HAPPY No, I've driven with him. He sees all right. He just doesn't keep his mind on it. I drove into the city with him last week. He stops at a green light and then it turns red and he goes. (*He laughs*)

BIFF Maybe he's color-blind.

HAPPY Pop? Why he's got the finest eye for color in the business. You know that.

BIFF (*sitting down on his bed*) I'm going to sleep.

HAPPY You're not still sour on Dad, are you, Biff?

BIFF He's all right, I guess.

WILLY (*underneath them, in the living-room*) Yes, sir, eighty thousand miles—eighty-two thousand!

BIFF You smoking?

HAPPY (*holding out a pack of cigarettes*) Want one?

BIFF (*taking a cigarette*) I can never sleep when I smell it.

WILLY What a simonizing job, heh!

HAPPY (*with deep sentiment*) Funny, Biff, y'now? Us sleeping in here again? The old beds. (*He pats his bed affectionately*) All the talk that went across those two beds, huh? Our whole lives.

BIFF Yeah. Lotta dreams and plans.

HAPPY (*with a deep and masculine laugh*) About five hundred women would like to know what was said in this room.

*They share a soft laugh.*

BIFF Remember that big Betsy something—what the hell was her name—over on Bushwick Avenue?

HAPPY (*combing his hair*) With the collie dog!

BIFF That's the one. I got you in there, remember?

HAPPY Yeah, that was my first time—I think. Boy, there was a pig! (*They laugh, almost crudely*) You taught me everything I know about women. Don't forget that.

BIFF I bet you forgot how bashful you used to be. Especially with girls.

HAPPY Oh, I still am, Biff.

BIFF Oh, go on.

HAPPY I just control it, that's all. I think I got less bashful and you got more so. What happened, Biff? Where's the old humor, the old confidence? (*He shakes* BIFF'S *knee.* BIFF *gets up and moves restlessly about the room*) What's the matter?

BIFF Why does Dad mock me all the time?

HAPPY He's not mocking you, he—

BIFF Everything I say there's a twist of mockery on his face. I can't get near him.

HAPPY He just wants you to make good, that's all. I wanted to talk to you about Dad for a long time, Biff. Something's—happening to him. He—talks to himself.

BIFF I noticed that this morning. But he always mumbled.

HAPPY But not so noticeable. It got so embarrassing I sent him to Florida. And you know something? Most of the time he's talking to you.

BIFF What's he say about me?

HAPPY I can't make it out.

BIFF What's he say about me?

HAPPY I think the fact that you're not settled, that you're still kind of up in the air . . .

BIFF There's one or two other things depressing him, Happy.

HAPPY What do you mean?

BIFF Never mind. Just don't lay it all to me.

HAPPY But I think if you just got started—I mean—is there any future for you out there?

BIFF I tell ya, Hap, I don't know what the future is. I don't know —what I'm supposed to want.

HAPPY What do you mean?

BIFF Well, I spent six or seven years after high school trying to work myself up. Shipping clerk, salesman, business of one kind or another. And it's a measly manner of existence. To get on that subway on the hot mornings in summer. To devote your whole life to keeping stock, or making phone calls, or selling or buying. To suffer fifty weeks of the year for the sake of a two-week vacation, when all you really desire is to be outdoors, with your shirt off. And always to have to get ahead of the next fella. And still—that's how you build a future.

HAPPY Well, you really enjoy it on a farm? Are you content out there?

BIFF (*with rising agitation*) Hap, I've had twenty or thirty different kinds of jobs since I left home before the war, and it always turns out the same. I just realized it lately. In Nebraska when I herded cattle, and the Dakotas, and Arizona, and now in Texas. It's why I came home now, I guess, because I realized it. This farm I work on, it's spring there now, see? And they've got about fifteen new colts. There's nothing more inspiring or—beautiful than the sight of a mare and a new colt. And it's cool there now, see? Texas is cool now, and it's spring. And whenever spring comes to where I am, I suddenly get the feeling, my God, I'm not gettin' anywhere! What the hell am I doing, playing around with horses, twenty-eight dollars a week! I'm thirty-four years old, I oughta be makin' my future. That's when I come running home. And now, I get here, and I don't know what to do with myself. (*After a pause*) I've always made a point of not wasting my life, and everytime I come back here I know that all I've done is to waste my life.

HAPPY You're a poet, you know that, Biff? You're a—you're an idealist!

BIFF No, I'm mixed up very bad. Maybe I oughta get married. Maybe I oughta get stuck into something. Maybe that's my trouble. I'm like a boy. I'm not married, I'm not in business, I just—I'm like a boy. Are you content, Hap? You're a success, aren't you? Are you content?

HAPPY Hell, no!

BIFF Why? You're making money, aren't you?

HAPPY (*moving about with energy, expressiveness*) All I can do now is wait for the merchandise manager to die. And suppose I get to be merchandise manager? He's a good friend of mine, and he just built a terrific estate on Long Island. And he lived there about two months and sold it, and now he's building another one. He can't enjoy it once it's finished. And I know that's just what I would do. I don't know what the hell I'm workin' for. Sometimes I sit in my apartment—all alone. And I think of the rent I'm paying. And it's crazy. But then, it's what I always wanted. My own apartment, a car, and plenty of women. And still, goddammit. I'm lonely.

BIFF (*with enthusiasm*) Listen, why don't you come out West with me?

HAPPY You and I, heh?

BIFF Sure, maybe we could buy a ranch. Raise cattle, use our muscles. Men built like we are should be working out in the open.

HAPPY (*avidly*) The Loman Brothers, heh?

BIFF (*with vast affection*) Sure, we'd be known all over the counties!

HAPPY (*enthralled*) That's what I dream about, Biff. Sometimes I want to just rip my clothes off in the middle of the store and outbox that goddam merchandise manager. I mean I can outbox, outrun, and outlift anybody in that store, and I have to take orders from those common, petty sons-of-bitches till I can't stand it any more.

BIFF I'm tellin' you, kid, if you were with me I'd be happy out there.

HAPPY (*enthused*) See, Biff, everybody around me is so false that I'm constantly lowering my ideals . . .

BIFF Baby, together we'd stand up for one another, we'd have someone to trust.

HAPPY If I were around you—

BIFF Hap, the trouble is we weren't brought up to grub for money. I don't know how to do it.

HAPPY Neither can I!

BIFF Then let's go!

HAPPY The only thing is—what can you make out there?

BIFF But look at your friend. Builds an estate and then hasn't the peace of mind to live in it.

HAPPY Yeah, but when he walks into the store the waves part in front of him. That's fifty-two thousand dollars a year coming through the revolving door, and I got more in my pinky finger than he's got in his head.

BIFF Yeah, but you just said—

HAPPY I gotta show some of those pompous, self-important executives over there that Hap Loman can make the grade. I want to walk into the store the way he walks in. Then I'll go with you, Biff. We'll be together yet, I swear. But take those two we had tonight. Now weren't they gorgeous creatures?

BIFF Yeah, yeah, most gorgeous I've had in years.

HAPPY I get that any time I want, Biff. Whenever I feel disgusted. The only trouble is, it gets like bowling or something. I just keep knockin' them over and it doesn't mean anything. You still run around a lot?

BIFF Naa. I'd like to find a girl—steady, somebody with substance.

HAPPY That's what I long for.

BIFF Go on! You'd never come home.

HAPPY I would! Somebody with character, with resistance! Like Mom, y'know? You're gonna call me a bastard when I tell you this. That girl Charlotte I was with tonight is engaged to be married in five weeks. (*He tries on his new hat*)

BIFF No kiddin'!

HAPPY Sure, the guy's in line for the vice-presidency of the store. I don't know what gets into me, maybe I just have an overdeveloped sense of competition or something, but I went and ruined her, and furthermore I can't get rid of her. And he's the third executive I've done that to. Isn't that a crummy characteristic? And to top it all, I go to their weddings! (*Indignantly, but laughing*) Like I'm not supposed to take bribes. Manufacturers offer me a hundred-dollar bill now and then to throw an order their way. You know how honest I am, but it's like this girl, see. I hate myself for it. Because I don't want the girl, and, still, I take it and—I love it!

BIFF Let's go to sleep.

HAPPY I guess we didn't settle anything, heh?

BIFF I just got one idea that I think I'm going to try.

HAPPY What's that?

BIFF Remember Bill Oliver?

HAPPY Sure, Oliver is very big now. You want to work for him again?

BIFF No, but when I quit he said something to me. He put his arm on my shoulder, and he said, "Biff, if you ever need anything, come to me."

HAPPY I remember that. That sounds good.

BIFF I think I'll go to see him. If I could get ten thousand or even seven or eight thousand dollars I could buy a beautiful ranch.

HAPPY I bet he'd back you. 'Cause he thought highly of you, Biff. I mean, they all do. You're well liked, Biff. That's why I say to come back here, and we both have the apartment. And I'm tellin' you, Biff, any babe you want . . .

BIFF No, with a ranch I could do the work I like and still be something. I just wonder though. I wonder if Oliver still thinks I stole that carton of basketballs.

HAPPY Oh, he probably forgot that long ago. It's almost ten years. You're too sensitive. Anyway, he didn't really fire you.

BIFF Well, I think he was going to. I think that's why I quit. I was never sure whether he knew or not. I know he thought the world of me, though. I was the only one he'd let lock up the place.

WILLY (*below*) You gonna wash the engine, Biff?
HAPPY Shh!

*Biff looks at Happy, who is gazing down, listening. Willy is mumbling in the parlor.*

HAPPY You hear that?

*They listen. Willy laughs warmly.*

BIFF (*growing angry*) Doesn't he know Mom can hear that?
WILLY Don't get your sweater dirty, Biff!

*A look of pain crosses Biff's face.*

HAPPY Isn't that terrible? Don't leave again, will you? You'll find a job here. You gotta stick around. I don't know what to do about him, it's getting embarrassing.
WILLY What a simonizing job!
BIFF Mom's hearing that!
WILLY No kiddin', Biff, you got a date? Wonderful!
HAPPY Go on to sleep. But talk to him in the morning, will you?
BIFF (*reluctantly getting into bed*) With her in the house. Brother!
HAPPY (*getting into bed*) I wish you'd have a good talk with him.

*The light on their room begins to fade.*

BIFF (*to himself in bed*) That selfish, stupid . . .
HAPPY Sh . . . Sleep, Biff.

*Their light is out. Well before they have finished speaking, Willy's form is dimly seen below in the darkened kitchen. He opens the refrigerator, searches in there, and takes out a bottle of milk. The apartment houses are fading out, and the entire house and surroundings become covered with leaves. Music insinuates itself as the leaves appear.*

WILLY Just wanna be careful with those girls, Biff, that's all. Don't make any promises. No promises of any kind. Because a girl, y'know, they always believe what you tell 'em, and you're very young, Biff, you're too young to be talking seriously to girls.

*Light rises on the kitchen. Willy, talking, shuts the refrigerator door and comes downstage to the kitchen table. He pours milk into a glass. He is totally immersed in himself, smiling faintly.*

WILLY Too young entirely, Biff. You want to watch your schooling first. Then when you're all set, there'll be plenty of girls for a boy like you. (*He smiles broadly at a kitchen chair*) That so? The girls pay for you? (*He laughs*) Boy, you must really be makin' a hit.

WILLY *is gradually addressing—physically—a point offstage, speaking through the wall of the kitchen, and his voice has been rising in volume to that of a normal conversation.*

WILLY I been wondering why you polish the car so careful. Ha! Don't leave the hubcabs, boys. Get the chamois to the hubcaps. Happy, use newspaper on the windows, it's the easiest thing. Show him how to do it, Biff! You see, Happy? Pad it up, use it like a pad. That's it, that's it, good work. You're doin' all right, Hap. (*He pauses, then nods in approbation for a few seconds, then looks upward*) Biff, first thing we gotta do when we get time is clip that big branch over the house. Afraid it's gonna fall in a storm and hit the roof. Tell you what. We get a rope and sling her around, and then we climb up there with a couple of saws and take her down. Soon as you finish the car, boys, I wanna see ya. I got a surprise for you, boys.

BIFF (*offstage*) Whatta ya got, Dad?

WILLY No, you finish first. Never leave a job till you're finished—remember that. (*Looking toward the "big trees"*) Biff, up in Albany I saw a beautiful hammock. I think I'll buy it next trip, and we'll hang it right between those two elms. Wouldn't that be something? Just swingin' there under those branches. Boy, that would be . . .

*Young* BIFF *and Young* HAPPY *appear from the direction* WILLY *was addressing.* HAPPY *carries rags and a pail of water.* BIFF, *wearing a sweater with a block "S," carries a football.*

BIFF (*pointing in the direction of the car offstage*) How's that, Pop, professional?

WILLY Terrific. Terrific job, boys. Good work, Biff.

HAPPY Where's the surprise, Pop?

WILLY In the back seat of the car.

HAPPY Boy! (*He runs off*)

BIFF What is it, Dad? Tell me, what'd you buy?

WILLY (*laughing, cuffs him*) Never mind, something I want you to have.

BIFF (*turns and starts off*) What is it, Hap?

HAPPY (*offstage*) It's a punching bag!

BIFF Oh, Pop!

WILLY It's got Gene Tunney's signature on it!

HAPPY *runs onstage with a punching bag.*

BIFF Gee, how'd you know we wanted a punching bag?

WILLY Well, it's the finest thing for the timing.

HAPPY (*lies down on his back and pedals with his feet*) I'm losing weight, you notice, Pop?

WILLY (*to* HAPPY) Jumping rope is good too.

BIFF Did you see the new football I got?

WILLY (*examining the ball*) Where'd you get a new ball?

BIFF The coach told me to practice my passing.

WILLY That so? And he gave you the ball, heh?

BIFF Well, I borrowed it from the locker room. (*He laughs confidentially*)

WILLY (*laughing with him at the theft*) I want you to return that.

HAPPY I told you he wouldn't like it!

BIFF (*angrily*) Well, I'm bringing it back!

WILLY (*stopping the incipient argument, to* HAPPY) Sure, he's gotta practice with a regulation ball, doesn't he? (*To* BIFF) Coach'll probably congratulate you on your initiative!

BIFF Oh, he keeps congratulating my initiative all the time, Pop.

WILLY That's because he likes you. If somebody else took that ball there'd be an uproar. So what's the report, boys, what's the report?

BIFF Where'd you go this time, Dad? Gee we were lonesome for you.

WILLY (*pleased, puts an arm around each boy and they come down to the apron*) Lonesome, heh?

BIFF Missed you every minute.

WILLY Don't say? Tell you a secret, boys. Don't breathe it to a soul. Someday I'll have my own business, and I'll never have to leave home any more.

HAPPY Like Uncle Charley, heh?

WILLY Bigger than Uncle Charley! Because Charley is not—liked. He's liked, but he's not—well liked.

BIFF Where'd you go this time, Dad?

WILLY Well, I got on the road, and I went north to Providence. Met the Mayor.

BIFF The Mayor of Providence!

WILLY He was sitting in the hotel lobby.

BIFF What'd he say?

WILLY He said, "Morning!" And I said, "You got a fine city here, Mayor." And then he had coffee with me. And then I went to Waterbury. Waterbury is a fine city. Big clock city, the famous Waterbury clock. Sold a nice bill there. And then Boston—Boston is the cradle of the Revolution. A fine city. And a couple of other towns in Mass., and on to Portland and Bangor and straight home!

BIFF Gee, I'd love to go with you sometime, Dad.

WILLY Soon as summer comes.

HAPPY Promise?

WILLY You and Hap and I, and I'll show you all the towns. America is full of beautiful towns and fine, upstanding people. And they know me, boys, they know me up and down New England. The finest people. And when I bring you fellas up, there'll be open sesame for all of us, 'cause one thing, boys: I have friends. I can park my car in any street in New England, and the cops protect it like their own. This summer, heh?

BIFF and HAPPY (*together*) Yeah! You bet!

WILLY We'll take our bathing suits.

HAPPY We'll carry your bags, Pop!

WILLY Oh, won't that be something! Me comin' into the Boston stores with you boys carryin' my bags. What a sensation!

BIFF *is prancing around, practicing passing the ball.*

WILLY You nervous, Biff, about the game?

BIFF Not if you're gonna be there.

WILLY What do they say about you in school, now that they made you captain?

HAPPY There's a crowd of girls behind him everytime the classes change.

BIFF (*taking* WILLY's *hand*) This Saturday, Pop, this Saturday—just for you, I'm going to break through for a touchdown.

HAPPY You're supposed to pass.

BIFF I'm takin' one play for Pop. You watch me, Pop, and when I take off my helmet, that means I'm breakin' out. Then you watch me crash through that line!

WILLY (*kisses* BIFF) Oh, wait'll I tell this in Boston!

BERNARD *enters in knickers. He is younger than* BIFF, *earnest and loyal, a worried boy.*

BERNARD Biff, where are you? You're supposed to study with me today.

WILLY Hey, looka Bernard. What're you lookin' so anemic about, Bernard?

BERNARD He's gotta study, Uncle Willy. He's got Regents next week.

HAPPY (*tauntingly, spinning* BERNARD *around*) Let's box, Bernard!

BERNARD Biff! (*He gets away from* HAPPY) Listen, Biff, I heard Mr. Birnbaum say that if you don't start studyin' math he's gonna flunk you, and you won't graduate. I heard him!

WILLY You better study with him, Biff. Go ahead now.

BERNARD I heard him!

BIFF Oh, Pop, you didn't see my sneakers! (*He holds up a foot for* WILLY *to look at*)

WILLY Hey, that's a beautiful job of printing!

BERNARD (*wiping his glasses*) Just because he printed University of Virginia on his sneakers doesn't mean they've got to graduate him, Uncle Willy!

WILLY (*angrily*) What're you talking about? With scholarships to three universities they're gonna flunk him?

BERNARD But I heard Mr. Birnbaum say—

WILLY Don't be a pest, Bernard! (*To his boys*) What an anemic!

BERNARD Okay, I'm waiting for you in my house, Biff.

BERNARD *goes off. The* LOMANS *laugh.*

WILLY Bernard is not well liked, is he?

BIFF He's liked, but he's not well liked.

HAPPY That's right, Pop.

WILLY That's just what I mean. Bernard can get the best marks in school, y'understand, but when he gets out in the business world, y'understand, you are going to be five times ahead of him. That's why I thank Almighty God you're both built like Adonises. Because the man who makes an appearance in the business world, the man who creates personal interest, is the man who gets ahead. Be liked and you will never want. You take me, for instance. I never have to wait in line to see a buyer. "Willy Loman is here!" That's all they have to know, and I go right through.

BIFF Did you knock them dead, Pop?

WILLY Knocked 'em cold in Providence, slaughtered 'em in Boston.

HAPPY (*on his back, pedaling again*) I'm losing weight, you notice, Pop?

LINDA *enters, as of old, a ribbon in her hair, carrying a basket of washing.*

LINDA (*with youthful energy*) Hello, dear!

WILLY Sweetheart!

LINDA How'd the Chevvy run?

WILLY Chevrolet, Linda, is the greatest car ever built. (*To the boys*) Since when do you let your mother carry wash up the stairs?

BIFF Grab hold there, boy!

HAPPY Where to, Mom?

LINDA Hang them up on the line. And you better go down to your friends, Biff. The cellar is full of boys. They don't know what to do with themselves.

BIFF Ah, when Pop comes home they can wait!

WILLY (*laughs appreciatively*) You better go down and tell them what to do, Biff.

BIFF I think I'll have them sweep out the furnace room.

WILLY Good work, Biff.

BIFF (*goes through wall-line of kitchen to doorway at back and calls down*) Fellas! Everybody sweep out the furnace room! I'll be right down!

VOICES All right! Okay, Biff.

BIFF George and Sam and Frank, come out back! We're hangin' up the wash! Come on, Hap, on the double! (*He and* HAPPY *carry out the basket*)

LINDA The way they obey him!

WILLY Well, that's training, the training. I'm tellin' you, I was sellin' thousands and thousands, but I had to come home.

LINDA Oh, the whole block'll be at that game. Did you sell anything?

WILLY I did five hundred gross in Providence and seven hundred gross in Boston.

LINDA No! Wait a minute, I've got a pencil. (*She pulls pencil and paper out of her apron pocket*) That makes your commission . . . Two hundred—my God! Two hundred and twelve dollars!

WILLY Well, I didn't figure it yet, but . . .

LINDA How much did you do?

WILLY Well, I—I did—about a hundred and eighty gross in Providence. Well, no—it came to—roughly two hundred gross on the whole trip.

LINDA (*without hesitation*) Two hundred gross. That's . . . (*She figures*)

WILLY The trouble was that three of the stores were half closed for inventory in Boston. Otherwise I woulda broke records.

LINDA Well, it makes seventy dollars and some pennies. That's very good.

WILLY What do we owe?

LINDA Well, on the first there's sixteen dollars on the refrigerator—

WILLY Why sixteen?

LINDA Well, the fan belt broke, so it was a dollar eighty.

WILLY But it's brand new.

LINDA Well, the man said that's the way it is. Till they work themselves in, y'know.

*They move through the wall-line into the kitchen.*

WILLY I hope we didn't get stuck on that machine.

LINDA They got the biggest ads of any of them!

WILLY I know, it's a fine machine. What else?

LINDA Well, there's nine-sixty for the washing machine. And for the vacuum cleaner there's three and a half due on the fifteenth. Then the roof, you got twenty-one dollars remaining.

WILLY It don't leak, does it?

LINDA No, they did a wonderful job. Then you owe Frank for the carburetor.

WILLY I'm not going to pay that man! That goddam Chevrolet, they ought to prohibit the manufacture of that car!

LINDA Well, you owe him three and a half. And odds and ends, comes to around a hundred and twenty dollars by the fifteenth.

WILLY A hundred and twenty dollars! My God, if business don't pick up I don't know what I'm gonna do!

LINDA Well, next week you'll do better.

WILLY Oh, I'll knock 'em dead next week. I'll go to Hartford. I'm very well liked in Hartford. You know, the trouble is, Linda, people don't seem to take to me.

*They move onto the forestage.*

LINDA Oh, don't be foolish.

WILLY I know it when I walk in. They seem to laugh at me.

LINDA Why? Why would they laugh at you? Don't talk that way, Willy.

WILLY *moves to the edge of the stage.* LINDA *goes into the kitchen and starts to darn stockings.*

WILLY I don't know the reason for it, but they just pass me by. I'm not noticed.

LINDA But you're doing wonderful, dear. You're making seventy to a hundred dollars a week.

WILLY But I gotta be at it ten, twelve hours a day. Other men—I don't know—they do it easier. I don't know why—I can't stop myself—I talk too much. A man oughta come in with a few words. One thing about Charley. He's a man of few words, and they respect him.

LINDA You don't talk too much, you're just lively.

WILLY (*smiling*) Well, I figure, what the hell, life is short, a couple of jokes. (*To himself*) I joke too much! (*The smile goes*)

LINDA Why? You're—

WILLY I'm fat. I'm very—foolish to look at, Linda. I didn't tell you, but Christmas time I happened to be calling on F. H. Stewarts, and a salesman I know, as I was going in to see the buyer I heard him say something about—walrus. And I—I cracked him right across the face. I won't take that. I simply will not take that. But they do laugh at me. I know that.

LINDA Darling . . .

WILLY I gotta overcome it. I know I gotta overcome it. I'm not dressing to advantage, maybe.

LINDA Willy, darling, you're the handsomest man in the world—

WILLY Oh, no, Linda.

LINDA To me you are. (*Slight pause*) The handsomest.

*From the darkness is heard the laughter of a woman.* WILLY *doesn't turn to it, but it continues through* LINDA's *lines.*

LINDA And the boys, Willy. Few men are idolized by their children the way you are.

*Music is heard as behind a scrim, to the left of the house.* THE WOMAN, *dimly seen, is dressing.*

WILLY (*with great feeling*) You're the best there is, Linda, you're a pal, you know that? On the road—on the road I want to grab you sometimes and just kiss the life outa you.

*The laughter is loud now, and he moves into a brightening area at the left, where* THE WOMAN *has come from behind the scrim and is standing, putting on her hat, looking into a "mirror" and laughing.*

WILLY 'Cause I get so lonely—especially when business is bad and there's nobody to talk to. I get the feeling that I'll never sell anything again, that I won't make a living for you, or a business, a business for the boys. (*He talks through* THE WOMAN's *subsiding laughter;* THE WOMAN *primps at the "mirror."*) There's so much I want to make for—

THE WOMAN Me? You didn't make me, Willy. I picked you.

WILLY (*pleased*) You picked me?

THE WOMAN (*who is quite proper-looking,* WILLY's *age*) I did. I've been sitting at that desk watching all the salesmen go by, day in, day out. But you've got such a sense of humor, and we do have such a good time together, don't we?

WILLY Sure, sure. (*He takes her in his arms*) Why do you have to go now?

THE WOMAN It's two o'clock . . .

WILLY No, come on in! (*He pulls her*)

THE WOMAN . . . my sisters'll be scandalized. When'll you be back?

WILLY Oh, two weeks about. Will you come up again?

THE WOMAN Sure thing. You do make me laugh. It's good for me. (*She squeezes his arm, kisses him*) And I think you're a wonderful man.

WILLY You picked me, heh?

THE WOMAN Sure. Because you're so sweet. And such a kidder.

WILLY Well, I'll see you next time I'm in Boston.

THE WOMAN I'll put you right through to the buyers.

WILLY (*slapping her bottom*) Right. Well, bottoms up!

THE WOMAN (*slaps him gently and laughs*) You just kill me, Willy. (*He suddenly grabs her and kisses her roughly*) You kill me. And thanks for the stockings. I love a lot of stockings. Well, good night.

WILLY Good night. And keep your pores open!

THE WOMAN Oh, Willy!

THE WOMAN *bursts out laughing, and* LINDA'S *laughter blends in.* THE WOMAN *disappears into the dark. Now the area at the kitchen table brightens.* LINDA *is sitting where she was at the kitchen table, but now is mending a pair of her silk stockings.*

LINDA You are, Willy. The handsomest man. You've got no reason to feel that—

WILLY (*coming out of* THE WOMAN'S *dimming area and going over to* LINDA) I'll make it all up to you, Linda, I'll—

LINDA There's nothing to make up, dear. You're doing fine, better than—

WILLY (*noticing her mending*) What's that?

LINDA Just mending my stockings. They're so expensive—

WILLY (*angrily, taking them from her*) I won't have you mending stockings in this house! Now throw them out!

LINDA *puts the stockings in her pocket.*

BERNARD (*entering on the run*) Where is he? If he doesn't study!

WILLY (*moving to the forestage, with great agitation*) You'll give him the answers!

BERNARD I do, but I can't on a Regents! That's a state exam! They're liable to arrest me!

WILLY Where is he? I'll whip him, I'll whip him!

LINDA And he'd better give back that football, Willy, it's not nice.

WILLY Biff! Where is he? Why is he taking everything?

LINDA He's too rough with the girls, Willy. All the mothers are afraid of him!

WILLY I'll whip him!

BERNARD He's driving the car without a license!

THE WOMAN'S *laugh is heard.*

WILLY Shut up!

LINDA All the mothers—

WILLY Shut up!

BERNARD (*backing quietly away and out*) Mr. Birnbaum says he's stuck up.

WILLY Get outa here!

BERNARD If he doesn't buckle down he'll flunk math! (*He goes off*)

LINDA He's right, Willy, you've gotta—

WILLY (*exploding at her*) There's nothing the matter with him! You want him to be a worm like Bernard? He's got spirit, personality . . .

*As he speaks,* LINDA, *almost in tears, exits into the living room.* WILLY *is alone in the kitchen, wilting and staring. The leaves are gone. It is night again, and the apartment houses look down from behind.*

WILLY Loaded with it. Loaded! What is he stealing? He's giving it back, isn't he? Why is he stealing? What did I tell him? I never in my life told him anything but decent things.

HAPPY *in pajamas has come down the stairs;* WILLY *suddenly becomes aware of* HAPPY'S *presence.*

HAPPY Let's go now, come on.

WILLY (*sitting down at the kitchen table*) Huh! Why did she have to wax the floors herself? Everytime she waxes the floors she keels over. She knows that!

HAPPY Shh! Take it easy. What brought you back tonight?

WILLY I got an awful scare. Nearly hit a kid in Yonkers. God! Why didn't I go to Alaska with my brother Ben that time! Ben! That man was a genius, that man was success incarnate! What a mistake! He begged me to go.

HAPPY Well, there's no use in—

WILLY You guys! There was a man started with the clothes on his back and ended up with diamond mines!

HAPPY Boy, someday I'd like to know how he did it.

WILLY What's the mystery? The man knew what he wanted and went out and got it! Walked into a jungle, and comes out, the age of twenty-one, and he's rich! The world is an oyster, but you don't crack it open on a mattress!

HAPPY Pop, I told you I'm gonna retire you for life.

WILLY You'll retire me for life on seventy goddam dollars a week? And your women and your car and your apartment, and you'll retire me for life! Christ's sake, I couldn't get past Yonkers today! Where are you guys, where are you? The woods are burning! I can't drive a car!

CHARLEY *has appeared in the doorway. He is a large man, slow of speech, laconic, immovable. In all he says, despite what he says, there is pity, and, now, trepidation. He has a robe over pajamas, slippers on his feet. He enters the kitchen.*

CHARLEY Everything all right?

HAPPY Yeah, Charley, everything's . . .

WILLY What's the matter?

CHARLEY I heard some noise. I thought something happened. Can't we do something about the walls? You sneeze in here, and in my house hats blow off.

HAPPY Let's go to bed, Dad. Come on.

CHARLEY *signals to* HAPPY *to go.*

WILLY You go ahead, I'm not tired at the moment.

HAPPY (*to* WILLY) Take it easy, huh? (*He exits*)

WILLY What're you doin' up?

CHARLEY (*sitting down at the kitchen table opposite* WILLY) Couldn't sleep good. I had a heartburn.

WILLY Well, you don't know how to eat.

CHARLEY I eat with my mouth.

WILLY No, you're ignorant. You gotta know about vitamins and things like that.

CHARLEY Come on, let's shoot. Tire you out a little.

WILLY (*hesitantly*) All right. You got cards?

CHARLEY (*taking a deck from his pocket*) Yeah, I got them. Someplace. What is it with those vitamins?

WILLY (*dealing*) They build up your bones. Chemistry.

CHARLEY Yeah, but there's no bones in a heartburn.

WILLY What are you talkin' about? Do you know the first thing about it?

CHARLEY Don't get insulted.

WILLY Don't talk about something you don't know anything about.

*They are playing. Pause.*

CHARLEY What're you doin' home?

WILLY A little trouble with the car.

CHARLEY Oh. (*Pause*) I'd like to take a trip to California.

WILLY Don't say.

CHARLEY You want a job?

WILLY I got a job, I told you that. (*After a slight pause*) What the hell are you offering me a job for?

CHARLEY Don't get insulted.

WILLY Don't insult me.

CHARLEY I don't see no sense in it. You don't have to go on this way.

WILLY I got a good job. (*Slight pause*) What do you keep comin' in here for?

CHARLEY You want me to go?

WILLY (*after a pause, withering*) I can't understand it. He's going back to Texas again. What the hell is that?

CHARLEY Let him go.

WILLY I got nothin' to give him, Charley. I'm clean, I'm clean.

CHARLEY He won't starve. None a them starve. Forget about him.

WILLY Then what have I got to remember?

CHARLEY You take it too hard. To hell with it. When a deposit bottle is broken you don't get your nickel back.

WILLY That's easy enough for you to say.

CHARLEY That ain't easy for me to say.

WILLY Did you see the ceiling I put up in the living-room?

CHARLEY Yeah, that's a piece of work. To put up a ceiling is a mystery to me. How do you do it?

WILLY What's the difference?

CHARLEY Well, talk about it.

WILLY You gonna put up a ceiling?

CHARLEY How could I put up a ceiling?

WILLY Then what the hell are you bothering me for?

CHARLEY You're insulted again.

WILLY A man who can't handle tools is not a man. You're disgusting.

CHARLEY Don't call me disgusting, Willy.

UNCLE BEN, *carrying a valise and an umbrella, enters the forestage from around the right corner of the house. He is a stolid man, in his sixties, with a mustache and an authoritative air. He is utterly certain of his destiny, and there is an aura of far places about him. He enters exactly as* WILLY *speaks.*

WILLY I'm getting awfully tired, Ben.

BEN'S *music is heard.* BEN *looks around at everything.*

CHARLEY Good, keep playing; you'll sleep better. Did you call me Ben?

BEN *looks at his watch.*

WILLY That's funny. For a second there you reminded me of my brother Ben.

BEN I only have a few minutes. (*He strolls, inspecting the place.* WILLY *and* CHARLEY *continue playing*)

CHARLEY You never heard from him again, heh? Since that time?

WILLY Didn't Linda tell you? Couple of weeks ago we got a letter from his wife in Africa. He died.

CHARLEY That so.

BEN (*chuckling*) So this is Brooklyn, eh?

CHARLEY Maybe you're in for some of his money.

WILLY Naa, he had seven sons. There's just one opportunity I had with that man . . .

BEN I must make a train, William. There are several properties I'm looking at in Alaska.

WILLY Sure, sure! If I'd gone with him to Alaska that time, everything would've been totally different.

CHARLEY Go on, you'd froze to death up there.

WILLY What're you talking about?

BEN Opportunity is tremendous in Alaska, William. Surprised you're not up there.

WILLY Sure, tremendous.

CHARLEY Heh?

WILLY There was the only man I ever met who knew the answers.

CHARLEY Who?

BEN How are you all?

WILLY (*taking a pot, smiling*) Fine, fine.

CHARLEY Pretty sharp tonight.

BEN Is Mother living with you?

WILLY No, she died a long time ago.

CHARLEY Who?

BEN That's too bad. Fine specimen of a lady, Mother.

WILLY (*to* CHARLEY) Heh?

BEN I'd hoped to see the old girl.

CHARLEY Who died?

BEN Heard anything from Father, have you?

WILLY (*unnerved*) What do you mean, who died?

CHARLEY (*taking a pot*) What're you talkin' about?

BEN (*looking at his watch*) William, it's half-past eight!

WILLY (*as though to dispel his confusion he angrily stops* CHARLEY'S *hand*) That's my build!

CHARLEY I put the ace—

WILLY If you don't know how to play the game I'm not gonna throw my money away on you!

CHARLEY (*rising*) It was my ace, for God's sake!

WILLY I'm through, I'm through!

BEN When did Mother die?

WILLY Long ago. Since the beginning you never knew how to play cards.

CHARLEY (*picks up the cards and goes to the door*) All right! Next time I'll bring a deck with five aces.

WILLY I don't play that kind of game!

CHARLEY (*turning to him*) You ought to be ashamed of yourself!

WILLY Yeah?

CHARLEY Yeah! (*He goes out*)

WILLY (*slamming the door after him*) Ignoramus!

BEN (*as* WILLY *comes toward him through the wall-line of the kitchen*) So you're William.

WILLY (*shaking* BEN's *hand*) Ben! I've been waiting for you so long! What's the answer? How did you do it?

BEN Oh, there's a story in that.

LINDA *enters the forestage, as of old, carrying the wash basket.*

LINDA Is this Ben?

BEN (*gallantly*) How do you do, my dear.

LINDA Where've you been all these years? Willy's always wondered why you—

WILLY (*pulling* BEN *away from her impatiently*) Where is Dad? Didn't you follow him? How did you get started?

BEN Well, I don't know how much you remember.

WILLY Well, I was just a baby, of course, only three or four years old—

BEN Three years and eleven months.

WILLY What a memory, Ben!

BEN I have many enterprises, William, and I have never kept books.

WILLY I remember I was sitting under the wagon in—was it Nebraska?

BEN It was South Dakota, and I gave you a bunch of wild flowers.

WILLY I remember you walking away down some open road.

BEN (*laughing*) I was going to find Father in Alaska.

WILLY Where is he?

BEN At that age I had a very faulty view of geography, William. I discovered after a few days that I was heading due south, so instead of Alaska, I ended up in Africa.

LINDA Africa!

WILLY The Gold Coast!

BEN Principally diamond mines.

LINDA Diamond mines!

BEN Yes, my dear. But I've only a few minutes—

WILLY No! Boys! Boys! (*Young* BIFF *and* HAPPY *appear*) Listen to this. This is your Uncle Ben, a great man! Tell my boys, Ben!

BEN Why, boys, when I was seventeen I walked into the jungle, and when I was twenty-one I walked out. (*He laughs*) And by God I was rich.

WILLY (*to the boys*) You see what I been talking about? The greatest things can happen!

BEN (*glancing at his watch*) I have an appointment in Ketchikan Tuesday week.

WILLY No, Ben! Please tell about Dad. I want my boys to hear. I want them to know the kind of stock they spring from. All I remember is a man with a big beard, and I was in Mamma's lap, sitting around a fire, and some kind of high music.

BEN His flute. He played the flute.

WILLY Sure, the flute, that's right!

*New music is heard, a high, rollicking tune.*

BEN Father was a very great and a very wild-hearted man. We would start in Boston, and he'd toss the whole family into the wagon, and then he'd drive the team right across the country; through Ohio, and Indiana, Michigan, Illinois, and all the Western states. And we'd stop in the towns and sell the flutes that he'd made on the way. Great inventor, Father. With one gadget he made more in a week than a man like you could make in a lifetime.

WILLY That's just the way I'm bringing them up, Ben—rugged, well liked, all-around.

BEN Yeah? (*To* BIFF) Hit that, boy—hard as you can. (*He pounds his stomach*)

BIFF Oh, no, sir!

BEN (*taking boxing stance*) Come on, get to me! (*He laughs*)

WILLY Go to it, Biff! Go ahead, show him!

BIFF Okay! (*He cocks his fists and starts in*)

LINDA (*to* WILLY) Why must he fight, dear?

BEN (*sparring with* BIFF) Good boy! Good boy!

WILLY How's that, Ben, heh?

HAPPY Give him the left, Biff!

LINDA Why are you fighting?

BEN Good boy! (*Suddenly comes in, trips* BIFF, *and stands over him, the point of his umbrella poised over* BIFF'*s eye*)

LINDA Look out, Biff!

BIFF Gee!

BEN (*patting* BIFF'*s knee*) Never fight fair with a stranger, boy. You'll never get out of the jungle that way. (*Taking* LINDA'*s hand and bowing*) It was an honor and a pleasure to meet you, Linda.

LINDA (*withdrawing her hand coldly, frightened*) Have a nice—trip.

BEN (*to* WILLY) And good luck with your—what do you do?

WILLY Selling.

BEN Yes. Well . . . (*He raises his hand in farewell to all*)

WILLY No, Ben, I don't want you to think . . . (*He takes* BEN'S *arm to show him*) It's Brooklyn, I know, but we hunt too.

BEN Really, now.

WILLY Oh, sure, there's snakes and rabbits and—that's why I moved out here. Why, Biff can fell any one of these trees in no time! Boys! Go right over to where they're building the apartment house and get some sand. We're gonna rebuild the entire front stoop right now! Watch this, Ben!

BIFF Yes, sir! On the double, Hap!

HAPPY (*as he and* BIFF *run off*) I lost weight, Pop, you notice?

CHARLEY *enters in knickers, even before the boys are gone.*

CHARLEY Listen, if they steal any more from that building the watchman'll put the cops on them!

LINDA (*to* WILLY) Don't let Biff . . .

BEN *laughs lustily.*

WILLY You shoulda seen the lumber they brought home last week. At least a dozen six-by-tens worth all kinds a money.

CHARLEY Listen, if that watchman—

WILLY I gave them hell, understand. But I got a couple of fearless characters there.

CHARLEY Willy, the jails are full of fearless characters.

BEN (*clapping* WILLY *on the back, with a laugh at* CHARLEY) And the stock exchange, friend!

WILLY (*joining in* BEN'S *laughter*) Where are the rest of your pants?

CHARLEY My wife bought them.

WILLY Now all you need is a golf club and you can go upstairs and go to sleep. (*To* BEN) Great athlete! Between him and his son Bernard they can't hammer a nail!

BERNARD (*rushing in*) The watchman's chasing Biff!

WILLY (*angrily*) Shut up! He's not stealing anything!

LINDA (*alarmed, hurrying off left*) Where is he? Biff, dear! (*She exits*)

WILLY (*moving toward the left, away from* BEN) There's nothing wrong. What's the matter with you?

BEN Nervy boy. Good!

WILLY (*laughing*) Oh, nerves of iron, that Biff!

CHARLEY Don't know what it is. My New England man comes back and he's bleedin', they murdered him up there.

WILLY It's contacts, Charley, I got important contacts!

CHARLEY (*sarcastically*) Glad to hear it, Willy. Come in later, we'll shoot a little casino. I'll take some of your Portland money. (*He laughs at* WILLY *and exits*)

WILLY (*turning to* BEN) Business is bad, it's murderous. But not for me, of course.

BEN I'll stop by on my way back to Africa.

WILLY (*longingly*) Can't you stay a few days? You're just what I need, Ben, because I—I have a fine position here, but I—well, Dad left when I was such a baby and I never had a chance to talk to him and I still feel—kind of temporary about myself.

BEN I'll be late for my train.

*They are at opposite ends of the stage.*

WILLY Ben, my boys—can't we talk? They'd go into the jaws of hell for me, see, but I—

BEN William, you're being first-rate with your boys. Outstanding, manly chaps!

WILLY (*hanging on to his words*) Oh, Ben, that's good to hear! Because sometimes I'm afraid that I'm not teaching them the right kind of— Ben, how should I teach them?

BEN (*giving great weight to each word, and with a certain vicious audacity*) William, when I walked into the jungle, I was seventeen. When I walked out I was twenty-one. And, by God, I was rich! (*He goes off into darkness around the right corner of the house*)

WILLY . . . was rich! That's just the spirit I want to imbue them with! To walk into a jungle! I was right! I was right! I was right!

BEN *is gone, but* WILLY *is still speaking to him as* LINDA, *in nightgown and robe, enters the kitchen, glances around for* WILLY, *then goes to the door of the house, looks out and sees him. Comes down to his left. He looks at her.*

LINDA Willy, dear? Willy?

WILLY I was right!

LINDA Did you have some cheese? (*He can't answer*) It's very late, darling. Come to bed, heh?

WILLY (*looking straight up*) Gotta break your neck to see a star in this yard.

LINDA You coming in?

WILLY Whatever happened to that diamond watch fob? Remember? When Ben came from Africa that time? Didn't he give me a watch fob with a diamond in it?

LINDA You pawned it, dear. Twelve, thirteen years ago. For Biff's radio correspondence course.

WILLY Gee, that was a beautiful thing. I'll take a walk.

LINDA But you're in your slippers.

WILLY (*starting to go around the house at the left*) I was right! I was! (*Half to* LINDA, *as he goes, shaking his head*) What a man! There was a man worth talking to I was right!

LINDA (*calling after* WILLY) But in your slippers, Willy!

WILLY *is almost gone when* BIFF, *in his pajamas, comes down the stairs and enters the kitchen.*

BIFF What is he doing out there?

LINDA Sh!

BIFF God Almighty, Mom, how long has he been doing this?

LINDA Don't, he'll hear you.

BIFF What the hell is the matter with him?

LINDA It'll pass by morning.

BIFF Shouldn't we do anything?

LINDA Oh, my dear, you should do a lot of things, but there's nothing to do, so go to sleep.

HAPPY *comes down the stairs and sits on the steps.*

HAPPY I never heard him so loud, Mom.

LINDA Well, come around more often; you'll hear him. (*She sits down at the table and mends the lining of* WILLY'*s jacket*)

BIFF Why didn't you ever write me about this, Mom?

LINDA How would I write to you? For over three months you had no address.

BIFF I was on the move. But you know I thought of you all the time. You know that, don't you, pal?

LINDA I know, dear, I know. But he likes to have a letter. Just to know that there's still a possibility for better things.

BIFF He's not like this all the time, is he?

LINDA It's when you come home he's always the worst.

BIFF When I come home?

LINDA When you write you're coming, he's all smiles, and talks about the future, and—he's just wonderful. And then the closer you seem to come, the more shaky he gets, and then, by the time you get here, he's arguing, and he seems angry at you. I think it's just that maybe he can't bring himself to—to open up to you. Why are you so hateful to each other? Why is that?

BIFF (*evasively*) I'm not hateful, Mom.

LINDA But you no sooner come in the door than you're fighting!

BIFF I don't know why. I mean to change. I'm tryin', Mom, you understand?

LINDA Are you home to stay now?

BIFF I don't know. I want to look around, see what's doin'.

LINDA Biff, you can't look around all your life, can you?

BIFF I just can't take hold, Mom. I can't take hold of some kind of a life.

LINDA Biff, a man is not a bird, to come and go with the springtime.

BIFF Your hair . . . (*He touches her hair*) Your hair got so gray.

LINDA Oh, it's been gray since you were in high school. I just stopped dyeing it, that's all.

BIFF Dye it again, will ya? I don't want my pal looking old. (*He smiles*)

LINDA You're such a boy! You think you can go away for a year and . . . You've got to get it into your head now that one day you'll knock on this door and there'll be strange people here—

BIFF What are you talking about? You're not even sixty, Mom.

LINDA But what about your father?

BIFF (*lamely*) Well, I meant him too.

HAPPY He admires Pop.

LINDA Biff, dear, if you don't have any feeling for him, then you can't have any feeling for me.

BIFF Sure I can, Mom.

LINDA No. You can't just come to see me, because I love him. (*With a threat, but only a threat, of tears*) He's the dearest man in the world to me, and I won't have anyone making him feel unwanted and low and blue. You've got to make up your mind now, darling, there's no leeway any more. Either he's your father and you pay him that respect, or else you're not to come here. I know he's not easy to get along with—nobody knows that better than me—but . . .

WILLY (*from the left, with a laugh*) Hey, hey, Biffo!

BIFF (*starting to go out after* WILLY) What the hell is the matter with him? (HAPPY *stops him*)

LINDA Don't—don't go near him!

BIFF Stop making excuses for him! He always, always wiped the floor with you. Never had an ounce of respect for you.

HAPPY He's always had respect for—

BIFF What the hell do you know about it?

HAPPY (*surlily*) Just don't call him crazy!

BIFF He's got no character—Charley wouldn't do this. Not in his own house—spewing out that vomit from his mind.

HAPPY Charley never had to cope with what he's got to.

BIFF People are worse off than Willy Loman. Believe me, I've seen them!

LINDA Then make Charley your father, Biff. You can't do that, can you? I don't say he's a great man. Willy Loman never made a lot of money. His name was never in the paper. He's not the finest character that ever lived. But he's a human being, and a terrible thing is happening to him. So attention must be paid. He's not to be allowed to fall into his grave like an old dog. Attention, attention must be finally paid to such a person. You called him crazy—

BIFF I didn't mean—

LINDA No, a lot of people think he's lost his—balance. But you don't have to be very smart to know what his trouble is. The man is exhausted.

HAPPY Sure!

LINDA A small man can be just as exhausted as a great man. He works for a company thirty-six years this March, opens up unheard-of territories to their trademark, and now in his old age they take his salary away.

HAPPY (*indignantly*) I didn't know that, Mom.

LINDA You never asked, my dear! Now that you get your spending money someplace else you don't trouble your mind with him.

HAPPY But I gave you money last—

LINDA Christmas time, fifty dollars! To fix the hot water it cost ninety-seven fifty! For five weeks he's been on straight commission, like a beginner, an unknown!

BIFF Those ungrateful bastards!

LINDA Are they any worse than his sons? When he brought them business, when he was young, they were glad to see him. But now his old friends, the old buyers that loved him so and always found some order to hand him in a pinch—they're all dead, retired. He used to be able to make six, seven calls a day in Boston. Now he takes his valises out of the car and puts them back and takes them out again and he's exhausted. Instead of walking he talks now. He drives seven hundred miles, and when he gets there no one knows him any more, no one welcomes him. And what goes through a man's mind, driving seven hundred miles home without having earned a cent? Why shouldn't he talk to himself? Why? When he has to go to Charley and borrow fifty dollars a week and pretend to me that it's his pay? How long can that go on? How long? You see what I'm sitting here and waiting for? And you tell me he has no character? The man who never worked a day but for your benefit? When does he get the medal for that? Is this his reward—to turn around at the age of sixty-three and find his sons, who he loved better than his life, one a philandering bum—

HAPPY Mom!

LINDA That's all you are, my baby! (*To* BIFF) And you! What happened to the love you had for him? You were such pals! How you used to talk to him on the phone every night! How lonely he was till he could come home to you!

BIFF All right, Mom. I'll live here in my room, and I'll get a job. I'll keep away from him, that's all.

LINDA No, Biff. You can't stay here and fight all the time.

BIFF He threw me out of this house, remember that.

LINDA Why did he do that? I never knew why.

BIFF Because I know he's a fake and he doesn't like anybody around who knows!

LINDA Why a fake? In what way? What do you mean?

BIFF Just don't lay it all at my feet. It's between me and him—that's all I have to say. I'll chip in from now on. He'll settle for half my pay check. He'll be all right. I'm going to bed. (*He starts for the stairs*)

LINDA He won't be all right.

BIFF (*turning on the stairs, furiously*) I hate this city and I'll stay here. Now what do you want?

LINDA He's dying, Biff.

HAPPY *turns quickly to her, shocked.*

BIFF (*after a pause*) Why is he dying?

LINDA He's been trying to kill himself.

BIFF (*with great horror*) How?

LINDA I live from day to day.

BIFF What're you talking about?

LINDA Remember I wrote you that he smashed up the car again? In February?

BIFF Well?

LINDA The insurance inspector came. He said that they have evidence. That all these accidents in the last year—weren't—weren't—accidents.

HAPPY How can they tell that? That's a lie.

LINDA It seems there's a woman . . . (*She takes a breath as . . .*)

BIFF (*sharply but contained*) What woman?

LINDA (*simultaneously*) . . . and this woman . . .

LINDA What?

BIFF Nothing. Go ahead.

LINDA What did you say?

BIFF Nothing. I just said what woman?

HAPPY What about her?

LINDA Well, it seems she was walking down the road and saw his car. She says that he wasn't driving fast at all, and that he didn't skid. She says he came to that little bridge, and then deliberately smashed into the railing, and it was only the shallowness of the water that saved him.

BIFF Oh, no, he probably just fell asleep again.

LINDA I don't think he fell asleep.

BIFF Why not?

LINDA Last month . . . (*With great difficulty*) Oh, boys, it's so hard to say a thing like this! He's just a big stupid man to you, but I tell you there's more good in him than in many other people. (*She chokes, wipes her eyes*) I was looking for a fuse. The lights blew out, and I went down the cellar. And behind the fuse box —it happened to fall out—was length of rubber pipe—just short.

HAPPY No kidding?

LINDA There's a little attachment on the end of it. I knew right away. And sure enough, on the bottom of the water heater there's a new little nipple on the gas pipe.

HAPPY (*angrily*) That—jerk.

BIFF Did you have it taken off?

LINDA I'm—I'm ashamed to. How can I mention it to him? Every day I go down and take away that little rubber pipe. But, when he comes home, I put it back where it was. How can I insult him that way? I don't know what to do. I live from day to day, boys. I tell you, I know every thought in his mind. It sounds so old-fashioned and silly, but I tell you he put his whole life into you and you've turned your backs on him. (*She is bent over in the chair, weeping, her face in her hands*) Biff, I swear to God! Biff, his life is in your hands!

HAPPY (*to* BIFF) How do you like that damned fool!

BIFF (*kissing her*) All right, pal, all right. It's all settled now. I've been remiss. I know that, Mom. But now I'll stay, and I swear to you, I'll apply myself. (*Kneeling in front of her, in a fever of self-reproach*) It's just—you see, Mom, I don't fit in business. Not that I won't try. I'll try, and I'll make good.

HAPPY Sure you will. The trouble with you in business was you never tried to please people.

BIFF I know, I—

HAPPY Like when you worked for Harrison's. Bob Harrison said you were tops, and then you go and do some damn fool thing like whistling whole songs in the elevator like a comedian.

BIFF (*against* HAPPY) So what? I like to whistle sometimes.

HAPPY You don't raise a guy to a responsible job who whistles in the elevator!

LINDA Well, don't argue about it now.

HAPPY Like when you'd go off and swim in the middle of the day instead of taking the line around.

BIFF (*his resentment rising*) Well, don't you run off? You take off sometimes, don't you? On a nice summer day?

HAPPY Yeah, but I cover myself!

LINDA Boys!

HAPPY If I'm going to take a fade the boss can call any number where I'm supposed to be and they'll swear to him that I just left. I'll tell you something that I hate to say, Biff, but in the business world some of them think you're crazy.

BIFF (*angered*) Screw the business world!

HAPPY All right, screw it! Great, but cover yourself!

LINDA Hap, Hap!

BIFF I don't care what they think! They've laughed at Dad for years, and you know why? Because we don't belong in this nut-house of a city! We should be mixing cement on some open plain, or—or carpenters. A carpenter is allowed to whistle!

WILLY *walks in from the entrance of the house, at left.*

WILLY Even your grandfather was better than a carpenter. (*Pause. They watch him*) You never grew up. Bernard does not whistle in the elevator, I assure you.

BIFF (*as though to laugh* WILLY *out of it*) Yeah, but you do, Pop.

WILLY I never in my life whistled in an elevator! And who in the business world thinks I'm crazy?

BIFF I didn't mean it like that, Pop. Now don't make a whole thing out of it, will ya?

WILLY Go back to the West! Be a carpenter, a cowboy, enjoy yourself!

LINDA Willy, he was just saying—

WILLY I heard what he said!

HAPPY (*trying to quiet* WILLY) Hey, Pop, come on now . . .

WILLY (*continuing over* HAPPY'S *line*) They laugh at me, heh? Go to Filene's, go to the Hub, go to Slattery's, Boston. Call out the name Willy Loman and see what happens! Big shot!

BIFF All right, Pop.

WILLY Big!

BIFF All right!

WILLY Why do you always insult me?

BIFF I didn't say a word. (*To* LINDA) Did I say a word?

LINDA He didn't say anything, Willy.

WILLY (*going to the doorway of the living-room*) All right, good night, good night.

LINDA Willy, dear, he just decided . . .

WILLY (*to* BIFF) If you get tired hanging around tomorrow, paint the ceiling I put up in the living-room.

BIFF I'm leaving early tomorrow.

HAPPY He's going to see Bill Oliver, Pop.

WILLY (*interestedly*) Oliver? For what?

BIFF (*with reserve, but trying, trying*) He always said he'd stake me. I'd like to go into business, so maybe I can take him up on it.

LINDA Isn't that wonderful?

WILLY Don't interrupt. What's wonderful about it? There's fifty men in the City of New York who'd stake him. (*To* BIFF) Sporting goods?

BIFF I guess so. I know something about it and—

WILLY He knows something about it! You know sporting goods better than Spalding, for God's sake! How much is he giving you?

BIFF I don't know, I didn't even see him yet, but—

WILLY Then what're you talkin' about?

BIFF (*getting angry*) Well, all I said was I'm gonna see him, that's all!

WILLY (*turning away*) Ah, you're counting your chickens again.

BIFF (*starting left for the stairs*) Oh, Jesus, I'm going to sleep!

WILLY (*calling after him*) Don't curse in this house!

BIFF (*turning*) Since when did you get so clean?

HAPPY (*trying to stop them*) Wait a . . .

WILLY Don't use that language to me! I won't have it!

HAPPY (*grabbing* BIFF, *shouts*) Wait a minute! I got an idea. I got a feasible idea. Come here, Biff, let's talk this over now, let's talk some sense here. When I was down in Florida last time, I thought of a great idea to sell sporting goods. It just came back to me. You and I, Biff—we have a line, the Loman Line. We train a couple of weeks, and put on a couple of exhibitions, see?

WILLY That's an idea!

HAPPY Wait! We form two basketball teams, see? Two water-polo teams. We play each other. It's a million dollars' worth of publicity. Two brothers, see? The Loman Brothers. Displays in the Royal Palms—all the hotels. And banners over the ring and the basketball court: "Loman Brothers." Baby, we could sell sporting goods!

WILLY That is a one-million-dollar idea!

LINDA Marvelous!

BIFF I'm in great shape as far as that's concerned.

HAPPY And the beauty of it is, Biff, it wouldn't be like a business. We'd be out playin' ball again . . .

BIFF (*enthused*) Yeah, that's . . .

WILLY Million-dollar . . .

HAPPY And you wouldn't get fed up with it, Biff. It'd be the family again. There'd be the old honor, and comradeship, and if you wanted to go off for a swim or somethin'—well, you'd do it! Without some smart cooky gettin' up ahead of you!

WILLY Lick the world! You guys together could absolutely lick the civilized world.

BIFF I'll see Oliver tomorrow. Hap, if we could work that out . . .

LINDA Maybe things are beginning to—

WILLY (*wildly enthused, to* LINDA) Stop interrupting! (*To* BIFF) But don't wear sport jacket and slacks when you see Oliver.

BIFF No, I'll—

WILLY A business suit, and talk as little as possible, and don't crack any jokes.

BIFF He did like me. Always liked me.

LINDA He loved you!

WILLY (*to* LINDA) Will you stop! (*To* BIFF) Walk in very serious. You are not applying for a boy's job. Money is to pass. Be quiet, fine, and serious. Everybody likes a kidder, but nobody lends him money.

HAPPY I'll try to get some myself, Biff. I'm sure I can.

WILLY I see great things for you kids, I think your troubles are over. But remember, start big and you'll end big. Ask for fifteen. How much you gonna ask for?

BIFF Gee, I don't know—

WILLY And don't say "Gee." "Gee" is a boy's word. A man walking in for fifteen thousand dollars does not say "Gee!"

BIFF Ten, I think, would be top though.

WILLY Don't be so modest. You always started too low. Walk in with a big laugh. Don't look worried. Start off with a couple of your good stories to lighten things up. It's not what you say, it's how you say it—because personality always wins the day.

LINDA Oliver always thought the highest of him—

WILLY Will you let me talk?

BIFF Don't yell at her, Pop, will ya?

WILLY (*angrily*) I was talking, wasn't I?

BIFF I don't like you yelling at her all the time, and I'm tellin' you, that's all.

WILLY What're you, takin' over this house?

LINDA Willy—

WILLY (*turning on her*) Don't take his side all the time, goddammit!

BIFF (*furiously*) Stop yelling at her!

WILLY (*suddenly pulling on his cheek, beaten down, guilt ridden*) Give my best to Bill Oliver—he may remember me. (*He exits through the living-room doorway*)

LINDA (*her voice subdued*) What'd you have to start that for? (BIFF *turns away*) You see how sweet he was as soon as you talked hopefully? (*She goes over to* BIFF) Come up and say good night to him. Don't let him go to bed that way.

HAPPY Come on, Biff, let's buck him up.

LINDA Please, dear. Just say good night. It takes so little to make him happy. Come. (*She goes through the living-room doorway, calling upstairs from within the living-room*) Your pajamas are hanging in the bathroom, Willy!

HAPPY (*looking toward where* LINDA *went out*) What a woman! They broke the mold when they made her. You know that, Biff?

BIFF He's off salary. My God, working on commission!

HAPPY Well, let's face it: he's no hot-shot selling man. Except that sometimes, you have to admit, he's a sweet personality.

BIFF (*deciding*) Lend me ten bucks, will ya? I want to buy some new ties.

HAPPY I'll take you to a place I know. Beautiful stuff. Wear one of my striped shirts tomorrow.

BIFF She got gray. Mom got awful old. Gee, I'm gonna go in to Oliver tomorrow and knock him for a—

HAPPY Come on up. Tell that to Dad. Let's give him a whirl. Come on.

BIFF (*steamed up*) You know, with ten thousand bucks, boy!

HAPPY (*as they go into the living-room*) That's the talk, Biff, that's the first time I've heard the old confidence out of you! (*From within the living-room, fading off*) You're gonna live with me, kid, and any babe you want just say the word . . .

*The last lines are hardly heard. They are mounting the stairs to their parents' bedroom.*

LINDA (*entering her bedroom and addressing* WILLY, *who is in the bathroom. She is straightening the bed for him*) Can you do anything about the shower? It drips.

WILLY (*from the bathroom*) All of a sudden everything falls to pieces! Goddam plumbing, oughta be sued, those people. I hardly finished putting it in and the thing . . . (*His words rumble off*)

LINDA I'm just wondering if Oliver will remember him. You think he might?

WILLY (*coming out of the bathroom in his pajamas*) Remember him? What's the matter with you, you crazy? If he'd've stayed with Oliver he'd be on top by now! Wait'll Oliver gets a look at him. You don't know the average caliber any more. The average young man today—(*he is getting into bed*)—is got a caliber of zero. Greatest thing in the world for him was to bum around.

BIFF *and* HAPPY *enter the bedroom. Slight pause.*

WILLY (*stops short, looking at* BIFF) Glad to hear it, boy.

HAPPY He wanted to say good night to you, sport.

WILLY (*to* BIFF) Yeah. Knock him dead, boy. What'd you want to tell me?

BIFF Just take it easy, Pop. Good night. (*He turns to go*)

WILLY (*unable to resist*) And if anything falls off the desk while you're talking to him—like a package or something—don't you pick it up. They have office boys for that.

LINDA I'll make a big breakfast—

WILLY Will you let me finish? (*To* BIFF) Tell him you were in the business in the West. Not farm work.

BIFF All right, Dad.

LINDA I think everything—

WILLY (*going right through her speech*) And don't undersell yourself. No less than fifteen thousand dollars.

BIFF (*unable to bear him*) Okay. Good night, Mom. (*He starts moving*)

WILLY Because you got a greatness in you, Biff, remember that. You got all kinds a greatness . . . (*He lies back, exhausted.* BIFF *walks out*)

LINDA (*calling after* BIFF) Sleep well, darling!

HAPPY I'm gonna get married, Mom. I wanted to tell you.

LINDA Go to sleep, dear.

HAPPY (*going*) I just wanted to tell you.

WILLY Keep up the good work. (HAPPY *exits*) God . . . remember that Ebbets Field game? The championship of the city?

LINDA Just rest. Should I sing to you?

WILLY Yeah. Sing to me. (LINDA *hums a soft lullaby*) When that team came out—he was the tallest, remember?

LINDA Oh, yes. And in gold.

BIFF *enters the darkened kitchen, takes a cigarette, and leaves the house. He comes downstage into a golden pool of light. He smokes, staring at the night.*

WILLY Like a young god. Hercules—something like that. And the sun, the sun all around him. Remember how he waved to me?

Right up from the field, with the representatives of three colleges standing by? And the buyers I brought, and the cheers when he came out—Loman, Loman, Loman! God almighty, he'll be great yet. A star like that, magnificent, can never really fade away!

*The light on* WILLY *is fading. The gas heater begins to glow through the kitchen wall, near the stairs, a blue flame beneath red coils.*

LINDA (*timidly*) Willy dear, what has he got against you?

WILLY I'm so tired. Don't talk any more.

BIFF *slowly returns to the kitchen. He stops, stares toward the heater.*

LINDA Will you ask Howard to let you work in New York?

WILLY First thing in the morning. Everything'll be all right.

BIFF *reaches behind the heater and draws out a length of rubber tubing. He is horrified and turns his head toward* WILLY'S *room, still dimly lit, from which the strains of* LINDA'S *desperate but monotonous humming rise.*

WILLY (*staring through the window into the moonlight*) Gee, look at the moon moving between the buildings!

BIFF *wraps the tubing around his hand and quickly goes up the stairs.*

*Curtain*

## ACT TWO

*Music is heard, gay and bright. The curtain rises as the music fades away.* WILLY, *in shirt sleeves, is sitting at the kitchen table, sipping coffee, his hat in his lap.* LINDA *is filling his cup when she can.*

WILLY Wonderful coffee. Meal in itself.

LINDA Can I make you some eggs?

WILLY No. Take a breath.

LINDA You look so rested, dear.

WILLY I slept like a dead one. First time in months. Imagine, sleeping till ten on a Tuesday morning. Boys left nice and early, heh?

LINDA They were out of here by eight o'clock.

WILLY Good work!

LINDA It was so thrilling to see them leaving together. I can't get over the shaving lotion in this house!

WILLY (*smiling*) Mmm—

LINDA Biff was very changed this morning. His whole attitude seemed to be hopeful. He couldn't wait to get downtown to see Oliver.

WILLY He's heading for a change. There's no question, there simply are certain men that take longer to get—solidified. How did he dress?

LINDA His blue suit. He's so handsome in that suit. He could be a—anything in that suit!

WILLY *gets up from the table.* LINDA *holds his jacket for him.*

WILLY There's no question, no question at all. Gee, on the way home tonight I'd like to buy some seeds.

LINDA (*laughing*) That'd be wonderful. But not enough sun gets back there. Nothing'll grow any more.

WILLY You wait, kid, before it's all over we're gonna get a little place out in the country, and I'll raise some vegetables, a couple of chickens . . .

LINDA You'll do it yet, dear.

WILLY *walks out of his jacket.* LINDA *follows him.*

WILLY And they'll get married, and come for a weekend. I'd build a little guest house. 'Cause I got so many fine tools, all I'd need would be a little lumber and some peace of mind.

LINDA (*joyfully*) I sewed the lining . . .

WILLY I could build two guest houses, so they'd both come. Did he decide how much he's going to ask Oliver for?

LINDA (*getting him into the jacket*) He didn't mention it, but I imagine ten or fifteen thousand. You going to talk to Howard today?

WILLY Yeah. I'll put it to him straight and simple. He'll just have to take me off the road.

LINDA And Willy, don't forget to ask for a little advance, because we've got the insurance premium. It's the grace period now.

WILLY That's a hundred . . . ?

LINDA A hundred and eight, sixty-eight. Because we're a little short again.

WILLY Why are we short?

LINDA Well, you had the motor job on the car . . .

WILLY That goddam Studebaker!

LINDA And you got one more payment on the refrigerator . . .

WILLY But it just broke again!

LINDA Well, it's old, dear.

WILLY I told you we should've bought a well-advertised machine. Charley bought a General Electric and it's twenty years old and it's still good, that son-of-a-bitch.

LINDA But, Willy—

WILLY Whoever heard of a Hastings refrigerator? Once in my life I would like to own something outright before it's broken! I'm always in a race with the junkyard! I just finished paying for the car and it's on its last legs. The refrigerator consumes belts like a goddam maniac. They time those things. They time them so when you finally paid for them, they're used up.

LINDA (*buttoning up his jacket as he unbuttons it*) All told, about two hundred dollars would carry us, dear. But that includes the last payment on the mortgage. After this payment, Willy, the house belongs to us.

WILLY It's twenty-five years!

LINDA Biff was nine years old when we bought it.

WILLY Well, that's a great thing. To weather a twenty-five year mortgage is—

LINDA It's an accomplishment.

WILLY All the cement, the lumber, the reconstruction I put in this house! There ain't a crack to be found in it any more.

LINDA Well, it served its purpose.

WILLY What purpose? Some stranger'll come along, move in, and that's that. If only Biff would take this house, and raise a family . . . (*He starts to go*) Good-by, I'm late.

LINDA (*suddenly remembering*) Oh, I forgot! You're supposed to meet them for dinner.

WILLY Me?

LINDA At Frank's Chop House on Forty-eighth near Sixth Avenue.

WILLY Is that so! How about you?

LINDA No, just the three of you. They're gonna blow you to a big meal!

WILLY Don't say! Who thought of that?

LINDA Biff came to me this morning, Willy, and he said, "Tell Dad, we want to blow him to a big meal." Be there six o'clock. You and your two boys are going to have dinner.

WILLY Gee whiz! That's really somethin'. I'm gonna knock Howard for a loop, kid. I'll get an advance, and I'll come home with a New York job. Goddammit, now I'm gonna do it!

LINDA Oh, that's the spirit, Willy!

WILLY I will never get behind a wheel the rest of my life!

LINDA It's changing, Willy, I can feel it changing!

WILLY Beyond a question. G'by, I'm late. (*He starts to go again*)

LINDA (*calling after him as she runs to the kitchen table for a handkerchief*) You got your glasses?

WILLY (*feels for them, then comes back in*) Yeah, yeah, got my glasses.

LINDA (*giving him the handkerchief*) And a handkerchief.
WILLY Yeah, handkerchief.
LINDA And your saccharine?
WILLY Yeah, my saccharine.
LINDA Be careful on the subway stairs.

*She kisses him, and a silk stocking is seen hanging from her hand.* WILLY *notices it.*

WILLY Will you stop mending stockings? At least while I'm in the house. It gets me nervous. I can't tell you. Please.

LINDA *hides the stocking in her hand as she follows* WILLY *across the forestage in front of the house.*

LINDA Remember, Frank's Chop House.
WILLY (*passing the apron*) Maybe beets would grow out there.
LINDA (*laughing*) But you tried so many times.
WILLY Yeah. Well, don't work hard today. (*He disappears around the right corner of the house*)
LINDA Be careful!

*As* WILLY *vanishes,* LINDA *waves to him. Suddenly the phone rings. She runs across the stage and into the kitchen and lifts it.*

LINDA Hello? Oh, Biff! I'm so glad you called, I just . . . Yes, sure, I just told him. Yes, he'll be there for dinner at six o'clock, I didn't forget. Listen, I was just dying to tell you. You know that little rubber pipe I told you about? That he connected to the gas heater? I finally decided to go down the cellar this morning and take it away and destroy it. But it's gone! Imagine? He took it away himself, it isn't there! (*She listens*) When? Oh, then you took it. Oh—nothing, it's just that I'd hoped he'd taken it away himself. Oh, I'm not worried, darling, because this morning he left in such high spirits, it was like the old days! I'm not afraid any more. Did Mr. Oliver see you? . . . Well, you wait there then. And make a nice impression on him, darling. Just don't perspire too much before you see him. And have a nice time with Dad. He may have big news too! . . . That's right, a New York job. And be sweet to him tonight, dear. Be loving to him. Because he's only a little boat looking for a harbor. (*She is trembling with sorrow and joy*) Oh, that's wonderful, Biff, you'll save his life. Thanks, darling. Just put your arm around him when he comes into the restaurant. Give him a smile. That's the boy . . . Good-by, dear. . . . You got your comb? . . . That's fine. Good-by, Biff dear.

*In the middle of her speech,* HOWARD WAGNER, *thirty-six, wheels on a small typewriter table on which is a wire-recording machine and proceeds to plug it in. This is on the left forestage. Light slowly fades on* LINDA *as it rises on* HOWARD. HOWARD *is intent on threading the machine and only glances over his shoulder as* WILLY *appears.*

WILLY Pst! Pst!
HOWARD Hello, Willy, come in.
WILLY Like to have a little talk with you, Howard.
HOWARD Sorry to keep you waiting. I'll be with you in a minute.
WILLY What's that, Howard?
HOWARD Didn't you ever see one of these? Wire recorder.
WILLY Oh. Can we talk a minute?
HOWARD Records things. Just got delivery yesterday. Been driving me crazy, the most terrific machine I ever saw in my life. I was up all night with it.
WILLY What do you do with it?
HOWARD I bought it for dictation, but you can do anything with it. Listen to this. I had it home last night. Listen to what I picked up. The first one is my daughter. Get this. (*He flicks the switch and "Roll out the Barrel" is heard being whistled*) Listen to that kid whistle.
WILLY That is lifelike, isn't it?
HOWARD Seven years old. Get that tone.
WILLY Ts, ts. Like to ask a little favor if you . . .

*The whistling breaks off, and the voice of* HOWARD'S *daughter is heard.*

HIS DAUGHTER "Now you, Daddy."
HOWARD She's crazy for me! (*Again the same song is whistled*) That's me! Ha! (*He winks*)
WILLY You're very good!

*The whistling breaks off again. The machine runs silent for a moment.*

HOWARD Sh! Get this now, this is my son.
HIS SON "The capital of Alabama is Montgomery; the capital of Arizona is Phoenix; the capital of Arkansas is Little Rock; the capital of California is Sacramento . . ." (*and on, and on*)
HOWARD (*holding up five fingers*) Five years old, Willy!
WILLY He'll make an announcer some day!
HIS SON (*continuing*) "The capital . . ."
HOWARD Get that—alphabetical order! (*The machine breaks off suddenly*) Wait a minute. The maid kicked the plug out.
WILLY It certainly is a—
HOWARD Sh, for God's sake!
HIS SON "It's nine o'clock, Bulova watch time. So I have to go to sleep."

WILLY That really is—

HOWARD Wait a minute! The next is my wife.

*They wait.*

HOWARD'S VOICE "Go on, say something." (*Pause*) "Well, you gonna talk?"

HIS WIFE "I can't think of anything."

HOWARD'S VOICE "Well, talk—it's turning."

HIS WIFE (*shyly, beaten*) "Hello." (*Silence*) "Oh, Howard, I can't talk into this . . ."

HOWARD (*snapping the machine off*) That was my wife.

WILLY That is a wonderful machine. Can we—

HOWARD I tell you, Willy, I'm gonna take my camera, and my bandsaw, and all my hobbies, and out they go. This is the most fascinating relaxation I ever found.

WILLY I think I'll get one myself.

HOWARD Sure, they're only a hundred and a half. You can't do without it. Supposing you wanna hear Jack Benny, see? But you can't be at home at that hour. So you tell the maid to turn the radio on when Jack Benny comes on, and this automatically goes on with the radio . . .

WILLY And when you come home you . . .

HOWARD You can come home twelve o'clock, one o'clock, any time you like, and you get yourself a Coke and sit yourself down, throw the switch, and there's Jack Benny's program in the middle of the night!

WILLY I'm definitely going to get one. Because lots of time I'm on the road, and I think to myself, what I must be missing on the radio!

HOWARD Don't you have a radio in the car?

WILLY Well, yeah, but who ever thinks of turning it on?

HOWARD Say, aren't you supposed to be in Boston?

WILLY That's what I want to talk to you about, Howard. You got a minute? (*He draws a chair in from the wing*)

HOWARD What happened? What're you doing here?

WILLY Well . . .

HOWARD You didn't crack up again, did you?

WILLY Oh, no. No . . .

HOWARD Geez, you had me worried there for a minute. What's the trouble?

WILLY Well, tell you the truth, Howard. I've come to the decision that I'd rather not travel any more.

HOWARD Not travel! Well, what'll you do?

WILLY Remember, Christmas time, when you had the party here? You said you'd try to think of some spot for me here in town.

HOWARD With us?

WILLY Well, sure.

HOWARD Oh, yeah, yeah. I remember. Well, I couldn't think of anything for you, Willy.

WILLY I tell ya, Howard. The kids are all grown up, y'know. I don't need much any more. If I could take home—well, sixty-five dollars a week, I could swing it.

HOWARD Yeah, but Willy, see I—

WILLY I tell ya why, Howard. Speaking frankly and between the two of us, y'know—I'm just a little tired.

HOWARD Oh, I could understand that, Willy. But you're a road man, Willy, and we do a road business. We've only got a half-dozen salesmen on the floor here.

WILLY God knows, Howard, I never asked a favor of any man. But I was with the firm when your father used to carry you in here in his arms.

HOWARD I know that, Willy, but—

WILLY Your father came to me the day you were born and asked me what I thought of the name of Howard, may he rest in peace.

HOWARD I appreciate that, Willy, but there just is no spot here for you. If I had a spot I'd slam you right in, but I just don't have a single solitary spot.

*He looks for his lighter.* WILLY *has picked it up and gives it to him. Pause.*

WILLY (*with increasing anger*) Howard, all I need to set my table is fifty dollars a week.

HOWARD But where am I going to put you, kid?

WILLY Look, it isn't a question of whether I can sell merchandise, is it?

HOWARD No, but it's a business, kid, and everybody's gotta pull his own weight.

WILLY (*desperately*) Just let me tell you a story, Howard—

HOWARD 'Cause you gotta admit, business is business.

WILLY (*angrily*) Business is definitely business, but just listen for a minute. You don't understand this. When I was a boy—eighteen, nineteen—I was already on the road. And there was a question in my mind as to whether selling had a future for me. Because in those days I had a yearning to go to Alaska. See, there were three gold strikes in one month in Alaska, and I felt like going out. Just for the ride, you might say.

HOWARD (*barely interested*) Don't say.

WILLY Oh, yeah, my father lived many years in Alaska. He was an adventurous man. We've got quite a little streak of self-reliance in our family. I thought I'd go out with my older brother and try to locate him, and maybe settle in the North with the old man. And I was almost decided to go, when I met a salesman in the Parker House. His name was Dave Singleman. And he was eighty-four years old, and he'd drummed merchandise in thirty-one states. And old Dave, he'd go up to his room, y'understand, put on his green velvet slippers—I'll never forget—and pick up his phone and call the buyers, and without ever leaving his room, at the age of eighty-four, he made his living. And when I saw that, I realized that selling was the greatest career a man could want. 'Cause what could be more satisfying than to be able to go, at the age of eighty-four, into twenty or thirty different cities, and pick up a phone, and be remembered and loved and helped by so many different people? Do you know? when he died —and by the way he died the death of a salesman, in his green velvet slippers in the smoker of the New York, New Haven and Hartford, going into Boston—when he died, hundreds of salesmen and buyers were at his funeral. Things were sad on a lotta trains for months after that. (*He stands up.* HOWARD *has not looked at him*) In those days there was personality in it, Howard. There was respect, and comradeship, and gratitude in it. Today, it's all cut and dried, and there's no chance for bringing friendship to bear—or personality. You see what I mean? They don't know me any more.

HOWARD (*moving away, to the right*) That's just the thing, Willy.

WILLY If I had forty dollars a week—that's all I'd need. Forty dollars, Howard.

HOWARD Kid, I can't take blood from a stone, I—

WILLY (*desperation is on him now*) Howard, the year Al Smith was nominated, your father came to me and—

HOWARD (*starting to go off*) I've got to see some people, kid.

WILLY (*stopping him*) I'm talking about your father! There were promises made across this desk! You mustn't tell me you've got people to see—I put thirty-four years into this firm, Howard, and now I can't pay my insurance! You can't eat the orange and throw the peel away—a man is not a piece of fruit! (*After a pause*) Now pay attention. Your father—in 1928 I had a big year. I averaged a hundred and seventy dollars a week in commissions.

HOWARD (*impatiently*) Now, Willy, you never averaged—

WILLY (*banging his hand on the desk*) I averaged a hundred and seventy dollars a week in the year of 1928! And your father came to me—or rather, I was in the office here—it was right over this desk—and he put his hand on my shoulder—

HOWARD (*getting up*) You'll have to excuse me, Willy, I gotta see some people. Pull yourself together. (*Going out*) I'll be back in a little while.

*On* HOWARD'S *exit, the light on his chair grows very bright and strange.*

WILLY Pull myself together! What the hell did I say to him? My God, I was yelling at him! How could I! (WILLY *breaks off, staring at the light, which occupies the chair, animating it. He approaches this chair, standing across the desk from it*) Frank, Frank, don't you remember what you told me that time? How you put your hand on my shoulder, and Frank . . .

*He leans on the desk and as he speaks the dead man's name he accidentally switches on the recorder, and instantly*

HOWARD'S SON ". . . of New York is Albany. The capital of Ohio is Cincinnati, the capital of Rhode Island is . . ." (*The recitation continues*)

WILLY (*leaping away with fright, shouting*) Ha! Howard! Howard! Howard!

HOWARD (*rushing in*) What happened?

WILLY (*pointing at the machine, which continues nasally, childishly, with the capital cities*) Shut it off! Shut it off!

HOWARD (*pulling the plug out*) Look, Willy . . .

WILLY (*pressing his hands to his eyes*) I gotta get myself some coffee. I'll get some coffee . . .

WILLY *starts to walk out.* HOWARD *stops him.*

HOWARD (*rolling up the cord*) Willy, look . . .

WILLY I'll go to Boston.

HOWARD Willy, you can't go to Boston for us.

WILLY Why can't I go?

HOWARD I don't want you to represent us. I've been meaning to tell you for a long time now.

WILLY Howard, are you firing me?

HOWARD I think you need a good long rest, Willy.

WILLY Howard—

HOWARD And when you feel better, come back, and we'll see if we can work something out.

WILLY But I gotta earn money, Howard. I'm in no position to—

HOWARD Where are your sons? Why don't your sons give you a hand?

WILLY They're working on a very big deal.

HOWARD This is no time for false pride, Willy. You go to your sons and you tell them that you're tired. You've got two great boys, haven't you?

WILLY Oh, no question, no question, but in the meantime . . .

HOWARD Then that's that, heh?

WILLY All right, I'll go to Boston tomorrow.

HOWARD No, no.

WILLY I can't throw myself on my sons. I'm not a cripple!

HOWARD Look, kid, I'm busy this morning.

WILLY (*grasping* HOWARD's *arm*) Howard, you've got to let me go to Boston!

HOWARD (*hard, keeping himself under control*) I've got a line of people to see this morning. Sit down, take five minutes, and pull yourself together, and then go home, will ya? I need the office, Willy. (*He starts to go, turns, remembering the recorder, starts to push off the table holding the recorder*) Oh, yeah. Whenever you can this week, stop by and drop off the samples. You'll feel better, Willy, and then come back and we'll talk. Pull yourself together, kid, there's people outside.

HOWARD *exits, pushing the table off left.* WILLY *stares into space, exhausted. Now the music is heard—*BEN's *music—first distantly, then closer, closer. As* WILLY *speaks,* BEN *enters from the right. He carries valise and umbrella.*

WILLY Oh, Ben, how did you do it? What is the answer? Did you wind up the Alaska deal already?

BEN Doesn't take much time if you know what you're doing. Just a short business trip. Boarding ship in an hour. Wanted to say good-by.

WILLY Ben, I've got to talk to you.

BEN (*glancing at his watch*) Haven't the time, William.

WILLY (*crossing the apron to* BEN) Ben, nothing's working out. I don't know what to do.

BEN Now, look here, William. I've bought timberland in Alaska and I need a man to look after things for me.

WILLY God, timberland! Me and my boys in those grand outdoors!

BEN You've a new continent at your doorstep, William. Get out of these cities, they're full of talk and time payments and courts of law. Screw on your fists and you can fight for a fortune up there.

WILLY Yes, yes! Linda, Linda!

LINDA *enters as of old, with the wash.*

LINDA Oh, you're back?

BEN I haven't much time.

WILLY No, wait! Linda, he's got a proposition for me in Alaska.

LINDA But you've got—(*To* BEN) He's got a beautiful job here.

WILLY But in Alaska, kid, I could—

LINDA You're doing well enough, Willy!

BEN (*to* LINDA) Enough for what, my dear?

LINDA (*frightened of* BEN *and angry at him*) Don't say those things to him! Enough to be happy right here, right now. (*To* WILLY, *while* BEN *laughs*) Why must everybody conquer the world? You're well liked, and the boys love you, and someday—(*to* BEN)—why, old man Wagner told him just the other day that if he keeps it up he'll be a member of the firm, didn't he, Willy?

WILLY Sure, sure. I am building something with this firm, Ben, and if a man is building something he must be on the right track, mustn't he?

BEN What are you building? Lay your hand on it. Where is it?

WILLY (*hesitantly*) That's true, Linda, there's nothing.

LINDA Why? (*To* BEN) There's a man eighty-four years old—

WILLY That's right, Ben, that's right. When I look at that man I say, what is there to worry about?

BEN Bah!

WILLY It's true, Ben. All he has to do is go into any city, pick up the phone, and he's making his living and you know why?

BEN (*picking up his valise*) I've got to go.

WILLY (*holding* BEN *back*) Look at this boy!

BIFF, *in his high school sweater, enters carrying suitcase.* HAPPY *carries* BIFF's *shoulder guards, gold helmet, and football pants.*

WILLY Without a penny to his name, three great universities are begging for him, and from there the sky's the limit, because it's not what you do, Ben. It's who you know and the smile on your face! It's contacts, Ben, contacts! The whole wealth of Alaska passes over the lunch table at the Commodore Hotel, and that's the wonder, the wonder of this country, that a man can end with diamonds here on the basis of being liked! (*He turns to* BIFF) And that's why when you get out on that field today it's important. Because thousands of people will be rooting for you and loving you. (*To* BEN, *who has again begun to leave*) And Ben! when he walks into a business office his name will sound out like a bell and all the doors will open to him! I've seen it, Ben, I've seen it a thousand times! You can't feel it with your hand like timber, but it's there!

BEN Good-by, William.

WILLY Ben, am I right? Don't you think I'm right? I value your advice.

BEN There's a new continent at your doorstep, William. You could walk out rich. Rich! (*He is gone*)

WILLY We'll do it here, Ben! You hear me? We're gonna do it here!

*Young* BERNARD *rushes in. The gay music of the Boys is heard.*

BERNARD Oh, gee, I was afraid you left already!

WILLY Why? What time is it?

BERNARD It's half-past one!

WILLY Well, come on, everybody! Ebbets Field next stop! Where's the pennants? (*He rushes through the wall-line of the kitchen and out into the living-room*)

LINDA (*to* BIFF) Did you pack fresh underwear?

BIFF (*who has been limbering up*) I want to go!

BERNARD Biff, I'm carrying your helmet, ain't I?

HAPPY No, I'm carrying the helmet.

BERNARD Oh, Biff, you promised me.

HAPPY I'm carrying the helmet.

BERNARD How am I going to get in the locker room?

LINDA Let him carry the shoulder guards. (*She puts her coat and hat on in the kitchen*)

BERNARD Can I, Biff? 'Cause I told everybody I'm going to be in the locker room.

HAPPY In Ebbets Field it's the clubhouse.

BERNARD I meant the clubhouse. Biff!

HAPPY Biff!

BIFF (*grandly, after a slight pause*) Let him carry the shoulder guards.

HAPPY (*as he gives* BERNARD *the shoulder guards*) Stay close to us now.

WILLY *rushes in with the pennants.*

WILLY (*handing them out*) Everybody wave when Biff comes out on the field. (HAPPY *and* BERNARD *run off*) You set now, boy?

*The music has died away.*

BIFF Ready to go, Pop. Every muscle is ready.

WILLY (*at the edge of the apron*) You realize what this means?

BIFF That's right, Pop.

WILLY (*feeling* BIFF'*s muscles*) You're comin' home this afternoon captain of the All-Scholastic Championship Team of the City of New York.

BIFF I got it, Pop. And remember, pal, when I take off my helmet, that touchdown is for you.

WILLY Let's go! (*He is starting out, with his arm around* BIFF, *when* CHARLEY *enters, as of old, in knickers*) I got no room for you, Charley.

CHARLEY Room? For what?

WILLY In the car.

CHARLEY You goin' for a ride? I wanted to shoot some casino.

WILLY (*furiously*) Casino! (*Incredulously*) Don't you realize what today is?

LINDA Oh, he knows, Willy. He's just kidding you.

WILLY That's nothing to kid about!

CHARLEY No, Linda, what's goin' on?

LINDA He's playing in Ebbets Field.

CHARLEY Baseball in this weather?

WILLY Don't talk to him. Come on, come on! (*He is pushing them out*)

CHARLEY Wait a minute, didn't you hear the news?

WILLY What?

CHARLEY Don't you listen to the radio? Ebbets Field just blew up.

WILLY You go to hell! (CHARLEY *laughs*) (*Pushing them out*) Come on, come on! We're late.

CHARLEY (*as they go*) Knock a homer, Biff, knock a homer!

WILLY (*the last to leave, turning to* CHARLEY) I don't think that was funny, Charley. This is the greatest day of his life.

CHARLEY Willy, when are you going to grow up?

WILLY Yeah, heh? When this game is over, Charley, you'll be laughing out of the other side of your face. They'll be calling him another Red Grange. Twenty-five thousand a year.

CHARLEY (*kidding*) Is that so?

WILLY Yeah, that's so.

CHARLEY Well, then, I'm sorry. Willy. But tell me something.

WILLY What?

CHARLEY Who is Red Grange?

WILLY Put up your hands. Goddam you, put up your hands!

CHARLEY, *chuckling, shakes his head and walks away, around the left corner of the stage.* WILLY *follows him. The music rises to a mocking frenzy.*

WILLY Who the hell do you think you are, better than everybody else? You don't know everything, you big, ignorant, stupid . . . Put up your hands!

*Light rises, on the right side of the forestage, on a small table in the reception room of* CHARLEY'S *office. Traffic sounds are heard.* BERNARD, *now mature, sits whistling to himself. A pair of tennis rackets and an overnight bag are on the floor beside him.*

WILLY (*offstage*) What are you walking away for? Don't walk away! If you're going to say something say it to my face! I know you laugh at me behind my back. You'll laugh out of the other side of your goddam face after this game. Touchdown! Touchdown! Eighty thousand people! Touchdown! Right between the goal posts.

BERNARD *is a quiet, earnest, but self-assured young man.* WILLY'S *voice is coming from right upstage now.* BERNARD *lowers his feet off the table and listens.* JENNY, *his father's secretary, enters.*

JENNY (*distressed*) Say, Bernard, will you go out in the hall?

BERNARD What is that noise? Who is it?

JENNY Mr. Loman. He just got off the elevator.

BERNARD (*getting up*) Who's he arguing with?

JENNY Nobody. There's nobody with him. I can't deal with him any more, and your father gets all upset everytime he comes. I've got a lot of typing to do, and your father's waiting to sign it. Will you see him?

WILLY (*entering*) Touchdown! Touch—(*He sees* JENNY) Jenny, Jenny, good to see you. How're ya? Working'? Or still honest?

JENNY Fine. How've you been feeling?

WILLY Not much any more, Jenny. Ha, ha! (*He is surprised to see the rackets*)

BERNARD Hello, Uncle Willy.

WILLY (*almost shocked*) Bernard! Well, look who's here! (*He comes quickly, guiltily, to* BERNARD *and warmly shakes his hand*)

BERNARD How are you? Good to see you.

WILLY What are you doing here?

BERNARD Oh, just stopped by to see Pop. Get off my feet till my train leaves. I'm going to Washington in a few minutes.

WILLY Is he in?

BERNARD Yes, he's in his office with the accountant. Sit down.

WILLY (*sitting down*) What're you going to do in Washington?

BERNARD Oh, just a case I've got there, Willy.

WILLY That so? (*Indicating the rackets*) You going to play tennis there?

BERNARD I'm staying with a friend who's got a court.

WILLY Don't say. His own tennis court. Must be fine people, I bet.

BERNARD They are, very nice. Dad tells me Biff's in town.

WILLY (*with a big smile*) Yeah, Biff's in. Working on a very big deal, Bernard.

BERNARD What's Biff doing?

WILLY Well, he's been doing very big things in the West. But he decided to establish himself here. Very big. We've having dinner. Did I hear your wife had a boy?

BERNARD That's right. Our second.

WILLY Two boys! What do you know!

BERNARD What kind of a deal has Biff got?

WILLY Well, Bill Oliver—very big sporting-goods man—he wants Biff very badly. Called him in from the West. Long distance, carte blanche, special deliveries. Your friends have their own private tennis court?

BERNARD You still with the old firm, Willy?

WILLY (*after a pause*) I'm—I'm overjoyed to see how you made the grade, Bernard, overjoyed. It's an encouraging thing to see a young man really—really— Looks very good for Biff—very— (*He breaks off, then*) Bernard—(*He is so full of emotion, he breaks off again*)

BERNARD What is it, Willy?

WILLY (*small and alone*) What—what's the secret?

BERNARD What secret?

WILLY How—how did you? Why didn't he ever catch on?

BERNARD I wouldn't know that, Willy.

WILLY (*confidentially, desperately*) You were his friend, his boyhood friend. There's something I don't understand about it. His life ended after that Ebbets Field game. From the age of seventeen nothing good ever happened to him.

BERNARD He never trained himself for anything.

WILLY But he did, he did. After high school he took so many correspondence courses. Radio mechanics; television; God knows what, and never made the slightest mark.

BERNARD (*taking off his glasses*) Willy, do you want to talk candidly?

WILLY (*rising, faces* BERNARD) I regard you as a very brilliant man, Bernard. I value your advice.

BERNARD Oh, the hell with the advice, Willy. I couldn't advise you. There's just one thing I've always wanted to ask you. When he was supposed to graduate, and the math teacher flunked him—

WILLY Oh, that son-of-a-bitch ruined his life.

BERNARD Yeah, but, Willy, all he had to do was go to summer school and make up that subject.

WILLY That's right, that's right.

BERNARD Did you tell him not to go to summer school?

WILLY Me? I begged him to go. I ordered him to go!

BERNARD Then why wouldn't he go?

WILLY Why? Why! Bernard, that question has been trailing me like a ghost for the last fifteen years. He flunked the subject, and laid down and died like a hammer hit him!

BERNARD Take it easy, kid.

WILLY Let me talk to you—I got nobody to talk to. Bernard, Bernard, was it my fault? Y'see? It keeps going around in my mind, maybe I did something to him. I got nothing to give him.

BERNARD Don't take it so hard.

WILLY Why did he lay down? What is the story there? You were his friend!

BERNARD Willy, I remember, it was June, and our grades came out. And he'd flunked math.

WILLY That son-of-a-bitch!

BERNARD No, it wasn't right then. Biff just got very angry, I remember, and he was ready to enroll in summer school.

WILLY (*surprised*) He was?

BERNARD He wasn't beaten by it at all. But then, Willy, he disappeared from the block for almost a month. And I got the idea that he'd gone up to New England to see you. Did he have a talk with you then?

WILLY *stares in silence.*

BERNARD Willy?

WILLY (*with a strong edge of resentment in his voice*) Yeah, he came to Boston. What about it?

BERNARD Well, just that when he came back—I'll never forget this, it always mystifies me. Because I'd thought so well of Biff, even though he'd always taken advantage of me. I loved him, Willy, y'know? And he came back after that month and took his sneakers—remember those sneakers with "University of Virginia" printed on them? He was so proud of those, wore them every day. And he took them down in the cellar, and burned them up in the furnace. We had a fist fight. It lasted at least half an hour. Just the two of us, punching each other down the cellar, and crying right through it. I've often thought of how strange it was that I knew he'd given up his life. What happened in Boston, Willy?

WILLY *looks at him as at an intruder.*

BERNARD I just bring it up because you asked me.

WILLY (*angrily*) Nothing. What do you mean, "What happened?" What's that got to do with anything?

BERNARD Well, don't get sore.

WILLY What are you trying to do, blame it on me? If a boy lays down is that my fault?

BERNARD Now, Willy, don't get—

WILLY Well, don't—don't talk to me that way! What does that mean, "What happened?"

CHARLEY *enters. He is in his vest, and he carries a bottle of bourbon.*

CHARLEY Hey, you're going to miss that train. (*He waves the bottle*)

BERNARD Yeah, I'm going. (*He takes the bottle*) Thanks, Pop. (*He picks up his rackets and bag*) Good-by, Willy, and don't worry about it. You know, "If at first you don't succeed . . ."

WILLY Yes, I believe in that.

BERNARD But sometimes, Willy, it's better for a man just to walk away.

WILLY Walk away?

BERNARD That's right.

WILLY But if you can't walk away?

BERNARD (*after a slight pause*) I guess that's when it's tough. (*Extending his hand*) Good-by, Willy.

WILLY (*shaking* BERNARD's *hand*) Good-by, boy.

CHARLEY (*an arm on* BERNARD's *shoulder*) How do you like this kid? Gonna argue a case in front of the Supreme Court.

BERNARD (*protesting*) Pop!

WILLY (*genuinely shocked, pained, and happy*) No! The Supreme Court!

BERNARD I gotta run. 'By, Dad!

CHARLEY Knock 'em dead, Bernard!

BERNARD *goes off.*

WILLY (*as* CHARLEY *takes out his wallet*) The Supreme Court! And he didn't even mention it!

CHARLEY (*counting out money on the desk*) He don't have to—he's gonna do it.

WILLY And you never told him what to do, did you? You never took any interest in him.

CHARLEY My salvation is that I never took any interest in anything. There's some money—fifty dollars. I got an accountant inside.

WILLY Charley, look . . . (*With difficulty*) I got my insurance to pay. If you can manage it—I need a hundred and ten dollars.

CHARLEY *doesn't reply for a moment; merely stops moving.*

WILLY I'd draw it from my bank but Linda would know, and I . . .

CHARLEY Sit down, Willy.

WILLY (*moving toward the chair*) I'm keeping an account of everything, remember. I'll pay every penny back. (*He sits*)

CHARLEY Now listen to me, Willy.

WILLY I want you to know I appreciate . . .

CHARLEY (*sitting down on the table*) Willy, what're you doin'? What the hell is goin' on in your head?

WILLY Why? I'm simply . . .

CHARLEY I offered you a job. You can make fifty dollars a week. And I won't send you on the road.

WILLY I've got a job.

CHARLEY Without pay? What kind of a job is a job without pay? (*He rises*) Now, look, kid, enough is enough. I'm no genius but I know when I'm being insulted.

WILLY Insulted!

CHARLEY Why don't you want to work for me?

WILLY What's the matter with you? I've got a job.

CHARLEY Then what're you walkin' in here every week for?

WILLY (*getting up*) Well, if you don't want me to walk in here—

CHARLEY I am offering you a job.

WILLY I don't want your goddam job!

CHARLEY When the hell are you going to grow up?

WILLY (*furiously*) You big ignoramus, if you say that to me again I'll rap you one! I don't care how big you are! (*He's ready to fight*)

*Pause.*

CHARLEY (*kindly, going to him*) How much do you need, Willy?

WILLY Charley, I'm strapped. I'm strapped. I don't know what to do. I was just fired.

CHARLEY Howard fired you?

WILLY That snotnose. Imagine that? I named him. I named him Howard.

CHARLEY Willy, when're you gonna realize that them things don't mean anything? You named him Howard, but you can't sell that. The only thing you got in this world is what you can sell. And the funny thing is that you're a salesman, and you don't know that.

WILLY I've always tried to think otherwise, I guess. I always felt that if a man was impressive, and well liked, that nothing—

CHARLEY Why must everybody like you? Who liked J. P. Morgan?

Was he impressive? In a Turkish bath he'd look like a butcher. But with his pockets on he was very well liked. Now listen, Willy, I know you don't like me, and nobody can say I'm in love with you, but I'll give you a job because—just for the hell of it, put it that way. Now what do you say?

WILLY I—I just can't work for you, Charley.

CHARLEY What're you, jealous of me?

WILLY I can't work for you, that's all, don't ask me why.

CHARLEY (*angered, takes out more bills*) You been jealous of me all your life, you damned fool! Here, pay your insurance. (*He puts the money in* WILLY's *hand*)

WILLY I'm keeping strict accounts.

CHARLEY I've got some work to do. Take care of yourself. And pay your insurance.

WILLY (*moving to the right*) Funny, y'know? After all the highways, and the trains, and the appointments, and the years, you end up worth more dead than alive.

CHARLEY Willy, nobody's worth nothin' dead. (*After a slight pause*) Did you hear what I said?

WILLY *stands still, dreaming.*

CHARLEY Willy!

WILLY Apologize to Bernard for me when you see him. I didn't mean to argue with him. He's a fine boy. They're all fine boys, and they'll end up big—all of them. Someday they'll all play tennis together. Wish me luck, Charley. He saw Bill Oliver today.

CHARLEY Good luck.

WILLY (*on the verge of tears*) Charley, you're the only friend I got. Isn't that a remarkable thing? (*He goes out*)

CHARLEY Jesus!

CHARLEY *stares after him a moment and follows. All light blacks out. Suddenly raucous music is heard, and a red glow rises behind the screen at right.* STANLEY, *a young waiter, appears, carrying a table, followed by* HAPPY, *who is carrying two chairs.*

STANLEY (*putting the table down*) That's all right, Mr. Loman, I can handle it myself. (*He turns and takes the chairs from* HAPPY *and places them at the table*)

HAPPY (*glancing around*) Oh, this is better.

STANLEY Sure, in the front there you're in the middle of all kinds a noise. Whenever you got a party, Mr. Loman, you just tell me and I'll put you back here. Y'know, there's a lotta people they don't like it private, because when they go out they like to see a lotta action around them because they're sick and tired to stay in the house by theirself. But I know you, you ain't from Hackensack. You know what I mean?

HAPPY (*sitting down*) So how's it coming, Stanley?

STANLEY Ah, it's a dog's life. I only wish during the war they'd a took me in the Army. I coulda been dead by now.

HAPPY My brother's back, Stanley.

STANLEY Oh, he come back, heh? From the Far West.

HAPPY Yeah, big cattle man, my brother, so treat him right. And my father's coming too.

STANLEY Oh, your father too!

HAPPY You got a couple of nice lobsters?

STANLEY Hundred per cent, big.

HAPPY I want them with the claws.

STANLEY Don't worry, I don't give you no mice. (HAPPY *laughs*) How about some wine? It'll put a head on the meal.

HAPPY No. You remember, Stanley, that recipe I brought you from overseas? With the champagne in it?

STANLEY Oh, yeah, sure. I still got it tacked up yet in the kitchen. But that'll have to cost a buck apiece anyways.

HAPPY That's all right.

STANLEY What'd you, hit a number or somethin'?

HAPPY No, it's a little celebration. My brother is—I think he pulled off a big deal today. I think we're going into business together.

STANLEY Great! That's the best for you. Because a family business, you know what I mean?—that's the best.

HAPPY That's what I think.

STANLEY 'Cause what's the difference? Somebody steals? It's in the family. Know what I mean? (*Sotto voce*) Like this bartender here. The boss is goin' crazy what kinda leak he's got in the cash register. You put it in but it don't come out.

HAPPY (*raising his head*) Sh!

STANLEY What?

HAPPY You notice I wasn't lookin' right or left, was I?

STANLEY No.

HAPPY And my eyes are closed.

STANLEY So what's the—?

HAPPY Strudel's comin'.

STANLEY (*catching on, looks around*) Ah, no, there's no—

*He breaks off as a furred, lavishly dressed girl enters and sits at the next table. Both follow her with their eyes.*

STANLEY Geez, how'd ya know?

HAPPY I got radar or something. (*Staring directly at her profile*) Oooooooo . . . Stanley.

STANLEY I think that's for you, Mr. Loman.

HAPPY Look at that mouth. Oh, God. And the binoculars.

STANLEY Geez, you got a life, Mr. Loman.

HAPPY Wait on her.

STANLEY (*going to the* GIRL'S *table*) Would you like a menu, ma'am?

GIRL I'm expecting someone, but I'd like a—

HAPPY Why don't you bring her—excuse me, miss, do you mind? I sell champagne, and I'd like you to try my brand. Bring her a champagne, Stanley.

GIRL That's awfully nice of you.

HAPPY Don't mention it. It's all company money. (*He laughs*)

GIRL That's a charming product to be selling, isn't it?

HAPPY Oh, gets to be like everything else. Selling is selling, y'know.

GIRL I suppose.

HAPPY You don't happen to sell, do you?

GIRL No, I don't sell.

HAPPY Would you object to a compliment from a stranger? You ought to be on a magazine cover.

GIRL (*looking at him a little archly*) I have been.

STANLEY *comes in with a glass of champagne.*

HAPPY What'd I say before, Stanley? You see? She's a cover girl.

STANLEY Oh, I could see, I could see.

HAPPY (*to the* GIRL) What magazine?

GIRL Oh, a lot of them. (*She takes the drink*) Thank you.

HAPPY You know what they say in France, don't you? "Champagne is the drink of the complexion"—Hya, Biff!

BIFF *has entered and sits with* HAPPY.

BIFF Hello, kid. Sorry I'm late.

HAPPY I just got here. Uh, Miss—?

GIRL Forsythe.

HAPPY Miss Forsythe, this is my brother.

BIFF Is Dad here?

HAPPY His name is Biff. You might've heard of him. Great football player.

GIRL Really? What team?

HAPPY Are you familiar with football?

GIRL No, I'm afraid I'm not.

HAPPY Biff is quarterback with the New York Giants.

GIRL Well, that is nice, isn't it? (*She drinks*)

HAPPY Good health.

GIRL I'm happy to meet you.

HAPPY That's my name. Hap. It's really Harold, but at West Point they called me Happy.

GIRL (*now really impressed*) Oh, I see. How do you do? (*She turns her profile*)

BIFF Isn't Dad coming?

HAPPY You want her?

BIFF Oh, I could never make that.

HAPPY I remember the time that idea would never come into your head. Where's the old confidence, Biff?

BIFF I just saw Oliver—

HAPPY Wait a minute. I've got to see that old confidence again. Do you want her? She's on call.

BIFF Oh, no. (*He turns to look at the* GIRL)

HAPPY I'm telling you. Watch this. (*Turning to the* GIRL) Honey? (*She turns to him*) Are you busy?

GIRL Well, I am . . . but I could make a phone call.

HAPPY Do that, will you, honey? And see if you can get a friend. We'll be here for a while. Biff is one of the greatest football players in the country.

GIRL (*standing up*) Well, I'm certainly happy to meet you.

HAPPY Come back soon.

GIRL I'll try.

HAPPY Don't try, honey, try hard.

*The* GIRL *exits.* STANLEY *follows, shaking his head in bewildered admiration.*

HAPPY Isn't that a shame now? A beautiful girl like that? That's why I can't get married. There's not a good woman in a thousand. New York is loaded with them, kid!

BIFF Hap, look—

HAPPY I told you she was on call!

BIFF (*strangely unnerved*) Cut it out, will ya? I want to say something to you.

HAPPY Did you see Oliver?

BIFF I saw him all right. Now look, I want to tell Dad a couple of things and I want you to help me.

HAPPY What? Is he going to back you?

BIFF Are you crazy? You're out of your goddam head, you know that?

HAPPY Why? What happened?

BIFF (*breathlessly*) I did a terrible thing today, Hap. It's been the strangest day I ever went through. I'm all numb, I swear.

HAPPY You mean he wouldn't see you?

BIFF Well, I waited six hours for him, see? All day. Kept sending my name in. Even tried to date his secretary so she'd get me to him, but no soap.

HAPPY Because you're not showin' the old confidence, Biff. He remembered you, didn't he?

BIFF (*stopping* HAPPY *with a gesture*) Finally, about five o'clock, he comes out. Didn't remember who I was or anything. I felt like such an idiot, Hap.

HAPPY Did you tell him my Florida idea?

BIFF He walked away. I saw him for one minute. I got so mad I could've torn the walls down! How the hell did I ever get the idea I was a salesman there? I even believed myself that I'd been a salesman for him! And then he gave me one look and—I realized what a ridiculous lie my whole life has been! We've been talking in a dream of fifteen years. I was a shipping clerk.

HAPPY What'd you do?

BIFF (*with great tension and wonder*) Well, he left, see. And the secretary went out. I was all alone in the waiting-room. I don't know what came over me, Hap. The next thing I know I'm in his office—paneled walls, everything. I can't explain it. I—Hap, I took his fountain pen.

HAPPY Geez, did he catch you?

BIFF I ran out. I ran down all eleven flights. I ran and ran and ran.

HAPPY That was an awful dumb—what'd you do that for?

BIFF (*agonized*) I don't know, I just—wanted to take something, I don't know. You gotta help me, Hap. I'm gonna tell Pop.

HAPPY You crazy? What for?

BIFF Hap, he's got to understand that I'm not the man somebody lends that kind of money to. He thinks I've been spiting him all these years and it's eating him up.

HAPPY That's just it. You tell him something nice.

BIFF I can't.

HAPPY Say you got a lunch date with Oliver tomorrow.

BIFF So what do I do tomorrow?

HAPPY You leave the house tomorrow and come back at night and say Oliver is thinking it over. And he thinks it over for a couple of weeks, and gradually it fades away and nobody's the worse.

BIFF But it'll go on forever!

HAPPY Dad is never so happy as when he's looking forward to something!

WILLY *enters.*

HAPPY Hello, scout!

WILLY Gee, I haven't been here in years!

STANLEY *has followed* WILLY *in and sets a chair for him.* STANLEY *starts off but* HAPPY *stops him.*

HAPPY Stanley!

STANLEY *stands by, waiting for an order.*

BIFF (*going to* WILLY *with guilt, as to an invalid*) Sit down, Pop. You want a drink?

WILLY Sure, I don't mind.

BIFF Let's get a load on.

WILLY You look worried.

BIFF N-no. (*To* STANLEY) Scotch all around. Make it doubles.

STANLEY Doubles, right. (*He goes*)

WILLY You had a couple already, didn't you?

BIFF Just a couple, yeah.

WILLY Well, what happened, boy? (*Nodding affirmatively, with a smile*) Everything go all right?

BIFF (*takes a breath, then reaches out and grasps* WILLY'S *hand*) Pal . . . (*He is smiling bravely, and* WILLY *is smiling too*) I had an experience today.

HAPPY Terrific, Pop.

WILLY That so? What happened?

BIFF (*high, slightly alcoholic, above the earth*) I'm going to tell you everything from first to last. It's been a strange day. (*Silence. He looks around, composes himself as best he can, but his breath keeps breaking the rhythm of his voice*) I had to wait quite a while for him, and—

WILLY Oliver?

BIFF Yeah, Oliver. All day, as a matter of cold fact. And a lot of —instances—facts, Pop, facts about my life came back to me. Who was it, Pop? Who ever said I was a salesman with Oliver?

WILLY Well, you were.

BIFF No, Dad, I was a shipping clerk.

WILLY But you were practically—

BIFF (*with determination*) Dad, I don't know who said it first, but I was never a salesman for Bill Oliver.

WILLY What're you talking about?

BIFF Let's hold on to the facts tonight, Pop. We're not going to get anywhere bullin' around. I was a shipping clerk.

WILLY (*angrily*) All right, now listen to me—

BIFF Why don't you let me finish?

WILLY I'm not interested in stories about the past or any crap of that kind because the woods are burning, boys, you understand? There's a big blaze going on all around. I was fired today.

BIFF (*shocked*) How could you be?

WILLY I was fired, and I'm looking for a little good news to tell your mother, because the woman has waited and the woman has suffered. The gift of it is that I haven't got a story left in my head, Biff. So don't give me a lecture about facts and aspects. I am not interested. Now what've you got to say to me?

STANLEY *enters with three drinks. They wait until he leaves.*

WILLY Did you see Oliver?

BIFF Jesus, Dad!

WILLY You mean you didn't go up there?

HAPPY Sure he went up there.

BIFF I did. I—saw him. How could they fire you?

WILLY (*on the edge of his chair*) What kind of a welcome did he give you?

BIFF He won't even let you work on commission?

WILLY I'm out! (*driving*) So tell me, he gave you a warm welcome?

HAPPY Sure, Pop, sure!

BIFF (*driven*) Well, it was kind of—

WILLY I was wondering if he'd remember you. (*To* HAPPY) Imagine, man doesn't see him for ten, twelve years and gives him that kind of a welcome!

HAPPY Damn right!

BIFF (*trying to return to the offensive*) Pop, look—

WILLY You know why he remembered you, don't you? Because you impressed him in those days.

BIFF Let's talk quietly and get this down to the facts, huh?

WILLY (*as though* BIFF *had been interrupting*) Well, what happened? It's great news, Biff. Did he take you into his office or'd you talk in the waiting-room?

BIFF Well, he came in, see, and—

WILLY (*with a big smile*) What'd he say? Betcha he threw his arm around you.

BIFF Well, he kinda—

WILLY He's a fine man. (*To* HAPPY) Very hard man to see, y'know.

HAPPY (*agreeing*) Oh, I know.

WILLY (*to* BIFF) Is that where you had the drinks?

BIFF Yeah, he gave me a couple of—no, no!

HAPPY (*cutting in*) He told him my Florida idea.

WILLY Don't interrupt. (*To* BIFF) How'd he react to the Florida idea?

BIFF Dad, will you give me a minute to explain?

WILLY I've been waiting for you to explain since I sat down here! What happened? He took you into his office and what?

BIFF Well—I talked. And—and he listened, see.

WILLY Famous for the way he listens, y'know. What was his answer?

BIFF His answer was—(*He breaks off, suddenly angry*) Dad, you're not letting me tell you what I want to tell you!

WILLY (*accusing, angered*) You didn't see him, did you?

BIFF I did see him!

WILLY What'd you insult him or something? You insulted him, didn't you?

BIFF Listen, will you let me out of it, will you just let me out of it!

HAPPY What the hell!

WILLY Tell me what happened!

BIFF (*to* HAPPY) I can't talk to him!

*A single trumpet note jars the ear. The light of green leaves stains the house, which holds the air of night and a dream. Young* BERNARD *enters and knocks on the door of the house.*

YOUNG BERNARD (*frantically*) Mrs. Loman, Mrs. Loman!

HAPPY Tell him what happened!

BIFF (*to* HAPPY) Shut up and leave me alone!

WILLY No, no! You had to go and flunk math!

BIFF What math? What're you talking about?

YOUNG BERNARD Mrs. Loman, Mrs. Loman!

LINDA *appears in the house, as of old.*

WILLY (*wildly*) Math, math, math!

BIFF Take it easy, Pop!

YOUNG BERNARD Mrs. Loman!

WILLY (*furiously*) If you hadn't flunked you'd've been set by now!

BIFF Now, look, I'm gonna tell you what happened, and you're going to listen to me.

YOUNG BERNARD Mrs. Loman!

BIFF I waited six hours—

HAPPY What the hell are you saying?

BIFF I kept sending in my name but he wouldn't see me. So finally he . . . (*He continues unheard as light fades low on the restaurant*)

YOUNG BERNARD Biff flunked math!

LINDA No!

YOUNG BERNARD Birnbaum flunked him! They won't graduate him!

LINDA But they have to. He's gotta go to the university. Where is he? Biff! Biff!

YOUNG BERNARD No, he left. He went to Grand Central.

LINDA Grand— You mean he went to Boston!

YOUNG BERNARD Is Uncle Willy in Boston?

LINDA Oh, maybe Willy can talk to the teacher. Oh, the poor, poor boy!

*Light on house area snaps out.*

BIFF (*at the table, now audible, holding up a gold fountain pen*) . . . so I'm washed up with Oliver, you understand? Are you listening to me?

WILLY (*at a loss*) Yeah, sure. If you hadn't flunked—

BIFF Flunked what? What're you talking about?

WILLY Don't blame everything on me! I didn't flunk math—you did! What pen?

HAPPY That was awful dumb, Biff, a pen like that is worth—

WILLY (*seeing the pen for the first time*) You took Oliver's pen?

BIFF (*weakening*) Dad, I just explained it to you.

WILLY You stole Bill Oliver's fountain pen!

BIFF I didn't exactly steal it! That's just what I've been explaining to you!

HAPPY He had it in his hand and just then Oliver walked in, so he got nervous and stuck it in his pocket!

WILLY My God, Biff!

BIFF I never intended to do it, Dad!

OPERATOR'S VOICE Standish Arms, good evening!

WILLY (*shouting*) I'm not in my room!

BIFF (*frightened*) Dad, what's the matter? (*He and* HAPPY *stand up*)

OPERATOR Ringing Mr. Loman for you!

WILLY I'm not there, stop it!

BIFF (*horrified, gets down on one knee before* WILLY) Dad, I'll make good, I'll make good. (WILLY *tries to get to his feet.* BIFF *holds him down*) Sit down now.

WILLY No, you're no good, you're no good for anything.

BIFF I am, Dad, I'll find something else, you understand? Now don't worry about anything. (*He holds up* WILLY's *face*) Talk to me, Dad.

OPERATOR Mr. Loman does not answer. Shall I page him?

WILLY (*attempting to stand, as though to rush and silence the Operator*) No, no, no!

HAPPY He'll strike something, Pop.

WILLY No, no . . .

BIFF (*desperately, standing over* WILLY) Pop, listen! Listen to me! I'm telling you something good. Oliver talked to his partner about the Florida idea. You listening? He—he talked to his partner, and he came to me . . . I'm going to be all right, you hear? Dad, listen to me, he said it was just a question of the amount!

WILLY Then you . . . got it?

HAPPY He's gonna be terrific, Pop!

WILLY (*trying to stand*) Then you got it, haven't you? You got it! You got it!

BIFF (*agonized, holds* WILLY *down*) No, no. Look, Pop. I'm supposed to have lunch with them tomorrow. I'm just telling you this so you'll know that I can still make an impression, Pop. And I'll make good somewhere, but I can't go tomorrow, see?

WILLY Why not? You simply—

BIFF But the pen, Pop!

WILLY You give it to him and tell him it was an oversight!

HAPPY Sure, have lunch tomorrow!

BIFF I can't say that—

WILLY You were doing a crossword puzzle and accidentally used his pen!

BIFF Listen, kid, I took those balls years ago, now I walk in with his fountain pen? That clinches it, don't you see? I can't face him like that! I'll try elsewhere.

PAGE'S VOICE Paging Mr. Loman!

WILLY Don't you want to be anything?

BIFF Pop, how can I go back?

WILLY You don't want to be anything, is that what's behind it?

BIFF (*now angry at* WILLY *for not crediting his sympathy*) Don't take it that way! You think it was easy walking into that office after what I'd done to him? A team of horses couldn't have dragged me back to Bill Oliver!

WILLY Then why'd you go?

BIFF Why did I go? Why did I go! Look at you! Look at what's become of you!

*Off left,* THE WOMAN *laughs.*

WILLY Biff, you're going to go to that lunch tomorrow, or—
BIFF I can't go. I've got no appointment!
HAPPY Biff, for . . .!
WILLY Are you spiting me?
BIFF Don't take it that way! Goddammit!
WILLY (*strikes* BIFF *and falters away from the table*) You rotten little louse! Are you spiting me?
THE WOMAN Someone's at the door, Willy!
BIFF I'm no good, can't you see what I am?
HAPPY (*separating them*) Hey, you're in a restaurant! Now cut it out, both of you! (*The girls enter*) Hello, girls, sit down.

THE WOMAN *laughs, off left.*

MISS FORSYTHE I guess we might as well. This is Letta.
THE WOMAN Willy, are you going to wake up?
BIFF (*ignoring* WILLY) How're ya, miss, sit down. What do you drink?
MISS FORSYTHE Letta might not be able to stay long.
LETTA I gotta get up very early tomorrow. I got jury duty. I'm so excited! Were you fellows ever on a jury?
BIFF No, but I been in front of them! (*The girls laugh*) This is my father.
LETTA Isn't he cute? Sit down with us, Pop.
HAPPY Sit him down, Biff!
BIFF (*going to him*) Come on, slugger, drink us under the table. To hell with it! Come on, sit down, pal.

*On* BIFF'*s last insistence,* WILLY *is about to sit.*

THE WOMAN (*now urgently*) Willy, are you going to answer the door!

THE WOMAN'*s call pulls* WILLY *back. He starts right, befuddled.*

BIFF Hey, where are you going?
WILLY Open the door.
BIFF The door?
WILLY The washroom . . . the door . . . where's the door?
BIFF (*leading* WILLY to the left) Just go straight down.

WILLY *moves left.*

THE WOMAN Willy, Willy, are you going to get up, get up, get up, get up?

WILLY *exits left.*

LETTA I think it's sweet you bring your daddy along.

MISS FORSYTHE Oh, he isn't really your father!

BIFF (*at left, turning to her resentfully*) Miss Forsythe, you've just seen a prince walk by. A fine, troubled prince. A hard-working, unappreciated prince. A pal, you understand? A good companion. Always for his boys.

LETTA That's so sweet.

HAPPY Well, girls, what's the program? We're wasting time. Come on, Biff. Gather round. Where would you like to go?

BIFF Why don't you do something for him?

HAPPY Me!

BIFF Don't you give a damn for him, Hap?

HAPPY What're you talking about? I'm the one who—

BIFF I sense it, you don't give a good goddam about him. (*He takes the rolled-up hose from his pocket and puts it on the table in front of* HAPPY) Look what I found in the cellar, for Christ's sake. How can you bear to let it go on?

HAPPY Me? Who goes away? Who runs off and—

BIFF Yeah, but he doesn't mean anything to you. You could help him—I can't! Don't you understand what I'm talking about? He's going to kill himself, don't you know that?

HAPPY Don't I know it! Me!

BIFF Hap, help him! Jesus . . . help him . . . Help me, help me, I can't bear to look at his face! (*Ready to weep, he hurries out, up right*)

HAPPY (*starting after him*) Where are you going?

MISS FORSYTHE What's he so mad about?

HAPPY Come on, girls, we'll catch up with him.

MISS FORSYTHE (*as* HAPPY *pushes her out*) Say, I don't like that temper of his!

HAPPY He's just a little overstrung, he'll be all right!

WILLY (*off left, as* THE WOMAN *laughs*) Don't answer! Don't answer!

LETTA Don't you want to tell your father—

HAPPY No, that's not my father. He's just a guy. Come on, we'll catch Biff, and, honey, we're going to paint this town! Stanley, where's the check! Hey, Stanley!

*They exit.* STANLEY *looks toward left.*

STANLEY (*calling to* HAPPY *indignantly*) Mr. Loman! Mr. Loman!

STANLEY *picks up a chair and follows them off. Knocking is heard off left.*

THE WOMAN *enters, laughing.* WILLY *follows her. She is in a black slip; he is buttoning his shirt. Raw, sensuous music accompanies their speech.*

WILLY Will you stop laughing? Will you stop?

THE WOMAN Aren't you going to answer the door? He'll wake the whole hotel.

WILLY I'm not expecting anybody.

THE WOMAN Whyn't you have another drink, honey, and stop being so damn self-centered?

WILLY I'm so lonely.

THE WOMAN You know you ruined me, Willy? From now on, whenever you come to the office, I'll see that you go right through to the buyers. No waiting at my desk any more, Willy. You ruined me.

WILLY That's nice of you to say that.

THE WOMAN Gee, you are self-centered! Why so sad? You are the saddest, self-centeredest soul I ever did see-saw. (*She laughs. He kisses her*) Come on inside, drummer boy. It's silly to be dressing in the middle of the night. (*As knocking is heard*) Aren't you going to answer the door?

WILLY They're knocking on the wrong door.

THE WOMAN But I felt the knocking. And he heard us talking in here. Maybe the hotel's on fire!

WILLY (*his terror rising*) It's a mistake.

THE WOMAN Then tell him to go away!

WILLY There's nobody there.

THE WOMAN It's getting on my nerves, Willy. There's somebody standing out there and it's getting on my nerves!

WILLY (*pushing her away from him*) All right, stay in the bathroom here, and don't come out. I think there's a law in Massachusetts about it, so don't come out. It may be that new room clerk. He looked very mean. So don't come out. It's a mistake, there's no fire.

*The knocking is heard again. He takes a few steps away from her, and she vanishes into the wing. The light follows him, and now he is facing* YOUNG BIFF, *who carries a suitcase.* BIFF *steps toward him. The music is gone.*

BIFF Why didn't you answer?

WILLY Biff! What are you doing in Boston?

BIFF Why didn't you answer? I've been knocking for five minutes, I called you on the phone—

WILLY I just heard you. I was in the bathroom and had the door shut. Did anything happen home?

BIFF Dad—I let you down.

WILLY What do you mean?

BIFF Dad...

WILLY Biffo, what's this about? (*Putting his arm around* BIFF) Come on, let's go downstairs and get you a malted.

BIFF Dad, I flunked math.

WILLY Not for the term?

BIFF The term. I haven't got enough credits to graduate.

WILLY You mean to say Bernard wouldn't give you the answers?

BIFF He did, he tried, but I only got a sixty-one.

WILLY And they wouldn't give you four points?

BIFF Birnbaum refused absolutely. I begged him, Pop, but he won't give me those points. You gotta talk to him before they close the school. Because if he saw the kind of man you are, and you just talked to him in your way, I'm sure he'd come through for me. The class came right before practice, see, and I didn't go enough. Would you talk to him? He'd like you, Pop. You know the way you could talk.

WILLY You're on. We'll drive right back.

BIFF Oh, Dad, good work! I'm sure he'll change it for you!

WILLY Go downstairs and tell the clerk I'm checkin' out. Go right down.

BIFF Yes, sir! See, the reason he hates me, Pop—one day he was late for class so I got up at the blackboard and imitated him. I crossed my eyes and talked with a lithp.

WILLY (*laughing*) You did? The kids like it?

BIFF They nearly died laughing!

WILLY Yeah? What'd you do?

BIFF The thquare root of thixthy twee is... (WILLY *bursts out laughing;* BIFF *joins him*) And in the middle of it he walked in!

WILLY *laughs and* THE WOMAN *joins in offstage.*

WILLY (*without hesitation*) Hurry downstairs and—

BIFF Somebody in there?

WILLY No, that was next door.

THE WOMAN *laughs offstage.*

BIFF Somebody got in your bathroom!

WILLY No, it's the next room, there's a party—

THE WOMAN (*enters, laughing. She lisps this*) Can I come in? There's something in the bathtub, Willy, and it's moving!

WILLY *looks at* BIFF, *who is staring open-mouthed and horrified at* THE WOMAN.

WILLY Ah—you better go back to your room. They must be finished painting by now. They're painting her room so I let her take a shower here. Go back, go back . . . (*He pushes her*)

THE WOMAN (*resisting*) But I've got to get dressed, Willy, I can't—

WILLY Get out of here! Go back, go back . . . (*Suddenly striving for the ordinary*) This is Miss Francis, Biff, she's a buyer. They're painting her room. Go back, Miss Francis, go back . . .

THE WOMAN But my clothes, I can't go out naked in the hall!

WILLY (*pushing her offstage*) Get outa here! Go back, go back!

BIFF *slowly sits down on his suitcase as the argument continues offstage.*

THE WOMAN Where's my stockings? You promised me stockings, Willy!

WILLY I have no stockings here!

THE WOMAN You had two boxes of size nine sheers for me, and I want them!

WILLY Here, for God's sake, will you get outa here!

THE WOMAN (*enters holding a box of stockings*) I just hope there's nobody in the hall. That's all I hope. (*To* BIFF) Are you football or baseball?

BIFF Football.

THE WOMAN (*angry, humiliated*) That's me too. G'night. (*She snatches her clothes from* WILLY, *and walks out*)

WILLY (*after a pause*) Well, better get going. I want to get to the school first thing in the morning. Get my suits out of the closet. I'll get my valise. (BIFF *doesn't move*) What's the matter? (BIFF *remains motionless, tears falling*) She's a buyer. Buys for J. H. Simmons. She lives down the hall—they're painting. You don't imagine—(*He breaks off. After a pause*) Now listen, pal, she's just a buyer. She sees merchandise in her room and they have to keep it looking just so . . . (*Pause. Assuming command*) All right, get my suits. (BIFF *doesn't move*) Now stop crying and do as I say. I gave you an order. Biff, I gave you an order! Is that what you do when I give you an order? How dare you cry! (*Putting his arm around* BIFF) Now look, Biff, when you grow up you'll understand about these things. You mustn't—you mustn't overemphasize a thing like this. I'll see Birnbaum first thing in the morning.

BIFF Never mind.

WILLY (*getting down beside* BIFF) Never mind! He's going to give you those points. I'll see to it.

BIFF He wouldn't listen to you.

WILLY He certainly will listen to me. You need those points for the U. of Virginia.

BIFF I'm not going there.

WILLY Heh? If I can't get him to change that mark you'll make it up in summer school. You've got all summer to—

BIFF (*his weeping breaking from him*) Dad . . .

WILLY (*infected by it*) Oh, my boy . . .

BIFF Dad . . .

WILLY She's nothing to me, Biff. I was lonely, I was terribly lonely.

BIFF You—you gave her Mama's stockings! (*His tears break through and he rises to go*)

WILLY (*grabbing for* BIFF) I gave you an order!

BIFF Don't touch me, you—liar!

WILLY Apologize for that!

BIFF You fake! You phony little fake! You fake! (*Overcome, he turns quickly and weeping fully goes out with his suitcase.* WILLY *is left on the floor on his knees*)

WILLY I gave you an order! Biff, come back here or I'll beat you! Come back here! I'll whip you!

STANLEY *comes quickly in from the right and stands in front of* WILLY.

WILLY (*shouts at* STANLEY) I gave you an order . . .

STANLEY Hey, let's pick it up, pick it up, Mr. Loman. (*He helps* WILLY *to his feet*) Your boys left with the chippies. They said they'll see you home.

*A second* WAITER *watches some distance away.*

WILLY But we were supposed to have dinner together.

*Music is heard,* WILLY'S *theme.*

STANLEY Can you make it?

WILLY I'll—sure, I can make it. (*Suddenly concerned about his clothes*) Do I—I look all right?

STANLEY Sure, you look all right. (*He flicks a speck off* WILLY'S *lapel*)

WILLY Here—here's a dollar.

STANLEY Oh, your son paid me. It's all right.

WILLY (*putting it in* STANLEY'S *hand*) No, take it. You're a good boy.

STANLEY Oh, no, you don't have to . . .

WILLY Here—here's some more, I don't need it any more. (*After a slight pause*) Tell me—is there a seed store in the neighborhood?

STANLEY Seeds? You mean like to plant?

*As* WILLY *turns,* STANLEY *slips the money back into his jacket pocket.*

WILLY Yes. Carrots, peas . . .
STANLEY Well, there's hardware stores on Sixth Avenue, but it may be too late now.
WILLY (*anxiously*) Oh, I'd better hurry. I've got to get some seeds. (*He starts off to the right*) I've got to get some seeds, right away. Nothing's planted. I don't have a thing in the ground.

WILLY *hurries out as the light goes down.* STANLEY *moves over to the right after him, watches him off. The other* WAITER *has been staring at* WILLY.

STANLEY (*to the* WAITER) Well, whatta you looking at?

*The* WAITER *picks up the chairs and moves off right.* STANLEY *takes the table and follows him. The light fades on this area. There is a long pause, the sound of the flute coming over. The light gradually rises on the kitchen, which is empty.* HAPPY *appears at the door of the house, followed by* BIFF. HAPPY *is carrying a large bunch of long-stemmed roses. He enters the kitchen, looks around for* LINDA. *Not seeing her, he turns to* BIFF, *who is just outside the house door, and makes a gesture with his hands, indicating "Not here, I guess." He looks into the living-room and freezes. Inside,* LINDA, *unseen, is seated,* WILLY'S *coat on her lap. She rises ominously and quietly and moves toward* HAPPY, *who backs up into the kitchen, afraid.*

HAPPY Hey, what're you doing up? (LINDA *says nothing but moves toward him implacably*) Where's Pop? (*He keeps backing to the right, and now* LINDA *is in full view in the doorway to the living-room*) Is he sleeping?
LINDA Where were you?
HAPPY (*trying to laugh it off*) We met two girls, Mom, very fine types. Here, we brought you some flowers. (*Offering them to her*) Put them in your room, Ma.

*She knocks them to the floor at* BIFF'S *feet. He has now come inside and closed the door behind him. She stares at* BIFF, *silent.*

HAPPY Now what'd you do that for? Mom, I want you to have some flowers—
LINDA (*cutting* HAPPY *off, violently to* BIFF) Don't you care whether he lives or dies?
HAPPY (*going to the stairs*) Come upstairs, Biff.
BIFF (*with a flare of disgust, to* HAPPY) Go away from me! (*To* LINDA) What do you mean, lives or dies? Nobody's dying around here, pal.

LINDA Get out of my sight! Get out of here!

BIFF I wanna see the boss.

LINDA You're not going near him!

BIFF Where is he? (*He moves into the living-room and* LINDA *follows*)

LINDA (*shouting after* BIFF) You invite him for dinner. He looks forward to it all day—(BIFF *appears in his parents' bedroom, looks around, and exits*)—and then you desert him there. There's no stranger you'd do that to!

HAPPY Why? He had a swell time with us. Listen, when I—(LINDA *comes back into the kitchen*)—desert him I hope I don't outlive the day!

LINDA Get out of here!

HAPPY Now look, Mom . . .

LINDA Did you have to go to women tonight? You and your lousy rotten whores!

BIFF *re-enters the kitchen.*

HAPPY Mom, all we did was follow Biff around trying to cheer him up! (*To* BIFF) Boy, what a night you gave me!

LINDA Get out of here, both of you, and don't come back! I don't want you tormenting him any more. Go on now, get your things together! (*To* BIFF) You can sleep in his apartment. (*She starts to pick up the flowers and stops herself*) Pick up this stuff, I'm not your maid any more. Pick it up, you bum, you!

HAPPY *turns his back to her in refusal.* BIFF *slowly moves over and gets down on his knees, picking up the flowers.*

LINDA You're a pair of animals! Not one, not another living soul would have had the cruelty to walk out on that man in a restaurant!

BIFF (*not looking at her*) Is that what he said?

LINDA He didn't have to say anything. He was so humiliated he nearly limped when he came in.

HAPPY But, Mom, he had a great time with us—

BIFF (*cutting him off violently*) Shut up!

*Without another word,* HAPPY *goes upstairs.*

LINDA You! You didn't even go in to see if he was all right!

BIFF (*still on the floor in front of* LINDA, *the flowers in his hand; with self-loathing*) No. Didn't. Didn't do a damned thing. How do you like that, heh? Left him babbling in a toilet.

LINDA You louse. You . . .

BIFF Now you hit it on the nose! (*He gets up, throws the flowers in the wastebasket*) The scum of the earth, and you're looking at him!

LINDA Get out of here!

BIFF I gotta talk to the boss, Mom. Where is he?

LINDA You're not going near him. Get out of this house!

BIFF (*with absolute assurance, determination*) No. We're gonna have an abrupt conversation, him and me.

LINDA You're not talking to him!

*Hammering is heard from outside the house, off right.* BIFF *turns toward the noise.*

LINDA (*suddenly pleading*) Will you please leave him alone?

BIFF What's he doing out there?

LINDA He's planting the garden!

BIFF (*quietly*) Now? Oh, my God!

BIFF *moves outside,* LINDA *following. The light dies down on them and comes up on the center of the apron as* WILLY *walks into it. He is carrying a flashlight, a hoe, and a handful of seed packets. He raps the top of the hoe sharply to fix it firmly, and then moves to the left, measuring off the distance with his foot. He holds the flashlight to look at the seed packets, reading off the instructions. He is in the blue of night.*

WILLY Carrots . . . quarter-inch apart. Rows . . . one-foot rows. (*He measures it off*) One foot. (*He puts down a package and measures off*) Beets. (*He puts down another package and measures again*) Lettuce. (*He reads the package, puts it down*) One foot— (*He breaks off as* BEN *appears at the right and moves slowly down to him*) What a proposition, ts, ts. Terrific, terrific. 'Cause she's suffered, Ben, the woman has suffered. You understand me? A man can't go out the way he came in, Ben, a man has got to add up to something. You can't, you can't—(BEN *moves toward him as though to interrupt*) You gotta consider, now. Don't answer so quick. Remember, it's a guaranteed twenty-thousand-dollar proposition. Now look, Ben, I want you to go through the ins and outs of this thing with me. I've got nobody to talk to, Ben, and the woman has suffered, you hear me?

BEN (*standing still, considering*) What's the proposition?

WILLY It's twenty thousand dollars on the barrelhead. Guaranteed, gilt-edged, you understand?

BEN You don't want to make a fool of yourself. They might not honor the policy.

WILLY How can they dare refuse? Didn't I work like a coolie to meet every premium on the nose? And now they don't pay off? Impossible!

BEN It's called a cowardly thing, William.

WILLY Why? Does it take more guts to stand here the rest of my life ringing up a zero?

BEN (*yielding*) That's a point, William. (*He moves, thinking, turns*) And twenty thousand—that *is* something one can feel with the hand, it is there.

WILLY (*now assured, with rising power*) Oh, Ben, that's the whole beauty of it! I see it like a diamond, shining in the dark, hard and rough, that I can pick up and touch in my hand. Not like—like an appointment! This would not be another damned-fool appointment, Ben, and it changes all the aspects. Because he thinks I'm nothing, see, and so he spites me. But the funeral— (*Straightening up*) Ben, that funeral will be massive! They'll come from Maine, Massachusetts, Vermont, New Hampshire! All the old-timers with the strange license plates—that boy will be thunder-struck, Ben, because he never realized—I am known! Rhode Island, New York, New Jersey—I am known, Ben, and he'll see it with his eyes once and for all. He'll see what I am, Ben! He's in for a shock, that boy!

BEN (*coming down to the edge of the garden*) He'll call you a coward.

WILLY (*suddenly fearful*) No, that would be terrible.

BEN Yes. And a damned fool.

WILLY No, no, he mustn't, I won't have that! (*He is broken and desperate*)

BEN He'll hate you, William.

*The gay music of the Boys is heard.*

WILLY Oh, Ben, how do we get back to all the great times? Used to be so full of light, and comradeship, the sleigh-riding in winter, and the ruddiness on his cheeks. And always some kind of good news coming up, always something nice coming up ahead. And never even let me carry the valises in the house, and simonizing, simonizing that little red car! Why, why can't I give him something and not have him hate me?

BEN Let me think about it. (*He glances at his watch*) I still have a little time. Remarkable proposition, but you've got to be sure you're not making a fool of yourself.

BEN *drifts off upstage and goes out of sight.* BIFF *comes down from the left.*

WILLY (*suddenly conscious of* BIFF, *turns and looks up at him, then begins picking up the packages of seeds in confusion*) Where the hell is that seed? (*Indignantly*) You can't see nothing out here! They boxed in the whole goddam neighborhood!

BIFF There are people all around here. Don't you realize that?

WILLY I'm busy. Don't bother me.

BIFF (*taking the hoe from* WILLY) I'm saying good-by to you, Pop. (WILLY *looks at him, silent, unable to move*) I'm not coming back any more.

WILLY You're not going to see Oliver tomorrow?

BIFF I've got no appointment, Dad.

WILLY He put his arm around you, and you've got no appointment?

BIFF Pop, get this now, will you? Everytime I've left it's been a fight that sent me out of here. Today I realized something about myself and I tried to explain it to you and I—I think I'm just not smart enough to make any sense out of it for you. To hell with whose fault it is or anything like that. (*He takes* WILLY's *arm*) Let's just wrap it up, heh? Come on in, we'll tell Mom. (*He gently tries to pull* WILLY *to left*)

WILLY (*frozen, immobile, with guilt in his voice*) No, I don't want to see her.

BIFF Come on! (*He pulls again, and* WILLY *tries to pull away*)

WILLY (*highly nervous*) No, no, I don't want to see her.

BIFF (*tries to look into* WILLY's *face, as if to find the answer there*) Why don't you want to see her?

WILLY (*more harshly now*) Don't bother me, will you?

BIFF What do you mean, you don't want to see her? You don't want them calling you yellow, do you? This isn't your fault; it's me, I'm a bum. Now come inside! (WILLY *strains to get away*) Did you hear what I said to you?

WILLY *pulls away and quickly goes by himself into the house.* BIFF *follows.*

LINDA (*to* WILLY) Did you plant, dear?

BIFF (*at the door, to* LINDA) All right, we had it out. I'm going and I'm not writing any more.

LINDA (*going to* WILLY *in the kitchen*) I think that's the best way, dear. 'Cause there's no use drawing it out, you'll just never get along.

WILLY *doesn't respond.*

BIFF People ask where I am and what I'm doing, you don't know, and you don't care. That way it'll be off your mind and you can start brightening up again. All right? That clears it, doesn't it?

(WILLY *is silent, and* BIFF *goes to him*) You gonna wish me luck, scout? (*He extends his hand*) What do you say?

LINDA Shake his hand, Willy.

WILLY (*turning to her, seething with hurt*) There's no necessity to mention the pen at all, y'know.

BIFF (*gently*) I've got no appointment, Dad.

WILLY (*erupting fiercely*) He put his arm around . . . ?

BIFF Dad, you're never going to see what I am, so what's the use of arguing? If I strike oil I'll send you a check. Meantime forget I'm alive.

WILLY (*to* LINDA) Spite, see?

BIFF Shake hands, Dad.

WILLY Not my hand.

BIFF I was hoping not to go this way.

WILLY Well, this is the way you're going. Good-by.

BIFF *looks at him a moment, then turns sharply and goes to the stairs.*

WILLY (*stops him with*) May you rot in hell if you leave this house!

BIFF (*turning*) Exactly what is it that you want from me?

WILLY I want you to know, on the train, in the mountains, in the valleys, wherever you go, that you cut down your life for spite!

BIFF No, no.

WILLY Spite, spite, is the word of your undoing! And when you're down and out, remember what did it. When you're rotting somewhere beside the railroad tracks, remember, and don't you dare blame it on me!

BIFF I'm not blaming it on you!

WILLY I won't take the rap for this, you hear?

HAPPY *comes down the stairs and stands on the bottom step, watching.*

BIFF That's just what I'm telling you!

WILLY (*sinking into a chair at the table, with full accusation*) You're trying to put a knife in me—don't think I don't know what you're doing!

BIFF All right, phony! Then let's lay it on the line. (*He whips the rubber tube out of his pocket and puts it on the table*)

HAPPY You crazy—

LINDA Biff! (*She moves to grab the hose, but* BIFF *holds it down with his hand*)

BIFF Leave it there! Don't move it!

WILLY (*not looking at it*) What is that?

BIFF You know goddam well what that is.

WILLY (*caged, wanting to escape*) I never saw that.

BIFF You saw it. The mice didn't bring it into the cellar! What is this supposed to do, make a hero out of you? This supposed to make me sorry for you?

WILLY Never heard of it.

BIFF There'll be no pity for you, you hear it? No pity!

WILLY (*to* LINDA) You hear the spite!

BIFF No, you're going to hear the truth—what you are and what I am!

LINDA Stop it!

WILLY Spite!

HAPPY (*coming down toward* BIFF) You cut it now!

BIFF (*to* HAPPY) The man don't know who we are! The man is gonna know! (*To* WILLY) We never told the truth for ten minutes in this house!

HAPPY We always told the truth!

BIFF (*turning on him*) You big blow, are you the assistant buyer? You're one of the two assistants to the assistant, aren't you?

HAPPY Well, I'm practically—

BIFF You're practically full of it! We all are! And I'm through with it. (*To* WILLY) Now hear this, Willy, this is me.

WILLY I know you!

BIFF You know why I had no address for three months? I stole a suit in Kansas City and I was in jail. (*To* LINDA, *who is sobbing*) Stop crying. I'm through with it.

LINDA *turns away from them, her hands covering her face.*

WILLY I suppose that's my fault!

BIFF I stole myself out of every good job since high school!

WILLY And whose fault is that?

BIFF And I never got anywhere because you blew me so full of hot air I could never stand taking orders from anybody! That's whose fault it is!

WILLY I hear that!

LINDA Don't, Biff!

BIFF It's goddam time you heard that! I had to be boss big shot in two weeks, and I'm through with it!

WILLY Then hang yourself! For spite, hang yourself!

BIFF No! Nobody's hanging himself, Willy! I ran down eleven flights with a pen in my hand today. And suddenly I stopped, you hear me? And in the middle of that office building, do you hear this? I stopped in the middle of that building and I saw—the sky. I saw the things that I love in this world. The work and the food and time to sit and smoke. And I looked at the pen and said to myself, what the hell am I grabbing this for? Why am I trying to become what I don't want to be? What am I doing in an office, making a contemptuous, begging fool of myself, when all I want is out there, waiting for me the minute I say I know who I am! Why can't I say that, Willy? (*He tries to make* WILLY *face him, but* WILLY *pulls away and moves to the left*)

WILLY (*with hatred, threateningly*) The door of your life is wide open!

BIFF Pop! I'm a dime a dozen, and so are you!

WILLY (*turning on him now in an uncontrolled outburst*) I am not a dime a dozen! I am Willy Loman, and you are Biff Loman!

BIFF *starts for* WILLY, *but is blocked by* HAPPY. *In his fury,* BIFF *seems on the verge of attacking his* FATHER.

BIFF I am not a leader of men, Willy, and neither are you. You were never anything but a hard-working drummer who landed in the ash can like all the rest of them! I'm one dollar an hour, Willy! I tried seven states and couldn't raise it. A buck an hour! Do you gather my meaning? I'm not bringing home any prizes any more, and you're going to stop waiting for me to bring them home!

WILLY (*directly to* BIFF) You vengeful, spiteful mut!

BIFF *breaks from* HAPPY. WILLY, *in fright, starts up the stairs.* BIFF *grabs him.*

BIFF (*at the peak of his fury*) Pop, I'm nothing! I'm nothing, Pop. Can't you understand that? There's no spite in it any more. I'm just what I am, that's all.

BIFF'S *fury has spent itself, and he breaks down, sobbing, holding on to* WILLY, *who dumbly fumbles for* BIFF'S *face.*

WILLY (*astonished*) What're you doing? What're you doing? (*To* LINDA) Why is he crying?

BIFF (*crying, broken*) Will you let me go, for Christ's sake? Will you take that phony dream and burn it before something happens? (*Struggling to contain himself, he pulls away and moves to the stairs*) I'll go in the morning. Put him—put him to bed. (*Exhausted,* BIFF *moves up the stairs to his room*)

WILLY (*after a long pause, astonished, elevated*) Isn't that—isn't that remarkable? Biff—he likes me!

LINDA He loves you, Willy!

HAPPY (*deeply moved*) Always did, Pop.

WILLY Oh, Biff! (*Staring wildly*) He cried! Cried to me. (*He is choking with his love, and now cries out his promise*) That boy —that boy is going to be magnificent!

BEN *appears in the light just outside the kitchen.*

BEN Yes, outstanding, with twenty thousand behind him.
LINDA (*sensing the racing of his mind, fearfully, carefully*) Now come to bed, Willy. It's all settled now.
WILLY (*finding it difficult not to rush out of the house*) Yes, we'll sleep. Come on. Go to sleep, Hap.
BEN And it does take a great kind of a man to crack the jungle.

*In accents of dread,* BEN'S *idyllic music starts up.*

HAPPY (*his arm around* LINDA) I'm getting married, Pop, don't forget it. I'm changing everything. I'm gonna run that department before the year is up. You'll see, Mom. (*He kisses her*)
BEN The jungle is dark but full of diamonds, Willy.

WILLY *turns, moves, listening to* BEN.

LINDA Be good. You're both good boys, just act that way, that's all.
HAPPY 'Night, Pop. (*He goes upstairs*)
LINDA (*to* WILLY) Come, dear.
BEN (*with greater force*) One must go in to fetch a diamond out.
WILLY (*to* LINDA, *as he moves slowly along the edge of the kitchen, toward the door*) I just want to get settled down, Linda. Let me sit alone for a little.
LINDA (*almost uttering her fear*) I want you upstairs.
WILLY (*taking her in his arms*) In a few minutes, Linda. I couldn't sleep right now. Go on, you look awful tired. (*He kisses her*)
BEN Not like an appointment at all. A diamond is rough and hard to the touch.
WILLY Go on now. I'll be right up.
LINDA I think this is the only way, Willy.
WILLY Sure, it's the best thing.
BEN Best thing!
WILLY The only way. Everything is gonna be—go on, kid, get to bed. You look so tired.
LINDA Come right up.
WILLY Two minutes.

LINDA *goes into the living-room, then reappears in her bedroom.* WILLY *moves just outside the kitchen door.*

WILLY Loves me. (*Wonderingly*) Always loved me. Isn't that a remarkable thing? Ben, he'll worship me for it!
BEN (*with promise*) It's dark there, but full of diamonds.

WILLY Can you imagine that magnificence with twenty thousand dollars in his pocket?

LINDA (*calling from her room*) Willy! Come up!

WILLY (*calling into the kitchen*) Yes! Yes. Coming! It's very smart, you realize that, don't you, sweetheart? Even Ben sees it. I gotta go, baby. 'By! 'By! (*Going over to* BEN, *almost dancing*) Imagine? When the mail comes he'll be ahead of Bernard again!

BEN A perfect proposition all around.

WILLY Did you see how he cried to me? Oh, if I could kiss him, Ben!

BEN Time, William, time!

WILLY Oh, Ben, I always knew one way or another we were gonna make it, Biff and I!

BEN (*looking at his watch*) The boat. We'll be late. (*He moves slowly off into the darkness*)

WILLY (*elegiacally, turning to the house*) Now when you kick off, boy, I want a seventy-yard boot, and get right down the field under the ball, and when you hit, hit low and hit hard, because it's important, boy. (*He swings around and faces the audience*) There's all kinds of important people in the stands, and the first thing you know . . . (*Suddenly realizing he is alone*) Ben! Ben, where do I . . . ? (*He makes a sudden movement of search*) Ben, how do I . . . ?

LINDA (*calling*) Willy, you coming up?

WILLY (*uttering a gasp of fear, whirling about as if to quiet her*) Sh! (*He turns around as if to find his way; sounds, faces, voices, seem to be swarming in upon him and he flicks at them, crying*) Sh! Sh! (*Suddenly music, faint and high, stops him. It rises in intensity, almost to an unbearable scream. He goes up and down on his toes, and rushes off around the house*) Shhh!

LINDA Willy?

*There is no answer.* LINDA *waits.* BIFF *gets up off his bed. He is still in his clothes.* HAPPY *sits up.* BIFF *stands listening.*

LINDA (*with real fear*) Willy, answer me! Willy!

*There is the sound of a car starting and moving away at full speed.*

LINDA No!

BIFF (*rushing down the stairs*) Pop!

*As the car speeds off, the music crashes down in a frenzy of sound, which becomes the soft pulsation of a single cello string.* BIFF *slowly returns to his bedroom. He and* HAPPY *gravely don their jackets.* LINDA *slowly walks out of her room. The music has developed into a dead march. The leaves of day are appearing over everything.* CHARLEY *and* BERNARD, *somberly dressed, appear and knock on the kitchen door.* BIFF *and* HAPPY *slowly descend the stairs to the kitchen as* CHARLEY *and* BERNARD *enter. All stop a moment when* LINDA, *in clothes of mourning, bearing a little bunch of roses, comes through the draped doorway into the kitchen. She goes to* CHARLEY *and takes his arm. Now all move toward the audience, through the wall-line of the kitchen. At the limit of the apron,* LINDA *lays down the flowers, kneels, and sits back on her heels. All stare down at the grave.*

## REQUIEM

CHARLEY It's getting dark, Linda.

LINDA *doesn't react. She stares at the grave.*

BIFF How about it, Mom? Better get some rest, heh? They'll be closing the gate soon.

LINDA *makes no move. Pause.*

HAPPY (*deeply angered*) He had no right to do that. There was no necessity for it. We would've helped him.
CHARLEY (*grunting*) Hmmm.
BIFF Come along, Mom.
LINDA Why didn't anybody come?
CHARLEY It was a very nice funeral.
LINDA But where are all the people he knew? Maybe they blame him.
CHARLEY Naa. It's a rough world, Linda. They wouldn't blame him.
LINDA I can't understand it. At this time especially. First time in thirty-five years we were just about free and clear. He only needed a little salary. He was even finished with the dentist.
CHARLEY No man only needs a little salary.
LINDA I can't understand it.
BIFF There were a lot of nice days. When he'd come home from a trip; or on Sundays, making the stoop; finishing the cellar; putting on the new porch; when he built the extra bathroom; and put up the garage. You know something, Charley, there's more of him in that front stoop than in all the sales he ever made.
CHARLEY Yeah. He was a happy man with a batch of cement.
LINDA He was so wonderful with his hands.
BIFF He had the wrong dreams. All, all, wrong.
HAPPY (*almost ready to fight* BIFF) Don't say that!
BIFF He never knew who he was.
CHARLEY (*stopping* HAPPY'S *movement and reply. To* BIFF) Nobody dast blame this man. You don't understand: Willy was a

salesman. And for a salesman, there is no rock bottom to the life. He don't put a bolt to a nut, he don't tell you the law or give you medicine. He's a man way out there in the blue, riding on a smile and a shoeshine. And when they start not smiling back—that's an earthquake. And then you get yourself a couple of spots on your hat, and you're finished. Nobody dast blame this man. A salesman is got to dream, boy. It comes with the territory.

BIFF Charley, the man didn't know who he was.

HAPPY (*infuriated*) Don't say that!

BIFF Why don't you come with me, Happy?

HAPPY I'm not licked that easily. I'm staying right in this city, and I'm gonna beat this racket! (*He looks at* BIFF, *his chin set*) The Loman Brothers!

BIFF I know who I am, kid.

HAPPY All right, boy. I'm gonna show you and everybody else that Willy Loman did not die in vain. He had a good dream. It's the only dream you can have—to come out number-one man. He fought it out here, and this is where I'm gonna win it for him.

BIFF (*with a hopeless glance at* HAPPY, *bends toward his mother*) Let's go, Mom.

LINDA I'll be with you in a minute. Go on, Charley. (*He hesitates*) I want to, just for a minute. I never had a chance to say good-by.

CHARLEY *moves away, followed by* HAPPY. BIFF *remains a slight distance up and left of* LINDA. *She sits there, summoning herself. The flute begins, not far away, playing behind her speech.*

LINDA Forgive me, dear. I can't cry. I don't know what it is, but I can't cry. I don't understand it. Why did you ever do that? Help me, Willy, I can't cry. It seems to me that you're just on another trip. I keep expecting you. Willy, dear, I can't cry. Why did you do it? I search and search and I search, and I can't understand it, Willy. I made the last payment on the house today. Today, dear. And there'll be nobody home. (*A sob rises in her throat*) We're free and clear. (*Sobbing more fully, released*) We're free. (BIFF *comes slowly toward her*) We're free . . . We're free . . .

BIFF *lifts her to her feet and moves out up right with her in his arms.* LINDA *sobs quietly.* BERNARD *and* CHARLEY *come together and follow them, followed by* HAPPY. *Only the music of the flute is left on the darkening stage as over the house the hard towers of the apartment buildings rise into sharp focus, and*

*The Curtain Falls*

## QUESTIONS

1. How well do you think Miller has succeeded in making a tragic hero out of Willy Loman? Discuss. Consider the rest of the questions in forming your answer.
2. How does your response to Willy compare with your response to Oedipus and/or Hamlet?
3. How does Miller's dramatization of Willy's hallucinations function?
4. What is the effect of teaming this unrealistic penetration into Willy's mind with the highly realistic language and plot?
5. How are social comment and family tensions interwoven in the play?

## EUGÈNE IONESCO (1912-    )

# *The Gap*

An English translation by Rosette Lamont

CHARACTERS

The Friend
The Academician
The Academician's Wife
The Maid

Set. *A rich bourgeois living room with artistic pretensions. One or two sofas, a number of armchairs, among which, a green, Régence style one, right in the middle of the room. The walls are covered with framed diplomas. One can make out, written in heavy script at the top of a particularly large one, "Doctor Honoris causa." This is followed by an almost illegible Latin inscription. Another equally impressive diploma states: "Doctorat honoris causa," again followed by a long, illegible text. There is an abundance of smaller diplomas, each of which bears a clearly written "doctorate."*

*A door to the right of the audience.*

*As the curtain rises, one can see* The Academician's Wife *dressed in a rather crumpled robe. She has obviously just gotten out of bed, and has not had time to dress.* The Friend *faces her. He is well dressed: hat, umbrella in hand, stiff collar, black jacket and striped trousers, shiny black shoes.*

THE WIFE Dear friend, tell me all.

THE FRIEND I don't know what to say.

THE WIFE I know.

THE FRIEND I heard the news last night. I did not want to call you. At the same time I couldn't wait any longer. Please forgive me for coming so early with such terrible news.

THE WIFE He didn't make it! How terrible! We were still hoping. . . .

THE FRIEND It's hard, I know. He still had a chance. Not much of one. We had to expect it.

THE WIFE I didn't expect it. He was always so successful. He could always manage somehow, at the last moment.

THE FRIEND In that state of exhaustion. You shouldn't have let him!

THE WIFE What can we do, what can we do! . . . How awful!

THE FRIEND Come on, dear friend, be brave. That's life.

THE WIFE I feel faint: I'm going to faint. (*She falls in one of the armchairs.*)

THE FRIEND (*holding her, gently slapping her cheeks and hands*) I shouldn't have blurted it out like that. I'm sorry.

THE WIFE No, you were right to do so. I had to find out somehow or other.

THE FRIEND I should have prepared you, carefully.

THE WIFE I've got to be strong. I can't help thinking of him, the wretched man. I hope they won't put it in the papers. Can we count on the journalists' discretion?

THE FRIEND Close your door. Don't answer the telephone. It will still get around. You could go to the country. In a couple of months, when you are better, you'll come back, you'll go on with your life. People forget such things.

THE WIFE People won't forget so fast. That's all they were waiting for. Some friends will feel sorry, but the others, the others. . . . (*The Academician comes in, fully dressed: uniform, chest covered with decorations, his sword on his side.*)

THE ACADEMICIAN Up so early, my dear? (*To* THE FRIEND.) You've come early too. What's happening? Do you have the final results?

THE WIFE What a disgrace!

THE FRIEND You mustn't crush him like this, dear friend. (*To* THE ACADEMICIAN.) You have failed.

THE ACADEMICIAN Are you quite sure?

THE FRIEND You should never have tried to pass the baccalaureate examination.

THE ACADEMICIAN They failed me. The rats! How dare they do this to me!

THE FRIEND The marks were posted late in the evening.

THE ACADEMICIAN Perhaps it was difficult to make them out in the dark. How could you read them?

THE FRIEND They had set up spotlights.

THE ACADEMICIAN They're doing everything to ruin me.

THE FRIEND I passed by in the morning; the marks were still up.

THE ACADEMICIAN You could have bribed the concierge into pulling them down.

THE FRIEND That's exactly what I did. Unfortunately the police were there. Your name heads the list of those who failed. Everyone's standing in line to get a look. There's an awful crush.

THE ACADEMICIAN Who's there? The parents of the candidates?

THE FRIEND Not only they.

THE WIFE All your rivals, all your colleagues must be there. All those you attacked in the press for ignorance: your undergraduates, your graduate students, all those you failed when you were chairman of the board of examiners.

THE ACADEMICIAN I am discredited! But I won't let them. There must be some mistake.

THE FRIEND I saw the examiners. I spoke with them. They gave me your marks. Zero in mathematics.

THE ACADEMICIAN I had no scientific training.

THE FRIEND Zero in Greek, zero in Latin.

THE WIFE (*to her husband*) You, a humanist, the spokesman for humanism, the author of that famous treatise "The Defense of Poesy and Humanism."

THE ACADEMICIAN I beg your pardon, but my book concerns itself with twentieth century humanism. (*To* THE FRIEND.) What about composition? What grade did I get in composition?

THE FRIEND Nine hundred. You have nine hundred points.

THE ACADEMICIAN That's perfect. My average must be all the way up.

THE FRIEND Unfortunately not. They're marking on the basis of two thousand. The passing grade is one thousand.

THE ACADEMICIAN They must have changed the regulations.

THE WIFE They didn't change them just for you. You have a frightful persecution complex.

THE ACADEMICIAN I tell you they changed them.

THE FRIEND They went back to the old ones, back to the time of Napoleon.

THE ACADEMICIAN Utterly outmoded. Besides, when did they make those changes? It isn't legal. I'm chairman of the Baccalaureate Commission of the Ministry of Public Education. They didn't consult me, and they cannot make any changes without my approval. I'm going to expose them. I'm going to bring government charges against them.

THE WIFE Darling, you don't know what you're doing. You're in your dotage. Don't you recall handing in your resignation just before taking the examination so that no one could doubt the complete objectivity of the board of examiners?

THE ACADEMICIAN I'll take it back.

THE WIFE You should never have taken that test. I warned you. After all, it's not as if you needed it. But you have to collect all the honors, don't you? You're never satisfied. What did you need this diploma for? Now all is lost. You have your Doctorate, your

Master's, your high school diploma, your elementary school certificate, and even the first part of the baccalaureate.

THE ACADEMICIAN There was a gap.

THE WIFE No one suspected it.

THE ACADEMICIAN But *I* knew it. Others might have found out. I went to the office of the Registrar and asked for a transcript of my record. They said to me: "Certainly Professor, Mr. President, Your Excellency. . . ." Then they looked up my file, and the Chief Registrar came back looking embarrassed, most embarrassed indeed. He said: "There's something peculiar, very peculiar. You have your Master's, certainly, but it's no longer valid." I asked him why, of course. He answered: "There's a gap behind your Master's. I don't know how it happened. You must have registered and been accepted at the University without having passed the second part of the baccalaureate examination."

THE FRIEND And then?

THE WIFE Your Master's degree is no longer valid?

THE ACADEMICIAN No, not quite. It's suspended. "The duplicate you are asking for will be delivered to you upon completion of the baccalaureate. Of course you will pass the examination with no trouble." That's what I was told, so you see now that I had to take it.

THE FRIEND Your husband, dear friend, wanted to fill the gap. He's a conscientious person.

THE WIFE It's clear you don't know him as I do. That's not it at all. He wants fame, honors. He never had enough. What does one diploma more or less matter? No one notices them anyway, but he sneaks in at night, on tiptoe, into the living room, just to look at them, and count them.

THE ACADEMICIAN What else can I do when I have insomnia?

THE FRIEND The questions asked at the baccalaureate are usually known in advance. You were admirably situated to get this particular information. You could also have sent in a replacement to take the test for you. One of your students, perhaps. Or if you wanted to take the test without people realizing that you already knew the questions, you could have sent your maid to the black market, where one can buy them.

THE ACADEMICIAN I don't understand how I could have failed in my composition. I filled three sheets of paper, I treated the subject fully, taking into account the historical background. I interpreted the situation accurately . . . at least plausibly. I didn't deserve a bad grade.

THE FRIEND Do you recall the subject?

THE ACADEMICIAN Hum . . . let's see. . . .

THE FRIEND He doesn't even remember what he discussed.

THE ACADEMICIAN I do . . . wait . . . hum.

THE FRIEND The subject to be treated was the following: "Discuss the influence of Renaissance painters on novelists of the Third Republic." I have here a photostatic copy of your examination paper. Here is what you wrote.

THE ACADEMICIAN (*grabbing the photostat and reading*) "The trial of Benjamin: After Benjamin was tried and acquitted, the assessors holding a different opinion from that of the President murdered him, and condemned Benjamin to the suspension of his civic rights, imposing on him a fine of nine hundred francs. . . ."

THE FRIEND That's where the nine hundred points come from.

THE ACADEMICIAN "Benjamin appealed his case . . . Benjamin appealed his case. . . ." I can't make out the rest. I've always had bad handwriting. I ought to have taken a typewriter along with me.

THE WIFE Horrible handwriting, scribbling and crossing out; ink spots didn't help you much.

THE ACADEMICIAN (*goes on with his reading after having retrieved the text his wife had pulled out of his hand*) "Benjamin appealed his case. Flanked by policemen dressed in zouave uniforms . . . in zouave uniforms. . . ." It's getting dark. I can't see the rest. . . . I don't have my glasses.

THE WIFE What you've written has nothing to do with the subject.

THE FRIEND Your wife's quite right, friend. It has nothing to do with the subject.

THE ACADEMICIAN Yes, it has. Indirectly.

THE FRIEND Not even indirectly.

THE ACADEMICIAN Perhaps I chose the second question.

THE FRIEND There was only one.

THE ACADEMICIAN Even if there was only that one, I treated another quite adequately. I went to the end of the story. I stressed the important points, explaining the motivations of the characters, highlighting their behavior. I explained the mystery, making it plain and clear. There was even a conclusion at the end. I can't make out the rest. (*To* THE FRIEND.) Can you read it?

THE FRIEND It's illegible. I don't have my glasses either.

THE WIFE (*taking the text*) It's illegible and I have excellent eyes. You pretended to write. Mere scribbling.

THE ACADEMICIAN That's not true. I've even provided a conclusion. It's clearly marked here in heavy print: "Conclusion or sanction . . . Conclusion or sanction. . . ." They can't get away with it. I'll have this examination rendered null and void.

THE WIFE Since you treated the wrong subject, and treated it badly, setting down only titles, and writing nothing in between, the mark you received is justified. You'd lose your case.

THE FRIEND You'd most certainly lose. Drop it. Take a vacation.

THE ACADEMICIAN You're always on the side of the Others.

THE WIFE After all, these professors know what they're doing. They haven't been granted their rank for nothing. They passed examinations, received serious training. They know the rules of composition.

THE ACADEMICIAN Who was on the board of examiners?

THE FRIEND For Mathematics, a movie star. For Greek, one of the Beatles. For Latin, the champion of the automobile race, and many others.

THE ACADEMICIAN But these people aren't any more qualified than I am. And for composition?

THE FRIEND A woman, a secretary in the editorial division of the review *Yesterday, the Day Before Yesterday, and Today.*

THE ACADEMICIAN Now I know. This wretch gave me a poor grade out of spite because I never joined her political party. It's an act of vengeance. But I have ways and means of rendering the examination null and void. I'm going to call the President.

THE WIFE Don't. You'll make yourself look even more ridiculous. (*To* THE FRIEND.) Please try to restrain him. He listens to you more than to me. (THE FRIEND *shrugs his shoulders, unable to cope with the situation.* THE WIFE *turns to her husband, who has just lifted the receiver off the hook.*) Don't call!

THE ACADEMICIAN (*on the telephone*) Hello, John? It is I... What?... What did you say?... But, listen, my dear friend... but, listen to me.. Hello! Hello! (*Puts down the receiver.*)

THE FRIEND What did he say?

THE ACADEMICIAN He said... He said.... "I don't want to talk to you. My mummy won't let me make friends with boys at the bottom of the class." Then he hung up on me.

THE WIFE You should have expected it. All is lost. How could you do this to me? How could you do this to me?

THE ACADEMICIAN Think of it! I lectured at the Sorbonne, at Oxford, at American universities. Ten thousand theses have been written on my work; hundreds of critics have analyzed it. I hold an *honoris causa* doctorate from Amsterdam as well as a secret university Chair with the Duchy of Luxembourg. I received the Nobel Prize three times. The King of Sweden himself was amazed by my erudition. A doctorate *honoris causa, honoris causa*... and I failed the baccalaureate examination!

THE WIFE Everyone will laugh at us!

THE ACADEMICIAN *takes off his sword and breaks it on his knee.*

THE FRIEND (*picking up the two pieces*) I wish to preserve these in memory of our ancient glory.

THE ACADEMICIAN *meanwhile in a fit of rage is tearing down his decorations, throwing them on the floor, and stepping on them.*

THE WIFE (*trying to salvage the remains*) Don't do this! Don't! That's all we've got left.

*Curtain*

## QUESTIONS

1. Although *The Gap* begins in an apparently normal setting, the action soon moves beyond that, to focus on a fantastic, absurd society. By what means is this progression created? What particular acts or speeches seem to you to mark notable points in the process?
2. How do you interpret this play? Compare it with the earlier brief comedy, *A Marriage Proposal.*
3. In a more serious vein, you could compare *The Gap* with *Death of a Salesman.* Both plays revolve around a hero who is forced to realize that he does not measure up to beliefs he has held about himself.
   a. How far do you think this comparison can be taken? What strengths and what weaknesses might it have? What aspects of the two plays would you cite in your arguments?
   b. Outline an essay along this theme. Be sure that it clearly shows your introduction, your various points of discussion, and your conclusion.

# *Index of Terms*

# *Index of Authors and Titles*

# *Index of First Lines*

1 2 3 4 5 6 7 8 9